# THE
# CONCORD
## DESK ENCYCLOPEDIA

The Concord Desk Encyclopedia

**VOLUME**

# 2
# F-N

### The Concord Desk Encyclopedia

Copyright © 1982 by Concord Reference Books, Inc. No portion of this book
may be reproduced in any form or by any means in whole or in part without
written permission of the publisher. Reproduction for use in electronic data
bases is also prohibited. Address all inquiries to the Rights and Permissions
Department, Concord Reference Books, Inc., 135 W. 50th St., New York,
N.Y. 10020.

Portions of this book were based on the University Desk Encyclopedia,
Copyright © 1977 by Elsevier Publishing Projects S.A., Lausanne.

ISBN 0-940994-01-1

Library of Congress Catalog Card 81-71378

Manufactured in the U.S.A.

The Concord Desk Encyclopedia is published by Concord Reference Books,
Inc., a subsidiary of Whitney Communications Corporation, 135 W. 50th St.,
New York, N.Y. 10020. (212) 307-1491. Kristin S. Loomis, President; Steven
E. Spaeth, Vice President & General Manager.

th letter of the English alphabet, and also of the Roman and early Greek alphabets. In science, F is the symbol for farad, the SI unit of capacitance, and °F for degrees Fahrenheit.

**FABERGE, Peter Carl** (1846–1920), Russian goldsmith famous for the jewelry he made for the Russian Tsars and other royalty, especially the bejeweled "Easter Eggs." He went into exile in 1917.

**FABIAN SOCIETY,** English society for the propagation of socialism, established 1883–84, taking its name from the delaying tactics of FABIUS CUNCTATOR. Fabians rejected violent revolution, seeking to change society gradually. They helped form the Labour Representation Committee which became the Labour Party in 1906. Leading Fabians were Sidney and Beatrice WEBB and G. B. SHAW.

**FABLE,** a fictional story, generally one illustrating a moral. The characters are often animals whose behavior caricatures human folly. Famous collections of fables are those by AESOP and Jean de LA FONTAINE.

**FACTOR, an** INTEGER which may be divided into another integer without remainder. Thus the factors of 12 are 1, 2, 3, 4 and 6, since each of these may be divided exactly into 12. In general it is of use to consider only the factors of a number which are NATURAL NUMBERS. The prime factors of a number are those PRIME NUMBERS which are its factors. The prime factors of 12 are 1, 2 (twice), and 3.

In ALGEBRA the factors of a POLYNOMIAL are found by a mixture of guesswork and rules of thumb. This is helped by certain standard rules:

$$x^2 - y^2 = (x + y)(x - y)$$
$$x^3 - y^3 = (x - y)(x^2 + xy + y^2)$$
$$x^3 + y^3 = (x + y)(x^2 - xy + y^2)$$
$$x^2 + 2xy + y^2 = (x + y)^2.$$

**FACTORY,** establishment for the manufacture of goods in quantity. In the US most goods are factory-made and almost 25% of the population is employed in factories. Factories as we know them originated in the INDUSTRIAL REVOLUTION and were soon focal points for overcrowding and slums caused by the massive influx of workers into urban areas. Working conditions were often bad and had to be improved by legislation. The factory today is attacked because of the POLLUTION it can cause, and because a town may become economically dependent on a few factories and so suffer disproportionately in a recession.

**FAEROE ISLANDS,** group of islands in the N Atlantic, self-governing since 1948 but linked with Denmark. They lie 190mi NW of the Shetlands and 250mi SE of Iceland. The islanders speak Faeroese, related to Old Norse. The economy rests on the fishing industry and on agriculture, especially sheep-raising. Pop 38,681.

**FAIENCE,** earthenware with a tin oxide glaze, made from a coarse clay and fired several times. The name, originally French, derives from the Italian town of FAENZA, famous for such earthenware since the 14th century. Egyptian blue-glazed ware is often also called faience.

**FAINTING,** or **syncope,** transient loss or diminution of consciousness associated with an abrupt fall in blood pressure. In the upright position, head and BRAIN are dependent on a certain blood pressure to maintain BLOOD CIRCULATION through them; if the pressure falls for any reason, inadequate flow causes consciousness to recede, often with the sense of things becoming more distant. The body goes limp and falls, so that, unless artificially supported, the effect of gravity on brain flow is lost and consciousness is rapidly regained. Fainting may result from sudden emotional shock in susceptible individuals, HEMORRHAGE, ANEMIA or occur with transient rhythm disorders of the HEART.

**FAIRBANKS, Douglas Sr.** (1883–1939), US film actor famous for his romantic and swashbuckling roles in films such as *Robin Hood* (1922) and *The Black Pirate* (1926). In 1919 he founded United Artists Studio with his wife Mary PICKFORD, Charlie CHAPLIN, and D. W. GRIFFITH.

**FAIR CAMPAIGN PRACTICES ACT (FEDERAL ELECTION CAMPAIGN ACT, 1972)** requires candidates for federal office, and their fund-raising committees, to report all contributions and expenditures of more than $100 (if their total is as much as $1,000). The law, which represented the first real attempt to control campaign financing since the CORRUPT PRACTICES ACT of 1925, was supplemented in 1974 by legislation providing for public financing of presidential primaries and elections, and setting ceilings on contributions and expenditures in house, senate, and presidential campaigns. Except in the case of presidential candidates who accept federal funds, the ceilings were ruled unconstitutional in 1976 by the US Supreme Court, which said they conflicted with the freedom of speech.

**FAIR DEAL,** domestic program put before Congress by President Truman 1945–48, covering civil rights, education, health services, agriculture and employment. Congress rejected many of the proposals as being too expensive, but the 1946 Employment Act and some other measures resulted.

**FAIR LABOR STANDARDS ACT,** passed in 1938 by the Roosevelt administration to ensure for most workers a minimum wage and a 44hr maximum working week. The act was subsequently extended and improved.

**FAIRS AND EXPOSITIONS,** gatherings at which goods from many areas are brought together for sale, or to foster trade and the prestige of the producing country. Fairs date from early times when they were accompanied by holidays and festivities, and some old fairs, such as the Frankfurt Book Fair, have survived until the present. Massive international fairs, or expositions, began with the Great Exhibition, held at the Crystal Palace, London, in 1851. The first large exposition in the US was the CENTENNIAL EXPOSITION at Philadelphia in 1876. Many other world fairs followed, such as Century 21 Expo at Seattle, Expo 67 at Montreal and Expo 70 in Tokyo.

**FAIRY TALE,** general term for a tale involving fantastic events and characters, not necessarily fairies. Many of these originate in myth and folklore, but an equal number have been written or collected to provide sophisticated adult entertainment, among them those by Charles PERRAULT, the brothers GRIMM, GOETHE, E. T. A. HOFFMANN and some by Hans Christian ANDERSEN. Many modern writers, such as J. R. R. TOLKIEN and C. S. LEWIS, invented and incorporated fairy-tale elements in their works.

**FAISAL,** or Feisal (1905–1975), king of Saudi Arabia from 1964, when his brother King Saud was forced to abdicate. A pious, moderate and able ruler, Faisal instituted a far-ranging program of social reform. Friendly to the West, he nevertheless joined the campaign against Israel and supported the Arab oil cartel. He was assassinated by a nephew in March 1975.

**FAISAL,** or Feisal, two kings of Iraq. **Faisal**

**I** (1885–1933), took part in the Arab revolt against the Ottoman Turks in 1915 and was king 1921–33. **Faisal II** (1935–58), reigned from 1939. His uncle, Abdul Ilah, ruled Iraq as regent till 1953. In 1958 they were both murdered in a revolution.

**FAITH,** confidence or trust, or that which is reliable and trustworthy. In Christianity "faith" is applied objectively to the content of Christian doctrine, the faith which is to be believed; and also, especially in St. Paul's theology, subjectively to the human response of acceptance of Divine truth by mind and will, and trust in Jesus Christ as savior. In the latter sense, faith is an act possible only by GRACE, leading to JUSTIFICATION and to obedience to God. Faith differs from belief in that while the former is absolute and unconditional, the latter, involving rational assent upon probable evidence, admits of degrees, and lies on a continuum with the shades of doubt.

**FAITH HEALING,** the treatment of DISEASE by the evocation of faith, usually induced during a public ceremony or meeting; chanting and laying on of hands are common accompaniments. Greatest success is often with disease that tends to remit spontaneously and in HYSTERIA; in some instances, patients are helped to come to terms with disease. Substantiation of cures is rare.

**FALCONRY,** the hunting of game using trained falcons and other birds of prey. An ancient sport, it was popular with the medieval nobility. Training a falcon is a long and difficult process; the bird must become familiar with its trainer, return to him after flights and learn not to eat its prey. Interest in falconry has recently revived after a period of decline.

**FALCONS,** name generally applied to about 60 species of hawk, though the true falcons of the family Falconidae number about 35 species. They are BIRDS OF PREY, feeding mainly on other birds which they kill in the air. They inhabit most parts of the world, making their nests on rocky ledges or tree forks. Falcons in the US include the Prairie falcon and the Sparrowhawk.

**FALKLAND ISLANDS,** self-governing British colony, a group of islands totalling 4,700sq mi in the S Atlantic about 480m NE of Cape Horn. Possession is disputed with Argentina. They number about 200 the largest of which are E Falkland and W Falkland. The inhabitants are mostly of British descent; the economy rests largely on sheep and cattle raising. The islands are noted for their abundant wild life. Capital Stanley. Pop 2,045.

**FALLA, Manuel de** (1876–1946), major Spanish composer. He studied in Madrid and Paris. His work was heavily influenced by RAVEL and native Andalusian folk music, evident in the famous ballets *El Amor Brujo* (1915) and *The Three-Cornered Hat* (1919). Other famous works are the opera *La Vida Breve* (1905) and *Nights in the Gardens of Spain* (1911–15), for piano and orchestra.

**FALLADA, Hans** (pseudonym of Rudolf Ditzen; 1893–1947), German novelist. His most popular books were *Little Man, What Now?* (1932) and *The World Outside* (1934).

**FALL LINE**, a line in the E US along which a number of rivers have WATERFALLS, marking the progress of the rivers from hard rock underlying the Piedmont to softer rock forming the Atlantic Coastal Plain. Since this marks the farthest inland point navigable from the sea, and because the falls can supply HYDROELECTRIC POWER, many important industrial centers have sprung up along fall lines, including Philadelphia, Baltimore and Washington, D.C.

**FALLOPIAN TUBE**, narrow tube leading from the surface of each ovary within the female PELVIS to the WOMB. Its abdominal end has fimbria which waft peritoneal fluid and eggs into the tube after ovulation. Fertilization may occur in the tube, and if followed by IMPLANTATION there, the PREGNANCY is ectopic and ABORTION, which may be life-threatening, is inevitable. In STERILIZATION, the tubes are divided.

**FALLOUT, Radioactive**, deposition of radioactive particles from the ATMOSPHERE on the earth's surface. Three types of fallout follow the atmospheric explosion of a nuclear weapon. Large particles are deposited as intense but short-lived local fallout within about 250km of the explosion; this dust causes radiation burns. Within a week, smaller particles from the TROPOSPHERE are found around the latitude of the explosion. Long-lived RADIOISOTOPES such as strontium-90, carried to the STRATOSPHERE by the explosion, are eventually deposited worldwide.

**FALN**, name by which the Puerto Rican terrorist group, Fuerzas Armadas de Liberación Nacional, was generally known. This pro-independence organization was blamed for 11 bombings in the US between 1974 and 1980, including one at historic Fraunces Tavern (1975) in which four persons were killed and 53 injured. In 1981 the reputed FALN leader was convicted of seditious conspiracy, armed robbery and other charges. Other arrests and convictions

in 1980 and 1981 crippled the organization.

**FALSTAFF, Sir John**, comic and half-tragic figure in Shakespeare's *Henry IV* and *The Merry Wives of Windsor*, companion of Prince Hal. A roguish and cowardly knight, he remains likeable because of his wit, good nature and humanity.

**FALWELL, Jerry** (1933–    ), US Baptist radio and television evangelist who preaches a politically oriented pro-family, pro-morality and pro-American gospel to millions of faithful followers. In 1979 he founded Moral Majority, Inc., which played an important role in electing conservatives, including Ronald Reagan, to office in the 1980 elections.

**FAMILY**, a social unit comprising a number of persons in most cases linked by birth or MARRIAGE. There are four main types of families: the conjugal or nuclear family, a single set of parents and their children; the extended or consanguine family, which includes also siblings and other relations and generations (e.g., brothers, grandparents, grandchildren, uncles and aunts); the corporate family, a group organized around an important activity such as hunting, sharing of shelter, religion or customs; and the experimental family, a group whose members are generally unrelated to each other genetically, but who choose to live together and perform the traditional roles of the nuclear or consanguine family. The *kibbutzim* of Israel and the commune are examples of experimental families.

The descent within a family is usually either patrilineal, through its male members, or matrilineal, through its female members. Occasionally descent is bilineal, through either male or female lines, or bilateral, through both males and females.

By far the most common forms of families are the nuclear and consanguine. There are sound reasons for this: psychological security through membership of a close, intimate group; ready sexual and emotional satisfaction between husband and wife; and physical security based on a family's sense of duty and willingness to protect its members. Moreover, it would seem that these types of families are the most efficient insofar as childrearing is concerned, with older generations or siblings acting as mentors during the child's formative years. In the West, the nuclear family has in recent years become generally more democratic, the male's absolute authority being tempered to permit wives and children greater freedom and responsibility.

**FAMILY PLANNING**, the practice of

regulation of family size by judicious use of CONTRACEPTION, STERILIZATION and, occasionally, induced ABORTION; increased survival of children and increasing world population have created the need for such an approach. Planning of numbers and timing to accord with economic and social factors are greatly aided by modern methods of contraception, so unwanted PREGNANCY should be a rarity. However, ignorance and neglect have prevented the realization of this ideal. ADOPTION, ARTIFICIAL INSEMINATION and treatment of infertility are used for parents unable to conceive.

**FANDANGO,** rapid Andalusian folk dance, probably of Moorish origin, in 3/4 or 6/8 time. Often accompanied by castanets, the dance is an expression of passion. A sung form of fandango exists, its melodies improvised within set rules.

**FANEUIL HALL,** given by Boston merchant Peter Faneuil (1700–1743) to Boston, Mass. Site of many events leading to the American Revolution, it is known as the "cradle of liberty." Famous speeches were later made here by Daniel WEBSTER and J. F. KENNEDY, among others.

**FANFANI, Amintore** (1908–   ), Italian Christian Democratic premier in 1954, 1958–59 and 1960–63. A supporter of the COMMON MARKET, he was foreign minister in 1965 and 1966–68. As premier, his "opening to the left," an alliance with the Socialists, constituted a realignment in Italian politics.

**FANON, Frantz Omar** (1925–1961), French black psychoanalyst and social philosopher. He condemned racism in his book *Black Skin, White Masks* (1952). In *The Wretched of the Earth* (1961) he advocated extreme violence against whites as a cathartic expression for black peoples.

**FANTIN-LATOUR, Ignace Henri Jean Théodor** (1836–1904), French painter known for his flower-paintings, his illustrations of the work of WAGNER and BERLIOZ, and his portraits of artistic celebrities as in the grouping in *A Studio at Batignolles* (1870).

**FARADAY, Michael** (1791–1867), English chemist and physicist, the pupil and successor of H. DAVY at the ROYAL INSTITUTION, who discovered BENZENE (1824), first demonstrated electromagnetic INDUCTION (see also HENRY, JOSEPH) and invented the dynamo (1831—see GENERATOR, ELECTRIC), and who, with his concept of magnetic lines of force, laid the foundations of classical field theory later built upon by J. Clerk MAXWELL. In the course of many years of researches, he also discovered the laws of ELECTROLYSIS which bear his name and, in showing that the plane of polarization of plane POLARIZED LIGHT was rotated in a strong magnetic field, demonstrated a connection to exist between LIGHT and MAGNETISM.

**FARCE,** comedy based on exaggeration and broad visual humor. Its traditional ingredients are improbable situations and characters developed to their limits. Farcical elements are present in the plays of ARISTOPHANES, PLAUTUS, SHAKESPEARE, MOLIÈRE and many others, but only through such 19th-century writers as Georges Feydeau and W. S. GILBERT did farce become a respectable theatrical form.

**FAREL, Guillaume** (1489–1565), French reformer, converted to REFORMATION doctrines c1520. A powerful preacher, he was a leader in the REFORMED CHURCHES of French-speaking Switzerland, and brought John CALVIN to Geneva. From 1538 he worked at Neuchâtel.

**FARGO, William George** (1818–1881), cofounder of Wells and Company (later Wells-Fargo), the pioneer express service, in 1844. In 1850 it merged with other companies to become the American Express Company, of which he was president until his death.

**FARM BUREAU FEDERATION,** US organization for promoting and protecting the interests of farmers. Founded in 1920, it was made up of voluntary organizations from most states. It has an effective Washington lobby and provides insurance and marketing, export and investment advice facilities, as well as various publications. The federation has more than 3 million members.

**FARM CREDIT ADMINISTRATION,** US federal agency formed in 1933 by President Franklin D. ROOSEVELT out of other agencies to provide adequate finance facilities to revive farming. Part of the Department of Agriculture 1939–53, it then became independent again.

**FARMER, Fannie Merritt** (1857–1915), US cookery instructor, author of the *Boston Cooking School Cook Book* (1896) which introduced standard level measurements. She served as the director of the Boston Cooking School 1891–1902, when she opened a school of her own.

**FARMER, James Leonard** (1920–   ), US civil rights leader who founded the Congress of Racial Equality and headed it 1942–66, utilizing nonviolent techniques of protest. He was assistant Secretary of Health, Education, and Welfare 1969–70.

**FARMERS ORGANIZATION, National** (NFO), US farmers' union which acts as a bargaining agent in negotiating farm produce prices. It was formed in Iowa in 1955.

**FAROUK I** (1920–1965), king of Egypt 1936–52. He was weak and incompetent, and his rule was marked by corruption, alienation of the military and many internal rivalries. This led to a military coup headed by Gamar Abdel NASSER. which forced Farouk's abdication.

**FARQUHAR, George** (1678–1707), English comic dramatist. His most successful plays, *The Recruiting Officer* (1706) and *The Beaux' Stratagem* (1707), are characterized by vigorous language and pungent satire, and more realism than was then fashionable.

**FARRAGUT, David Glasgow** (1801–1870), US admiral, a Civil War hero. In 1862 he captured New Orleans, a Confederate supply center, by a bold maneuver. In 1863 he gained control of the Mississippi R. In a daring attack on Mobile Bay, Ala., in 1864 he gave the now proverbial command "Damn the torpedoes! Full speed ahead!"

**FARRAR, Geraldine** (1882–1967), US soprano. She studied with Lilli LEHMANN and made her debut in 1901 as Marguerite in FAUST in Berlin. Her famous roles included Mimi in LA BOHÈME, Carmen and Cio-Cio-San in *Madame Butterfly*, and in 1921 she introduced Charpentier's *Louise* at the Metropolitan.

**FARRELL, James Thomas** (1904–1979), US writer. He is known for his social novels, particularly the *Studs Lonigan* trilogy (1932–35), which depicts the often harsh life of the Irish on the Chicago South Side.

**FARSIGHTEDNESS.** See HYPEROPIA.

**FASCISM**, strictly, the political social system of Italy under MUSSOLINI 1922–45; (the name is derived from the FASCES); more generally, an authoritarian and antidemocratic political philosophy placing the corporate society, as embodied in the party and the state, above the individual, and stressing absolute obedience to a glorified leader. It is a reaction against the achievements of the ENLIGHTENMENT, the FRENCH REVOLUTION and LIBERALISM. It rejects both the 19th-century neutral state based on economic laissez-faire and also socialism, because fascism denies to separate social groups any independent political and economic activity. Instead it promotes an organic social order whereby the individual will find his own place in family, profession and society according to his character and ability. Nationalism and militarism are its logical products and thus it has close ties with NAZISM. "Fascist" has

become a term of abuse for many because of the ugly aspects of fascism, and is often used of anyone whose views are right wing.

The roots of fascism in Italy lie in the stagnant political situation with its chronic poverty, social unrest and manifold dissensions, worsened by the fact that the country had "won the war (WWI) but lost the peace." In 1919 Mussolini founded the *Fasci Italiani di Combattimento*, mainly ex-soldiers in black shirts who strove to overthrow the government by means of street fighting units. Regular fights ensued during 1921 between them and the communists. On 28 Oct. 1922, Mussolini, with four companions and followed by thousands of supporters, marched on Rome from Naples, where the king refused the prime minister's request for extraordinary powers, thus making way for Mussolini's first cabinet three days later.

Fascist movements spread to most western countries between WWI and WWII following in the wake of the economic crisis. Dollfuss and Schuschnigg headed a fascist government in Austria from 1933 until its incorporation into Germany in 1938, Horthy led one in Hungary, Pilsudski in Poland, Metaxas in Greece and Perón in Argentina. The longest surviving fascist regimes were in Portugal under Salazar and in Spain under Franco and the Falange.

**FASHION**, the prevailing style of dress, particularly new designs representing changes from previous seasons. Fashion in both dress and interior design is believed to have originated in 14th-century Europe and was set by monarchs and other prominent persons, with descriptions conveyed by travelers or in letters. The fashion doll was a popular means of transmitting the latest costume designs until the emergence of the first fashion magazine, thought to have originated in late 16th-century Germany. In the US, *Godey's Ladies' Book*, a precursor of *Vogue, Harper's Bazaar* and *Mademoiselle*, was established in 1830. For many decades it was the leading US source of fashion news, bringing to American women the latest creations from Paris, the leading arbiter of fashion since the Renaissance. By the mid-19th century, designer-dressmakers became prominent in the fashion world for the first time, and this coincided with a certain decline in the influence of celebrities. Fashion houses became the trend setters in female styles, Paris taking its place as the undisputed capital of *haute couture*, a distinction it continues to hold despite inroads by Italian, English, and, most recently, American designers. London led the way in men's fashions in the early 1800s, when such Regency dandies as Beau BRUMMELL were widely emulated, and briefly became a women's fashion leader in the mid-1960's with the Carnaby Street look, characterized by the popular mini-skirt. By the late 1970s, US designers had begun to compete successfully with Paris fashion greats and such names as HALSTON, BLASS and GALANOS were rivaling those of DIOR and SAINT-LAURENT in lustre.

**FASHODA INCIDENT**, confrontation between the French and British (Sept. 18, 1898), at the small town of Fashoda in the Sudan, over the desire of both nations to consolidate their African territories. The British under KITCHENER forced the French to relinquish claims to the region.

**FAST, Howard Melvin** (1914–   ), US writer of historical fiction, known for his strong stand on social issues. His works include *Citizen Tom Paine* (1943) and *Spartacus* (1952), and *April Morning* (1961). A one-time communist, he was imprisoned in 1947 for refusing to cooperate with the House Un-American Activities Committee and then blacklisted. In *The Naked God* (1957) he recounted his disillusion with communism.

**FATHER DIVINE**, pseudonym of George Baker (c1877–1965), black US religious leader whose Peace Mission sect, popular on the East Coast in the 1930s, demanded worship of him as God incarnate and communal celibate living.

**FATIMA**, village and sanctuary in central Portugal, famous for its shrine of the Virgin Mary. The shrine was created after several apparitions of the Virgin were reported here in 1917.

**FATS**, ESTERS of CARBOXYLIC ACIDS with GLYCEROL which are produced by animals and plants and form natural storage material. Fats are insoluble in water and occur naturally as either liquids or solids; those liquid at 20°C are normally termed oils and are generally found in plants and fishes. Oils generally contain esters of OLEIC ACID which can be converted to esters of the solid STEARIC ACID by HYDROGENATION in the presence of finely divided nickel. This process is basic to the manufacture of MARGARINE. Fats are the most concentrated sources of energy in the human diet, giving over twice the energy of STARCHES. Diets containing high levels of animal fats have been implicated as causative factors in heart disease, and substitution of animal fat by plant oils (e.g., peanut oil, sunflower oil) has been suggested. Fats particularly of fish and plant origin represent important items of commerce, and world production in 1976 reached 49 million tons. Of major importance are soybean oil (9–10 million tons), sunflower, palm, peanut, cottonseed, rapeseed and coconut oil (2.5–4 million tons each) and olive and fish oil (over 1 million tons each). Major producers include the US (soybean oil), the USSR (sunflower oil and cottonseed oil) and India (peanut oil).

**FAULKNER, William** (1897–1962), major US writer, known for his vivid characterization and complex, convoluted style in novels and short stories set in the fictional Yoknapatawpha Co., Miss. His best works are the novels *The Sound and the Fury* (1929), an experimental work influenced by James JOYCE, and *Light in August* (1932) and the haunting short story "A Rose for Emily." He painted a vivid picture of the decadent and dying South, seeing in it a microcosm of human destiny. In 1949 he was awarded the Nobel Prize for Literature. He also won two Pulitzer prizes (1955 and 1963).

**FAULT**, a fracture in the earth's crust along which there has been relative movement and displacement. *Dip-slip faults* involve movement up or down an inclined fault plane. Thus, *normal faults* result from tensional stress and involve a downward relative displacement of overlying rocks with respect to rocks underlying the fault plane. A *reverse* or *thrust fault* involves relative displacement upward of the overlying rocks and results from compressive stress. *Strike-slip faults* involve horizontal displacement and result from shearing stress. In PLATE TECTONICS, an important type of strike-slip fault that trends at right angles to and offsets plate boundaries along an oceanic ridge is called a *transform fault. Oblique-slip faults* are also known. The sudden release of accumulated long-term stresses through sudden rupturing of rock either creates a new fault or involves renewed displacement along an existing fault, a process responsible for most EARTHQUAKES.

**FAURÉ, Gabriel Urbain** (1845–1924), influential French composer, director of the Paris Conservatory 1905–20, where his pupils included RAVEL and ENESCO. He is famous for his songs, chamber music and large-scale works such as the *Requiem* (1887).

**FAUVISM**, art movement that developed in early 20th-century France, characterized by its bold use of brilliant color and rhythmic line. Hostile critics dubbed the group of artists painting in the style "*fauves,*" wild beasts. Its main members were MATISSE, DERAIN, BRAQUE, ROUALT,

VLAMINCK and DUFY. The movement, lasting c1898–c1908, was largely transitional; some Fauvists moved on to CUBISM.

**FAWKES, Guy** (1570–1606), Roman Catholic Englishman, hired by the GUNPOWDER PLOT conspirators as an explosives expert while he was serving in the Spanish army. Arrested while setting explosives beneath the House of Lords, he was tortured and hanged. In England he is burnt in effigy on Guy Fawkes Day, Nov. 5.

**FEBRUARY,** the second month of the year. Before Julius Caesar decreed that the year should begin in January, February was the last month of the year. The name is from the Latin *februarius*, purification; the month was then a time of religious purification for the new year.

**FEDERAL ARTS PROJECTS,** four projects begun by the US Work Projects Administration in 1935 to relieve the economic plight of many US people in the arts. The Art Project (1935–43) had around 5,000 employees, and produced artwork for public buildings and exhibitions. The Music Project (1935–43) operated many orchestras, bands and other organizations. The Theater Project (1935–39) put on performances of many old and new works, but was disbanded for its political bias. The Writers' Project (1935–39) produced hundreds of books on all aspects of US life.

**FEDERAL AVIATION ADMINISTRATION (FAA),** an agency of the US Department of Transportation created in 1958 to regulate air traffic. It shares responsibility with the CIVIL AERONAUTICS BOARD. The agency's main responsibility is the operation and maintenance of the national air traffic control system in the interests of efficiency and safety. In 1981 the FAA terminated the services of some 2,000 air controllers who struck in violation of federal law, and it began to hire and train new employees as controllers of the nation's reduced aircraft traffic. (See AIR TRAFFIC CONTROLLERS' ORGANIZATION.)

**FEDERAL BUREAU OF INVESTIGATION (FBI),** investigative branch of the US Department of Justice. Established in 1908, it is headed by a director appointed by the president, subject to Senate confirmation. Its headquarters are in Washington, D.C. In general, the FBI is responsible for the investigation of possible violations of all federal laws except those for which enforcement is specifically assigned to another agency, and is also concerned with internal security, counterespionage, organized crime and corruption (see ABSCAM). FBI history was dominated by J. Edgar HOOVER, director 1924–72, a conservative

figure who held the post until his death. Its first permanent director after Hoover was Clarence M. Kelley, who served 1973–78 and modernized the bureau's procedures. William H. Webster (1924–    ), exfederal judge and FBI director 1978, restructured the bureau in the light of revelations that its agents had committed illegal acts during Hoover's tenure (see COINTELPRO).

**FEDERAL COMMUNICATIONS COMMISSION (FCC),** an independent agency of the federal government, directly responsible to the US Congress, which regulates communication by radio, television, wire and cable. Created in 1934, it has seven members appointed by the president. Its most important functions are the licensing of commercial radio and television stations, the assignment of broadcasting frequencies, the supervision of other radio services and regulation of interstate communications services.

**FEDERAL CROP INSURANCE CORPORATION,** agency of the US Department of Agriculture, created by the 1938 Crop Insurance Act. It insures farmers against crop loss caused by natural hazards; loss through bad farming is not so covered and profit is not guaranteed.

**FEDERAL DEPOSIT INSURANCE CORPORATION (FDIC),** federal corporation which insures almost all bank deposits in the US, created by the 1933 Banking Act. All FEDERAL RESERVE SYSTEM banks must insure with FDIC. In the case of failure of an insured bank, the FDIC reimburses each depositor up to a maximum sum. It also acts as a watchdog over banking practices.

**FEDERAL ENERGY REGULATORY COMMISSION,** independent five-member commission within the US Department of Energy. Retaining many functions of the Federal Power Commission, it sets rates for transportation of oil by pipeline, levies charges for the transportation and sale of natural gas and electricity, and licenses hydroelectric power plants.

**FEDERAL HALL NATIONAL MEMORIAL,** stands on Wall and Nassau streets, Manhattan Island, New York City. The site was first occupied by the colonial city hall, which became the first US capitol 1781–89; it was rebuilt as Federal Hall. The present building was completed in 1842 and designated a national memorial in 1955.

**FEDERALIST PAPERS,** collection of American political essays written in support of the proposed US Constitution, published serially 1787–88. Written anonymously by Alexander HAMILTON, James MADISON and John JAY, the papers were later collected in book form and published under the title *The Federalist*. They provide a classic exposition of the US federal system.

**FEDERALIST PARTY,** first true US political party. Founded by Alexander HAMILTON c1789, it was in general supported by prosperous citizens who wanted a strong central government. It dominated the government 1794–1800 but lost support among the lower middle class to Thomas JEFFERSON's Democratic Republican Party. After Jefferson won the election of 1800, the Federalist Party endured until 1816 only, remaining as a New England party until the 1820s.

**FEDERAL NATIONAL MORTGAGE ASSOCIATION** (FNMA, or "Fanny Mae"), government-sponsored corporation which acts as a secondary mortgage market for banks. Created by Congress in 1938, Fanny Mae helped make mortgage funds widely available in the post-WWII housing surge.

**FEDERAL POWER COMMISSION** (FPC), independent regulatory agency which oversees the electricity and natural gas industries. The FPC regulates rates and business practices of all public utilities and wholesale supplies of gas and electricity in interstate commerce. It is also responsible for regulating hydroelectric projects.

**FEDERAL RESERVE SYSTEM,** central US banking authority, created by the Federal Reserve Act of 1913. It consists of a board of governors, 12 Federal Reserve banks, the Federal Open Market Committee and Advisory Council, and the member banks, which account for about 85% of the country's banking. All national banks must belong to the System; state banks may also join. The System is the basic arm of the monetary side of national economic management. By buying securities it expands bank reserves, enabling banks to expand loans and stimulate economic activity. When it sells, it contracts bank reserves, reducing lending and slowing the economy (these are called open-market operations). The System may also affect the volume of banks' lending by changing the statutory amount of reserves they must hold and by changing the rate at which member banks may borrow from the System.

**FEDERAL STYLE,** in architecture and the decorative arts, the dominant style in the US from c1790 to c1830. Like the COLONIAL STYLE but more developed and often more monumental, it is based on French and Italian Renaissance designs as well as English Palladian precedents. Graceful in proportions and delicate in design, the federal style is typified by slender, fluted columns; large, freestanding porticoes brick walls trimly accented with white at the openings; entrances topped by fanlights and, in general, curvilinear decorative forms. Major exponents were Charles BULFINCH in Boston and Samuel McIntire in Salem, Mass. The style is seen in many state capitols.

**FEDERAL TRADE COMMISSION** (FTC), a federal agency established in 1914 to prevent unfair business practices, particularly monopolies, and to maintain a competitive economy. Its five commissioners are appointed by the president subject to Senate confirmation. The FTC studies the effects of business mergers and price agreements, issuing cease and desist orders if their effects prove undesirable. It also attempts to prevent misleading advertising and protect public health.

**FEEDBACK,** the use of the output of a system to control its performance. Many examples of feedback systems can be found in the life sciences, particularly in ecology biochemistry and physiology. Thus the population of a species will grow until it overexploits its food supply. Malnutrition then leads to a reduction in population. In the design of machines, SERVOMECHANISMS and GOVERNORS also exemplify feedback systems. The most important application of the feedback concept in modern technology comes in ELECTRONICS where it is common practice to feed some of the output of an AMPLIFIER back to the input to help reduce NOISE, distortion or instability. Most often used is "negative feedback" in which the effect of the feedback is to reduce the amplifier's output while stabilizing its performance. The howling that can occur when too much sound from a LOUDSPEAKER enters the MICROPHONE of a public address system is an example of positive feedback Feedback plays an essential role in CYBERNETICS. (See also MECHANIZATION AND AUTOMATION.)

**FEIFFER, Jules** (1929–    ), US cartoonist whose sparsely drawn neurotic characters reflect the insecurities of contemporary urban America. His strip, *Feiffer* appeared in the *Village Voice* (from 1956) and in several books. He also wrote the play *Little Murders* (1967) and the screenplay for *Carnal Knowledge* (1971).

**FEININGER, Lyonel** (1871–1956), US artist. Influenced by CUBISM, his style is based on interpenetrating prismatic planes of color that create geometric designs. He lived in Germany 1887–1936, teaching at the BAUHAUS 1919–32. Also a caricaturist, he produced a memorable weekly comic page for the Chicago *Tribune* in 1906–07.

**ELLER, Robert William Andrew** (1919– ), US baseball star, a pitcher with the Cleveland Indians 1936–42 and 1944–56. In 1946 he set a season record of 48 strike-outs. He was elected to the Baseball Hall of Fame in 1962.

**ELLINI, Federico** (1920– ), Italian film director. His early films, such as *La Strada* (1954) and *La Dolce Vita* (1960), portray human disillusionment in a corrupt society. Later films such as *8½* (1963), *Juliet of the Spirits* (1964), *Satyricon* (1970) and *Amarcord* (1974), have a more personal style, often dream-like and fantastic.

**ELONY,** a criminal offense more serious than a MISDEMEANOR. In US law the distinction between the two categories is generally the severity of the prescribed penalty for the offense. HOMICIDE, ROBBERY, BURGLARY, THEFT and RAPE are the main felonies.

**EMINISM.** See WOMEN'S RIGHTS.

**ENCING,** sport of combat with swords. It descended from the DUEL, but in fencing the object is only to touch, not to wound, one's opponent. Fencers wear protective clothing and masks. Three weapons are used; the light, rectangular foil, the stiffer, triangular épée and the triangular two-edged saber. Only the tip of the foil and épée may be used to score hits; saber scores may be made with the point or by a cut. In foil and saber fencing hits may only be made in certain parts of the body. Matches take place on a measured strip or *piste*. In men's bouts the first to be hit five times loses, in women's four times.

**ENIAN BROTHERHOOD,** Irish-American revolutionary society, founded in 1858 by Irish exile John O'Mahony. The movement achieved little in Ireland but made sporadic terrorist attacks in Canada 1866–71. It collapsed with O'Mahony's death in 1877.

**ERBER, Edna** (1887–1968), US author famous for her epic popular novels set in the 19th- and 20th-century US, such as *So Big* (1924), for which she won a 1925 Pulitzer Prize, *Show Boat* (1926), *Cimarron* (1930), *Saratoga Trunk* (1941) and *Giant* (1952).

**ERDINAND,** name of three kings of Spain. **Ferdinand II of Aragon** (1452–1516), married Isabella of Castile in 1469, becoming her consort in Castile in 1474. In 1492 he conquered the Moorish kingdom of Granada, becoming effective king of Spain. A supporter of the Spanish Inquisition, he expelled the Jews from Spain. Isabella, rather than he, was COLUMBUS' sponsor. **Ferdinand VI** (1713–1759), came to the throne in 1746. A capable ruler and patron of the arts, he carried out many administrative reforms and managed to keep Spain neutral during the SEVEN YEARS' WAR. **Ferdinand VII** (1784–1833), acceded in 1808 when his father Charles IV was deposed by a revolt; he was himself deposed by Napoleon two months later and imprisoned until his restoration in 1814. A cruel and repressive absolutist, he was deposed 1820–23 and only restored by a French army. Of limited ability, he was unable to prevent the complete loss of Spain's American possessions.

**FERENCZI, Sándor** (1873–1933), Hungarian psychoanalyst, and an early colleague of FREUD, best known for his experiments in PSYCHOTHERAPY, in course of which he broke away from Freud's classic psychoanalytic theory. (See PSYCHOANALYSIS.)

**FERLINGHETTI, Lawrence** (1919– ), US poet of the BEAT GENERATION, founder of the City Lights bookstore and publishing house. His poetry was generally a means of political expression. The best known collection is *A Coney Island of the Mind* (1958).

**FERMAT, Pierre de** (1601–1665), French mathematician best remembered for **Fermat's Principle,** that the path of light traveling between two points by REFLECTION is that taking least time; and **Fermat's Last Theorem,** that $x^n + y^n - z^n = 0$, where $x$, $y$, $z \neq 0$ and $n > 2$, is impossible for integral $x$, $y$, $z$ and $n$. (See NUMBERS, THEORY OF.)

**FERMENTATION,** the decomposition of CARBOHYDRATES by microorganisms in the absence of air. Louis PASTEUR first demonstrated that fermentation is a biochemical process, each type being caused by one species. It is an aspect of bacterial and fungal METABOLISM, in which GLUCOSE and other sugars are oxidized by ENZYME catalysis to pyruvic acid (see CITRIC ACID CYCLE). Pyruvic acid is then reduced to LACTIC ACID or degraded to carbon dioxide and ETHANOL. Considerable energy is released in this process: some is stored as the high-energy compound ATP (see NUCLEOTIDES), and the rest is given off as heat. Fermentation by YEAST has been used for centuries in BREWING and making bread and wine; fermentation by lactic acid bacteria is used to make cheese. Special fermentations are used industrially for the manufacture of ACETONE, butanol (see ALCOHOLS), GLYCEROL, CITRIC ACID, glutamic acid (see MONOSODIUM GLUTAMATE) and many other compounds. (See also RESPIRATION.)

**FERMI, Enrico** (1901–1954), Italian

atomic physicist who was awarded the 1938 Nobel Prize for Physics. His first important contribution was his examination of the properties of a hypothetical gas whose particles obeyed Pauli's EXCLUSION PRINCIPLE; the laws he derived can be applied to the ELECTRONS in a metal, and explain many of the properties of metals. Later he showed that NEUTRON bombardment of most elements produced their RADIOISOTOPES. He built the world's first NUCLEAR REACTOR (1942).

**FERNS,** nonflowering plants of the class Filicineae having creeping or erect RHIZOMES or an erect aerial stem and large conspicuous leaves. Spores are produced on the underside of the leaf within sporangia and germinate to form the GAMETOPHYTE or sexual stage of the life cycle. Ferns are widely distributed throughout the world, but the majority grow in the tropics. Many ferns are popular house plants, e.g. *Nephrolepis* (Boston ferns), *Pteris* (maidenhair ferns), *Platycerium* (staghorn ferns) and *Asplenium* (bird's nest ferns). Indoors they require a reasonably bright position but avoiding direct sunlight; they flourish under fluorescent lighting. They grow best at temperatures between 16°C and 21°C (60°F and 70°F) and will tolerate temperatures as high as 24°C (75°F) so long as the air is fresh and humid. They should be watered often enough to keep the soil evenly moist and most benefit from daily misting. They can be propagated from spores, but normally by division of the plant or by rhizome cuttings.

**FERRARA,** historic capital city of Ferrara province, N Italy. Always an agricultural center, it has become industrialized since WWII. It contains a number of medieval and Renaissance structures, including the Cathedral of San Giorgio (1185), the Castello Estense (begun in 1385), the Palazzo del Commune and the Palazzo della Ragione.

**FERRET** *Mustelo furo*, a domesticated POLECAT, normally about 350mm (13.8in) long, which is bred in Europe to kill vermin and, in hunting, to drive rabbits from burrows. The wild, black-footed ferret of the western US is a close relative.

**FERRY, Jules François Camille** (1832–1893), French statesman. A republican opponent of the Second Empire, he held many offices in the Third Republic, becoming premier 1880–81 and 1883–85. He sought to exclude the clergy from education, and directed the acquisition of many colonies.

**FERTILE CRESCENT,** area in the Middle East, extending in an arc or crescent from the N coast of the Persian Gulf to the E coast of the Mediterranean. Natural irrigation made this semi-arid land fertile; i gave birth to the Sumerian, Phoenician and Hebrew civilizations. (See also MESOPOTA MIA.)

**FERTILIZATION,** the union of two GAMETES, or male and female sex cells, to produce a CELL from which a new individual animal or plant, develops. The sex cells contain half the normal number o CHROMOSOMES, and fertilization therefore produces a cell with the normal number o chromosomes for any particular species Fertilization may take place outside the organism's body (external fertilization), o inside the female (internal fertilization) as a result of copulation.

**FERTILIZERS,** materials added to the soil to provide elements needed for plant NUTRITION, and so to enable healthy growth of crops with high yield. The element needed in large quantities are NITROGEN PHOSPHORUS, POTASSIUM, SULFUR, CALCIUM and MAGNESIUM; the last three are usually adequately supplied in the soil o incidentally in other fertilizers. Small amounts of TRACE ELEMENTS are also needed and usually supplied in fertilizers. The choice of compounds or materials containing nitrogen, phosphorus and potassium depends mainly on cost. The traditional natural fertilizers—BONE MEAL, GUANO and MANURE—are now too expensive to be much used outside HORTICULTURE. Potassium is supplied as potassium chloride, widely available as SYLVITE. Phosphorus fertilizers are obtained from mineral PHOSPHATES especially APATITE; some is used as such, but most is converted to ammonium phosphate or superphosphate (see PHOSPHATES Nitrogen is supplied as AMMONIA (injected under pressure), ammonium salts, NITRATE (ammonium nitrate being most useful) and UREA (see also NITROGEN CYCLE; NITROGEN FIXATION). Fertilizers in excess may harm crops and cause EUTROPHICATION.

**FETUS,** the developing intrauterine form of an animal, loosely used to describe it from the development of the fertilized egg (EMBRYO), but strictly referring in man to the period from three months gestation to BIRTH. During fetal life, organ development is consolidated and specialization extended so that function may be sufficiently mature at birth; some organs start to function before birth in preparation for independent existence. During the fetal period most increase in size occurs, both in the fetus and in the PLACENTA and WOMB. The fetus lies in a sac of AMNIOTIC FLUID which protects and allows it to move about. Blood

CIRCULATION in the fetus is adapted to the placenta as the source of OXYGEN and nutrients and site for waste excretion, but alternative channels are developed so that within moments of birth they may take over. Should the fetus be delivered prematurely, immaturity of the LUNGS may cause respiratory distress, that of the LIVER, resulting in JAUNDICE.

**FEUDALISM,** system of social, economic and political relationships that shaped society in medieval Europe. It originated in the 8th century and flourished from the 10th to the 13th centuries. Thereafter it declined, although in Europe and Russia many feudal institutions persisted into the 19th century. The system rested on the obedience and service of a vassal to his lord in return for protection, maintenance and, most particularly, a tenancy of land (a *fief*). The duty owed by a vassal included military service, counsel and attendance at court, and contribution towards the lord's extraordinary expenditures such as ransoms or dowries. At the apex of the social pyramid was the king, vassal only to God. His vassals were his great nobles, holding land or some other source of income in fief from him. They in turn invested, or *enfeoffed* (so, "feodal" or "feudal") their own vassals, the lords of the manor. At the base of the pyramid were the serfs, or villeins, permanently tied to the land. They worked both for the lord and for themselves, unpaid; serfdom offered a degree of security in that if a serf could not leave the land, neither could it be taken from him.

In effect feudalism tended to allow vassal lords unrestricted freedom, at least in their own holdings. With the tendency towards centralized government this liberty was curbed. The system assumed a subsistence economy; the growth of trade and of economically powerful towns attacked it, and by the 15th century it was dying out.

**FEUERBACH, Ludwig Andreas** (1804–1872), German materialist philosopher, a major influence on MARX. He rejected HEGEL's Idealism, and in such works as *The Essence of Christianity* (1841) he analyzed the Christian concept of God as an illusory fulfillment of human psychological needs.

**FEVER,** raising of body TEMPERATURE above normal (37°C or 98.6°F in man), usually caused by DISEASE. Infection, INFLAMMATION, heat stroke and some TUMORS are important causes. Fever is produced by pyrogens, which are derived from cell products, and alter the set level of temperature-regulating centers in the HYPOTHALAMUS. Fever may be continuous, intermittent or remittent, the distinction helping to determine the cause. Anti-inflammatory drugs (e.g., ASPIRIN) reduce fever; STEROIDS mask it.

**FEZ,** or Fés, historic city in N Morocco, long important as a trading center and as a center for Islamic studies. It has over 100 mosques, of which the Qarawiyin, dominating the university, is reputedly the largest in Africa. The old city was founded in 808. Pop 325,327.

**FIANNA FÁIL,** Irish political party, formed in 1926 in opposition to the terms of the 1921 Anglo-Irish treaty. Led by Eamonn DE VALERA, it came to power in 1932 and, except for brief periods it remained the dominant party in Ireland.

**FIBER,** a thin thread of natural or artificial material. **Animal fibers** include wool, from the fluffy coat of the sheep, and silk, the fiber secreted by the silkworm LARVA to form its cocoon. **Vegetable fibers** include COTTON, FLAX, HEMP, JUTE and SISAL: they are mostly composed of LIGNIN, though CELLULOSE is also important. **Mineral fibers** are generally loosely termed ASBESTOS. These fibrous mineral SILICATES are mined in South Africa, Canada and elsewhere. **Man-made fibers** are of two types: regenerated fibers, extracted from natural substances (e.g., rayon is cellulose extracted from wood pulp); and SYNTHETIC FIBERS. Most PAPER is made from wood fiber. (See also COTTON GIN; SPINNING; WEAVING.)

**FIBERGLASS,** GLASS drawn or blown into extremely fine fibers that retain the tensile strength of glass while yet being flexible. The most used form is fused QUARTZ, which when molten can be easily drawn and which is resistant to chemical attack. Most often, the molten glass is forced through tiny orifices in a platinum plate, on the far side of which the fine fibers are united (though not twisted) and wound onto a suitable spindle. Fiberglass mats (**glass wool**) are formed from shorter fibers at random directions bonded together with a thermo-setting RESIN; they may be pressed into predetermined shapes. Known in ancient Egypt, fiberglass is now used in INSULATION, automobile bodies, etc.

**FIBONACCI, Leonardo,** or **Leonardo of Pisa** (c1180–c1240), Italian mathematician whose *Liber Abaci* (1202) was probably the first European account of the mathematics of India and Arabia, including some material on ALGEBRA. He also devised the FIBONACCI SEQUENCE.

**FICHTE, Johann Gottlieb** (1762–1814), German philosopher, an early exponent of ethical idealism, for whom the ego was the primary metaphysical and epistemological principle. His work influenced HEGEL and SCHOPENHAUER, among others. Some of his theories prefigured socialism; his concept of the nation as a manifestation of divine order, combined with his fanatical patriotism, stimulated German nationalism.

**FICINO, Marsilio** (1433–1499), Italian philosopher who headed the Renaissance revival of Platonism. He translated all of PLATO into Latin, and under the aegis of Cosimo de MEDICI taught a form of Platonism reconciled with Christianity.

**FIEDLER, Arthur** (1894–1979), US conductor, famous for his concerts and records of high quality light music with the Boston Pops Orchestra. A player in the Boston Symphony Orchestra 1915–30, he was the Pops conductor from 1930 until his death.

**FIEDLER, Leslie A(aron)** (1917–    ), US social historian and literary critic, noted for his provocative opinions in such works as *An End to Innocence: Essays on Culture and Politics* (1955). Among his other works are *The Jew in the American Novel* (1959), *Being Busted* (1969) and *Collected Essays* (1971). He has also written stories, novels, and poetry.

**FIEGUEREDO, João** (1918–    ), Brazilian general and president (1979–    ). Head of the Brazilian national intelligence service 1974–78, he became the fifth military man to succeed to the presidency since the army seized power in 1964. Despite his regime's reputation for human rights abuses, he promised a gradual restoration of democracy.

**FIELD**, US family prominent in law and industry in the 19th century. **Cyrus West Field** (1819–1892), an industrialist, financed the laying of the first permanently operational transatlantic telegraph cable in 1866. His elder brother **David Dudley Field** (1805–1894), a jurist, was appointed by N.Y. in 1857 to draw up civil, political and penal codes, the last of which was subsequently adopted. Other states adopted all three. In 1873, he became the first president of the International Law Association. A third brother, **Stephen Johnson Field** (1816–1899), was also a distinguished jurist. He rose to become chief justice of Cal. and in 1863 was appointed to the US Supreme Court.

**FIELD**, influential US mercantile and publishing family. **Marshall Field I** (1834–1906) established one of the world's first and largest department stores. His donations established the U. of Chicago and the city's Art Institute and Field Museum of Natural History. **Marshall Field III**

(1893–1956), publisher and philanthropist, began the *Chicago Sun* (later Sun-Times) in 1941, and published the *World Book Encyclopedia*, and various magazines. **Marshal Field IV** (1916–1965), expanded and increased the Field publishing concerns.

**FIELD HOCKEY**, a stick and ball game played on a field by two teams of eleven. Each team defends its own goal and the object of the game is to hit the 5½ oz white ball into the opponent's goal as many times as possible. The game, of uncertain origin, was nationally organized in England in 1886. It was introduced into the US in 1902, and is today a popular sport in over 70 countries.

**FIELDING, Henry** (1707–1754), English novelist, dramatist and essayist. His satirical comedies angered the Whig premier Sir Robert WALPOLE, and Fielding had to abandon the stage and turn to the law. He then wrote two novels, *Joseph Andrews* (1742) and *Tom Jones* (1749). Boisterous, picaresque works, they burlesque the stilted sentimentality then fashionable. He became a magistrate in 1748; he helped organize the Bow Street Runners, an early police force.

**FIELD-ION MICROSCOPE**, an instrument producing very beautiful pictures of the arrangement of individual ATOMS in materials drawn out into, or evaporated on to, a fine tip, typically 40nm in radius. Invented by Erwin Wilhelm Müller (1911–    ) in 1936, the microscope is lensless, the image being produced on a fluorescent screen by IONS created in a low pressure gas by the intense ELECTRIC FIELD at the tip when it is positively charged to a few kilovolts.

**FIELDS, W. C.** (pseudonym of Claude William Dukenfield, 1880–1946), US comedian and actor, characterized both on and off stage as a cantankerous but witty misogynist and child-hater. He began in VAUDEVILLE as a juggler but rose to fame in movies, many of which, such as the classic farce *The Bank Dick* (1940), he wrote himself. He was acclaimed for his portrayal of Mr. Micawber in *David Copperfield* (1935).

**FIJI**, since 1970 an independent state within the British Commonwealth, an island group in the SW Pacific. It contains around 100 inhabited islands, of which the largest are Viti Levu, with the capital city Suva, and Vanua Levu. The larger islands are volcanic in origin, the rest are coral atolls or reefs. The climate is tropical, rainfall averaging over 100in a year and temperatures 65°–95°F. The original

**Official name:** Fiji
**Capital:** Suva
**Area:** 7,055sq mi
**Population:** 618,979
**Languages:** Fijian; Hindustani; English
**Religions:** Christian, Hindu
**Monetary unit(s):** 1 Fiji dollar = 100 cents

Melanesian and Polynesian inhabitants are now only 40% of the population, outnumbered by Indian immigrants.

Sugarcane and coconuts are the main crops; dairying is increasingly important. Tourism, sugar milling and copra processing are major industries. First visited by Abel TASMAN in 1643 and James COOK in 1774, the islands were offered to Britain by a chieftain in 1858 but not accepted until 1874.

**FILARIASIS,** a group of PARASITIC DISEASES of warm climates, transmitted by MOSQUITOS, causing FEVER, LYMPH node enlargement, ABSCESSES, epididymal inflammation and signs of ALLERGY: ELEPHANTIASIS may result. A specific type, onchocerciasis, or river blindness, leads to SKIN rash, EYE disease, sometimes causing BLINDNESS, and muscle pains or nodules. Some cause LUNG disease and increased BLOOD eosinophils. Diagnosis is by special staining of blood films and skin tests. Treatment and prevention are with diethylcarbamine; mosquito control is needed.

**FILENE, Edward Albert** (1860–1937), US merchant who, as president of William Filene's Sons, Boston, pioneered such new methods of retailing as the "bargain basement." He was also a founder of the US Chamber of Commerce.

**FILIGREE,** a form of fine-wire decoration usually made of gold or silver. It may be applied to a background or used as open lacework. Gold and silver are preferred because they lend themselves readily to the forming of intricate designs when reduced to thin wires. Filigree decoration was practiced in ancient Greece, China and Egypt. Fine examples of filigree may be found today in Israel and Mexico.

**FILLMORE, Millard** (1800–1874), 13th US president. Fillmore stepped into office on the death of President Zachary Taylor in 1850. He served only 2½ years and assumed the role of moderator in the fierce national and congressional debates of the pre-Civil War period.

Born in Summerhill, N.Y., and trained as a lawyer, Fillmore was first elected to the US House of Representatives in 1832, serving from 1833–35 and again from 1837–43. In 1848 he was elected to the vice-presidency on the Whig ticket under Taylor. His principal achievement as president 1850–53 was a trade agreement with Japan. He supported the COMPROMISE OF 1850 as avoiding a North–South clash, although himself against slavery. This damaged his reelection chances, and on March 4, 1853, Fillmore left office after failing to win renomination with the Whig party. He finally retired from public life in 1856 after an unsuccessful candidacy for the KNOW-NOTHING Party.

**FILM.** See MOTION PICTURES.

**FINCHES,** small seed-eating birds of the family Fringillidae—canaries, grosbeaks, sparrows, cardinals, crossbills and buntings. Finches are characterized by their conical bills, used for opening seeds. Many members of the family number among the familiar song-birds of town and country.

**Official name:** Finland
**Capital:** Helsinki
**Area:** 130,094sq mi
**Population:** 4,780,000
**Languages:** Finnish, Swedish, Lappish
**Religions:** Evangelical Lutheran Church
**Monetary unit(s):** 1 Markka = 100 penni

**FINLAND,** independent republic in N Europe, bordered by arms of the Baltic Sea in the SW and W, by the USSR in the E and by Norway and Sweden in the N and NW. An independent country only since 1917, it has made great contributions to European culture, among them the music of Jan SIBELIUS and the work of architects Alvar AALTO and Eliel and Eero SAARINEN.

**Land.** The central plateau, glacial relatively recently, is low-lying. Lakes, which cover about 9% of the whole country, extend over about 20%–50% of the central lakeland, creating a labyrinth of waterways. The N uplands, about 40% of the country, pass from forest into swamplands, and then into barren Arctic tundra; 30% of the country lies above the Arctic circle. The coastal lowlands are fertile, with a mild climate fostered by the Gulf Stream. The major cities, Turku and Helsinki, are situated here, as is most of the country's farmland. The coastal archipelago is largely barren.

**People.** The Lapps, nomadic reindeer herders, live in the N, numbering only about 1,500. There is a Swedish-speaking minority along the coasts, but the remaining 92% of the people are Finns. Around 60% of the population is now urban, compared with 9% in 1880. Educational standards have long been high and illiteracy is minimal; there are five universities. Most of the population belongs to the Lutheran National Church. Government is by elected president and single-chamber parliament.

**Economy.** Before WWII Finland remained predominantly agricultural, but manufacturing has now expanded until agriculture and forestry account for around only 8% of the national output. The economy is largely managed by private enterprise, but the government has often intervened because of capital shortage. Forests remain the most important national resource, covering 70% of the total land area.

**History.** Finland was colonized from the S, and by the 9th century formed three tribal states, Karelia, Tavastenland and Suomi. Sweden progressively colonized the area and after the 14th century Finland became a Swedish grand duchy. In 1809 Sweden was forced to cede it to Russia. Tsar Alexander I maintained the country as a grand duchy but allowed it considerable autonomy under a governor-general. This period saw the rise of nationalism: the Swedish language was replaced by Finnish, particularly after the publication of the national folk-epic, the KALEVALA. In 1863 the legislative Diet was revived and political parties developed. Under Alexander III a policy of "Russification" was adopted and generally bitterly resisted until WWI. In 1917 the parliament declared independence from the new regime in Russia, and Bolshevik forces were defeated in a brief civil war. In 1919 a republic was declared. In 1939, in breach of a non-aggression pact, the USSR invaded Finland, but was stalled by fierce resistance. For the German aid Finland then received it was made to pay massive postwar reparations to the USSR and lost S Karelia. During the postwar period, the Finnish government, dominated by the Social Democratic Party and the Agrarian Party under KEKKONEN, has sought a peaceful rapprochement with the USSR, despite much Soviet interference in Finnish affairs.

**FINNEY, Albert** (1936–    ), English stage and film actor, notable for the range of his talents. His films include *Saturday Night and Sunday Morning* (1960), *Tom Jones* (1963) and *Death on the Nile* (1978). He played Macbeth, Martin Luther and Coriolanus on the stage.

**FINNISH,** the most important of the UGRO-FINNIC LANGUAGES, spoken by around 5 million people in Finland. It has a written tradition dating from the 16th century but only achieved official status in the 19th century.

**FIRBANK, (Arthur Annesley) Ronald** (1886–1926), English novelist known for his eccentric and often innovative style and his fluent verbal wit. Among his best-known works are *Vainglory* (1915), *Inclinations* (1916) and *Valmouth* (1919).

**FIRDAUSI,** penname of the great Persian poet Abul Qasim Mansur (c940–1020), author of the *Shah-Nameh* (Book of Kings), Persia's national epic. The poem, 60,000 verses long, took him 35 years and appears to have ruined him financially.

**FIRE ANTS,** mainly tropical ants with extremely painful stings. Two species, one introduced from Argentina, are found in the southern US, and are a pest in fruit plantations.

**FIREARMS,** weapons in which missiles are projected by firing explosive charges. They are classified as either ARTILLERY or small arms. The latter seem to have originated in 14th-century Europe in the form of metal tubes, closed at one end, into which GUNPOWDER and the missile were packed, the charge being ignited via a touch hole. The heavy **harquebus** was one of these. The 15th century saw the introduction of the **matchlock** in which a spring-loaded lever mechanism was used to introduce a smoldering match (a hemp cord soaked in SALTPETER) to the powder. This was superseded in the next century by the **wheel lock**. In this a serrated wheel rotated against a flint and ignited the powder with a spark. In the 17th century the **flintlock** was introduced. Here a flint held in a spring-loaded arm, or cock, struck a metal hammer, or frizzen, to produce the spark. The perfecting of the gas-tight breechblock and the modern percussion lock in the early 19th century led to the development of the breech-loading RIFLE and the repeating pistol (see REVOLVER). By the end of the century, MACHINE GUNS were in an advanced state of development. SHOTGUNS, used mainly for sport, fire a cartridge containing numerous small pellets. (See also AIR GUN; AMMUNITION; PISTOL.)

**FIRE CONTROL,** the techniques and operations ensuring that a missile, shell or depth charge lands on target. When the target is visible and stationary the problem is relatively simple (see BALLISTICS), and accurate sights, firing tables, etc., are used. Such devices as RADAR, SONAR, RADIO and TELEPHONE communications and COMPUTER control have become parts of increasingly complex and sophisticated systems. Artillery guns can now be trained by computer. Laser systems allow pinpoint accuracy in target location.

**FIREDAMP.** See DAMP.

**FIRE EXTINGUISHER,** a portable appliance for putting out small fires. Extinguishers work either by cooling or by depriving the fire of OXYGEN (as typified by the simplest, a bucket of water or bucket of sand), and most do both. The **soda-acid extinguisher** contains a SODIUM bicarbonate solution and a small, stoppered bottle of SULFURIC ACID: depression of a plunger shatters the bottle, mixing the chemicals so that CARBON dioxide ($CO_2$) gas is generated, forcing the water out of a nozzle. **Foam extinguishers** employ a foaming agent (usually animal PROTEIN or certain detergents) and an aerating agent: they are effective against oil fires, as they float on the surface. **Carbon dioxide extinguishers** provide a smothering blanket of $CO_2$; and **dry chemical extinguishers** provide a powder of mainly sodium bicarbonate, from which the fire's heat generates $CO_2$.

**FIREFLIES,** mainly tropical soft-bodied BEETLES which produce an intermittent greenish light in their abdominal organs. The light is created by the oxidation of luciferin under the influence of an ENZYME, luciferase. In some species females are without wings and are known as **glowworms**. The lights serve to attract mates.

**FIRE PROTECTION,** the prevention and control of fires, one of the most essential community services. Volunteer firefighting organizations are known to have existed in ancient Egypt, Rome and many other countries, but the first attempts to cope with fires in the modern fashion began after the Great Fire of London in 1666. After this the first regulations controlling building materials and techniques to avoid fire risks were passed. Also at this time the flourishing fire insurance companies set up brigades with pumps mounted on handcarts, to attend to their customers only. In the early 19th century fast horsecarts were used to carry the pumps, and soon after steam-driven pumps were introduced. The extensible ladder was developed c1800, and the wheeled escape ladder in 1837. In 1865 the communal fire department of the insurance companies was taken over and expanded into the London Metropolitan Fire Brigade, ancestor of modern brigades. In the US the trend was similar. The first volunteer fire organization in America was founded by Benjamin Franklin in Philadelphia in 1736. In the US also it was the insurance companies which established fire brigades, and these were eventually taken over by the municipalities. Small towns, however, often still have a wholly or partly volunteer service.

**FIRESTONE, Harvey Samuel** (1868–1938), US industrialist, founder of one of the largest rubber companies in the world, the Firestone Tire & Rubber Company. His million acre rubber plantation in Liberia played a large role in the country's economic development from 1926.

**FIREWORKS,** combustible or explosive preparations used for entertainment, probably first devised in ancient China to frighten off devils. Their initial European use was as weaponry (see GREEK FIRE) and not until after about 1500 were they employed for entertainment. Compounds of CARBON, POTASSIUM and SULFUR are the prime constituents in fireworks, colors being produced by metallic salts (e.g., blue, COPPER; yellow, SODIUM; red, LITHIUM or STRONTIUM; green, BARIUM), sparks and crackles by powdered IRON, CARBON or ALUMINUM, or by certain LEAD salts. (See also EXPLOSIVES; GUNPOWDER.)

**FIRST AID,** treatment that can be given by minimally-trained people for accident, injury and sudden illness, until more skilled persons arrive or the patient is transferred to hospital. Recognition of the injury or the nature of the illness and its gravity are crucial first measures, along with prevention of further injury to the patient or helpers. Clues such as medical bracelets or cards, tablets, lumps of sugar, alcohol and evidence of external injury should be sought and appropriate action taken. Arrest of breathing should be treated as a priority by clearing the airway of dentures, gum, vomit and other foreign material and the use of ARTIFICIAL RESPIRATION; likewise CARDIAC massage may be needed to restore BLOOD CIRCULATION if major PULSES cannot be felt. In traumatic injury, FRACTURES must be recognized and splinted to reduce pain; the possibility of injury to the spine must be considered before moving the patient to avoid unnecessary damage to the SPINAL CORD. External HEMORRHAGE should be arrested, usually by direct pressure on the bleeding point; tourniquets are rarely needed and may be dangerous. Internal hemorrhage may be suspected if SHOCK develops soon after collapse or trauma without obvious bleeding. BURNS AND SCALDS should be treated by immediately cooling the burnt surface to reduce the continuing injury to SKIN due to retained heat. The use and, if necessary, improvisation of simple dressings, bandages, splints and stretchers should be known; simple methods of moving the injured, should this be necessary, must also be understood. Accessory functions such as contacting ambulances or medical help, direction of traffic and different aspects of resuscitation should be delegated by the most experienced person present. The inquisitive should be kept away and a calm atmosphere maintained.

Prevention as a part of first aid includes due care in the home: avoiding highly polished floors and unfixed carpets, obstacles on or near stairs, loose cords, overhanging saucepan handles, unlabeled bottles of poison and DRUG cupboards accessible to children. Attention to fireguards, adequate lighting and suitable education of children are also important. Effective first aid depends on prevention, recognition, organization and, in any positive action, adherence to the principle of "do no harm."

**FISCHER, Bobby** (Robert James Fischer; 1943–     ), US chess player. In 1958, he became the youngest player (age 15) to attain the rank of international grand master. In 1972 in Iceland, he became the first American to win the world championship, defeating the Russian Boris Spassky in a widely-publicized tournament. He subsequently refused to defend his title, which was awarded to Anatoly KARPOV in 1975.

**FISCHER-DIESKAU, Dietrich** (1925–     ), German baritone. He achieved international fame in the 1950s as an opera singer and an interpreter of German lieder (see SONG), notably those of SCHUBERT and WOLF.

**FISH AND WILDLIFE SERVICE,** US federal agency within the Department of the Interior, created in 1956, concerned with conservation and development of fish and wildlife resources, wilderness areas and river basins. It maintains waterfowl refuges and fish hatcheries, prepares federal hunting regulations, performs research for the fishing industry, protects threatened wildlife, manages the fur seal herds of Alaska and administers international agreements.

**FISHER, John** (c1469–1535), English cardinal, saint and martyr. As bishop of Rochester (1504–34), he refused to recognize Henry VIII's claim to royal ecclesiastical supremacy, was imprisoned in the Tower and later beheaded.

**FISHER, John Arbuthnot Fisher, 1st Baron** (1841–1920), British admiral, who as second (1892–97) and then first sea lord (1902–10), introduced wide-ranging naval reforms, including the encouragement of submarine development. His measures helped ensure British naval superiority in WWI.

**FISHER, Sir Ronald Aylmer** (1890–1962), British scientist who was a pioneer in the application of statistical techniques to biological experimentation. He also helped reconcile MENDEL's theory of GENES with DARWIN's theory of NATURAL SELECTION.

**FISHERIES,** the commercial harvesting of marine and freshwater animals (and some plants) to provide food for men and animals. The main catch is of FISHES, but shellfish and marine mammals including seals and whales are also important. The world harvest now totals about 70 million tons per year, and has risen annually by about 6% since WWII. About 75% is caught in the cold and temperate zones of the Northern Hemisphere. The chief fishing nations are Peru, China, the USSR, Norway, Japan and the US; in the next rank are Canada, India, Spain, Great Britain and Iceland. Inland fisheries—in lakes, rivers and ricefields—account for less than 10% of recorded catches. The most important groups of fish caught are herring and its relatives, and cod and its relatives. Modern fishing vessels are equipped with radar, depth sounders and echo sounders to locate fish shoals; increasingly used are factory ships which process the fish and freeze or can them. Modern nets are very strong, being made from synthetic fibers. Trawlers draw a bag-shaped net behind them; drift nets are fastened to a buoy; lining involves trailing many-hooked lines in deep water; and in seining a large net encircles the fish and is gradually closed as it is drawn in. The supply of fish can no longer be regarded as practically inexhaustible: it is depleted by the vast catches of efficient modern fishing and also by POLLUTION. Conservation is therefore important, and there are international agreements against overfishing and to regulate the meshes of nets so that young fish can escape. Fish farming is also being developed. International disputes have often arisen over fishing rights in coastal waters.

**FISHES,** a large group of cold-blooded aquatic vertebrates that breathe by means of GILLS, and whose bodies bear a vertical tail fin. Most fishes fall within this definition, but a few breathe atmospheric air by means of a lung or lung-like organ, some species have a body temperature slightly above that of the surrounding water and in certain fishes the tail may be missing or reduced to a filament. There are four classes of fish-like vertebrates: the jawless fishes (Agnatha); the placoderms (Placodermi); the cartilaginous fishes (Chondrichthyes), and the bony fishes (Pisces).

The AGNATHA are now represented solely by the lampreys and hagfishes. When they first appeared, during the Ordovician period 530 million years ago, they were fish-like in shape, but had poorly formed fins and lacked jaws.

The Placoderms are now entirely extinct. They are known only as fossils, mainly from rocks of Devonian age (about 400 million years old). They had jaws and paired fins, and ossified skeletons.

The Chondrichthyes include the SHARKS, RAYS and CHIMAERAS as well as certain fossil forms. They are characterized by skeletons that are composed of cartilage, gills that are located in pouches and tooth-like scales.

The most widespread class comprises the Pisces or bony fish, which include the COELACANTH, LUNGFISHES and ray-finned fishes. Ray-finned fishes contain the chondrosteans (bichirs, sturgeons and one entirely fossil order); the holosteans (bowfins and five fossil orders), and finally the teleosteans. The overwhelming majority of present-day fishes are teleosts. There are at least 20,000 different species of teleosts and countless millions of individuals inhabiting the seas, lakes and rivers of the world. They show an amazing diversity of form, from eels to the sea horse, but have a number of characteristics in common. They range in size from a total length of over 6m (20ft) in the oarfish and a weight of over 2 tons in the ocean sunfish, to an adult length of only 13mm (½in) in a Philippine goby *Paudaka pygmaea*), the latter qualifying as the smallest of all vertebrates. Typically, the body is streamlined, rising smoothly from the head and tapering gently to the tail, but in particular cases the body shape reflects the mode of life of the fish. In most fishes swimming is achieved by throwing the body into a series of lateral undulations which travel along the length of the body growing in amplitude toward the tail. The tail provides the final thrust and evens out the oscillations of the body. One characteristic (but not invariable) feature of fishes is the presence of scales on the body.

**FISHING,** the catching of fish for consumption or for sport. It is one of the world's most popular participant sports. There are millions of fishermen (almost 30 million in the US alone), or anglers, who fish for recreation or in competition. World records by weight, length and girth exist for every type of fish. The first fishing club in America was the Schuylkill Fishing Company of Philadelphia (established 1732). There are three main types of sports fishing: game, coarse and sea angling, or deep-sea fishing. Game anglers fish trout, salmon and other fish in fast-moving streams which require accurate casting of the right lure. Coarse anglers fish in slow, deep rivers. Sea anglers generally fish for shark, tuna, tarpon or barracuda.

**FISK, James** (1834–1872), US financial speculator, notorious for stock manipulation. With Jay GOULD he engaged in a brutal stock market struggle for control of the Erie Railroad and together their attempt to corner the gold market in 1869 led to the BLACK FRIDAY scandal. He was shot by a business associate and rival for the affections of an actress.

**FISSION,** the division of CELLS, or sometimes multicellular organisms, to produce identical offspring. Binary fission results in the production of two equal parts and multiple fission in the production of more than two equal parts. The term is normally applied to the reproduction of multicellular organisms such as members of the phylum PROTOZOA.

**FISSION, Nuclear,** the splitting of the nucleus of a heavy ATOM into two or more lighter nuclei with the release of a large amount of ENERGY. Fission power is used in NUCLEAR REACTORS and the ATOMIC BOMB.

**FISTULA,** an abnormal communication between two internal organs, or from an organ to the outside of the body. Infection, inflammatory disease (e.g. Crohn's disease—see ENTERITIS), TUMORS, trauma and SURGERY may lead to fistula. The GASTROINTESTINAL TRACT (particularly DUODENUM), PANCREAS, BLADDER and female genital tract are particularly susceptible.

**FITCH, John** (1743–1798), US inventor and engineer who built the first practical steamboat (1787), larger vessels being launched in 1788 and 1790. All were paddle-powered; his later attempt to introduce the SCREW PROPELLER was a commercial failure.

**FITZGERALD, Edward** (1809–1883), English poet and scholar. FitzGerald is famous for his "translation" of OMAR KHAYYAM's *Rubaiyat* (1859) in which he managed to capture the spirit of the original while at the same time creating a new masterpiece using his own images and structure.

**FITZGERALD, Ella** (1918–    ), US jazz singer. Internationally known as a great original interpreter of jazz and blues, she possessed a clear, powerful voice, an exceptional sense of pitch and unique rhythmic control. She began her career in the 1930s as a band vocalist.

**FITZGERALD, F. Scott** (Francis Scott Key Fitzgerald; 1896–1940), US novelist and short story writer. The "spokesman" of the Jazz Age in the 1920s, his works deal with the frenetic life style of the post-WWI generation and the spiritual bankruptcy of the so-called American Dream. His celebrated novel *The Great Gatsby* (1925) explores the ruthless society of the 1920s. *Tender is the Night* (1934) draws upon his experience of American expatriates in Paris and upon the schizophrenic gaiety and breakdown of his wife, Zelda. He spent his last years as a Hollywood scriptwriter.

**FITZSIMMONS, Robert Prometheus** (called "Bob" or "Ruby Robert"; 1863–1918), English world boxing champion. Middleweight (1891–97), heavyweight (1897–99) and light-heavyweight (1903–05) champion of the world, he fought in New Zealand and Australia and in the US from 1890.

**FIVE CIVILIZED TRIBES,** term for the CHEROKEE, CHICKASAW, CHOCTAW, CREEK and SEMINOLE Indian tribes of North America. Between about 1830–50 they were forced to settle in INDIAN TERRITORY but were recognized as domestic, dependent nations with constitutions and laws based on those of the US. After the Civil War they were restricted to areas in E Okla. and the US followed a detribalization policy which left the five with little autonomy.

**FLAG DAY,** June 14, anniversary of the adoption in 1777 of the Stars and Stripes as the US flag.

**FLAGG, James Montgomery** (1877–1960), US painter and illustrator famous for a WWI recruiting poster showing a beckoning Uncle Sam who says "I want YOU." Flagg also drew homely scenes of American life in a vigorous pen-and-ink technique for several popular magazines.

**FLAGLER, Henry Morrison** (1830–1913), US financier who helped develop Fla. In partnership with John D. Rockefeller, he helped form the Standard Oil Company in 1870, then built hotels and railways that made Fla. a vacation center.

**FLAGSTAD, Kirsten** (1895–1962), Norwegian singer, one of the greatest Wagnerian sopranos. She made her New York debut as Sieglinde in *Die Walküre* in 1935 and retired from public singing in 1953, though she continued making records.

**FLAHERTY, Robert Joseph** (1884–1951), US pioneer documentary filmmaker. He is chiefly famous for *Nanook of the North* (1922), a study of Eskimo life, and *Man of Aran* (1934), about life on the Aran Islands of Ireland.

**FLAMENCO,** type of sensuous folk music and dancing from Andalusia in S Spain, performed especially by gypsies. Dancers, stamping and clapping, interpret songs, accompanied by forceful guitar playing. It is probably of Moorish origin.

**FLAMETHROWER,** device—basically a SYRINGE—that propels a petroleum fuel, commonly NAPALM, through a nozzle, igniting it as it emerges, so that a burning stream lands on the enemy. Compressed air provides the driving force. A portable flamethrower has a range of 50m, and a mechanized flamethrower 150m. (See also CHEMICAL AND BIOLOGICAL WARFARE.)

**FLAMINGO,** several species of colorful water birds, of the family Phoenicopteridae, related to HERONS. They have long spindly legs and necks, and large bills with bristles which they use to sift their food from the water. Their plumage is white, pink and black. They live in large flocks on alkaline lakes in America, Africa and S Eurasia.

**FLANAGAN, Edward Joseph** (1886–1948), Irish-born US Roman Catholic priest who founded BOYS TOWN, a self-governing community of homeless boys, near Omaha, Neb., in 1917. After WWII he helped organize youth facilities abroad for the US government.

**FLANDERS,** medieval county on the coast of NW Europe, largely corresponding to N Belgium, with smaller portions in the Netherlands and France. In the 14th and 15th centuries, wealth from trade and textile manufacture enriched the chief towns (Antwerp, Ypres, Bruges and Ghent) and made Flanders a major cultural center. Its famous artists included Bruegel, Rubens and Van Dyck.

**FLANNER, Janet** (pen name Genêt; 1892–1978), US writer known for her "Letter from Paris" column which appeared in the *New Yorker* from 1925. Containing news of French politics, her "letters" were collected in various volumes including *An American in Paris* (1940) and *Paris Journal* (1965–71).

**FLASH PHOTOLYSIS,** technique for

investigating very fast chemical reactions. A very intense flash of light of very short duration (from a LASER or flash lamp) is passed through a reaction mixture, usually gaseous. Instant dissociation occurs, producing FREE RADICALS, whose subsequent fast reactions are followed by automatic spectroscopy.

**FLATFOOT**, deformity of FOOT in which the longitudinal or transverse arches of the feet are flattened or lost; this results in loss of spring and the inefficient use of the feet in walking or running. It may result from muscle weakness or be congenital. Corrective exercises and shoe wedges may relieve the condition.

**FLATHEAD INDIANS**, North American tribe of the Salish linguistic family inhabiting W Mont. The name derives from the head-flattening practiced by tribes from whom the Flatheads took slaves. The Flatheads were early converts to Christianity, and most now live at Flathead Lake, Mont.

**FLAUBERT, Gustave** (1821–1880), French novelist; a scrupulous observer and stylist, whose work influenced much subsequent French writing. His first work, *Madame Bovary* (1856–57), brought him immediate fame. The vividly naturalistic tragedy of a provincial wife who attempts to live out her fantasies, it was unsuccessfully prosecuted as an offense against public morality in 1857. The exotic Carthaginian setting of *Salammbô* (1862) showed an equal mastery of Romantic style. His *Three Tales* (1877), set in modern, medieval and ancient times, combined both Romanticism and realism.

**FLAXMAN, John** (1755–1826), English sculptor and illustrator, chief exponent of the Neoclassical style in England. He illustrated works by Homer, Dante and Aeschylus, designed pottery for Wedgwood and produced monumental sculpture.

**FLEAS**, wingless INSECTS with legs developed for jumping, and a laterally compressed body. They suck the blood of host animals, and can carry such diseases as the bubonic PLAGUE. The flea survives its early stages in insanitary conditions; when newly emerged, adults leap onto passing hosts.

**FLEMING, Ian (Lancaster)** (1908–1964), English novelist and journalist. He created the fictional British secret-service agent James Bond—who became a popular cult figure.

**FLEMING, Sir Alexander** (1881–1955), British bacteriologist, discoverer of lysozome (1922) and penicillin (1928). Lysozome is an ENZYME present in many

body tissues and lethal to certain bacteria; its discovery prepared the way for that of ANTIBIOTICS. His discovery of PENICILLIN was largely accidental; and it was developed as a therapeutic later, by Harold FLOREY and Ernst CHAIN. All three received the 1945 Nobel Prize for Physiology or Medicine for their work.

**FLEMISH**, the form of DUTCH traditionally spoken in N Belgium. Given official equality with French in 1898, it became the official language of N Belgium in 1934.

**FLETCHER, John.** See BEAUMONT, FRANCIS AND FLETCHER, JOHN.

**FLEXNER, Abraham** (1866–1959), US educator who profoundly changed medical teaching in the US. His survey of medical schools (1910) led to drastic reorganization. He was founder and first director (1930–39) of the Institute for Advanced Study, Princeton, N.J.

**FLIES**, members of the INSECT order Diptera which number about 85,000 species, and whose second pair of wings has been reduced to a pair of halteres or balancing organs which act as GYROSCOPES. These give flies great agility. They have two compound eyes; the antennae act as tactile, and possibly also smelling and hearing, organs. Their mouths are adapted either for sucking (as in the House fly), or piercing (as in mosquitoes). Their larvae are called MAGGOTS, and live on plants or decaying flesh. Adults feed on NECTAR, other insects, decaying matter or animal blood. The MOSQUITO and TSETSE FLY carry MALARIA and SLEEPING SICKNESS respectively.

**FLIGHT**, the ability to travel through the air for long periods. The only animals that are capable of sustained flight are the extinct PTERODACTYLS; some insects; a few fish; bats; and most birds. Very few insects are completely wingless, and most have two pairs of wings that flap together. In flies and beetles one pair is modified. Usually muscles distort the thorax, forcing the wings up and down at rates of up to 1,000 beats per second in midges.

So-called flying fishes in fact glide. In birds, power for flying comes from the breast muscles, which control both the up and down strokes of the wing. Wing shape depends on the kind of flight; narrow for gliding and broad for soaring.

**FLIGHT, History of.** LEONARDO DA VINCI was the first man to attempt the scientific design of flying machines. But in his time no motor was available which was powerful enough to lift a man into the air. Man's first ascents from the ground had to await the late 18th century and the invention of the MONTGOLFIER brothers' hot-air BALLOON and

J, CHARLES' hydrogen balloon (1783). The addition of steam engines to the balloon gave the first maneuverable AIRSHIP (1852). Meanwhile G. CAYLEY designed and built flying GLIDERS (1810–1853) and William Henson designed a steam-powered model airplane with twin PROPELLERS (1842). It was not until the advent of the gasoline INTERNAL-COMBUSTION ENGINE, though, that the powered heavier-than-air machine became a practical possibility. The first successful controlled airplane flight was made by the WRIGHT BROTHERS near Kitty Hawk, N.C., on December 17, 1903 and within a few years there were many competing manufacturers and fliers of airplanes. Airplane technology was greatly stimulated by WWI and after 1919 commercial aviation developed rapidly. Meanwhile, the AUTOGIRO was invented by J. de la CIERVA (1923), to be followed by SIKORSKY'S HELICOPTER in 1939. JET PROPULSION was developed in several countries during WWII and by the mid-1950s had come to be used in the majority of military and commercial airplanes. RADAR navigation systems came into general use in this period. The early 1970s saw the introduction of widebodied jet airliners (jumbo jets) with vastly increased carrying capacity and the development of the first supersonic jet airliners. (See also AIR TRANSPORTATION.)

**FLINT,** or **chert,** sedimentary rock composed of microcrystalline QUARTZ and CHALCEDONY. It is found as nodules in LIMESTONE and CHALK, and as layered beds, and was mainly formed by alteration of marine sediments of siliceous organisms, and by replacement, preserving many FOSSIL outlines. A hard rock, flint may be chipped to form a sharp cutting edge, and was used by STONE AGE man for their characteristic tools.

**FLINTLOCK,** firearm developed in the 17th century and named for its use of flint ignition. It had a cock or hammer containing a piece of flint. When the trigger was pulled the flint struck a steel *frizzen* and the resulting spark ignited the charge. It was superseded by the percussion system which was introduced in the 19th century.

**FLOATING EXCHANGE RATE,** in international finance, the exchange rate for a national currency as determined by SUPPLY AND DEMAND and not by fixed PARITY. It is sometimes used to allow a currency to find a stable level. (See also GOLD STANDARD.)

**FLOODS AND FLOOD CONTROL.** River floods are one of mankind's worst enemies. In 1887, when the Hwang Ho overflowed, around 900,000 lost their lives; and, as recently as 1970, 200,000 died in E Pakistan when a cyclone struck the Ganges delta. Clearly the development of ways to control and contain floods must be a preoccupation of man.

Often floods are caused by unusually rapid thawing of the winter snows: the river, unable to hold the increased volume of water, bursts its banks. Heavy rainfall may have a similar effect. Coastal flooding may result from an exceptionally high TIDE combined with onshore winds, or, of course, from a TSUNAMI.

River floods can be forestalled by artificially deepening and broadening river channels or by the construction of suitably positioned DAMS. Artificial levees may also be built (in nature, levees occur as a result of sediment deposited while the river is in flood; they take the form of built-up banks). Vegetation planted on uplands helps to reduce surface runoff.

Flood control can create new problems to replace the old. In Egypt the Aswan Dam has halted the once regular flooding of the Nile, thus robbing farmlands of a rich annual deposit of silt. But flood control made possible the civilization of ancient Mesopotamia and plays a vital role in modern water conservation. (See also RIVERS AND LAKES.)

**FLORENCE** (Firenze), historic city in central Italy, capital of Firenze province, on the Arno R at the foot of the Apennines. A town on the Cassian Way during Roman times, it grew to become a powerful medieval republic, dominating Tuscany. Florence was a major commercial and artistic center during the Renaissance. It retains many architectural and other art treasures which, together with the proximity of the Apennines, serve to make the city an important tourist center. The great art museums of Florence include the Uffizi Gallery, the Pitti Palace and the Accademia. Famous figures associated with Florence include BRUNELLESCHI, DANTE, GIOTTO, MACHIAVELLI, MASACCIO, MICHELANGELO and SAVONAROLA. Glass and leatherware, pottery, furniture and precision instruments are among its products. In 1966 floods seriously damaged many of Florence's art treasures. Pop 463,000.

**FLOREY, Howard Walter, Baron** (1898–1968), Australian-born British pathologist who worked with E. B. CHAIN and others to extract PENICILLIN from *Penicillium notatum* mold for use as a therapeutic drug (1934–44). He shared with Chain and Alexander FLEMING the 1945 Nobel Prize for Medicine.

**Name of state:** Florida
**Capital:** Tallahassee
**Statehood:** Mar. 3, 1845 (27th state)
**Familiar name:** Sunshine State
**Area:** 58,560sq mi
**Population:** 9,739,992
**Elevation:** Highest—345ft, in Walton Co.
Lowest—sea level, Atlantic Ocean
**Motto:** In God We Trust
**State flower:** Orange blossom
**State bird:** Mockingbird
**State tree:** Sabal palm
**State song:** "Swanee River"

**FLORIDA,** state, SE US, bounded to the E by the Atlantic Ocean, to the W by the Gulf of Mexico, and to the N and NW by Ga. and Ala. It is a major resort area and one of the fastest growing states in the US.
**Land.** The greater part of the state consists of a low 400mi-long peninsula between the Gulf of Mexico and the Atlantic, with the Straits of Florida skirting its S coast. Sandbars and islands flank the smooth E coast. The string of islands known as the Florida Keys and the Dry Tortugas Islands extend SW from Biscayne Bay on the S coast. The W coast is indented and swampy. The central plains run from the NW to central Florida. Big Cypress Swamp and the EVERGLADES are situated in the marshlands of the S. There are some 30,000 lakes, including the 700sq mi OKEECHOBEE, and numerous rivers. Florida enjoys a subtropical climate.
**People.** More than 80% of the people live in rapidly expanding urban areas, such as Miami, Palm Beach, St. Petersburg and Fort Lauderdale. The state is administered by a governor elected for 4 years, a 40-member Senate and a 120-member House of Representatives. The state's numerous institutions of higher learning include the U. of Florida and Miami U.
**Economy.** Tourism, manufacturing (processed foods, paper, chemicals, electrical products) and agriculture, which produces a large proportion of the nation's citrus fruit, are the three leading industries. Mining and fishing are also important economically.

Florida's transportation system includes international airports, interstate bus, rail and road systems and a number of deepwater harbors. Lake Okeechobee links the ATLANTIC INTRACOASTAL WATERWAY to the Gulf of Mexico, via the Caloosahatchee and St. Lucie canals and rivers.
**History.** Juan PONCE DE LEÓN discovered and named Florida in 1513 and claimed the territory for Spain. Early European settlements met with failure, but in 1565 Spain founded Saint Augustine, which survives as the oldest permanent white settlement in the US. Spain soon controlled all Florida. Britain held it from 1763 until 1783 when it was returned to Spain. American colonists began moving in and in 1819 Spain ceded Florida to the US. Resistance to white settlement by Seminole Indians culminated in the brutal Seminole War (1835–42). Admitted to the Union in 1845, Florida seceded in 1861. It was readmitted in 1868. Major economic growth began only late in the 19th century when an expanding railroad system encouraged the development of tourism and of the citrus fruit industry. Economic expansion has been phenomenal since WWII, putting increasing strains upon social services, public utilities, transportation and the dwindling tracts of subtropical wilderness. In the decade of the 1970s, Florida experienced a 43% growth rate, and it was the leading point of entry for Caribbean refugees, especially from Cuba. In the early 1980s, amid a variety of pressing problems, including an abrupt rise in urban crime and a critical drop in ground-water level, Floridians were looking to the federal government for help with refugees and to local governments for better management of resources and growth.
**FLORIDA KEYS,** chain of about 20 small coral islands off S Fla. Their arc curves SW from Biscayne Bay S of Miami to KEY WEST. Causeways bearing some 160mi of highway link most of the islands, which support fishing and farming and attract vacationers.
**FLORISSANT FOSSIL BEDS NATIONAL MONUMENT,** area of 5,998 acres in central Col., noted for its Oligocene fossils and petrified trees. It was authorized in 1969.
**FLOUNDERS,** edible FLATFISHES of the Pacific and Atlantic. They include members of the family which have eyes on the left side of the body, and the Pleuronectidae which have eyes on the right side.
**FLOUR,** fine powder ground from the grains or starchy portions of WHEAT, RYE,

CORN, RICE, POTATOES, BANANAS or BEANS. Plain white flour is produced from wheat; soft wheat produces flour used for cakes and hard wheat, with a higher GLUTEN content, makes flour used for bread. Flour is made from the endosperm, which constitutes about 84% of the grain; the remainder comprises the BRAN, which is the outer layers of the grain, and the germ, which is the embryo. Grain used to be milled by hand between two stones, until the development of wind, water or animal driven mills. In modern mills, the grain is thoroughly cleaned and then tempered by bringing the water content to 15%, which makes the separation of the bran and germ from the endosperm easier. The endosperm is broken up by rollers and the flour graded and bleached. It may then be enriched with VITAMINS. Byproducts are used mainly for cattle food, although wheat germ is an important source of vitamin E.

**FLOWER,** the part of an ANGIOSPERM that is concerned with REPRODUCTION. There is a great variety of floral structure, but the basic organs and structure are similar. Each flower is borne on a stalk or pedicel, the tip of which is expanded to form a receptacle that bears the floral organs. The sepals are the first of these organs and are normally green and leaflike. Above the sepals there is a ring of petals, which are normally colored and vary greatly in shape. The ring of sepals is termed the calyx and the ring of petals the corolla. Collectively the calyx and corolla are called the perianth. Above the perianth are the reproductive organs comprising the male organs, the stamens (collectively known as the androecium) and female organs, the carpels (the gynoecium). Each stamen consists of a slender stalk, or FILAMENT, which is capped by the pollen-producing anther. Each carpel has a swollen base, the ovary, which contains the ovules that later form the seed. Each carpel is connected by a style to an expanded structure called the stigma. Together, the style and stigma are sometimes termed the pistil.

There are three main variations of flower structure. In hypogynous flowers (e.g. BUTTERCUP) the perianth segments and stamens are attached below a superior ovary, while in perigynous flowers (e.g. ROSE) the receptacle is cuplike enclosing a superior ovary, with the perianth segments and stamens attached to a rim around the receptacle. In epigynous flowers (e.g. DANDELION) the inferior ovary is enclosed by the receptacle and the other floral parts are attached to the ovary. In many plants, the flowers are grouped together to form an INFLORESCENCE.

Pollen produced by the stamens is transferred either by insects or the wind to the stigma where POLLINATION takes place. Many of the immense number of variations of flower form are adaptations that aid either insect or wind pollination. (See also PLANT KINGDOM.)

**FLU.** See INFLUENZA.

**FLUID,** a substance which flows (undergoes a continuous change of shape) when subjected to a tangential or shearing FORCE. LIQUIDS and GASES are fluids, both taking the shape of their container. But while liquids are virtually incompressible and have a fixed volume, gases expand to fill whatever space is available to them.

**FLUIDICS,** application of fluid flow to perform such functions as sensing, control, actuation, amplification and information processing. Many of these functions can also be accomplished by electronic circuitry, but fluidic devices are preferable in certain hostile environments where electronic components would fail, such as under conditions of excessive heat, humidity or vibrations. A fluidic device is especially efficient for systems in which the flow of fluid plays an integral part, such as certain chemical-engineering processes and automotive fuel systems.

**FLUID MECHANICS,** the study of moving and static FLUIDS, dealing with the FORCES exerted on a fluid to hold it at rest and the relationships with its boundaries that cause it to move. The scope of the subject is wide, ranging from HYDRAULICS, concerning the applications of fluid flow in pipes and channels, to aeronautics, the study of airflow relating to the design of AIRPLANES and ROCKETS. Any fluid process, such as flow around an obstacle or in a pipe, can be described mathematically by a specific equation that relates the forces acting, the dimensions of the system and its properties such as TEMPERATURE, PRESSURE and DENSITY. Newton's laws of motion and VISCOSITY, the first and second laws of THERMODYNAMICS and the laws of conservation of MASS, ENERGY and MOMENTUM are applied as appropriate. Much use is also made of experimental evidence from models, wind tunnels, etc., to determine the process equation. Many types of flow occur: in laminar flow in a closed pipe, distinct layers of fluid slide over each other, their velocity decreasing to zero at the pipe wall; in turbulent flow the fluid is mixed by eddies and vertices and a statistical treatment is needed. (See also ARCHIMEDES; BERNOULLI; PASCAL'S LAW; REYNOLDS NUMBER.)

**FLUKES,** parasitic FLATWORMS, some of which are important disease carriers. The sheep liver fluke lives in the bile duct of mammals. Its eggs pass out of the intestine into water, where the larvae infect water snails, then wait on vegetation to be eaten by mammals. The blood fluke is responsible for the disease SCHISTOSOMIASIS, which is thought to affect 250 million people throughout the world.

**FLUORIDATION,** addition of small quantities of fluorides (see FLUORINE) to public water supplies, bringing the concentration to 1 ppm, as in some natural water. It greatly reduces the incidence of tooth decay by strengthening the teeth. Despite some opposition, many authorities now fluoridate water. Toothpaste containing fluoride is also valuable.

**FLUORINE** (F), the lightest of the HALOGENS, occurring naturally as FLUORITE, CRYOLITE and fluorapatite (see APATITE). A pale-yellow toxic gas, fluorine is made by electrolysis of potassium fluoride in liquid HYDROGEN FLUORIDE. It is the most reactive, electronegative and oxidizing of all elements, reacting with almost all other elements to give fluorides (see HALIDES) of the highest possible oxidation state. It displaces other nonmetals from their compounds. Most nonmetal fluorides are highly reactive, but sulfur hexafluoride (used as an electrical insulator) and carbon tetrafluoride are inert (see STEREOCHEMISTRY). Fluorine is used in rocket propulsion, in URANIUM production, and to make FLUOROCARBONS. (See also FLUORIDATION.) AW 19.0, mp—220°C, bp—188°C.

**FLUOROCARBONS,** HYDROCARBONS in which hydrogen atoms are replaced (wholly or in part) by fluorine. Because of the stability of the carbon-fluorine bond, they are inert and heat-resistant. Thus they can be used in artificial joints in the body, and where hydrocarbons would be decomposed by heat, such as in spacecraft heatshields, the coating of nonstick pans or as lubricants. Liquid fluorocarbons are used as refrigerants. (See also TEFLON; FREON.)

**FLUOROSCOPE,** device used in medical diagnosis and engineering quality control which allows the direct observation of an X-RAY beam which is being passed through an object under examination. It contains a fluorescent screen which converts the X-ray image into visible light (see LUMINESCENCE) and, often, an image intensifier.

**FLUTE,** reedless woodwind instrument of ancient origin. The modern concert flute is a transverse or side-blown instrument, the earlier form being, like the RECORDER, end-blown. It was in widespread use by the end of the 18th century. The C flute with a three octave range is the standard instrument. Other types include the bass flute and the piccolo, about half the size of the flute and the highest pitched instrument in the orchestra. The piccolo is widely used in military bands.

**FLUXIONS,** term used by NEWTON for CALCULUS. In his terminology, later abandoned in favor of that of LEIBNIZ, what we now call a FUNCTION was called a fluent, its derivative a fluxion.

**FLYING FISHES,** members of the family Exocoetidae, tropical fish which propel themselves out of the sea by an elongated lobe of the tail. They can glide on their fins for over 0.4km (0.25mi) but the flights are usually 55m (180ft) or less. The reason for flying is to escape predatory fish.

**FLYING SAUCER,** popular term for Unidentified Flying Object (UFO). UFOs have been reported for many years, but only caught the public imagination in the 1950s "Saucer Scare." Most sightings are obviously erroneous but a number by reliable observers remain unexplained.

**FLYNN, Errol** (1909–1959), Tasmanian-born US film actor who won international fame as a swashbuckling hero in such Hollywood films as *Captain Blood* (1935), *The Charge of the Light Brigade* (1936) and *The Adventures of Robin Hood* (1938). Adventure, trials and suspicions of spying marked his private life.

**FOCH, Ferdinand** (1851–1929), outstanding French army marshal. His courageous stand against the Germans at the Marne in 1914 led to further commands and (1917) becoming chief of the French general staff. He commanded the Allied armies in France, April–Nov., 1918, launching the Aisne-Marne offensive which ended WWI.

**FOKINE, Michel** (1880–1942), Russian-born US dancer and choreographer, a founder of modern ballet. Influenced by the work of Isadora DUNCAN, he stressed the total effect of expressive dancing, costume, music and scenery. He worked in Paris as chief choreographer of DIAGHILEV's Ballets Russes 1909–14, and from 1925 directed his own company in the US.

**FOKKER, Anthony Herman Gerard** (1890–1939), Dutch-American pioneer in aircraft design. In WWI he designed pursuit planes for Germany, developing a synchronizer mechanism by which guns could be fired from directly behind a plane's propeller blades. In 1922 Fokker emigrated to the US where he designed for the Army Air Corps and built transport planes, such as the Fokker T-2, which in 1923 made the first nonstop flight across the US.

**FOLD,** a buckling in rock strata. Folds convex upward are called **anticlines;** those convex downward, **synclines.** They may be tiny or up to hundreds of kilometers across. Folds result from horizontal pressures in the EARTH's crust and result in crustal shortening. The upper portions of anticlines have often been eroded away. (See also GEOSYNCLINE.)

**FOLGER, Henry Clay** (1857–1930), US lawyer and industrialist, founder of Washington D.C.'s Folger Shakespeare Library (1932). He was president of the Standard Oil Company of New York 1911–23 and chairman 1923–28.

**FOLGER SHAKESPEARE LIBRARY,** Washington, D.C., institution possessing the world's largest collection of Shakespeariana, including 79 First Folios, and a host of material on the Tudor and Stuart periods. Opened in 1932, the collection was assembled initially by American philanthropist Hen y Clay FOLGER (1857–1930) and his wife.

**FOLIES BERGÈRE,** Paris music hall. It opened in 1869 and featured pantomime and light opera, but soon became (and remains) famous for lavish spectacles featuring nude or seminude female performers. The American singer Josephine BAKER once descended a staircase attired in bananas, which she then tossed to the spectators.

**FOLK DANCING,** traditional popular dancing, often stylistically peculiar to a nation or region. Folk dances derive variously from ancient magic and religious rituals and also from the sequences of movement involved in certain forms of communal labor. Famous national dances include the Irish JIG, Italian TARANTELLA and Hungarian CZARDAS. The American Folk Dancing Society popularizes American folk dances, notably the SQUARE DANCE where an expert "caller" gives rhyming instructions. Many US dances have European origins, but their barn dance setting is authentically American. (See also DANCE.)

**FOLKLORE,** a culture's traditional beliefs, customs and superstitions handed down informally in fables, myths, legends, proverbs, riddles, songs and ballads. Folklore studies were developed in the 1800s, largely through collection and collation of material by the GRIMM brothers, and folklore societies were set up in Europe and the US. The American Folklore Society was founded in 1888. The extent to which folktale themes are echoed and paralleled among distinct and isolated cultures is truly remarkable. One of the major studies of this phenomenon is Sir James FRAZER's *Golden Bough* (1890). (See also FABLE; MYTHOLOGY.)

**FOLK MUSIC,** traditional popular music stylistically belonging to a regional or ethnic group. Compositions are usually anonymous and, being in the main orally transmitted, often occur in several different versions. Folk music of the US includes the English ballads of Kentucky, Mexican music of the Southwest, and Black music of the South. Among classical composers influenced by folk music are Béla Bartók, Zoltán Kodaly, Aarón Copland and Ralph Vaughan Williams.

**FOLLICLE-STIMULATING HORMONE,** or FSH, a pituitary-gland GONADOTROPHIN, concerned with ovarian follicle and SPERM development in females and males.

**FOLSOM CULTURE,** prehistoric (c8000 BC) American Indian culture named for Folsom, N. M., where stone arrow or spearheads were discovered in the 1920s in close association with the bones of an extinct breed of bison. Other tools, such as stone scrapers, bone needles, etc., have been found; and it is thought that the culture was a nomadic, hunting one.

**FONDA,** family of US actors. **Henry Fonda** (1905–    ) made many major Hollywood films including *The Grapes of Wrath* (1940) and *Twelve Angry Men* (1957) and starred in several plays, notably *Mister Roberts* (1949). His daughter **Jane Fonda** (1937–    ) starred in *Cat Ballou* (1964), *They Shoot Horses Don't They* (1969), *Nine to Five* (1981) and *Klute* (1971), for which she won an Academy Award. She was also a political activist who campaigned vigorously against the Vietnam War. Her brother **Peter Fonda** (1939–    ) co-produced, coauthored and starred in *Easy Rider* (1969).

**FONTAINEBLEAU,** French town 37mi SSE of Paris, in the department Seine-et-Marne. A tourist center in the Forest of Fontainebleau, it is best known for its magnificent, mainly 16th-century chateau which was once a royal residence and is now a presidential summer home. Pop 20,580.

**FONTANA, Domenico** (1543–1607), Italian architect and civil engineer. As chief architect to Pope Sixtus V he completed the dome of St. Peter's (1585–90) and designed the Lateran Palace and the Vatican Library (1588).

**FONTEYN, Dame Margot** (Dame Margot Fonteyn de Arias; 1919–    ), English prima ballerina of the Royal Ballet. Before WWII she had danced leads in *Giselle,*

*Swan Lake* and *The Sleeping Beauty*, and ASHTON had begun choreographing works for her. She retired from the Royal Ballet in 1959, but continued to appear as a guest star and in 1962 formed a dance partnership with NUREYEV that won new international fame for both of them.

**FOOD AND AGRICULTURE ORGANIZATION** (FAO), agency of the UN, established in 1945, with headquarters in Rome. It provides member nations with information on food and agricultural problems and with technical and financial aid.

**FOOD AND DRUG ADMINISTRATION,** US, Federal agency in the Department of Health, Education and Welfare, set up in 1940 to enforce the laws maintaining standards in the sale of food and drugs. Originally concerned largely with preventing adulteration and poor food hygiene, the FDA is now also involved in testing the safety, reliability and usefulness of drugs and chemicals, and assessing the effects on health of "accidental additives" such as PESTICIDES.

**FOOD FOR PEACE,** program originally intended under Public Law 480 of 1954 for disposing of US farm surpluses; restructured and expanded under the Food for Peace Act of 1966, it provides for low-interest loans to other nations to enable them to purchase American farm products. The program diminished in importance in the 1970s, with most of the shipments going to two countries—South Vietnam and Cambodia. Proposals for ending the program were made by the Reagan administration, but in July 1981 it was used to extend a $55 million credit to Poland.

**FOOD POISONING,** disease resulting from ingestion of unwholesome food, usually resulting in COLIC, VOMITING DIARRHEA and general malaise. While a number of VIRUS, contaminant, irritant and allergic factors may play a part in some cases, three specific types are common: those due to STAPHYLOCOCCUS, Clostridium and SALMONELLA bacteria. Inadequate cooking, allowing cooked food to stand for long periods in warm conditions and contamination of cooked food with bacteria from humans or uncooked food are usual causes. **Staphylococci** may be introduced from a BOIL or from the NOSE of a food handler; they produce a TOXIN if allowed to grow in cooked food. Sudden vomiting and abdominal pain occur 2–6 hours after eating. *Clostridium* poisoning causes colic and diarrhea, 10–12 hours after ingestion of contaminated meat. *Salmonella* enteritis causes colic, diarrhea, vomiting and often fever, starting 12–24 hours after eating; poultry and human carriers are the usual sources. BOTULISM is an often fatal form of food poisoning. In general, food poisoning is mild and self-limited and symptomatic measures only are needed; ANTIBIOTICS rarely help.

**FOOD PRESERVATION,** a number of techniques used to delay the spoilage of food. There are two main causes of spoilage: one is the PUTREFACTION that follows the death of any plant or animal; the other over-ripening, the result of the action of certain plant ENZYMES. Heating destroys these enzymes and the BACTERIA responsible for putrefaction but, before it cools, the food must be isolated in cans or bottles from air-borne bacteria. Freezing slows the enzyme action and the REPRODUCTION of the bacteria and preserves flavor better. DEHYDRATION, IRRADIATION and preservatives are also used. Traditional means of preservation include smoking, salting and pickling (see VINEGAR). (See also FOOD POISONING; REFRIGERATION.)

**FOOD STAMPS,** a locally administered, federally funded US program that enables poverty-level families to buy a greater variety and quantity of food. Households receive stamps in proportion to total net income and the number of people comprising them. The program helps feed about 22 million people. For 1981–82, its budget was $11.3 billion, making it the largest federal welfare program.

**FOOT, Michael** (1913–    ), British political leader. A member of Parliament for 30 years, Foot served first as deputy leader and then as leader of the Labour Party (1980–    ).

**FOOTBALL,** popular US sport, played with a leather-covered oval-shaped ball, by two teams of 11 players. The football gridiron or field is 120 yd long by 53 yd 1 ft wide, with two end zones 10 yd deep, each with an H-shaped goal post having a crossbar 10 ft high. Playing time for men is 60 min, divided into two halfs of two quarters each. To score, a team must run or pass the football over the opponent's goal line, or kick it through the uprights of the goal post. A touchdown (running or passing the ball over the goal line) scores six points, a field goal (kicking the ball over the goal post) three points, and after a touchdown an extra point or conversion (usually by kicking the ball over the crossbar) one point. Possession of the ball is the key to scoring; the offensive team has four plays, or downs, to advance 10 yd and keep possession of the ball by gaining a new first down. The defense obtains the ball by stopping the offense from gaining 10 yd within four downs, by intercepting a pass or by recovering a fumble (dropped ball).

Early US football was similar to SOCCER, but today's game evolved from RUGBY, which permits handling of the ball. In the 1880s the main rules and tactics of American football were devised by Yale U's Walter CAMP, the "father" of the game. The new college sport soon became popular, but public criticism of its physical violence brought about a meeting of President Theodore Roosevelt with college team representatives in 1906 that resulted in banning mass formations and other dangerous practices. Forward passing of the ball was legalized, opening up the strategy and tactics of the game.

Organized professional football began in 1921 with formation of the National Football League, although the Depression of the 1930s and WWII retarded the NFL's development. After the war the televising of the pros' faster, more skillful and hard-hitting style of play contributed to making the sport extremely popular. The two major pro leagues merged in 1966 into the NFL's American and National conferences, each having 14 teams in the early 1980s; a Super Bowl championship game between the conference winners has been played every January since 1967. Canadian football more closely resembles the US game than it does either soccer or rugby.

**FORAMINIFERA,** single-celled sea animals. Each species has a limy shell which sinks when the foraminifer dies. These shells form deposits of Foraminiferan ooze which cover one third of the ocean floor.

**FORBIDDEN CITY,** walled enclosure in Peking, China, containing the imperial palace, its grounds, reception halls and state offices. In imperial times, the Forbidden City was closed to the public.

**FORCE,** in mechanics, the physical quantity which, when it acts on a body, either causes it to change its state of motion (i.e., imparts to it an ACCELERATION), or tends to deform it (i.e., induces in it an elastic strain—see MATERIALS, STRENGTH OF). Dynamical forces are governed by NEWTON's laws of motion, from the second of which it follows that a given force acting on a body produces in it an acceleration proportional to the force, inversely proportional to the body's MASS and occurring in the direction of the force. Forces are thus VECTOR quantities with direction as well as magnitude. They may be manipulated graphically like other vectors, the sum of two forces being known as their resultant. The SI UNIT of force is the newton, a force of one newton being that which will produce an acceleration of 1cm/sec² in a mass of 1 gram.

**FORD, Ford Madox** (1873–1939), influential English man of letters, born Ford Madox Hueffer. His novels *The Good Soldier* (1915) and *Parade's End* (1924–28), a tetralogy, described the decline of the English upper classes before WWI. As first editor of *The English Review* (1908–11), he encouraged such writers as Conrad (with whom he also collaborated), Pound, Frost and D. H. Lawrence.

**FORD, Gerald Rudolph, Jr.** (1913–    ), 38th president of the US. Born Leslie King, Jr., in Omaha, Neb., Ford was adopted and renamed before he was two by his mother's second husband. Ford grew up in Grand Rapids, Mich., graduated from the U. of Michigan, where he had been a star football player, worked his way through Yale U. Law School as a coach, and returned home to practice law in 1941. He served four years in the Navy during WWII, becoming a lieutenant-commander.

At the urging of Senator Arthur VANDENBERG, Ford ran for Congress in 1948 and won. He arrived on Capitol Hill in 1949 with a new bride, Elizabeth Bloomer. He became a hard-working Congressman and remained in the House of Representatives for 25 years. He obtained a seat on the powerful House Appropriations Committee and was known as a conservative and an internationalist. Slowly he became a prominent Republican spokesman. In 1963 he was appointed to the WARREN COMMISSION investigating President Kennedy's assassination. In 1964 Ford became Republican Minority Leader of the House.

Several times Ford was considered as a possible vice-presidential nominee, but he remained in the House; the highest office in the US came to him unexpectedly and unsought. On Oct. 12, 1973, President Nixon nominated Ford to succeed Spiro Agnew as vice-president. On Aug. 9, 1974, Nixon resigned the presidency over the WATERGATE crisis and Ford took the oath of office, declaring, "Our long national nightmare is over . . . Our Constitution works." Ford proved himself to be a competent president, but lost popularity because of his pardon of Nixon and because of inflation and economic recession. The US-supported regime in Vietnam was overthrown by the communists. Ford worked for détente with the USSR. In 1976 he narrowly lost a bid for reelection to Jimmy Carter.

**FORD, Henry** (1863–1947), American

automobile production pioneer. He produced his first automobile in 1896 and established the Ford Motor Company, Dearborn, Mich., in 1903. By adopting mass-assembly methods, and introducing the moving assembly line in 1913, Ford revolutionized automobile production. Ford saw that mass-produced cars could sell at a price within reach of the average American family. His Model T sold 15 million (1908–26). Ford was a paradoxical and often controversial character. Although a proud anti-intellectual, he set up several museums and the famous FORD FOUNDATION. A violent anti-unionist, he reduced the average working week, introduced profit-sharing and the highest minimum daily wage of his time. In 1938 he accepted a Nazi decoration and became a leading isolationist. At the outbreak of war, however, he built the world's largest assembly plant, to produce B-24 bombers.

**FORD, Henry II** (1917–   ), US automotive executive, the grandson of Henry Ford. He revivified the ailing Ford Motor Co. during the 1940s and 1950s and served as its chief executive officer from 1960 to 1979.

**FORD, John** (1586–1640?), English dramatist. Three tragedies, *'Tis Pity She's a Whore* (c.1627), *The Broken Heart* (c.1629) and *Love's Sacrifice* (1630), are his best-known works. Considered decadent by earlier critics because of his lack of moral comment, Ford's insight into human passion has been admired in the 20th century.

**FORD, John** (1895–1973), US motion picture director. One of the great masters of his craft, he began directing the first of his more than 125 films in 1917. He won Academy Awards for *The Informer* (1935), *The Grapes of Wrath* (1941), *How Green Was My Valley* (1942), and *The Quiet Man* (1953). In later years, his principal output was Westerns, a form he had pioneered with such early films as *The Iron Horse* (1924) and *Stagecoach* (1939).

**FORD FOUNDATION,** philanthropic corporation founded by Henry Ford in 1936. With assets of over $3 billion, it is the world's largest philanthropic trust. The foundation uses its funds for educational, cultural, scientific and charitable purposes in the US and abroad.

**FOREIGN AID PROGRAMS,** financial and other aid given by one country to another. The first major foreign aid programs were loans from the US to Europe during and after WWII. The LEND-LEASE program provided over $40 billion to US allies. After the war the MARSHALL PLAN strengthened the weakened economies of Western Europe. In 1949 the POINT FOUR PROGRAM initiated US aid to under-developed countries, particularly in Asia. Credit facilities were set for these nations in 1957 with the creation of the DEVELOPMENT LOAN FUND. The 1960s saw a diversification of US aid programs (in Asia, Africa and Latin America), and establishment of the PEACE CORPS and the ALLIANCE FOR PROGRESS.

Since 1945 US foreign aid has totaled over $150 billion and was continuing at about $5 billion a year in the 1980s. Apart from bilateral aid, the US is involved in multilateral aid programs, acting with other countries through the UN and other agencies. Member-countries of the Organization for Economic Cooperation and Development provide $6-7 billion per year in aid. Increasingly, the nations of Western Europe and Canada, Japan, Australia and the US have been coordinating their foreign aid programs, through such agencies as the WORLD BANK, to help narrow the gap between rich and poor nations. By the early 1980s the developing countries were becoming more assertive in calling for greater aid from wealthier nations.

**FOREIGN LEGION,** elite mercenary army created in 1831 by the French to save manpower in Algeria. The legion fought mainly outside France until Algerian independence (1962): in Morocco, Madagascar, Spain, Mexico, the Crimea and Indochina.

**FOREIGN SERVICE,** diplomatic and consular employees of the US Department of State. They staff embassies and consulates, promote friendly relations between the US and countries where they serve, advise on political and economic matters, protect and aid US citizens abroad and deal with aliens seeking entry to the US. (See also STATE, US DEPARTMENT OF.)

**FORENSIC MEDICINE,** the branch of MEDICINE concerned with legal aspects of DEATH, DISEASE or injury. Forensic medical experts are commonly required to examine corpses found in possibly criminal circumstances. They may be asked to elucidate probable cause and approximate time of death, to investigate the possibility of POISONING, trauma or suicide, to analyse links with possible murder weapons and to help to identify decayed or mutilated bodies.

**FORESTER, Cecil Scott** (1899–1966), English novelist, best known for his popular Captain Hornblower novels set in the Napoleonic period. An earlier novel, *The African Queen* (1935), was made into an Academy Award-winning film in 1951.

**FORESTRY,** management of forests for productive purposes. In the US, a forestry program emerged in the 1890s because of fears of a "timber famine" and following exploitation of the Great Lakes pine forests. Congress authorized the first forest reserves in 1891; creation of the FOREST SERVICE in 1905 put forestry on a scientific basis.

The most important aspect of forestry is the production of lumber. Because of worldwide depletion of timber stocks, it has become necessary to view forests as renewable productive resources, and because of the time scale and area involved in the growth of a forest, trees need more careful planning than any other crop. Forestry work plans for a continuity of timber production by balancing planting and felling. Other important functions are disease, pest, fire and flood control. The forester must control the density and proportions of the various trees in a forest and ensure that man does not radically disturb a forest's ecological balance.

The science of forestry is well advanced in the US, which is the world's largest timber producer and has more than 25 forestry schools across the country. However, only 20% of the world's forests are being renewed, and timber resources are declining.

**FOREST SERVICE, US,** Department of Agriculture agency, created in 1905 to manage and protect the national forests. Nearly 190 million acres of national forests and grasslands, as well as 480 million acres of forests and watersheds belonging to state and local governments and private owners, benefit from the service's conservation, research, development and advisory programs.

**FORGERY,** in law, the making or altering of a written instrument with intent to defraud. As a general term it is used of anything, such as a work of art or literature, made or altered with intent to deceive whether fraudulently or not. This is usually not criminal unless done for some kind of gain. Art forgeries are common, but are easier to detect than is commonly supposed; literary forgeries, such as CHATTERTON's "Rowley" poems, have seldom survived for long. Forgeries are usually detected through errors in either content or material. It is almost impossible, for example, to age paper or canvas artificially. The most successful modern art forger, however, the Dutchman Hans van Meegeren, was detected only when he confessed to forgery to escape a charge of selling art treasures to the Nazis. The term for forgery of money is COUNTERFEITING.

**FORGING,** the shaping of metal by hammering or pressing, usually when the workpiece is red hot (about 400–700C) but sometimes when it is cold. Unlike CASTING, forging does not alter the granular structure of the metal, and hence greater strength is possible in forged than in cast metals. The most basic method of forging is that of the blacksmith, who heats the metal in an open fire (forge) and hammers it into shape against an anvil. Today, metals are forged between two DIES, usually impressed with the desired shape. Techniques include: **drop forging,** where the workpiece is held on the lower, stationary die, the other being held by a massive ram which is allowed to fall; **press forging,** where the dies are pressed together; and **impact forging,** where the dies are rammed horizontally together, the workpiece between. (See also METALLURGY.)

**FORMALDEHYDE** (HCHO), colorless, acrid, toxic gas; the simplest ALDEHYDE, more reactive than the others. It is made by catalytic air oxidation of METHANOL vapor or of NATURAL GAS. Formaldehyde gas is unstable, and is usually stored as its aqueous solution, **formalin,** used as a disinfectant and preservative for biological specimens; on keeping, formalin deposits a polymer, **paraformaldehyde,** which regenerates formaldehyde on heating. Formaldehyde is condensed with UREA and PHENOLS to make PLASTICS. It is also used in TANNING and textile manufacture. MW 30.0, mp −92°C bp −21°C.

**FORMOSA.** See CHINA, REPUBLIC OF.

**FORMULA, Chemical,** a symbolic representation of the composition of a MOLECULE. The **empirical formula** shows merely the proportions of the atoms in the molecule, as found by chemical ANALYSIS, e.g., water $H_2O$, acetic acid $CH_2O$. (The subscripts indicate the number of each atom if more than one.) The **molecular formula** shows the actual number of atoms in the molecule, e.g., water $H_2O$, acetic acid $C_2H_4O_2$. The atomic symbols are sometimes grouped to give some idea of the molecular structure, e.g., acetic acid $CH_3COOH$. This is done unambiguously by the **structural formula,** which shows the chemical BONDS and so distinguishes between ISOMERS. The **space formula** shows the arrangement of the atoms and bonds in three-dimensional space, and so distinguishes between STEREOISOMERS; it may be drawn in PERSPECTIVE or represented conventionally.

**FORREST, Edwin** (1806–1872), prominent American tragedian; the first US actor actively to encourage native playwrights. His feud with English actor William Macready led to a notorious riot at New

York's Astor Place Opera House on May 8, 1849.

**FORSTER, E. M.** (1879–1970), Edward Morgan Forster, a major English novelist of the early 20th century. His novels are *Where Angels Fear to Tread* (1905), *The Longest Journey* (1907), *A Room with a View* (1908), *Howard's End* (1910), *A Passage to India* (1924) and *Maurice* (1971). Forster's major themes concern conflict in human relations—between truth and falsehood, "culture" and instinct or emotion, and the inner and outer life. His *Aspects of the Novel* (1927) was an influential critical work.

**FORSYTH, Frederic** (1938– ), British author. A reporter and staff member of the BBC before turning to fiction, he has produced novels of political intrigue and suspense, including *The Day of the Jackal* (1971), *The Odessa File* (1972) and *The Devil's Alternative* (1980).

**FORT . . .** Forts usually appear alphabetically under their identifying names, except when part of a city's or national monument's name.

**FORTIFICATION**, military construction for defense or protection. Two main types are permanent fortification (forts, castles, defense zones), usually built in peacetime, and field works, temporary defense systems in combat zones. Permanent structures such as walls, forts or castles have been important in most countries thoughout world history. Artillery revolutionized fortification: walls and towers became lower and thicker; bastions and gun platforms were set at calculated angles in walls; and concrete came into use (see MAGINOT LINE). Field works can be hasty (fox or shell hole, shallow trench) or deliberate (rampart, trench, bunker, obstacles such as mines or wire), and have been used in war since ancient times.

**FORT KNOX,** is a US military reservation in N Hardin Co., N central Ky., 33,000 acres in size and established in 1917 as a training camp. It has been a permanent military post since 1932, and the site of the US Gold Bullion Depository since 1936. Godman Air Force Base is also there.

**FORT McHENRY NATIONAL MONUMENT AND HISTORIC SHRINE,** fort in Baltimore harbor, Md. During the War of 1812, it withstood overnight bombardment by a British fleet. This inspired Francis Scott Key, a spectator, to write the words to *The Star-Spangled Banner,* which became the US national anthem.

**FORTRAN** (*formula trans*lation), one of the most widely used COMPUTER languages. Originally developed for purely scientific work, it is now, as Fortran IV, used also in commerce and elsewhere.

**FORT SUMTER NATIONAL MONUMENT,** site of a US fort in Charleston harbor, S.C., where the first shots in the Civil War were fired on April 12, 1861. When S.C. seceded from the Union (1860), US Maj. Robert Anderson received a rebel summons to surrender his garrison. He refused, Sumter was fired upon, and the war had begun. The fort was retaken when Confederates evacuated Charleston in Feb. 1865.

**FORTUNE TELLING,** prediction of future events by nonscientific or mystical means. ASTROLOGY, PALMISTRY, crystal gazing, the reading of TAROT and other cards and of tea leaves and coffee grounds, and various methods of DIVINATION such as clairvoyance are popular methods of attempting to foretell the future. In recent times there has been a popular resurgence in fortune telling, despite scientific skepticism, and some methods (such as clairvoyance) have been considered subjects for serious research.

**FOSS, Lukas (Lukas Fuchs,** 1922– ), German-born US composer who developed a method of simultaneous improvisation, and experimented with electronic effects, the use of prerecorded tape, and aleatory composition, as in *Echoi* (1961–63) and *Cello Concerto* (1966). He championed contemporary music as conductor of the Buffalo Philharmonic (1964–70) and Brooklyn Philharmonia (from 1971).

**FOSSE, Bob** (1927– ), US dancer and choreographer who staged dance sequences for such popular musicals as *The Pajama Game* (1954), *Damn Yankees* (1955) and *Redhead* (1959). He also choreographed and directed the films *Sweet Charity* (1966), *Cabaret* (1972) and the autobiographical fantasy *All That Jazz* (1979).

**FOSSILS,** evidences of ancient life preserved in sediment or rock. The preservation of most **body fossils** usually requires the possession of hard skeletal parts and rapid burial of the organism so as to prevent its decay and/or destruction. Common skeletal materials include bone, calcium carbonate, opaline silica, chitin and tricalcium phosphate. Preservation of an organism in its entirety (i.e., unaltered hard and soft parts together) is exceptional, e.g. MAMMOTHS in Siberian PERMAFROST. Unaltered hard parts are common in post-MESOZOIC sediments but become increasingly scarcer further back in geologic time.

**Petrification** describes two ways in which the shape of hard parts of the organism may be preserved. In **permineralization,** the pore spaces of the hard parts are infilled by certain minerals (e.g., SILICA, PYRITE, CALCITE) that infiltrate from the local GROUNDWATER. The resulting fossil is thus a mixture of mineral and organic matter. In many other cases, substitution (or replacement) occurs, where the hard parts are dissolved away but the form is retained by newly deposited minerals. Where this has happened very gradually, even microscopic detail may be preserved; but generally only the outward form remains.

Often the skeletal materials are dissolved entirely, leaving either internal or external molds. The filling of a complete mold may also occur, forming a cast. The complete filling of a hollow shell interior may form a core or steinkern such as the corkscrewlike filling of a coiled snail shell.

In the process of carbonization, the tissues decompose leaving only a thin residual CARBON film that shows the outline of the organism's flattened form. In addition to interest in body fossils, there is also much interest in trace fossils (See PALEOICHNOLOGY), which include more indirect evidences of the former presence of an organism.

**FOSTER, Stephen Collins** (1826–1864), US composer of over 200 songs and instrumental pieces. His *Oh! Susannah, My Old Kentucky Home* and *Old Black Joe* and other Southern dialect songs are essentially so simple that they are often considered folk music.

**FOSTER, William Zebulon** (1881–1961), US communist leader, organizer of the 1919 steel strike. He joined the Communist Party (c1921) and was its candidate for president (1924; 1928; 1932) and for governor of N.Y. (1930).

**FOUCAULT, Michel** (1926–  ), French philosopher best known for his social history and epistomology. His works include *Madness and Civilization* (1965), *The Order of Things* (1971), *The Archeology of Knowledge* (1972) and *The History of Sexuality* (1978).

**FOUNTAIN,** a device which allows water to flow into a basin, or a more complex system from which water is forced into the air through a jet or jets. Fountains were used in ancient Greece as shrines and as public water supply points and by the Romans both to supply water and as civic decoration. The Italian Renaissance opened a new era of grandeur in fountain design. These featured tiered basins and elaborate sculptures and tableaus. BERNINI's Baroque Fountain of the Rivers (1648–51) and the Trevi Fountain (1762) are among Rome's many famous fountains. Other fine examples are those by LE NÔTRE at VERSAILLES in France, and by the modern designer Carl MILLES in New York and Chicago.

**FOUNTAIN OF YOUTH,** a rejuvenating spring located according to legend on the BIMINI ISLANDS off the coast of Fla. The Spaniard PONCE DE LEON discovered Florida in 1513, probably on an expedition to find the fountain.

**FOUQUET, Jean** (c1420–1480), French painter who helped bring the Italian Renaissance style to France. His miniatures, panels, portraits and manuscript illuminations are realistic and precisely detailed. One of his finest works is the *Melun Diptych* (c1450).

**FOUR FREEDOMS,** freedom of speech, freedom of worship, freedom from want, freedom from fear. These principles were first presented by President Roosevelt in 1941 as a basis for world peace. After WWII the freedoms became enshrined in the UN Charter. (See DECLARATION OF HUMAN RIGHTS.)

**FOUR-H CLUBS,** educational organizations for young people from 9–19 years, who live primarily in rural areas. Started in 1914 by the US Department of Agriculture, the clubs undertake projects in farming, home economy, science and community services. The four "H's" are contained in the oath: "I pledge my *head* to clearer thinking, my *heart* to greater loyalty, my *hands* to larger service and my *health* to better living, for my club, my community and my country."

**FOUR HORSEMEN OF NOTRE DAME,** a famous football backfield. Quarterback Harry Stuhldreher, halfbacks Don Miller and Jim Crowley, and fullback Elmer LAYDEN weighed an average of only 160 pounds each, but were devastating as a unit from 1922 to 1924, when they led their Notre Dame team to a national championship, beating Stanford 27–10 in the Rose Bowl game.

**FOUR HORSEMEN OF THE APOC-ALYPSE,** allegorical biblical figures in the book of Revelation (often called the Apocalypse) 6:1-8. The red horse's rider represents war, the black's famine, the pale horse's rider death, while the rider on the white horse is usually taken to represent Christ.

**FOURIER, François Marie Charles** (1772–1837), French Utopian socialist. Rejecting CAPITALISM, he devised a social system based on cooperative, primarily farming COMMUNES of about 400 families. Fourierism gained considerable following in France and the US, but attempts to put his theories into practice, as at BROOK FARM, were short-lived. (See also UTOPIA.)

**FOURIER, Jean Baptiste Joseph, Baron** (1768–1830), French mathematician best known for his equations of HEAT propagation and for showing that all periodic OSCILLATIONS can be reduced to a SERIES of simple, regular WAVE MOTIONS, as represented by Fourier Series, which have the general form

$$\tfrac{1}{2}a_0 + \sum_{n=1}^{\infty} (a_n \cos nx + b_n \sin nx).$$

**FOURTEEN POINTS,** war objectives for the US, proposed by President Wilson in Jan. 1918, incorporated in the armistice of Nov. 1918. The points were that there should be: open covenants of peace; freedom of the seas; abolition of trade barriers; general disarmament; settlement of colonial claims; evacuation of conquered Russian territories; evacuation and restoration of Belgium; return of Alsace-Lorraine to France; readjustment of Italian frontiers; autonomy for the subject peoples of Austria and Hungary; guarantees for the integrity of Serbia, Montenegro and Rumania; autonomy for the subject peoples of the Ottoman Empire; an independent Poland; and a general association of nations. These points formed the basis of the Treaty of VERSAILLES and the LEAGUE OF NATIONS.

**FOURTH DIMENSION.** See SPACE-TIME.

**FOWLER, Henry Watson** (1858–1933), distinguished English lexicographer, best-known for his masterly *A Dictionary of Modern English Usage* (1926). Fowler collaborated with his brother on several books, including *The Concise Oxford Dictionary of Current English* (1911).

**FOWLES, John** (1926–   ), English novelist. Often attempting to reconcile the Victorian novel form with more philosophical concerns, he has written such passionate, sometimes difficult works as *The Magus* (1966; rev. version, 1978), *The French Lieutenant's Woman* (1969) and *Daniel Martin* (1977).

**FOX, Charles James** (1749–1806), English statesman and orator, champion of political and religious freedom and fierce opponent of George III and the power of the crown. He served in Parliament from 1768 as a Tory and as a Whig, both in and out of government. He championed the colonists in the REVOLUTIONARY WAR (1775–83) and in the 1790s supported the French Revolution.

**FOX, George** (1624–1691), English religious leader, founder of the Society of Friends or QUAKERS (1652). Although frequently harassed and imprisoned by the authorities, Fox traveled widely in Europe and North America preaching his doctrine—derived from his conversion experience (1646)—that truth comes through the inner light of Christ in the soul. (See also MYSTICISM.)

**FOXES,** small members of the dog family Canidae, noted for their cunning and solitary habits; foxes feed mainly on small mammals. The common Red fox of the N Hemisphere is the quarry of British fox-hunts; American foxes include the Gray fox, the desert Kit fox and the now rare Swift fox. The Arctic fox lives in northern tundras and has a white winter coat. Africa offers the insect-eating Bat-eared fox and South America the Crab-eating fox.

**FOXHOUND,** versatile, strong, fast hunting dog standing up to 25in at the shoulder, weighing up to 70lb, with a short coat that may be a mixture of black, tan and white.

**FOX HUNTING,** popular sport among horsemen in Britain, with some following in North America and elsewhere. Members of a hunt, led by a pack of foxhounds, pursue a wild fox to the death. The excitement of a chase comes from pitting the wits of the hounds against the fox. Hunts are often opposed by animal welfare and anti-blood-sports groups.

**FOX TALBOT, William Henry.** See TALBOT, WILLIAM HENRY FOX.

**FOX TERRIER,** dog bred in smooth and wirehaired varieties, originally used in the 19th century by English fox hunters to pursue its quarry into its lair. It stands around 15in at the shoulder and is predominantly white, marked with black or tan.

**FOXX, James Emory** (1907–1967), US baseball player. Jimmy "the Beast" Foxx played (1926–45) for the Philadelphia Athletics, Boston Red Sox, Chicago Cubs and Philadelphia Phillies, hitting 534 home runs. He was elected to the Baseball Hall of Fame in 1951.

**FOXX, Red** (John Elroy Sanford, 1922–   ), US comedian. After a successful career playing black nightclubs, he achieved national attention in the TV series "Sanford & Son" (1972–77).

**FOY, Eddie** (1856–1928), US entertainer. A comic in Chicago revues in the 1880s and 1890s, he went on to star in Broadway musical comedies such as *The Earl and the Girl* (1905) and *Over the River* (1911–13). From 1913 to 1923 he was a vaudeville favorite with his children, the "Seven Little Foys."

**FOYT, A.J.** (1935–   ), US race car driver. He won the Indianapolis 500 a record four times, and was US Auto Club national champion five times, also a record.

He was the first driver to win more than 100 USAC races.

**FRA ANGELICO.** See ANGELICO, FRA.

**FRACTURES,** mechanical defects in BONE caused by trauma or underlying DISEASE. Most follow sudden bending, twisting or shearing forces, but prolonged stress (e.g., long marches) may lead to small fractures. Fractures may be *open*, in which bone damage is associated with SKIN damage, with consequent liability to infection; or *closed*, in which the overlying skin is intact. Comminuted fractures are those in which bone is broken into many fragments. Greenstick fractures are partial fractures where bone is bent, not broken, and occur in children. Severe pain, deformity, loss of function, abnormal mobility of a bone and HEMORRHAGE, causing swelling and possibly SHOCK, are important features; damage to nerves, ARTERIES and underlying viscera (e.g., LUNG, SPLEEN, LIVER and BRAIN) are serious complications. Principles of treatment are: reduction, or restoring the bone to satisfactory alignment, by manipulation or operation; immobilization with plaster, splints or internal fixation with metal or bone prostheses, until bony healing has occurred, and rehabilitation, which enables full recovery of function in most cases. Early recognition and appropriate treatment of associated soft tissue injury is crucial. **Pathological fractures** occur when congenital defect, lack of mineral content, TUMORS etc. weaken the structure of bone, allowing fracture with trivial or no apparent injury.

**FRAGONARD, Jean-Honoré** (1732–1806), French ROCOCO painter and noted portraitist. His work is characterized by a lightness of touch and a use of radiant color. Among his masterpieces are *The Swing* (1766) and *Fête at St. Cloud* (1775), which convey the atmosphere of erotic playfulness and gaiety cultivated at the court of Louis XV.

**FRAME, Janet** (1924–    ), New Zealand short-story writer, poet and novelist whose works reflect her history of mental illness and love of her native landscape. Among her best works are the novels *Faces in the Water* (1961) and *Intensive Care* (1970) and poetry *A Pocket Mirror* (1967).

**FRANCE,** officially the French Republic, the largest country in W Europe, covering some 211,000sq mi. It is bordered on the N by the English Channel; on the NE by Belgium and Luxembourg; on the E by West Germany, Switzerland and Italy; on the S (where Monaco forms a small enclave) by the Mediterranean, Spain and Andorra; and on the W by the Atlantic Ocean; and it includes the island of Corsica. The whole area is known as metropolitan France, and is divided administratively into 95 departments grouped into 22 regions. In addition, the former colonies of Guadeloupe, French Guiana, Martinique and Réunion rank as overseas departments.

**Land.** More than 50% of metropolitan France is lowlying and less than 25% is highland. The main mountain ranges form natural frontiers: the Pyrenees in the SW, the French Alps (with Mont Blanc, 15,781ft, the highest peak in W Europe) in the SE, and the Jura and Vosges (separated by the Belfort Gap, an important routeway) in the E. A major physical feature is the Massif Central (central plateau) W of the Saône and Rhône rivers and terminated in the S by the Cévennes Mts. Its features include lava plateaus and *puys* (ash and lava cones). In the NW is the small and much lower Armorican Massif. The lowlands are mainly in the N and W and include the Paris Basin (about 29,000sq mi) between the English Channel and the Massif Central, the Ile-de-France, a fertile plateau and the triangular Aquitaine lowland in the SW.

Draining the country are five major river systems: the Seine (historically and commercially France's most important river), Loire, Garonne-Gironde, Rhône-Saône, and Rhine. Most have important canal links and some provide hydroelectric power, notably the Rhône. Coastal features include the *rias* (long inlets) of the Armorican Massif, the sand dunes and lagoons of the Landes in the SW, and the marshy lagoons of the Rhône delta.

The climate is mainly mild but has many regional variations. More than half of France has less than 80 days with frost annually and most areas average 20-50in of rain yearly. The Riviera and Corsica have a typically Mediterranean climate. Vegetation ranges from the beech and oak of N and central France to the drought-resistant scrub and wild olives of Mediterranean areas.

**People.** Due to invasions by Romans, Celts, Franks and Mediterranean peoples, the French are of mingled racial types. Distinctive groups include the Celtic Bretons of Brittany and the Basques living along the Spanish frontier. The population of almost 54,000,000 also includes more than 750,000 Algerians and some 3,500,000 migrant workers, including many Spaniards and Italians. More than 70% of the population lives in the cities and towns; the largest is Paris, the capital. The Paris megalopolis has more than 15% of the total population. Other large conurbations are Lyons, Marseilles and Lille-Roubaix-Tourcoing. People are increasingly moving from the rural areas into the towns.

Most French people are baptized Roman Catholic, but many are not practicing Catholics. Minority groups include Protestants, Jews and Muslims. The French are proud of their education system; illiteracy is negligible. French culture has had worldwide influence on social intercourse, diplomacy, arts, crafts and architecture since the Middle Ages.

**Economy.** France is a major agricultural and industrial country, leading W Europe in food production, especially grain, beef, sugar beets and wine. Leading crops include wheat (especially in the Paris Basin and Flanders), oats, rye and corn, sugar beets (Brittany and Flanders), rice (the Camargue) and all kinds of fruits. Millions of beef and dairy cattle, sheep and hogs are reared. The NW is known for its dairy products. France is the world's third-largest silk-producer and leads in the production of high-quality wines from such areas as Champagne, Bordeaux and lower Burgundy. About 20% of the land is forested, and fisheries, centered on such ports as Boulogne and Lorient, are important. France has coal (Nord, Pas de Calais, Lorraine), oil (Parentis), natural gas (Lacq), abundant iron ore (mainly Lorraine but also in Normandy), bauxite and other minerals. Industry includes iron and steel production, mainly in the N and E (especially Dunkerque) but also in the S (Fos-sur-Mer), oil refining (mainly of imported oil) and petrochemicals, aircraft

**Official name:** The French Republic
**Capital:** Paris
**Area:** 211,208sq mi
**Population:** 53,710,000
**Languages:** French
**Religions:** Catholic, Protestant, Jewish
**Monetary unit(s):** 1 French franc=100 centimes

and automobiles, textiles (Lyons, Roubaix, Lille, Tourcoing, Castres). Paris is the chief manufacturing center. Tourism is important, and so is the production of high fashion clothing, gloves, perfume, jewelry and watches.

**History.** Among early inhabitants were the Stone Age hunter-painters of such caves as Lascaux (Dordogne) and the megalith builders in Brittany. Greeks founded Marseilles about 600 BC. The country was progressively settled and unified under the Gauls, Romans and Franks. On Charlemagne's death (814 AD) the Frankish Empire disintegrated and feudal rulers became powerful. Their territories were increasingly welded together under the CAPETIANS' (987–1328), and the HUNDRED YEARS WAR (1338–1453) saw the eviction of the English. Under Louis XI (1461–83) and later monarchs, royal power was strengthened, reaching its zenith with Louis XIV (1643–1715). Continuing royal extravagance culminated in the FRENCH REVOLUTION (1789), the execution of Louis XVI and the establishment of the First Republic. The Bourbon restoration following on the downfall of NAPOLEON (1815) was short-lived and Louis Philippe was put on the throne (July Revolution, 1830). After his deposition, Louis NAPOLEON headed the Second Republic (1848), then made himself Emperor NAPOLEON III (1852). Defeat in the Franco-Prussian War (1870) led to his downfall and to the Third Republic. WWI left France victorious but devastated and in WWII the country was occupied by Germany (1940). The Fourth Republic (1946) proved unstable and Gen. Charles DE GAULLE was recalled to head the Fifth Republic (1958). He established a strong presidential government, gave independence to most French possessions (notably Algeria, 1962) but pursued conservative policies at home, and stressed greater independence from the United States in foreign policy. After De Gaulle resigned over a constitutional issue (1969), his conservative policies were maintained by his successors Georges POMPIDOU and Valéry GISCARD D'ESTAING. In 1981 François Mitterrand, a socialist, was elected president, promising substantial changes in French domestic policy.

**FRANCE, Anatole** (Jacques Anatole François Thibault; 1844–1924), French novelist and critic, a renowned stylist. Though he believed in and worked for social justice, his work is deeply pessimistic. Among his best-known books are *Penguin Island* (1908) and *The Revolt of the Angels*

(1914). He won the 1921 Nobel literature prize.

**FRANCIS,** name of two Holy Roman Emperors. **Francis I** (1708–1765), Holy Roman Emperor from 1745, was consort of Maria Theresa of Austria from 1736. **Francis II** (1768–1835), last Holy Roman Emperor (1792–1806) and first emperor of Austria (from 1804). Defeated by Napoleon in 1796, 1805 (AUSTERLITZ) and 1809, he then sided with him until 1813, when he joined the anti-Napoleonic side. At the CONGRESS OF VIENNA, through the diplomacy of METTERNICH, he regained most of the Austrian territories.

**FRANCIS,** two kings of France. **Francis I** (1494–1547), king from 1515, strengthened royal power at the expense of the nobility. He conducted costly wars against the Hapsburgs, including abortive Italian campaigns. He suppressed Protestantism but fostered Renaissance ideals; he was a great patron of art and letters, and a great builder of palaces. **Francis II** (1544–1560), king from 1559, first husband of MARY QUEEN OF SCOTS. A weak-willed man, he was dominated by the House of Guise and his mother, Catherine de MEDICIS.

**FRANCISCANS,** largest order in the Roman Catholic Church. Three orders were founded by St. FRANCIS OF ASSISI between 1209 and 1224. They were called Grey Friars for the color of their habits; modern habits are dark brown. Dissension within the First Order divided it into three main branches, the Observants, Conventuals and CAPUCHINS. The Second Order are nuns, known as Poor Clares for their foundress St. Clare. The Third Order is mainly a lay fraternity, though some members live in community under vows.

**FRANCIS OF ASSISI, Saint** (c1181–1226), Italian Roman Catholic mystic, founder of the FRANCISCANS. In 1205 he turned away from his extravagant life and wealthy merchant family to a wandering religious life of utter poverty. With his many followers he preached and ministered to the poor in Italy and abroad, stressing piety, simplicity and joy in creation, and the love of all living things. Given oral sanction by Pope Innocent III, his order expanded beyond the control of its founder; he relinquished the leadership in 1221. His feast day is Oct. 4.

**FRANCIS OF SALES, Saint** (1567–1622), Roman Catholic bishop of Geneva-Annecy from 1603. Author of popular works such as *Introduction to the Devout Life* (1608), he was respected even by the Calvinists for his good nature and humility. He helped found the Order of the Visitation (1610). His feast

day is Jan. 24.

**FRANCIS XAVIER, Saint** (1506–1552), Spanish missionary. A friend of St. Ignatius LOYOLA, he was a founder member of the JESUITS. In 1541 he set out as a missionary, reaching the East Indies, Goa, India, Malacca and Ceylon. In 1549 he established a Jesuit mission in Japan and in 1552 sought to extend his work to China, but died before he reached there. His feast day is Dec. 3.

**FRANCIUM (Fr),** a radioactive ALKALI METAL, resembling CESIUM, which has been obtained only in tracer quantities. Its most stable isotope, $Fr^{223}$, has a half-life of 21 minutes.

**FRANCK, César Auguste** (1822–1890), Belgian French composer. Organist of St. Clotilde, Paris, from 1858, he became a professor at the Paris Conservatory in 1872. Though at first little appreciated, his compositions greatly influenced French Romantic music. Among his famous works are the tone poem *The Accursed Hunter* (1882) and the *Symphony in D minor* (1888).

**FRANCO, Francisco** (1892–1975), Spanish general, *caudillo* (Spanish: leader, head of state) of Spain from 1939. Kept in foreign commands by leftwing governments, he joined the 1936 military revolt in Spain from Morocco and in 1937 became leader of the FALANGE party and head of the anti-republican army. After the fall of leftist-held Madrid he became head of state. Although he had been aided against the Soviet-backed Loyalists by Germany and Italy he remained neutral in WWII. In the postwar period his rule became less totalitarian but he retained all his power. In the late 1960s increasing unrest caused him to harden the regime once more; he remained in control until shortly before his death, when he was succeeded by Prince JUAN CARLOS as king.

**FRANCO-PRUSSIAN WAR** (July 1870–May 1871), arose from BISMARCK's desire to unify the German states against a common enemy and NAPOLEON III's fear of an alliance against him if a Prussian prince succeeded to the Spanish throne. Provoked by the EMS DISPATCH, France declared war; the more efficient Prussians trapped a large French army at Metz, and in Sept. 1870 captured the main French army and Napoleon himself at Sedan. The Second Empire fell and Paris was besieged; despite vigorous resistance led by Leon GAMBETTA -it capitulated in Jan. 1871. William II of Prussia was declared German emperor at Versailles. The PARIS COMMUNE revolt followed. In the treaty, France lost

Alsace-Lorraine and incurred crushing indemnities.

**FRANK, Anne** (1929–1945), German Jewish girl who with her family lived in hiding from the Nazis in Amsterdam 1942–44; betrayed and sent to a concentration camp, she died there of typhus. Her diary, published in 1947, provided the material for a popular play and film.

**FRANKENSTEIN,** novel by Mary SHELLEY. In an attempt to recreate life, its title character makes a hideous, suffering creature who wavers between good and evil and finally kills his creator. The name has become attached to the creature, particularly as portrayed on film by Boris KARLOFF.

**FRANKENTHALER, Helen** (1928–    ), US painter whose work is considered transitional between abstract expressionism and color-field painting. She often used stains and diluted paints to achieve her effects.

**FRANKFORT,** city in central Ky., capital of the commonwealth and seat of Franklin Co. It has various industries, especially whiskey distilling, and is the trading center of the surrounding agricultural area. Pop 25,973.

**FRANKFURT AM MAIN,** historic city on the Main R in West Germany, since medieval times a world center of commerce, industry and finance. Its prosperity was founded on the textile trade, and on the great medieval trade fairs; the city remained independent until taken by Prussia in 1866. It was largely devastated in WWII but some old buildings, including its Gothic cathedral, still survive. A major river port, it is a rail and road junction with Germany's busiest airport. It has a wide range of industries. Pop 628,200.

**FRANKFURTER, Felix** (1882–1965), US Supreme Court Justice 1939–62, legal adviser to presidents Wilson and F. D. Roosevelt. Known for his liberal views, he advocated the doctrine of judicial restraint, minimizing the judiciary's role in the process of government; he was equally opposed to attempts to obstruct "progressive" legislation and to attempts to further it by undue interpretation.

**FRANKINCENSE,** an aromatic gum produced from the trunks of trees of the genus *Boswellia*. It is used as INCENSE, for fumigation and in perfumes, and was once thought to have medicinal properties. It was one of the MAGI's gifts to the infant Jesus.

**FRANKLIN, Aretha** (1942–    ), US singer. The daughter of a Baptist minister, she grew up surrounded by the gospel singing of revival meetings. Her struggle for recognition ended in 1967 with "I Never Loved a Man (The Way I Love You)," the first of her many great hits.

**FRANKLIN, Benjamin** (1706–1790), American writer, printer, philosopher, scientist and statesman of the American revolution. Tolerant, urbane and intellectual, he combined the spirit of the ENLIGHTENMENT with his puritan upbringing. Born of a poor family in Boston, Mass., he moved to Philadelphia (1723) and married Deborah Read, by whom he had two children. By his own efforts he made enough money as a publisher and printer to retire at the age of 42 and devote himself entirely to writing, science and public life. His writings include letters, journals, satires, economic and social essays, a revealing *Autobiography* and the aphoristic *Poor Richard's Almanack* (1732). A founder of the American Philosophical Society (1743), he was an enthusiastic researcher and inventor. Experiments in electrostatics (1750–51) led to his famous kite experiment, which proved that lightning was a form of electricity; from this he invented the lightning conductor. He also invented bifocal spectacles, the glass harmonica and the efficient Franklin stove, and developed theories of electricity, heat absorption, meteorology and ocean currents.

In Philadelphia's civic affairs he helped found an insurance company, a hospital, a public library, a night watch and in 1747 the first militia. He served as deputy postmaster general of the colonies 1753–1754 and in 1754 organized defenses in the FRENCH AND INDIAN WARS. As Pennsylvania's delegate to the Albany Congress, he was largely responsible for a plan to unite the colonies under the British crown. He was an important influence for conciliation in pre-Revolutionary years when he acted as Pennsylvania's agent in London.

When he returned home, he helped draft the Declaration of Independence. He was the rebel colonies' commissioner in the French court from 1776 and his diplomatic skill gained them vital French support in the war. He led the independence negotiations and returned home in 1785 to serve as president of the Pennsylvania Executive Council. Franklin supported the abolition of slavery and at 81 became a member of the Constitutional Convention, where despite ill-health he helped formulate the compromise that made the US Constitution possible.

**FRANKS,** Germanic tribes, living originally E of the Rhine. In the 3rd–5th centuries AD they repeatedly invaded Gaul and finally overran it. CLOVIS I united the disparate tribes under his rule, founding the Christian MEROVINGIAN dynasty; this was weakened by internal conflict, and finally deposed by the CAROLINGIANS in the 8th century. Under the rule of CHARLEMAGNE the Franks reached the height of their power. France and Franconia in Germany are named for them.

**FRANZ FERDINAND** (1863–1914), Archduke of Austria and heir to the Austro-Hungarian Empire. His children's right of succession was forfeited by his morganatic marriage to Sophie Chotek of the lesser nobility. Their assassination at Sarajevo triggered off WWI.

**FRANZ JOSEF** (1830–1916), Emperor of Austria from 1848 and King of Hungary from 1867. He came to the throne in a year of revolutions and was at first highly absolutist. He suppressed a Hungarian revolt in 1849, but in 1867 further unrest forced him to create the Dual Monarchy, giving Hungary internal autonomy. Alliance with Germany (1879) and Italy (1882) created the TRIPLE ALLIANCE. His harsh policies against Serbia were among the causes of WWI. A conservative autocrat but a patron of arts and learning, he was generally liked and respected by his subjects.

**FRASER, Malcolm** (1930– ), Australian prime minister (1975– ). First elected to Parliament in 1955, he served in various posts in Liberal Party governments 1966–71. In 1975 he became Liberal leader and later prime minister. His party easily won reelection in 1977. He pursued a policy of cutbacks in public expenditures in order to halve the inflation rate; however, a high unemployment rate continued in the country.

**FRASER, Simon** (1776–1862), Canadian fur-trader who in establishing a chain of trading posts explored the interior of British Columbia. In 1808 he sailed down most of the British Columbia R (now the FRASER RIVER). In 1816 he was acquitted of the massacre at the RED RIVER SETTLEMENT.

**FRAUNCES TAVERN**, historic building in New York City. A tavern in Revolutionary times, it was named for its owner, the West Indian "Black Sam" Fraunces. A rendezvous for patriot groups, it was the scene of Washington's farewell to his officers in Dec. 1783. Since 1904 it has been a museum run by the Sons of the Revolution.

**FRAZER, Sir James George** (1854–1941), British social anthropologist. In *The Golden Bough: A Study in Magic and Religion* (1890; enlarged 1907–15) he proposed a parallel evolution of thought in all peoples:

from magic through religion to science, each with its distinct notion of cause and effect. Despite the apparent error of his conclusions, his work in surveying primitive customs and beliefs was of great value to cultural anthropology.

**FRAZIER, Edward Franklin** (1894–1962), US sociologist. A prominent black educator, he specialized in socioeconomic studies of the black community and wrote *Black Bourgeoisie* (1957).

**FRAZIER, Joe** (1944– ), US boxer declared world champion in 1970 after Muhammad Ali's deposition. His title was disputed, but he defeated Ali in the ring in 1971. In 1973 he lost the title to George Foreman.

**FREDERICK**, name of three Holy Roman Emperors. **Frederick I Barbarossa** (c1123–1190) was elected king of Germany in 1152. Having pacified Germany, where he promoted learning and economic growth, he occupied Lombardy and was crowned king of Italy in 1154 and Holy Roman Emperor in 1155. He was drowned while leading the Third Crusade, and passed into legend as Germany's savior. **Frederick II** (1194–1250) became king of Sicily in 1198 and of Germany in 1211. He was crowned Holy Roman Emperor in 1220. Made titular king of Jerusalem in 1227, he acquired territory in the Holy Land and was crowned in 1229. He was continually at odds with the papacy and was excommunicated three times. A capable administrator, scholar and patron of the arts, he went into a decline after a serious defeat at Parma in 1248. **Frederick III** (1415–1493) was chosen king of Germany in 1440 and obtained election as Holy Roman Emperor in 1452 by making concessions to the papacy, weakening the Empire.

**FREDERICK WILLIAM** (1620–1688), Elector of Brandenburg from 1640, known as the Great Elector. By skillful shifting of alliances in an attempt to establish a balance of power he was able to shield his country from the worst of the THIRTY YEARS WAR and add Prussia to Brandenburg. This and the modern army he created laid the foundations for the country's future predominance in Germany.

**FREDERICK WILLIAM**, name of four kings of Prussia. **Frederick William I** (1688–1740), king from 1713, centralized and radically reformed his administration. He spent freely on building up a powerful army but was otherwise frugal to the point of miserliness. **Frederick William II** (1744–1797), reigned from 1786. Nephew of Frederick the Great, he lacked his uncle's military and administrative skill, being most noted as a patron of the arts. Prussia made large territorial gains in his reign, however, by inheritance and through the partition of Poland. **Frederick William III** (1770–1840), reigned from 1797. He resisted demands for internal reforms until the collapse of Prussia in the Napoleonic Wars. **Frederick William IV** (1795–1861), reigned from 1840, a time of unrest and the growth of the movement for German unity. He resisted most demands for reform until forced by the 1848 revolution to make drastic changes.

**FREDERICTON,** capital city of New Brunswick, Canada, and seat of York Co. An administrative and trade center, it also has some light industry. The U. of New Brunswick is here. Pop 24,254.

**FREED, Arthur** (Arthur Grossman; 1894–1973), US film producer who led a unit at MGM which produced (1939–60) many of the greatest American movie musicals, including *The Wizard of Oz* (1939), *Singin' in the Rain* (1952) and the Academy Award winners *An American in Paris* (1951) and *Gigi* (1958).

**FREEDMEN'S BUREAU,** the US Bureau of Refugees, Freedmen and Abandoned Lands (1865–72), established during RECONSTRUCTION to act as a welfare agency for freed slaves in the South. It was headed by Major O. O. HOWARD. Handicapped by inadequate funding and personnel, the bureau nevertheless built Negro hospitals, schools and colleges. It had little success in improving civil rights, due to judicial and congressional hostility; its influence had declined by the time it was dissolved.

**FREEDOM OF INFORMATION ACT** **(FOIA)** gives the public right of access to governmental records. Enacted in 1966 and strengthened in 1974, FOIA provides that agencies must respond to requests for information within 10 working days; appeals are supposed to be settled in another 20. FOIA has helped reporters gather material for such important stories as those on the MY LAI massacre and the FBI's illegal harassment of domestic political groups. Most requests under the act come from businesses seeking information in governmental files about their competitors. Some records are exempted from the act, including confidential files of law enforcement and intelligence agencies and information gained by the Federal Trade Commission through subpoenas. In 1981 the Reagan administration proposed that such exemptions be broadened.

**FREEDOM OF RELIGION,** right to believe and worship freely, without legal restraint. Religious practices considered contrary to public interest, however, e.g. polygamy, snake handling, and withholding medical treatment from minors, are usually forbidden in the US.

**FREEDOM OF SPEECH,** right to express facts and opinions without legal restraint. In practice this is usually limited by the laws of libel, and, in extreme cases, sedition. (See also BILL OF RIGHTS; FOUR FREEDOMS.)

**FREEDOM OF THE PRESS,** right of private individuals to print and distribute information and opinions without interference, subject only to laws against indecency, libel and in extreme cases sedition. (See also BILL OF RIGHTS.)

**FREEDOM RIDES,** bus trips from the North to the South organized in 1961, originally by the CONGRESS OF RACIAL EQUALITY (CORE), for the purpose of protesting and breaking racial-segregation practices in Southern interstate bus terminals. After the first black and white Freedom Riders encountered violence in Ala., other civil rights groups joined the movement, and ugly confrontations between Freedom Riders and racist crowds and local officials continued for some months. In Nov. 1961, the Interstate Commerce Commission banned such segregation.

**FREE ENTERPRISE SYSTEM,** economic doctrine advocating unrestricted freedom for individuals and companies to determine what they produce and how. It relies upon competition and the discrimination of the consumer market to check abuses of this freedom. (See also CAPITALISM.)

**FREEMAN, Douglas Southall** (1886–1953), US journalist and historian. The conservative editor of the Richmond *News Leader* (1915–49), he was an authority on Civil War military history. He wrote *Lee's Lieutenants* (3 vols., 1942–44) and won Pulitzer Prizes for a biography of Robert E. Lee (4 vols., 1934), and a biography of George Washington (7 vols., 1949–57).

**FREEMASONRY.** See MASONRY.

**FREER, Charles Lang** (1856–1919), US industrialist and art collector. He built the Freer Gallery in Washington, D.C., to house the magnificent art collection, including the world's largest collection of WHISTLER's works, that he gave to the SMITHSONIAN INSTITUTION in 1906.

**FREE SILVER,** 19th-century US political issue started by Western silver interests in an attempt to boost the price of silver, which had been hit by world prices and demonetization in 1873. The idea of "free silver" as an economic panacea was nonsensical but had great appeal among the economically ignorant and those whose debts would be lessened by a cheaper dollar. After the 1893 depression (which it in fact helped precipitate) it became the major issue of the 1896 presidential campaign, with William Jennings BRYAN as its most fervent advocate.

**FREE SOIL PARTY,** a short-lived US coalition party (including the BARN BURNERS), formed in N.Y. in 1848 to oppose the extension of slavery into the territories. It attracted many famous men, including President Martin VAN BUREN but polled few votes in the 1848 and 1852 elections, and most members merged with the Republican Party in 1854.

**FREE TRADE,** international commerce, free from tariffs, quotas or other legal restriction, except nonrestrictive tariffs levied for revenue only. The opposite of free trade is PROTECTIONISM. Among early advocates of free trade were the PHYSIOCRATS, Adam SMITH, David RICARDO and J. S. MILL. Modern economists generally accept free trade but advocate varying degrees of protection to safeguard employment and developing industries, as in the theories of J. M. KEYNES. The US has traditionally been protectionist but since WWII has become committed to freer trade.

**FREE VERSE** (from French *vers libre*), verse without conventional rhythm or meter, relying instead upon the cadences of the spoken language. It was first developed in 19th-century France as a reaction to the extreme formality of accepted styles. Among its many exponents in English are Walt WHITMAN, D. H. LAWRENCE, Ezra POUND and T. S. ELIOT.

**FREE WILL,** in philosophy, a faculty of originating an action or decision man is alleged to require if he is to be able to make moral choices. Philosophical theories in which man is assumed to have free will formally conflict with those in which his actions are considered to be determined by causes beyond his control. However, the choice between theories of free will and DETERMINISM may admit of other, intermediate alternatives.

**FREGE, Gottlob** (1848–1925), German logician, father of mathematical LOGIC. Inspired by the earlier work of LEIBNIZ, he tried to show that all mathematical truths could be derived logically from a few simple axioms. After RUSSELL's criticism that his system allowed at least one paradox, he wrote little more; but his work influenced later thinkers such as PEANO, RUSSELL and WHITEHEAD. (See also LOGICAL POSITIVISM.)

**FRÉMONT, John Charles** (1813–1890), US explorer, general, politician and popular hero. He mapped much of the territory between the Mississippi valley and the Pacific during the early 1840s. He was caught up in the struggle with Mexico over California, being at one time appointed military governor and the next convicted of mutiny (1847–48), a sentence later commuted by President Polk. Frémont stood as the Republican Party's first presidential candidate (1856) but was defeated by James BUCHANAN. He had to resign as commander of the Department of the West during the Civil War for exceeding his office by declaring martial law. He was governor of Arizona territory 1878–83.

**FRENCH,** Romance language spoken in France and parts of Belgium, Switzerland, Canada and former French and Belgian colonies; it is the official language of 21 countries. It developed from Latin during and after the Roman occupation of Gaul and also from Celtic and Germanic elements. By the 11th century two dialects had developed: in the south the *langue d'oc*, in the north the *langue d'öil*. From the latter came *francien*, the Paris dialect which became modern French as spoken and written since the 17th century.

**FRENCH, Daniel Chester** (1850–1931), US sculptor best known for his monumental statuary, such as his first work, *The Minute Man* (1875) in Concord, Mass., and the seated *Lincoln* (1922) in the Lincoln Memorial, Washington, D.C.

**FRENCH, John Denton Pinkstone, 1st Earl of Ypres** (1852–1925), British field marshal, commander of the British Expeditionary Force at the beginning of WWI. He was relieved of his command after the costly retreat from Mons and the battles of Ypres and Loos 1914–15.

**FRENCH AND INDIAN WARS,** struggle for supremacy in North America between the British and French and their respective Indian allies. Both countries sought to expand from their initial settlements; their clashes reflected European wars but in general arose from local problems. The first three wars were named for the British monarch of the day.

**FRENCH SOUTHERN AND ANTARCTIC TERRITORIES,** French overseas territory (established 1955) in Antarctica and the South Indian Ocean, comprising the Kerguelen and Crozet archipelagoes, the islands of St. Paul and Nouvelle-Amsterdam, and the Adélie Coast. Pop 180.

**FRENCH GUIANA,** French overseas department on the NE coast of South America. The chief town is Cayenne. It is bounded by Suriname on the W and Brazil on the E and S, and consists of a strip of lowland along the 200mi Atlantic coastline and a hilly interior stretching c225mi inland. Its economy rests on the timber trade from its massive forests, and on shrimp fishing. Pop 64,400.

**FRENCH HORN.** See HORN.

**FRENCH POLYNESIA,** French overseas territory in the Pacific, consisting of about 120 islands in the Society, Gambier, Austral, Marquesas, and Tuamotu archipelagoes. They export copra, cultured pearls and fruit. French nuclear tests have been conducted here since 1966. The capital is Papeete, on Tahiti in the Society Islands. Pop 137,382.

**FRENCH REVOLUTION** (1789), the first major revolution of modern times. It overthrew the most famous monarchy in Europe, executed the Royal Family, ended the privileged position of the nobility and replaced the traditional institutions of France with new ones based upon popular sovereignty and democratic rights. Subsequently through its wars, the Revolution spread the explosive ideas of the sovereignty of the people, liberty of the individual and equality before the Law throughout Europe. Although the immediate sequel to the Revolution was the establishment of the Napoleonic empire, its impact survived the Napoleonic interlude, and inaugurated the liberal and democratic movements of the 19th century.

By 1788, in a time of rapid economic growth and the consequent rise of the middle classes the country was still ruled by the privileged nobility and clergy, the two upper Estates of the STATES-GENERAL. The tax burden fell on the Third Estate, made up of the middle classes and the landowning peasantry; this was further increased by the corruption of the fiscal system. Into this situation the philosophy of the ENLIGHTENMENT introduced the ideal of progress, scientific materialism and the concepts of constitutional monarchy and republicanism on the British and American models. When the nobility thwarted attempts by the royal ministers to reform government finance the king was forced to summon the Estates-General for the first time since 1614. The Third Estate, which outnumbered the other two chambers, demanded that votes be counted individually and not by chamber, giving them a majority; when this was not immediately granted the Third Estate, with sympathetic members of the other two, declared itself the National Assembly on June 20, 1789. Louis XVI agreed to this, but brought troops to Versailles; mobs stormed the BASTILLE prison on July 14, and pillaged the nobility's country estates. On Aug. 4 the Assembly abolished the feudal system and approved the DECLARATION OF THE RIGHTS OF MAN; the royal family was threatened by mobs, the Church disestablished and largely suppressed. The royal family fled in June, hoping to join their sympathizers who had fled abroad, but were arrested at Varennes and returned to Paris. In Oct. 1791 the Legislative Assembly convened under a new constitution, and became increasingly radical in form. Threat of attack from abroad precipitated the FRENCH REVOLUTIONARY WARS. In the face of this crisis the mob again threatened the king, forcing him to replace the Assembly with a radical Convention elected in Sept. 1792, during mob massacres of jailed royalists. The king was tried for treason and executed in Jan. 1793. In the face of royalist insurrection and foreign hostility the JACOBINS now seized power from the more moderate GIRONDINS, transferring power from the Convention to arbitrary bodies such as the Committees for Public Safety and General Security. Dominated by DANTON and ROBESPIERRE, these brought about the REIGN OF TERROR. This ended with Robespierre himself being executed by the Convention in July 1794. The Convention then introduced a new constitution, setting up the DIRECTORY, which proved ineffectual and corrupt. In 1799 it was overthrown by the army, led by the popular general NAPOLEON. He established the CONSULATE, effectively ending the revolutionary period.

**FRENCH REVOLUTIONARY WARS,** waged by Revolutionary France before the accession of NAPOLEON I. In 1789 France preemptively declared war on and defeated Austria. The First Coalition (Austria, Britain, Prussia, Russia, Spain, and the Netherlands) was defeated 1793–95, France showing surprising if costly military strength. The Second Coalition of Britain, Austria and Russia was defeated 1799–1800, although Napoleon's strike at British-held Egypt failed.

**FRENCH WEST AFRICA,** federation of eight French overseas territories, 1895–1958. Its members were Dahomey, Guinea, Ivory Coast, Mauritania, Niger, Senegal, Sudan (now Mali) and Upper Volta.

**FRENCH WEST INDIES,** comprises two islands: MARTINIQUE and GUADELOUPE. They were French colonies until 1946.

**FREQUENCY MODULATION (FM).** See RADIO.

**FRESCO,** type and technique of wall

painting common in ancient Crete and China, and in Europe from the 13th to the 17th centuries. In true fresco, dry earth pigments mixed with water were painted on fresh wet lime-plaster, setting with it. Preparatory drawings (*sinopia*) were often done in red paint on an underlying layer. In *fresco secco* (dry fresco) varnishes are painted on a smooth, non-absorbent surface. Among famous fresco painters are GIOTTO and MICHELANGELO.

**FRESCOBALDI, Girolamo** (1583–1643), Italian organist, an early master of organ and instrumental composition. His style is bold but logical. He was organist of St. Peter's, Rome, 1608–28 and from 1634.

**FRESNEL, Augustin Jean** (1788–1827), French physicist who evolved the transverse-wave theory of LIGHT through his work on optical INTERFERENCE. He worked also on REFLECTION, REFRACTION, DIFFRACTION and POLARIZATION, and developed a compound LENS system still used for many lighthouses.

**FREUD, Anna** (1895–    ), Austrian-born British pioneer of child psychoanalysis. Her book *The Ego and Mechanisms of Defense* (1936) is a major contribution to the field. After escaping with her father Sigmund FREUD from Nazi-occupied Austria (1938), she established an influential child-therapy clinic in London.

**FREUD, Sigmund** (1856–1939), Austrian neurologist and psychiatrist, founder and author of almost all the basic concepts of PSYCHOANALYSIS. He graduated as a medical student from the University of Vienna in 1881; and for some months in 1885 he studied under J. M. CHARCOT. Charcot's interest in HYSTERIA converted Freud to the cause of psychiatry. Dissatisfied with HYPNOSIS and electrotherapy as treatment techniques, he evolved the psychoanalytic method, founded on DREAM analysis and FREE ASSOCIATION. Because of his belief that sexual impulses lay at the heart of NEUROSES, he was for a decade reviled professionally, but by 1905 disciples such as Alfred ADLER and Carl Gustav JUNG were gathering around him; both were later to

break away. For some thirty years he worked to establish the truth of his theories, and these years were especially fruitful. Fleeing Nazi anti-Semitism, he left Vienna for London in 1938, and there spent the last year of his life before dying of cancer.

**FREYA,** in Norse myth the goddess of love, beauty and fertility, sister of FREY. Portrayed unfavorably in some tales, in others she is a patroness of heroes equal to ODIN.

**FREYRE, Gilberto de Mello** (1900–    ), Brazilian anthropologist, historian, man of letters, and statesman. His most famous work is *The Masters and the Slaves* (1933), the first part of a tetralogy on the history of Brazil.

**FRIAR,** member of any of the medieval Roman Catholic mendicant orders. Friars were forbidden to hold property in common, not bound to one convent, and enjoyed various controversial ecclesiastical privileges. Some were distinguished by the color of their habits as Black Friars (DOMINICANS), Grey Friars (FRANCISCANS) and White Friars (CARMELITES); Augustinians or Austin Friars were the other main order.

**FRICK, Henry Clay** (1849–1919), US industrialist and art collector. He started a coke business in 1868, and in 1882 he became an associate of Andrew CARNEGIE and managed his steel company 1889–99. He bequeathed his extensive art collection, housed in his New York mansion, for public exhibition.

**FRICTION,** resistance to motion arising at the boundary between two touching surfaces when it is attempted to slide one over the other. As the FORCE applied to start motion increases from zero, the equal force of "static friction" opposes it, reaching a maximum "limiting friction," just before sliding begins. Once motion has started, the "sliding friction" is less than the limiting. Friction increases with the load pressing the surfaces together, but is nearly independent of the area in contact. For a given pair of surfaces, limiting friction divided by load is a dimensionless constant known as the coefficient of friction. LUBRICATION is used to overcome friction in the BEARINGS of machines.

**FRIEDAN, Betty** (1921–    ), US feminist leader. Her book *The Feminine Mystique* (1963) challenged attitudes which had led women to become housewives and mothers at the expense of more ambitious careers. She was founding president of the NATIONAL ORGANIZATION FOR WOMEN (1966–70) and helped organize the National Women's Political Caucus

(1971). *It Changed My Life* (1976) concerns her participation in the women's movement.

**FRIEDMAN, Bruce Jay** (1930– ), US novelist, short story writer and playwright noted for his zany black humor. His works include the novels *Stern* (1962) and *A Mother's Kisses* (1964) and the play *Scuba Duba* (1968).

**FRIEDMAN, Milton** (1912– ), US economist, a proponent of the monetarist theory; this regards the money supply as the central controlling factor in economic development. He was a professor at the University of Chicago from 1946 and has written many books, including *A Monetary History of the U.S.: 1867–1960* (1963) and *Free to Choose* (1980; with Rose Friedman), a defense of free market capitalism. He was awarded the 1976 Nobel Prize in Economic Science.

**FRIEDRICH, Caspar David** (1774–1840), German Romantic painter, known for the land and seascape compositions he imbued with rich light effects and deep religious symbolism, such as *Cross in the Mountains* (1807) and *Man and Woman Gazing at the Moon* (1809).

**FRIENDLY ISLANDS.** See TONGA.

**FRIENDS, Society of.** See QUAKERS.

**FRIGATE**, originally a fast, three-masted vessel used in the 18th and 19th centuries for cruising and scouting, with its main gun battery on the upper deck only. Applied to a British escort vessel in WWII, the name is now given to larger missile carriers.

**FRIML, (Charles) Rudolf** (1879–1972), Czech-born US composer of widely popular operettas and film scores. His best-known works include *The Firefly* (1912), *Rose Marie* (1924) and *The Vagabond King* (1925).

**FRISCH, Karl von** (1886– ), Austrian zoologist best known for his studies of bee behavior, perception and communication, discovering the "Dance of the Bees." With TINBERGEN and LORENZ he was awarded the 1973 Nobel Prize for Physiology or Medicine for his work.

**FRISCH, Max** (1911– ), Swiss architect, journalist and playwright best known for his play *The Firebugs* (1958) and the novels *Stiller* (1954), *Homo Faber* (1957) and *Man in the Holocene* (1980). His dominant theme is the destructive effect of modern society upon individuals.

**FRISIAN ISLANDS**, chain of about 30 islands in the North Sea, from 3mi to 20mi off the coasts of the Netherlands, Germany and Denmark. Their economy is largely agricultural, often on land reclaimed from the sea.

**FROEBEL, Friedrich Wilhelm August** (1782–1852), German educator noted as the founder of the kindergarten system. He believed in play as a basic form of self-expression, and in the innate nature of mystical understanding. Though much criticized, he has profoundly influenced later educators.

**FROGS**, jumping, tailless AMPHIBIA. Strictly, the name applies only to true frogs, members of the family Ranidae, but other members of the order Anura (which also includes the TOADS) are sometimes called frogs. True frogs are characterized by shoulder-girdles that are fused down the midline. They are found throughout the world except in the southern parts of South America and Australia.

**FROISSART, Jean** (c1338–1410?), French poet and chronicler who traveled widely in search of material for his *Chronicles of France, England, Scotland and Spain*, which present a colorful picture of events between 1325 and 1400. His poetry ranges from light verse to the romance *Meliador*.

**FROMM, Erich** (1900–1980), German-born US psychoanalyst who combined many of the ideas of Freud and Marx in his analysis of human relationships and development in the context of social structures and in his suggested solutions to problems such as alienation. His books include *Escape from Freedom* (1941), *The Art of Loving* (1956) and *The Anatomy of Human Destructiveness* (1973).

**FRONDE,** a series of uprisings against the French crown 1648–53. At first largely popular uprisings against heavy taxation, they were later fomented by the *parlements* and discontented members of the aristocracy, such as Prince Louis II de Condé, against the autocratic chief minister, Cardinal MAZARIN whose decisive intervention in 1653 finally crushed the Fronde.

**FRONTENAC, Louis de Buade, Comte de Palluau et de** (1622–1698), French soldier who became governor of New France in 1672. He badly mismanaged Indian relations, and damaged the fur trade. Recalled to France in 1682, he returned in 1689 and in King William's War successfully held Quebec against the English. He maintained the French position in New France up to the Treaty of RYSWICK (1697).

**FRONTIER**, in American history, the boundary between the settled and unsettled areas of the country. It was constantly expanding as the descendants of the original settlers of the 13 Colonies spread out N, S and especially W. In the early days expansion was slow, consisting largely of migrations into the Appalachian area and into what is now Pa. By the time of Independence, Ky. had been settled and the frontier was in Tenn. The new government provided for surveying, settlement and administration of new areas. The frontier moved steadily W, and new states were formed in quick succession until by 1846 Mexico had been forced to cede the SW, and settlement had begun on the W coast. The Indians suffered badly under the government's policy of moving them to make way for settlers, and struggled to resist it. After the Civil War, Indian wars broke out again, but by the 1870s and 1880s the growth of cities and the enclosure of much of the land meant that the settlers were firmly established. In 1890 the Bureau of the Census officially declared the frontier closed; its way of life and the peculiar mythology it created have had a great influence on American culture.

**FROST, Robert** (1874–1963), eminent US poet. For most of his life he supported himself by farming and part-time academic work. His first two volumes of poetry *A Boy's Will* (1913) and *North of Boston* (1914) were published during a stay in England. His reputation grew in America, and he won many honors, including four Pulitzer prizes. His style is individual, clearly influenced by rural life, religion and much personal tragedy. Frost's complete poems were published in 1967.

**FROSTBITE,** damage occurring in SKIN and adjacent tissues caused by freezing. (The numbness caused by cold allows considerable damage without pain.) DEATH of tissues follows and they separate off. Judicious rewarming, pain relief and measures to maximize skin blood flow may reduce tissue loss.

**FRUIT FLIES,** small FLIES of the genus *Drosophila*, which feed on decaying vegetation and ripe fruit, sometimes causing great damage to crops. Some species are used for genetics experiments because they breed rapidly. As a result, the fruit fly is one of the most studied animals in the world today.

**FRUMENTIUS, Saint,** 4th century bishop of Aksum, a native of Tyre. He and his brother St. Aedesius established the COPTIC CHURCH in Ethiopia.

**FRY, Christopher** (1907–    ), British verse dramatist, whose plays, although often in ancient or medieval settings, deal with contemporary themes. His best-known play, *The Lady's Not For Burning* (1948), is a dry comedy centering on witchcraft hysteria. *A Sleep of Prisoners* (1951) and *The Dark is Light Enough* (1955) are essentially religious plays.

**FRY, Elizabeth Gurney** (1780–1845), British Quaker philanthropist whose inspections of prisons throughout Britain and Europe led to great advances in the treatment of the imprisoned and the insane. Her proposed reforms of London's notorious Newgate prison, including segregation of the sexes and the provision of employment and religious instruction, were largely accepted.

**FRY, Roger Eliot** (1866–1934), British art critic and painter. A member of the London group, he was among the first to champion CÉZANNE and POSTIMPRESSIONISM. In 1933 he was appointed Slade Professor of Fine Art at Cambridge.

**FUAD I** (1868–1936), modern Egypt's first monarch, son of the khedive Ismail Pasha. He became sultan on his brother's death in 1917 and assumed the title of king when the British protectorate ended in 1922.

**FUCHS, Klaus** (1911–    ), German-born physicist and convicted spy. During WWII, Fuchs—by then a British citizen and active Soviet agent—worked on the top-secret, atomic-bomb project in the US (1943–45). He supplied the Russians with designs for both the uranium and plutonium bombs. Released from a British prison in 1959, he returned to East Germany.

**FUCHS, Sir Vivian Ernest** (1908–    ), British geologist and explorer, who led the British Commonwealth Trans-Antarctic expedition that made the first overland crossing of Antarctica 1957–58.

**FUEL,** a substance that may be burned (see COMBUSTION) to produce heat, light or power. Traditional fuels include dried dung, animal and vegetable oil, wood, PEAT and COAL, supplemented by the manufactured fuels CHARCOAL, COAL GAS, COKE and WATER GAS. In this century PETROLEUM and NATURAL GAS have come into widespread use. The term "fuel" has also been extended to include chemical nuclear fuels (see FUEL CELL; NUCLEAR ENERGY), although these are not burned. Specialized high-energy fuels such as HYDRAZINE are used in ROCKET engines. The chief property of a fuel is its calorific value—the amount of heat produced by complete combustion of a unit mass or volume of fuel. Also of major importance is the proportion of incombustibles—ASH and moisture—and of sulfur and other compounds liable to cause AIR POLLUTION.

**FUGGER,** German family of merchant bankers. The business was founded in Augsburg in the 14th century by Johann Fugger, a Swabian weaver. The fortunes of his descendants flourished during the 15th and 16th centuries. Jakob Fugger (1459–1525) materially assisted Charles V's election as Holy Roman Emperor. The family included many distinguished soldiers, statesmen and clerics.

**FUGITIVE SLAVE ACTS,** laws passed by Congress in 1793 and 1850 to deter slaves from fleeing to Abolitionist states. The 1793 act denied runaway slaves the benefit of jury trial. The 1850 measure was a reaction to the growing opposition this provoked. It imposed severe fines and imprisonment on US marshals and citizens who helped or failed to apprehend runaway slaves. The acts only hardened opposition and were another divisive factor between North and South.

**FUGUE,** a musical form in which two or more parts (voices) combine in introducing and developing a theme. The principal idea behind fugal composition is that of developing contrasts which produce a specific texture and density. The fugue's history dates from the 16th century CANON and round. The greatest achievements in this form are by J. S. BACH whose unfinished *The Art of Fugue* (1748–50) is a major study of fugal form.

**FUJI, Mount** (or Fujiyama), highest mountain in Japan (12,388ft), long considered sacred by the Japanese and a source of inspiration to artists and poets. A dormant volcano crowned by a wide crater, it last erupted in 1707.

**FULANI,** an ancient people of W Africa found over a wide area from Senegambia to W Sudan. They include nomadic pastoralists as well as settled communities. The Fulani have a deep-rooted culture based on Islam and have strong ties with the HAUSA. They number some 7 million.

**FULBRIGHT, James William** (1905– ), US political leader and lawyer, initiator of the FULBRIGHT SCHOLARSHIPS. After teaching law at Arkansas U. Fulbright was elected to the House of Representatives in 1942, and served in the Senate 1944–75. He was chairman of the Senate Foreign Relations Committee 1959–74, becoming an outspoken critic of US policy in Vietnam.

**FULLER, John Frederick Charles** (1878–1966), British soldier and military historian. In WWI he directed the first successful use of tanks in battle, at Cambrai n 1917. He pioneered the concept known as BLITZKRIEG. His chief work is *Military History of the Western World* (1954–56).

**FULLER, Margaret** (1810–1850), influential American critic and advocate of female emancipation. A friend of EMERSON, she edited the Transcendentalist magazine *The Dial* 1840–42. She became literary critic for the New York *Tribune* in 1844 and in the following year published *Woman in the Nineteenth Century.* She was drowned with her husband and child in a shipwreck off FIRE ISLAND.

**FULLER, Richard Buckminster** (1895– ), US inventor, philosopher, author and mathematician. He has been a prolific source of original ideas, many of which have had important consequences. He is best known for his concept "Spaceship Earth" and for inventing the GEODESIC DOME.

**FULTON, Robert** (1765–1815), US inventor who improved both the submarine and the steamboat. His submarine *Nautilus* was launched at Rouen, France (1800), with the aim of using it against British warships: in fact, these repeatedly escaped and the French lost interest. His first steamship was launched on the Seine (1803), and after this success he returned to the US, launching the first commercially successful steamboat (see FITCH, John) the *Clermont,* from New York (1807). He built several other steamboats and the *Demologus,* the first steam warship (launched 1815).

**FUNCTION,** a rule by which each element of one set (see SET THEORY), for example the real NUMBERS, is assigned an element of another set. (The two sets may share some or all elements.) The same element of the second set may be assigned to more than one element of the first set. In CARTESIAN COORDINATES a function of one real VARIABLE may be plotted by setting $x$ along one axis and $f(x)$ (read "function of $x$") along the other. (See also ANALYTIC GEOMETRY; GRAPH.) If the rule defining the function is SQUARE the number, add twice the number and subtract three, this is expressed as $f(x) = x^2 + 2x - 3$. If a function of one variable is plotted as a graph or curve as above, it is said to be **continuous** if the curve has no breaks. More precisely, it is continuous if any two points $f(x)$ and $f(x')$ can be brought as close together as desired by bringing $x$ and $x^1$ sufficiently close together. This definition can be extended to sets of any kind (not necessarily numbers) provided a meaning can be given to "close" (see TOPOLOGY).

**FUNCTIONALISM,** the principle that all design should be dictated by the function of what is being designed, all unnecessary elements being discarded. This was derived from a dictum of the architect Louis SULLIVAN, "form follows function," and was a moving principle of the BAUHAUS school. Functionalism influenced many modern architects, notably Frank Lloyd WRIGHT and LE CORBUSIER.

**FUNDAMENTALISM,** US conservative Protestant movement, upholding EVANGELICALISM against MODERNISM, which has flourished, particularly in the South, since the early 20th century. Its chief doctrines, set out in a series of pamphlets, *The Fundamentals* (1910–1912), are Christ's virgin birth, physical resurrection and second coming, the substitutionary theory of the atonement, and the absolute infallibility of the Bible. The last led to a denial of biblical criticism and the theory of evolution. Leading advocates of the movement included W. J. BRYAN and the theologian John Gresham Machen. Modern fundamentalism is mostly anti-intellectual, dispensationalist, pietist and revivalist.

**FUNDY, Bay of,** an arm of the Atlantic Ocean between New Brunswick and Nova Scotia about 94mi long and about 50mi at its widest. It is remarkable for a massive fluctuation in tidal level, which has reached 70ft. Its chief harbor is St. John, in New Brunswick.

**FUNGAL DISEASES,** DISEASES caused by FUNGI which, apart from common SKIN and nail ailments such as ATHLETE'S FOOT, tinea cruris and RINGWORM, develop especially in people with disorders of IMMUNITY or DIABETES and those on certain DRUGS (STEROIDS, immunosuppressives, ANTIBIOTICS). THRUSH is common in the MOUTH and vagina but rarely causes systemic disease. Specific fungal diseases occur in some areas (e.g., HISTOPLASMOSIS, blastomycosis) while aspergillosis often complicates chronic LUNG disease. In addition, numerous fungi in the environment lead to forms of ALLERGY and lung disease.

**FUNGI,** a subdivision (Eumycotina) of the PLANT KINGDOM which comprises simple plants that reproduce mostly by means of SPORES and which lack CHLOROPHYLL, hence are either SAPROPHYTES or PARASITES.

The closely related SLIME MOLDS produce naked (no cell walls) amoeboid states, and the YEASTS are single-celled, but the majority of true fungi produce microscopic filaments (hyphae) that group together in an interwoven weft, the mycelium or spawn. REPRODUCTION is sometimes by budding (yeasts) but more normally by the production of asexual and sexual spores. Some fungi produce large fruit bodies, which are the structures commonly associated with fungi. The classification of fungi is complicated and several systems have evolved, mostly based on the types of spore produced. Fungi belong to the division MYCOTA, which also includes the Myxomy-

cetes or slime molds. The true fungi are divided into a number of classes, the main ones being: the Chytridomycetes, which produce motile gametes or zoospores that have a single flagellum; the Oomycetes, which have biflagellate zoospores and produce dissimilar male and female reproductive organs and gametes; Zygomycetes, which do not produce motile zoospores and reproduce sexually by fusion of identical gametes; the Ascomycetes, including yeasts, which reproduce asexually by budding or by the production of spores (conidia) and sexually by the formation of ascospores within sac-like structures (asci) that are often enclosed in a fruiting body or ascocarp; the Basidiomycetes, including BRACKET FUNGI and AGARICS in which the sexual spores are produced, or enlarged cells called basidia, that often occur on large fruiting bodies; and the Deuteromycetes, or Fungi Imperfecti, which are only known to reproduce asexually, although sexual forms are often classified in the Ascomycetes and Basidiomycetes. (See also FUNGAL DISEASES; MOLD; PLANT DISEASES; RUST; SMUT.)

**FUNGICIDE,** substance used to kill FUNGI and so to control FUNGAL DISEASES in man and plants. In medicine some ANTIBIOTICS, SULFUR, CARBOXYLIC ACIDS and potassium iodide are used. In agriculture a wide variety of fungicides is used, both inorganic—BORDEAUX MIXTURE and sulfur—and organic—many different compounds, generally containing sulfur or nitrogen. They are applied to the soil before planting or around seedlings, or are sprayed or dusted onto foliage. (See also PESTICIDE.)

**FUR,** the soft, dense, hairy undercoat of certain mammals. Fur is an excellent heat insulator and protects against the cold of the northern regions where most furbearing animals are found. It is generally interspersed with guard HAIRS, longer and stiffer, that form a protective outer coat and prevent matting. Skins or pelts are cleaned, softened and converted to a leatherlike state by "dressing," a process resembling TANNING. In some cases the guard hairs are sheared or plucked. The pelt is then dyed or bleached and then glazed, chemically or by heat, to give it a lustrous sheen. To make the furs into a garment, they are matched for color and texture, cut to shape, sewn together, and finally dampened and nailed to the pattern to dry smooth and the exact shape wanted. Fur clothing has long been valued for its beauty and warmth, and was an aristocratic luxury until the discovery of America, in whose exploration and economic development trapping and fur trading played a major role. Demand is still high, threatening some furbearing species with extinction; this has led to fur-farming of suitable animals such as mink and to the development of artificial furs made of synthetic fibers.

**FURSTENBERG, Diane Von** (1947– ), Belgian-born US designer whose popular wrap-around print dresses launched her venture into the fashion world in the early 1970s. Cosmetics, perfume and home furnishings later bore the famous Von Furstenberg monogram.

**FURTWANGLER, Wilhelm** (1886–1954), German conductor whose free, passionate style made him one of the great interpreters, particularly of Beethoven and Wagner.

**FUSE,** safety device placed in an electric circuit to prevent overloading. It usually comprises a wire of low-melting-point metal mounted in or on an insulated frame. Current passing through the wire heats it (see RESISTANCE); and excessive current heats it to the point where it melts, so breaking the CIRCUIT. In most domestic plugs, the fuse consists of a cylinder of glass, capped at each end by metal, with a wire running between the metal caps. Similar, but larger, cartridge fuses are used in industry.

**FUSELI, Henry** (1741–1825), Anglo-Swiss painter and writer, appointed professor of painting at the Royal Academy in 1799. His paintings, of which the most famous is probably *The Nightmare* (1782), are highly stylized and have an often sinister sensuality.

**FUSION, Nuclear,** a nuclear reaction in which the nuclei of light ATOMS combine to produce heavier, more stable nuclei, releasing a large quantity of ENERGY. Fusion reactions are the energy source of the SUN and the HYDROGEN BOMB. If they could be controlled and made self-sustaining man would have a safe and inexhaustible energy source using DEUTERIUM or TRITIUM extracted from seawater. Only small amounts of fuel would be needed and the products are not radioactive. But if they are to fuse, the light, positively charged nuclei must collide with sufficient energy to overcome their electrostatic repulsion. This can be done by using a particle ACCELERATOR, but to get a net energy release the material must be heated to very high temperatures (around $10^9$K) when it becomes a PLASMA. However, plasmas are difficult to contain and, as yet, no apparatus has been designed which allows more energy to be extracted than is used in heating and containing the plasma. (See also NUCLEAR ENERGY.)

**FUTURISM,** 20th-century Italian art movement based on two manifestos of Futurist poetry and painting, issued in 1909 and 1910 by the poet Filippo MARINETTI and an allied group of artists. It sought to express the speed, violence and dynamism of a mechanical age.

**FUTUROLOGY,** the study of the probable evolution of technology and culture based on projections from the present. Although these studies may be simply predictive, those done in recent years tend to concentrate on the consequences of various courses of action, thus aiding policymakers in choosing wisely from among current options. The field was engendered by the increasingly rapid rate of social and technological change since WWII. Rapid population growth and the depletion of natural resources have further spurred the development of these studies. Herman KAHN, author of *The Next 200 Years*, is a prominent futurologist, and the RAND CORPORATION and Hudson Institute are "think tanks" active in the field. The Office of Technology Assessment, set up by Congress, seeks to identify areas of future change that should be of concern to legislators.

7th letter of the English alphabet, developed from the Semitic *ghimel* and a differentiated form of the Greek *gamma*. English has a hard "g" sound as in "go" and a soft "g" sound, mostly before e, i, and y, as in "gentle." In music G is the fifth note in the scale of C.

**GABIN, Jean** (1904–1976), French film actor who often played tough but decent heroes. The most popular French star of the 1930s, his most memorable films include *Pépé le Moko* (1936) and *La Grande Illusion* (1937).

**GABLE, Clark** (1901–1960), US film star, winner of a 1934 Academy Award for a comedy role in *It Happened One Night*. His most famous role was Rhett Butler in *Gone with the Wind* (1939). Called "the King," he was a leading box-office "draw" for more than two decades.

**GABO, Naum** (born Naum Pevsner; 1890–1977), Russian sculptor, a pioneer of

CONSTRUCTIVISM. With his brother Anton PEVSNER, he issued the *Realist Manifesto* (1920). He left Russia and taught at the BAUHAUS (1922–32). In 1946 he emigrated to the US. He is noted for his kinetic sculptures and geometrical constructions in metal, plastic and nylon.

**Official name:** Gabon Republic
**Capital:** Libreville
**Area:** 103,088sq mi
**Population:** 546,000
**Languages:** French, Fang, Bantu
**Religions:** Roman Catholic, Animist, Muslim
**Monetary unit(s):** 1 CFA franc=100 centimes

**GABON,** small republic on the Atlantic coast of W Africa.

**Land.** Most of the country, lying across the Equator, is rain forest; a mountain range separates the narrow coastal area from the heartland plateaus. The climate is hot and humid, with heavy rainfall.

**People.** Gabon's relatively small population has a wide range of ethnic groups: the largest, the Fang, constitutes about 30% of the population and dominates politics and industry; the Omyene are a small but important coastal group. Most of the people are village dwellers, but about 30% live in the main towns of Libreville, Port-Gentil and Lambarene, site of Albert SCHWEITZER's famous hospital. There is a strong emphasis on education and a large number of children attend school.

**Economy.** Gabon is the richest country in sub-Saharan Africa in terms of per capita income, and the second richest in all of Africa, after Libya. Oil dominates Gabon's export earnings; manganese and uranium are also exported. Agricultural output is low and much food is imported from France, a main trading partner. Despite national wealth, living standards are generally low.

**History.** Gabon became an important slave-trade center after discovery by the Portuguese in the 15th century. The Omyene peoples dominated Gabon until gradually displaced by the Fang in the 19th century. France maintained a naval base on the coast from 1843, but occupied the country only when its economic possibilities became apparent. A French colony from 1886, in 1946 it became an overseas territory of France. It achieved self-government in 1958, independence in 1960, and became a one-party state in 1968.

**GABOR, Dennis** (1900–    ), Hungarian-born UK physicist who invented HOLOGRAPHY, for which he was awarded the 1971 Nobel Prize for Physics. He had developed the basic technique in the late 1940s, but practical applications had to wait for the invention of the LASER (1960) by C. H. TOWNES.

**GADDI, Taddeo** (c1300–1366), Florentine painter, a pupil of GIOTTO, whom he succeeded as decorator of S. Croce in Florence. His frescoes of the lives of Christ, St. Francis and St. Bonaventure, are perhaps his greatest works.

**GADSDEN PURCHASE,** Mexican territory bought by the US in 1853, to add to lands acquired in the war of 1848. The extra land, some 45,000 sq mi, cost $10 million. It provided a rail route through the conquered land to the Pacific. The purchase was negotiated by James GADSDEN.

**GAELIC,** or Goidelic, group of CELTIC LANGUAGES, native to Ireland (Irish Gaelic), the Isle of Man (Manx) and the Scottish Highlands (Scottish Gaelic).

**GAELIC LITERATURE,** writings in the Gaelic language. There are two main traditions. Irish Gaelic is divided into three periods, Old Irish (up to c10th century), Middle Irish (up to mid-15th century) and Modern Irish. The early literature consists chiefly of lyric verse and sagas, of which the *Ulster Cycle* is a famous example. Scottish Gaelic diverged from the Irish tradition in c1300 and developed an impressive body of poetry, with some prose work. (See also OSSIAN; MACPHERSON, JAMES.)

**GAGARIN, Yuri Alekseyevich** (1934–1968), Soviet astronaut, first man in space. His capsule was launched on April 12, 1961, and orbited the earth once. A deputy to the Supreme Soviet from 1962, he died in a plane crash.

**GAINSBOROUGH, Thomas** (1727–1788), English portraitist and landscape painter. He painted numerous society portraits; in 1780 he was commissioned to portray George III and Queen Charlotte. Many of his portraits are actually set in landscapes, which were his primary interest. His work influenced CONSTABLE and English landscape painting in the 19th century.

**GALÁPAGOS ISLANDS,** group of volcanic islands in the Pacific, on the equator W of Ecuador. They were named for the giant tortoises found there in 1535 by the Spaniard Thomas de Berlanga. They have unique vegetation and wildlife, the study of which confirmed Charles DARWIN in his theory of evolution. There are large marine and land iguanas, scarlet crabs, penguins, a flightless cormorant, unique finches and the giant tortoises, now rare. The main islands are Isabella, Santa Cruz, Fernandina, San Salvador and San Cristobal; they are now a national park and wildlife sanctuary.

**GALATIANS, Epistle to the,** ninth book of the NEW TESTAMENT, a letter written by St. Paul to the Christians in N or S Galatia to counter the influence of Judaizers who taught that Christians must keep all the law of Moses. It sets forth the basis of Christian freedom, man's union with Christ through faith.

**GALAXY,** the largest individual conglomeration of matter, containing stars, gas, dust and planets. Galaxies start life as immense clouds of gas, out of which stars condense. Initially a galaxy is **irregular** in form; that is, it has neither a specific shape nor any apparent internal structure. It contains large amounts of gas and dust in which new stars are constantly forming. It rotates and over millions of years evolves into a **spiral** form, looking rather like a flying saucer, with a roughly spherical nucleus surrounded by a flattish disk and orbited by GLOBULAR CLUSTERS. In the nucleus there is little gas and dust and a high proportion of older stars; in the spiral arms a great deal of gas and dust and a high proportion of younger stars (our SUN lies in a spiral arm of the MILKY WAY). Over further millions of years the spiral arms "fold" toward the nucleus, the end result being an **elliptical** galaxy containing a large number of older stars and little or no gas and dust. The ultimate form of any galaxy is a sphere, after which it possibly evolves into a BLACK HOLE. The nearest external galaxy to our own is the ANDROMEDA Galaxy. Similarly spiral, though rather larger, it has two satellite galaxies which are elliptical in form. Originally it was thought to be a NEBULA within our own galaxy, but in 1924 HUBBLE showed that it was a galaxy in its own right. Study of the Andromeda Galaxy is important as it enables us better to understand our own, most of which is obscured from us by clouds of gas and dust. Galaxies emit radio waves, and the strongest sources are known as **radio galaxies**. One group of these, spiral with active nuclei, are named **Seyfert galaxies** for the US astronomer Carl Seyfert. (See also PULSAR; QUASAR.) Galaxies tend to form in clusters. The Milky Way and the Andromeda Galaxy are members of a cluster of around 20 galaxies.

**GALBRAITH, John Kenneth** (1908–    ), US economist and author, ambassador to India 1961–63. In *American Capitalism* (1952) he introduced the concept of COUNTERVAILING POWER. In *The Affluent Society* (1958) he argued that resources used in the production of superfluous consumer goods should be diverted into public and social sectors. A Harvard professor (1949–75) and activist in the liberal wing of the Democratic Party, he also wrote *The New Industrial State* (1967), *Money* (1975) and *The Age of Uncertainty* (1977).

**GALILEE, Sea of** (Lake Tiberias), lake in N Israel, 696ft below sea level and 104sq mi in area, fed by the Jordan R. The only body of fresh water in Israel, it has been a fishing center since biblical times. Many sites on its shores are associated with Jesus' ministry.

**GALILEO GALILEI** (1564–1642), Italian mathematical physicist who discovered the laws of falling bodies and the parabolic motion of projectiles. The first to turn the newly invented TELESCOPE to the heavens, he was among the earliest observers of SUNSPOTS and the phases of Venus. A talented publicist, he helped to popularize the pursuit of science. However, his quarrelsome nature led him into an unfortunate controversy with the Church. His most significant contribution to science was his provision of an alternative to the Aristotelian dynamics. The motion of the earth thus became a conceptual possibility and scientists at last had a genuine criterion for choosing between the Copernican and Tychonic hypotheses in ASTRONOMY.

**GALLATIN, (Abraham Alfonse) Albert** (1761–1849), Swiss-born American statesman and diplomat. As congressman 1795–1801 he defended US relations with France during the XYZ AFFAIR. Secretary of the treasury 1801–13, he objected to the drain on national economy caused by the War of 1812 and helped negotiate the Treaty of GHENT, 1814. He was minister to France 1816–23 and Britain 1826–27.

**GALLAUDET, Thomas Hopkins** (1787–1851), US educator of the deaf. After study at the Royal Institute for Deaf-Mutes in Paris, he founded the first free school for the deaf in the US at Hartford, Conn. (1817).

**GALL BLADDER,** small sac containing BILE, arising from the bile duct which leads from the LIVER to DUODENUM. It lies beneath the liver and serves to concentrate bile. When food, especially fatty food, reaches the STOMACH, local HORMONES cause gall bladder contraction and bile enters the

GASTROINTESTINAL TRACT. In some people the concentration of bile favors the formation of gallstones, usually containing CHOLESTEROL. These stones may cause no symptoms; they may obstruct the gall bladder causing biliary COLIC or INFLAMMATION (cholecystitis), or they may pass into the bile duct and cause biliary obstruction with JAUNDICE or, less often, pancreatitis. Acute episodes are treated with ANALGESICS, antispasmodics and ANTIBIOTICS, but SURGERY is frequently necessary later. Recent advances suggest that in some instances stones may be dissolved by DRUG therapy.

**GALLIC WARS,** a series of campaigns by Julius CAESAR, 58–51 BC. The name is derived from Caesar's *Commentaries on the Gallic War* (c50 BC). As governor of Transalpine Gaul, Caesar carried out a combined strategy of driving out invading German tribes and in the process occupying more territory in Gaul, until almost the whole country was in Roman hands (55 BC). In 53–52 BC he put down revolts by the chieftains Ambiorix and VERCINGETORIX. The latter's defeat at Alesia (52 BC) effectively ended the wars, with the Romans in control.

**GALLIPOLI PENINSULA,** a 50mi long strip of land in European Turkey between the Aegean Sea and the Dardanelles. A strategic point of defense for Istanbul, it was fought over during the Crimean War and WWI. In 1915 an Allied expedition of British, Australian, French and New Zealand forces failed to dislodge Turkish troops in an effort to gain control of the Dardanelles.

**GALLSTONES.** See GALL BLADDER.

**GALLUP, George Horace** (1901–    ), American pollster. In 1935 he established the American Institute of Public Opinion which undertakes the Gallup polls, periodic samplings of public opinion on current issues. His several books include *The Pulse of Democracy* (1940) and *The Gallup Poll: Public Opinion,* 1935–71 (1972).

**GALSWORTHY, John** (1867–1933), English novelist and playwright. His works, especially the famous cycle of novels *The Forsyte Saga* are concerned with the life and attitudes of the wealthier English middle classes, typified by the "man of property" Soames Forsyte. He was awarded the Nobel Prize for Literature in 1932.

**GALTON, Sir Francis** (1822–1911), British scientist, the founder of EUGENICS and biostatistics (the application of statistical methods to animal populations); the coiner of the term "anticyclone" and one of the first to realize their meteorological significance; and the developer of one of the first FINGERPRINT systems for identification.

**GALVANI, Luigi** (1737–1798), Italian anatomist who discovered "animal electricity" (about 1786). The many varying accounts of this discovery at least agree that it resulted from the chance observation of the twitching of frog legs under electrical influence. A controversy with VOLTA over the nature of animal electricity was cut short by Galvani's death.

**GAMA, Vasco da** (c1469–1524), Portuguese navigator whose discovery of a new sea-route around the Cape of Good Hope and destruction of the Muslim trade monopoly made possible large-scale European trade with the East. In his first voyage (1497–99) his trade negotiations in India were thwarted by Muslim merchants. On his second voyage (1502–03) his fleet established Portuguese supremacy in the area by a ruthless destruction of the Malabar Muslim fleet. Later appointed viceroy to India, he died soon after his arrival there.

**Official name:** Republic of the Gambia
**Capital:** Banjul
**Area:** 4,361sq mi
**Population:** 600,000
**Languages:** English, French, Mandinka, Wolof
**Religions:** Muslim, Animist
**Monetary unit(s):** 1 dalasi = 100 butut

**GAMBIA,** republic in W Africa, smallest state on the continent.
**Land.** It extends for around 200mi from the W coast narrowly along the Gambia R, almost bisecting Senegal. A low-lying country, it ranges from coastal mangrove areas to interior scrublands.
**People and Economy.** The Mandingo peoples constitute around 40% of the population; others are the Fulani, Wolof, Jola and Sarahule. Most are small farmers, producing millet, corn and rice for local consumption. Goats and sheep are raised, and the Fulani breed cattle. Peanuts and peanut oil are the main exports. Britain is the principal trade partner. There is little industry.

**History.** In ancient times Gambia was part of the Mali Empire. During the 1400s Portuguese began trading for slaves along the coast. Gambia was born of the struggle between Britain and France for supremacy in W Africa. The French territory became Senegal and the British territory became Gambia. The first legislative assembly was elected in 1960; independence came in 1965. The country became a republic within the Commonwealth in 1970, with Sir Dawda Jawara as its first head of state.

**GAMETE,** or germ cell, a sexual reproductive CELL capable of uniting with a gamete of the opposite sex to form a new individual or ZYGOTE; this process is termed FERTILIZATION. Each gamete contains one set of dissimilar chromosomes and is said to be HAPLOID. Thus when gametes unite, the resultant cell contains a DIPLOID or paired set of CHROMOSOMES. The gametes of some primitive organisms are identical cells capable of swimming in water, but in most species only the male gamete (sperm) is mobile while the female gamete (ovary or egg) is a larger static cell. In higher PLANTS the male gametes or pollen are produced by the anthers and the female gametes (ovules) by the ovary. In animals gametes are produced by the GONADS, namely the testes in the male and ovaries in the female.

**GAME THEORY,** an application of mathematics to decision-making in games and, by extension, in commerce, politics and warfare. In singular games (e.g., solitaire) the player's strategy is determined solely by the rules. In dual games (e.g., chess, football) one side's strategy must take into account the possible strategies of the other. Dual games are usually zero-sum: one side's gain exactly equals the other's loss. In practical situations, however, they may be non-zero-sum, as where two conflicting nations negotiate a truce that benefits both. A player in a zero-sum dual game, knowing that whatever he does his opponent will maximize his own gain, should play in such a way as to maximize his minimum gain. VON NEUMANN showed in his **minimax theorem** that if both players follow this principle, then, if they use "mixed strategies" in which their moves are chosen at random but with certain probabilities in each situation, the game has a determinate result (as a long-run average, because of the chance element) in which each player achieves his optimum result in the sense defined above. Games with more than two players are more difficult to analyze.

**GAMMA GLOBULIN,** the fraction of BLOOD PROTEIN containing antibodies (see ANTIBODIES AND ANTIGENS). Several types are recognized. Although they share basic structural features they differ in size, site, behavior and response to different antigens. Absence of all or some gamma globulins causes disorders of IMMUNITY, increasing susceptibility to infection, while the excessive formation of one type is the basis for **myeloma,** a disease characterized by BONE pain, pathological FRACTURES and liability to infection. Gamma globulin is available for replacement therapy, and a type from highly immune subjects is sometimes used to protect against certain diseases (e.g., serum hepatitis, TETANUS). (See also GLOBULINS.)

**GAMOW, George** (1904–1968), Russian-born US physicist and popular science writer, best known for his work in nuclear physics, especially related to the evolution of STARS; and for his support of the "big bang" theory of COSMOLOGY. In GENETICS, his work paved the way for the discovery of the role of DNA.

**GANDHI, Indira Priyadarshini** (1917– ), first woman prime minister of India. Daughter of Jawaharlal NEHRU, she became president of the Congress Party in 1959. As prime minister (1966–77) she became more friendly with the USSR and less so with the US, and defeated Pakistan in a war. In 1975, she was found guilty of electoral malpractice. During the ensuing constitutional crisis she declared a state of emergency and jailed nearly 700 political opponents. The Indian Supreme Court overruled the verdict against her and upheld her electroral and constitutional changes. Briefly turned out of office, she regained the premiership in 1980.

**GANDHI, Mohandas Karamchand "Mahatma"** (1869–1948), Indian nationalist leader. After studying law in London, he went to South Africa, where he lived until 1914 becoming a driving force in the Indian community's fight for civil rights. During this campaign he developed the principle of SATYAGRAHA, nonviolent civil disobedience, and held to it despite persecution and imprisonment. When he returned to India he had achieved substantial improvements in civil rights and labor laws. In India he became leader of the Congress Party, initiating the campaign which led to the independence of India after WWII. He was assassinated by a Hindu fanatic who disapproved of his tolerance of Muslims.

**GANGES RIVER,** in India the most sacred Hindu river, believed to be the reincarnation of the goddess Ganga. It rises in the Himalayas and flows through N and NE India, following a SE course across the plain of India. It joins the Brahmaputra R in Bangladesh, then continues through the vast Ganges delta to empty through several mouths (Meghna, Tetulia, Hooghly) into the Bay of Bengal. The river waters irrigate a populous agricultural area. Many cities line the river's banks, including the holy Indian cities of Váránasi (Benares), Alláhábád, and Calcutta, and Dacca (Bangladesh) on the delta.

**GANG OF FOUR,** a group of supporters of China's Mao Tse-tung who, after Mao's death, were tried and convicted of many offenses. China's new leaders blamed them for the excesses of the Cultural Revolution of the late 1960s. Principal charges included plotting to kill Mao and overthrow the state and persecuting more than 30,000 persons. Mao's widow, Chiang Ch'ing, was identified as the group's leader. Ten persons in all were tried in 1980. Two, including Chiang Ch'ing, were sentenced to death, subject to repentance, and the others received prison sentences.

**GANGRENE,** DEATH of tissue following loss of blood supply, often after obstruction of ARTERIES by trauma, THROMBOSIS or EMBOLISM. **Dry** gangrene is seen when arterial block is followed by slow drying, blackening and finally separation of dead tissue from healthy. Its treatment includes improvement of the blood flow to the healthy tissue and prevention of infection and further obstruction. **Wet gangrene** occurs when the dead tissue is infected with BACTERIA. **Gas gangrene** involves infection with gas-forming organisms (*Clostridium*) and its spread is particularly rapid ANTIBIOTICS, HYPERBARIC CHAMBERS and early AMPUTATION are often required.

**GANNETT, Frank** (1876–1957), US newspaper publisher who founded (1906) a communications empire that eventually included radio and television stations and twenty-two urban newspapers. An anti-New Deal conservative, he ran unsuccessfully for the 1940 Republican presidential nomination.

**GARAMOND, Claude** (c1480–1561), French type designer and publisher. He created typefaces which helped establish roman in place of Gothic or black letter as standard type. His royal Greek and italic types were also highly influential. (See also TYPOGRAPHY.)

**GARBO, Greta** (1905–   ), Swedish-American film actress, born Greta Lovisa Gustafsson. She was a talented actress known for her aura of glamour and mystery; her 24 films included *Anna Christie* (1930), *Camille* (1937) and *Ninotchka* (1939). She retired in 1941, and was given an Academy Award in 1954.

**GARCIA LORCA, Frederico.** See LORCA, FREDERICO GARCIA.

**GARCIA y IÑIGUEZ,** (1839–1898), Cuban revolutionary. He commanded Cuban forces in the Ten Years War (1868–78) against Spain. After being imprisoned in Spain, he helped lead the Cuban revolt in 1895–98 which led to the SPANISH-AMERICAN WAR. His name became a famous byword in the US after publication of a magazine article, *A Message to Garcia* (1899), dealing with an incident in the war

**GARDEN, Mary** (1877–1967), Scottish-US soprano. She made her debut in 1900 at the Opéra-Comique in Paris in Charpentier's *Louise* and later became famous as Mélisand in Debussy's *Pelléas and Mélisand* and in Massenet's *Thaïs*. She was a member (1910–31) of the Chicago Opera

**GARDENS,** land cultivated for flowers, herbs, trees, shrubs and vegetables. Early man made the first gardens when he discovered he could plant and then harvest edible roots, greens and fruits. The Hanging Gardens of Babylon (about 600 BC) were considered one of the seven wonders of the ancient world. Ancient Greek, Roman and medieval monastic gardens cultivated herbs for medicinal uses. The Greeks had the first potted plant gardens and the Romans planted roof gardens. The elaborate gardens of Renaissance Italy were copied in Tudor England. The formal gardens of Versailles were the most impressive of 17th century French LANDSCAPE ARCHITECTURE. In 18th and 19th century England, idealized natural landscapes were created by landscape gardeners such as Lancelot "Capability" BROWN. The US tended to imitate English and European garden design, but after WWI emphasis was on private suburban gardens. "Garden apartments" with shared parklike facilities became increasingly common after WWII. (See also BOTANICAL GARDENS; HORTICULTURE.)

**GARDNER, Erle Stanley** (1889–1970), US

ystery writer, creator of lawyer-detective Perry Mason. Gardner wrote over 140 ovels under his own name and the seudonym A. A. Fair.

**GARDNER, Isabella Stewart** (1840–1924), US art collector. Her home in Boston, Mass., was built as a 15th-century Venetian palace; it was opened in 1903 as a public museum to display her collection which includes works by Cellini, Raphael, Rembrandt and Titian.

**GARDNER, John William** (1912–    ), US public offical. He taught psychology before joining the Carnegie Corporation, which he served as president (1955–65). He was secretary of health, education and welfare (1965–68) and founded and headed Common Cause (1970–77), a non-partisan citizen's lobby working for political reforms and legislation on national problems.

**GARFIELD, James Abram** (1831–1881), 20th president of the US, the second to be assassinated in office. He was born in a log cabin near Orange in Cuyahoga Co., Ohio, the son of pioneer farmers. In his youth he worked as a farmer and on canal boats. He graduated from Williams College in 1856 and then became a teacher and principal of Hiram College (Ohio), and was admitted to the bar. A distinguished officer of Ohio volunteers in the Civil War, he was commissioned major general in the Union army (1863). He resigned to take a seat in the House of Representatives (1863–80). During his years in Congress he was chairman of the House appropriations committee (1871–75), Republican House leader and helped establish an Office of Education (1867), served as a Smithsonian institution regent and helped create the US Geological Survey. He favored a conservative policy on money, fought inflation and supported RECONSTRUCTION measures against the South. In 1880 he was elected to the Senate, but the same year was chosen as compromise Republican presidential candidate and defeated W. S. HANCOCK in the election. Garfield's brief term of office was notable for the start of friendlier US–Latin American relations under Secretary of State James G. BLAINE and for exposure of TAR ROUTE mail frauds in the W. He gained prestige by asserting presidential power in a patronage struggle with New York state Republican Party boss Roscoe CONKLING. When the president was shot, the nation was outraged, and the postal and civil service reforms he had advocated were hastened supported by his successor Chester A. ARTHUR). (See also SPOILS SYSTEM.)

**GARIBALDI, Giuseppe** (1807–1882), Italian patriot and general, one of the creators of modern Italy. As a young man he joined the republican Young Italy society set up by MAZZINI. In 1834 he first fought in a republican uprising in Genoa and then fled to South America. There he became famous as a guerrilla leader in revolutions in Brazil and Uruguay. In 1848, the "year of revolutions," he returned to Italy to fight against Austrian, French and Neapolitan armies in support of Mazzini's short-lived Roman Republic. On its collapse, Garibaldi fled to the US until 1854. Again returning to Italy, from 1859–62 he led brilliant guerrilla campaigns against Austria and captured Sicily and Naples (see KINGDOM OF THE TWO SICILIES) with a volunteer army, his famous "Red Shirts," in the most decisive campaign of the RISORGIMENTO. He surrendered the territories to King VICTOR EMMANUEL, which effectively unified Italy. Twice (in 1862 and 1867) Garibaldi unsuccessfully tried to capture Rome from the pope. Subsequently he fought for the French against Prussia (1870). In 1874 he was elected to the Italian parliament, but retired in 1876.

**GARLAND, (Hannibal) Hamlin** (1860–1940), US writer. His fiction portrays pioneering Middle Western farm life with bitterness and realism. Among his best work is the story collection *Main Travelled Roads* (1891) and his autobiographical "Middle Border" stories (4 vols., 1917–1928).

**GARLAND, Judy** (1922–1969), US singer and movie actress, born Frances Gumm. Famous for her performances of popular songs such as "You Made Me Love You," she starred in *The Wizard of Oz* (1939) and *A Star is Born* (1954).

**GARNER, Erroll** (1921–    ), US jazz musician and composer. He created a piano style of spread chords and melodic variations on popular tunes. His most famous recording was that of his own ballad "Misty."

**GARNER, John Nance** (1868–1967), US vice-president, 1933–40 under Franklin ROOSEVELT. A Democratic member of the US House of Representatives (1903–33) and its speaker 1931–33, he was a skillful behind-the-scenes political legislator. He ran unsuccessfully for the Democratic presidential nomination in 1940.

**GARRICK, David** (1717–1779), English actor-manager and dramatist. He introduced a more natural acting style to the English stage in roles such as Hamlet and partially restored the original versions of Shakespeare's plays. From 1747–1776 he was manager of the DRURY LANE THEATRE.

**GARRISON, William Lloyd** (1805–1879),

US leader of the abolitionist movement. From 1831–65 he published *The Liberator*, an influential crusading journal which opposed slavery, war and capital punishment and supported temperance and women's rights. (See ABOLITIONISM; see also EMANCIPATION PROCLAMATION.)

**GARROWAY, Dave** (1913–    ), US television personality who created and was the first host of TV's popular *Today Show* (1952–61).

**GARTER, Order of the,** the highest order of British knighthood, established in the mid-14th century by King Edward III. It consists of the sovereign, the Prince of Wales, 25 knights companions and such foreign rulers and others as the monarch may name. Its patron is St. George and its famous motto is *Honi soit qui mal y pense* ("Shame to him who thinks ill of it").

**GARTER SNAKES,** harmless snakes of the genus *Thamnophis*. They are the most common snakes of North America, growing usually to a length of 500–750mm (20–30in) and feeding on frogs or salamanders. Some are aquatic or semiaquatic and kept as pets.

**GARVEY, Marcus Moziah** (1887–1940), US Negro leader, born in the British West Indies. In 1914 he founded the Universal Negro Improvement Association in Jamaica and in 1916 introduced it to the US where it gained a widespread following. It emphasized the kinship of all Negroes and a "back to Africa" movement. He promoted the Black Star Line, a shipping company for trade with Africa but in 1925 was convicted of mail fraud in connection with its funds. His sentence commuted by President Coolidge (1927), he was deported to Jamaica.

**GARY, Elbert Henry** (1846–1927), US lawyer and industrialist. He organized the US Steel Corporation and was its chairman, 1901–27. He founded the city of GARY, Ind., named for him, and promoted good working conditions, but opposed unions.

**GARY, Romain** (1914–1980), French novelist of Russian origin, born Romain Kacev. He fought in WWII and was a diplomat. His works include *The Roots of Heaven* (1956) and *Promise at Dawn* (1960).

**GAS,** one of the three states (solid, liquid, gas) into which nearly all matter above the atomic level can be classified. Gases are characterized by a low DENSITY and VISCOSITY; a high compressibility; optical transparency; a complete lack of rigidity, and a readiness to fill whatever volume is available to them and to form molecularly homogeneous mixtures with other gases.

Air and STEAM are familiar examples. A sufficiently high temperatures, all material vaporize, though many undergo chemica changes first. Gases, particularly steam an CARBON dioxide, are common products o COMBUSTION, while several available natur ally or from PETROLEUM or COAL (e.g. HYDROGEN, METHANE) are used as fuel themselves. The great bulk of the universe i gaseous, in the form of interstella hydrogen. Gases will often dissolve in liquids, the solubility rising with PRESSUR and falling with TEMPERATURE; a littl dissolved carbon dioxide is responsible fo the bubbles in soda.

In contrast to solids and liquids, th MOLECULES of a gas are far apart compare with their own size, and move freely an randomly at a wide range of speeds of th order of 100m/s. For a given temperatur and pressure, equal volumes of gas contai the same number of molecule ($2.7 \times 10^{25}$m$^{-3}$ at room temperature an atmospheric pressure). The impacts of th molecules on the walls of the container ar responsible for the pressure exerted b gases.

For a given mass of an ideal gas (i.e., on in which the molecules are of negligible siz and exert no forces on each other), th product of the pressure (P) and the volum (V) is proportional to the absolut temperature (T):

$$PV = RT \text{ (the general gas laws).}$$

The constant of proportionality ($R$) i known as the **universal gas constant** and ha the value 8.314 joules/kelvin-mole. Th general gas law and most of the othe properties of gases can be explained i terms of the KINETIC THEORY withou reference to the internal structure of th molecules. Real gases deviate from thi ideal behavior because of the actua presence of small intermolecular forces.

**GAS, Fuel,** combustible GAS used as FUEL fo domestic or industrial heating, furnace engines, etc. The main types are NATURA GAS, coal gas, producer gas and water ga (blue gas). Town gas, now little used, is mixture of coal gas and water gas. (See als BOTTLED GAS.)

**GASCONY,** historic region of SW France Once occupied by the Romans and settle by the Basques, it was semi-independent o France until the 17th-century.

**GASKELL, Elizabeth Cleghorn (Stevenson** (1810–1865), English novelist. Her mos famous works are *Cranford* (1853), abou middle-class village life, *North and Sout* (1855), a social portrayal of industria

wns, and *The Life of Charlotte Brontë*
857).

**ASOHOL,** a nine-to-one mixture of
.soline with ethanol (ethyl or grain
cohol) or with methanol (methyl or wood
cohol), each of which can be produced
om certain agricultural waste products.
he alcohol increases the octane rating of
ie gasoline, reduces gasoline-produced
ollutants and is considered promising in
igmenting gasoline supplies.

**ASOLINE,** or petrol, a mixture of volatile
rDROCARBONS having 4 to 12 carbon atoms
r molecule, used as a FUEL for
ITERNAL-COMBUSTION ENGINES, and as a
lvent. Although gasoline can be derived
om oil, coal and tar, or synthesized from
irbon monoxide and hydrogen, almost all
produced from PETROLEUM by refining,
RACKING and ALKYLATION, the fractions
:ing blended to produce fuels with desired
laracteristics. Motor gasoline boils
tween 30°C and 200°C, with more of the
w-boiling components in cold weather for
isy starting. If, however, the fuel is too
olatile, vapor lock can occur—i.e., vapor
ibbles form and hinder the flow of fuel.
.viation gasoline contains less of both low-
id high-boiling components. The structure
` gasoline components is also carefully
ontrolled for maximum power and
'ficiency, as reflected in the OCTANE rating;
iis may be further improved by ANTIKNOCK
DDITIVES. Other additives include lead
cavengers (ethylene dibromide and
ichloride), antioxidants, metal deactiva-
rs (which remove metal ions that catalyze
xidation) anti-icing agents, and
etergents.

**ASPÉ PENINSULA,** mountainous pen-
isula, c170mi long, in SE Quebec, Canada,
rojecting into the Gulf of St. Lawrence.
cenic and popular with tourists, it has a
rested interior with lakes and rivers that
rovide excellent hunting and fishing.

**ASTROENTERITIS,** group of conditions,
sually due to viral or bacterial infection of
pper GASTROINTESTINAL TRACT, causing
IARRHEA, VOMITING and abdominal COLIC.
Vhile these are mostly mild illnesses, in
oung infants and debilitated or elderly
dults, dehydration may develop rapidly
id fatalities may result. (See also
NTERITIS; FOOD POISONING.)

**ASTROINTESTINAL SERIES,** X-RAY
xamination of the GASTROINTESTINAL TRACT
sing radio-opaque substances, usually
arium salts. In barium swallow and meal,
n emulsion is taken and the ESOPHAGUS,
rOMACH and DUODENUM are X-rayed. A
llow-through may be performed later to
utline the small intestine. For **barium**

enema, a suspension is passed into rectum
and large intestine. CANCER, ULCERS,
diverticulae and forms of ENTERITIS and
COLITIS may be revealed.

**GASTROINTESTINAL TRACT,** or gut, or
alimentary canal, the anatomical pathway
involved in the DIGESTIVE SYSTEM of animals.
In man it starts at the PHARYNX, passing into
ESOPHAGUS and STOMACH. From this arises
the small intestine, consisting of the
DUODENUM and the great length of the
jejunum and ileum. This leads into the large
bowel, consisting of the cecum (from which
the vermiform APPENDIX arises), colon and
rectum. The parts from the stomach to the
latter part of the colon lie suspended on a
MESENTERY, through which they receive
their blood supply, and lie in loops within
the peritoneal cavity of the ABDOMEN. In
each part, the shape, muscle layers and
epithelium are specialized for their
particular functions of secretion and
absorption. Movement of food in the tract
occurs largely by PERISTALSIS, but is
controlled at key points by SPHINCTERS.
There are many gastrointestinal tract
diseases. In GASTROENTERITIS, ENTERITIS and
COLITIS, gut segments become inflamed.
Peptic ULCER affects both the duodenum
and stomach, while CANCER of the
esophagus, stomach, colon and rectum are
relatively common. Disease of the small
intestine tends to cause malabsorption.
Methods of investigating the tract include
GASTROINTESTINAL SERIES, and endoscopy, in
which viewing tubes are passed in via the
mouth or anus to examine the gut
epithelium.

**GAS TURBINE,** a heat ENGINE in which hot
gas, generated by burning a fuel or by heat
exchange from a nuclear reactor, drives a
TURBINE and so supplies power. Straight-
forward and reliable, they were developed in
the late 1930s, and are now used to power
aircraft, ships and locomotives, to generate
electricity and to drive compressors in
pipelines. The fuel used may be fuel GAS,
gasoline, kerosine or even powdered coal.
Some gas turbines are external-combustion
engines, the working gas being heated in a
heat exchanger and passed round the
system in a closed cycle. Most, however, are
INTERNAL COMBUSTION ENGINES working on
an open cycle: in the combustors fuel is
injected into compressed air and ignited; the
hot exhaust gases drive the turbines and are
vented to the atmosphere, heat exchangers
transferring some of their heat to the air
from the compressors. (See also JET
PROPULSION.)

**GATES, Horatio** (c1727–1806), American
Revolutionary War general. As a com-

mander of the Army of the North he gained credit for the defeat of General Burgoyne at the battle of SARATOGA in 1777, after which the CONWAY CABAL plotted unsuccessfully to replace Washington by Gates as commander-in-chief. Gates took command in the South in 1780 and was badly defeated at CAMDEN, by General Cornwallis.

**GATEWAY NATIONAL RECREATION AREA,** urban recreational area established 1972 and officially opened 1974, in N.Y. and N.J. It comprises three units in N.Y.—Breezy Point (W Rockaway Peninsula, Jacob Riis Park and Fort Tilden), Jamaica Bay (Jamaica Bay Wildlife Refuge, Frank Charles Memorial Park, Canarsie Pier, Plumb Beach and Floyd Bennett Field), and Staten Island (Great Kills Park, Miller Field Park, Hoffman and Swinburne Islands)—and Sandy Hook in N.J.

**GAUCHO,** cowboy of the South American pampas who flourished in the 18th and 19th centuries. Gauchos were skilled riders, and were usually employed to herd cattle. Their function ceased with the fencing of the pampas and reorganization of the cattle industry, but like the US COWBOY they survived as local folk heroes.

**GAUDÍ, Antonio** (1852–1926), Spanish architect, born Antonio Gaudí i Cornet. The fluidity, intricacy and bizarre aspect of his designs are an expression of ART NOUVEAU. He used glazed tiles to color his architecture. He worked mostly in Barcelona where he created the Milá House, the Güel Park and the Church of the Holy Family.

**GAUDIER-BRZESKA, Henri** (1891–1915), French sculptor, born Henri Gaudier, who worked in England. His abstract animal sculptures attracted the interest of Ezra POUND and Wyndham LEWIS and he became an exponent of VORTICISM. He was killed in WWI.

**GAUGUIN, Paul Eugéne Henri** (1848–1903), French post-impressionist painter noted for his pictures of Polynesian life. After painting in a symbolist style at Pont-Aven, Brittany and working with VAN GOGH, he went to Tahiti and the Marquesas in 1891 where he lived for the rest of his life. He painted scenes in brilliant colors and flattened, simplified forms. His concept of primitivism in art influenced EXPRESSIONISM.

**GAUL,** ancient designation for a region in W Europe comprising present-day France, Belgium, western Germany and northern Italy. The region was named for the invaders the "Galli" (Celts) who conquered it. Northern Italy, *Cisalpine Gaul* (Gaul

this side of the Alps), was conquered in th 5th century BC by Celts who were subjecte by Rome in 222 BC. The inhabitants wei given Roman citizenship in 49 BC *Transalpine Gaul* (Gaul the other side the Alps), now France and parts Germany, Belgium, Holland and Switze land, was gradually conquered by the Cel from the 8th to the 5th century BC However, by 121 BC Rome had occupie the S portion. In his GALLIC WARS, 58–5 BC, Julius Caesar defeated incursions Germanic tribes and conquered all th Gallic tribes. Under Roman dominion Ga prospered; roads were built and citie founded. In the 5th century AD it wa overrun by Germanic tribes.

**GAUSS, Johann Karl Friedrich** (1777 1855), German mathematician who di covered the method of LEAST-SQUARES (fo reducing experimental errors), made mar contributions to the theory of NUMBEF (including the proof that all algebra equations have at least one root of the form $(a+ib)$ where $i$ is the IMAGINARY OPERATC and $a$ and $b$ are real numbers), an discovered a NON-EUCLIDEAN GEOMETRY. H won fame when he showed how to rediscove the lost ASTEROID Ceres (1801), and late (1831) turned to the study of MAGNETISM particularly terrestrial magnetism. He also remembered for his contributions STATISTICS and CALCULUS.

**GAUTIER, Theophile** (1811–1872 French poet, novelist and critic. He was supporter of the aesthetic movement, "a for art's sake," which he explained in th preface to his novel *Mademoiselle c Maupin* (1835–36). He wrote outstandir art, drama and ballet criticism. His volum of verse include *Enamels and Camee* (1852).

**GAY, John** (1685–1732), English poet ar dramatist, author of *The Beggar's Oper* (1728). Using English ballads for th music, he satirized Italian operatic form and contemporary politics in this comedy highwaymen, thieves and prostitute BRECHT based his THREEPENNY OPERA on *Th Beggar's Opera.*

**GAY ACTIVISM,** a movement b homosexuals to obtain full legal and civ rights. They contend that persons known be or suspected of being "gay" (homose: ual) were subjected to discrimination employment and housing, and that ga were often harassed by police and physical attacked by violence-prone individual Though they generally had sought to avo public attention, gays became more militai in the 1970s after a series of incident including a police raid on a Greenwic

Village (New York City) bar in 1969 and the slaying of a gay San Francisco city supervisor in 1978. Activists usually work at state and local levels to repeal discriminatory legislation—including laws prohibiting certain kinds of sexual conduct among consenting adults—and to win adoption of laws affirming full rights regardless of an individual's sexual preference. Opponents argue that homosexuality is a sin condemned by the Bible and that permitting gays to teach, for example, would jeopardize young children. In 1977, singer Anita Bryant led a successful fight to repeal a Dade County (Fla.) gay rights ordinance.

**GAZA STRIP,** narrow piece of land in the former SW Palestine, about 26 mi long, 4–5 mi wide. After the Arab–Israeli war in 1948, it was granted to Egypt and many Arab refugees fled there. Israel occupied the area in 1967. Some of the Arab population has been resettled. Although the Israeli-Egyptian peace treaty (1979) provided for negotiations on self-rule in Gaza, the area continued to be a subject of acrimonious disagreement.

**GAZELLE,** a slender, graceful ANTELOPE of Asia and Africa. Males are horned; females may have short spikes. They are usually 600–900mm (2–3ft) high at the shoulder, swift and light-footed. They inhabit dry open country. Thompson's and Grant's gazelles live in Africa; the Goitered gazelle, so called from a swelling in the throat, in Asian deserts; Speke's gazelle, with an inflatable nose, in Somali deserts. The gerenuk or Giraffe-necked gazelle has a long neck and legs.

**GECKOES,** small lizards living in warm climates all over the world. They appear in the US in Fla. and Cal. They are about 150mm (6in) long, eat insects and are able to climb vertical surfaces by means of suction pads and minute hairs on the feet. Some can change color to match their background. Most live in trees, but some are found in the desert.

**GEDDES, Norman Bel** (1893–1958), US industrial and stage designer famous for his "streamlined" style. He designed over 200 stage and film sets, and, after the 1920s, theaters, trains and automobiles.

**GEESE,** water birds of 14 species closely related to DUCKS and SWANS. There are two natural groups of true geese: Gray geese of the genus *Anser*, and Black geese (genus *Branta*). They are all confined to the N Hemisphere, breeding in arctic or subarctic regions. They are gregarious, feeding and migrating in large flocks. In flight a flock usually adopts a characteristic V-formation. Geese feed by grazing on the banks of rivers and lakes, or may fly quite a distance from water to feed on grain or in stubble. Domestic geese are derived from the Graylag goose, *A. anser*.

**GEHRIG, "Lou"** (Henry Louis; 1903–1941), US baseball player, known as the "Iron Man." As first baseman for the New York Yankees he set a record by playing 2,130 consecutive games. He had a .361 batting average in seven world series, a lifetime average of .341 and 493 home runs. He died of a rare muscle-wasting disease that now bears his name.

**GEIGER COUNTER,** or **Geiger-Müller tube,** an instrument for detecting the presence of and measuring radiation such as ALPHA PARTICLES, BETA-, GAMMA- and X-RAYS. It can count individual particles at rates up to about 10,000/s and is used widely in medicine and in prospecting for radioactive ores. A fine wire ANODE runs along the axis of a metal cylinder which has sealed insulating ends, contains a mixture of ARGON or NEON and METHANE at low pressure, and acts as the CATHODE, the potential between them being about 1kV. Particles entering through a thin window cause ionization in the gas; ELECTRONS build up around the anode and a momentary drop in the inter-electrode potential occurs which appears as a voltage pulse in an associated counting circuit. The methane quenches the ionization, leaving the counter ready to detect further incoming particles.

**GEISEL, Ernesto** (1908–    ), president of Brazil 1974–79. A retired general, he continued the tradition of military presidents after the 1964 coup that ended civilian rule. He supported some reforms in the authoritarian regime.

**GEISEL, Theodor.** See SEUSS, DR.

**GEISHA,** Japanese professional female entertainer, especially for businessmen's parties in restaurants. The name means "art person" and a Geisha's accomplishments include singing, dancing, playing instruments and conversation, ranging in subject from a knowledge of history to contemporary gossip. Geishas are not prostitutes. Training for the profession, which has existed since the 18th century, begins early with a highly-organized apprenticeship.

**GELL-MANN, Murray** (1929–    ), US physicist awarded the 1969 Nobel Prize for Physics for his work on the classification of SUBATOMIC PARTICLES (notably K-mesons and hyperons) and their interactions. He (and independently G. Zweig) proposed the quark as a basic component of most subatomic particles.

**GEMINI** (the Twins), a constellation on the

ECLIPTIC named after its two brightest stars, Castor and Pollux. The third sign of the ZODIAC, Gemini gives its name to the Geminid METEOR shower.

**GEMINI MISSIONS,** US space program designed to develop docking and rendezvous procedures, a vital preparation for the Apollo Project (see SPACE EXPLORATION). Gemini 1 was launched April 8, 1964; 3 (the first manned), March 23, 1965; 12 (the last), Nov. 11, 1966. From Gemini 4 E.H. White II became the 2nd man ever to float free in space.

**GENEALOGY,** the study of the origins and history of families, by means of pedigree charts showing lines of descent. It is a skilled profession, also a hobby, which developed after 1500. Genealogy is a tool of the historian and is useful for determining legal cases involving inheritance. It is fundamental to such hereditary organizations as the DAUGHTERS OF THE AMERICAN REVOLUTION.

**GENE POOL,** the total amount of information present at any time in the GENES of the reproductive members of a biological population. The frequency of any particular gene in the gene pool changes owing to NATURAL SELECTION, MUTATION and GENETIC DRIFT. This change forms the basis of evolutionary change.

**GENERAL ACCOUNTING OFFICE (GAO),** an independent agency of the US Congress, created in 1921 for auditing government spending. Headed by the US Comptroller General, it sets up accounting and management standards, settles claims for or against the government, collects debts and assesses the practicability and legality of public expenditures of most government agencies.

**GENERAL AGREEMENT ON TARIFFS AND TRADE (GATT),** a set of agreements which aim to abolish quotas and reduce tariffs and other restrictions on world trade, originally agreed to by 23 countries in 1947. By the 1970s there were 78 nations participating in GATT. The "Kennedy round" of GATT negotiations in 1964–67 provided for a reduction in import duties over five years. Tariffs among steel-producing countries were agreed upon, export prices for grain controlled and an international anti-dump code established.

**GENERAL SERVICES ADMINISTRA-TION (GSA),** an independent US federal agency, established 1949, to maintain government property and records. Its five branches deal with quality-controlled supplies for government use, emergency stockpiles of strategic materials, erection and management of public buildings,

transportation and telecommunications and the preserving of historical records and archives.

**GENERATOR, Electric,** or **dynamo,** a device converting mechanical ENERGY into electrical energy. Traditional forms are based on inducing ELECTRIC FIELDS by changing the MAGNETIC FIELD lines through a circuit (see ELECTROMAGNETISM). All generators can be, and sometimes are, run in reverse as electric MOTORS.

The simplest generator consists of a permanent magnet (the **rotor**) spun inside a coil of wire (the **stator**); the magnetic field is thus reversed twice each revolution, and an AC voltage is generated at the frequency of rotation (see also MAGNETO). In practical designs, the rotor is usually an ELECTROMAGNET driven by a direct current obtained by rectification of a part of the voltage generated, and passed to the rotor through a pair of CARBON brush/slip ring contacts. The use of three sets of stator coils 120° apart allows generation of a three-phase supply. (See also ARMATURE.)

Simple DC generators consist of a coil rotating in the field of a permanent magnet: the voltage induced in the coil alternates at the frequency of rotation, but it is collected through a **commutator** —a slip ring broken into two semicircular parts, to each of which one end of the coil is connected, so that the connection between the coil and the brushes is reversed twice each revolution—resulting in a rapidly pulsating direct voltage. A steadier voltage can be achieved through the use of multiple coil/commutator arrangements and except in very small generators, the permanent magnet is again replaced by an electromagnet driven by part of the generated voltage.

For large-scale generation, the mechanical power is usually derived from fossil-fuel-fired steam TURBINES, or from dam-fed water turbines, and the process is only moderately efficient. The magneto-hydrodynamic generator, currently under development, avoids this step, and has no moving parts either. A hot conducting fluid (treated coal gas, or reactor-heated liquid metal) passes through the field of an electromagnet, so that the charges are forced in opposite directions producing a DC voltage. In another device, the electrogasdynamic generator, the voltage is produced by using a high speed gas stream to pump charge from an electric discharge, against the electric field, to a collector. (See also ELECTROSTATIC GENERATOR.)

Generators originated with the discovery of induction by M. FARADAY in 1831; the considerable advantages of electromagnets over permanent magnets were first exploited by E. W. von SIEMENS in 1866.

**GENES,** the carriers of the genetic information which is passed on from generation to generation by the combination of GAMETES. Genes consist of chain-like molecules of NUCLEIC ACIDS, DNA in most organisms and RNA in some VIRUSES. The genes are normally located on the CHROMOSOMES found in the nucleus of the CELL. The genetic information is coded by the sequences of the four bases present in nucleic acids, with a differing 3-base code for each AMINO ACID so that each gene contains the information for th synthesis of one PROTEIN chain.

**GENESIS** (Greek: origin or generation), the first book of the OLD TESTAMENT and of the PENTATEUCH. It tells of the creation, the Fall (see ORIGINAL SIN), the Flood (see NOAH), the origins of the HEBREWS, and the early PATRIARCHS with whom God made his COVENANT. The book accounts for the Israelites' presence in Egypt, and so leads into EXODUS.

**GENET, Jean** (1910– ), French playwright and novelist. He spent much of his life in prisons. His writing concerns the homosexual underworld of France and the borderline between acceptable and unacceptable social behavior. His works include the novel *Our Lady of the Flowers* (1944), *The Thief's Journal* (1948) and the plays *The Balcony* (1956) and *The Blacks* (1958).

**GENETIC ENGINEERING,** manipulation of genetic material, or DNA, to effect a particular result. Gene splicing, which creates RECOMBINANT DNA, has been the most prominent technique of genetic engineering since 1973; it promises to revolutionize any number of enterprises from pharmaceuticals to agriculture; for example, by implanting an insulin-producing gene into a DNA ring of the common bacterium *E. coli*, one can create (given the rapid reproduction of these bacteria) a virtual insulin factory. Similarly, with such gene transference, one should be able to develop new characteristics in plants selectively and immediately, as opposed to the time-consuming, imprecise method of cross-breeding. The scientists who developed the basic techniques of gene splicing are the 1980 Nobel Prize winner Paul Berg of Stanford University, first to make recombinant DNA, and Stanley N. Cohen of Stanford University and Herbert W. Boyer of the University of California at San Francisco.

**GENETICS,** the branch of biology dealing with HEREDITY, which studies the way in which GENES operate and the way in which they are transmitted from parent to offspring. Genetics can be subdivided into a number of more specialized subjects including classical genetics (which deals with the inheritance of parental features in higher animals and plants), cytogenetics (which deals with the cellular basis of genetics), microbial genetics (which deals with inheritance in microorganisms), molecular genetics (which deals with the biochemical basis of inheritance) and human genetics (which deals with inheritance of features of social and medical importance in man). Genetic counselling is a branch of human genetics of growing importance. Here couples, particularly those with some form of inherited defect, are advised on the chances that their children will have similar defects.

**GENEVA,** city and capital of Geneva canton, SW Switzerland, on Lake Geneva at the Rhône R outlet. It is the headquarters of the WORLD HEALTH ORGANIZATION, the INTERNATIONAL LABOR ORGANIZATION, and the International RED CROSS. It is an important cultural, scientific, theological, industrial and banking city and the center of the Swiss watchmaking industry. The Collèg de Genève was founded (1559) by John CALVIN. Pop 151,000; met pop 327,100.

**GENEVA, Lake,** or Lac Léman, largest Alpine lake in Europe, at an altitude of 1,200ft, between SW Switzerland and SE France and the Jura Mts. The Rhône R enters at the E end of the beautiful crescent-shaped lake, emerging at Geneva.

**GENEVA CONVENTIONS,** four international agreements for the protection of soldiers and civilians from the effects of war, signed by 58 nations and the Holy See in Aug. 1949, at Geneva, Switzerland. Convention I derived from a conference in 1864 in which the work of Jean DUNANT, founder of the RED CROSS, led to an agreement to improve conditions for sick and wounded soldiers in the field. Convention II deals with armed forces at sea, Convention III with treatment of prisoners of war and Convention IV with protection of civilians.

**GENGHIS KHAN** (1167?–1227), Mongol ruler of one of the greatest empires in world history, born Temujin. After 20 years of tribal warfare, he was acknowledged Genghis Khan (Universal Ruler) in 1206. He campaigned against the CH'IN empire in N China (1213–15) and in 1218–25 he conquered Turkistan, Iran, Afghanistan and S Russia until his empire stretched from the Caucasus Mts to the Indus R and from the Caspian Sea to Peking. He was not only a fearsome warrior, but also a skilled political leader. (See MONGOL EMPIRE.)

**GENOA,** capital of Genoa province and of the region of Liguria, NW Italy, 71mi SSW of Milan. It is Italy's largest port and is second only to Marseilles on the Mediterranean. In ancient times it was the headquarters of the Roman fleet. In the 12th and 13th centuries it was an independent republic with its own fleet and possessions in the LEVANT. The city's principal industries include shipbuilding, iron and steel making and oil and sugar refining. Pop 789,100.

**GENOCIDE,** (from Greek *genos,* race), the deliberate extermination of a racial, ethnic, political or religious group of people. The term is widely credited to the Polish–American scholar Raphael Lemkin. He believed that Nazi persecution of the Jews and other groups called for an international code on the subject. This was achieved when the UN General Assembly in 1948 approved the Convention on the Prevention and Punishment of the Crime of Genocide. (See also ANTISEMITISM.)

**GENOTYPE,** the total genetic makeup of a particular organism consisting of all the GENES received from both parents. For any individual the genotype determines their strengths and weaknesses during their whole life and is unique and constant for each individual. Duplication of the genotype except in identical twins is statistically impossible except in the simplest organisms. (See also PHENOTYPE.)

**GENRE,** form of painting which takes its subjects from everyday life. The term derives from the French *de tout genre* (of every kind). Dutch, Flemish and Italian genre schools flourished in the 16th and 17th centuries. Among the great artists of the genre are Pieter BRUEGEL, VERMEER, WATTEAU, LONGHI and CHARDIN. The 19th and 20th centuries saw their own genre movements, such as the American ASHCAN SCHOOL.

**GENTILE DA FABRIANO** (c1370–1427), Italian painter, a major exponent of the international Gothic style. His rich, exotic manner with its profusion of color and gilt is seen in his masterpiece, the *Adoration of the Magi* (1423), an altarpiece now in the Uffizi in Florence.

**GENUS.** See TAXONOMY.

**GEOCHEMISTRY,** the study of the CHEMISTRY of the EARTH (and other planets). Chemical characterization of the earth as a whole relates to theories of planetary formation. Classical geochemistry analyzes rocks and MINERALS. The study of PHASE

EQUILIBRIA has thrown much light on the postulated processes of ROCK formation. (See also GEOLOGY.)

**GEODESIC DOME,** architectural dome-like structure composed of polygonal (usually triangular) faces of lightweight material. It was developed by Buckminster FULLER. A geodesic dome housed the US exhibit at Expo '67 (Montreal).

**GEODESY,** an area of study concerned with the determination and explanation of the precise shape and size of the EARTH. The first recorded measurement of the earth's circumference that approximates to the correct value was that of ERATOSTHENES in the 3rd century BC. Modern geodesists use not only the techniques of SURVEYING but also information received from the observations of artificial SATELLITES.

**GEOGRAPHY,** the group of sciences concerned with the surface of the earth, including the distribution of life upon it, its physical structures, etc. Geography relies on surveying and mapping, and modern cartography (mapmaking) has rapidly adapted to the new needs of geography as it advances and develops. (See MAP; SURVEYING.) **Biogeography** is concerned with the distribution of life, both plant and animal (including man), about our world. It is thus clearly intimately related to BIOLOGY and ECOLOGY. **Economic geography** describes and seeks to explain the patterns of the world's commerce in terms of production, trade and transportation, and consumption. It relates closely to economics. **Mathematical geography** deals with the size, shape and motions of the EARTH, and is thus linked with ASTRONOMY (see also GEODESY). **Physical geography** deals with the physical structures of the earth, also including CLIMATOLOGY and OCEANOGRAPHY, and is akin to physical GEOLOGY. **Political geography** is concerned with the world as nationally divided; **regional geography** with the world in terms of regions separated by physical rather than national boundaries. **Historical geography** deals with the geography of the past: PALEOGEOGRAPHY at one level, exploration or past political change or settlement at another. **Applied geography** embraces the applications of all these branches to the solution of socioeconomic problems. Its subdivisions include urban geography and social geography; and it contributes to the science of SOCIOLOGY. (See also ETHNOLOGY HYDROLOGY; METEREOLOGY.) **Development of Geography.** Geography had its origins in the Greek attempts to understand the world in which they found themselves. Once it was realized that the earth was round, the next step was to estimate its size. This was achieved in the 3rd century BC by ERATOSTHENES. The classical achievement in geography, like that in astronomy, was summed up by Claudius PTOLEMY. His world MAP was used for centuries. Geographical knowledge next leapt forward in the age of exploration that opened with the voyages of Dias and Columbus. The 17th-century saw continuing discovery and greatly improved methods of survey. The earliest modern geographical treatises, including that of Varenius, also appeared in this era. The 19th-century brought with it the works of F. H. A. von HUMBOLDT and Karl Ritter, the former stressing physical and systematic geography, the latter the human and historical aspects of the science. Encompassing so many different studies, geography since the mid-19th century has become a battleground for the strife between different schools of geographers. While some have encouraged a regional approach, others have preferred to develop a landscape-concept. Others have stressed the study of the physical environment while others still have concentrated on political and economic factors. Perhaps the most recent group to come to the fore favors the collection of precise numerical data. With this they try to build mathematical models of geographic phenomena.

**GEOLOGICAL SURVEY,** US government bureau, within the Dept. of the Interior, established in 1879, responsible for the location and control of water and mineral resources on federal land, and for the chartering of water resources and the location of potential problem areas. It carries out and supervises research in the earth sciences.

**GEOLOGY,** the group of sciences concerned with the study of the earth, including its structure, long-term history, composition and origins.

**Physical Geology** deals with the structure and composition of the EARTH and the forces of change affecting them. The sciences that make up physical geology thus include structural geology, petrology, mineralogy, GEOMORPHOLOGY, GEOPHYSICS, geochemistry, and environmental geology. Much of modern physical geology is based on the theory of PLATE TECTONICS.

**Historical Geology** deals with the physical history of the earth in past ages, and with the EVOLUTION of life upon it. It embraces such sciences as PALEOCLIMATOLOGY, GEOGRAPHY, PALEONTOLOGY and STRATIGRAPHY, and attempts to integrate these with the accumulated data of physical geology in a plate tectonics-oriented

reconstruction of earth history embracing some 4.5-5 billion years of geologic time.

**Economic Geology** lies between these two, and borrows from both. Concerned with the location and exploitation of the earth's natural resources (see ORE), it includes such disciplines as petroleum geology, mining geology, and groundwater geology, and utilizes modern **Geology of other Planets.** Except for the MOON, it is not yet possible to examine the rocks of other planets, but telescopic and spectroscopic examinations and unmanned probes have revealed much. VOLCANISM is known on the moon and MARS (one volcano is some 600km across), and "moonquakes" have been detected.

**Development of Geology.** Most early geological knowledge came from the experience of mining engineers, some of the earliest geological treatises coming from the pen of Georgius AGRICOLA. The interest of the 16th-century in FOSSILS was also reflected in the writings of K. von GESNER. In the 17th-century the biblical timescale of about 6,000 years from the Creation to the present largely constrained the many speculative "Theories of the Earth" that were issued. The century's most notable geological observations were made by N. STENO. The late 18th-century saw the celebrated controversy between A. G. WERNER'S "Neptunists" and J. HUTTON'S "Plutonists" as to the origin of rocks. The first decades of the 19th-century witnessed the decline of speculative geology as field observations became ever more detailed. William Smith (1769–1839), the "father of stratigraphy," showed how the succession of fossils could be used to index the stratigraphic column, and he and others produced impressive geological maps. C. LYELL'S classic *Principles of Geology* (1830-33) restated the Huttonian principle of UNIFORMITARIANISM and provided the groundwork for much of the later development of the science. L. AGASSIZ pointed to the importance of glacial action in the recent history of the earth (1840), while mining engineering continued to contribute to the pool of geologic data. The most significant recent development in the earth sciences has been the acceptance of the theory of PLATE TECTONICS, foreshadowed by A. WEGENER'S 1912 theory of CONTINENTAL DRIFT.

**GEOMETRY,** the branch of MATHEMATICS which studies the properties both of space and of the mathematical constructs—lines, curves, surfaces and the like—which can occupy space. Today it divides into ALGEBRAIC GEOMETRY; ANALYTIC GEOMETRY; DESCRIPTIVE GEOMETRY; DIFFERENTIAL

GEOMETRY; EUCLIDEAN GEOMETRY; and PROJECTIVE GEOMETRY, but many of these divisions have grown up only in the last few hundred years. The name geometry reminds us of its earliest use—for the measurement of land and materials. The Babylonian and Egyptian civilizations thus gained great empirical knowledge of elementary geometric figures, including how to construct a right-angled triangle. The Greek philosophers transformed this practical art into an intellectual pastime through which they sought access to the secrets of nature. About 300 BC EUCLID collected together and added to the Greek rationalization of geometry in his *Elements*. Later Alexandrian geometers began to develop TRIGONOMETRY. The revival of interest in life-like painting in the Renaissance led to the development of projective geometry, though it is to the philosopher–scientist DESCARTES that we owe the invention of the algebraic (coordinate) geometry which allows algebraic FUNCTIONS to be represented geometrically. The next new branch of geometry to be developed followed fast upon the invention of CALCULUS: differential geometry. The greatest upset in the history of geometry came in the 19th century. Men such as J. K. F. GAUSS, N. I. LOBACHEVSKI and JÁNOS BOLYAI began to question the Euclidean parallel-lines axiom and discovered hyperbolic geometry, the first non-Euclidean geometry. The elliptic non-Euclidean geometry of G. F. B. RIEMANN aided EINSTEIN in the development of the theory of general RELATIVITY.

**GEOPHYSICS,** the physics of the EARTH, as such including studies of the LITHOSPHERE, e.g. SEISMOLOGY, GEOMAGNETISM, GRAVITY, RADIOACTIVITY, ELECTRIC PROPERTIES, HEAT FLOW. Also included are studies of the ATMOSPHERE and hydrosphere. Geophysical techniques are used extensively in the search for mineral deposits, an area known as *exploration geophysics* or geophysical PROSPECTING. (See also HYDROLOGY; OCEANOGRAPHY; METEOROLOGY.)

**GEOPOLITICS,** the study of politics in relation to geography and demography. The term was originally applied to the theories of the biologist and geographer Friedrich RATZEL, who sought to apply evolutionary theory to the rise and fall of nations. In the 1900s the British geographer Sir Halford MACKINDER extended these, seeing the international struggle for survival as hanging on control of the heartlands, or interior lands, of the world's great landmasses, particularly the "World Island" of Eurasia. The German Karl HAUSHOFER combined these theories to preach the eventual regeneration of Germany through her inevitable demand for *Lebensraum* (German: living space, space to expand), which would have to be sacrificed by the seaboard countries to the more dynamic countries of the heartland. This was seized upon by Adolf Hitler and became a cornerstone of Nazi doctrine, thus entirely discrediting the theory.

**GEORGE,** name of six kings of Britain. **George I** (1660–1727), Elector of Hanover from 1698, came to the throne in 1714. Shrewd and not very popular, he never learned English; this left much power in the hands of his chief minister Sir Robert WALPOLE. **George II** (1683–1760), born in Hanover, succeeded his father, George I, in 1727. He was considerably more popular. Strongly in favor of peace, he allowed the country to be drawn into the War of Austrian Succession (1740–48), losing influence and prestige. After 1750 he took little interest in politics, becoming a great patron of musicians such as HANDEL; Parliament was dominated by the Whigs WALPOLE and PITT the elder. **George III** (1738–1820), king from 1760. Much of his reign was spent in conflict with the Whig oligarchy in Parliament, which had become entrenched under his father's rule. Ironically, he became the American colonists' principal symbol of English oppression although Whig policy was really responsible. Before the onset of insanity in his later years, George III was a well-meaning ruler in a time of great stress abroad and at home. **George IV** (1762–1830), regent from 1811 and king from 1820. A loose-living dandy, he cared little about government. The scandal surrounding his divorce from Caroline of Brunswick lowered public esteem of the monarchy. **George V** (1865–1936), ascended the throne in 1910. He was immediately thrown into a constitutional crisis over the power of the House of Lords, in which he played a moderating role. He proved a popular monarch in WWI, seeking to unify the country; he later played an important part in the formation of a coalition government in the economic crisis of 1931 **George VI** (1895–1952), ascended the throne after the abdication crisis of 1936. He and his consort did much to restore confidence in the monarchy; during WWI they were a tireless example of devotion to duty. In 1939 George VI became the first reigning monarch to visit the US.

**GEORGE, Henry** (1839–1897), US journalist whose *Progress and Poverty* (1879) saw the prime cause of inequality as the possession of land. His proposed SINGLE TAX on land was never endorsed by economists but won him popular support.

**GEORGE, Saint,** the patron saint of England. He is an obscure figure, possibly a Christian convert martyred in 303. Many medieval legends became connected with his name, including his rescue of a maiden from a dragon. His feast day was April 23, but since 1969 the Roman Catholic Church has merely commemorated him on Jan. 1.

**GEORGE WASHINGTON BRIDGE,** suspension bridge across the Hudson R linking New York City and Fort Lee, N.J. Designed by Othmar AMMANN, it was completed in 1931.

**GEORGE WASHINGTON CARVER NATIONAL MONUMENT,** estate in Mo., birthplace and childhood home of the famous chemist, botanist and educator G. W. CARVER. The monument was established in 1951.

**Name of state:** Georgia
**Capital:** Atlanta
**Statehood:** Jan. 2, 1788 (4th state)
**Familiar name:** Peach State, Empire State of the South
**Area:** 58,876sq mi
**Population:** 5,464,265
**Elevation:** Highest—4,784ft, Brasstown Bald Mountain. Lowest—Sea level, Atlantic Ocean
**Motto:** Wisdom, Justice and Moderation
**State flower:** Cherokee rose
**State bird:** Brown thrasher
**State tree:** Live oak
**State song:** "Georgia On My Mind"

**GEORGIA,** state in SE US, bordered to the E by the Atlantic Ocean and S.C., to the S by Fla., to the W by Ala., and to the N by Tenn. and N.C.

**Land.** More than half the state consists of plains which extend from the Atlantic coast to the Piedmont region. The rest consists of rolling hill country. On the coastal plains, average temperatures range from a winter low of 54°F to a summer high of 82°F; the Piedmont is a little cooler in winter.

**People.** The majority of Georgians live in urban areas—over one million live within the urban area of Atlanta, the capital. Until the late 1950s Georgia was primarily rural in character, but today fewer than 10% of Georgians live on farms, and most of the rural population commute to work in the towns.

**Economy.** The structure of Georgia's economy has changed radically in the last 40 years; the volume of manufacturing has grown markedly since WWII. Leading manufactures include textiles, transportation equipment, processed foods, clothing, paper and wood products, chemicals and cigarettes. Agriculture still accounts for about a quarter of the state's income. No longer totally dependent on cotton, however, it produces peanuts, peaches, tobacco and chickens; cattle and hog raising is also of importance.

**History.** The first permanent settlement in Georgia was made by the English in 1733. In 1749 a ban on the importation of slaves was removed and Georgia quickly prospered. Before the Civil War Georgia was one of the world's leading cotton producers and by 1860 a large proportion of the state's inhabitants were black slaves. Georgia seceded from the Union on Jan. 19, 1861, and suffered greatly in the Civil War. After the war, resentment aroused by harsh RECONSTRUCTION measures ensured Democratic control over the state's politics for a century. Little changed fundamentally until the combined effects of crop destruction by the boll weevil and low cotton prices in the 1920s and 1930s drove thousands of smaller farmers from the land. Since WWII Georgia has enjoyed rapid industrialization. In 1976, the former Governor of Georgia, Jimmy Carter, was elected President of the US, and in 1981 his onetime ambassador to the UN, Andrew Young, was elected mayor of Atlanta. While the state's population increased 19.1% in the 1970s, Atlanta grew more slowly, signaling a shift of political power to the suburbs. Along with the prospect of greatly reduced federal aid for economic and social programs, the political power shift is likely to aggravate Atlanta's problems as it attempts to reduce a persistent poverty level of almost 25% among its citizens.

**GEORGIA,** or Georgian Soviet Socialist Republic, constituent republic of the USSR since 1936. The Caucasus Mts run across the N of the republic. Georgia has a subtropical climate and the lowland areas near the Black Sea produce tea, fruit, wine, tobacco and cereals. Georgia provides the Soviet Union with petroleum and many essential minerals. There is much heavy industry, with steel and other metals, textiles and chemicals the main products.

Around two-thirds of the population still work on the land. The Georgian people have a long cultural history. The ancient kingdom of Georgia, ravaged by Turkey and Persia, was annexed to Russia in 1801; an attempt to regain independence after the Revolution was crushed in 1921. Georgia was the home of STALIN. (See USSR.)

**GEORGIAN              ARCHITECTURE,** 18th-century architectural style in Britain and the British North American colonies. In Britain it refers to the classically formal and elegant style, influenced by the Italian PALLADIO, popular during the reigns of the first three Georges. In the US it refers to the style prevailing between 1700 and the Revolution, deriving more from WREN and the baroque; Palladian influences entered later. Fine examples are INDEPENDENCE HALL, Philadelphia (1745) and King's Chapel in Boston (1754).

**GEORGIAN BAY ISLANDS NATIONAL PARK,** about 30 islands in Georgian Bay, Ontario, Canada. The area's dense woodlands and the good fishing have made the park a popular tourist area.

**GERANIUM,** genus of cosmopolitan hardy perennial herbs, some of which are cultivated in gardens and as house plants. Geranium is also the name given to popular pot and bedding plants of the genus *Pelargonium*. Common or zonal geraniums (hybrid races derived from *Pelargonium zonale*) have white, salmon pink or red, flowers single or semidouble, some with bronze or maroon zones on the leaves. A range of dwarf or miniature varieties are available in this group. Another decorative-leaved variety is the ivy-leaved geranium (*P. peltatum*). Indoors, geraniums grow well in sunny south-facing windows, and the miniature varieties are particularly suited to ˇfluorescent-light gardens. Ideally, geraniums should grow at temperatures between 16°C and 21°C (60°F and 70°F) and they should be well watered whenever the soil surface becomes nearly dry, making sure that the soil never completely dries out. Propagation is by seeds and taking shoot tip cuttings. Family: Geraniaceae.

**GERBILS,** small RODENTS found in arid areas of Africa and Asia. Known as sand rats, they have fine, dense fur, long tails and can move fast by hopping.

**GERIATRICS,** the branch of MEDICINE specializing in the care of the elderly. Although concerned with the same DISEASES as the rest of medicine, the different susceptibility of the aged and a tendency for multiple pathology make its scope different. In particular the psychological problems of old age differ markedly from those encountered in the rest of the population and require special management. The social and medical aspects of long-term care involve the coordination of family, voluntary and hospital services; the geriatrician must nevertheless seek to maximize the individuality and freedom available to the geriatric patient.

**GÉRICAULT, (Jean Louis André) Théodore** (1791–1824), French painter whose style combined a massive, dynamic romanticism with a minutely detailed realism. As seen in such well-known works as his studies of lunatics, his horse paintings and the *Raft of the Medusa* (1818–19), Géricault's daringly revolutionary approach helped eclipse the classical school in French painting.

**GERMAN,** official language of Germany and Austria and an official language of Switzerland and Luxembourg, native tongue of more than 100 million people. Modern German is descended from two main forms. Low German, spoken mainly in the N, is the ancestor of both Dutch and Flemish. High German, spoken in central and S Germany is, historically, the classical German. A large part of medieval German literature, such as the 12th and 13th century epics, is in Middle High German. Today the written language is standardized but there are still great differences between spoken N and S German. Modern German is a highly inflected language with three genders and four cases, and requires agreement in number, gender and case, as in Latin. Many words are formed by compounding.

**GERMAN DEMOCRATIC REPUBLIC.** See GERMANY, EAST.

**GERMAN FEDERAL REPUBLIC.** See GERMANY, WEST.

**GERMAN MEASLES,** or rubella, mild VIRUS infection, usually contracted in childhood and causing FEVER, SKIN rash, malaise and LYMPH node enlargement. Its importance lies in the fact that infection of a mother during the first three months of PREGNANCY leads to infection of the EMBRYO via the PLACENTA and is associated with a high incidence of congenital DISEASES including CATARACT, DEAFNESS and defects of the HEART and ESOPHAGUS. VACCINATION of intending mothers who have not had rubella is advisable. If rubella occurs in early pregnancy, ABORTION may be induced to avoid the BIRTH of malformed children.

**GERMAN SHEPHERD (or Alsatian),** a breed of dog developed in Germany, known for its strength, loyalty and intelligence. It has a long body, with black and tan or grey hair, and a rather wolf-like head. It is much used by police and military and as a guide dog for the blind.

**GERMANY,** nation in western Europe now divided into two effectively independent states, East and West Germany. It occupies the heartland of Europe and is composed of the North German Plain in the N, and highlands in the center and S. West Germany has a maritime climate with average temperatures in July 64°F and in January 32°F. In East Germany the temperature varies more widely. About 28% of Germany is still forest and about 39% is farmland; the soil, however, is fairly poor in most areas.

**The People.** The German people are of two distinct strains: the tall, fair-skinned, blue-eyed Nordic people of the N, and the darker, stockier Alpine types of the S; the two types are well-mingled throughout the country. About three-quarters of the population now lives in urban areas. Germans are known for their liking of outdoor sports and also for their folk traditions. German culture has made major contributions to European art, thought, science, and especially music, through such composers as BEETHOVEN and WAGNER.

**Economy.** Germany's greatest natural asset has been her coal. The soft coal mines of the Ruhr supply much of the fuel needed for the whole W European steel industry. Other important minerals are salt, potash, silver, copper, lead, zinc and nickel. The Ruhr is still one of the centers of heavy industry in W Europe. More traditional industries include the making of fine clocks, toys and cameras.

**History.** Although Rome conquered the left bank of the Rhine, the Teutonic tribes of central Germany were never brought into the empire. CHARLEMAGNE united most of the territory of modern France and Germany into the Frankish empire, which was eventually divided among his three grandsons; the area E of the Rhine went to Louis the German. From the 10th to the 13th centuries attempts to retain a united Germany were unsuccessful, and until the 19th century Germany was composed of independent states, loosely united in name only as the Holy Roman Empire. The Protestant Reformation, launched by Luther in the 16th century, influenced much of Europe, but German disunity was intensified by strife between Catholic and Protestant states, culminating in the devastating Thirty Years' War (1618–48). The foundation of modern Germany was largely the work of Otto von BISMARCK, prime minister of Prussia from 1862. After defeating Austria in 1866 and France in

1871, he unified Germany in a Prussian-dominated empire. In the last decades of the 19th century there was massive industrial development in Germany; she began to compete with Britain and France, a competition that culminated in WWI. Germany was defeated and the WEIMAR REPUBLIC was declared on Nov 9, 1918. However, resentment aroused by the harsh Treaty of VERSAILLES (1919), economic chaos in the 1920s and 1930s and lack of democratic traditions all served to undermine support for the Republic.

HITLER became chancellor in 1933 and quickly established a dictatorial, one-party regime. His aggressive expansionist policies led to WWII in Sept. 1939 and although German armies overran most of Europe in 1939 and 1940, the war in Europe ended with Germany's unconditional surrender, May 7–8, 1945. The US, France, Britain and the USSR divided the defeated country into four zones of occupation, the first three of which became West Germany, the fourth, Russian zone becoming East Germany. The former capital, Berlin, although situated in East Germany, was divided between the Western powers and East Germany. (See also GERMANY, EAST and GERMANY, WEST.)

**Official name:** German Democratic Republic
**Capital:** East Berlin
**Area:** 41,768sq mi
**Population:** 16,740,000
**Language:** German
**Religions:** Protestant; Roman Catholic
**Monetary unit(s):** 1 Mark (M)=100 pfennige

**GERMANY, East,** customary name for the German Democratic Republic. The population has dropped by around two million since 1948 due to emigration to West Germany before the erection of the Berlin Wall in 1961. The standard of living is much lower than that in West Germany. East Germany's free educational system stresses science, mathematics, sports and public service.

**Economy.** The East German economy is

socialized, though there are private firms in the retail trade and in handicrafts. Over 90% of industrial output comes from state-owned establishments. East Germany is now a major industrial nation. Important industries include chemicals, electronics, textiles and metallurgy. Trade is oriented towards the USSR, which accounts for more than one third of the country's imports and exports. Agriculture is now highly mechanized; main products are rye, wheat, barley, potatoes and sugar beet. Livestock is also important.

**History.** The German Democratic Republic came into being in 1949. It lacked popular support and a revolt in 1953 by students and workers was violently suppressed with the help of Soviet troops. East Germany was not recognized by many Western countries in the 1950s and 1960s and there were continual crises, particularly over the status of West Berlin. The 1970s saw important steps towards improvements of relations between East Germany and the rest of the world, and in Sept. 1973, East Germany was admitted to the UN. (see also GERMANY and GERMANY, WEST.)

**Official name:** Federal Republic of Germany
**Capital:** Bonn
**Area:** 95,985sq mi
**Population:** 61,560,000
**Languages:** German
**Religions:** Protestant; Roman Catholic
**Monetary unit(s):** 1 Deutsche Mark (DM) = 100 pfennige

**GERMANY, West,** customary name for the Federal Republic of Germany, a member of NATO and the COMMON MARKET. The country has a federal constitution: power is shared between the central government in Bonn and the 10 state governments. West Germany has a well-developed state educational system; there are very few private schools.

**Economy.** The country's economic progress since WWII has been so striking that it has become known as the *Wirtschaftswunder* (economic miracle). West Germany now has one of the highest living standards in the world. This is the result of the German capacity for hard work, injections of American capital in the COLD WAR period and a good supply of immigrant labor. West Germany's vast and diverse industries include automobiles, electronics, oil refining, textiles, chemicals and shipbuilding. Industrial products, especially machinery and transport equipment, play a central part in West Germany's highly successful export trade. The country has to import many of her foodstuffs.

**History.** The Federal Republic of Germany came into being in 1949. The Christian Democratic Party leader, Konrad ADENAUER, became chancellor, and held office for 14 years. In the early years West Germans hoped above all for the reunification of their country, and to this end refused to recognize East Germany. In recent years, however, the existence of two German states has come to be seen as an inescapable reality at least for the time being. The government of Willy Brandt in 1969 took the first steps towards improving relations with East Germany. This resulted in a nonaggression pact with the USSR (1970) and a treaty recognizing East Germany (1972). In 1973 West Germany was admitted to the UN. (See also GERMANY and GERMANY, EAST.)

**GERM CELL.** See GAMETE.

**GERMICIDES.** See ANTISEPTICS.

**GERMINATION,** the resumption of growth of a plant embryo contained in the SEED after a period of reduced metabolic activity or dormancy. Conditions required for germination include an adequate water supply, sufficient oxygen and a favorable temperature. Rapid uptake of water followed by increased rate of respiration are often the first signs of germination. During germination, stored food reserves are rapidly used up to provide the energy and raw materials required for the new growth. The embryonic root and shoot which break through the seed coat are termed the radicle and plumule, respectively. There are two general forms of germination: hypogeal and epigeal. In the former, the seed leaves, or COTYLEDONS, remain below the ground, as in the broad bean, while in the latter they are taken above the ground and become the first photosynthetic organs, as in the castor oil seed.

**GERM PLASM,** a special type of PROTOPLASM present in the reproductive cells or gametes of plants and animals which A. WEISMANN suggested passed on unchanged from generation to generation. Although it gave rise to the body cells, it remained distinct and unaffected by the

offspring.

**GERONIMO** (1829–1909), greatest war leader of the APACHE INDIANS of Ariz. When his tribe was forcibly removed to a barren reservation he led an increasingly large band of hit-and-run raiders 1876–86. Twice induced to surrender by Lt.-Col. George CROOK, he was driven to escape again by maltreatment. Persuaded to surrender a third time by Gen. Nelson MILES, he was summarily exiled to Fla. and resettled in Okla., where he became a farmer.

**GERRYMANDER,** an unfair practice usually employed by a party in power, involving a redivision of electoral boundaries in its favor. The term originated during Elbridge GERRY's governorship of Mass. in 1812, when the state senatorial districts were reapportioned to produce a majority in his party's favor.

**GERSHWIN, George** (1898–1937), US composer. From a Jewish immigrant family, he rose to fame first as a songwriter and then with musical shows such as *Lady Be Good!* (1924), his first Broadway success, and the satirical *Of Thee I Sing* (1931), among many others. He also wrote highly regarded orchestral pieces, *Rhapsody in Blue* (1924), *Piano Concerto* (1925), *An American in Paris* (1928), and and an opera *Porgy and Bess* (1935), noted for its unusual lyricism and emotional power. These works show the influence of RAVEL, STRAVINSKY and, especially, American jazz.

**GERSHWIN, Ira** (1896–    ), US lyricist known primarily for his collaborations with his brother George in the 1920s and 1930s on many shows, songs and the opera *Porgy and Bess* (1935). After George's death he collaborated with Kurt WEILL and others.

**GESTALT PSYCHOLOGY,** a school of psychology concerned with the tendency of the human (or PRIMATE) mind to organize PERCEPTIONS into "wholes"; for example, to hear a symphony rather than a large number of separate notes of different tones. Gestalt psychology, whose main proponents were WERTHEIMER, KÖFFKA and KÖHLER, maintained that this was due to the mind's ability to complete patterns from the available stimuli.

**GESTAPO,** abbreviated form of *Geheime Staatspolizei* (Secret State Police) the executive arm of the Nazi police force 1936–45, with almost unlimited power. Under the overall control of Heinrich HIMMLER, it shared responsibility for internal security and administered the concentration camps. It was declared a criminal organization at the NUREMBERG TRIALS.

**GESUALDO, Don Carlo** (1560–1613), Italian composer, a master of the MADRIGAL form. Of his five collections (1594–1611) the last two are noted for their revolutionary use of harmony and their handling of chromaticism and dissonance.

**GETHSEMANE** (from Hebrew *gat semanim*, oil press), the garden across the Kidron valley, on the Mount of Olives, E of the old city of Jerusalem, where Jesus prayed on the eve of his crucifixion, and was betrayed. Gethsemane was probably an olive grove; its precise location is disputed.

**GETTY, John Paul** (1892–1976), US business tycoon who made his first million in oil by the age of 21. He owned or controlled many companies, including Getty Oil; by the 1960s he was regarded as the world's richest man.

**GETTYSBURG, Battle of,** the major conflict of the US Civil War, fought July 1–3, 1863. In a daring maneuver Confederate General Robert E. LEE struck deep into Union territory, reaching Pa. in June 1863. He and the Union Army of the Potomac, under Gen. George S. MEADE, converged upon Gettysburg, Pa. On July 1 and 2 there were many inconclusive attacks and counterattacks; Union reinforcements arrived on July 2. On July 3 suicidal Confederate attacks broke the Union line on Cemetery Ridge, but were driven back in disorder. On July 4, after a day of stalemate, Lee retreated under cover of night and rain. Union losses were over 23,000, around 25%; Confederate losses were around 20,000, a similar percentage. The costly battle marked a reversal in the fortunes of the Confederacy which paved the way for the eventual Union victory.

**GETTYSBURG ADDRESS,** speech delivered by President LINCOLN at the dedication of the national cemetery at Gettysburg, Pa., on Nov. 19, 1863. A brief masterpiece of oratory, it combined the themes of grief for the dead with the maintenance of the principles they had died to uphold.

**GETZ, Stanley** (1927–    ), US jazz musician, a tenor saxophonist with Woody HERMAN, Benny GOODMAN and Stan Kenton. In the 1950s, playing with smaller groups, he helped to popularize a Brazilian style of jazz.

**GEYSER,** a hot spring, found in currently or recently volcanic regions (see VOLCANISM), that intermittently jets steam and superheated water into the air. It consists essentially of a system of underground fractures analogous to an irregular tube leading down to a heat source. GROUNDWATER accumulates in the tube, that near the bottom being kept from boiling by the PRESSURE of the cooler layers above. When the critical temperature is reached, bubbles rise, heating the upper layers which expand and well out of the orifice. This reduces the pressure enough for substantial STEAM formation below, with subsequent eruption. The process then recommences. The famous Old Faithful used to erupt every 66½min, but has recently become less reliable. (See also FUMAROLE; HOT SPRINGS; SPRING.)

**Official name:** Republic of Ghana
**Capital:** Accra
**Area:** 92,100sq mi
**Population:** c12,129,000
**Languages:** English; Twi; Fanti; Ga; Hausa and others
**Religions:** Christian; animist; Muslim
**Monetary unit(s):** 1 New cedi=100 pesewas

**GHANA**, republic in West Africa, on the Gulf of Guinea, formerly the British colony of the Gold Coast.
**Land.** Generally a low-lying country, it is characterized by tropical rain forests in the S, a central inland plateau that forms a divide between the White Volta and the Black Volta rivers, and rolling savanna in the N. Lake Volta, in central Ghana, is one of the world's largest man-made lakes. Ghana has a hot climate with, generally, one rainy season in the N and two in the S.
**People.** The population is made up of various tribal groups. Compared with other African states, Ghana has a high level of education with 10 years of free and compulsory basic schooling and subsidized further education. Most Ghanians still live on the land, but large numbers have moved to the cities.
**Economy.** Once one of the most prosperous countries in Africa, Ghana underwent serious economic decline in the 1970s, falling from first to third place among the world's producers of cocoa, which accounts for more than half of its export earnings. Forest products are the second-most-important export. Principal mineral exports are gold, industrial diamonds,

manganese and bauxite. The manufacturing sector is well developed but has declined because of its heavy reliance upon imported oil and spare parts.
**History.** In 1482 the Portuguese began trading at Elmina in gold, ivory and then slaves. The Gold Coast was then controlled by the French, Dutch, and finally the British, under whom the economy expanded, bringing prosperity. Ghana was the first West African country to become independent, on March 6, 1957, with Kwame NKRUMAH as premier. In 1960 he declared the country a republic, with himself as life president. While he made reforms in education, transportation and other social services, during his rule political opponents were jailed and government became increasingly inefficient and corrupt. In 1966 Nkrumah was deposed by a coup that had popular support. In 1969 Kofi Busia was elected premier; he was deposed in 1972. Following a series of coups, civilian rule was restored in 1979.

**GHANA, Ancient Empire of,** former empire in West Africa, located between the Niger and Senegal rivers. Founded in the 4th century AD, it reached its height in the 10th century, but was eclipsed by the rise of the Mali empire in the 13th century. At one point, the Ghanaian empire stretched from the Atlantic as far as Timbuktu.

**GHATS, Eastern and Western,** two mountain ranges forming the E and W boundaries of the Deccan Plateau of peninsular India. The Western Ghats receive between 200in and 400in of rain a year from the monsoons and are the source of several rivers. Both ranges are between 3,000 and 5,000ft high, and about 1000mi long.

**GHAZZALI, AL-** (1058–1111), important medieval Muslim philosopher and mystic who taught at Baghdad. His system evidences his mistrust of purely intellectual inquiry in theology; for a time he gave up philosophy to seek certainty as a Sufi mystic, an experience he attempted to reconcile with orthodox Islamic teachings.

**GHENT, Treaty of,** concluded on Dec. 24, 1814, in Ghent, Belgium, formally ending the WAR OF 1812 between Britain and the US. Because the war had developed into a military stalemate, the treaty was essentially a return to prewar status. No concession was made over the impressment of former British citizens from US ships, a major US grievance, but the resulting British withdrawal from interference in the affairs of the American Northwest opened the frontier to westward expansion.

**GHIBERTI, Lorenzo** (c1378–1455),

Italian sculptor, goldsmith, painter, writer and architect. A Florentine, he was one of the leading figures of the early Renaissance. His most famous work is probably his second pair of bronze doors for the Florence baptistery, known as the *Gates of Paradise* (1425–52).

**GHIRLANDAIO, Domenico** (1449–1494), Florentine Renaissance painter said to have taught MICHELANGELO. Probably his most famous frescoes are those of *Saint Jerome* (1480) and the *Last Supper* (1480), both in the Church of Ognissanti, Florence. He is also noted for his portraits, among them *Grandfather and Grandson*.

**GHOSE, Aurobindo** (1872–1950), Indian nationalist leader and mystic philosopher. Arrested by the British as the head of a secret terrorist organization opposed to the 1905 Partition of Bengal, he underwent a religious transformation in jail. Upon his release (1910), he renounced politics, established a religious retreat in India, and gained a large following. He devoted his life to the study of Hindu philosophy and became known as Sri Aurobindo. His writings include *The Synthesis of Yoga* (1948) and *The Divine Life* (1949).

**GHOST DANCE,** millenarian cult originating among the PAIUTE INDIANS in W Nev. in 1870, named for its ceremonial dance. It was led by WOVOKA who prophesied the rebirth of the dead and the restoration of the Indians to their lands. The massacre of Ghost Dance believers at WOUNDED KNEE in 1890 did much to suppress the cult.

**GIACOMETTI, Alberto** (1901–1966), Swiss-born sculptor and painter who spent most of his life in Paris. He is best known for his elongated and skeletal human figures which convey a sense of extreme spiritual isolation. His early work was influenced by primitive art and SURREALISM.

**GIANNINI, Amadeo Peter** (1870–1949), US banker, founder (1930) of the Bank of America National Trust and Savings Association. One of the largest US banks, it was based on the Transamerica chain which Giannini built up after founding his Bank of Italy in San Francisco (1904).

**GIANT'S CAUSEWAY,** spectacular rock structure near Portrush, Northern Ireland, formed by cooling LAVA. Initially, generally hexagonal cracks appeared on the surface, formed by localized contractions toward discrete centers: these developed downward, forming 38,000 basalt columns. According to folk legends, it was formed by giants as part of a roadway to Staffa, the site of a similar structure.

**GIBBON,** the smallest of the apes, distinguishable by its very long arms. It is the only ape to walk upright with ease. There are six species living in SE Asia from Borneo to Assam. They can leap over 9m (30ft) and swing along the branches of trees in which they live without pausing between bounds. (See also ANTHROPOID APES.)

**GIBBON, Edward** (1737–1794), English historian, author of the *History of the Decline and Fall of the Roman Empire* (1776–88), the greatest historical work of the 18th century and a literary masterpiece. The *Decline and Fall* is particularly well known for its skeptical treatment of Christianity. Gibbon served somewhat unsuccessfully as a member of Parliament (1774–82).

**GIBBONS, Grinling** (1648–1721), English carver and sculptor. While still a young man he was engaged by WREN to work on St. Paul's Cathedral. His wood carvings decorate many of England's country houses, among the most notable being at Petworth, Sussex.

**GIBBS, James** (1682–1754), Scottish architect, designer of the present church of St. Martin's-in-the-Fields, London, and the Radcliffe Camera, Oxford. Trained in Rome, he developed a simple but striking style unlike the then fashionable Palladian architecture. His *Book of Architecture* (1728) was a major influence in the 18th century.

**GIBBS, Josiah Willard** (1839–1903), US physicist best known for his pioneering work in chemical THERMODYNAMICS, and his contributions to *Statistical Mechanicals*. In *On the Equilibrium of Heterogeneous Substances* (2 vols., 1876 and 1878) he states Gibbs' Phase Rule, for chemical systems. In the course of his research on the electromagnetic theory of LIGHT, he made fundamental contributions to the art of VECTOR analysis.

**G.I. BILL OF RIGHTS,** the Serviceman's Readjustment Act of 1944, which provided government aid for demobilized servicemen. It was designed to prevent a repetition of the social problems that had resulted after WWI. It provided financial aid for the purchase of houses, farms and businesses, and for veterans' hospitals; unemployment benefits; and vocational training. Most significant, however, was the educational aid, which in effect paid for four years of college education, including basic living expenses. Veterans from the Korean and Vietnam wars also received benefits.

**GIBRALTAR,** self-governing British colony, 2.5sq mi in area, on the Rock of Gibraltar at the S tip of the Iberian peninsula. The population is mixed; natives are of English, Genoese, Portuguese and Maltese descent. The economy rests on light industry, shipping and tourism, and on the important British naval and airbases. Gibraltar was captured from Spain in 1704. A 1967 referendum showed overwhelming opposition to a return to Spanish rule. Pop 29,760.

**GIBRAN, Kahlil** (1883–1931), Lebanese–American essayist, philosopher–poet and painter who blended elements of Eastern and Western mysticism. He was influenced by BLAKE and NIETZSCHE. His best-known work is *The Prophet* (1923).

**GIBSON, Althea** (1927–    ), US tennis player. She was the first black player to win the US women's championship singles (1957), was British champion the same year, and retained both titles in 1958.

**GIBSON, Charles Dana** (1867–1944), US artist, a fashion illustrator who created the "Gibson Girl." Based on his wife, she was an elegant and high-spirited figure who came to typify the ideal of American womanhood in the early 20th century.

**GIDE, André Paul Guillaume** (1869–1951), French writer and moralist, whose relentless examination of his own standards and assumptions, and the resulting inner conflicts, made him one of the foremost figures in French literature in the first half of the 20th century. In 1947 he was awarded the Nobel Prize for Literature. Among his best-known works are the novels *The Immoralist* (1902) and *The Counterfeiters* (1925) and four volumes of *Journals* (1889–1949).

**GIDEON VS. WAINWRIGHT**, case involving the right of a defendant in a criminal case to legal counsel. In 1963 the US Supreme Court ruled that Clarence Gideon, an indigent convicted of burglary by a Fla. court, had been wrongfully imprisoned because, not being able to afford a lawyer, he had defended himself. The Supreme Court held that all defendants in criminal cases are entitled to counsel, and that attorneys must be provided for defendants who are indigent.

**GIELGUD, Sir (Arthur) John** (1904–    ), British actor, producer and director, famous early in his career for his Shakespearean roles, especially Hamlet and Richard III. He made his debut in 1921 at the Old Vic theater in London. Famous for his versatility, he created many modern roles in his maturity in numerous stage, film and television appearances.

**GIEREK, Edward** (1913–    ), first secretary of the Polish Communist Party (1970–80). A Politburo member since 1956, he was appointed to improve the standard of living following food riots in late 1970. A failing economy and massive national labor unrest led to his fall from power in 1980.

**GIESEKING, Walter** (1895–1956), German pianist who was best known for his refined interpretations of the works of DEBUSSY and RAVEL.

**GIGANTISM**, or abnormally large stature starting in childhood, may be caused by a constitutional trait or by HORMONE disorders during growth. The latter are usually excessive secretion of growth hormone or thyroid hormone before the EPIPHYSES have fused.

**GIGLI, Beiamino** (1890–1957), Italian tenor, who made his debut in 1914. After bowing at the Metropolitan Opera in 1920 as Faust in Arrigo Boito's *Mefistofele* he was a principal tenor of the company until 1932, assuming many of the roles formerly sung by Enrico CARUSO.

**GILA CLIFF DWELLINGS NATIONAL MONUMENT**, Pueblo Indian CLIFF DWELLER settlement in SW N.M., about 30mi N of Silver City. Dating from the 10th century, it was built in natural cavities of a 150ft cliff; it was made a national monument in 1907.

**GILA MONSTER**, stout-bodied lizard, up to 0.6m (2ft) long. It and the related BEADED LIZARD, are the only poisonous lizards. Both live in the deserts of the SW states and in Mexico. The gila monster is so rare that it is protected by law.

**GILBERT, Cass** (1859–1934), US architect most famous for the Woolworth Building in New York (1913). His characteristic neoclassical style appears also in his other designs, such as the Supreme Court Building in Washington, D.C.

**GILBERT, Sir Humphrey** (c1537–1583), English soldier and explorer who founded England's first North American colony, at St. John's, Newfoundland (1583). He was granted a royal charter to colonize unclaimed lands in North America (1578). His first expedition had to turn back after being attacked by the Spanish. He went down with his ship while returning from his second, otherwise successful voyage.

**GILBERT, Walter** (1932–    ), US microbiologist who shared the 1980 Nobel Prize in Chemistry for his development of procedures for rapidly determining the precise chemical makeup of subunits of DNA, the carrier of genetic traits.

**GILBERT, Sir William Schwenck** (1836–1911), English author and humorist who collaborated with Sir Arthur SULLIVAN on the cycle of comic operettas named for them. He combined facetiousness with a mordant wit in satires more vigorous in their day than they appear to modern audiences.

**GILBERT, William** (1544–1603), English scientist, the father of the science of MAGNETISM. Regarding the earth as a giant magnet, he investigated its field in terms of dip and variation (see EARTH), and explored many other magnetic and electrostatic phenomena. The GILBERT is named for him.

**GILBERT AND ELLICE ISLANDS.** See TUVALU.

**GILBERT AND SULLIVAN.** See GILBERT, SIR WILLIAM SCHWENCK; SULLIVAN, SIR ARTHUR SEYMOUR; D'OYLY CARTE, RICHARD.

**GILDED AGE,** sardonic name for the post-Civil War period up to around 1880 in the US, a time of rampant corruption in politics and commerce. The term derives from the title of a novel by Mark TWAIN and C. D. WARNER.

**GILELS, Emil Grigorevich** (1916– ), Russian pianist, winner of the Stalin Prize in 1946 and the Lenin Prize in 1962. Noted for his crystalline technique, he was one of the first Soviet artists to tour the US (1955) after WWII.

**GILGAMESH, Epic of,** the earliest known epic poem, written in the Akkadian language and originating in Mesopotamia in the 3rd millennium BC. The fullest surviving text, carved on tablets, was found in a 7th-century BC library at Nineveh in 1872. The poem tells of the semi-divine hero Gilgamesh (a historical 3rd-millennium king of Uruk), and of his friend Enkidu. They clash with the gods, who cause Enkidu's death. Gilgamesh then goes on a quest to find the secret of eternal life, which in the end eludes him. The epic contains a flood story with close parallels to that in Genesis (see NOAH).

**GILL, Eric** (1882–1940), English sculptor, engraver and typographic designer, famous for the *Perpetua* (1925) and *Gill Sans Serif* (1927) faces. His *Stations of the Cross* (1914–18), bas-reliefs for Westminster Cathedral, are perhaps his most famous sculptures.

**GILLESPIE, (John Birks) "Dizzy"** (1917– ), US jazz trumpeter and composer who in the 1940s pioneered, with Charlie PARKER, the BOP style. He is noted for his technically brilliant and original style. He became in 1956 the first jazz musician to have a foreign tour sponsored by the US government.

**GILLRAY, James** (1757–1815), English caricaturist whose violent and often scurrilous cartoons both expressed and influenced public opinion in his time. He reduced all the major political figures of his day, including George II and the royal family, to ridiculous grotesques.

**GILLS,** the respiratory organs of many aquatic animals. They take in OXYGEN from the water and give off CARBON dioxide waste. They are thin-walled so that gases pass easily through and usually take the form of thin flat plates or finely divided feathery filaments. The higher invertebrates, crabs and lobsters for instance, have gills protected by an EXOSKELETON and maintain an adequate oxygen supply by pumping water over them. The gills of most fish are protected by a bony operculum and movements of the throat provide a water current over them. (See RESPIRATION.)

**GIN,** liquor distilled from grain flavored with juniper berries. Sometimes coriander, orange or lemon peel, cardamon and orris roots are added as flavoring agents. It contains 40–47% alcohol (80–94 US Proof). It originated in the Netherlands, apparently from a juniper-berry medicine. (See ALCOHOLIC BEVERAGES.)

**GINASTERA, Alberto** (1916– ), leading Argentinian composer. Despite his advanced techniques he is an essentially nationalistic composer, making much use of local idioms. His best-known work is his opera *Don Rodrigo* (1964).

**GINGIVITIS,** or gum INFLAMMATION, due to BACTERIAL INFECTION (e.g., VINCENT'S ANGINA) or disease of the TEETH and poor mouth hygiene.

**GINSBERG, Allen** (1926– ), US poet. An outspoken member of the BEAT GENERATION, his works include *Howl* (1956), *Kaddish and Other Poems* (1961) and *The Yage Letters* (an exchange with William BURROUGHS; 1963).

**GIORGIONE** (c1478–1510), Renaissance painter and student of Giovanni BELLINI who is regarded as the founder of the Venetian school in Italian art of the 1500s. Painting with a soft subordination of line to light and color, he achieved a unity of human figures with landscape which greatly influenced TITIAN and several other painters of note. Among the works attributed to him are *The Tempest* (c1505), *Madonna and Child Enthroned* (1504) and *The Three Philosophers* (1510).

**GIOTTO** (Giotto di Bondone; c1266–1337), Italian painter and architect of the Florentine school. He had a profound influence on his own time and on future generations of artists throughout Europe. Breaking away from the Byzantine style of graceful but static representation, he painted monumental figures dramatically and emotionally, giving his vast FRESCO scenes a sense of movement and spatial depth. Among his famous works are frescoes in Padua, Florence and the Church of St. Francis at Assisi.

**GIPP, George** (1895–1920), US football player. An elusive running back, he played for Notre Dame from 1917–20, leading the college team to two undefeated seasons. He died of a throat infection in December 1920 and was immortalized eight years later when Notre Dame coach Knute ROCKNE urged his team to "Win one for the Gipper."

**GIRAFFE,** *Giraffa camelopardalis,* the tallest living mammal, reaching 5.5m (18ft) in the male, some 2m (6.6ft) of which are taken up by the head and extremely long neck. Its coat is a neutral buff color spotted with red-brown patches. A short, rather bristly mane runs along its spine from head to tail. Giraffes live by grazing, often on trees, aided by their long necks and tongues. They are speedy runners. Giraffes are related to deer as is evidenced by their short horns.

**GIRAUDOUX, (Hippolyte) Jean** (1882–1944), French playwright. Known for his imaginative, satirical dramas, his major works include *Tiger at the Gates* (1935) and *Electra* (1937), both based on Greek mythology, and *The Mad Woman of Chaillot* (1945).

**GIRL SCOUTS AND GIRL GUIDES,** organizations in almost 70 countries which form an international movement, The World Association of Girl Guides and Girl Scouts. The Girl Guides were founded in England (1909) by Lord BADEN-POWELL, who also founded the BOY SCOUTS, in Canada in 1910 and in the US (as Girl Scouts) in 1912 by Juliette Gordon LOW. Girls learn to become good citizens, they practice useful skills, develop self-reliance and enjoy a continuing, well-rounded program of companionship, work, service to others and play, from age seven through the late teens.

**GIRONDINS,** or Girondists, French political group of republicans, representing the middle classes and favoring a federal republic, prominent in the FRENCH REVOLUTION. The group's original members came from the Gironde department in SW France. They came into power under the 1791 Constitution but lost ground to the JACOBINS. In June 1793, a Jacobin-led mob forced the expulsion of 29 Girondins from the National Convention; many Girondins were guillotined in the REIGN OF TERROR.

**GISCARD D'ESTAING, Valéry** (1926– ), president of France 1974–81. At 29 he became a member of the national assembly. In 1959, under President DE GAULLE, he became deputy finance minister.

From 1962–66 he was minister of finance, a post he resumed (1969) under Georges POMPIDOU, supporting the Common Market and closer ties with the US. He ran for president as an independent Republican with Gaullist support. His austerity program failed to solve problems related to inflation, unemployment, and the balance of payments. He was defeated for reelection by the Socialist candidate, François Mitterand.

**GISH, Lillian Diana** (1896– ), and **Dorothy** (1898–1968), American sisters, famous stage and screen actresses who appeared in the pioneering epics of D. W. GRIFFITH. In *The Birth of a Nation* (1915), Lillian won world fame; later she appeared in many notable plays, including *All the Way Home* (1960) and *Uncle Vanya* (1973).

**GISSING, George Robert** (1857–1903), English novelist. He is noted for his starkly realistic studies of late Victorian lower and middle class life. His most famous novel *New Grub Street* (1891), depicts much of the drudgery and hardship he himself experienced as an aspiring writer.

**GIULIO ROMANO** (born Giulio Pippi; c1492–1546), Italian painter and architect in the style of MANNERISM. RAPHAEL'S pupil, his masterpiece is the Palazzo del Té, Mantua, where his architecture is highly fanciful and the frescoes exciting examples of illusionism.

**GIVENCHY, Hubert de** (1927– ), French fashion designer. With BALENCIAGA'S encouragement he opened his own firm in 1951. His elegant, classic designs were seen on devotees such as Audrey Hepburn.

**GIZZARD,** part of the alimentary canal developed by a variety of animals for the mechanical breakdown of food. Situated before the main digestive region of the gut, it has very muscular walls. Fragmentation of the food may be by chitinous "teeth" in the inner wall or by stones and grit, swallowed expressly for this purpose.

**GLACIER,** a large mass of ice formed from the burial, compaction and recrystallization of snow, which is flowing or has flowed in the past under the influence of gravity. There are three recognized types of glacier: ice sheets and caps; mountain or valley glacier; and piedmont glaciers. Glaciers form wherever conditions are such that annual PRECIPITATION of snow, sleet and hail is greater than the amount that can be lost through evaporation, melting, or otherwise. The occurrence of a glacier also depends much on the position of the lower limit of perennial snow (*snowline*), which generally

...ries with latitude (see LATITUDE and ...NGITUDE) and also on local topography: ...ere are several glaciers at high elevations ... the Equator. The world's largest glacier ... the ice sheet which covers over 90% of the ...ntarctic continent and has ice thicknesses ...ceeding 3,000m. Mountain glaciers are ...ore numerous and are found in the Alps, ...imalayas, Andes and other high ranges of ...e world, including about 50 in the NW ...S (excluding Alaska). **Mountain glaciers** ...ually result from snow accumulated in ...owfields which grow to form glaciers and ...ccupy mountain valleys originally formed ...rough stream erosion; and **piedmont** ...aciers occur when such a glacier spreads ...t of its valley into a contiguous lowland ...ea. (See also DRIFT; DRUMLIN; EROSION; ...KER; FJORD; ICE; ICE AGES; ICEBERG; MORAINE; ...ÉVÉ; TILL.)

**GLACIER NATIONAL PARK,** wilderness ...ea of over 1 million acres in the Rocky ...ts, NW Mont. Part of the Waterton-...lacier International Peace Park, it is noted ...r its spectacular peaks and glacier-fed ...kes. It was established in 1910.

**GLACKENS, William James** (1870–1938), ...S illustrator and painter. A member of the ...SHCAN SCHOOL in New York City, he ...inted GENRE subjects and landscapes. ...mong his works are *Hammerstein's Roof ...arden* (1901) and *Chez Mouqin* (1905).

**GLADIATORS,** warrior-entertainers of ...ncient Rome. They fought in public arenas ...ainst each other and against wild beasts ...ith a variety of weapons including swords ...atin *gladius*, a short sword), three-...ronged tridents and nets, for the favor of ...e crowds. They were recruited from ...isoners of war, slaves, criminals and ...metimes freemen. The tradition survived ...to the 5th century AD.

**GLADSTONE, William Ewart** (1809–...898), British statesman; four times prime ...inister (1868–74; 1880–85; 1886; ...892–94). Originally a TORY, he later ...ominated the LIBERAL PARTY, 1868–94. He ...as a powerful and popular orator, a ...edicated social reformer and a deeply ...ligious man. Among his many accom-...ishments from the time he entered ...arliament (1832) were the introduction of ...e secret ballot, the extension of the ...anchise, the abolition of sales of army ...ncessions, the first Education Act, the ...ish Land Act and the disestablishment of ...e Anglican Church in Ireland. (See also ...EFORM BILLS.)

**GLANDS,** structures in animals and plants ...ecialized to secrete essential substances. ... plants they may discharge their ...cretions to the outside of the plant (via glandular hairs), or into special secretory canals. External secretions include NECTAR and insect attractants; internal secretions, PINE resin and RUBBER latex. In animals they are divided into ENDOCRINE GLANDS, which secrete HORMONES into the BLOOD stream, and **exocrine glands** which are the remainder, usually secreting materials via ducts into internal organs or onto body surfaces. LYMPH nodes are sometimes termed glands. In man, SKIN contains two types of gland: *sweat glands*, which secrete watery fluid (PERSPIRATION) and *sebaceous glands* which secrete sebum. *Lacrimal glands* secrete TEARS. The cells of mucous membranes or the EPITHELIUM of internal organs secrete MUCUS, which serves to lubricate and protect the surface. *Salivary glands* (parotid, submandibular and sublin-gual) secrete SALIVA to facilitate swallow-ing. In the GASTROINTESTINAL TRACT, mucus-secreting glands are numerous, particularly in the STOMACH and colon, where solid food or feces need lubrication. Other stomach glands secrete hydrochloric acid and pepsin as part of the DIGESTIVE SYSTEM. Small-intestinal juices containing ENZYMES are similarly secreted by minute glandular specializations of the epithelium. The part of the PANCREAS secreting enzyme-rich juice into the DUODENUM may be regarded as an exocrine gland. Analysis of gland secretion may be helpful in diseases of digestion, of the EYES and salivary glands and in CYSTIC FIBROSIS.

**GLASGOW,** Scotland's largest city and principal port, on the Clyde R. It is a major commercial and industrial center for shipbuilding, metal working and manufac-turing of locomotives, machinery, chemicals, paper, leather, whisky and textiles. Glasgow U. was founded in 1451. Pop 792,600.

**GLASGOW, Ellen Anderson Gholson** (1873–1945), US novelist, winner of the Pulitzer Prize in 1941 for *In This Our Life*. Her realistic novels about the American South satirized the code of Southern chivalry. They include *The Descendants* (1897) and *Barren Ground* (1925).

**GLASHOW, Sheldon** (1933–    ), US physicist who shared the 1979 Nobel Prize in Physics for detailing the role of the "charmed quark," a fundamental unit of nature.

**GLASS,** material formed by the rapid cooling of certain molten liquid so that they fail to crystallize (see CRYSTAL) but retain an amorphous structure. Glasses are in fact supercooled LIQUIDS which, however, have such high viscosity that they behave like solids for all practical purposes. Some glasses may spontaneously crystallize or devitrify. Few materials form glasses, and almost all that are found naturally or used commercially are based on SILICA and the SILICATES. Natural glass is formed by rapid cooling of MAGMA, producing chiefly OBSIDIAN, or rarely by complete thermal metamorphism (see also TEKTITES). The earliest known manufactured glass was made in Mesopotamia in the 3rd millennium BC. Glass was shaped by molding or core-dipping, until the invention of glassblowing by Syrian craftsmen in the 1st century BC. Essentially still used, the process involved gathering molten glass on the end of a pipe, blowing to form a bubble, and shaping the vessel by further blowing, swinging, or rolling it on a surface. They also blew glass inside a shaped mold; this is now the chief process used in mechanized automatic glassblowing. Modern glass products are very diverse, including windows, bottles and other vessels, optical devices, building materials, fiberglass products, etc. Most are made of soda-lime glass. Although silica itself can form a glass, it is too viscous and its melting point is too high for most purposes. Adding soda lowers the melting point, but the resultant sodium silicate is water-soluble (see WATER GLASS), so lime is added as a stabilizer, together with other metal oxides as needed for decolorizing etc. The usual proportions are 70% $SiO_2$, 15% $Na_2O$, 10% CaO. Crown glass, used in optical systems for its low DISPERSION, is of this type, with BARIUM oxide (BaO) often replacing the lime. Flint glass, or crystal, is a brilliant clear glass with high optical dispersion, used in high-quality glassware and to make lenses and prisms. It was originally made from crushed flints to give pure, colorless silica; later, sand was used, with increasing amount of lead (II) oxide. For borosilicate glass, used where high thermal stresses must be withstood, see PYREX. The manufacture of the various kinds of glass begins by mixing the raw materials—sand, limestone, sodium nitrate or carbonate, etc.—and melting them in large crucibles in a furnace. The molten glass, having been refined (free from bubbles) by standing, is formed to the shape required and then annealed (see ANNEALING). Some SAFETY GLASS is not annealed, but rapidly cooled to induce superficial compressive stresses which yield greater strength. Plate glass is made by passing a continuous sheet of soft glass between rollers, GRINDING AND POLISHING it on both sides, and cutting it up so as to eliminate flaws. A newer method (the float glass process) involves pouring the

molten glass onto molten metal, such as tin, and to allow it to cool slowly: the surface touching the metal is perfectly flat and needs no polishing. Special glass products include foam glass, made by SINTERING a mixture of glass and an agent that gives off a gas on heating, used for insulation; photosensitive glass, which darkens reversibly in bright light; and FIBERGLASS. (See also ENAMEL.)

**GLASTONBURY**, historic town in Somerset, SW England, famous for its abbey. It stands on a peninsula which is alleged to be the Isle of Avalon of ARTHURIAN LEGEND. Tradition and legend also suggest that JOSEPH OF ARIMATHEA founded England's first Christian church here. Pop 6,571.

**GLAUCOMA**, raised fluid pressure in the EYE, leading in chronic cases to a progressive deterioration of VISION. It arises from a variety of causes, often involving block to aqueous humor drainage. Glaucoma is relieved using drugs or surgically.

**GLAZER, Nathan** (1923–    ), US sociologist who collaborated on two classics of American sociology, *The Lonely Crowd* (1950; with David Riesman) and *Beyond the Melting Pot* (1963; with Daniel Moynihan). A professor at Harvard from 1969, he became increasingly conservative and wrote the controversial *Affirmative Discrimination* (1975), which attacked government-enforced racial quotas.

**GLAZUNOV, Aleksandr Konstantinovich** (1865–1936), Russian composer. A pupil of RIMSKY–KORSAKOV, with whom he worked on the completion of Borodin's *Prince Igor*, he was director 1906–17 of the St Petersburg Conservatory. He wrote eight symphonies and numerous other work including the ballet *The Seasons* (1889).

**GLEASON, Jackie** (1916–    ), US comedian. A former musical comedy performer, he starred in *The Jackie Gleason Show* on TV in the 1950's and 1960's, becoming one of the medium's best-known personalities. He also appeared in films.

**GLEN CANYON DAM**, dam on the Colorado R in N Ariz. Completed in 1964, it is 710ft high and is one of the highest concrete dams in the world; it regulates the river flow and generates electricity.

**GLENDOWER, Owen** (c1354–c1416), the last independent prince of Wales, a Welsh national hero. He led one of the last Welsh rebellions against English rule (1400–13) exploiting baronial unrest in England against Henry IV. His gains were finally recovered by Henry V.

**GLENN, John Herschel, Jr.** (1921–    ) first US astronaut to orbit the earth. He served as a pilot in WWII and in the Korean War. On Feb. 20, 1962, in the space capsule *Friendship 7*, he orbited the earth three times. Active in Ohio politics, he became a Democratic senator in 1974.

**GLIDER,** or **sailplane,** nonpowered airplane which, once launched by air or ground towing, or by using a winch, is kept aloft by its light, aerodynamic design and the skill of the pilot in exploiting "thermals" and other rising air currents. Sir George CAYLEY built his first model glider in 1804 and in 1853 he persuaded his coachman to undertake a short glide—the first manned heavier-than-air flight. Otto LILIENTHAL made many successful flights in his hang gliders (planes in which the pilot hangs underneath and controls the flight by altering his body position, hence moving the craft's CENTER OF GRAVITY) from 1891 until his death in a gliding accident in 1896. Later, the WRIGHT brothers developed gliders in which control was achieved using moving control surfaces, as a prelude to their experiments with powered flight. Gliding as a sport was born in Germany after WWI and is now popular throughout the world. Recent years have seen a particular resurgence of interest in hang gliding.

**GLIERE, Reinhold Moritzovich** (1875–1956), Russian composer whose pupils included PROKOFIEV. Among his works are the ballet *The Red Poppy* (1927) and *Symphony No. 3* (1911).

**GLINKA, Mikhail Ivanovich** (1804–1857), Russian composer. His two operas, *A Life for the Tsar* (1836) and *Russlan and Ludmilla* (1842), marked the start of a nationalistic Russian school of music.

**GLOBE THEATRE,** the principal public theater of the Elizabethan acting company, the Lord Chamberlain's Men, where most of SHAKESPEARE's plays were first performed. It was an open-air theater with three galleries and a platform stage and stood on the S bank of the Thames. Built in 1598, it was destroyed by fire in 1613, rebuilt in 1614 and finally destroyed in 1644 by the Puritans.

**GLOBULAR CLUSTERS,** apparently ellipsoidal densely packed clusters of up to a million stars orbiting a GALAXY. The MILKY WAY and the ANDROMEDA Galaxy have each around 200 such clusters. They contain high proportions of cool red stars and RR Lyrae ARIABLE STARS. Study of the latter enables the distances of the clusters to be calculated.

**GLORIOUS REVOLUTION,** or the Bloodless Revolution, events of 1688–89, which drove King James II from England and brought William III of Orange and his wife Mary to the throne. Distrusting Parliament, the Catholic James had kept a large standing army. The birth of his son threatened to turn England into a permanently Catholic monarchy. This finally caused the Whigs and Tories to unite and invite the Dutch prince and his wife to become joint rulers. James fled to France after his army deserted him. In 1689, Parliament redefined and restricted royal powers in the BILL OF RIGHTS.

**GLOSSOLALIA,** speech in an unknown or fabricated language uttered by individuals under HYPNOSIS, suffering from certain MENTAL ILLNESSES or in trance, or by groups undergoing religious ecstasy. In the Christian Church, glossolalia has sometimes accompanied revivals, and characterizes the PENTECOSTAL CHURCHES. A spiritual gift (see CHARISMA) common in the early Church, its use was regulated by St. Paul.

**GLUBB, Sir John Bagot** (1897– ), British soldier. As commander of the Arab Legion for nearly 20 years, "Glubb Pasha" was a stabilizing influence on Jordanian affairs and a symbol of Britain's influence in the Middle East until the beginning of the 1956 ARAB-ISRAELI WAR.

**GLUCK, Christoph Willibald von** (1714–1787), German operatic composer. His first 10 operas were produced in Italy, and he traveled extensively in Europe before he settled in Vienna. In *Orfeo ed Euridice* (1762) he discarded many of the static operatic conventions of the previous hundred years and made the opera a dramatic musical work. In the preface to *Alceste* (1767) he set out his ideas for operatic reform which considerably influenced later operatic composers such as MOZART.

**GLUTEN,** a mixture of two proteins (gliadin and glutenin) found in wheat and other cereal flours. In the rising of BREAD gluten forms an elastic network which traps the carbon dioxide, giving a desirable crumb structure on baking. The proportion of gluten in wheat flour varies from 8% to 15%. The level determines the suitability of the flour for different uses. The high gluten content of hard wheat is right for bread and pasta, while soft wheat (low gluten) is used for biscuits.

**GNEISS,** a type of coarse-grained METAMORPHIC ROCKS with a banded, foliated structure and poor CLEAVAGE (see also SCHIST). Their composition is variable, but often approximates to that of GRANITE.

**GNOSTICISM,** syncretic religious system of numerous pre-Christian and early heretical Christian sects. A form of DUALISM, Gnosticism held that matter (created by the Demiurge) is evil and spirit good, and that salvation comes from secret knowledge (gnosis) granted to initiates. A large Gnostic library was found in Egypt in 1945. The sources of Gnostic beliefs range from Babylonian, Egyptian and Greek mythology to the CABALA and ZORO-ASTRIANISM. Gnosticism threatened early Christianity, but declined after the 2nd century AD. (See also MANICHAEISM.)

**GNU.** See WILDEBEEST.

**GOA**, former Portuguese colony on the W coast of India. Since Dec. 1961 it has been part of the Union Territory of Goa, Daman and Diu in the Republic of India.

**GOATS**, members of the Bovidae closely related to SHEEP. Goats are widely kept as domestic stock and, as browsers (feeding on the twigs and leaves of bushes), they can be kept in areas not suitable for other domestic stock. They will eat anything, and the barrenness of many Mediterranean countries is largely due to overgrazing by goats. Probably the earliest-domesticated ruminant, the domestic goat is derived from the wild goat (*Capra aegagrus*) of Western Asia.

**GOBELIN**, French family of clothmakers and dyers. Their workshops, established in the mid-15th century, were bought by Louis XIV (1662) whose finance minister COLBERT created from them a factory to make fine TAPESTRY and furniture. The Gobelin factory is still state-controlled.

**GOBI**, vast desert in central Asia, which lies mainly in Mongolia, but extends to N China. It covers about 500,000sq mi in the Mongolian plateau and has an average altitude of between 3,000ft and 5,000ft. Parts of the desert's steppeland fringes are inhabited by Mongol herdsmen.

**GOD**, a supernatural being worthy of worship; especially, the supreme being who is the creator of the universe and on whom all else depends. Many religions are based on POLYTHEISM, having a pantheon of many gods which are generally local, tribal or which have particular functions. Behind some such pantheons lies a more or less explicit belief in a supreme being, which idea comes to fruition in the MONOTHEISM of Judaism, Christianity and Islam; and, in a different form, in the Good Power of DUALISM, who is not merely one of many gods, yet not wholly supreme. Many scholars have supposed that religions evolve from ANIMISM through polytheism to monotheism. In monotheistic religions and philosophies the knowledge of God (absent from AGNOSTICISM—and impossible in ATHEISM) has been approached via reason, in particular the classical arguments for the existence of God (see NATURAL THEOLOGY) via God's self-disclosure (see REVELATION) or via an existential encounter in which th knowledge is personal rather than intellec tual. The attributes of God as held b traditional monotheism— though now ofte questioned—are derived partly fron revealed scripture, partly from the results o controversy with pagans, and partly fron Greek philosophy. God is described as one eternal, all-powerful, all-knowing, omnipre sent, self-existent, unchangeable, an perfectly good, just, holy and true. Bein infinite, his nature is ineffable, and th human mind is incapable of fully graspin it. The relation of God to the world i differently held in DEISM, PANTHEISM an THEISM; theism, as in orthodox Christianity balances God's IMMANENCE and transcen dence. Christianity also teaches that God i a TRINITY—that the one God exists as thre Persons—a doctrine which in early an modern Christianity has been controversia and which is rejected by Jews, Muslims an Unitarians as being inconsistent with th absolute unity of God. (See also RELIGION THEOLOGY.)

**GODARD, Jean-Luc** (1930–    ), Frenc film director. His film *Breathless* (1959 pioneered the French "new wave" school c the cinema. Godard's personal use c imagery and innovative camera work wer highly influential on films in the late 1960s

**GODDARD, Robert Hutchings** (1882 1945), US pioneer of rocketry. In 1926 h launched the first liquid-fuel rocket. Som years later, with a Guggenheim Foundatic grant, he set up a station in N.M., ther developing many of the basic ideas c modern rocketry: among over 200 paten was that for a multistage rocket. He die before his work received US Governmer recognition.

**GODDEN, (Margaret) Rumer** (1907    ). British author whose novels, poem and children's books are distinguished t their warm characterization and lyric styl Her novels of life in India include *Blac Narcissus* (1939) and *The River* (1946).

**GÖDEL, Kurt** (1906–1978), Austrian-bo US mathematician who in 1931 propose GÖDEL'S THEOREM, one of the mo significant mathematical achievements the 20th century.

**GODEL'S THEOREM**, showing the futili of attempting to set up a comple axiomatic formalization of mathematic GÖDEL proved (1931 onward) that a consistent mathematical system must incomplete; i.e., that in any syste formulae must be constructed that can neither proved nor disproved within th system. Moreover, no mathematical system can be proved consistent without recourse to axioms beyond that system. Gödel's Theorem has had profound effects on attitudes toward the foundations of MATHEMATICS. (See also LOGIC.)

**GODEY, Louis Antoine** (1804–1878), US magazine publisher. *Godey's Lady's Book*, founded in Philadelphia in 1830, contained notable fiction and fashion pictures in color, and was the first successful US periodical for women.

**GODFREY, Arthur** (1903–   ), US radio and TV personality. His early success in radio (from 1934), where his early morning how was broadcast to 40 million listeners a week, led to a career in television as host of *Arthur Godfrey's Talent Scouts* (1948–58).

**GODIVA, Lady** (c1040–80), noted for her legendary ride through Coventry, England. Her husband Leofric, Earl of Mercia, promised to reduce the people of Coventry's heavy taxes if she rode naked through the city streets on a white horse. "Peeping Tom" alone essayed to gaze upon the spectacle.

**GODUNOV, Aleksandr** (1950–   ), Soviet dancer who defected to the West in 1978. A member of the BOLSHOI Ballet from 1971, he became partner to Maya PLISETSKAYA in 1974. He has danced classical and modern roles with the American Ballet Theatre and appeared as guest with other companies.

**GODUNOV, Boris Fedorovich** (c1551–1605), tsar of Russia (1598–1605). A close adviser to IVAN IV ("the Terrible") and regent for Feodor I, Ivan's son and heir, Boris was virtual ruler of Russia. On Feodor's death (1598), Boris was elected tsar and continued Ivan IV's policies of subjugating the BOYARS and expanding Russian boundaries. His life is the subject of a drama by PUSHKIN upon which MUSSORGSKY based his famous opera.

**GODWIN, William** (1756–1836), English political theorist and novelist. In his *Enquiry Concerning Political Justice* (1793) and in his novels such as *The Adventures of Caleb Williams* (1794), Godwin rejected all government as corrupting and expressed his belief that humans are rational beings able to live without laws and institutions. He was the father of Mary SHELLEY.

**GODWIN-AUSTEN, Mount.** See K2.

**GOEBBELS, Paul Joseph** (1897–1945), German Nazi propaganda chief. He had a brilliant academic career before joining the Nazi party. Appointed minister of propaganda by Hitler in 1933, Goebbels

skillfully organized political campaigns and used the mass media to promote NAZISM throughout Germany until the end of WWII. He committed suicide with his family in Berlin in 1945.

**GOERING, Hermann Wilhelm** (1893–1946), German political leader and Hitler's deputy, 1939–45. He organized the STORM TROOPS and the GESTAPO and, as commander of the German Air Force, prepared for the aerial *blitzkrieg* campaigns of WWII. By 1936 Goering was economic dictator of Germany, but his power dwindled when he failed to stop Allied air attacks. Convicted of WAR CRIMES at the NUREMBERG TRIALS in 1946, he poisoned himself in his prison cell.

**GOETHALS, George Washington** (1858–1928), US army engineer who completed construction of the PANAMA CANAL, 1907–14. Apart from solving the complicated technical problems of the project, Goethals successfully overcame unexpected difficulties caused by the climate, disease and the labor force. He served as governor of the Canal Zone, from 1914–16.

**GOETHE, Johann Wolfgang von** (1749–1832), German poet, novelist and playwright, one of the giants of world literature, and perhaps the last European to embody the ideal of the Renaissance man. His monumental work ranges from poems, novels, plays, and a famous correspondence with SCHILLER to 14 volumes of scientific studies and is crowned by *Faust* (part I, 1808; part II, 1833), written in stages during 60 years, in which he synthesized his life and art in a poetic and philosophical statement of man's search for complete experience and knowledge.

Born in Frankfurt-am-Main, Goethe achieved national recognition with his STURM UND DRANG play *Götz von Berlichingen* (1773) and the romantic novel *The Sorrows of Young Werther* (1774). From 1775 until his death, he lived at the ducal court of Saxe-Weimar, where he published, among many other works, *The Apprenticeship of Wilhelm Meister* (1795–96), a novel of the maturing artist to which he later wrote a sequel. A visit to Italy in 1786–88 gave Goethe inspiration for the plays *Iphigenie auf Tauris* (1787) and *Egmont* (1788). Thomas CARLYLE is among his notable English translators; the Weimar edition of Goethe's complete works was published in 133 volumes, 1887–1919.

**GOGARTY, Oliver St. John** (1878–1957), Irish physician and writer associated with the Irish Renaissance. An acquaintance of Yeats, Joyce and Russel (AE), Gogarty recalled his youthful days in Dublin in his memoirs *As I Was Going Down Sackville Street* (1937) and *Tumbling in the Hay* (1939). The character of Buck Mulligan in Joyce's *Ulysses* is based on him.

**GOGH, Vincent van.** See VAN GOGH, VINCENT.

**GOGOL, Nikolai Vasilievich** (1809–1852), Russian short story writer, novelist and dramatist. Considered the father of Russian realism, his comic stories of Ukrainian peasant life and later more bizarre and intense tales set in St. Petersburg, such as *The Overcoat* (1872), put him among the most original of Russian authors. Adverse reaction in Russia to his satirical drama *The Inspector-General* (1836) drove Gogol into a self-imposed exile abroad, where he wrote more macabre stories and also his masterpiece, the picaresque novel, *Dead Souls* (1834–52), of which only the first part survives.

**GOITER,** enlargement of the THYROID gland in the neck, causing swelling below the LARYNX. It may represent the smooth swelling of an overactive gland in **thyrotoxicosis** or more often the enlargement caused by multiple CYSTS and nodules without functional change. Endemic goiter is enlargement associated with IODINE deficiency, occurring in certain areas where the element is lacking in the soil and water. Rarely, goiter is due to CANCER of the thyroid. If there is excessive secretion or pressure on vital structures SURGERY may be needed, although DRUG or RADIATION THERAPY for excess secretion are often adequate.

**GOLD, Thomas** (1920–    ), Austrian-born US cosmologist who, with Hermann BONDI, proposed (1948) the steady-state model of the universe (see COSMOLOGY).

**GOLD (Au),** yellow NOBLE METAL in Group IB of the PERIODIC TABLE; a TRANSITION ELEMENT. Gold has been known and valued from earliest times and used for jewelry, ornaments and coinage. It occurs as the metal and as tellurides, usually in veins of QUARTZ and PYRITE; the chief producing countries are South Africa, the USSR, Canada and the US. The metal is extracted with CYANIDE or by forming an AMALGAM, and is refined by electrolysis. The main use of gold is as a currency reserve (see GOLD STANDARD). Like SILVER, it is used for its high electrical conductivity in printed circuits and electrical contacts, and also for filling or repairing teeth. It is very malleable and ductile, and may be beaten into GOLD LEAF or welded in a thin layer to another metal (rolled gold). For most uses pure gold is too soft, and is alloyed with other noble metals, the proportion of gold being

measured in CARATS. Gold is not oxidized in air, nor dissolved by alkalis or pure acids, though it dissolves in AQUA REGIA or cyanide solution because of LIGAND complex formation, and reacts with the HALOGENS. It forms trivalent and monovalent salts. Gold (III) chloride is used as a toner in photography. AW 197.0, mp 1063°C, bp 2966°C, sg 19.32 (20°C).

**GOLDBERG, Arthur Joseph** (1908–    ) US labor lawyer and public servant. He served as secretary of labor, (1961–62) associate justice of the Supreme Court (1962–65) and US representative to the United Nations (1965–68). Goldberg was instrumental in the 1955 merger of the AMERICAN FEDERATION OF LABOR and the Congress of Industrial Organizations (AFL-CIO).

**GOLDBERG, "Rube"** (Reuben Lucius Goldberg; 1883–1970), US cartoonist and sculptor. Known for his bizarre "inventions" of ridiculously complicated machinery to perform everyday tasks. In 1948 he won the Pulitzer Prize for political cartoons.

**GOLD COAST.** See GHANA.

**GOLDEN, Harry** (1902–1981), US writer. A Northern Jewish liberal who moved to the South, he published the *Carolina Israelite* (1941–68), through which he presented his humorous analyses of Southern racism and other topics. His collections of reminiscences and observations, *Only in America* (1958) and *For 2¢ Plain* (1959), were best-sellers.

**GOLDEN GATE BRIDGE,** bridge spanning the entrance to San Francisco Bay, Cal., built in 1933–37. Its 4,200ft central span, between two 746ft towers, is the second longest in the world and carries six traffic lanes 220ft above the water.

**GOLDEN HORDE,** name for the Mongol rulers of much of Russia from the 13th to the 15th century, and their *khanate* or empire. Led by BATU KHAN, the horde swept across Russia in 1237–40. The *khanat* slowly came under Turkish influence, but at the end of the 14th century was reconquered by TAMERLANE. (See also MONGOL EMPIRE; TARTARS.)

**GOLDEN RETRIEVER,** breed of hunting dog, popular as a gundog in the US and UK. First bred in Scotland c1870, it has a thick golden tan coat. Adults may stand up to 24in high at the shoulder and weigh from 60–75lb.

**GOLDEN RULE,** the precept stated by Jesus in the SERMON ON THE MOUNT: "Always treat others as you would like them to treat you." The name, implying that this is the chief ethical principle, has been used since the 16th century. The golden rule is not peculiarly Christian, and is also found (in a negative form) in Jewish writers, Confucius, Aristotle, Plato, Isocrates and Seneca.

**GOLDFISH,** *Carassius auratus*, a common pet fish related to the CARP. In the wild state, the goldfish—native to the rivers and streams of China—is dull brown in color. Chance MUTATION produces a form in which all pigments are missing except red (a form of albinism [see ALBINO] well-known in carp-like species). Such mutants breed true, and goldfish have now been kept as pets for over 2,000 years.

**GOLDING, William (Gerald)** (1911– ), English novelist. His powerful allegorical works explore the nature of mankind, and include *Lord of the Flies* (1954), *The Inheritors* (1955), *The Spire* (1964) and *Darkness Visible* (1979).

**GOLD LEAF,** thin GOLD foil produced by beating gold ribbon placed between vellum and animal skins until the leaf is only $0.1\mu$ thick. It is used for decorative gilding, lettering on leather-bound books, and for coating artificial satellites, etc., to reflect infrared radiation.

**GOLDMAN, Emma** (1869–1940), Russian-born anarchist who worked in the US c1890–1917. She was imprisoned (1893, 1916, 1917) for inciting riots, advocating birth control and obstructing the draft. She was temporarily deported (1919) and later lived in England and Canada and was active in the Spanish civil war, 1936.

**GOLDMARK, Peter Carl** (1906–1977), Hungarian-born US engineer and inventor who, at CBS Laboratories, developed the first practical color TELEVISION (1940) and the first long-playing PHONOGRAPH record. He was also a pioneer in the field of educational television and in the development of electronic video recording.

**GOLDONI, Carlo** (1707–1793), Italian dramatist. His type of character comedy led to the decline in popularity of the rival COMMEDIA DELL' ARTE. Goldoni directed the Comédi Italienne in Paris, 1762–64. Among his 150 comic plays are *The Mistress of the Inn* (1753) and *The Fan* (1763).

**GOLD RUSH,** general term for an influx of gold prospectors following the discovery of a new gold field. From 1848–1915, in the Americas, Australia and South Africa, there were numerous gold rushes. Three main North American gold strikes attracted thousands of prospectors: in California (1849; see FORTY-NINERS), Colorado (1858–59) and the Klondike (1897).

**GOLDSMITH, Oliver** (c1730–1774), Anglo-Irish man of letters. His best-known works are the novel *The Vicar of Wakefield* (1766), the comedy *She Stoops to Conquer* (1773) and the pastoral poem *The Deserted Village* (1770). An unsuccessful physician, he achieved both a considerable literary reputation and widespread popularity in his day. His works attacked pedantry and sentimentalism and stressed the simple virtues of humility, courage and humor.

**GOLD STANDARD,** a monetary system in which a standard currency unit equals a fixed weight of gold and central banks must be prepared to exchange currency for gold and vice versa. In an *internal* gold standard system, gold coins circulate in a country as LEGAL TENDER. In an *international* system, gold (or gold-based currency) is used for making international payments. Since WWII most countries no longer have an internal gold standard, but do use a limited international standard in which they convert their currencies into gold or US dollars for international payments. The US went on the gold standard in 1900, but the Gold Reserve Act of 1934 prohibited the redemption of dollars into gold. And in 1970 the US Treasury ended its requirement that Federal Reserve notes be backed 25% by gold deposits, in effect taking the US completely off the gold standard.

**GOLDWATER, Barry Morris** (1909– ), leading US conservative senator from Ariz. since 1952. As Republican presidential candidate in 1964, Goldwater won only six states in the running against Lyndon B. JOHNSON. Goldwater's writings include *The Conscience of a Conservative* (1960) and *Why Not Victory?* (1962). An Air Force officer in WWII, he became an authority on defense issues in the Senate.

**GOLDWYN, Samuel** (1882–1974), Polish-born US motion picture pioneer. He produced over 70 films and in 1916 founded a unit in the future Metro-Goldwyn-Mayer film company, though he worked as an independent producer after 1924. He won an Academy Award (1947) for *The Best Years of Our Lives.*

**GOLEM,** in Jewish medieval legend, an effigy (often of clay) magically endowed with life. The golem was a faithful mechanical servant, protecting its owner in times of danger. The most famous golem, supposedly created by Rabbi Löw in 16th-century Prague, was a forerunner of the creature FRANKENSTEIN.

**GOLF,** the most popular outdoor sport in the US, a game in which individual competitors drive a small hard ball with variously-shaped clubs towards and into a hole. A game consists of playing into either 9 or 18 consecutive holes spread over an extensive ground known as a golf course or links. The winner of individual stroke (or medal) play is the player who holes his ball in the fewest strokes over the course; in match play the winner is the player who wins the most individual holes. Playing a hole involves driving the ball from a raised peg or *tee* across the fairway towards the distant closely-mown *putting green* around the hole (which may be 100 to 600yd from the tee). The player seeks to keep the ball on the intervening mown fairway, avoiding the flanking "rough"—water and sand trap hazards. A player's score is based on *par*, the number of strokes an expert golfer would need to hit the ball from the tee into the hole in a given distance and course difficulty. Par varies from three to six strokes per hole. An expert golfer would average a score of 72 strokes for 18 holes—or an average of four per hole.

Written records of golf date from the 15th century in Scotland, where the traditional international rulemaking body, the Royal and Ancient Club of St. Andrews, was founded (1754). Early Scottish colonists probably introduced golf to the US in the 17th century. The game slowly gained popularity, and the Professional Golfers' Association (PGA) championship began in 1916. American golfers have tended to dominate the world game, from Bobby JONES to Ben HOGAN, Arnold PALMER and Jack NICKLAUS. More than 10 million Americans play golf, which is a multi-million dollar leisure business.

**GOMORRAH.** See SODOM AND GOMORRAH.

**GOMPERS, Samuel** (1850–1924), pioneer American labor leader. A leader in the cigar makers' union, he helped found and became first president, 1886–94, 1896–1924, of the AMERICAN FEDERATION OF LABOR (AFL). Gompers led the labor fight for higher wages, shorter working hours and more freedom. He opposed militant political unionism and as head of the War Committee on Labor (WWI), he greatly helped organized labor gain respectability in the US.

**GOMULKA, Wladyslaw** (1905–    ), Polish communist leader. He helped organize communist underground resistance in WWII, became Poland's deputy premier, 1945–49, and cochairman of the COMINFORM (from 1947). A Polish nationalist, he opposed Russian domination and was imprisoned, 1951–54. After the Poznan uprising (1956) he became first secretary of the Polish Communist Party (1956–70), encouraging some social and economic freedoms for Poles while maintaining close ties with the USSR. He resigned following food price riots.

**GONCHAROV, Ivan Aleksandrovich** (1812–1891), Russian novelist. His novel, *Oblomov* (1859), satirized realistically the indolence of Russian landed gentry in the 1860s. As a result, the Russian word *oblomovism* was coined to describe the hero's typical aristocratic laziness.

**GONCOURT,** two French brothers, known as "les deux Goncourt," art historians and pioneer authors of the naturalist school of fiction. **Edmond Louis Antoine Huot de Goncourt** (1822–1896) and **Jules Alfred Huot de Goncourt** (1830–1870) wrote novels exploring aspects of French society, notably *Germinie Lacerteux* (1864), a study of working-class life. They also wrote perceptively on art and social history and published a famous journal depicting Parisian society, 1851–95. Edmond provided money in his will for the Goncourt Academy which annually awards the prestigious literary Goncourt Prize.

**GÓNGORA Y ARGOTE, Luis de** (1561–1627), Spanish poet. Often called the greatest poet of Spain's cultural Golden Age, he created an ornate, difficult poetic style called Gongorism. His greatest work *Las Soledades* (1613), led to long controversy over his grandiose and abstruse yet technically skilled and never dull style.

**GONORRHEA.** See VENEREAL DISEASES.

**GONZALES, Richard Alonzo "Pancho"** (1928–    ), American tennis champion. One of the great world-class players, he won the US amateur men's singles championship (1948, 1949), and subsequently the professional championship, remaining an active player through the 1960s.

**GOOD FRIDAY,** the Friday in HOLY WEEK before Easter, observed in most Christian churches as a day of fasting and repentance in commemoration of the CRUCIFIXION OF Jesus Christ, of which it is the anniversary. Its observance dates from the 2nd century.

**GOOD HOPE, Cape of.** See CAPE OF GOOD HOPE.

**GOODMAN, Benny (Benjamin D** 1909–    ), American clarinetist and band leader. One of the most famous jazz soloist and danceband leaders of the 1930s and 1940s "swing" era. His virtuoso playing inspired classical compositions for the clarinet, notably *Contrasts* (1938) by Béla BARTÓK and concertos by COPLAND and HINDEMITH.

**GOODMAN, Paul** (1911–1972), US psychotherapist, poet, novelist, essayist and social critic. He came to prominence with the publication of *Growing Up Absurd*

(1960), which strongly attacked US culture and defended American youth. Among his many works are *Communitas* (1947), *The Community of Scholars* (1962) and *Collected Poems* (1974).

**GOOD NEIGHBOR POLICY,** pact signed at the 1933 Pan-American conference by the US and Latin American countries, as outlined by President Franklin D. ROOSEVELT. Ending the "gun-boat diplomacy" long practiced by the US to protect its interests in Latin America, the policy stated that no nation would interfere in another's affairs. Exchange programs were set up for teachers and technical experts and the US agreed to help develop Latin American agriculture, business, education and health facilities. (See also ALLIANCE FOR PROGRESS.)

**GOODWILL INDUSTRIES OF AMERICA,** nonprofit welfare organization, founded 1902, to provide training and employment for the handicapped in the US, Canada and Mexico. Clothing and appliances donated by the public and reconditioned in Goodwill workshops are resold in more than 150 Goodwill stores in the US.

**GOODYEAR, Charles** (1800–1860), US inventor of the process of VULCANIZATION (patented 1844). In 1839 he bought the patents of Nathaniel Manley Hayward (1808–1865), who had had some success by treating RUBBER with SULFUR. Working on this, Goodyear accidentally dropped a rubber/sulfur mixture onto a hot stove, so discovering vulcanization.

**GOPHERS,** the name applied in North America to any burrowing rodent, but properly referring to the Pocket gophers, a group confined to arid areas of North America. Gophers are solitary animals feeding on bulbs and roots collected in their underground tunnels. They possess furlined cheek pouches for storing food, which open on the outside of each cheek.

**GORDIAN KNOT,** in Greek mythology, an intricate knot by which King Gordius of Phrygia joined the yoke and pole of an oxcart. A prophecy held that anyone undoing the knot would rule all Asia. The knot defied all comers until the conqueror ALEXANDER THE GREAT severed it with his sword. Hence, "cutting the Gordian knot" describes any problem solved by bold, unorthodox action.

**GORDON, Charles George** (1833–1885), British soldier, popularly known as "Chinese Gordon." He helped suppress the TAIPING REBELLION (1863–64) in China, was governor of the Sudan (1877–80), where he established law, improved communications

and attempted to suppress the slave trade. In 1885 he defended Khartoum against the MAHDI's forces for 10 months, but was killed on Jan. 26 before relief arrived on Jan. 28. British indignation over his abandonment led to the collapse of GLADSTONE'S government.

**GOREN, Charles** (1901–    ), US bridge expert who won more than 30 US national championships. His books popularized the point-count bidding system.

**GORGAS, William Crawford** (1854–1920), US Army sanitarian. After Walter REED'S commission had proved (1900) Carlos FINLAY'S theory that YELLOW FEVER is transmitted by the MOSQUITO, Gorgas conducted in Havana a massive control program; he repeated this in Panama (1904–1913), facilitating the digging of the Panama Canal.

**GORGIAS** (c483–376 BC), Greek sophist and teacher of rhetoric. He believed that objective truth or knowledge was impossible, and hence that the ability to argue on either side of a question was of prime value to an educated man. He is a central figure of Plato's *Gorgias* dialogue. (See SOPHISTS; SKEPTICISM.)

**GORILLA,** (*Gorilla gorilla*) the largest of the PRIMATES, with a scattered distribution throughout central Africa. They live in groups with a single dominant "silverback" male, feeding on vast quantities of vegetable material as they wander over their range of 25–40km$^2$ (10–15sq mi). Gorillas are quadrupedal, rising to two legs only when displaying. They spend most of their time on the ground, but may make nests on the ground or in trees to sleep in at night. Though huge apes, (a male weighs 160–200kg (350–440lb) they are peaceable and will not attack unprovoked. The well-known chest-beating display is not a threat, but an intraspecific social signal.

**GORKI, Maxim** (1868–1936), pen name of Aleksey Maksimovich Peshkov, Russian author recognized as the father of SOCIALIST REALISM. His works, noted for their stark naturalism, include the play *The Lower Depths* (1902), the novel *Mother* (1906) and the autobiographical trilogy *Childhood* (1914), *In the World* (1915) and *My Universities* (1923). After the Revolution, Gorki headed state publishing up to 1921 and later served as propagandist for the Stalin regime.

**GORKY,** (also Gorkii and Gorkiy) city in the Russian SFSR, USSR about 250mi E of Moscow, capital of Gorky oblast. It is a major industrial center at the confluence of the Volga and Oka rivers. It produces planes, automobiles, machinery and plastics. Formerly Nizhny Novgorod, the city was renamed for Maxim GORKY in 1932. Pop 1,358,000.

**GORKY, Arshile** (1904–1948), Armenian-born US painter, a pioneer of ABSTRACT EXPRESSIONISM. His seemingly spontaneous, organic abstracts influenced the work of Jackson POLLOCK and Willem DE KOONING.

**GOSPEL MUSIC,** folk music in which a religious text is sung in a blues style, created originally by blacks in the S US. Mahalia JACKSON was the best known singer of gospel.

**GOSPELS, The,** first four books of the NEW TESTAMENT, named for their reputed authors: Matthew, Mark, Luke and John. Each is a collection of the acts and words of Jesus. Didactic in intention rather than biographical, they were written to help spread the gospel ("good news") of Christian salvation. All broadly cover the key events of Jesus' life, death and resurrection, but narrative styles and details, and intended readership, differ. The Gospel— an excerpt from the Gospels—is one of the readings at Holy COMMUNION. (See also SYNOPTIC GOSPELS.)

**GÖTEBORG,** city in SW Sweden on the Kattegat. Sweden's leading seaport and second largest city, it is linked to Stockholm by canal. Shipbuilding is a major industry and timber, iron, steel products, textiles and porcelain are also made. There is a university and a cathedral. Pop 437,000.

**GOTHIC ART AND ARCHITECTURE.** The Gothic style of art and architecture flourished in Europe, particularly in France, from the mid-12th century to the end of the 15th century. The style was first referred to as "gothic" in the Renaissance by artists and writers who sought to condemn it as barbaric.

Gothic architecture in fact to barrel vault and the stone rib to produce its most characteristic feature, the rib vault. This was first perfected at the Abbey Church of St. Denis near Paris, in 1140. It made possible a lighter, almost skeletal building. The flying buttress, also characteristic, was first used at Notre Dame in Paris. During the 13th century, High Gothic was perfected and cathedrals with higher vaults and more slender columns and walls were constructed, as at Chartres and Reims in France, Salisbury in England and Cologne in Germany. In the 14th and 15th centuries Gothic became more elaborate and ornate. (See DECORATED STYLE; FLAMBOYANT STYLE; PERPENDICULAR STYLE.)

Sculptural decoration was an essential part of Gothic architecture, as were stained glass windows, among the most notable examples of which are at Chartres. The period is also noted for its manuscript illumination in missals, books of hours, Bibles and psalters.

**GOTHIC NOVEL,** genre of fiction whose terror-laden stories are usually set against a menacing, medieval background. Famous early examples of the genre are Horace WALPOLE's *Castle of Otranto* (1765) and Ann RADCLIFFE's *The Mysteries of Udolpho* (1794). The term now embraces a wide range of popular fiction, including formulaic historical romances.

**GOTHIC REVIVAL,** 18th- and 19th-century revival of interest in medieval culture, chiefly in England and the US. It involved a somewhat dilettante liking for such phenomena as the GOTHIC NOVEL and pseudomedieval country houses, but there was also a more serious appeal to the standards of the Middle Ages, as by the architect Pugin and by John RUSKIN.

**GOTHS,** ancient Germanic peoples, reputed to have originated in S Scandinavia, who invaded and settled in Roman Spain and Italy in the 5th century AD. In the 2nd century AD, they settled on the N and NW Black Sea coast and during the next century occupied the Roman province of DACIA. The Goths in Dacia became known as VISIGOTHS and those around the Black Sea as OSTROGOTHS.

**GOTTFRIED VON STRASSBURG,** 13th century German poet famous for his masterpiece *Tristan* (c1210), an epic based on Celtic legend, and stressing the ennobling ideals of courtly love. Richard WAGNER used the work as the basis of his opera *Tristan and Isolde* (1859).

**GOTTLIEB, Adolph** (1903–1974), US artist. His oversized abstract-expressionist landscapes, featuring bursts of color, gained him much popularity in the 1950s. He derived his early style from "pictographs," arranging abstract symbols in grids.

**GOUDSMIT, Samuel** (1902–1978), Dutch-born US physicist who, with George Uhlenbeck, formulated the theory of electron SPIN (1925), which explained certain puzzling features of atomic spectra. He was senior scientist at the Brookhaven National Laboratory (1948–70) and edited the influential journal *Physical Review* (1951–62).

**GOUJON, Jean** (c1510–1568?), French sculptor and architect. He is famous for his elongated and elegant statues. His finest work, part of which is in the Louvre in Paris, is generally agreed to be the *Fontaine des Innocents* (1547–49).

**GOULD, Glenn** (1932– ), Canadian virtuoso pianist, famous for his performances of BACH, BEETHOVEN and BRAHMS. From the late 1960s he abandoned live performances, making records and documentary films.

**GOULD, Jay** (1836–1892), US railroad speculator. He denied Cornelius VANDERBILT control of the Erie Railroad by selling stock illegally. With James FISK he tried cornering the gold market (1869) and triggered the BLACK FRIDAY panic. From 1872 he built up the Gould railroad system in the SW, which included the Union Pacific. He also gained a controlling interest in the Western Union Telegraph Company.

**GOULD, Morton** (1913–    ), US composer, conductor and pianist who began his wide-ranging career as a teenage pianist and later composed works blending popular American themes and classical forms, such as *Cowboy Rhapsody* (1942). He also composed music for films, musical comedies and ballet.

**GOUNOD, Charles François** (1818–1893), French composer, best known for the operas *Faust* (1859) and *Romeo and Juliet* (1867). He wrote 10 other operas, as well as oratorios, masses, songs and piano pieces in a melodic and often sentimental style.

**GOUT,** a DISEASE of PURINE metabolism characterized by elevation of uric acid in the BLOOD and episodes of ARTHRITIS due to uric acid crystal deposition in SYNOVIAL FLUID and the resulting INFLAMMATION. Deposition of urate in CARTILAGE and subcutaneous tissue (as *tophi*) and in the KIDNEYS and urinary tract (causing stones and renal failure) are other important effects. The arthritis is typically of sudden onset with severe pain, often affecting the great toe first and large JOINTS in general. Treatment with allopurinol prevents recurrences.

**GOUZENKO, Igor** (1919–    ), Russian defector who as a cipher clerk at the Soviet embassy in Ottawa had copied over 100 secret documents in a bid to gain political asylum in Canada in 1945. Dismissed as a fraud by government officials, he was forced to turn this information over to a neighbor, a Royal Canadian Air Force sergeant. The information he provided disclosed the identities of Soviet spies throughout North America.

**GOVERNMENT PRINTING OFFICE** (GPO), US government agency in Washington D.C., one of the world's largest printing establishments. Created in 1860, it prints and publishes official documents and supplies writing materials to other government agencies.

**GOWON, Yakubu** (1934–    ), Nigerian general, head of state (1966–75). He crushed secessionist BIAFRA in a bloody civil war (1967–70), then announced an amnesty and launched a reconciliation program. He was deposed in a bloodless coup and took up residence in England.

**GOYA Y LUCIENTES, Francisco José de** (1746–1828), Spanish painter and etcher, famous as much for his delightful paintings and portraits for the Spanish court as for his grim depictions of the French invasion of Spain in 1808–14. During the 1790s he painted some of his most delicately and brilliantly colored portraits, including *La Tirana* (1794) and, after he became first court painter in 1799, the *Family of Charles IV* (1800). The etchings *Caprices* (1793–98) and *Disasters of War* (1810–14) are scenes of absurd and savage human behavior.

**GOZZOLI, Benozzo** (Benozzo di Lese; 1420–1497), Italian painter and goldsmith. He assisted Fra ANGELICO and is best known for the frescoes in which he treated contemporary Florentine life. His finest work is in the Medici Palace chapel, Florence.

**GRACCHUS,** family name of two Roman brothers, reformers and statesmen, known as the Gracchi. **Tiberius Sempronius** (163–133 BC), was elected a tribune of Rome in 133 and proposed a law redistributing public land (largely farmed by rich senators) to landless citizens to restore the middle class of small independent farmers. To push his law through he illegally renominated himself. He was killed in an election riot. **Gaius Sempronius** (154–121 BC) was elected a tribune in 123 and 122. He, too, tried to restrict the powers of the Senate and to help the poor and the underprivileged middle class—for instance by issuing cheap grain, establishing overseas colonies and proposing Roman citizenship for all free Italians and Latins. The Senate moved to revoke his bills, fighting broke out, and Sempronius was killed in a riot.

**GRACE,** in Christian theology, the undeserved favor shown by God towards needy and sinful men through Jesus Christ. In biblical thought, especially in St. Paul, grace is at the heart of SALVATION, and is necessary for faith and good works; the relation between them has been controversial (see ARMINIANS; AUGUSTINE; CALVINISM; PELAGIANISM). The "means of grace" include holy scripture, the sacraments, prayer and Christian fellowship. The term is also applied to a formal thanksgiving for food.

**GRAFFITI** or **graffito**, from Italian, "scratchings", a term generally used to mean a casual writing on an interior or exterior wall. Graffiti are found in great numbers on ancient Egyptian monuments, the walls of Pompeii, etc., and are of special interest in PALEOGRAPHY as they show the corruptions and transmutations of alphabetical characters. Ancient graffiti, like their modern counterparts, are mainly of a political or obscene nature. In some US urban centers in the 1970s, the use of spray-paint cans added a new dimension to the practice. In the fine arts, **graffito** designates a technique in which a second covering of color is partially scraped away to reveal a primary covering of color below.

**GRAFTING,** the technique of propagating plants by attaching the stem or bud of one plant (called the scion) to the stem or roots of another (the stock or rootstock). Only closely related varieties can be grafted. ROSES and fruit trees are often grafted so that good flowering or fruiting varieties have the benefit of strong roots.

**GRAHAM, Billy** (1918–    ), William Franklin Graham, US evangelist. Ordained a Southern Baptist minister, 1939, he gained national prominence on the revivalist circuit about 1949 and went on to establish an international reputation as a leader of mass religious rallies. He was friendly with Presidents Eisenhower and Nixon.

**GRAHAM, Katherine Meyer** (1917–    ), US publisher. One of the most influential women in the US, she was publisher of the *Washington Post* (1968–78) and head of its parent company, which also controlled *Newsweek* magazine and several television stations.

**GRAHAM, Martha** (1895–    ), US dancer and choreographer, a major pioneer of modern dance. Influenced by Isadora DUNCAN, Ruth SAINT DENIS and Ted SHAWN, she made her solo concert debut in 1926. She choreographed over 100 works, most notably *Appalachian Spring* (1944) and *Clytemnestra* (1958). In 1976 she was awarded the US Medal of Freedom.

**GRAHAME, Kenneth** (1859–1932), British writer, author of the famous children's story *The Wind in the Willows* (1908), featuring animals with appealingly human characteristics.

**GRAIN,** or caryopsis, a dry one-seeded FRUIT, usually containing a high percentage of starch, produced by, for example, CORN, OATS, BARLEY, RYE and other CEREAL CROPS. Grain crops have a high food value, store well and are a primary food stuff, contributing over half the world's calorie intake. (See also FLOUR.)

**GRAINGER, Percy Aldridge** (1882–1961), Australian-born composer and pianist, a naturalized American from 1919. Influenced by his friend GRIEG, he collected and edited English folk music, basing short orchestral pieces upon it.

**GRAMMAR,** the structures of language and of its constituents; and the science concerned with the study of those structures. The grammarian concentrates on three main aspects of language: syntax, the ways that words are put together to form sentences; accidence, or morphology, the ways that words alter to convey different senses, such as past and present or singular and plural (see INFLECTION); and phonology, the ways that sounds are used to convey meaning.

**Syntax.** In English, the simplest sentence has a noun followed by a verb: "Philip thinks." More complicated is "Philip thinks little," where the verb is qualified by an adverb. In both of these, order is important: in "Little Philip thinks" the change in order has brought about a change in meaning. In contrast, sentences of widely different outward form may have the same meaning (for example, using active and passive forms of the verb), and this suggests to many grammarians that superficial structure is not ultimately important, that there is a deep-lying structure of language which can be resolved into a few basic elements whose combinations can be used to produce an infinite number of sentences. Here grammatical studies are probing at the very roots of the human psyche; and ethnographical studies of the syntaxes of different languages, primitive and civilized, have been of primary importance in cultural ANTHROPOLOGY. (See also CHOMSKY; ETHNOGRAPHY.)

**Accidence.** Most English nouns have different endings for singular and plural: "knight" and "knights." Again, there is a change of ending for the genitive (possessive) case: "knight's" (the obsolete full form is "knightes") and "knights'." Most other cases are dealt with by prepositions: "to the knight" (dative); "from the knight" (ablative). Similarly, verb-endings are changed for two tenses only, past and present, the remainder being dealt with by use of the "auxiliary" verbs "to be" and "to have." Most other languages have a profusion of noun and verb endings to deal with different cases and tenses, and so have a lesser flexibility than English.

**Phonology.** Much of our speech depends for meaning on our tone of voice: "Philip is thinking" may have several meanings, depending on the stress placed on each of the words. These stresses are thus an important part of grammar, less so in English than in many other tongues: in the Sino-Tibetan languages, for example, a word may have two utterly different meanings depending upon the tone of voice in which it is said. (See also ETYMOLOGY; LANGUAGE; LINGUISTICS; MORPHEME; PHILOLOGY; PHONEME; PHONETICS; PRONUNCIATION; PUNCTUATION; SEMANTICS.)

**GRANADA, Kingdom of,** medieval Moorish kingdom in S Spain. Founded 1238 by the Nasrid Dynasty, who made GRANADA its capital, the state pursued an independent Moorish policy, and was a center of Moorish culture. In the 15th century internal dissensions furthered Castile's slow conquest, completed when BOABDIL surrendered to Ferdinand and Isabella in 1492.

**GRANADOS, Enrique** (1867–1916), Spanish composer and pianist who helped create a distinctively Spanish musical style. He is best known for his songs and the *Goyescas* piano pieces (1912–14), inspired by Goya's paintings, and used in one of Granados' seven operas.

**GRAN CHACO,** lowland region in central S America, occupying 300,000sq mi between the Amazon forests and Argentinian pampa. Prone to droughts and flooding, it is mostly scrub with areas of swamp, grassland and desert.

**GRAND ARMY OF THE REPUBLIC (GAR),** fraternal society of Union Civil War veterans, founded 1866. It helped veterans and their families, and by 1890 had 400,000 members forming a powerful political pressure group that secured the Disability Pension Act. The last member died in 1956.

**GRAND BANKS,** underwater plateau in the N Atlantic Ocean, extending 350mi off Newfoundland, where the Labrador Current and Gulf Stream meet. Averaging 240ft in depth, the shallow waters abound in plankton that directly and indirectly support millions of food fish, notably cod. This is one of the world's richest fishing grounds.

**GRAND CANYON,** spectacular gorge cut by the Colorado R in NW Ariz. It is about 217mi long, 4–18mi wide, up to 1mi deep, and flanked by a plateau 5,000–9,000ft above sea level. The main canyon contains smaller canyons, peaks and mesas, and is walled by colorful, horizontal rock strata dating back to the PRECAMBRIAN era. It is an important geological site, contains a wealth of animal and plant life, and attracts 1,500,000 visitors a year. The most impressive part forms the 673,575-acre Grand Canyon National Park.

**GRAND COULEE DAM,** concrete dam on the Columbia R, Wash., 85mi WNW of Spokane. Built 1934–42, it is one of the world's largest hydroelectric generating plants with an ultimate capacity of 10,080 megawatts resulting from expansion work during the 1980s.

**GRANDFATHER CLAUSE,** legal device used in Southern states to deny blacks the vote, by giving it to males with high literacy and property qualifications or to those whose fathers and grandfathers had been qualified to vote on Jan. 1, 1867 (before the 15th Amendment had enfranchised Southern blacks). First used in S.C. in 1895, it was declared unconstitutional in 1915.

**GRAND GUIGNOL,** a theater in Paris that presented plays with horror themes. Ingenious devices were invented to simulate the flow of blood and to give verisimilitude to depictions of murder, torture, and other kinds of violence in order to shock and amuse the audience. Founded in 1897, the theater closed in 1962, but has given its name to any play that makes use of its distinctive themes.

**GRAND NATIONAL,** most famous steeplechase in horse-racing, held annually since 1834 at the Aintree race course in England. The difficult and dangerous 4½mi course includes 30 jumps, and many participants fail to finish.

**GRAND TETON NATIONAL PARK,** spectacular area of the Rocky Mts in NW Wyo., just S of Yellowstone National Park. It comprises major peaks of the TETON RANGE and the valley of JACKSON HOLE from which the peaks rise abruptly. Created in 1929, the park occupies c500sq mi. It is a major tourist area and wildlife preserve.

**GRANGE, The,** American farmers' organization, officially the National Grange of the Patrons of Husbandry. Founded as a fraternal order in 1867, in the 1870s it led the Granger Movement to protect farmers against the railroad monopolies, who fixed high prices on freight and storage. Soon individual states pioneered laws to curb these charges. Upheld in the GRANGER CASES, such laws led to government regulation of transportation and utilities. The Grange united farmers throughout the country as a political force, encouraged technical and educational exchanges and laid a basis for farm cooperatives. It is now a social and educational organization, still representing farmers' interests when necessary. (See also FARMERS' ALLIANCE.)

**GRANGE, (Harold Edward) "Red"** (1903– ), American football player, one of the most prolific scorers of touchdowns. He played for the University of

Illinois, Chicago Bears and New York Yankees, and was All-American halfback 1923–24, and quarterback 1925.

**GRANITE,** coarse- to medium-grained plutonic IGNEOUS ROCK, composed of FELDSPAR (orthoclase and microcline predominating over plagioclase) and QUARTZ, often containing BIOTITE and/or amphibole. It is the type of the family of **granitic rocks,** plutonic rocks rich in feldspar and quartz, of which the CONTINENTS are principally made. Most granite was formed by crystallization of MAGMA, though some may be METAMORPHIC, formed by "granitization" of previously existing sedimentary rock. It occurs typically as large plutonic masses called BATHOLITHS. A hard, weather-resistant rock, usually pink or gray, granite is used for building, paving and road curbs.

**GRANT, Cary** (1904–       ), English-born US actor, a dapper leading man for more than five decades. His films include *She Done Him Wrong* (1933), *Bringing Up Baby* (1938), *The Philadelphia Story* (1940), *To Catch a Thief* (1955) and *North By Northwest* (1959).

**GRANT, Duncan James Corrowr** (1885–1978), Scottish painter and designer, whose pictures are characterized by bright colors and bold brushwork. He was influenced by POSTIMPRESSIONISM and his friendship with the BLOOMSBURY GROUP.

**GRANT, Ulysses Simpson** (1822–1885), 18th president of the US 1869–77, and military leader who secured Union victory in the Civil War. A man of great personal integrity, he led an administration infiltrated by corruption.

**Army career.** Son of an Ohio farmer and tanner, he entered West Point in 1839, graduated four years later and first saw action in 1846 as a second lieutenant in the MEXICAN WAR. He then returned to St. Louis, and married his fiancée, Julia Dent. Though made a captain in 1853, he resigned from the army in 1854, disheartened by an uncongenial posting. For the next seven years he wandered from job to job, but on the outbreak of the Civil War became

colonel of the 21st Illinois Regiment. Promoted to brigadier general, he fought at Paducah, Ky. (1861), then won victories at forts Henry and Donelson (1862)—the first major Union successes. His subsequent victories at Shiloh, Vicksburg and Chattanooga eventually cut the Confederacy in two. Lincoln made Grant a lieutenant-general in 1864, with command of the entire Union Army and control of the Virginia campaign that eventually ended the war.

**The politician.** Created a full general in 1866, Grant was now a national hero. He impressed Republicans by opposing President Johnson's unpopular attempt to oust Edwin M. Stanton as secretary of war and to put Grant in his place. Becoming the Republican presidential candidate, Grant defeated Democrat Horatio Seymour in the 1868 election by a small popular majority. He was reelected in 1872, defeating Horace Greeley. As president, Grant pursued a lenient RECONSTRUCTION policy, reduced the national debt and worked to prevent a currency crisis. His administration improved relations with Britain (see WASHINGTON, TREATY OF). But Grant's scheme to annex Santo Domingo foundered, and his FORCE ACTS failed to help Southern Negroes. Above all, corruption affected the government—partly because the inexperienced Grant chose personal friends rather than the most able Republicans to fill government offices. Grant's own brother-in-law helped in an attempt to corner the gold market that led to the 1869 business panic (see BLACK FRIDAY). BELKNAP resigned as secretary of war to avoid impeachment for taking bribes. The CRÉDIT MOBILIER OF AMERICA frauds and the WHISKEY RING were among other scandals, though none of these touched Grant personally. After leaving the presidency, Grant undertook a world tour, then lost all his capital in an investment swindle. Virtually penniless and suffering from throat cancer, he wrote two volumes of Civil War memoirs that helped to ensure his family's financial security.

**GRANVILLE-BARKER, Harley** (1877–1946), English actor, director, playwright and seminal Shakespeare critic. He produced several of G. B. SHAW's plays for the first time. His best-known plays include *The Voysey Inheritance* (1905), *Waste* (1907) and *The Madras House* (1910).

**GRAPHS,** plottings of sets of points whose coordinates are of the form $(x, f[13(x))$, where $f[13(x)$ is a FUNCTION of $x$ (see ANALYTIC GEOMETRY). These points may define a CURVE or straight LINE. Graphs are a powerful tool of STATISTICS, since it is often profitable to plot one variable (such as age) along one axis, against another (such as height) plotted along the other (see also NORMAL DISTRIBUTION): the points on statistical graphs need not define a continuous curve (see HISTOGRAM). The AXES on a graph are not always marked off regularly: in some cases it is useful to mark off one or both on a nonlinear scale—e.g., using logarithmic (see LOGARITHM) or exponential (see EXPONENT) scales.

**GRASS, Günter Wilhelm** (1927–    ), German novelist and playwright. His works, deeply affected by the post-WWII sense of national guilt, are usually centered around grotesque motifs and have a strong moral content. His best-known works include the novels *The Tin Drum* (1959), *Local Anaesthetic* (1969) and *The Flounder* (1977) and the controversial play *The Plebeians Rehearse the Uprising* (1965).

**GRASSE, François Joseph Paul, Comte de** (1722–1788), French naval commander whose fleet made possible Washington's decisive victory over the British at the siege of YORKTOWN (1781). Grasse landed 3,000 troops to aid the siege, and remained off Chesapeake Bay to keep the British fleet from aiding the British force under Cornwallis.

**GRASSES,** large group of ANGIOSPERMS that are of great importance to man. Strictly speaking grasses only include those species belonging to the family Gramineae, but the name applies to any plant with a similar growth habit. Grasses are wind- or self-pollinated and have hollow or pithy, jointed stems, bearing lanceolate leaves. The fruit is a GRAIN. Grasses include CEREAL CROPS, such as WHEAT, RICE and CORN, SUGARCANE, SORGHUM, MILLET and BAMBOO.

**GRASSHOPPERS,** active jumping INSECTS related to the CRICKETS. The hindlegs are greatly enlarged for jumping. Adults usually have two pairs of fully developed wings; these are lacking in immature stages. Many grasshoppers can produce sounds by rubbing the hind legs against the folded wings. Grasshoppers feed entirely on grasses and other plants. A few species form large migratory swarms; certain of these species are known as LOCUSTS.

**GRASSO, Ella** (1919–1981), first US woman governor (Connecticut, 1975–81) elected in her own right, not in succession to a husband. Previously Connecticut secretary of the state (1959–71) and a member of the US House of Representatives (1971–75), she cut spending to revive the state's economy. She resigned because of ill health.

**GRATEFUL DEAD,** a major ROCK MUSIC band whose free San Francisco concerts in the 1960s opened the era of the giant rock music event. Their first album, *The Grateful - Dead*, was released in 1967. Originators of acid and country rock, the Dead have lately attracted a large cult following.

**GRAVES, Morris Cole** (1910–    ), US painter whose interest in Eastern art and American Indian mythology is seen in his delicate images of, for example, blind birds, pine trees and waves. His best-known work is probably the *Little Known Bird of the Inner Eye* (1941).

**GRAVES, Robert Ranke** (1895–    ), English poet and novelist, best known for his novels set in imperial Rome, *I. Claudius* (1934) and *Claudius the God* (1934). Less popular but equally successful were *Goodbye to All That* (1929), describing his experiences in WWI and *The Long Week-End* on the interwar period. He was professor of poetry at Oxford from 1961–66.

**GRAVITATION,** one of the fundamental forces of nature, the force of attraction existing between all MATTER. It is much weaker than the nuclear or electromagnetic forces and plays no part in the internal structure of matter. Its importance lies in its long range and in its involving all masses. It plays a vital role in the behavior of the UNIVERSE: the gravitational attraction of the SUN keeps the PLANETS in their orbits, and gravitation holds the matter in a STAR together. NEWTON'S **law of universal gravitation** states that the attractive FORCE $F$ between two bodies of MASSES $M_1$ and $M_2$ separated by distance $d$ is $F = GM_1 M_2/d^2$ where $G$ is the **Universal Gravitational Constant** $(6.670 \times 10^{-11}$ $Nm^2 kg^{-2})$. The force of gravity on the earth is a special case of all attraction between masses and causes bodies to fall toward the center of the earth with a uniform ACCELERATION $g = GM/R^2$ where $R$ and $M$ are the radius and mass of the earth. Assuming, with Newton, that the inertial mass of a body (that which is operative in the laws of motion) is identical with its gravitational mass, application of a body of mass $m$, the force with which the earth attracts that body, as $mg$. Bodies on the earth and moon thus have the same mass but different weights. Again, the gravitational force on a body is proportional to its mass but is independent of the type of material it is. Newton's theory explains most of the observed motions of the planets and the TIDES and is still sufficiently accurate for most applications. The Newtonian analysis of gravitation remained unchallenged until, in the early 20th century, EINSTEIN introduced radically new concepts in his theory of general RELATIVITY. According to this, mass deforms the geometrical properties of the space around it. Einstein reaffirmed Newton's assumption regarding the equivalence of gravitational and inertial mass, proposing that it was impossible to distinguish experimentally between an accelerated coordinate system and a local gravitational field. From this he predicted that LIGHT would be found to be deflected a certain amount toward massive bodies by their gravitational fields and this effect indeed was observed for starlight passing close to the sun. It was also predicted that accelerated matter should emit gravitational waves with the velocity of light but the existence of these has not as yet been demonstrated.

**GRAVURE.** See PRINTING.

**GRAY, Asa** (1810–1888), the foremost of 19th-century US botanists. Being a prominent Protestant layman, his advocacy of the Darwinian thesis carried special force. However, he never accepted the materialist interpretation of the evolutionary mechanism and taught that NATURAL SELECTION was indeed consistent with a divine TELEOLOGY.

**GRAY, Elisha** (1835–1901), US inventor whose claim to have invented the device used by BELL in his telephone led to a famous legal battle. The invention appears to have been almost simultaneous; Gray's device was in fact the more practical of the two, but the legal battle was won by Bell.

**GRAY, Thomas** (1716–1771), English poet. His *Elegy Written in a Country Churchyard* (1750) is one of the most popular English poems; among his other main works are the odes *The Progress of Poesy* and *The Bard* (both 1757).

**GRAY PANTHERS,** organization founded 1971 in Philadelphia, Pa., to further the well-being of older people in the US. It sponsors workshops, conferences, and seminars in the field of gerontology, produces educational films, and provides consultation services.

**GRAZIANO, Rocky** (1922–   ), US boxer, the world welterweight and middleweight champion in the mid-1940s. A popular, rough-and-tumble fighter, he is especially remembered for his three bloody championship contests with middleweight Tony ZALE.

**GREAT AMERICAN DESERT,** a term applied to the desert areas of SW US and N Mexico. Beginning in S Cal., it stretches N along the E side of the Sierra Nevada into Ida. and Ore. It continues E to the Rockies and S into Mexico where the Lower California peninsula and the E shore of the Gulf of California are desert.

**GREAT AWAKENING,** an intense and widespread religious REVIVAL in 18th-century America, forming part of the EVANGELICAL REVIVAL. Starting in N.J. (c1726), the movement quickly spread across New England. In reaction to the prevailing rationalism and formalism, its leaders—notably Jonathan EDWARDS and George WHITEFIELD—preached evangelical CALVINISM and discouraged excessive emotionalism. The 1740s saw the zenith of the Awakening, which led to the rapid growth of the Presbyterian, Baptist and Methodist churches, continuing to the end of the century. A similar revival beginning in the 1790s is known as the Second Great Awakening.

**GREAT BARRIER REEF,** series of massive coral reefs off the NE coast of Australia, extending for about 1,250mi. The reef, which is the world's largest coral formation, can only be safely crossed at certain passages, the chief of which is Raines Inlet.

**GREAT BASIN,** desert region in the W US between the Wasatch and Sierra Nevada Mts and parts of adjacent states. A subdivision of the Basin and Range physiographic province, the Great Basin of Nev. contains Death Valley, Reno, Las Vegas, and Salt Lake City. Mineral mining and agriculture are the main industries.

**GREAT BEAR** (Ursa Major), a large N Hemisphere constellation containing the seven bright stars known as the Plow or Big Dipper. Two of these, the Pointers, form roughly a straight line with POLARIS and are hence of navigational importance. Five stars of the Plow are, with SIRIUS, members of a widely separated GALACTIC CLUSTER.

**GREAT BRITAIN,** name of the main island of the British Isles comprising England, Scotland and Wales. (See UNITED KINGDOM.)

**GREAT DANE,** breed of large dog, standing up to 36in at the shoulder and weighing up to 150lb. The Great Dane, first developed in Germany, has a short smooth coat and is bred in blue, black, brindle, fawn and black-and-white.

**GREAT DEPRESSION,** a period of US and world economic depression during the 1930s which was immediately precipitated by the disastrous stockmarket collapse in Wall Street on BLACK FRIDAY, Oct. 29, 1929. This heralded a period of high unemployment, failing businesses and banks and falling agricultural prices. Millions of workers were unemployed during the period (some 16 million in the US alone in 1933).

here were many causes of the depression: easy credit had led to widespread stock peculation; the world had not completely recovered from WWI; US economic policies under President HOOVER had created domestic overproduction and less foreign trade. Franklin ROOSEVELT, elected president in 1932, brought in the NEW DEAL measures, but full recovery of the economy only occurred with the beginnings of defense spending immediately prior to WWII.

**GREAT DIVIDE.** See CONTINENTAL DIVIDE.

**GREAT LAKES,** chain of five large freshwater lakes in North America, forming the largest lake group in the world and covering an area of 95,170sq mi. From E to W the lakes are: Ontario, Erie, Huron, Michigan and Superior. They are connected by several channels, including the St. Lawrence R, Niagara R, and Lake St. Clair and the Welland Canal, Sault Sainte Marie (Soo) Canals and St. Lawrence Seaway and are now navigable by ocean-going vessels from Duluth, Minn., on Lake Superior to the Atlantic. The lake system is used for the transportation of iron ore, steel, petroleum, coal, grain and heavy manufactured goods. Trading ports on the waterways include Duluth, Chicago, Detroit, Cleveland, Buffalo, Port Arthur, Toronto and Montreal. In recent years, the lakes, particularly Lake Erie, have suffered from serious pollution.

**GREAT PLAINS,** large plateau in W central North America, extending for over 2,500mi from the Saskatchewan R in NW Canada to the Rio Grande in Mexico and the Gulf coastal plain in the S US. The plateau slopes gently downwards from the Rockies in the W, extending about 400mi E. The natural vegetation is buffalo grass, and the area generally has hot summers and cold winters with an average annual rainfall of 20in. The plains are known as the "granary of the world" owing to their vast wheat production; livestock is also important.

**GREAT RIFT VALLEY,** a large downfaulted depression extending more than 3,000mi from SE Africa to N Syria. In Africa, its W course is partly occupied by lakes Malawi (Nyasa), Tanganyika, Kivu and Edward (Mobutu Sese Seko); its E course by Lake Turkana. In Asia, the Sea of Galilee, the Jordan R, the Gulf of Aqaba, the Red Sea and the Gulf of Aden are in the Great Rift Valley. Volcanic and seismic activity are common throughout the length of the rift, tending to support the hypothesis that the rift represents an early stage in the development of an ocean that will in the geologic future separate E Africa from the rest of the continent. (See also PLATE TECTONICS; SEA-FLOOR SPREADING.)

**GREAT SALT LAKE,** a shallow saline inland sea in NW Ut., about 5mi NW of Salt Lake City. Its size and depth vary yearly, but on average the lake is 72mi long and 30mi across at its widest point, with a maximum depth of 27ft. It is the largest brine lake in North America. Industrial plants along the shore extract some 300,000 tons of salt from the lake every year, and plans are under way for tapping other mineral resources.

**GREAT SAND DUNES NATIONAL MONUMENT,** about 37,000 acres in S Col., in San Luis Park, Sangre de Cristo Mts, containing the largest, highest inland sand dunes in the US. The monument was established in 1932.

**GREAT SCHISM,** two divisions in the Christian Church. The first was the breach between the EASTERN CHURCH and the WESTERN CHURCH. Long-standing divergences in tradition, combined with political and theological disputes, came to a head in 1054 when Pope Leo IX sent legates to refuse the title of Ecumenical Patriarch to the Patriarch of Constantinople and to demand acceptance of the *filioque* ("and from the Son") clause in the Nicene Creed (see HOLY SPIRIT). The Patriarch refused and rejected the claim of papal supremacy. Reciprocal excommunications and anathemas followed. Later Councils were unsuccessful in healing the breach.

The second Great Schism was the division within the Roman Catholic Church from 1378 to 1417, when there were two or three rival popes and antipopes (see PAPACY), each with his nationalistic following. The Council of Constance ended the schism by electing Martin V sole pope.

**GREAT SLAVE LAKE,** large lake in the Northwest Territories, Canada. Fed by the Slave and Hay rivers and drained by the Mackenzie, it covers about 11,000sq mi. Lead, gold and zinc mines are located on its shores, and there are important fisheries.

**GREAT SMOKY MOUNTAINS,** range of the Appalachian Mts, forming the border between N.C. and Tenn. The "Great Smokies" are almost entirely within the 800sq mi Great Smoky Mountains National Park, established 1934. The mountain valleys are often filled with a smoky-blue haze, from which the name of the range derives.

**GREAT SOCIETY,** collective name for the domestic programs of President Lyndon B. JOHNSON. It derives from his aim (first stated in a speech in 1964) to build a great society in the US. Such a society, as

Johnson envisioned it, would offer "abundance and liberty for all" and an "end to poverty and racial injustice."

**GREAT TREK,** a migration between 1835 and 1845, of about 14,000 Afrikaners out of Cape Colony, South Africa, to escape British domination. They set up Natal but when in 1843 it was taken by Britain, they trekked on across the Drakensberg Mts to form the ORANGE FREE STATE and the TRANSVAAL.

**GREAT WALL OF CHINA,** the world's longest wall fortification, N China. It extends over 1,500mi, roughly following the S border of the Mongolian plain. Construction was begun in the CH'IN dynasty to defend China against invasion from the N and mostly completed during the MING dynasty. Its average height is 25ft; it is wide enough (about 12ft) for horsemen to ride along it.

**GREBES,** a group of highly specialized aquatic birds all closely related; family: Podicipedidae. They are diving birds of lakes or coastal waters; the feet are not webbed but "lobed" with flaps along the toes. Many of the grebes are highly ornamental birds, brightly colored and bearing tufts or crests. Courtship displays are often complex and extremely spectacular. All grebes eat quantities of their own feathers which collect around fishbones in the gut allowing these indigestible remains to be formed into a pellet and cast.

**GRECO, El** (1541–1614), one of the greatest and most individual Spanish painters and religious subjects, born Domenikos Theotokopoulos. First in Venice, where he was influenced by TINTORETTO, and later in Toledo, Spain, he developed his distinctive style of painting characterized by dramatically elongated figures and contrasting colors. Among his most famous works are *The Burial of the Count of Orgaz* (1586), the *Portrait of Cardinal Niño de Guevara* (c1600), and *View of Toledo* (1608).

**Official name:** Greece
**Capital:** Athens
**Area:** 50,943sq mi

**Population:** 9,600,000
**Language:** Greek
**Religions:** Greek Orthodox; Muslim
**Monetary unit(s):** 1 Drachma = 100 leptae

**GREECE,** a European republic which occupies the S part of the Balkan peninsula and the surrounding islands in the Ionian Mediterranean and Aegean seas. Of the country's total land area, almost 20% is accounted for by islands, among them Corfu, the Ionian Isles, Crete, the Cyclades Sporades and Dodecanese. Over 75% of the land is mountainous; the Pindus range runs SE down the length of the country and then continues S into the Peloponnesus. The S and coastal areas of Greece have hot summers and mild winters, but Macedonia and the mountainous northern interior have cold winters. Much of Greece receives only about 15in of rain a year, but W Greece can receive as much as 50in.

**People and Economy.** The Greek people who call themselves Hellenes, are a racial mixture of the many peoples who invaded the Balkans before and after classical times. Language and culture, rather than race, define the Greeks. Half of Greece's population lives in rural communities of fewer than 2,000 inhabitants, and about 40% is engaged in agriculture. In the last two decades there has been a trend toward urbanization. The capital, Athens, with its port Piraeus, is the largest city. The official language is Modern Greek. Religious life is dominated by the Greek Orthodox Church. Elementary and secondary education are free, but private secondary schools are widespread. The country's two biggest universities are at Athens and Salonika.

The leading farm products are fruit and vegetables, wheat, cotton, tobacco, wine and olive oil. Both sheep and goats are raised in large numbers. The country is rich in mineral resources which have not been fully exploited. The bulk of the country's manufacturing is located in or near Athens but efforts are being made to develop industrialization and thus provide a wide economic base for future growth. Greece has traditionally had a prosperous shipping industry; in 1978 its merchant fleet ranked third in the world. In recent years tourism has become increasingly important to Greece's economy. In 1981 Greece joined the European Economic Community.

**History.** Conquered by the Turks in the 15th century, Greece fought a successful War of Independence (1821–29) and established a constitutional monarchy. Thereafter Greece was characterized by political instability and conflict between monarchists and republicans. In WWI the country fought against Germany and Turkey. During WWII Greece was invaded by Germany in 1941 and occupied until Oct. 1944. A civil war was fought between 1944 and 1949, and US intervention was a major factor in ensuring the victory of the monarchists over communist and other left-wing groups. Political instability continued during the 1950s and 1960s leading to a military coup and eventual dictatorship in April 1967. The monarchy was abolished in July 1973, and another military coup in Nov. of that year overthrew the dictatorship. In 1974 the Greek people voted for a constitutional republic rather than a restoration of the monarchy and a new constitution was adopted in June 1975.

**GREECE, Ancient,** the independent cities and states of classical times occupying the Balkan peninsula and the surrounding islands. The name Greece comes from the Greek *graikoi*—the original inhabitants of the area around Dodona, the most ancient shrine of ZEUS. The Greeks called their land Hellas and themselves Hellenes. Ancient Greek culture is recognized as profoundly significant for Western man, for it provided the foundation of civilization in the West.

Greece was settled by about 3500 BC, and the Greek people probably moved into the area around 2000 BC. These settlers were strongly influenced by the MINOAN CIVILIZATION on the island of Crete. In the next few centuries the Mycenaean Civilization (named after the city of Mycenae on the mainland; see AEGEAN CIVILIZATION) flourished (1600–1200 BC). The writings of HOMER provide a vivid picture of Mycenaean times. In the period between 1200–750 BC (known as the "Dark Ages" of Greek history), Dorian invaders overwhelmed the culture of Mycenae, bringing with them the knowledge of working with iron. In the 8th and 7th centuries BC the first Greek CITY-STATES emerged, generally consisting of a fortified hilltop such as the Athenian ACROPOLIS and the surrounding market town and countryside. Trade with Egypt, Syria and Phoenicia grew and the city-states formed colonies throughout the Mediterranean area. From the 6th century ATHENS and SPARTA became the two most powerful city-states, embodying, respectively, a liberal and an authoritarian approach to government and society. Athens became a DEMOCRACY; Sparta became a military state. The 5th century BC began with attempted invasions of Greece by the Persians. The Persians were defeated on land at the Battles of Marathon (490 BC) and Plataea (479 BC) and at sea near Salamis. Athens emerged as

the undisputed leader of Greece and led a number of Ionian cities in the formation of the DELIAN LEAGUE, whose purpose was to protect commerce and resist any further Persian invasions. From this league the Athenian empire emerged. The latter half of the 5th century, especially during PERICLES' leadership, was the Golden Age of Athens—a period of unparalleled cultural activity ranging from the building of the PARTHENON (see also PHIDIAS) to the ideas of SOCRATES. However, growing resentment against Athenian power led eventually to Athens' defeat by Sparta in the PELOPONNESIAN WAR (431–404 BC).

In the 4th century BC Athens' artistic and intellectual achievements continued to flourish under PLATO, ARISTOTLE, the sculptor PRAXITELES and others. However, in 338 BC Philip of Macedon became ruler of Greece, depriving the people of political liberty they were not to regain for more than 2,000 years. Philip's son Alexander the Great (356–323 BC) carried out a plan of conquest which would have far reaching effects on the world. In the period that followed his death, the HELLENISTIC AGE, Greek culture and civilization spread over all the known world. Macedonia controlled Greece for more than a hundred years, although some city-states joined two confederations to restore a measure of their lost power: the Aetolian League (see AETOLIA) and the Achaean League (see ACHAEANS).

Rome first became involved in Greek affairs in 220 BC in support of the Aetolian League against Macedonia, and in 197 BC the leagues helped the Romans defeat Macedonia. The Romans were hailed as liberators, but after the revolt of the Achaean League against Rome (146 BC), Greece was dominated by Rome and in 27 BC became the Roman province of Achaea. Greece still remained the cultural and intellectual center of the Mediterranean world, but economically and politically was unable to regain her former power. From 395 AD when the Roman Empire was divided into W and E, Greece was incorporated into the BYZANTINE EMPIRE (395–1453 AD). In the DARK AGES (from the 4th to the 9th centuries), Greece suffered from barbarian incursions, and after the fall of Constantinople in 1453 it became part of the Turkish OTTOMAN EMPIRE.

**GREEK,** the language of ancient and modern Greece, one of the oldest INDO-EUROPEAN LANGUAGES. The ancient and modern tongues use the same alphabet (which the Greeks adopted from the Phoenicians in the 8th century BC), but differ greatly in grammar, vocabulary and pronunciation. The earliest known records of ancient Greek date from around 1400 BC and use a form of writing known as MINOAN LINEAR SCRIPT. Classical Greek is based on Athenian dialects spoken from the 6th to the 4th centuries BC. During Hellenistic times a simplified Greek known as Koine became the common language of the civilized world. There are two forms of modern Greek: Koine for everyday use and an official state language which incorporates classical forms and words.

## GREEK ART AND ARCHITECTURE.

The art of ancient Greece was the tangible expression of its religion and philosophy. Greek culture is essentially humanist, and the expressive possibilities of the human figure played a preeminent part in Greek art. Gods took human forms and abstract qualities were personified.

**Sculpture.** The Greeks first began to carve large scale marble sculptures around 650 BC. Their finest achievements date from the Classical Age beginning about 480 BC—idealized majestic figures of great harmony and fluidity. Notable examples are MYRON's *Discus Thrower*, POLYCLITUS' *Spearbearer* and PHIDIAS' PARTHENON sculptures and his *Zeus*, a 40ft statue of gold and ivory at Olympus, one of the seven wonders of the ancient world. From the 4th century, Greek sculpture embodied emotional appeal, as in PRAXITELES' *Aphrodite of Cnidus*, the Hellenistic *Venus de Milo* and *Winged Victory of Samothrace*.

**Vase Painting.** The history of Greek painting in which portraiture and perspective were skilfully developed is illustrated primarily from painted pottery which has survived from about 900 BC. The earliest Dipylon vases, decorated with human figures in funeral and battle scenes, were grave markers. In the 7th century BC black-figure ware appeared, with carefully incised silhouette forms. In the mid-6th century BC Athenian red-figure ware appeared with carefully painted-on details and scenes which conformed to the shape of the pottery.

**Architecture.** Classical Greek architecture, which flourished in the 5th century BC, had its origins in the 6th century when stone and then marble replaced wood in civic buildings and temples. Greek architecture is characterized by harmony and symmetry. There are three specific styles of decoration: the earliest Doric style has great columns with wide flutes as in the Parthenon of Athens; the later Ionic and Corinthian styles have slenderer columns with more elaborate capitals (see CLASSICAL ORDERS).

**GREEK REVIVAL,** a movement in art and architecture, in Europe and America during the late 18th and 19th centuries characterized by renewed interest in classical antiquity. Private and public buildings were modeled on Classical designs. Notable examples include the U. o Va. by Thomas JEFFERSON and the WASHINGTON MONUMENT. (See also NEOCLASSICISM.)

**GREELEY, Horace** (1811–1872), US journalist and reformer, founder and editor of the popular New York *Tribune* (1841). One of the most influential figures of the pre-Civil War period, he endorsed abolitionism, helped found the Republican Party and was instrumental in the candidature and election of Lincoln. However, his popularity was diminished during and after the Civil War by his confused attitude towards the South, and by his pleas for total amnesty for the Confederacy. He was defeated for the presidency in 1872.

**GREEN, Thomas Hill** (1836–1882) English idealist philosopher at Oxford who was the leading critic of the empiricis philosophies of J. S. MILL and H. SPENCER in mid-Victorian England. His influence long survived his death, declining only with the resurgence of the empirical approach in the 20th century.

**GREEN, William** (1873–1952), American labor leader. A union official from an early age, he served as president of the AMERICAN FEDERATION OF LABOR (1924–52).

**GREENBACK PARTY,** US political group active between 1876 and 1884. Founded largely by farmers, its main aim was to expand the circulation of GREENBACK currency to bring about inflation, and thus end the depressed agricultural prices and make debts easier to pay. In 1878 the party sent 14 congressmen to Washington but it rapidly declined in the 1880s. Many of the party's supporters and leaders turned to POPULISM in the 1890s.

**GREENBERG, Hank,** (1911–    ), American League baseball batting champion. He played 15 seasons at first base with the Detroit Tigers (1933–47), four times leading the league in home runs and runs batted in. He was elected to the Baseball Hall of Fame in 1956.

**GREENE, Graham** (1904–    ), British novelist, best known for the works he defined as "entertainments," such as *The Third Man* (1950) and *Our Man in Havana* (1958). His more serious work is influenced by Roman Catholicism, expressing the need for faith and the possibility of personal salvation, as in *Brighton Rock* (1938), *The*

*Power and the Glory* (1940), *The Heart of the Matter* (1948) and *The End of the Affair* (1951). Greene has also written short stories, several plays and the autobiographical volumes *A Sort of Life* (1971) and *Ways of Escape* (1980).

**GREENE, Nathanael** (1742–1786), American military commander in the REVOLUTIONARY WAR. Washington's second-in-command, he became general of the Southern army in 1780. His strategy at the battles of Guildford Court House, Hobkirk's Hill and Eutaw Springs in 1781 did not bring outright victory, but wore out the British forces.

**GREENFIELD VILLAGE**, in Dearborn, Mich., 15mi W of Detroit, is a collection of about 100 restored homes and workshops of famous Americans. Founded by Henry FORD in 1929 as a tribute to his friend Thomas EDISON, it includes Edison's laboratory complex from Menlo Park, N.J., and the bicycle shop where the WRIGHT BROTHERS planned their first airplane.

**GREENHOUSE EFFECT**, a phenomenon whereby the temperature at the earth's surface is some 18C° warmer than would otherwise be the case. Sunlight radiated at visible and near-ultraviolet wavelengths provides most of the earth's incoming energy. After absorption it is reradiated, but at longer, infrared wavelengths, the earth being much cooler than the sun (see BLACKBODY RADIATION). Although the ATMOSPHERE is transparent to the incoming solar radiation, that reradiated from the earth's surface is strongly absorbed by atmospheric water vapor and carbon dioxide. That absorbed is again reradiated, the majority back toward the surface. The analogy of the atmosphere and glass in a greenhouse is now considered erroneous, but the usage persists.

**GREENLAND**, the world's largest true island, part of the kingdom of DENMARK. It is located mainly N of the Arctic Circle, to the NE of Canada. An ice cap which may reach a depth of over 1mi covers four-fifths of the island; the only habitable areas are two small coastal strips. Vegetation is sparse, but there is a variety of Arctic fauna such as musk ox and caribou. About 90% of the population live on the SW coast, near the capital Godthaab. Greenlanders have in general a blend of ESKIMO and Danish blood, but enjoy a distinct racial identity and have their own language. W Greenland has local government; the country sends two representatives to the Danish parliament. Health services and education are free. Known mineral resources are now largely exhausted and the economy rests on fishing and agriculture.

It is uncertain when Eskimo tribes first arrived from N Canada. VIKINGS, led by ERIC THE RED, established a colony in Greenland in around 982, but the settlers appear to have died out in the 14th century. Greenland was rediscovered in the 16th century; it became a Danish colony in 1815 and a Danish settlement was established in 1894. The island was made an integral part of Denmark in 1953. It was defended by the US during WWII. There is still a US airbase and research station at Thule in the NW.

**GREEN MOUNTAIN BOYS**, organization formed in the Green Mountains of what is now Vt. in the 1760s. Led by Ethan ALLEN, its original purpose was to assault and rob N.Y. state officials and settlers in areas disputed between N.Y. and N.H. In the REVOLUTIONARY WAR the Green Mountain Boys directed their activities against the British, and helped take Crown Point and Fort Ticonderoga.

**GREEN REVOLUTION**, an agricultural trend of recent years which has greatly increased crop production in India, Pakistan and Turkey. It is based on the introduction of new varieties of crops and is dependent on the use of large quantities of PESTICIDES and FERTILIZERS. It was once hoped that the Green Revolution could solve the problem of feeding the world's increasing population, but these hopes have faded in the face of high prices and of secondary ecological effects. (See POLLUTION.)

**GREENWICH OBSERVATORY**, Royal, observatory established in 1675 at Greenwich, England, by Charles II to correct the astronomical tables used by sailors and otherwise to advance the art of NAVIGATION. Its many famous directors, the "astronomers royal" have included J. FLAMSTEED (the first), E. HALLEY and Sir George Airy. The original Greenwich building, now known as Flamsteed House and run as an astronomical museum, was designed by Sir C. WREN. The observatory is presently sited at Herstmonceux, Sussex, where it moved in the late 1940s. The observatory itself is thus no longer sited on the Greenwich meridian, the international zero of longitude.

**GREENWICH VILLAGE**, area between Spring and West 14th Streets in New York City, famous since the 19th century as an "artist's colony." The area's Bohemian atmosphere has made it a popular tourist attraction.

**GREER, Germaine** (1939–    ), Australian feminist author. In *The Female*

*Eunuch* (1970), she charged that society tried to force women into passive, insipid feminine roles that they should reject. In Britain and the US she has taught literature at Sussex and Tulsa universities.

**GREGG, John Robert** (1867–1948), inventor of the Gregg system of shorthand, using the phonetic principle and the forms of ordinary handwriting. Easy to learn, it is now taught in most US schools, and is adopted for use in 20 languages.

**GREGORIAN CHANT.** See PLAINSONG.

**GREGORY,** name of 16 popes. **Saint Gregory I** (c540–604), called Gregory the Great, was pope 590–604. His papacy laid the foundation for the political and moral authority of the medieval papacy. He reorganized the vast papal estates scattered all over Italy, providing an economic foundation for the Church's power. In 596 he sent St. AUGUSTINE to Britain, beginning its conversion to Christianity. His feast day is March 12. **Saint Gregory II** (c669–731, pope 715–731. Held office at a time of increasing conflict between Rome and Byzantium, and eventually excommunicated Patriarch Anastasius of Byzantium. His feast day is Feb. 11. **Saint Gregory III** (d. 741), pope 731–41, continued to be involved in conflicts with Byzantium, excommunicating Byzantine Emperor Leo III. His feast day is Nov. 28. **Saint Gregory VII** (c1025–1085), called Hildebrand, was pope 1073–85. One of the great medieval reform popes; he attacked corruption in the Church, insisted on the celibacy of the clergy and on the sole right of the Church to appoint bishops and abbots. These reforms threatened the power of the German monarchy, leading to disputes and war with Henry IV of Germany. In 1084 Henry seized Rome, forcing Gregory to flee. His feast day is May 25. **Gregory IX** (c1170–1241), pope 1227–41. His papacy was marked by conflict with Holy Roman Emperor Frederick II, leading eventually to war in Italy between Imperial and papal factions. **Gregory XI** (1329–1378), was pope 1370–78. Elected pope in Avignon, he managed to return the papal court to Rome in 1377. **Gregory XIII** (1502–1585), pope from 1572–85, promoted the COUN-TER-REFORMATION through his pledge to execute the decrees of the Council of Trent. A patron of the Jesuits, he is remembered for the calendar reform he sponsored and for his lavish building program, which emptied the papal treasury. He celebrated the massacre of the Huguenots on St. Bartholomew's Day, 1572, with a *Te Deum*. **Gregory XVI** (1765–1846), pope 1831–46, strengthened the papacy, aligning it with

Austria under METTERNICH, with whose help he suppressed a revolt in the Papal States. He opposed the introduction of gas lighting and railways.

**GREGORY, Lady Isabella Augusta** (1852–1932), Irish dramatist and director largely responsible for the production of YEATS's and SYNGE's plays at the famous ABBEY THEATRE in Dublin. Their works have tended to overshadow her own plays, such as *The Rising of the Moon* and *The White Cockade* (1904–08).

**Official name:** Grenada
**Capital:** St. George's
**Area:** 133 sq mi
**Population:** 110,400
**Languages:** English, French-African patois
**Religions:** Roman Catholic, Anglican
**Monetary Unit(s):** 1 East Caribbean dollar = 10 cents

**GRENADA,** is the smallest independent country in the Western Hemisphere.
**Land.** Grenada is the southernmost of the Windward Islands in the West Indies, 90m N of Trinidad. The state consists of the main island, which is mountainous, and of the S group of the GRENADINES. The climate is semitropical.
**People and economy.** Over half of the population are Negroes, about 45% mulattoes, and 1% whites. Exports include nutmeg, cocoa, mace, sugar, cotton, coffee, lime oil and bananas. Tourism is becoming an important source of income, but Grenada is still a very poor country.
**History.** Discovered by COLUMBUS in 1498, Grenada was first colonized by the French but became British in 1762. It achieved internal self-government in 1967 and became fully independent within the Commonwealth in 1974. After a bloodless coup in 1979 a left-wing Revolutionary People's Government was installed.

**GRENADINES,** a group of c600 small islands, part of the WINDWARD ISLANDS in the West Indies, between Grenada and St Vincent. The N group, and the N part of Carriacou (the largest island) belong to St Vincent. The S Group belongs to Grenada.

**GRENFELL, Sir Wilfred Thomas**

(1865–1940), English physician, missionary and author who devoted himself to establishing hospitals, nursing stations and schools in Labrador and Newfoundland. He founded the International Grenfell Association. His books include *Forty Years for Labrador* (1932).

**GRENVILLE, George** (1712–1770), English statesman who tried to impose internal taxation on the American colonies by means of the STAMP ACT, which was a precipitant of the American Revolution. He was prime minister 1763–65.

**GRENVILLE, Sir Richard** (1542–1591), Elizabethan "sea dog." He commanded RALEIGH's first expedition (1585) to colonize Roanoke Island, N.C. When his ship the *Revenge* became isolated from the rest of the fleet in a Brittish attempt (1591) to intercept Spanish treasure ships off the coast of the Azores, Grenville held an entire Spanish fleet in combat for 15 hours before he was mortally wounded and captured.

**GRESHAM'S LAW**, the economic principle (erroneously attributed to Sir Thomas Gresham) that "bad money drives out good." This means that when coins of the same face-value but of different market-value circulate together, the coins of higher market-value will disappear from circulation to be hoarded or used as an open-market commodity.

**GREUZE, Jean-Baptiste** (1725–1805), French painter who started a vogue with his sentimental and moralistic GENRE painting, e.g. *The Village Bride* (1761). He is also known for his popular erotic studies of young girls, such as *The Broken Pitcher* (c1773).

**GREY, Charles, 2nd Earl Grey** (1764–1845), English prime minister responsible for the passage of the REFORM BILL (1832), which extended the franchise to the middle classes. A long-time leader of the liberal Whig party in opposition, he was in office from 1830 to 1834.

**GREY, Zane** (1875–1939), US author of sagas about the American West. His 54 novels, of which *Riders of the Purple Sage* (1912) is the most popular, have sold over 15 million copies.

**GREYHOUND**, hunting dog bred originally for speed, and to hunt by sight rather than scent, and today raced for sport. The family existed in ancient Egypt, and includes many varieties, as for example the SALUKI. Greyhounds have an arch-backed slender body with a narrow waist and long wiry legs. The coat is short and may be various colors. Adults can weigh up to 70lb.

**GREY OF FALLODEN, Edward Grey, Viscount** (1862–1933), British foreign secretary 1905–16 who brought about a conference of the Great Powers to negotiate a settlement of the BALKAN WARS, and attempted similarly to avert WWI after the assassination of Archduke Ferdinand. He was responsible for the Treaty of London that brought Italy into WWI in 1915.

**GRIEG, Edvard Hagerup** (1843–1907), Norwegian composer who based his work on traditional national folk music. He wrote many songs and piano pieces. His best known orchestral works are: the *Piano Concerto* (1869), the *Peer Gynt* suites (1876) and the *Holberg Suite* (1885).

**GRIFFITH, Arthur** (1872–1922), Irish nationalist who founded SINN FEIN, a major force in Ireland's struggle for independence from England. He led the Irish delegation in negotiating the treaty (1921) that established the Irish Free State. He was the first vice-president of the Dáil Éireann and, in 1922, briefly succeeded De Valera as its president.

**GRIFFITH, D. W.** (David Wark Griffith; 1880–1948), US silent film director and producer, often considered the father of modern cinema. His immensely popular *Birth of a Nation* (1915) introduced major principles of film technique. Griffith also pioneered the film "spectacular." Among his other films are *Intolerance* (1916), *Way Down East* (1920) and *Orphans of the Storm* (1922).

**GRILLPARZER, Franz** (1791–1872), Austria's foremost dramatist. His poetic tragedies introduced a new realism to the romantic tradition out of which they grew. His major works include *Hero and Leander* (1831), and *A Dream is Life* (1834).

**GRIMALDI, Joseph** (1779–1837), English clown. Born of a family of pantomimists, he first appeared on stage at age two. His legendary success (1806) in *Mother Goose* established him as one of the comic masters of all time.

**GRIMKÉ, Angelina Emily** (1805–1879), and **Sarah Moore** (1792–1873), US abolitionists and women's rights crusaders. Angelina's *An Appeal to the Christian Women of the South* and Emily's *An Epistle to the Clergy of the Southern States* (both 1836) urged opposition to slavery.

**GRIMM, Jakob** (1785–1863) and **Wilhelm** (1786–1859), German philologists, most famous for their collections of folk tales, notably *Grimm's Fairy Tales* (1812–1815). Jakob's *German Grammar* (1819–37) formulated a linguistic law (Grimm's Law) explaining the systematic sound-changes of consonants in the Germanic languages from their Indo-European roots. In 1838 the brothers began work on the great *German*

Dictionary, completed only in 1960.

**GRIMMELSHAUSEN, Hans Jakob Christoffel von** (1625–1676), German novelist whose picaresque romance *Simplicissimus* (1669), set in the Thirty Years' War, ranks as the great 17th-century German novel.

**GRIS, Juan** (1887–1927), Spanish cubist painter, born José Victoriano González. A follower of PICASSO, he developed the style known as Synthetic CUBISM, which he applied to still lifes in increasingly free compositions.

**GRIVAS, Giorgios** (1898–1974), Greek-Cypriot leader of the guerrilla army known as EOKA, which fought (1955–59) to end British rule in Cyprus. Favoring union with Greece (ENOSIS), he actively opposed President MAKARIOS.

**GRIZZLY BEAR,** *Ursus arctos horribilis,* one of the largest of the North American brown bears. The name refers to the grizzled coat rather than to the beast's temper, but despite this the grizzly has more or less been exterminated in the US. Though classed with the CARNIVORA, the grizzly is largely vegetarian and rarely eats flesh. An imposing, even terrifying, animal, the grizzly plays a big role in the legends of the North American pioneers.

**GROFÉ, Ferde** (1892–1972), US composer and pianist. His best-known works are the *Mississippi Suite* (1924) and the *Grand Canyon Suite* (1931) and the orchestration of George GERSHWIN'S *Rhapsody in Blue* (1924).

**GROMYKO, Andrei Andreyevich** (1909–      ), Soviet diplomat. In a rapid rise after Stalin's purges, he became ambassador to the US in WWII and UN representative of the USSR after the war. Named foreign minister in 1957, he held that post for more than 20 years during periods of cold war, disarmament talks, détente and incidents of Soviet military interventions in several countries.

**GROPIUS, Walter** (1883–1969), German-American architect and teacher who originated the profoundly influential BAUHAUS style, characterized by a marriage of form and function, and the use of modern materials (especially glass). His designs include the Bauhaus in Dessau (1926) and (in collaboration) the Pan Am Building in New York.

**GROPPER, William** (1897–1977), US satirical cartoonist and painter whose theme was social and economic injustice. In the 1930s his expressionist paintings won widespread recognition. He also painted murals in important public buildings.

**GROSSETESTE, Robert** (c1168–1253), English scholar and prelate whose teaching and writings turned Oxford into a major institution of learning and helped lay the basis for medieval SCHOLASTICISM. Grosseteste translated and commented on Aristotle and wrote scientific works on mathematics, physics, and astronomy. Bishop of Lincoln from 1235, he vigorously defended the rights of the Church against the monarchy and chastised his superiors in Rome for corruption.

**GROSS NATIONAL PRODUCT (GNP),** the total value of goods and services produced by a national economy before any deduction has been made for depreciation (the *net national product*). The annual growth of the GNP is often taken as an indicator of the state of a country's economy, but its significance is limited because it does not take inflation into account. Its chief purpose is to indicate a nation's comparative national wealth.

**GROSZ, George** (1893–1959), German-American satirical artist. He was an early member of the DADA movement. His caricatures, especially those attacking corruption and militarism in post-WWI Germany, are among the most persuasive expressions of misanthropy in the 20th century. He moved to the US in 1933.

**GROTIUS, Hugo** (1583–1645), Dutch jurist, considered the father of international law. In 1619 he was condemned to life imprisonment for his political activity, but he escaped to Paris. There he wrote *On the Law of War and Peace* (1625). This was a study of all the laws of mankind with an emphasis on rules of conduct applying to states, nations and individuals.

**GROUNDHOG,** a familiar North American member of the ground squirrels popularly referred to as the WOODCHUCK.

**GROUNDHOG DAY,** in US tradition Feb. 2. On this day, according to legend, the groundhog emerges from hibernation. If he does not see his shadow when he first pokes his head out of the hole then spring has come. If he does, he is supposed to jump back in fright and sleep for six more weeks and spring is delayed until he awakens again.

**GROUNDNUT.** See PEANUT.

**GROUNDWATER,** water accumulated beneath the earth's surface in the pores of rocks, spaces, cracks, etc. Most underground water is *meteoric* and originates as precipitation that sinks into soil and rocks. Permeable, water-bearing rocks are AQUIFERS; rocks with pores small enough to inhibit the flow of water through them are aquicludes. Build-up of groundwater pressure beneath an aquiclude makes possible construction of an ARTESIAN WELL

The uppermost level of groundwater saturation is the water table. (See also PERMAFROST; SPRING; WELL.)

**GROUP,** a set of algebraic elements in which there is an operation * such that: (1) for all elements *a*, *b*, in the set, * is associative (see ALGEBRA) and *a*b* is a member of the set; (2) there is an identity element *e* defined by *a*e=a* for every element *a* of the set; (3) every element *a* has an inverse $a^{-1}$, also a member of the set, where *a*a* 03$^{W1}$=e*. If *a*b=b*a* for every *a* and *b*, the group is said to be commutative, or abelian. Groups are important in pure and applied mathematics partly because many sorts of operations, for example all the rotations of space or all the ways of rearranging a set of objects, form groups. See SYMMETRY; ALGEBRA, ABSTRACT.

**GROUP,** in psychology and sociology, a collection of individuals that can be regarded as a single unit. The behavior of a group (usually a social unit) or an individual acting in response to his membership of the group is termed **group behavior.** The study of group behavior and group consciousness is termed **group psychology** or **social psychology:** important factors include the presence of an exterior common enemy, and identification of the individual with not only the group but also another individual within it regarded as leader. An application of this to social psychology is **group dynamics,** whose chief proponent was LEWIN. Key concepts include cohesiveness (the field of forces binding each member to the group), and communication between members, the nature and extent of which determines the group's structures, hierarchy and cohesiveness. **Group therapy** is a technique of PSYCHOANALYSIS in which several patients are treated by an analyst simultaneously, with the aim that individuals within the group will assist each other in the treatment; recent amateur applications have tended to bring the technique into popular disrepute. The term "group" is also used in GESTALT PSYCHOLOGY to describe a pattern of PERCEPTIONS. Found in primitive societies (see PRIMITIVE MAN) and occasionally more advanced ones is **group marriage,** where a number of individuals of each sex marry in common.

**GROUP THEATER,** New York City theatrical organization that from 1929–41 produced new plays, largely on contemporary social themes. It laid great emphasis on the STANISLAVSKI method in acting, and was a revitalizing influence on US theater, presenting such plays as Clifford ODETS' *Golden Boy* for the first time.

**GROUSE,** a family (Tetraonidae) of game birds usually brown, gray or black in plumage. They are ground birds living on open moorland or heath, and are well-camouflaged. Three species moult into a white or parti-colored winter plumage for camouflage in snow. Grouse feed largely on plant material—shoots, buds and fruits—but will also eat insects. In many species males perform elaborate courtship displays at established display grounds, or "leks." These lek species, and many others, are polygamous.

**GROVE, Lefty** (1900–1975), US baseball player. Born Robert Moses Grove, he got his nickname from his left-handed pitching. He played with the Philadelphia Athletics 1925–33 and the Boston Red Sox 1934–41, totaling 300 victories. He was elected to the Baseball Hall of Fame in 1947.

**GROVES, Leslie Richard** (1896–1970), US army officer who headed the MANHATTAN PROJECT to develop the atomic bomb, and was responsible for the vast construction program involved. Before the war he supervised all US military construction, including the building of the PENTAGON.

**GROWTH,** the increase in the size of an organism, reflecting either an increase in the number of its CELLS, or one in its protoplasmic material, or both. Cell number and protoplasmic content do not always increase together; cell division can occur without any increase in PROTOPLASM giving a larger number of smaller cells. Alternatively, protoplasm can be synthesized with no cell division so that the cells become larger. Any increase in protoplasm requires the synthesis of cell components such as nuclei, mitochondria, thousands of enzymes, and cell membrane. These require the synthesis of macromolecules such as PROTEINS, NUCLEIC ACIDS and polysaccharides from AMINO ACIDS, SUGARS and fatty acids. These subunits must be synthesized from still simpler substances or obtained from the environment. **Growth curves,** which plot time against growth (such as the number of cells in a bacterial culture, the number of human beings on earth, the size or weight of a plant seedling, an animal or an organ of an animal) all have a characteristic S-shape. This curve is divided into three parts: the lag phase, during which cells prepare for growth; the exponential phase when actual growth occurs, and the stationary phase when growth ceases. The time any particular cell or group of cells remains in any phase depends on their type and the particular condition prevailing. The *lag phase* represents a period of rapid growth of protoplasm so that the cells become larger without any increase in their number. The duration of the lag phase depends on the resynthesis of the enzyme systems required for growth and the availability of the necessary raw materials. Basically each original cell must obtain sufficient components to form two new cells. During the *exponential phase*, each cell gives rise to two cells, the two to four and so on, so that the number of cells after $n$ generations is $2^n$. The generation or doubling time for any particular cell is constant throughout the exponential phase. The time for organisms to double their mass ranges from 20 min for some bacteria to 180 days for a human being at birth. If exponential growth were unlimited, one bacterial cell in 24 hours would give rise to some 4,000 tonnes of bacteria. However, the exponential growth usually ceases (giving the *stationary phase*) either because of lack of an essential nutrient or because waste products produced by the cells pollute the environment. Again, in higher animals population growth is often slowed by parasite-carried epidemics.

The S-type growth pattern can be readily seen in unicellular organisms. Although growth in organisms containing different types of cells obeys the same basic rules, the relationships of the different types of cells complicate the pattern. But although all parts of a multicellular organism do not grow at the same rate or stop growing at the same time, the overall growth curve is still S-shaped.

**GRÜNEWALD, Mathias** (c1475–1528), German painter who, with his contemporary DÜRER, is considered one of the two great masters of the German Renaissance. His most characteristic theme is the crucifixion, a subject in which he combined beauty and delicacy of style with a savage and harrowing realism. His masterpiece is the altarpiece for St. Anthony's monastery at Isenheim, with subjects such as the *Resurrection* and the *Temptation of St. Anthony* (1513–15).

**GUADALCANAL,** largest of the SOLOMON ISLANDS in the S Pacific. Volcanic in nature, it supports extensive coconut plantations which are the economic mainstay; copra and timber are the main exports. The island was the scene of a decisive battle of WWII in 1943, when it was recaptured by Allied troops from the Japanese. Pop 46,619.

**GUADALUPE HIDALGO, Treaty of,** was signed by the US and Mexico at this Mexican town in 1848 to end the Mexican War. Mexico agreed to cede what are now Tex., Cal., Utah., Nev., and parts of N.M., Ariz., Col., and Wyo. to the US in return for $15 million and other benefits. The treaty guaranteed Mexicans' land rights, but these were not respected.

**GUADALUPE MOUNTAINS NATIONAL PARK,** covers 128.6sq mi of Tex. E of El Paso. An area of geological interest, particularly for its limestone formations, it contains prehistoric Indian ruins and a wide variety of wildlife; established 1966.

**GUADELOUPE,** overseas department of France composed of two islands in the E Caribbean Sea, Grande-Terre and Basse-Terre. With some smaller islands they cover a total area of 687sq mi. A French settlement since 1635, it was captured by the British in the Seven Years' War and confirmed as French in 1815; the largely Negro population speaks a French patois. Bananas, coffee, cacao and vanilla are produced. Pop 330,160.

**GUAM,** largest and southernmost of the MARIANA ISLANDS, in the Pacific Ocean 6,000mi W of San Francisco. A US territory since 1898 and an important US naval and air base, Guam was captured by the Japanese in 1941, and was recaptured by the US in 1944.

**GUANTÁNAMO BAY,** large natural harbor in Cuba, site of a US naval base strategically placed with access to the Caribbean and Panama. It has been leased to the US since 1903 but since 1960 has been isolated and harassed by the hostile Castro regime.

**GUARANI INDIANS,** group of primitive South American tribes, linked by language, who once lived in an area now covered by parts of Paraguay, Brazil and Argentina. Conquered by Spain in the 16th century, their numbers have been reduced by disease. Their language, however, is now the second language of Paraguay.

**GUARDI, Francesco** (1712–1793), Venetian landscape, architectural and figure painter, noted for his romantic, visionary views of Venice executed with a high degree of individualism and ellipticism in a style inspired by CANALETTO. His characteristic work, typified by his *Feast of the Ascension at Venice* (c1763), was done in later life.

**GUARINI, Guarino** (1624–1683), influential Italian architect, one of the masters of the Baroque. Most of his major works were churches and palaces in Turin, such as San Lorenzo, the Capella della Sacra Sindone and the Palazzo Carignano.

**GUARNERI,** family of violin makers of Cremona in Italy. Andrea (c1626–1698) with STRADIVARI an apprentice of AMATI founded the dynasty. His sons Giuseppe (1666–1739?) and Pietro Giovanni (1655–c1740), and Pietro (1695–c1765), a grandson, continued the trade, but the most renowned member of the family was the eccentric and experimental **Giuseppe "del Gesù'** (c1687–1745).

**Official name:** Republic of Guatemala
**Capital:** Guatemala City
**Area:** 42,042sq mi
**Population:** 7,262,400
**Languages:** Spanish; Maya-Quiché dialects
**Religions:** Roman Catholic
**Monetary unit(s):** 1 Quetzal=100 centavos
**GUATEMALA,** northernmost republic in Central America.

**Land.** Guatemala is a mountainous country composed largely of volcanic highland at altitudes of 2,000–6,000ft, although mountain peaks such as Mount Tajumulco (13,845ft) rise much higher. The E and W highlands are not very fertile, lacking the rich volcanic soils of the coast or the cooler climate and high rainfall of the N central area. To the N is the Petén, a rain forest plateau with areas of savanna covering a third of the country. The climate varies from the tropical Petén and coastal areas to the subtropical and temperate highlands.

**People.** The native Indians moved into the highland areas as Spanish colonizers occupied the valleys, and many of them still live there. Today they account for over 54% of the population, only 4% being white; the remainder are mestizos (*Ladinos*).

The Indians maintain a traditional family-oriented village culture, speaking mainly their own dialects.

**Economy.** Coffee plantations account for almost half the nation's revenues. Cotton is also an important product, having superseded banana cultivation since the 1930s. Other exports are tobacco, vegetables, fruit and beef. Guatemala has only limited mineral resources: nickel, chromate, silver, lead and zinc are produced. Manufacturing industries are mainly devoted to the processing of local produce, but they are steadily expanding. Although Guatemala joined the Central American Common Market in 1961, the US remains its principal trading partner, taking over 30% of its exports and providing about 40% of its imports.

**History.** The Indian MAYAS ruled the area from about 300 AD, but their civilization declined and they were unable to offer much resistance to the invading Spaniards under ALVARADO in 1524. With the breakup of the Spanish New World, Guatemala became independent in 1821, and subsequently was a member of the Central American Federation (1824–39). The post-WWII governments, especially under Jacobo Arbenz Guzmán, had socialist tendencies. After a military coup in 1954 Guatemala has been plagued by left- and right-wing terrorism and political assassinations. An earthquake in 1976 caused heavy casualties and left about 1 million people homeless.

**GUATEMALA CITY,** capital of Guatemala and largest city in Central America, the country's political, cultural and commercial hub. In the center of an agricultural region, it has a wide range of light industries. Founded in 1776, the city was razed by earthquakes 1917–18 and has been largely rebuilt. Pop 700,504.

**GUDERIAN, Heinz** (1888–1954), German army officer whose tank warfare and *blitzkrieg* techniques were successful in the German invasion of Poland (1939) and of France (1940).

**GUELPHS AND GHIBELLINES,** two opposing political factions in 13th- and 14th-century Italy. The Guelphs supported the pope, while the Ghibellines backed imperial Germany. Both originated in 12th century Germany, in opposition over territories of the Holy Roman Empire. After 1268, the rivalries became purely political between cities and families. In Florence the ruling Guelphs split into rival groups of Whites and Blacks.

**GUERICKE, Otto von** (1602–1686), German physicist credited with inventing the vacuum pump. His best-known experiment was with the Magdeburg hemispheres (1654): he evacuated a hollow sphere composed of two halves placed together, and showed that two 8-horse teams were insufficient to separate the halves. (See PUMPS.) He is also credited with inventing the first electric GENERATOR.

**GUERNICA,** town in N Spain in the Basque province, destroyed by bombing in 1937 by German planes fighting for FRANCO in the Spanish Civil War. PICASSO's picture commemorating the event is in the Prado in Madrid. Pop 14,678.

**GUERRILLA WARFARE,** is waged by irregular forces in generally small-scale operations, often in enemy-held territory. The term (Spanish: little war) originally applied to the tactics of Spanish–

Portuguese irregulars in the Napoleonic Wars. Traditional guerrilla warfare is generally waged against larger and better-equipped conventional forces; it is usually part of a wider strategy, as for example the activities of the resistance movements in Nazi-occupied Europe, which were part of overall Allied strategy. Guerrilla fighters must avoid open battle as much as possible, exploiting the mobility gained from lack of equipment and supply lines. To compensate for these they must have a wide degree of popular support. They must rely on hit-and-run tactics, ambush, sabotage and the psychological effects of unpredictable attack.

Communist efforts in Cuba and Angola attested to the effects of inciting and supporting guerrilla campaigns far from home at relatively low cost. Recent years have seen the development of the "urban guerrilla," whose desire is not to expel an invader by a general insurrection but to so disorganize the fabric of society that a faction can seize power without relying on popular support. To this end ambush, hijacking and bombing, directed both at specific targets and simply at the populace at large, have become increasingly common. Such revolutionary guerrilla warfare tends to be offensive rather than defensive. It is ideological rather than patriotic in nature. More centralized than conventional guerrilla fighting, it is easier to suppress in the earlier stages.

With the advent of the nuclear age, guerrilla warfare is perceived to have distinct advantages. No longer relegated to the underdog, it avoids large-scale confrontations which might lead to escalation, is less expensive for aggressors than all-out war and can be easier to disclaim. In an era of nuclear stalemate, it is likely to grow increasingly important.

**GUEVARA, Che** (Ernesto Guevara de la Serna; 1928–1967), Argentinian-born Cuban communist revolutionary and guerrilla leader, who helped organize CASTRO'S coup in 1959. After serving as president of the Cuban national bank and minister of industry, he went to Bolivia in 1966 to direct the guerrilla movement there. He was captured by the Bolivian army and executed.

**GUGGENHEIM,** name of a family of US industrialists and philanthropists. **Meyer** (1828–1905), emigrated to Philadelphia from Switzerland in 1847 and set up a business importing Swiss lace. Aided by his seven sons he later established large smelting and refining plants. One son, **Daniel** (1856–1930) extended the concern

internationally and set up an aeronautics research foundation. Another son, **Simon** (1867–1941), was a senator for Col. and established a memorial foundation awarding fellowships to artists and scholars. The sixth son **Solomon Robert** (1861–1949), founded the GUGGENHEIM MUSEUM.

**GUGGENHEIM, Peggy** (1898–1979), US art collector who founded Guggenheim Jeune, the famous Parisian gallery of contemporary art, and the equally renowned Art of This Century gallery in New York. Her vast personal art collection is at her palazzo in Venice.

**GUGGENHEIM MUSEUM,** museum of modern art in New York. It was set up in 1939 and in 1959 moved to the building designed by Frank Lloyd WRIGHT which centers around a spiral ramp gallery.

**GUIANA, British.** See GUYANA.

**GUIANA, Dutch.** See SURINAM.

**GUIANA, French.** See FRENCH GUIANA.

**GUIDE DOG.** See SEEING-EYE DOG.

**GUIDO D'AREZZO** (c990–1050), Italian musical theorist and monk whose great work *Micrologus* (c1025) reformed musical notation. He introduced a four-line staff so that certainty of pitch in notation was established.

**GUILD,** association of merchants or craftsmen in the same trade or craft to protect the interests of its members. Guilds had both economic and social purposes and flourished in Europe in the Middle Ages. Merchant guilds were often very powerful, controlling trade in one area, or in the case of the HANSEATIC LEAGUE much of N Europe. The guilds of individual craftsmen such as goldsmiths, weavers or shoemakers, regulated wages, quality of production and working conditions for APPRENTICES. Wealthy guilds built extensive headquarters for themselves, some of which still stand. The guild system declined from the 16th century because of changing trade and work conditions.

**GUILD SOCIALISM,** the English version of SYNDICALISM, calling for the organization of industry in independent workercontrolled guilds. In the early 20th century, guild socialists, led by S. G. Hobson and G. D. H. Cole, rejected the violent general strike in favor of parliamentary methods and, although the guilds themselves disappeared, strongly influenced the growth of the modern British LABOUR PARTY.

**GUILLEMIN, Roger** (1924–    ), French-born US medical researcher who discovered and synthesized hormones produced by the HYPOTHALAMUS which govern the action of the pituitary gland. For his research, which revolutionized the study of brain control over body chemistry, he shared the 1977 Nobel Prize in Physiology or Medicine.

**GUILLOTINE,** French method of beheading; an oblique blade between two upright posts falls, when a supporting cord is released, onto the victim's neck below. It came into use during the French Revolution in response to J. I. Guillotin's call for a more humane form of execution. Used for the last time in France in 1971, it was abolished with the elimination of the nation's death penalty in 1981.

**GUIMARD, Hector** (1867–1942), French ART NOUVEAU architect and designer. He is famous for the Castel Béranger (1894–98), an apartment building in Paris, and the Paris métro station's decorative cast-iron gates (c1900).

**GUINAN, Texas** (Mary Louise Guinan; d. 1933), US entertainer and nightclub owner who reigned as Broadway's "Queen of the Nightclubs" during the Prohibition era of the 1920s. She was known for greeting patrons with the phrase, "Hello Sucker."

**Official name:** Republic of Guinea
**Capital:** Conakry
**Area:** 95,000sq mi
**Population:** c5,422,000
**Languages:** French; Soussou; Manika
**Religions:** Muslim; Animist; Christian
**Monetary unit(s):** 1 Sily = 100 corilles
**GUINEA,** West African republic, between Guinea-Bissau and Sierra Leone, and with frontiers with Senegal, Mali, Ivory Coast and Liberia.
**Land.** It is a tropical country. The Atlantic coastline has many estuaries and mangrove swamps, which have been reclaimed for the cultivation of rice and bananas. Behind the narrow coastal plain is the high and extensive Fouta Djallon plateau, the slopes of which are densely forested. Mt Nimba in the SE is the highest peak (5,800ft). The annual rainfall is especially heavy in the coastal region, the average being 169in. The climate and vegetation support a richly varied wildlife.
**People and Economy.** The population is made up of about 16 ethnic groups, notably the Fulani, Malinke, Soussou and Kissi. The majority of Guineans are Muslims, but many are animist. Most of the people live in villages. Although most Guineans are illiterate, free education is having a strong impact. Besides the capital Conakry, the principal towns are Kankan and Kindia. Agriculture is central to the country's economy, engaging some 85% of the work force and accounting for about 30% of the gross domestic product. Traditional export crops, including palm kernels, coffee, pineapple and bananas, have been declining in recent years, and aluminum, bauxite, iron ore and diamonds play an increasingly important role in the economy. Manufacturing is negligible. Large herds of small Ndama cattle are bred on the plateau.

**History.** Portuguese exploration began in the 15th century and by the 17th there was extensive trade with Europe. Guinea became independent in 1958, whereupon France stopped supplying aid, which was subsequently accepted from both communist and non-communist countries. Politics are dominated by the president and there is only one political party, the Democratic Party of Guinea. Several unsuccessful attempts have been made to overthrow the regime, and many Guineans are in exile.

**Official name:** Republic of Guinea-Bissau
**Capital:** Bissau
**Area:** 13,948sq mi
**Population:** 777,200
**Languages:** Cape Verde-Guinean Crioulo; Portuguese
**Religions:** Animist, Muslim
**Monetary unit(s):** 1 Guinea peso = 100 centavos
**GUINEA-BISSAU** (formerly Portuguese Guinea), a republic in W Africa, is wedged between Senegal to the N and the Republic of Guinea to the E and S, with various coastal islands and an offshore archipelago in the Atlantic.
**Land.** Low-lying and crossed by many rivers, the mainland consists of coastal swamps, a heavily forested central plain, and savanna grazing land to the E. The climate is hot and humid, with heavy rains

May–Oct.

**People and Economy.** Africans form 98% of the population; most are engaged in agriculture, on which the economy is based. The chief export is peanuts; the main food crop, rice. Seafood is an increasingly important export. Industry is limited, but expanding. The largest town and main port is Bissau, the capital.

**History.** First visited by the Portuguese in 1446–47, the country became a Portuguese colony and a center of the slave trade. It became an overseas province of Portugal in 1951, and in 1963 nationalists started a war of independence which continued for 10 years. The independence of Guinea-Bissau was proclaimed in 1973 and recognized by Portugal in 1974. Guinea-Bissau and Cape Verde have close ties.

**GUINEA PIG,** *Cavia porcellus,* a domestic pet related to the CAVIES of South America. The plump body, absence of tail and extremely short legs are quite distinctive.

**GUINNESS, Sir Alec** (1914–    ), English stage and screen actor, remarkable for his versatility in both comic and serious roles. His films include *Kind Hearts and Coronets* (1950) and *The Bridge on the River Kwai* (1957), for which he won an Academy Award.

**GUITAR,** stringed musical instrument, related to the lute, played by plucking. Its curved sides form a waisted shape. The Moors introduced the guitar into Spain about the 13th century, and the Spanish guitar with five strings evolved in the 1500s, becoming the Spanish national musical instrument. The modern guitar has six, sometimes metal, strings.

**GUITRY, Sacha** (1885–1957), Russian-born French actor, playwright and film producer. His prolific output included 130 comedies. His best-known films are *The Comedian* (1921) and *The Cheat* (1935).

**GUJARATI,** INDO-ARYAN LANGUAGE of the Indian states of Gujarat and Maharashtra. Spoken by around 20,000,000 people, it is written in a form of Devanāgái script.

**GULBENKIAN, Calouste Sarkis** (1869–1955), Turkish-born British financier, industrialist and philanthropist. One of the richest men of the 20th century, he helped establish, 1911, the Turkish Petroleum Company (later called the Iraq Petroleum Company), which was the first to exploit the Iraqi oil fields. He also owned one of the world's greatest art collections.

**GULF INTRACOASTAL WATERWAY,** system of navigable waterways, both natural and man-made, running about 1,100mi along the Gulf of Mexico from Apalachee Bay, Fla., to Brownsville, Tex.

**GULF OF CALIFORNIA,** 700mi arm of the Pacific Ocean separating Baja (Lower) California, Mexico, from the Mexican states of Sonora and Sinaloa to the E.

**GULF OF MEXICO,** off the SE coast of North America between the US and Mexico, and bounded to the E by Cuba. It is linked to the Atlantic by the Strait of Florida and to the Caribbean by the Strait of Yucatan. Extensive petroleum deposits are worked offshore.

**GULF OF SAINT LAWRENCE,** gulf on the Atlantic coast of Canada, extending 250mi from Newfoundland across the mouth of the St. Lawrence R to New Brunswick and Nova Scotia. Containing many islands, it is linked to the Atlantic by the Strait of Belle Isle and by the Cabot and Canso Straits.

**GULF OF TONKIN RESOLUTION,** put before the US Congress on Aug. 4, 1964 by President Lyndon B. JOHNSON, following unprovoked attacks by North Vietnamese vessels on US destroyers in the Gulf. The resolution declared the maintenance of peace in SE Asia to be essential to US interests and therefore gave the president power to take measures necessary to repel other attacks and prevent aggression. The resolution was later seen as the beginning of full-scale US involvement in the VIETNAM WAR and was attacked for giving excessive power to the president. In July 1970 the Senate voted to revoke its authorizations.

**GULLAH,** descendants of freed slaves who settled in the coastal districts of S.C. and Ga. The name is also used for their Creole dialect, a blend of various African languages and English; it resembles neither very closely.

**GULLS,** strong-flying and swimming seabirds forming the subfamily Larinae. The plumage is basically white with darker wings and back. Some species develop a dark hood in the breeding plumage. There are altogether some 40 species of gulls and the group is widespread. Gulls are a very successful and adaptable group and many species have now become common inland as scavengers on refuse, or on plowed land.

**GUMBO.** See OKRA.

**GUM TREES.** See EUCALYPTUS.

**GUN CONTROL.** Guns are used to kill some 10,000 Americans annually, and since the assassination of President John F. Kennedy in 1963 by gunshot, there have been repeated calls at all levels of government for controls over gun sales. But although such controls are approved by the majority of citizens, they have been vigorously and effectively opposed by the NATIONAL RIFLE ASSOCIATION. In the Crime

Control Act of 1968 are some useful provisions, including limits on mail-order gun sales and required licensing of gun dealers; also, N.Y. and Mass. have strong gun control laws. In general, though, legislation and enforcement have been feeble nationwide. There are now estimated to be at least 50 million handguns in the US; homicide by shooting continues to rise, and murders and gun assaults on public figures have become commonplace, with the victims including Martin Luther King, Jr. (d 1968), Robert F. Kennedy (d 1968), George Wallace (shot and paralyzed, 1972), John Lennon (d 1980) and Ronald Reagan (shot, 1981).

**GUNPOWDER, or black powder,** a low EXPLOSIVE, the only one known from its discovery in the West in the 13th century until the mid-19th century. It consists of about 75% POTASSIUM (or SODIUM) nitrate, 10% SULFUR and 15% CHARCOAL; it is readily ignited and burns very rapidly. Gunpowder was used in fireworks in 10th-century China, as a propellant for firearms from the 14th century in Europe and for blasting since the late 17th century. It is now used mainly as an igniter, in fuses and in fireworks.

**GUNPOWDER PLOT,** conspiracy of a group of English Roman Catholics led by Robert Catesby to blow up King James I, his family and government in the Houses of Parliament on Nov. 5, 1605. Guy FAWKES was arrested while setting charges under the Houses of Parliament and under torture disclosed the names of the conspirators, who were executed. In England Nov. 5 is celebrated with bonfires, fireworks and the burning of effigies.

**GUNTHER, John** (1901–1970), US journalist and author. His background as a foreign correspondent enabled him to write the highly successful "Inside" books, the first being *Inside Europe* (1936); in describing various countries these blended personal observation with historical and economic analysis to provide a vivid picture.

**GUPTA DYNASTY,** N Indian dynasty which ruled c320–550 AD, a period which produced some of the finest Indian art and literature. From a small area in the Ganges valley their power spread out to most of India, and under CHANDRAGUPTA II (385–414) scholarship, law and art reached new heights. The White Hun invasion c450 reduced the Gupta empire to a portion of Bengal.

**GURKHAS,** dominant Hindu race in Nepal, and its ruling dynasty. The name has become attached to the Nepalese soldiers serving in the British army. Gurkha

regiments are famous for their great courage, endurance, discipline and loyalty. The Gurkhas carry the famous *kukhri*, a long knife with a hooked blade.

**GUSTON, Philip** (c1913–    ), Canadian-born US painter, a follower of ABSTRACT EXPRESSIONISM; his *White Painting* series is often reminiscent of MONET.

**GUTENBERG, Johann** (c1400–1468), German printer, usually considered the inventor of PRINTING from separately cast metal types. By 1450 he had a press in Mainz, financed by Johann Fust (c1400–c1466) but in 1455 he handed over the press (and his invention) to Fust in repayment of debts. By now the Gutenberg (or Mazarin) Bible was at least well under way: each page has two columns of 42 lines. Gutenberg possibly founded another press some time later.

**GUTHRIE, Sir (William) Tyrone** (1900–1971), influential British stage director, famous for his experimental approach to traditional works. His Shakespeare productions and his vigorous and realistic opera productions, such as *Peter Grimes* (1946) and *Carmen* (1949 and 1952), set new standards in their time. The establishment in 1963 of the Tyrone Guthrie Theater at Minneapolis, Minn., under his direction, spurred the development of REGIONAL THEATER in the US.

**GUTHRIE, Woody** (Woodrow Wilson Guthrie; 1912–1967), US folksinger whose compositions and guitar style have had enormous influence on modern folk music. He developed the characteristic themes of his "protest" songs as a migrant worker in the 1930s.

**Official name:** Co-operative Republic of Guyana
**Capital:** Georgetown
**Area:** 83,000sq mi
**Population:** 850,000
**Languages:** English, Hindi, Chinese; Portuguese also spoken
**Religions:** Christian, Hindu, Muslim
**Monetary: unit(s):** 1 Guyana dollar=100 cents

**GUYANA,** independent republic on the NE

coast of South America, largest of the three countries in the Guiana region.

**Land.** The sparsely settled interior is largely massive sandstone plateaus, up to 500ft in height, sloping up to the Guiana Highlands in the S. Much of the more densely populated coastal strip, 10–40mi in width, lies below sea level; some of it is reclaimed land. About 85% of the country is tropical rain forest. Heat is constantly around 80°F with average humidity of about 75%; rainfall at the coast is around 90in a year.

**People.** More than 90% of the population lives along the coast. The main ethnic groups are East Indians (descendants of imported labor), 55%, and Negroes, 36%; there are also about 30,000 Amerindians. Many of the professional classes are European or Chinese. Education is compulsory between 6 and 14, and literacy is around 85%.

**Economy** rests on agriculture, especially sugarcane grown on plantations near the coast. Rice is the other major crop. Important mineral reserves include bauxite (Guyana's chief export), diamonds and manganese. Hardwood from the enormous forests is also becoming an important resource.

**History.** Guyana's original inhabitants were CARIB and ARAWAK Indians. The Dutch were the first to colonize the area, setting up POLDERS to reclaim land and importing Negro slaves to cultivate sugar and tobacco. The region became British in 1815 and was subsequently known as British Guiana. East Indian labor was imported in the 19th century. Amid political, economic and racial unrest Guyana achieved internal self-rule in 1961 and full independence in 1966. The country has long-standing border disputes with Venezuela and Suriname. In 1979, a mass suicide-execution of 911 members of Rev. Jim Jones's People's Temple cult took place in the Guyana jungle.

**GWYN, Nell** (1650–1687), English actress, favorite mistress of Charles II from 1669. Daughter of a brothel-keeper, she became an orange-seller in the King's theater, and 1666–69 its most popular actress. She bore Charles two sons.

**GYMNASTICS,** a system of exercise designed not only to maintain and improve the physique, but also as a sport. In ancient Greece gymnastics were important in education, including track and field athletics and training for boxing and wrestling. Competitive gymnastics are a series of exercises on set pieces of apparatus: parallel bars, horizontal bar, side and vaulting horses, beam and asymmetric bars.

The US system, derived from the German, is designed to assist physical growth; the Swedish system aims at rectifying posture and weak muscles; and the Danish system seeks general fitness and endurance.

**GYMNOSPERMS,** the smaller of the two main classes of seed-bearing plants, the other being the ANGIOSPERMS. Gymnosperms are characterized by having naked seeds usually formed on open scales produced in cones. All are perennial plants and most are EVERGREEN. There are several orders, the main ones being the Cycadales, the CYCADS or sago palms; the Coniferales, including PINE, LARCH, FIR and REDWOOD; the Ginkgoales, the GINKGO; and the Gnetales, tropical shrubs and woody vines.

**GYNECOLOGY,** branch of MEDICINE and SURGERY, specializing in diseases of women, specifically disorders of female reproductive tract; often linked with OBSTETRICS. CONTRACEPTION, ABORTION, STERILIZATION, infertility and abnormalities of MENSTRUATION are the commonest problems. The early recognition and treatment of CANCER of the WOMB cervix after PAPANICOLAOU smears have become important. Other TUMORS of womb or ovaries, benign or malignant, and disorders of genital tract or closely related BLADDER following PREGNANCY, commonly require gynecological surgery. Dilatation of the cervix and curettage of womb endometrium (D and C) is used frequently for diagnosis and sometimes for treatment of menstrual disorders or postmenopausal bleeding. HYSTERECTOMY or removal of the womb is the commonest major operation of gynecologists.

**GYPSIES,** nomadic people of Europe, Asia and North America. They are believed to have originated in India; their language, ROMANY, is related to Sanskrit and Prakrit. The gypsies probably began their westward migration about 1000 AD. By the 15th century they had penetrated the Balkans, Egypt and North Africa. In the 16th century they were to be found throughout Europe. Often known as thieves and tricksters, they have met with little toleration. In WWII many European gypsies were executed by the Nazis. There is a strong gypsy tradition of folklore, legend and song, and this, combined with the independence of their lives, has inspired the romantic imagination of many musicians, artists and writers.

**GYPSY MOTH,** *Porthetria dispar*, a pretty moth originating in Europe and later introduced to North America. Here, in the absence of natural enemies, it has become a serious pest: the caterpillars feed on the leaves of deciduous trees, particularly fruit trees, and their occasional mass outbreaks can lead to complete defoliation.

**GYROCOMPASS,** a continuously-driven GYROSCOPE which acts as a COMPASS. It is unaffected by magnetic variations and is used for steering large ships. As the earth rotates the gyroscope experiences a TORQUE if it is out of the meridian. The resulting tilting is sensed by a gravity sensing system which itself applies a torque to the gyroscope which returns it to the N–S meridian. The sensitivity of such instruments decreases with latitude away from the equator.

**GYROPILOT,** an automatic device for keeping a ship or airplane on a given course using signals from a gyroscopic reference. The marine version operates a ship's rudder by displacement signals from the GYROCOMPASS. In an airplane, the device is usually known as an **automatic pilot** and consists of sensors to detect deviations in direction, pitch and roll, and pass signals via a computer to alter the controls as necessary.

**GYROSCOPE,** a heavy spinning disk mounted so that its axis is free to adopt any orientation. Its special properties depend on the principle of the conservation of angular MOMENTUM. Although the scientific gyroscope was only devised by FOUCAULT in the mid-19th century, the child's traditional spinning top demonstrates the gyroscope principle. The fact that it will stay upright as long as it is spinning fast enough demonstrates the property of **gyroscopic inertia:** the direction of the spin axis resists change. This means that a gyroscope mounted universally, in double gimbals, will maintain the same orientation in space however its support is turned, a property applied in many navigational devices. If a FORCE tends to alter the direction of the spin axis (e.g., the weight of a top tilting sideways), a gyroscope will turn about an axis at right-angles to the force for as long as it is applied; this movement is known as **precession.** Instrument gyroscopes usually consist of a wheel having most of its mass concentrated at its rim to ensure a large moment of inertia - and which is kept spinning in frictionless bearings by an electric motor. Once the wheel is set spinning its response to applied TORQUES can be monitored or used in control servomechanisms.

**GYROSTABILIZER,** a gyroscopic device for stabilizing a ship, airplane or instrument mounting. Originally giant gyroscopes (up to 4m in diameter) were used to counteract roll in ships, but they were found to be too cumbersome. Now fins protruding from the ship's hull are moved hydraulically to oppose roll under the control of signals from small GYROSCOPES that sense roll angle and velocity.

**H** 8th letter of the English alphabet, derived from the Semitic letter *cheth.* Usually a glottal spirant, it is silent in many Romance languages. In thermodynamics it is the symbol for enthalpy.

**HAAKON VII** (1872–1957), king of Norway from 1905. A Danish prince, he was elected constitutional monarch when Norway became independent of Sweden. He resisted the German invasion in 1940; forced to flee to England, he reigned from there until 1945, becoming the much-respected symbol of his country's resistance.

**HAAS, Ernst** (1921–    ), Austrian-born US photographer whose work was chosen by the Museum of Modern Art (1962) for its first exhibition of color photography. He created a cubist style through the use of multiple color exposures.

**HABAKKUK, Book of,** the eighth of the Old Testament MINOR PROPHETS, dated probably late 7th century BC. Nothing is known of Habakkuk himself. The first part explores the problem of God's using the evil Chaldeans to punish Judah, and includes the influential statement, "The righteous shall live by his faith." The final chapter is a psalm.

**HABEAS CORPUS** (Latin: you have the body), in COMMON LAW a writ issued by the judiciary to compel a person held in custody to be brought before a court, so that it may determine whether or not the detention is lawful. Habeas corpus originated in medieval England, becoming a major civil right through the 1679 Habeas Corpus Act. Embodied in the US Constitution, it may not be suspended except in cases of rebellion or invasion. President Lincoln suspended it in 1861, at the onset of the Civil War. The writ may also be used in some non-judicial cases, as by an inmate in a mental hospital.

**HABERMAS, Jürgen** (1929–    ), German philosopher who expanded the scope of "critical theory" first propounded by Marxist scholars at the Frankfurt Institute for Social Research in the 1920s. He was best known for his work on epistemology, communication theory, the legitimation function of science and the theory of capitalist crisis. He taught at the University of Frankfurt and headed the Max Planck Institute.

**HADASSAH,** US Zionist women's organization. Founded in 1912, it supports educational and charitable work in the US and relief and refugee welfare in Israel.

**HADDOCK,** *Melanogrammus aeglefinus*, a cod-like fish found throughout the N Atlantic. Economically among the most important food fishes of countries fishing the North Sea, they live in shoals on sandy bottoms, feeding on shellfish, urchins and small fish. The black spot on the side of the haddock is said to be the thumbprint of St. Peter.

**HADES,** in Greek mythology, the pitiless god of the underworld, ruling with PERSEPHONE his queen over the dead. The term *hades* is used in the Greek Old Testament to render the Hebrew *sheol*, and so in late Judaism and Christianity means the realm of departed spirits. (See also HELL.)

**HADRIAN** (76–138), Publius Aelius Hadrianus, Roman emperor from 117, successor of TRAJAN. He traveled the empire for 12 years, reforming and restoring imperial rule. An able administrator, builder and soldier, he was a talented poet and an admirer of Greek civilization. He was responsible for construction (120–123) of Hadrian's Wall to defend Britain against the Picts. His plan to build a new city at Jerusalem, however, sparked off a Jewish revolt 132–135, which he savagely repressed. His later years were saddened by the death of his favorite, Antinoüs.

**HAGANAH,** (Hebrew: defense) Jewish volunteer militia in Palestine, formed after WWI to protect the Jewish community there. Although outlawed by the British, it was moderate and well-disciplined. It fought alongside the Allies in WWII and against the Arabs in 1947; in 1948 it was made into the Israeli national army.

**HAGGAI, Book of,** the tenth of the Old Testament MINOR PROPHETS, dated 520–519 BC. It consists of four oracles urging the Jews to rebuild the Temple at Jerusalem and attributing their economic plight to their delay in doing so, and prophesying the glories of the Messianic Age.

**HAGIA SOPHIA,** or Santa Sophia, massive cathedral raised at Constantinople (now Istanbul) by JUSTINIAN I; completed in 537, it became a mosque after the Turkish conquest (1453). Now a museum, the domed basilica, richly decorated, is the finest remaining example of Byzantine architecture.

**HAGUE, The** (Dutch's Gravenhage or Den Haag), historic city, seat of government of the Netherlands and capital of South Holland province. It has many ancient buildings and is one of the country's handsomest cities, with many parks and woodland areas. The Binnenhof palace houses the two chambers of the legislature. The economy rests more on administration than on industry. The city is also an educational and cultural center. Pop 456,900.

**HAGUE TRIBUNAL,** an international Permanent Court of Arbitration. Established by the first HAGUE PEACE CONFERENCE (1899), it is now supported by 71 nations, each of which may appoint up to four jurists. The court will supply arbitrators to decide international disputes submitted to them by international agreement. After WWI it was supplemented by the World Court and later the INTERNATIONAL COURT OF JUSTICE.

**HAHN, Otto** (1879–1968), German chemist awarded the 1944 Nobel Prize for Chemistry for his work on nuclear FISSION. With Lise MEITNER he discovered the new element PROTACTINIUM (1918); later they bombarded URANIUM with NEUTRONS, treating the uranium with ordinary barium. Meitner showed that the residue was radioactive BARIUM formed by the splitting (fission) of the uranium nucleus.

**HAIFA,** city in NE Israel, on the Mediterranean, the country's principal port. It existed in the 1st century BC and probably earlier. It is now a flourishing industrial center, especially in the port area; the city's upper region, on Mt Carmel, is largely residential. The population includes Muslim and Christian minorities, and is the world headquarters of the BAHA'I FAITH. Pop 229,000.

**HAIG, Alexander** (1924–   ), US general and secretary of state (1981–   ). After serving in the KOREAN and VIETNAM WARS, he became a deputy to Henry KISSINGER on the National Security Council in 1969. He rose to become chief of staff in the NIXON White House and presided over the final days of the WATERGATE events (1974). He then served as supreme commander of NATO forces in Europe until he retired in 1979. He returned to the US to serve as president of United Technologies Corp., then was appointed secretary of state by President Reagan.

**HAIG, Douglas Haig, 1st Earl** (1861–1928), field-marshal, British commander in WWI. He has been unfairly blamed for the misconduct of the Somme and Ypres campaigns 1916–17. Hampered by the hostility of British premier LLOYD GEORGE, he was denied effective command until 1918, when he displayed far greater generalship.

**HAILE SELASSIE** (1892–1975), reignname of Ras Tafari, emperor of Ethiopia 1930–74. A benevolent despot, he won great popularity by his determined resistance to the Italian invasion of Ethiopia 1935–41, when British forces restored him to his throne. Efficient at first, his autocracy degenerated in later years. In the face of a nationwide famine he was deposed by his army in 1974 and died in captivity.

**HAILEY, Arthur** (1920–    ), English-born Canadian scriptwriter and popular novelist, best known for *Airport* (1968), which was made into a successful movie that spawned several sequels. Noted for their meticulous detail and many subplots, his other novels include *Hotel* (1965), *Wheels* (1971), *The Moneychangers* (1975) and *Overload* (1979).

**HAIR,** nonliving filamentous structure made of KERATIN and pigment, formed in the skin hair FOLLICLES. Facial and genetic factors determine both coloring and shape (by heat-labile sulfur bridges). In man all skin surfaces except the palms and soles are covered with very fine hair. This assists in TOUCH reception. In the cold, these hairs are erected to create extra insulation. Scalp hair is prominent in man. Pubic and axillary hair develop at PUBERTY in response to sex HORMONES and their patterns differ in the sexes; facial hair is ANDROGEN-dependent. Hair growth is more rapid in the summer. Hormone abnormalities alter hair distribution, while BALDNESS follows hair OSS.

**Official name:** Republic of Haiti
**Capital:** Port-au-Prince
**Area:** 10,712sq mi
**Population:** 4,918,695
**Languages:** French; Creole spoken by majority

**Religions:** Roman Catholic, voodoo
**Monetary unit(s):** 1 Gourde = 100 centimes

**HAITI,** independent republic in the Caribbean Sea, the W portion of the island of Hispaniola, which it shares with the Dominican Republic.

**Land.** Haiti is mainly mountainous; the coastline has beaches, coral reefs, mangrove swamps and cliffs. The climate is tropical, with two rainy seasons. There are extensive forests in the interior and many coffee and fruit plantations on the coast.

**People.** The people are mostly of African descent, with a powerful mulatto minority. The official language is French, but the main tongue is CREOLE. The official religion is Roman Catholicism but VOODOO dominates the life of the people. Only about 20% of the population is literate and education, although theoretically compulsory, is scant. The standard of living is low; government, army and professions are in the hands of the mulattoes.

**Economy.** The economy is poor, based on subsistence agriculture. Coffee is the major cash crop and some sisal, sugarcane, cotton and cocoa is processed and exported, as are wood and, on a small scale, minerals. The tourist trade is the second-largest source of foreign exchange.

**History.** COLUMBUS claimed Haiti for Spain in 1492. Spanish exploitation wiped out the aboriginal ARAWAK INDIANS. The island was ceded to France in 1697, and became a plantation center to which African slaves were imported. In 1804 a slave revolt led by TOUSSAINT L'OUVERTURE and Jacques DESSALINES finally won independence. Political chaos then continued until the US occupation 1915–47. In 1957 François DUVALIER became dictator, and with the brutal backing of his *tontons macoutes* (secret police) held power until his death in 1971; he was succeeded by his son, Jean-Claude, under whom the regime became slightly less repressive. That in turn led to better foreign relations, increased foreign investment and more tourism. Severe drought brought a widespread famine in 1977, and in 1979 Haiti was severely damaged by Hurricane David.

**HAKLUYT, Richard** (c1552–1616), pioneering British geographer. He published many early accounts of the Americas and a major account of English voyaging and discoveries. He lectured on geography at Oxford.

**HALAS, George** (called "Poppa George;" 1896–    ), US football coach and owner. He was player-coach, 1920–32, of the Chicago Bears, a team he came to own. He is considered one of the chief founders of professional football.

**HALDANE, John Burdon Sanderson** (1892– 1964), British geneticist whose work, with that of Sir Ronald Aylmer Fisher (1890–1962) and Sewall WRIGHT, provided a basis for the mathematical study of population GENETICS.

**HALDANE, Richard Burdon Haldane, 1st Viscount** (1856–1928), British statesman and lawyer, a Liberal member of Parliament 1885–1911. As secretary of state for war 1905–12 he introduced sweeping army reforms, founding the Territorial Army and national and imperial general staffs. He was Lord Chancellor 1912–15 and in 1924. A founder of the London School of Economics (1895), he wrote several philosophical works.

**HALE, George Ellery** (1868–1938), US astronomer who discovered the magnetic fields of SUNSPOTS, and who invented at the same time as Henri Alexandre Deslandres (1853–1948) the Spectroheliograph (c1892). His name is commemorated by HALE OBSERVATORIES.

**HALE, Nathan** (1755–1776), American revolutionary. A former schoolteacher, he was caught in disguise behind the British lines on Long Island, and hanged as a spy on Sept. 22, 1776. His last words are said to have been that he regretted having but one life to lose for his country; the quotation actually comes from Joseph ADDISON's play *Cato.*

**HALEVI, Jehuda.** See JUDAH HA-LEVI.

**HALEY, Alex** (1921–    ), US author best known for *Roots* (1976), the story of Haley's ancestor, Kunta Kinte, who was enslaved in The Gambia and brought to Maryland before the American Revolution. Described as a "factional" novel—semifictional, semifactual—*Roots* became a publishing sensation and record-setting television drama in 1977.

**HALEY, William John** ("Bill," 1927–1981), US musician. At age 15, he formed his band, the Comets, which recorded some of the biggest hits of the rock-and-roll era, including "Shake Rattle and Roll" (1954) and "Rock Around The Clock" (1955).

**HALF-LIFE,** the time taken for the activity of a radioactive sample to decrease to half its original value, half the nuclei originally present having changed spontaneously into a different nuclear type by emission of particles and energy. After two half-lives, the radioactivity will be a quarter of its original value and so on. Depending on the type of nucleus and mode of decay, half-lives range from less than a second to

over $10^{10}$ years. The half-life concept can also be applied to other systems undergoing random decay, e.g. certain biological populations.

**HALFTONE,** reproduction of a photograph or other picture containing a range of continuous tones, by using dots of various sizes but uniform tone. The dots are small enough to blend in the observer's vision to give the effect of the original. The picture is photographed through a screen on which a fine rectangular grid has been scribed (2 to 6 lines/mm); the dots arise by DIFFRACTION. From the screened negative is made a halftone plate used for PRINTING by all processes.

**HALIBUT,** *Hippoglossus hippoglossus,* largest of the N Atlantic flatfishes, reported to reach 2.7m (9ft) and to weigh up to 270kg (600lb). The related Pacific halibut (*H. stenolepsis*) is somewhat smaller. Halibut are carnivorous, feeding on other fishes, squids and crabs. Important as a food fish, the halibut is the subject of one of the most successful fish-management projects.

**HALIFAX,** port city, capital of Nova Scotia, E Canada. A major British military base from 1749, it was taken over by Canada in 1906 and remained a naval base in WWI and WWII. It now has various industries, many connected with the port, and is a cultural and educational center. Pop 117,885.

**HALIFAX, Edward Frederick Lindley Wood, 1st Earl of** (1881–1959), British statesman, a Conservative member of Parliament 1910–25. As viceroy of India 1925–31 he was sympathetic to the independence movement. Foreign secretary 1938–40, he advocated APPEASEMENT of Hitler, helping to negotiate the MUNICH PACT. He was ambassador to the US 1941–46.

**HALL, Granville Stanley** (1844–1924), US psychologist and educator best known for founding the *American Journal of Psychology* (1887), the first US psychological journal. He was first president of the American Psychological Institute (1894), a body whose foundation he had assisted.

**HALL, Gus** (Arvo Kusta Halberg; 1910–    ), secretary-general of the US Communist Party (from 1959). Under his leadership the party closely followed the Soviet line.

**HALLEY, Edmund** (1656–1742), English astronomer. In 1677 he made the first full observation of a transit of Mercury; and in 1676–79 prepared a major catalog of the S-hemisphere stars. He persuaded NEWTON to publish the *Principia,* which he financed.

In 1720 he succeeded FLAMSTEED as Astronomer Royal. He is best known for his prediction that the comet of 1680 would return in 1758 (see HALLEY'S COMET), based on his conviction that COMETS follow elliptical paths about the sun.

**HALLEY'S COMET,** the first periodic comet to be identified (by HALLEY, late 17th century) and the brightest of all recurring comets. It has a period of about 76 years. Records of every appearance of the comet since 240 BC, except that of 163 BC, are extant; and it is featured on the BAYEUX TAPESTRY. It will next reappear in 1986.

**HALLOWEEN,** festival on Oct. 31, eve of All Saints' Day or Hallowmas, originally a Celtic festival to mark the new year, welcoming the spirits of the dead and assuaging supernatural powers. It was introduced to the US by Scots and Irish immigrants, and is now a children's festival famous for "trick-or-treat."

**HALLUCINATION,** an experience similar to a normal PERCEPTION but with the difference that sensory stimulus is either absent or too minor to explain the experience satisfactorily. Certain abnormal mental conditions (see MENTAL ILLNESS) produce hallucinations, as does the taking of HALLUCINOGENIC DRUGS. Hallucinations may also result from exhaustion or FEVER; or may be experienced while falling asleep (hypnogogic) or waking (hypnopompic), and also by individuals under HYPNOSIS.

**HALLUCINOGENIC DRUGS,** DRUGS which cause hallucinations or illusions, usually visual, together with personality and behavior changes. The last may arise as a result of therapy, but more usually follow deliberate exposure to certain drugs for their psychological effects ("trip"). Lysergic acid diethylamide (LSD), HEROIN, MORPHINE and other OPIUM NARCOTICS, MESCALINE and PSILOCYBIN are commonly hallucinogenic and cannabis sometimes so. The type of hallucination is not predictable and many are unpleasant ("bad trip"). Recurrent hallucinations may follow use of these drugs; another danger is that altered behavior may inadvertently cause death or injury. Although psychosis may be a result of their use, it may be that recourse to drugs represents rather an early symptom of SCHIZOPHRENIA.

**HALS, Frans** (c1580–1666), Dutch painter, one of the great portraitists. In his time he was not especially famous and known mainly in his native Haarlem. Many of his greatest works, such as the *Lady Governors of the Old Men's Home* (1664), are civic portraits. His later works have a somber serenity, but many portraits and genre scenes, such as *Banquet of the Officers of St. George* (1616) and the so-called *Laughing Cavalier* (1624), are infused with a rich joviality. Working freely and rapidly without wasting a brush stroke, he was able to capture the reality of his subjects on canvases that sparkle with color and light.

**HALSEY, William Frederick "Bull," Jr.** (1882–1959), US admiral, WWII. After commanding a Pacific carrier division with great distinction 1940–42, he took command of the Pacific theater. As commander of the 3rd Fleet he helped destroy the Japanese fleet at LEYTE GULF in 1944. He resigned as fleet admiral in 1947 and entered business.

**HAMBLETONIAN STAKE,** premier harness racing event in the US. Limited to three-year-old trotters, it has been held annually since 1926 and, since 1978, has been contested at New Jersey's Meadowlands. The victor must win two one-mile heats. The race is named for a trotting horse called *Rydyk's Hambletonian* (1849–76), the ancestor of most modern trotters.

**HAMBURG,** historic seaport, now the largest city in West Germany, near the mouth of the Elbe R. Probably founded by CHARLEMAGNE, it was a dominant member of the HANSEATIC LEAGUE, and always a flourishing commercial center. Devastated in WWII, it has been rebuilt and now has shipyards and a wide range of industries. A transport hub, it is the center of the country's fishing industry. Pop 1,653,000.

**HAMILL, Dorothy** (1956–    ), US figure skater. She gave an almost flawless performance to win the gold medal at the 1976 Olympics. She was considered the finest freestyle skater in the world in the mid-1970s.

**HAMILTON, Alexander** (c1755–1804), a founding father of the US. Successively a revolutionary, first secretary of the treasury, founder of the first American political party, adviser to Washington and a powerful statesman, he was one of the most important figures in the new nation. His hauteur and elitist political outlook antagonized many people, but his integrity was beyond doubt. The young republic would have had less chance of surviving without his determination to make it fiscally sound with a strong central government.

A pamphleteer for the Revolution, he joined the army and became Washington's aide-de-camp in 1777. After the war he campaigned for central government, and served in the Continental Congress and the New York legislature, becoming its delegate to the ANNAPOLIS CONVENTION and the Constitutional Convention of 1787. With John JAY and MADISON he wrote the *Federalist Papers* (1787–88), still considered classics of political theory. Not a democrat, he advocated an intellectual aristocracy maintained by the "enlightened self-interest" of the wealthy. This brought him into conflict with JEFFERSON, who supported the French Revolution and sought to abolish privilege. As first secretary to the treasury from 1789, Hamilton created the Bank of the United States (1791) and became leader of the Federalist Party; Jefferson and Madison led the Republicans, the Hamiltonians becoming the Federalists. Hamilton left the cabinet in 1795 but he continued to influence the executive from behind the scenes until John ADAMS became president. When the latter lost his bid for reelection, an electoral tie occurred between Aaron BURR and Jefferson. The Federalists in Congress wanted Burr, but Hamilton intervened in favor of his old opponent and Burr lost. Burr challenged him to a duel, in which Hamilton was killed.

**HAMILTON, Alice** (1869–1970), US physician and social reformer. The first woman on the faculty of the Harvard Medical School (1919–35), she was the first researcher to study industrial diseases and industrial hygiene in the US. Her work was instrumental in the passage of WORKMEN'S COMPENSATION laws.

**HAMILTON, Edith** (1867–1963), US educator and classical scholar. Founder and headmistress of Bryn Mawr school for girls in Baltimore, she interpreted classical civilizations in such influential books as *The Greek Way* (1930), *The Roman Way* (1932) and *The Echo of Greece* (1957).

**HAMILTON, Emma, Lady** (1765–1815), celebrated beauty who became the mistress of Lord NELSON. A blacksmith's daughter, she was the wife of Sir William Hamilton, British envoy in Naples. She exercised great influence over Nelson. After his death she died in poverty.

**HAMITIC LANGUAGES,** a group within the **Hamito-Semitic** language family, including Berber, Cushite and Ancient Egyptian (the former two still being spoken today). Other Hamito-Semitic Languages include SEMITIC and Chadic. (See also LANGUAGE.)

**HAMLET,** Danish prince in SHAKESPEARE'S tragedy of that name. The story is that of Amleth, whose vengeance on his usurping uncle is recounted in SAXO GRAMMATICUS' *History of Denmark* (12th century). The legend of the prince who feigns madness to outwit a tyrant, however, has origins in

Roman and Eastern legend. Shakespeare probably found the story in François de Belleforest's *Histoires Tragiques* (1570) or in Thomas KYD's play, now lost, drawn from it.

**HAMMARSKJÖLD, Dag (Hjalmar Agne Carl)** (1905–1961), Swedish statesman and economist, UN secretary general 1953–61. He greatly increased UN power and prestige. He was instrumental in negotiations over the Korean War truce and the Suez crisis of 1956. In 1960 he directed UN attempts to end the fighting in the Congo, and his actions were condemned by the USSR. He refused to resign, but was killed in an aircrash in the Congo. He was posthumously awarded the 1961 Nobel Peace Prize.

**HAMMERSTEIN,** name of two US theatrical producers. **Oscar Hammerstein I** (1846–1919) was a German-born tobacco magnate who became an opera impresario, opening theaters in New York, London and Philadelphia. **Oscar Hammerstein II** (1895–1960), his grandson, became famous as a writer and producer of musical comedies in partnership with Richard RODGERS and others. Among his successes with Rodgers were *Oklahoma!* (1943), *Carousel* (1945), *South Pacific* (1949), *The King and I* (1951) and *The Sound of Music* (1959).

**HAMMER THROWING.** See TRACK AND FIELD.

**HAMMETT, (Samuel) Dashiell** (1894–1961), US detective-story writer and left-wing political activist. His novels are "hard-boiled" and realistic. His main character, Sam Spade, became the prototype of the fictional American detective, especially as portrayed by Humphrey Bogart in the film of Hammett's best-known work, *The Maltese Falcon* (1930). *The Thin Man* (1932) featured more amiable detectives, Nick and Nora Charles.

**HAMMURABI,** more correctly Hammurapi (d. 1750 BC or 1686 BC), 6th king of the 1st dynasty of Babylon, from 1792 BC or 1728 BC. Over many years of wars and alliances he conquered and united Mesopotamia, though his empire did not long survive him. An able administrator, he was responsible for the Code of Hammurabi, a compilation and expansion of earlier laws which is the fullest extant collection of Babylonian laws. The best source of the code is a black diorite stela found at Susa, Iran, in 1901.

**HAMPDEN, John** (1594–1643), English Parliamentary leader. He provoked a test case by refusing to pay ship money, a royal tax not approved by Parliament, in 1636. King Charles I's attempted seizure of him and other Parliamentary leaders in 1642 was one of the incidents which provoked the English Civil War, in which Hampden was killed.

**HAMPDEN, Walter** (1879–1955), US actor who began his career with a British Shakespearean company, winning critical acclaim for his portrayal of Hamlet (1905). In America he appeared in more than 150 plays by Shakespeare, Ibsen, Arthur Miller and others, and was noted for his portrayal of Cyrano de Bergerac, performed over 1000 times.

**HAMPTON, Lionel** (1913–    ), the first jazz vibraphone virtuoso, widely heard in the 1930s as a member of Benny Goodman's Quartet, and leader of his own band since the 1940s.

**HAMPTON, Wade** (1818–1902), US politician and soldier. Although opposed to secession, he joined the Confederate army, becoming famous as General LEE's cavalry commander. He advocated postwar reconciliation, and in his 1876 gubernatorial campaign led the "Red Shirt" movement which ended RECONSTRUCTION in S.C. He was a senator 1879–91.

**HAMSTERS,** short-tailed RODENTS of Europe and Asia. Living in dry areas—STEPPE country or the edge of deserts—hamsters feed chiefly on cereals, but also on fruits, roots and leaves. Large cheek pouches are used for carrying food back to their nests—where it may be stored against the winter. The most familiar species, the Golden hamster, *Mesocricetus auratus*, makes an attractive pet, though both it and the related Common hamster, *Cricetus cricetus*, are nocturnal.

**HAMSUN, Knut** (1859–1952), Norwegian novelist. In his youth he led a wandering life, which became the theme of many of his novels, such as *Hunger* (1890). His masterpiece, *Growth of the Soil* (1917), brought him the Nobel Prize for Literature in 1920.

**HANCOCK, John** (1737–1793), American Revolutionary leader. President of the Continental Congress (1775–77) and first signer of the Declaration of Independence, he used much of his inherited wealth to support the American cause. First governor of Mass. 1780–93, he presided over the convention that ratified the US Constitution in 1788.

**HAND, (Billings) Learned** (1872–1961), prominent US jurist noted for his profoundly reasoned rulings in almost 3,000 cases. He served 52 years as a New York federal district judge and, from 1924,

member and later chief of the federal Court of Appeals. Although never a Supreme Court justice, he was greatly influential.

**HANDBALL,** court game played between two or four people; it requires both stamina and coordination. There are one-wall and four-wall versions of the game. Players attempt to hit a hard rubber ball against one or more walls so as to prevent opponents from returning it before it bounces twice on the floor. The ball is only 7/8in in diameter and reaches very high speeds. The game is popular in the US; it was probably imported from Ireland in the 1880s. The first world championship, won by the US, was staged in New York City in 1964.

**HANDEDNESS** refers to the side of the body, and in particular to the hand, that is most used in motor tasks. Most people are right-handed and few are truly ambidextrous (either-handed). In the BRAIN, the paths for sensory and motor information are crossed, so the right side of the body is controlled by the left cerebral hemisphere and vice versa. The left hemisphere is usually dominant and also contains centers for speech and calculation. The nondominant side deals with aspects of visual and spatial relationships, while other functions are represented on both sides. In some left-handed people, the right hemisphere is dominant. Suppression of left-handedness may lead to speech disorder.

**HANDEL, George Frederick** (1685–1759), German-born composer who settled in England in 1712. He is considered one of the greatest composers of the baroque period; he enjoyed both public favor and royal patronage in his lifetime. Established as an opera composer in Germany and Italy, he turned to oratorio to suit British taste. His most famous such works are *Saul* (1739), *Israel in Egypt* (1739), *The Messiah* (1742) and *Belshazzar* (1745). Among the rest of his vast output, the *Water Music* (1717) and the *Music for the Royal Fireworks* (1749) are best known. His career was ended by blindness in 1751–52.

**HANDLIN, Oscar** (1915–    ), US social historian. A professor at Harvard (from 1939), he specialized in the history of immigration to the US and the role of immigrants in US life. His best-known works include the Pulitzer Prize-winning *The Uprooted* (1951) and *The Americans* (1963).

**HANDY,    W(illiam)    C(hristopher)** (1873–1958), US songwriter, band leader and jazz composer. He conducted his own band 1903–21. In 1912 he published one of the first popular blues songs, *Memphis Blues*, and in 1914 wrote the famous *St.*

*Louis Blues.* He became a music publisher in the 1920s.

**HAN DYNASTY,** powerful Chinese dynasty lasting from 206 BC to 220 AD. Usually divided into Western Han and the later Eastern Han, it was founded by Liu Pang after a period of oppressive centralized rule under the Chi'in dynasty. At the height of its expansion, the dynasty extended from Korea and Vietnam to Uzbekistan, and presided over a period of great cultural growth.

**HANG GLIDING,** a new sport in which participants "sky surf" in hang gliders, which are basically large kites with suspended seats. At the US Hang Gliding Association national championships, competitors are judged on distance, form, turns, soaring ability and landing accuracy.

**HANGING,** method of execution in which the victim is hanged by the neck from a noose. In primitive forms, death results from slow strangulation. In more sophisticated methods, the victim is dropped through a trap, and the resultant jerk dislocates the cervical vertebrae, causing almost immediate unconsciousness. One of the most common methods of execution, hanging is employed by four states of the US, but it has not been used since the 10-year hiatus in US executions ended in 1977.

**HANNA, Marcus Alonzo "Mark"** (1837–1904), US Republican politician and industrialist whose financial backing of William MCKINLEY helped bring about the latter's victory over William Jennings BRYAN in the 1896 presidential elections. Hanna was appointed and subsequently elected US Senator from Ohio 1897–1904 and remained a close presidential adviser.

**HANNA-BARBERA,** cartoon producers who popularized the stripped-down animation techniques used in such TV series as *The Flintstones, Yogi Bear* and *Huckleberry Hound.* Producer William D. Hanna and cartoonist Joseph Barbera created MGM's prize-winning *Tom & Jerry* cartoons before forming their own company in 1957.

**HANNIBAL** (247–183 BC), brilliant Carthaginian general who almost defeated Rome in the Second PUNIC WAR. Son of the great general HAMILCAR BARCA. he commanded Carthaginian forces in Spain against a city allied to Rome. When Rome declared war in 218 BC, he set off across the Pyrenees with around 40,000 seasoned troops and a force of elephants. In an extraordinary feat of organization, he took his forces across the Alps in wintry conditions and defeated Roman forces under SCIPIO at the Trebia R, then won great victories at Lake Trasimene (217 BC) and at CANNAE (216 BC). Rome then detained him by harassing tactics while Roman armies reduced Carthaginian possessions in Spain and began to strike at Carthage itself. Hannibal was recalled, only to be defeated at Zama in 202 BC. Driven into exile c195 BC, he joined Syrian operations against Rome. When the defeated Syrians had to promise to surrender him to Rome, he poisoned himself.

**HANOI,** capital of North Vietnam 1954–76 and of Vietnam from 1976. Dating from the 7th century, it is an important shipping, industrial and transport center on the Red R., part European and part Annamese in style. The city suffered from US bombings during the VIETNAM WAR. Pop 2,571,000.

**HANOVER, House of,** reigning family of Hanover, in Germany, and of Great Britain (1714–1901). In 1658 the 1st Elector of Hanover married Sophia, granddaughter of James I, named heir to the British throne by the ACT OF SETTLEMENT, 1701. Her son became GEORGE I of Britain. By Salic law, Victoria could not become queen of Hanover, and from 1837 the thrones separated. On Edward VII's accession the family name became Saxe-Coburg (after Prince Albert) and in 1917 was changed to WINDSOR.

**HANSBERRY, Lorraine** (1930–1965), US playwright, first black woman to have a play produced on Broadway. *A Raisin in the Sun* (1959) won the New York Drama Critics' Circle Award, and was later made into a film and a musical, *Raisin* (1973).

**HANSEATIC LEAGUE,** a medieval confederation (c1157–1669) organized by N German towns and merchants to protect their trading interests in the Baltic Sea and throughout Europe. The town of Lübeck on Germany's N coast was the League's administrative center. Diets were held there to decide on monopolies, trading rights and other policy matters. From the late 13th to 14th centuries, the *hanse* (or guild) had over 100 members and exercised wide commercial powers, backed by monopoly and boycott, and strong political influence. Members of the *hanse* established commercial centers in numerous foreign towns such as Bergen (Norway), London and Novgorod (Russia). The League's strength declined with the rise of nationalism in Europe.

**HANSON, Howard** (1896–1981), US conductor, teacher and composer in the Romantic tradition. He won a Prix de Rome (1921) and was director of the Eastman School of Music, Rochester, N.Y.,

1924–64. Hanson's Fourth Symphony won a Pulitzer Prize in 1944.

**HANUKKAH,** Jewish Feast of Dedication in Nov.–Dec., which marks the rededication (164 BC) of the Temple in Jerusalem after Judas Maccabaeus' victory over Antiochus IV (see MACCABEES, BOOK OF). This "Festival of Lights" is celebrated by lighting candles, one on the first night, two on the second and so forth, for eight days.

**HAPPENING,** in art, a performance combining prepared and random effects, aural as well as visual, frequently including some degree of audience participation. The happening may make use of any materials and take place in any environment, from an art gallery or theater to a gym or city street. John CAGE's pieces in the 1950s, combining music with other media, provided the inspiration for the art form, but the term itself comes from painter Allan Kaprow's *18 Happenings in 6 Parts,* first performed in 1959 at New York City's Reuben Gallery.

**HAPSBURG, House of,** European dynasty from which came rulers of Austria (1278–1918), the HOLY ROMAN EMPIRE (1436–1806), Spain (1516–1700), Germany, Hungary, Bohemia and other countries. Count Rudolf, elected king of Germany in 1273, founded the imperial line. Thereafter Hapsburg power and hereditary lands grew until under CHARLES V they included most of Europe (excepting France, Scandinavia, Portugal and England). After Charles, the Hapsburgs were divided into Spanish and imperial lines. When the Spanish line died out, Charles V's granddaughter, MARIA THERESA, gained the Austrian title. Her husband, Francis I (Duke of Lorraine), became Holy Roman Emperor (1745); the Hapsburg-Lorraine line ruled the Holy Roman Empire until its demise. The last Hapsburg ruler, Charles I, emperor of Austria and king of Hungary, abdicated in 1918.

**HARA-KIRI,** or *seppuku,* ancient Japanese act of ceremonial suicide, in which a short sword was used to slash the abdomen from left to right, then upwards; used by warriors to escape capture by the enemy, and also by the Samurai (warrior) class to avoid dishonorable execution after breaking the law. The Japanese favored hara-kiri to avoid capture even during WWII.

**HARBIN,** industrial port in NW China, capital of Heilungkiang (Heilongjiang) province, on the S bank of the Sungari R. Largely built by Russians engaged in construction of a railroad from Siberia to Vladivostock, Harbin is architecturally similar to Leningrad. It produces machin-

ery, steel, chemicals, textiles, paper, foodstuffs and forest products in over 1,000 factories. Pop 2,000,000.

**HARD-EDGE PAINTING,** a modern school of painting that stresses the optical relationships between flat areas of color arranged with geometrical precision. Josef ALBERS' works, such as *Homage to The Square,* are well-known examples. See MINIMALISM.

**HARDENING OF THE ARTERIES.** See ARTERIOSCLEROSIS.

**HARDIE, James Keir** (1856–1915), pioneer British socialist and first leader of the Labour Party. A mine worker from age 10, he was elected the first independent Labour member of Parliament (1892) and helped form the Labour Party in 1906.

**HARDING, Warren Gamaliel** (1865–1923), 29th president of the US. He died after only 30 months in office, during which his administration was marred by high-level corruption, culminating in the TEAPOT DOME oil reserve scandal, which involved Secretary of the Interior Albert B. Fall accepting large bribes.

Born in Ohio and educated at a backwater college, Harding became part owner of the Marion, Ohio, *Star* (1884), which he turned into a successful small-town daily. In 1891 he married Mrs. Florence Kling DeWolfe; their domestic life was unhappy and led to Harding's involvement in liaisons which hurt his personal reputation. A genial man with a flair for vague rhetoric, Harding entered politics, becoming a Republican state senator and Ohio's lieutenant-governor. Defeated in the 1910 gubernatorial race, but elected US Senator in 1914, he was a conservative and popular member of Congress though he did little of consequence.

In 1920 he was adopted as a presidential candidate when the Republican convention became deadlocked over the leading contenders. He won a sweeping victory on a "return to normalcy" platform, appealing to a nation weary of wartime restraints. Many of Harding's political appointments were disastrous; he rewarded political cronies with office, and their corruption and dishonesty seriously damaged both his administration and the reputation of the Republican Party. Harding's cabinet did include some distinguished political figures: Charles Evans Hughes (State), Herbert Hoover (Commerce), Andrew Mellon (Treasury) and Henry C. Wallace (Agriculture). He also appointed former President Taft as chief justice and created the Bureau of the Budget, introducing modern budgetary systems into government. Determined that America should join the League of Nations' World Court, despite Congressional disapproval, Harding set out on a cross-country tour to take the issue to the people. Already suffering from a serious heart condition, Harding died in San Francisco on Aug. 2, 1923, during the tour. After his death, the scandals of his administration and personal life that came to light destroyed his reputation. Harding is now recognized as a well-intentioned, ingenuous man who did not have the leadership capabilities to fulfill the office of president.

**HARDNESS**, the resistance of a substance to scratching, or to indentation under a blow or steady load. Resistance to scratching is measured on the **Mohs' scale**, named for Friedrich Mohs (1773–1839), who chose 10 MINERALS as reference points, from TALC (hardness 1) to DIAMOND (10). The **modified Mohs' scale** is now usually used, with 5 further mineral reference points. Resistance to indentation is measured by, among others, the Brinell, Rockwell and Vickers scales. (See also MATERIALS, STRENGTH OF.)

**HARD WATER**, water containing CALCIUM and MAGNESIUM ions and hence forming scum with soap and depositing scale in boilers, pipes and kettles. **Temporary hardness** is due to calcium and magnesium BICARBONATES; it is removed by boiling, which precipitates the carbonates. **Permanent hardness** (unaffected by boiling) is due to the sulfates. Hard water may be softened by precipitation of the metal ions using CALCIUM hydroxide and SODIUM carbonate, followed by sodium PHOSPHATE; or by a Zeolite or ION-EXCHANGE column, which exchanges the calcium and magnesium ions for sodium ions.

**HARDWICK, Elizabeth** (1916–    ), US novelist and essayist who often deals with issues of interest to women. Her works include the novels *The Ghostly Lover* (1945) and *Sleepless Nights* (1979) and the essays *Seduction and Betrayal: Women and Literature* (1974).

**HARDY, Thomas** (1840–1928), English novelist and poet. Born in Dorset (Wessex in his novels), he practiced architecture until the popular success of his novel *Far From the Madding Crowd* (1874). Nine novels, including *The Return of the Native* (1878) and *Tess of the d'Urbervilles* (1891), appeared in the next 20 years. *Jude the Obscure* (1894), partially autobiographical, so offended Victorian morality that Hardy abandoned writing novels and continued writing poetry. His heroic verse-drama *The Dynasts* (1903–08) and later lyric poetry

are as highly regarded as his novels. The "last of the great Victorians," Hardy directly influenced 20th-century English literature. His view of life was essentially tragic; his characters often seem victims of malignant fate, especially if they rebel against "nature." Hardy is almost unsurpassed in his skill at describing rustic life and the English countryside.

**HARE KRISHNAS**, popular name for members of a strict monastic order (the International Society for Krishna Consciousness), famous for their orange robes, shaved heads, public chanting of "Hare Krishna" (in praise of the Hindu god Krishna), and aggressive begging. The movement was founded in 1965 in New York City by A. C. Bhaktivedanta Swami Prabhupada. Among the group's international string of residences and temples is the Palace of Gold, on 2,000 acres in W. Va., opened in 1980.

**HARELIP**, a congenital DISEASE with a cleft defect in the upper lip due to impaired facial development in the EMBRYO, and often associated with CLEFT PALATE. It may be corrected by plastic SURGERY.

**HARES**, *Lepus spp*, animals resembling RABBITS and including the JADE RABBITS, adapted for swift running and characterized by long ears, long, powerful hindlegs and feet and short tails. Hares are herbivorous, living entirely above ground in grasslands in Eurasia, Africa and North America and, by introduction, in South America, Australia and New Zealand. Various species molt into a white pelage over winter. Male European hares indulge in wild boxing matches during the rut—the origin of the expression "Mad as a March hare." Young hares, leverets, are born well-developed, alert and capable of independent movement.

**HARLAN**, two associate justices of the US Supreme Court, grandfather and grandson. **John Marshall Harlan** (1833–1911), appointed in 1877, served 34 years. A court independent, he is best known for his 1896 dissenting opinion that Jim Crow laws which established the principle of "separate but equal" racial segregation, in fact deprived black citizens of equal protection of the law. **John Marshall Harlan** (1899–1971), was appointed to the court by President Eisenhower in 1955. He had been an assistant US attorney, chief counsel to the N.Y. State Crime Commission and member of the US Court of Appeals.

**HARLEM**, densely populated, primarily Black and Hispanic community, in the N part of Manhattan borough, New York City. A Dutch settlement from 1658 (Nieuw Haarlem), it was a rural and then a fashionable residential area. From the 1920s it became chiefly black; overcrowding helped turn Harlem into a notorious slum. Government-funded programs since the 1960s have attempted to improve conditions there.

**HARLEM GLOBETROTTERS,** famous US professional basketball team, first organized in 1927 by Abe Saperstein. The squad has toured the US and abroad, playing exhibitions against college All-Star and professional teams. Their "games" have been widely televised, and their popularity is due to adroit handling of the ball and extraordinary clowning on the playing court.

**HARLEM RENAISSANCE,** period of cultural development among US blacks, centered on Harlem, New York City, in the 1920s. In this period black American literature changed from works in dialect and imitations of white writers to penetrating analyses of black culture and protests, displaying racial pride. Notable writers included Countee CULLEN, Langston HUGHES and Jean TOOMER.

**HARLOW, Jean** (1911–1937), US film actress who was the voluptuous Hollywood sex symbol of the 1930s. Her films included *Hell's Angels* (1930), *Platinum Blonde* (1932) and *China Seas* (1935).

**HARMONICA,** or mouth organ, a wind instrument with metal reeds inside a small flat box. The player moves the box horizontally across the lips, inhaling or exhaling air to produce musical tones and chords.

**HARMONICS,** vibrations at FREQUENCIES which are INTEGER multiples of that of a fundamental vibration: the ascending notes $C$, $C$, $G$, $C'$, $E'$, $G'$ comprise a fundamental with its first five harmonics. Apart from their musical consonance, they are important because any periodically repeated signal—a vowel sound, for example—can be produced by superimposing the harmonics of the fundamental frequency, each with the appropriate intensity and time lag.

**HARMONIUM,** or reed organ, portable keyboard instrument, related to the organ and resembling a small upright piano, with pedals to pump air past single metal reeds. It was popular in the late 19th century.

**HARMONY,** in music, the simultaneous sounding of two or more tones or parts; also the structure, relation and progression of chords and the rule governing their relationship. Traditional harmony is based upon a triad, a three-tone musical structure, with notes named for their position on the musical SCALE: the lowest tone is called the root, the middle tone is called the third (located a third scale tone above the root), the next is called the fifth (a fifth scale tone above the root). The triad becomes a chord in four-part writing when one tone is doubled. Chords can be erected on any note of the traditional eight-note scale. In the 20th century, harmonic rules and standards, developed over the preceding 400 years, were largely discarded. (See also ATONALITY; HARMONICS; PROGRESSION.)

**HARMONY SOCIETY,** or Rappites, religious group of 600 German immigrants to the US, led by George RAPP, which established Utopian communities in Pa. and Ind. (1804–1906). They held property in common and believed in Christ's imminent coming. The celibate society prospered until Rapp's death (1847), but thereafter attracted few converts.

**HARNESS RACING.** See HORSE RACING.

**HAROLD II** (c1020–1066), last Anglo-Saxon king of the English, son of GODWIN and earl of East Anglia, Wessex and Kent. Harold accepted the crown on the death of Edward the Confessor. Nine months later, he was killed at the Battle of HASTINGS when William, duke of Normandy, began his conquest of England.

**HARP,** stringed instrument, usually triangular in shape, with a resonating chamber nearly perpendicular to the plane of the strings. The harp is of ancient origin, although the Greeks and Romans favored the LYRE. The modern "double-action" harp, developed in 1800, is chromatic throughout its range. To alter their pitch, strings are shortened by means of seven pedals.

**HARPERS FERRY,** town in NE W.Va., scene of John BROWN's raid in Oct. 1859. Its location at the confluence of the Potomac and Shenandoah rivers made it an important Civil War strongpoint. It changed hands many times; its spirited resistance in 1862 seriously delayed Robert E. LEE's march N. The Civil War sites are preserved in the Harpers Ferry National Historical Park.

**HARPSICHORD,** keyboard instrument in which the strings are plucked, rather than hit as in a piano. The range is small, but tonal effects are achieved by stops or "registers." Larger harpsichords have two keyboards. The harpsichord was very popular from c1550 until the advent of the piano in the early 1800s, and much great music was written for it, most notably by Bach, Couperin and Scarlatti. It is now enjoying renewed popularity.

**HARRIMAN,** father and son prominent in US commerce and government. **Edward**

**Henry Harriman** (1848–1909), formed syndicates to buy the Union Pacific railroad in 1898 and the Southern Pacific in 1901, and created a Wall Street panic in his fight for the Northern Pacific in 1901. His son, **William Averell Harriman** (1891–    ), board chairman of Union Pacific 1933–46, served under Franklin D. Roosevelt in the NATIONAL RECOVERY ADMINISTRATION, and carried on lend-lease negotiations in Britain 1941–42. Named US ambassador to Moscow in 1943, he took part in all the major wartime conferences. Ambassador to London in 1946, he became secretary of commerce 1946–48 and governor of N.Y. 1955–59. As ambassador-at-large he was instrumental in the Laos peace talks 1961–62 and in achieving the limited test ban treaty in 1963. In 1968–69 he took part in the Vietnam peace talks.

**HARRINGTON, Michael** (1928–    ), US socialist leader and writer; his book *The Other America* (1962) described the "invisible poor" in the contemporary US and was credited with inspiring the federal antipoverty programs of the 1960s. He was chairman of the Socialist Party (1968–72) and the Democratic Socialist Organizing Committee (from 1973).

**HARRIS, Frank** (1856–1931), British writer, editor of three London newspapers 1892–98. A prolific writer, he is best remembered for his biographies of Shakespeare, Oscar Wilde and G. B. Shaw, and for his humorous, erotic and unreliable autobiography *My Life and Loves* (1925–29).

**HARRIS, Joel Chandler** (1848–1908), US journalist and author. His tales of plantation life, many featuring the old slave and folk philosopher Uncle Remus, are noted for their charming narrative style rendered in authentic dialect.

**HARRIS, Julie** (1925–    ), US stage, film and TV actress. She won critical acclaim at 24 for her portrayal of 12-year-old Frankie Adams in Carson McCullers' *The Member of the Wedding* (1950). She also appeared in *I Am a Camera* (1951), *The Belle of Amherst* (1976), and more than 25 other Broadway plays.

**HARRIS, Louis** (1921–    ), US pollster who founded Louis Harris and Associates (1956), one of the most influential public opinion polling organizations in the US.

**HARRIS, Marvin** (1927–    ), US anthropologist. A professor at Columbia U (from 1952), he was a major advocate of the theory of cultural materialism. His widely read books include *The Rise of Anthropological Theory* (1968), *Cows, Pigs,*

*Wars, and Witches* (1974) and *Cultural Materialism* (1979).

**HARRIS, Patricia Roberts** (1924–    ), US educator and public official. A former dean of the Howard U. School of Law, she held two Cabinet positions under President Carter: secretary of housing and urban development (1977–79) and secretary of health, education and welfare (1979–81).

**HARRIS, Roy Ellsworth** (1898–1979), US composer who studied in Paris with Nadia BOULANGER. Well known as a teacher, he was twice awarded the Guggenheim Fellowship (1927–28). The *Third Symphony* (1937) is perhaps his best-known work.

**HARRIS, Seymour Edwin** (1897–1974), US economist. A leading exponent of Keynesian economics, he taught at Harvard 1922–63 and was a key economic adviser to Presidents John F. Kennedy and Lyndon Johnson.

**HARRISBURG SEVEN**, group of Roman Catholic, anti-Vietnam War activists tried in Harrisburg, Pa., in 1972 on charges of conspiring to kidnap Secretary of State Henry Kissinger and otherwise disrupt the US war effort. The jury deadlocked 10–2 in favor of acquitting all defendants on the conspiracy charges, but Father Philip BERRIGAN and Sister Elizabeth McAlister were convicted of smuggling letters in and out of Lewisburg, Pa., prison, where he was then incarcerated. This was the last of a series of "numbered" trials involving Father Berrigan. In 1968, he was part of "the Baltimore Four" and "the Catonsville (Md.) Nine," groups that were convicted of destroying governmental property (i.e., draft records). Their actions inspired "the Milwaukee Fourteen," another Roman Catholic group, half of them priests, who were found guilty in 1969 of destroying draft records.

**HARRISON, Benjamin** (1833–1901), 23rd president of the US (1889–93). Grandson of William Henry Harrison, 9th president, he studied law in Cincinnati, and in 1854 began practice in Indianapolis. There he became active in the new Republican Party, was elected city attorney in 1857, and became reporter of the Ind. Supreme Court in 1860. During the Civil War, he served heroically in Sherman's Atlanta campaign of 1864. He returned to his law practice and politics, supporting Garfield in 1880 and entering the US Senate in 1881. There he backed high tariffs, helped to create the Interstate Commerce Commission and worked to expand the national park system. In 1888 he won the Republican presidential nomination, to oppose the then president

Grover Cleveland. The ensuing election was fought largely on the tariff issue; Harrison defeated Cleveland in the electoral vote, although trailing in the popular vote. As president, Harrison pursued a vigorous foreign policy. US claims to Samoa were established; the first and highly successful Pan American conference was held in Washington. A dispute with the UK over Bering Sea fur-seal exploitation went to arbitration. He had less influence over domestic legislation, although he signed the HERMAN ANTITRUST ACT and the McKinley Tariff Act, convinced that the nation wanted high import duties. In 1890, the Democrats captured Congress, due to low farm prices, the rise of the Populist party and the rising cost of living. This made Harrison's last years in office unfruitful and lost him personal popularity; he was reluctantly renominated in 1892. His wife died two weeks before the election. Growing agrarian unrest and bitter labor disputes helped to give Cleveland an easy victory; Harrison returned to Indianapolis to pursue a distinguished legal career.

**HARRISON, Rex** (1908–    ), British stage and screen actor. A debonair leading man, he appeared in such films as *School for Scandal* (1930) and *Blithe Spirit* (1945). He played Professor Higgins in the Broadway musical *My Fair Lady* (1956) and in the film (1964), for which he won an Academy Award.

**HARRISON, William Henry** (1773–1841), 9th president of the US (March 4–April 4, 1841). Born on a Va. plantation and son of a former state governor, Harrison entered the army on his father's death in 1791 and fought in Indian campaigns in the Northwest Territory. He finally settled in North Bend, Ohio, and in 1800 became governor of the new Indiana Territory. In treaties with the Indians, Harrison opened up 133,650sq mi of Ohio and Ind. to white settlement. During the 1811 Indian uprising, led by TECUMSEH, Harrison's troops repulsed an Indian attack at the battle of TIPPECANOE; he became a national hero, "Old Tippecanoe." When the War of 1812 began, he was made brigadier-general in charge of the Northwestern army, and major-general in 1813. At the war's end in 1814, he entered politics, serving in the Ohio Senate 1819–21 and in Congress 1816–19 and 1825–28. First minister to Colombia 1828–29, he retired to North Bend when Jackson took office.

In 1839 Harrison won the Whig presidential nomination at its first national convention on the strength of his military record and broad political views. He and his running mate, John Tyler, were launched by a campaign more colorful than any yet seen in the US. With the famous slogan, "Tippecanoe and Tyler, too," Harrison was put forward as a war hero and a son of the people with simple tastes. This image appealed to a country caught in a serious economic depression and he won by an overwhelming electoral vote. He appointed an able cabinet, headed by Daniel WEBSTER, and called a special session of Congress to act on the nation's financial difficulties. He delivered his inaugural address in pouring rain, however, and caught a cold which quickly turned to pneumonia. He died one month to the day after taking office.

**HART, Lorenz Milton** (1895–1943), US lyricist who collaborated with Richard RODGERS on 29 musical comedies. The most famous are *A Connecticut Yankee* (1927), *The Boys from Syracuse* (1938) and *Pal Joey* (1940).

**HART, Moss** (1904–1961), US dramatist and director. With George S. KAUFMAN, he wrote *You Can't Take It With You* (1936) and *The Man Who Came to Dinner* (1939). He directed the Broadway hits *My Fair Lady* (1956) and *Camelot* (1960).

**HART, William S.** (1870–1946), US film actor and director who was the first cowboy film star. Playing an austere, humorless hero, he starred in such movies as *The Disciple* (1915), *The Covered Wagon* (1923) and *Wild Bill Hickok* (1923).

**HARTE, Bret** (1836–1902), influential US writer. His short stories of frontier life helped create the mythology of the West. Among the stories that brought him worldwide fame are *The Luck of Roaring Camp* (1868) and *The Outcasts of Poker Flat* (1869). When his popularity in America declined, he settled in Britain.

**HARTFORD**, capital and largest city of Conn., on the Connecticut R. Founded in 1635, it has always been a cultural and educational center, and has many financial institutions. Its economy rests upon various industries, of which the most important are precision manufactures such as machine tools, computers, typewriters and firearms, and on its flourishing commerce. Pop 136,392.

**HARTFORD WITS**, a literary circle who met in Hartford, Conn., during the last quarter of the 18th century. Mostly Yale men, they were all Federalists; their main product was political satire, typified by the *Anarchiad*, a jointly-written mock verse epic. A collection of their work, *Echo*, was published in 1807.

**HARTLEY, David** (1705–1757), English physician and a founder of the school of psychology known as ASSOCIATIONISM. In his *Observations on Man* (1749), he taught that sensations were communicated to the brain via vibrations in nerve particles and that the repetition of sensations gave rise to the association of ideas in the mind.

**HARTLEY, Marsden** (1877–1943), US artist who abandoned an early interest in abstraction to produce impressionistic depictions of natural scenes. He was best known for paintings of his native Maine.

**HARTMAN, Heinz** (1894–1970), Austrian-born US psychologist who was a leader of the second generation of Freudians and was best known for the expansion of the basic theory of the EGO. He wrote *Essays in Ego Psychology* (1964) and collaborated on the annual *Psychoanalytic Study of the Child*.

**HARUN-AL-RASHID** (c766–809), fifth ABBASID caliph of Baghdad, from 786, whose rule extended from N Africa to the Indus R in India; he exacted tribute from the Byzantine Empire. His reign marked both the height and decline of the caliphate, and is remembered in the ARABIAN NIGHTS as a golden age.

**HARVARD, John** (1607–1638), American clergyman, first benefactor of Harvard College. Born in London, he emigrated to Mass. in 1637 to become Charlestown's minister. In 1638 he bequeathed half his estate and his library to the college, which was named for him in 1639.

**HARVARD UNIVERSITY,** founded by the General Court of Mass. in 1636, is the oldest university in the US. It has long been influenced by European patterns of education, but under the 40-year presidency of C. W. ELIOT developed a distinctive character of its own, especially in the growth of graduate schools. It now has nine faculties, administering 17 departments and nearly 200 allied institutions such as libraries, laboratories, museums and observatories.

**HARVEY, William** (1578–1657), British physician who discovered the circulation of the blood. He showed that the HEART acts as a pump and that the blood circulates endlessly about the body; that there are valves in the heart and VEINS so that blood can flow in one direction only; and that the necessary pressure comes only from the lower left-hand side of the heart. His discoveries demolished the theories of GALEN that blood was consumed at the body's periphery and that the left and right sides of the heart were connected by pores. He also made important studies of the development of the EMBRYO.

**HARZ MOUNTAINS,** range in N Germany on the border between lower Saxony and East Germany. In medieval times it was a major mining center for various metals, but the area's economy now rests on tourism, especially for winter sports. The range's highest point is BROCKEN peak.

**HASEK, Jaroslav** (1883–1923), Czech novelist whose *The Good Soldier Schweik* (1920–23) satirizes the WWI Austrian military machine. Schweik became the archetypical "little man," who outwits authority despite apparent stupidity.

**HASHEMITE DYNASTY,** Arab royal family claiming descent from the grandfather of the prophet MOHAMMED, hereditary sherifs of MECCA from the 11th century until 1919. After WWI the Hashemites FAISAL I and ABDULLAH IBN HUSSEIN became kings of IRAQ and JORDAN respectively. Abdullah's grandson HUSSEIN I is the present king of Jordan.

**HASHISH, or cannabis,** a drug produced from a resin obtained from the HEMP plant (*Cannabis sativa*), particularly from its flowers and fruits. It is a non-addictive drug whose effects range from a feeling of euphoria to fear. Hashish is mainly produced in the Middle East and India, and has been in use for many centuries although it is still illegal in many countries. (See MARIJUANA.)

**HASIDISM,** Jewish pietistic movement established in 18th-century Poland by Israel ben Eliezer. Reacting against emphasis on rabbinical learning and strict observance of the law, he stressed the ecstatic, joyous element in religion. The movement became grouped around tzadikkim, holy men or saints. Hasidism still flourishes in Israel and New York. In Hebrew, *hasidim* means "the pious ones." It is also applied to fiercely orthodox sectarians who fought in the 2nd-century BC Maccabaean wars.

**HASSAM, Childe** (1859–1935), US painter and graphic artist. He studied in Paris, and was one of the first US artists to adopt IMPRESSIONISM, painting many New York and New England landscapes.

**HASSAN II** (1929–    ), king and spiritual head of Morocco since 1961. He initiated partial democratization in 1962 but has retained effective absolute power despite an abortive coup in 1971–72. A protracted war (from 1976) to gain control of the former Spanish Sahara strained the Moroccan economy.

**HASTINGS, Battle of,** the prelude to the Norman conquest of England, fought between King HAROLD II and Duke William of Normandy on Oct. 14, 1066. Delayed at

nmer by unfavorable winds, William was
ally able to cross the English Channel
st when Harold was in N England
feating a Norwegian invasion. Forced
arches brought Harold south with an
hausted and depleted force to meet
illiam at Senlac (renamed Battle), near
astings. Harold's axmen were only swept
m a strong hilltop position, and Harold
led, when William, after a day's fighting,
ccessfully managed a feigned retreat.

**ASTINGS, Warren** (1732–1818), first
vernor-general of British India (1772–
). Starting as a clerk in 1750, he rose high
the British East India Company and as
vernor fought corruption and banditry,
t also amassed a large personal fortune.
iticized in England as an aggressive and
casionally arbitrary governor, he resigned
d was impeached. Despite fierce
osecution speeches, notably by Edmund
RKE, during the celebrated trial
788–95), Hastings was honorably
quitted.

**ATHAWAY, Anne** (c1556–1623), wife of
illiam Shakespeare. Eight years his
nior, she married him in 1582, bearing
n three children. Her family home,
nne Hathaway's Cottage," is at
ottery, near Stratford-upon-Avon.

**ATSHEPSUT,** queen of Egypt, 18th
nasty (15th century BC). She ruled with
r husband and half-brother THUTMOSE II.
coming regent to his son and then
suming the powers and titles of a pharaoh.
e presided over a period of prosperity,
d built the great temple of Deir el-Bahri
ar Thebes.

**AUPTMANN, Gerhart** (1862–1946),
rman author and playwright who
oneered naturalism in the German
eater. His first play, *Before Dawn* (1889),
aling with social problems, won him
ernight fame, and was followed—among
ers—by *The Weavers* (1892), a drama
working-class life. He won the Nobel
ize for Literature, 1912.

**AUSA,** a people of NW Nigeria and
ghboring Niger, numbering about 7
llion and Muslim since the 14th century.
rly in the 19th century they were mostly
nquered by the FULANI, who are still
minant in Hausaland. Their language is
ich used in W African trade.

**AUSHOFER, Karl Ernst** (1869–1946),
rman theoretician of geopolitics. His
velopment of earlier theories of
*bensraum* or "living space" influenced
tler's ideas. Under investigation as a war
minal, he committed suicide.

**AUSSMANN, Georges-Eugène, Baron**
809–1891), French civic official

(1853–70) responsible for planning and
rebuilding central Paris under Napoleon
III. Besides the famous boulevards, he laid
out improved water and sewage systems.

**HAVANA,** (La Habana), capital of
Cuba, on the Gulf of Mexico. One of the
largest cities in the West Indies, it was
founded by the Spanish in c1515. The U. of
Havana was opened in 1728. It has an
excellent harbor. Tobacco from the
neighboring Vuelta Abajo is used for the
famous Havana cigars. Until Fidel CASTRO's
revolution (1959), the city's economy rested
on gambling and tourism controlled from
the US. Since then Havana has been
subordinated to the general economy of
Cuba. Pop 1,986,500.

**Name of state:** Hawaii
**Capital:** Honolulu
**Statehood:** Aug. 21, 1959 (50th state)
**Familiar name:** Aloha State
**Area:** 6,450sq mi
**Population:** 965,000
**Elevation:** Highest—13,796ft., Mauna Kea.
Lowest—sea level, Pacific Ocean
**Motto:** Ua mau ke ea o ka aina i ka pono
(The Life of the Land is Perpetuated in
Righteousness)
**State flower:** Hibiscus
**State bird:** Né-né (Hawaiian goose)
**State tree:** Kukui (Candlenut)
**State song:** "Hawaii Ponoi" (Hawaii's
Own)

**HAWAII,** 50th state of the US in the North
Pacific Ocean, a chain of some 130 islands,
over 1,500mi long.

**Land.** The main islands, at the SE end of the
chain and about 2,400mi from the
mainland, are Hawaii, Maui, Kahoolawe,
Lanai, Molokai, Oahu, Kauai and Niihau.
Oahu is the most developed, and contains
the naval base at Pearl Harbor, the capital
Honolulu, and more than three-fourths of
the state's population.

MAUNA LOA, MAUNA KEA and KILAUEA,
active volcanoes on Hawaii Island, still
cause frequent damage. Prevailing trade
winds give an equable climate with daytime
temperatures of 75°–80°F.

**People.** Settled by Polynesians c400–800
AD, it now has a population of mixed
descent, more than half E Asian. Remnants
of the old culture, such as the *lei*
(flower-necklace), the *hula* dance and the
*luau* or Hawaiian feast, survive as tourist
attractions.

**Economy.** Besides the more than 1 million
tourists annually, agriculture based on
pineapple and sugarcane, and military
spending, are mainstays of the economy.
Industry is largely devoted to food
processing and the manufacture of clothing.

**History.** In 1778 Captain James Cook discovered the islands, and the arrival of the US missionaries from 1820 began the process of westernization. They introduced writing and new political concepts and opened the way to trade. Treaties (1875, 1887) freed Hawaiian sugar of duty but also gave the US Pearl Harbor as a way station. Agitation by US residents brought the fall of the monarchy in 1893 and in 1898 the US annexed the new republic. In 1908 Pearl Harbor became a US naval base and the Japanese attack on it (Dec. 7, 1941) brought the US into WWII. An expanding postwar economy and resentment at taxation by the US without representation fueled agitation for admission to the Union. Statehood was granted on Aug. 21, 1959 under a constitution amended in 1958. Since then, Hawaii has continued to grow (with a more than 20% increase in population) and to remain prosperous. Inflation, however, has recently diminished the tourist business; this, along with problems characteristic of many other states (a rise in crime, a debasement of the environment), has led Hawaii into a period of self-examination and reevaluation of goals.

**HAWAII VOLCANOES NATIONAL PARK,** on Hawaii Island, established 1916, has among the largest and most active volcanoes in the world. MAUNA LOA (13,680ft) has the Mokuaweoweo crater on its summit, and KILAUEA crater on its E slope which is 4,090ft high and over 4sq mi in area with a fiery floor called Halemaumau. Area of Park: 317sq mi.

**HAWKES, John** (1925–    ), US avant-garde novelist noted for his dreamlike narratives that reject the traditional elements of plot, character, setting and theme. Among his works are *The Cannibal* (1949), *The Lime Twig* (1961), *The Blood Oranges* (1971) and *The Passion Artist* (1979).

**HAWKING, Stephen** (1942–    ), British theoretical physicist and cosmologist who has applied general RELATIVITY and QUANTUM MECHANICS to the theory of BLACK HOLES in novel ways and produced results of great originality.

**HAWKINS, Coleman** (1904–1969), US jazz virtuoso on the tenor saxophone who established the instrument in the classic "hot" jazz of the 1920s. His style became increasingly subtle and complex in the 1930s and 1940s, influencing the younger instrumentalists who founded BOP.

**HAWKINS, Sir John** (1532–1595). Elizabethan sea captain and, as treasurer of the navy, sponsor of reforms in ship design

and gunnery which contributed to victor over the Spanish ARMADA (1588). H commanded one of the English squadron In 1562–63 he had captained the fir English slaving voyage, breaking th Spanish West Indies trade monopoly.

**HAWKS,** fast-flying, diurnal BIRDS OF PRE The name is properly restricted to the gen *Accipiter,* though, especially in Nor America, it is taken as a general name f any bird of prey. True hawks ar broad-winged birds of woodland or fores the shape of the wings and the long ta enabling them to maneuver rapidly amon trees. They prey mostly on small bird approaching behind cover and making swift dash to kill. (See also GOSHAWK.)

**HAWKS, Howard** (1896–1977), US fil director whose productions ran the gamu from sophisticated comedies to gangst stories and westerns. His best-know movies included *Scarface* (1932), *Bringin Up Baby* (1938), *To Have and Have N* (1944), *The Big Sleep* (1946), and *Re River* (1948).

**HAWKSMOOR, Nicholas** (1661–1736 English baroque architect. He achieve dramatic and massive designs, notably th Castle Howard Mausoleum.

**HAWTHORNE, Nathaniel** (1804–1864 major US novelist and short story write born in Salem, Mass. At first unable to ea a living by writing, he worked at the Bosto custom house. Later he was US consul Liverpool (1853–57). His great novels, *Th Scarlet Letter* (1850) and *The House of th Seven Gables* (1851), set in Puritan Ne England, are masterpieces of psychologic portraiture and dark atmosphere. His sho stories collected in *Twice-Told Tale* (1842) and *Mosses from an Old Mans* (1846) mark him as a master of that genre

**HAY, John** (Milton) (1838–1905), U statesman and author, and when youn President Lincoln's secretary (1860–65 Secretary of State under McKinley ar Roosevelt (1898–1905), he established U sovereignty over Hawaii and the Philip pines, negotiated the HAY-PAUNCEFO TREATIES and the HAY-BUNAU-VARILL TREATY which together ensured US contr of the Panama Canal, and evolved the OPE DOOR POLICY in China. His writings includ *Pike County Ballads* (1871) and (with J. ( NICOLAY) *Abraham Lincoln: A History* (1 vols., 1890).

**HAYDEN, Carl** (1877–1972), US politic leader. A Democrat, he became Arizona first Congressman, from statehood in 19 to 1926, when he was elected to the Senat serving until 1969, the longest Congressio al career of any man in American history.

power in the Senate for decades, he was chairman of the Appropriations Committee 1957–69 and president pro tem 1957–69.

**HAYDEN, Thomas Emmet** (1940– ), American political activist and writer, signing himself "Tom Hayden." He was a co-founder of Students for a Democratic Society, a defendant in the Chicago 8 trial, and founded the California-based Committee for Economic Democracy. He is married to actress and political activist Jane Fonda.

**HAYDN, Franz Joseph** (1732–1809), Austrian composer who established the accepted classical forms of the symphony, string quartet and piano sonata. The architect of classicism, Haydn nevertheless drew inspiration from folk music in many of his works. His greatest music combines vigor, lyricism and poignancy with frequent flashes of wit. For 48 years court musician to the Esterhazy family, his huge output includes 107 symphonies, hundreds of chamber works as well as violin and piano concertos, some 25 operatic works, a number of great masses, notably the *Nelson* mass, and other great religious works, such as the oratorio *The Creation*. In the 1790s he visited England, where he won great acclaim for his 12 "London" or "Salomon" symphonies, which were commissioned by the impresario Salomon.

**HAYEK, Friedrich August von** (1899– ), Vienna-born British economist (naturalized 1938). From 1931 Prof. of Economic Sciences in London U.; 1950–62 U. of Chicago, and 1962–69 U. of Freiburg. He has written prolifically on monetary theory and the history of capitalism. He shared the Nobel Prize for Economics with Gunnar MYRDAL in 1974.

**HAYES, Helen** (1900– ), US actress, born Helen Hayes Brown. Beginning at age five, she grew to become one of America's most versatile and admired performers, associated with numerous interpretations that were often definitive and always memorable, and winner of numerous awards for stage, screen, radio and television. She married Charles MAC-ARTHUR. A New York theater has been named after her.

**HAYES, Rutherford Birchard** (1822–1893), 19th president of the US who won office in the most bitterly contested of all presidential elections. Born in Delaware, Ohio, he graduated from Harvard Law School in 1845 to begin a successful legal career. In the Civil War he was four times wounded in action and rose to become a major general of volunteers. Elected to Congress while on active service (1865) he later won three terms as governor of Ohio

(1867–75). At the Republican Convention of 1876 he won the nomination from the better known James G. BLAINE. In the election, the Democrat reform governor of New York, Samuel J. TILDEN, revived his party's fortunes to win a popular majority. But disputed results in S.C., Fla., La. and Ore. led to the formation of a special electoral commission with a Republican majority, which awarded all the disputed votes to Hayes.

**President.** Hayes' contribution as president has undoubtedly been underrated. Following pre-inaugural pledges to Southern Democrats for their acquiescence in the commission's decision, he recalled Federal troops from the South, thus ending 11 years of Republican military RECONSTRUCTION. Despite opposition in his own party, he appointed ex-Confederates to administration posts and began a much-needed reform of the civil service by insisting upon recruitment by competitive examination rather than political patronage. In economic affairs, although his hard money policies were modified, even overridden by Congress, he has been credited with restoring business confidence. Hayes, whose personal integrity was never impugned, refused to stand for a second term. Yet he had slowly mollified opposition resentment over the "stolen" election and he had helped to repair Republican credibility after the corruption and scandals of Grant's presidential terms. His achievements were certainly equal to those of other, better-known presidents.

**HAY FEVER,** common allergic disease causing RHINITIS and CONJUNCTIVITIS on exposure to allergen. The prototype is ALLERGY to grasses, but pollens of many trees, weeds and grasses (e.g., ragweed, Timothy grass) may provoke seasonal hay fever in sensitized individuals. Allergy to FUNGI or to the house-dust mite may lead to perennial rhinitis; animal fur or feathers may also provoke attacks. Susceptibility is often associated with ASTHMA, ECZEMA and ASPIRIN sensitivity in the individual or his family. Treatment consists of allergen avoidance, desensitizing INJECTIONS and cromoglycate, ANTIHISTAMINES or STEROID sprays in difficult cases.

**HAYMARKET AFFAIR,** violent confrontation between labor organizers and police in Chicago's Haymarket Square on May 4, 1886. After several workers had been killed or injured on May 3, a protest meeting was held. During the meeting a bomb was thrown at the police who intervened, and rioting started; four workers and seven policemen died. Of the eight anarchists later sentenced to death for murder, four were hanged, one committed suicide and three, in 1893, were pardoned.

**HAYS, William Harrison** (1879–1954), US politician, famous for administering the motion-picture moral code of 1934 known as the "Hays Code." He was president of the Motion Picture Producers and Distributors of America, 1922–45.

**HAYWOOD, William Dudley** (1869–1928), US labor leader and principal organizer of the INDUSTRIAL WORKERS OF THE WORLD (1905). His membership in the Socialist party ended with expulsion because of his advocacy of sabotage and violence. In WWI he was convicted of sedition but escaped to Russia in 1921.

**HAZLITT, William** (1778–1830), one of England's greatest literary critics and essayists. His perceptive and sympathetic observations of culture, politics and English manners, appeared in *Characters of Shakespeare's Plays* (1817) and *Lectures on the English Comic Writers* (1819). His wit and versatility are reflected in the miscellaneous essays of *Table Talk* (1821–22) and *The Spirit of The Age* (1825).

**H.D.** See DOOLITTLE, HILDA.

**HEADACHE,** the common symptom of an ache or pain affecting the head or neck, with many possible causes including FEVER, emotional tension (with spasm of neck MUSCLES) or nasal SINUS infection. **Migraine,** due to abnormal reactivity of blood vessels, is typified by zig-zag or flashing visual sensations or tingling in part of the body, followed by an often one-sided severe throbbing headache. This may be accompanied by nausea, VOMITING and sensitivity to light. There is often a family history. **Meningeal inflammation,** as in MENINGITIS and subarachnoid HEMORRHAGE, may also cause severe headache. The headache of RAISED INTRACRANIAL PRESSURE is often worse on waking and on coughing and may be a symptom of brain TUMOR, ABSCESS or HYDROCEPHALUS. Headaches are often controlled by simple ANALGESICS, while migraine may need drugs that act on blood vessels (e.g., ERGOT derivatives).

**HEAD START,** US government program, set up in 1964 by the Economic Opportunity Act, to prepare "culturally deprived" children of preschool age for school, and to involve parents and local communities in the effort. The "Head Start" program was so popular that "Follow Through" programs for children in kindergarten were added in 1967.

**HEALEY, Denis** (1917–    ), British political leader. He served as secretary of state for defense (1964–70) and chancellor of the Exchequer (1974–79) in Labour governments. He lost a contest for party leader (1980), serving as deputy leader thereafter.

**HEALTH AND HUMAN SERVICES, Department of** (HHS), US executive department established 1939 as the Federal Security Agency and reestablished 1953 as the Department of Health, Education and Welfare. It was designated the Department of Health and Human Services in 1979, when the Office of Education became a new department. As the second-largest federal department (after the Department of Defense), HHS is responsible for over 300 federal health and human service programs, including the Offices of Human Developmental Services, Public Health Service, Social Security Administration and Child Support Enforcement.

**HEARN, Lafcadio** (1850–1904), US writer of Irish-Greek origin. His move to Japan in 1890 and naturalization as a Japanese citizen brought about his best work: *In Ghostly Japan* (1899), *Shadowings* (1900), *Kwaidan* (1904) and *Japan: An Attempt at Interpretation* (1904).

**HEARST, Patricia** (1954–    ), US heiress to the HEARST publishing empire who in Feb. 1974 was allegedly kidnapped by the SYMBIONESE LIBERATION ARMY (SLA), a group of urban guerrillas then operating out of San Francisco. Following a two-month indoctrination period, she participated in a bank robbery staged by SLA members. She was apprehended 16 months later, arrested and sentenced (1976) to seven years in prison; she served 22 months before her sentence was commuted by presidential order.

**HEARST, William Randolph** (1863–1951), US publisher, head of a vast newspaper empire. His early success as a newspaper publisher in "yellow journalism" was largely due to his papers' sensationalism, low prices, the introduction of color cartoons, banner headlines and Sunday supplements. In 1895 he bought the New York *Journal* and engaged in an epic circulation war with Joseph PULITZER's *World.* Both were accused of having helped to bring on the 1898 war with Spain to increase circulation. He also pursued a largely unsuccessful political career.

**HEART,** vital organ in the CHEST of animals, concerned with pumping the BLOOD, thus maintaining the BLOOD CIRCULATION. The evolution of the vertebrates shows a development from the simple heart found in fish to the four-chambered heart of mammals. In man, the circulation may be regarded as a figure-of-eight, with the heart at the cross-over point, but keeping the two systems separate by having two parallel sets of chambers. The pumping in the two sets, right and left, is coordinated, ensuring a balance of flow. Each set consists of an atrium, which receives blood from the LUNGS (left) or body (right), and a ventricle. The atria pump blood into the ventricles, which pump it into the lungs (right) or systemic circulation (left). The bulk of the heart consists of specialized MUSCLE fibers which contract in response to stimulation from a pacemaker region relayed via special conducting tissue. Between each atrium and ventricle are valves, the mitral (left) and tricuspid (right). Similarly, between the ventricles and their outflow tracts are aortic and pulmonary valves. The heart is lined by PERICARDIUM and receives its blood supply from the AORTA via the coronary ARTERIES. The cells in the right atrium have an inbuilt tendency to depolarize and thus to set up an electrical impulse in the conducting tissue. In heart action this passes to both atria, which have already filled with blood from the systemic or pulmonary veins. Blood is then pumped by atrial contraction into the ventricles, though much of it passes into the latter before the atria contract. The same electrical impulse is conducted to both ventricles and there sets up a coordinated contraction (*systole*), which leads to the forceful expulsion of blood into the aorta or pulmonary artery and to the closure of the mitral and tricuspid valves. When the contraction ceases (*diastole*), the pressure in the ventricle falls, and the aortic and pulmonary valves close. The force generated by systole is propagated into the major arteries, providing the driving force for the circulation. Heart output may be increased (e.g., in EXERCISE) through several agencies including increased rate (*tachycardia*) and force of contraction (mediated by the sympathetic NERVOUS SYSTEM and ADRENALINE), and the increased return of venous blood (effected by a muscle pumping action on the valved, collapsible VEINS). **Disorders of the heart** include: *Congenital disorders* of the structure of the chambers or valves (e.g., BLUE BABY), and disease following RHEUMATIC FEVER, leading to stenosis or incompetence of the valves, especially the mitral and aortic. These disorders may be improved by DRUG treatment but they frequently require cardiac SURGERY to correct or repair defects or to insert PROSTHETICS (e.g., artificial heart valves). *Coronary thrombosis* causes DEATH or injury to areas of heart muscle. This may lead to defects in pumping and

heart failure, rhythm disorder, ANEURYSM or, rarely, cardiac rupture. *Rhythm disturbance* may follow damage to conducting tissue (where abnormal conducting or pacemaker tissue exists), in certain metabolic disorders (thyrotoxicosis—see THYROID GLAND), and in valve disease. *Bradycardia* is very slow heart rate. This may be due to disease but can be normal in fit athletes in whom it indicates increased heart efficiency. Rhythm disorders are often treated with drugs including DIGITALIS, sympathetic-nervous-system stimulants or blockers, ATROPINE, and certain agents used in local ANESTHESIA. *Heart failure*, in which inadequate pumping leads to imbalance between the two parts of the circulation or the failure of both, may be due to coronary thrombosis, cardiac muscle disease or fluid overload. It causes pulmonary EDEMA with shortness of breath on exercise or on lying flat, or peripheral edema. DIURETICS and digitalis are the cornerstones of treatment, relieving edema and increasing pump efficacy. *Infection of abnormal valves* with BACTERIA or FUNGI is a serious disease causing FEVER and other systemic manifestations including EMBOLISM, heart failure and valve destruction. Its prevention, in high-risk patients, and treatment involve careful use of selected ANTIBIOTICS. Valve replacement may also be needed. Investigation of the heart can involve the use of the ELECTROCARDIOGRAPH, chest X-RAY or cardiac CATHETER (to study ANATOMY and flow) and the study of serum ENZYME levels.

**HEART ATTACK.** See CORONARY THROMBOSIS.

**HEARTBURN,** or esophagitis, burning sensation of "indigestion" localized centrally in the upper ABDOMEN or lower CHEST. It is frequently worse after large meals or on lying flat, especially with hiatus HERNIA. Acid STOMACH contents irritate the esophageal EPITHELIUM and may lead to ULCER; relief is with ANTACIDS. Heartburn is also losely applied to other pains in the same situation.

**HEART MURMUR,** abnormal sound heard on listening to the CHEST over the HEART with a STETHOSCOPE. Normally there are two major heart sounds due to valve closure, separated by silence. Murmurs arise in the disease of heart valves, with narrowing (stenosis) or leakage (incompetence). Holes between chambers, valve roughening and high flow also cause murmurs.

**HEAT,** the form of ENERGY that passes from one body to another owing to a TEMPERATURE difference between them; one of the basic functions in THERMODYNAMICS.

The energy residing in a hot body is also loosely called heat, but is better termed internal energy, since it takes several different forms. Despite an earlier view by some philosophers that heat was a form of agitation, in the 18th century the CALORIC THEORY OF HEAT predominated, until disproved by the experiments of Sir Humphry Davy and Count RUMFORD (1798) showing that mechanical WORK could be converted to heat. James JOULE confirmed this by many ingenious experiments and found a consistent value for the **mechanical equivalent of heat** (the ratio of work done to heat produced). In the mid-18th century Joseph BLACK first clearly distinguished heat from temperature, a conceptual advance which allowed heat to be measured (see CALORIMETRY) in terms of the temperature rise of a known mass of water, the unit being the CALORIE (or the BRITISH THERMAL UNIT). In SI UNITS heat is measured, as a form of energy, in JOULES. A given mass $m$ of any substance shows a characteristic temperature rise $\theta$ when an amount of heat $Q$ is supplied: $Q=ms\theta$ where $s$ is the SPECIFIC HEAT of the substance. If the substance changes its state, however, by melting, freezing, boiling or condensing, LATENT HEAT is absorbed or produced without any temperature change, the internal energy being changed by altering the molecular interrelations, not merely their degree of motion. Heat is commonly produced as required for space heating or to power ENGINES, by conversion of chemical energy (burning fuel—see COMBUSTION), electrical energy or nuclear energy. There are three processes by which heat flows from a hotter to a cooler body: CONDUCTION and CONVECTION, in which molecular motion is transferred, and radiation, in which INFRARED RADIATION is emitted and propagates through space. Heat transfer may be hindered by means of thermal INSULATION. **Newton's law of cooling** states that the rate of loss of heat by a body in a draft (forced convection) is proportional to its temperature difference from its surroundings.

**HEATH, Edward Richard George** (1916–    ), British prime minister 1970–74. He was elected to parliament in 1950, and after holding Conservative Party positions, he became party leader in 1965. As prime minister, he brought Britain into the Common Market. He employed austerity measures to fight inflation and resorted to a 3-day work week to save fuel during a miners' strike. In 1975, a year after being turned out of office, he resigned as party leader.

**HEAT RASH.** See PRICKLY HEAT.

**HEATTER, Gabriel** (1890–1972), US newscaster who dramatically and optimistically reported the news over the radio from 1932 to 1965. He habitually found the brighter side of any event and was especially popular during WWII.

**HEAVEN,** the celestial regions in which the heavenly bodies—sun, moon, stars and planets—exist; the abode of God, angels and the righteous after death. These two concepts have been progressively differentiated, especially since the 16th-century scientific revolution made the three-decker universe archaic. In the Old Testament, God, who dwells in heaven, also transcends it. Not until late Judaism was heaven generally regarded as the abode of the righteous; the dead were previously believed to have a shadowy existence in *sheol* (see HADES). In Christian thought, heaven is the eternal home of true believers, or the state of living in full union with Christ, which the perfected soul enters after death—or, in Roman Catholic doctrine, after PURGATORY—there "to glorify God, and to enjoy him for ever," an experience sometimes known as the beatific vision. In Islam likewise heaven is the joyful dwelling-place of faithful Muslims after death. Similar concepts are found in some other religions (see ELYSIAN FIELDS; VALHALLA). (See also ASCENSION; ESCHATOLOGY; HELL; RESURRECTION.)

**HEAVISIDE, Oliver** (1850–1925), British physicist and electrical engineer best known for his work in telegraphy, in course of which he developed operational calculus, a new mathematical system for dealing with changing wave-shapes. In 1902, shortly after A. E. Kennelly, he proposed that a layer of the atmosphere was responsible for reflecting RADIO waves back to earth. This, the E layer of the IONOSPHERE, was found by E. V. Appleton and others (1924), and is often called the **Kennelly-Heaviside Layer**, or **Heaviside Layer.**

**HEAVY WATER,** or DEUTERIUM oxide ($D_2O$), occurs as 0.014% of ordinary WATER, which it closely resembles. It is used as a moderator in nuclear reactors and as a source of deuterium and its compounds. It is toxic in high concentrations. Water containing TRITIUM or heavy isotopes of oxygen ($O^{17}$ and $O^{18}$) is also called heavy water, mp 3.8°C, bp 101.4°C.

**HEBREW,** the Semitic language in which the Old Testament was written and which is now the official language of Israel. The earliest extant Hebrew writings date from at least the 11th century BC, since when there has been a continuous Hebrew literature. Hebrew is now a sacred tongue and a common written language for religious Jews of all nationalities. Hebrew died out as a spoken language by the 3rd century BC. It was revived as the language of the modern Jewish nation, largely owing to Eliezer Ben Jehudah, who compiled a Hebrew dictionary in the 19th century. Hebrew script, written from right to left, was influenced by ARAMAIC, and adopted the square letters still used in writing Hebrew.

**HEBREWS.** See JEWS; JUDAISM.

**HEBREWS, Epistle to the,** a NEW TESTAMENT book of unknown authorship, though traditionally ascribed to Paul. Addressed to Jewish converts to Christianity who were in danger of apostasy, it explains the fulfillment in Christ of the Old Testament.

**HEBRIDES,** or Western Islands, a group of about 500 islands off the NW coast of Scotland, fewer than 100 of them inhabited. The Outer Hebrides include Harris, Lewis, North and South Uist, Benbecula and Barra, while Skye, Mull and Iona lie among the Inner Hebrides. Apart from tourism, industries include fishing, farming, sheepraising, distilling, quarrying and weed-making.

**HECHT, Ben** (1894–1964), US dramatist, short story writer and novelist. After working as a journalist he collaborated with Charles MACARTHUR on the highly successful plays *The Front Page* (1928), and *Twentieth Century* (1932). He also worked on the filmscripts of *Gunga Din* (1938), *Wuthering Heights* (1939), and *Notorious* (1946). His autobiography is *A Child of the Century* (1954).

**HECTOR,** prince of TROY and in the ILIAD the greatest Trojan warrior in the TROJAN WAR. Son of PRIAM and HECUBA, a favorite of APOLLO, he was brutally killed by ACHILLES. (See also HOMER.)

**HEDGEHOGS,** small, spine-covered insectivores of Asia, Africa and Europe. The Eurasian species is the Common hedgehog, *Erinaceus europaeus*. Nocturnal mammals, they wander about searching the ground for worms, beetles and slugs. Each spine is a modified hair about 25mm (1in) long. Hedgehogs are able to roll up for protection against predators, and become entirely enclosed by the spiny part of the skin.

**HEDONISM,** a philosophical theory which regards pleasure as the ultimate good for man. The view of the CYRENAICS and Aristippus was that the sentient pleasure of the moment was the only good. EPICURUS thought man's aim should be a life of lasting pleasure best attained by the guidance of reason. The 19th-century theory of UTILITARIANISM, for "the greatest good of the greatest number," was a revival of hedonism. Hedonism has often been attacked, for instance by Joseph Butler who saw pleasure as a bonus when a desire is fulfilled, not as an end in itself.

**HEFNER, Hugh** (1926–    ), US publisher who in 1953 founded *Playboy* magazine, the first sexually oriented mass-market magazine in the US. He also established a network of private nightclubs and resorts throughout the country.

**HEGEL, Georg Wilhelm Friedrich** (1770–1831), German philosopher of IDEALISM who had an immense influence on 19th and 20th-century thought and history. During his life he was famous for his professorial lectures at the University of Berlin and he wrote on logic, ethics, history, religion and aesthetics. The main feature of Hegel's philosophy was the dialectical method by which an idea (*thesis*) was challenged by its opposite (*antithesis*) and the two ultimately reconciled in a third idea (*synthesis*) which subsumed both. Hegel found this method both in the workings of the mind, as a logical procedure, and in the workings of the history of the world, which to Hegel was the process of the development and realization of the World Spirit (*Weltgeist*). Hegel's chief works were *Phenomenology of the Mind* (1807) and *Philosophy of Right* (1821). His most important follower was MARX.

**HEIDEGGER, Martin** (1889–1976), German philosopher. Influenced by KIERKEGAARD and HUSSERL, he was concerned with the problem of how man's awareness of himself is dependent on a sense of time and his impending death. Heidegger rejects traditional metaphysics and criticizes many aspects of modern technological and mass culture as a "forgetfulness of being." His major work *Being and Time* (1927) has been fundamental in the development of existentialism, although Heidegger denied he was an existentialist. (See also EXISTENTIALISM; PHENOMENOLOGY.)

**HEIDELBERG,** historic city in West Germany, in Baden-Württemberg on the Neckar R. Overlooking the city is the ruined castle of the former Electors of the Palatinate. Heidelberg has the oldest German university (1386). The city is European headquarters of the US army. Pop 129,000.

**HEIDEN, Eric** (1958–    ), US speed skater. He set a Winter Olympics record with five gold medals in 1980. His eight consecutive international titles in three years (1977–80) made him the first world-famous US speed skater.

**HEIFETZ, Jascha** (1901– ), Russian-born US violinist. He was a child prodigy, giving concerts by 1911, and his virtuosity and technique have been compared to those of PAGANINI. He has transcribed many works for the violin and made many recordings.

**HEINE, Heinrich** (1797–1856), German romantic lyric poet and essayist. His best-known work, *Book of Songs* (1827), was influenced by German folk songs. His prose writings such as *Travel Pictures* (1827–31), although poignant, were often very satirical. His poems have been set to music by such composers as SCHUMANN, SCHUBERT and MENDELSSOHN.

**HEINLEIN, Robert Anson** (1907– ), US science-fiction writer, a trained physicist and engineer known for such books as *Starship Troopers* (1959) and *Stranger in a Strange Land* (1961).

**HEISENBERG, Werner Karl** (1901–1976), German mathematical physicist generally regarded as the father of QUANTUM MECHANICS, born out of his rejection of any kind of model of the ATOM and use of mathematical MATRICES to elucidate its properties. His famous UNCERTAINTY PRINCIPLE (1927) overturned traditional physics.

**HEISMAN TROPHY**, the John W. Heisman Memorial Trophy, awarded annually since 1935 to the best college football player. It is most often bestowed on a running back.

**HEJAZ**, NW province in Saudi Arabia, on the E coast of the Red Sea, the holy land of Islam. The cities of MECCA and MEDINA are the most important Muslim pilgrimage sites. Saudi Arabia annexed Hejaz in 1924.

**HELD, John Jr.** (1889–1958), US cartoonist and illustrator who captured the mood of the 1920s with his famous line drawings of bobbed-haired flappers and their raccoon-coated escorts. His work appeared frequently in such sophisticated magazines as *The New Yorker, Smart Set* and *Vanity Fair.*

**HELENA**, city in W central Mont., state capital and the seat of Lewis and Clark Co. Its industries are mining and the manufacture of concrete, paint and machine parts. Pop 23,938.

**HELEN OF TROY**, the most beautiful of all women, according to Greek mythology. Daughter of ZEUS and LEDA, she was wife of MENELAUS, king of Sparta, from whom PARIS abducted her to Troy, thus provoking the TROJAN WAR. After the war she returned to Greece with Menelaus.

**HELICOPTER**, exceptionally maneuverable aircraft able to take off and land vertically, hover, and fly in any horizontal direction without necessarily changing the alignment of the aircraft. Lift is provided by one or more rotors mounted above the craft and rotating horizontally about a vertical axis. Change in the speed of rotation or in the pitch (angle of attack) of all the blades at once alters the amount of lift; cyclic change in the pitch of each blade during its rotation alters the direction of thrust. Most helicopters have only a single lift rotor, and thus have also a tail-mounted vertical rotor to prevent the craft from spinning around (see TORQUE); change in the speed of this rotor is used to change the craft's heading.

Helicopter toys were known to the Chinese and in medieval Europe, but, because of problems with stability, it was not until 1939, following the success of the AUTOGIRO (1923), that the first fully successful helicopter flight was achieved by SIKORSKY. Used in combat in Vietnam, the helicopter has become increasingly important in military use. It has given ground forces entree to areas hitherto inaccessible. Its firepower and maneuverability permit close air support of ground forces. Its extreme mobility allows evasive action and the potential to surprise the enemy. Its capacity to hover makes it a relatively stable weapons platform.

In civilian use, helicopters have proved valuable for city-to-airport and city-to-suburb transportation and for such uses as monitoring traffic, spotting forest fires, patrolling pipelines, and rescue work. (See also AERODYNAMICS; VERTICAL TAKEOFF AND LANDING AIRCRAFT.)

**HELIUM (He)**, one of the NOBLE GASES, lighter than all other elements except hydrogen. It is a major constituent of the SUN and other STARS. The main source of helium is natural gas in Tex., Okla. and Kan. ALPHA PARTICLES are helium nuclei. Helium is lighter than air and nonflammable, so is used in balloons and airships. It is also used in breathing mixtures for deep-sea divers, as a pressurizer for the fuel tanks of liquid-fueled rockets, in helium-neon LASERS, and to form an inert atmosphere for welding. Liquid helium $He^4$ has two forms. Helium I, stable from 2.19K to 4.22K, is a normal liquid, used as a refrigerant (see CRYOGENICS; SUPERCONDUCTIVITY). Below 2.18K it becomes helium II, which is a superfluid with no VISCOSITY, the ability to flow as a film over the side of a vessel in which it is placed, and other strange properties explained by QUANTUM THEORY. $He^3$ does not form a superfluid. Solid helium can be produced only at pressures above 25atm. AW 4.0, mp 1.1K (25atm) bp 4.22K.

**HELL,** the abode of evil spirits (see DEMON; DEVIL) and of the wicked after death, usually thought of as an underworld or abyss. In many ancient religions hell is merely the dark, shadowy abode of the dead—HADES or its equivalent—and the word is so used when Christ is said to have descended into hell. Zoroastrianism and many Eastern religions saw it as a place of chastisement and purification, resembling the Roman Catholic PURGATORY. In later Judaism, Christianity and Islam, hell is the place of eternal punishment of unrepentant sinners condemned at the LAST JUDGMENT. The New Testament describes hell (or GEHENNA) as a place of corruption and unquenchable fire and brimstone—images which have often been taken literally. Modern theology usually regards hell as ultimate separation from God, the confirmation of the sinner's own choice. Many Christians deny the eternity or the existence of hell (see UNIVERSALISM). (See also LIMBO.)

**HELLENISTIC AGE,** the period in which Greco-Macedonian culture spread through the lands conquered by Alexander the Great. It is generally accepted to run from Alexander's death (323 BC) to the annexation of the last Hellenistic state, Egypt, by Rome (31 BC) and the death of Cleopatra VII, last of the Ptolemies (30 BC). After Alexander's death, and despite the temporary restraint imposed by Antipater, his empire was split by constant warring between rival generals eager for a share of the territory. Even after the accomplishment of the final divisions (Egypt, Syria and Mesopotamia, Macedonia, the Aetolian and Achaean Leagues in Greece, Rhodes and Pergamum), Greek remained the international language throughout most of the known world and a commercial and cultural unity held sway. The age was marked by cosmopolitanism, sharply contrasting with the parochialism of the earlier Greek era, and by advances in the sciences (see ARCHIMEDES; ARISTARCHUS; ERATOSTHENES; EUCLID; THEOPHRASTUS). The art was powerfully naturalistic if occasionally bathetic. Traditional religious cults weakened and were superseded by others either imported from the east or increasing in influence; such as the cults of Isis, Sarapis, Cybele and Mithras. The Hellenistic age saw the emergence of Stoicism (see ZENO) and Epicureanism (see EPICURUS).

**HELLER, Joseph** (1923– ), US novelist and playwright best known for *Catch-22* (1961), a grotesquely humorous novel about an American bombardier's "deep-seated survival anxieties" during WWII. Other satiric works include the play *We Bombed in New Haven* (1967) and the novel *Good as Gold* (1979).

**HELLMAN, Lillian** (1905– ), US playwright, screenwriter, and autobiographer. A mordant social critic, her plays, such as *The Children's Hour* (1934), *The Little Foxes* (1939) and *Watch on the Rhine* (1941), studied the evil effects of ruthless ambition and exploitation in personal, social and political situations. Her books of reminiscences, such as *An Unfinished Woman* (1969, National Book Award 1970) and *Scoundrel Time* (1976), are fascinating for their portraits of famous people and events.

**HELL'S ANGELS,** classic black-leather-jacketed motorcycle gang of the sort portrayed in the 1953 film *The Wild Ones*, starring Marlon Brando. Although identified as a public menace as early as 1957 by the Cal. attorney general, and the subject of numerous investigations and trials, the gang still persists, with clubs on both coasts. (See also ALTAMOUNT FESTIVAL.)

**HELLS CANYON,** also Grand Canyon of the Snake, gorge of the Snake R on the Ida.–Ore. boundary. At a depth of 7,900ft it is the deepest in North America. An area of great natural beauty, it extends for 40 mi.

**HELMHOLTZ, Hermann Ludwig Ferdinand von** (1821–1894), German physiologist and physicist. In course of his physiological studies he formulated the law of conservation of ENERGY (1847), one of the first to do so. He was the first to measure the speed of nerve impulses (see NERVOUS SYSTEM), and invented the OPHTHALMOSCOPE (both 1850). He also made important contributions to the study of ELECTRICITY and NON-EUCLIDEAN GEOMETRY.

**HELMONT, Jan Baptista van** (1580–1644), Flemish chemist and physician, regarded as the father of biochemistry. He was the first to discover that there were airlike substances distinct from air, and first used the name "gas" for them.

**HÉLOÏSE.** See ABÉLARD, PETER.

**HELPMANN, Robert** (1909– ), Australian dancer, choreographer and actor. From 1933 to 1950 he was a leading dancer with the Sadler's Wells Ballet, often partnering Margot FONTEYN. He choreographed several ballets and has been active in theater as well as film. He appeared in *The Red Shoes* (1948) and *Tales of Hoffman* (1950).

**HELSINKI,** capital of Finland, situated on a rocky peninsula. Called "white city of the north" because much of it is built of local white granite, it is Finland's chief industrial center and seaport. Its main industries are shipyards, foundries, textiles and paper and machinery manufacture. Chief exports are timber, pulp and metal goods. Founded by GUSTAVUS Vasa in 1550, its Swedish name is Helsingfors. Pop 483,200.

**HELSINKI ACCORDS.** On Aug. 1, 1975, the US, Canada, the USSR and 35 European countries signed this document as the final act of the Conference on Security and Cooperation in Europe that began in 1972. Though nonbinding, it outlines a broad basis for peaceful relations in Europe. It includes the promise to give 21 days notice of military maneuvers by more than 25,000 men by either the East or West bloc, respect for human rights and recognition of existing European frontiers. Each side later accused the other of violating these accords.

**HELVÉTIUS, Claude Adrien** (1715–1771), French philosopher and Encyclopedist whose *The Mind* (1758), considered godless, caused a furor in France. He was attacked by his fellow Encyclopedists, VOLTAIRE and ROUSSEAU, but his work later influenced UTILITARIANISM.

**HEMINGWAY, Ernest** (1899–1961), influential US novelist and short story writer whose terse prose style was widely emulated. His first major novel, *The Sun Also Rises* (1926), chronicled the postwar experiences of what his friend Gertrude STEIN called the "lost generation" of WWI. *A Farewell to Arms* (1929) and *For Whom the Bell Tolls* (1940) were based on his own experiences in WWI and the Spanish Civil War respectively and added greatly to his reputation as a writer. *The Old Man and the Sea* (1952) won a 1953 Pulitzer Prize and he won the Nobel Prize for Literature the next year. Increasingly depressed and ill in later years, he committed suicide.

**HEMOGLOBIN,** respiratory pigment found in the BLOOD of many animals including man. It contains heme, an iron-containing molecule, and globin, a large protein, and occurs in red blood cells. The whole molecule has a high affinity for oxygen, being converted to oxyhemoglobin. In the LUNG capillaries, hemoglobin is exposed to a high oxygen concentration and oxygen is taken up. The redder blood then passes via the HEART into the systemic circulation. In the tissues the oxygen concentration is low, so oxygen is released from the ERYTHROCYTES and reduced hemoglobin returns to the lungs. Carbon monoxide has an even higher affinity for hemoglobin than oxygen and thus acts as a poison by displacing oxygen from hemoglobin, causing ANOXIA. Abnormal hemoglobin structures occur in certain races and may cause red-cell destruction and anemia. Lack of hemoglobin, regardless of cause, produces ANEMIA.

**HEMOPHILIA,** inherited disorder of CLOTTING in males, carried by females who do not suffer from the disease. It consists of inability to form adequate amounts of a clotting factor (VIII) essential for the conversion of soluble fibrinogen in blood to form fibrin. Prolonged bleeding from wounds or tooth extractions, HEMORRHAGE into JOINTS and MUSCLES with severe pain are important symptoms. Bleeding can be stopped by giving PLASMA concentrates rich in factor VIII and, if necessary, BLOOD TRANSFUSION. Similar diseases of both sexes are **Christmas disease** (due to lack of factor IX) and **von Willebrand's disease** (factor VIII deficiency with additional CAPILLARY defect).

**HEMORRHAGE,** acute loss of BLOOD from any site. Trauma to major ARTERIES, VEINS or the HEART may lead to massive hemorrhage. GASTROINTESTINAL TRACT hemorrhage is usually accompanied by loss of altered blood in vomit or feces and may lead to SHOCK; ULCERS and CANCER of the bowel are important causes. **Antepartum hemorrhage** is blood loss from the WOMB in late PREGNANCY and may rapidly threaten life of both mother and FETUS; **postpartum hemorrhage** is excessive blood loss after BIRTH due to inadequate womb contraction or retained PLACENTA. STROKE due to BRAIN hemorrhage may damage vital structures and cause COMA, while *subarachnoid bleeding* around the brain from ANEURYSM or malformation causes severe HEADACHE. FRACTURES may cause sizeable hemorrhage into soft tissues. Blood loss may be replaced by TRANSFUSION, and any blood clots may need to be removed.

**HEMORRHOIDS,** or **piles,** enlarged VEINS at the junction of the rectum and anus, which may bleed or come down through the anal canal, usually on defecation, and which are made worse by CONSTIPATION and straining. Sentinal pile is a SKIN tag at the anus. Bleeding from the rectum may be a sign of bowel CANCER and this may need to be ruled out before bleeding is attributed to piles.

**HEMP,** *Cannabis sativa*, tall herbaceous plant native to Asia, but now widely cultivated for fiber, oil and a narcotic drug called **cannabis,** HASHISH or MARIJUANA. The fibers are used in the manufacture of rope. They are separated from the rest of the plant by a process called RETTING (soaking) during which BACTERIA and FUNGI rot away all but the fibers, which are then combed out. Hemp oil obtained from the seed is used in the manufacture of PAINTS, VARNISHES and SOAPS. (See also DRUGS.)

**HENDERSON, Fletcher** (1898–1952), US jazz musician who introduced written orchestration into big band jazz. After college he began as a pianist with W. C. HANDY and accompanied such singers as Bessie Smith. In 1923 he became a bandleader, and built up his band to very high standards.

**HENDRIX, Jimi** (James Marshall, 1942–1970), US singer. An accomplished guitarist from Seattle who worked with the Isley Brothers and Little Richard, he formed his own group in 1966. His influential style, combining driving rhythm and electronic feedback, won him great popularity before his death of a drug overdose at the age of 28.

**HENIE, Sonja** (1912–1969), Norwegian figure skater. From 1927–36 she won 10 consecutive world titles and three Olympic gold medals. She introduced dance choreography to skating in her Olympic debut in 1924, as a 12-year-old. She was a film star from 1937–48.

**HENLEY ROYAL REGATTA,** the oldest major event in rowing. It was begun in 1839 at Henley-on-Thames, England, and is now held annually over four days in early July. The eight oars and single scullers cups are the most coveted awards in rowing.

**HENNINGS, Doug** (1947–    ), US illusionist. He starred in numerous television and casino shows and in two magic-and-rock musicals, *Spellbound* (1973–74) and *The Magic Show* (1974–75). He is also the author of a book on HOUDINI.

**HENRI, Robert** (1865–1929), US painter and art teacher, founder of the ASHCAN SCHOOL of realistic painters. He studied and traveled in Europe 1888–1900, then taught in New York, where he organized the 1908 exhibition of THE EIGHT and the 1910 Independent Artists Exhibition.

**HENRY,** name of eight kings of England. **Henry I** (1068–1135), reigned 1100–35. Son of William I, he seized the English throne on the death of his brother William II and became Duke of Normandy in 1106. **Henry II** (1133–1189), reigned 1154–89, the first of the ANGEVIN kings. By marrying Eleanor, Duchess of Aquitaine in 1152, he acquired vast lands in France. His policy of establishing royal authority in England led to Thomas à BECKET's murder. Henry made many legal and judicial reforms. **Henry III** (1207–1272), reigned 1216–72. His unpopular rule was marked by administrative and diplomatic incompetence and by the

revolts of nobles who forced him to yield power to them. **Henry IV** (1366–1413), reigned 1399–1413, known as Henry of Bolingbroke, the first ruler of the House of LANCASTER. He usurped the throne after forcing Richard II to abdicate. His reign was marked by struggles with Owen GLENDOWER and Sir Henry PERCY. **Henry V** (1387–1422), reigned from 1413, son of Henry IV. He defeated the French at AGINCOURT in 1415, married Catherine of Valois and became successor to the French throne. He established civil order in England and was a great popular hero. **Henry VI** (1421–1471), reigned 1422–61 and 1470–71. A weak, unstable ruler, he was frequently dominated by factions and this led to the dynastic Wars of the ROSES. He was deposed for nine years, and finally murdered. **Henry VII** (1457–1509), reigned 1485–1509, the first of the TUDOR rulers. He killed Richard III in the last battle of the Wars of the ROSES and united the houses of LANCASTER and YORK by marrying Elizabeth of York. He restored order to England and Wales, and promoted efficient administration. **Henry VIII** (1491–1547), son of Henry VII, reigned 1509–47, one of the most powerful and formative rulers in British history. His religious policies led to the Act of Supremacy (1534) in which Parliament renounced papal authority and established

the Church of England with the king as supreme head. He replaced feudal authority with a central system of government, albeit despotic at times, and he created a navy which was to become the basis of British power for centuries to come. His matrimonial problems arose originally from his search for a male heir; he was married successively to CATHERINE OF ARAGON, whom he divorced for Anne BOLEYN (mother of ELIZABETH I) whom he beheaded, Jane SEYMOUR (mother of Edward VI), ANNE OF CLEVES (divorced within a year), Catherine HOWARD (beheaded) and Catherine PARR, who survived him.

**HENRY,** name of four kings of France. **Henry I** (c1008–1060), reigned 1031–60. His rule was disturbed by feudal conflicts organized by his mother and brother. One of his chief enemies was the future William I of England. **Henry II** (1519–1559), reigned 1547–59. In 1533 he married Catherine de Médici but he was dominated by his mistress Diane de Poitiers and his military commander, the Duc de Montmorency. A fanatic Catholic, he persecuted the HUGUENOTS and continued the war against the Holy Roman Emperor and Spain. **Henry III** (1551–1589), reigned 1574–89. He collaborated with his mother Catherine de Médici in the SAINT BARTHOLOMEW'S DAY Massacre (1572). He was dominated by the GUISE family, and his reign was unstable. He was assassinated by a Jacobin friar. **Henry IV** (1553–1610), reigned 1589–1610, king of NAVARRE 1572–1610, the first French BOURBON king. A Protestant leader of the HUGUENOTS, he converted to Roman Catholicism in 1593, granting religious freedom with the Edict of NANTES (1598). He brought unity and economic stability to France, but was assassinated by a Catholic extremist.

**HENRY, Joseph** (1797–1878), US physicist best known for his electromagnetic studies. His discoveries include INDUCTION and self-induction; though in both cases FARADAY published first. He also devised a much improved ELECTROMAGNET by insulating the wire rather than the core; invented one of the first ELECTRIC MOTORS; helped MORSE and Wheatstone devise their telegraphs; and found SUNSPOTS to be cooler than the surrounding photosphere. The HENRY is named for him.

**HENRY, O.** (1862–1910), pseudonym of William Sidney Porter, US short story writer noted for the "surprise ending." He began writing stories while imprisoned in Ohio for embezzlement, and was already popular when released. He moved to New York City in 1902, and wrote over 300 stories, collected in *The Four Million* (1906), *The Voice of the City* (1908) and many other books. His last years were marred by an unhappy second marriage, financial difficulties and alcoholism.

**HENRY, Patrick** (1736–1799), statesman, orator and prominent figure of the American Revolution. A lawyer, he came to public notice with his defense of the Va. legislature over a law repealed by King George II as unjust. Elected to the legislature himself in 1765, he persuaded it to reject the Stamp Act, then joined the first CONTINENTAL CONGRESS in 1774. In a speech at Va.'s second revolutionary convention in 1775, advocating war rather than negotiations, he coined the famous phrase "Give me liberty, or give me death!" He served as

governor of Va. 1776–79 and 1784–86, bu furiously opposed the ratification of the US CONSTITUTION in 1788.

**HENRY THE NAVIGATOR** (1394–1460) Portuguese prince, third son of King John o Portugal, whose active interest inaugurate Portuguese maritime exploration an expansion overseas. He sponsored th exploration and mapping of the W coast o Africa, and his expeditions discovered the Madeiras and the Azores and rounded Cap Verde.

**HENSON, Jim** (1936–    ), US puppetee who created the MUPPETS, a community o fanciful, foam-rubber, puppet-marionett creations, featuring such beloved character as Miss Piggy, Big Bird, Kermit the Frog Oscar the Grouch and the Cookie Monster.

**HENZE, Hans Werner** (1926–    ) German composer known for his symphon ies, concertos and operas, which includ *Elegy for Young Lovers* (1961), for whic W. H. AUDEN and Chester Kallman wrot the libretto.

**HEPATITIS**, INFLAMMATION of the LIVER usually due to VIRUS infection, causin nausea, loss of appetite, FEVER, malaise JAUNDICE and abdominal pain; liver failur may result. It can occur as part of a systemi disease (e.g. YELLOW FEVER, MONO NUCLEOSIS). In two forms infection i restricted to the liver: **infectious hepatitis** i an EPIDEMIC form, transmitted by feces an is of short INCUBATION; it is rarely serious o prolonged. **Serum hepatitis** is transmitte by BLOOD (e.g., used needles and syringe TRANSFUSION), it develops more slowly bu may be more severe, causing death. It i common among drug addicts; carriers ma be detected by blood tests and immuniza tion of those at risk may be helpful Amebiasis and certain DRUGS can also caus hepatitis.

**HEPBURN, Katharine** (1909–    ), US stage and film actress. She is famous fo many performances during a long caree which includes several films with Spence TRACY, and has won three Academy awards Her films include *Bringing up Baby* (1938) *The Philadelphia Story* (1940), *Th African Queen* (1951) and *Long Day Journey Into Night* (1962).

**HEPPLEWHITE, George** (d. 1786) famous English furniture-maker an designer, influenced by Robert ADAM. In th *Cabinet-maker and Upholsterer's Guid* (1788), his furniture is characterized b elegant, fine carved forms and painted o inlaid wood.

**HEPWORTH, Dame Barbar** (1903–1975), British sculptor, and one o the most famous woman artists of the 20t century. Her abstract work, in stone and bronze, like that of Henry MOORE, is concerned with surface textures and the contrast of space and mass.

**HERACLITUS** (c540–c480 BC), Greek philosopher from Ephesus, called "the Obscure" for his cryptic style. He is known to us through some 125 fragments of his own work and by comments of later authors. Believing in universal impermanence ("everything is in flux") and that all things (notably opposites) were interrelated, he considered fire the fundamental element of the universe. His view of the transience of all things exerted a strong influence on PLATO.

**HERALDRY**, the system of devising and granting armorial designs or insignia, and of establishing family genealogies. The designs are displayed on shields or coats of arms and identify individuals or families (in which case they are hereditary), towns, universities, military regiments and nations. The term derives from the work of the heralds of the Middle Ages who announced tournaments and became expert in identifying the armorial bearings of the participants. The practice of bearing coats of arms was adopted by the crusaders and spread through Europe in the 12th century. The arrangement of the devices on the shields was subject to strict conventions. Coats of arms became so general in England that Richard III established the Herald's College (1483) to regulate their adoption.

**HERBERT, George** (1593–1633), English poet and clergyman. His poetry, generally termed Metaphysical, deals for the most part with his own intense religious experiences, expressed in a complex but elegant, sometimes witty style. His work was first published posthumously in a collection entitled *The Temple* (1633).

**HERBERT, Victor** (1859–1924), Irish-American operetta composer and conductor, famous for *Babes in Toyland* (1903) and *Naughty Marietta* (1910). He also wrote two grand operas and a cello concerto.

**HERBICIDES**, chemical compounds used to kill plants. Originally, general herbicides were used in agriculture to kill weeds, but these dangerous substances have been largely superseded since WWII by a host of selective weedkillers, complex organic compounds which at suitable dosage are much more toxic to the prevailing weeds than to the crop. These chemicals have also proved to be dangerous to human and animal life and must be used with great care. (See also DEFOLIANTS.)

**HERBLOCK.** See BLOCK, HERBERT

LAWRENCE.

**HERCULANEUM,** ancient Roman city at the foot of Mt Vesuvius in Italy. Like nearby POMPEII, it was destroyed in 79 AD, by the eruption of Vesuvius which engulfed it in volcanic mud that hardened and preserved even wood and textiles. Rediscovered in 1709, it is still being excavated.

**HERCULES** (Heracles), Greek mythological hero famed for his strength and courage. The son of ZEUS, he performed twelve seemingly impossible labors. He killed the NEMEAN LION and the HYDRA; captured the wild boar of Mt Erymanthus and the hind of Arcadia, a deer with golden antlers; killed the man-eating birds of the Stymphalian marshes; cleaned, in one day, the AUGEAN STABLES; captured the savage bull of King MINOS of Crete and the man-eating mares of King DIOMEDES of Thrace; obtained the girdle of the Amazon queen HIPPOLYTA; seized the cattle of the monster GERYON; fetched the golden apples of the Hesperides and brought CERBERUS from the underworld.

**HERDER, Johann Gottfried von** (1744–1803), German philosopher and literary critic in the STURM UND DRANG movement. He initiated the study of comparative folk literatures and in his *Outlines of the Philosophy of Man* (1784–91) he developed the influential concept of the evolution of human culture and the singularity of each historical epoch.

**HEREDITY**, the process whereby progeny resemble their parents in many features but are not, except in some microorganisms, an exact duplicate of their parents. Patterns of heredity for a long time puzzled biologists and it was not until the researches of Gregor MENDEL, an Austrian monk, that any numeric laws of heredity were discovered. Although Mendel's work was published in the mid-1860s, it went ignored by the majority of biologists until the opening of the 20th century.

Mendel showed that hereditary characteristics are passed on in units called GENES. When GAMETES (reproductive cells) are formed by MEIOSIS, the genes controlling any given characteristic "segregate" and become associated with different gametes. Thus, if the height of a pea plant is controlled by the genes $T$ (for tallness) and $t$ (for shortness) and pollen from a pure-breeding dwarf strain (of genotype $tt$) is used to fertilize ovules of a pure-breeding tall strain (of genotype $TT$), the resulting plants (of the "first filial"—$F_1$—generation), are of genotype $Tt$. Now the gametes of the $F_1$ generation contain equal numbers of genes $T$ and $t$, both in the pollen and the ovules. The second filial ($F_2$) generation thus contains 50% of the "heterozygote" $Tt$, together with 25% each of the "homozygotes" $TT$ and $tt$. In many cases, the heterozygote is indistinguishable from one of the homozygotes. In this case the gene that is expressed in the heterozygous condition is called a *dominant* gene; that which only manifests itself when homozygous is termed *recessive*. In the case of Mendel's peas, since $T$ was dominant and $t$ recessive, in the $F_1$ generation (100% $Tt$) all the plants were tall, while in the $F_2$ generation 75% were of the tall phenotype (i.e., the 25% $TT$ and the 50% $Tt$) and 25% (the $tt$) of the short one.

Mendel also showed that when two or more pairs of genes segregate simultaneously the distribution of any one is independent of the distribution of the others. This work was done by crossing peas pure-breeding for round yellow seeds ($RRYY$) with peas pure-breeding for wrinkled green seeds ($rryy$). All the first-cross seeds were round yellow showing that round is dominant over wrinkled and yellow over green. The possible number of GENOTYPES is 16 but only 4 PHENOTYPES appeared: in the ratio of 9 round yellow seeds to every 3 round green, 3 wrinkled yellow and 1 wrinkled green. This "independent segregation" applies only to genes on different CHROMOSOMES; genes on the same chromosome are "linked" and do not segregate independently.

It is now known the genes are normally located on the chromosomes in the nucleus of the CELL. Each chromosome carries many genes which may be transmitted together and are said to be in *coupling*. However, genes are exchanged between chromosome pairs so that RECOMBINATION occurs. Because of the occurrence of recombination the LINKAGE of genes is not complete.

In the vast majority of animals and higher plants sex is determined by a special sex chromosome which in humans is the XY chromosome. Men are XY and women XX so that all ova are X while a sperm is either X or Y. Therefore there should be an equal number of males and females in a population. In practice Y-bearing sperm are more successful in fertilizing ova than X, so that more boys are born than girls.

Genes not only replicate themselves to pass on genetic information and direct the synthesis of PROTEINS within individual cells, they also interact with each other both directly at the chromosomal level and indirectly through gene products. Although a particular characteristic of an organism is probably under the control of a single gene, the characteristic may be modified by a

large number of other genes. For example mice have a gene which can either slightl shorten the tail or result in early deat through kidney failure, depending on th presence of other genes. Other genes exis for the sole function of suppressing th effects of another gene. The translocation c genes on chromosomes probably plays a important part in gene interaction.

In most organisms the majority c abnormal or mutant genes are recessive But in man mutant genes tend either to b dominant or show no dominance. A humans generally avoid marrying clos relatives, different combinations of gene are always being formed which give rise t the great variation seen among huma beings. A reduction of variability occurs i thoroughbred animals where matings ar controlled so as to select for desired constar features.

It has been estimated that throughou EVOLUTION there have been over 500 millio different species of plants and animal therefore there must have been at least 50 million different genes. Genes are compose of DNA (see NUCLEIC ACIDS) which capable of an enormous number c variations. A sequence of 15 nucleotide composed of four different bases is capabl of over 500 million alternatives. It possible using the four different nucleotide in DNA to construct a code of 6 three-nucleotide sequences capable c indicating all the differing AMINO ACIDS (se CODON).

**HERMAN, Woody** (Woodrow Charle Herman; 1913–    ), US jazz musicia and bandleader. A clarinetist, he forme several big bands, including the famou "Herman Herd" of the WWII era, one c the most distinguished of all jaz orchestras.

**HERMAPHRODITE,** any organism i which the functions of both sexes ar combined. Usually, an individual functior in only one sexual role at a time, but in a fe species, e.g., earthworms, each of a pair c partners fertilizes the other durin copulation. Hermaphrodite plants ar usually referred to as being bisexual.

**HERMITAGE,** Soviet art museum i Leningrad, one of the world's mo outstanding art collections. The hug collection was begun by Empress Catherir II in the 18th century. It has art treasure from all over the world and masterpieces b Rembrandt, Picasso and Matisse.

**HERMIT CRABS,** a group of crustacear with soft bodies which occupy the empt shells of sea snails. Most members of th group occupy spiral WHELK shells and in a of them, the appendages on the right side of he abdomen are not developed. Detritus eeders, hermit crabs have well-developed incers and two pairs of walking legs, and an withdraw into their borrowed shells if attacked. Not infrequently the shell is hared by one or more SEA-ANEMONES, commensal with the hermit crab (see COMMENSALISM).

**HERNIA**, protrusion of abdominal contents through the abdominal wall in the inguinal or femoral part of the groin, or through the DIAPHRAGM (**hiatus hernia**). Hernia may occur through a congenital defect or through an area of MUSCLE weakness. Bowel and omentum are commonly found in hernial sacs and if there is a tight constriction at the neck of the sac (the hernia is "strangulated"), the bowel may be obstructed or suffer GANGRENE. In hiatus hernia, part of the STOMACH lies in the CHEST. Hernia may need SURGERY to reposition the bowel and close the defect, but this is rare in hiatus hernia.

**HEROD**, family name of a dynasty in Palestine which ruled for nearly 150 years around the time of Christ. They were clients of Rome.

**Herod the Great** (c73–4 BC), first important ruler of the dynasty, king of Judaea from 37 BC. He strengthened his position by keeping on good terms with the Romans, including MARK ANTONY and Augustus. Although an able ruler and generous builder (especially the Temple at Jerusalem) he was hated for his ruthlessness. He was responsible for the deaths of many of his family and according to the New Testament, ordered the massacre of the Innocents.

**Herod Antipas** (c21 BC–39 AD), son of Herod the Great, ruler of Galilee at the time of Christ's crucifixion. He was tricked by his wife and her daughter Salome, into having John the Baptist executed.

**Herod Agrippa I** (c10 BC–44 AD), grandson of Herod the Great, king of Judaea 41–44 AD. Helped in his career by his friendship with the Roman emperors Caligula and Claudius, he earned the support of the Jews by his adherence to Jewish tradition.

**Herod Agrippa II** (c27–93 AD), son of Herod Agrippa I, king of Chalcis, last important ruler of the Herodian dynasty. Lacking his father's tact in the treatment of the Jews, he contributed to their discontent, and sided with the Romans in the Jewish revolt 66–70 AD.

**HERODOTUS** (c484–425 BC), Greek historian, renowned as "the Father of History" for his work seeking to describe and explain the causes of the Greco-Persian wars of 499–479 BC. This involved him in a monumental survey of the whole of mankind's previous history, collected from the stories he had heard during his extensive travels. He is also famed as a geographer and ethnologist.

**HEROIN**, OPIUM alkaloid with narcotic ANALGESIC and euphoriant properties, a valuable DRUG in severe pain of short duration (e.g., CORONARY THROMBOSIS) and in terminal malignant disease. It is abused in DRUG ADDICTION, taken intravenously for its psychological effects and later because of physical addiction. SEPTICEMIA and hepatitis may follow unsterile INJECTIONS and early death is common.

**HERONS**, long-billed and long-legged wading birds of the subfamily Ardeinae, and including the EGRETS. Herons are the only birds that fly with the neck tucked back and the head between the shoulders. Gregarious at nesting time, most species disperse after breeding. Waterside or marsh birds, they feed on frogs, fish, eels and watervoles, stabbing with their heavy bills.

**HERO OF ALEXANDRIA** (c62 AD), or **Heron**, Greek scientist best known for inventing the aeolipile, a steam-powered engine that used the principle of jet propulsion, and many other complex steam-and water-powered toys. Other works ascribed to him deal with MENSURATION, optics (containing an early version of FERMAT's Principle) and MECHANICS.

**HEROPHILUS** (c300 BC), Alexandrian physician regarded as the father of scientific ANATOMY, and one of the first dissectors. He distinguished nerves from tendons and partially recognized their role. His work survives only through GALEN's writings.

**HERPES SIMPLEX.** See COLD SORE.

**HERPES ZOSTER.** See SHINGLES.

**HERRICK, Robert** (1591–1674), English lyric poet. Writing in the classical tradition of the Latin lyricists, he was also greatly influenced by the dramatist Ben JONSON. Most of his poems are concerned with the pleasures of nature, wine and love, and he is probably best known for the line "Gather ye rosebuds while ye may."

**HERRINGS**, or clupeid fishes, a large family of important food fishes of worldwide distribution, characterized by a forward extension of the swimbladder into the skull forming two small capsules associated with the ears, and a short, deep lower jaw. Shoaling fishes, some species are found in enormous numbers: shoals of herring may be 15km (9mi) across. The herring family includes the round herrings, SHADS and MENHADEN.

**HERRIOT, Édouard** (1872–1957), French statesman and scholar, leader of the Radical Socialists from 1919. Mayor of Lyon from 1905, he became a senator in 1912. He was a minister, premier of France three times and president of the Chamber of Deputies. In 1942 he was imprisoned by the Germans for opposition to the Vichy government. After WWII he became president of the National Assembly, 1947–54.

**HERSCHEL**, family of British astronomers of German origin. **Sir Frederick William Herschel** (1738–1822) pioneered the building and use of reflecting TELESCOPES, discovered URANUS (1781), showed the sun's motion in space (1783), found that some DOUBLE STARS were in relative orbital motion (1793), and studied NEBULAE. His sister **Caroline Lucretia** (1750–1848) assisted him and herself discovered eight COMETS. His son **Sir John Frederick William Herschel** (1792–1871), with BABBAGE and Peacock helped establish Leibnitzian CALCULUS notation in Britain, was the first to use SODIUM thiosulfate (hypo) as a photographic fixer, studied POLARIZED LIGHT and made many contributions to ASTRONOMY, especially that of the S Hemisphere.

**HERSEY, John Richard** (1914–    ), US author who won a Pulitzer Prize with his first novel, *A Bell for Adano* (1944). His experiences as a war correspondent provided him with material for his books, which include *Hiroshima* (1946) and *The Wall* (1950).

**HERSKOVITS, Melville Jean** (1895–1963), US anthropologist. He was particularly interested in culture change and African ethnology, and in 1927 he founded the first US university course in African studies at Northwestern U.

**HERTZ, Heinrich Rudolph** (1857–1894), German physicist who first broadcast and received RADIO waves (c1886). He showed also that they could be reflected and refracted (see REFLECTION; REFRACTION) much as light, and that they traveled at the same velocity though their wavelength was much longer (see ELECTROMAGNETIC RADIATION). In doing so he showed that light (and radiant heat) are, like radio waves, of electromagnetic nature.

**HERTZSPRUNG, Ejnar** (1873–1967), Danish astronomer who showed there was a relation between a STAR's brightness and color: the resulting **Hertzsprung–Russell Diagram** (named also for Henry RUSSELL) is important throughout astronomy and cosmology. He also conceived and defined absolute MAGNITUDE; and his work on CEPHEID VARIABLES has provided a way to measure intergalactic distances.

**HERZEGOVINA.** See BOSNIA AND HERZEGOVINA.

**HERZL, Theodore** (1860–1904), Austrian writer and founder of the political Zionist movement. He worked for a Palestine homeland for the Jews in the face of mounting anti-Semitism in Europe. The fund and bank he established became essential elements in the founding of Israel.

**HESCHEL, Abraham Joshua** (1907–1972), Polish-born US Jewish philosopher and theologian whose influential philosophy of a dialogue between man and God was influenced by the work of Martin BUBER. His major works included *Man Is Not Alone* (1951), *God in Search of Man* (1955) and *The Prophets* (1962).

**HESIOD** (8th century BC), Greek epic poet. His major works are the didactic *Theogeny*, describing the gods and heroes of Greek mythology, and *Works and Days*, which departed from the heroic tradition of Homer in dealing with the everyday life of a farmer.

**HESS, Dame Myra** (1890–1965), British pianist noted for her interpretations of Bach, Mozart and Scarlatti. She is especially remembered for her morale-boosting lunch-time concerts in London's National Gallery during WWII.

**HESS, Rudolf** (1894–    ), German Nazi leader and Hitler's deputy, 1933–39. Depressed by his loss of influence, in 1941 he flew to Scotland to try personally to arrange a settlement between Germany and Britain. Arrested and interned in Britain during the war, he was condemned to life imprisonment for war crimes at the NUREMBERG TRIALS in 1946. He eventually became the only inmate in Berlin's Spandau Prison. The USSR rejected appeals for his release.

**HESSE, Hermann** (1877–1962), German-born Swiss poet and novelist. The duality of man's nature, particularly with regard to the artist, is a recurrent theme in his work with a later emphasis on symbolism and psychoanalytic insights. His novels include *Demian* (1919), *Siddhartha* (1922), *Steppenwolf* (1927) and *The Glass Bead Game* (1943). In 1946 he won the Nobel Prize for Literature.

**HESSIANS**, German mercenaries, mostly from Hesse-Kassel, who fought with distinction on the British side during the American REVOLUTIONARY WAR. They suffered a serious defeat at Trenton, N.J., in Dec. 1776. After the war many settled in he US and Canada.

**IESTON, Charlton** (1924–    ), US film
ctor, most famous for playing larger-
han-life figures in Biblical and historical
pics. His films include *The Ten
'ommandments* (1956), *Ben Hur* (1959),
*'he Agony and the Ecstasy* (1965) and
*'lanet of the Apes* (1967).

**IEYDRICH, Reinhard** (1904–1942),
otoriously cruel German Nazi leader,
eputy head of the Gestapo 1934–39, then
ut in charge of all security. He became
nown as "the Hangman," and was
ssassinated while acting as "protector" in
Czechoslovakia (see LIDICE).

**IEYERDAHL, Thor** (1914–    ), Nor-
vegian ethnologist famous for his expedi-
ions to prove the feasibility of his theories
f cultural diffusion, and for his books. On
he **Kon-Tiki**, a primitive balsawood raft, he
nd his crew sailed from the W coast of
outh America to Polynesia, demonstrating
he possibility that the Polynesians
riginated in South America (1947). On
**ta**, a facsimile of an ancient Egyptian
apyrus reed boat, he and his cosmopolitan
rew succeeded at the second attempt in
ailing from Morocco to Barbados, showing
he possibility that the pre-Columbian
ultures of South America were influenced
y Egyptian civilization (Ra I, 1969, Ra II,
970). On **Tigris**, another primitive reed
essel, he demonstrated that the ancient
iumerians of Mesopotamia could have
eached the Indus Valley and Africa by sea
1977–78).

**IEYWARD, DuBose** (1885–1940), US
uthor, best known for his novel *Porgy*
1925), on which GERSHWIN based his opera
*'orgy and Bess*. Much of his work deals
vith the plight of Southern blacks.

**IEYWOOD, Thomas** (c1574–1651), En-
lish dramatist and actor. He was a prolific
vriter, claiming over 200 dramas, but only
bout 20 have survived. Excelling at themes
ased on everyday life, often set in London,
is best known play is *A Woman Kilde with
'indnesse* (1607).

**IIBERNATION**, a protective mechanism
vhereby certain animals reduce their
ctivity and apparently sleep throughout
vinter. At its most developed it is a
haracteristic of warm-blooded animals but
comparable phenomenon, **diapause**, is
ound in cold-blooded forms. Diapause is a
irect physiological response to cold
emperatures: metabolic activity in cold-
looded animals is entirely dictated by
xternal temperature. In hibernating
nimals, internal preparations, such as
aying down a store of fat, begin several
veeks before the onset of hibernation. Then,

when temperatures drop, the animal goes to
sleep. Pulse rate and breathing drop to a
minimum. With metabolism reduced, the
animal can live on food stored in its body till
spring. Winter food supplies would not be
sufficient to maintain the animal in a
fully-active state. When an animal remains
torpid throughout the summer, this is
known as **aestivation**.

**HICCUP**, brief involuntary contraction of
the DIAPHRAGM that may follow dietary or
alcoholic excess and rapid eating. It may
also be a symptom of UREMIA, mineral
disorders and brain-stem disease. Rebreath-
ing into a paper bag or repeated swallowing
are effective remedies; chlorpromazine also
suppresses hiccups.

**HICKOK, Wild Bill** (1837–1876), American scout and frontier law officer. During
the Civil War he was a Union scout and spy.
As US marshal at Hays City and Abilene,
Kan. (1869–71), both lawless frontier
towns, he won a reputation for marksman-
ship and daring which he demonstrated in
1872–73 on tour with BUFFALO BILL.

**HICKS, Edward** (1780–1849), US primitive painter. A Quaker preacher, he is best
known for his illustrations of biblical
passages, including over 50 versions of *The
Peaceable Kingdom*, based on Isaiah's
prophecy of peace among all creatures.

**HICKS, Elias** (1748–1830), US Quaker
preacher, one of the first advocates of the
abolition of slavery in the US. His idea that
beliefs could be continually revised caused a
split among the Friends, and his liberal
followers became known as Hicksites.

**HICKS, Granville** (1901–    ), US writer,
critic and editor of the *New Masses*. A
member of the Communist Party until
1939, he wrote a Marxist interpretation of
American literature since the Civil War,
*The Great Tradition* (1933), and, later,
*Literary Horizons: A Quarter Century of
American Fiction* (1970).

**HIDALGO Y COSTILLA, Miguel**
(1753–1811), Mexican revolutionary,
known as "the father of Mexican
independence." A village priest, when
Napoleon annexed Spain he plotted
independence from Spain. The plot
discovered (1810), he rang his church bells
and shouted the famous *grito* (cry) *de
Dolores*, demanding revolution against
Spain. He led a peasant revolt which after
initial success was suppressed in 1811.
Hidalgo was executed, but the anniversary
of his *grito* (Sept. 16) is celebrated as
Mexico's Independence Day.

**HIEROGLYPHICS**, system of writing
using pictorial characters (hieroglyphs),
especially that found on Egyptian mon-

uments. Egyptian hieroglyphics are first found from c3000 BC, their use declining during the 3rd century AD. Initially there were a fairly limited number of hieroglyphs. This was followed by a rapid expansion of the number of characters in order to reduce ambiguity, and by a further expansion around 500 BC. There were two derived cursive scripts, hieratic and demotic. **Hieratic script**, initially used only for sacred texts, coexisted with true hieroglyphics from early on until c100 AD. The less legible, more cursive **demotic script** appeared around 660 BC and disappeared around 450 AD. The writings of other ancient peoples, e.g., the Hittites and Mayas, are also termed hieroglyphics. (See also ROSETTA STONE.)

**HIGH BLOOD PRESSURE.** See BLOOD CIRCULATION.

**HIGH-FIDELITY,** an adjective applicable to systems carrying a signal with very little distortion, such as a good CAMERA or RADIO transmitter, but also a generic noun ("Hi-Fi") for a wide range of domestic equipment for SOUND REPRODUCTION. The input signal may arise from a phonograph disc, in which case a high-compliance (flexibility) stylus following a groove produces a piezoelectric (see PIEZOELECTRICITY) or induced (see ELECTROMAGNETISM) voltage; from magnetic tape, on which the signal is recorded in the variations of magnetization of a ferromagnetic (see MAGNETISM) coating, produced by a finely focused ELECTROMAGNET (the recording head) and inducing a voltage in the small playback head coil; or from a radio receiver which detects the slight variations in intensity (AM) or frequency (FM) of a broadcast electromagnetic wave. The resulting voltage is amplified electronically and passed to a LOUDSPEAKER, consisting typically of a paper cone, vibrated by an electromagnet, in an enclosure which attempts to compensate for the uneven response of the cone for different directions and frequencies. The most important measures of the overall faithfulness are the frequency response (the range of frequencies passed with intensities unchanged within a quoted tolerance), the harmonic distortion (the change in the balance of the HARMONICS of a signal— particularly a boost in the high harmonics), the hum and NOISE levels (in the absence of a signal), and the flutter and wow (fluctuations in speed of record or tape decks).

**HIGH JUMP.** See TRACK AND FIELD.

**HIGH SEAS,** in maritime law, the sea beyond territorial waters. Since the 19th century freedom of the seas has been recognized as a rule of international law, but recently the discovery of minerals under the sea and the importance of the airspace above it have made the concept crucial. Attempts by any state to extend its jurisdiction, for example, to protect fishing rights, should be ratified by international agreement, but various UN conferences have failed in attempts to codify or enforce the law.

**HIGHWAY,** major road, often with controlled access. The term goes back to the Roman roads which were on a mound (hence "high way"), made by earth from the side ditches thrown into the center. The first roads were probably Mesopotamian, but the earliest recorded long-distance road was the Persian Royal Road stretching c1,775mi from Susa to Smyrna. The Romans were the best of the ancient road-builders, and their greatest road, the APPIAN WAY, begun 312 BC, set the standard for road-building for 2,000 years.

Until the 18th century European roads were neglected and hard to travel, but Pierre Marie Jérôme Trésaguet (1716–93) in France and John Metcalf (1777–1810) in England pioneered modern road-building. The Scots, Thomas TELFORD and John Loudon McAdam, developed lightweight road construction, and the MACADAM road relied on a compacted subgrade with a thin surface of broken stone to support the load, as opposed to the heavy Roman system.

The composition was improved in the 20th century by the addition of tar, or bitumen as a binder. The coming of the automobile and increasing loads meant that totally new requirements were introduced. It became necessary for highway systems to be integrated, so although local roads are usually still the responsibility of cities, major highways are administered on a national basis to ensure continuity and uniformity. In the US this is seen to by the Federal Highway Administration. Finances are supplied by the user, with motor-fuel taxes as the main single source of revenue. Vehicles are usually licensed on the basis of weight, and toll roads are popular in areas of high demand. In road construction the major operation is earth moving, and the soil then has to be suitably prepared to make the roadbed. The pavement, or road surface laid on the roadbed, will depend on the traffic anticipated and the nature of the ground.

First-class highways, especially designed for fast-moving traffic, are variously described as expressways, superhighways, throughways or freeways, and parkways are uilt in park-like country and are often ndscaped. The growing numbers of utomobiles and the increase in road usage emands a constant rethinking of highway olicy. Compromise is often necessary to void conflicts with community or nvironmental amenities.

**IJACKING,** illegal seizure of a vehicle in ransit for a political or criminal purpose. he word, first used for the theft of ruckloads of illegal liquor during ROHIBITION, now includes the takeover of hips, trains and planes. The first hijacking f a plane in the US was in 1961, to Cuba, nd the spate of hijacking that followed, for oth political and personal motives, has rced international measures to deal with e problem. (See also SKYJACKING.)

**ILBERT, David** (1862–1943), German aathematician whose most important ontributions were in the field of aathematical LOGIC. With the advent of the ON-EUCLIDEAN GEOMETRIES it had become ear that the axiomatic basis of EUCLID's ork needed further examination. This ilbert did, establishing a logical axiomatic stem for geometry.

**ILL, Joe** (born Joseph Hillstrom; 879–1915), Swedish-American labor rganizer for the INDUSTRIAL WORKERS OF HE WORLD in California. He wrote many bor songs. Tried and executed on a urder charge, his funeral was attended by bout 30,000 people.

**ILLARY, Sir Edmund Percival** 1919– ), New Zealand explorer and ountaineer. In 1953 he and Tenzing orkay, a Sherpa from Nepal, became the rst men to reach the summit of Mount VEREST, the world's highest mountain.

**ILLEL** (d. 10 AD), Jewish scholar, who as one of the great founders of rabbinic udaism, and ethical leader of his eneration. He was opposed by SHAMMAI, nother teacher. His "Seven Rules" of xegesis laid the groundwork for a liberal ther than literal interpretation of riptural law.

**ILLMAN, Sidney** (1887–1946), US labor ader. A Lithuanian immigrant, Hillman ecame the first president of the malgamated Clothing Workers of Amer- a (1914). He was a powerful supporter of dustrial unions, a founder of the Congress * Industrial Organizations (CIO) whose olitical Action Committee he directed, nd a government adviser on labor relations. See also AMERICAN FEDERATION OF LABOR.)

**ILTON, Conrad Nicholson** (1887–1979), S businessman who built up one of the rgest hotel chains in the world. His first otel was a 50-room hotel in Cisco, Tex.,

purchased in 1919.

**HILTON, James** (1900–1954), English popular novelist. His books include *Lost Horizon* (1933), and *Random Harvest* (1941), which were made into films.

**HIMALAYAS,** the highest mountain system in the world, over 1,500mi long, extending from NW Pakistan and across Kashmir, N India, S Tibet, Nepal, Sikkim, Bhutan to the bend of the Tsangpo-Brahmaputra R. The Himalayas consist of a series of parallel ranges that are thought to have originated when the Indian subcontinent moved N and collided with Eurasia (see PLATE TECTONICS). The Great Himalayas lie in the N, then the Lesser Himalayas, and the Outer Himalayas in the S. The average elevation is 20,000ft in the Great Himalayas, where Mt Everest rises to 29,028ft and there are 11 other mountains of over 26,000ft. The Himalayas protect S and W China from the moisture-laden monsoons which strike Bhutan, Sikkim and Nepal, but this results in semiarid and desert conditions in those parts of China. The Indus, Sutlej, Brahmaputra and Ganges rivers all rise in the mountains.

**HIMES, Chester (Bomar)** (1909–    ), US author of novels and detective fiction which he began writing while imprisoned for armed robbery (1928–35). Focusing on US violence and racial problems, his works include *If He Hollers Let Him Go* (1945), *Pinktoes* (1961) and *Cotton Comes to Harlem* (1965).

**HIMMLER, Heinrich** (1900–1945), Nazi leader, police chief and politician. Head of the SS from 1929 and the GESTAPO from 1936, he was largely responsible for the CONCENTRATION CAMPS and the murder of millions of Jews and others considered undesirable to the Nazi regime in the 1930s and 1940s. He became interior minister in 1943, but fell from Hitler's favor in 1945. After the German defeat in 1945 he committed suicide.

**HINDEMITH, Paul** (1895–1963), influential German composer and teacher. Considered a modernist because of his dissonant harmonies and counterpoint, he nevertheless embraced the classical musical forms of Bach and Mozart in a modern idiom. He viewed the composer as a craftsman who ought to write music for specific uses (*Gebrauchsmusik*). Among his many major works are the opera and symphony *Mathis der Maler* (1934) and *Symphonic Metamorphoses on Themes of Carl Maria von Weber* (1943).

**HINDENBURG, Paul von** (Paul Ludwig Hans Anton von Hindenburg und Beneck-endorff; 1847–1934), German general, military hero of WWI and president of Germany (1925–34). Together with LUDENDORFF he directed the German WWI effort and military strategies. As president he was chiefly a figurehead, becoming increasingly senile. During his presidency the Nazis gradually gained popular support until HITLER became chancellor in 1933.

**HINDI,** the official language of India, a written form of HINDUSTANI. It is written in Devanagari script (or SANSKRIT), reading from left to right.

**HINDUISM,** one of the major world religions: the civilization, in all its aspects, of the Hindus, the people of India and neighboring countries, with outposts elsewhere in SE Asia and Africa. A comprehensive culture embracing diverse beliefs and practices, it tolerates almost any belief, but regards none as essential. Even other religions are accepted, though not their exclusivism. Thus Hinduism has no dogma, and is almost indefinable. It had neither beginning nor founder, and has no hierarchy or source of authority. Abstract philosophies co-exist with magic, animism, pantheism, polytheism, mysticism, asceticism and cultic sexuality. Nevertheless there are some characteristics common to most Hindus. These include belief in BRAHMAN, the One that is the All, the absolute and ultimate principle which is the Self of all living things. Brahman is sometimes personified as BRAHMA, a background figure who, with SHIVA and VISHNU, forms the Trimurti, in some ways analogous to the Christian TRINITY. This element of monotheism plays almost no part in popular Hinduism, where countless gods are worshiped. Hindus have great respect for all life, many being vegetarian and revering and protecting the cow. The upper-caste class of Brahmins is respected as sacrosanct. The doctrine of TRANSMIGRATION OF SOULS in an endless cycle, under the law of KARMA, is universally believed. The three paths of escape from the cycle are duty, knowledge (sought by meditation and YOGA) and devotion to God. Hinduism has its roots in Vedism, the religion of the early Indo-Aryans who settled in India in the late 2nd millennium BC. The authority of the VEDA is still generally recognized, though in practice the Veda is hardly known. Vedism, a chiefly ritual system, developed into BRAHMANISM, in which, from about 700 BC, philosophy developed and was enshrined in the UPANISHADS. A period of great change followed, in which the sects (as they were at first) of BUDDHISM and JAINISM arose. True Hinduism began in the 2nd century BC,

marked by the BHAGAVAD-GITA (found in the epic MAHA'BHA'RATA); the cults of Vishnu and Shiva developed, becoming major sects, and were followed by the cult of SHAKTI, often associated with TANTRA, esoteric practices both ritual and sensual. Modern Hinduism has seen the rise of innumerable reform movements and sects, some influenced by Islam or Christianity. Although in present-day India traditional Hindu social structures (see CASTE SYSTEM) are weakened, Hinduism is readily adapting to modern conditions. (See also KRISHNA; RAMAKRISHNA; RAMAYANA.)

**HINDU KUSH,** mountain range in Asia, stretching from NE Afghanistan to N Pakistan. High altitude passes cross the range. The range's highest peak is Tirich Mir (25,260ft).

**HINDUSTANI,** the most widespread language of N India, particularly of the Hindu-speaking areas. It is the spoken form of HINDI and URDU, and derives from the Prakrits (vernacular forms of classical Sanskrit). Hindustani grammar is less complex than Sanskrit in that it avoids noun inflections, gender agreement and irregular forms, and instead of prepositions it has postpositions, which explain the grammatical function of preceding words. GANDHI, at the time of India's independence in 1947, wanted Hindustani to be adopted as the national Indian language, because of its simple grammar and since it can be written in Devanagari or Urdu. However, Hindi was adopted as the official language.

**HINE, Lewis** (1874–1940), US photographer who documented social conditions among European immigrants as they arrived at Ellis Island and settled into the tenements and factories of American cities. His *Charities and the Commons* (1908) was the first "photo-story," and his *Child Labor in the Carolinas* (1909) influenced social legislation.

**HINES, Earl "Fatha"** (1905– ), US jazz musician, born Earl Kenneth Hines. A member of Louis ARMSTRONG's "Hot Five" group (1948–51), he formed his own group in 1957. He is considered one of the great jazz pianists and has influenced modern jazz.

**HIPPARCHUS** (c130 BC), Greek scientist, the father of systematic ASTRONOMY who compiled the first star catalog and ascribed stars MAGNITUDES, made a good estimate of the distance and size of the moon, probably first discovered PRECESSION, invented many astronomical instruments, worked on plane and SPHERICAL TRIGONOMETRY, and suggested ways of determining LATITUDE AND LONGITUDE.

**HIPPOCRATES** (c460–c377 BC), Greek physician generally called "the Father of Medicine" and the probable author of at least some of the **Hippocratic Collection**, some 60 or 70 books on all aspects of ancient MEDICINE. The authors probably formed a school centered around Hippocrates during his lifetime and continuing after his death. The **Hippocratic Oath**, traditionally regarded as the most valuable statement of medical ethics and good practice, probably represents the oath sworn by candidates for admission to an ancient medical guild.

**HIPPOPOTAMUS**, *Hippopotamus amphibius*, one of the largest living terrestrial mammals, distantly related to pigs. With a massive body set on short legs, each with our toes with hoof-like nails, the hippo spends the day submerged in water, coming to land at night to graze a strip extending up to 10km (6mi) inland. Highly adapted to its daytime life in water, the hippo has its sense organs, nose, eyes and ears, on top of its head, so that they are the last parts to submerge. Indeed it rarely submerges completely, and then only for short periods. The common hippopotamus is still widespread in the lakes and rivers in Africa.

**HIROHITO** (1901– ), emperor of Japan from 1926 and a distinguished marine biologist. After WWII his status dramatically changed from a god-like position to being a "symbol of the state and unity of the people," without political or sovereign power. In 1971 he visited Alaska and Europe in the first trip abroad for a reigning emperor.

**HIROSHIGE, Ando** (1797–1858), Japanese painter and printmaker of the *ukiyo-e* (popular) school led by HOKUSAI. He is famous for his sets of woodblock color prints depicting atmospheric landscapes of snow, rain, mist and moonlight. These inspired a number of his contemporaries in the West, including MANET and WHISTLER. Among his works is *53 Stages of the Tokaido Highway* (1833), a series of landscapes.

**HIROSHIMA**, industrial city on SW Honshu Island, Japan, located on a bay in the Inland Sea. As a thriving industrial and commercial center, it was chosen as the target for the US atomic bomb attack of Aug. 6, 1945, which caused enormous havoc and destruction, killing over 800,000 people, and wounding 600,000. It has been largely rebuilt since 1950 and is again an important industrial marketing center. Pop 92,300.

**HIRSHHORN, Joseph** (1899–1981), Latvian-born US financier and art collector who founded the renowned Joseph H. Hirshhorn Museum and Sculpture Garden in Washington, D.C. He donated his collection of American and European art to the US government in 1974.

**HISPANIOLA**, second largest island in the West Indies, located W of Puerto Rico and E of Cuba. The island is shared between the Republic of Haiti and the Dominican Republic.

**HISS, Alger** (1904– ), US public official accused of spying for Russia. Hiss was an adviser to the US State Department on economic and political affairs. In 1948 he was brought before the House Committee of Un-American Activities, and in 1950 was convicted of perjury. He served four years in prison. Maintaining his innocence, Hiss devoted the rest of his life to clearing his name. Legal scholars were sharply divided on his guilt. (See also Whittaker CHAMBERS.)

**HISTAMINE**, AMINE concerned with the production of INFLAMMATION, and particularly of HIVES and the allergic spasm of the BRONCHI in ASTHMA and ANAPHYLAXIS; it enhances STOMACH acid secretion and has several effects on BLOOD CIRCULATION. ANTIHISTAMINES and cromoglycate can interfere with its release; ADRENALINE counteracts its serious effects.

**HISTOLOGY**, the study of the microscopic ANATOMY of parts of organisms after DEATH (autopsy) or removal by SURGERY (BIOPSY). Tissue is fixed by agents that denature PROTEINS, preventing autolysis and bacterial degradation; they are stained by dyes that have particular affinity for different structures. Histology facilitates the study both of normal tissue and of DISEASED organs, or pathological tissue.

**HITCHCOCK, Alfred Joseph** (1899–1980), English film director known for his skillful suspense and macabre humor. He made over 50 films, among the best of which were *The Thirty-Nine Steps* (1935), *The Lady Vanishes* (1938) and, in Hollywood, *Rebecca* (1940), *Spellbound* (1945), *Notorious* (1946), *Rear Window* (1954) and *Psycho* (1960).

**HITCHCOCK, Lambert** (1795–1852), US cabinetmaker who in 1818 established a furniture factory in Barkhamsted, Conn. Here he manufactured "Hitchcock chairs," which combined simplicity with elegance. They are now collector's pieces.

**HITLER, Adolf** (1889–1945), Austrian-born dictator of Germany 1933–45. Hitler will for a long time remain a highly controversial figure. He was without doubt an evil man, coarse and unstable by nature, but he had political genius and was one of the phenomena of the 20th century. He hardly put a foot wrong politically between

1931 and 1941, and conquered an area of Europe larger than NAPOLEON did. He was the first man to understand and exploit the politics of the mass age and set up a radicalism of the right which won mass support and beat the radicals of the left on their own ground, something which earlier conservative and reactionary parties had failed to do. A powerful orator, he was one of the first to understand how to use political propaganda, including the propaganda value of violence and terror. He was indeed one of the inventors of the politics of violence from which recent decades have suffered.

The son of a customs official, he grew up near Linz, Austria. He left school at 16 and made a scanty living as a hack artist 1908–13. Drafted in WWI, he was twice awarded the Iron Cross. In 1919 he joined the small German Workers' Party, which he turned into the National Socialist Workers' (NAZI) Party. In 1923, after an abortive coup against the Bavarian government, he served nine months in prison; there he wrote *Mein Kampf*, setting out his plans for restoring greatness to Germany. He then began to make the Nazis into a national party, and by 1932, aided by unemployment and economic chaos, he made it the largest party in the country. In 1933 he became chancellor, and in 1934 secured his position by liquidating potential opponents within the party. He took full credit for the economy's recovery and prepared it for war. He paid little further attention to domestic affairs, except to intensify persecution of the Jews. After 1935 he turned increasingly to foreign affairs.

In 1936 he reoccupied the Rhineland, in 1938 annexed Austria, and in 1939 seized parts of Czechoslovakia. On September 1 his invasion of Poland began WWII. At first his conduct of the war was effective, but his invasion of Russia in 1941 was precipitate and proved disastrous. Unable to maintain two fronts, German forces lost N Africa and were pushed back on both sides after D-Day. Hitler maintained popular support despite an assassination attempt in 1944, but became increasingly ill and unbalanced. In 1945 he retreated to his Berlin bunker. After marrying his mistress, Eva BRAUN, he committed suicide with her on April 30, 1945.

**HITTITES,** important Indo-European people of the Middle East in the second millennium BC.

**History.** Of unknown origin, they appear to have first settled in southern Turkey c1900 BC; they conquered central Turkey and became a dominant power. By c1650 BC they had established a kingdom of city states (the Old Kingdom), with its capital at Hattusas (BOĞAZKÖY), just E of modern Ankara. Mursilis I overran Syria and even Babylon c1600 BC, but lost them almost at once.

The Hittite Empire proper starts with Tudhaliyas II (c1450 BC), who regained much lost territory. A period of decline followed but by the mid-14th century BC more lasting conquests were made by SUPPILULIUMAS, who finally controlled Syria as far as the Euphrates and the Lebanon, and all Anatolia. At the battle of KADESH c1285 BC the Hittites under Muwatallis drove off Egyptians under RAMSES II, but were seriously weakened. The final downfall of the Hittite empire came c1200 BC, when it was overrun and fragmented by a vast migration of uncertain origin, called by the Egyptians "peoples of the sea." Individual states continued to flourish, however, until SARGON II of Assyria captured CARCHEMISH in 715 BC.

**Culture.** Much of what we know about the Hittites comes from clay tablets, some written in CUNEIFORM and some in Hittite HIEROGLYPHICS, which were part of the royal archives. The main Hittite language is Indo-European in origin, though other non-Indo-European tongues were apparently also current.

The Old Kingdom was a league of city states controlled by a royal governor. Each king nominated his successor. The society was essentially feudal, consisting of nobles (the land-owning warrior caste), artisans, peasants and also slaves, who had some rights, such as owning property and marriage with free persons.

During the Hittite empire the ruler became absolute and hereditary; regarded as the representative of the weather-god, the supreme god in the polytheistic Hittite religion, he was deified at his death. The Hittite legal system was in some ways more just and liberal than the Mesopotamian and Mosaic codes. Prices were regulated, and silver pieces were used as money. The economy was based on agriculture: the mai crops were wheat and barley. As well as livestock, bees were kept and horses bred for the chariotry that was the basis of the Hittite army. Copper, lead and silver were mined; iron smelting was well developed, at first for religious objects and later for military purposes. Much of Hittite architecture and art is powerful and vigorous rather than beautiful. Their surviving literature, excluding political texts, is largely religious and folkloric in nature; many epics were translated and adapted from foreign sources.

**HIVES**, or **urticaria**, an itchy SKIN condition characterized by the formation of weals with surrounding ERYTHEMA, and due to HISTAMINE release. It is usually provoked by ALLERGY to food (e.g., shellfish, nuts, fruits), pollens, FUNGI, DRUGS (e.g., PENICILLIN) or parasites (SCABIES, worms). But it may be symptomatic of infection, systemic disease or emotional disorder. **Dermographism** is a condition in which slight skin pressure may produce marked hives, as in the linear marks which appear after writing on the skin.

**HOARE, Sir Samuel, Viscount Templewood,** (1880–1959), British political leader. A Conservative member of Parliament (from 1910) and holder of many cabinet posts, he helped build the British air force as air secretary 1922–29. He was criticized for supporting the Munich agreement of 1938 and for the Hoare-Laval Pact. As ambassador to Spain (1940–44), he was instrumental in keeping Spain neutral during WWII.

**HOBBEMA, Meindert** (1638–1709), Dutch landscape painter, taught by Jacob van RUISDAEL. His early atmospheric river landscapes and his later forest and road scenes, such as The Avenue at Middelharnis (1689), had little influence in their time but foreshadowed CONSTABLE and others.

**HOBBES, Thomas** (1588–1679), English political philosopher who sought to apply rational principles to the study of human nature. In both the physical and moral sciences reasoning was to proceed from cause to effect: certain knowledge could only flow from deductive reasoning based upon known principles. Hobbes' view of man was materialistic and pessimistic—men's actions were motivated solely by self-interest. This led Hobbes to consider that the existence of a sovereign authority in state was the only way to guarantee its stability. Leviathan (1651), which gave voice to this opinion, was his most celebrated work. Hobbes saw matter in motion as the only reality: even consciousness and thought were but the outworkings

of the motion of atoms in the brain. During and after his lifetime, Hobbes was well known as a materialist and suspected as an atheist, but in the 20th century his reputation as an able thinker has overshadowed his former notoriety.

**HOBBY, Oveta Culp** (1905– ), US publisher and public servant. Director of the Women's Army Corps, 1942–45, she became the first secretary of health, education and welfare under EISENHOWER 1953–55 and was editor and president of the Houston Post 1938–42 and from 1955.

**HOBSON, John Atkinson** (1858–1940), British economist, a forerunner of KEYNES. He believed that the root cause of depression was a predominance of savings at the expense of consumption, with a resultant drop in production. He wrote many books, most notably The Physiology of Industry (1889).

**HOCHHUTH, Rolf** (1931– ), controversial German playwright whose first play, The Deputy (1963), attacked Pope Pius XII for his stand on the Jews in WWII and whose second, Soldiers (1967), portrayed Churchill as a murderer.

**HO CHI MINH** (1890–1969), Vietnamese political leader, president of North Vietnam from 1954 until his death. His early life is obscure until his arrival in Europe in 1914. Active in revolutionary politics, he settled in Paris in 1917, then went to study in Moscow in 1923, where he was trained as a Comintern agent. He helped organize subversion in Indochina, operating from Hong Kong. In 1941 he settled in Tonkin, China, and began to organize the Vietminh, who in 1945 proclaimed him president of Vietnam, confirming this by their crushing defeat of the French at DIEN BIEN PHU in 1954. As president of North Vietnam he trained and equipped the Vietcong forces in the VIETNAM WAR.

**HO CHI MINH CITY,** formerly Saigon, city in Vietnam, 60mi from the South China Sea, on Saigon R. It is an industrial center and river port with a trade in rice and textiles. It was established as an Annamese settlement in the 17th century and was taken by the French in 1859. The city was capital of South Vietnam (1954–75) and suffered considerable damage during the VIETNAM WAR. Pop 3,420,000.

**HOCKEY.** See FIELD HOCKEY; ICE HOCKEY.

**HOCKNEY, David** (1937– ), British artist whose emphasis on figurative work and brilliant color, often using acrylic paints, brought him immediate fame. One of his most characteristic paintings, A Bigger Splash (1967), was also the title of a semi-autobiographical documentary film made in 1974.

**HODGKIN, Dorothy Mary Crowfoot** (1910–    ), British chemist awarded the 1964 Nobel Prize for Chemistry for determining the structure of VITAMIN B₁₂.

**HODGKIN'S DISEASE,** the most important type of LYMPHOMA or malignant proliferation of LYMPH tissue. Usually occurring in young adults, it may begin with lymph node enlargement, weight loss, FEVER or malaise; the SPLEEN, LIVER, LUNGS and BRAIN may be involved. Treatment has radically improved the outlook in a proportion of cases; it consists of local RADIATION THERAPY or systemic intermittent CHEMOTHERAPY with a combination of agents and STEROIDS.

**HOFFA, James Riddle** (1913–1975), US labor leader, president of the International Brotherhood of Teamsters from 1957. After an investigation, led by Robert F. KENNEDY, into his underworld links, Hoffa was convicted in 1964 of tampering with a jury over a bribery charge and jailed 1968–71. In 1975 he disappeared mysteriously and is thought to have been murdered.

**HOFFER, Eric** (1902–    ), self-educated US author and philosopher. A migratory worker and longshoreman until 1967, he won immediate acclaim with his first book, *The True Believer* (1951), a study of mass movements. *The Passionate State of Mind* (1955), a volume of maxims, followed.

**HOFFMAN, Abbie** (1937–    ), US counter-culture figure. An outspoken opponent of the Vietnam War and leader of the Youth International Party ("Yippies"), he and other defendants were convicted of crossing state lines to incite riots at the 1968 Democratic National Convention. The convictions were overturned. He jumped bail in a drug case in 1974, concealed his identity and became a magazine writer and environmentalist, then surrendered in 1980 and was imprisoned briefly.

**HOFFMAN, Dustin** (1937–    ), US film actor who achieved stardom in *The Graduate* (1967) and went on to distinguish himself in a wide variety of roles in such films as *Midnight Cowboy* (1969), *Lenny* (1974) and *Kramer vs. Kramer* (1978), for which he won the Academy Award.

**HOFFMANN, Ernst Theodor Amadeus** (1776–1822), German romantic author, composer, man of the theater and critic. He is best remembered today for his fantastic short stories, which inspired POE and others, and an opera, *Tales of Hoffmann*, by OFFENBACH.

**HOFFMANN, Josef** (1870–1956), Austrian architect who championed ART NOUVEAU in Austria and who was appointed city architect of Vienna in 1920. His masterpiece was the Stoclet House (1905–11) in Brussels.

**HOFMAN, Josef** (1876–1957), Polish-born US pianist who made a spectacular debut in New York City at the age of 11 and was noted for his authoritative interpretations of the works of CHOPIN and LISZT. He directed the Curtis Institute of Music in Philadelphia.

**HOFMANN, Hans** (1880–1966), German-American artist and teacher, prominent in the ABSTRACT EXPRESSIONISM movement. His vigorous and colorful style, inspired by KANDINSKY, is exemplified by *The Gate* (1959). In 1934 he opened his influential Eighth Street School in New York.

**HOFMANNSTHAL, Hugo von** (1874–1929), Austrian neo-romantic poet and dramatist. His early style was influenced by Stefan GEORGE and the Pre-Raphaelites. An adaptation of Sophocles' *Elektra* (1903) was made into an opera by Richard STRAUSS in 1909, beginning a long collaboration on such operas as *Der Rosenkavalier* (1911), *Ariadne auf Naxos* (1912), *Die Frau ohne Schatten* (1919) and many others. Poems, plays such as *Jedermann* (1911), and his opera librettos make him a major figure of Austrian literature.

**HOGAN, Ben** (1912–    ), US professional golfer. He won the US Open championship 1948, 1950, 1951 and 1953 and the Professional Golfers Association championship 1946 and 1948. He won the Masters in 1951 and 1953 and the British Open in 1953.

**HOGARTH, William** (1697–1764), English painter and engraver, best known for his three series of moralistic and satirical engravings, *The Harlot's Progress* (1732), *The Rake's Progress* (1735) and *Marriage à la Mode* (1745). His first success was as a portraitist. Some of his finest work, such as *Captain Thomas Coram* (1740), is in this field. A master of the early ROCOCO style, he foreshadowed his later style in such work as *The Shrimp Girl* (c1760).

**HOGS,** or **pigs,** or **swine,** members of the hog family (Suidae), including the BABIRUSA, wild BOAR, bushpig and WARTHOG. They are usually sociable animals, but older boars tend to be solitary. The upper or lower canines are developed in all species to form slashing tusks. Hogs live in forests or thickets, though the warthog is more commonly found in more open country, feeding on a variety of vegetable foodstuffs—grass, roots and tubers, fallen fruits and nuts—and, in addition, insects, earthworms, eggs and other animal material. The many varieties of domesti-

ig are all descended from the European oar (*Sus scrofa*). Pigs are bred primarily ither for their fat (lard) or for their meat bacon and pork). China has the largest umber of domestic swine in the world; in he US they are concentrated in the corn elt.

**HOHENZOLLERN,** German ruling ynasty that first rose to prominence in the 2th century. In 1192 Frederick III of Zollern became the ruler of Nuremburg, nd his descendants founded the Swabian nd Franconian lines. From the latter were escended the electors of Brandenburg and he dukes and kings of Prussia, who ruled as mperors of Germany, 1871–1918.

**HOKKAIDO,** northernmost major island of apan, second largest but least populated. ts aboriginal inhabitants are the AINU. Its conomy rests on mining, crop agriculture nd fisheries. Its main town is Sapporo.

**HOKUSAI, Katsushika** (1760–1849), apanese painter, printmaker and book llustrator, greatest master of the Japanese *kiyo-e* (popular) school. Interested in very aspect of life, Hokusai worked under a umber of different names in a variety of tyles, producing over 30,000 drawings of reat imagination, compositional mastery nd technical excellence. The most famous ollections are *36 Views of Fuji* (1823–29) nd *Mangwa*, or *Ten Thousand Sketches* 1814–18), many of which were admired in 'aris and London as well as the Far East.

**HOLBACH, Paul Henri Dietrich, Baron d'** 1723–1789), French encyclopedist and naterialist philosopher, best known for *The ystem of Nature* (1770), published as by J. B. Mirabeau," which included a cathing attack on religion. He translated rticles for DIDEROT's *Encyclopédie*.

**HOLBEIN,** name of two German painters. **Hans Holbein the Elder** (c1465–1524) was a ierman Gothic painter of great distinction, est known for his many altarpieces and ther church decorations, such as the Kaisheim altar (1502). His middle and later vork may have been influenced by iRÜNEWALD. **Hans Holbein the Younger** c1497–1543), a religious painter and ortraitist, is generally considered the reater of the two. He lived in many European countries and later entered the ervice of Henry VIII of England, whose nost famous portraits are by him.

**HÖLDERLIN, Johann Christian Friedrich** 1770–1843), among the greatest of ierman lyric poets, notable for the randeur of his images, usually deriving rom classical Greek themes. Among his est-known poems are *Bread and Wine, The Rhine* and the *Empedocles* poems.

*Hyperion* (1797–99) is a semi-autobiographical prose novel. Suffering from extreme emotional pressures, he finally went mad in 1806.

**HOLIDAY, "Billie"** (1915–1959), US jazz singer, born Eleanora Fagan. She started her career at 16, singing in Harlem cafés and night spots. Her highly individual style was soon recognized, and she sang with many famous bands and small groups in the 1930s and 1940s. In later years she suffered from heroin addiction.

**HOLINESS CHURCHES,** group of fundamentalist Protestant churches. Their central dogma is that a state of perfection—"holiness"—may be achieved in this life through "sanctification," a religious experience similar to but following conversion.

**HOLINSHED'S CHRONICLES,** purported histories of England, Scotland and Ireland, largely edited by Raphael Holinshed (c1525–c1580). Colorful, imaginative and inaccurate, they provided plots for many Elizabethan dramatists, including SHAKESPEARE.

**HOLLAND,** former countship in the W NETHERLANDS, roughly corresponding to the present provinces of North and South Holland. Outside the Netherlands the term is frequently applied to the whole country.

**HOLLAND TUNNEL,** second-longest underwater vehicular tunnel in the US. Its twin tubes, each 29½ft in diameter and 9,250ft long, pass beneath the Hudson R to link Jersey City, N.J., with downtown New York City. Begun in 1919, it was completed in 1927.

**HOLLY, Buddy** (Charles Harden Holly, 1936–1959), ROCK MUSIC artist whose first hit, "That'll Be The Day," was recorded in 1957. Holly died two years later, leaving a body of work that colored the music of later rock groups, among them, the Beatles.

**HOLLYWOOD,** district of Los Angeles, Cal. Its name became synonymous with the US film industry in the 1920s. Few films are made there, but it now produces a very large percentage of US television material.

**HOLM, Hanya** (1898– ), German-US dance teacher and choreographer. In Europe she studied Dalcroze EURYTHMICS and attended the Mary WIGMAN school. In 1930 she came to the US where, with Martha GRAHAM, Doris HUMPHREY and Charles WEIDMAN, she helped develop the modern dance movement.

**HOLMES, Larry** (1949– ), US heavyweight boxing champion. After winning the World Boxing Commission crown from Ken Norton in 1978, he tied a record set by Joe LOUIS by knocking out seven consecutive challengers.

**HOLMES, Oliver Wendell** (1809–1894), US author and physician, best known for his light essays and poems which appeared in the *Atlantic Monthly* from 1857, and in book form as *The Autocrat of the Breakfast Table* (1858) and three sequels. He taught at Harvard, 1847–82; his paper *The Contagiousness of Puerperal Fever* (1843) is considered the first major contribution to medicine by an American.

**HOLMES, Oliver Wendell, Jr.** (1841–1935), US jurist, Supreme Court justice 1902–32. He is often called "the great dissenter," - but this reflects the significance rather than the number of his dissenting judgments. In *Lochner v. New York* (1905) and *Hammer v. Dagenhart* (1918) he reinforced arguments for legislative checks on the economy. His dissent in *Abrams v. United States* (1919) was a powerful defense of free speech.

**HOLMES, Sherlock.** See DOYLE, SIR ARTHUR CONAN.

**HOLOCAUST,** term applied to the systematic execution of 6,000,000 European Jews by the German Nazi regime 1933–45. Hitler had exploited anti-Semitic feelings on his rise to power and later called for a "final solution to the Jewish question." Most Jews in countries overrun by the Nazis who did not emigrate in time were victims of the Holocaust, which effectively obliterated the Jewish secular and religious life that had flourished in Europe for centuries.

**HOLOCENE,** also known as the Recent, the later epoch of the QUATERNARY Period, representing the time since the last ICE AGE (PLEISTOCENE Epoch) up to and including the present; i.e., about the last 10,000 years. (See also GEOLOGY.)

**HOLOGRAPHY,** a system of recording LIGHT or other waves on a photographic plate or other medium in such a way as to allow a three-dimensional reconstruction of the scene giving rise to the waves, in which the observer can actually see around objects by moving his head. The apparently unintelligible plate, or **hologram**, records the INTERFERENCE pattern between waves reflected by the scene and a direct reference wave at an angle to it; it is viewed by illuminating it from behind and looking through rather than at it. The high spatial coherence needed prevented exploitation of the technique, originated in 1948 by D. GABOR, until the advent of LASERS. Color holograms are possible, and three-dimensional TELEVISION may ultimately be feasible.

**HOLST, Gustav Theodore** (1874–1934), English composer. He is best known for *The*

*Planets* (1918), a massive symphonic suite each piece representing a planet character ized in myth and astrology. Its popularit has overshadowed his other work, such a the opera *Savitri* (1908).

**HOLT, Victoria** (1906–    ), author o best-selling gothic novels, among them *Mistress of Mellyn* (1960), *The Queen' Confession* (1968) and *My Enemy th Queen* (1978).

**HOLY ALLIANCE,** collective securit agreement created at the CONGRESS O VIENNA in 1815 by Russia, Austria an Prussia and later joined by most othe powers except Britain, Turkey and th Vatican. Its avowed aim was to conduc mutual relations according to Christia principles. It had little importance in itsel except as a symbol of reaction; revolts i Spain and Naples in the 1820s wer suppressed in its name.

**HOLY GHOST.** See HOLY SPIRIT.

**HOLY GRAIL,** legendary talisman, give various forms in various versions of the tale In his *Conte del Graal* (c1180) CHRÉTIEN D TROYES made it the chalice from whic Christ drank at the Last Supper and whic was used to catch His blood on the Cros The knight Perceval, who in the poem b WOLFRAM VON ESCHENBACH became *Parziva* (c1210), seeks the Grail to redeem himsel and others. The *Queste del Saint Gra* (c1200) linked the Grail with th ARTHURIAN LEGENDS, and was the source c MALORY's *Morte d'Arthur* (c1470). Th Grail legends have inspired such moder writers as T. H. WHITE, T. S. ELIOT an TENNYSON, and also WAGNER's opera *Lohengrin* (1848) and *Parsifal* (1882).

**HOLY ROMAN EMPIRE,** Europea empire centered in Germany which endure from medieval times until 1806. Fir founded by Charlemagne, it was effective established in 962 when the pope crowne OTTO I, king of Germany, emperor at Rom At its height in the 10th and 11th centurie it included all the German lands, Austri and modern W Czechoslovakia, Switze land, the Low Countries, E France and and central Italy. The emperor was usuall the dominant German sovereign, elected b the princes and, until Maximilian crowned by the pope. The empire wa originally seen as a universal monarch modeled on the Roman Empire, th temporal equivalent and ally of the papac From the 11th to the 13th centurie however, it clashed continually with th papacy for European supremacy. At th Reformation a further split develope between the Catholic emperor ar Protestant princes, whose sovereignty wa confirmed by the Treaty of Westphalia in 1648, leaving the Emperor no more than a figurehead. The empire endured in name until Napoleon, as Emperor of the French, ceased to recognize it in 1806; Francis II of Austria then abdicated the imperial title.

**HOLY SEPULCHRE** (officially, Church of the Resurrection), multidenominational church in the Old City of Jerusalem, on what is traditionally the site of the tomb of Jesus. The first church was built by CONSTANTINE THE GREAT c336 AD, but it has been destroyed and rebuilt many times.

**HOLY SPIRIT, or Holy Ghost,** in Christian theology, the third Person of the TRINITY, proceeding from the Father and the Son (according to Western churches; Eastern churches reject the phrase "and the Son," Latin *filioque*). In the Old Testament the idea unfolds of the Spirit as God in action, both in creation and in man: the Spirit, bringing wisdom and holiness, was bestowed especially on the prophets, and was promised to dwell in the MESSIAH and to characterize the coming Messianic age. The New Testament shows the Holy Spirit as empowering Jesus Christ throughout his life, and at PENTECOST descending on the apostles, filling them with power and inaugurating the Christian Church as such. The Holy Spirit is basic to the Christian life, being the agent of new (spiritual) birth, given through BAPTISM and CONFIRMATION, and producing in the Church Christian character and charismatic gifts (emphasized by PENTECOSTAL CHURCHES). By the title **Paraclete** (Greek *parakletos*) the Holy Spirit is described as a comforter and advocate.

**HOLY WEEK,** in the CHURCH YEAR, the week preceding EASTER, observed in most churches as a time of solemn devotion to the passion of Christ. From the 4th century the events of the week of the crucifixion have been liturgically re-enacted, now especially on PALM SUNDAY, MAUNDY THURSDAY, GOOD FRIDAY, Holy Saturday and Easter Day.

**HOMELANDS, or** "black states," areas set aside for black South Africans. Bantustans was the original name for these areas. In theory, the homelands, which are delineated on the basis of tribal language, were created to enable the "separate" economic and political development of blacks in areas outside "white" SOUTH AFRICA, where blacks are excluded from the general franchise. In practice, the homelands are poverty-stricken, generally poor in soil and in natural resources, depending to a large extent on South African aid and revenues generated by commuter workers, those who work in white areas but reside in homelands.

According to plan, each of the homelands, of which there are ten, is to become an "independent" nation. Transkei, Bophuthatswana and Venda have become independent, although they are not recognized by any country other than South Africa. The Ciskei's independence was slated for late 1981. The other homelands are Gazankulu, KwaZulu, Lebowa, Qwaqwa, Ndebele and KaNgwane. Together, the homelands encompass only about 13% of the total land area of South Africa, and population density is high. Critics of the homelands concept contend that it is a separatist structure enabling further entrenchment of white rule in South Africa.

**HOMEOPATHY,** system of treatment founded in the early 19th century by C. F. S. HAHNEMANN, based on a theory that DISEASE is cured by DRUGS whose effects mimic it and whose efficacy is increased by the use of extremely small doses, achieved by multiple dilutions.

**HOMER,** Greek epic poet, probably of the 8th century BC, to whom are ascribed the ILIAD and ODYSSEY. Nothing is known of his life, nor even of the genesis of the poems. Since they were probably composed orally and based on traditional tales of real events in Bronze Age Greece, it is hard to say whether Homer actually was the author; most scholars now hold, though, that one man gave a final shape to each poem, and that it was the same man in both cases. Homer has come to represent, for many different ages and tastes, the epitome of poetry; this is still true in the 20th century, as witness his influence on POUND and JOYCE.

**HOMER, Winslow** (1836–1910), US painter who often worked in watercolor, best known for his landscapes and sea studies of New England and Florida, such as *Gulf Stream* (1899). Originally an illustrator, he recorded the Civil War for *Harper's Weekly*. His quasi-Impressionist paintings revolutionized the style of American painting in the 1880s and 1890s.

**HOME RULE, Irish,** movement to win Ireland control over its domestic affairs. The movement began in the early 1870s, and was initially peaceful despite the PHOENIX PARK MURDERS. As a result of the influence of Charles PARNELL, the Liberal Party under GLADSTONE adopted it as policy in 1886. Opposed by the Conservatives, nothing came of this; two Home Rule Bills in 1886 and 1893 foundered, and increasingly the Home Rule movement was dominated by violent radicals uninterested in constitutional solutions. A third bill was finally passed in 1914 but its implementation was postponed until after WWI. In

1916, however, extremists, fearful of losing influence, precipitated the EASTER RISING, which created lasting bitterness. LLOYD GEORGE, in 1922, finally overcame Ulster's objections by agreeing to partition. S Ireland then became completely independent as the Republic of EIRE.

**HOMESTEADING,** the claiming and settling of federal lands under the Homestead Act (1862), which proved crucial in developing the US West. From independence, settlers in the West had complained at being charged for virgin lands which, they said, were valueless before being developed by their labor. The homestead movement, for the free distribution of such land, had won wide support by the 1830s and advocacy from such popular figures as Thomas Hart BENTON and Horace GREELEY. The 1862 act awarded land patents on 160-acre plots to individual settlers who paid a nominal registration fee, built a homestead and cultivated the land for five years. Despite much subsequent legislation there were flaws. The best lands were generally outside the provisions while loopholes left scope for bulk acquisition by railroads and speculators. Of the 250 million acres homesteaded by the 1950s, much was in large aggregates.

**HOMESTEAD NATIONAL MONUMENT,** established in 1939, consists of 162.73 acres of land in Gage Co., SE Nebraska. It commemorates the site of the first homestead entered under the General Homestead Act of 1862 (see HOMESTEADING).

**HOMESTEAD STRIKE,** bitter labor dispute (1892) between steel workers and the Carnegie Steel Company, in Homestead, Pa., a landmark in the history of the US labor movement. A clash between strikers and the company's 300 PINKERTON guards left 10 dead. The national guard was sent in and the strike was broken, but at a high cost to the union movement and to the reputations of Carnegie and President Benjamin Harrison.

**HOMING PIGEON,** a bird of the family Columbidae able to return to its loft from vast distances, and selectively crossbred to combine speed and ever greater stamina. Although the bird's navigational methods are still not fully understood, man has used the homing pigeon since ancient times, particularly to communicate over long distances. The racing of homing pigeons has been a popular sport since the 19th century. A well-trained bird may travel over 1000mi; the record flight is over 2,300mi.

**HOMO SAPIENS.** See PREHISTORIC MAN; RACE.

**HOMOSEXUALITY,** sexual activity or inclination involving members of the same sex; in women it is termed *lesbianism.* Almost every aspect of homosexuality is fraught with misinformation, misunderstanding and scientific uncertainty. Furthermore, it is difficult to generalize about homosexual behavior; for example, one homosexual, particularly a man, may engage in hundreds of sexual encounters, while others, in a trend that appears to be gaining, establish long-term relationships resembling conventional marriages. Likewise, some homosexuals practice a wide variety of activity, perhaps including sadomasochism, while others abstain from any kind of relationship because of inhibitions or social disapproval. Some homosexuals who are also attracted to the opposite sex and able to function heterosexually marry and have children.

Freud believed that children pass through a homoerotic phase and that some persons retain and amplify their feelings from that period. While few specialists believe that anyone is "born homosexual," no one can fully explain why some persons and not others become disposed toward homosexuality. One theory holds that a boy or girl with a weak father and a dominant mother may become so inclined, but many cases do not fit this pattern. The explanation does not seem to lie in differences in chromosomes or hormones. Some evidence suggests that a predisposition to homosexuality occurs when the child is quite young and that the tendency may be initiated or enforced if the child, for whatever reason, has low self-esteem or concern about his or her ability to fulfill the role society expects of a member of that sex. Homosexuals include a wide range of personality types and may be found in all professions. Psychiatrists generally reject the idea that homosexuals are, per se, emotionally disturbed. Homosexuality has been tolerated in certain societies, as in ancient Greece, but it has encountered hostility among fundamentalist Christians, who believe it to be proscribed by the Bible. In many countries, homosexual acts are not a crime, but the reverse is true in most states of the US. (See also GAY ACTIVISM.)

Despite occasional claims of success by psychotherapists and their patients, the likelihood of an individual being able to "change" to heterosexuality is slim, although a strong desire to change plus previous heterosexual experience may be helpful. For some, therapy offers a means for the individual to learn to accept his situation.

**Official name:** Republic of Honduras
**Capital:** Tegucigalpa
**Area:** 43,300sq mi
**Population:** 3,140,800
**Language:** Spanish
**Religions:** Roman Catholic
**Monetary unit(s):** 1 Lempira = 100 centavos

**HONDURAS,** the second-largest and most mountainous Central American republic.
**Land.** Mountain ranges, high open valleys and plateaus cover Honduras. The hot and humid low-lying areas are the lower reaches of the Ulúa and Chamelecón rivers, the swampy coastal plain in the NE and the narrow coastal plain on the Gulf of Fonseca. Rainfall varies from less than 40in to 120in. The terrain renders communications difficult.
**People.** Spanish-Indian *mestizos* compose 90% of the population; there are white, Indian and Negro minorities. Most people are concentrated in the rural areas of the central highlands. Illiteracy runs to 40%. Poverty is endemic: most Hondurans occupy poor subsistence farms.
**Economy.** US-owned banana plantations dominate the economy, and the bulk of the population works on the land. Coffee replaced bananas as the main export in 1975; other exports are timber, meat, cotton and tobacco. The mineral resources, which include silver and gold, are poorly exploited. There is little industry and poor transport facilities.
**History.** From the 4th to the 7th centuries AD the ancient city of Copán was a center of the civilization of the MAYAS, but when COLUMBUS touched the Honduran coast on his 1502 voyage the country was inhabited only by semi-nomadic Indian tribes. As a Spanish colony for almost 300 years, Honduras was mostly governed from Guatemala; in 1821 it won independence from Spain to become part of the Mexican empire. Subsequently, Honduras joined the Central American Federation of which the Honduran patriot Francisco Morazán was president until its dissolution in 1838. As an independent republic since that time, its history has been generally marked by conflicts, revolutions and military rule. In 1969 El Salvador invaded Honduras in a dispute over Salvadoran laborers in Honduras and the fighting left tens of thousands homeless. In April 1975 General Oswaldo López Arellano (proclaimed as president in 1965) was ousted following charges of accepting bribes from a US print company to reduce export levies on bananas. A civilian president was elected in 1980 and the government raised minimum wages and initiated a literacy campaign.

**HONDURAS, British.** See BELIZE.

**HONEGGER, Arthur** (1892–1955), Swiss-French composer, member of the French Les SIX group, best known for his popular *Pacific 231* (1923) and his oratorio *King David* (1921–23).

**HONEY,** a sweet, sticky confection, formed of partially-digested SUGARS. NECTAR, collected from flowers by foraging worker BEES, is returned to the hive, mixed with digestive "saliva" and often a little pollen, and stored in the cells of a wax honeycomb to act as a winter food supply for the hive. Combs, with their familiar hexagonal cells are used for a variety of purposes in the hive, and honeycombs are not always distinct from combs of grubs. Where honey is taken from domestic hives for man's use, the beekeeper must replace the food supply by feeding sugar throughout the winter. (See BEEKEEPING.)

**HONG KONG,** British crown colony on the S China coast, consisting of mainland territories and numerous offshore islands. Hong Kong island was ceded to the British after the OPIUM WAR in 1842. Mainland Hong Kong includes Kowloon, acquired in 1860, and the New Territories (360sq mi of the colony's total area), leased to Britain for 99 years in 1898. China, while not recognizing British sovereignty, still accepts these arrangements as convenient to its international trade.

Of the rocky land surface, 75% is unsuitable for building and a mere 14% urbanized, accommodating 90% of the population. Since the early 1900s refugees from China's political upheavals have swelled the colony's population. During Japanese wartime occupation (1941–45) the trend was briefly reversed but since then the population has increased rapidly and necessitated reclamation since 1945 of about 6sq mi of land along the harbor. Hong Kong is a free trade area and one of the world's principal ports. There is much light industry, particularly textiles and electrical goods. The colony depends on China for most of its food and water.

**Official name:** The Crown Colony of Hong Kong
**Capital:** Victoria
**Area:** 420.8sq mi
**Population:** 5,017,000
**Languages:** English, Cantonese, Mandarin
**Religions:** Buddhist, Taoist, Christian, Muslim, Hindu
**Monetary unit(s):** 1 Hong Kong dollar = 100 cents

**HONOLULU,** capital and chief seaport of Hawaii, seat of Honolulu Co. It is located on the SE coast of Oahu Island. Honolulu grew from a fishing village in 1820 to the capital of independent Hawaii, and then territorial capital when Hawaii was annexed to the US. It is important as a shipping center, for sugar and pineapple processing and as the tourist hub of Hawaii. Pop 365,048.

**HONORIUS,** name of four popes and one antipope. **Honorius I** (d. 638), pope from 625–638 AD, ably administered the Church and promoted missions, but was later pronounced a heretic (681) for seeming to support MONOTHELITISM in a correspondence with the patriarch of Constantinople. **Honorius III** (d. 1227), pope from 1216–1227, recognized the Dominican and Franciscan orders and also helped the young Henry III of England to secure his crown against French intervention.

**HONSHU,** the largest island of Japan, about 89,000sq mi in area. It is Japan's prime industrial and agricultural region, containing the country's six major cities. Narrow coastal plains surround a mountainous interior of which Mt Fuji (12,388ft) is the highest peak.

**HOOCH, Pieter de,** or **Hoogh** (c1629–c1684), Dutch painter best known for his portrayals of the domestic life of the wealthy burghers of Delft, similar in style to the works of his contemporary VERMEER.

**HOOD, Mount,** extinct volcano in the Cascade Mts, about 50mi E of Portland, Ore. The peak (11,245ft) is the center of Mount Hood National Forest, an all-season recreation area of over a million acres.

**HOOF AND MOUTH DISEASE,** or foot and mouth disease, a VIRUS infection of cattle and pigs, rarely affecting domestic animals and man. Vesicles of the SKIN and mucous membranes, and FEVER are usual. It is highly contagious and EPIDEMICS require the strict limitation of stock movements and the slaughter of affected animals.

**HOOKE, Robert** (1635–1703), English experimental scientist whose proposal of an inverse-square law of gravitational attraction (1679) prompted NEWTON into composing the *Principia*. From 1655 Hooke

was assistant to R. BOYLE but he entered into his most creative period in 1662 when he became the ROYAL SOCIETY OF LONDON's first curator of experiments. He invented the compound MICROSCOPE, the universal joint and many other useful devices. His microscopic researches were published in the beautifully illustrated *Micrographia* (1665), a work which also introduced the term "cell" to biology. He is best remembered for his enunciation in 1678 of **Hooke's Law.** This states that the deformation occurring in an elastic body under stress is proportional to the applied stress (SEE MATERIALS, STRENGTH OF).

**HOOKER, Richard** (c1554–1600), English theologian—a man of wide learning—whose eight-volume work, *Of the Laws of Ecclesiastical Polity,* in masterly English prose defended the Elizabethan religious settlement against both Roman Catholics and PURITANS. A landmark of ANGLICAN theology, it acknowledged the authority of the Bible, but gave authority to the Church and reason when Scripture was silent or unclear. Hooker's political theories, modern in tendency, influenced John LOCKE.

**HOOKER, Thomas** (1586–1647), early American Puritan and founder of HARTFORD, Conn. A religious exile from England, he came to Massachusetts via Holland (1633), and became minister at the New Town (now Cambridge) settlement. But conflicts with the Massachusetts leaders drove him and his congregation to Connecticut (1635–36). He wrote the FUNDAMENTAL ORDERS for the new settlements there (1639).

**HOOKWORMS,** intestinal PARASITES of man and his domestic animals, belonging to the nematodes (see ROUNDWORMS). The life cycle involves a free-living larval stage and direct infection of the final HOST. No intermediate host is involved. The parasitic adults are blood feeders and attack vessels in the wall of the intestine. Each worm may cause the loss of up to 0.25ml of blood a day.

**HOOTON, Earnest Albert** (1887–1954), US physical anthropologist best remembered for his attempts to relate behavior to physical or racial type, and for books such as *Up From the Ape* (1931) and *The American Criminal* (1939).

**HOOVER, Herbert Clark** (1874–1964), 31st US president, 1929–33. Born in West Branch, Ia., he graduated as a mining engineer from Stanford U. in 1895, and managed mining operations in various parts of the world until 1914. Already a millionaire, he then became chairman of the voluntary Commission for Relief in

Belgium and in 1917 was appointed US Food Administrator, responsible for increasing production and conservation of supplies. This he did with considerable success, providing large supplies for war-stricken Europe. He became secretary of commerce under Warren G. Harding in 1921. A national figure, he had already been considered as a Republican presidential nominee, but it was not until 1928 that he won the nomination. He ran on a conservative platform, proposing a program for "The New Day" to realize the country's full economic potential.

In Oct. 1929 the Wall Street crash began the Depression. In the belief that the root cause was psychological he tried to restore business confidence by cutting public expenditure and balancing the budget. He stressed the responsibility of states for relief programs and would allow the government to help only indirectly. The RECONSTRUCTION FINANCE CORPORATION was formed in 1932 and, in its first year, lent $1½ billion to help businesses survive. In the same year, Hoover lost a great deal of popularity over his harsh handling of the BONUS MARCH. Clearly unable to cope with the economic situation, he suffered a crushing defeat by F. D. Roosevelt in the 1932 election. His foreign policy had been more successful; he had done much to assure the Latin American states that the US would not intervene in their affairs. The London Naval Treaty (1930) had improved European relations. He retired from public life until he helped organize European relief after WWII. He also headed two "Hoover Commissions" on the organization of the executive branch of government in 1947–49 and 1953–55. These recommended many measures to improve efficiency and management, which Congress accepted.

**HOOVER, John Edgar** (1895–1972), first director of the FEDERAL BUREAU OF INVESTIGATION (FBI). A lawyer in the Department of Justice 1919–29, he became director of the then Bureau of Investigation in 1924, at a time when it enjoyed a bad reputation for political corruption. Effectively ridding it of political appointees, he instituted rigorous selection and training methods. He established the world's largest fingerprint file and introduced the most up-to-date scientific criminology and research programs. Hoover held the directorship until his death at the age of 77. His prestige, so great that he could not be displaced, was seriously declining at his death, and with it that of the FBI.

**HOOVER COMMISSION,** familiar name of the Commission on the Organization of the Executive Branch of the US government, after Herbert C. Hoover, 31st president of the US, who served as its chairman in 1947–49. This commission, and a second commission, which sat in 1953–55, recommended ways for increasing the efficiency of the government, many of which were embodied in the Reorganization Act of 1949 and later laws.

**HOOVER DAM,** formerly Boulder Dam, on the Colorado R in Ariz. It is 726ft high and 1,244ft in length; while providing flood control and irrigation it supplies electricity to S Cal., Ariz., and Nev. and water supplies to several cities. Built 1931–35, it began operating in 1936; it was named for President Herbert Hoover.

**HOP,** *Humulus lupulus* and related species, tall, perennial twining vine, the female INFLORESCENCE of which is used to flavor BEER. Hops are cultivated throughout the world, the US, Germany and England being the leading producers. Family: Cannabinaceae.

**HOPE, Bob** (1903–    ), stage name of Leslie Townes Hope, British-born US actor and comedian. He began in vaudeville and rose to fame with the Ziegfeld Follies and in Broadway musical comedies. Of his many films the *Road* series, beginning with *The Road to Singapore* (1940), is best known; he starred in them with Bing CROSBY and Dorothy Lamour.

**HOPE, John** (1868–1936), US educator and civil rights leader. Son of a black mother and white father, he could have lived as a white but threw in his lot with the black community, advocating advanced education at a time when Booker T. WASHINGTON was inclined to restrict Negro education to the purely technological. First Negro president of Morehouse College in Atlanta, Ga., in 1906, he became the first president of Atlanta U. in 1929.

**HOPI** (or Moki), Pueblo Indian tribe of NE Ariz. An agricultural people, they have a complex society based on clans organized around matrilineal extended households. They are peaceful and deeply religious, the *kachina*, or beneficial spirit, being the center of their way of life. Around 6,000 Hopis survive today.

**HOPKINS, Gerard Manley** (1844–1889), English poet and Jesuit priest. Largely misunderstood in his lifetime, Hopkins' work was experimental. It exploits natural speech rhythms, using what he called "sprung rhythm" rather than a syllable count, and is highly mimetic, as for example in the poem *The Windhover* and the more unconventional *Harry Ploughman*. His work was published posthumously in 1918.

By the 1930s Hopkins had become a major influence on modern poetry.

**HOPKINS, Harry Lloyd** (1890–1946), US administrator under F. D. Roosevelt who did much to implement the NEW DEAL. He was successively administrator of the Federal Emergency Relief Administration (1933), director of the Works Project Administration (1935), secretary of commerce (1938) and US Lend-Lease administrator (1941). He was Roosevelt's aide throughout WWII, and at its close carried out important negotiations with Russia for President Truman.

**HOPKINS, Johns** (1795–1873), US financier and philanthropist. A Quaker, he made his fortune as a wholesale grocer. He bequeathed $7 million to endow Johns Hopkins U. and Johns Hopkins Hospital.

**HOPKINS, Mark** (1813–1878), US railroad tycoon, who worked as a commission merchant until 1853, when he became a partner of Collis P. HUNTINGTON, with whom he founded the Central Pacific Railroad.

**HOPPE, William Frederick** (1887–1959), US billiards champion, winner of 51 world championships. A masterly player from the age of eight, he is regarded as the finest in the history of the game.

**HOPPER, Edward** (1882–1967), US painter and engraver. First recognized for his etchings, he returned to painting late in life, and became known for large, quiet urban studies that revealed a subtle sense of composition and often reflected his feeling of loneliness and alienation.

**HORACE** (65–8 BC), Quintus Horatius Flaccus, Roman lyric poet and satirist. At first supported by the rich patron Maecenas, he later became the favored poet of AUGUSTUS. Horace's surviving work includes four books of *Odes*, two of *Satires*, two of *Epistles* and his *Epodes*. These and the *Art of Poetry* have been a profound and lasting influence on European literature.

**HORMONES**, substances produced in living organisms to affect GROWTH, differentiation, METABOLISM, digestive function, mineral and fluid balance, and usually acting at a distance from their site of origin. Plant hormones, AUXINS and GIBBERELLINS, are particularly important in growth regulation. In animals and man, hormones are secreted by ENDOCRINE GLANDS, or analogous structures, into the BLOOD stream which carries them to their point of action. The rate of secretion, efficacy on target organs and rate of removal are all affected by numerous factors including FEEDBACK from their metabolic effects, mineral or sugar concentration in the blood, and the action of controlling hormones. The latter usually originate in the PITUITARY GLAND and those controlling the pituitary in the HYPOTHALAMUS. Important hormones include INSULIN, THYROID hormone, ADRENALINE, STEROIDS, PARATHYROID GLAND hormone, GLUCAGON, GONADOTROPHINS, ESTROGEN, PROGESTERONE, ANDROGENS, pituitary growth hormone, VASOPRESSIN, thyroid stimulating hormone, adrenocorticotrophic hormone, GASTRIN and SECRETIN.

**HORMUZ, STRAIT OF**, strategically important waterway and only maritime exit from the Persian Gulf. Most tanker-borne Middle East oil exports pass through the strait, which is commanded by Qishm Island (Iran) and three other islands—Greater Tunb, Lesser Tunb and Abu Musa—currently held by Iran but claimed also by the United Arab Emirates.

**HORN**, in music, a brass wind instrument. It is derived from the primitive horns—actual animal horns—used by primitive societies. Metal was found to produce a better tone, and horns became increasingly sophisticated and complex. The principal modern horn, the French horn, which is derived from hunting horns, blends well in small brass or woodwind ensembles and is frequently combined with violin and piano. Horns were introduced into orchestral music in the early 18th century. Valved horns were developed in the 19th century.

**HORNE, Marilyn** (1934–    ), US mezzo-soprano. A pupil of Lotte LEHMANN's, she appeared in 1960 with the San Francisco Opera and soon began thrilling audiences with her brilliance in difficult BELLINI and ROSSINI operas. She made her Metropolitan Opera debut in 1970 as Adalgisa in Bellini's NORMA.

**HORNETS**, large WASPS which, unlike the commoner YELLOW JACKETS which nest underground, build their nests in trees or in human dwellings. The nest is enclosed in a paper shell and consists of a series of horizontal combs. The papery material used is manufactured by the hornets by chewing woody plant matter. Hornets can inflict an extremely painful sting. Family: Vespidae.

**HORNEY, Karen** (1885–1952), German-born US psychoanalyst who stressed the importance of environment in character development, thus rejecting many of the basic principles of FREUD's psychoanalytic theory, especially his stress on the LIBIDO as the root of personality and behavior (see PSYCHOANALYSIS).

**HORNS**, strictly, keratinous structures (see KERATIN) with a bony core, borne on the 'orehead of many UNGULATES. They show a variety of forms. Horns are usually permanent structures though the antlers (which are all bone) of many DEER are cast and regrown annually. Horns appear occasionally to be purely ornamental, but usually they are used for defense or in ntra-specific AGGRESSION. In such species horns are borne only by the males.

**HORNSBY, Rogers** (1896–1963), US baseball player-manager, one of the greatest right-handed batters in the game's history. His greatest successes were with the St. Louis Cardinals from 1915. He was elected to the Baseball Hall of Fame in 1942.

**HOROWITZ, Vladimir** (1904– ), Russian-born US virtuoso pianist. After a brilliant debut at Kiev (1922), he toured Russia and Europe (1924) and the US (1928). He became a US citizen in 1944.

**HORSEFLIES**, biting flies, so called because they bite horses as well as other mammals, including man. Only the females bite, piercing the skin with specialized mouthparts and sucking blood. Like MOSQUITOES female horseflies require a blood-meal before laying eggs. They transmit a few diseases, but their main importance as a pest is in the pain of their bite.

**HORSE RACING**, sometimes called the sport of kings, is among the most popular spectator sports in existence. It is watched by millions of people in many different countries, but chiefly in North America, Western Europe, Australasia and South America. Its interest as a spectator sport is considerably enlarged by the practice of on-and off-track betting.

The oldest stake race in the world is the English St. Leger, first run in 1776. In America the most famous race is the KENTUCKY DERBY, first run in 1875. Today the three premier stake races in the US are the Derby, the Preakness Stakes and the Belmont Stakes, all for three-year-olds. Besides flat racing there are also STEEPLECHASING and harness racing. In the latter, special trotting horses known as trotters or pacers are used. They pull carts called sulkies and are trained not to break into a gallop. The major annual event in US harness racing is the HAMBLETONIAN.

**HORSES**, single-toed, ungulate, herbivorous mammals. Wild horses occurred in prehistoric times over most of Eurasia. True wild horses are represented now only by Przewalski's horse (*Equus przewalskii*) of Siberia, Mongolia and western China. These live in groups of 10–15 led and protected by a stallion. Many feral strains

of the domestic breeds have however become established—the famous herds of the Camargue and of Sable Island off Nova Scotia. Domestic horses (*E. caballus*) are bred in many different races and can be grouped as ponies, heavy draft horses, lightweight draft and riding horses. Barbs and Arabs, the two most popular riding horses, originated from N African stock. Thoroughbreds are descended from Arabs and both are used widely in breeding light draught and riding horses. The ponies, especially the Icelands, are considered to be descendants of a Celtic stock of domestic horses, while heavy draft animals—Belgians, Percherons, Clydesdales, Shires and Suffolks—come from a breeding stock of central and west Europe. The fossil record of the horse family is so well documented that it provides a classic example of EVOLUTION in action. The earliest animal which can be placed in the family was *Hyracotherium*, or *Eohippus*, from the EOCENE of Europe and North America. This was a small animal the size of a fox terrier with three toes of equal size on each hindfoot and four toes on the forefeet. The development of the single-toed foot of modern horses—an adaptation to running on hard dry grassland (while the side toes represented by splint bones in the foot of the modern horse provided a flatter foot for the marshy habitat of *Hyracotherium*); the change in tooth pattern to allow the animal to eat grasses, a very abrasive food, and the increase in size, may be followed through a continuous series of intermediate stages through to the present day.

**HORTHY DE NAGYBÁNYA, Miklós** (1868– 1957), Hungarian admiral and politician. In 1919 he headed the counter-revolutionary army which overthrew the communist and socialist coalition under Béla KUN. From 1920–44 he acted as regent, preventing Emperor Charles I from regaining his throne. He joined the Axis powers in WWII, but in 1944, after trying to make peace with Russia, was imprisoned in Germany. He was freed by US forces in 1949 and settled in Portugal.

**HORTICULTURE**, branch of agriculture concerned with producing fruit, flowers and vegetables. It can be divided into pomology (growing fruit), olericulture (growing vegetables) and floriculture (growing shrubs and ornamental plants). About 3% of US cropland is devoted to horticulture. It was originally practiced on a small scale, but crops such as the POTATO and TOMATO are now often grown in vast fields.

**HORUS**, ancient Egyptian god. Originally a sky god, depicted as a falcon or as falcon-headed, he became thought of as the son of ISIS and OSIRIS. He avenged his father's murder by defeating SET, the spirit of evil, and succeeded Osiris as king.

**HOSEA, Book of,** the first of the Old Testament MINOR PROPHETS. Its material originated in the prophecies of Hosea, delivered in ISRAEL in the 8th century BC. It compares God's abiding love for idolatrous Israel to Hosea's love for his prostitute wife, whom he divorced but remarried.

**HOSPITAL,** institution for the care of the sick or injured. Early hospitals and medical schools were usually attached to the temples of certain gods, for example, AESCULAPIUS and HYGEIA in Greece, and the association with religion continued; many hospices and hostels were founded by Christian religious orders, such as the KNIGHTS OF ST. JOHN. As refuges for the sick poor, hospitals tended to spread disease rather than prevent or cure it. Only in the 19th century did they improve and then they did so dramatically, as a result of Louis PASTEUR's work on germ theory, LISTER's on infection and aseptic surgery and Florence NIGHTINGALE's organization of the nursing profession. Charitable, voluntary subscription and church hospitals increased greatly in number in Europe and North America from the 18th century, while the 19th saw new government hospitals for the old, sick poor and insane.

Modern hospitals are often large, complex institutions. In most countries the majority are government-owned, but in the US only a third (mostly long-stay hospitals for the mentally ill) are government-owned. Most general hospitals in the US and over half the total are "voluntary," run by religious and other non-profit bodies. Because most charge for treatment, many people take out medical insurance. One in seven hospitals is privately run and makes a profit from fees. There are over 7,000 hospitals in the US with 1,650,000 hospital beds. Every year they admit over 30 million sick people, who stay on average just over one week. General hospitals (over 80% of hospitals) may have equipment for diagnosis (including X-rays), a pharmacy, laboratory, maternity division, operating and recovery rooms, and departments for physical and occupational therapy, for outpatients and emergencies. While larger hospitals may cover sophisticated surgery and intensive care, training of medical staff, and research, there is increased emphasis everywhere on health checks, short stays and outpatient treatment.

**HOSTAGE CRISIS.** On Nov. 4, 1979, militants in Iran stormed the US embassy, taking as hostages 66 members of the diplomatic and military staff. The action was precipitated by the decision of President Jimmy CARTER, some two weeks earlier, to allow Shah Reza Pahlevi, the former ruler of Iran, to enter the US for medical treatment. The militants, supported by the Ayatollah Ruhollah KHOMEINI, the new political and religious leader of Iran, demanded in exchange for the hostages the extradition of the Shah to stand trial for alleged crimes against the Iranian people. The US refused to comply. President Carter, already unpopular, was widely criticized for indecisiveness in his reaction, especially following the failure of a military rescue attempt on April 25. Eight members of the mission died in the Iranian desert, diplomatic negotiations were disrupted, and Secretary of State Cyrus Vance resigned. Toward the end of the year, with the help of the Algerian government, Deputy Secretary of State Warren M. Christopher worked out an agreement that called for the return to Iran of $12 billion in Iranian assets (frozen on Nov. 4) and the prohibition of retaliatory law suits against Iran in US courts in exchange for the hostages. Their release was effected on Jan. 20, 1981, a few minutes after Ronald REAGAN was inaugurated president. The 52 hostages (14 had been let go earlier) came home to a joyous nation bedecked in the yellow ribbons that had become a symbol of commitment to obtaining their safe return.

**HOT LINE,** direct White House–Kremlin emergency communications link, established 1963. It aims to reduce the risk of war occurring by mistake or misunderstanding. Telegraphic and radio circuits run via London, Copenhagen, Stockholm and Helsinki.

**HOT ROD,** automobile with improved engine or body design, giving greater acceleration and speed. Following WWII, a cult of street racing developed in the US, consisting of acceleration races between traffic lights. In the 1950s, "drag racing" on special tracks was encouraged by police departments to try to prevent this. The term "hot rod" now includes recognized "stock" sedans and especially designed "dragsters."

**HOT SPOTS OR THERMAL CENTERS,** sites of unusually high heat flow, and frequently of volcanic activity, thought to represent the surface expression of columns ("plumes") of partially molten material rising from the earth's MANTLE. (See also PLATE TECTONICS, PLUME, EARTH.)

**HOT SPRINGS NATIONAL PARK,** in the Ouachita Mts, central Ark. It is a popular tourist and health resort noted for its 47 thermal springs. The park, created in 1921, comprises 3,535 acres.

**HOTTENTOTS,** people of South Africa similar to the Bushmen. Small in stature, they have brown skins, prominent cheekbones, broad noses, coarse hair and pointed chins, and are dolichocephalic (see CEPHALIC INDEX) and commonly steatopygic (see STEATOPYGIA). Originally known to themselves as the Khoikhoin, they were nomadic herdsmen and farmers, but this way of life has largely disappeared.

**HOUDINI, Harry** (1874–1926), born Erich Weiss, US magician and escapologist. He was world famous for his escapes from seemingly impossible situations, as for example from a sealed chest underwater. He also pursued a campaign of exposing fake mediums and spiritualists.

**HOUDON, Jean-Antoine** (1741–1828), French sculptor famous for his portraits. His sitters included Catherine the Great (1773), Voltaire (1781) and Benjamin Franklin (1791). The best known of his mythological works is *Diana* (1777).

**HOUPHOUËT-BOIGNY, Félix** (1905– ), president of the Ivory Coast since it gained independence (1960). He was elected to a new term in 1980. In 1946 he helped found the Rassemblement Démocratique Africain (RDA), which paved the way for independence of the French West African colonies. He was a French minister of state 1956–57.

**HOUSE, Edward Mandell** (1858–1938), US diplomat and adviser to President Woodrow Wilson. He helped Wilson secure the 1912 Democratic nomination. In WWI, he acted for Wilson in Europe, and was responsible for arranging the peace conference and acceptance of Wilson's FOURTEEN POINTS. In 1919, his conciliatory approach during the Treaty of Versailles negotiations led to a rift with Wilson.

**HOUSE COMMITTEE ON UN-AMERICAN ACTIVITIES** (HUAC), a committee of the US House created in 1938 to investigate fascist, communist and other organizations deemed to be "un-American." Its chairmen, beginning with Martin Dies (Democrat, Texas), were conservatives, and they directed much of their attention to the bureaucracies created by the New Deal. Although the committee was criticized for abusing witnesses and for proceeding on the basis of flimsy or dubious evidence, its status was changed from temporary to permanent in 1945. When 10 prominent film-industry figures (the "Hollywood 10") refused to provide information on alleged communist infiltration, they were imprisoned for contempt. It

was before this committee that Alger Hiss gave the testimony for which he was subsequently convicted of perjury. A new name, the House Committee on Internal Security, was adopted in 1969, but a changing political climate led to the committee's abolition in 1975.

**HOUSE OF COMMONS,** lower house of the British parliament. It consists of 635 M.P.s elected by simple majority in single-member constituencies. It is the assembly to which the government is ultimately responsible; it legitimizes legislation, votes money and acts as a body in which complaints can be raised. Proceedings are regulated by the SPEAKER, and a majority of members must assent before a bill becomes law. (See also PARLIAMENT.)

**HOUSE OF LORDS,** upper house of the British parliament. Members consist of the Lords Temporal: hereditary peers, life peers and ex-officio law lords, and Lords Spiritual: the 2 archbishops and 24 most senior bishops. Of over 1,100 members, only about 200 attend regularly. It is the highest court of appeal and can delay the passage of a Commons bill for up to a year. (See also PARLIAMENT.)

**HOUSING AND URBAN DEVELOPMENT, US Department of** (HUD), executive department of the federal government, established 1965, to coordinate programs relating to housing problems. It took over the Housing and Home Finance Agency (HHFA). The department supervises the federal aid programs of both the Model Cities Program and the 1965 Housing and Urban Development Act. Its other programs include urban renewal and planning, mortgage insurance, housing for the elderly, low rent public housing and community facilities.

**HOUSMAN, Alfred Edward** (1859–1936), English poet and classical scholar. His poetry, narrow in range but at its best intensely felt and always craftsmanlike, is collected in *A Shropshire Lad* (1896), *Last Poems* (1922) and *More Poems* (1936).

**HOUSTON,** city and seat of Harris Co. in SE Tex., a major US seaport. It is situated about 25mi SW of Galveston Bay on the HOUSTON SHIP CHANNEL. Founded in 1836 and named for Sam HOUSTON, it remained relatively unimportant until 1901 when oil was discovered in the area. It is now a prosperous industrial, manufacturing and wholesale distribution center. Major industries include chemicals and petroleum refineries, and the NASA Manned Spacecraft Center (1961) has contributed to the growth of medical and technological research. Houston is a cultural center with museums, a symphony orchestra and several colleges and universities, including the U. of Houston. Pop 1,594,086.

**HOUSTON, Sam (Samuel)** (1793–1863), American frontiersman and politician, leader in the struggle against Mexico to create an independent Texas (1835–36). He commanded a force of fewer than 800 settlers in a decisive battle at San Jacinto (1836) and went on to become the first president of the Republic of Texas 1836–38. During a second term as president 1841–44 he worked to bring Tex. into the Union (1845). Houston served as US senator 1846–59 and was governor of Tex. 1859–61. He was deposed after refusing to support the Confederacy.

**HOUSTON SHIP CHANNEL,** or Houston Ship Canal, major waterway between Houston, Tex., and the Gulf of Mexico. Built 1912–14, it is 57mi long, 200ft wide and 34ft deep.

**HOVHANESS, Alan** (1911–    ), US composer noted for his innovative use of Eastern musical materials. He is of Armenian descent, and this is evidenced in his works, among the best-known of which are *Mysterious Mountain* (1955) and *Magnificat* (1957).

**HOVING, Thomas P.** (1931–    ), US art administrator who was the controversial, innovative director of New York's Metropolitan Museum of Art 1967–77. He wrote *Tutankhamen, The Untold Story* (1978) and *King of the Confessors* (1981).

**HOWARD, Roy Wilson** (1883–1964), US journalist and publisher. One of the most powerful newspapermen of the 20th century, Howard was board chairman (1921–36) and president (1936–52) of United Press and of the Scripps-McRae (later Scripps-Howard) newspaper chain. He edited the New York *World-Telegram* (later the *World-Telegram and Sun*) from 1927 to 1960.

**HOWARD, Sidney** (1891–1939), US playwright whose work is noted for its realism. He won the 1925 Pulitzer Prize with *They Knew What They Wanted* (1924). Other well-known plays include *Lucky Sam McCarver* (1925) and *The Silver Cord* (1926).

**HOWE,** name of two brothers who were British commanders in the American War of Independence. **Richard, Earl Howe** (1726–1799), commanded the British fleet in America 1776–78 but is best known for his victory over the French off Ushant (1794) as commander of the Channel Fleet. **William, 5th Viscount Howe** (1729–1814), was a commander in the British army 1775–78. He won two major victories in 1777 at BRANDYWINE and GERMANTOWN.

**HOWE, Gordie** (1928–    ), record-setting US ice hockey player. He played 26 seasons in the NHL and holds career records for most games, goals, assists and points. He was selected as an all-star 22 times and, as a 52-year-old grandfather, played on the same team as his sons.

**HOWELLS, William Dean** (1837–1920), US author, critic and chief editor of the *Atlantic Monthly* (1871–81). He was a pioneer of American social fiction; his finest and most famous novel is *The Rise of Silas Lapham* (1885). Among those influenced by his work were Stephen CRANE and Theodore DREISER.

**HOWITZER,** medium-range cannon. Between a gun and a mortar in length, it fires medium-velocity shells in a curved trajectory. Howitzers are used to hit targets shielded by obstacles that normal high-velocity, low-trajectory fire cannot negotiate.

**HOXHA, Enver** (1908–    ), Albanian leader. He helped found the Albanian Communist Party in 1941 and was the first premier of the new communist government (1944–54). Continuing as party secretary after 1954 he remained a Stalinist and fell out with the USSR during the latter's destalinization phase. Hoxha became allied with Communist China in the early 1960s. Later this friendship cooled when China moved toward closer ties with the West.

**HOYLE, Edmond** (1672–1769), English authority on card and board games, especially whist. He wrote *A Short Treatise on the Game of Whist* (1742), as well as treatises on other games, including chess and backgammon. The expression "according to Hoyle," meaning according to the rules, derives from his name.

**HOYLE, Sir Fred** (1915–    ), British cosmologist best known for formulating with T. GOLD and H. BONDI the steady state theory (see COSMOLOGY); and for his important contributions to theories of stellar evolution, especially concerning the successive formation of the elements by nuclear FUSION in STARS. He is also well known as a science fiction writer and for his popular science books such as *Frontiers of Astronomy* (1955).

**HRDLICKA, Aleš** (1869–1943), Bohemian-born US physical anthropologist best known for expounding the theory that the AMERINDS are of Asiatic origin, which is still generally accepted today.

**HUAC.** See HOUSE, COMMITTEE ON UN-AMERICAN ACTIVITIES.

**HUA KUO-FENG** (c1920–    ), Chinese political leader, Communist Party chairman from 1976. Achieving swift promotion during the Cultural Revolution, he was made premier following CHOU EN-LAI's death, and then succeeded MAO TSE-TUNG. As China turned toward more pragmatic policies, Hua's close identification with Mao proved a handicap, and he fell from power in 1981.

**HUANG HUA** (1913–    ), Chinese public official. He served as China's representative to the UN (1971–76) and as foreign minister 1976–  .

**HUBBELL, Carl** (1903–    ), US baseball player. A left-handed pitcher for the New York Giants (1928–43), he won 253 games including 20 or more victories for five straight years (1933–37). He was inducted into the Baseball Hall of Fame in 1947.

**HUBBLE'S CONSTANT,** ratio between the distance of a GALAXY and the rate at which it is receding from us. HUBBLE first calculated this as around 500km/s per Mpc; however, he incorrectly estimated the distances of the galaxies, and the constant has been more recently calculated to be about 75km/s per Mpc.

**HUBERT, Saint** (c655–727), patron saint of hunters, and of Liège and also Belgium. Hubert is reputed to have been converted after seeing a stag with a cross between its antlers. He became bishop of Maastricht (c708), later moving his diocese to Liège.

**HUDSON, Henry** (d. 1611), English navigator and explorer who gave his name to the Hudson R, Hudson Strait and Hudson Bay. After voyages for the English Muscovy Company to find a northeast passage to China (1607 and 1608), Hudson turned to the west where, with Dutch and then once more English backing (1609 and 1610), he made his most successful voyages. He reached the river known as the Hudson in 1609 and the following year entered Hudson Strait and Hudson Bay, establishing an English claim to the area. After the bitter winter, he was set adrift by a mutinous crew and left to die.

**HUDSON, William Henry** (1841–1922), English author and naturalist, born in Argentina. Of his early books, romances set in the South American pampas, the best-known is *Green Mansions* (1904). He also wrote studies of bird life and books on the English countryside, such as *A Shepherd's Life* (1910).

**HUDSON BAY,** shallow, epicontinental sea in N Canada, named for Henry HUDSON. Up to about 850mi long and 600mi wide, it is linked to the Atlantic by the Hudson Strait and to the Arctic Ocean by Foxe Channel. James Bay, the largest inlet, extends southwards between Ontario and Quebec provinces. Hudson Bay shipping is restricted since the bay freezes over in winter. (See also HUDSON'S BAY COMPANY.)

**HUDSON RIVER,** American river rising in the Adirondacks, flowing generally S for 315mi through N.Y., and emptying into the Atlantic at New York City. It was discovered in 1524, but only explored fully by Henry HUDSON in 1609. It is an important commercial waterway, being navigable by ocean ships as far upstream as Albany. A canal system links it to the Great Lakes. A major program was begun in 1975 to prevent further pollution and make the river safe for fishing and swimming.

**HUDSON RIVER SCHOOL,** group of 19th-century American landscape painters. The founders were Thomas COLE, Thomas DOUGHTY and Asher DURAND, who were especially interested in the Hudson River Valley and New England. The school later included artists who took their inspiration from other parts of the US.

**HUDSON'S BAY COMPANY,** mercantile corporation established by the British in 1670 for trading in the Hudson Bay region. The original intention was also to colonize the area and seek a northwest passage, but the company's major activity was furtrading with the Indians. It played an important part during the next two centuries in opening up Canada. Although its vast lands were sold to the Dominion in 1870, it is still a major fur-trading company and one of Canada's chief business firms with holdings in metal ores, oil, gas and timber.

**HUERTA, Victoriano** (1854–1916), Mexican general and dictator (1913–14). After first supporting President Porifiro DÍAZ and then Francisco MADERO, he rebelled, proclaimed himself president in February 1913 and had Madero and his vicepresident murdered. A combination of revolution at home and hostility from the US finally forced him into exile.

**HUGHES, Charles Evans** (1862–1948), US jurist and statesman. He was Republican governor of New York 1906–10 and narrowly missed becoming president in 1916 when Woodrow Wilson was elected. He served as secretary of state 1921–25 and as chief justice 1930–41 during the NEW DEAL.

**HUGHES, Howard Robard** (1905–1976), US industrialist, aviator and film producer. President of the Hughes Aircraft Company and of the Hughes Tool Company, he was a billionaire who in his later years became an eccentric recluse. Years of litigation over his will followed his death.

**HUGHES, Langston** (1902–1967), black

US poet and writer. He is best known for adapting the rhythms of Afro-American music to his poetry. His works include *The Weary Blues* (1926) and *Not Without Laughter* (1930).

**HUGHES, Richard** (1900–1976), English writer. His works include plays, poems, novels and short stories but he is best known for his novel *A High Wind in Jamaica* (1929), published in the US as *The Innocent Voyage*, and for *The Fox in the Attic* (1961), part of a projected long novel *The Human Predicament*.

**HUGHES, Ted** (1930–    ), English poet whose work is noted for its brutal, often violent animal imagery. Among his many collections are *The Hawk in the Rain* (1957), *Lupercal* (1960), *Crow* (1970), *Selected Poems: 1957–1967* (1972) and *Moortown* (1980). He was married to Sylvia PLATH.

**HUGHES, Thomas** (1822–1896), English jurist, reformer and novelist. He wrote *Tom Brown's School Days* (1857) which, through its emphasis on the Christian virtues and on athletic ability, did much to shape the popular image of the English public school.

**HUGO, Victor Marie** (1802–1885), major French novelist, playwright and poet, best known for his historical novel *The Hunchback of Notre Dame* (1831). Among his several important collections of verse are *Les Feuilles d'automne* (1831) and *Les Châtiments* (1853). Hugo went into exile when Napoleon III became emperor (1851), and during this period produced his famous, socially committed novel *Les Misérables* (1862). He spent his last years in France, recognized as one of his country's greatest writers and republicans.

**HUGUENOTS**, French Protestants, followers of John CALVIN's teaching. The Huguenot movement originated in the 16th century as part of the REFORMATION and found support among all sections of French society, despite constant and severe persecution. (See ST. BARTHOLOMEW'S DAY MASSACRE.) Some respite was provided by Henry IV's Edict of NANTES (1598) but this was revoked in 1685 and many thousands of Huguenots were forced into exile. Full civil and religious liberty was not granted to Huguenots until 1789.

**HULA**, traditional Hawaiian folk-dance. Its undulating, sensuous movements offended missionaries; despite their attempts to suppress it, it remains popular. The accompanying chants have now been influenced by Western music, but the subtle, graceful hand gestures that are part of the hula have remained basically unchanged.

**HULL, Cordell** (1871–1955), American statesman, secretary of state 1933–44 under ROOSEVELT. He developed the "Good Neighbor" policy in relations with South American states and helped maintain relations with the USSR in WWII. He was a Congressman 1907–21 and 1923–30 and senator 1931–33. After the war he was a major force behind US acceptance of the UN, for which he was awarded the 1945 Nobel Peace Prize.

**HULL HOUSE**, one of the first US social settlement houses. Founded in Chicago in 1889 by Jane ADDAMS and Ellen Gates Starr, it provided community services and recreational facilities to a poor community.

**HUMAN ENGINEERING**, or ergonomics, research into physical and psychological human characteristics with particular reference to the environments in and the tools with which people work, and the application of the information so received to the design of equipment, factories, etc. In fact, the techniques of human engineering are now applied to a wide range of other problems involving humans and technology; e.g. POLLUTION control.

**HUMANISM**, originally, the RENAISSANCE revival of the study of classical (Latin, Greek and Hebrew) literature for its own sake, rather than of medieval SCHOLASTICISM. In a broader sense it has come to mean a philosophy centered on man and human values, exalting human free will and superiority to the rest of nature; man is made the measure of all things. Renaissance thinkers such as PETRARCH began a trend towards humanism which embraced such diverse figures as BOCCACCIO, MACHIAVELLI, Thomas MORE and ERASMUS and which became the ancestor of much subsequent secular thought and literature, as well as—in another direction—of the REFORMATION. Modern humanism tends to be nontheistic (see AGNOSTICISM; ATHEISM), emphasizing the need for man to work out his own solutions to life's problems, but has a strong ethic similar to that of Christianity. Both Roman Catholic and Protestant theologians (such as Karl BARTH) have sought to show that Christian beliefs embody true humanism.

**HUMANITIES**, branches of learning concerned with culture, excluding the sciences. Originally the term was limited to the study of ancient Greek and Roman literature, but has been extended to include all languages, literature, religion, philosophy, history and the arts.

**HUMBOLDT, Friedrich Heinrich Alexander, Baron von** (1769–1859), German naturalist. With the botanist **Aimé Jacques Alexandre Bonpland** (1773–1858) he traveled for five years through much of South America (1799–1804), collecting plant, animal and rock specimens and making geomagnetic and meteorologic observations. Humboldt published their data in 30 volumes over the next 23 years. In his most important work, *Kosmos* (1845–62), he sought to show a fundamental unity of all natural phenomena.

**HUMBOLDT, Karl Wilhelm, Baron von** (1767–1835), German philologist regarded as the father of comparative PHILOLOGY. He maintained both that the nature of language reflects the culture of which it is a product, and that man's perception of the world is governed by the language available to him.

**HUMBOLDT CURRENT, or Peru Current,** cold OCEAN CURRENT originating in the S Pacific, and flowing N along the coasts of N Chile and Peru, whose climates it moderates, before turning W to join the S EQUATORIAL CURRENT.

**HUME, David** (1711–1776), Scottish Enlightenment philosopher, economist and historian, whose *Treatise of Human Nature* (1739–40) is one of the key works in the tradition of British EMPIRICISM. But it was his shorter *Enquiry Concerning Human Understanding* (1748) which prompted KANT to his most radical labors. His influential *Dialogues Concerning Natural Religion* were published posthumously in 1779, long after their composition. In EPISTEMOLOGY Hume argued that men had no logical *reason* to associate distinct impressions as cause and effect; if they did so, it was only on the basis of custom or psychological habit. His SKEPTICISM in this respect has always been controversial. In his own day, Hume's most popular work was his *History of England* (1754–63).

**HUMIDITY,** the amount of water vapor in the air, measured as mass of water per unit volume or mass of air, and is also called the DEW point. Saturation of the air occurs when the water vapor pressure reaches the VAPOR PRESSURE of liquid water at the TEMPERATURE concerned; this rises rapidly with temperature. Relative humidity, expressed as a percentage, is the amount of water in the air at any given time compared with the amount the air could hold at that temperature before becoming saturated. The physiologically tolerable humidity level falls rapidly with temperature, as humidity inhibits body cooling by EVAPORATION of sweat.

**HUMMEL, Johann Nepomuk** (1778–1837), Austro-Hungarian composer and pianist. A child prodigy, he studied with MOZART. After some years of European travel and further study in Vienna under HAYDN, he became court conductor at Weimar in 1819, and remained there till his death. He wrote masses, ballets, operas and piano works; the latter influenced CHOPIN and SCHUMANN. His *Pianoforte School* (1828), a new fingering method, influenced subsequent keyboard techniques.

**HUMMINGBIRDS,** an enormous family (Trochilidae) of tiny nectar-feeding birds of the New World, which take their name from the noise of their rapid wingbeats—up to 70 a second in smaller species—as they hover at flowers to feed. Colorful birds, the body size in most species is 50mm (2in) or less. With their small size and fierce activity, hummingbirds must feed about once every 10–15 min. Highly adapted to flight, hummingbirds have short legs and little feet, used only for perching. They can hover in one place and are the only birds capable of flying backwards.

**HUMPERDINCK, Engelbert** (1854–1921), German composer. He was much influenced by WAGNER, whom he assisted at the Bayreuth Festival. He wrote several operas; only one, *Hansel and Gretel* (1893) is widely performed today, although *The Royal Children* (1910) is revived from time to time.

**HUMPHREY, Doris** (1895–1958), US dancer and choreographer, a leader in modern dance. Influenced by Ruth SAINT DENIS and Ted SHAWN, under whom she studied before setting up her own school with Charles WEIDMAN in 1928, she broke away to develop her own expressive style, based upon her theories of movement and her concept of dance as an expression of human dignity.

**HUMPHREY, Hubert Horatio** (1911–1978), US political leader, who was vice president 1965–1969. A Democrat, he was mayor of Minneapolis, then was elected Senator from Minnesota in 1948. Identified with many liberal causes, as vice president under Lyndon Johnson, he vocally supported US Vietnam policy. Unsuccessful as the Democratic candidate for president (1968) he returned to the Senate (1970) until his death.

**HUNCHBACK, or** kyphosis, deformity of the spine causing bent posture with or without twisting (SCOLIOSIS) and abnormal bony prominences. TUBERCULOSIS of the spine may cause sharp angulation, while congenital diseases, ankylosing spondylitis, vertebral collapse and spinal TUMORS cause smooth kyphosis.

**HUNDRED YEARS' WAR,** sporadic series of wars fought mainly between England and

France 1337–1453. They originated in disputes over English possessions in France, and the claims of Edward III of England to the throne of France. In 1337 he invaded Gascony and won the battles of Sluis (1340) CRÉCY (1346) and POITIERS (1356) and seized Calais, gaining important concessions at the Treaty of Brétigny (1360). The French under Charles V regained much of their lost territory 1369–75 and attacked the English coast. Henry V of England destroyed the resulting uneasy truce when he invaded France in 1415, in pursuit of a vainglorious dream of establishing himself as monarch of Britain and France; he captured Harfleur and defeated a superior French force at AGINCOURT. At the Treaty of Troyes (1420) Henry V was recognized as heir to the French throne and from 1422 his infant son, Henry VI, ruled the dual monarchy, with John, Duke of Bedford as French regent. His able rule won French support, and only the resurgence led by JOAN OF ARC in 1429 halted English gains. Although the Dauphin was crowned Charles VII at Reims in 1429, the English position was not assailed until 1435, when PHILIP THE GOOD of Burgundy recognized Charles VII as king of France. After 1444 the English were driven back until they held only Calais (until 1558) and the Channel Islands.

**HUNGARIAN,** or *Magyar*, one of the UGRO-FINNIC LANGUAGES in the Uralic group. It is spoken mainly in Hungary, but also by groups in Czechoslovakia, Romania and Yugoslavia. It has many loan-words from the non-Uralic tongues within it, but retains its own distinct identity. Its six dialects do not differ widely; Standard Hungarian is the speech of the Budapest area.

**Official name:** People's Republic of Hungary
**Capital:** Budapest
**Area:** 35,911sq mi
**Population:** 10,710,000
**Languages:** Hungarian
**Religions: Roman Catholic; Protestant**
**Monetary unit(s):** 1 Forint = 100 fillér
**HUNGARY,** People's Republic in central

Europe, bordered by Czechoslovakia on the N, the USSR and Romania on the E, Yugoslavia on the S and Austria on the W.
**Land** is mainly low plain, the Kisalföld (Little Plain) in the NW and the Nagyalföld (Great Plain) in the center and E. Crossing the country are two major rivers, the Danube and Tisza, the area between the two (Cumania) being sandy plateau and reclaimed marsh. Other plains lie E of the Tisza including the Hortobagy with its dry steppes (*puszta*). In the W and SW is the more rolling Mezoföld (Middle Plain), and in the S the forested Mecsek massif. Lake Balaton (about 230sq mi) is Europe's largest natural lake. Highlands include the Bakony Forest, Vértes, Gerecse and Pilis hills, and the Carpathian foothills (Kékes 3,330ft, Hungary's highest peak). Winters are cold and summers hot and dry. Rainfall is heavier in the W and floods can occur in spring and early summer, though the E and S can have serious summer droughts.
**People.** Most of the people are Magyars (Hungarians) who speak a Finno-Ugrian language distantly related to Finnish. There are German, Slovak, Croat, Serb and Romanian minorities. A cultured people, their distinctive language is distantly related to Finnish. About half of the population are urban-dwelling, the largest cities being Budapest, the capital (2,060,000), Miskolc, Debrecen, and Szeged.
**Economy** it has expanded as a result of the "New Economic Mechanism" (inaugurated 1968). But mineral resources, including coal, oil, natural gas and iron ore are relatively poor, though bauxite is plentiful. Industrial centers include Budapest (engineering and transportation equipment) and Dunáujvaros (iron and steel). There are important electrical, chemical, food-processing and textile plants. Most of the farmland is owned by the state or by cooperatives. Leading crops include corn, wheat, oats, rye, potatoes, sunflowers and sugar beets. Apricots, vines, paprika and tobacco are also grown, and hogs, sheep and cattle reared.
**History.** The area was conquered by the Magyars under Arpád about 896 AD and Christianized in the 900s. Resistance to Turkish invasion ended with the defeat of King Lewis II at Mohács (1526), and most of the country was divided between the Ottoman Empire and Austria, the W and N coming under Hapsburg rule in 1687. A bid for independence led by Lajos Kossuth (1848) failed, but led to the Dual Monarchy (1867), the Austrian Emperor Francis

Joseph I being crowned King of Hungary. After WWI, ruled by regent Admiral Horthy, Hungary came under German influence and was Nazi Germany's ally in WWII. Occupied by Russia (1945), Hungary soon turned communist (1949). An uprising against the repressive regime was crushed by Russia (1956) and a puppet government under János Kádár set up. In 1968 Hungary helped other Warsaw Pact countries crush the Dubček regime in Czechoslovakia.

**HUNGER STRIKE,** the dramatic use of fasting by prisoners to achieve certain demands. British suffragettes used this weapon in the early 20th century to create sympathy for their cause. The first death of an imprisoned IRISH REPUBLICAN ARMY member occurred in 1920; three more starved themselves in the 1940s; and in 1981, beginning with Bobby SANDS, 10 IRA members incarcerated in Maze Prison, Belfast, fasted to death in an unsuccessful attempt to force the British to grant them political prisoner status.

**HUNS,** nomadic, probably Mongolian, race who invaded SE Europe during the 4th and 5th centuries. They crossed the Volga R in c372 and attacked the Germanic Goth tribes. By 432 they had invaded the Eastern Empire. Under their great leader ATTILA, they threatened the Roman Empire, unsuccessfully invading Gaul in 451. In 452 their Italian invasion was halted at Lake Garda. After Attila's death in 453, the Hun empire gradually disintegrated.

**HUNT, Haroldson Lafayette** (1889–1974), US oilman who in 1937 founded the Hunt Oil Company, which became the largest independent producer of oil and gas in the US. One of the world's richest men, H. L. Hunt broadcast his ultraconservative views on radio and television during the 1960s and published numerous right-wing political tracts. His sons, **(Nelson) Bunker Hunt** (1926–    ) and **W. Herbert** (1928–    ), caused financial panic on US stock exchanges March 1980 by cornering about a third of the world's silver supply, worth $3 billion; they were later reprimanded by the Securities & Exchange Commission.

**HUNT, Leigh** (1784–1859), English critic, journalist and poet. Editor of the liberal *Examiner,* 1808–22, and later of other journals, Hunt was a friend of the leading literary figures of his day, notably Keats and Shelley whose poetic careers he furthered, Lamb, Hazlitt, Byron and eventually Carlyle. His most highly regarded works are *Lord Byron and Some of His Contemporaries* (1828), his *Autobiography* (1850) and the short lyric

poems "Abou Ben Adhem" (1834) and "Jenny Kissed Me" (1844). His literary and dramatic criticism is considered first-rate.

**HUNT, William Holman** (1827–1910), English painter who helped to found the PRE-RAPHAELITE movement. His work is noted for its brilliant coloring and accurate details. His best-known painting is *The Light of the World* (1853).

**HUNTINGTON,** name of two US railroad tycoons. **Collis Potter Huntington** (1821–1900) was chief promoter of the first railroad company in the West, the Central Pacific (1861). In 1884 he established the Southern Pacific. His nephew and heir, **Henry Edwards Huntington** (1850–1927), formed an outstanding art collection and library at San Marino, Cal. It specializes in English 18th-century art and literature and is now a research center.

**HUNTLEY, Chet** (1911–1974) and **BRINKLEY, David** (1920–    ), US broadcast journalists who anchored the nightly news program on NBC television (1956–70) and gained the highest ratings of any news show. After Huntley's death, Brinkley remained an NBC newscaster and analyst until 1981, when he joined ABC.

**HURDY-GURDY,** lute-shaped, stringed musical instrument popular during the Middle Ages. It has 2–4 drone strings sounded by a wheel which is rotated by means of a handle at the base of the instrument. The melody is played on one or more strings by means of keys. The BARREL ORGAN, also turned by a handle, has been erroneously called a hurdy-gurdy.

**HUROK, Sol** (1888–1974), Russian-born US impresario who discovered, promoted and presented to American audiences many of the world's greatest performing artists, including almost all of the Soviet musicians and dancers who appeared in the US from the 1950s through the 1970s.

**HURON, Lake,** the second largest of the GREAT LAKES, covering some 23,010sq mi, with Canada to the N and E, and Mich. to the S and W. It belongs to the Great Lakes–St. Lawrence Seaway navigation passage. Its principal ports are Sarnia, Owen Sound and Midland in Canada; Alpena, Port Huron and Bay City in the US. Georgian Bay is the largest inlet.

**HURON INDIANS,** league of four North American Indian tribes who lived in S Ontario and in c1615 numbered some 20,000. They belonged to the Iroquoian language group, and lived by agriculture. In 1650 the Iroquois virtually destroyed the league. Small numbers of Hurons remain in Quebec and in Okla.

**HURRICANE, a tropical cyclone** of great

intensity. High-speed winds spiral in toward a low-pressure core of warm, calm air (the eye); winds of over 300km/hr have been measured. The direction of spiral is clockwise in the S Hemisphere, counter-clockwise in the N (see CORIOLIS EFFECT). Hurricanes form over water (usually between latitudes 5° and 25°) when there is an existing convergence of air near sea level. The air ascends, losing moisture as precipitation as it does so. If this happens rapidly enough, the upper air is warmed by the water's LATENT HEAT of vaporization. This reduces the surface pressure, so accelerating air convergence. Since they require large quantities of moist warm air, hurricanes rarely penetrate far inland. Hurricanes of the N Pacific are often called typhoons. (See also CYCLONE; WIND.)

HUS, Jan (c1370–1415), Bohemian religious reformer and Czech national hero. Influenced by John WYCLIFFE, Hus attacked Church and papal abuses. He defended his ideas at the Council of CONSTANCE in 1414, where he was arrested, tried and burned at the stake as a heretic. His followers, the Hussites, demanded many reforms in the Roman Catholic Church with which they were involved in a series of wars in Bohemia in the 15th century.

HUSAK, Gustav (1913– ), premier of Czechoslovakia. Taking a pro-Moscow line after 1968, he replaced DUBČEK as secretary of the Czech Communist Party in 1969. He was named president in 1975.

HUSEIN IBN ALI (c1854–1931), sharif of Mecca 1908–16, and king of Hejaz 1916–24. In 1916 he led the WWI Arab revolt against the Turks, and proclaimed himself king of all Arabia. Assisted by T. E. LAWRENCE, he drove the Turks from Syria, Northern Arabia and Transjordan. In 1924 IBN SAUD forced him to abdicate, and he died in exile.

HUSSEIN IBN TALAL (1935– ), King of Jordan since 1953. His policies are generally pro-Western and he is a spokesman for moderation in the conflict between the Arab nations and Israel. Jordan's loss of the West Bank in the 1967 ARAB–ISRAELI WAR led to civil war in 1970 when King Hussein gained firmer control over the country. He declined to endorse the Camp David agreements between Israel and Egypt. His fourth wife, Elizabeth Halaby, an American, whom he married in 1978, became Queen Noor.

HUSSERL, Edmund (1859–1938), Czech-born German philosopher who founded PHENOMENOLOGY. Professor at the Göttingen and Freiburg universities, he was concerned with what constitutes acts of consciousness

and how they relate to experience. He held that consciousness is "intentional" in that it is always "consciousness of" an object. Husserl's investigations of consciousness strongly influenced HEIDEGGER, SARTRE, and other thinkers of twentieth-century EXISTENTIALISM.

HUSTON, the name of two film personalities. Walter Huston (1884–1950), Canadian-born American actor, is best known for his roles in the play *Dodsworth* (1936), the musical comedy *Knickerbocker Holiday* (1938) and the film *The Treasure of Sierra Madre* (1947) directed by his son John Huston (1906– ), Hollywood writer, then director, whose films include *The Maltese Falcon* (1941), *The Asphalt Jungle* (1950), *The African Queen* (1951), *Beat the Devil* (1954) and *Moby Dick* (1956).

HUTCHINS, Robert Maynard (1899–1977), influential US educator, president of Chicago U. 1929–45, chancellor 1945–51. He advocated the integration and synthesis of academic disciplines. In 1959 he founded the Center for the Study of Democratic Institutions as an ideal "Community of Scholars." His books include *The Higher Learning in America* (1936) and *University of Utopia* (1953).

HUTCHINSON, Anne (c1600–1643), English Puritan religious leader, one of the founders of Rhode Island. She emigrated to Mass. in 1634 where she preached that faith alone could achieve God's salvation. She opposed obedience to the strict laws of the Puritan community. In 1638 she and her followers were banished and they established a settlement on Aquidneck island (now Rhode Island). She was killed by Indians.

HUTCHINSON, Thomas (1711–1780), American colonial governor of Massachusetts, 1770–74. A political enemy of Samuel ADAMS, he opposed American independence, and enforced the STAMP ACT (1765) although considering the act unwise. In 1773 he insisted that duty be paid on tea cargoes at Boston, which led to the BOSTON TEA PARTY. In 1774 he went to England where he served George III as an adviser.

HUTTERITES, or Hutterian Brethren, Protestant sect found primarily in S.D., and Canada. Like the MENNONITES, they believe in common ownership of goods and are pacifists. The sect originated in 1533 as a branch of the ANABAPTISTS and takes its name from Jacob Hutter, martyred in 1536.

HUTTON, James (1726–1797), Scottish geologist who proposed, in *Theory of the Earth* (1795), that the earth's natural

...atures result from continual processes, ...ccurring now at the same rate as they have ...the past (see UNIFORMITARIANISM). These ...ews were little regarded until LYELL's work ...me decades later. (See also ...ATASTROPHISM.)

...UXLEY, distinguished British family. ...homas Henry Huxley (1825–1895) is best ...nown for his support of DARWIN's theory of ...VOLUTION, without which acceptance of the ...eory might have been long delayed. Most ...his own contributions to paleontology and ...oology (especially taxonomy), botany, ...cology and anthropology were related to ...is. He also coined the word "agnostic". ...is son Leonard Huxley (1860–1933), a ...stinguished man of literature, wrote *The* ...*ife and Letters of Thomas Henry Huxley* ...900). Of his children, three earned fame. ...r Julian Sorell Huxley (1887–1975) is ...est known as a biologist and ecologist. His ...arly interests were in development and ...owth, genetics and embryology. Later he ...ade important studies of bird behavior, ...udied evolution and wrote many popular ...ientific books. Aldous Leonard Huxley ...894–1963) was one of the 20th century's ...remost novelists. Important works include ...*rome Yellow* (1921), *Antic Hay* (1923) ...nd *Point Counter Point* (1928), character-...ed by their wit and attitude toward lofty ...retensions, and the famous *Brave New* ...*orld* (1932) and *Eyeless in Gaza* (1936). ...fter experimenting with hallucinogenic ...rugs he became interested in mysticism. ...ater works include *The Devils of Loudon* ...952), *The Doors of Perception* (1954) ...nd *Island* (1962). Andrew Fielding Huxley ...917–    ) shared the 1963 Nobel Prize ...r Physiology or Medicine with A. L. ...ODGKIN and Sir J. ECCLES for his work with ...lodgkin on the chemical basis of nerve ...mpulse transmission (see NERVOUS ...YSTEM).

...UYGENS, Christiaan (1629–1695), ...utch scientist who formulated a wave ...eory of LIGHT, first applied the PENDULUM ...the regulation of CLOCKS, and discovered ...e surface markings of MARS and that ...ATURN has rings. In his optical studies he ...ated Huygens' Principle, that all points on ...wave front may at any instant be ...nsidered as sources of secondary waves ...aat, taken together, represent the wave ...ont at any later instant.

...YDE PARK, small residential village in ...E N.Y., on the Hudson R, birthplace and ...urial site of President F. D. Roosevelt; ...amed for Edward Hyde, the British ...vernor of New York (1702–08). The ...oosevelt home, adjacent to the Roosevelt ...ibrary, and the Vanderbilt home are national historic sites.

**HYDRAS,** freshwater CHIDARIA, perhaps the most familiar of the HYDROZOA. Occurring only as polyps, hydras have no medusoid, or jelly-fish, stage; they are found in ponds, lakes and streams throughout the world. The body is an elongated column with a mouth at one end surrounded by tentacles. Normally attached by the other end to the substrate, hydras can move by "looping" across a plane surface or by free-swimming. Hydras reproduce by asexual budding when food is abundant. When food is scarce, ovaries and testes develop on the column, and sexual REPRODUCTION gives rise to resistant, dormant, embryos.

**HYDRAULICS,** application of the properties of liquids (particularly WATER), at rest and in motion, to engineering problems. Since any machine or structure that uses, controls or conserves a liquid makes use of the principles of hydraulics, the scope of this subject is very wide. It includes methods of WATER SUPPLY for consumption, IRRIGATION or navigation and the design of associated DAMS, canals and pipes; HYDROELECTRICITY, the conversion of water power to electric energy using hydraulic TURBINES; the design and construction of ditches, culverts and hydraulic jumps (a means of slowing down the flow of a stream by suddenly increasing its depth) for controlling and discharging FLOOD water, and the treatment and disposal of industrial and human waste. Hydraulics applies the principles of HYDROSTATICS and HYDRODYNAMICS and is hence a branch of FLUID MECHANICS. Any hydraulic process, such as flow of liquid through a turbine, may be described mathematically in terms of four basic equations derived from the conservation of ENERGY, MASS, MOMENTUM and the relationship between the specific FORCES and internal mechanics of the problem. In hydraulic machines which transmit energy through liquids and convert it into mechanical power, three principles of liquid behavior that have been known for centuries are applied. TORICELLI's law states that the speed of liquid flow from a hole in the side of a vessel increases with the depth of the hole below the surface of the liquid in it. PASCAL's law states that the PRESSURE (force per unit area) in an enclosed body of liquid is transmitted equally in all directions. (This law is applied directly in a hydraulic press, in which a force applied over a small area by a piston is transmitted through the liquid filling the system to another piston with a larger area on which a much larger force will be exerted.) BERNOULLI's law states that at any point in a tube through which liquid is flowing, if no work is done, the sum of energies due to the pressure, motion (kinetic energy) and elevation (potential energy) of the liquid is constant. Thus by increasing the cross-section of the tube and slowing the flow down, kinetic energy is converted to pressure energy. The development of pumps in the 19th century, which converted mechanical to hydraulic energy and produced greater fluid velocities and pressures than had previously been obtainable, meant that hydraulic principles could usefully be applied to operate a wide variety of machines. Self-contained hydraulic units consisting of an engine, a pump, control valves, a motor to convert hydraulic to mechanical energy, and a load were soon developed for use in industry and transportation. Hydraulics is now one of the main technologies for transmitting energy, comparing well with mechanical and electrical systems and having the advantages of being fast and accurate and good at multiplying forces. Hydraulic systems containing water, oil or special fire-resistant fluids are now used in AIRPLANE landing systems, AUTOMOBILE braking systems and many other industrial applications.

**HYDROCARBONS,** organic compounds (see ORGANIC CHEMISTRY) composed of CARBON and HYDROGEN only. Other organic compounds may be said to derive formally from the various hydrocarbon structures by the addition of FUNCTIONAL GROUPS and by the substitution of other groups or ELEMENTS. Hydrocarbons can be divided into aliphatic, alicyclic, and aromatic compounds. **Aliphatic** hydrocarbons, which are made of carbon atoms linked in straight or branched chains, can be further subdivided into **alkanes** (paraffins), which are *saturated* hydrocarbons, in which all possible sites for hydrogen atoms are filled; **alkenes** (olefins), *unsaturated* hydrocarbons in which one or more double bonds exist between the carbon atoms; and **alkynes** (acetylenes), also unsaturated, but with a triple bond between carbon atoms. **Alicyclic** hydrocarbons are made of carbon atoms that are linked to form one or more rings, and in general resemble analogous aliphatic structures. **Aromatic** compounds also contain one or more rings, but have a more stable structure than alicyclic compounds, and in many cases include a BENZENE ring. Some hydrocarbons occur in plant oils, but by far the largest sources of all kinds of hydrocarbons are PETROLEUM, NATURAL GAS, and COAL GAS. They are used as FUELS, for LUBRICATION, and as starting materials for a wide variety of industrial

syntheses.

**HYDROCEPHALUS,** enlargement of th BRAIN ventricles with increase CEREBROSPINAL FLUID (CSF) within th SKULL. In children it causes a characteris enlargement of the head. Brain tissue attenuated and damaged by long-standin hydrocephalus. It may be caused by block CSF drainage in the lower ventricles brain stem aqueduct (e.g., by TUMOR ar malformation, including those seen wi SPINA BIFIDA), or by prevention of i reabsorption over the brain surface (e.g following MENINGITIS). Apart from atte tion to the cause, treatment may inclu draining CSF into the atrium of the HEART

**HYDRODYNAMICS,** the branch of FLU MECHANICS dealing with the FORCES, ENERG and PRESSURE of FLUIDS in motion. mathematical treatment of ideal frictionle and incompressible fluids flowing arour given boundaries is coupled with a empirical approach in order to sol practical problems.

**HYDROELECTRICITY,** or **hydroelectr power,** the generation of ELECTRICITY usir water power, is the source of about a third the world's electricity. Although the pow station must usually be sited in th mountains and the electricity transmitt over long distances, the power is still chea since water, the fuel, is free. Moreove running costs are low. An exciting mode development is the use in coastal regions the ebb and flow of the tide as a source electric power. Hydroelectric power uses flow of water to turn a TURBINE which itse drives a GENERATOR.

Convenient heads of water sometim occur naturally (see WATERFALL), but mo often must be created artificially b damming a river (see DAM); an add advantage is that the reservoir that forr behind the dam may be tapped for drinki or irrigation water.

The powerhouse, which contains t turbines and generators, may be at the fo of the dam or some distance away, the wat then being transported in tunnels and lor pipelines called **penstocks.** The turbines a of two main types: impulse (e.g., the Pelt wheel) and reaction (e.g., the Francis a Kaplan wheels. The Pelton wheel h buckets about its edge, into which jets water are aimed, so turning the wheel. T Francis wheel has spiral vanes: water ente from the side and is discharged along t axis. The Kaplan wheel is rather like a hu propeller immersed in the water.

**HYDROFOIL,** a structure which, whe moved rapidly through water, generates li in exactly the same way and for the sar

asons as does the AIRFOIL (see also
ERODYNAMICS). It is usually mounted
neath a vessel (also called a hydrofoil).
Much of a conventional boat's power is
ent in overcoming the drag (resistance) of
e water; as a hydrofoil vessel builds up
eed, it lifts out of the water until only a
nall portion of it (struts, hydrofoils and
OPELLER) is in contact with the water.
hus drag is reduced to a minimum.
ydrofoils can exceed 125km/h as
mpared with conventional craft, whose
aximum speeds rarely approach 80km/h.

YDROGEN (H), the simplest and lightest
ement, a colorless, odorless gas. Hydrogen
oms make up about 90% of the UNIVERSE,
d it is believed that all other elements
ave been produced by fusion of hydrogen
ee STAR; FUSION, NUCLEAR). On earth most
ydrogen occurs combined with oxygen as
ATER and mineral HYDRATES, or with
rbon as HYDROCARBONS (see PETROLEUM).
ydrogen is produced in the laboratory by
e action of a dilute ACID on zinc or other
ectropositive metals. Industrially it is
ade by the catalytic reaction of
ydrocarbons with steam, or by the WATER
AS process, or as a by-product of some
ECTROLYSIS reactions. Two-thirds of the
ydrogen manufactured is used to make
nmonia by the HABER PROCESS. It is also
ed in HYDROGENATION, PETROLEUM
fining, and metal smelting. METHANOL
d HYDROGEN CHLORIDE are produced from
ydrogen. Being flammable, it has now
en largely superseded by helium for
lling BALLOONS and AIRSHIPS. Hydrogen is
ed in oxy-hydrogen WELDING; liquid
ydrogen is used as fuel in rocket engines, in
BBLE CHAMBERS, and as a refrigerant (see
YOGENICS). Hydrogen is fairly reactive,
ving HYDRIDES with most other elements
a heating, and a moderate reducing agent.
belongs in no definite group of the
RIODIC TABLE, but has some resemblance
the HALOGENS in forming the ion H⁻, and
the ALKALI METALS in forming the ion H⁺
ee ACIDS); it is always monovalent. (See
SO HYDROGENATION; HYDROGEN BONDING.)
hydrogen atom consists of one ELECTRON
biting a nucleus of one PROTON. A
ydrogen molecule is two atoms combined
$_2$). In parahydrogen both the protons
ve the same SPIN: in orthohydrogen the
otons have opposite spin. They have
ghtly different properties. At room
mperature, hydrogen is 75% orthohy-
ogen, 25% parahydrogen. DEUTERIUM
$I^2$) and TRITIUM (H³) are ISOTOPES of
drogen. (See also HYDROGEN BOMB.) AW
008, mp −259°C, bp −253°C.

YDROGEN BOMB, or thermonuclear

bomb, very powerful BOMB whose explosive
energy is produced by nuclear FUSION of two
DEUTERIUM atoms or of a deuterium and a
TRITIUM atom. The extremely high temperatures required to start the fusion reaction
are produced by using an ATOMIC BOMB as a
fuse. Lithium-6 deuteride (Li⁶D) is the
explosive; neutrons produced by deuterium
fusion react with the Li⁶ to produce tritium.
The end products are the isotopes of HELIUM
He³ and He⁴. In warfare hydrogen bombs
have the advantage of being far more
powerful than atomic bombs, their power
being measured in megatons (millions of
tons) of TNT, capable of destroying a large
city. In defensive and peaceful uses they can
be modified so that the radioactivity
produced is reduced. Hydrogen bombs were
first developed in the US (1949–52) by
Edward TELLER and others, and have been
tested also by the USSR, Great Britain,
China and France.

**HYDROGEN PEROXIDE.** See PEROXIDES.

**HYDROGEN SULFIDE.** See SULFIDES.

**HYDROLOGIC CYCLE,** the circulation of
the waters of the earth between land, oceans
and atmosphere. Water evaporates from the
oceans into the ATMOSPHERE, where it may
form CLOUDS (see also EVAPORATION). Much
of this water is precipitated as RAIN (or
snow, sleet, hail) back to the earth's surface.
Of this, some is returned to the atmosphere
by the TRANSPIRATION of plants, some joins
rivers and is returned to the sea, some joins
the GROUNDWATER and eventually reaches a
sea, lake or river, and some evaporates back
into the atmosphere from the surface of the
land or from rivers, streams, lakes, etc. Over
97% of the earth's water is in the oceans.
(See also HYDROLOGY.)

**HYDROLOGY,** the branch of geophysics
concerned with the HYDROSPHERE (all the
waters of the EARTH), with particular
reference to water on and within the land.
The science was born in the 17th century
with the work of Pierre Perrault and Edme
MARIOTTE. (See also HYDROLOGIC CYCLE.)

**HYDROLYSIS,** a double decomposition
effected by WATER, according to the general
equation

$$XY + H_2O \rightarrow XOH + YH.$$

If $XY$ is a salt of a weak ACID or a weak BASE,
the hydrolysis is reversible, and affects the
pH of the solution (see BUFFER). Reactive
organic compounds such as ACID CHLORIDES
and ACID ANHYDRIDES are rapidly
hydrolyzed by water alone, but others
require acids, bases, or ENZYMES as catalysts
(see also DIGESTION). Industrial hydrolysis
processes include the alkaline saponifica-
tion of oils and fats to glycerol and SOAP, and
the acid hydrolysis of starch to glucose.

**HYDROPHOBIA.** See RABIES.

**HYDROPONICS,** the technique by which plants are grown without soil. It is also known as soil-less culture. All the minerals required for plant growth are provided by nutrient solutions in which the roots are immersed. The technique has been highly developed as a tool in botanical research, but commercial exploitation is limited primarily because of the difficulty of aerating the water and providing support for the plants. Gravel culture has overcome these problems to some extent and is used to grow some horticultural crops.

**HYDROSTATICS.** (See FLUID MECHANICS).

**HYENAS,** three species of carnivorous mammals of essentially African distribution. They are distinctive in having the shoulders considerably higher than the hindquarters and have also an unusual gait, moving both limbs on one side of the body together. All three species have massive heads with powerful jaws. Though reviled as scavengers and carrion-feeders, hyenas are active and skilful predators in their own right, hunting in packs of up to 20. Family: Hyaenidae.

**HYGROMETER,** device to measure HUMIDITY (the amount of water vapor the air holds). Usually, hygrometers measure relative HUMIDITY, the amount of moisture as a percentage of the SATURATION level at that temperature. The **hair hygrometer**, though of limited accuracy, is common. The length of a hair increases with increase in relative humidity. This length change is amplified by a lever and registered by a needle on a dial. Human hair is most used. The **wet and dry bulb hygrometer** (psychrometer) has two THERMOMETERS mounted side by side, the bulb of one covered by a damp cloth. Air is moved across the apparatus (e.g., by a fan) and evaporation of water from the cloth draws LATENT HEAT from the bulb. Comparison of the two temperatures, and the use of tables, gives the relative humidity. The **dewpoint hygrometer** comprises a polished container cooled until the DEW point is reached: this temperature gives a measure of relative humidity. The **electric hygrometer** measures changes in the electrical RESISTANCE of a hygroscopic (water-absorbing) strip.

**HYKSOS,** kings of Egypt, Asian invaders who formed the 15th and 16th dynasties. They introduced the Asian light horse and chariot, bronze weapons and the compound bow. (See also EGYPT, ANCIENT.)

**HYPERBARIC CHAMBER,** chamber built to withstand and be kept at pressures above atmospheric. The high OXYGEN pressures achieved in them may destroy t[...] anaerobic bacteria (*Clostridia*) responsib[...] for gas GANGRENE; SURGERY may be done [...] the chamber. It is also used f[...] AEROEMBOLISM in decompression.

**HYPERBOLA.** See CONIC SECTIONS.

**HYPEROPIA,** or hypermetropia or far-longsightedness, a defect of VISION in whi[...] light entering the EYE from nearby objec[...] comes to a focus behind the retina. T[...] condition may be corrected by use of converging spectacle LENS.

**HYPERTENSION.** See BLO[...] CIRCULATION.

**HYPERTHYROIDISM.** See THYRO[...] GLAND.

**HYPNOSIS,** an artificially induced ment[...] state characterized by an individual's loss [...] critical powers and his consequent openne[...] to SUGGESTION. It may be induced by [...] external agency or by the individual hims[...] (**autohypnosis**). Hypnotism has been wide[...] used in medicine and especially PSYCHIATRY and PSYCHOTHERAPY. Here, t[...] particular value of hypnosis is that, while [...] trance, the individual may be encouraged [...] recall deeply repressed memories (s[...] MEMORY; REPRESSION) that may be the caus[...] for example, of a COMPLEX; once such caus[...] have been elucidated, therapy can proceed[...]

Hypnosis seems to be as old as ma[...] However, the first definite information on [...] comes from the late-18th-century with t[...] work of MESMER, who held that disease w[...] the result of imbalance in the patien[...] "animal magnetism", and hence attempt[...] to cure by use of magnets. In fact, some [...] his patients *were* cured, presumably [...] suggestion; and the term **mesmerism** is st[...] sometimes used for hypnotism. Ear[...] psychotherapeutic uses include that [...] CHARCOT and his pupil FREUD, though Fre[...] later rejected hypnosis and instead used [...] own technique, FREE ASSOCIATION. Little [...] known of the nature or root cause [...] hypnosis, and its amateur use is dangerous[...]

**HYPOCHONDRIA,** or **hypochondrias**[...] involves undue ANXIETY about real [...] supposed ailments, usually in the belief th[...] these are incurable. Hypochondriacs m[...] unconsciously, or even consciously, use th[...] symptoms to gain attention and sympathy[...]

**HYPOTHALAMUS,** central part of t[...] base of the BRAIN, closely related to t[...] PITUITARY GLAND. It contains vital cente[...] for controlling the autonomic NERVO[...] SYSTEM, body temperature and water a[...] food intake. It also produces HORMONES f[...] regulating pituitary secretion and tw[...] systemic hormones (e.g., VASOPRESSIN).

**HYSTERECTOMY,** or surgical removal [...] the WOMB, with or without the OVARIES a[...]

LLOPIAN TUBES. It may be performed via
ther the ABDOMEN or the vagina and is
ost often used for fibroids, benign TUMORS
womb muscle, CANCER of the cervix or
dy of womb, or for diseases causing heavy
ENSTRUATION. If the ovaries are preserved,
RMONE secretion remains intact, though
riods cease and infertility is inevitable.

YSTERIA, psychiatric disorder char-
terized by exaggerated responses, emo-
nal lability with excess tears and
ughter, over-activity and hyperventila-
n. It is often a manifestation of
tention-seeking behavior. **Conversion
stems** or mimicry of organic disease are
ten termed hysterical; the simulation of a
rticular disorder fulfills some
ychological need in response to certain
resses and results in an unconscious gain
release from anxiety.

h letter of the English alphabet. It derives
om a Semitic form adopted into the Greek
phabet as *iota*. The dot above the
wer-case *i* was introduced in the 11th
ntury. With the advent of printing *j* was
rmally distinguished from *i*.

ERT, Jacques (1890–1962), French
mposer of piano pieces, orchestral works,
mphonic poems and operas. Among his
ell-known works are a cantata, *Le Poète et
Fée* (Prix de Rome, 1919), a ballet based
Oscar Wilde's *Ballad of Reading Gaol*
922), the orchestral suites *Escales* (1922)
d *Divertissement* (1930) and the light
era for radio *Barbe-bleue* (1943).

EX, seven species of wild goats which
ffer from true GOATS in their flattened
reheads and usually broad-fronted horns.
lways found in mountainous areas, ibex
ve for most of the year in separate-sexed
rds, with the males only forming harems
ring the 7–10-day rut.

ISES, stork-like birds of moderate size,
aracterized by long thin downward-
rving bills. Ibises have a worldwide
stribution in tropical, subtropical and
mperate regions, and are usually found
ar fresh water, feeding on small aquatic
imals. Ibises are gregarious and
equently raucous. The best known species

are the sacred ibis (*Threskiornis
aethiopica*), honored in ancient Egypt, and
the scarlet ibis, *Eudocimus ruber*, a
Caribbean species with scarlet plumage.

**IBN BATTUTA** (1304–1368?), greatest
Arab traveler of the Middle Ages. Born in
Tangier, Morocco, he spent about 25 years
traveling in Africa, the Middle East, Persia,
India and the Far East. His notes (the
*Rihlah* or *Travels*) provide a priceless
account of life in the oriental world before
the rise of Europe.

**IBN SAUD** (c1880–1953), creator of the
kingdom of Saudi Arabia in 1932 and its
first ruler. As a young man he set up the
Ikhwan, a fanatical brotherhood of
Muslims. With the Ikhwan's help in the
1920s, he conquered and united the small
kingdoms which now make up SAUDI ARABIA.
Saud was one of the first Arab leaders to
exploit Middle East oil. (See also MUSLIMS.)

**IBO**, African ethnic group of SE Nigeria
numbering several million. After independence (1963) they came to dominate the
civil service and commerce of Nigeria.
Hostilities between Ibo and other tribal
groups led to the secession of BIAFRA, the Ibo
homeland, in 1967. In the civil war which
followed, about 2 million Ibos died in battle
or from starvation.

**IBSEN, Henrik Johan** (1828–1906),
Norwegian playwright and poet. The
pioneer of modern drama, his work
developed from national Romanticism (*The
Vikings at Helgoland*; 1858) to the realistic
and effective presentation of contemporary
social problems and moral dilemmas in such
plays as *A Doll's House* (1879) and *Ghosts*
(1881), *The Wild Duck* (1884), *Hedda
Gabler* (1890). Very different, but as
important to his philosophy, are his
verse-dramas *Brand* (1866) and *Peer Gynt*
(1867).

**ICE**, frozen WATER: a colorless crystalline
solid in which the strong, directional
HYDROGEN BONDING produces a structure
with much space between the molecules.
Thus ice is less dense than water, and floats
on it. The expansion of water on freezing
may crack pipes and automobile radiators.
Since dissolved substances lower the
freezing point, ANTIFREEZE is used. For the
same reason, seawater freezes at about
−2° (see OCEAN). Ice has a very low
coefficient of FRICTION, and some fast-
moving sports (ICE HOCKEY, ICE SKATING and
ICEBOATING) are played on it; however,
slippery, icy roads are dangerous. Ice
deposited on AIRPLANE wings reduces lift.
Ice is used as a refrigerant, and to cool some
beverages. (See also GLACIER; HAIL; ICE AGES;
ICEBERG; ICEBREAKER; SNOW.) mp 0°C, sg

0.92 (0°C).

**ICE AGES,** periods when glacial ice covers large areas of the earth's surface that are not normally covered by ice. Ice ages are characterized by fluctuations of climatic conditions: a cycle of several glacial periods contains interglacial periods, perhaps of a few tens of thousands of years, when the climate may be as temperate as between ice ages. It is not known whether the earth is currently between ice ages or merely passing through an interglacial period.

There seem to have been several ice ages in the PRECAMBRIAN, and certainly a major one immediately prior to the start of the CAMBRIAN. There were a number in the PALEOZOIC, including a major ice age with a complicated cycle running through the MISSISSIPPIAN, PENNSYLVANIAN and early PERMIAN. The ice age that we know most about, however, is that of the QUATERNARY, continuing through most of the PLEISTOCENE and whose last glacial period ended about 10,000 years ago, denoting the start of the HOLOCENE. (See GEOLOGY.) At their greatest, the Pleistocene glaciers covered about a third of the earth's surface, or some 45 million km², and may have been up to 3km thick in places. They covered most of Canada, N Europe and N Russia, N parts of the US, Antarctica, parts of South America, and some other areas in the Southern Hemisphere.

Theories about the cause of ice ages include that the SUN's energy output varies, that the earth's axis varies in its inclination and in the shape and eccentricity of its orbit, that CONTINENTAL DRIFT and polar wandering may alter global climatic conditions, and that volcanic dust or dust produced by meteorite impact in the ATMOSPHERE could reduce the amount of solar heat received by the surface. (See EARTH; GLACIER; VOLCANO.)

**ICEBERG,** a large, floating mass of ice. In the S Hemisphere, the Antarctic ice sheet overflows its land support to form shelves of ice on the sea; huge pieces, as much as 200km across, break off to form icebergs. In the N Hemisphere, icebergs are generally not over 150m across. Most are "calved" from some 20 GLACIERS on Greenland's W coast. Small icebergs (growlers) may calve from larger ones. Some 75% of the height and over 85% of the mass of an iceberg lies below water. Northern icebergs usually float for some months to the Grand Banks, off Newfoundland, there melting in a few days. They endanger shipping, the most famous tragedy being the sinking of the *Titanic* (1912). The International Ice Patrol now keeps a constant watch on the area.

**ICE CREAM,** popular frozen dairy foo whose main constituents are sugars, mi products, water, flavorings and air. I cream has a high caloric value, and a ve high VITAMIN A content, as well as bein protein and calcium-rich. It is also a sour of, in smaller quantities, iron, phosphoru riboflavin and THIAMIN. Water ices, whi contain no milk products, have been know since ancient times in Europe and Asia. I cream probably reached the US in the 17 century, and was first commercial manufactured by Jacob Fussel (1851 Today, the US is the world's large producer and consumer.

**ICE HOCKEY,** modern version of fie hockey played on ice. Two teams of s skaters each attempt to score goals usir wooden sticks to hit a hard rubber disk (t puck) into a small cage (the opponent goal). Ice hockey is an exciting game whi places a premium on speed, strengt mobility and stamina. The game originate in Canada, where it is a national spo Canada and the US provide teams for t North American professional organizatio the National Hockey League (NHL). T International Ice Hockey Federatio governs amateur groups in North Ameri and Europe. Television has made ice hock popular. (See also ICE SKATING.)

**Official name:** Republic of Iceland
**Capital:** Reykjavik
**Area:** 39,758sq mi
**Population:** 230,000
**Languages:** Icelandic
**Religions:** Lutheran
**Monetary unit(s):** 1 Króna = 100 aurar
**ICELAND,** island republic in the Atlantic Ocean just touching on the Arct Circle. Geologically young and volcanic origin, the island is still being molded volcanic activity. Surtsey, a new island o the S coast, first emerged from the sea 1963, and Heimay had to be evacuate when the Helgafell volcano erupted 1973.
**Land.** Iceland is mainly a high inlan plateau surrounded by mountain

vannadalshnjúku is the highest peak ,952ft) and Hekla (4,747ft) is the st-known volcano. Large surface areas e covered by cooled laval flows and there e many glaciers, eroded valleys and rds. Numerous geysers and hot springs e used for central heating and irrigation. he climate is cool and temperate, and the eather very changeable. Temperatures at eykjavik average 30°F in Jan. and 52°F July; rainfall averages 34in yearly at eykjavik, but is heavier in the SE. egetation is mainly mosses, lichens and casional small trees and shrubs, with me coastal grassland. Soils are thin.

eople. The population of Iceland lives ainly in small towns along the coast, in N lleys and the SE lowlands. The largest wn is Reykjavik, the capital, chief port d cultural center. Icelanders are a mogenous mixture of Nordic and Celtic cial stock. Their language, ICELANDIC, veloped from Old Norse, and has changed tle over the centuries. Iceland has a rich erary tradition of heroic medieval sagas d bardic poems which are still read by the ople today. Education is free and mpulsory from age 7 to 15; illiteracy is actically nonexistent.

conomy. Fishing (especially cod, haddock d herring) and fish-processing are the ainstay industries and provide two thirds Iceland's exports. A long dispute with reat Britain over fishing rights in the aters off Iceland led to a series of "cod ars." In 1975 Iceland extended its conomic" sea limits to 200mi, and the xt year broke diplomatic relations with 'itain temporarily. There is some small ale agriculture (cattle, sheep, potatoes, rnips) and manufacturing (fertilizer, pliances, food, clothing and books). eland has vast resources of natural energy her rivers, hot streams and geysers as well important volcanic mineral potential. hese natural resources are only beginning be exploited for industrial and mmercial purposes.

istory. Discovered by Norsemen c870 D, Iceland was under Norwegian rule om 1262, and under the Danes from 1380. he tradition of democratic government .tes from 930 AD when the Althing, the rld's oldest parliament, was established. eland was entirely self-governing from '18, and became a fully independent public in 1944.

'ELANDIC, the official language of eland, developed from Old Norse, which as brought to Iceland from W Norway in e 9th and 10th centuries. Although onunciation and spelling have changed,

the old grammatical structure has remained. Icelanders are still able to read their medieval literature and the SAGAS.

ICE SKATING, movement over ice on steel blades fastened to shoe soles; a popular sport in Canada, the US and N Europe. Originally confined to frozen lakes and rivers, the sport has been widely popularized by the introduction of artificial ice rinks. Skating is not difficult, but it takes many years to become a skilled professional. Competitive ice skating is divided into figure skating and speed skating. Figure skating is really ballet on skates, demanding great body control and a feel for music. Speed skating demands strength, stamina and fitness. The first US skating club was formed in Philadelphia (1849), but only in the last 50 years has the sport achieved national and international popularity. (See also ICE HOCKEY.)

I CHING, or Book of Changes, ancient Chinese literary classic dating to c12th century BC. It consists of a set of symbols and texts for DIVINATION. There has been a revival of interest in the *I Ching* in recent years.

ICKES, Harold LeClair (1874–1952), US government official, secretary of the interior, 1933–46, and head of the Public Works Administration 1933–39. An able and responsible administrator, he was a central figure in Roosevelt's NEW DEAL.

ICONOCLASTIC CONTROVERSY, Christian dispute over the popular use of ICONS within the Eastern Orthodox (Byzantine) Church. With public support from Emperor Leo III the iconoclasts (Greek for "image breakers") succeeded (726) in destroying works of art and in persecuting icon worshipers for idolatry and heresy. Under Empress Irene icon veneration was officially restored (787), an event still celebrated in the Eastern Church as the Feast of Orthodoxy. (See also BYZANTINE ART.)

ID, according to Freudian theory, the formless collection of all parts of the mind present at birth, part of which develops to form the EGO. The id thus contains such parts of the psychic makeup as EMOTIONS and INSTINCTS. (See also PSYCHOANALYSIS; UNCONSCIOUS.)

IDAHO, state, NW US, in the Rocky Mts, bounded by Mont. and Wyo. to the E, Utah and Nev. to the S, Wash. and Ore. to the W, and Canada to the N.

Land. Idaho contains about 81 mountain ranges, over 2,000 lakes and 10 major rivers, including the Clearwater, Salmon and Snake (a tributary of the Columbia R), which flows across the entire southern part of the state. The climate is widely varied with dry heat in the S, cold in the snow-laden Rockies and warm moist air from the Pacific in the N. Average July temperatures are 75°F–70°F; average Jan. temperatures are 30°F–16°F. Snowfall ranges from 14in (SW) to more than 200in (in the mountains). Rain varies from below 10in in the Snake R plains to 30in in the Panhandle. Evergreen forests cover two-fifths of Idaho. Wildlife is abundant, and includes elk, antelope, black bear, beaver, muskrat, game and other birds and fish.

**People.** Population density is one of the lowest in the US; 70% of all Idahoans live within about 30mi of the Snake R in the fertile agricultural areas. The people are about 98% native-born Americans with about 1% non-Caucasian residents; about 6,000 descendants of French and Spanish Basques live in metropolitan Boise. Some 100 local school districts provide free public elementary and secondary education. The U. of Idaho (at Moscow), Idaho State U. (at Pocatello), and the College of Idaho (at Caldwell) are among the state's institutions of higher education.

**Economy.** Farming (Idaho potatoes are famous), tourism, mining (silver, lead, gold, zinc, copper and phosphates), livestock raising, manufacturing (especially food processing); lumbering and tourism are the state's chief sources of wealth. Sun Valley is a famous vacation resort. Other attractions include HELLS CANYON, one of the deepest gorges in North America, Craters of the Moon National Monument; fish and game

**Name of state:** Idaho
**Capital:** Boise
**Statehood:** July 3, 1890 (43rd state)
**Familiar name:** Gem State
**Area:** 83,557sq mi
**Population:** 943,935
**Elevation:** Highest—12,662ft., Borah Peak. Lowest—710ft, Snake River at Lewiston
**Motto:** Esto Perpetua (It is Forever)
**State flower:** Syringa (mock orange)
**State bird:** Mountain bluebird
**State tree:** Western white pine
**State song:** "Here We Have Idaho"

reserves and designated "wilderness" area[s] The state has vast water resources and hu[ge] dams on the rivers provide hydroelectr[ic] power and water for irrigation.

**History.** The LEWIS AND CLARK expediti[on] crossed the area in 1805. Fur traders a[nd] missionaries arrived in the next fe[w] decades. Discovery of gold (1860) brough[t a] rush of prospectors followed by lumberme[n,] farmers and ranchers. Idaho became [a] territory (with Wyo. and Mont.) in 186[ ] The territorial area was transformed [into] present-day boundaries, and in 1890 Ida[ho] became the Union's 43rd state. In the 20[th] century, Idaho has been prosperous, a[nd] during the 1970s the population increas[ed] by 30%. Early in the 1980s, significa[nt] problems occupying the state governme[nt] related to water pollution, waste dispos[al,] energy and conservation, management [of] natural resources, and rising unemplo[y]ment. In 1980, a large section of the N pa[rt] of the state was covered with volcanic a[sh] from MOUNT SAINT HELENS.

**IDEALISM,** name adopted by sever[al] schools of philosophy, all of which in so[me] way assert the primacy of ideas, either [as] the sole authentic stuff of reality or as t[he] only medium through which we can ha[ve] knowledge or experience of the worl[d.] Idealisms are commonly contrasted bo[th] with the various types of REALISM and wi[th] philosophical MATERIALISM. They are oft[en] associated with methodological RATIONA[L]ISM because they usually seem to owe mo[re] to reasoning upon a PRIORI principles than [to] any appeal to experience. The idealism [of] PLATO, in which ideas were held to have a[n] external objectivity, is unrepresentative [of] modern varieties, of which that of BERKEL[EY] is archetypal. KANT and HEGEL we[re] foremost in the German idealist traditio[n,] while T. H. GREEN, F. H. Bradley and [ ] ROYCE were representative of more rece[nt] English-speaking idealists. Idealism ha[s,] however, been in eclipse in the 20th century.

**IDEOGRAM,** a written symbol whi[ch] directly conveys an idea or represents [a] thing, rather than representing a spoke[n] word, phrase or letter. **Logograms,** symbo[ls] that each represent an entire word, are al[so] often called ideograms. Egyptian HIER[O]GLYPHICS comprised a writing system part[ly] ideogramic, partly logogrammatic a[nd] partly phonetic. (See also WRITING, HISTO[RY] OF.)

**IDRIS I** (1890– ), king of Liby[a] 1951–69; chief of the powerful Musli[m] brotherhood, Sanusi. From Egyptian ex[ile] (1923–49), he led the struggle against t[he] Italian occupation, and became king wh[en]

Libya gained independence. He was deposed when a military junta proclaimed the Libyan Arab Republic.

**IGNEOUS ROCKS,** one of the three main classes of rocks, those whose origin is the solidification of molten material, or detrital volcanic material. They crystallize from LAVA at the earth's surface (extrusion) or from MAGMA beneath (intrusion). There are two main classes: **Volcanic rocks** are extruded (see VOLCANISM), typical examples being LAVA and PYROCLASTIC ROCKS. **Plutonic rocks** are intruded into the rocks of the EARTH's crust at depth, a typical example being GRANITE: those forming near to the surface are sometimes called **hypabyssal rocks.** Types of intrusions include BATHOLITHS, DIKES, SILLS and LACCOLITHS. As plutonic rocks cool more slowly than volcanic, they have a coarser texture, more time being allowed for crystal formation. (See also ROCKS.)

**IGOR** (1151–1202), Russian prince. He led a disastrous expedition into the Don steppes to try to keep the Polovtskys (CUMANS) from marauding in S and W Russia; described in the famous Russian epic poem *Tale of the Host of Igor* (c1187) and BORODIN's opera.

**IGUAÇU FALLS,** also Iguazu, spectacular series of waterfalls on the Argentina-Brazil border. They are located on the Iguaçu R 14mi above its confluence with the Paraná R. The falls have a total fall of only 230ft but rank fourth among world waterfalls in total volume of water with an estimated flow of 61,00 cubic ft per second or slightly less than one-third that of Niagara Falls.

**IGUANAS,** the largest and most elaborately marked lizards of the New World. The family (Iguanidae) includes insectivorous, carnivorous and herbivorous forms. Many species are territorial. Iguanas characteristically show ornamental scales and a dorsal fringe, and bear tubercles on the head and body. Some species have an erectile throat fan. There are two major groups: Ground iguanas and Green iguanas; there is also one species of marine iguana. All species are hunted for food, although this is greatly depleting their numbers.

**ILE-DE-FRANCE,** historic name for the limestone plains area of the Paris basin, N central France— between the Oise, Aisne, Marne and Seine rivers—the traditional political power center of France.

**ILEITIS,** INFLAMMATION of the ileum; part of small intestine (see ENTERITIS; GASTROINTESTINAL TRACT).

**ILIAD,** ancient Greek epic poem of 24 books in hexameter verse, attributed to HOMER; internal references suggest it was composed in the mid-8th century BC. It describes a quarrel during the siege of Troy between the Greek warrior-hero Achilles and King Agamemnon which results in Achilles' brutal slaying of Hector, the Trojan warrior-prince. A companion to the ODYSSEY, the *Iliad* is one of the world's greatest tragic works of literature.

**ILLICH, Ivan** (1926–    ), Austrian-born educator and social critic of modern Western industrial society. He founded (1961) and directed the Intercultural Center of Documentation (Cuernavaca, Mexico), a "think tank" for those seeking radical social, economic and political change in Latin America. His best known book is *De-Schooling Society* (1971).

**Name of state:** Illinois
**Capital:** Springfield
**Statehood:** Dec. 3, 1818 (21st state)
**Familiar name:** Land of Lincoln, Prairie State
**Area:** 56,400sq mi
**Population:** 11,418,461
**Elevation:** Highest—1,241ft, Charles Mound. Lowest—269ft, Mississippi River at Cairo
**Motto:** State Sovereignty, National Union
**State flower:** Native violet
**State bird:** Cardinal
**State tree:** Oak
**State song:** "Illinois"

**ILLINOIS,** state, in NE central US, at the heartland of US transportation with a vast network of railroads, highways, airways, lake and river routes. CHICAGO, its largest city, is the crossroads of America.

**Land.** Illinois is bounded in the N by Wis., in the E by its 60mi shoreline on Lake Michigan, Ind., and the Wabash R, in the SE by the Ohio R and Ken. and in the SW and W by Mo., Ia., and the Mississippi R. Flat prairies and fertile deep black soil plains cover the central and northern areas with rolling hills in the S. Some 4 million acres of forest exist in the S, mostly in Shawnee National Forest. The climate is temperate with summers averaging 70°F (in the S) and 77°F (in the N); cold, snowy winters average 22°F (in the N) and 37°F (in the S). Rainfall averages 32–48in (N) and 48–64in (S). Plant life is varied, with N and S tree varieties ranging from oak, white pine and hickory to cypress and tupelo gum. The state has large numbers of waterfowl, game birds, small animals and fish.

**People.** The first wave of settlers moved into the Ohio R valley from the E and S. They pushed the local Indians (after whom the state is named) westward by the 1820s. Since the Civil War the state has had a steady influx of blacks primarily from the South; and of European immigrants, among them Germans, Poles, and Italians. Regionalism has always been a characteristic of Illinois; the population is divided in outlook and political attitudes between the metropolitan Chicago area and "downstate" (the smaller cities and rural areas towards the S). More than 80% of the state's people live in urban areas.

**Economy.** About one-third of the labor force is employed in manufacturing industries, based mainly in the Chicago area and in the East St. Louis area. A leading agricultural state, it produces corn, hogs, cattle and soybeans. Industry is exceptionally varied and includes the manufacture of machinery, electrical and electronic equipment, processsed foods, metal products and chemicals. Illinois is a leading coal producer and also has significant oil resources.

There is a large system of free public schools; over 100 institutions of higher learning include Northwestern U., the U. of Illinois, U. of Chicago and Illinois Institute of Technology. Unofficially named "the Land of Lincoln," the state's many tourist attractions include Abraham Lincoln's home and tomb in Springfield and a reconstruction of his earlier home in New Salem.

**History.** The state was first explored by fur traders and then by JOLIET and MARQUETTE (1673) and by LASALLE (1680). The British took the area from the French after the French and Indian Wars (1763). Following the American Revolution, Illinois became part of the NORTHWEST TERRITORY (1787). In 1818 Illinois was admitted to the Union as a state. The people split over the question of states' rights and slavery at the time of the Civil War. After the war, construction of railroads aided industrial expansion. Through the later part of the 19th and early 20th centures, Illinois was the scene of labor unrest and bitter strikes, but the result was that the state became a leader in social welfare legislation and progressive labor-employer relations. Following the 1930s depression, industrialization in "downstate" Illinois accelerated enormously. In recent years, Illinois has suffered from the economic shift to the Sun Belt. There was less than 3% growth in the population in the 1970s; in 1980–81, unemployment was high. Illinois has been a major stumbling block for the Equal Rights Amendment, which it has repeatedly rejected. In 1980, Ronald Reagan became the first native of Illinois to be elected US president.

**ILLINOIS WATERWAY,** major waterway in NE Ill. linking Lake Michigan with the Mississippi R. at Grafton, Ill. It is a heavily-used bargeway consisting of the Chicago R. (its flow reversed), the canalized Des Plaines and Illinois rivers and a canal, 327mi in all.

**ILLUMINATION, Manuscript,** the decoration of a handwritten text with ornamental design, letters and paintings, often using silver and gold leaf. Illumination flourished between the 5th and 16th centuries AD. The art was highly developed in the Near East, the Orient and in Christian Europe where monks and others skilled in CALLIGRAPHY and painting often devoted their lifetimes to embellishing manuscripts of all kinds, particularly religious. Among the most celebrated manuscripts are the Irish BOOK OF KELLS, the Carolingian *Utrecht Psalter* and the *Très riches heures* commissioned by Jean duc de Berry from the LIMBOURG brothers.

**ILLUSION,** an erroneous perception of reality, often the result of misinterpretation by the brain of information received by the SENSES. Most commonly the sense involved is sight: one of the exploitations of optical illusion is the use by artists of PERSPECTIVE. Optical illusions may also have external causes, such as REFRACTION, which produces a faulty impression. Examples of auditory illusions include BEATING and the apparent change in pitch of a railroad train's whistle as it passes (see DOPPLER EFFECT). Rather different classes of illusion are HALLUCINATIONS and EIDETIC IMAGES. The unconscious falsification of the MEMORY of a past experience is also termed an illusion.

**IMAGINARY NUMBERS.** See COMPLEX NUMBERS.

**IMAGISTS,** a group of poets writing in the early 20th century in the US and England who rebelled against the artificiality and sentimentality of much 19th-century poetry. Free, idiomatic verse, unusual rhythms and sharp, clear imagery were characteristics of their work which was influenced by French SYMBOLISM. The movement embraced Ezra POUND, Hilda DOOLITTLE (H.D.), Amy LOWELL, D. H. LAWRENCE and James JOYCE.

**IMHOTEP,** ancient Egyptian architect of

the Step Pyramid at Saqqara. Chief minister, priest and scribe to Pharaoh ZOSER (3rd millennium BC), Imhotep's fame spread and after his death he became a god of medicine. He is considered the first doctor known to history by name.

**IMMACULATE CONCEPTION,** Roman Catholic dogma, officially defined in 1854, that the Virgin MARY was conceived free from ORIGINAL SIN, owing to a special act of redemptive grace. It implies that Mary was always perfectly sinless.

**IMMIGRATION,** the movement of people from one country or area of the world to another to establish a new permanent residence. People become immigrants primarily for economic, political or religious reasons. MIGRATIONS in ancient times spread people throughout the world, although they tended to migrate within the same continent; Asians stayed in Asia, Africans stayed in Africa. In the first centuries AD Europe suffered successive waves of barbarian migrations from the N and E. After Columbus discovered the New World, the pattern of immigration changed and Europeans began to leave for other lands. Without modern immigration large habitable areas of the world (the USA, Canada, South America, Australia and New Zealand) would otherwise be underpopulated.

The US has received more diverse immigrant groups than any other country—about 38 million from the 1820s to 1930s, and is thus known as a "melting pot" of the world's nations. Its growth and prosperity were stimulated by great waves of immigrants in the 19th and 20th centuries. Immigration accelerated economic development by providing an abundant labor supply, while for the newcomers, America offered hope of a freer and more prosperous life. After the arrival of the original colonists and of African slaves, who accounted for 20% of the population by 1790, there was an era of "old" and then "new" immigration. In the "old" era from 1820 to 1880 the population multiplied more than five times with the arrival of peoples from N and W Europe. In the "new" period (1880–1921) immigrants came primarily from S and E Europe.

Until WWI the US maintained more or less an open-door policy towards immigrants, but social and economic conflicts between various ethnic groups and between the older and newer immigrants led to a major policy reversal. Restrictions were placed on Chinese and Japanese and other so-called "undesirables" before WWI (see KNOW-NOTHING PARTY; GENTLEMEN'S AGREEMENT). In 1917 a literacy test was made compulsory for all immigrants. In 1921 and 1924 quotas were fixed which favored immigration from N Europe, especially the UK, but which imposed an overall limit of 150,000 European immigrants a year. In 1952 the MCCARRAN-WALTER ACT banned communists and other subversives, removed racial exclusions, and strengthened the quota system's ethnic and national system. A 1965 act abolished the quotas discriminating between nationalities. The criteria became professional qualifications and skills and kinship with US citizens or resident aliens. Provision, too, was made for political refugees. The collapse of US-supported regimes in SE Asia brought in new waves of immigrants in the 1970s. In the same decade, Mexicans, seeking higher wages, arrived in much greater numbers.

Immigration elsewhere in the world has had different patterns. South America received large numbers of immigrants before the 1930s. Portuguese, Germans, Swiss, Italians and Japanese went to Brazil. The Spanish migrated to Argentina and other parts of Latin America. Since WWII an entirely new phase of immigration has taken place within Europe itself. West Indians, Asian Indians and Pakistanis have settled in the UK claiming their rights as members of the COMMONWEALTH. Since 1962, the British government has introduced new laws reducing this trend. W and N Europe have admitted large numbers of immigrants from the less developed parts of S Europe. The COMMON MARKET (EEC) requires all its member countries to allow free movement of labor across their borders. (See also EMIGRATION).

**IMMORTALITY,** the life of the soul after death. This belief is found in both primitive and advanced cultures. It was important in Greek philosophy, notably that of PLATO. Immortality is a fundamental tenet of Christianity and of Islam and is generally accepted in Judaism. Their doctrines of eternal life include the RESURRECTION of the body. Hinduism, Buddhism and Jainism do not recognize individual immortality but believe souls can reach an immortal state or NIRVANA. (See also ESCHATOLOGY; HEAVEN; HELL; SPIRITUALISM.)

**IMPALA,** *Aepyceros melampus*, one of the most abundant African antelopes. They are about 1m (39in) high and red-brown in color; males have long, black, lyre-shaped horns. Animals of the woodland edge, impala live in big herds in the dry season, breaking up into single male harems in the wetter months for breeding. Impala herds often associate with BABOONS for protection against predators.

**IMPEACHMENT,** a formal accusation of a crime or other serious misconduct brought against a public official by a legislature. The term sometimes includes the trial by the legislature which follows. Impeachment began in England as a way of putting officials on trial who were derelict in their duties. The impeachment of Warren HASTINGS (1785–95) was a famous English case. Under US constitutional procedure the House of Representatives has the power to impeach; the Senate tries the impeached officials. Grounds for impeachment are: "Treason, Bribery or other high Crimes and Misdemeanors," generally interpreted as being limited to demonstrably criminal acts in the US. Conviction requires a two-thirds vote of all senators present and voting, providing there is a quorum, and entails automatic removal from office. The Chief Justice of the US presides. In US history Congress has impeached 11 officials and convicted four. President Andrew JOHNSON was impeached but acquitted in the Senate by one vote. In 1974, after the House Judiciary Committee recommended his impeachment, Richard M. NIXON resigned as president of the US.

**IMPERIALISM,** policy of one country or the people, usually "developed," to extend its control or influence over other territories or peoples, usually "under-developed" ones. There are many different kinds of imperialism—political, financial, economic, military and cultural. The justification for imperialism has been that backward countries were advanced technologically, economically and culturally by the influence of more developed nations. However, imperialist policies have also restricted individual and national freedoms and have often exploited undeveloped natural resources and native populations. (See also COLONIALISM; COLONIZATION.)

**IMPERIAL VALLEY,** important agricultural area in the low-lying SE Cal. desert, extending into Mexico, called the "Winter Garden" of America. Since the construction of the 80mi-long All-American irrigation canal and soil reclamation projects in the 1940s and 1950s, the valley has become a highly fertile farm region producing alfalfa, melons, tomatoes, lettuce and sugar beets. Even the January temperature averages 53°F.

**IMPETIGO,** superficial SKIN infection, usually of the FACE, caused by STREPTOCOCCUS or STAPHYLOCOCCUS. It starts with small vesicles which burst and leave a characteristic yellow crust. It is easily spread by fingers from a single vesicle to affect several large areas and may be transmitted to others. It is common in children and requires ANTIBIOTIC creams, and systemic PENICILLIN in some cases.

**IMPLANTATION,** the earliest stage of EMBRYO development in which the embryo invades the WOMB. After fertilization by SPERM, the EGG divides into a small ball of cells, whose outer layer is specialized to invade the endometrium, which is itself prepared for implantation. The interface between embryo and endometrium develops into the PLACENTA. The term is also used to refer to the placing of DRUGS, PROSTHETICS or grafts in the body in treatment of DISEASE.

**IMPLIED POWERS,** powers exercised by the US federal government which are not explicitly delegated to it by the CONSTITUTION or reserved to the individual states (see STATES' RIGHTS) or the people. This authority is implied in the so-called "elastic clause" (Article I, Section 8, Clause 18), which empowers the Congress to enact such laws as are "necessary and proper" to the execution of the government's specified powers. The doctrine of implied powers has been widely used to enable Congress to legislate in the areas of labor relations, health, public welfare, commerce and finance.

**IMPRESSIONISM,** dominant artistic movement in France from the mid-1860s to c1890. The Impressionist painters, who include MANET, MONET, PISSARRO, and others, painted landscapes and scenes of leisure in contemporary Paris. They usually worked out-of-doors, recording the scenes before them spontaneously and directly. Their pictures were executed in bright contrasting colors in order to convey the impression of light and they emphasized the individual brushstrokes. The term "impressionist" was first used as a criticism of Monet's *Impression: Soleil levant* (*Sunrise*), 1874. The artists organized eight independent exhibitions for their pictures. The American painters CASSATT and HASSAM were influenced by the Impressionists. Impressionism also describes other art forms, notably literature which uses symbolic imagery (see RILKE) and music which expresses mood and feeling (see DEBUSSY).

**IMPRESSMENT,** the seizure of persons or property for the purpose of placing them in public SERVICE. Common in many countries, impressment was used by the British to obtain seamen until the 19th century. Impressment of British deserters and US citizens from American ships aroused public indignation in the US and was one of he causes of the WAR OF 1812.

**NBREEDING,** the breeding of individual plants or animals that are closely related. nbreeding tends to bring together recessive GENES with, usually, deleterious effects. This is because recessive genes are often harmless in the heterozygous condition but harmful in the homozygous condition (see GENETICS). For this reason, inbreeding has ong been regarded as a practice to be discouraged; in human cultures, consanguinity is frequently forbidden by law or discouraged by custom.

**NCA,** title of the ruler of an empire in W South America which, at the time of the Spanish conquest, occupied what is now Peru, parts of Ecuador, Chile, Bolivia and Argentina. It extended some 3,000mi from N to S, stretching back between 150 and 250mi from the narrow Pacific coastal plain nto the high Andes. Communications were maintained along brilliantly engineered and extensive roads, carried over the sheer Andean gorges by fiber cable suspension bridges. Trained relay runners carried messages 150mi a day and the army had quick access to trouble spots. Restive subject tribes were resettled near Cuzco, the capital. Detailed surveys of new conquests were recorded by *quipu,* a mnemonic device using knotted cords. Writing, like draft animals and wheeled transport, was unknown; so too was monetary currency. Taxation and tribute were levied in the form of labor services. In other respects the culture was highly advanced. At sites such as. MACHU PICCHU Inca architects raised some of the world's finest stone structures; precious metals from government-controlled mines were worked by supremely-skilled goldsmiths; bronze was also used; ceramic and textile design was outstanding. Agriculture was based on elaborate irrigation and hillside terracing.

**NCARNATION,** embodiment of a deity as a human or animal. In Hindu belief, VISHNU has manifested himself in different incarnations or *avatara.* In Christianity the doctrine of the incarnation is that the Son of God (see TRINITY) took human nature and was born as JESUS CHRIST, who was thus fully God and fully man. This doctrine, much debated in the early Church, was finally defined at the Council of CHALCEDON 451. By the incarnation, redeemed mankind is in Christ united to God.

**NCHON LANDING,** amphibious landing Sept. 15, 1950, during the Korean War, by 1st Marine and 7th Infantry divisions at Inchon, port for South Korea's capital, Seoul, then some 150 miles behind enemy North Korean lines. At the same time, the American Eighth Army broke out from the perimeter around Pusan, in southeastern Korea, to which it had been confined. The two forces advanced toward each other, cutting North Korean lines of communication and capturing thousands of enemy soldiers. The Inchon landing was one of the most brilliant achievements of Gen. Douglas MacArthur's long career.

**INCOME DISTRIBUTION,** refers to a body of economic theory that attempts to explain the causes for income differences among the various economic groups in a society. The term also refers to the actual spread of incomes. In the US, for example, income distribution has slowly tended toward a greater equality as an expanding economy, a relatively progressive income tax, and a widespread welfare system have lifted the incomes of the lowest economic groups.

**INCOME TAX,** the major source of government revenue. As opposed to EXCISE taxes levied on goods, it is a direct tax on the incomes of individuals, proportionate to their wealth, or on corporations. At first imposed only to meet extraordinary expenditures such as war financing, income tax became permanent in Britain in 1874. In the US it was levied during the Civil War, but an attempt to make it a permanent federal tax was ruled unconstitutional. The 16th Amendment (1913) authorized the federal government to levy the tax and since 1919 most states have also adopted this mode of revenue raising. It is assessed on net income after allowances have been deducted for family dependents, contributions to charities and certain other expenditures. Incomes below a certain level are entirely tax exempt; above this level the rate rises progressively. The 1981 tax law sets a minimum tax rate of 14% and a maximum of 50%. The new law also provides for inflation indexing after 1985; from that year higher incomes will not automatically put taxpayers into higher tax brackets, which require them to pay higher tax rates, but the brackets themselves will be linked to the inflation rate. A "negative" income tax has been proposed as one solution to the welfare problem by permitting the poor to receive rather than make income-related payments.

**INCUBATION,** a method of keeping microorganisms such as BACTERIA or VIRUSES warm and in an appropriate medium to promote their growth (e.g., in identification of the organisms causing DISEASE); also, the period during which an organism is present in the body before causing DISEASE. INFECTIOUS DISEASE is contracted from a source of infective microorganisms. Once these have entered the body they divide and spread to different parts and it is some time before they cause symptoms due to local or systemic effects. This incubation period may be helpful in diagnosis and in determining length of QUARANTINE periods.

**INDEPENDENCE DAY (US),** the Fourth of July, the principal non-religious holiday which commemorates the signing of the DECLARATION OF INDEPENDENCE (July 4, 1776).

**INDEPENDENCE NATIONAL HISTORICAL PARK,** Philadelphia, Pa., established by the federal government in 1948 to preserve the area and structures associated with the period of the Revolutionary War and the growth of the US. INDEPENDENCE HALL and many other historic buildings stand here.

**INDETERMINACY PRINCIPLE.** See UNCERTAINTY PRINCIPLE.

**INDEX OF FORBIDDEN BOOKS** (*Index Librorum Prohibitorum*), official list of books banned by the Roman Catholic Church as being in doctrinal or moral error. A book could be removed from the Index by expurgation of offending passages, and permission could be given to read prohibited books. The index ceased publication in 1966.

**Official name:** Republic of India
**Capital:** New Delhi
**Area:** 1,269,420sq mi
**Population:** 666,753,000
**Languages:** Hindi, English; fourteen other official national languages
**Religions:** Hindu, Muslim, Christian, Sikh, Buddhist, Jain
**Monetary unit(s): 1 Rupee** = 100 paisa
**INDIA,** a federal republic of 22 states and nine union territories, in S Asia. It occupies a land mass ranging from the Himalayas southward to Cape Cormorin on the Indian Ocean, and shares the triangular-shaped Indian subcontinent with PAKISTAN, NEPAL, BHUTAN and BANGLADESH. The world's second most populous country, India has sought development aid wherever it is offered, and follows a policy of non-alignment.

**Land.** The chief geographical regions of N India are the Thar Desert along the Pakistan border; the mountain valleys of KASHMIR (disputed with Pakistan); the fertile plains of the GANGES and Brahmaputra rivers; and the Himalaya Mts, with Nanda Devi (25,645ft), India's highest peak. The mountains shield India from the cold winter winds of central Asia. The Deccan plateau, bordered by the Western and Eastern Ghats mountain ranges, occupies most of S India. Here rivers flow sluggishly to the Eastern Ghats, then descend through broad valleys to the Bay of Bengal. The rich volcanic soil is used mainly for cotton-growning, though there are important mineral deposits. Most of the country has a tropical MONSOON climate, temperatures reaching 120°F in the hot season on the Northern Plains and, in the cool season, falling below freezing point in the mountains. The monsoon rains are especially heavy on the Western Ghats and in NE India and some places average more than 426in of rain a year. The rainy season lasts from May to September.

**People.** In 1980, India's population was over 666 million; despite birth control programs it is still rapidly expanding. The ethnic composition is complex, but there is a basic division between the light-skinned INDO-ARYANS in the N and the darker DRAVIDIANS in the S. About 80% of the population live in small villages, though the towns are growing fast. The chief cities are the seaports of BOMBAY, CALCUTTA and MADRAS and the capital NEW DELHI. The dominant religion is HINDUISM which through its CASTE system, profoundly affects the nation's social structures. Most Indians live on the poverty line in crowded slums or primitive villages, eating a mainly vegetarian diet.

**Economy.** India is an importer of food and industrial goods and an exporter of raw materials. Two-thirds of the labor force is engaged in agriculture. Rice, beans, peas, tea, sugarcane, jute, pepper and timber are the main agricultural products. Output, despite recent increases, is relatively low overall. Improvements are being sought by irrigation, land reclamation projects and the introduction of improved strains of crops and fertilizers. There are iron and steel mills, and electronic and engineering plants, but about 45% of the industrial manpower works in the jute, cotton and other textile mills. Mineral resources include oil, iron ore, coal, natural gas, copper, bauxite, manganese and mica, but are poorly exploited. Energy requirements are supplemented by hydroelectric plants and India's first atomic power station, at Tarapur, came into operation in 1969.

**History.** The INDUS VALLEY CIVILIZATION, in modern Pakistan, was the first great culture on the subcontinent. It succumbed c1500 BC to Aryan peoples invading through the NW mountain passes; they brought the SANSKRIT language and Hinduism to India. The MAURYA EMPIRE and GUPTA dynasties represented high points of Buddhist and Hindu rule, but India was never united and from the 10th century AD, Muslim invaders added to the warring states. In the 14th century the Delhi Muslim sultanate and the Hindu kingdom of Vijayanagar in the S were dominant; in the 1520s the Muslim empire of the MOGULS was founded. Europeans also began to exert influence in the Indian subcontinent. In 1510 the Portuguese took Goa, and soon the Dutch, British and French were vying for Indian trade. In the 18th century English and French interests contested for control of the by then moribund empire. Victory went to the British EAST INDIA COMPANY whose first governor-general of India was Warren HASTINGS (1774). After the **Sepoy Rebellion** 1857–58), the British government took over rule of much of the country and the remaining independent princes, both Muslim and Hindu, recognized British paramountcy. The British did nothing to weaken religious rivalries but did give the subcontinent a unified code of law, a single administrative language and the world's greatest railroad network. In 1885, the Indian National CONGRESS PARTY was set up; under Mahatma GANDHI and Jawaharlal NEHRU it led the movement for independence. JINNAH led the MUSLIM LEAGUE urging partition into India and Pakistan on religious grounds. Many thousands died in fierce communal riots following partition in 1947.

India achieved sovereign status in 1948. The constitution (1949) provided for a bicameral democratically-elected parliament and a cabinet government with a prime minister and a president. The Congress Party has been the ruling party, first under Nehru and (since 1966) under his daughter Indira GANDHI. Domestic politics have been concerned with the vast problem of food supply, the drive towards large-scale industrialization, the mitigation of the worst injustices of the caste system and, since the late 1960s, tension between the central and provincial governments. Foreign policy was long overshadowed by the dispute with Pakistan over Kashmir, which flared into war in 1965. A frontier war in 1962 also emphasized the strained relations between India and China. In 1975 Mrs. Gandhi, convicted of irregularities in an election, declared a state of emergency, jailed her opponents and began to rule by decree. SIKKIM became an Indian state in 1975. Mrs. Gandhi's party was defeated in the general elections in 1977 by the Janata Party, a coalition. The new government dismantled the state of emergency. The coalition, however, began to disintegrate, and in 1980 Mrs. Gandhi again became prime minister. Charges against her (for abusing power) were dropped.

**Name of state:** Indiana
**Capital:** Indianapolis
**Statehood:** Dec. 11, 1816 (19th state)
**Familiar name:** Hoosier State
**Area:** 36,291 sq mi
**Population:** 5,490,179
**Elevation:** Highest—1,257ft, Wayne County. Lowest—320ft, Ohio River in Posey County
**Motto:** The Crossroads of America
**State flower:** Peony
**State bird:** Cardinal
**State tree:** Tulip Tree (yellow poplar)
**State song:** "On the Banks of the Wabash"

**INDIANA,** state, in NE central US, it was created from the NORTHWEST TERRITORY, and is bounded to the N by Mich. and Lake Michigan, on the E by Ohio, on the S by the Ohio R, which forms the border with Ky., and on the W by Ill.

**Land.** There are three main regions in Indiana. In the N are the Great Lakes Plains, in the center the Till Plains, and to the S the Southern Hills and Lowlands. Glacial cover created many small lakes and left rich soil in the N and center. Main rivers are the Wabash, Kankakee and Maumee. The climate is humid, with summer temperatures from 65°F to 90°F typical; in winter it can be as low as 27°F, with heavy snow in the N.

**People.** Indiana's population swelled after statehood, driving out the Indians by about 1840. Since WWI it has become increasingly urbanized with the growth of industry and in 1980 more than 65% of the population lived in urbanized areas. Under the constitution of 1851 the bicameral legislature is headed by a governor and lieutenant-governor elected for four-year terms. The 1816 constitution was the first to specifically provide free public education; the state now has state universities and many private institutions of higher education.

**Economy.** Before WWI the state's economy rested on agriculture, but it then expanded and is now among the top ten industrial states. Its largest industry is steel and other metal production, particularly in the Lake Michigan area, which also has major oil refineries. The cities, especially Indianapolis, are manufacturing centers, where transportation equipment, electrical and electronic products, machinery, chemicals and processed foods are produced. Agriculture remains important, however; the major crops are corn and soybeans, and the most plentiful livestock are hogs, cattle and poultry.

**History.** Algonkin, Iroquois and Delaware Indians occupied the area when French fur traders explored it in the 17th century. After the FRENCH AND INDIAN WARS, the area passed to the British (1763) and to the US after the Revolution. In 1800 it became a territory, with William Henry HARRISON as governor. Initial Indian resistance to white settlement ended after the battle of FALLEN TIMBERS, but revived under the Shawnee chief TECUMSEH until the battle of TIPPECANOE (1811). In 1816 Indiana became a state, although its settlements were too isolated to form a coherent political body until about 1850. In the Civil War it supported the Union, but despite this and the growth of industrialization it remained a rural and reactionary state. In the 20th century, increased prosperity was accompanied by social and cultural advances, but the state has been hard hit recently by the general decline in industry in the Midwest, especially in the automotive industry. Between 1970 and 1980, Indiana's population grew at half the national average. In 1980, more than 10% of the non-agricultural work force was unemployed while farmers were also struggling; the state gave a $39 million loan to Chrysler to try to save some 15,000 jobs, and in the 1980 elections it virtually led the national Republican landslide.

**INDIANA, Robert** (Robert Clark; 1928– ), US artist whose pseudonym is his home state. His use of verbs and numbers as artistic symbols won him fame in the 1960s. His poster design, "Love," appeared on 400 million US postage stamps.

**INDIAN AFFAIRS, Bureau of,** US federal agency, part of the Department of the Interior, set up in 1824 to safeguard the welfare of American Indians. It acts as trustee for tribal lands and funds, supervises the reservations and provides welfare and education facilities.

**INDIANAPOLIS,** city in central Ind., state capital and seat of Marion Co. Situated on the White R, the city is the market center for a rich agricultural region. The economy rests on its manufacturing industries among the largest are airplane and truck engines, and meat-packing. The city is famous for the annual "Indy 500" motor race. Pop 700,807.

**INDIANAPOLIS 500,** the premier American automobile race. The 500-mile event has been held annually on Memorial Day at Indianapolis (Ind.) Speedway since 1911.

**INDIAN ART AND ARCHITECTURE.** The classical tradition begins after the fall of the INDUS VALLEY CIVILIZATION, c1500 BC and the establishment of the Indo-Aryan culture based on HINDUISM. The naturalistic Aryan pantheon assimilated local deities and concepts to produce a complex system celebrated in the sacred Hindu texts called VEDAS. Statues, paintings and temples, often lavishly embellished with sculpture, both symbolize and embody the gods and their attributes or powers. Cosmic symbols and a profuse, intricate language of imagery in form and gesture, present the divine aspects of meditation, courage, mercy, erotic love, war, death and life. The spread of BUDDHISM under ASOKA (d. 232 BC) brought a new emphasis. In architecture, the stupa was a round, brick- or stone-faced earth mound containing a relic or tomb and surrounded by a square stone railing. Painting and sculpture, notably in the AJANTA caves and the art of Gandhara (influenced by Hellenism), portray episodes in the physical and spiritual life of the Buddha. The golden age of Indian culture came during the GUPTA DYNASTY (320–c500 AD). Resurgent Hinduism soon adapted the Buddhist cella and porch temples to the classic porch, pillared hall and cella of the Hindu temple, often surmounted by massive conical spires, as at Khajuraho (c1000 AD). In the 13th century S India perfected the Dravidian pyramidal temple and produced superb bronze sculptures such as the famous dancing Siva. Indian Muslim art reached its peak under the MOGULS (see also TAJ MAHAL).

**INDIAN CLAIMS COMMISSION,** independent federal agency, set up in 1946 to decide on all Indian claims of unjust land dealings by the government. The commission's decisions may be appealed against in the Court of Claims.

**INDIAN OCEAN**, at about 28,350,000sq mi the world's third largest ocean. It is bounded by Antarctica to the S, Africa to the W, and Australia and Indonesia to the E. The Indian subcontinent divides the N part of the ocean into two great arms, the Arabian Sea to the W and the Bay of Bengal to the E. Largest of its many islands are Madagascar and Sri Lanka; others include Zanzibar, Mauritius and the Seychelles. Major inflowing rivers include the Limpopo, Zambezi, Ganges and Indus. The deepest recorded point is in the Java or Sunda Trench (25,344ft).

**INDIANS, American**, name given by European explorers to the aboriginal inhabitants of the Western Hemisphere. It is generally believed that the ancestors of these first Americans migrated from Asia c26,000 years ago across a land bridge (now the Bering Strait) between Siberia and Alaska. A less popular theory suggests that the native Americans evolved on the American continent. It is certain that by 6000BC the Indians were distributed widely throughout North and South America.

**Central and South American Indians** are, like their counterparts in the N, believed to be of Asiatic origin. The major Indian groups in Central and N South America at the beginning of the European conquest (16th century) included the CARIBS, ARAWAKS, AZTECS, MAYAS and INCAS. The Maya civilization had reached its zenith some 700 years before, but the Inca and Aztec were at their peak. The three cultures had developed complex political and religious structures, built great temples, roads and bridges and achieved sophisticated astronomical and calendrical calculations, yet writing was rudimentary and wheeled transport unknown. The cultures were overthrown and millions of Indians killed by warfare and disease during the 16th-century Spanish conquest. The Spanish government proclaimed the Indians to be subjects and not slaves, but the settler community treated them as chattels and subjected them to forced labor. The situation was little better in Portuguese Brazil, though Jesuit-run plantations here and elsewhere treated their Indians humanely. Where they were able to, Indians withdrew physically and psychologically from European culture. South American independence in the 19th century did little to improve their status. Atrocities committed against them by rubber barons in the early 20th century brought a degree of government protection. In Mexico Indian influence in the 1910–17 revolution, the restitution of certain Indian property rights and some integration between Indian and European cultures greatly improved the status of Indians in contemporary Mexico.

In South America progress is fitful, however, for cultural more than racial reasons. Indian tribal values lay more emphasis on the communal good and the sanctity of the soil; they cannot be easily integrated into a money economy. There is still a good deal of exploitation and maltreatment of remote tribes, often by government officials; they are still sometimes brutally driven off their lands, or simply massacred.

**North American Indians.** By the time of the European incursion, there appeared to have been about 900,000 Indians N of the Rio Grande. European weapons, diseases and destruction of natural resources took their toll, however, and the Indian population declined rapidly. The Indians had hundreds of peoples and nations, with as many languages. These may be divided into six broad culture areas: Eastern Woodlands, Plains, Southwest, Plateau, Northwest Coast and North or Sub-Arctic; the ESKIMOS are treated separately.

Early inhabitants of the Eastern Woodlands region in the E US were the Mound Builders (see MOUNDS) of the Mississippi Valley. Later tribes in the area belonged to the great ALGONQUIAN and IROQUOIAN linguistic families; they included Cherokee, Chickasaw, Choctaw and Creek. In the SE the SEMINOLE were the dominant tribe. The IROQUOIS confederacy had effective political structures which were strengthened when the colonists appeared. Their main occupations were farming, tribal warfare and religious ceremonial.

The vast Plains area lay between the Mississippi R and the Rocky Mts. It was uninhabited until the 1600s, when the introduction of horses and guns by settlers made it possible for tribes to live as nomadic buffalo hunters. These included the Apache, Cheyenne, Sioux, Comanche, Blackfoot and Arapaho. The buffalo herds supplied food, fuel, bone utensils and skin for shelter and clothing. Status was achieved by success in warfare, often in defense of hunting grounds. The Plains Indians maintained a long resistance to white encroachment with skill and courage.

The original inhabitants of the Southwest, what is now Ariz., N.M., S Col. and S Ut., included a group called the BASKET MAKERS (100–700 AD), who may have been the ancestors of the PUEBLO INDIANS. The peace-loving Pueblo peoples depended on agriculture for food, while their neighbors, tribes of the Apache and Navaho, relied on hunting and marauding. The Apaches were seminomadic, whereas the Navaho lived, and still live, in wooden HOGANS. Today there are about 200,000 sheep-farming Navaho on their reservation in Ariz., the largest existing Indian group.

The plateau region included most of what is now Cal. and the Great Basin between the Rocky Mts and the Sierra Nevada Ranges. Food was plentiful in the W part, and most tribes lived simply by gathering. Their culture was not sophisticated and there was little warfare. The dietary staple was acorn flour; rabbits, deer, elk and caribou were hunted, and there was fishing in the N.

The tribes of the Northwest Coast, notably the HAIDA, KWAKIUTL and NOOTKA, lived along the Pacific coast from S Alaska to N Cal. The area was rich in food, principally fish, freeing the tribes to develop an elaborate and sophisticated culture. Art, particularly carving, was complex and developed; it still flourishes today, often commanding high prices. Social status was based on the surplus wealth available, mainly through the POTLATCH ceremony, in which office or status was gained by the distribution or destruction of wealth. The N tribes retain much of their culture today.

The peoples of the sparse North region from Newfoundland to Alaska belonged to the ATHABASCAN language group in the W and the ALGONQUIAN group around Hudson Bay. Warfare played small part in their seminomadic life styles; too much energy went into the search for food.

**Religion.** Most Indian religion, even the fasts and self-mortification of the Plains Indian SUN DANCE, reveals a deep-felt communion with nature and a belief in a divine power. Individuals and kin groups of many tribes had spiritual ties with particular "totem" birds and animals. Shamans performed sacred rituals and treated the sick. The 1880s saw the tragic rise and fall of another Indian religion, the millenarian GHOST DANCE.

**Indians and the Whites.** The paternalistic attitudes of the first English colonists did not stop their encroachment on Indian lands (see INDIAN WARS). Indians were caught up in British and French rivalry in the FRENCH AND INDIAN WARS. Unscrupulous land speculators hardened mistrust. With the NORTHWEST ORDINANCE (1787) the newly independent US, in need of Indian support, proclaimed a policy of peaceful coexistence, yet with new expansion hostilities increased. The Indian Removal Act of 1830 (see INDIAN TERRITORY) was followed from 1850

by campaigns against Plains Indians which ended in the massacre of Indians at Wounded Knee, S.D., in 1890. In 1871 Congress ceased to recognize the Indian nation's independent rights; the Dawes Act (1887), by breaking up tribal land into individual grants, deprived the Indians of around 86 million acres, more than half their territory. A decline in the Indian population due to disease, war and starvation led to a belief that Indians were "naturally" dying out by natural selection; no long-term provision was therefore made for them. Reform began with the Indian Reorganization Act of 1934, aimed at increasing Indian autonomy and improving their economic position; it restored some lands. Other reforms followed, but poverty, poor education and unemployment are still a terrible problem on the reservations where the majority of about 800,000 US Indians still live. However, there is now a strong revival of Indian culture and an increasing awareness of their political and social identity. In the late 1970s some Indian tribes instituted lawsuits to recover their original tribal lands. In 1980, Congress approved an Indian Land Claims bill authorizing Maine's Indians to receive $81 million in federal funds in order to buy land from private owners. And in 1981 the US Supreme Court cleared the way for Conn.'s Mohegan tribe to sue the state for recovery of its ancestral lands.

**INDIAN WARS,** the continuing struggle between the North American Indians and white colonizers from the earliest colonial times to the late 19th century. The first permanent English settlement was established at JAMESTOWN, Va., in 1607; despite peaceful trade with the Indians under POWHATAN, hostilities began in 1622 and by 1644 the Indians had been crushed. In New England, early relations between Puritan settlers and local Indians were good; but in 1636 war broke out with the PEQUOT tribe, resulting in their massacre. With the end of KING PHILIP'S WAR in 1678 Indian resistance in New England was broken.

The FRENCH AND INDIAN WARS (1689–1763) involved the NE tribes in constantly shifting alliances. In the long struggle for possession of North America both France and Britain offered guns and liquor to win tribal allies. In 1763 the tribal alliance headed by PONTIAC resulted in British recognition of Indian territorial and hunting rights. This was ignored and flouted by the colonists and corrupt officials.

With the Revolutionary War in 1775 the colonists needed Indian allegiances, and trade regulations were introduced to protect the Indians from exploitation. Trade and land companies continued to cheat the Indians, however, provoking uprisings which government troops were sent in to crush. In 1811 an alliance of southern and western tribes under the SHAWNEE chieftain TECUMSEH was defeated at the Tippecanoe R by William Henry HARRISON; Tecumseh's death in 1813, after an abortive alliance with the British in the WAR OF 1812, virtually ended Indian resistance in this area. The SEMINOLE in Fla., however, continued hostilities until 1816. In 1830 the Indian Removal Act, passed by President JACKSON, authorized the transfer of SE tribes to land W of the Mississippi. Indian resistance was met by illegal force; Jackson even ignored a Supreme Court order upholding the land rights of the CHEROKEES.

In 1855, the defeated NEZ PERCÉ tribes were given land in the NW states, but when gold was found in the area they were again forced to move. Chief JOSEPH led an unsuccessful revolt against this in 1877. The Cal. GOLD RUSH also led to the overrunning of Indian lands and to the deaths of thousands of Indians 1848–58. The second half of the 19th century saw the final suppression of the Indians. The NAVAHO, holding the land between the Rio Grande and Cal., were defeated by Kit CARSON in 1863 and transferred to NW Ariz. After the Civil War attempts were made to restrict the Apaches, though COCHISE and others resisted; their last war chief, GERONIMO, surrendered in 1886. In 1871 the government ceased to recognize Indian tribes as independent nations.

The Great Plains, home of the SIOUX, APACHE and CHEYENNE, were subdued 1870–90 by a combination of military force and the depletion of buffalo herds. The Indian victory at the battle of LITTLE BIGHORN only hastened their defeat; it was marked by the surrender of CRAZY HORSE in 1877, and the suppression of the GHOST DANCE in 1890.

**INDIVIDUAL RETIREMENT ACCOUNT (IRA),** a retirement plan established by the 1974 Employee Benefit Security Act. It was originally intended only for employees who were not covered by an employer's retirement plan, but under President Ronald Reagan the plan was extended to permit anyone to own a personal retirement account. The maximum annual investment was raised to $2,000, or 15% of annual income, whichever is less.

**INDO-ARYAN LANGUAGES,** group of languages of the family of INDO-EUROPEAN LANGUAGES, spoken on the Indian sub-continent. The oldest known is SANSKRIT, from which the others are directly or indirectly descended. Most widely spoken today are Hindi-Urdu, Bengali, Marathi, Punjabi, Gujarati, Oriya, Bihari and Rajasthani. Romany, the language of the Gypsies, is known to be descended from an Indo-Aryan original.

**INDOCHINA,** political term for peninsular SE Asia between China and India. It was formerly French Indochina, now divided into VIETNAM, LAOS and KAMPUCHEA. The area contains two densely-peopled, rice-rich deltas (Red R in the N, Mekong R in the S) separated by Annamite Mt. chain. Thais, Laos and Annamese (Vietnamese) settled Indochina from the N. From the second century AD, many states and cultures, affected by India and China, rose and fell there, including FUNAN, the KHMER EMPIRE, CHAMPA and ANNAM. European penetration began in the 16th century; France concluded a treaty with Annam in 1787, annexed COCHIN CHINA in 1862 and by 1900 had welded separate states into the single political unit of French Indochina. WWII and militant nationalism destroyed France's authority and in 1949 Cambodia and Laos gained independence. The communist Vietminh drove the French out of Vietnam; the US continued France's anti-communist role in the long VIETNAM WAR, but by 1976 Indochina was effectively under communist control.

**INDO-EUROPEAN LANGUAGES,** one of the most important language families, spoken throughout most of Europe and much of Asia, and descended from a hypothetical common ancestor, Proto-Indo-European, extant more than 5,000 years ago. There are two main branches, Eastern, with six main groups, and Western, with four. The Eastern branch includes the extinct Anatolian and Tocharian groups, as well as Albanian, Armenian, Balto-Slavic and Indo-Iranian (with its important sub-group, the INDO-ARYAN LANGUAGES). The Western branch includes Celtic, Greek, Romance or Italic (Latin and the languages derived from it) and Teutonic or Germanic (one of which is English). Until the beginning of the 20th century it was thought that SANSKRIT inscriptions represented the oldest written form of any of the family; however, both ancient Hittite and Linear B (see MINOAN LINEAR SCRIPTS), which have since been deciphered, are older. (See also LANGUAGE.)

**INDO-IRANIAN LANGUAGES,** easternmost branch of the INDO-EUROPEAN family of languages, and itself divided into two subgroups: 1) Indo-Iranian (Indic), sometimes called INDO-ARYAN, includes ancient Vedic-SANSKRIT, and the modern languages HINDI, BENGALI-Assamese, Punjabi, GUJARATI, SINHALESE (spoken in Sri Lanka), URDU (spoken in Pakistan), Nepali and others; this subgroup represents some 400 million speakers in India and neighboring countries; the Gypsy language, ROMANY, also belongs to this group. 2) Indo-Iranian (Iranian) includes Old Persian and modern PERSIAN (Fārsī), Pashto (spoken especially in Afghanistan), Kurdish and others spoken by some 50 million people in Iran and neighboring countries.

**Official name:** Republic of Indonesia
**Capital:** Jakarta
**Area:** 735,358sq mi
**Population:** 139,376,400
**Languages:** Bahasa Indonesia
**Religions:** Muslim, Christian, Buddhist
**Monetary unit(s):** 1 Rupiah=100 sen

**INDONESIA,** republic in SE Asia, occupying most of the enormous Malay Archipelago.

**Land.** Indonesia consists of more than 13,000 islands and islets strung out along the equator from Sumatra to New Guinea. There are three main island groups: the Greater Sunda Islands, including JAVA, SUMATRA, Indonesian Borneo (KALIMANTAN) and SULAWESI (Celebes); the Lesser Sunda Islands, including BALI, FLORES, Lombok, Sumba, Sumbawa and Timor; and the MOLUCCAS (Maluku), including Ambon, Aru Island, Banda Islands, Buru, Ceram, Halmahera and the Tanimbar Islands. Indonesia also has Irian Jaya (W New Guinea). The islands are mountainous and volcanic (many actively so), with tropical rain forests nourished by a hot, wet equatorial climate. There is abundant wild life, including many marsupials and the KOMODO DRAGON.

**People.** Two-thirds of the population live on Java, site of the capital and chief port, Jakarta. The population can be broadly divided into Malays and Papuans, with Chinese, Arabs and others; Bahasa Indonesia is the official language but over 250 other languages are spoken. Education is compulsory and most Indonesians are literate. There are more than 50 universities and technological institutes.

**Economy.** Some 70% of the population are farmers, producing rice, coconuts, cassava, corn, peanuts, sweet potatoes, spices, and coffee and raising cattle, goats, hogs and chickens. Forest products include hardwoods, rubber, palm oil, quinine and kapok. The economy rests largely on agriculture, forestry and fisheries, but mineral resources are being increasingly exploited. Coal, bauxite, copper, manganese, nickel and precious metals are mined. Indonesia's most important products are oil, its chief export, and tin, of which it is one of the world's major producers. In general raw materials are exported and manufactured goods imported. There is some light manufacturing, mostly centered on Java. The multitude of islands, most of them rugged and mountainous, hinder transportation; air links are important.

**History.** Primitive man existed on Java c1 million years ago. Civilization grew under Indian influence after the 4th century AD; several kingdoms flourished from the 12th to 14th centuries. Islam spread swiftly in the 15th century. European impact began in 1511 when the Portuguese captured Malacca. But Portugal eventually kept only E Timor, losing control to the competing English and Dutch. The victorious Dutch EAST INDIA COMPANY founded Batavia (Jakarta) in 1619 and dominated the so-called Dutch East Indies until the Netherlands assumed control in 1798. Britain occupied the islands (1811–16) during the Napoleonic Wars, then returned them to the Dutch, who greatly expanded cash-crop exports during the 19th century. Nationalist movements emerged in the early 1900s, and after Indonesia's occupation by Japanese forces in WWII (1942–45), SUKARNO proclaimed Indonesia an independent republic; the Dutch were forced to grant independence in 1949. President Sukarno's dictatorial, anti-Western regime and extravagant spending damaged the economy; General SUHARTO deposed Sukarno in 1968. He suppressed left-wing groups; severed links with communist China and restored relations with the West. He sought to stabilize the economy, and in 1971 held the first free elections since 1955. In 1975 after Portugal withdrew from East Timor, Indonesian troops invaded, and in 1976 the region was proclaimed a province of Indonesia, a move not recognized by the UN.

**INDUCTION, Electromagnetic,** the phenomenon in which an ELECTRIC FIELD is generated in an electric circuit when the number of MAGNETIC FIELD lines passing through the circuit changes; independently discovered by M. FARADAY and J. HENRY. The voltage induced is proportional to the rate of change of the field, and large voltages can be produced by switching off quite small magnetic fields suddenly. Frequently, the magnetic field is itself generated by an electric current in a coil, in which case the voltage induced is proportional to the rate of change of the current (see INDUCTANCE). The principle finds numerous applications in electric GENERATORS and MOTORS, TRANSFORMERS, MICROPHONES, and engine ignition systems.

**INDULGENCE,** in the Roman Catholic Church, a remission of the temporal punishment (on earth or in PURGATORY) that remains due for sin even after confession, absolution and doing penance. In consideration of prayers and good works, the Church may grant plenary (full) or partial indulgences by administering the merits of Christ and the saints. Sale of indulgences was denounced by the Protestant reformers, and the abuse was abolished by the Council of TRENT.

**INDUS RIVER,** rising in the Himalayas of W Tibet and flowing 1,800mi through Kashmir and Pakistan to its 75mi-long delta on the N Arabian Sea. Cradle of the ancient INDUS VALLEY CIVILIZATION, it is now an important source of hydroelectric power and irrigation.

**INDUSTRIAL REVOLUTION,** in a country's history a period of rapid transition from an agrarian to an industrial society; specifically, the prototype of such periods, the late 18th and early 19th centuries in the UK. This period saw Britain transformed from a predominantly agricultural society into the world's first industrial nation. In the 18th century, British expansionism, inventiveness, economic sophistication and natural resources combined to provide unique opportunities for building business fortunes. The growth of capitalism developed the FACTORY system to harness new inventions that cheaply mass-produced textiles to exploit the expanding world market for British cloth. Key inventions in textile production included KAY's flying shuttle, HARGREAVES' spinning jenny, ARKWRIGHT's water frame and CARTWRIGHT's powered loom. In 1709 Abraham DARBY had learned to smelt iron with coke; in 1781, James WATT patented a steam engine producing rotary motion. Soon many factories were using steam-powered iron machinery. Canals and, from the 1830s, railroads and steamships provided a transportation network linking new industrial cities with sources of supply and markets. The urban masses were supported by increasingly efficient agriculture, due to scientific advances and the stimulus to self-sufficiency of the NAPOLEONIC WARS. Largely through improvements in food supply, sanitation and medicine Britain's population rose from under 7 million in 1750 to over 20 million in 1850, creating both an increased labor force and escalating consumer demand. Factory workers endured appalling conditions before legislation brought improvements. The wealth they had created, however, made possible a more general prosperity.

**INDUSTRIAL WORKERS OF THE WORLD** (IWW), American labor organization, founded 1905 by revolutionary socialists to radicalize the labor movement. It reached its greatest influence 1912–17, with a policy of confrontation, often violent; at its peak it had almost 100,000 members. Unlike the American Federation of Labor (AFL) it aimed not at improving labor conditions but at revolution. It lost support by attempting to exploit WWI; its strikes were considered treasonable. IWW leaders were imprisoned and the movement almost wholly suppressed.

**INDUS VALLEY CIVILIZATION,** centered round the Indus R in India and Pakistan, the earliest known urban culture of the Indian subcontinent. Superimposed on earlier stone- and bronze-using (see STONE AGE; BRONZE AGE) cultures dating from c4000 BC, the Indus Valley civilization, centered around HARAPPA and MOHENJO-DARO, lasted from c2500 to c1750 BC. About 100 of its towns and villages, some with fortified citadels, have been identified.

**INERT GASES,** former name for the NOBLE GASES.

**INERTIA,** property of all MATTER, representing its resistance to any alteration of its state of MOTION. The MASS of a body is a quantitative measure of its inertia; a heavy body has more inertia than a lighter one and needs a greater FORCE to set it in motion. NEWTON's laws of motion depend on the concept of inertia. In EINSTEIN's theory of RELATIVITY, inertia, or mass, is equivalent to ENERGY.

**INFALLIBILITY, Papal. See** PAPACY.

**INFANTILE PARALYSIS. See** POLIOMYELITIS.

**INFANTILE SEXUALITY,** general term embracing those aspects of sexuality (see SEX) exhibited by most children under five years. They do not in general persist into adulthood, though the adult may suffer from a COMPLEX caused by GUILT concerning them. The articulation of infantile sexuality is considered one of FREUD'S greatest contributions.

**INFANTRY,** body of soldiers who fight on foot using light weaponry, such as rifles, machine guns, bazookas, mortars and grenades. Despite the mechanization of warfare, infantry units still form the largest combat branch of most armies. In the US army an infantry division consists of about 15,000 infantrymen and normally comprises eight infantry battalions and two supporting armored battalions equipped with tanks and heavy weapons.

**INFERIORITY COMPLEX,** term used by ADLER and now mainly by psychoanalysts to describe the COMPLEX of fears and EMOTIONS arising out of feelings of inferiority or inadequacy, particularly those concerned with (usually imagined) inferiority of the sexual organs. (See SUPERIORITY COMPLEX.)

**INFINITY** ($\infty$), a quantity greater than any finite quantity. In modern mathematics infinity is viewed in two ways. In one, the word infinity has a definite meaning; and with TRANSFINITE CARDINAL NUMBERS, for example, it may have a plurality of meanings. In the other, infinity is seen as a LIMIT: to say that parallel lines intersect at infinity, for example, means merely that the point of intersection of two lines may be made to recede indefinitely by making the lines more and more nearly parallel. Similarly, in $f(x) = 1/x$, it is meaningful to say that $f(x)$ tends to infinity as $x$ tends to zero; again, the SEQUENCE $1,2,3,...,n$, tends to infinity since, however large $n$ is chosen, there is an $(n+1)$ greater than it. In advanced SET THEORY an infinite set is defined as one whose elements can be put in a one-to-one correspondence with those of a proper subset of the set (i.e., a subset that is not the whole set).

**INFLAMMATION,** the complex of reactions established in body TISSUES in response to injury and infection. It is typified by redness, heat, swelling and pain in the affected part. The first change is in the CAPILLARIES, which dilate, causing ERYTHEMA, and become more permeable to cells and PLASMA (leading to EDEMA). White BLOOD cells accumulate on the capillary walls and pass into affected tissues; foreign bodies, dead tissue and bacteria are taken up and destroyed by phagocytosis and ENZYME action. Active substances produced by white cells encourage increased blood flow and white cell migration into the tissues. LYMPH drainage is important in removing edema fluid and tissue debris. ANTIBODY AND ANTIGEN reactions, ALLERGY and other types of IMMUNITY are concerned with the initiation and perpetuation of inflammation. Inflammatory DISEASES comprise VIRAL and BACTERIAL DISEASE, PARASITIC DISEASE and disorders in which the inflammatory response is activated inappropriately (e.g., by autoimmunity) causing tissue damage.

**INFLATION,** economic phenomenon characterized by rising prices of goods and services which result in the diminished purchasing power of a nation's money. It is the opposite of DEFLATION, where prices and costs are falling. Inflation in the US is measured by the CONSUMER PRICE INDEX, which reflects price changes of a "market basket" of goods and services commonly purchased by householders and which indicates the cost of living. Inflation is generally considered unfavorable because (1) it may lead to undesirable redistribution of real income where people with fixed incomes or whose money income rises more slowly than the rate of inflation suffer a loss in their purchasing power; (2) unless interest rates rise, saving is discouraged as the sum saved falls in value over time; (3) higher prices and costs make a nation's exports less competitive in the international market, thus adversely affecting domestic production, employment and the balance of payments. The two principal theories on the causes of inflation are the Cost-Push theory, which explains inflation as stemming from higher costs of production leading to higher prices, and the Demand-Pull theory, which attributes inflation to excessive aggregate demand caused by an excess volume of money relative to the available supply of goods and services, driving up prices. Remedies for inflation depend on which of these two theories is accepted. Demand-Pull theorists advocate use of fiscal and monetary policies (control over money supply) to restrain aggregate demand. Cost-Push theorists, by contrast, would either allow unemployment to rise or would intervene in wage negotiations to curtail inflationary wage claims.

**INFLUENZA, grippe,** or **'flu,** a group of VIRAL diseases causing mild respiratory symptoms, FEVER, malaise, muscle pains and HEADACHE, and often occurring in rapidly spreading EPIDEMICS. GASTROINTESTINAL TRACT symptoms may also occur. Rarely, it may cause a severe viral PNEUMONIA. A characteristic of influenza viruses is their property of changing their antigenic nature frequently, so that IMMUNITY following a previous attack ceases to be effective. This also limits the usefulness of influenza VACCINATION.

**INFORMATION RETRIEVAL,** a branch of technology of ever-increasing importance as man attempts to cope with the "information explosion." To store and have reference to the vast amount of printed matter produced annually is impossible for most libraries. The problem can be solved by microphotography. Pages are photographed at a reduction (typically to about ⅟₂₀) and stored on 35mm or 16mm film (microfilm), on transparent cards measuring about 100×150mm (microfiches) or as positive prints on slighly smaller cards (microcards). VIDEOTAPE is also used. Reference may be manual or by machine, usually computer. The information must be classified so that the user may gain rapid access *either* to a particular book or paper or to all the relevant material on a particular subject.

In COMPUTERS, information retrieval involves a reverse of those operations used for data storage. The operator inserts a classification which the computer matches with the classification in its memory.

**INFORMATION THEORY,** or communication theory, a mathematical discipline that aims at maximizing the information that can be conveyed by communications systems, at the same time as minimizing the errors that arise in the course of transmission. The information content of a message is conventionally quantified in terms of "bits" (binary digits). Each bit represents a simple alternative—in terms of a message, a yes-or-no; in terms of the components in an electrical circuit, that a switch is opened or closed. Mathematically, the bit is usually represented as a 0-or-1. Complex messages can be represented as series of bit alternatives. Five bits of information only are needed to specify any letter of the alphabet, given an appropriate code. Thus able to quantify "information," information theory employs statistical methods to analyze practical communications problems. The errors that arise in the transmission of signals, often termed NOISE, can be minimized by the incorporation of redundancy. Here more bits of information than are strictly necessary to encode a message are transmitted, so that if some are altered in transmission, there is still enough information to allow the signal to be correctly interpreted. Clearly, the handling of redundant information costs something—a reduced speed of or capacity for transmission, but the reduction in message errors compensates for this loss. Information theoreticians often point to an analogy between the thermodynamic concept of ENTROPY and the degree of misinformation in a signal.

**INFRARED RADIATION,** ELECTROMAGNETIC RADIATION of wavelength between 780nm and 1mm, strongly radiated by hot objects and also termed heat radiation. Detected using PHOTOELECTRIC CELLS, bolometers and photography, it finds many uses—in the home for heating and cooking and in medicine in the treatment of muscle and skin conditions. Infrared absorption SPECTROSCOPY is an important analytical tool in organic chemistry. Military applications (including missile-detection and guidance systems and night-vision apparatus) and infrared PHOTOGRAPHY (often FALSE-COLOR PHOTOGRAPHY) exploit the **infrared window**, the spectral band between 7.5 and 11m in which the ATMOSPHERE is transparent. This and the high infrared reflectivity of foliage give infrared photographs their striking, often dramatic clarity, even when exposed under misty conditions.

**INGE, William** (1913–1973), US playwright, noted for psychological studies of life in small Midwest towns, in such plays as *Come Back, Little Sheba* (1950), *Picnic* (1953) which won a Pulitzer Prize, *Bus Stop* (1955) and *A Loss of Roses* (1959).

**INGRES, Jean Auguste Dominique** (1780–1867), French neoclassical painter renowned for his mastery of line and superb draughtsmanship. *The Vow of Louis XIII* (1824) won him acclaim as the foremost classicist of his time, but today he is better known for portraits and nude studies such as the *Odalisque* (1814). A disciple of RAPHAEL, he was a determined opponent of the romantic movement and an inspiration to many later artists, including DEGAS, RENOIR, and PICASSO.

**INHERITANCE TAX,** levy or assessment on property bequeathed by a deceased person to a specific legatee. It thus differs from an estate tax, levied on a deceased person's estate as a whole. In the US most states levy both estate and inheritance taxes; since 1916 the federal government has levied only an estate tax.

**INHIBITION,** according to Freudian theory, the action of a mental process or function in restraining the expression of another mental process or function; e.g., fear of social condemnation inhibiting fulfilment of sexual desire. Most often the EGO or SUPEREGO inhibits instinctual behavior (see INSTINCT.) (See also REPRESSION.)

**INITIATIVE, REFERENDUM AND RECALL,** methods by which a country's citizens may directly intervene to influence government policy between elections.

Initiative, provided for in most US states, is a procedure whereby a new law is proposed in a petition, then submitted to a vote by the legislature or electorate or both. Laws so passed are generally not subject to veto. Referendum allows citizens a direct vote on proposed laws and policies. A referendum may be demanded by petition, but in most US states it is mandatory for measures such as constitutional amendments and bond issues. Recall, adopted by many cities and some states, provides for the removal of an elected official by calling a special election. Such an election must usually be demanded in a petition whose signers number at least 25% of the votes originally received by the official. Recall has rarely succeeded at state level.

**INKBLOT TEST.** See RORSCHACH, H.

**INNATE IDEAS,** the theory that knowledge is inherent rather than acquired by means of sense experience to which reason is then applied. Derived from PLATO (c427–347 BC), the theory was vigorously denied by John LOCKE (1632–1704), who held the mind to be a *tabula rasa* or clean slate, and other ENLIGHTENMENT philosophers.

**INNER MONGOLIA** (also Nei Monggol), autonomous region in N China, 440,657sq mi in area. Its NW area is part of the Gobi desert, bordering the Mongolian People's Republic; the rest is steppe plateau. The economy is mainly based on animal husbandry. Agriculture is important as are mineral deposits; gold, zinc, silver, coal, copper. Pop 11,000,000.

**INNES, George** (1825–1894), US landscape painter. His best-known work, such as *The Lackawanna Valley* (1855), shows the influence of COROT and the BARBIZON SCHOOL. His later work, such as *The Home of the Heron* (1893) is less realistic and more atmospheric.

**INNSBRUCK,** capital of Tyrol province, Austria, situated on the Inn R between steep Alpine ranges. An important medieval trading post (chartered 1233), Innsbruck has many historic buildings, including the Imperial Palace, the Franciscan Church, and the Cathedral. It is a popular tourist center. Pop 115,000.

**INNS OF COURT,** the four legal societies in London which, since the Middle Ages, have controlled admissions to the English bar. They are Lincoln's Inn, Gray's Inn, the Inner Temple and the Middle Temple.

**INONO, Ismet** (1884–1973), Turkish statesman, twice prime minister between 1923 and 1937, and second president of Turkey (1938–50). Militarily and political-

ly second in command to ATATURK, he helped found the republic. In 1950 he held free elections, his own party being defeated. Following the military coup of 1960, he won further terms as premier (1961–65).

**INORGANIC CHEMISTRY,** major branch of CHEMISTRY comprising the study of all the elements and their compounds, except carbon compounds containing hydrogen (see ORGANIC CHEMISTRY). The elements are classified according to the PERIODIC TABLE. Classical inorganic chemistry is largely descriptive, synthetic and analytical; modern theoretical inorganic chemistry is hard to distinguish from PHYSICAL CHEMISTRY.

**INPUT-OUTPUT ANALYSIS,** a technique of economics which analyzes in detail the interdependence of the productive sectors and units of an economy. By showing how given products function not only as units of consumption, but also in the production of further goods, input-output tables assist the planning of production or consumption goals.

**INQUISITION,** a medieval agency of the Roman Catholic Church to combat heresy, first made official in 1231, when Pope Gregory IX appointed a commission of Dominicans to investigate heresy among the ALBIGENSIANS of S France. It aimed to save the heretic's soul, but a refusal to recant was punished by fines, penance or imprisonment, and often by confiscation of land by the secular authorities. Later the penalty was death by burning. Torture, condemned by former popes, was permitted in heresy trials by Innocent IV (d. 1254). The accused was not told the name of his accusers but could name his known enemies so that their hostile testimony might be discounted. Often the Inquisition was an object of political manipulation. In 1542 it was reconstituted to counter Protestantism in Italy; its modern descendant is the Congregation of the Doctrine of the Faith.

The Spanish Inquisition, founded in 1478 by Ferdinand V and Isabella, was a branch of government and was distinct from the papal institution. Its first commission was to investigate Jews who had publicly embraced Christianity but secretly held to Judaism. Under the grand inquisitor TORQUEMADA, it became an agency of official terror—even St. Ignatius Loyola was investigated. It was extended to Portugal and South America and not dissolved until 1820.

**INSANITY,** In psychology and psychoanalysis, a loose synonym for PSYCHOSIS. In criminal law, insanity is defined as an individual's inability to distinguish right from wrong and, therefore, to assume responsibility for his acts.

**INSECTICIDE,** any substance toxic to INSECTS and used to control them in situations where they cause economic damage or endanger the health of man and his domestic animals. There are three main types: **stomach insecticides,** which are ingested by the insect with their food; **contact insecticides,** which penetrate the cuticle, and **fumigant insecticides,** which are inhaled. Stomach insecticides are often used to control chewing insects like CATERPILLARS and sucking insects like APHIDS. They may be applied to the plant prior to attack and remain active in or on the plant for a considerable time. They must be used with considerable caution on food plants or animal forage. Examples include ARSENIC compounds which remain on the leaf, and organic compounds which are absorbed by the plant and transported to all its parts (systemic insecticides). Contact insecticides include the plant products NICOTINE, derris and PYRETHRUM, which are quickly broken down, and the synthetic compounds such as DDT (and other chlorinated HYDROCARBONS, organophosphates [malathion, parathion] and carbamates. Polychlorinated biphenyls (PCBs) are added to some insecticides to increase their effectiveness and persistence. Highly persistent insecticides may be concentrated in food chains and exert harmful effects on other animals such as birds and fish (see ECOLOGY).

**INSECTIVORA,** an order of small insectivorous MAMMALS, regarded as the most primitive group of placental mammals, having diverged little from the ancestral form. The skull is generally long and narrow, with a primitively large complement of unspecialized teeth in the jaw. Ears and eyes are small and often hidden in fur or skin. The group includes SHREWS, HEDGEHOGS, TENRECS, and MOLES.

**INSECTIVOROUS PLANTS,** or **carnivorous plants,** specialized plants whose leaves are adapted to trap and digest insects. They normally live in boggy habitats or as EPIPHYTES. The insects may be caught in vase-like traps (see PITCHER PLANT), by leaves that spring shut by a trapdoor (see BLADDERWORT) or on sticky leaves (see SUNDEW). The captured insects are broken down by ENZYMES secreted from the plants and the products absorbed.

**INSECTS,** animals having an external skeleton of chitin, characterized by having the body divided into three distinct sections: head, thorax and abdomen. The thorax typically bears two pairs of wings and three pairs of legs. This last is the most diagnostic feature and gives them their alternative name: Hexapoda. The insects are by far the most diverse class of invertebrates, and many are highly specialized. In terms of numbers they are undoubtedly the most successful group in the ANIMAL KINGDOM: the number of species alone exceeds that of all other groups of animals combined. The head bears the mouth, complex mouthparts, the antennae and eyes. The mouthparts above all reflect the diversity of the group. Although they are composed of the same six basic structures in all species, the mouthparts show incredible modifications to specialized modes of feeding. Primitively distinct, heavy, serrated, structures for chewing and crushing in the COCKROACH, they form piercing stylets in MOSQUITOES and APHIDS, with animal or plant juices drawn up a central groove. The long, coiled proboscis of BUTTERFLIES and MOTHS, adapted for sucking NECTAR, is also a tube—but one formed from the modification of different mouthparts. In WASPS and BEES some of the mouthparts have formed a tube for drawing up nectar, while others have retained their chewing form, for handling wax and pollen. The thorax also reflects the great diversity of the insects. Though typically of three segments each bearing a pair of legs, and the last two segments each with a pair of wings, wings are absent in some primitive forms (the Apterygota) and modified in others. In the BEETLES, and other groups, one pair of wings loses its flight function and forms a protective case for the other, flying wings. In the FLIES the second pair of wings are modified as balancing organs. Insects have highly-developed sense organs: on the head are COMPOUND EYES and antennae, which are covered with little "hairs" sensitive to the chemical stimuli of smell and taste. Little hairs over the body are sensitive to touch and smell. The life history of insects usually involves a larval stage. As the LARVA grows, it passes through a series of molts before it reaches the adult stage, each time shedding the existing, rigid EXOSKELETON, after laying down another, larger one within. The new cuticle is at first soft and can be extended. It hardens on contact with air. Larvae are of two types: those which, with each succeeding molt not only increase in size, but also show a progressive development of adult features; and those which remain totally unlike the adult during growth, but pass through a resting stage or PUPA, when the internal and external structures are completely reorganized to form the adult insect (see METAMORPHOSIS). Some insects, such as grasshoppers, instead of a larval stage have a nymph stage in which they already resemble the adult insect.

**INSIDE PASSAGE,** shipping route, some 950mi long, sheltered by a chain of islands along the W coast of North America. Its main ports are Seattle, Wash., Vancouver, B.C., and Juneau and Skagway in Alaska.

**INSTINCT,** a phenomenon whose effects can be observed in animals and man. In general, one can say that instinctive behavior comprises those fixed reactions to external stimuli that have not been learned, such as the sucking instinct or fear of smothering in infants. In fact, such behavior seems to stem from a complex of hereditary and environmental factors characteristic of their species. Animals placed from birth in artificial environments display some, but not all, instinctive reactions characteristic of their species. Numbered among the instincts are the sex drive, AGGRESSION, TERRITORIALITY and the food urge; but much debate surrounds such classification. In psychoanalysis, "instinct" (sometimes called drive) has a similar meaning, with special emphasis on the response as a complex one (see REFLEX). Frustration of, or conflict between, instincts engenders NEUROSES. FREUD suggested the existence of two fundamental instincts: the life instinct, rather akin to the LIBIDO; and its opposite, the death instinct.

**INSTITUTE FOR ADVANCED STUDY,** research center in Princeton, N.J., founded for graduate study in various fields. It has long specialized in the physical sciences and social studies. It was opened in 1933 and one of its first members was Albert Einstein.

**INSULIN,** HORMONE important in METABOLISM, produced by the islets of Langerhans in the PANCREAS, which act as an ENDOCRINE GLAND. Insulin is the only hormone which reduces the level of SUGAR in the BLOOD and is secreted in response to a rise in blood sugar (e.g., after meals, or in conditions of stress); the sugar is converted into GLYCOGEN in the cells of MUSCLE and the LIVER under the influence of insulin. Absence or a relative failure in secretion of insulin occurs in DIABETES, in which blood sugar levels are high and in which sugar overflows into the urine. The isolation of insulin as a pancreatic extract by F. G. BANTING and C. H. BEST in 1921 was a milestone in medical and scientific history. It is a PROTEIN made up of fifty AMINO ACIDS as two peptide chains linked by sulfur bridges. Because it is destroyed in the GASTROINTESTINAL TRACT, it has to be taken by subcutaneous INJECTION by diabetics with severe insulin lack. Its use in diabetics has revolutionized treatment of this disease; the aim in its administration is to be as close to natural secretion patterns as possible. If insufficient insulin is taken, diabetic COMA may result, while in excess hypoglycemia supervenes; both require prompt medical treatment.

**INSURANCE,** method of financial protection by which one party undertakes to indemnify another against certain forms of loss. An insurance company pools the payments for this service and invests them to earn further funds. Each insured person pays a relatively small amount, the *premium,* for a stated period of cover. In return the company will, subject to an assessment of his claim, reimburse him for loss caused by an event covered in the policy. Forms of insurance have existed since the earliest civilizations. Modern insurance began with the medieval GUILDS, which sometimes insured members against trade losses. The specialized fields of fire and maritime insurance (see LLOYDS OF LONDON) developed in the 17th and 18th centuries. The development of PROBABILITY theory allowed the statistical likelihood of damage to be calculated, making insurance as a business possible.

**INTEGRATION.** See CALCULUS.

**INTEGRATION, Racial,** the right to equal access for people of all races to such facilities as schools, churches, housing and public accommodations. It became an issue of public importance in the US after the Civil War and the passage of the 13th, 14th and 15th Amendments to the Constitution, 1864–70, which declared the Negro free and equal, and the Civil Rights Act of 1866. Although slavery was ended as a legal institution state laws were passed during the reaction against RECONSTRUCTION to enforce the physical segregation of blacks and whites. Tennessee adopted the first "Jim Crow" law in 1875, segregating public transportation. In 1896 the Supreme Court approved "separate but equal" accommodations for blacks, following which segregation laws proliferated. In the North segregation in housing created the black slum ghettos; while less common than in the South it still continued in factories, unions and restaurants. In 1910 the NATIONAL ASSOCIATION FOR THE ADVANCEMENT OF COLORED PEOPLE (NAACP) was founded in New York, followed by the National URBAN LEAGUE in 1911. Several activist groups were formed in the 1940s, including the CONGRESS OF RACIAL EQUALITY (CORE). The NAACP won its greatest legal victories in 1954 and 1955, when the Supreme Court outlawed segregation in the public schools and ordered that integration be implemented "with all deliberate speed." Among black leaders advocating passive resistance to discriminatory local laws was Martin Luther KING, Jr. His SOUTHERN CHRISTIAN LEADERSHIP CONFERENCE and the more radical STUDENT NON-VIOLENT COORDINATING COMMITTEE exerted political pressure to enact the Civil Rights Act of 1964 and Voting Rights Act of 1965. Integration was more generally accepted during the 1970s, although serious unrest occurred over busing practices to end school segregation in Boston and other northern cities. See also CIVIL RIGHTS ACT (1957, 1964, 1968).

**INTELLIGENCE,** the general ability to solve problems. Since man is the animal of highest intelligence, most investigations of intelligence have been carried out in human beings. Intelligence tests are structured upon the following bases: numerical ability (the speed and accuracy with which the individual can solve problems of simple arithmetic); verbal fluency; verbal meaning (the ability to understand words); the ability to remember; the speed of perception; and, most importantly, the ability to reason. Such tests are of considerable use, though their limitations must be recognized. Disagreement about whether intelligence tests validly measure intelligence has led some psychologists to define human intelligence as "that which can be measured by intelligence tests."

Throughout the animal kingdom, there is a good correlation between the intelligence of an animal and the size of its brain relative to that of its body. There is an even better one when the surface area of the BRAIN is considered: the higher mammals have a more convoluted cortex (outer layer) than do the lower. After man, the most intelligent animal is the DOLPHIN. Perhaps surprisingly, ANTS show an ability to solve mazes that compares with that of some mammals.

The ways in which animals solve problems are a useful indication of their intelligence. The two important ways are trial-and-error, which is a LEARNING process dependent upon intelligence, and insight. This latter is displayed only by the higher animals.

The evolution of intelligence is unclear, though obviously it has had a profound effect on the emergence of man as earth's dominant animal. Equally obviously, intelligence is a considerable aid to species survival. Much effort has been expended in recent years to examine how much of an individual's intelligence is determined by hereditary factors, how much by environmental factors. Although results have not been conclusive, it would seem that about half the difference in intelligence between people is determined by inheritance, the remainder by early environmental conditions. (See also HEREDITY.)

**INTELLIGENCE QUOTIENT.** See IQ.

**INTELSAT I,** or Early Bird, launched Apr. 6, 1965, the first commercial communications satellite to be put in synchronous orbit, 22,300 miles above the equator, where it revolved at just the right speed to remain stationary over one point on the earth's surface. Intelsat I was built by Hughes Aircraft Co. and launched at cost by NASA for Comsat, the American company that manages the International Telecommunications Satellite Consortium. Intelsat I was orbited over the Atlantic; later satellites were placed in synchronous orbits over the Pacific and Indian Oceans. Intelsat III-D, launched May 21, 1969, completed the first global network of commercial communications satellites.

**INTEREST,** money paid for the use of money loaned. It is generally expressed as a percentage of the principal (sum loaned) per period (usually per year or per month). In "simple" interest, where the principal does not change, the interest can be calculated by the formula $I = prt$, where $I$ is interest, $p$ is principal (the amount borrowed), $r$ the rate of interest and $t$ the time. "Compound" interest is added periodically to the principal; interest is subsequently paid on the resulting compound total. The formula for this is $S = p(1 + r/k)^n$ where $S$ is the final amount, $p$ and $r$ are as before, $k$ is the time interval between compounding and $n$ is the number of times the interest is compounded.

Medieval Christian law forbade the taking of interest on moral grounds as "usury," but Jewish businessmen were freely used as bankers; in the face of this the Church was eventually forced to relax its attitude. Today, with credit playing a major economic role worldwide, interest rates affect the viability of every sort of economic venture, from buying a family home to the exploration of space. In the US, interest rates have skyrocketed in recent years, driven upward by government deficits, inflation and the tight-money policy of the Federal Reserve Board. The prime rate—the interest rate set by banks for their best customers—has gone up from the 7–8% range in 1976–77 to around 20% in 1980–81.

**INTERFERENCE,** the interaction of two

or more similar or related WAVE MOTIONS establishing a new pattern in the AMPLITUDE of the waves. It occurs in all wave phenomena including SOUND, LIGHT and water waves. In most cases the resulting amplitude at a point is found by adding together the amplitudes of the individual interfering waves at that point. Interference patterns can only result if the interfering waves are of related wavelength and exhibit a definite PHASE relationship.

**Optical interference.** Light from ordinary sources is "incoherent"—there is no definite relationship between the phases of the waves associated with different PHOTONS. Until recently the only way to demonstrate optical interference was to use light from a single source which had been divided and led to the interference zone along paths of differing length, thus ensuring that the interfering beams were coherent at least with each other. In this way Thomas YOUNG in 1801 first demonstrated optical interference, showing, because interference effects cannot be explained on either ray or particle models, that light was indeed to be regarded as a wave phenomenon. Young passed light from a single pinhole source through two parallel pinholes in an opaque screen and found that interference fringes—alternate bands of light and dark—were formed on another screen placed beyond the slits. The bright bands resulted from the constructive interference of the two beams, the wave amplitude of each reinforcing the other; the dark bands, destructive interference, the amplitude of one wave canceling the effect of that of the other because the difference in path length was such that the "peaks" of one wave coincided with the "troughs" of the other. Newton's rings, colored fringes seen in thin transparent films, are a similar interference effect. In recent years LASERS (which produce coherent light—radiation having a uniform and controllable phase structure) have enabled physicists to produce optical interference effects much more easily, an important application being HOLOGRAPHY. (See also INTERFEROMETER.)

**INTERFEROMETER,** any instrument employing INTERFERENCE effects used: for measuring the wavelengths of LIGHT, RADIO, SOUND or other wave phenomena; for measuring the refractive index (see REFRACTION) of gases (Rayleigh interferometer); for measuring very small distances using radiation of known wavelength, or, in ACOUSTICS and RADIO ASTRONOMY, for determining the direction of an energy source. In most interferometers the beam of incoming radiation is divided in two, led along paths of different but accurately adjustable lengths and then recombined to give an interference pattern. Perhaps the best known optical instrument is the Michelson interferometer devised in 1881 for the MICHELSON-MORLEY EXPERIMENT. More accurate for wavelength measurements is the Fabry-Perot interferometer in which the radiation is recombined after multiple partial reflections between parallel lightly-silvered glass plates.

**INTERFERON,** substance produced by living tissues following infection with VIRUSES, BACTERIA etc., which interferes with the growth of any organism. It is responsible for a transient and mild degree of nonspecific IMMUNITY following infection.

**INTERIOR, US Department of the,** executive branch of the federal government, headed by the secretary of the interior. Founded in 1849, its original task was to administer the census and Indian affairs, and to regulate the exploitation of natural resources. In recent years, however, it has been increasingly exercised by the need for conservation of resources and protection of the environment. Today it has five major areas of responsibility, each in the charge of an assistant secretary. These are Fish, Wildlife, Parks and Marine Resources; Mineral Resources; Water and Power Development; Water Quality and Research; and Public Land Management, which as well as agencies responsible for federally owned lands includes the Office of the Territories, which administers US territories and trust territories, and the Bureau of INDIAN AFFAIRS.

**INTERIOR DECORATION,** the design and arrangement of decorative elements in a home or public building. Until relatively recently, architectural and interior styles were almost inseparable and the names used to characterize each period applied both to the architecture of buildings and their interior decor.

In medieval Europe attention to interior display was confined largely to churches which, by late medieval times, exemplified the Gothic. It was only with the Renaissance that important styles of interior design began to emerge. Italian Renaissance design took classical architecture and ornament as its model, and Italian influences were soon seen throughout Europe, especially in the great French chateaus of the time and in the English Tudor, Elizabethan and Jacobean styles, which combined earlier Gothic with Italian forms. Baroque (c1600–1750) accented the grandiose and elaborate. Rococo (1700s, especially in France and Germany) was smaller-scale, with a generous use of curves. The Baroque-Rococo era also saw the development of the Louis period styles of interior decoration. Neoclassicism in France and Georgian in England (18th and early 19th centuries) both returned to the lighter forms reminiscent of classical design. Directoire and Empire were influential post-revolutionary French styles. In England, the Victorian period was undistinguished except for the attempt of artist William MORRIS and his Arts and Crafts Movement to return to the simpler hand-crafted forms of the past. In America, early utilitarian colonial designs were succeeded by the Georgian-influenced Federal style that characterizes the beginning 1800s. The early 1900s saw the curvilinear forms of ART NOUVEAU, and the later, more geometric work of the ART DECO movement. The BAUHAUS style of the 1920s, which emphasized simplicity and functional design, is still influential today. Through the years, the major furniture designers, such as CHIPPENDALE, HEPPLEWHITE, SHERATON, PHYFE and EAMES have also greatly influenced decorative styles.

**INTERNAL-COMBUSTION ENGINE,** type of ENGINE—the commonest now used—in which the fuel is burned inside the engine and the expansion of the combustion gases is used to provide the power. Because of their potential light weight, efficiency and convenience, internal-combustion engines largely superseded STEAM ENGINES in the early 20th century. They are used industrially and for all kinds of transport, notably to power AUTOMOBILES. There are three classes of internal-combustion engine: RECIPROCATING ENGINES, which include the **gasoline engine** the DIESEL ENGINE and the FREE-PISTON ENGINE; rotary engines, including the GAS TURBINE, the turbojet (see JET PROPULSION) and the WANKEL ENGINE; and ROCKET engines and non-turbine jet engines, working by reaction. Although originally coal gas and even powdered coal were used as fuel, now almost all fuels used are PETROLEUM products: diesel oil, GASOLINE, BOTTLED GAS and NATURAL GAS. The first working (though not usable) internal-combustion engine was a piston engine made by HUYGENS (1680) that burned gunpowder. In 1794 Robert Street patented a practicable though inefficient engine into which the air had to be pumped by hand. In 1876 N. A. OTTO built the first four-stroke engine, using the principles stated earlier by Alphonse Beau de Rochas. The cycle is (1) intake of fuel/air mixture; (2) compression of mixture; (3) ignition (see IGNITION

SYSTEM) and expansion of burned gases; (4) expulsion of gases as exhaust. Only the third stroke is powered, but the engine is highly efficient, and modern gasoline engines are basically the same. Generally four, six or eight cylinders are linked to provide balanced power. The engine is cooled by water circulating through pipes or by air from a fan. The fuel/air mixture is produced in the CARBURETOR; greater power is given by **supercharging**, by which the proportion of air and the initial pressure of the mixture are increased. The two-stroke engine, giving greater power for a given size, but less efficient in fuel use, does not usually have valves, but an inlet and an exhaust port in the cylinder, blocked and uncovered in turn by the piston. At the end of the powered stroke, the piston drives fresh fuel mixture from the crankcase into the cylinder, pushing out the exhaust gases. The EFFICIENCY of an internal-combustion engine increases with the COMPRESSION RATIO; if this is too high, however, "knocking" occurs due to irregular burning and detonations. It is avoided by using fuel of high OCTANE number, and by using ANTIKNOCK ADDITIVES. (See also AIR POLLUTION.)

**INTERNAL REVENUE SERVICE (IRS),** agency of the US Department of the Treasury. Created by Congress in 1789, it assesses and collects domestic or "internal" taxes. These include federal taxes on goods and services, income taxes and corporate taxes, as well as gift and estate taxes. The service is headed by a commissioner of internal revenue appointed by the president. Its headquarters are in Washington, D.C., and it has seven regional and 58 district offices.

IRS rules are based on the Internal Revenue Code, a huge compilation of tax laws passed by Congress and interpreted through regulations issued by the IRS. As administered by the agency, the tax system has been called inequitable and inefficient by some critics who claim that IRS regulations are intricate, confusing and frequently not fully understood even by the IRS itself. To gain the full benefit of the tax laws, taxpayers must frequently buy the services of expert tax accountants. In addition, the IRS has been accused of trying to influence policies unrelated to tax law, as in its recent attempt to deny tax-exempt status to segregated private schools.

**INTERNATIONAL, The,** common name of a number of socialist-communist revolutionary organizations. Three of these have had historical significance. The First International, officially the International

Working Men's Association, was formed under the leadership of Karl MARX in London in 1864 with the aim of uniting workers of all nations to realize the ideals of the *Communist Manifesto*. Divisions grew up between reformers and violent revolutionaries; these became increasingly bitter, culminating in the expulsion of the faction led by Mikhail BAKUNIN after a leadership struggle in 1872. The association broke up in 1876. The Second, commonly called the Socialist International was founded in Paris in 1889 by a group of socialist parties that later made their headquarters in Brussels. The leading social democratic parties, including those of Germany and Russia were represented. Among representatives were Jean JAURÈS, Ramsay MACDONALD, LENIN and TROTSKY. It influenced international labor affairs until WWI, when it broke up. The Third or . Communist International, generally known as the Comintern, was founded by Lenin, following his seizure of power in Russia in 1919, in an attempt to win the leadership of world socialism; ZINOVIEV was its first president. Soviet-dominated from the outset, it aimed, in the 1920s, to foment world revolution. In the 1930s, under STALIN, it sought contacts with less extreme left-wing groups abroad, to assuage foreign hostility. Stalin dissolved it in 1943 as a wartime conciliatory gesture to the Allies.

**INTERNATIONAL ATOMIC ENERGY AGENCY (IAEA)**, intergovernmental agency closely related to the UN. Established in 1957, it promotes and conducts research into peaceful uses of atomic energy and seeks to ensure adequate safety standards. It is particularly concerned that agency assistance should not be used for military purposes.

**INTERNATIONAL COMMUNICATION AGENCY (ICA)**, independent federal agency established in 1953 under the name of the United States Information Agency (USIA). The ICA replaced the USIA in 1978. Its purpose is to convince people of other countries "that the objectives and policies of the US are in harmony with and will advance their legitimate aspirations for freedom, progress, and peace." ICA offices in some 100 countries work through press, TV and radio (see VOICE OF AMERICA) and provide information pamphlets and English classes.

**INTERNATIONAL COURT OF JUSTICE**, highest judicial organ of the UN, founded in 1946 to provide a peaceful means of settling international disputes according to the principles of INTERNATIONAL LAW. Like its predecessor

under the LEAGUE OF NATIONS, the World Court, it sits at the Hague. In practice its authority is limited by frequent refusals to accept its decisions.

**INTERNATIONAL DEVELOPMENT ASSOCIATION (IDA)**, organization affiliated to the WORLD BANK. It was established in 1960 to make loans for development projects to member countries on less economically burdensome terms than World Bank loans; a service charge is substituted for interest. IDA has more than 120 member nations.

**INTERNATIONAL LABOR ORGANIZATION (ILO)**, UN agency with headquarters in Geneva, formed in 1919 to develop and improve working conditions worldwide. In 1934 the US joined; in 1946 the organization became affiliated to the UN.

**INTERNATIONAL LADIES' GARMENT WORKERS' UNION**, AFL-CIO union in the US women's and children's clothing industry. It was founded in 1900 by AMERICAN FEDERATION OF LABOR charter. Strikes in New York 1909–10 led to Louis BRANDEIS' Protocol of Peace, which set a pattern for labor-management cooperation. Under David DUBINSKY (president 1932–66) the ILGWU grew fast in the 1930s, was active in the AFL-CIO debate and pioneered union welfare schemes. Its membership totals 348,000 (1980).

**INTERNATIONAL LAW**, body of laws assumed to be binding among nations by virtue of their general acceptance. Although customary rules on maritime matters and on ambassadorial immunity had long existed, the real beginnings of international law lay in attempts to humanize the conduct of war. The seminal work of Hugo GROTIUS, *On the Law of War and Peace* (1625), was one such, but he also formulated several important principles, including a legal basis for the sovereignty of states. The works of Grotius and his successors were widely acclaimed but never officially accepted; however, legal principles were increasingly incorporated into international agreements such as the Congress of VIENNA as well as into the constitution of the UNITED NATIONS. International laws may arise through multilateral or bilateral agreements, as with the GENEVA CONVENTION, or simply by long-established custom, as with a large part of MARITIME LAW. In some cases, as with the war crimes rulings of the NUREMBERG TRIALS, they may be said to arise retrospectively. Because few nations are willing to relinquish any sovereignty, the law lacks a true legislative body and an effective executive to enforce it. The

INTERNATIONAL COURT OF JUSTICE is the international judicial body; the UN in the process of compiling an international legal code, is the nearest thing to a legislature, but all these bodies are limited by the willingness of states to accept their decisions, as was the LEAGUE OF NATIONS in the 1930s. These difficulties have led some theorists to deny international law true legal status, but this is an extreme view; the need for international rules is widely recognized, as shown by the increasing tendency to anticipate problem areas such as space exploration and exploitation of seabed resources and to attempt to develop international rules to regulate them.

**INTERNATIONAL MONETARY FUND (IMF)**, international organization, affiliated to the UN, existing to develop international monetary cooperation, in particular to stabilize exchange rates by providing international credit. Members cannot make changes greater than 10% in the exchange rate of their national currency without consulting the Fund. Established by the BRETTON WOODS CONFERENCE, it began operating in 1947. Operating funds are subscribed by its 141 member governments; the Group of Ten (US, UK, Belgium, Canada, France, West Germany, Italy, Japan, Netherlands and Sweden) are pledged to lend further funds if necessary. (See also WORLD BANK.)

**INTERNATIONAL RELATIONS**, relationships between nations, through politics, treaties, military confrontation or cooperation, economics or culture. Peacetime contact is generally maintained through DIPLOMACY; each nation maintains embassies in other countries it recognizes as nations. Even when states do not maintain mutual embassies, however, they may find it desirable to keep contacts open, often through the offices of a third nation. The other primary link is through membership in international organizations, either for global politics as with the UNITED NATIONS, defense as with NATO or the WARSAW PACT, or simply mutual convenience, as with the UNIVERSAL POSTAL UNION. From 1946 on international relations were dominated by the concept of the COLD WAR, in which the complications of world diplomacy were reduced to an oversimplified model of an ideological contest between two global antagonists, the communist and capitalist systems as personified by the USSR and US. In the 1960s the rise of the Third World countries negated this simple division, though many of these took one or the other side. In the 1970s relations between the US and USSR improved, largely through trade

and nuclear limitation agreements and also because of the rise of China as a rival superpower. The endurance and value of the resulting detente, however, remained in dispute. (See also INTERNATIONAL LAW; INTERNATIONAL TRADE.)

**INTERNATIONAL STYLE**, architectural style, best defined in its widest sense as the dominant trend in large-scale buildings in industrialized countries since the 1920s. It emphasizes a clean functionalism, open space with large areas of glass, and reinforced concrete construction. Among pioneering exponents were Walter GROPIUS, MIES VAN DER ROHE, LE CORBUSIER, Pier Luigi NERVI and in the US Philip C. JOHNSON and R. I. NEUTRA.

**INTERNATIONAL TRADE**, or world trade, the exchange of goods and services between nations. Since the 18th century it has become a vital element in world prosperity. One reason for this is that it is generally thought more profitable for countries to specialize in making those things in which such factors as natural resources, climatic conditions, availability of raw materials, a skilled labor force or low labor costs give them a special advantage. This is known as the international division of labor. Some countries, such as the UK, rely largely on exports; US exports amount to 15% of the world total, but are less vital to its economy.

Even in prehistoric times the amber route carried trade between tribes thousands of miles apart. The ancient Greeks, Romans and Phoenicians were active traders. Chinese merchants penetrated most of Asia, and Arabs operated trade routes on the Indian Ocean and in Africa. Most explorers before the 20th century sought to open trade routes. Early trade was largely in goods yielding high prices on small amounts because of the difficulty of transportation. Only with modern transport did international trade become economically vital.

The financing of world trade relies on the foreign exchange market where an importer can buy the necessary currency to pay his foreign supplier. Most countries keep a record of their BALANCE OF PAYMENTS with foreign trading partners; a large surplus or deficit in this is often a good economic indicator.

After WWII efforts were made to promote free trade throughout the world. In 1948 the US and 23 other nations made an agreement within the framework of the UN known as the GENERAL AGREEMENT ON TARIFFS AND TRADE (GATT). In 1962 Congress passed the Trade Expansion Act, enabling President Kennedy to lower or remove tariffs affecting the European COMMON MARKET countries. Subsequently, a series of tariff reductions have been negotiated under what is known as the "Kennedy Round." The Common Market had as its main aim free trade between its members, but it also created a system of common external tariffs in agriculture, a source of continual controversy. (See also EFTA, COMECON.)

One of the biggest unsolved problems of international trade is the balance between industrialized and developing countries of the Third World. Since they export mainly food and raw materials, which rise only slowly in price, and import manufactured goods, their expansion is much slower than that of rich countries.

**INTERPOL,** contraction of the International Criminal Police Organization, established in 1923. Its headquarters are now in Paris. It is a clearing house for police information and specializes in the detection of counterfeiting, smuggling and trafficking in narcotics.

**INTERSTATE COMMERCE,** commercial transactions that cross state boundaries or concern more than one state. By Article I, section 8 of the US Constitution, Congress is empowered to regulate commerce among foreign nations and the various states. The Interstate Commerce Act of 1887 created the INTERSTATE COMMERCE COMMISSION (ICC) to prevent discriminatory practices in interstate transportation. In 1914 Congress created the FEDERAL TRADE COMMISSION, and since then other similar agencies have been established: the Civil Aeronautics Board, the Federal Aviation Administration, the Federal Communications Commission and the Federal Power Commission. The Civil Rights Act of 1964, forbidding racial discrimination in public accommodation, was also based on the widespread powers of Congress over interstate commerce.

**INTOLERABLE ACTS,** also known as Coercive Acts, five acts of the British Parliament passed in 1774 to penalize dissidents in Mass. The Boston Port Act closed the harbor in default of compensation for the BOSTON TEA PARTY. The Massachusetts Bay Regulating Act suspended many of the colony's original rights. The Impartial Administration of Justice Act ordained that British officials accused of crimes within the colonies should be tried in other colonies or in England. The Quartering Act required colonists to shelter and feed British troops. The QUEBEC ACT extended Quebec's boundary S to the Ohio R. These strong measures were widely protested throughout the colonies and led to the calling of the First Continental Congress and hence the REVOLUTIONARY WAR.

**INTOXICATION,** state in which a person is overtly affected by excess of a DRUG or poison. It is often used to describe the psychological effects of drugs and particularly ALCOHOL, in which behavior may become disinhibited, facile, morose or aggressive and in which judgment is impaired. Late stages of intoxication affecting the BRAIN include stupor and COMA. Ingestion of very large amounts of water causes water intoxication and may lead to coma and death. POISONING with TOXINS and drugs may cause intoxication of other organs (e.g., HEART with DIGITALIS overdosage).

**INTROVERSION AND EXTRAVERSION,** terms coined by JUNG for two opposite character traits. Introverts are shy, introspective, "ingoing"; extraverts sociable, little concerned with their own inner thoughts and feelings, "outgoing." Most people display both traits, one or the other dominating at different times. Jung suggested that conflict between them was a cause of NEUROSIS.

**INVESTMENT,** the productive employment of resources (*capital*) or the transformation of savings into active wealth (*capital formation*), also the use of funds to obtain dividends, for example, from corporate stock or government bonds.

Investment is now one of the prime areas of concern for governments seeking to influence or control the progress of their economies. Planned investment in modern industry is achieved through an elaborate system of institutions and intermediaries including stock markets, investment banks, industrial finance corporations and commercial banks. This system enables individual investors to handle their assets easily and to choose the degree of risk they are willing to take.

Foreign investment can take two forms: *portfolio* investment, the purchase of the stock of foreign corporations, and *direct* investment, the establishment or expansion of an investor-controlled corporation in a foreign country. (See also BANKING; CAPITAL; ECONOMICS; STOCKS AND STOCK MARKET.)

**INVESTMENT BANKING,** system of banking that enables companies—and sometimes countries—to raise capital by selling new issues of stocks and bonds to investors. Investment bankers often join together to try and sell these substantially priced securities to insurance companies, pension funds, commercial banks and members of the investing public.

**IODINE (I),** the least reactive of the HALOGENS, forming black lustrous crystals which readily sublime to pungent violet vapor. Most iodine is produced from calcium iodate ($Ca[IO_3]_2$), found in CHILE SALTPETER. In the US, much is recovered from oil-well brine, which contains sodium iodide (NaI). Chemically it resembles BROMINE closely, but has a greater tendency to covalency and positive oxidation states. It is large enough to form 6-coordinate oxy-anions. Most plants (especially seaweeds) contain traces of iodine; in the higher animals it is a constituent of the thyroxine hormone secreted by the THYROID GLAND. Iodine deficiency can cause GOITER. Iodine and its compounds are used as antiseptics, fungicides and in the production of dyes. The RADIOISOTOPE $I^{131}$ is used as a tracer and to treat goiter. Silver iodide, being light-sensitive, is used in PHOTOGRAPHY. (See also HALIDES.) AW 126.9, mp 113.5°C, bp 184°C, sg 4.93 (20°C).

**ION,** an ATOM or group of atoms that has become electrically charged by gain or loss of negatively-charged ELECTRONS. In general, ions formed from metals are positive (CATIONS), those from nonmetals negative (ANIONS). CRYSTALS of ionic compounds consist of negative and positive ions arranged alternately in the lattice and held together by electrical attraction (see BOND, CHEMICAL). Many covalent compounds undergo ionic DISSOCIATION in solution. Ions may be formed in gases by radiation or electrical discharge, and occur in the IONOSPHERE (see also ATMOSPHERE). At very high temperatures gases form PLASMA, consisting of ions and free electrons. (See ELECTROLYSIS; ION EXCHANGE; IONIZATION CHAMBER; IONIZATION POTENTIAL; ION PROPULSION.)

**IONESCO, Eugène** (1912– ), Rumanian-born French playwright, a leading figure in the so-called theater of the absurd. Among his best-known works are *The Bald Soprano* (1950), *Rhinoceros* (1959) and *Exit the King* (1962).

**ION EXCHANGE,** chemical reaction in which IONS in a solution are replaced by others of like charge. An insoluble solid is used that has an open, netlike molecular structure: a zeolite, or a synthetic organic polymer called an **ion-exchange resin**, whose composition and properties can be tailored for the use required. The solid has attached anionic groups, which are neutralized by small mobile cations in the interstices. It is these cations which are exchanged for others when a solution is passed through. The principle of anion exchange is similar. Ion exchange is used for softening HARD WATER, purifying sugar, and concentrating ores of uranium and the NOBLE METALS. Ion-exchange CHROMATOGRAPHY is used to separate the RARE EARTHS, and in chemical ANALYSIS.

**IONIAN ISLANDS,** group of islands off the SW mainland of Greece, chief of which are Cephalonia, Cerigo, Corfu, Ithaca, Leukas, Paxos and Zante. A Byzantine province in the 10th century, the islands passed through periods of Venetian, French, Russian and British control before becoming part of Greece in 1864. Exports include wine, cotton, olives and fish.

**IONIAN SEA,** arm of the Mediterranean Sea, between SE Italy and W Greece. It is connected to the Adriatic by the Strait of Otranto and the Tyrrhenian Sea by the Strait of Messina.

**IONOSPHERE,** the zone of the earth's ATMOSPHERE extending outward from about 75km above the surface in which most atoms and molecules exist as electrically charged IONS. The high degree of ionization is maintained through the continual ABSORPTION of high-energy solar radiation. Several distinct ionized layers, known as the D, E, $F_1$, $F_2$ and G layers, are distinguished. These are somewhat variable, the D layer disappearing and the $F_1$, $F_2$ layers merging at night. Since the free ELECTRONS in these layers strongly reflect RADIO WAVES, the ionosphere is of great importance for long-distance radio communications.

**ION PROPULSION,** or **ion drive,** drive proposed for spacecraft on interstellar or longer interplanetary trips. The vaporized propellant (liquid CESIUM OR MERCURY) is passed through an ionizer, which strips each atom of an ELECTRON. The positive IONS so formed are accelerated rearward by an ELECTRIC FIELD. The resultant thrust is low, but in the near-vacuum of space may be used to build up huge velocities by constant acceleration over a long period of time. The drive has been tested in orbit.

**Name of state:** Iowa
**Capital:** Des Moines
**Statehood:** Dec. 28, 1846 (29th state)

**Familiar name:** Hawkeye State
**Area:** 56,290sq mi
**Population:** 2,913,387
**Elevation:** Highest—1,675ft, Ocheyedan Mound. Lowest—480ft, Mississippi River in Lee County
**Motto:** Our Liberties We Prize and Our Rights We Will Maintain
**State flower:** Wild Rose
**State bird:** Eastern Goldfinch
**State tree:** Oak
**State song:** "The Song of Iowa"

**IOWA,** state, in central US, bounded to the E by Wis. and Ill., to the S by Mo., to the W by Neb. and S.D. and to the N by Minn. It lies E-W between the Mississippi and Missouri rivers, which have contributed to its development, as routes first for exploration and then commerce.

**Land.** Iowa consists of a gently rolling plain, sloping towards the SE, about two-thirds of which lies at 800–1,400ft. It is crossed by several large rivers, tributaries of the Mississippi and the Missouri. From 85% to 90% of the state's area is suitable for cultivation.

**People.** The first settlers came to Iowa from the states in the E and S, but from the 1840s many Europeans, particularly those with farming experience, joined them. Major ethnic groups include the Germans, Scandinavians, English and Dutch. More than 55% of the population lives in urban areas.

**Economy.** The state's income from agriculture is one of the nation's highest. Cattle and hogs are the most important livestock, and the major crops are corn and soybeans. After the sharp decline in farm prices in the 1930s, Iowa began a drive to diversify its economy. Principal manufactures include farm implements, electronic goods, appliances, furniture, chemicals and automobile parts. Mineral production is relatively small, but the state is one of the nation's leading producers of gypsum. A good railroad and road system have contributed to the growth of industry.

**History.** French explorers visited the region in 1673, and by 1682 France had claimed the area, naming it Louisiana for the French king. The territory W of the Mississippi was ceded to Spain (1762–1800), but in 1803 France sold the area to the US under the LOUISIANA PURCHASE. From 1804 to the early 1830s it was Indian land, not open to legal settlement but by 1851 the entire area had been opened to settlers. The Territory of Iowa was created in 1838, and it became the 29th state of the US in 1846. In 1857 a second constitution was adopted and the state capital established at Des Moines. In the 20th century, Iowa has remained stable, prosperous, and still essentially agricultural. Recently, the state government has experienced fiscal troubles and there have been painful cutbacks in government spending, but the economy has remained relatively sound.

**IPHIGENIA,** in Greek mythology, daughter of AGAMEMNON and CLYTEMNESTRA. During the TROJAN WAR the goddess ARTEMIS requested the sacrifice of Iphigenia. In one version she consented to die for the glory of Greece, in another Artemis put a stag in Iphigenia's place at the very last moment and had her carried off to the land of Tauris. Both versions are treated by the classical Greek dramatist EURIPIDES.

**IPPOLITOV-IVANOV, Mikhail Mikhailovich** (1859–1935), Russian composer and conductor. His work, which includes orchestral pieces, chamber music and operas, bridges Russian pre-revolutionary and post-revolutionary music.

**IQ** (*I*ntelligence *Q*uotient), a measure of an individual's INTELLIGENCE. IQ's are determined by an individual's performance on a variety of verbal, mathematical, perceptual and problem-solving tasks. Each individual's performance is considered in relation to average scores achieved by others of the same age group. IQ scores between 90 and 109 are considered average the MEAN score being defined as 100; scores of 130 and above are considered very superior; while scores of 69 and below indicate mentally defective functioning. IQ scores of children vary moderately during childhood and adolescence as a result of environmental and emotional factors. (See also PSYCHOLOGICAL TESTS; JENSENISM.)

**IRAN,** known as Persia until 1935, a republic in SW Asia, a major oil-exporting country. It is bordered by the USSR and the Caspian Sea in the N, Afghanistan and Pakistan in the E and by Turkey and Iraq in the W. The Perisan Gulf and the Gulf of Oman lie to the S.

**Land.** Most of the country is a high mountainous plateau above 4,000ft, with an interior desert which contains a salt waste about 200mi long and half as wide. The climate ranges from subtropical to subpolar. About 11% of the land is forested.

**People.** Iran is multi-lingual and culturally diverse. The Kurds are an independent and nomadic people living in the W mountains, where about 350,000 Lurs, thought to be aboriginal Persians, also live. Other smaller nomadic tribal groups inhabit the mountainous fringes and ethnic Arabs live in the SW. There are Armenians, who are primarily concerned with commerce and

**Official name:** Islamic Republic of Iran
**Capital:** Teheran
**Area:** 636,296sq mi
**Population:** 38,940,000
**Languages:** Persian (Farsi) Kurdish; Luri;
Turkish; Arabic; French
**Religion:** Muslim
**Monetary unit(s):** 1 Iranian Rial=100
dinars

live in big cities, and groups of Turks and
Jews. About 50% speak Persian and
although the Turkish groups are small,
about 26% of Iranians speak Turkish—
there was a long period of Turkish rule in
the N. About 98% of the people are Shi'ite
Muslims, although most of the tribal
minorities are Sunnites.
**Economy.** In the early 1970s Iran's growth
rate was one of the highest in the developing
countries, because of profits from the oil
industry. Agriculture remains important,
employing about one-third the economically active population. Crops include cereals,
cotton, tobacco and olives, and livestock is
raised. In the late 1970s Iran was the
world's fourth largest producer of oil.
Natural gas was becoming important,
though Iran's other mineral resources,
including coal, chromium, lead and copper,
were largely undeveloped. In 1954 the
government instituted a major drive for
self-sufficiency, and by the 1970s manufactures included machine tools, textiles, steel
and automobiles.
**History.** Iran's history before 650 AD is
treated under the entry on Ancient PERSIA.
In 1055 Iran was invaded by the Turks, who
in turn were overthrown by the Mongol
leader GENGHIS KHAN in 1219. Between 1381
and 1404 there were frequent attacks by
TAMERLANE, and it was not until 1501 that
the Safavid dynasty, which ruled until 1736,
was established in 1795 and ruled until
1925. During this time Iran was dominated
politically and economically by the
European powers, especially Britain and
Russia. After WWI Reza Khan, an army
officer, overthrew the Shah and as REZA
SHAH PAHLAVI founded the Pahlavi dynasty.

In 1941 under pressure from the Western
powers, he abdicated in favor of his son,
Mohammed Reza Pahlavi. In 1951 Prime
Minister Mohammed Mossadegh nationalized the oil industry, precipitating a crisis
in which the US and European powers
backed the Shah and Mossadegh was
deposed. The Shah assumed complete
control of the government in 1963. His
regime—supported by the US—became
increasingly repressive, and popular opposition, which grew in 1977–78, forced the
Shah to leave the country in 1979. The
exiled Islamic fundamentalist leader,
Ayatollah Ruhollah Khomeini, returned,
establishing an islamic republican government under his effective control. Militants
seized the US embassy in Nov. 1979,
holding its staff hostage until Jan. 1981.
The new regime was also at war with Iraq in
the oil-producing Gulf area beginning in
Sept. 1980, which reduced oil output. The
government, facing increasing violence and
dissent from ethnic minorities, moderates
and militant leftists, stepped up its
repressive measures.

**Official name:** Republic of Iraq
**Capital:** Baghdad
**Area:** 168,928sq mi
**Population:** 12,029,700
**Language:** Arabic
**Religions:** Muslim; Christian
**Monetary unit(s):** 1 Iraqi dinar=1,000 fils
IRAQ, independent Arab republic in SW
Asia, a major oil-producing state. It is
bounded by Turkey in the N, Iran in the E,
and Syria and Jordan in the W. The S
border is with Kuwait, the Persian Gulf and
Saudi Arabia.
**Land.** Iraq consists of a largely level region
between the Tigris and Euphrates rivers,
whose waters are utilized for irrigation. In
the south the rivers join to form the SHATT
AL-ARAB, flowing through extensive marshlands. There are two climatic regions, a hot
arid lowland in the W and SW desert and a
damper area in the NE where rain is
sufficient for crops. In the N and E there is
steppe vegetation with bushes and thorns,
but the S and W support only salt-resistant

shrubs.

**People.** Most Iraqis are Sunnite Muslim Arabs. The principal minority is the tribal Kurds, who comprise less than 15% of the population and live in the Zagros Mts of the N, and adjacent portions of Turkey and Iran. They have long demanded independence. Other minorities include small groups of Iranians and Turkomans and other tribes, and a Christian minority. The government has devoted considerable oil wealth to raising the standard of living, and primary education is now widely available.

**Economy.** Although agriculture employs 43% of the labor force, oil production, begun in 1928, dominates the economy, and among Middle Eastern oil exporters Iraq is surpassed only by Saudi Arabia. Oil from the Zubayr and Rumaila fields (near Basra) is shipped by tanker through the Persian Gulf, and there is an overland pipeline to the Mediterranean from the Kirkuk oilfield. Until 1961 the industry was monopolized by the Iraq Petroleum Company, largely British owned, but the government then took over much of I.P.C.'s holdings and the industry was nationalized in 1972. The government is using oil revenues to diversify the underdeveloped industrial sector and such traditional industries as food processing and textiles have been joined by electronics, petrochemicals, steel, and pharmaceuticals. Air and road transport are becoming increasingly important.

**History.** For the history of the region before the 7th century see under the entries ASSYRIA, BABYLONIA and MESOPOTAMIA. When the Arabs settled in the area now known as Iraq in the 7th century AD, they brought about a cultural and scientific revival. Baghdad became the capital of the ABBASID caliphate. After the Mongol invasion in the 13th century the country was impoverished and continuing political instability prevented its rebuilding. Ottoman control was solidified in 1638 although Iraq often maintained some autonomy. Iraq's modern history begins in 1914, with the British invasion during WWI. It was not until 1932, after years of violence and unrest, that the British granted independence to Iraq. Unrest continued, particularly over Kurdish demands for self-government. In 1945 Iraq joined the ARAB LEAGUE but then in 1955 joined the Baghdad Pact (see CENTRAL TREATY ORGANIZATION). The Arab socialist Baath Party took control of the government in 1968, nationalizing much of the economy. Violent conflict with the Kurds erupted in 1962 and despite a 1975 peace treaty,

conflict continues. By 1975 Iraq had aligned with the USSR, which now provides considerable technical aid. War between Iran and Iraq erupted in the S in 1980.

**IRAQI-IRANIAN WAR,** a conflict that broke out in Sept. 1980 after months of border clashes. Iraq, invading Iran, alarmed the world because the continued availability of vast amounts of oil was jeopardized. The downfall of the shah of Iran, regarded as a regional protector of the peace, may have offered Iraq, concerned about possible persecution of the Arab minority in Iran, an excuse to invade. Iraq was also concerned about unrest among its Shi'ite Muslims, the sect that dominated Iran. Sporadic fighting, without military distinction, led to a stalemate.

**IRELAND, Northern,** comprises six counties of Ulster in NE Ireland. Since 1922 it has been a province of the UK. Covering 5,452sq mi, it has a predominantly Protestant population with a Roman Catholic minority swelled in recent years to around 30%. The largest towns are the capital, Belfast and Londonderry. Major manufactures include machinery and shipbuilding, textiles (man-made fibers and linen) and electronics.

**History.** The Ulster counties chose to remain British after Ireland (Eire) became independent in 1922 and maintained this resolve despite occasional outbreaks of terrorism by the IRISH REPUBLICAN ARMY. Discrimination against the growing Catholic minority in politics led them to form a civil rights movement (1968), which was used to justify renewed IRA terrorism. The resulting violence and civil unrest led the UK government to suspend the Northern Ireland Parliament at Stormont (1972) and assume direct rule of the province. Though a new Northern Ireland Assembly was elected (1975) in an effort to promote power-sharing, neither Catholic nor Protestant extremists accepted it; violence by both sides continued. Pop 1,538,800.

**Official name:** Irish Republic
**Capital:** Dublin
**Area:** 26,599sq mi

**Population:** 3,368,200
**Languages:** Irish, English
**Religions:** Roman Catholic, Protestant
**Monetary unit(s):** 1 pound (punt) = 100
pence

**IRELAND, Republic of,** or Eire, independent country in the British Isles occupying all of the island of Ireland except the NE (see IRELAND, NORTHERN).

**Land.** The chief physical feature is the broad central limestone plain; seldom rising above 400ft, it is marked by numerous *loughs* (lakes) and large peat bogs. Rimming the plain are groups of hills and mountains, the most extensive being the Wicklow Mts in the E. The country's highest peak, Carrantuohill (3,414ft), rises in Macgillycuddy's Reeks in the SW near the beautiful Lakes of Killarney. The chief river is the Shannon (240mi), longest in the British Isles; like the Erne R it is harnessed for hydroelectric power. The long Shannon estuary is one of many inlets of the much-indented W coast, which is fringed by many islands. The climate is mild and damp, with annual rainfall ranging from 30–40in in the lowlands to over 60in in the W uplands. This has helped create the lush green pastures which have made Ireland "the Emerald Isle." Rainfall and high winds are more frequent in the W and N than in the sunnier E.

**People.** In 1845 about 8.5 million people lived in Ireland. A century later, the whole island had about half that many inhabitants. This unique demographic decline resulted from the POTATO FAMINE of 1845–48 and subsequent emigration especially from the rural W. Today the population of the republic is concentrated mainly in or near the cities, the largest of which are Dublin, the capital, Cork and Limerick. The Irish are a Celtic people; since 1922 the government has encouraged the revival of the Irish language (often known as Gaelic), although English remains the principal language. About 95% of the people are Roman Catholics; about 5% are Protestants, of whom the largest denomination is the Church of Ireland.

**Economy.** It is based mainly on small mixed farms rearing cattle or engaged in dairying (especially in the S), with barley, wheat, oats, potatoes, turnips and sugar beets as the chief arable crops. Ireland is relatively poor in minerals, but some coal is mined, along with recently-discovered deposits of lead, zinc, copper and silver. Peat from the bogs is a valuable fuel, used for home heating and electricity generation. Industries include food-processing, distilling, brewing, tobacco products, textiles, clothing and small-scale engineering. Foreign manufacturers, mainly W German and Japanese, have been encouraged to set up export-oriented plants, and tourism is important.

**History.** In the 4th century BC the GAELS evolved a Celtic civilization which in its full flowering, after St. PATRICK introduced Christianity in the 5th century, produced superb works of art (see BOOK OF KELLS) and sent religious and cultural missionaries to the rest of Europe (see CAROLINGIAN REVIVAL). It was severely damaged by the VIKINGS in the 9th and 10th centuries, until their defeat by BRIAN BORU in 1041. In 1166 the Anglo-Normans invaded Ireland and thereafter the English tried constantly to assert their authority over the native Irish and the settlers, who quickly became assimilated with them. The Tudors and Stuarts promoted English and Scottish settlement (see ULSTER), and tried to anglicize the country in wars constantly embittered by religious differences, until Oliver CROMWELL's pacification. Roman Catholic gentry fled when Protestant ascendency was confirmed by WILLIAM III's victory at the Boyne (1690). In the Rebellion of 1798 the Irish peasantry, roused by such patriots as Wolfe TONE, rebelled, but were ruthlessly suppressed. The Act of Union (1801) ended parliamentary independence from England; nevertheless, despite the POTATO FAMINE and FENIAN violence, a measure of independence by constitutional means was slowly attained through agitation for Catholic Emancipation and the emergence of leaders like Daniel O'CONNELL and C. S. PARNELL. One result was the cultural CELTIC REVIVAL of the 1890s. The inability of British governments to implement HOME RULE led to the bitter EASTER RISING (1916), and the armed struggle after WWI resulted in Britain's grant of dominion status to the IRISH FREE STATE (1921), but the civil war was continued on a terrorist basis by the IRISH REPUBLICAN ARMY until 1923. Eamonn DE VALERA, in power from 1932, broke with the British Crown and renamed the country Eire (1937). In 1949 it left the British Commonwealth as the Republic of Ireland. In the 1960s and 1970s the six counties of Ulster which remained part of the UK were the scene of renewed IRA terrorism. In 1973 Ireland joined the EEC.

**IRISH FREE STATE,** the forerunner of the Republic of IRELAND, constituted by the Irish Free State (Agreement) Act, 1922, as a British dominion under a governor general, representing the monarch. The first president of the executive council

(1922–32) was W. T. Cosgrave.

**IRISH LITERATURE.** See GAELIC LITERATURE.

**IRISH REPUBLICAN ARMY (IRA),** illegal revolutionary force operating in Ireland. The IRA evolved from militant remnants of the Irish Volunteers, who planned and fought the Easter Rising (1916). Refusing to accept the separation of Northern Ireland, it became a secret terrorist organization responsible for bombings and raids on both sides of the border. Loss of popular support because of its violence and pro-German activities in WWII, and strong repressive action by the government reduced its role until the 1960s.

In 1969 the IRA split into the anti-terrorist "officials" and the terrorist "Provisionals," who rely on Irish-American financial aid. The Provisionals then launched a campaign of indiscriminate bombings and assassinations in Northern Ireland and in England. IRA terrorists were responsible for the murder of Lord Mountbatten in 1979. Imprisoned IRA gunmen resorted to hunger strikes, sometimes fatal, to gain attention for their cause in 1981.

**IRISH SETTER,** an exuberant red working dog, oldest of the setter family. It has a narrow head, long feathery body and tail. An elegant and gentle dog, it is used extensively as a game dog and retriever in both England and the US.

**IRISH TERRIER,** a red or red-gold dog of about 0.45m (18in) descended from the ancient terrier-type known as Madadh. Though popular as a pet, it is a working strain, used for flushing and killing vermin.

**IRISH WOLFHOUND,** a dog originally used, as its name suggests, for wolf or elk-hunting. The dogs are at least 790mm (31in) high and weigh a minimum of 55kg (120lb). They have a rough hard coat, gray or brown in color.

**IRON AGE,** the stage of man's material cultural development, following the STONE AGE and BRONZE AGE, during which iron is generally used for weapons and tools. Though used ornamentally as early as 4000 BC in Egypt and Mesopotamia, iron's difficulty of working precluded its general use until efficient techniques were developed in Armenia, c1500 BC. By c500 BC the use of iron was dominant throughout the known world, and by c300 BC the Chinese were using cast iron. Some cultures, as those in America and Australia, are said never to have had an iron age.

**IRONCLADS,** the first armored warships, wooden-hulled ships with iron plate armor, developed by the French and British in the CRIMEAN WAR. The first engagement between ironclads came in the US Civil War, involving the famous MONITOR. Iron-hulled ships superseded ironclads in the 1890s.

**IRON CURTAIN,** term for the self-imposed exclusion of the communist countries, especially during the Stalinist era. The term was popularized by Sir Winston CHURCHILL in a speech at Fulton, Mo., on March 5, 1946.

**IRON (Fe),** silvery-gray, soft, ferromagnetic (see MAGNETISM) metal in Group VIII of the PERIODIC TABLE; a TRANSITION ELEMENT. Metallic iron is the main constituent of the earth's core (see EARTH), but is rare in the crust; it is found in meteorites (see METEORS). Combined iron is found as HEMATITE, MAGNETITE, LIMONITE, SIDERITE, GEOTHITE, TACONITE, CHROMITE and PYRITE. It is extracted by smelting oxide ores in a BLAST FURNACE to produce PIG IRON which may be refined to produce CAST IRON or WROUGHT IRON, or converted to STEEL in the OPEN-HEARTH PROCESS or the BESSEMER PROCESS. Many other iron ALLOYS are used for particular applications. Pure iron is very little used; it is chemically reactive, and oxidizes to RUST in moist air. It has four allotropes (see ALLOTROPY). The stable oxidation states of iron are $+2$ (ferrous), and $+3$ (ferric), though $+4$ and $+6$ states are known. The ferrous ion ($Fe^{2+}$) is pale green in aqueous solution; it is a mild GEOTHITE, TACONITE, CHROMITE and PYRITE. It **Iron(II) sulfate** ($FeSO_4 7H_2O$), or **green vitriol,** or **copperas,** green crystalline solid, made by treating iron ore with sulfuric acid, used in tanning, in medicine to treat iron deficiency, and to make ink, fertilizers, pesticides and other iron compounds, mp 64°C. The ferric ion ($Fe^{3+}$) is yellow in aqueous solution; it resembles the ALUMINUM ion, being acidic and forming stable LIGAND complexes, especially with CYANIDES (see PRUSSIAN BLUE). **Iron(III) oxide** ($Fe_2O_3$), red-brown powder used as a pigment and as jewelers' rouge (see ABRASIVES); occurs naturally as HEMATITE; mp 1565°C. (See also ALUM; SANDWICH COMPOUNDS.) In the human body, iron is a constituent of HEMOGLOBIN and the CYTOCHROMES. Iron deficiency causes ANEMIA. AW 55.8, mp 1535°C, bp 2750°C, sg 7.874 (20°C).

**IRON GATE,** at 2,600ft the deepest gorge in Europe, 2mi long. It lies on the Danube R at the Romania-Yugoslavia border; the two countries run a joint hydroelectric project in the gorge.

**IROQUOIAN,** family of languages spoken by North American Indians chiefly in what

now N N.Y. The languages of the first
ve confederated IROQUOIS tribes and
Wyandot, the Huron language, are the most
osely related. The two southern languages
e Tuscarora and Cherokee.

ROQUOIS, North American Indian tribes
the IROQUOIAN linguistic family, members
the Iroquois League. This political union
the Mohawk, Oneida, Onondaga,
ayuga and Seneca tribes was founded in
e 16th century by the Onondaga chief
AWATHA and Dekanawida, formerly a
uron. Villages and tribes were sometimes
lopted into the League, as with the
uscarora in 1722. Hunters and farmers,
e Iroquois tribes lived in stockaded
llages of *longhouses*; families were
atrilineal, and belonged to an intertribal
an system. In the 1600s they were
upplied with firearms and metal weapons
y the Dutch, and became supreme in the
E. During the FRENCH AND INDIAN WARS
e Iroquois supported the British, but the
ague split over the REVOLUTIONARY WAR.

RAWADDY RIVER, main waterway of
urma, formed by the confluence of the
Iali and Nmai rivers. It flows S for about
350mi to empty into the Bay of Bengal. Its
lta is one of the world's richest
ce-growing areas.

REDENTISM (from *Italia irredenta*:
nredeemed Italy), Italian nationalist
ovement begun after unification (1866) to
cquire Italian-speaking lands still under
reign rule, an end achieved after WWI.
ne term is now used for any movement
tempting to free territory from foreign
ntrol.

RRIGATION, artificial application of
ater to soil to promote plant growth.
rigation is vital for agricultural land with
adequate rainfall. The practice dates back
least to the canals and reservoirs of
ncient Egypt. Today over 320 million acres
farmland throughout the world are
rigated, notably in the US, India,
akistan, China, Australia, Egypt and the
SSR. There are three main irrigation
chniques: **surface irrigation**, in which the
il surface is moistened or flooded by water
owing through furrows or tubes; **sprinkler
rigation**, in which water is sprayed on the
nd from above; and **subirrigation**, in which
nderground pipes supply water to roots.
ne amount of water needed for a
articular project is called the **duty of water**,
pressed as the number of acres irrigated
y 1cu ft of water per second.

TYSH RIVER, main tributary of the Ob
in W central Asia. Rising in glaciers of
e Altai Mts of China, it flows 2,760mi W
Lake Zaisan, then NW to Siberia.

IRVING, John Winslow (1942–    ), US
novelist, author of the best-sellers *The
World According to-Garp* (1978) and *The
Hotel New Hampshire* (1981). His writing
stresses the passionate, comic and grotesque
aspects of life.

IRVING, Sir Henry (1838–1905), stage
name of John Henry Brodribb, greatest
British actor and actor-manager of his day.
At the Lyceum Theater, London,
1878–1902, he staged spectacular Shakespeare productions, often with Ellen TERRY
as his leading lady.

IRVING, Washington (1783–1859), first
US writer to achieve international acclaim.
Born in N.Y., he became a casual writer and
publisher; he went to Europe in 1815 on
business and remained there until 1832. His
most famous stories, *Rip Van Winkle* and
*The Legend of Sleepy Hollow*, appeared in
*The Sketch Book of Geoffrey Crayon*
(1820). None of his later works approached
the success of this collection. He served as
minister to Spain 1842–46, but spent the
rest of his life at Tarrytown, N.Y., near the
setting of many of his tales.

ISAAC, in the Old Testament, second of the
Hebrew patriarchs. Son of Abraham and
Sarah, he was spared at the last moment
from being sacrificed as proof of his father's
faith. He married REBECCA and fathered
ESAU and JACOB, who cheated Esau out of
Isaac's last blessing.

ISABELLA, name of two queens of Spain.
**Isabella I** (1451–1504), was queen of
Castile from 1474 and of Aragon from 1481
by marriage to the future Ferdinand II of
Aragon (1469). The marriage unified
Christian Spain; royal power was strengthened and the INQUISITION reestablished,
Isabella supporting its call for the expulsion
of Spanish Jews. She financed COLUMBUS'
expedition in 1492. She helped direct the
conquest of Moorish Granada. **Isabella II**
(1830–1904), was queen of Spain 1833–68,
under a regency until 1843. Her succession
was disputed by the Carlists, provoking civil
war 1833–39; after the regency was ended
by a revolt her personal rule proved
arbitrary and ineffectual. Promiscuous and
irresponsible, she was ousted in 1868 and
abdicated in 1870.

ISAIAH, great Hebrew prophet of the 8th
century BC, for whom the Old Testament
Book of Isaiah is named; probably only the
first 36 chapters represent his teachings, the
remainder (often known as Deutero—and
Trito—Isaiah) being additions by his
followers. Isaiah condemns the decadence
of Judah, foretelling coming disaster; he
warns against trusting in foreign alliances
rather than in God and heralds the

Messiah.

**ISHERWOOD, Christopher William Bradshaw** (1904–    ), English-born novelist and playwright who settled in the US in 1939. His best-known novels are *Mr. Norris Changes Trains* (1935) and *Goodbye to Berlin* (1939), set in the decaying Germany of the 1930s, later adapted by others into plays and films (*I Am a Camera* and *Cabaret*). He collaborated with W. H. AUDEN on three plays, the best-known being *The Ascent of F-6* (1936).

**ISIS,** in ancient Egyptian mythology the dominant mother goddess, protectress of living and dead. Sister and wife of OSIRIS, she temporarily restored him to life after his murder and dismembering by SET, and so conceived HORUS. Her cult spread from Lower Egypt throughout the Roman world as one of the MYSTERIES.

**ISLAM** (Arabic: Submission to God), major world religion, founded by Mohammed in the 7th century AD; a monotheistic faith, it incorporates elements of Judaic and Christian belief. Today there are more than 400 million MUSLIMS ("ones who submit"), mainly in the Arab countries and SW Asia, and in N and E Africa, Turkey, Iran, Afghanistan, Pakistan, India, SE Asia and the USSR. The Prophet MOHAMMED was a merchant of Mecca in the early 7th century; on his journeys he came into contact with Jews and Christians. Inspired by a vision of the archangel Gabriel, he began to preach the worship of the one true God (Arabic: *Allah*), and to denounce idolatry. In his lifetime Mecca was converted to Islam. In the century after his death (632 AD) Muslim armies forged an Arab Empire extending from Spain to India.

**Teachings.** The KORAN, the holy book of Islam, sets forth the fundamental tenets of Islam as revealed by God to Mohammed. These include the five basic duties of Muslims and also rules for their social and moral behavior. Muslims also study the prophet's teachings, or *Sunna,* collected in the *Hadith* ("traditions"). A legal system, the *Shari'a,* based on the Koran and the Sunna, has been the law of many Muslim countries.

**Worship.** Public worship takes place in MOSQUES; these are often highly decorated in abstract patterns, because representational art is forbidden as idolatrous. (See ISLAMIC ART AND ARCHITECTURE.) Before entering a mosque, Muslims must ritually cleanse themselves. Special services are held at midday on Friday. Devout Muslims must pray five times daily, facing in the direction of Mecca. Islam has no priests as such; worship is led by a lay leader, the *imam.* A *muezzin* calls the faithful to prayer from a rooftop or MINARET. Other leaders in Muslim communities include the *ulema,* experts on the *Shari'a,* who give guidance and may even decide legal disputes.

**ISLAMABAD,** newly-built capital of Pakistan, 8mi NE of Rawalpindi. Begun in 1961, it is largely a governmental and administrative center, but also houses educational, scientific and cultural institutions. Pop 250,000.

**ISLAMIC ART AND ARCHITECTURE,** art that grew out of the Islamic way of life. Because there was no strong tradition of Arab art, it adapted the Byzantine, Sassanian and Coptic styles of Muslim-dominated lands. Arab influence added a sense of visual rhythm and an interest in astronomy and mathematics. Interpretations of the Prophet's sayings, however, forbade portrayals of people or animals either in religious art or elsewhere. Figures appeared in the book illustration and miniature work at which Persian and Indian artists excelled, and (in Persia only) in the decoration of some mosques. In general, however, designs relied on abstract and mathematical forms, as well as the calligraphic rendering of Koranic texts, often every available piece of a building may be so decorated.

Early examples of Islamic architecture are the KAABA and the Dome of the Rock in Jerusalem. The dominant style of MOSQUE, with a minaret tower, was introduced under the Omayyad dynasty. A characteristic feature of Islamic buildings is the arch, in horseshoe, trefoil and zigzag forms. The greatest Muslim mausoleum is the TA MAHAL. The Moorish ALHAMBRA in Granada, Spain, is the most famous palace in the Islamic style. In craftwork there is also a distinctive Islamic tradition; as well as its famous rugs and textiles, the Islamic world developed beautiful pottery, including luster-glazed ceramics, and metalwork inventing DAMASCENING.

**ISLE ROYALE NATIONAL PARK,** wildlife reserve, established in 1940, comprising more than 100 islands in NW Lake Superior, N Mich. Isle Royale itself (229sq mi) is the site of pre-Columbian Indian copper mines; its wildlife include moose, timber wolves and diverse bird life.

**ISMAILIS,** Muslim SHI'ITE sect sometimes known as Seveners because they venerate the religious leader Ismail (d. 760) as the seventh IMAM. Among branches of the Ismaili faith were the ASSASSIN sects of Iran and Syria. The Ismaili spiritual leader today is the Harvard-educated AGA KHAN IV.

**ISOLATIONISM,** national policy of avoiding entanglement in foreign affairs, a recurrent phenomenon in US history. In 1823 the MONROE DOCTRINE tried to exclude European powers from the Americas. The US entered WWI reluctantly, stayed out of the League of Nations it helped create and entered WWII only when attacked. Thereafter it joined the UN and international defense pacts (NATO, SEATO) and played an active role in international affairs. British policy was essentially isolationist in the period between the wars.

**ISOMORPHISM,** the formation by different compounds or MINERALS of CRYSTALS having closely similar external forms and lattice structure. Isomorphous compounds have similar chemical composition—ions of similar size, charge, and ionization potential being substituted for each other—and form mixed crystals. Cations are usually involved in the interchange, although anions may also replace each other. A mineral series showing a continuous isomorphous change between end members constitutes a *solid solution* as in the plagioclase feldspars where sodium and calcium are the cations involved.

**ISOTOPES,** ATOMS of a chemical ELEMENT which have the same number of PROTONS in the nucleus, but different numbers of NEUTRONS, i.e., having the same atomic number but different MASS NUMBER. Isotopes of an element have identical chemical and physical properties (except those determined by atomic mass). Most elements have several stable isotopes, being found in nature as mixtures. The natural proportions of the isotopes are expressed in the form of an **abundance ratio**. Because some isotopes have particular properties (e.g., 0.015% of HYDROGEN atoms have two neutrons and combine with oxygen to form HEAVY WATER, used in NUCLEAR REACTORS), mass-dependent methods of separating these out have been devised. These include MASS SPECTROSCOPY, DIFFUSION, DISTILLATION and ELECTROLYSIS. A few elements have natural radioactive isotopes (RADIOISOTOPES) and others of these can be made by exposing stable isotopes to RADIATION in a reactor. These are widely used therapeutically and industrially; their radiation may be employed directly, or the way in which it is scattered or absorbed by objects can be measured. They are useful as tracers of a process, since they may be detected in very small amounts and behave virtually identically to other atoms of the same element. They may also be used to

"label" particular atoms in complex molecules, in attempts to work out chemical reaction mechanisms.

**Official name:** State of Israel
**Capital:** Jerusalem
**Area:** 7,848sq mi
**Population:** 3,855,000
**Languages:** Hebrew, Arabic
**Religions:** Judaism, Muslim, Christian
**Monetary unit(s):** 1 shekel = 100 new agorot

**ISRAEL,** Jewish republic on the E extremity of the Mediterranean. Founded in 1948, it is surrounded on its landward sides by Arab countries who, with the exception of Egypt, are largely hostile. Although small in itself Israel captured large territories from Egypt, Syria and Jordan in various wars including the Golan Heights, WEST BANK of the Jordan R., GAZA STRIP, Sinai Desert, from which Israel began to withdraw in 1979. The other territories are the subject of continual international controversy.

**Land.** Israel has a long straight Mediterranean coastline, and to the S access to the Red Sea from the port of Elath through the Gulf of Aqaba. There are three main regions, the mountainous but fertile Galilee area in the N, the more fertile coastal plain in the W and in the S the Negev Desert, barren but with important mineral resources. In the E a depression contains the Huleh Valley, Sea of Galilee, Jordan R., and Dead Sea. Summers are hot and dry, winters mild; rainfall (mainly in winter, or Nov.–April) varies from 40in in the N to almost nil in the S. Because much of Israel's potential farmland lacks water supplies a vast irrigation program has been put into operation; huge areas of formerly barren land are now productive. Available water resources, however, are already almost fully exploited.

**People.** About 85% of Israelis are Jews, and most of these are immigrants, notably from central and E Europe, the Middle East, N Africa and the USSR. Minorities include Christian and Muslim Arabs, DRUSES, CIRCASSIANS and SAMARITANS. The official language is HEBREW, but Arabic is also important and English, French, German and Yiddish are widely spoken. Elementary schooling is free and compulsory and there are seven institutions of higher learning. Most of the population is urban, living mostly in Tel Aviv, Jaffa, Haifa and Jerusalem. There are 230 *kibbutzim*, collective agricultural settlements, and 384 *moshavim*, cooperative farming villages.

**Economy.** Heavy defense expenditure, immigration and limited natural resources have produced an unstable economy; assistance has come from American aid, German reparation and Jews abroad. Many immigrants bring technical and administrative skills. Land reclamation and irrigation have nearly trebled the cultivated area since 1955 and the country produces most of its own food. Major crops include citrus fruit, grains, olives, melons, grapes. Mineral resources include gypsum, natural gas, oil and phosphates; potash, magnesium and bromine come from the Dead Sea. Light industry is developing, and manufactures include chemicals, textiles and paper. Citrus fruits, diamonds, chemicals and textiles are major exports. Tourism is a major industry. Because of heavy defense spending and reliance on imported oil, Israel suffers from severe payments deficits and one of the world's highest inflation rates, exceeding 100% per year.

**History.** (For the early history of the Jews in Palestine see JEWS; PALESTINE.) In 1947 the UN voted to divide Palestine (then under British mandate) into Jewish and Arab states. After the subsequent British withdrawal, Palestine Arabs and Arab troops from neighboring countries immediately tried to eradicate Israel by force, but the Israelis defeated them, capturing almost all Palestine (see ARAB-ISRAELI WARS). Arab refugees, settled in S Lebanon, the West Bank, and Gaza Strip in UN-administered camps, are a continuing social and political problem; also, refugee camps have proved a fruitful recruiting area and cover for Palestinian guerrilla groups. When Egypt nationalized the SUEZ CANAL in 1956 it closed it to Israeli shipping; Israeli troops then overran Gaza and Sinai, winning the right of passage from Elath to the Red Sea. In the Six-Day War (1967) Israel acquired large tracts of its neighbors' territories including the West Bank and East Jerusalem; these it refused to return without a firm peace settlement. It lost some of these in the Yom Kippur War (1973). Relations with Egypt improved; in 1978 the two countries reached the so-called CAMP DAVID AGREEMENT and Israel began returning the Sinai to Egypt. Subsequent meetings between Egypt and Israel on Palestinian autonomy have met with little success, however, partly because of new West Bank settlements established by Jewish extremists. In 1978 and 1981 Israeli troops invaded S Lebanon in retaliation for Palestinian attacks in Israel, and Israeli bombers destroyed an alleged atomic bomb plant in Iraq in 1981.

**ISRAEL, Kingdom of,** Hebrew kingdom, first as united under Saul, David and Solomon c1020 BC–922 BC, and then the breakaway state in the N founded by JEROBOAM I in the territory of the 10 tribes. In 722 BC this was overrun by the Assyrians; the tribes were apparently killed, enslaved or scattered. (See also TWELVE TRIBES OF ISRAEL.)

**ISTANBUL,** largest city in Turkey, divided by the Bosporus. Until 1930 its official name was Constantinople, of which Istanbul was originally a contraction. Built on the site of a former Greek town, BYZANTIUM, in 330 AD by CONSTANTINE I, it became the capital of the BYZANTINE EMPIRE; it reached its cultural height under JUSTINIAN I in the 6th century. The city was taken and sacked by the Fourth Crusade in 1204; after years of decay it was taken by the Ottoman Turks in 1453, and was rebuilt as the Turkish capital, which it remained until 1923 when the capital was moved to Ankara. It is still the economic and cultural heart of Turkey, a port, transport hub and manufacturing center. Pop 2,853,539.

**ISTRIA,** mountainous peninsula in NW Yugoslavia, on the N Adriatic Sea. It became part of Yugoslavia in 1947. Its population's chief occupations are fruit growing, fishing and mining.

**ITALIAN,** one of the ROMANCE LANGUAGES, spoken in Italy and in parts of Switzerland, France and Yugoslavia. It derives from colloquial LATIN. The Tuscan dialect established as a literary language by Dante, Petrarch and Boccaccio became the foundation of modern Italian. Since the Renaissance, words from other Romance languages have been added. There are regional dialects.

**ITALO-ETHIOPIAN WAR** (1935–36), Fascist Italy's conquest of Ethiopia, launched from Italian-held Eritrea and Somalia. Refusing to accept the League of Nations proposals for settling border disputes, Mussolini used planes, guns and poison gas to overwhelm the ill-equipped Ethiopians, and to forge a new empire. Too weak to halt aggression, the League merely voted economic sanctions against Italy, which simply left the League.

**ITALY,** republic in S Europe comprising a

ong, narrow peninsula and nearby Sicily, Sardinia and smaller Mediterranean islands. Italy is a land of great natural beauty, with an immensely rich historical and artistic heritage. It made a phenomenal economic recovery after the devastation suffered during WWII.

Italy is predominantly mountainous. In the N is the great curve of the Alps, while the Apennine chain forms the peninsula's spine. Between the two lies the N plain containing the Po R—Italy's largest natural waterway, flowing E to the Adriatic Sea. The Arno and Tiber flow W from the Apennines, respectively to the Ligurian and Tyrrhenian seas. Except in the cooler, wetter mountains, summers are hot and dry, winters mild and rainy. Forest and scrub cover much of the mountains; the lowlands are largely cultivated.

**People.** People of short, dark, Mediterranean stock predominate in the S; in the N live taller, fair-haired peoples of Celtic and Alpine origin. Italy is densely populated, with the highest concentrations in the industrial cities of the N, the Po Valley, Rome and Naples. About half the population is urban. Rural poor from the underdeveloped S migrate to the N and abroad. Italian is the official language, but French and German are spoken respectively in the extreme NW and N. Over 90% of Italians profess Roman Catholicism. Education is free and compulsory for ages 6-14 and more than 40 cities and towns have university centers.

**Economy.** Foreign aid and founder membership of the European Common Market vastly boosted Italy's postwar economy before the 1973-74 oil crisis damaged it. Increased industrial output (steel, chemicals, automobiles, typewriters, machinery, textiles and shoes) enriched the N, but a faltering agriculture kept the S poor. The main farm products are grapes, citrus fruits, olives, grains, vegetables and cattle. Mineral resources are limited, but Italy has hydroelectric power, natural gas and oil. There are also a few nuclear power stations. Tourism helps the trade balance. Italy has an advanced system of roads and railroads.

**History.** The Romans—a Latin people of central Italy—held most of the peninsula by 200 BC, absorbing the ETRUSCAN CIVILIZATION in the N and Greek colonies dating from the 8th century BC) in the S. (See ROME, ANCIENT.) In the 5th–6th centuries AD, barbarian tribes (VISIGOTHS, OSTROGOTHS and LOMBARDS) overran Italy, forming Germanic kingdoms. These kingdoms were disputed by the Byzantine Empire, whose lands in Italy became the core of the PAPAL STATES. Italy was to remain divided for over 1,000 years, although nominally part of Charlemagne's empire from 774 and part of the Holy Roman Empire from 962.

In the Middle Ages the S came under Norman rule (see NAPLES, KINGDOM OF). Powerful rival city-states (see GUELPHS AND GHIBELLINES) emerged in the center and N, from the late Middle Ages under the MEDICI and other dynasties. Italy pioneered the RENAISSANCE, but Spain (from the late 1400s) and Austria (from the early 1700s) controlled much of the land until the RISORGIMENTO culminated in unity and independence under Victor Emmanuel II (1861). Italy gained Eritrea, Italian Somaliland and Libya in Africa, and fought alongside the Allies in WWI. In 1922 the Fascist dictator Benito MUSSOLINI seized power, later conquering Ethiopia and siding with Nazi Germany in WWII. Defeated Italy emerged from the war as a republic shorn of its overseas colonies and firmly allied with the West.

**Official name:** Republic of Italy
**Capital:** Rome
**Area:** 116,303sq mi
**Population:** 57,040,000
**Languages:** Italian
**Religions:** Roman Catholic
**Monetary unit(s):** 1 lire=100 centesimi

**ITURBIDE, Agustín de** (1783–1824), Mexican revolutionary, emperor of Mexico 1822–23. A royalist officer, he united the revolutionaries with his Plan of Iguala (1821), which proclaimed Mexican independence. Exploiting political divisions, he became emperor of independent Mexico. But opposition to his capricious rule brought abdication, exile and (on his return) execution.

**IVAN,** name of six Russian rulers. **Ivan I Kalita** (c1304–1340), was grand prince of Moscow 1328–40. **Ivan II Krasnyi** (1326–1359), was grand prince of Moscow 1353–59. **Ivan III the Great** (1440–1505), was grand prince of Moscow 1462–1505. He paved the way for a unified Russia by annexing land, repelling the Tatars, strengthening central authority over the Church and nobility, and revising the law code. **Ivan IV the Terrible** (1530–1584), was grand prince from 1533 and the first tsar of Russia 1547–84. He annexed Siberia, consolidated control of the Volga R, and established diplomatic and trading relations with Europe. He strengthened the law and administration, but was notoriously cruel. **Ivan V** (1666–1696), was co-tsar (with Peter I) 1682–96. **Ivan VI** (1740–1764), was tsar 1740–41.

**IVANOV, Vsevolod** (1895–1963), Russian writer: Born in Siberia, he often used it as a setting for his stories. His most popular novels, *The Guerillas* (1921) and *Armored Train* (1922), treat the Russian Revolution and Civil War in epic fashion.

**IVES, Burl** (1909–   ), folk singer and actor whose records and radio show, "The Wayfaring Stranger," made him nationally famous. He gave award-winning performances in *Cat on a Hot Tin Roof* (play, 1955; film, 1959) and *The Big Country* (1958).

**IVES, Charles Edward** (1874–1954), US composer, a major 20th-century innovator. His music (mostly pre-1915) incorporated popular songs and hymn tunes, and exploits dissonance, polytonality and polymetric construction. Ignored by his contemporaries, he influenced later composers. His best-known works include *Three Places in New England* (1903–14) and the *Second (Concord) Piano Sonata* (1909–15). His *Third Symphony* (1904–11) won a 1947 Pulitzer Prize.

**IVORY,** hard white substance obtained from the tusks of ELEPHANTS, HIPPOPOTAMUSES, WALRUSES and NARWHALS. It is no more than a thickened form of dental enamel, yet carved ivory has been greatly prized—and priced—for centuries. Elephant ivory is the most sought-after, due to its greater length and finer grain; the poaching of elephants for their tusks threatens their existence in Africa. A vegetable ivory is also produced, from the nuts of the DOUM PALM.

**Official name:** Republic of Ivory Coast

**Capital:** Abidjan
**Area:** 124,502sq mi
**Population:** 8,032,000
**Languages:** French, African languages
**Religions:** Animist, Muslim, Roman Catholic
**Monetary unit(s):** 1 CFA franc=100 centimes

**IVORY COAST,** one of the most prosperous West African republics, located on the N coast of the Gulf of Guinea and bordering Liberia, Guinea, Mali, Upper Volta and Ghana.

One-third of the country is covered by dense rain forest, with a grassy and wooded plateau to the N and mountains to the NW. The climate is hot and rainy in the S, drier and cooler in the N. Wildlife includes African big game animals.

**People.** There are some 60 tribal groups and about 15,000 foreigners—mainly French. Over 20% of the population is urban. Tribal languages and animist faiths predominate. Some two-fifths of the population is aged under 15, and spending on basic education is relatively high. There is a university at Abidjan.

**Economy.** Farming, forestry and fisheries provide most of the gross national product. Major cash crops are cotton, coffee and cocoa. Palm-oil, pineapples and bananas are also exported, as are hardwoods including mahogany, iroko, satinwood and teak. Diamonds and manganese are mined. An expanding manufacturing industry produces palm-oil, instant coffee, fruit juices and textiles. Trade is chiefly with European Common Market countries and the US. Exports usually exceed imports in value.

**History.** In the 16th century the Portuguese traded in slaves and ivory along the coast. In the 18th century Ashanti peoples entered the region, while French trade and missionary activity increased in the E. France began systematic occupation in 1870, declaring a protectorate in 1893. A railroad built in 1903 made the Ivory Coast potentially the most prosperous colony in FRENCH WEST AFRICA. In 1946 Félix HOUPHOUET-BOIGNY founded an all-African political party. He became president of the Ivory Coast upon independence (1960). His government's policies encouraged foreign investment, exploited natural resources and raised living standards.

**IWO JIMA,** Japanese island in the NW Pacific, scene of a fierce battle in WWII Largest of the Volcano Islands (about 8sq mi), it was annexed by Japan in 1891 and captured by US marines in Feb.–March 1945 at the cost of over 21,000 US

casualties. US administration ended in 1968.

**IWW.** See INDUSTRIAL WORKERS OF THE WORLD.

**IZMIR** (formerly Smyrna), city in W Turkey on the Gulf of Izmir, capital of Izmir province. Founded by the Greeks contemporaneously with Troy; it was refounded by Alexander the Great, and became successively part of the Roman, Byzantine and Ottoman empires. During the Roman Empire, it was the site of an important school of medicine and a library. Turkey's third-largest city and chief Asian port, it exports figs, raisins, olives, wheat, opium, tobacco, carpets and silk. Pop 753,442.

# J

10th letter of the English alphabet, a variant of the letter *i*, from which it became formally distinguished with the advent of printing. It has a *y* sound in most European languages but French influence has given it a *dzh* sound in modern English.

**JACKALS,** carnivorous mammals closely related to DOGS and wolves. The four species are distributed throughout Africa and S Asia. All are extreme opportunists—although often considered to be primarily scavengers, they will also hunt and kill birds, hares, mice and insects. Small packs may be formed temporarily, but they are usually solitary animals.

**JACK RABBITS,** true HARES of the genus *Lepus.* All seven species are found in Central and W North America. Jack rabbits have enormously large ears functional in body temperature control. Found in open, comparatively arid plains they actually flourish in drought-stricken, overgrazed areas. Among the most abundant of American LAGOMORPHA, they constitute a considerable pest in agricultural areas.

**JACKSON,** capital city of Miss. and a seat of Hinds Co., on Pearl R. It was devastated during the Civil War, but is now a major manufacturing and transport center. Site of several colleges, it holds an annual Arts Festival. Pop 153,968.

**JACKSON, Andrew** (1767–1845), seventh president of the US. The first from W of the Alleghenies, he was a self-made statesman championing the common man against monopoly and privilege.

Born in a log cabin in the Waxhaw settlement, S.C., Jackson had a minimal education; he joined the militia at 13 and was briefly captured by the British in 1781. He decided to study law, was admitted to the N.C. bar in 1787 and began his political career in 1796 as a member of the Tenn. constitutional convention. He became the first congressman from Tenn. 1796–97, senator from Tenn. 1797–98 and a superior court judge in Nashville 1798–1804. In the WAR OF 1812 he became a national hero as commander of the Tenn. militia; at the Battle of Horseshoe Bend he forced the Creek Indians to yield 23 million acres, opening much of the South for settlement. In 1815 he led a decisive victory over the British at the battle of NEW ORLEANS. Jackson's rough personality and leadership earned him the epithet "Old Hickory." As commander of the US army in the South he campaigned against the SEMINOLE Indians, entering and raiding Spanish-owned Florida; this accelerated the sale of Florida to the US (1819). Military governor of the Florida Territory in 1821, he was reelected to the US Senate from Tenn. in 1823. A presidential candidate in 1824, Jackson received the most electoral votes but no overall majority, and the House of Representatives chose runner-up John Quincy Adams. Jackson considered this a "corrupt bargain"; bitter personal attacks disfigured the campaign for the 1828 election, which Jackson resoundingly won.

Inaugurated in 1829, he attempted to root out corruption in the bureaucracy by dismissing over 2,000 government employees and appointing his political supporters in their place; he thus created the SPOILS SYSTEM. He also built up a KITCHEN CABINET of personal advisers. Opposition to his powerful executive control eventually produced the Whig Party, revitalizing the two-party system. In 1832 Jackson vetoed a bill to recharter the BANK OF THE UNITED

STATES, denouncing the bank as an unconstitutional monopoly. Making the bank a presidential campaign issue, Jackson easily defeated Henry CLAY and won reelection in 1832. Later that year Jackson prepared to send troops to S.C. to prevent secession, after it had rejected federal tariff laws. The president paid off the national debt in 1835 and his SPECIE CIRCULAR (1836) helped halt land speculation. In 1837 Jackson retired to the Hermitage, his estate near Nashville. He had helped found the modern Democratic Party, strengthened respect for democratic government, and established the role of the president as a popular leader.

**JACKSON, Glenda** (1936–    ), British actress, acclaimed for her performances in *Marat/Sade* (Broadway, 1966; film, 1967) and the film *Sunday, Bloody Sunday* (1971). She won Academy Awards for her portrayals in *Women in Love* (1970) and *A Touch of Class* (1973).

**JACKSON, Helen (Maria) Hunt** (1831–1885), US author who publicized the mistreatment of Indians. *A Century of Dishonor* (1881) condemned governmental malpractice; the novel *Ramona* (1884) described the plight of California's mission Indians.

**JACKSON, Henry Martin** (1912–    ), US political leader, Democratic senator from Washington from 1952; he was a congressman 1940–52. Chairman of the committee on energy and natural resources, as ranking Democrat on the armed forces committee he became a major spokesman on national defense issues. In foreign affairs, he was a leading advocate of the US interventionist policy in Vietnam and was an articulate ally of Israel. In 1972 he sought Democratic presidential nomination.

**JACKSON, Jesse Louis** (1941–    ), US clergyman and Chicago-based black activist who directed Operation Breadbasket (1968) and founded People United to Save Humanity (PUSH), organizations set up to improve the economic and educational standards of blacks in the US.

**JACKSON, Mahalia** (1911–1972), US black gospel singer with a powerful and expressive contralto voice; her concerts and recordings gained worldwide recognition for Negro religious music. In the 1960s she was active in the civil rights movement.

**JACKSON, Reggie** (1946–    ), US baseball player. Known as "Mr. October" for his World Series heroics, he led the Oakland As and the N.Y. Yankees to a total of four World Series championships. In 1977, with the Yankees, he hit a record three homeruns in one Series game and five in the entire Series.

**JACKSON, Robert Houghwout** (1892–1954), US Supreme Court justice from 1941, chief US prosecutor in the NUREMBERG TRIALS. A supporter of the NEW DEAL, he served as solicitor general 1938–40 and attorney general 1940–41.

**JACKSON, Shirley** (1919–1965), US author. Her best-known works, such as *The Haunting of Hill House* (1959) and the short story *The Lottery* (1948), blend Gothic horror with psychological insight. Autobiographical works such as *Raising Demons* (1957) are in a contrastingly humorous vein.

**JACKSON, Thomas Jonathan "Stonewall"** (1824–1863), brilliant Confederate general, one of America's greatest commanders. After service in the MEXICAN WAR he was given command of a regiment at the outbreak of the Civil War. As a brigadier-general at the First Battle of BULL RUN, 1861, he was nicknamed "Stonewall" for his stand against Union troops. After his bold tactics in the 1862 Shenandoah Valley campaign he fought brilliantly at the battles of Richmond, the Seven Days' Battles, Cedar Mt, the Second Battle of Bull Run, Antietam and Fredericksburg. At CHANCELLORSVILLE he was accidentally mortally wounded by his own troops.

**JACKSON, William Henry** (1843–1942), US photographer and painter, known for his post-Civil War documentation of the scenery and historic events of the Wild West. His photos of Yellowstone for the US Geological Survey led to its being named the first national park. He worked as a painter after 1924.

**JACOB**, in the Old Testament, son of ISAAC and REBECCA, progenitor of the Israelites. He fled after tricking his elder brother Esau out of his birthright; he settled in Mesopotamia, where he married, then returned to Canaan. In a vision he wrestled with and overcame an angel, and was honored with the name Israel. In a time of famine he migrated to Egypt, where he died, after a period of staying with his favorite son JOSEPH.

**JACOBINS**, powerful political clubs during the FRENCH REVOLUTION, named for the former Jacobin (Dominican) convent where the leaders met. Originally middle-class, they became increasingly radical advocates of terrorism. After they seized power in 1793 the extremists, led by ROBESPIERRE instituted the REIGN OF TERROR. In the THERMIDOR reaction the clubs were suppressed, to revive under the Directory and be finally put down by NAPOLEON.

**JACOBITE CHURCH,** or Syrian Orthodox Church, Christian church of Syria, India and Iraq. One of the MONOPHYSITE CHURCHES, it was founded in the 6th century Syria by Jacobus Baradaeus. Its head is the patriarch of Antioch, who now resides at Damascus, and its ritual language is Syriac. An offshoot of the Jacobites is the Syrian Catholic Church, one of the UNIATE CHURCHES.

**JACOBITES,** supporters of that branch of the House of Stuart exiled by the GLORIOUS REVOLUTION of 1688; a large number were Highland Scots. Jacobites sought to regain the English throne for JAMES II and his descendants, notably James Edward Stuart (1699–1766), "The Old Pretender," and CHARLES EDWARD STUART, "Bonnie Prince Charlie." After rebellions in 1715, 1719 and 1745 they were effectively crushed at the battle of CULLODEN MOOR (1746).

**JACOBS, Hirsch** (1904–1970), US racehorse trainer, the most successful in US racing history. He had 3,596 wins and won more than $12 million in purses.

**JACOBSEN, Jens Peter** (1847–1885), major Danish writer, known for his early Romantic poetry and his translation of DARWIN'S works. He later turned to NATURALISM in the novels *Marie Grubbe* (1876) and *Niels Lyhne* (1880), developing a rich style despite suffering from serious tuberculosis after 1873.

**JACQUES-DALCROZE, Émile**. (1865–1950), Swiss composer and educator, best known for his invention of EURHYTHMICS as a teaching aid for musicians.

**JADE,** either of two tough, hard minerals with a compact interlocking grain structure, commonly green but also found as white, mauve, red-brown or yellow; used as a GEM stone to make carved jewelry and ornaments. Jade carving in China dates from the 1st millennium BC, but the finest examples are late 18th century AD. **Nephrite,** the commoner form of jade, is an AMPHIBOLE, a combination of tremolite and actinolite, occurring in China, the USSR, New Zealand and the western US. **Jadeite,** rarer than nephrite and prized for its more intense color and translucence, is a sodium aluminum found chiefly in upper Burma.

**JAFFA** (formerly Joppa), ancient port for Jerusalem on the Mediterranean coast of Israel. Dating from at least the 15th century BC, it was occupied by the Philistines and later by David and Solomon, changing hands among the Persians, Greeks, Syrians, and Romans. It was captured during the Crusades by Richard the Lion Heart, but was won back by the Turks. It was finally taken over by Israel in 1948 and incorporated into TEL AVIV in 1949.

**JAFFE, Rona** (1932–   ), US author. Her popular novels about the lives of contemporary collegiates and upper-middle-class women include *The Other Woman* (1972) and *Class Reunion* (1979).

**JAGUAR,** *Panthera onca,* the only true "big cat" of the American continent. The coat bears black spots arranged in rosettes on a background varying from almost white and buff, through black, where the rosettes appear only as a variation in texture. It lives in thick cover in forests or swamps and although an accomplished swimmer, hunts mostly on the ground or in trees.

**JAI ALAI,** very fast ball game, similar to SQUASH, popular in parts of the US, Cuba, Mexico and Spain, where it is called *pelota.* It is played in a three-walled court; each player has a wicker racket (*cesta*) strapped to his wrist. With this he tries to bounce a small hard rubber ball off a wall, beyond his opponent's reach.

**JAINISM,** philosophy and religion—an offshoot of HINDUISM—largely confined to India, with 2 million adherents. It was founded alongside BUDDHISM, which it resembles, in about the 6th century BC by Mahavira, an ascetic saint who taught the doctrine of *ahimsa* or non-injury to all living creatures. Jains do not believe in a creator God but see in the universe two independent eternal categories: "Life" and "Non-life" (see DUALISM), maintaining that man can reach perfection only through ascetic, charitable and monastic discipline.

**JAKARTA** (formerly Batavia), capital and largest city of Indonesia, in NW Java. It is the country's commercial, transport and industrial center, manufacturing automobiles, textiles, chemicals and iron products, and processing lumber and food. Much of Indonesia's external trade passes through the port. The city is also the administrative center and the home of the University of Indonesia. It grew out of the Dutch East India company settlement of Batavia (1614–19) and became British 1811–14. With independence in 1949 it was made national capital and renamed Djakarta, now officially spelled Jakarta. Pop 5,690,000.

**JAKOBSON, Roman** (1896–   ), Russian-born US linguist and philologist best known for his pioneering studies of the Slavic languages.

**JAMAICA,** island republic in the Caribbean.
**Land.** The body of the island is a limestone plateau with an E–W backbone of mountains and volcanic hills. The climate is

**Official name:** Jamaica
**Capital:** Kingston
**Area:** 4,244sq mi
**Population:** 2,137,300
**Language:** English
**Religions:** Protestant, Roman Catholic
**Monetary unit(s):** 1 Jamaican dollar=100 cents

tropical, with heavy rainfall.

**People.** The majority of Jamaicans are of African descent, but there are East Indians, Chinese and Europeans also. As a result of a literacy campaign in the 1970s, only about 10% of the population remains illiterate.

**Economy.** The economy is largely agricultural, relying on sugar processing for its major industry. Bauxite and gypsum mining has become important, as has tourism.

**History.** Discovered by COLUMBUS in 1494, Jamaica was a Spanish settlement until captured by the British in 1655. The original ARAWAK INDIANS had been wiped out and the British, under such governors as Sir Henry MORGAN, accelerated the importation of Negro slaves to man the sugar industry. After the full emancipation of former slaves in 1838 the sugar industry declined and poverty, unemployment and overpopulation led to serious unrest in the 19th and 20th centuries. Crop diversification and reforms improved conditions. Full internal self-government came in 1959, within the WEST INDIES FEDERATION and full independence within the British Commonwealth in 1962. Under Prime Minister Michael Manley (1972–80), the government initiated a number of social reforms and took control of mining and the sugar industry.

**JAMES,** name of two saints, both Apostles. **St. James the Greater** (d. c43 AD), son of Zebedee and brother of St. John, was killed by Herod Agrippa I. There is a famous shrine to him at SANTIAGO DE COMPOSTELA. **St. James the Less** (1st century AD) was possibly the son of Alphaeus and Mary.

**JAMES,** name of two kings of England and Scotland. **James I and VI** (1566–1625), was king of Scotland from 1567, after his mother MARY QUEEN OF SCOTS was forced to abdicate, and king of England from 1603. James gained control over the nobles who sought to dominate him in 1583. Anxious to be Elizabeth I's heir, he condoned her execution of his mother. Early popularity in England, reinforced when he escaped the GUNPOWDER PLOT, waned as James sought autocratic control over Parliament, bolstered by his belief in the DIVINE RIGHT OF KINGS. His extravagance and dubious personal life alienated many, as did the execution of Sir Walter RALEIGH, part of a pro-Spanish policy. He was, however, scholarly and in some ways progressive. He established a large Presbyterian settlement in IRELAND and encouraged the first English colonies in America. He wrote the treatise on government *Basilikon Doron* and commissioned the Authorized Version of the Bible (1611). **James II** (1633–1701), reigned 1685–88. Although able, he sought to disregard Parliament and alienated many by his attempt to introduce toleration of Roman Catholicism. It was suspected—perhaps correctly—that he intended to make it the state religion. His Dutch son-in-law William of Orange was invited to invade Britain, deposing James in the GLORIOUS REVOLUTION. James' forces were driven out of Ireland also at the battle of the BOYNE.

**JAMES, Epistle of,** 20th book of the NEW TESTAMENT, traditionally attributed to St James, kinsman of Jesus and first bishop of Jerusalem. One of the Catholic (general) Epistles, it is primarily a homily or Christian ethics.

**JAMES, Henry** (1843–1916), American born novelist and critic, brother of William JAMES. He settled in London (1876) and became a British citizen in 1915. A recurring theme in his work is the corruption of innocence, particularly as shown by the contrast between sophisticated and corrupt Europe and brash, innocent US society. His most famous works distinguished by subtle characterization and a precise, complex prose style, including *The Americans* (1877), *Daisy Miller* (1878), *The Portrait of a Lady* (1881), *The Turn of the Screw* (1898) and *The Golden Bowl* (1909).

**JAMES, Jesse Woodson** (1847–1882), US outlaw. A member of the William QUANTRILL's raiders in the Civil War, he and his brother Frank led the "James Gang" 1866–79, robbing banks and trains from Ark. to Col. and Tex. Living as an ordinary citizen in St. Joseph, Mo., he was murdered for reward by gang member Robert Ford.

**JAMES, William** (1842–1910), US philosopher and psychologist, the originator of the doctrine of PRAGMATISM, brother of Henry JAMES. His first major contribution was *The Principles of Psychology* (1890). Turning his attention to questions of religion, he published in 1902 his Gifford Lectures, *The Varieties of Religious Experience*, which has remained his best-known work.

**JAMESTOWN,** former village in SE Va. on the James R., the first permanent English settlement in North America. Founded in 1607 by colonists from the LONDON COMPANY led by John SMITH, it was named for King James I. Lord DE LA WARR reinforced it in 1610 and John ROLFE introduced tobacco cultivation in 1612. In 1619 the House of Burgesses, the first representative government of the colonies, met here. It is now part of Colonial National Historical Park.

**JANÁČEK, Leoš** (1854–1928), major Czech composer and collector of Moravian folk music, best known for the *Sinfonietta* (1926) and the opera *Jenufa* (1904). Other operas include *Mr. Brouček* (1920), *Katya Kabanova* (1921), *The Cunning Little Vixen* (1924), *The Makropoulos Case* (1926), and *From the House of the Dead* (1928). First professor of composition at Prague Conservatory (1919), he wrote many songs, chamber and choral works, especially the *Glagolitic Mass* (1926).

**JANET, Pierre Marie Félix** (1859–1947), French psychologist and neurologist, best known for his studies of HYSTERIA and NEUROSIS. He played an important role in bringing the theories of psychology to bear on the clinical treatment of mental disease.

**JANIS, Sidney** (1896–      ), US art dealer whose New York gallery featured the work of important contemporary artists such as Jackson POLLOCK and Mark ROTHKO. He wrote several books about art and donated his impressive personal collection to New York's Museum of Modern Art in 1967.

**JANISSARIES** (Janizaries), elite Turkish infantry of the 14th–19th centuries, conscripted from prisoners of war and Christian children abducted and reared as fanatical Muslims. From c1600 Turks gradually infiltrated the highly privileged corps, which became increasingly corrupt. Unruly and rebellious, it was massacred by order of Sultan MAHMUD II in 1826.

**JANNINGS, Emil** (1884–1950), German actor best remembered for his character roles in American films. His films include *The Way of All Flesh* (1927), for which he won the Academy Award, and *The Blue Angel* (1930).

**JANOV, Arthur** (1924–      ), US psychologist who devised PRIMAL SCREAM THERAPY, a form of treating neuroses through the reenactment of traumatic childhood experiences. He wrote *The Primal Scream* (1970) and *Primal Man* (1975).

**JANSENISM,** French and Flemish Roman Catholic reform movement, based on the ideas of the Flemish theologian Cornelius Jansen (1585–1638) and centering on the convent of PORT-ROYAL. Jansen stressed St. Augustine's teaching of redemption by divine grace and also accepted PREDESTINATION; opponents charged his followers with CALVINISM. Cultivated at first by French statesmen because it opposed the Catholic establishment, Jansenism and its prominent leaders, Antoine ARNAULD and Blaise PASCAL, were condemned by Pope INNOCENT. In the 18th century persecution in France, especially under Louis XIV, drove much of the movement into the Netherlands, where there are still Jansenist bishops (now OLD CATHOLICS). In France it survived mainly as a school of thought within the church.

**JANSKY, Karl Guthe** (1905–1950), US engineer, whose discovery of radio waves emanating from the Milky Way, while studying static interference for the Bell Telephone Laboratories (1931), led to the development of radio astronomy.

**JANUARY,** first month of the year in the Julian calendar, named for the god JANUS.

**Official name:** Japan
**Capital:** Tokyo
**Area:** 142,726.5sq mi
**Population:** 126,309,000
**Language:** Japanese
**Religions:** Shinto, Buddhism
**Monetary unit(s):** 1 Yen

**JAPAN** (Nippon), an island country off the E Asian coast, now a leading industrial superpower.

**Land.** The Japanese archipelago, about 2,000mi long, comprises some 3,500 islands. The four major islands are HOKKAIDO, HONSHU, SHIKOKU and KYUSHU. Around 80% of the country is mountainous, and there are more than 190 active volcanoes; earth tremors and quakes are frequent. Many of the fast-flowing rivers are harnessed for hydroelectric power. Lowland is scarce, consisting mainly of coastal plains, including the 5,000sq mi Kanto plain on Honshu. About 70% of the land is forested, only 16% cultivable. The monsoonal climate is moderated by latitude and the sea. Winters are very cold, summers hot and humid with frequent typhoons. Rainfall is high and winter snowfall heavy.

**People.** The Japanese are basically a Mongoloid race. Japan is the world's most densely populated country in terms of arable land per person. Most Japanese live in the non-mountainous areas and more than 66% in cities like Tokyo, the capital, Osaka and Yokohama. The population includes about 15,000 aboriginal AINUS and more than 737,000 foreigners, mostly Koreans. The literacy rate is the highest in Asia. Buddhism and Shintoism are the chief religions, but Japanese thought has also been greatly influenced by Confucianism.

**Economy.** Since 1945 Japan has become a leading industrial power, with a record annual real growth rate (since 1955) of more than 10%. Products range from ships and automobiles to electronic equipment, cameras and textiles for world markets, notably the US. Imports include coal, petroleum and industrial raw materials; Japan has few mineral resources. Agriculture, once the mainstay, continues to decline; rice is still the chief crop. Because of inaccessibility, only 27% of Japan's forests are commercially exploited. It has extensive fisheries, including a controversially large whaling fleet.

**History.** Artifacts dating from at least 4000 BC have been found in Japan. Asiatic invaders drove the aboriginal Ainus into the extreme N. The first Japanese state was ruled by the Yamato clan, from whom the present imperial house supposedly descends.

Japan was subject to powerful cultural influences from China through Korea. Rice cultivation had been introduced from China c250 BC and Buddhism from Korea (c538 AD). Under the Taika Reforms (646–702 AD) the Chinese ideographic script (somewhat adapted to Japanese) and T'ANG DYNASTY administrative system was adopted. Clan chiefs became imperial officials and land became the property of the emperor, who distributed it according to rank. The powerful FUJIWARA family tried to maintain strong government centered on a figurehead emperor, and were dominant from the 9th to the 12th century; theirs was a classical age in art and literature.

In 1192 YORITOMO Minamoto seized power as SHOGUN (military dictator). Successive *shoguns* ruled absolutely with the emperors relegated to purely ritual functions. Power was based on a vassal class of warrior knights, SAMURAI. Feudal warfare (1300–1573) brought the rise of powerful lords, often free of *shogun* rule. In 1543 the Portuguese visited Japan and other European traders followed; Christianity, introduced by St. Francis Xavier (1549) became involved with politics and was banned in 1614, with savage persecution. A policy of isolation (*sakoku*) closed Japan to all foreigners except a few Dutch and Chinese traders until 1853–54, when US Commander Matthew PERRY negotiated a trade treaty. Similar treaties with Britain, France, the Netherlands and Russia followed. The shogunate collapsed in 1867 and under Emperor MEIJI (1867–1912) Tokyo became the capital; a program of westernization began. A new constitution (1889) established a parliamentary system under the divine emperor, and finance, industry and trade were developed by the *zaibatsu*, powerful family corporations.

Japan's spectacular victories over Russia and China (see RUSSO-JAPANESE WAR and SINO-JAPANESE WARS) won her recognition as a world power, as did her support of the Allies in WWI. In the 1930s a militarist regime took power after an economic crisis; Japan then built a large Asian colonial empire. The regime increasingly favored Nazi Germany, signing an Anti-Comintern Pact in 1936. Japan entered WWII with the surprise attack on PEARL HARBOR in 1941; war brought economic ruin and finally nuclear devastation at HIROSHIMA and NAGASAKI. Following the Japanese surrender (1945), Japan was occupied by US troops. A new democratic constitution was introduced (1947) and full sovereignty and independence restored by the San Francisco Peace Treaty (1951). With US aid the economy was rebuilt, making Japan a vast industrial giant. Japan was admitted to the UN in 1956. The economic boom slowed considerably in the middle 1970s only to pick up again as the decade ended. Because of WWII Japan has maintained a low diplomatic and military profile in the world, concentrating on economic development at which it has become so successful that other nations now use Japan as a model.

**JAPANESE,** language probably related to the ALTAIC group. Written Japanese originally used only adapted Chinese characters (*kanji*) despite their suitability; in the 8th century phonetic characters (*kana*) were added. Since 1945 both types have been simplified, their number reduced and romanized writing introduced.

**JAPANESE ART AND ARCHITECTURE** has been influenced by China, Korea and India, particularly through Buddhism from the 6th and 7th centuries. Japanese Buddhist temple architecture is subtler than Chinese in proportion and decoration. Early Buddhist sculpture reflects the Chinese Wei and T'ang styles (3rd–9th centuries), but tends toward naturalism and clear proportioning. Colored wall paintings in temple interiors show Indian influence.

In the FUJIWARA period (886–1160) fortified castles and palaces with moats and massive walls were built. Wood was the major temple and domestic building material. Domestic interior design is based on multiples of the *tatami*, a straw mat 3ft wide by 6ft long. Houses are built on wooden frames with sliding interior walls and doors opening onto a landscaped garden. Historical and landscape painting (*Yamato-e*) decorated palace walls and screens. Hand scrolls (*makimono*) were a popular medium. The Chinese-derived black and white *Sumi* style, inspired by ZEN, was exemplified by SESSHU (1420–1506). In the 16th century *ukiyo-e*, taking subjects from everyday life, was perfected in block prints (see UTAMARO, HOKUSAI, HIROSHIGE). Little regarded in Japan, these popular prints influenced late 19th-century European art. Modern Japanese art has often been an uneasy compromise with Western influence.

**JAPANESE BEETLE,** *Popillia japonica*, a pest beetle in the family *Scarabaeidae*. The grubs feed on the roots of grasses, especially in lawns. Adults feed on almost all kinds of green vegetation, flowers and fruits. Trees and shrubs may be severely defoliated. Introduced to N.J. about 1916, the adults have a shiny bronze-green head and deep tan wing covers. They are about 13mm (0.5in) long.

**JAPANNING,** a means of varnishing articles of wood, metal or glass in imitation of Japanese lacquerwork. The varnish is usually resin-based with a variety of pigments; it is applied in successive layers which are heat-dried.

**JARRELL, Randall** (1914–1965), US poet and influential critic. His poetry is emotional and often pervaded with a sense of tragedy and alienation; best-known collections are *Selected Poems* (1955), *The Woman at the Washington Zoo* (1960) and *The Lost World* (1965). *Poetry and the Age* (1953) is the first of three collections of his criticism.

**JARRY, Alfred** (1873–1907), eccentric French poet and dramatist whose *Ubu* plays (1896–1902) anticipated SURREALISM, DADA and the theater of the absurd. Brilliant but disordered, Jarry became an alcoholic while still young. The revoltingly gross, comic but sinister Ubu embodies his view of the bourgeoisie.

**JASON,** in Greek myth the leader of the ARGONAUTS on the quest for the GOLDEN FLEECE. He gained it with the aid of the sorceress MEDEA, whom he married and later deserted. In old age he was killed when the prow of his ship, the *Argo*, fell on him.

**JASPERS, Karl Theodor** (1883–1969), German philosopher, noted for his steadfast opposition to National Socialism and his acute yet controversial analyses of the state of German society. Early work in psychopathology led him into the Heidelberg philosophical faculty in 1913. He there became one of Germany's foremost exponents of EXISTENTIALISM.

**JAUNDICE,** yellow color of the SKIN and sclera of the EYE caused by excess bilirubin pigment in the BLOOD. HEMOGLOBIN is broken down to form bilirubin which is excreted by the LIVER in the BILE. If blood is broken down more rapidly than normal (hemolysis), the liver may not be able to remove the abnormal amount of bilirubin fast enough. Jaundice occurs with liver damage (HEPATITIS, late CIRRHOSIS) and when the bile ducts leading from the liver to the DUODENUM are obstructed by stones from the GALL BLADDER or by CANCER of the PANCREAS or bile ducts.

**JAURÈS, Jean** (1859–1914), French pacifist politician, one of the founders of the French Socialist Party (1905). He was a member of the Chamber of Deputies 1885–88, 1893–98 and 1902–14; in 1904 he founded the socialist journal *Humanité*. Jaurès who opposed war with Germany in 1914, was assassinated by a fanatic.

**JAVELIN.** See TRACK AND FIELD.

**JAVITS, Jacob Koppel** (1904–    ), US lawyer and political leader. He was a Republican congressman 1946–54, New York attorney-general 1955–57; and senator from N.Y., 1957–81. In the Senate he became known for his liberal views on social issues.

**JAY, John** (1745–1829), American statesman. An attorney, he drafted the N.Y. state constitution in 1777. In 1778 he was elected president of the Continental Congress and in 1779 first minister to Spain. In 1782, with Benjamin FRANKLIN and John ADAMS, he negotiated peace with Britain, resulting in the Treaty of PARIS (1783). As secretary for foreign affairs 1784–89 he supported the new Constitution, believing in the need for a strong central government. He was the first Chief Justice of the Supreme Court 1789–95. In 1794 he negotiated the unpopular JAY TREATY. A conservative member of the FEDERALIST PARTY, he served as governor of N.Y. 1795–1801.

**JAYS,** a diverse group of birds in the crow family, Corvidae, many of which are brightly-colored, with screeching, raucous voices. Adaptable and omnivorous, they have evolved to fill a variety of ecological roles and habitats. The original bearer of the name is the European jay, *Garrulus glandarius*, found in the woodlands of most of Europe and Asia, a striking bird with a pinkish body, black, white and blue wings and a white rump. There are in addition some 30 species of New World jays.

**JAY TREATY,** agreement between the US and Britain negotiated by John JAY, 1794. The British held forts in US territory and were inciting Indians against American settlers. Some American ships trading with the French were being seized and American seamen impressed. The Jay Treaty provided for British evacuation of NW forts, compensation for confiscated shipping, American repayment to Britain of prewar debts and limited trading concessions to the US. No mention was made of impressment, incitement of the Indians or compensation for abducted slaves. The treaty, considered a capitulation to the British, made Jay and the FEDERALIST PARTY unpopular. It led France to break its alliance with America and to pursue an undeclared naval war (1798–1800), but it averted a potentially crippling war with Britain.

**JAZZ,** form of music which grew out of Southern US black culture. Rhythmically complex, with a strong emphasis on syncopation, it is often highly improvisatory. Jazz may be said to have been born in the work songs, laments and spirituals of slaves and Southern black communities and to derive ultimately from African music. It was popularized by street bands that played for special occasions, particularly in New Orleans. By the 1900s such early forms as Stomp and RAGTIME had developed, and the BLUES had begun to evolve.

In the 1920s jazz moved north with the black populations to the cities, notably Chicago and New York. With increasing musical sophistication, new styles developed, and jazz found a wider audience through radio and phonograph. Big bands developed a commercialized jazz called Swing in the 1930s and 1940s. In the early 1940s black musicians pioneered a vivid new style, BOP. "West Coast" and "cool" styles appeared in the 1950s and 1960s, which saw the development of "free form" jazz.

Among early jazz musicians were "King" OLIVER, Sidney BECHET, "Jelly Roll" MORTON, Louis ARMSTRONG, "Fats" WALLER and "Bix" BEIDERBECKE. "Duke" ELLINGTON and "Count" BASIE led bands from the 1930s and Glenn MILLER, Benny GOODMAN and Woody HERMAN dominated the "swing era" (c1937–1947). Bessie SMITH and "Billie" HOLIDAY are considered two of the greatest jazz singers. Among more modern artists are Lester YOUNG, Charlie PARKER, Dizzy GILLESPIE, Miles DAVIS, John COLTRANE and the "free-form" pioneers Ornette COLEMAN and Cecil Taylor.

**JEANS, Sir James Hopwood** (1877–1946), British mathematician and astrophysicist who applied mathematical principles to his studies of physics and astronomy. He contributed to the KINETIC THEORY of gases, researched the origin of binary STARS and (after 1929) wrote several popular books explaining astronomy and the philosophy of science to the layman.

**JEFFERS, (John) Robinson** (1887–1962), American poet. His powerful poetry is violently disillusioned, seeing man as a mere doomed animal and glorifying nature. *Tamar and Other Poems* (1924) is his best-known collection, but his chief success was a searing adaptation of EURIPIDES' *Medea* (1946).

**JEFFERSON, Thomas** (1743–1826), third president of the US. The son of a Va. planter, he was admitted to the bar in 1767. He entered politics in 1769 as a member of the Va. House of Burgesses. In reply to the INTOLERABLE ACTS of 1774 he wrote *A Summary View of the Rights of British America*, in which he entirely denied Britain any right of government in the colonies. In 1775 he was a delegate to the second Continental Congress. In 1776, as leading member of a five-man committee, he wrote most of the DECLARATION OF INDEPENDENCE.

Jefferson was governor of Va. 1779–81

and after a short retirement was elected to Congress. In 1785 he succeeded Benjamin FRANKLIN as minister to France and secured trade concessions for the US there. From 1789 to 1793 he was secretary of state under Washington. Two parties, the Democratic-Republicans and the Federalists, formed respectively around Jefferson—who believed in agrarian egalitarianism based on the rationality of man—and Alexander HAMILTON, secretary of the treasury, who favored a strong central government led by a wealthy and able aristocracy.

In 1796 Jefferson ran as presidential candidate against the Federalist John ADAMS. Though he received the larger popular vote he lost by three electoral votes and became vice-president. During this time he wrote a *Manual of Parliamentary Practice*, and, with James MADISON, the KENTUCKY AND VIRGINIA RESOLUTIONS, protesting against the Federalists' ALIEN AND SEDITION ACTS which restricted freedom of speech and the press. From these resolutions there evolved the doctrines of STATES' RIGHTS and NULLIFICATION.

In 1800 Jefferson ran against Adams again and, gaining the same number of electoral votes as his opponent Aaron BURR, was chosen president by Congress. His administration was notable in foreign affairs and domestic expansion. He negotiated the LOUISIANA PURCHASE in 1803 and sent out the LEWIS AND CLARK EXPEDITION. He balanced the budget and reduced the national debt.

He was reelected in 1804 and during his second term tried to maintain US neutrality during the Napoleonic wars. He attempted to combat the seizure of ships and impressment of seamen with the EMBARGO ACT of 1807, prohibiting American export, but this damaged American agricultural and commercial interests and violated his principle of individual liberty. He repealed it in 1809, and in that year retired to his home, MONTICELLO. A noted scholar, he founded the U. of Virginia (1819–25).

**JEFFERSON CITY,** capital city of Mo. and seat of Cole Co., on the Missouri R. A trading center, it also has industries including printing and publishing and the manufacture of shoes, clothing and electrical appliances. Pop 33,619.

**JEFFERSON MEMORIAL,** monument in Washington, D.C., dedicated in 1943 to the memory of Thomas Jefferson. A white marble structure in classical style, it was designed by John Russell Pope and contains a statue of Jefferson by Rudulph Evans.

**JEFFRIES, James J.** (1875–1953), US heavyweight boxer who won the champion-ship from Bob Fitzsimmons in 1899. He retired undefeated in 1905; returning to the ring in 1910 he was defeated by Jack Johnson.

**JEHOVAH,** variant of the Old Testament personal name for God. The sacred name YHWH, probably pronounced "Yahweh," was not used by the Jews after about 300 BC for fear of blaspheming. Hence in reading the Hebrew Bible *Adonai* (Lord) was substituted. Medieval translators combined the consonants of one name with the vowels of the other, arriving at "Jehovah."

**JEHOVAH'S WITNESSES,** religious movement founded in 1872 by Charles Taze Russell in Pittsburgh, Pa. There is no formal church organization. Their central doctrine is that the Second Coming is at hand; they avoid participation in secular government which they see as diabolically inspired. Over a million members proselytize by house-to-house calls and through publications such as *The Watchtower* and *Awake*, issued by the Watchtower Bible and Tract Society.

**JELLYFISH,** familiar marine cnidarians (see CNIDARIA) with a pulsating "jelly" bell and trailing tentacles. Many cnidarian classes display ALTERNATION OF GENERATIONS, where a single species may be represented by a polyp form, usually asexual, and a medusoid, sexually reproductive stage. These medusoid forms are frequently referred to as jellyfish. The true jellyfish all belong to the class Scyphozoa, where the medusa is the dominant phase and the polyp or hydroid is reduced or absent. Jellyfish are radially symmetrical. Rings of muscle around the margin of the bell contract to expel water and propel the jellyfish forward.

**JENKINS' EAR, War of,** a conflict between England and Spain, 1739–41. The allegation by ship's master Robert Jenkins that a Spanish coast guard in the West Indies had cut off his ear while pillaging his ship was exploited to foment popular anger in England.

**JENNER, Bruce** (1949–    ), US decathlon champion. He set a record in the 1976 Olympics with 8,618 points. He subsequently embarked on a show business career.

**JENNER, Edward** (1749–1823), British pioneer of VACCINATION. He examined in detail the country maxim that dairymaids who had had COWPOX would not contract SMALLPOX: in 1796 he inoculated a small boy with cowpox and found that this rendered the boy immune from smallpox.

**JENSEN, Johannes Vilhelm** (1873–1950), Danish winner of the 1944 Nobel Prize for

Literature. His main works are a series of more than 100 tales entitled *Myths* (1907–44) and a six-volume novel cycle on the rise of man, *The Long Journey* (1908–22).

**JEREMIAH** (c650–c570 BC), prophet of Judah, and the primary author of the Old Testament Book of Jeremiah, a collection of his oracles. He prophesied the subjugation of Judah by Babylon and the destruction of Jerusalem and the Temple, and called for submission to the conquerors as God's agents in punishing idolatry. He was distressed by his message, but endured imprisonment for treason and threats to his life.

**JERICHO**, village in Jordan, 14mi ENE of Jerusalem, built 825ft below sea level. Dating possibly from 9000 BC, it was captured from the Canaanites by Joshua in 1400 BC. It has regularly been destroyed and rebuilt; HEROD the Great built a Jericho 1mi S of the Old Testament city. In 1967 it was occupied by Israel. Pop 6,829.

**JEROME, Saint** (Sophronius Eusebius Hieronymus; c347–c420), biblical scholar, one of the first theologians to be called a Doctor of the Christian Church. After being educated in classical studies he fled to the desert as a hermit in 375 to devote himself to prayer. He was subsequently papal secretary and translated the Old Testament into Latin (see VULGATE) and wrote New Testament commentaries.

**JERSEY**, largest and southernmost bailiwick of the British CHANNEL ISLANDS. Its main industries are tourism and agriculture. It contains numerous remnants of prehistoric life, and was known to the Romans as Caesarea. Interesting features include the Mont Orgueil castle and La Corbiere Lighthouse, along with the zoological gardens founded by Gerald Durrell. It is a British Crown dependency, but the official language is French.

**JERUSALEM**, capital of Israel, and holy city for Jews, Christians and Muslims. The city stands on a ridge at an altitude of 2,500ft, W of the Dead Sea and 35mi from the Mediterranean. It retains many grandiose shrines and the cobbled streets of the Old City.

The city dates from possibly the 4th millennium BC. In c1000 BC King DAVID captured the city from the Jebusites and made it his capital. The great Temple was built by his son SOLOMON c970 BC. David's dynasty was ended by the invasion of King NEBUCHADNEZZAR in 586 BC, who sacked the Temple and deported most of the Jews to Babylon. The Jews were allowed to return by CYRUS II of Persia, and the Temple was rebuilt. Jerusalem subsequently bacame part of Syria, but in 165 BC JUDAS MACCABEUS freed the city and it was ruled by the HASMONEAN dynasty. From 37 BC the HEROD family led the state under the aegis of the Roman Empire. The Jewish revolts, in 66 AD and 132 AD led to the destruction of the Temple and complete subjugation to the Romans until the 4th century, when Christianity became the religion of the Byzantine Roman Empire.

The city was captured by the Persian king KHOSRAU II in 614, from whom it passed to the religiously tolerant rule of the Muslim Omar. In 1099 the knights of the First Crusade took Jerusalem and set up the Latin Kingdom of Jerusalem. However in 1187 the Muslims under SALADIN recaptured the city. The MAMELUKES and then the Ottoman emperor SULEIMAN I restored Jerusalem. The city declined as a religious and economic center from the 16th to the 19th century. It was conquered by the British in 1917 and became the capital of Palestine. The 1947 UN resolution máde it an international city, but in the 1948 Arab–Israeli conflict it was divided, the Old City being under Jordanese administration, and the New City becoming the capital of Israel. In the 1967 ARAB-ISRAELI WAR, Israel took the Old City and all Jerusalem was placed under unified administration.

There are traditional Armenian, Christian, Jewish and Muslim quarters in the Old City. Government, tourism and religious activity dominate life in Jerusalem. Pop 420,000.

**JESUITS**, name given to members of the Society of Jesus, an order of the Roman Catholic Church dedicated to foreign missions, education and studies in the humanities and sciences. Jesuit life is regulated by the constitutions written by the founder of the Society, St. Ignatius LOYÓLA. Vows of obedience, poverty, chastity and obedience to the pope are taken, and training may last up to 15 years. After its foundation in 1540 they undertook notable missions in the Far East under St. FRANCIS XAVIER, and in Europe worked for Counter-Reformation. Their influence and power eventually led to their expulsion from many countries, and in 1773 Pope CLEMENT XIV dissolved the Society, but it was restored in 1814. Today there are about 31,000 Jesuits.

**JESUS CHRIST**, or Jesus of Nazareth (c6 BC–c33 AD), the founder of CHRISTIANITY. The four GOSPELS, embodying early Christian tradition, are the primary sources for his life. Born in Bethlehem, Judaea, to MARY (see VIRGIN BIRTH), Jesus grew up with

s parents in Nazareth in Galilee. Little is
...own of his life before he began his public
...inistry at the age of about 33; this was
...augurated when he was baptized in the
...rdan R by JOHN the Baptist. For the next
...ree years he journeyed, mainly in Galilee,
...thering a band of disciples, in particular
...e 12 APOSTLES, teaching and training
...em, preaching to large crowds and
...aling the physically and mentally ill. His
...imely parables are memorable teaching
...ds; the MIRACLES, few but significant, had
...e same function. The chief theme of Jesus'
...aching was the imminent coming of the
...ingdom of God and his own central role as
...e agent of God, bringing redemption and
...quiring commitment. He disavowed the
...pular wish for a political Messiah (see
...ALOTS), but made claims in which he
...ansformed the traditional idea of the
...ESSIAH; toward the end of the three years,

...he and his disciples traveled to
...rusalem, he introduced teaching about his
...ming humiliation, suffering and death.
...ppealing throughout to the Old Tes-
...ment, he antagonized the Scribes and
...arisees by denouncing their legalism. In
...e last week of his life he entered
...rusalem and taught there; after the LAST
...PPER he was betrayed by JUDAS ISCARIOT
...d arrested in the garden of GETHSEMANE.
...ne Jewish authorities handed him over to
...e Roman governor, Pontius Pilate, who
...d him executed by CRUCIFIXION. Two days
...ter his tomb was found to be empty, and
...any recognizable appearances of Jesus to
...s disciples convinced them of his
...SURRECTION. According to the Acts of the
...postles, 40 days later he ascended to
...aven (see ASCENSION). The early Church
...on crystallized its beliefs about Jesus,
...cepting him as Messiah, Lord and Son of
...od (see also INCARNATION; TRINITY), and as
...e Savior who by dying redeemed mankind
...ee ATONEMENT). Muslims believe Jesus to
...ve been the greatest prophet before
...ohammed, but deny his deity.

...T PROPULSION, the propulsion of a
...hicle by expelling a fluid jet backward,
...nose MOMENTUM produces a reaction that
...parts an equal forward momentum to the
...hicle, according to NEWTON's third law of
...otion. The squid uses a form of jet
...opulsion. Jet-propelled boats, using water
...r the jet, have been built, and air jets have
...en used to power cars, but by far the chief
...e is to power AIRPLANES and ROCKETS,
...ce to attain high speeds, jet propulsion is
...sential. The first jet engine was designed
...d built by Sir Frank WHITTLE (1937), but
...e first jet-engine aircraft to fly was
...erman (Aug. 1939). Jet engines are

INTERNAL-COMBUSTION ENGINES. The
**turbojet** is the commonest form. Air enters
the inlet diffuser and is compressed in the
Dair compressor, a multistage device
having sets of rapidly rotating fan blades. It
then enters the combustion chamber, where
the fuel (a kerosene/gasoline mixture) is
injected and ignited, and the hot, expanding
exhaust gases pass through a TURBINE that
drives the compressor and engine accessor-
ies. The gases, sometimes heated further in
an AFTERBURNER, are expelled through the
jet nozzle to provide the thrust. The nozzle
converges for subsonic flight, but for
supersonic flight one that converges and
then diverges is needed. The fanjet or
turbofan engine uses some of the turbine
power to drive a propeller fan in a cowling,
for more efficient subsonic propulsion; the
**turboprop**, similar in principle, gains its
thrust chiefly from the propeller. The
**ramjet** is the simplest air-breathing jet
engine, having neither compressor nor
turbine. When accelerated to supersonic
speeds by an auxiliary rocket or turbojet
engine, the inlet diffuser "rams" the air and
compresses it; after combustion the exhaust
gases are expelled directly. Ramjets are
used chiefly in guided missiles.

**JEVONS, William Stanley** (1835–1882),
English economist and logician. In 1862 he
introduced the marginal utility theory of
value, stating that value was determined by
utility. His most famous work was *Theory
of Political Economy* (1871).

**JEWETT, Sarah Orne** (1849–1909), US
novelist and writer of realistic short stories
based on small-town life in upper New
England. Her best-known work is *The
Country of the Pointed Firs* (1896).

**JEWISH AGENCY,** international Zionist
organization founded in 1929 by Chaim
WEIZMANN to help Jewish immigrants settle
in Palestine. After WWII it represented the
Jewish cause in the negotiations for the
foundation of Israel.

**JEWS,** a people who share common racial
origins, history and culture and who date
from at least 1500 BC. It is nevertheless
very difficult to define what constitutes
Jewishness. In Israel there are Jews from
many origins and races, but most Jews in
Israel are not observant or practicing
religious Jews.

According to the Old Testament the
history of the Jewish people begins with
ABRAHAM, who led his family from
Mesopotamia to Canaan. The Egyptians
reduced the Israelites to captivity, until
MOSES led his people into the wilderness of
Sinai. After 40 years of wandering the
tribes reached and conquered Canaan.

External threats forced the 12 tribes to unite under SAUL, whose successor, King DAVID, brought peace and prosperity to the country. Under the rule of David's grandson, JEROBOAM, however, the northern 10 tribes seceded to form the kingdom of Israel. Israel was defeated in 721 BC by the Assyrians and these tribes lost their identity in captivity. The southern kingdom, Judah, was defeated by the Babylonians in 586 BC and the people were sent into exile in Babylon, where they later introduced the SYNAGOGUE as a place of study and prayer. Babylon was conquered by the Persian CYRUS THE GREAT in 538 BC; he allowed the Jews to return to Judah. Their later conquest by ALEXANDER THE GREAT meant a gradual imposition of Greek culture, until a rebellion under JUDAS MACCABAEUS in 165 BC led to the foundation of the HASMONEAN dynasty. The religious strife and disagreement between the SADDUCEES, PHARISEES and such sects as the ESSENES brought about Roman intervention in 53 BC when POMPEY's legions entered Jerusalem and Palestine became a Roman province. In c33 AD Jesus was executed because he was regarded as a threat to the security of the Roman rule. A Jewish revolt in 66 led to the destruction of Jerusalem by the Romans; after a further revolt in 131 led by BAR COCHBA the Jewish state was completely crushed by the Romans, Judah was renamed Syria Palestina, and Jews were forbidden to enter Jerusalem. Fearing the loss of their religion, Jewish scholars and rabbis codified the oral law into the MISHNAH and the TALMUD.

Many Jews moved to Western Europe and their culture flourished, particularly in Spain. However, the CRUSADES led to widespread suppression of the Jews and throughout Western Europe there were laws confining them to GHETTOS, excluding them from most trades and professions other than that of money-lending, and barring them from owning land. From the end of the 13th century they were in turn banished from England, France and from Spain where they were persecuted by the INQUISITION. By the end of the Middle Ages only small parts of Germany and Italy still allowed Jews within their borders. Many of the exiles perished; some of the descendants of the Spanish Jews, the SEPHARDIM, settled in the Ottoman Empire, while others, the MARRANOS, reestablished Jewish communities in England, France and the Netherlands in the 17th century. In 1654, twenty-three Dutch Jews founded the first Jewish congregation at New Amsterdam (New York). The descendants of German Jews, the ASHKENAZIM, took refuge in E Europe, in Poland and Lithuania, but many found themselves trapped in ghettos and persecuted by the Russians. Some adopted HASIDISM, a form of religious mysticism.

In Western Europe tolerance for the Jew increased after the French Revolution, and Jewish communities grew. Nevertheless there was considerable opposition to the Jewish race and religion, as manifested by the DREYFUS AFFAIR in France. Between 1880 and 1922 harsh conditions in E Europe and the Russian POGROMS brought about both a massive Jewish emigration from E Europe, especially to the US, and the modern movement of ZIONISM led by Theodor HERZL and Chaim WEIZMANN who hoped to reestablish a state of Jewry in Palestine. In Palestine most new Jewish immigrants from Europe settled on the land. The 1917 BALFOUR DECLARATION guaranteed "a national home for the Jewish people" in Palestine but increasing Jewish settlement aroused the hostility of the Arab inhabitants whose own national aspirations were beginning to awaken.

From the 1930s NAZISM brought virulent ANTISEMITISM in Germany; before the outbreak of WWII the Nazis were systematically murdering European Jews and by 1945 they had exterminated over six million. Many Jews moved to Palestine after the war and world reaction to the WWII catastrophes led to the establishment of the state of ISRAEL in 1948. Its presence, however, has resulted in continuous hostility and warfare between Israel and other Arab countries. (See ARAB-ISRAELI WARS.) The majority of Jews now live in Israel, in the US, and in Russia where their cultural and religious life is seriously restricted.

**JEWS FOR JESUS,** evangelistic body of Jews converted to a belief in Jesus Christ as the expected Messiah of Israel. Founded in 1973 by Moishe Rosen, the organization has no connection with any Christian denomination, and employs a variety of modern proselytizing techniques. Headquarters are in San Francisco.

**JIM CROW,** name for a system of laws and customs in the Southern US to segregate Negroes from white society. The name comes from a minstrel song. The laws dated from the 1880s and applied to schools, transportation, theaters and parks. After the mid-1950s, Supreme Court rulings overturned the legislation. (See CIVIL RIGHTS AND LIBERTIES; INTEGRATION.)

**JIMÉNEZ, Juan Ramón** (1881–1958) major Spanish poet. At first influenced by SYMBOLISM, in *Diary of a Poet and the Sea*

(1917) he developed a free, direct style of his own, *poesía desnuda* (Spanish: naked poetry). After the Spanish Civil War he moved to Puerto Rico. He received the Nobel Prize for Literature in 1956.

**JINNAH, Mahomed Ali** (1876–1948), Indian Muslim lawyer and statesman, founder of Pakistan. At first a member of the Indian CONGRESS PARTY, he resigned in 1921 because of its Hindu bias. From 1934 head of the MUSLIM LEAGUE, he campaigned for Muslim rights in an independent state, and in 1947 became Pakistan's first head of state.

**JITTERBUG,** a fast, strenuous dance to swing or jazz music, popular in the 1930s and 1940s. The basic jitterbug step, a variation of the earlier Lindy Hop, was often embellished with swings, twirls and leaps that required considerable athletic ability.

**JOAN OF ARC, Saint** (c1412–1431), French heroine of the HUNDRED YEARS WAR, a peasant girl from Domrémy, Lorraine, who heard "voices" telling her to liberate France from the English. Given command of a small force by the Dauphin Charles, she inspired it to victory at Orléans and in the surrounding region in 1429. She stood beside the Dauphin when he was crowned Charles VII that year, but failed to relieve besieged Paris because he denied her adequate forces. Captured at Compiègne (1430), she was tried for heresy by French clerics who sympathized with the English, and burnt at the stake. The verdict was reversed in 1456 and she was canonized in 1920.

**JOB,** 18th book of the OLD TESTAMENT. It seeks to show that suffering need not be God's penalty for sin. God permits Satan to torment the virtuous Job with the loss of family, wealth and health. Finding small comfort in wife and friends, Job is bitterly questioning but remains faithful, and is restored to good fortune in old age.

**JOB CORPS,** program established under the Economic Opportunity Act of 1964 to provide training and work experience for disadvantaged young people; the trainees were originally housed in residential treatment centers. The program was cut back under President Richard M. Nixon and stopped entirely in 1981 by the Reagan administration when its funding under CETA was eliminated as the result of drastic federal budget cuts.

**JODL, Alfred** (1890–1946), German soldier, chief of operations staff in WWII. He signed the surrender at Rheims, May 7, 1945. Convicted of war crimes at the NUREMBERG TRIALS, he was executed.

**JOEL,** second book of the Minor Prophets in the OLD TESTAMENT. Messianic in nature, it forecasts the Day of the Lord in apocalyptic terms. Its prophecy of the outpouring of the Spirit upon all flesh is regarded by the Christian Church as fulfilled at PENTECOST.

**JOFFRE,          Joseph-Jacques-Césaire** (1852–1931), commander-in-chief of the French army 1914–16. He underestimated German power at the start of WWI, but shared with GALLIENI credit for the victory on the MARNE. After the mismanagement of VERDUN he resigned, but was immediately made a marshal of France.

**JOFFREY, Robert** (1930–     ), US dancer and choreographer. He founded his school, the American Ballet Center, in 1953 and his first company, the Robert Joffrey Theater Dancers, in 1956. By 1976, when it became the Joffrey Ballet, it was one of the most highly regarded of US companies. The touring Joffrey II Company was formed in 1970 to develop young dancers.

**JOHANNESBURG,** city in South Africa, one of the largest in Africa and the country's economic center. It was founded in 1886 as a gold-mining camp; its economy still rests on gold and diamonds, but there is also a wide range of industries. Pop 1,432,643.

**JOHN,** name of 22 popes and 2 antipopes. **Saint John I** (d. 526), pope from 523, was sent to Constantinople by THEODORIC to win toleration for ARIANISM from the emperor; Theodoric imprisoned him when he failed. **John II** (d. 535) reigned from 533. **John VII** (d. 707) reigned from 705. **John VIII** (d. 882), reigned from 872. He sought political power for the papacy, intervening, with mixed success, in the rivalries of the CAROLINGIAN imperial house and ex-communicating his opponent FORMOSUS. In 877 he had to bribe SARACEN raiders to spare Rome. He resolved a dispute with the Eastern Church by recognizing PHOTIUS as patriarch of Constantinople in 879. He was assassinated by a household conspiracy. **John XXII** (c1249–1334) reigned from 1316. The second pope at Avignon, he filled the college with French cardinals. A skillful administrator, he lost popularity for his persecution of the Spiritual FRANCISCANS, who sought to observe a strict rule of evangelical poverty. He contested the election of Emperor LOUIS IV; Louis attempted to have him declared a heretic, but John imprisoned the antipope Louis appointed, NICHOLAS V. **John XXIII** was first taken as a name by Baldassare Cossa (d. 1419), schismatic antipope 1410–15. He promoted the council of PISA (1408) to end the Great SCHISM. Elected pope by the Pisa cardinals, he defended Rome against his rival GREGORY XII. Prompted by Emperor Sigismund, he convened the Council of CONSTANCE. At this he agreed to abdicate if his two rivals did, but reneged; the Council deposed all three. Cossa was made a cardinal-bishop in 1419. The name **John XXIII** was therefore taken by Angelo Giuseppe Roncalli (1881–1963), who reigned from 1958. Of peasant stock, he was an army chaplain in WWI. He was made a titular archbishop in the Vatican diplomatic corps 1925–35 and nuncio 1925–53, serving in Turkey, the Balkans and France; in this post he won great popularity. Made cardinal in 1953, he was elected pope, in 1958. He revolutionized the church, promoting cooperation with other Christian churches and other religions in the face of world problems; the encyclical *Mater et Magister* (1961) advocated social reform in underdeveloped areas of the world. In 1962 he called the influential Second VATICAN COUNCIL.

**JOHN, Augustus Edwin** (1878–1961), leading British painter, famous for his portraits of contemporary celebrities such as George Bernard SHAW, Dylan THOMAS and James JOYCE. He is noted for his vigorous use of rich color and his excellent draughtsmanship.

**JOHN, Epistles of,** three NEW TESTAMENT epistles ascribed to St. John the Apostle. The first and longest seeks to strengthen Christians by giving the signs of the faith; the second attacks gnostic denials of Christ's incarnation; the third urges an obstinate church leader to receive genuine missionaries.

**JOHN, Gospel of,** the fourth GOSPEL in the New Testament, written c100 AD and traditionally ascribed to St. John the Apostle. Based on a series of long discourses by Jesus, it has little in common with the SYNOPTIC GOSPELS; it emphasizes Jesus' deity, and is spiritual and theological in tone. (See also LOGOS.)

**JOHN, Saint** (called the Evangelist or the Divine), son of Zebedee and brother of James, is usually thought to be the author of three New Testament Epistles and possibly the fourth GOSPEL.

**JOHN, Saint** (d. c30 AD), called John the Baptist, the preacher who proclaimed the coming of Christ and urged repentance, baptizing his followers in the Jordan R. He denounced HEROD Antipas for marrying Herodias, wife of Herod's brother, and was beheaded at her instigation. (See also SALOME.)

**JOHN** (1167–1216), king of England from 1199. Youngest son of HENRY II, he succeeded his brother Richard I. John refused to accept a papal nominee as archbishop of Canterbury, and so was excommunicated in 1209; he faced invasion by Philip II of France, to whom he had lost England's French possessions. Expensive military provisions had alienated the barons, already curbed by Henry II; in 1215 they rose in revolt and forced John to sign the MAGNA CARTA, confirming their feudal rights. John later repudiated it and waged a new war against the barons, who summoned French support. John died while the issue was still in doubt.

**JOHN BIRCH SOCIETY,** US organization founded in 1958 by businessman Robert Welch. Named for a US officer murdered by the communist Chinese in 1945, it seeks to combat the spread of communist influence in the US, urging abandonment of welfare legislation and withdrawal from the UN.

**JOHN BULL,** personification, favorable or otherwise, of the typical Englishman, usually portrayed as a burly good-natured farmer or tradesman wearing a Union Jack waistcoat. The name derives from a satire by John ARBUTHNOT.

**JOHN OF GAUNT** (1340–1399), fourth son of Edward III, became duke of Lancaster in 1362. Born at Ghent (hence "Gaunt"), he was a commander in France 1367–74, during the HUNDRED YEARS WAR. From 1371 he ruled England for his senile father and young nephew RICHARD II; his economic policies and alliance with John WYCLIF made him unpopular in many quarters, as did his unsuccessful campaigns to claim the Castilian throne 1369–73. His eldest son became HENRY IV.

**JOHN OF SALISBURY** (c1110–1180), English churchman and leading SCHOLASTIC philosopher. Friend and secretary to Archbishop Thomas à Becket, he shared his exile 1163–70. John, who studied under Peter ABELARD, was a principal theorist of REALISM.

**JOHN OF THE CROSS, Saint** (1542–1591), Spanish poet and mystic, founder of a reformed Carmelite order. Influenced by St. TERESA OF AVILA, he is remembered for poems such as *The Dark Night of the Soul.* Canonized in 1726, he was made a CHURCH DOCTOR in 1926.

**JOHN PAUL I** (Albino Luciani; 1912–1978), Italian-born pope. A moderate tradionalist of humble village background, he was cardinal and patriarch of Venice when elected pope in 1978. He died of a heart attack one month later, ending the shortest papal reign in nearly 400 years.

**JOHN PAUL II** (Karol Jozef Wojtyla; 1920– ). Polish-born Roman Catholic Pope who was the first non-Italian to be elected pontiff (1978) in 455 years. A personable world traveler, he has maintained a theologically conservative position on such controversial issues as birth control and abortion. He survived an assassination attempt in 1981.

**JOHNS, Jasper** (1930– ), US painter, a leading exponent of POP ART in such works as *Flag* (1958), a copy of the US flag, and *Painted Bronze* (1960), two cast beer cans.

**JOHNSON, Andrew** (1808–1875), 17th President of the US. He was born in Raleigh, N.C., of a poor family and at 10 apprenticed to a tailor. In 1826 he moved to Greenville, Tenn., where in 1827 he married Eliza McCardle; she taught him writing and arithmetic. He took an active part in public life, and after becoming mayor was elected to the Tenn. House of Representatives and then the state Senate. A Democrat, he served 10 years as a US congressman. Governor of Tenn. 1853–57, he was then elected to the Senate. Though supporting some measures by the pro-slavery South he introduced a HOMESTEADING bill which was opposed by slave owners and most Southern congressmen. After Lincoln became president in 1860, Tenn. seceded; Johnson, the only Southern senator not to join the Confederate cause, was made military governor of Tenn., establishing a working basis for civilian rule. In 1865 he was elected vice-president, but six weeks later became president when Lincoln was assassinated. He inherited the problems of RECONSTRUCTION. On May 29, 1865, with Congress adjourned, he issued a proclamation of amnesty, allowing Southern states the right to adopt new constitutions and elect governments. His policy offended radical Republicans because it threatened their absolute control of Congress and robbed them of the chance of holding office in the South. In a mid-term election characterized by a vicious and emotive campaign by Johnson's opponents, they were returned with a two-thirds majority. On March 2, 1867 the first radical reconstruction act was passed. To further restrict Johnson Congress passed, over his veto, the Tenure of Office Act, forbidding the dismissal of certain federal officeholders. Despite this he dismissed the secretary of war, Edwin Stanton, and in March 1868 Johnson was impeached. The vindictiveness of the radical attack won him sympathy and he escaped conviction by one vote. He failed to capture the Democratic nomination, and attempts to reenter Congress failed until he was elected senator from Tenn. in 1874. He served a short session in 1875 and died of a stroke soon after.

**JOHNSON, Howard Deering** (1896–1972), US businessman and pioneer in franchising (1929) who transformed a run-down soda fountain into a giant chain of white clapboard restaurants featuring 28 flavors of ice cream. Building restaurants on many new turnpikes created after WWII, he developed "Howard Johnson's" into the largest private US food distributor.

**JOHNSON, Jack** (1878–1946), US boxer. In 1908 he became the first black to win the world heavyweight championship. Unpopular with the white boxing world, he jumped bail on serious charges and fled abroad (1912). He lost the title to Jess Willard in Havana in 1915.

**JOHNSON, John Harold** (1918– ), leading US publisher of popular magazines for blacks, including *Ebony, Tan, Jet* and *Black World*. He was also president of a major black-run insurance company, and served on many government committees.

**JOHNSON, Lyndon Baines** (1908–1973), 36th President of the US. He became chief executive on Nov. 22, 1963, after the assassination of John F. KENNEDY.

Johnson was born on a farm near Stonewall, SW Tex., of a prominent local family. He did not go to college until 1927, and taught after graduating in 1930. In 1931 he became secretary to the Republican congressman Richard Kleberg. In 1934 he married Claudia Alta Taylor, nicknamed "Lady Bird." He was Texan administrator of the NEW DEAL National Youth Administration 1935–37, and was elected to Congress as a Democratic New Deal supporter 1937–48, with a period of naval service 1941–42; he served on the House Naval and later Armed Services Committees. Elected to the Senate in 1948, he became the youngest majority leader in its history when the Democrats regained control in 1954. He used his influence and mastery of procedure to secure a unanimous Democratic condemnation of Senator J. R. MCCARTHY and passage of important CIVIL RIGHTS bills. After losing the presidential nomination in 1960 Johnson became vice-president under John F. Kennedy, despite prior disagreements. He influenced committee decisions on space projects and civil rights and traveled abroad as a kind of roving ambassador, but remained in the background politically.

After Kennedy's assassination Johnson quickly and capably assumed his presidential responsibilities. With the same cabinet and presidential staff he implemented the faltering Kennedy tax reform and civil rights programs, as well as a massive anti-poverty program of his own. Winning a landslide victory in 1964, with Hubert HUMPHREY as vice-president, Johnson pushed through extensive liberal legislation to build the "Great Society," including the MEDICARE PROGRAM and the Voting Rights Act. He equally vigorously extended Kennedy's policy of US involvement in the VIETNAM WAR, despite mounting hostility from sections of the public. Campus demonstrations and general civil unrest caused three years of turbulence rarely equalled in US history. On Mar. 31, 1968, Johnson announced that he would neither seek nor accept renomination, and retired to his home in Tex., where early in 1973 he suffered a fatal heart attack.

**JOHNSON, Philip Cortelyou** (1906–   ), US architect, a major exponent of the INTERNATIONAL STYLE. His "Glass House" (1949) at New Canaan, Conn., won him international recognition. In the 1950s he worked with MIES VAN DER ROHE on the Seagram Building, New York. His later work is less severely functional.

**JOHNSON, Samuel** (1709–84), English man of letters, poet, critic, essayist and lexicographer. After failing as a schoolmaster he supported himself in London by journalism and hack writing. He published the poems *London* (1738) and *The Vanity of Human Wishes* (1749). From 1746 to 1755 he prepared his pioneering *Dictionary of the English Language* (1755), an idiosyncratic but brilliant work which won him a wide reputation. The satirical *Rasselas* (1759) was produced as a quick moneymaker. In 1763 he met James BOSWELL, his biographer, who recorded much of Johnson's fiery but polished conversation. The critical works, particularly the edition of Shakespeare (1765) and *Lives of the Most Eminent English Poets* (1781) combine excellent writing and insight with, often, what many consider eccentric judgments.

**JOHNSON, Walter Perry** called "Big Train" (1887–1946), US baseball pitcher famous for his speed. With the Washington Senators 1907–27 he won 414 games and in 1913 pitched 56 consecutive scoreless innings. In 1936 he was one of the first five players elected to the Baseball Hall of Fame.

**JOLIET, Louis** (c1645–c1700), French-Canadian explorer who, with Father MARQUETTE, led the first expedition down the Mississippi R. In 1672–73 they reached its confluence with the Arkansas R, but turned back when they found it led not to the Pacific but into the Spanish-held Gulf of Mexico.

**JOLIOT-CURIE, Irène** (1897–1956), French physicist, the daughter of Pierre and Marie CURIE. She and her husband, **Jean Frédéric Joliot** (1900–1958), shared the 1935 Nobel Prize for Chemistry for their discovery of artificial RADIOACTIVITY. Both later played a major part in the formation of the French atomic energy commission but, because of their communism, were removed from positions of responsibility there (Frédéric 1950, Irène 1951). Like her mother, Irène died from LEUKEMIA as a result of prolonged exposure to radioactive materials.

**JOLSON, Al** (1886–1950), Russian-born US singer, blackface comedian and songwriter, famous for sentimental songs such as *Mammy* and *Sonny Boy*. After starring in various Broadway musicals and talking pictures he appeared in *The Jazz Singer* (1927), the first full-length talking picture.

**JONAH, Book of,** fifth book of the MINOR PROPHETS, unique in its entirely narrative form. Jonah is portrayed as so intolerant of Gentiles that he disobeys God's command to convert the city of Nineveh. Thwarted in the "great fish" episode, he obeys God but, still resentful, has the necessity of mercy demonstrated to him.

**JONES, Alfred Ernest** (1897–1958), British psychoanalyst who played a major role in gaining recognition for PSYCHOANALYSIS in Britain and North

America. His 3-volume biography of FREUD (1953–57) became a classic.

JONES, Bob (1883–1968), US evangelist who spent his life spreading an old-time fundamentalist Protestant religion. He established his first Bob Jones College in Fla. (1927), trained ministers and missionaries, published books at the school's press and preached over the school's radio.

JONES, Bobby (Robert Tyre Jones; 1902–1971), US amateur golfer, only man to have won the US and British amateur and open championships—the "Grand Slam"—in the same year (1930).

JONES, Inigo (1573–1652), English architect who introduced the classical style to England. While staying in Italy he had been influenced by the works of PALLADIO. Surveyor of the King's Works 1615–44, his masterpieces include the Queen's House at Greenwich, Whitehall Banqueting Hall and St. Paul's Church, Covent Garden. His sets and costumes for court MASQUES greatly influenced subsequent stage design.

JONES, James (1921–1977), US novelist. His first book, From Here to Eternity (1951), portrayed the degradation of army life on the eve of WWII. Other works include Some Came Running (1957), The Pistol (1959) and The Thin Red Line (1962).

JONES, James Earl (1931–    ), US actor who won a Tony Award for his performance in The Great White Hope (1968; film 1970), based on the life of black heavyweight champion Jack Johnson. He was also noted for his performances as Shakespeare's Othello and King Lear. He provided the voice of Darth Vader in the Star Wars films.

JONES, Jesse (1874–1956), US public official. A prominent New Deal administrator, he was chairman of the Reconstruction Finance Corporation (1933–39), administrator of the Federal Loan Agency (1939–45) and Secretary of Commerce (1940–45). Controlling billions of federal dollars, he was one of the most powerful financial figures in the US.

JONES, John Paul (1747–1792), US naval hero, born John Paul in Kirkudbrightshire, Scotland. Serving at first in British ships, he killed one of his crew (1773) and deserted to America. In the Revolution he joined the Continental navy, taking command of the Alfred in 1775, in 1776 the Providence, and in 1777 the Ranger. His successes against British Atlantic shipping won him command of the French-donated Bon Homme Richard (1779). After petty raiding around the Scottish and Irish coasts he attacked a convoy escorted by the British

ship Serapis. In a fierce battle the Richard was irreparably damaged, but Jones refused to surrender with the famous words "I have not yet begun to fight!" He managed to capture the Serapis as the Richard sank. Service in the Russian navy 1788–89 left him physically and mentally broken, and he died in Paris.

JONES, LeRoi. See BARAKA, IMAMU AMIRI.

JONES, Robert Edmond (1887–1954), US stage designer whose "new stagecraft," featuring spare and abstract sets, lighting and costumes, revolutionized the American theater. He designed notable Shakespearean productions, many of Eugene O'Neill plays, and the popular Lute Song (1946) and Green Pastures (1951).

JONESTOWN, settlement in Guyana established in 1977 by Rev. Jim Jones for himself and nearly 1,000 members of his church, the People's Temple (formerly based in San Francisco, Cal., and originally concerned with helping the poor). On Nov. 19, 1978, the bodies of almost all the Jonestown residents (913 men, women and children) were discovered in the village, the result of cyanide poisoning; Jones had died of a bullet wound in the head. A charismatic but tyrannical and megalomaniacal leader, Jones had persuaded, deceived and coerced his followers into mass suicide, done by drinking cyanide mixed in Kool-Aid. Jones had ordered this carnage on Nov. 18, directly after the murder by several of his assistants of US Congressman Leo J. Ryan and four others at a nearby airport. Ryan was heading a team investigating reports of abuses and crimes committed in Jonestown.

JONG, Erica (1942–    ), US feminist poet and novelist best known for her popular erotic novel Fear of Flying (1973). Her collections of poetry include Fruits and Vegetables (1971), Half-Lives (1973) and Loveroot (1975). Fanny, a mock 18th-century picaresque novel, appeared in 1980.

JONGKIND, Johann Barthold (1819–1891), Dutch painter, a precursor of IMPRESSIONISM. Resident in France from 1846, he met COROT there and painted in Normandy with Boudin. His landscapes and seascapes continued the Dutch tradition with a new exploration of light and atmospheric effects, a major influence on MONET.

JONSON, Ben (1572–1637), English dramatist and lyric poet. He served in the Dutch wars in the 1590s, returning to London to act and write for the stage. Every Man in his Humour (1598) established him as a playwright. His tragedies Sejanus (1603) and Catiline (1611) are still admired, but it is the comedies that are most often performed, especially *Volpone* (1606) and *The Alchemist* (1610); both of these are sardonic depictions of human gullibility before the lure of gold. Under James I Jonson and Inigo JONES collaborated on masques for the court, but he fell from favor under Charles I.

**JOPLIN, Janis** (1943–70), US singer involved with the 1960s hippie subculture of San Francisco. She gained recognition for her electric performance at the 1967 Monterey Rock Festival with the group Big Brother and the Holding Company. She was best known for her passionate blues ballads such as "Me and Bobby McGee." She died at the age of 27 of a heroin overdose.

**JOPLIN, Scott** (1868–1917), US black composer who in lyrical and elegant pieces such as *Maple Leaf Rag* (1899) sought to establish RAGTIME as serious music. When ambitious ventures such as the opera *Treemonisha* (1911) failed, Joplin declined into mental illness. In the 1970s his works enjoyed a great revival.

**JORDAENS, Jacob** (1593–1678), Flemish baroque painter. Influenced by RUBENS, with whom he studied, he painted religious and allegorical scenes, genre works and portraits in a vigorous if occasionally crude style. Among his best-known works is *The King Drinks* (1638).

**Official name:** Hashemite Kingdom of Jordan
**Area:** 37,738sq mi (including Israeli-occupied West Bank)
**Population:** 2,864,173 (including Israeli-occupied West Bank)
**Languages:** Arabic
**Religions:** Islam
**Monetary unit(s):** 1 Jordanian dinar = 1,000 fils

**JORDAN,** Arab HASHEMITE monarchy in the Middle East, bordered to the E by Saudi Arabia, the N by Syria and Iraq, and the W by Israel.
**Land.** Jordan is bisected by the GREAT RIFT VALLEY through which flows the JORDAN R. The E region has 94% of the land area but under 50% of the population, being largely a desert plateau rising to greener highlands.

In the SW is the capital, Amman, and the only port, Aqaba. The W area, known as the West Bank, is smaller but much more fertile, especially in the N. The climate ranges from Mediterranean in the highlands to subtropical in the Jordan valley; the desert receives minimal rainfall.
**People and Economy.** The population is mainly Arab, but there is a wide cultural gulf between the traditionally nomadic BEDOUIN of the E region and the Palestinians including about 800,000 refugees from Israel, most of whom live either in U.N.-administered camps on the WEST BANK, or in the large urban centers, Amman, Irbid, and Zarqa. Almost 95% of the people are Sunni Muslims, the remainder Christians. Jordan's economy is largely agricultural, with wheat, barley, and fruits the principal crops; outside the irrigated Jordan valley yields are low due to reliance on sometimes insufficient rainfall. Most industry is limited to food processing and textiles although there is some oil refining, and cement and fertilizer manufacturing. Phosphate is mined. The economy was greatly disrupted by the loss of the West Bank and Jordan relies heavily on foreign aid, mostly from Saudi Arabia and the US.
**History.** In biblical times the West Bank was settled by the Israelites, the E region by their enemies the AMMONITES, MOAB and EDOM. This region later became the NABATEAN empire, its capital at PETRA. Later ruled by Rome and Byzantium, it was conquered by the Arabs in the 7th century. Jordan was part of the OTTOMAN EMPIRE from 1516 until the 20th century, but during World War I a Hashemite Arab revolt was backed by the British forces (see FAISAL I; LAWRENCE, T. E.). In 1923 it was made into the British-supervised state of Transjordan, ruled by the Emir ABDULLAH. Its army, the Arab Legion, was trained by British officers led by Sir John GLUBB. In 1946 Transjordan won full self-government as Jordan, Abdullah becoming king; in 1948 the Arab Legion conquered the West Bank. In 1951 Abdullah, who had made a truce with Israel, was assassinated; his grandson HUSSEIN I was enthroned in 1953. Jordan, which maintained strong ties with the United Kingdom and had troubled relations with the Palestinians, was often in conflict with its neighbors Egypt (until a 1967 mutual defense pact) and Syria. Jordan's subsequent involvement in the Six-Day War cost her the West Bank, occupied by Israel, and the Palestinian Liberation Organization (PLO) was expelled. In 1970 the growing power of the Palestine

guerrillas in Jordan led to a short civil war in which they were defeated. In 1974 Hussein recognized the PLO as the sole legitimate representative of the Palestinian people and has since enjoyed better relations in the Arab world.

**JORDAN, David Starr** (1851–1931), US scientist and educator who was a prominent ichthyologist and first president of Stanford U. 1891–1913. As director of the World Peace Foundation 1910–1914, he opposed US participation in WWI, then became president of the World Peace Congress (1915). He wrote more than 50 books on fish, education, peace and world federalism.

**JORDAN RIVER,** starts at a confluence in the Hula basin N Israel, and flows about 200mi S through the Sea of Galilee and the Ghor valley to the Dead Sea. It occupies the Asian continuation of the GREAT RIFT VALLEY. Honored in the Christian, Moslem and Jewish religions, it is an important source of water in an arid region.

**JOSEPH,** name of two Holy Roman Emperors. **Joseph I** (1678–1711) reigned from 1705, during the War of the SPANISH SUCCESSION and a Hungarian revolt led by Francis RAKOCZY. **Joseph II** (1741–1790), reigned from 1765, but until 1780 with his mother, MARIA THERESA. When she died he began to institute a massive social reform program on ENLIGHTENMENT principles, abolishing serfdom and attacking feudal, class and property systems. His religious, administrative, and language reforms made him unpopular in Austria and caused revolts abroad. His attempt at enlightened despotism was hindered by his tactless autocracy, and few of his reforms survived him.

**JOSEPH,** Jewish patriarch, favorite son of JACOB. His jealous brothers sold him into slavery in Egypt. There he won favor with Pharaoh by correctly interpreting premonitory dreams, and was eventually made chief minister. He forgave his brothers and rescued the family from famine.

**JOSEPH, Chief** (c1840–1904), Nez Percé Indian chief. In 1877, faced with forcible resettlement under a basically fraudulent treaty, he led his people in a mass flight from their Oregon lands to Canada. The Nez Percé were defeated only 30mi from the frontier; Joseph won popular sympathy for his heroic and brilliant resistance.

**JOSEPH, Saint,** husband of Mary, mother of Jesus. A carpenter, he was a descendant of David. Warned by God, he took Mary and the infant Jesus into Egypt to escape the wrath of Herod. He is honored as patron saint of the Roman Catholic Church.

**JOSEPHSON, Brian David** (1940–     ),

British physicist awarded, with I. GIAEVER and L. ESAKI, the 1973 Nobel Prize for Physics for his discovery of the **Josephson Effect,** the passage of ELECTRICITY through an insulator between two superconductors (see SUPERCONDUCTIVITY). Pairs of ELECTRONS form in the superconductors and tunnel (see WAVE MECHANICS) through the insulating layer.

**JOSHUA,** sixth book of the OLD TESTAMENT. It describes the conquest of CANAAN by the Israelites under Joshua, associate of and successor to MOSES, and its division among the TWELVE TRIBES OF ISRAEL.

**JOSQUIN DES PRÉS** (c1450–1521), major Flemish composer. He traveled widely in Europe; much of his work was done in Italy. Technically brilliant, his music ranges from the almost mystical fervor in his 20 masses and 90 motets to the gaiety and elegance of his secular songs. His music has enjoyed a revival since the 1950s.

**JOULE, James Prescott** (1818–1889), British physicist who showed that HEAT energy and mechanical energy are equivalent and hinted at the law of conservation of ENERGY. From 1852 he and Thomson (later Lord KELVIN) performed a series of experiments in THERMODYNAMICS, especially on the Joule–Thomson effect (see CRYOGENICS). The JOULE (unit) is named for him.

**JOWETT, Benjamin** (1817–1893), English classical scholar, master of Balliol College, Oxford from 1870 and vice-chancellor of Oxford University, 1882–86. His translations of PLATO's *Dialogues* (1871) and *Republic* (1844) are literary and scholastic masterpieces.

**JOYCE, James Augustine Aloysius** (1882–1941), Irish novelist and poet whose novel *Ulysses* (1922) is a seminal work of 20th-century literature. Within the framework of Homeric myth he dissects his characters' thoughts and actions in the course of a single day through STREAM OF CONSCIOUSNESS techniques and the creation of an allusive private language. This he developed in *Finnegans Wake* (1939), a complex cyclical exploration of dream consciousness. Dublin, where Joyce grew up, is central to his writing as in *Dubliners* (1914), and the autobiographical *A Portrait of the Artist as a Young Man* (1916), but from 1904 he lived abroad, in Paris, Trieste and Zurich, where he died. (For the *Ulysses* case see PORNOGRAPHY.)

**JOYCE, William** (1906–1946), US-born Nazi propagandist, named "Lord Haw-Haw" for the affected and sneering tone he adopted in broadcasts to Britain in WWII. Captured in 1945, he was hanged for treason.

**JUANA INÉS DE LA CRUZ** (1651–1695), Mexican-Spanish poet and scholar. As a girl she left court to become a nun. Criticized for her "unwomanly" studies, she defended women's education in a vigorous letter to her bishop (1691). Her lyric poems, especially the sonnets, are among the finest in Spanish. She died nursing epidemic victims in Mexico City.

**JUAN CARLOS** (1938–      ), king of Spain from Nov. 1975, after the death of Gen. FRANCO. Educated as Franco's successor, he was so named in 1969 in preference to his father Don Juan, son of ALFONSO XIII. In 1962 he married Princess Sophia of Greece, by whom he had three children. On becoming king, he proved to be an unexpectedly strong force for stability and democracy. Personally popular, he was instrumental in thwarting an attempted right-wing military coup in 1981.

**JUAREZ, Benito Pablo** (1806–1872), Mexican national hero, effective ruler from 1861. Of Indian descent, he was imprisoned and exiled as a liberal 1853–55, when he was made justice minister in the administration that ousted SANTA ANNA (1855). His reforms attacked privilege in the Church and the army, precipitating civil war 1855–61. In 1861 he was elected president. The French incursion under MAXIMILIAN 1864–67 forced him to conduct a guerrilla campaign, which he won with US backing. He continued to serve as president from 1867 until his death, but his last years in office saw insurrections.

**JUDAH, Kingdom of**, territory in S Palestine, held by the tribes of Judah and Benjamin, after the breakup of SOLOMON's kingdom under REHOBOAM, c931 BC. The house of David ruled Judah until the destruction of Jerusalem in 587 BC.

**JUDAH HA-LEVI** (c1075–1141), Jewish rabbi, philosopher and poet who lived and worked in Muslim Spain. His *Sefer ha-Kuzari* remains his monument.

**JUDAISM**, the religion of the Jews, the most ancient of the world's surviving monotheistic religions and as such deeply influential on CHRISTIANITY and ISLAM. It sees the world as the creation of a living god and the Jews as his chosen people. Central is the idea of the COVENANT made between God and Abraham, ancestor of the Jews. This was sealed and is commemorated by the ceremony of male CIRCUMCISION; it was reaffirmed at the time of the EXODUS by the PESACH or Passover. Abraham bound himself and his descendants to carry the message of one God to the world in return for His protection. The relationship between God and His chosen people is the great theme of the Hebrew Bible.

Its first five books, the PENTATEUCH, constituted the TORAH, or law, which is the foundation of the religion. It contains a history of the Jews until the death of MOSES, the Ten Commandments and a corpus of ritual and ethical precepts. The Torah is supplemented by a body of oral traditions and interpretations and instructions, set down in the 1st century and known as the Mishnah. With a commentary on it, known as the Gemara, it is part of the TALMUD. Yet doctrinally Judaism is not a dogmatic religion. No analytical statement of the nature of God exists, the concept of the afterlife is undefined, and there is no formulaic creed of beliefs.

The faith was many times in danger of destruction by conquest or corruption from within. Its survival was, often, due to great kings, but principally to great spiritual leaders (among whom Moses ranks almost as a second founder), great PROPHETS and great scholars. Until the conquest of Jerusalem by Babylon in 586 BC the Temple built by SOLOMON was the great religious center. Its destruction and the dispersion of Jewish communities through the ancient world made the SYNAGOGUE, or local meeting, increasingly important. Judaism survived the catastrophic destruction of the second Temple and depopulation of Jerusalem by Romans in 70 AD, thank largely to JOHANAN BEN ZAKKAI. His emphasis on the Torah, with the consolidation of the synagogue, provided Judaism with the intellectual and communi ty strongholds in which to withstand the persecution of ensuing centuries. Also important was the ancient concept of th MESSIAH, a descendant of the house of Davi to be sent by God to restore and rule triumphant Israel, and the strict observanc of Judaic rituals and customs. (See BA MITZVAH; KOSHER.) An important festival the weekly SABBATH; others are ROSI HASHANAH, YOM KIPPUR, SHAVUOT HANNUKAH, TISHAH B'AV.

**JUDAS ISCARIOT** (d.c30 AD), th APOSTLE who betrayed Jesus. For 30 piece of silver he identified Jesus to the soldiers a GETHSEMANE by a kiss of greeting According to MATTHEW he later repente and hanged himself.

**JUDAS MACCABEUS** (d. 160 BC Jewish leader of the HASMONEAN dynasty He defeated Antiochus IV, a SELEUCID kin seeking to force paganism on the Jews, an in 165 BC reconsecrated the Temple. Th event is commemorated by the festival HANNUKAH.

# The Concord World Atlas

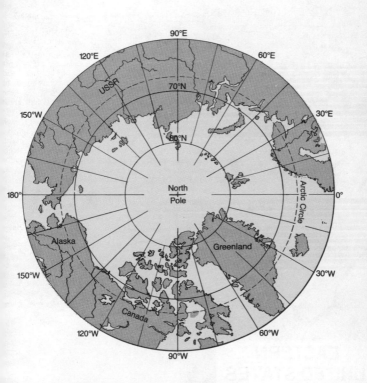

# EASTERN
# UNITED STATES

- ◉ **CITY** population more than 1,000,000
- ◎ **CITY** population more than 500,000
- ○ **CITY** population more than 100,000
- • **City** population more than 50,000
- ○ **City** population less than 50,000
- —— railroads
- highways

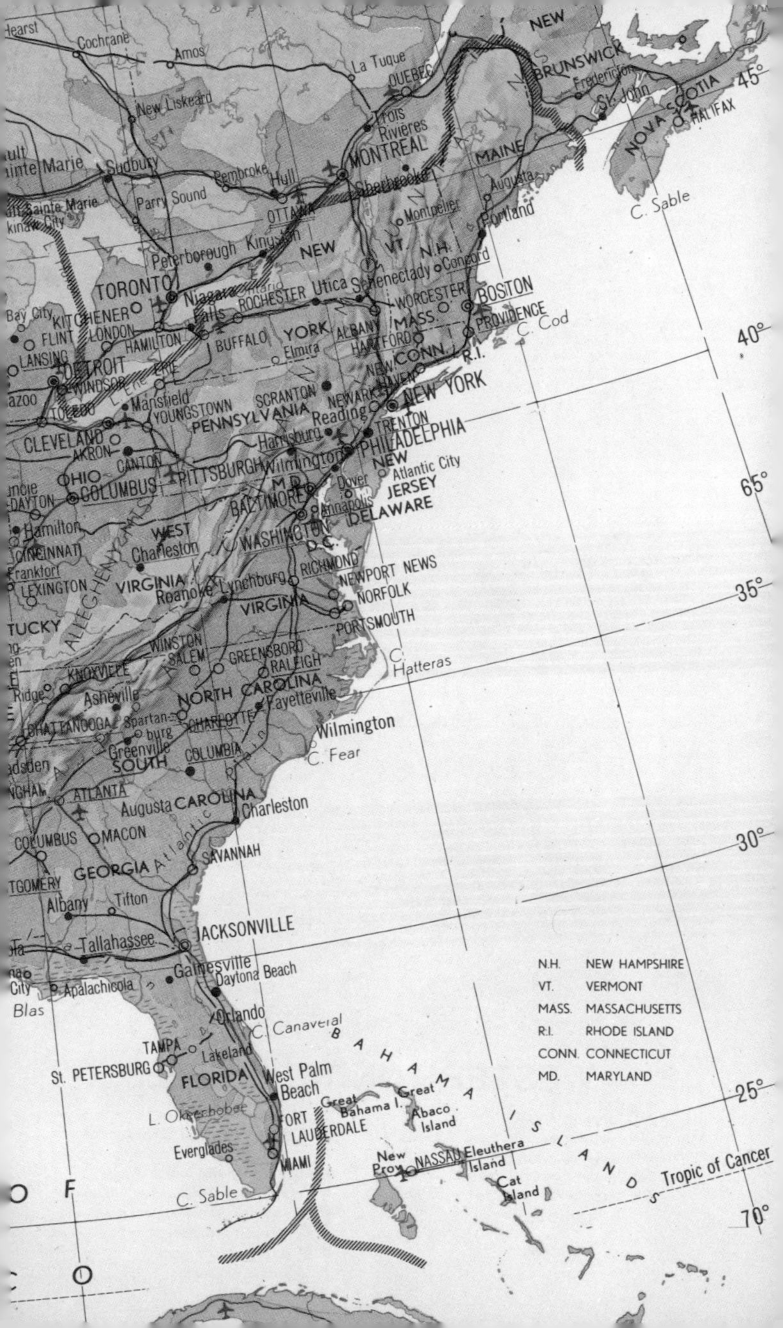

NEW
BRUNSWICK
Fredericton
St. John
NOVA SCOTIA
HALIFAX
45°
C. Sable
Cochrane
Amos
La Tuque
QUEBEC
Trois
Rivières
MONTREAL
MAINE
New Liskeard
Sainte Marie
Sudbury
Parry Sound
Pembroke
Hull
OTTAWA
Sherbrooke
Augusta
Montpelier
Portland
Peterborough Kingston
NEW
VT. N.H.
Concord
C. Sable
TORONTO
Niagara
Falls
ROCHESTER
Utica Schenectady
WORCESTER
BOSTON
40°
KITCHENER
Bay City
Marie
HAMILTON
BUFFALO
YORK
ALBANY
MASS.
PROVIDENCE
FLINT
LONDON
Elmira
HARTFORD
CONN.
R.I.
C. Cod
DETROIT
Lansing
WINDSOR
Erie
NEW
NEW YORK
65°
Mansfield
YOUNGSTOWN
SCRANTON
NEWARK
Toledo
PENNSYLVANIA
Reading
CLEVELAND
Harrisburg
TRENTON
AKRON
PHILADELPHIA
OHIO
CANTON
PITTSBURGH
Wilmington
NEW
COLUMBUS
Dover
Atlantic City
Hamilton
DAYTON
BALTIMORE
Annapolis
JERSEY
DELAWARE
WEST
WASHINGTON
CINCINNATI
Charleston
35°
Frankfort
LEXINGTON
VIRGINIA
Lynchburg
RICHMOND
NEWPORT NEWS
Roanoke
NORFOLK
TUCKY
VIRGINIA
PORTSMOUTH
Ridge
KNOXVILLE
WINSTON
SALEM
GREENSBORO
RALEIGH
Hatteras
Asheville
NORTH CAROLINA
Fayetteville
CHATTANOOGA
Spartan-
burg
CHARLOTTE
Greenville
COLUMBIA
Wilmington
SOUTH
C. Fear
ATLANTA
CAROLINA
COLUMBUS
MACON
Augusta
Charleston
30°
GEORGIA
SAVANNAH
MONTGOMERY
Albany
Tifton
JACKSONVILLE
Tallahassee
Gainesville
Daytona Beach
P. Apalachicola
Orlando
C. Canaveral
Blas
TAMPA
Lakeland
ST. PETERSBURG
FLORIDA
West Palm
Beach
N.H.      NEW HAMPSHIRE
VT.       VERMONT
MASS.     MASSACHUSETTS
R.I.      RHODE ISLAND
CONN.     CONNECTICUT
MD.       MARYLAND
L. Okeechobee
FORT
LAUDERDALE
Great
Bahama I.
Great
Abaco
Island
25°
Everglades
MIAMI
New
Prov.
NASSAU
Eleuthera
Island
OF
C. Sable
Cat
Island
Tropic of Cancer
70°

# WESTERN UNITED STATES

| | |
|---|---|
| ● CITY population more than 1,000,000 | ▢ snow- and icecaps |
| ◉ CITY population more than 500,000 | ▢ tundras and high mountain flora |
| ○ CITY population more than 100,000 | ▢ mixed forest of the temperate zone |
| • City population more than 50,000 | ▢ tropical rain forest |
| ○ City population less than 50,000 | ▢ monsoon forest and thorn scrub |
| — railroads | ▢ steppe- and mountain grassland |
| | ▢ desert and semi-desert |
| highways | ▢ cultivated areas |
| | ▢ irrigated areas |
| | ▢ swamp |

# CENTRAL AMERICA

| | | |
|---|---|---|
| ● | **CITY** | population more than 1,000,000 |
| ◉ | **CITY** | population more than 500,000 |
| ○ | CITY | population more than 100,000 |
| ● | City | population more than 50,000 |
| ○ | City | population less than 50,000 |

— railways
— roads
✈ airport

| | |
|---|---|
| | irrigated areas |
| | mixed forest of the temperate zone |
| | tropical rain forest |
| | monsoon forest and thorn scrub |
| | steppe- and mountain grassland |
| | desert and semi-desert |
| | cultivated areas |
| | swamp |

scale 1: 20,000,000

0 — 250 — 500 st. miles

# NORTHERN SOUTH AMERICA

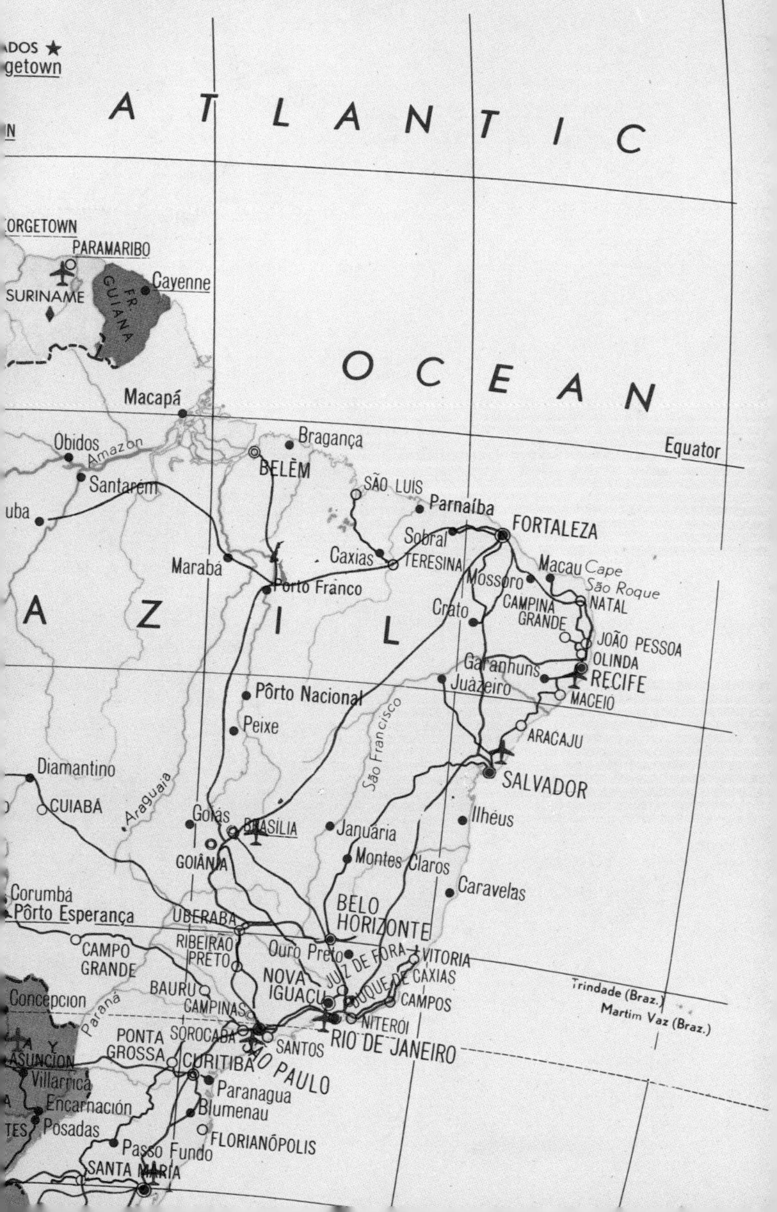

DOS ★
getown

N

A T L A N T I C

ORGETOWN
PARAMARIBO
Cayenne
SURINAME
FR. GUIANA

O C E A N

Macapá

Equator

Obidos
Amazon
Santarém

uba

Bragança

BELÉM
SÃO LUIS
Parnaíba
FORTALEZA

Caxias
Sobral
TERESINA
Macau Cape
São Roque
NATAL

Marabá
Pôrto Franco
Mossoro
CAMPINA
GRANDE
JOÃO PESSOA
OLINDA
RECIFE

A Z I L
Crato

Pôrto Nacional
Garanhuns
Juàzeiro
MACEIO

Peixe

ARACAJU

Diamantino
Januaria
SALVADOR

CUIABÁ
Golás
BRASILIA
Ilhéus

GOIÂNIA
Montes Claros
Caravelas

Corumbá
Pôrto Esperança
UBERABA
BELO
HORIZONTE

CAMPO
GRANDE
RIBEIRÃO
PRETO
Ouro Preto
VITORIA

Concepcion
BAURU
CAMPINAS
NOVA
IGUAÇU
JUIZ DE FORA
DUQUE DE CAXIAS
CAMPOS
Trindade (Braz.)
Martim Vaz (Braz.)

Y
ASUNCION
Villarica
PONTA
GROSSA
SOROCABA
SANTOS
NITEROI
RIO DE JANEIRO
SÃO PAULO

TES
Encarnación
Posadas
CURITIBA
Paranagua
Blumenau
FLORIANÓPOLIS

Passo Fundo
SANTA MARIA

São Francisco

Araguaia

Paraná

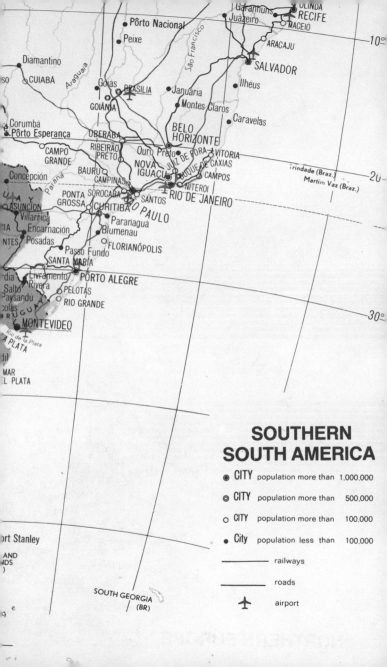

# SOUTHERN SOUTH AMERICA

◉ **CITY** population more than 1,000,000

◎ **CITY** population more than 500,000

○ **CITY** population more than 100,000

• **City** population less than 100,000

―――― railways

―――― roads

✈ airport

**NORTHERN EUROPE**

# NORTHERN AFRICA

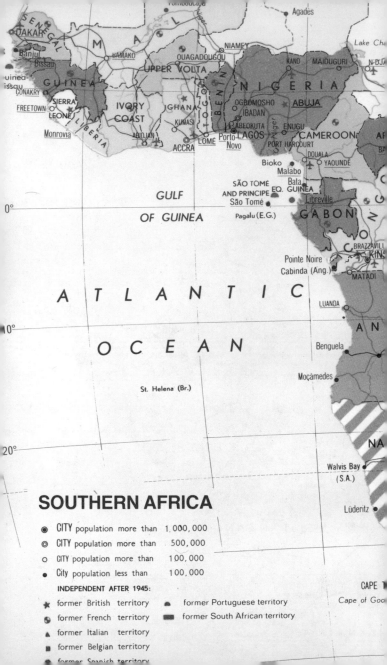

SENEGAL
DAKAR
Banjul
Bissau
uinea-
issau
CONAKRY
FREETOWN
SIERRA
LEONE
Monrovia
LIBERIA

MALI
BAMAKO
Tombouctou
Agades
NIAMEY
Lake Cha
OUAGADOUGOU
UPPER VOLTA
GUINEA
IVORY
COAST
GHANA
KUMASI
ABIDJAN
ACCRA
LOMÉ
BENIN
TOGO
Porto LAGOS
Novo
KANO
MAIDUGURI
N-DJA
N I G E R I A
OGBOMOSHO
IBADAN
ABEOKUTA
ENUGU
PORT HARCOURT
ABUJA
CAMEROON
DOUALA
YAOUNDÉ
AF
BA
Bioko
Malabo
Bata
EQ. GUINEA
SÃO TOMÉ
AND PRINCIPE
São Tomé
Pagalu (E.G.)
Libreville
GABON
G
G
C

GULF

OF GUINEA

0°

A T L A N T I C

0°

O C E A N

St. Helena (Br.)

Pointe Noire
Cabinda (Ang.)
MATADI
BRAZZAVILL
KIN
LUANDA
AN

Benguela

Moçâmedes

20°

NA
Walvis Bay
(S.A.)

Lüderitz

# SOUTHERN AFRICA

- ⊙ CITY population more than 1,000,000
- ◎ CITY population more than 500,000
- ○ CITY population more than 100,000
- • City population less than 100,000

INDEPENDENT AFTER 1945:

- ★ former British territory
- ⑤ former French territory
- ▲ former Italian territory
- ■ former Belgian territory
- ● former Spanish territory
- ▬ former Portuguese territory
- ▬ former South African territory

CAPE T
Cape of Goo

**SOUTH AND WEST ASIA**

# EAST ASIA

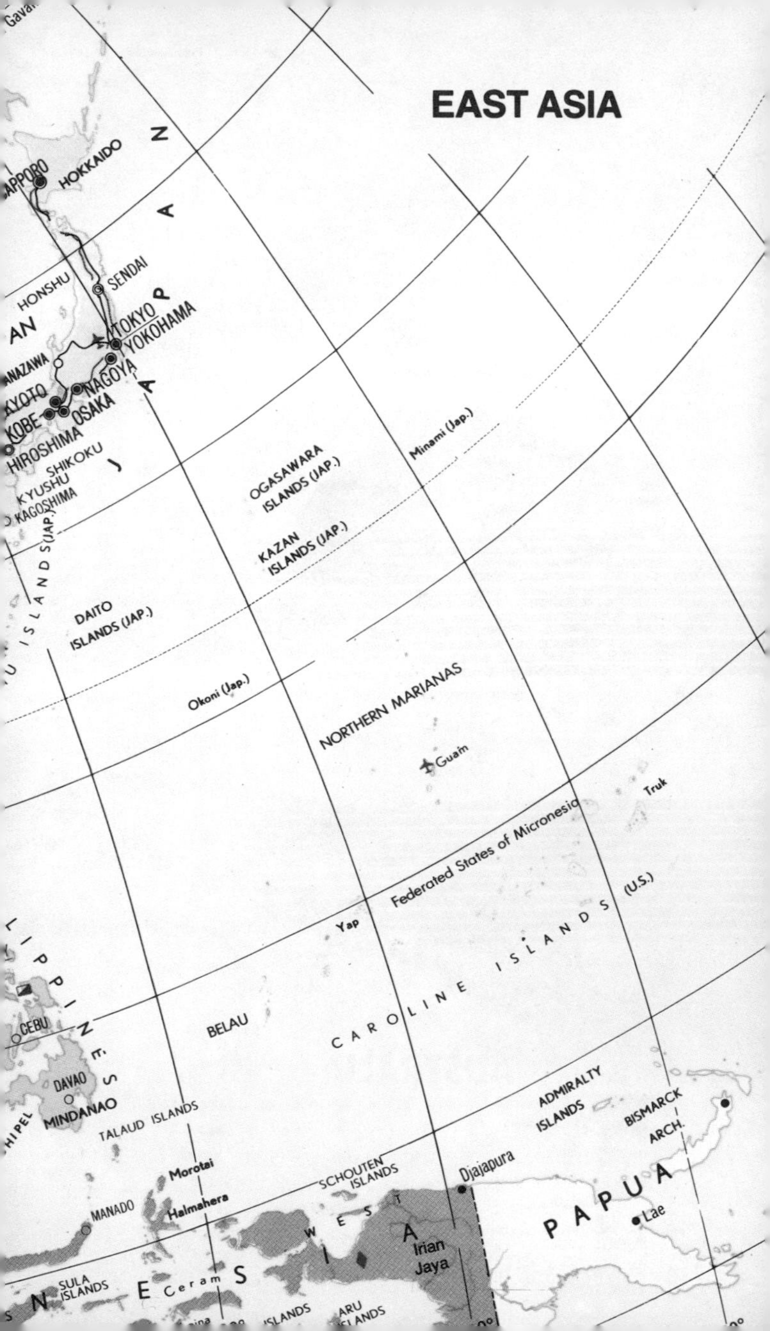

SAPPORO
HOKKAIDO

HONSHU
SENDAI

KANAZAWA
TOKYO
YOKOHAMA

KYOTO
NAGOYA
KOBE
OSAKA
HIROSHIMA
SHIKOKU
KYUSHU
KAGOSHIMA

DAITO
ISLANDS (JAP.)

Okoni (Jap.)

OGASAWARA
ISLANDS (JAP.)

KAZAN
ISLANDS (JAP.)

Minami (Jap.)

NORTHERN MARIANAS

Guam

Truk

Federated States of Micronesia

Yap

CAROLINE ISLANDS (U.S.)

CEBU

BELAU

DAVAO
MINDANAO

TALAUD ISLANDS

ADMIRALTY
ISLANDS

BISMARCK
ARCH.

Morotai

SCHOUTEN
ISLANDS

Djaiapura

PAPUA

MANADO
Halmahera

Lae

SULA
ISLANDS
Ceram

Irian
Jaya

ARU
ISLANDS

# AUSTRALIA

| | | |
|---|---|---|
| | steppe grassland | |
| | savannah and bush woodlands | |
| | irrigated areas | |
| | cultivated areas | |
| | mixed woodlands | |
| | tropical rain forest | |
| | high mountain flora | |
| | desert and semi-desert | |

| | | |
|---|---|---|
| ⊙ | CITY | population more than 1,000,000 |
| ◎ | CITY | population more than 500,000 |
| ○ | CITY | population more than 100,000 |
| ● | City | population more than 50,000 |
| ○ | City | population less than 50,000 |
| | | roads |
| | | railways |
| ✈ | | airport |

scale 1 : 20,000,000

0          250          500 st. miles

**Map labels:**

TIMOR SEA · Melville Island · Bathurst Island · Cape Londonderry · Joseph Bonaparte Gulf · Darwin · Rum Jungle · Pine Cr · Kathe · Ar · Collier Bay · KIMBERLEY PLATEAU 3000 · ARNHEM LAND · Wyndham · Victoria · Nave Hill · Broome · Derby · Mt. Wells · Hall's Creek · NORTH · TERR · Sturt Creek · Great Sandy Desert · The Granites · Dampier · Roebourne · Port Hedland · Marble Bar · Lake Mackay · Preston · Prestoria · Mt. Macpherson 1205 · Lake Macdonald · Northwest Cape · Onslow · HAMERSLEY RANGE · De Grey · Lake Disappointment · MACDON · Mt. Brockman · Mount Tom Price · Mt. Newman · Lake Amadeus · Salt Lake · Mt. Augustus 3627 · Gibson Desert · 3507 Mt. Olga · Carnarvon · WESTERN AUSTRALIA · 3238 · MUSGRAVE RANGES · Lake Carnegie · Mt. Aloysius · Wiluna · Great · 1705 Mt. Murchison · Meekatharra · Sandstone · Victoria Dese · Mount Magnet · Laverton · Noman's Land · S · AUS · Geraldton · Dongara · Lake Barlee · Menzies · Forrest · Tarcoola · Moore · Lake Moore · Kalgoorlie · Nullarbor Plain · Eucla · Northam · Coolgardie · Lake Cowan · PERTH · Mt. William · Perth-Fremantle · 1910 · Narrogin · Norseman · GREAT AUSTRALIAN · BIG · Collie · Bunbury · Esperance · Augusta · Manjimup · Cape Leeuwin · Albany

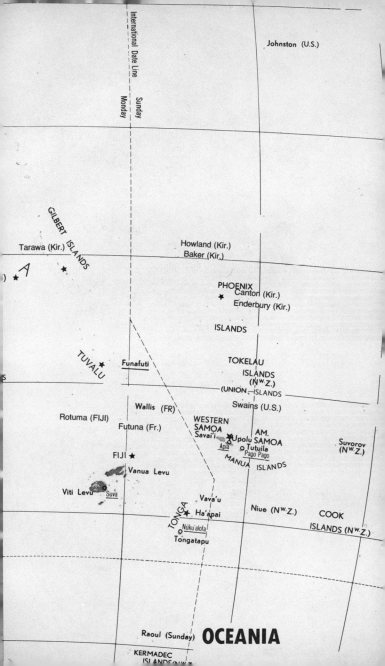

Johnston (U.S.)

International Date Line

Sunday Monday

GILBERT ISLANDS

Tarawa (Kir.)

Howland (Kir.)
Baker (Kir.)

PHOENIX
Canton (Kir.)
Enderbury (Kir.)

ISLANDS

TUVALU

Funafuti

TOKELAU

ISLANDS
(N.Z.)
(UNION ISLANDS)

Wallis (FR)

Swains (U.S.)

Rotuma (FIJI)

Futuna (Fr.)

WESTERN
SAMOA
Savai'i

AM.
SAMOA

Upolu

Apia

Tutuila

Pago Pago

Suvorov
(N.Z.)

FIJI

Vanua Levu

MANUA ISLANDS

Viti Levu

Suva

Vava'u

Niue (N.Z.)

COOK

TONGA

Ha'apai

Nuku'alofa

ISLANDS (N.Z.)

Tongatapu

Raoul (Sunday)

**OCEANIA**

KERMADEC
ISLANDS (N.Z.)

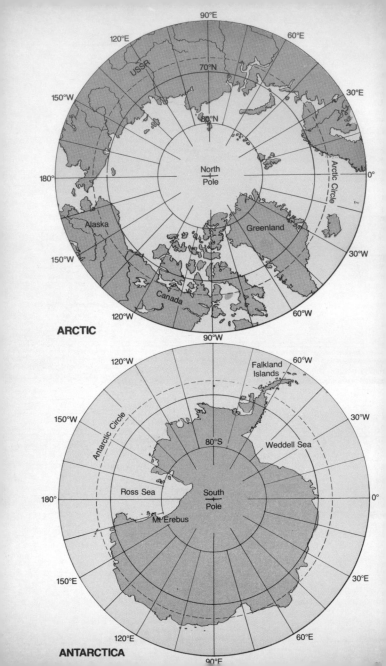

**ARCTIC**

**ANTARCTICA**

**JUDE, Saint,** one of the APOSTLES, possible author of the New Testament Epistle of Jude, which combats heresy. Jude is an anglicized form of Judas, to distinguish him from JUDAS ISCARIOT.

**JUDGES,** seventh book of the Old Testament. It recounts the exploits of military leaders, known as "judges," between the time of Joshua and the birth of Samuel. Israel's successive apostasies from God are punished by enemy oppression, until God sends a judge to deliver the people. The main judges are Barak, DEBORAH, GIDEON, Abimelech, Jephthah and SAMSON.

**JUDICIAL REVIEW.** See SUPREME COURT OF THE UNITED STATES; UNITED STATES CONSTITUTION.

**JUDITH,** book of the Old Testament APOCRYPHA. During an Assyrian invasion a young Jewish widow, Judith, seduces the Assyrian general Holofernes in order to murder him. She shows his head to the Jewish army, which routs its leaderless enemy.

**JUDO,** a form of unarmed combat, a sport developed by Jigoro Kano in 1882 as a less violent form of Japanese *jujitsu.* It uses grappling and throwing holds, combined with a skillful use of balance and timing, to turn an opponent's strength against him; judo can thus enable a weaker person to overcome a stronger. Colored belts, ranging from white for beginners to black for experts, denote proficiency grades. Introduced into the US in 1902, it has been regulated by the Amateur Athletic Union since 1952, and has been featured in the OLYMPIC GAMES since 1964.

**JUDSON, Arthur Leon** (1881–1975), US impresario who managed many of the great conductors, violinists and pianists of his time. He inaugurated classical concerts on radio (1926) and established a chain of radio stations which became the Columbia Broadcasting System in 1928. His Columbia Management Corp (founded 1930) was the pioneer in bringing world-class musicians to small-town America.

**JUGENDSTIL,** German ART NOUVEAU style 1890–c1910. Centering particularly on Munich and Vienna, it was named for the magazine *Die Jugend* (Youth). Among major exponents was Henry VAN DER VELDE.

**JUILLIARD STRING QUARTET,** musical group founded in 1946 by William SCHUMAN, then president of the Juilliard School of Music, New York City. In 1962 it became "quartet in residence" at the Library of Congress. The group has given premieres of many American compositions.

**JUJITSU.** See JUDO.

**JULIANA** (1909– ), queen of the Netherlands (1948–80) following the abdication of her mother Queen Wilhelmina. In 1937 she married Prince Bernhard of Lippe-Biesterfeld; they had four daughters. She abdicated (1980) in favor of her daughter Princess Beatrix.

**JULIUS II** (1443–1513), pope who reigned from 1503. As Cardinal Giuliano della Rovere he dominated INNOCENT VIII but went into exile 1492–1503 when his bitter enemy Rodrigo Borgia became pope as ALEXANDER VI. As pope, Julius commanded the armies that reconquered the papal states, and led the HOLY LEAGUE against France (1510). The Fifth LATERAN Council, which he assembled, criticized the French Church and attacked Church corruption. Patron of RAPHAEL, MICHELANGELO and BRAMANTE, he laid the foundation stone of the new SAINT PETER'S BASILICA.

**JULY,** the seventh month of the year, named for Julius Caesar, who reorganized the CALENDAR. It has 31 days.

**JULY REVOLUTION,** popular rising in France, July 26–30, 1830, against the reactionary aims of King Charles X. Middle-class opposition was aroused when the ultraroyalist POLIGNAC ministry published the July Ordinances, which suspended freedom of the press, dissolved the Chamber and reduced the small electorate by 75%. Rioting broke out on July 27, and by July 29 most of Paris was in insurgent hands; on July 30 Charles repealed the Ordinances, but was forced to abdicate. His cousin the duke of Orleans became king as LOUIS PHILIPPE.

**JUNE,** sixth month of the year, named for the Roman goddess Juno; it has 30 days.

**JUNEAU,** capital city of Alaska, sited in the Panhandle area. Its ice-free harbor and its airport make it a trade center; lumbering and fishing are also important, as is tourism. Mt Juneau and Mt Roberts overlook the city. Pop 19,528.

**JUNG, Carl Gustav** (1875–1961), Swiss psychiatrist who founded analytical psychology. He studied PSYCHIATRY at Basel University, his postgraduate studies being of PARAPSYCHOLOGY. After working with BLEULER and JANET, he met FREUD (1907), whom he followed for some years. His disagreement with Freud's belief in the purely sexual nature of the LIBIDO, however, led to a complete break between the two in 1913. In *Psychological Types* (1921) he expounded his views on INTROVERSION AND EXTRAVERSION. Later he investigated anthropology and the occult, which led to his theory of ARCHETYPES, or universal symbols present in the COLLECTIVE UNCONSCIOUS. (See also ANIMA AND ANIMUS; PERSONA; PSYCHOANALYSIS; PSYCHOLOGY.)

**JUNGFRAU**, third-highest mountain in the Bernese Alps, S central Switzerland, 13,642ft high. A railroad runs up to the Jungfraujoch, the mountain's saddle, the site of the highest observatory in Europe, at about 11,000ft.

**JUNKER**, Prussian landowner of the middle aristocracy. The junkers were powerful in the Prussian bureaucracy and army from the 17th century. In the 19th century the name was applied to German aristocratic conservatives generally.

**JUNO.** See HERA.

**JUPITER.** See ZEUS.

**JUPITER**, the largest and most massive planet in the solar system (diameter about 143Mm, mass 317.8 times that of earth), fifth of the major planets from the sun. Jupiter is larger than all the other planets combined and, with a mean solar distance of 5.20AU and a "year" of 11.86 earth-years, is the greatest contributor to the solar system's angular MOMENTUM. Jupiter is believed to consist mainly of solid, liquid and gaseous HYDROGEN. Its disk, observed at close range by two US VOYAGER space probes in 1979, is marked by prominent cloud-belts paralleling its equator. These are occasionally interrupted by stormlike turbulences and particularly the **Great Red Spot**, an elliptical area 40Mm long and 13Mm wide: unlike most other features of Jupiter's disk, which have a lifetime of a few days, it has been observed for about 150 years. Another long-term feature, the **South Tropical Disturbance**, was first observed in 1901 and disappeared in 1939. Jupiter's day is about 9.92h, and this high rotational velocity causes a visible flattening of the poles: the equatorial diameter is some 7% greater than the polar diameter. Jupiter has 16 known moons, the two largest of which, Callisto and Ganymede, are larger than MERCURY. Io exhibits volcanism, probably because of tidal action resulting from its close proximity to Jupiter. The planet also has a ring system, much fainter than that of Saturn and invisible from earth. Jupiter radiates energy, possibly because of nuclear reactions in its core or a gravitational contraction of the planet.

**JURA MOUNTAINS**, range in W Europe. It runs from the Rhône R to the Rhine R on the Swiss-German border, a series of heavily forested ridges crossed by gorges and with fertile valleys. The highest peak is Crêt de la Neige (5,652ft).

**JURASSIC**, the middle period of the MESOZOIC era, lasting from about 190 to 135 million years ago. (See also GEOLOGY.)

**JURISPRUDENCE.** See LAW.

**JURY**, in COMMON LAW, body of people responsible for deciding points of fact in legal proceedings such as inquests and trials. The jury, probably a product of the Norman practice of calling character witnesses, was adopted from English law into the US system; the 6th and 7th Amendments to the Constitution provide for jury trial in most criminal and civil cases. A grand jury, usually of 23 persons, hears evidence and decides whether it should go for trial; a petit (small) jury of 12 persons sits at the trial proper and its verdict was until recently required to be unanimous. In 1970 and 1971, however, the Supreme Court held that six-person juries and less-than-unanimous verdicts were permissible in state (but not federal) criminal trials.

**JUSTICE, US Department of,** federal executive department created by Congress in 1870. Headed by the ATTORNEY GENERAL, its functions are to enforce federal laws, administer federal prisons and supervise district attorneys and marshals. It also represents the federal government in legal matters and legally advises the president.

**JUSTIFICATION BY FAITH,** Pauline doctrine that justification is given freely by God on the grounds of Christ's ATONEMENT and by imputation of his righteousness. Justification is God's declaration that a person is righteous. The sinner is justified through believing in Jesus Christ, not by his own works. The Reformers, especially LUTHER, emphasized the doctrine in opposition to the popular medieval Roman Catholic belief in justification by works. It is no longer controversial.

**JUSTINIAN I** (483–565), Byzantine emperor 527–565, the last to rule in the West. His generals BELISARIUS and NARSES reconquered Italy and North Africa 533–534. Justinian's attempts to impose heavy taxation and religious Orthodoxy on the diverse peoples and sects of the empire, especially the MONOPHYSITES, caused periodic unrest. In 532 political rivalries in the capital caused the Nika riots, quelled only by the decisiveness of the empress THEODORA. Justinian commissioned the great *Digest* of Roman law (see CORPUS JURIS CIVILIS) and built such great churches as HAGIA SOPHIA and SAN VITALE.

**JUTES**, Germanic people who originated in Scandinavia, probably in Jutland. With the ANGLES and SAXONS they invaded Britain in the 5th century AD, settling in S and SE England. Their national identity was soon lost, although some cultural influence seems to have survived in Kent.

**JUTLAND,** peninsula in NW Europe, comprising continental Denmark and N Schleswig-Holstein state, West Germany. The name is usually applied only to the Danish territory.

**JUTLAND, Battle of,** only major naval battle in WWI, fought between the British and German fleets off the coast of Jutland on May 31, 1916, for domination of the North Sea. The British fleet under Admiral JELLICOE lost more ships but won a tactical victory.

**JUVENAL,** (c60–130 AD), Roman poet whose 16 *Satires* (100–128 AD) are scathing attacks on the corruption of social and political life in Rome, which he contrasts with older standards. Many of his epigrammatic sayings—for example, "A sound mind in a sound body"—have passed into everyday use.

**JUVENILE DELINQUENCY,** term for crime committed by minors. Illegal activity by juveniles appears to be increasing throughout the world, although it may be that it is simply attracting more attention. In the US 50% of those arrested for theft are under eighteen years of age. Personal factors such as poor health, environmental factors such as cultural deprivation and the general emotional crises of adolescence are all seen as contributing to juvenile delinquency. Young offenders in the US are dealt with in JUVENILE COURTS. Often their sentences may depend on reports from a social worker, psychiatrist or welfare worker, the policy being to "cure" rather than suppress criminal tendencies, but in extreme cases offenders may be sent to correctional institutions.

11th letter of the English alphabet, from the Semitic *kaph*, representing the palm of the hand, and the ancient Greek *kappa*. K stands for *King* in chess.

**K2** (also, unofficially, Mt Godwin Austen or Dapsang), at 28,250ft the world's second highest peak after Mt Everest. Situated in the Karakoram Range in N Kashmir, it was first climbed in 1954.

**KAABA,** most sacred shrine of ISLAM, in the courtyard of the Great Mosque at Mecca, Saudi Arabia. Pilgrims must circle the flat-roofed Kaaba seven times and at its E corner kiss the Black Stone, which is said to have been given to Adam on his fall from paradise.

**KABALEVSKY, Dmitri** (1904–    ), Russian composer and critic. His work includes symphonies, ballet, chamber music and operas such as *Colas Breugnon* (1938) and *The Taras Family* (1949).

**KABUKI,** traditional Japanese popular theater which developed in the 17th century in contrast to the aristocratic NOH theater. A blending of dance, song and mime, the kabuki dramatized both traditional stories and contemporary events in a stylized but exuberant fashion. It remains popular today and has influenced much Western theatrical thought.

**KABUL,** capital and largest city of Afghanistan, lying in a mountain valley (elev. 5,900ft) on both banks of the Kabul R. The city is a commercial and manufacturing center with cement and textile industries. Founded in ancient times, Kabul fell to many conquerors because of its strategic location near important mountain passes. It was occupied by Russian troops in 1979. Pop 913,200.

**KADÁR, János** (1912–    ), Hungarian politician, premier in 1956–58 and 1961–65 and first secretary of the Socialist Workers' Party. As leader of the counter-revolutionaries during the 1956 anti-Soviet uprising, he had many rebel leaders executed. In power, while remaining close to the USSR, he allowed a slightly flexible "goulash communism" to evolve.

**KAFKA, Franz** (1883–1924), German-language writer born in Prague of Jewish parents. Most of Kafka's stories confront his protagonists with nightmarish situations which they cannot resolve or escape from. They reflect his profound sense of alienation, and his inhibitions and shortcomings, particularly in relation to the powerful figure of his father. Kafka died of tuberculosis at age 40. His friend and executor Max BROD ignored his instructions to destroy all his work, and subsequently published Kafka's many short stories and his novels *The Trial* (1925), *The Castle* (1926) and *Amerika* (1927).

**KAHN, Herman** (1922–    ), US physicist and futurologist who wrote two widely read, controversial works on modern warfare, *On Thermonuclear War* (1960) and *Thinking About the Unthinkable* (1962). He established his own think tank, the Hudson Institute (1961), which produced studies on national security and social issues. He coauthored two volumes of futurology, *The Year 2000* (1967) and *The Next 200 Years* (1976).

**KAHN, Louis Isadore** (1901–1974), US architect, noted for his work on housing projects and university buildings, particularly the Richards Medical Research Laboratories at the U. of Pennsylvania, where he was a professor.

**KAHN, Otto Hermann** (1867–1934), German-born US banker and patron of the arts. As a member of the New York Metropolitan Opera Company board he instituted many reforms, and appointed TOSCANINI as principal conductor.

**KAISER, Henry John** (1882–1967), US industrialist, founder of the Kaiser-Frazer Corporation. He contributed greatly to the Allied war effort in WWII by his development of faster production techniques for ships, aircraft and military vehicles, especially the famous "jeep."

**KALAHARI DESERT**, arid plain of some 100,000sq mi in S Africa. It lies mainly in Botswana but extends into Namibia and South Africa. The region has low annual rainfall and only seasonal pasture for sheep. It is inhabited only by Bushmen. There is a wide variety of game.

**KALI** (Hindi: black mother), Hindu goddess of fearsome aspect, associated with the god SHIVA (her husband) in his role as destroyer of evil by death and disease, and once propitiated with blood sacrifice. (See also THUGS.)

**KALININ, Mikhail Ivanovich** (1875–1946), Russian revolutionary leader. A loyal Stalinist, Kalinin was chairman of the central executive (now the presidium) from 1919 and a member of the Politburo from 1925.

**KALMUCKS**, a Mongol people who now inhabit parts of W China and the USSR, especially the Kalmuck SSR along the Volga R. Exiled by the Soviet government in 1945, they were returned to their lands in 1957. Famous as horsemen and soldiers, they are traditionally nomadic, but many have now turned to agriculture and settled down.

**KALTENBORN, H. V.** (1878–1965), US journalist who was a pioneer radio news analyst (1922). Famous for his knowledgeable commentaries as well as his rapid delivery and dignified diction, he was a full-time broadcaster for CBS (1929–40) and NBC (1940–55).

**KAMCHATKA PENINSULA**, land area and oblast in the USSR which extends about 750mi S from NE Siberia to separate the Sea of Okhotsk from the Bering Sea. It is largely tundra and pine forest, and has

Siberia's highest peak, Klyuchevskaya Sopka (15,584ft) and includes 22 active volcanoes, along with geysers and hot springs. Its main city is Petropavlovsk-Kamchatsky.

**KAMEHAMEHA I** (c1738–1819), Hawaiian monarch from 1790, a benevolent despot who united the islands (1810). He encouraged foreign contact and trade, but always sought to preserve the independence of his country and its people.

**KAMPALA**, capital of Uganda on the largest lake in Africa, Victoria Nyanza. A communications and business center, it produces foodstuffs, shoes and textiles. Pop 458,000.

**Official name:** Democratic Kampuchea
**Capital:** Phnom Penh
**Area:** 69,892sq mi
**Population:** 6,000,000
**Languages:** Khmer
**Religions:** Hinayana Buddhist
**Monetary unit(s):** 1 Riel = 100 sen

**KAMPUCHEA,** formerly Cambodia, republic in SE Asia, known as the KHMER REPUBLIC, 1970–75. Laos lies to the N, South Vietnam to the E and Thailand to the W and N.

**Land.** About half of Kampuchea is covered by tropical forest; at the center of the country the Mekong R flows from N to S, providing 900mi of navigable waterways. During the rainy season, May-Oct., the river backs up to the Tonle Sap Lake, vastly increasing its size and leaving rich fertile silt, excellent for rice production. There are two mountain ranges: the Dong Rek to the N and the Cardamom to the SW.

**People.** About 85% of the population are Khmers, with sizeable minorities of Chinese and Vietnamese, and smaller groups of Cham-Malays, Mayao-Polynesian and Austro-Asian hill tribes. The official language is Khmer but many people speak French. Kampuchea is one of the few countries in SE Asia which is sparsely populated and the majority of the people work in agriculture. The capital and largest city is Phnom Penh.

**Economy.** The economy, which is overwhelmingly agricultural, was severely disrupted during most of the 1970s; famine was widespread in 1979 after warfare had prevented the planting of the rice crop. In normal times the principal product is rice. Other crops are corn, tobacco, sugar and pepper, and fishing is locally significant. Rubber cultivation was very important to the Cambodian economy and, like rice, was one of the largest exports. The rubber plantations were badly damaged in the fighting in the early 1970s and production has not recovered. Forests are extensive but underexploited. Mineral reserves, including phosphates and iron ore, are limited.

**History.** The FUNAN kingdom was established in Kampuchea for the first six centuries AD, but late in the 6th century the Funans were overcome by the Khmers from the neighboring Chenla state who founded the powerful KHMER EMPIRE. This empire, with its capital at ANGKOR, extended to modern Laos, Thailand and S Vietnam and lasted until the 15th century. From the 14th to the 19th centuries Cambodia's area was reduced by Thai conquests in the N and by the Annamese in the S. In 1863 Cambodia asked for, and was placed under, French protection. This lasted until 1954 when Cambodia became independent, largely owing to Prince Norodom SIHANOUK's negotiations. Sihanouk, as head of state from 1960, tried to keep Cambodia neutral in the VIETNAM WAR but this proved increasingly difficult. He broke off relations with the US, 1965–69, and allowed the Vietnamese communists to use Cambodia as a supply base. The Cambodian communists (Khmers Rouges) emerged by 1970 as a powerful political group with a standing army of 3,000 men. In 1970 General Lon Nol staged a military coup and established the Khmer Republic, supported by the US. In alliance with the Khmers Rouges, Sihanouk formed an exile government—the National United Front of Cambodia—in Peking. Civil war raged between Lon Nol's government forces and the Khmers Rouges, who by 1973 numbered 30,000 and were gaining control of the country despite intensive US bombing until 1973. Fighting was especially heavy at the beginning of 1975; in April Phnom Penh was besieged and surrendered to the Khmers Rouges. "The Royal Government of the National Union of Cambodia (Kampuchea)" returned from exile under Sihanouk. Following the resignation of Sihanouk in 1976, Pol Pot became prime minister of the newly named Democratic Kampuchea. The regime enacted harsh measures, evacuating all cities and suppressing opposition. In 1978 Vietnam launched attacks against Kampuchea, and in 1979 Vietnamese troops captured Phnom Penh and proclaimed the People's Republic of Kampuchea. Pol Pot, as commander-in-chief of the Khmers Rouges forces, continued to fight the Vietnamese from unoccupied parts of the country. The UN called for the withdrawal of all foreign troops from Kampuchea (1979); few countries have recognized the legitimacy of the People's Republic of Kampuchea.

**KANDINSKY, Wassily** (1866–1944), Russian painter, widely regarded as one of the fathers of ABSTRACT ART. A founder (1911) of the BLAUE REITER group of artists, he taught at the BAUHAUS design school 1922–33. His works, largely abstract, are characterized by their dynamic color and style.

**KANGAROOS,** MARSUPIAL mammals with large hind feet, strong hind limbs and a tail. Normally quadrupedal, they rise to a bipedal stance when moving quickly, progressing in huge leaps. The tail in true kangaroos is heavily built and serves to balance the body in bipedal locomotion. It may also be used as a prop during fighting when a kangaroo can kick with both hind feet together. Female kangaroos have a pouch containing the teats, in which the young, born singly and at a very "premature" stage, are raised. Kangaroos are herbivorous; the alimentary canal shows strong similarities to the stomach of placental, ruminant mammals. A diverse group, kangaroos include true kangaroos, WALLABIES, Tree kangaroos and Rat kangaroos.

**KANSAS,** state, central US, bounded to the E by Mo., to the S by Okla., to the W by Col. and to the N by Neb. The state's name was derived from the Kansas or KANSA INDIANS, earliest inhabitants of the area.

**Land.** Kansas is not all prairie, as is sometimes thought. Its soils are generally dark, fertile loam, irrigated by a system of over 100 artificial lakes. The two major river systems are the Kansas and the Arkansas, with their tributaries. Kansas has cold winters and warm to hot summers. Rainfall averages about 40in in the SE and under 18in in the W.

**People.** The population is concentrated in the E of the state and, reflecting the change from a farm to a mixed farm-factory economy, nearly two-thirds live in urban areas. Kansas is still governed under its original constitution of 1859. The legislature now has a Senate of 40 members and a House of Representatives, comprising 125

**Name of state:** Kansas
**Capital:** Topeka
**Statehood:** Jan. 29, 1861 (34th state)
**Familiar name:** Sunflower State.
**Area:** 82,264sq mi
**Population:** 2,363,208
**Elevation:** Highest—4039ft.,
Mt. Sunflower. Lowest—680ft.,
Verdigris River in Montgomery County
**Motto:** Ad Astra per Aspera
(To the Stars through Difficulties)
**State flower:** Sunflower
**State bird:** Western meadowlark
**State tree:** Cottonwood
**State song:** "Home on the Range"

members.

**Economy.** Since WWII manufacturing has developed rapidly and is now the state's chief money earner. Kansas is the nation's largest wheat producer, and livestock, dairy products and poultry account for a major proportion of agricultural income. Petroleum, natural gas and helium are important mineral resources. Principal manufactures include processed foods, aerospace equipment, farm machinery and petroleum products.

**History.** The Kansas area remained in European hands for some time, but in 1803 the US acquired most of Kansas under the LOUISIANA PURCHASE and used the region for Indian resettlement from the E. The cutting of the SANTA FE TRAIL (1821) and the OREGON TRAIL (1830) led to the first permanent white settlements. In 1854 the KANSAS-NEBRASKA ACT made the territory the focus of the growing slavery problem, a dispute which resulted in virtual civil war. Anti-slavery forces finally gained control and in 1861 Kansas achieved statehood. After the Civil War came rapid settlement and economic expansion, aided by railroad construction and cattle ranching in the W; mineral exploitation in WWI and growth in manufacturing industries after WWII gave Kansas a solid industrial, agricultural and mining economy. Going into the 1980s, Kansas continued to be strong in the production of wheat and aerospace

equipment. It enjoyed a low unemployment rate (4.9%) and a high annual average per capita income ($9,233).

**KANSAS CITY,** city in W Mo., opposite Kansas City, Kan. It was founded in 1833 and became the eastern terminus of the Santa Fe trail. It is an important port of entry and industrial center and has extensive stockyards. Pop 448,159.

**KANSAS-NEBRASKA ACT,** bill passed by Congress in 1854 which upset the balance of power between slave and free states and helped bring on the Civil War. It established Kansas and Nebraska with a provision that each territory, and subsequent ones, could decide for itself whether or not to introduce slavery. Settlers were poured in by both North and South in an attempt to establish control. The act upset the MISSOURI COMPROMISE (1820–21) and led to the formation of the REPUBLICAN PARTY.

**KANT, Immanuel** (1724–1804), German philosopher, one of the world's greatest thinkers. He was born and lived in Königsberg (Kaliningrad). The starting point for Kant's "critical" philosophy was the work of David HUME, who awakened Kant from his "dogmatic slumber" and led him to make his "Copernican revolution in philosophy." This consisted of the radical view found in *Critique of Pure Reason* (1781) that objective reality (the phenomenal world) can be known only because the mind imposes the forms of its own intuitions—time and space—upon it. Things that cannot be perceived in experience (noumena) cannot be known, but as Kant says in *Critique of Practical Reason* (1788) their existence must be presumed in order to provide for man's free will (see CATEGORICAL IMPERATIVE). In his third major work, *Critique of Judgment* (1790), he makes aesthetic and teleological judgments serve to mediate between the sensible and intelligible worlds which, he divided sharply in the first two *Critiques*.

**KAPITZA, Peter Leonidovich** (1894– ), Russian physicist best known for his work on low-temperature physics (see CRYOGENICS), especially his discovery of the SUPERFLUIDITY of HELIUM II. During the 1920s and early 1930s he worked at England's Cavendish Laboratory and directed the Institute for Physical Problems after he returned to the USSR (1934). He was an outspoken advocate of freedom of thought and scientific exchange and was awarded the 1978 Nobel Prize for Physics.

**KARACHI,** former capital (1947–59) and largest city of Pakistan. The country's major port and industrial center, it stands on the Arabian Sea near the Indus Delta in Sind province, of which it is the capital. Among its manufactures are automobiles, steel, petroleum products and textiles. Karachi began to develop as a trading center in the early 18th century. Pop 3,498,000.

**KARAJAN, Herbert von** (1908–    ), Austrian conductor. He directed the Berlin State Opera 1938–45; the Vienna State Opera 1954–64 and concurrently from 1954 the Berlin Philharmonic Orchestra.

**KARAMANLIS, Constantine** (1907–    ), Greek statesman who in 1974 returned to national acclaim as prime minister and leader of the New Democratic Party after the overthrow of the Colonels' junta (1967–74). A lawyer, Karamanlis held several ministries 1946–55 and was premier 1955–63, apart from March–May 1958 and Sept.–Nov. 1961. Parliament (1975) approved a new republican constitution supported by Karamanlis. In 1980 he was elevated to the presidency.

**KARLOFF, Boris** (1887–1969), stage name of William Henry Pratt, British actor who rose to fame with his sympathetic portrayal of the monster in the film *Frankenstein* (1930). He infused villainous roles with a subtly understated sense of evil.

**KARMA**, Sanskrit term denoting the inevitable effect of man's actions on his destiny in successive lives, central to Buddhist and Hindu thought. (See also TRANSMIGRATION OF SOULS.)

**KARMAN, Theodore von** (1881–1963), Hungarian-born US aeronautics engineer best known for his mathematical approach to problems in aeronautics (especially in jet engineering) and astronautics.

**KARPOV, Anatoly** (1951–    ), a Russian chess prodigy who became the Soviet champion in his early twenties. He was awarded the world chess championship in 1975, after reigning champion Bobby FISCHER of the US had repeatedly refused to defend his title. In 1981, Karpov defeated his principal challenger, Viktor KORCHNOI, for the second time.

**KARSH, Yousuf** (1908–    ), Turkish-Armenian born Canadian portrait photographer, whose company used the professional name Karsh of Ottawa. In 1935 he was appointed the Canadian government's official photographer.

**KASAVUBU, Joseph** (c1915–1969), African politician, first president of the Republic of Congo (now Zaire) 1960–65. He ousted Premier Patrice LUMUMBA but was himself supplanted (1965) by Col. Joseph MOBUTU.

**KASHMIR**, territory administered since 1972 by India (Jammu and Kashmir) and Pakistan (Azad Kashmir), bordered by those countries and by Afghanistan and China. Ever since Indian partition in 1947 the territory, which was formerly one of India's largest princely states, has been a cause of conflict between India and Pakistan, with some interference from China 1959–63, cease-fire lines being drawn and redrawn repeatedly. An agreement in 1972 confirmed the positions held by both sides at the end of the 1971 war. The Jhelum R forms the rich and scenically beautiful Vale of Kashmir. The region is mainly agricultural but also produces timber, medicines, silk, carpets and perfume oil. The chief cities are Srinagar (Jammu) and Muzaffarabad (Azad).

**KATANGA.** See SHABA.

**KATTEGAT**, strait between Denmark and Sweden, linked by the Skagerrak to the North Sea and in the E to the Baltic. It is about 140mi long and 40–100mi wide.

**KATYN FOREST**, site in the USSR of a massacre of some 4,250 Polish officers in WWII. The mass grave was reported in 1943 by the Germans, who accused the Russians, who in their turn accused the Germans. Stalin refused a Red Cross enquiry; the Polish government in exile in London took this as an admission of Russian guilt.

**KAUFFMANN, (Maria Ann) Angelica** (1741–1807), Swiss artist of the neoclassical school. She worked in England in 1766–81 and was a friend of Sir Joshua REYNOLDS. She is noted for her portraits but is best remembered as a designer for Robert and James ADAM.

**KAUFMAN, George Simon** (1889–1961), US dramatist who collaborated on several successful plays noted for their dry satirical humor. Among his works are, with Marc Connelly, *Beggar on Horseback* (1924); and with Moss Hart *You Can't Take it With You* (1936). He won Pulitzer prizes in 1932 and 1937.

**KAUNDA, Kenneth David** (1924–    ), first president of Zambia, from 1964. From 1953 he worked ardently for African rule in the then British colony of N Rhodesia, suffering exile and imprisonment. Released in 1960, he headed the new United National Independence Party. Kaunda maintained a hard line against white regimes in southern Africa.

**KAUTSKY, Karl Johann** (1854–1938), German Marxist. Influenced by Eduard BERNSTEIN, and a friend of ENGELS, he was a great popularizer of MARXISM. After the revolution in Russia (1917) he became a staunch opponent of BOLSHEVISM

**KAVAFIS, Konstantinos Petrou,** or Constantine Cavafy (1863–1933), Greek poet. He spent most of his life in his native Alexandria. His ironic poetry, of great breadth and dramatic power, has proved widely influential since his death.

**KAWABATA, Yasunari** (1899–1972), Japanese novelist. He is noted for his impressionistic, lyrical style and a preoccupation with loneliness and death; he finally committed suicide. One of his best-known works is *Snow Country* (1947). He was awarded the 1968 Nobel Prize for Literature.

**KAYE, Danny** (1913–    ), US comedian and entertainer. His best-known films are *The Secret Life of Walter Mitty* (1946), and *Hans Christian Anderson* (1952). A favorite with children, he was active as a fund-raiser for the UN Children's Fund.

**KAZAKHSTAN,** constituent republic of the USSR. In central Asia, it runs from the Caspian Sea in the W to the Chinese frontier in the E. Over 45% of the population is Russian and Ukrainian, the Kazakhs forming nearly 35%. Rich in coal, tungsten, oil, copper, lead, manganese and zinc, it is one of Russia's leading industrial and agricultural areas, providing various grain crops. It is the launching place of Soviet space flights. (See USSR.)

**KAZAN, Elia** (1909–    ), Turkish-born US film and stage director best known for realistic films on social issues, such as *On the Waterfront* (1954). Among his many other films are *A Streetcar Named Desire* (1951) and *Viva Zapata!* (1952). He wrote and directed *The Arrangement* (1967) and *The Assassins* (1972).

**KAZANTZAKIS, Nikos** (1883?–1957), prolific Greek writer and statesman, minister of public welfare 1919–27 and minister of state 1945–46. Among his best-known works are the novels *Zorba the Greek* (1946) and *The Greek Passion* (1951) and his epic poem *The Odyssey: A Modern Sequel* (1938).

**KAZIN, Alfred** (1915–    ), influential US critic. His book *On Native Grounds* (1942) was a major study of contemporary US prose literature. His autobiographical *Walker in the City* (1951) is an evocation of a Brooklyn Jewish childhood.

**KEAN, Edmund** (1787–1833), leading English actor of his time. His greatest roles were in Shakespearian tragedy, notably as Othello, to which he introduced a dynamic naturalistic style.

**KEATON, (Joseph Frank) Buster** (1895–1966), US silent-film comedian. In such films as *The Navigator* (1924), and

*The General* (1926) now considered masterpieces of comic inventiveness, he created the character of an innocent in conflict with malevolent machinery. His apparently deadpan face was actually subject to a considerable range of subtle expressions.

**KEATS, John** (1795–1821), one of the greatest English Romantic poets. He gave up medicine in 1816 to devote himself to poetry. His earlier poems and the Spenserian epic *Endymion* (1817) attracted little attention except politically motivated abuse. In 1817 his brother Tom died of tuberculosis, and his own health suffered after a long walking tour. The epic *Hyperion*, the ballad *La Belle Dame sans Merci* and *The Eve of St. Agnes* were written at this time. A developing romance with Fanny Brawne was offset by serious financial troubles caused by his guardian. In May 1819 he wrote the four great odes—*To a Nightingale*, *On a Grecian Urn*, *On Melancholy*, and *On Indolence*. *Lamia* and *To Autumn*, effectively his last works, followed that summer. In Jan. 1820 he developed definite tuberculosis symptoms. Taken to winter in Italy, he died in Rome, where he is buried.

**KEKKONEN, Urho Kaleva** (1900–    ), Finnish statesman, head of the Agrarian Party. President for three terms from 1956, he was elected for a fourth time in 1978. In 1981 he resigned because of poor health.

**KEKULE VON STRADONITZ, Friedrich August** (1829–1896), German chemist regarded as the father of modern ORGANIC CHEMISTRY. At the same time as Archibald Scott Couper (1831–1892) he recognized the quadrivalency of CARBON and its ability to form long chains. With his later inference of the structure of BENZENE (the "benzene ring"), structural organic chemistry was born.

**KELLER, Helen Adams** (1880–1968), US author and lecturer. Born blind, deaf and dumb, she became famous for her triumph over her disabilities. Taught by Anne SULLIVAN from 1887, she learned to read, write and speak, and graduated from Radcliffe College, Cambridge, Mass., with honors in 1904. Her books include *The Story of My Life* (1902) and *Helen Keller's Journal* (1938).

**KELLOGG, Will Keith** (1860–1951), US industrialist and philanthropist. He made his fortune through the breakfast cereal industry he established in 1906 at Battle Creek, Mich., originally to manufacture the cornflakes developed as a health food by his physician brother.

**KELLOGG-BRIAND PACT,** agreement

signed on Aug. 27, 1928, by 15 nations (later observed by 64 others) renouncing "war as an instrument of national policy." Conceived by Aristide BRIAND of France and F. B. KELLOGG of the US, it left many loopholes, and ultimately proved ineffectual.

**KELLY, Emmett** (1898–1979), US circus clown. He created "Weary Willie," the mournful clown who chased elusive spotlights and "cleaned" the ring with a frayed old broom. He appeared with circuses throughout Britain and the US.

**KELLY, Gene** (1912– ), US film actor and dancer who choreographed and starred in such classic musicals as *An American in Paris* (1951) and *Singin' in the Rain* (1952). From the late 1950s he also directed movies.

**KELLY, Grace** (1929– ), US film and stage actress, Oscar winner for *Country Girl* (1954). After such films as *The Swan* (1956) and *High Society* (1956), she married Prince Ranier III of Monaco.

**KELLY, Walt** (1913–1973), US cartoonist who created the popular comic strip *Pogo*, featuring a talking opossum and his Okefenokee Swamp friends. The strip, which sometimes featured pointed political commentary, was carried by more than 450 newspapers.

**KELVIN, William Thomson, 1st Baron** (1824–1907), British physicist who made important contributions to many branches of physics. In attempting to reconcile CARNOT's theory of heat engines and JOULE's mechanical theory of HEAT he both formulated (independently of CLAUSIUS) the 2nd Law of THERMODYNAMICS and introduced the ABSOLUTE temperature scale, the unit of which is called KELVIN for him. His and FARADAY's work on ELECTROMAGNETISM gave rise to the theory of the the electromagnetic field, and his papers, with those of Faraday, strongly influenced J. Clerk MAXWELL's work on the electromagnetic theory of LIGHT (though Kelvin himself rejected Maxwell's over-abstract theory). His work on wire-telegraphic signaling played an essential part in the successful laying of the first ATLANTIC CABLE.

**KENNAN, George Frost** (1904– ), US diplomat, one of the main authors of the US postwar policy of "containment" of Russian expansionism. Ambassador to the USSR 1952 and Yugoslavia in 1961–63, he wrote *Russia Leaves the War* (1956), for which he received the Pulitzer Prize, and *Memoirs, 1925–1950* (1968), which won another Pulitzer.

**KENNEDY, Edward Moore** (1932– ),

US political leader. The brother of President John Kennedy, he was elected to the Senate from Massachusetts in 1962. With the deaths of his brothers John and Robert, he became a national leader of the Democratic party and an articulate advocate of liberal causes. His career suffered (1969) when a woman companion drowned after he drove his car off a bridge on Chappaquiddick Island. He challenged President Carter for the 1980 presidential nomination, but failed.

**Born:** May 29, 1917
**Died:** November 22, 1963
**Term of office:** January 20, 1961–November 22, 1963
**Political party:** Democratic

**KENNEDY, John Fitzgerald** (1917–1963), 35th president of the US, was the youngest man to be elected president and the fourth president to be assassinated. The second son of Joseph P. KENNEDY, he was brought up in Boston and New York. Popular but undistinguished at school, he was overshadowed by his older brother Joseph Jr., upon whom their father's ambition focused. In his senior year at Harvard in 1939, however, his thesis on British policies leading to the MUNICH PACT was well-received and published as *Why England Slept* (1940). He joined the US Navy in 1941; when his torpedo boat was sunk by the Japanese in 1943 he led survivors to safety, himself towing an injured man three miles through rough seas. His already bad health was seriously weakened by a back injury and malaria, and he was discharged in 1945 with the Purple Heart and the Navy and Marine Corps medal. His brother Joseph had been killed in 1944 and the family ambition now rested on him. In 1952 he became junior senator for Mass., taking a position on the moderate right. In 1953 he married Jacqueline Bouvier (see ONASSIS, JACQUELINE). While convalescing after operations on his injured back he wrote *Profiles in Courage* (1956); a study of US statesmen who put national interest before party, it won the Pulitzer Prize for biography in 1957. By 1957 he was becoming known for his liberal views on race, social and foreign issues.

Narrowly missing the 1956 vice-presidential nomination, in 1960 he was nominated as Democratic presidential candidate, running with Lyndon B. Johnson, and defeated Richard M. Nixon in the election. The abortive BAY OF PIGS invasion of Cuba in 1961 rocked the new administration, but the action was supported by both parties. More serious was the growing confrontation with the USSR under Khrushchev over West Berlin. Kennedy met the Russian challenge with equal obstinacy and the crisis was gradually defused, despite the construction of the BERLIN WALL. A more serious confrontation threatened in Oct., 1962, when aerial reconnaissance revealed Russian missile bases under construction in Cuba. Kennedy immediately imposed a quarantine on all weapons shipments to Cuba, threatening to search and turn back any such consignments. After a week of tense confrontation the USSR capitulated, a considerable victory for Kennedy, as was his part in persuading the USSR to sign a limited nuclear test-ban treaty, a significant check to COLD WAR policies. A massive foreign aid program for Latin America and his support of the European COMMON MARKET won him considerable support abroad. At the height of his popularity he was shot dead by Lee Harvey OSWALD in a motorcade through Dallas, Tex. Theories of a conspiracy are unsupported by evidence.

**KENNEDY, Joseph Patrick** (1888–1969), US businessman and diplomat. Having amassed a fortune in banking, the stock market and other areas in the 1920s, he was active in government and served as US ambassador to Britain 1937–40. His sons John Fitzgerald and Robert Francis were both assassinated in high office; his fourth son, Edward, continues to represent the family in politics.

**KENNEDY, Robert Francis** (1925–1968). Younger brother of John F. KENNEDY, he served as US attorney general 1961–64 and was senator for New York from 1965. After his brother's death, he became a popular leader of the liberal wing of the Democratic Party and ran as presidential candidate in 1968. On June 4, 1968, the evening of his victory in the Cal. primary, he was assassinated by Sirhan SIRHAN.

**KENNY, Sister Elizabeth** (1886–1952), Australian nurse best known for developing the treatment of infantile paralysis (see POLIOMYELITIS) by stimulating and reeducating the muscles affected.

**KENSINGTON RUNE STONE,** found in 1898 on a farm near Kensington, Minn. Inscribed in RUNES dated 1362 is an account of Norse exploration of the Great Lakes of North America. The stone is in a special museum in Alexandria, Minn., but most scholars now think it to be a forgery.

**KENT, Rockwell** (1882–1971), US writer and artist. He is best known for his illustrations of popular classics and his own works, which include *Wilderness* (1921) and *This is My Own* (1940).

**KENT STATE SHOOTING.** On May 4, 1970, National Guardsmen patrolling the campus of Kent State University in Ohio fired upon a crowd of students protesting the Cambodian "incursion," an apparent widening of the Vietnam War. The guardsmen thus killed four students and injured nine more; subsequent investigations discovered no evidence that the soldiers had been in danger, although some students had been throwing rocks. The event touched off nationwide expressions of sorrow; however, no indictments were brought in this case until 1974, and these resulted in acquittals.

**Name of state:** Kentucky
**Capital:** Frankfort
**Statehood:** June 1, 1792 (15th state)
**Familiar name:** Bluegrass State
**Area:** 40,395sq mi
**Population:** 3,661,433
**Elevation:** Highest—4,145ft, Black Mountain. Lowest—257ft, Mississippi River in Fulton County
**Motto:** United We Stand, Divided We Fall
**State flower:** Goldenrod
**State bird:** Cardinal
**State tree:** Kentucky coffee tree
**State song:** "My Old Kentucky Home"

**KENTUCKY,** state, E central US, bounded to the E by W.V. and Va., to the S by Tenn. to the W by Mo. and to the N by Ill., Ind and Ohio.

**Land.** The state is roughly triangular in shape and may be divided into three regions. In the W, the land slopes down to the Jackson Purchase Area, including swamp land flanking the Mississippi R. The Interior Low Plateau consists of the W coalfield and the gently rolling Bluegrass Region, where there are rich soils and where the largest cities and major industries are also situated. The blue blossoms of the grasses around Lexington, in this region, have given Kentucky its nickname. The third land region, the Appalachian Plateau, is a mountainous area of narrow valleys, in which the CUMBERLAND GAP is one of the few natural passes to the West. The most important rivers are the Ohio and the Tennessee, dammed at Gilbertsville to create KENTUCKY LAKE. Kentucky has a mild climate with warm summers and cool winters.

**People.** The majority of Kentuckians now live in urban areas, the drift to the cities having been considerable through the past 50 years. Louisville and Lexington are the chief cities.

**Economy.** Industry is concentrated along the Ohio R and the chief products are foodstuffs, machinery, textiles, metal products and cigarettes, of which Kentucky produces one quarter of the US total. Other important products are burley tobacco, coal, gas, oil, livestock, grains and bourbon whiskey. Kentucky, home of the world-famous KENTUCKY DERBY, ranks first in the US in thoroughbred racehorse breeding.

**History.** The first permanent settlement was established by James HARROD in 1774 after Daniel BOONE's expeditions over the Appalachians 1769–71. After the Revolutionary War, new settlers flowed in. In 1792 a constitution for the Commonwealth of Kentucky was adopted and in the same year Kentucky became the 15th state in the Union. On the eve of the Civil War, Kentucky had vast tobacco plantations worked by slaves, but as much of the land was occupied by small farmers raising corn and hogs, the state was divided during the war. The legislature declared allegiance to the Union although a good number of Kentuckians enlisted in the Confederate armies.

After the war, burley tobacco became the mainstay of Kentucky's agriculture, though the new railroads opened up the coalfields of the Appalachians. Following the depression years of the 1930s, WWII brought economic recovery and since then industrial expansion has continued. Despite general prosperity, however, pockets of poverty still exist, notably in the E coalmining regions of the Appalachians. Also, at the start of the 1980s, layoffs of industrial workers, especially in Louisville, caused a rise in unemployment. Renewed economic development became a major state priority.

**KENTUCKY AND VIRGINIA RESOLU-**
TIONS, passed by the legislatures of Ky. and Va. in 1798 and 1799, after the Federalist-controlled Congress had passed the ALIEN AND SEDITION ACTS. The Kentucky Resolutions, drafted by Thomas JEFFERSON, claimed that the federal government was the result of a compact between the states. If it assumed powers not specifically delegated to it, the states could declare any acts under these powers unconstitutional. The Virginia resolutions, drafted by James MADISON, declared the same theory in milder form. The resolutions were concerned principally with individual civil liberties, but John CALHOUN and other Southern leaders used them as the basis for the doctrines of NULLIFICATION and SECESSION.

**KENTUCKY DERBY,** famous US horse-race. It is an annual classic for three-year-olds run over a course of 1¼mi at Churchill Downs, Louisville, Ky. It was founded in 1875 by Col. M. Lewis Clark. (See also HORSE RACING.)

**Official name:** Republic of Kenya
**Capital:** Nairobi
**Area:** 224,960sq mi
**Population:** c16,393,000
**Languages:** English, Swahili, Kikuyu, Luo widely spoken
**Religions:** Animist, Christian, Muslim, Hindu
**Monetary unit(s):** 1 Kenya shilling=100 cents

**KENYA,** East African republic, bounded by the Sudan, Ethiopia, Somalia, Uganda and Tanzania, famous for its national parks and game reserves.

**Land.** The country straddles the equator and has four main regions: the narrow fertile coastal strip, with rain forests and mango swamps; the vast dry scrubland pastures of the Niyika, crossed by Kenya's two chief rivers, the Tana and the Athi; the highlands, cut by the Great Rift Valley, where Mt Kenya (17,058ft) and Mt Elgon (14,178ft) stand and where the rich volcanic soil, moderate temperatures and ample rainfall provide most farm crops; the western (Nyanza) plateau, stretching to

Lake Victoria, an area of farmlands, forests and grasslands.

**People.** Nearly 98% of the population is African, comprising more than 40 ethnic groups, chief among which are the KIKUYU. There are also Indian, Arab and European (primarily British) communities. More than eight million Kenyans live in the SW, mainly in the highlands where Nairobi, the capital and largest city, is situated.

**Economy.** Agriculture is the major occupation with coffee, tea, timber, fruit and vegetables the main exports. Chief industries center around food processing, textiles, footwear, and clothing. There is also a large livestock industry. Kenya has few natural resources and its reliance upon imported oil places a strain on the economy. Hydroelectric power sources and a geothermal power project are being developed. Tourism is also important.

**History.** Until 1887 the coast was under Arab control; the British then opened the interior with imported Indian labor and encouraged European settlement. In 1944 the first African nationalist party was set up, Jomo KENYATTA becoming its leader in 1947. Discontent led to the formation of the MAU MAU terrorist organization. Pacified by reforms, Kenya gained independence in 1963, becoming a republic in 1964 under Kenyatta's presidency. In 1978 Kenyatta died. A new leader was elected unopposed.

**KENYATTA, Jomo** (1893?–1978), Kenya's first president, (1964–78). His early political career was concerned with rights of his Kikuyu people. In 1953 he was imprisoned on charges of leading the MAU MAU. His release came in 1961 following pressure from African nationalists. Kenyatta was one of the most influential of the early African nationalist leaders and his policies preserved Kenya's stability and prosperity.

**KEPLER, Johannes** (1571–1630), German astronomer who, using BRAHE'S superbly accurate observations of the planets, advanced COPERNICUS' heliocentric model of the SOLAR SYSTEM in showing that the planets followed elliptical paths. His three laws (see KEPLER'S LAWS) were later the template about which NEWTON formulated his theory of GRAVITATION. Kepler also did important work in optics, discovering a fair approximation for the law of REFRACTION.

**KEPLER'S LAWS**, three laws formulated by Johannes KEPLER to describe the motions of the planets in the solar system. (**1**) Each planet orbits the sun in an ELLIPSE of which the sun is at one focus. (**2**) The line between a planet and the sun sweeps out equal areas in equal times: hence the planet moves faster when closer to the sun than it does when farther away. (**3**) The square of the time taken by a planet to ORBIT the sun is proportional to the cube of its mean distance from the sun.

**KERENSKY, Alexander Feodorovich** (1881–1970), Russian moderate revolutionary leader and head of the provisional government July to Oct. 1917. Overthrown in the Bolshevik Revolution (October 1917), he emigrated to Western Europe and in 1940 went to the US. His books include *The Catastrophe* (1927) and *The Kerensky Memoirs* (1966).

**KERN, Jerome David** (1885–1945), US composer. His most famous work is the score of *Show Boat* (1927) which includes the song "Ol' Man River." Among his classic songs are "Smoke Gets in Your Eyes" and "The Song is You."

**KERNER COMMISSION**, appointed by President L. B. Johnson in 1967 to investigate the causes of the race riots of the mid-1960s. The commission, headed by Gov. Otto Kerner of Ill., put most of the blame on "white racism." It concluded that the US was moving towards two societies, one black and one white—"separate but unequal." It suggested improvements in schools and housing and better police protection for residents of black ghettoes.

**KEROSENE**, or paraffin oil, a mixture of volatile HYDROCARBONS having 10 to 16 carbon atoms per molecule, used as a FUEL for jet engines (see JET PROPULSION), for heating and lighting and as a solvent and paint thinner. Although it can be derived from oil, coal and tar, most is produced from PETROLEUM by refining and CRACKING—it was the major product until gasoline's ascendancy. Kerosene boils between 150°C and 300°C.

**KEROUAC, Jack** (1922–1969), US novelist. His best-known book is *On the Road* (1957), describing his life of freedom from conventional middle-class ties and values. He was a leading figure of the BEAT GENERATION.

**KESEY, Ken** (1935–    ), US author best known for his first novel *One Flew Over the Cuckoo's Nest* (1962), a dark satire about life in a mental institution.

**KESSELRING, Albert** (1885–1960), German field marshal of WWII. He became commander in chief in Italy (1943) and in the West (1945). He was convicted of war crimes (1947) and sentenced to life imprisonment, but was released in 1952.

**KETTERING, Charles Franklin** (1876–1958), US inventor of the first electric cash register and the electric self-starter, who made many significant contributions to

AUTOMOBILE technology.

**KETTLEDRUM.** See TIMPANI.

**KEY,** in music, the prescribed system of tones forming a major or minor scale, often used synonomously with TONALITY. It includes all the tones in the scale, and the chords built upon them, and receives its name from the lowest note of the scale to which it belongs. Thus the key of C Major has C as its principal note. In musical notation the key of a piece of music is shown at the beginning by the key signature, composed of the sharps and flats necessary for that particular key.

**KEY, Francis Scott** (1779–1843), American lawyer who wrote the words to the STAR-SPANGLED BANNER. He wrote it after witnessing the night bombardment of Fort McHenry by the British in September 1814. It became the national anthem of the US by act of Congress (1931).

**KEYBOARD INSTRUMENTS,** musical instruments played by depressing a row of levers called keys. The organ has keyboards for both hands and feet but the term usually refers to instruments like the harpsichord and piano which have a keyboard consisting of long keys covered with ivory, and short keys covered with ebony, which when pressed by the fingers hit or pluck a string to produce a note. Since WWII, the name has also been applied to instruments with keyboards that produce piano-like or organ-like notes electrically.

**KEY LARGO,** island S of Miami off the coast of Fla. About 30mi long, it is the largest of the FLORIDA KEYS.

**KEYNES, John Maynard, 1st Baron of Tilton** (1883–1946), British economist at Cambridge University, a major pioneer in the development of modern economics. He resigned in protest as treasury representative at the VERSAILLES PEACE CONFERENCE, stating his objections to the possible outcome of the treaty in *The Economic Consequences of the Peace* (1919). His chief work, *The General Theory of Employment, Interest, and Money* (1936), formed the basis of the "new" or Keynesian economics. It argued against the traditional idea that the economy was best left to run itself and showed how government policies could maintain high levels of economic activity and employment. He attended the BRETTON WOODS CONFERENCE. Keynes was a prominent member of the BLOOMSBURY GROUP. (See also KEYNESIAN ECONOMICS.)

**KEYNESIAN ECONOMICS,** economic theories of John Maynard KEYNES and other theories derived from them. In analyzing the causes of the GREAT DEPRESSION, Keynes focused on the relationship among demand, production, and unemployment. He concluded that when national demand falls critically short of productive capacity, this leads to a state of economic depression—high unemployment, low prices, business stagnation—that may last indefinitely. In the Keynesian view, the cure is to create demand by government spending and low taxes; excessive demand, by contrast, leads to inflation and should be curbed by tight-budget policies.

**KHACHATURIAN, Aram Ilich** (1903–1978), Soviet-Armenian composer, greatly influenced by the folk music of Armenia and other Soviet nationalities. He is famous for the *Violin Concerto* (1940) and the "Saber Dance" in his ballet *Gayne* (1942).

**KHALID IBN ABDUL-AZIZ** (1913– ), King of Saudi Arabia. Appointed Crown Prince in 1965, he acceded to the throne in 1975 on the death of his brother FAISAL. His regime showed some restraint on oil prices and otherwise took cautious positions on Middle East issues.

**KHARTOUM,** capital of Sudan, at the junction of the White and Blue Niles, a cotton trading center linked by rail and river to Egypt and Port Sudan. General GORDON was killed here in 1885 defending the city against the MAHDI. Pop 1,000,000.

**KHMER EMPIRE,** ancient Cambodian empire dating from the 6th century, which at its acme under the Angkors occupied much of modern Laos, Thailand and South Vietnam. The capital, Angkor Thom, and the Hindu temple of Angkor Wat (12th century) were architectural masterpieces. After the empire fell to the Thais in 1434 the court moved to Phnom Penh. (See also ANGKOR.)

**KHOMEINI, Ayatollah Ruhollah** (1901– ), spiritual and political leader of Iran. In 1962 he was recognized as one of the six grand ayatollahs (religious leaders) of Iranian Shi'ite Islam. The next year he was forced into exile because of his opposition to the rule of the SHAH. In exile in Turkey, Iraq and France he emerged as the leader of the anti-shah forces, which overthrew the Pahlevi regime. He returned to Iran in Jan. 1979 to become absolute leader of his new Islamic republic. Increasingly he ruled through violence and terror in order to eliminate his opponents.

**KHORANA, Har Gobind** (1922– ), Indian-born US biochemist who shared with HOLLEY and NIRENBERG the 1968 Nobel prize for Physiology or Medicine for his major contributions toward deciphering the genetic code (see GENETICS).

**KHRUSHCHEV, Nikita Sergeyevitch** (1894–1971), Ukrainian-born Soviet statesman and premier of the USSR, 1958–64. He rose in the communist hierarchy to membership of the Presidium (1952). On STALIN's death he succeeded him as party secretary, but at the 20th Party Congress (1956) denounced STALINISM. He ousted the other members of the "collective leadership" to assume sole power (1958). His rule saw the launching of SPUTNIK, the break with China and a rapprochement with the West, but the failure of his farm policy and loss of face in the Cuban missile crisis led to his fall.

**KHUFU** (or Cheops), Egyptian pharaoh of the 4th dynasty, reigned 23 years, early 26th century BC. He built the great pyramid at GIZA, the largest single structure ever erected.

**KHWARIZMI, Muhammad ibn-Musa al-,** or **al-Khwarizmi,** 9th-century Arab mathematician. The title of his treatise on the solution of many basic mathematical problems contained the word *al-jabr*, from which comes the modern English term, ALGEBRA.

**KHYBER PASS,** mountain pass on the Pakistan border between PESHAWAR and KABUL, Afghanistan, historically crucial for the control of India, now a strategic military road and railroad. It is about 28mi long.

**KIBBUTZ,** type of cooperative farming settlement in Israel jointly owning or leasing land. All work, economic and municipal activities are done communally. Kibbutzim provide food, accommodation, nursery and elementary education. They began in Israel in the early 20th century.

**KIDD, William** (c1645–1701), famous British pirate. Settling in New York, he was employed in 1696 by the British governor there to privateer against French ships in KING WILLIAM'S WAR. He later plundered the British in the Indian Ocean and was hanged in London for murder and piracy.

**KIDNEYS,** two organs concerned with the excretion of waste products in the urine and the balance of salt and water in the body. They lie behind the peritoneal cavity of the ABDOMEN and excrete urine via the ureters, thin tubes passing into the PELVIS to enter the BLADDER. The basic functional unit of the kidney is the *nephron*, consisting of a glomerulus and a system of tubules; these feed into collecting ducts, which drain into the renal pelvis and ureter. BLOOD is filtered in the glomerulus so that low-molecular-weight substances, minerals and water pass into the tubules; here most of the water, sugar and minerals are reabsorbed, leaving behind wastes such as urea in a small volume of salt and water. Tubules and collecting ducts are concerned with the regulation of salt and water reabsorption, which is partly controlled by two HORMONES (VASOPRESSIN and aldosterone). Some substances are actively secreted into the urine by the tubules and the kidney is the route of excretion of many DRUGS. Hormones concerned with ERYTHROCYTE formation and regulation of aldosterone are formed in the kidneys, which also take part in protein METABOLISM. DISEASES affecting the kidney may result in acute NEPHRITIS, including BRIGHT'S DISEASE, the nephrotic syndrome (EDEMA, heavy protein loss in the urine and low plasma albumin) or acute or chronic renal failure. In acute renal failure, nephrons rapidly cease to function, often after prolonged SHOCK, SEPTICEMIA, etc. They may, however, recover. In chronic renal failure, the number of effective nephrons is gradually and irreversibly reduced so that they are unable to excrete all body wastes. Nephron failure causes UREMIA. Disease of the kidneys frequently causes hypertension (see BLOOD CIRCULATION). Advanced renal failure may need treatment with DIETARY FOODS, dialysis and renal TRANSPLANT.

**KIEL CANAL,** German canal 61mi long from the Elbe R mouth to Holtenau near Kiel. It opened in 1895 and as a major commercial-naval canal cut 300mi off the sea route between the North and Baltic Seas. After WWI it was internationalized until 1936.

**KIERKEGAARD, Sören Aabye** (1813–1855), Danish religious philosopher, precursor of EXISTENTIALISM. Opposing HEGEL, he emphasized that man has free will and can pass from the aesthetic (or material) to the ethical point of view and finally, through "a leap of faith," to the religious. His attack on systematic philosophy and rational religion was ignored in the 19th century but has influenced 20th-century Protestant theology and much modern literature and psychology. His main works are *Either/Or* (1843) and *Philosophical Fragments* (1844).

**KIESINGER, Kurt Georg** (1904–    ), West German Christian Democrat chancellor of the Federal Republic 1966–69. He governed in coalition with the Social Democrats, and generally pursued the West-oriented policies of his predecessors ADENAUER and ERHARD, with particular emphasis on Franco-German relations.

**KIEV,** third largest city in the USSR and capital of the Ukraine, on the Dnieper R. Known in Russia as "the mother of cities," it was founded before the 9th century and was the seat of the Russian Orthodox Church from 988. Much of Kiev (more than 40%) was destroyed in WWII, but after extensive reconstruction it is now a flourishing industrial, communications and cultural center. Pop 2,192,000.

**KILAUEA,** world's largest active volcano, located on SE Hawaii island, Hawaii. Its elevation is 4,090ft, and it is 2mi wide, 3mi long and over 700ft deep. Kilauea last erupted in 1979.

**KILIMANJARO,** Africa's highest mountain, in NE Tanzania, near the Kenyan border. It is an extinct volcano and its highest peak, Kibo, reaches 19,340ft and is snow-capped.

**KILLER WHALE,** or *Orcinus orca,* a true DOLPHIN, but lacking a beak. Fast and voracious predators, they eat dolphins, porpoises, seals and fish. They may hunt in small groups or form packs of 40 or more, driving their prey into shallow water where escape is impossible. Huge animals, average length about 6m (20ft), Killer whales are found throughout the world.

**KILLY, Jean-Claude** (1943– ), the second skier ever to win three gold medals in one Olympic meeting (1968). He won the first two World Cups ever contested (1967–68).

**KILMER, Joyce** (1886–1918), US poet remembered for his sentimental poem *Trees* (1913). He was killed in WWI.

**KIM IL SUNG** (1912– ), North Korean political leader. A Communist, he fought the Japanese, received training in Russia, and returned to Korea as head of a provisional government, supported by the Russians, in 1946. Invading South Korea, he precipitated the Korean War, and only Chinese intervention saved his regime. He then launched a vast industrial and military buildup. In 1972 he gave up the premiership and became president.

**KINDERGARTEN,** school for children aged 4–6, conceived by FROEBEL in 1837. The school aims to develop a child's self-expression and sociability through games, play and creative activities. One of the first American schools was opened in 1860 by Elizabeth PEABODY. Over 50% of children aged five in the US are enrolled in kindergartens.

**KINETIC ART,** style of art concerned with movement. There are several forms: OP ART involving dynamic optical effects; mobiles whose structure moves randomly and unaided; and works which are mechanically powered and use lights, water or electromagnets. The style first evolved about 1910.

**KINETIC ENERGY.** See ENERGY.

**KINETIC THEORY,** widely used statistical theory based on the idea that matter is made up of randomly moving ATOMS or MOLECULES whose kinetic ENERGY increases with TEMPERATURE. It is closely related to STATISTICAL MECHANICS, and predicts macroscopic properties of solids, liquids and gases from motions of individual particles using MECHANICS and PROBABILITY theory. Gases are particularly suited to treatment by kinetic theory, and the basic laws connecting their pressure, temperature, density, diffusion and other properties have been deduced with its aid. (See GAS; DIFFUSION.)

**KING, B.B.** (1925– ), blues singer and guitarist noted for the use of brass and string instruments in his arrangements. His work has had a major influence on ROCK MUSIC.

**KING, Billie Jean Moffitt** (1943– ), US tennis player, a prominent figure in the international game, whose efforts have done much to improve the lot of women in tennis. She took her sixth Wimbledon women's singles title in 1975, and was US women's winner 1971 and 1972.

**KING, Ernest Joseph** (1878–1956), US admiral, the only officer who was both commander of the US fleet and naval operations chief in WWII. His stress on the superiority of aircraft carriers to battleships led to Japan's naval defeat.

**KING, Martin Luther, Jr.** (1929–1968), American black clergyman and civil rights leader, recipient of the 1964 Nobel Peace Prize for his work for racial equality in the US. Born in Atlanta, Ga., King organized the boycott of the Montgomery, Ala. transit company in 1955 to force desegregation of the buses. Under his leadership in the late 1950s and 1960s civil disobedience and non-violent tactics, like the Washington March of 250,000 people in 1963, brought about the Civil Rights Act and Voting Rights Act in 1965. Black militants challenged his methods in 1965 but in 1966 he extended his campaign to slum conditions in the N cities of the US and set up the Poor People's Campaign in 1968. He was less successful in this area since the Vietnam War distracted national attention from the civil and urban rights issues. He was assassinated in Memphis, Tenn. (See also CIVIL RIGHTS AND LIBERTIES.)

**KING, Stephen Edwin** (1947–   ), US novelist and short story writer. His best-selling occult thrillers about children and families threatened by amlevolent supernatural forces include *Carrie* (1974), *The Shining* (1976) and *Cujo* (1981).

**KING, William Lyon Mackenzie** (1874–1950), Canadian statesman, three times Liberal prime minister. In his first term, 1921–26, he established Canada's right to act independently in international affairs; in his second, 1926–30, he introduced old age pensions—Canada's first national social security scheme; and in his third, 1935–48, he united Canada as the "arsenal of democracy" in WWII making the national economy a federal responsibility.

**KINGFISHERS**, a family, Alcedinidae, found worldwide, of brightly-colored fish-eating birds of rivers, lakes and streams. When hunting, the bird watches from a perch until prey is sighted, then dives arrowlike into the water to take the fish. Certain African species do not frequent water, and are insectivorous.

**KING PHILIP'S WAR** (1675–76), last Indian resistance to the whites in S New England. In 1675, the Plymouth colony executed three Indians for an alleged murder. Metacom, a WAMPANOAG chief also called "King Philip," led an alliance of tribes in fierce guerilla raids. The whites replied in kind and Metacom was killed when his secret refuge was betrayed. The colonists then drove most of the Indians from S New England.

**KINGS, Books of,** two books of the OLD TESTAMENT (one book in Hebrew), numbered as 1 and 2 Kings by Protestants, but as 3 and 4 Kings by Roman Catholics (see SAMUEL, BOOKS OF). Related to DEUTERONOMY and religious in aim, they cover Israelite history from the reign of Solomon through the period of the two kingdoms of Israel and Judah to the destruction of Judah by the Babylonians.

**KINGS CANYON NATIONAL PARK**, area of about 460,330 acres in the Sierra Nevada, S central Cal., established as a national park in 1940. The canyon is formed by the Kings R and is noted for its surrounding snow-covered peaks and rich wildlife.

**KINGSLEY, Charles** (1819–1875), English writer and clergyman and an ardent advocate of social reform. His early novel, *Alton Locke* (1850) is a sympathetic study of working class life. He also wrote historical novels, notably *Westward Ho!* (1855) and the famous children's fantasy *The Water Babies* (1863).

**KINGSLEY, Sidney** (1906–   ), US playwright noted for his treatment of social problems. His first play, *Men in White* (1933), won a Pulitzer Prize.

**KINSEY, Alfred Charles** (1894–1956), US zoologist best known for his statistical studies of human sexual behavior, published as *Sexual Behavior in the Human Male* (1948) and *Sexual Behavior in the Human Female* (1953).

**KIPLING, Rudyard** (1865–1936), English writer, born in India. Kipling is perhaps now most admired for his short stories about Anglo-Indian life, as in the collection *Plain Tales from the Hills* (1888), and for his verse, including such pieces as *Mandalay* and *Gunga Din*, while his children's stories, among them *Kim* (1901) and the *Just So Stories* (1902), are perennial favorites. After an English education he worked as a journalist in India 1882–89. He lived in Vt. 1892–96 and in England from 1900. Kipling was enormously popular in his day. He was the first English winner of the Nobel Prize for Literature (1907).

**KIRCHHOFF, Gustav Robert** (1824–1887), German physicist best known for his work on electrical conduction, showing that current passes through a conductor at the speed of light, and deriving KIRCHHOFF'S LAWS. With BUNSEN he pioneered spectrum analysis (see SPECTROSCOPY), which he applied to the solar spectrum, identifying several elements and explaining the FRAUNHOFER LINES.

**KIRCHHOFF'S LAWS**, two laws governing electric circuits involving Ohm's-law conductors and sources of electromotive force, stated by G. R. KIRCHHOFF. They assert that the sums of outgoing and incoming currents at any junction in the circuit must be equal, and that the sum of the current-resistance products around any closed path must equal the total electromotive force in it.

**KIRCHNER, Ernst Ludwig** (1880–1938), German expressionist graphic artist and painter, cofounder of the Brücke (Bridge) movement (1905–13). He is noted for his powerful, savagely expressive woodcuts and, in his painting, for his vigorous distorted use of color and form. His work condemned by the Nazis as degenerate, Kirchner committed suicide.

**KIRIBATI**, independent island republic in the central Pacific, consists of three groups

**Official name:** Republic of Kiribati
**Capital:** Tarawa
**Area:** 278sq mi
**Population:** 58,108
**Languages:** Kiribatian, English
**Religion:** Christian
**Monetary unit(s):** 1 Australian dollar = 100 cents

of coral atolls astride the equator.

**Land.** The 33 atolls of Kiribati include the 16 Gilbert Islands, Banaba Island and eight each in the Phoenix and Line island groups. There are no rivers but most of the atolls enclose a lagoon. Because scanty soil covers the coral, little vegetation grows on the atolls. Temperatures are high and vary little during the year. Rainfall occurs between Oct. and Mar.

**People.** The administrative center is on Tarawa, the most populous and westernized island, where over 30% of the total population lives. Most of the inhabitants of Kiribati are Micronesian. English is the official language.

**Economy.** Fishing constitutes the mainstay of the subsistence economy, supplemented by the cultivation of taro and fruits. Coconuts are cultivated, and copra is virtually the only export since phosphate mining on Banaba ceased in 1979.

**History.** Most European exploration occurred between 1765 and 1826. In 1892 the British declared the islands a protectorate. During World War II some of the fiercest fighting between Japanese and US forces took place, and much of the native population died or was deported by the Japanese. Independence from the UK, achieved in 1979, had been slowed because Banaba had initially demanded separate status.

**KIRKLAND, (Joseph) Lane** (1922–    ), US labor leader. Joining the AFL in 1948, he became executive assistant to President George Meany in 1960 and secretary-treasurer of the AFL-CIO in 1969. Succeeding Meany as president in 1979, he became known as a strong supporter of civil rights and national defense.

**KIRKPATRICK, Jeane** (1926–    ), US ambassador to the UN (1981–    ). A professor of political science at Georgetown University, she was a charter member of the conservative Coalition for a Democratic Majority, a group that advocated a tougher American foreign policy.

**KIRSTEIN, Lincoln** (1907–    ), US ballet promoter who persuaded George BALANCHINE to come to the US and helped him organize the School of American Ballet in New York, 1934, and the New York City Ballet, 1948. Kirstein has also written several books on ballet.

**KISSINGER, Henry Alfred** (1923–    ), German-born US adviser on foreign affairs and one of the most influential men in government. He was professor at Harvard when his book *Nuclear Weapons and Foreign Policy* (1957) brought him international recognition. Kissinger served as special assistant for national security affairs (1969–75) and secretary of state (1973–77) under presidents Nixon and (after 1974) Ford. He was instrumental in initiating the STRATEGIC ARMS LIMITATION TALKS on disarmament (1969), in ending US involvement in Vietnam and opening US policies toward China. In 1974–75 he made major peace initiatives in the Middle East and in 1976, in southern Africa. His policy of détente toward the USSR came under criticism from political conservatives. He received the Nobel Peace Prize in 1973.

**KITASATO, Shibasaburo** (1852–1931), Japanese bacteriologist who discovered, independently of YERSIN, the PLAGUE bacillus; and with BEHRING discovered that graded injections of toxins could be used for immunization (see ANTITOXINS).

**KITCHEN CABINET,** popular name for an unofficial body of advisers to President Andrew Jackson (1829–31). It included politicians, editors and government officials.

**KITCHENER, Horatio Herbert, Earl** (1850–1916), British field marshal, secretary of state for war in WWI. In the Sudan in 1898, he defeated the MAHDI at Omdurman and retook Khartoum. He was commander in chief in the Boer War, 1900–02, and in India to 1909. At the outbreak of WWI he foresaw a long war and his appeals raised thousands of patriotic volunteers. He died when a ship taking him to Russia hit a mine and sank.

**KITES,** a diverse assemblage of BIRDS OF PREY, worldwide in distribution but especially developed in America and Australia. The name is properly restricted to Old World Fork-tailed kites of the genus *Milvus* but it is also used for 25 other species. Most kites are mainly or entirely insectivorous. A few species are scavengers: the Black and Red kites of Europe were formerly common scavengers of city streets.

**KIWANIS INTERNATIONAL,** US service association, founded 1915 to promote the Golden Rule, higher standards in business and participation in community affairs. It sponsors the Key Club International for high school boys and Circle K International for college men.

**KIWI,** the genus *Apteryx*, three species of flightless New Zealand birds about 460mm (18in) high, lacking a tail and, unlike most flightless birds, even lacking visible wings. The feathers are gray-brown and hairlike in texture. The long slender bill is adapted for probing into soil as they feed at night on worms, insects and berries. Birds of damp forests, they are extremely shy and rarely seen.

**KLAMATH MOUNTAINS,** mountain range of the Pacific Coast Ranges in SW Ore. and NW Cal. It has peaks and ridges reaching 9,000ft.

**KLAPROTH, Martin Heinrich** (1743–1817), German chemist noted for his pioneering work in chemical analysis. He discovered the elements ZIRCONIUM (1789) and URANIUM (in fact, uranium oxide: 1789), and rediscovered and named TITANIUM (1795).

**KLEE, Paul** (1879–1940), Swiss painter and graphic artist. In Munich, from 1906, he exhibited with the BLAUE REITER group, and developed a subtle color sense. In 1920–31 he taught at the BAUHAUS, publishing an important textbook on painting. Sensitive line, color and texture are combined in Klee's varied paintings with wit and fantasy.

**KLEIN, Lawrence** (1920–    ), US economist, known as "the father of econometric model-making." A professor at the Wharton School of the U. of Pa. from 1958, he was an adviser to President Jimmy Carter (1976–81) and winner of the 1980 Nobel Prize in Economic Science.

**KLEIN, Melanie** (1882–1960), Austrian-born psychoanalyst whose development of a psychoanalytic therapy for small children radically affected techniques of child psychiatry and theories of child psychology.

**KLEIST (Bernd) Heinrich (Wilhelm) von** (1777–1811), German dramatist and writer of novellas, known for his power and psychological insight. His works include the plays *Penthesilea* (1808) and *Prince Friedrich of Homburg* (1821), and the novels *Michael Kohlhaas* and *The Marquis of O* (1810–11).

**KLEMPERER, Otto** (1885–1973), German conductor. As director of the Kroll opera house Berlin (1927–33) he introduced many modern works and new interpretations of classics. After a period of crippling illness he revived his career from 1947, notably as an interpreter of BEETHOVEN and MAHLER.

**KLIMT, Gustav** (1862–1918), Austrian painter and designer, a leader of the Vienna Secession (1897) who was noted for his lavishly ornamented, mosaic-patterned style. His interior designs, as for the Palais Stoclet, Brussels, and in Vienna, influenced JUGENDSTIL.

**KLINE, Franz Joseph** (1910–1962), US abstract expressionist painter. His huge, stark, black-and-white compositions influenced the "calligraphic" style of the 1950s New York school. Later, Kline reintroduced color into his works.

**KLOPSTOCK, Friedrich Gottlieb** (1724–1803), German poet. His *Der Messias* (1749–73), on Christ's salvation of mankind, an epic modelled on Milton and Homer, freed German poetry from the conventions of French classicism.

**KLUCKHOHN, Clyde** (1905–1960), US anthropologist, best known for his studies of the Navaho Indians and work on the theory of culture and personality. A professor at Harvard (1935–60), he wrote several books including *Mirror for Man* (1949).

**KNELLER, Sir Godfrey** (1646–1723), German-born English portrait painter, a court painter from 1688. He founded the first English painting academy (1711); his finest works are the 42 portraits of members of the Kit-Cat Club, a London political and literary group.

**KNIGHTS OF COLUMBUS,** US organization for Roman Catholic men, started in 1882 in Conn. It sponsors deserving causes and disseminates religious information to its members, who number over a million.

**KNIGHTS OF LABOR,** early US labor group, precursor of the American Federation of Labor. Founded in 1869 to organize all workers in one union, it led successful strikes in 1884–86, but declined after the HAYMARKET AFFAIR.

**KNIGHTS OF PYTHIAS,** US social and charitable organization founded 1864. It has over 3,000 lodges and several auxiliary organizations.

**KNIGHTS OF SAINT JOHN** (officially, Order of the Hospital of St. John of Jerusalem; also known as Hospitalers, Knights of Rhodes, and Knights of Malta), religious order founded by papal charter (1113) to tend sick pilgrims in the Holy Land. It became a military order as well c1140, and after the fall of Jerusalem was based successively on Cyprus (1291),

Rhodes (1309) and Malta (1530) to provide a defense against Muslim seapower. Expelled from Malta by Napoleon in 1798, the Knights have been established at Rome since 1834 in their original humanitarian role.

**KNIGHTS OF THE GOLDEN CIRCLE,** semimilitary US secret society organized in the Midwest states during the Civil War to set up proslavery colonies in Mexico, to help the South against the North. It merged with the Order of American Knights, later the Sons of Liberty, and disbanded in the 1860s.

**KNIGHTS OF THE WHITE CAMELLIA,** southern US secret society to sustain white supremacy after the Civil War. It was dissolved in the 1870s.

**KNIGHTS TEMPLAR,** Christian military order founded c1118, with its headquarters on the site of Solomon's Temple in Jerusalem, to protect pilgrims. It provided elite troops for the kingdom of Jerusalem. Its immense riches from endowments and banking excited the greed of Philip IV of France, who (1307–14) confiscated its property, forced the pope to suppress the order and executed the Grand Master and other knights. What remained of its possessions in France and elsewhere were transferred to the KNIGHTS OF ST. JOHN.

**KNOPF, Alfred Abraham** (1892– ), US publisher. He founded Alfred A. Knopf, Inc. (1915) which published many Nobel Prize-winning authors and became perhaps the most prestigious publishing house in the US. He also co-founded and edited (1924–34) the magazine *American Mercury*.

**KNOSSOS,** ancient city near Candia on the N coast of Crete, center of the MINOAN CIVILIZATION. Excavations by Sir Arthur Evans revealed settlements from the 3rd millennium and the great 2nd-millennium palace, now partly restored. Associated with the mythological King MINOS, it comprises more than five acres of halls, ceremonial rooms and staircases. It has magnificent fresco decorations, advanced sanitation and every amenity of luxury. Fire destroyed it c1400 BC.

**KNOW-NOTHING PARTY,** US political party formed to restrict immigration and exclude naturalized citizens and Roman Catholics from politics. It won success in the 1854 election as the American Party, but split irremediably in 1856 over the slavery issue. Its name came from its members' habit of saying they "knew nothing" of the movement.

**KNOX, John** (c1514–1572), Scottish Protestant Reformation leader, preacher and chronicler of the Scottish Reformation. A converted Roman Catholic priest, Knox was active in the English Reformation, but fled in 1554 from the Roman Catholic regime of Queen Mary I to Geneva, where he was a follower of CALVIN. He returned to Scotland in 1559 ardently preaching Protestantism. When it became the state religion (1560) Knox gained great political influence, opposing Mary Queen of Scots. His fiery prose includes a history of the Reformation in Scotland and the *First Blast of the Trumpet Against the Monstrous Regiment of Women* (1556–58). He also wrote the *Book of Common Order*, which regulated Scottish worship.

**KOALA,** *Phascolarctos cinereus*, a large, arboreal, superficially bear-like MARSUPIAL of eastern Australia. It feeds on the foliage of *Eucalyptus* and a few other trees. Alone among the marsupials but for the WOMBATS, koalas have a true allantoic placenta, though the young are brooded in a marsupial pouch. The koala has been considered an endangered species but is now increasing in numbers again.

**KOCH, Edward I.** (1924– ), US Democratic congressman from New York 1969–77, elected mayor of New York City 1977. He steered the city through a severe fiscal crisis by cutting city expenditures while trying to maintain essential services. A popular, hard-working mayor, Koch won both the Democratic and Republican party nominations for reelection in 1981.

**KOCH, Robert** (1843–1910), German medical scientist regarded as a father of BACTERIOLOGY, awarded the 1905 Nobel Prize for Physiology or Medicine for his work. He isolated the ANTHRAX bacillus and showed it to be the sole cause of the disease; devised important new methods of obtaining pure cultures; and discovered the bacilli responsible for TUBERCULOSIS (1882) and CHOLERA (1883).

**KÖCHEL, Ludwig von** (1800–1877), Austrian musicologist (and also scientist), whose 1862 catalogue of Mozart's compositions, though revised, is still standard. The works are usually identified with a "K" number.

**KODÁLY, Zoltán** (1882–1967), Hungarian composer and, with BARTÓK, an ardent researcher of Hungarian folk music. Folk influences are evident in such works as the cantata *Psalmus Hungaricus* (1923), the opera *Háry János* (1925–26) and the orchestral *Peacock Variations* (1938–39).

**KOESTLER, Arthur** (1905– ), Hungarian-born British writer. His novel *Darkness at Noon* (1940), based on his own experience in a Spanish death cell, analyzed the psychology of victims of Stalin's 1930s purges. Many later works on philosophical and scientific subjects include *The Sleepwalkers* (1964), *The Case of the Midwife Toad* (1971) and *The Thirteenth Tribe* (1978).

**KOHLER, Wolfgang** (1887–1967), German-born US psychologist, a founder of GESTALT PSYCHOLOGY. He devoted much of his career to studying problem-solving among chimpanzees.

**KOKOSCHKA, Oskar** (1886–1980), Austrian painter and writer who was a leader of German EXPRESSIONISM. He is known for such psychologically acute portraits as *The Tempest* (1914), a self-portrait with Alma Mahler, and for his lyric landscapes and townscapes. He became a naturalized British subject in 1947.

**KOLFF, Willem** (1911–   ), Dutch-born US physician who developed an artificial kidney (dialysis) machine and perfected a complete artificial heart.

**KOLMOGOROV, Andrei Nikolayevich** (1903–   ), Soviet mathematician. Considered to be the most influential Soviet mathematician of the 20th century, he made fundamental contributions to the theory of functions, TOPOLOGY, PROBABILITY theory, CYBERNETICS and INFORMATION THEORY.

**KONEV, Ivan Stepanovich** (1897–1973), USSR field marshal of WWII, who drove the Germans from the Ukraine, captured Prague and took part in the fall of Berlin. He headed the Warsaw Pact armies 1955–60.

**KONOYE, Prince Fumimaro** (1891–1945), Japanese premier 1937–39 and 1940–41. A moderate, he appeased the military extremists and so furthered expansionism. He killed himself when listed for trial as a war criminal.

**KON-TIKI.** See HEYERDAHL, THOR.

**KOO, V. K. Wellington** (1888–   ), Chinese diplomat and political leader. By 1920 he had been minister to Mexico, the US, Britain and the League of Nations. He was minister of foreign affairs twice and prime minister 1926–27. He was ambassador to France, Britain again, and the US again 1946–56. He also represented China at the UN founding conference in San Francisco (1945).

**KOPIT, Arthur (Lee)** (1937–   ), US playwright noted for his wry imagination in depicting "the rotten underside of life from below" in such plays as *Oh Dad, Poor Dad, Mama's Hung You in the Closet and I'm Feelin' So Sad* (1960), *Indians* (1969) and *Wings* (1978).

**KORAN,** sacred scripture of the religion of ISLAM, regarded by Muslims as God's actual words revealed to the prophet MOHAMMED in the 7th century AD. A canonical text was established in 651–52 AD, and Arabic itself was molded and preserved by its highly-charged, poetic language. Comprising laws, moral precepts and narrative, the Koran is divided into 114 *suras* or chapters, arranged according to length from the longest to the shortest except for the brief opening prayer. The Koran demands total surrender to the will of Allah (God), and stresses Allah's compassion and mercy. It contains much in common with the Judeo-Christian tradition, and indeed all Christians and Jews are regarded as believers since they accept the existence of one God. Today Islam places a greater emphasis on the spirit than on the letter of Koranic laws which govern, for instance, moral behavior and social life. The Koran remains, however, the inspiration and guide for millions of Muslims and is the supreme authority of the Islamic tradition.

**KORBUT, Olga** (1955–   ), Russian gymnastics star. As a 5ft, 1in, 84lb 17-year-old, she won three gold medals and one silver at the 1972 Olympics.

**KORDA, Sir Alexander** (1893–1956), Hungarian-born British film producer and director. His historical extravaganzas, such as *The Private Life of Henry VIII* (1933), *The Scarlet Pimpernel* (1934), *Rembrandt* (1936) and *The Four Feathers* (1939), enhanced the international status of the British film industry. He was the first filmmaker to be knighted (1942).

**Official name:** Democratic People's Republic of Korea
**Capital:** Pyongyang
**Area:** 47,225sq mi
**Population:** 19,279,000
**Language:** KOREAN
**Religions:** No official religion
**Monetary unit(s):** 1 Won = 100 jun

**KOREA,** 600mi-long peninsula of E Asia, separating the Yellow Sea from the Sea of Japan. It is bounded N by China and the

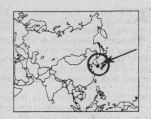

**Official name:** Republic of Korea
**Capital:** Seoul
**Area:** 38,452sq mi
**Population:** 39,766,000
**Language:** Korean
**Religions:** Buddhism,
Confucianism, Christianity,
Shamanism, Chondokyo
**Monetary unit(s):** 1 Won = 10 hwan

USSR, and S by Korea Strait. Korea is two countries: the communist Democratic People's Republic (North Korea) and the Republic of Korea (South Korea). The division, which runs along 38°N, was made in 1945 and formalized in 1948. Korea is mostly mountainous, with coastal plains in the W. Most rivers flow W and S from the mountains to the Yellow Sea. The climate is varied and includes extremes of cold and humidity.

**People.** South Korea, though smaller, has more than twice the population of North Korea. The Koreans are mostly agricultural workers, and less than a third of the people live in towns. In the North, as in other communist countries, religious belief is discouraged. In the South, Buddhism, Confucianism and Christianity coexist.

**Economy.** Agricultural crops are still of primary importance in Korea, but in the 1960s rapid industrial expansion, facilitated by foreign aid, profoundly altered the economy of both North and South. The North especially is now highly industrialized, and produces large quantities of iron and steel. Farming is cooperative and mechanized. The North also has the dominant share of the country's mineral wealth and is one of the world's few totally self-sufficient nations. The South has widely mixed industry including plywood, chemicals and textiles and is largely export-oriented.

**History.** After more than 1,000 years of Chinese settlements among the Korean tribes, the first of several native kingdoms arose, in the N, c100 AD. Korea was not united until the 7th century. Most of its early civilization was destroyed by the Mongol invasions of the 13th century; but

with the establishment (1392) of the Yi dynasty, Korea entered an age of stability and outstanding cultural achievement which included the first known printing with moveable metal type. In 1592 Japan invaded the peninsula, followed soon after by the Manchu. Korea became a Chinese vassal state, entirely cut off from the world. Commercial contact with Japan in the late 1800s foreshadowed Japan's annexation of Korea in 1910. After Japan's 1945 capitulation in WWII Korea was divided into a Russian zone of occupation in the N and a US zone in the S. Negotiations to unite the country failed, and in 1948 separate regimes were established. The North became a communist state under the former guerrilla leader, KIM IL SUNG. Elections in the South produced a republic under Syngman RHEE. On June 25, 1950, the communists of the North invaded South Korea, thus beginning the KOREAN WAR. The heavy fighting was eventually stopped (July 1953) by an armistice. In the South, Syngman Rhee's increasingly autocratic and corrupt regime was displaced (1960). A military coup in 1961 brought General PARK CHUNG HEE to power. President under a new constitution after 1963, he gained wider powers and the right to unlimited terms of office in 1972. In July 1979 he was assassinated and replaced by General Chun Doo Hwan who established his own autocratic rule forbidding political freedom. In North Korea, Kim Il Sung began grooming his son, Kim Jong Il, as his heir apparent against strong internal opposition. Unification of the country remains a remote possibility and unlikely in this generation.

**KOREAN,** language spoken by the Korean people, numbering about 47 million. Of uncertain origin, Korean is considered by some to belong to the ALTAIC LANGUAGES. The official script has a simple phonetic alphabet called *hankul*, with 11 vowels and 14 consonants.

**KOREAN WAR** (1950–1953), a conflict between forces of the United Nations (primarily the US and South Korea) on one side and forces of North Korea and (later) communist China on the other. KOREA had been divided along latitude 38°N in 1945, Russia becoming the occupying force N of this line, and the US S of it. The war began when, having attempted to topple the government of the south by indirect means, North Korea launched a surprise invasion. UN forces were sent to assist South Korea under General Douglas MACARTHUR. By July the UN forces had been pushed SE to a small area around Pusan, but MacArthur's surprise landing at Inchon, near the captured capital Seoul, altered the complexion of the war. The UN forces destroyed the North Korean army in the south, retook Seoul, and advanced into North Korea. By November 1950 they were approaching the Yalu R on the Chinese border. At this point nearly 300,000 Chinese troops went into action and there was another major reversal as the UN forces were beaten back into South Korea. They recovered, and the fighting moved back and forth over the 38th parallel. MacArthur, urging a direct attack on China herself, was replaced in April 1951 by General RIDGWAY. Two years of negotiations, begun in July, achieved only an armistice (signed at Panmunjom on July 27, 1953). By then the communists had suffered about 2,000,000 casualties and the UN nearly 1,500,000. A peace treaty has never been signed and Korea remains divided as before.

**KORNBERG, Arthur** (1918–    ), US biochemist awarded with OCHOA the 1959 Nobel Prize for Physiology or Medicine for discovering an ENZYME (DNA polymerase) that could produce from a mixture of NUCLEOTIDES exact replicas of DNA molecules. He thus extended Ochoa's related work.

**KORNGOLD, Erich Wolfgang** (1897–1957), Austrian-US composer. The Metropolitan Opera presented his *Die Tote Stadt* in 1921 and *Violanta* in 1927. In the 1930s he began composing scores for such films as *Anthony Adverse* and *The Adventures of Robin Hood*.

**KORNILOV, Lavr Georgeyevich** (1870–1918), Russian general placed in command of the armies after the February Revolution of 1917. His efforts to restore military discipline led KERENSKY to suspect him of planning an army takeover. Imprisoned, he escaped to lead the anti-Bolsheviks after the October Revolution and died in battle.

**KORZYBSKI, Alfred Habdank Skarbek** (1879–1950), Polish-born US scientist who formulated the philosophical linguistic system, General SEMANTICS.

**KOSCIUSKO, Thaddeus** (1746–1817), Polish soldier and patriot who fought as a volunteer in the American Revolution. As colonel of engineers he helped build defense works at Saratoga and West Point. He was given US citizenship and made brigadier general. Returning to Poland in 1784, he instigated and led (1794) an unsuccessful fight for independence and unification. He died in exile in Switzerland.

**KOSINSKI, Jerzy** (1933–    ), Polish-born US writer best known for his semi-autobiographical novel *The Painted Bird* (1965), which with vivid, often shockingly brutal imagery deals with "daily life among the violations of the spirit and body of human beings." Among his other works are *Steps* (1968), for which he won a National Book Award, and *Being There* (1971).

**KOSSUTH, Lajos** (1802–1894), Hungarian patriot and statesman who campaigned against Austrian rule and led the Hungarian revolution of 1848–49. A minister in the government which was set up in April 1848, he engineered Hungary's declaration of independence as a republic the following year, and became president. Austria, with the aid of Russian troops, forced a surrender, and Kossuth fled. Received as a hero in the US and England, where he lived many years, he died in Italy.

**KOSYGIN, Aleksei Nikolaevich** (1904–1980), Soviet premier, elected 1964. He joined the Communist Party in 1927, and by 1939, with much industrial-managerial experience behind him, was on the Central Committee. In 1948 he was made a full Politburo member and in 1960 became first deputy to Khrushchev, whom he succeeded. Sharing leadership with others from 1964, Kosygin concentrated on modernizing industry and agriculture. He resigned as premier in 1980, just before his death.

**KOUFAX, Sandy** (Sanford Koufax; 1935–    ), US left-handed baseball pitcher who played with the Dodgers in Brooklyn and Los Angeles (1955–66). He established many records and was the first major leaguer to pitch four no-hit games.

**KOUMISS. See** KUMISS.

**KOUSSEVITSKY, Serge** (1874–1951), Russian-US conductor. He left Russia in 1920 and settled in the US as conductor of the Boston Symphony Orchestra (1924–49). In 1940 he established the Berkshire Music Center at Stockbridge, Mass. He is remembered as a champion of contemporary composers.

**KOVACS, Ernie** (1919–1962), US comedian, actor and television personality whose *Ernie Kovacs Show* during the 1950s was one of the more technically and comedically inventive of the early TV programs. He also acted in several films before dying in a car crash at the height of his career.

**KOVALEVSKI, Sonya** (1850–1891), Russian mathematician and novelist who made important contributions to the theory of DIFFERENTIAL EQUATIONS. Her brother-in-law, **Alexandr Onufrievich Kovalevski** (1840–1901) did pioneering work in

EMBRYOLOGY.

**KRAFFT-EBING, Richard, Baron von** (1840–1902), German psychologist best known for his work on the psychology of SEX. He also showed there was a relation between SYPHILIS and general PARALYSIS.

**KRAKATOA,** volcanic island in the Sunda Strait, Indonesia. The eruption of Aug. 1883, one of the most violent ever known, destroyed most of the island, caused a tidal wave killing 36,000 people in neighboring Java and Sumatra, and threw debris as far as Madagascar.

**KRAKÓW,** or Cracow, city in S Poland on the Vistula R, administrative center of Krakó province. Capital of Poland from 1320 to 1609, the city has much outstanding architecture, including that of Jagiellonian U. (founded 1364). Still today a center of culture and learning, modern Kráków is also a major industrial city. Notable products are iron, steel, machinery and chemicals. Pop 706,100.

**KRAMER, Jack** (1921–    ), US tennis player who helped organize the professional circuit after WWII. He captured the US championship twice (1946–47), and the British title once (1947).

**KRAZY KAT,** a comic strip by George Herriman (1880–1944) which chronicled the adventures of a lovesick cat, a mischievous mouse and an authoritarian but philosophical canine police officer. Never a commercial success, the strip was a favorite of many intellectuals, including President Woodrow WILSON.

**KREISLER, Fritz** (1875–1962), world-renowned Austrian-US violinist of great brilliance and elegance of style. His compositions included musical forgeries of various 17th- and 18th-century composers, which he later admitted were his own. He lived in the US from 1943.

**KREMLIN,** medieval fortified center of a Russian city, especially that of MOSCOW. The Moscow Kremlin's great wall, built in the 15th century, encloses magnificent palaces and churches from the time of the tsars. The Kremlin is the administrative and political center of the Soviet Union.

**KRENEK, Ernst** (1900–    ), Austrian-US composer of the jazz opera *Johnny Strikes Up* (1926), and of TWELVE TONE MUSIC such as the *Fourth Symphony* (1947). He moved to the US in 1938.

**KRETSCHMER, Ernst** (1888–1964), German psychiatrist and neurologist who developed a "constitutional theory of personality" which linked behavior and psychological disorders to physical stature.

**KREUGER, Ivar** (1880–1932), Swedish industrialist, financier and swindler. Known as the "Match King," he lent governments large sums of money in exchange for a monopoly over their match production, controlling about half the world's match production by 1928. After his suicide it was discovered that his empire was based on forgery and financial manipulation, and that he had perpetrated perhaps the greatest fraud in financial history.

**KRISHNA,** or **Govinda** or **Gopala,** major deity in later Hinduism, depicted as a blue-skinned, sportive youth generally playing the flute; he is worshiped as an incarnation of VISHNU. He is the hero of the MAHABHARATA; his teachings, related in the BHAGAVAD-GITA', advocate selfless action.

**KRISHNAMURTI, Jiddu** (1895–    ), Hindu religious thinker and teacher. His meeting (1909) with Annie BESANT led to claims that he was the reincarnation of Buddha, which he later denied. Since 1969 he has led the Krishnamurti Foundation in Cal.

**KRISTOL, Irving** (1922–    ), American neoconservative political writer, co-editor of *The Public Interest*. He taught at New York University.

**KROC, Ray** (1902–    ), US restaurateur. Purchasing a California hamburger stand from two brothers named McDonald who had developed assembly-line techniques, in 1955 he started to franchise McDonald's drive-in restaurants, which became the largest chain in the fast-food industry.

**KROEBER, Alfred Louis** (1876–1960), US anthropologist who made contributions to many areas of cultural ANTHROPOLOGY and ARCHAEOLOGY, particularly with reference to the AMERINDS. His books include *The Nature of Culture* (1952) and *Style and Civilization* (1957).

**KRONSTADT,** fortress and naval base in the USSR, on Kotlin Island in the Gulf of Finland. For most of the 18th and 19th centuries it was of primary importance, both as port and as garrison, to the then Russian capital of St. Petersburg (present-day Leningrad). The scene of several mutinies (the last, in 1921, against the Soviets) it also played a significant part in WWII.

**KROPOTKIN, Peter Alexeyevich, Prince** (1842–1921), Russian theorist of ANARCHISM whose writings, especially *Mutual Aid* (1902), won international respect. An established geographer, he abandoned (1871) career and social position to pursue revolutionary activities. Imprisoned (1874) in Russia, he escaped to Europe, where after a further spell of imprisonment in France (1883–86) he lived in England and devoted himself to studying, writing and lecturing. He returned to Russia in 1917, but denounced the October (Bolshevik) Revolution and lived in retirement until his death.

**KRUGER, Paul** (Stephanus Johannes Paulus Kruger; 1825–1904), South African Boer leader. He opposed the annexation (1877) of the Transvaal by the British and played a leading part in the Boer rebellion of 1880. Elected president of the new selfgoverning Transvaal Republic (1883), he attempted to extend the frontiers of Transvaal territory, and his pursuit of anti-British policies ultimately led to the second BOER WAR (1899–1902). In 1900 he went to Europe and sought vainly for support for the Boers. He died in Switzerland.

**KRUGER NATIONAL PARK,** game reserve in South Africa, NE Transvaal Province. Founded by Paul KRUGER in 1898, it was expanded and established as a national park in 1926. Its 8,000sq mi contain almost all native species of wildlife.

**KRUPA, Gene** (1909–1973), US jazz musician and outstanding virtuoso drummer. He played with Chicago bands until 1935, when he joined the Benny Goodman orchestra. He had his own band from 1938 to 1951.

**KRUPP,** family of German industrialists famous as armaments makers and long associated with German militarism. The Essen firm was founded in 1811 by **Friedrich Krupp** (1787–1826) with a small steel casting factory, and under his son **Alfred** (1812–1887), became the largest cast steel enterprise in the world. It played a key role in the FrancoPrussian War, WWI and WWII. The Krupps clung to family ownership and opposed unionism. After WWII, **Alfred Krupp von Bohlen und Halbach** (1907–1967), head of the firm from 1943, was imprisoned (1948–51) for war crimes. The company, reorganized but retaining much of its holdings, now concentrates on heavy industrial equipment.

**KRUPSKAYA, Nadezhda Konstantinovna** (1869–1939), Soviet revolutionary and educationist. She married LENIN in 1898 while both were exiled in Siberia, thereafter sharing his life in Europe and his return (1917) to Russia. An opponent of Stalin, she lost her considerable influence in the Communist Party after Lenin's death.

**KRUTCH, Joseph Wood** (1893–1970), US literary critic, social critic and naturalist, author of many books in all three fields. An early environmentalist, he began to concentrate on nature studies when he moved to Arizona in 1950. His subsequent

books include *The Great Chain of Life* (1957).

**KUALA LUMPUR,** capital and largest city of Malaysia, on the S Malay Peninsula. It is Malaysia's commercial, transportation, cultural and educational center. Founded as a mining camp in 1957, the city owed much of its subsequent rapid growth to the local abundance of tin and rubber. During WWII the city was occupied (1942–45) by the Japanese. Pop 451,986.

**KUBELIK, Rafael** (1914–   ), Czech conductor and composer. He was musical director of the Chicago Symphony Orchestra (1950–53), of the Covent Garden Opera (1955–58) and of the Metropolitan Opera (1973–74).

**KUBITSCHEK, Juscelino** (1902–1976), president of Brazil 1956–61. He encouraged scientific and industrial progress, but economic problems followed the building of the new capital BRASILIA. In 1964 he was accused of corruption and went into exile for some years.

**KUBLAI KHAN** (c1216–1294), Mongol emperor from 1259, founder of the Mongol Yüa dynasty of China and grandson of GENGHIS KHAN. By 1279, the last resistance of the Chinese SUNG dynasty crushed, his empire reached from the Pacific to the Volga R and into Poland. Under his skilled and tolerant rule China flourished both economically and culturally. His new capital Cambuluc, described by MARCO POLO, became the nucleus of modern Peking.

**KUBRICK, Stanley** (1928–   ), US film director noted for his technical brilliance and thematic daring. His films include *Paths of Glory* (1958), *Spartacus* (1960) *Lolita* (1962), *Dr. Strangelove* (1964) *2001:A Space Odyssey* (1968), *A Clockwork Orange* (1971) and *Barry Lyndon* (1975).

**KUHN, Walt** (1877–1949), US painter and sculptor. As organizer of New York's 1913 Armory show, he brought leading postimpressionists and cubists, such as MATISSE, VAN GOGH and PICASSO, to the attention of the American public. His own painting career began in 1925, and his best-known canvases feature clowns and acrobats in posed situations.

**KUIPER, Gerard Peter** (1905–1973) Dutch-born US astronomer who discovered CARBON DIOXIDE in the atmosphere of MAR (1948) and satellites of URANUS and NEPTUNE (1948–49), and contributed to the theory of planetary genesis.

**KU K'AI-CHIH** (c344–406 AD), reputedly the first great Chinese painter, noted especially for his portraits and also for landscapes. They are known only from ancient writings and from paintings thought to be copies. Of these last the most famous is *The Admonitions of the Instructress to the Palace Ladies* (7th century).

**KU KLUX KLAN,** secret organization originally begun (1866) to conduct a campaign of terror against newly enfranchized blacks. Founded by Confederate veterans, it spread from Tenn. throughout the South. Its members adopted an arcane hierarchy and dressed in hoods and white sheets to play on their victims' belief in vengeful ghosts. Its emblem was a fiery cross. It was officially disbanded in 1869, although many members remained active throughout RECONSTRUCTION and beyond. The second Klan, organized in 1915, extended its hostilities to Jews, Catholics, pacifists, the foreign born, radicals and labor unions. A membership of nearly 5,000,000 was claimed in the 1920s and its political power extended to some northern states. Officially disbanded once more in 1944, the Klan again revived in recent years as a response to desegregation and was involved in several violent confrontations with anti-Klan and civil rights groups in the early 1980s.

**KULAKS,** term for the historical class of prosperous peasants in Russia: those, e.g., who owned large farms and could employ labor. Stalin designated the Kulaks an anachronism in a state-planned economy; they were dispossessed (1929–34) and deported en masse to labor camps.

**KUN, Béla** (1886–c1939), Hungarian politician and communist premier of Hungary for four months in 1919. Forced to flee by counterrevolutionists, Kun settled in Moscow, returning briefly to Hungary in 1928 to attempt another revolution. He was liquidated in Russia during the 1930s purges.

**KUNIYOSHI, Yasuo** (1893–1953), Japanese-born US painter. Undertones of his Oriental heritage surface through somber tones and rich symbolism that pervade his still lifes. This style replaced the whimsy of his early work, which featured fantastic landscapes, mischievous boys and the like.

**KUNLUN MOUNTAINS,** great chain of mountain ranges in China, on the N extremity of the Tibetan plateau, extending E–W for over 1,800mi. Because they are the longest continuous mountain chain in Asia, they are called the "Backbone of Asia." The highest peak is Ulugh Mus Tagh (25,340ft).

**KUOMINTANG** (Chinese: National People's Party), political party of CHINA founded (1912) by SUN YAT-SEN to stand for an independent Chinese republic with a moderate socialist reform program. In 1924 Sun's "Three People's Principles" (nationalism, democracy and work for all) were accepted by a coalition that included the communists. After Sun's death (1925) CHIANG KAI-SHEK took over the leadership and in 1927 expelled the communists. Most of China was under Kuomintang rule until 1947, but corruption and galloping inflation hastened communist victory (1949). The Kuomintang survives in TAIWAN.

**KUPKA, Frank (Frantisek Kupka;** 1871–1957), Czech-born French painter who was among the first "nonobjective" artists. He was noted for the use of bright colors and geometric shapes.

**KURCHATOV, Igor Vasilevich** (1903– ), Russian nuclear physicist largely responsible for the development of Soviet nuclear armaments and for the first Soviet nuclear power station. The Soviets have named RUTHERFORDIUM *kurchatovium* for him.

**KURDS,** people of KURDISTAN in W Asia, estimated to number about 8,000,000. Traditionally nomadic, most Kurds today are settled farmers. Almost all are Muslims. Kurds have fought vigorously against various rulers for an independent Kurdistan. In Iraq the 1960s and 1970s saw much warfare between the Kurds and Iraqi troops over the issue of self-government.

**KURIL ISLANDS,** USSR, chain of 56 volcanic islands, stretching from the Kamchatka Peninsula of Siberia to Hokkaido Island, Japan. Sparsely inhabited, the islands are the subject of a territorial dispute between Japan and the USSR following Russian occupation during WWII. They remain the only Japanese land still under foreign occupation and consequently the major obstacle to close Russo-Japanese economic and diplomatic ties.

**KUROSAWA, Akira** (1910– ), Japanese movie director whose outstanding talent and originality have been internationally recognized. His films include *Rashomon* (1950), the widely-distributed epic *Seven Samurai* (1954), *Throne of Blood* (1957), a Japanese interpretation of *Macbeth*, and *Kagemusha* (1981).

**KURUSU, Saburo** (1886–1954), Japanese diplomat. He held a number of foreign posts (1910–45), including ambassador to Germany, in which position he signed (1940) the Axis pact between Japan, Germany and Italy. In the US in 1941 he and Ambassador Nomura negotiated with Secretary of State Cordell Hull before the

Pearl Harbor attack. After war was declared, he was interned in the US until exchanged for US diplomats in 1942.

**KUTUZOV, Mikhail Illarionovich, Prince** (1745–1813), Russian field marshal in charge of the forces opposing NAPOLEON I's invasion of Russia in 1812. After a heavy defeat at BORODINO Kutuzov successfully adopted evasive tactics, then hounded Napoleon during the retreat from Moscow.

**Official name:** State of Kuwait
**Capital:** Kuwait
**Area:** 6,880
**Population:** 1,355,837
**Languages:** Arabic, English
**Religions:** Muslim
**Monetary unit(s):** 1 Kuwait dinar=100 fils

**KUWAIT,** independent Arab state on the NW coast of the Persian Gulf, bounded S by Saudi Arabia and N and W by Iraq. The country is nearly all desert and the bulk of the population lives in the cities, chief of which is Kuwait, the capital and major port. Only about half the population is Kuwaiti; the rest are mostly Palestinian, Pakistani and Iranian. A major oil-producer since the 1940s, Kuwait is now a leading economic power with an estimated 20% of the world's oil reserves. Oil revenues finance free education and medical care for all, housing, power stations and water supplies, as well as providing Kuwait with the highest per capita income in the world. Since its foundation in the 18th century, Kuwait has been ruled by the al-Sabah dynasty. Even when a part of the Ottoman Empire, Kuwait retained independence, relying upon the port of Kuwait as its main source of income. A British protectorate from 1899 to 1961, Kuwait has successfully resisted territorial claims from both Saudi Arabia and Iraq; oil revenues from the so-called Partitioned Zone are now divided between Saudi Arabia and Kuwait. In 1975 the oil industry was completely nationalized. Kuwait is now an influential member of the ARAB LEAGUE.

**KUZNETS, Simon Smith** (1901–    ), Russian-born US economist. He pioneered development of a conceptual basis for national income accounts in the US, for which he won the Nobel Prize for Economics in 1971. He is noted for studies of structural changes in economic development and growth of nations. Since 1960, he has been a professor of economics at Harvard U.

**KUZNETSOV, Anatoli** (1929–1979), Soviet novelist best known for his documentation of the annihilation of Russian Jews by the Nazis in *Babi Yar* (1970). He defected to England in 1969.

**KWASHIORKOR,** PROTEIN malnutrition simultaneous with the maintenance of relatively adequate calorie intake. In affected children it causes EDEMA, SKIN and HAIR changes, loss of appetite, DIARRHEA, LIVER disturbance and apathy. Its name derives from its occurrence in children rejected from the breast at the birth of the next sibling. Treatment involves rehydration, treatment of infection and a balanced diet with adequate protein.

**KYD, Thomas** (1558–1594), English dramatist, whose *The Spanish Tragedy* (c1586) was a prototype of the Elizabethan and Jacobean revenge tragedy. The work is partly modeled on Seneca but is both more lurid and more psychologically acute. Kyd may have written a version of the Hamlet story.

**KYOTO,** city in Japan, Honshu Island, about 25mi NE of Osaka. The national capital from its foundation in 794 AD until supplanted by Tokyo in 1868, Kyoto is rich in architectural relics and art treasures. Still today a cultural and religious center, it also has leading educational establishments and large-scale mixed industry with manufactures that include electrical equipment, cameras, chemicals, silk and porcelain. Pop 1,467,700.

**KYUSHU,** most southerly of the four major islands which make up JAPAN. Area 16,205sq mi.

L

12th letter of the English alphabet, derived from the Semitic *lamedh* and the Greek *lambda*. In Roman numerals, L represents 50. The symbol £, a form of L, is an abbreviation of the Latin *libra*, a pound in

' 'eight.

**LABOR,** the act of physical work or the social group that does-it, namely the LABOR FORCE; also an economic term applied to any kind of service that commands an economic return. The economic concept of labor was developed in the mid-18th century by Adam SMITH, and later by MALTHUS and above all by MARX in his LABOR THEORY OF VALUE.

In ancient civilizations manual laborers were generally slaves. In medieval Europe agriculture was carried on by SERFS while other productive processes came to be controlled by master craftsmen, who formed GUILDS largely consisting of journeymen. Apprentices were used for simple preparatory operations. Such distribution of production tasks is found even in primitive economies, but it was the mechanization of the INDUSTRIAL REVOLUTION that made division of labor fundamental. This breaks down a given production process into as many simple, repetitive functions as possible, to minimize time-consuming skill and judgment. The immediate result was improved productivity, but also the degradation of work from a potentially creative act to a tedious chore. At the same time, regular hours were needed to get maximum output from machinery, and, because of the fluctuating demand patterns of a growth economy, labor had to be available or dismissible at will. The notion of "free labor" evolved. This replaced the master-servant relationship with a simple implied contract in which the wages, paid only for work done, became full quittance for the laborer's service. The day-laborer, the exception in early civilizations, became the norm. The labor contract released the employer from even notional responsibility for the laborer, but gave the laborer a highly limited freedom to contract where he would.

Labor UNIONS grew from employees' determination to force employers to observe the labor contract, to acknowledge obligations of humanity in terms of pay and working conditions, and then to improve these terms and conditions. Working hours have diminished from about 70 hours per week (c1800) to about 40 hours in industrialized countries by the 1980s. In many countries organized labor has come to be represented by political parties.

**LABOR, US Department of,** federal department, independent since 1913, responsible for US workers' welfare. Headed by the secretary of labor, a cabinet member, it is concerned with the enforcement of federal laws regulating hours, wages and safety measures; it collects and issues industrial statistics; it administers job-training programs and provides information in labor disputes. It has several specialized divisions.

**LABOR DAY,** official holiday in the US and Canada since 1894, held on the first Monday in September. In socialist countries and most others, labor is honored on MAY DAY.

**LABOR UNIONS.** See UNIONS.

**LABOUR PARTY, British,** political party founded in 1900 by trade unions and socialist groups—the Independent Labour Party (1893) and the FABIAN SOCIETY—with Keir HARDIE its first leader. It gained nationwide support after WWI, first coming to power under Ramsay MACDONALD in 1924. His second administration, 1929–31, ended in coalition with the Conservatives, division within the party and electoral defeat. The first effective socialist program was implemented by the Labour government of Clement ATTLEE (1945–51): the National Health Service was instituted, and the Bank of England and major industries were nationalized. Attlee was followed as leader by Hugh GAITSKELL who was succeeded at his death (1963) by Harold WILSON. Prime minister in four Labour governments, he was succeeded by James Callaghan in 1976. Callaghan, turned out as prime minister in 1979, yielded leadership to Michael Foot, a member of the party's left wing. As Labour became deeply embroiled in factionalism, several leaders resigned to form the new Social Democratic Party.

**LABRADOR.** See NEWFOUNDLAND.

**LA BRUYÈRE, Jean de** (1645–1696), French moralist. His *Les Caractères* (1688) is partly a translation of THEOPHRASTUS, but mostly his satirical impressions of contemporary society.

**LACE,** fine openwork decorative fabric made by braiding, looping, knotting or twisting thread, usually linen or cotton, sometimes silver and gold. Before 19th-century mechanization, it was handmade either by needlepoint or with bobbins. Lace was developed in 16th-century Italy and Flanders and became highly popular. Some towns, such as Brussels, gave their names to their particular styles of lace. (See also CROCHET; NEEDLEWORK.)

**LACHAISE, Gaston** (1882–1935), French-born US sculptor who was best known for his heavy-set nudes, often sculpted larger than life size.

**LACQUERWARE,** articles treated with lacquer, a colored, usually opaque VARNISH. The process originated in the Far East some 2,000 years ago, the sap of the sumac tree

*Rhus vernicifera* being used as varnish. The basis of much lacquerwork is SHELLAC. Many layers of varnish were applied to form a hard bright surface suitable for decorative painting. The process of JAPANNING arose in imitation of oriental lacquerware. Modern synthetic lacquers are widely used for protective coating.

**LACROSSE,** team game derived by French settlers from the North American Indians' game of baggataway, and now the national game of Canada. It is played with a stick called a cross having a net at one end, and a hard rubber ball. The cross is used to catch, throw and carry the ball with the aim of sending it into the opposing goal. In men's lacrosse, played in Canada, the US and the UK, each team has 10 members. Women's lacrosse is usually played with 12 to a side.

**LACTATION,** the production of MILK by female mammals. Shortly before the birth of her young, hormonal changes in the mother result in increased development of the mammary glands and teats. Glandular cells in the body of the mammaries secrete milk which is released to the young when the teats are stimulated. Lactation and the feeding of young on milk are characteristic of the MAMMALS.

**LADYBUGS,** or **ladybirds,** small brightly-colored beetles with 5,000 species of worldwide distribution. In length 2.5–7.5mm (0.1–0.3in), they are harlequin-patterned insects with, commonly, black spots on a red background or yellow spots on black. The colors are borne on the wingcases, modified forewings covering the true flying wings. Ladybugs and their larvae feed on plant aphids and have considerable economic value in controlling pest populations.

**LAETRILE,** alleged anticancer drug created from an extract of apricot pits in 1926 by Ernst Krebs, Sr., and refined by his son Ernst, Jr., who patented it in 1949. Though considered worthless by the medical establishment and banned by the US Food and Drug Administration, laetrile's advocates had managed to have it legalized in 14 states by 1978 when a US appeals court ruled that the drug could not be withheld from terminally ill people since the government's criteria of "safety" and "effectiveness" had no meaning in their case.

**LA FARGE, Christopher Grant** (1862–1938), US architect, best known as a designer of churches, particularly of the early plans of the Cathedral of St. John the Divine in New York City.

**LA FARGE, John** (1835–1910), influential US artist noted for his fine mural painting and stained glass, chiefly executed for churches such as the mural *Ascension* in the Church of the Ascension, New York. These works are held to be unequaled of their kind in the US. He also produced fine watercolors and drawings and was known for his writing and lectures.

**LAFAYETTE, Marie Joseph Paul Yves Roch Gilbert du Motier, Marquis de** (1757–1834), French soldier and statesman who fought in the American Revolution and worked for French–American alliance. He came to America 1777, joined Washington's staff as major general and fought in the campaigns of 1777–78 and at Yorktown (1781). On a visit to France (1779) he persuaded Louis XVI to send troops and a fleet to aid the colonists. In the French Revolution he supported the bourgeoisie, helped set up the National Assembly, drafted the Declaration of the Rights of Man, and commanded the National Guard, but fell from power after ordering his troops (July 1791) to fire on the populace. In 1824 he revisited the US, hailed as a hero. He was one of the leaders of the JULY REVOLUTION (1830).

**LAFFITTE, Jean** (c1780–1825?), also **Lafitte,** French pirate and smuggler who attacked Spanish ships S of New Orleans. He and his men received a pardon from President Madison in return for aiding Andrew Jackson against the British in 1815, but later went back to piracy. When he attacked US ships (1820) the navy sailed against him, and he set out in his favorite ship the *Pride,* never to be seen again.

**LA FOLLETTE, Robert Marion, Sr.** (1855–1925), US statesman and reform legislator. He served in the House of Representatives 1885–91. He became Wis. governor (1901–06), supported by progressive Republicans, and initiated the "Wisconsin idea" reform program, proposing direct primaries and a state civil service. He served as senator (1906–25), founded the PROGRESSIVE PARTY, opposed US entry to WWI and the League of Nations, and ran for president 1924.

His son **Robert Marion La Follette, Jr.** (1895–1953), was senator 1925–47, and another son, **Philip Fox La Follette** (1897–1965), was twice governor of Wis.

**LA FONTAINE, Jean de** (1621–1695), French writer, remembered especially for his *Fables* (1668–94), moral tales drawn from AESOP and oriental sources which he used to comment satirically on contemporary society; and for his humorous, bawdy *Tales* (1664–66).

**LAGERLÖF, Selma Ottiliana Lovisa** (1858–1940), Swedish novelist, the first woman to win a Nobel Prize for Literature (1909). Her works, rooted in legend and the folklore of her native Värmland, include *Gösta Berlings Saga* (1891).

**LAGOS,** chief port of Nigeria, and national capital (until ABUJA, the new capital is completed), on the Bight of Benin. The city takes up four islands and part of the mainland. It produces textiles and metal goods, and exports palm products, groundnuts and cocoa. It houses Lagos U. Pop 1,060,848.

**LAGRANGE, Joseph Louis** (1736–1813), French mathematician who made important contributions to CALCULUS, DIFFERENTIAL EQUATIONS and especially the application of techniques of ANALYSIS to MECHANICS. He worked also on celestial mechanics, in particular explaining the MOON's libration.

**LA GUARDIA, Fiorello Henry** (1882–1947), US statesman and reforming mayor of New York. A Progressive member of Congress 1916–17 and 1923–33, he supported liberalizing and pro-labor measures, including the Norris–La Guardia Act forbidding the use of injunctions in labor disputes. As mayor 1933–45 he instituted major reforms in New York and fought corruption.

**LAHR, Bert** (1895–1967), US entertainer, a successful vaudeville comic before appearing in Broadway comedies such as *Du Barry Was a Lady* (1939). He was acclaimed for his dramatic performance in *Waiting for Godot* (1956), but is best remembered as the cowardly lion in the film *The Wizard of Oz* (1939).

**LAKE, Simon** (1866–1945), US naval architect and engineer who was known as the "father of the modern SUBMARINE." He built the first experimental underwater boat (1894) and the first submarine to be operated successfully in open waters, the gasoline-powered *Argonaut* (1897).

**LAKE DISTRICT,** region in NW England, since 1951 a national park. It contains the highest mountain in England (Scafell Pike, 3,210ft) and 15 lakes including Windermere, Ullswater and Derwentwater. Its scenic beauty has made it a popular walking and tourist area. William and Dorothy Wordsworth, Samuel Coleridge, and Robert Southey all made their homes here in the early 19th century. (See also LAKE POETS.)

**LAKE POETS,** name given to the English poets WORDSWORTH, COLERIDGE and SOUTHEY, who lived in the LAKE DISTRICT for a time and were described by the critic Jeffrey as constituting the "Lake school of poetry." Although all three were friends, they do not really form a group, for Southey's style differed widely from the others'.

**LALO, Édouard** (1823–1892), French composer. A fine orchestrator, he is remembered for his *Symphonie espagnole* (1875) for violin and orchestra, the ballet *Nanouma* (1882) and the opera *Le roi d'Ys* (1888).

**LAMAISM,** popular term for Tibetan BUDDHISM (Mahayana), a distinctive form that evolved from the 7th century AD; it incorporated strict intellectual disciplines, YOGA and ritual, and large monastic orders as well as the shamanistic features of the old folk-religion. Spiritual and temporal power combined in the DALAI LAMA and PANCHEN LAMA, and the continuity provided by reincarnating Lamas created an intensely religious society which remained unchanged until the Chinese invasion (1959). Like Hinduism, Lamaism has innumerable deities with consorts and families to represent symbolically the inner life. It survives in Bhutan, Sikkim, S Siberia, Nepal and Mongolia, and, since 1959, has been gaining new converts in the West.

**LAMAR, Mirabeau Buonaparte** (1798–1859), vice-president (1836–38) and president (1838–41) of the Republic of Texas. While in office he resisted union with the US, though he later supported it. He set up a system of public education in Texas.

**LAMARCK, Jean Baptiste Pierre Antoine de Monet, Chevalier de** (1744–1829), French biologist who did pioneering work on taxonomy (especially that of the INVERTEBRATES) which led him to formulate an early theory of EVOLUTION. Where DARWIN was to propose NATURAL SELECTION as a mechanism for evolutionary change, Lamarck felt that organisms could develop new organs in response to their need for them, and that ACQUIRED CHARACTERISTICS could be inherited.

**LAMARTINE, Alphonse Marie Louis de** (1790–1869), French poet and statesman, briefly head of government after the 1848 revolution (see REVOLUTIONS OF 1848). His collection *Poetic Meditations* (1820) was a landmark of French Romantic literature; lyric evocations of love and nature are underlaid by gentle melancholy and religious feeling.

**LAMB, Charles** (1775–1834), English essayist and critic. With his sister Mary he wrote *Tales from Shakespeare* (1807) for children. His famous *Essays of Elia* (1823, 1833) contain personal comments on many subjects written with humor and pathos. He helped revive interest in Elizabethan drama with *Specimens of English Dramatic Poets* (1808).

**LAMENTATIONS,** book of the OLD TESTAMENT, traditionally ascribed to Jeremiah, though this is disputed by modern scholars. It consists of a series of five poems in dirge meter (the first four are acrostics) lamenting the fall of Jerusalem at the hands of the Babylonians (586 BC).

**LA METTRIE, Julien Offray de** (1709–1751), French physician and philosopher who took the idea of "man as machine" to its extreme. He held that all mental phenomena resulted from organic changes in the NERVOUS SYSTEM.

**L'AMOUR, Louis** (1908–    ), US writer of dozens of best-selling western adventure novels based on historical sources and Old West folklore. Several of his works were made into Hollywood movies, including *Hondo* (1953) and *How the West Was Won* (1962).

**LAMPEDUSA, Giuseppe di** (1896–1957), Italian novelist. A Sicilian prince, he won critical and popular acclaim with *The Leopard*, posthumously published in 1958.

**LAMPREYS,** one of the two remaining groups of jawless fishes, AGNATHA, found both in freshwater and in the sea. The body is eel-like and there is a round, sucking mouth with horny teeth with which they rasp away at their prey. Many species are parasitic when adult, feeding on the flesh of living fishes. The blind, worm-like, filter-feeding larva or ammocoete, is totally unlike the adult, and lives only in freshwater. Sea lampreys migrate into fresh waters to breed.

**LANCASTER, House of,** English royal family which produced the kings HENRY IV, HENRY V and HENRY VI. Edmund Crouchback, second son of HENRY III, was first earl of Lancaster (1267); his son Thomas (d. 1322) led baronial opposition to EDWARD II. JOHN OF GAUNT became duke of Lancaster by marriage in 1362, and his son became HENRY IV in 1399. The Lancastrians were deposed by the house of YORK during the WARS OF THE ROSES, but the heir to their claims, Henry TUDOR, reestablished the line in 1485 as HENRY VII.

**LAND, Edwin Herbert** (1909–    ), US physicist and inventor of Polaroid, a cheap and adaptable means of polarizing light (1932), and the Polaroid Land Camera (1947). In 1937 he set up the Polaroid Corporation to manufacture scientific instruments and antiglare sunglasses incorporating Polaroid.

**LANDAU, Lev Davidovich** (1908–1968), Soviet physicist who made important contributions in many fields of modern physics. His work on CRYOGENICS was rewarded by the 1962 Nobel Prize for Physics for his development of the theory of liquid HELIUM and his predictions of the behavior of liquid He³.

**LAND-GRANT COLLEGES,** US colleges set up with the proceeds of land sales. By the Morrill Act of 1862 Congress granted the states federal lands to be sold to establish agricultural and mechanical arts colleges. There are some 70 land-grant colleges in existence today, including many state universities.

**LANDIS, Kenesaw Mountain** (1866–1944), US judge and baseball commissioner. A well-known judge, he was appointed the first baseball commissioner in 1920 after the "Black Sox" bribery scandal and ruled the game with uncompromising integrity until his death.

**LANDOR, Walter Savage** (1775–1864), English poet and prose writer. He wrote epics, dramatic fragments, lyrics and epigrams, but is best known for his *Imaginary Conversations* (1824–53), a series of 150 stylish and amusing dialogues between notable characters from different ages.

**LANDOWSKA, Wanda** (1877–1959), Polish harpsichord virtuoso, largely responsible for the modern revival of the harpsichord. Living in Paris 1900–40, and then in the US, she was famous as a performer, teacher and authority on early music.

**LANDSAT,** originally Earth Resources Technology Satellite (ERTS), developed by NASA to make pictures of the earth at different wavelengths. The first Landsat was orbited in May 1972. (See also REMOTE SENSING.)

**LANDSCAPE ARCHITECTURE,** the art of modifying land areas to make them more attractive, useful and enjoyable. Highly developed in the ancient civilizations—in China and Japan it had symbolic significance—the art was neglected in Europe after the fall of Rome, but was revived in Renaissance Italy and spread through Europe. The French stress on geometric formality, as at VERSAILLES, was superseded in early 18-century England by picturesque and dramatic, yet apparently natural hills and lakes and vistas, often over large areas; this style shaped the US tradition. Today landscaping is used in parks, highways and other public amenities. (See also BROWN, CAPABILITY; OLMSTEAD, FREDERICK LAW; REPTON, HUMPHREY.)

**LANDSEER, Sir Edwin Henry** (1802–1873), English artist whose sentimental animal paintings, such as *The Monarch of the Glen* (1851), were enormously popular and frequently reproduced as engravings. He also modeled the lions around Nelson's Column in Trafalgar Square, London.

**LANG, Andrew** (1844–1912), Scottish writer and scholar. He pioneered the use of anthropology in folklore in *Custom and Myth* (1884) and *Myth, Literature and Religion* (1887), as well as publishing translations of Homer, popular fairy tale collections, poetry and historical and miscellaneous works.

**LANG, Fritz** (1890–1976), Austrian film director, one of the masters of EXPRESSIONISM in the silent film. *Metropolis* (1926) was a bleak futuristic drama; in the *Doctor Mabuse* films (1922, 1932, 1960) and above all *M* (1931), about a child murderer, Lang explored the psychology of evil. He left Germany in 1933, and his Hollywood films include the social drama *Fury* (1936), westerns, *Clash by Night* (1952) and *Beyond a Reasonable Doubt* (1956).

**LANGDON, Harry,** (1884–1944), one of the great comedians of the silent screen. An obscure US vaudeville performer, he shot to fame with such films as *Tramp, Tramp, Tramp* (1926), *The Strong Man* (1926) and *Long Pants* (1927), in which he played an innocent, stupid but lovable character.

**LANGE, Dorothea** (1895–1965), US documentary photographer. Her powerful, stark pictures of Depression victims, migrant workers and the rural poor created a profound impression and greatly influenced subsequent photojournalistic technique. In 1939 she published *An American Exodus.*

**LANGER, Susanne Knauth** (1895–    ), US philosopher whose *Philosophy in a New Key* (1942) propounded for the nondiscursive symbolism of art a meaning and significance equal to that of the discursive symbolism of language and science. Other works include *Mind: An Essay on Human Feeling* (2 vols., 1967, 1972).

**LANGER, William Leonard** (1896–1977), US diplomatic historian whose major works were *European Alliances and Alignments, 1871–1890* (1931) and *The Diplomacy of Imperialism, 1890–1902* (1935). He edited the *Rise of Modern Europe* series (1934–    ). As the chief of research and analysis of the OSS (1942–45), he prepared a secret psychological study of Hitler, published as *The Mind of Adolf Hitler* (1973).

**LANGLAND, William** (c1332–c1400), presumed poet of *The Vision of Piers Plowman*, a religious allegory representing a dream-vision of the Christian life and one of the finest examples of Middle English alliterative verse.

**LANGMUIR, Irving** (1881–1957), US physical chemist awarded the 1932 Nobel Prize for Chemistry for his work on thin films on solid and liquid surfaces (particularly oil on water), which gave rise to the new science of surface chemistry.

**LANGTON, Stephen** (c1155–1228), English cardinal, whose appointment as archbishop of Canterbury (1207) led to a quarrel between Pope INNOCENT III and King JOHN. Despite a papal INTERDICT, John kept him out of his see until 1213. Langton led baronial opposition to the king, and his is the first signature on the MAGNA CARTA. He was a distinguished theologian, noted for his Old Testament commentaries, and helped to develop English canon law and the autonomy of the English Church.

**LANGTRY, Lillie** (1853–1929), British actress, known as the "Jersey Lily." A famous beauty, she was a mistress of King EDWARD VII.

**LANGUAGE,** the spoken or written means by which man expresses himself and communicates with others. The word "language" comes from the Latin *lingua,* tongue, demonstrating that speech is the primary form of language and writing the secondary. Language comprises a set of sounds that symbolize the content of the message to be conveyed. It is, on this planet, peculiar to man, constituting as it does a formal system with rules whereby complex messages can be built up out of simple components (see GRAMMAR). Languages are the products of their cultures, arising from the cooperative effort required by societies. There are some 3,000 different languages spoken today, added to which are many more regional dialects. Languages may be classified into families, groups and subgroups. To us the most important language family is the Indo-European, to which many Asian and most European languages (including English) belong. Other important families are the Hamito-Semitic, Altaic, Sino-Tibetan, Austro-Asiatic and Dravidian, among others. (See also ETYMOLOGY; LINGUISTICS; PHILOLOGY; PRONUNCIATION; SEMANTICS; SEMIOLOGY; SHORTHAND; SIGN LANGUAGE; WRITING, HISTORY OF.)

**LANGUEDOC,** historic region of S France, W of the Rhône R. Montpellier and Nîmes are the main cities, and the chief product wine. Its name comes from *langue d'oc,* the language of the PROVENÇAL culture. Languedoc was the center of the ALBIGENSIAN heresy, and later of French Protestantism.

**LANIER, Sidney** (1842–1881), US poet

and musician. A Southerner who fought in the Civil War (recalled in his novel *Tiger-Lilies*, 1867), he practiced law, and became a professional flutist. After publication of his *Poems* (1877) he became a lecturer at Johns Hopkins U.

**LANSING**, state capital of Mich., at the junction of Grand R and Cedar R. It is a transportation and commercial center, with an important automobile industry. Pop 130,414.

**Official name:** Lao People's Democratic Republic
**Capital:** Vientiane
**Area:** 91,428sq mi
**Population:** 3,633,000
**Languages:** Lao; French widely used
**Religions:** Buddhist, animist
**Monetary unit(s):** 1 kip≈100 at

**LAOS**, landlocked kingdom of SE Asia, bordered by China to the N, Vietnam to the E, Kampuchea (Cambodia) to the S and Thailand and Burma to the W.

**Land.** Laos is dominated by mountain chains and plateaus, which are cut by deep, narrow valleys. The terrain is covered by forests interspersed with grassland. In the S, limestone plateaus slope W to rice-growing plains along the Mekong R, which forms the border with Burma and most of the border with Thailand and is for 300mi the main transport route of Laos. The wet season of the monsoon climate is from May to Oct., while Nov. to April is a time of near drought. Average temperature in the valleys is above 70°F. Animal life includes elephants, used for lumbering, draft buffalo, and tigers.

**People.** The Lao, by far the largest ethnic group, are a Thai people; Hinayana (Theravada) Buddhism is the religion of their chiefly valley communities. Animist cults predominate among the mountain peoples, the Meo (Hmong) and Yao (in the N) and Kha (S). In the Mekong towns Chinese and Vietnamese traders are important minorities. Vientiane, the capital, is the only sizeable city.

**Economy.** Laos has few manufactures (some silk and silver products). Tin (found

in central Laos) and timber (teak from the largely unexploited N forests) are the main exports. Opium poppies have traditionally been cultivated as a cash crop in the N. In the valleys in the center and S rice is the chief crop though tobacco, cotton, tea and coffee are also grown. There are some hydroelectric and irrigation schemes and, in the NW, unexploited iron-ore deposits.

**History.** Part of the KHMER EMPIRE, the territory was settled from the 10th to 13th centuries by Thai Lao, forced out of Yünnan S China. By the 17th century a powerful Lao kingdom, based on Khmer culture and Buddhism, had emerged; but in the early 1700s it split into the principalities of Luang Prabang in the N and Vientiane in the S. Civil wars invited foreign dominance, notably from Siam, but in 1893 France established hegemony. After WWII national insurgency of various factions (including the Communist PATHET LAO with Vietnamese support) won the country independence within the French Union in 1949; it remained in the French Union until 1954. In 1959 renewed civil war between the neutralist premier Souvanna Phouma and right- and left-wing rivals brought intervention from the great powers. A coalition government was formed in 1973. In May 1975 the right-wing was toppled in an almost bloodless coup; in Dec. 1975 the king abdicated, the country becoming a Communist republic under the Pathet Lao.

**LAO-TSE**, or Lao-Tsu ("Old Master"), Chinese philosopher of the 6th century BC, said to be the founder of TAOISM and the author of *Tao Te Ching*. His actual existence is uncertain, but he was allegedly a librarian at the Chou court. Tao, or the Way, emphasizes simplicity, naturalness and spontaneity in all the essentials of life.

**LA PAZ**, largest city and administrative capital of Bolivia (the legal capital is Sucre). Founded in 1548 by the CONQUISTADORS, it is located in the La Paz river valley, some 12,000ft above sea level, the world's highest capital. Local products include cement, glass, textiles and consumer goods. Pop 1,768,867.

**LAPLACE, Pierre Simon, Marquis de** (1749–1827), French scientist known for his work on celestial mechanics, especially for his NEBULAR HYPOTHESIS, for his many fundamental contributions to mathematics, and for his PROBABILITY studies.

**LAPLAND**, region in the extreme N of Europe, the homeland of the LAPPS. Within the Arctic Circle, it embraces parts of Norway, Sweden, Finland and Russia, with an area of about 150,000sq mi. It has tundra vegetation.

**LAPPS,** a people of N Europe who speak a Finno-Ugric language and may have come originally from central Asia. They number about 30,000 and live mostly in N Norway. Many · are nomads who live off their wandering reindeer herds; others engage in fishing, hunting, forestry and agriculture, and live in settled communities.

**LARDNER, "Ring"** (Ringgold Wilmer Lardner; 1885–1933), US sports journalist and short-story writer. Stories in racy sports idiom, as in *You Know Me, Al* (1916), satirize vulgarity and greed in US life and the success cult. With G. S. Kaufman, he wrote the comedy *June Moon* (1929).

**LARIONOV, Mikhail** (1881–1964), Russian painter and illustrator. He was the originator of the "rayonist" movement which attempted to combine elements of pointillism and cubism. In 1914 he moved permanently to Paris and designed for DIAGHILEV's Ballet Russe, 1914–29.

**LARKS,** small terrestrial songbirds of Europe, Asia, India and Africa, forming the family, Alaudidae. Streaked brown birds, they feed on insects and seeds, walking or running at great speed along the ground. Larks are renowned for their beautiful songs, usually delivered on the wing.

**LA ROCHEFOUCAULD, François, Duc de** (1613–1680), French writer known for his *Memoirs* (1662) of the FRONDE, and his *Maxims* (1665), a collection of more than 500 moral reflections and epigrams, generally paradoxical, often pessimistic, usually acute.

**LARYNX,** specialized part of the respiratory tract used in VOICE production (see SPEECH AND SPEECH DISORDERS). It lies above the TRACHEA in the neck, forming the Adam's apple, and consists of several CARTILAGE components linked by small MUSCLES. Two folds, or *vocal cords*, lie above the trachea and may be pulled across the airway so as to regulate and intermittently occlude air flow. It is the movement and vibration of these that produce voice.

**LA SALLE, René Robert Cavelier, Sieur de** (1643–1687), French explorer and fur trader in North America, who claimed the Louisiana territory for France. In Canada from 1666, he commanded Fort Frontenac, sailed across Lake Michigan (1679) and explored the Illinois R and followed the Mississippi R to its mouth on the Gulf of Mexico. In 1684, sailing to plant a colony there, his fleet was wrecked by storms and Spanish raiders. He was killed by a mutinous crew.

**LA SCALA,** world-famous opera house in Milan, Italy. Built 1776–78, it can seat 3,600. TOSCANINI was its artistic director

1898–1907, 1921–31.

**LAS CASAS, Bartolomé de** (1474–1566), Spanish missionary in the West Indies, South and Central America. He exposed the oppression of the Indians, notably the forced labor of the ENCOMIENDA system, persuaded Madrid to enact the New Laws for Indian welfare (1542) and in his monumental *History of the Indies* recorded data valuable to modern anthropology.

**LASCAUX CAVE,** cave near Montignac, France, containing many outstanding examples of AURIGNACIAN cave paintings. Opened to the public in 1940, deterioration of the paintings led to its being closed in 1963. (See also ALTAMIRA.)

**LASCH, Christopher** (1932–    ), US social historian. A professor at the U. of Rochester from 1970, he wrote many provocative books, including *The Agony of the American Left* (1969) and *The Culture of Narcissism* (1978).

**LASER,** a device producing an intense beam of parallel LIGHT with a precisely defined wavelength. The name is an acronym for "*l*ight *a*mplification by *s*timulated *e*mission of *r*adiation." It works on the same principle as the MASER, but at visible rather than microwave frequencies.

The light produced by lasers is very different from that produced by conventional sources. In the latter, all the source atoms radiate independently in all directions, whereas in lasers they radiate in step with each other and in the same direction, producing **coherent light**. Such beams spread very little as they travel, and provide very high capacity communication links. They can be focused into small intense spots, and have been used for cutting and WELDING—notably for refixing detached retinas in the human EYE. Lasers also find application in distance measurement by INTERFERENCE methods, in SPECTROSCOPY and in HOLOGRAPHY.

The principles of laser operation are described under MASER. The active material is enclosed between a pair of parallel MIRRORS, one of them half-silvered; light traveling along the axis is reflected to and fro and builds up rapidly by the stimulated emission process, passing out eventually through the half-silvered mirror, while light in other directions is rapidly lost from the laser.

In pulsed operation, one of the end mirrors is concealed by a shutter, allowing a much higher level of pumping than usual; opening the shutter causes a very intense pulse of light to be produced—up to 100MW for 30ns—while other pulsing techniques can achieve $10^{13}$ W in picosecond pulses.

Among the common laser types are ruby lasers (optically pumped, with the polished crystal ends serving as mirrors), liquid lasers (with RARE EARTH ions or organic dyes in solution), gas lasers (an electric discharge providing the high proportion of excited states), and the very small SEMICONDUCTOR lasers (based on electron-hole recombination).

**LASKI, Harold Joseph** (1893–1950), English political theorist, economist and author, active in the FABIAN SOCIETY and the Labour Party. From 1920 he lectured at the London School of Economics and was a visiting lecturer in many countries. In the 1930s he moved from political pluralism to Marxism. His books include *Democracy in Crisis* (1933) and *Liberty in the Modern State* (1948).

**LASKY, Jesse** (1880–1958), US film production pioneer who, in partnership with Samuel GOLDWYN and Cecil B. DE MILLE, produced Hollywood's first feature-length film, *The Squaw Man* (1914). He was a co-founder of Paramount Pictures and directed production of more than 1,000 movies.

**LASSALLE, Ferdinand** (1825–1864), German socialist and lawyer, co-founder (1863) of the General German Workers' Association, later the Social Democratic Party, the first labor party in Germany. A Hegelian influenced by Marx's economic theories, he nevertheless favored state action, not revolution, as the way to socialism.

**LASSUS, Roland de,** or **Orlando di Lasso** (c1530–1594), Flemish Renaissance composer. He was choirmaster at St. John Lateran, Rome, and from 1556 director of music at the ducal court at Munich. His vast and varied output includes religious motets, secular chansons and the great *Penitential Psalms of David* (1584). His expressive integration of music and text anticipated the BAROQUE.

**LASSWELL, Harold Dwight** (1902–1978), US political scientist who adapted Freudian concepts to political studies and emphasized the personal and sexual dimensions of political leadership. A professor at Chicago 1922–38 and Yale 1946–71 universities, he wrote *Psychopathology and Politics* (1930), *World Politics and Personal Insecurity* (1935) and *Power and Personality* (1948).

**LAST JUDGMENT,** in Christian theology, the judgment of all men by God at the end of the world. According to the New Testament, at Christ's SECOND COMING the dead will be raised (see RESURRECTION) and, with those then living, assembled before God to be judged by what they have done: the unrighteous thrown into HELL with Satan, the righteous admitted to HEAVEN. (See also ESCHATOLOGY; PURGATORY.)

**LAS VEGAS,** city in SE Nev., seat of Clark Co.; world-renowned for "The Strip" with its casinos (state-legalized gambling), luxury hotels, bars and night clubs. The city is also a mining and cattle-farming center. There are artesian springs nearby. Pop 164,674.

**LATENT HEAT,** the quantity of HEAT absorbed or released by a substance in an isothermal (constant-temperature) change of state, such as FUSION or vaporization. The temperature of a heated lump of ice will increase to 0°C and then remain at this temperature until all the ice has melted to water before again rising. The heat energy absorbed at 0°C overcomes the intermolecular forces in the ordered ice structure and increases the kinetic ENERGY of the water molecules.

**LATERAN,** district of SE Rome, given to the church by Emperor Constantine I in 311. The Lateran palace—the papal residence until 1309—was rebuilt in the 16th century. The basilica of St. John Lateran is the cathedral church of the pope as bishop of Rome. Of the five Lateran ECUMENICAL COUNCILS the fourth, convened by INNOCENT III, was of major importance.

**LATERAN TREATY,** concordat between the papacy and the government of Italy, signed 1929 in the Lateran palace and confirmed by the 1948 Italian constitution. It established Roman Catholicism as Italy's state religion and VATICAN CITY as an independent sovereign state.

**LATEX.** See RUBBER.

**LATIN,** INDO-EUROPEAN LANGUAGE of the Italic group, the language of ancient Rome and the ancestor of the ROMANCE languages. Originating in LATIUM c8th century BC, Latin spread with Roman conquests throughout the Empire, differentiating into vulgar Latin and classical (literary) Latin. It is a logical and highly inflected language that has furnished scientific and legal terminology and is still used in the Roman Catholic Church. It was the international language of scholarship and diplomacy until the 18th century. About half of all English words are Latin in origin, many derived through Old French.

**LATIN AMERICA,** traditionally twenty independent republics in MIDDLE and SOUTH AMERICA where Romance languages are spoken: Spanish in Mexico, Cuba, Dominican Republic, Costa Rica, El Salvador, Guatemala, Honduras, Nicaragua, Panama, Argentina, Bolivia, Chile,

Colombia, Ecuador, Paraguay, Peru, Uruguay, and Venezuela; Portuguese in Brazil; and French in Haiti. Sometimes the term includes Guyana, Suriname, and French Guiana in South America, and, less often, also all the Caribbean Islands.

**People.** About 320 million people living in Latin America have Indian, European, Negro and white ancestry. The population growth of almost 3% per year is one of the highest in the world. Differences in educational levels and social structure are great—the predominantly white, literate, middle-class populations of Argentina, Uruguay, and Costa Rica have little in common with traditional Indian communities of Mexico, Bolivia, Peru, and Ecuador. Despite educational campaigns, illiteracy rates remain high, especially in remote highlands. The universities, which are seldom technologically oriented, suffer from lack of full-time teaching staffs. After World War II, large numbers of people moved from rural to urban areas in search of employment and most large cities are now surrounded by extensive squatter colonies. Housing, social, and medical services are usually inadequate.

**Economy.** Historically, Latin American economies depended on one export commodity—oil, copper, tin, coffee, bananas, livestock, fish—to earn foreign currency. In several countries there have been efforts at diversification, but economic development is hampered by poor transport, political instability, and burdensome effects of foreign aid. Persistent unequal income distribution and urban unemployment (reaching up to 50%) are two great problems that still defy solution. Although about half of the people work on the land, agriculture is mostly primitive and inefficient. Important changes in recent decades include the emergence of Brazil as a leading industrial power, and use of oil revenues in Mexico and Venezuela to finance economic growth.

**History.** Before the arrival of COLUMBUS in 1492, several highly developed civilizations flourished in the region, most notably the MAYAS, AZTECS and INCAS. During the conquest the indigenous populations were decimated by war and European diseases. Spanish and Portuguese colonial rule lasted about three hundred years, and by 1825 most of the colonies, inspired by the leadership of BOLÍVAR and SAN MARTÍN, gained their independence. Power and wealth, however, remained in the hands of tiny minorities, and political life was marked by corruption and instability. In the 20th century, several countries (Mexico,

Chile, Costa Rica, Uruguay) enjoyed long peaceful periods of constitutional rule, but during the 1960s and 1970s the region witnessed an upsurge of military dictatorships.

**LATITUDE AND LONGITUDE,** the coordinate system used to locate points on the earth's surface. Longitude "lines" are circles passing through the poles whose centers are at the center of the earth; they divide the earth rather like an orange into segments. Longitudes are measured $0°-180°E$ and W from the line of the GREENWICH OBSERVATORY. Assuming the EARTH to be a sphere, we can think of the latitude of a point as the ANGLE between a line from the center of the earth to the point and a line from the center to the equator at the same longitude. Each pole, then, has a latitude of $90°$, and so latitude is measured from $0°$ to $90°$ N and S of the EQUATOR. latitude "lines" being circles parallel to the equator that get progressively smaller towards the poles. (See CELESTIAL SPHERE.)

**LA TOUR, Georges de** (1593–1652), French painter of religious and genre subjects. Renowned in his lifetime, he was virtually forgotten until 1915. Influenced indirectly by CARAVAGGIO, his work exploited indirect lighting sources and candle light and was characterized by simple forms and warm colors. (See also CHIAROSCURO.)

**LATROBE, Benjamin Henry** (1764–1820), English-born US architect and engineer. His work includes the S wing of the Capitol in Washington and Baltimore's Roman Catholic cathedral. A pioneer of the Classical revival, he was the first major professional architect in the US.

**LATTER-DAY SAINTS, Church of Jesus Christ of.** See MORMONS.

**LATTER-DAY SAINTS, Reorganized Church of Jesus Christ of,** sect which split from the main body of MORMONS when Brigham Young became leader at the death of Joseph Smith. They chose Smith's son as their leader, becoming formally organized in 1852. They follow the main Mormon beliefs but admit blacks as priests. The headquarters are at Independence, Mo.

**LATTIMORE, Owen** (1900–    ), US authority on the Far East. He taught at Johns Hopkins, edited the quarterly *Pacific Affairs*, and, during WWII, served as an adviser to Chiang Kai-shek and in the US Office of War Information. Sen. Joseph McCarthy created a sensation by accusing Lattimore of being a Soviet agent, but the latter was cleared by a Senate investigation.

**LATVIA,** a republic of the USSR, bordering on the Baltic Sea, between

Estonia and Lithuania; its capital is RIGA. It is a lowland country, covering some 24,600sq mi, with a moderate continental climate. Nearly a third of the people are Russians but the majority are Letts, an ancient Baltic people. Cattle and dairy farming, fishing and lumbering are still important but there are highly developed industries, including steel, shipbuilding, engineering, textiles, cement and fertilizers. Christianized by the German Livonian Knights in the 13th century, Latvia was ruled by Poles, Swedes and, from the 18th century, Russians. From 1920 to 1940, when it was reabsorbed in Russia, it enjoyed a precarious independence. (See USSR.)

**LATVIAN LANGUAGE.** See LETTISH.

**LAUDER, Sir Harry** (1870–1950), Scottish singer and comedian who performed in traditional kilts and was a beloved entertainer in British music halls and US vaudeville houses. He was known for his recitations and his singing of quaint Scottish songs, many of which he wrote.

**LAUE, Max Theodor Felix von** (1879–1960), German physicist awarded the 1914 Nobel Prize for Physics for his prediction (and, with others, subsequent experimental confirmation) that X rays can be diffracted by crystals (see X-RAY DIFFRACTION).

**LAUGHTON, Charles** (1899–1962), English-born actor, a US citizen from 1950. Films include the award-winning *The Private Life of Henry VIII* (1933) and *The Hunchback of Notre Dame* (1939). He directed *Night of the Hunter* (1955).

**LAUREL AND HARDY,** famous Hollywood comedy team. The English-born Stan Laurel (Arthur Stanley Jefferson; 1890–1965) and the American Oliver Hardy (1892–1957), thin man and fat man, simpleton and pompous heavy, made over 200 films between 1927 and 1945 in a style, shaped by Laurel, which ranged from slapstick to slow-paced comedy of situation and audience anticipation.

**LAURENTIAN MOUNTAINS,** or Laurentides, range in S Quebec, Canada. One of the oldest in the world; it rises almost 4,000ft. Heavily forested, the area's economy rests on wood and the tourist industry.

**LAURIER, Sir Wilfrid** (1841–1919), first French-Canadian Prime Minister of Canada 1896–1911. Leader of the federal Liberal party 1887–1919, he encouraged provincial autonomy while seeking to unite the country. Many of his attempts to better the rights of French-Canadians, particularly in education, met with little success. Defeated in the 1911 election, he was supported by Quebec and rejected by the rest of Canada in the 1917 election, a divisive result he worked against.

**LAVA,** both molten ROCK rising to the earth's surface through VOLCANOES and other fissures, and the same after solidification. Originating as MAGMA deep below the surface, most lavas (e.g., BASALT) are basaltic (subsilicic) and flow freely for considerable distances. Lavas of intermediate silica content are called andesite. SILICA-rich lavas such as RHYOLITE are much stiffer. Basaltic lavas solidify in a variety of forms, the commonest being *aa* (Hawaiian, rough) or block lava, forming irregular jagged blocks, and *pahoehoe* (Hawaiian, satiny) or ropy lava, solidifying in ropelike strands. Pillow lava, with rounded surfaces, has solidified under water, and slowly-cooled basalt may form hexagonal columns.

**LAVAL, Pierre** (1883–1945), French politician who collaborated with the Germans in WWII. A socialist and pacifist, he served three unsuccessful terms as premier 1931–32, 1932 and 1935–36. Believing that Nazi victory was inevitable, he allowed himself to be installed as a Nazi puppet premier 1942–44. He fled abroad, returned for trial (1945) and was executed.

**LAVER, Rod** (1938–    ), Australian tennis player, the only man to win the Grand Slam (Australian, British, French, US championships) both as an amateur (1962) and a professional (1969). The left-hander was the first tennis player to earn $200,000 in one season.

**LAVOISIER, Antoine Laurent** (1743–1794), French scientist who was foremost in the establishment of modern CHEMISTRY. He applied gravimetric methods to the process of COMBUSTION, showing that when substances burned, they combined with a component in the air (1772). Learning from J. PRIESTLEY of his "dephlogisticated air" (1774), he recognized that it was with this that substances combined in burning. In 1779 he renamed the gas *oxygène,* because he believed it was a component in all acids. Then, having discovered the nature of the components in water, he commenced his attack on the PHLOGISTON theory, proposing a new chemical nomenclature (1787), and publishing his epoch-making *Elementary Treatise of Chemistry* (1789). In the years before his tragic death on the guillotine, he also investigated the chemistry of RESPIRATION, demonstrating its analogy with combustion.

**LAW,** body of rules governing the relationship between the members of a community and between the individual and the state. In England, the British

Commonwealth and the US the law is based upon statute law, laws enacted by legislative bodies such as Congress, and upon COMMON LAW, the body of law created by custom and adherence to rules derived from previous judgments. This also covers the body of law created by EQUITY. The other main system, CIVIL LAW, derives from the laws of ancient Rome and relies not on precedent but on a code of rules established and modified only by statute. This is the dominant system in most of Europe and in many other countries of the world. In fact the division is not absolute. Many areas of the common law are codified by statute for convenience; there is often unofficial but very real reliance on previous decisions in civil law countries.

All major bodies of law break down into two divisions, public law and private law (often called civil law also). Public law governs matters which concern the state. CRIMINAL LAW is public because a crime is an offense against the state; other kinds of public law are ADMINISTRATIVE LAW, INTERNATIONAL LAW and CONSTITUTIONAL LAW. Private law governs the relationship between individuals (including corporate bodies such as companies) in such matters as CONTRACT, and the law of TORT; this covers damaging acts done by one individual to another which are not necessarily crimes.

**History of law.** The first legal system of which we have any detailed knowledge is that of the Babylonian King HAMMURABI in c1700 BC, a complex code linking crime with punishment and regulating the conduct of everyday affairs. Like the Hebrew Mosaic Law, it treated law as a divine ordinance; the ancient Greeks were probably the first to regard law as made by man for his own benefit. Roman law was based on the Twelve Tables, compiled c451–450 BC; it developed a complex equity system when these became outdated. The emperor JUSTINIAN produced the last definitive code in an attempt to clear up resulting difficulties. Much medieval law was based on Church law, although an independent system arose quite early in England. This grew into the common law and spread outwards with the growth of the British Empire. Napoleon revised Roman law as the basis for his CODE NAPOLÉON, the model for most subsequent civil law codes. US law grew out of the common law, but has been much modified by the federal system. (See also LEGAL PROFESSION.)

**LAW, Andrew Bonar** (1858–1923), Canadian-born Scottish politician. He succeeded BALFOUR as leader of the Conservative Party in 1911. Colonial secretary in the 1915 war cabinet, he was chancellor of the exchequer under LLOYD GEORGE 1916–18 and prime minister 1922–23.

**LAW OF THE SEA CONFERENCE,** an international assembly that first met in Geneva in 1958. Issues relating to control of the high seas include the extent of national off-shore territory and free passage of foreign ships through international straits. The most important and difficult matter is the access to valuable minerals on the ocean floor, especially manganese nodules, which contains deposits of cobalt, copper and manganese. A draft accord was reached in 1980 by some 150 nations, but the US announced (1981) it was not ready to sign.

**LAWRENCE, D(avid) H(erbert)** (1885–1930), major English author. He combined a vivid prose style with a solid background of ideas and intense human insight. Stressing the supremacy of instinct and emotion over reason in human relationships, he advocated absolute sexual candor; his novel *Lady Chatterley's Lover* (1928) is known for this to the exclusion of its other themes. Perhaps his best works are *The Rainbow* (1915) and *Women in Love* (1920). From a working-class background (reflected in *Sons and Lovers*, 1913), he was for some years a teacher. He died of pleurisy at Vence in France.

**LAWRENCE, Ernest Orlando** (1901–1958), US physicist awarded the 1939 Nobel Prize for Physics for his invention of the CYCLOTRON (1929; the first successful model was built in 1931).

**LAWRENCE, Gertrude** (1898–1952), versatile and sophisticated English actress and singer. Her first great success was in her friend Noel COWARD's *Private Lives* (1930). Famous in London and on Broadway, her last appearance was in *The King and I* (1951).

**LAWRENCE, James** (1781–1813), US naval officer, captain of the frigate *Chesapeake*, sunk by the British frigate *Shannon* off Boston in 1813. He was mortally wounded; his dying words "Don't give up the ship!" have become proverbial.

**LAWRENCE, Sir Thomas** (1769–1830), English painter, the most fashionable portraitist of his time. President of the Royal Academy from 1820, he never had the success he wished for as a history painter. His style is richly colorful, fluid and vigorous, but occasionally careless.

**LAWRENCE, T(homas) E(dward)** called "Lawrence of Arabia" (1888–1935), English scholar, writer and soldier, legendary guerrilla fighter with the Arabs against the Turks in WWI. As a British Intelligence officer he carried out with Prince FAISAL a successful guerrilla campaign against Turkish rail supply lines, and was with the Arab forces that captured Damascus in 1918. In *The Seven Pillars of Wisdom* (1926) he described his wartime experiences and his personal philosophy. A neurotic, lonely man, he joined the Royal Air Force and Royal Tank Corps under assumed names 1923–25 and again 1925–35. He was killed in a motorcycle crash.

**LAWSON, Ernest** (1873–1939), US Impressionist painter. One of the EIGHT, he exhibited at their controversial ARMORY SHOW. Seeking a greater degree of naturalism, he specialized in serene landscapes, often rendered in glowing colors, such as *Winter* (1914) and *High Bridge* (1939).

**LAXNESS, Halldór Kiljan** (1902– ), Iceland's greatest modern writer. He became famous with his novel *Salka Valka* (1934). This and later books such as *The Atom Station* (1945) are harsh but compassionate descriptions of Icelandic rural life and post-WWII problems. He was awarded the Nobel Prize in 1955.

**LAZARUS, Emma** (1849–1887), US poet best known for the sonnet *The New Colossus* engraved at the base of the Statue of Liberty. Of a Sephardic Jewish family, she based much of her work on Jewish culture and supported Jewish nationalism.

**LEACH, Edmund Ronald** (1910– ), British anthropologist who researched kinship and mythology in southeast Asia and made notable theoretical contributions to structural anthropology. His books include *Political Systems of Highland Burma* (1954) and *Rethinking Anthropology* (1961).

**LEACOCK, Stephen Butler** (1869–1944), Canadian political scientist and humorist. Head of Economics and Political Science at McGill U., Montreal, 1908–36, he wrote 57 books, the majority humorous. *Literary Lapses* (1910), his first, was made an immediate success by its dry, observant and witty style.

**LEADBELLY.** See LEDBETTER, HUDDIE.

**LEAD (Pb)**, soft, bluish-gray metal in Group IVA of the PERIODIC TABLE, occurring as GALENA, and also as CERUSSITE and anglesite (lead sulfate). The sulfide ore is converted to the oxide by roasting, then smelted with coke. Lead dissolves in dilute nitric acid, but is otherwise resistant to corrosion, because of a protective surface layer of the oxide, sulfate etc. It is used in roofing, water pipes, coverings for electric cables, RADIATION shields, ammunition, storage BATTERIES, and alloys, including solder (see SOLDERING), PEWTER, BABBITT METAL and type metal. Lead and its compounds are toxic (see LEAD POISONING). AW 207.2, mp 327.5°C, bp 1740°C, sg 11.35 (20°C).

Lead forms two series of salts; the lead(II) compounds are more stable than the lead(IV) compounds. **Lead(II) Oxide** (PbO), or **Litharge**, yellow crystalline solid, made by oxidizing lead; used in lead-acid storage batteries, glass and glazes; mp 888°C. **Lead(IV) Oxide** ($PbO_2$), brown crystalline solid, a powerful oxidizing agent used in matches, fireworks, and dyes; it decomposes at 290°C. **Trilead Tetroxide** ($Pb_3O_4$), or **Red Lead**, orange-red powder, made by oxidizing litharge, used in paints, inks, glazes and magnets. **Lead Tetraethyl** ($Pb[C_2H_5]_4$), colorless liquid, made by reacting a lead/sodium alloy with ethyl chloride. It is used as an ANTIKNOCK ADDITIVE to GASOLINE.

**LEAD POISONING,** DISEASE caused by excessive LEAD levels in TISSUES and BLOOD. It may be taken in through the industrial use of lead, through AIR POLLUTION due to lead-containing fuels or, in children, through eating old paint. BRAIN disturbance with COMA or CONVULSIONS, peripheral NEURITIS, ANEMIA and abdominal COLIC are important effects. Chelating agents (see CHELATE) are used in treatment but preventative measures are essential.

**LEAF,** green outgrowth from the stems of higher plants and the main site of PHOTOSYNTHESIS. The form of leaves varies from species to species but the basic features are similar. Each leaf consists of a flat blade or lamina, attached to the main stem by a leaf stalk or petiole. Leaf-like stipules may be found at the base of the petiole. The green coloration is produced by CHLOROPHYLL which is sited in the CHLOROPLASTS. Most leaves are covered by a waterproof covering or cuticle. Gaseous exchange takes place through small openings called STOMATA, through which water vapor also passes (see TRANSPIRATION). The blade of the leaf is strengthened by veins which contain the vascular tissue that is responsible for conducting water around the plant and also the substances essential for METABOLISM.

In some plants the leaves are adapted to catch insects (see INSECTIVOROUS PLANTS), while in others they are modified to reduce water loss (see SUCCULENTS; XEROPHYTE). Leaves produced immediately below the

FLOWERS are called bracts and in some species, e.g., POINSETTIA, they are more highly colored than the flowers.

**LEAGUE OF NATIONS** (1920–46), the first major international association of countries; a total of 63 states were members, although not all simultaneously. In WWI Allied leaders, particularly President WILSON, became convinced of the need for an international organization to resolve conflicts peacefully and avert another devastating war. The charter of the proposed League of Nations was incorporated in the Treaty of VERSAILLES. Ironically, however, Wilson was unable to persuade the US Senate to ratify the Treaty and thus join the League; this may have been the League's greatest weakness. The Covenant embodied the principles of collective security against an aggressor, arbitration of international disputes, disarmament and open diplomacy.

Established at Geneva, Switzerland, the League grew during the 1920s, taking in many new members, but it never had much influence. It could do little to stop the Italian invasion of Corfu in 1923 or the CHACO WAR. It did no more than investigate and protest the Japanese invasion of Manchuria in 1931. Its failure to take decisive action against Italy over the invasion of Ethiopia in 1934 was the final blow to its prestige; WWII proved it a failure. Its subsidiary organizations, however, such as the INTERNATIONAL LABOR ORGANIZATION and the INTERNATIONAL COURT OF JUSTICE, have endured, as have the public health bodies it created.

**LEAGUE OF WOMEN VOTERS,** non-partisan organization with over 130,000 members in the US and Puerto Rico, founded in 1920 by members of the National American Women Suffrage Association (see WOMEN'S RIGHTS). Apart from political education for its members, the league studies and campaigns on economic and social issues. It does not sponsor electoral candidates or political parties.

**LEAKEY, Louis Seymour Bazett** (1903–1972), British archaeologist and anthropologist best known for his findings of human FOSSILS, especially in the region of Olduvai Gorge, Tanzania, and for his (sometimes controversial) views on their significance. His son Richard continued his work.

**LEAN, David** (1908–    ), British film director responsible for several memorable English films, including *Great Expectations* (1946), *Brief Encounter* (1946) and *Oliver Twist* (1948). He later won Academy Awards for *Bridge on the River Kwai* (1957) and *Lawrence of Arabia* (1962).

**LEANING TOWER OF PISA,** white marble bell tower or *campanile* in Pisa, Italy. Building was started in 1174, reputedly by Bonanno Pisano, but the foundations were unsound and the 184.5ft tower had already begun to lean by the time of its completion in the 14th century. It now tilts more than 17ft from the perpendicular.

**LEAP YEAR.** See CALENDAR.

**LEAR, Edward** (1812–1888), English artist, traveler and versifier, best known for his LIMERICKS and nonsense rhymes. *The Owl and the Pussy-Cat* is a famous example. His landscapes and illustrated journals are highly regarded.

**LEAR, Norman** (1922–    ), US television producer who pioneered American production of adult situation comedies, including *All in the Family* and *Mary Hartman, Mary Hartman*. Originally a comedy writer, he managed to interject controversial social and political issues into TV programming.

**LEARNING,** refers to the acquisition of new knowledge and new responses. If it were not for early school learning you would be able neither to read these words nor to understand them. The concepts of learning and MEMORY are closely related, though learning is usually considered to be the result of practice, which in itself is encouraged by a particular stimulus. The simplest learned response is the conditioned REFLEX. The most powerful learning stimulus is the satisfaction of instinctive drives (see INSTINCT). For example, a dog might learn that if he sits up and "begs" he will be fed by his owner. Here the stimulus is positive, in that the result of his response is a reward, rather than negative, where the correct response earns only escape from punishment: positive stimuli are more effective encouragements to learning than are negative. All animals display the ability to learn, and even some of the most primitive have the ability to become bored with the tests of experimenters (where the reward is not an adequate stimulus). In humans, learning ability depends to a great extent on INTELLIGENCE, though social and environmental factors clearly play a part. (See also CONDITIONING; HABIT; IMPRINTING.)

**LEASE, Mary Elizabeth** (1853–1933), American barrister, better known as an agrarian protester and temperance advocate. An active supporter of POPULISM in the 1890s, she earned the nickname Mary "Yellin' " Lease, urging farmers to "raise less corn and more hell."

**LEAVIS, F. R.** (Frank Raymond Leavis; 1895–1978), influential English literary critic and lecturer. Leavis judged works by their moral standpoint and condemned low standards in modern culture. He edited the quarterly review *Scrutiny* (1932–53) and wrote *New Bearings in English Poetry* (1932), *The Great Tradition* (1948) and *The Common Pursuit* (1952).

**LEAVITT, Henrietta Swan** (1868–1921), US astronomer who headed the photographic PHOTOMETRY department of the Harvard College Observatory. Her measurement and analysis of the luminosity of STARS were used to determine stellar distances and to map the MILKY WAY.

**Official name:** Republic of Lebanon
**Capital:** Beirut
**Area:** 4,015sq mi
**Population:** 3,205,000
**Languages:** Arabic; French and English widely used
**Religions:** Muslim, Christian
**Monetary unit(s):** 1 Lebanese pound=100 piastres

**LEBANON,** Mediterranean republic in SW Asia, a small Arab state bordered by Syria and Israel.

**Land.** The four main regions, paralleling the sea, are the flat, fertile, coastal strip; the Lebanon Mountains; the narrow, fertile Bekaa (Biqa) Valley and the Anti-Lebanon Mountains. Lebanon has more rain (15–50in per year) and a more moderate climate than its neighbors. Only a few groves of the famous 'Cedars of Lebanon' remain on the once-forested mountains.

**People.** Lebanon is an Arab state, but about half of the people are Christian, mainly MARONITE. Most of the remainder are SUNNITE MUSLIMS, though the DRUZES, a small Muslim sect, are historically of great importance. The uneasy balance of power maintained by Muslims and Christians over the centuries has been upset by an influx of Palestinian refugees since 1948, many of whom subsequently settled in various refugee camps in the S.

The level of education is highest in the Middle East, with about 85% of the population literate. There are five universities, including the American University in Beirut (1866) which has an international reputation.

**Economy.** About half the labor force works in agriculture, producing grains, olives and citrus fruits. Until the 1975–76 civil war the country had a service-oriented economy, with Beirut the financial and banking capital of the Middle East. Although the city has not regained its preeminence, Beirut is once again a major transshipment port, and Iraqi oil is refined there. Remittances sent home by Lebanese working abroad are a major source of income.

**History.** The site of ancient PHOENICIA, Lebanon is a land of great antiquity and resilience. Although engulfed by successive invaders—Greek, Roman, Arab and Turkish—it preserved some degree of autonomy. Lebanon's inaccessible mountains were an early refuge for persecuted religious groups, especially Christians, whose influence was entrenched during the CRUSADES. Freed from Turkish rule after WWI, the country passed into French hands, becoming effectively independent in 1943. During the early Arab-Israeli conflicts Lebanon was able to steer a course of noninvolvement. Civil war erupted in 1975 between the conservative Christian Phalangists and leftist Muslim and Palestinian militias, including the PALESTINE LIBERATION ORGANIZATION, supported by Syrian troops in 1976 who have remained as part of an Arab peace-keeping force. Despite a 1976 ceasefire, sporadic fighting has continued, mostly in Beirut. In the late 1970s and early '80s S Lebanon was the scene of fighting between Palestinian guerillas and Israeli troops.

**LE BRUN, Charles** (1619–1690), French artist, "first painter" to Louis XIV and virtual dictator of the arts in France 1662–83. He directed the GOBELIN tapestry works and decorated the Palace of Versailles.

**LECLERC, Jacques Philippe** (1902–1947), name assumed by Jacques Philippe, Vicomte de Hauteclocque, WWII Free French commander. He led his forces from French Equatorial Africa 1,500mi across the Sahara to Tunisia 1942–43. In 1944 he received the surrender of Paris.

**LECONTE DE LISLE, Charles Marie René** (1818–1894), French poet and translator of classical verse. Established by his *Poésies barbares* (1862) as chief among the PARNASSIANS, he succeeded Victor HUGO at the Académie Française (1886).

LE CORBUSIER (1887–1965), professional name of Charles-Édouard Jeanneret: Swiss-born, French-trained architect, a founder of the INTERNATIONAL STYLE. His austere, rectangular designs made in the 1920s and 1930s reflected his view of a house as a "machine to live in." Later influential designs (featuring reinforced concrete) include apartments at Marseilles, a chapel at Ronchamp and CHANDIGARH, in India.

LEDBETTER, Huddie ("Leadbelly") (c1888–1949), American Negro blues and folk singer and guitarist, born in La. His repertoire and powerful singing style impressed the folk historian and archivist John Avery LOMAX, who became his patron. Leadbelly sang in New York nightclubs in the 1940s.

LEDERBERG, Joshua (1925–   ), US geneticist awarded with G. W. BEADLE and E. L. TATUM the 1958 Nobel Prize for Physiology or Medicine for his work on bacterial genetics. With Tatum, he showed that the offspring of different mutants of *Escherichia coli* had genes recombined from those of the original generation, thus establishing the sexuality of *E. coli*. Later he showed that genetic information could be carried betwen *Salmonella* by certain bacterial viruses. (See also BACTERIA; GENETICS; VIRUS.)

LEDUC, Violette (1907–   ), French writer, best known for the autobiographical *La Bâtarde* (1964).

LEE, Bruce (1940–1973), US film actor and martial arts expert who starred in a series of low-budget, Hong Kong-made kung fu movies and became an international cult hero. His films included *Fist of Fury* (1972) and *Enter the Dragon* (1973).

LEE, Charles (1731–1782), American major general in the Revolutionary War. He refused orders from George Washington (1776), planned betrayal while in British captivity (1776–78), and retreated at the battle of MONMOUTH (1778), robbing Washington of a victory. He was court-martialed, deprived of his command and later dismissed.

LEE, Gypsy Rose (Rose Louise Hovick; 1914–1970), US entertainer who was the most famous striptease artist in the US. After her retirement (1937) she wrote two bestselling mystery novels and an autobiography, *Gypsy* (1957), which became the basis of a musical play and a film.

LEE, Henry ("Light Horse Harry"; 1756–1818), dashing American cavalry officer in the Revolutionary War, highly praised by George Washington. He was governor of Va. 1791–94 and a representative in Congress 1799–1801. Civil War general Robert E. LEE was his son.

LEE, Richard Henry (1732–1794), American Revolutionary statesman from Va., member of the CONTINENTAL CONGRESS 1774–79, 1784–87, president 1784–85. On June 7, 1776, he introduced the motion that led to the DECLARATION OF INDEPENDENCE. He opposed ratification of the US Constitution, fearing its effects on states' rights. As a US senator from Va., 1789–92, he helped secure adoption of the BILL OF RIGHTS.

LEE, Robert E. (Edward) (1807–1870), American general who commanded the Confederate armies in the American Civil War. Son of Henry LEE, he was born at Stratford, Va., graduated from WEST POINT (1829) and served brilliantly as a field engineer in the MEXICAN WAR 1846–48. He was superintendent of West Point 1852–55, and in 1859 arrested John BROWN at HARPERS FERRY. Lee opposed slavery and secession, but from loyalty to his native Va., declined Lincoln's offer of command of the Union armies in 1861 and reluctantly accepted a Confederate post. He became a full general in May 1861 and a year later gained command of the Army of Northern Virginia. His first great success was the defense of Richmond in the SEVEN DAYS' BATTLE (June 26–July 2, 1862). After the Confederate victory at the second Battle of BULL RUN, Lee invaded Maryland but was halted at ANTIETAM. Victory at CHANCELLORSVILLE encouraged a further offensive into Pa., but he was turned back at the Battle of GETTYSBURG. Lee finally surrendered to Ulysses S. GRANT at APPOMATTOX COURT HOUSE on April 9, 1865. Universally respected for his personal qualities and brilliant generalship, he ended his days as a college president.

LEE, Tsung Dao (1926–   ), Chinese-born US physicst who shared with YANG the 1957 Nobel Prize for Physics for their demonstration that the principle of PARITY had not been shown to be valid in certain interactions of SUBATOMIC PARTICLES. It was soon shown experimentally to be invalid in those interactions, first by c. s. wu.

**LEECHES,** annelid worms, segmented, with a prominent attachment sucker at the posterior end and another sucker around the mouth. Leeches are hermaphroditic. Freshwater or semiterrestrial animals, they feed by sucking the blood or other body fluids of mammals, small invertebrates, worms, insect larvae or snails. The crop is capable of great distention to enable large meals to be taken as occasion permits, for, with many species, meals are available only at intervals, and then only by chance. A fully-grown Medicinal leech can survive for a whole year on a single blood meal.

**LEE KUAN YEW** (1923–   ), prime minister of the Republic of Singapore, since its secession from Malaysia in 1965. After training as a lawyer in England, where he was called to the bar, he returned to Singapore and became leader of the People's Action Party (PAP)—since 1968 the only official party.

**LEEUWENHOEK, Anton van** (1632–1723). Dutch microscopist who made important observations of CAPILLARIES, red BLOOD corpuscles and SPERM cells, and who is best known for being the first to observe BACTERIA and PROTOZOA (1674–6), which he called "very little animalcules." (See also MICROSCOPE.)

**LEEWARD ISLANDS,** chain of about 15 islands and many islets in the West Indies, northernmost group of the Lesser Antilles. They include Antigua, St. Kitts-Nevis, and Anguilla; Montserrat and the British Virgin Islands (British colonies); St. Eustatius, Saba and S St. Martin (Dutch); Guadeloupe and dependencies (French); and the Virgin Islands of the US.

**LEFT-HANDEDNESS.** See HANDEDNESS.

**LE GALLIENNE, Eva** (1899–   ), British-born US actress and director, who translated and directed works by Ibsen and Chekhov and became known for her performances in them. She founded and ran the Civic Repertory Theater (1926–32). In 1981 she appeared on Broadway in *To Grandmother's House We Go*.

**LEGAL PROFESSION,** body of people concerned with the interpretation and application of the law. The first law school in the US was started at Harvard U. in 1817. Students wishing to qualify as attorneys must usually complete at least two years of college, graduate from law school and pass a state bar examination. Since requirements vary from state to state, a lawyer may usually practice only in the state in which he qualified. There are different types of legal careers. Lawyers may enter private practice, where they will advise individuals or firms on matters ranging from criminal defense to divorce, income tax, wills, contracts, trusts, mortgages and claims for injury. Then there are law firms that specialize in corporation law, and advise clients on such matters as labor laws, antitrust laws, tax laws and corporate organization and finance. Large corporations often possess their own legal department. State and federal governments employ lawyers as city attorneys, judges, prosecutors and in LEGAL AID organizations. Most lawyers belong to a professional legal association, the largest of which is the AMERICAN BAR ASSOCIATION. Many states have their own bar association. The other main branch of the legal profession is the bench. A JUDGE is a member of the bench just as a lawyer is a member of the bar. Judges serve at all levels from district and municipal courts to the Supreme Court. Federal judges are appointed by the president with the Senate's advice and consent and may only be removed by impeachment. State judges are elected and serve for a given number of years. The legal profession in England differs chiefly in retaining the official separation of barrister and solicitor. (See also JUDICIARY.)

**LEGENDRE, Adrien Marie** (1752–1833) French mathematician best known for his work on elliptic integrals; for first publishing the method of LEAST SQUARES (1806); and for deriving the Legendre functions, which find many applications in physics.

**LEGER, Fernand** (1881–1955), French painter. A Cubist, he used strong colors and geometrical shapes and introduced such objects as cogwheels and pistons. His preoccupation with the machine age may be seen in such paintings as *The City* (1919) He designed huge murals for the UN in New York. (See also CUBISM.)

**LEGIONNAIRE'S DISEASE,** a mysterious pneumonia-like illness that broke out among people who attended an American Legion convention in July 1976 at Philadelphia's Bellevue Stratford Hotel. The disease got national attention as the number of deaths mounted, eventually reaching 29, and as doctors searched frantically for its cause and cure. Not until Jan. 18, 1977, was Dr. Joseph E. McDade, scientist at the government's Center for Disease Control in Atlanta, Ga., able to report that he had traced the illness to bacterium that, though probably widely spread and the cause of other, earlier outbreaks of fatal pneumonia, had not previously been identified. The most effective treatment was found later to be erythromycin, an antibiotic.

**LEGION OF HONOR,** a French order created by Napoleon Bonaparte in 1802 to reward distinguished service in military or civil life.

**LEGUMINOUS PLANTS,** general name for plants of the PEA family (Leguminosae) the fruit of which are called LEGUMES (pods). In terms of number of species, this family is second in size only to the COMPOSITAE. There are many economically important species including ACACIA, ALFALFA, BEAN, LENTIL, PEA and SOYBEAN. The roots of leguminous plants produce nodules containing nitrogen-fixing bacteria.

**LEHÁR, Franz** (1870–1948), Hungarian composer famous for Viennese-style light opera. His most successful work was the melodious operetta *The Merry Widow* (1905).

**LEHMAN, Herbert Henry** (1878–1963), American statesman. As Democratic governor of New York (1932–42) he supported widespread social legislation. Later he was director (1943–46) of the United Nations Relief and Rehabilitation Administration, and a leading liberal senator (1949–56) and opponent of Joseph MCCARTHY.

**LEHMANN, Lotte** (1888–1976), German-US soprano. She sang with the Vienna State Opera (1914–38) and in the US at the Metropolitan (1934–45). Famous for her Marschallin in DER ROSENKAVALIER, she created roles in other Richard STRAUSS operas and was a skilled interpreter of lieder.

**LEHMBRUCK, Wilhelm** (1881–1919), German sculptor noted for his images of pathos and heroism of spirit. Influenced by Gothic sculpture and the modern works of PICASSO and MODIGLIANI, he depicted his human subjects as ascetic, angular figures.

**LEIBNIZ, Gottfried Wilhelm von** (1646–1716), German philosopher, historian, jurist, geologist and mathematician, codiscoverer of the CALCULUS and author of the theory of monads. His discovery of the calculus was independent of though later than that of NEWTON, yet it is the Leibnizian form which predominates today. He devised a calculating machine and a symbolic mathematical logic. His concept of the universe as a "pre-established harmony," his analysis of the problem of evil, his epistemology, logic, and philosophy of nature place him in the foremost rank of philosophers and helped mold the mind of the ENLIGHTENMENT.

**LEICESTER, Robert Dudley, Earl of** (c1532–1588), favorite and one-time suitor of Elizabeth I of England. Although his political and military performances were poor and his reputation was marred by suspicions of treason, wife-murder and bigamy, he wielded great power and was made a privy councillor and army commander.

**LEINSDORF, Erich** (1912– ), Austrian conductor who began his career as assistant to Bruno Walter and Arturo Toscanini at the Salzburg festival in 1934. By 1940 he had become a principal conductor at New York's Metropolitan Opera and was its director 1957–62. He directed the Boston Symphony Orchestra 1962–69.

**LELONG, Lucien** (1889–1958), French fashion designer whose elegant, understated designs had an enthusiastic following among the wealthy. Christian DIOR was among his students.

**LELY, Sir Peter** (1618–1680), Dutch-English portrait painter, born Pieter van der Faes. He moved to England about 1641 and became court painter to Charles I and Charles II. His works include portrait series of court beauties and English admirals.

**LEM, Stanisław** (1921– ), Polish doctor and the most widely respected contemporary science-fiction writer. Among his many works are *Solaris* (1961) and *The Invincible* (1964).

**LEMAITRE, Georges Édouard** (1894–1966), Belgian physicist who first proposed the "big bang" model of the universe, explaining the RED SHIFTS of the galaxies as due to recession (SEE DOPPLER EFFECT), thereby inferring that the universe is expanding. The theory holds that the origins of the universe lie in the explosion of a primeval atom, the "cosmic egg." (See also COSMOLOGY.)

**LEMMINGS,** small rodents, 75–150mm (3–6in) long, closely related to voles. They are the characteristic rodents of the arctic tundra and are well adapted to severe conditions. Like many small mammals of simple ecological systems lemmings show periodic fluctuations in numbers with a periodicity of 3–4 years. These result in spectacular mass migrations whereby surplus animals in a high population area emigrate to find new ranges.

**LEMMON, Jack** (1925– ), US film actor. Best known for light comedy roles in such films as *Mister Roberts* (1955) and *Some Like It Hot* (1959), he was also acclaimed as a dramatic actor in *Days of Wine and Roses* (1962), *The China Syndrome* (1978), and *Save The Tiger* (1973), for which he received an Academy

Award.

**LEMURS,** cat-sized primates found on Madagascar and small islands nearby, related to primitive ancestors of the whole primate group of monkeys and apes. They are nocturnal and strictly arboreal, feeding on insects, fruit, even small mammals. The family Lemuridae includes two subfamilies: the Cheirogaleinae or Mouse lemurs, and the Lemurinae, true lemurs.

**LEND-LEASE,** program by which the US sent aid to the Allies in WWII, during and after neutrality. President Roosevelt initiated the program in 1941 to help countries "resisting aggression." Total aid exceeded 50 billion dollars and not only bolstered Allied defense but developed the US war industries and helped mobilize public opinion.

**L'ENFANT, Pierre Charles** (1754–1825), French-American engineer and architect who fought in the Revolutionary War and was commissioned (1791) to plan Washington, DC. Because of opposition his plans were shelved and L'Enfant was long dead when they were revived (1901) the basis for the development of the city. L'Enfant also designed Federal Hall in New York City.

**LENIN, Vladimir Ilyich** (1870–1924), Russian revolutionary, founder of the Bolshevik (later Communist) Party, leader of the Bolshevik Revolution of 1917 and founder of the Soviet state. Born Vladimir Ilyich Ulyanov, Lenin became a revolutionary after his elder brother was executed (1887) for participating in a plot to assassinate the tsar. By then a follower of Karl MARX, Lenin was exiled to Siberia (1887–90) for his activities and on his release he went to W Europe. In 1902 he published his famous pamphlet *What is to be Done?* arguing that only professional revolutionaries trained to lead a proletarian-peasant rising could bring Marxist socialism to Russia. Subsequent factional disputes between proponents of Lenin's BOLSHEVISM and the less radical MENSHEVIKS were interrupted only by the abortive Russian revolution of 1905, when

Lenin and his fellow Marxists returned briefly to Russia. Lenin's confidence in the imminence of revolution was profoundly shaken by the rush of the socialist parties of Europe to support their own governments at the outbreak of WWI, and news of the 1917 RUSSIAN REVOLUTION, when it came, was sudden and unexpected. Lenin returned at once to Russia with German aid and within six months the Bolsheviks controlled the state. Against overwhelming odds, and at the massive cost of the German-Russian treaty of BREST-LITOVSK, Lenin maintained and consolidated power. The history of his remaining years is that of the birth of Soviet RUSSIA herself.

Lenin influenced COMMUNISM more than anyone else except Karl Marx. He adapted Marxist theory to the realities of Russia's backward economy but displayed his continuing hope of world-wide socialist revolution by founding the COMINTERN. Before his death from a series of strokes he warned against STALIN's growing ambition for power.

**LENINGRAD,** second largest city and chief port of the USSR, on the Gulf of Finland, capital of Leningrad oblast and former Russian capital (as St. Petersburg 1712–1914, Petrograd 1914–24). Founded (1703) by Peter the Great and linked by its port with W Europe, it rapidly became a cultural and commercial center. Industrial expansion during the 19th century was followed by a temporary decline during WWI and the RUSSIAN REVOLUTION. The city was renamed for Lenin in 1924. There was great destruction and loss of life in the German siege (1941–44) during WWII, since when Leningrad has been restored and enlarged. Today industries include heavy machinery manufacturing, shipbuilding, chemicals and textiles. The city has a university, outstanding libraries and art galleries, museums and palaces. Pop 4,638,000.

**LE NOTRE, André** (1613–1700), French landscape architect who dominated European garden design for many years. His strictly geometrical creations, including the gardens of VERSAILLES, featured splendid vistas and radiating paths.

**LENS, Optical,** a piece of transparent material having at least one curved surface and which is used to focus light radiation in CAMERAS, GLASSES, MICROSCOPES, TELESCOPES and other optical instruments. The typical thin lens is formed from a glass disk, though crystalline minerals and moulded plastics are also used and, as with spectacle lenses, shapes other than circular are quite common.

The principal axis of a lens is the perpendicular to its surface at its center. Lenses which are thicker in the middle than at the edges focus a parallel beam of light traveling along the principal axis at the principal focus, a point on the axis on the far side of the lens from the light source. Such lenses are converging lenses. The distance between the principal focus and the center of the lens is known as the focal length of the lens; its focal power is the reciprocal of its focal length and is expressed in diopters $(m^{-1})$.

A lens thicker at its edges than in the middle spreads out a parallel beam of light passing through along its principal axis as if it were radiating from a virtual focus one focal length out from the lens center on the same side as the source. Such a lens is a diverging lens.

Lens surfaces may be either inward curving (concave), outward bulging (convex) or flat (plane) and it is the combination of the properties of the two surfaces which determines the focal power of the lens. In general, IMAGES of objects produced using single thin lenses suffer from various defects including spherical and chromatic aberration (see ABERRATION, OPTICAL), coma (in which peripheral images of points are distorted into pear-shaped spots) and astigmatism. The effects of these are minimized by designing compound lenses in which simple lenses of different shapes and refractive indexes (see REFRACTION) are combined. ACHROMATIC LENSES reduce chromatic aberration; aplanatic lenses reduce this and coma, and anastigmatic lenses combat astigmatism. (See also CONTACT LENS; LIGHT.)

**LENYA, Lotte** (1900–1981), Austrian-born US singer and actress. She performed on the stage in Berlin 1920–33, notably in *The Three-Penny Opera* (1928), composed by her husband, Kurt WEILL, in collaboration with BRECHT. In the US after 1933 she sang and acted in productions of several Weill works, including a 1954 revival of *The Three-Penny Opera*. She also appeared in motion pictures.

**LEO** (the Lion), a constellation on the ECLIPTIC and fifth sign of the ZODIAC. It contains the bright star REGULUS (apparent magnitude $+1.35$). Leo gives its name to the annual Leonid METEOR shower.

**LEON, Juan Ponce de.** See PONCE DE LEÓN, JUAN.

**LEONARD, "Sugar Ray"** (1956–   ), US boxing champion. He won the light welterweight Olympic gold medal in 1976. In 1980 he won the WBC welterweight title, defending it successfully in bouts against Roberto Duran (1980) and Thomas Hearns (1981).

**LEONARDO DA VINCI** (1452–1519), Italian RENAISSANCE painter, sculptor, architect, engineer and naturalist celebrated as history's outstanding "Renaissance Man." Born in Vinci, Tuscany, the illegitimate son of a notary, he studied painting with VERROCCHIO in Florence. He worked at Ludovico SFORZA's court in Milan as an architect, military engineer, inventor, theatrical designer, sculptor, musician, scientist, art theorist and painter. His fresco, *The Last Supper* (c1495), in Milan, is noted for its innovative composition and variety of gesture. He thought that painting should express the laws of light and space and of sciences like anatomy, botany and geology, and this he attempted in *Virgin of the Rocks* (c1506). He made thousands of sketches and notes in connection with his investigations into the laws of nature; his growing sense of awe of the world is reflected in the painting *Mona Lisa* (c1514), now in the Louvre, Paris. In Rome, 1513–16, he was preoccupied by the dynamic movement to be found in nature. He spent his last years at the French court of FRANCIS I, venerated as a genius.

**LEONARDO OF PISA.** See FIBONACCI, LEONARDO.

**LEONCAVALLO, Ruggiero** (1858–1919), Italian opera composer. He wrote many operas, of which only the melodramatic *I Pagliacci* (The Clowns, 1892) is now widely known.

**LEONTIEF, Wassily** (1906–   ), Russian-born US economist, who developed the techniques of INPUT-OUTPUT ANALYSIS. He came to New York in 1931 and subsequently worked at Harvard U. and New York U. In 1973 he won the Nobel Memorial Prize in Economics.

**LEOPARD**, *Panthera pardus*, a big cat similar to the JAGUAR, with a yellow coat marked with black rosettes. Found in a variety of habitats across Africa and Asia, they are agile cats which rely when hunting on their power to spring quickly. The leopard is well known for its habit of dragging its kill up into a tree out of the reach of jackals and hyenas. The kill may weigh more than the leopard itself.

**LEOPARDI, Giacomo, Count** (1798–1837), Italian poet and philosopher, one of the foremost writers of his time. Acutely unhappy almost all his life, he expressed himself most fully in his brilliant, supple, lyric poetry of which the major volume is *Songs* (1836). *Moral Essays* (1827) reveals his bleak philosophy.

**LEOPOLD**, name of three kings of

Belgium. **Leopold I** (1790–1865), a Saxe-Coburg, was elected king by the Belgians in June 1831. He did much to create national unity and carried out some reforms. He was the uncle of England's Queen Victoria. **Leopold II** (1835–1909), his son, reigned from 1865. He promoted exploration in Africa and in 1885 established the Congo Free State (see ZAÏRE), which he exploited for personal gain until it was taken over by the Belgian government in 1908. There was great commercial and industrial growth in Belgium during his reign. **Leopold III** (1901–    ), reigned 1934–51. He lost popularity by ordering surrender to the Nazis in 1940, and was compelled to abdicate in favor of his son BAUDOUIN I.

**LEPANTO, Battle of,** Christian naval victory over the Muslim Turks, Oct. 7, 1571. JOHN OF AUSTRIA led combined Spanish, Venetian and papal fleets which crushed the Turkish fleet in the Gulf of Patras near Lepanto, Greece. The battle somewhat moderated the power of the OTTOMAN EMPIRE.

**LEPIDOPTERA,** the insect order that includes the BUTTERFLIES and MOTHS. Their bodies and wings are covered with minute scales of chitin often pigmented to produce the colors and patterns characteristic of these insects. The mouthparts of the adults are formed into a *proboscis*, a tube for sucking up liquid such as the NECTAR from flowers. The life history includes the egg, a LARVA or CATERPILLAR, a PUPA or CHRYSALIS and the usually winged adult. The caterpillar is totally different in structure and habit from the adult, feeding with chewing mouthparts on a variety of vegetable materials, completely separated ecologically from the adult. Caterpillars feed voraciously and those of many species are agricultural pests. In the chrysalis, a resting stage, the structure of the adult insect is organized (see METAMORPHOSIS).

**LEPROSY,** or **Hansen's disease,** chronic disease caused by a mycobacterium and virtually restricted to tropical zones. It leads to SKIN nodules with loss of pigmentation, mucous membrane lesions in NOSE and PHARYNX, and NEURITIS with nerve thickening, loss of pain sensation and patchy weakness, often involving FACE and intrinsic HAND muscles. Diagnosis is by demonstrating the organisms in stained scrapings or by skin or nerve BIOPSY. The type of disease caused depends on the number of bacteria encountered and basic resistance to the disease. Treatment is with sulfones (Dapsone).

**LERMONTOV, Mikhail Yurevich** (1814–

1841), Russian poet and novelist. Initially influenced by BYRON, he wrote outstandingly fine lyric and narrative poetry. His prose masterpiece is the novel *A Hero of our Time* (1840), an early example of psychological realism. He died in a duel.

**LERNER, Alan Jay** (1918–    ), US musical comedy lyricist. With Frederick LOEWE he created such famous musicals as *Brigadoon* (1947), *Paint Your Wagon* (1951), *My Fair Lady* (1956) and *Camelot* (1960).

**LE SAGE, Alain René** (1668–1747), French novelist and dramatist. His picaresque masterpiece *Gil Blas* (1715–35) greatly influenced the development of the realistic novel in France. It is a witty satirical account of all levels of French society.

**Official name:** Kingdom of Lesotho
**Capital:** Maseru
**Area:** 11,720sq mi
**Population:** 1,390,000
**Languages:** Sesotho, English
**Religions:** Christian, Animist
**Monetary unit(s):** 1 Loti = 100 cents

**LESOTHO** (formerly Basutoland), landlocked kingdom surrounded by, and economically dependent on, the white-ruled Republic of South Africa.

**Land.** Part of the great plateau of S Africa, Lesotho lies mainly between 8,000ft and 11,000ft. In the E and N is the Drakensberg mountain range. The chief rivers are the Orange R and its tributaries. Annual rainfall averages under 30in and temperatures vary seasonally from 93°F to 30°F. Sparsely forested, Lesotho is mainly dry grassland.

**People and Economy.** The Basuto, who comprise all but 1% of the population, are chiefly rural. Education is mainly in the hands of missionaries; there is a literacy rate of about 50% and about 70% of the people are Christian. An agricultural country, Lesotho is heavily dependent on livestock and food crops such as wheat and maize. Poor farming techniques have resulted in a shortage of good land. Although Lesotho is opposed to apartheid, it depends heavily upon South Africa for trade and employment.

**History.** The nation was established c1829 by Chief Moshoeshoe I, who secured British protection from Boer encroachment. As Basutoland, it was under British rule from 1884, gaining independence in 1966. Chief Lebua Jonathan has been prime minister since independence.

**LESSEPS, Ferdinand Marie, Vicomte de** (1805–1894), French diplomat whose idea for a canal to cross the isthmus of Suez resulted in the SUEZ CANAL. Lesseps supervised the building of it (1859–69) himself. His later plans for a Panama canal failed.

**LESSING, Doris** (1919– ), British novelist, and short story writer, raised in Southern Rhodesia, who has dealt perceptively with the struggles of intellectual women for political, sexual, and artistic integrity. Her major works include *The Golden Notebook* (1962), *The Four-Gated City* (1969) (part of *The Children of Violence* series) and *Shikasta* (1979).

**LESSING, Gotthold Ephraim** (1729–1781), German playwright, critic and philosopher, founder of a new national literature. He rejected French classicism and pioneered German bourgeois tragedy with *Miss Sara Sampson* (1755). He also wrote the influential comedy *Minna von Barnhelm* (1767), the prose tragedy *Emilia Galotti* (1772) and the dramatic poem *Nathan the Wise* (1779). The treatise *Laokoön* (1766) critically contrasted the natures of poetry and painting.

**LETTISH,** or Latvian, language spoken by some 2,000,000 people, chiefly in LATVIA. One of the Baltic groups of Indo-European languages, Lettish preserves many archaic features, and has changed little since books were first printed in it in the 16th century.

**LEUKEMIA,** malignant proliferation of white blood cells in BLOOD or BONE MARROW. It may be divided into acute and chronic forms for both granulocytes and lymphocytes. In acute forms, primitive cells predominate and progression is rapid with ANEMIA, bruising and infection. Acute lymphocytic leukemia is commonest in young children. Chronic forms are present in adult life with mild systemic symptoms, susceptibility to infection and enlarged LYMPH nodes (lymphatic) or SPLEEN and LIVER (granulocytic). Cancer CHEMOTHERAPY and ANTIBIOTICS have greatly improved survival prospects.

**LEUTZE, Emanuel** (1816–1868), US historical painter. His large-scale, patriotic works include *Westward the Course of Empire Takes its Way* and *Washington Crossing the Delaware*.

**LEVANT,** the E Mediterranean countries, from Turkey to Egypt (inclusive), so named from the French *lever* (to rise), Levant implying lands of the sunrise, that is, of the east.

**LEVELLERS,** radical reformers of the English Civil War and Commonwealth period. Their leader, John LILBURNE, advocated a republic, economic reforms and political and religious equality. Oliver Cromwell, to whom they were bitterly opposed, broke their power.

**LEVER,** the simplest MACHINE, a rigid beam pivoted at a *fulcrum* so that an *effort* acting at one point of the beam may be used to shift a *load* acting at another point on the beam. There are three classes of lever: those with the fulcrum between the effort and the load; those with the load between the fulcrum and the effort, and those with the effort between the fulcrum and the load. The part of the beam between the load and the fulcrum is the load arm; that between the effort and the fulcrum, the effort arm. The effort multiplied by the length of the effort arm equals the load multiplied by the length of the load arm: a load of 50kg, 5m from the fulcrum, may be moved by any effort 10m from the fulcrum greater than 25kg (the longer the effort arm, the less effort required). Load divided by effort gives the mechanical advantage; in this case 2. A first-class lever (e.g., a crowbar) has a mechanical advantage greater, less than or equal to 1; a second-class (e.g., a wheelbarrow), always more than 1; a third-class (e.g., the human arm), always less than 1. (See also ARCHIMEDES; MECHANICS.)

**LEVIATHAN,** in the Bible, the name of a primordial monster, or, as in the Book of Job, a sea monster, perhaps a whale. The name is commonly used for anything massive, particularly ships. It was used by HOBBES as an allegorical title for the state.

**LEVIN, Ira** (1929– ), US novelist and playwright. His occult, mystery and espionage thrillers include such best-selling novels as *Rosemary's Baby* (1969) and *The Boys From Brazil* (1976) and the plays *Veronica's Room* (1973) and *Deathtrap* (1978).

**LEVINE, David** (1926– ), US caricaturist whose blend of outrageous exaggeration and careful draughtsmanship in a series of portraits published in the *New York Review of Books* in the 1960s and 1970s made him preeminent in his field.

**LEVINE, Jack** (1915– ), US satirical painter. Believing that art must have some social significance, he rejects abstract art in favor of a satirically distorted realism, seen in such works as *Feast of Pure Reason* (1937), *Welcome Home* (1946) and *Gangster Funeral* (1953).

**LEVINE, James** (1943–  ), US pianist, conductor and opera executive. In 1964–70 he was an apprentice conductor of the Cleveland Symphony Orchestra under George Szell and then assistant conductor. In 1972 he became principal conductor at the Metropolitan Opera, where he was appointed music director in 1975.

**LEVI-STRAUSS, Claude** (1908–  ), Belgian–born French social anthropologist, best known for his advocacy of *structuralism*, an analytical method whereby different cultural patterns are related so that the universal logical substructure underlying them may be elicited. His writings include *Structural Anthropology* (1958) and *The Savage Mind* (1962).

**LEVITICUS**, in the Old Testament, third of the five books of the PENTATEUCH. It is essentially a collection of liturgical and ceremonial laws.

**LEWIN, Kurt** (1890–1947), German-born US psychologist, an early member of the GESTALT PSYCHOLOGY school, best known for his development of field theory and especially the concept of group dynamics.

**LEWIS, Cecil Day** (1904–1972), English poet and critic, POET LAUREATE from 1968. *The Magnetic Mountain* (1933) is his best known work from the 1930s, but his style matured fully after 1945. He wrote novels under his own name and detective novels as "Nicholas Blake."

**LEWIS, C.S.** (Clive Staples Lewis; 1898–1963), British author, literary scholar and Christian apologist. Of more than 40 books his best-known is *The Screwtape Letters* (1942), a diabolical view of humanity. *The Allegory of Love* (1936), his major critical work, was a study of love in medieval literature. He also wrote a well-known science-fiction trilogy and the *Narnia* fantasies for children.

**LEWIS, Gilbert Newton** (1875–1946), US chemist who suggested that covalent bonding consisted of the sharing of valence-electron pairs. His theory of ACIDS and bases involved seeing acids (Lewis acids) as substances which are able to accept electron pairs from bases which are electron-pair donating species (Lewis bases). In 1933, Lewis became the first to prepare HEAVY WATER ($D_2O$).

**LEWIS, Jerry** (1926–  ), US comedian who teamed with singer Dean Martin, 1946, to form the popular Martin and Lewis comedy duo. After making 16 films, the team broke up (1956) and Lewis went on to

direct and star in a series of slapstick comedies, including *The Bellboy* (1960) and *The Nutty Professor* (1963).

**LEWIS, John Llewellyn** (1880–1969), colorful American labor leader, president of the United Mine Workers of America 1920–60. He organized the Congress of Industrial Organizations in 1935 as a rival to the AMERICAN FEDERATION OF LABOR, beginning a bitter rivalry; he resigned as president of CIO in 1940.

**LEWIS, Meriwether** (1774–1809), American explorer and commander of the LEWIS AND CLARK EXPEDITION, which penetrated to the NW Pacific coast 1804–06. In 1808 he became governor of the Louisiana Territory, but was badly affected by the pressures of the post. En route for Washington, he was found dead at a lonely inn in Tenn., either by murder or suicide.

**LEWIS, Oscar** (1914–1970), US anthropologist. He presented the controversial thesis of the "culture of poverty" in notable biographical accounts of impoverished Latin Americans such as *Five Families* (1959), *The Children of Sanchez* (1961) and *La Vida* (1966).

**LEWIS, Sinclair** (1885–1951), US novelist, best known for five novels satirizing small-town life in the Middle West, an environment in which he himself grew up and only escaped from at college. *Main Street* (1920) was his first major success. *Babbitt* (1922), a satire on the provincial small businessman, is perhaps his best-known book. He refused a Pulitzer Prize for *Arrowsmith* (1925); it was followed by *Elmer Gantry* (1927) and *Dodsworth* (1929). In 1930 he became the first American to win the Nobel Prize for Literature, but his work declined thereafter.

**LEWIS, Wyndham** (1882–1957), controversial English painter, critic and writer, the founder of VORTICISM. He is best known for his savage satirical novel *The Apes of God* (1930).

**LEWIS AND CLARK EXPEDITION,** first overland American expedition to the NW Pacific coast under the command of Meriwether LEWIS and William CLARK, with Sacagawea, the Indian wife of an expedition member, acting as interpreter and guide. Setting out from St. Louis in May, 1804, the expedition pushed westwards through the Rockies, reaching the Pacific Ocean at the mouth of the Columbia R in Nov., 1805. They returned to St. Louis in Sept., 1806.

The expedition was dispatched by President Jefferson to explore the newly-purchased Louisiana Territory which expanded America's borders to the

Continental Divide. It caught the popular imagination and played a major part in establishing the view that it was the "Manifest Destiny" of the US to expand to the Pacific Ocean.

LEXINGTON, Battle of, first engagement of the American REVOLUTIONARY WAR on April 19, 1775. A force of around 700 British troops marching to destroy illegal military stores at Concord, Mass., were met at Lexington by 70 MINUTEMEN. These obeyed an order to disperse, but one fired a shot which was returned by a volley, killing eight Americans and wounding ten. The British marched on unopposed, but were turned back at the battle of CONCORD.

LEYDEN JAR, the simplest and earliest form of CAPACITOR, a device for storing electric charge. It comprises a glass jar coated inside and outside with unconnected metal foils, and a conducting rod which passes through the jar's insulated stopper to connect with the inner foil. The jar is usually charged from an electrostatic generator. The device is now little used outside the classroom.

LEYTE GULF, Battle of, a major air-sea battle off Leyte Island in the Philippines on Oct. 25–26, 1944, in which the Japanese were decisively defeated in an attempt to decoy the US 3rd Fleet N and attack the landing on Leyte it was protecting.

LHASA, also Lasa, former capital of Tibet, now capital of the Tibetan Autonomous Region of China. Western visitors were discouraged before the 20th century, and Lhasa became known as the "Forbidden City." Centered around a massive Buddhist temple, it is dominated by the Potala, former citadel of the DALAI LAMA, on a 400ft hillside above the city. It was a trading center before it was occupied by the Communist Chinese in 1951. Most of the former inhabitants have been resettled and the population is now substantially Chinese. Some light industry has also been developed. Pop 175,000.

LHEVINNE, Josef (1874–1944), Russian-born US pianist noted for his brilliant performances of the music of CHOPIN and CHAIKOVSKY. He and his wife, Rosina (1880–1976), also a concert pianist, emigrated in 1919 to the US, where both joined the faculty of the Juilliard School of Music in New York. Rosina Lhevinne became one of the century's most celebrated teachers of piano.

LIBBY, Willard Frank (1908–1980), US chemist awarded the 1960 Nobel Prize for chemistry for discovering the technique of radiocarbon dating (1947), the first method of RADIOISOTOPE DATING.

LIBBY PRISON, notorious Confederate prison for Union officers in Richmond, Va., 1863–64. A converted warehouse, it lacked heat, ventilation and sufficient sanitation. Up to 1,200 prisoners were confined there, and when food supplies became inadequate many died in the bad conditions.

LIBEL, a false and malicious statement in writing or other durable form (such as on film), tending to injure the reputation of a living person, or blacken the memory of the dead. In US law the truth of the statement creates a valid defense in an action for libel. The 1st Amendment to the US Constitution shields the press against certain libel suits unless malice or reckless disregard for truth is proved.

LIBERACE (1919–    ), US pianist and popular entertainer. Dressed in sequined suits, he played popular and semiclassical melodies on his candelabra-lit piano in nightclubs and on television.

LIBERAL ARTS, term now applied to college curriculums covering such subjects as languages, philosophy, history, literature and pure science, when these are studied as the basis of a general or liberal education, and not as professional or vocational skills. (See also SEVEN LIBERAL ARTS.)

LIBERALISM, a political philosophy that stresses individual liberty, freedom and equality of opportunity. Liberalism tends to place its faith in progress. Classical liberalism developed in Europe in the 18th century, characterized by a rational critique of traditional institutions and a distrust of state power over individuals and interference in the economy (see LAISSEZ-FAIRE). Modern liberalism accepts state interference in the economy, but is still very concerned with social issues such as civil rights and equality of opportunity. In the US, a degree of liberalism has been the dominant creed of both major political parties.

LIBERAL PARTY, British, a political party, powerful from about 1832 to 1922. With its origins in the traditional Whig Party, the Liberal Party was associated with such policies as free trade, LAISSEZ-FAIRE economics, religious liberty and anti-imperialism. Under great leaders like GLADSTONE, ASQUITH and LLOYD GEORGE, the Liberal Party enjoyed a golden age, but it was unable to adjust to the rise of socialism, and was replaced in the 1920s by the Labour Party as the chief opposition to the Conservative Party. In 1981 the party combined forces with the new Social Democratic Party to offer an alternative to the Labour and Conservative parties.

LIBERAL REPUBLICAN PARTY, a

party formed during the administration of President U. S. GRANT, seeking reconciliation with the South and action against corruption in government and public service. In 1872 the Liberal Republicans nominated Horace GREELEY for president, but when he was soundly defeated the party effectively broke up.

**Official name:** Republic of Liberia
**Capital:** Monrovia
**Area:** 43,700sq mi
**Population:** 1,715,973
**Languages:** English; tribal
**Religions:** Protestant, Roman Catholic; Muslim; Animist
**Monetary unit(s):** 1 Liberian dollar = 100 cents

**LIBERIA**, oldest black republic in Africa. It is on the W coast of Africa, bordered by Sierra Leone, Guinea and the Ivory Coast. Its land area is only slightly larger than that of Ohio. Beyond a narrow coastal plain it consists of tropical rain forests, with mountainous plateaus in the interior. The climate is hot and humid, with an average temperature of 80°F, and up to 150in of rain a year.

**People.** Liberia was settled in the early 19th century as a haven for freed American slaves, whose descendants dominated the country's economy and politics until recently. Called Americo-Liberians, they are Christian, English-speaking and generally live in coastal urban areas. Literacy is high among this group, many of whom are professionals. Indigenous Africans, 90% of the population, generally speak tribal languages and live in rural areas, engaging in subsistence farming. There are 16 principal tribes. Most practice traditional African religions, although about 15% adhere to Islam and 10% to Christianity; most are illiterate.

**Economy.** The Liberian economy is still underdeveloped. Its main industries are rubber plantations, established in the 1920s, and the mining of iron ore, dating from the 1950s. Both of these have been run and maintained by US firms. Apart from iron ore and rubber, Liberia exports several crops including coffee, sugarcane, bananas and cocoa. Valuable foreign exchange is also earned by registering foreign ships under extremely lax rules; this practice has made the Liberian merchant navy appear to be one of the world's largest.

**History.** The first repatriated slaves arrived from the US in 1822 under the aegis of the American Colonization Society. The settlement was named Monrovia in honor of US President James Monroe. In 1847 the settlers declared their independence. Liberia gradually extended its territory by signing treaties with local chiefs, or by buying or claiming land. Inequities in wealth and political power have caused antagonisms between Americo-Liberians and indigenous Africans over the years. William V. S. Tubman was president from 1944 until his death in 1971. His successor, William R. Tolbert, Jr., was assassinated in 1980 by soldiers of indigenous origin who assumed control of the government.

**LIBERTARIAN PARTY,** US political party which stresses individual rights. It favors the unfettered right of private property and a laissez-faire, free-market economy. Libertarians regard the state as the greatest threat to liberty and oppose government snooping in private lives and the use of taxes for war preparations. Founded in 1971, the party grew rapidly. In 1980 its presidential candidate, Ed Clark, was on the ballot in every state and polled 921,188 votes, or 1.1% of the total cast.

**LIBERTY, Statue of,** or in full, *Liberty Enlightening the World,* a 300ft bronze female figure on Liberty Island in New York Harbor. The statue, designed by Frédér-BARTHOLDI, was given to the US by France on the 100th anniversary of US independence.

**LIBERTY BELL,** famous American bell housed in Independence Hall, Philadelphia. It was cast in London and arrived in America in 1752. It rang on many historic occasions, including the announcement of the Declaration of Independence on July 8, 1776; having been twice recast, it reputedly cracked while tolling for the funeral of Chief Justice John Marshall in 1835.

**LIBERTY PARTY,** antislavery political party founded in 1839 by J. G. BIRNEY and other abolitionists. In 1840 and 1844 it put up presidential candidates, but in 1848 the party united with other groups to form the FREE SOIL PARTY.

**LIBIDO,** originally and still popularly, the sexuality or general SEX drive of the individual. In PSYCHOANALYSIS, following FREUD, the libido, with its source in the ID, a type of mental energy (though it may, as n sexuality, generate physiological energy r activity) responsible for all human onstructive action.

**IBRA** (the Scales), an average size onstellation on the ECLIPTIC, the seventh ign of the ZODIAC.

**IBRARY.** The earliest libraries were kept y the ancient peoples of Mesopotamia; nscribed clay tablets have been found going ack to about 3500 BC. The most famous ibrary of the ancient world was begun at Alexandria by Ptolemy I Soter (305–283 BC) and destroyed in various fires. The Roman Empire had many libraries, but uring the Dark Ages the Church alone ept the library tradition alive in Europe. The Renaissance saw the formation of many new libraries such as the Vatican Library (1447), and the growth of libraries vas further stimulated by the invention of rinting in the 15th century. The Bodleian Library, Oxford, dates from 1602, but it vas the 18th century that saw the formation f many of the great national libraries: the British Museum Library (1753), Italy's National Central Library at Florence 1741), and Russia's Saltykov-Shchedrin Library in Leningrad.

**The United States.** The oldest library in the US originated in the 320 books bequeathed y John HARVARD (1638), Harvard U.'s hief benefactor. The present LIBRARY OF CONGRESS originated in 1815 in a purchase f JEFFERSON's personal library by Congress. The first tax-supported public library was stablished in New Hampshire in 1833. The American Library Association was founded n 1876. An important figure in library istory is Melvil DEWEY whose decimal lassification system has now been adopted n many countries. In the late 19th century reat industrialists such as Andrew CARNEGIE were often benefactors of braries. In the 20th century the public ibrary system has been extended and onsolidated. There are many types of ibraries, ranging from the great university esearch libraries to school libraries, usiness libraries and area public libraries. See also INFORMATION RETRIEVAL.)

**IBRARY OF CONGRESS,** national brary of the US, located to the E of the Capitol in Washington, D.C. Originally stablished by Congress in 1800, it now ontains more than 58 million items, cluding over 14 million books and amphlets. Since 1870 the library has been ntitled to two free copies of all material opyrighted in the US. The library's atalog, the National Union Catalog, lists ooks in libraries all over the US and Canada.

**Official name:** Socialist People's Libyan Arab Jamahiriya
**Capital:** Tripoli
**Area:** 679,358sq mi
**Population:** 3,245,000
**Languages:** Arabic; Italian used
**Religion:** Muslim
**Monetary unit(s):** 1 Libyan dinar = 1,000 dirhams

**LIBYA,** independent republic in North Africa, a historic state once an important part of the Roman empire. Most of the country is in the Sahara Desert, although there is a fertile strip along the Mediterranean coast where 90% of the population lives, with an average rainfall of 10in and a warm Mediterranean climate.

**People.** The population is predominantly Arab, but there are many Berbers—the original inhabitants—of Hamitic stock, with a strong negroid strain. They live by small-crop, primitive farming along the Mediterranean coast and in the desert to the S. There are also Bedouins and Tuaregs in the Sahara regions. Sunnite Muslims predominate and Islam is the state religion. Only about 30% of the total population live in urban areas, the largest of which is the capital, Tripoli, located on the coast. Although 60% of Libyans still cannot read or write, there have been great educational advances in recent years funded from oil revenues and primary education is free and compulsory.

**Economy.** In 1959 the discovery of vast petroleum reserves in the desert revolutionized the economy. New homes, power stations, roads, irrigation projects, schools and hospitals have been built, and from 1962 to 1975, GNP increased twentyfold. Though the economy now depends on the export of crude oil, which accounts for 99% of export revenue, agriculture employs 50% of the labor force. In the coastal area barley, wheat, millet, oranges, olives, almonds and groundnuts are grown. Dates are plentiful in the desert oases, and nomads raise livestock. Libya consumes much of her agricultural produce, and is a net importer of foodstuffs. Petrochemicals have been added to the traditional textile and leather industries.

**History.** Because of Libya's strategic position on the Mediterranean coast, it has been occupied by many foreign powers throughout its history—the ancient Greeks, Egyptians, Romans, Arabs and Ottoman Turks controlled the country successively. In 1912 Italy annexed Libya, although it was not able to end Libyan armed opposition until 1932. In WWII Libya was an Axis military base and the scene of desert fighting between the Axis powers and the British. In 1951 the UN declared Libya an independent sovereign state under the rule of King Idris I. He was overthrown on Sept. 1, 1969, by a military coup led by Colonel Muammar al-Qaddafi who proclaimed Libya a republic; it is in effect an Islamic military dictatorship. In 1973 he launched a "cultural revolution," running the country along socialist lines, including nationalization of key industries. A prominent follower of pan-Arabism, he had attempted to unite Libya with Egypt (1973), Tunisia (1974), Syria (1980), and intervened militarily in Chad (1980). A fervent opponent of Israel, he is a strong supporter of such groups as the PALESTINIAN LIBERATION ORGANIZATION, and relations with neighboring Egypt have remained tense since that country signed a peace accord with Israel (1978). A member of the ORGANIZATION OF PETROLEUM EXPORTING COUNTRIES, Libya has consistently favored higher prices for crude oil.

**LICE,** wingless parasitic insects of two orders: Mallophaga, Bird lice or Biting lice, and Anoplura, Mammalian or Sucking lice. Dorsoventrally flattened with a broad, clearly-segmented abdomen, lice are well-adapted to moving between hair or feathers, and are usually host-specific. Bird lice feed with chewing mouthparts on feather fragments or dead skin, occasionally biting through the skin for blood. Mammalian lice feed purely on blood obtained with needle-like sucking mouthparts. The human lice are instrumental in the spread of several diseases.

**LICHTENSTEIN, Roy** (1923– ), US painter prominent in the POP ART movement of the early 1960s. He depicted comic strip frames and used commercial art techniques, such as Benday dots, in his work.

**LIDDELL HART, Basil Henry** (1895–1970), English military authority and writer. Among his works is the redrafted *British Infantry Training Manual* (1920). An advocate of tank warfare, he put forward a strategy developed by General GUDERIAN into the Nazi BLITZKRIEG; his far-seeing ideas were not accepted by the British army in his time.

**LIDICE,** Czech village, about 16mi NW of Prague, destroyed by the Gestapo in 1942 as a reprisal for the assassination of Reinhard HEYDRICH, the Nazi governor of Bohemia. A new village has been built near the site which is now a national memorial.

**LIE, Trygve Halvdan** (1896–1968), Norwegian statesman, first secretary-general of the United Nations 1946–53. He believed in the UN as an effective peace agency, and incurred Russian hostility by his support for UN action in Korea. He resigned in 1953 to ease the tension over Korea. Returning to Norway, he served in ministerial and ambassadorial posts, and as governor of Oslo.

**LIEBERSON, Goddard** (1911–1978), British-born US businessman who developed the long-playing record (1948). As president of Columbia Record (1956–66; 1973–75) he recorded original Broadway shows and pioneered the recording of serious 20th-century music.

**LIEBIG, Baron Justus von** (1803–1873), German chemist who with WÖHLER proposed the radical theory of organic structure. This suggested that groups of atoms such as the benzoyl radical ($C_6H_5CO-$), now known as the benzoyl group, remained unchanged in many chemical reactions. He also developed methods for organic quantitative analysis and was one of the first to propose the use of mineral fertilizers for feeding plants. (See also MIRROR.)

**LIEBKNECHT, Karl** (1871–1919), German socialist leader, one of the founders of the German Communist Party. He was mainly known as a campaigner against militarism. With Rosa LUXEMBURG he took part in the SPARTACUS LEAGUE's abortive uprising in 1919, after which he was arrested and shot.

**LIEBLING, A(bbott) J(oseph)** (1904–1963), US journalist. A staff writer for the *New Yorker* for 28 years, he wrote with humor and affection of the New York he loved. He is best remembered for his incisive commentaries on the American press, collected in *The Wayward Pressman* (1947) and *The Press* (1964).

**LIECHTENSTEIN,** tiny European principality in the mountains between Switzerland and Austria. Industry has developed rapidly since WWII. Precision instruments are exported. Because of low taxes and bank secrecy, Liechtenstein is the nominal headquarters of thousands of international corporations. The mild climate and attractive scenery make Vaduz, the capital, a thriving tourist center. Independent since 1719, Liechtenstein was closely linked with

**fficial name**: Principality of Liechtenstein
**apital**: Vaduz
**rea**: 61.8sq mi
**opulation**: 25,800
**anguage**: German
**eligion**: Roman Catholic
**onetary unit(s)**: 1 Swiss franc = 100
**appen**

ustria until 1919; since then it has been
ed to Switzerland.

**IEDER**. See SONG.

**IE DETECTOR**, or **polygraph**, device
hich gives an indication of whether or not
ा individual is lying. Though much used in
iminal investigation, its results are not
dmissible as legal evidence. Its use is based
า the assumption that lying produces
notional, and hence physiological (see
MOTION), reactions in the individual. It
sually measures changes in BLOOD
ressure, PULSE rate and RESPIRATION;
metimes also muscular movements and
RSPIRATION. Success varies with the
dividual.

**IFE**, the property whereby things live.
espite the vast knowledge that has been
ained about life and the forms of life, the
rm still lacks any generally accepted
efinition. Indeed, biologists tend to define
in terms that apply only to their own
ecialisms. Physiologists regard as living
ny system capable of eating, metabolizing,
creting, breathing, moving, growing,
producing and able to respond to external
imuli. Metabolically, life is a property of
ay object which is surrounded by a definite
undary and capable of exchanging
aterials with its surroundings. Bio-
emically, life subsists in cellular systems
ntaining both NUCLEIC ACIDS and
OTEINS. For the geneticist, life belongs to
stems able to perform complex transfor-
ations of organic molecules and to
nstruct from raw materials copies of
emselves which are more or less identical,
though in the long term capable of
OLUTION by natural selection. In terms of
ERMODYNAMICS, it has been said that life
exhibited by localized regions where net
der is increasing (or net ENTROPY

decreasing). But the scientist has no
monopoly over the use of the term, and for
poets, philosophers and artists, it carries
another myriad significations.

**Life on Earth** is manifest in an incredible
variety of forms—over 1 million species of
animals and 350,000 species of plants. Yet,
despite superficial differences, all organisms are closely related. The form and
matter of all life on earth is essentially
identical, and this implies that all living
organisms shared a common ancestor and
that life on earth has originated only once.

**LIFTON, Robert Jay** (1926–    ), US
psychiatrist. His unusual studies applied the
insights of psychiatry and history to the
background of US involvement in Asia. His
works include *Thought Reform and the
Psychology of Totalism* (1961), a study of
Chinese brainwashing during the Korean
War; *Death in Life: Survivors of
Hiroshima* (1968); and *Home From the
War: Vietnam Veterans* (1973).

**LIGHT**, ELECTROMAGNETIC RADIATION to
which the human EYE is sensitive. Light
radiations occupy the small portion of the
electromagnetic SPECTRUM lying between
wavelengths 400nm and 770nm. The eye
recognizes light of different wavelengths as
being of different COLORS, the shorter
wavelengths forming the blue end of the
(visible) spectrum, the longer the red. The
term light is also applied to radiations of
wavelengths just outside the visible
spectrum, those of energies greater than
that of visible light being called ultraviolet
light, those of lower energies, infrared. (See
ULTRAVIOLET   RADIATION;   INFRARED
RADIATION.) White light is a mixture of
radiations from all parts of the visible
spectrum. Bodies which do not themselves
emit light are seen by the light they reflect
or transmit. In passing through a body or on
reflection from its surface, particular
wavelengths may be absorbed from white
light, the body consequently displaying the
colors which remain. Objects which reflect
no visible light at all appear black.

For many years the nature of light
aroused controversy among physicists.
Although HUYGENS had demonstrated that
REFLECTION and REFRACTION could be
explained in terms of waves—a disturbance
in the medium—NEWTON preferred to think
of light as composed of material corpuscles
(particles). YOUNG'S   INTERFERENCE
experiments reestablished the wave hypothesis and FRESNEL gave it a rigorous
mathematical basis. At the beginning of the
20th century, the nature of light was again
debated as PLANCK and EINSTEIN proposed
explanations of blackbody radiation and the

PHOTOELECTRIC EFFECT respectively, which assumed that light comes in discrete quanta of ENERGY (see PHOTON). Today physicists explain optical phenomena in terms either of waves (reflection, REFRACTION, DIFFRACTION, INTERFERENCE) or quanta (blackbody radiation, photoelectric emission) as is required by each case (see QUANTUM MECHANICS).

Light from the sun is the principal source of energy on earth, being absorbed by plants in PHOTOSYNTHESIS. Many other chemical reactions involve light (see CHEMILUMINESCENCE; PHOTOCHEMISTRY; PHOTOGRAPHY) though few artificial light sources are chemical in nature. Most light sources employ radiation emitted from bodies which have become hot or have been otherwise energetically excited (see ENERGY LEVEL; LASER; LUMINESCENCE). Light can be converted into electricity using the PHOTOELECTRIC CELL. Light used for illumination is the subject of the science of photometry. (See also OPTICS.)

**LIGHTHOUSE**, tower with a light at its head, erected on or near the coast, or on a rock in the sea, as a warning to ships. One of the earliest lighthouses was on the PHAROS peninsula at Alexandria, built in the 3rd century BC, and one of the "Seven Wonders of the World." In modern lighthouses, the lantern usually consists of a massive electric light with an elaborate optical system, producing intense beams which sweep the horizon. Radio signals may be transmitted, and foghorns are sometimes used. Where conditions make it difficult to build a lighthouse, an anchored lightship may be used. Most lighthouses are operated by small teams of men who may live isolated in the lighthouse for weeks at a time.

**LIGHTING, Artificial**, the illumination of sectors of man's physical environment in the absence of natural LIGHT. In the course of EVOLUTION, EYES sensitive to the solar radiation penetrating the earth's atmosphere to the surface developed in many of the planet's animals. Man's eyes are thus sensitive to light of these same wavelengths, so artificial light sources must be designed to produce radiations having an intensity SPECTRUM similar to that of natural sunlight.

Oil lamps, brushwood torches and candles formed man's earliest means of artificial lighting, developments leading towards the KEROSENE lamp of the late 19th century (see also ARGAND BURNER). Gas lighting dates from 1792 when the British engineer William Murdock used coal gas to light his Cornish home. The modern portable camping lamp burns BUTANE gas to heat an incandescent mantle.

In the 20th century the industrialized nations have come to use ELECTRICITY for most lighting purposes because it offers an instant source of bright, clean, fume-free light. One of the earliest electrical lighting sources was the ARC LAMP which utilizes the flame arcing between two pointed carbon electrodes maintained with a moderate voltage between them. Successful incandescent filament lamps date from 1879 when Sir Joseph William Swan and EDISON demonstrated lamps in which a carbon filament enclosed in an evacuated glass bulb was heated electrically until it glowed. After 1913 these gave way to lamps having tungsten filaments, coiled to improve efficiency (from 1918), and filled with an unreactive gas such as nitrogen. In 1937 efficiency was further improved by coiling the coiled filament (coiled-coil lamp). A more recent development is the tungsten halogen lamp (an early type of which was the quartziodine lamp) in which efficiency is improved and life extended by filling the bulb with a HALOGEN with which tungsten evaporating from the filament can combine, preventing deposition of the metal on the envelope (which is sometimes made of quartz). Because discharge lamps (in which a glow discharge is set up in mercury or sodium vapor—glowing bluegreen and yellow respectively) do not produce light in all parts of the solar spectrum they find their greatest use in highway rather than domestic lighting. More recent high-pressure sodium lamps, however, offer a fuller light spectrum. Cold-discharge tubes containing neon (glowing red) or argon (glowing blue) are contorted into exotic shapes for use in advertising signs. Fluorescent lamps produce light similar to sunlight by using a PHOSPHOR coating on the inside of the tube to convert ultraviolet light produced in a mercury-vapor discharge. Although they require more complex circuitry than filament lamps, they are much more efficient and last longer. Other light sources such as light-emitting diodes (LEDs—see SEMICONDUCTORS) and electroluminescent panels find use in instrument display panels. (See also FIREWORKS; FLASHBULB; PHOTOMETRY.)

**LIGHTNING**, a discharge of atmospheric electricity resulting in a flash of light in the sky. Flashes range from a few km to about 150km in length, and typically have an energy of around 300kWh and an electromotive force around 100MV.

Cloud-to-ground lightning usually appears forked. A relatively faint light moves towards the ground at about 125km/s in steps, often branching or forking. As this first pulse (leader stroke) nears the ground, electrical discharges (streamers) arise from terrestrial objects; where a streamer meets the leader stroke, a brilliant, high-current flash (return stroke) travels up along the ionized (see ION) path created by the leader stroke at about 100Mm/s (nearly ⅓ the speed of light). Several exchanges along this same path may occur. If strong wind moves the ionized path, ribbon lightning results.

Sheet lightning occurs when a cloud either is illuminated from within or reflects a flash from outside, in the latter case often being called heat lightning (often seen on the horizon at the end of a hot day). Ball lightning, a small luminous ball near the ground, often vanishing with an explosion, and bead lightning, the appearance of luminous "beads" along the channel of a stroke, are rare.

Lightning results from a buildup of opposed electric charges in, usually, a cumulonimbus CLOUD, negative near the ground and positive on high (see ELECTRICITY). There are several theories which purport to explain this buildup. Understanding lightning might help us probe the very roots of life, for lightning was probably significant in the formation of those organic chemicals that were to be the building blocks of life.

**LIGHT YEAR,** in astronomy, a unit of distance equal to the distance traveled by light in a vacuum in one sidereal year, equal to 9,461Tm (about 6 million million miles). The unit has largely been replaced by the PARSEC (1 1y=0.3069pc).

**LIGNITE,** or brown coal. See COAL.

**LI HUNG-CHANG** (1823–1901), Chinese general and westernizing statesman. He helped crush the TAIPING REBELLION (1850–64). As governor general of the capital province, Chihli (1870–95), he tried to modernize the army and introduce western industries, and was virtually in charge of conducting China's relations with the West.

**LILBURNE, John** (c1614–1657), English pamphleteer and leader of the LEVELLERS. Imprisoned 1638–40, he became a commander in the CIVIL WAR (1640–45), but was then persecuted, spending much time in prison or exile. He remained popular, however, and was twice (1649, 1653) acquitted of treason by a London jury.

**LILIENTHAL, David Eli** (1899–1981), US lawyer and government official. He was a director (from 1933) and chairman (1941–46) of the TENNESSEE VALLEY AUTHORITY. As chairman (1946–50) of the ATOMIC ENERGY AUTHORITY, he championed civilian control of atomic energy.

**LILIENTHAL, Otto** (1848–1896), German pioneer of aeronautics, credited with being the first to use curved, rather than flat, wings, as well as first to discover several other principles of AERODYNAMICS. He made over 2,000 glider flights, dying from injuries received when one of his gliders crashed. (See also FLIGHT, HISTORY OF.)

**LILITH,** female demon of Jewish folklore (from the Assyrian demon Lilit, "night monster"), killer of children and legendary first wife of Adam.

**LILIUOKALANI** (1838–1917), queen of Hawaii, who reigned 1891–93. She succeeded her brother King Kalakaua. When she tried to assert her royal powers, Americans living in Hawaii fostered a revolt in which she lost her throne. She wrote the well-known farewell song "Aloha Oe."

**LILLEHEI, Clarence Walton** (1918–    ), US heart surgeon. A pioneer in the field of open-heart surgery, he was a coinventor of the heart-lung machine, and the first to use prosthetic plastic devices to replace damaged heart valves and to implant successfully an electronic heart pacemaker.

**LILLIE, Beatrice** (1894–    ), Canadian-born British actress, singer and comedienne who was best known for her rollicking performances in musical revues in London and New York. She often appeared with Noel Coward and Gertrude Lawrence.

**LIMA,** historic capital and largest city of Peru, about 8mi inland from the port of Callao. Founded 1535, Lima was the chief residence of the Spanish viceroys. Earthquakes in 1687 and 1746 destroyed most of the city, but it still retains its old character. The university dates from 1551. Rapidly expanding, Lima has many industries, including textiles, chemicals, oil refining and food processing. Pop 2,862,197; Met Pop 3,158,417.

**LIMBO,** in Roman Catholic theology, the abode of those excluded from HEAVEN but not punished in HELL or PURGATORY. The Old Testament saints were in limbo until Christ's coming; the unbaptized who die in infancy remain there forever. Limbo's existence is not an officially defined dogma.

**LIMBOURG, Pol de** (d. 1416?), Flemish manuscript illuminator, one of three brothers who after 1404 worked for the Burgundian duc de Berry. Their renowned devotional book of hours, the *Très riches heures du duc de Berry*, shows courtly life and landscape in brilliant detail and dazzling color. (See also ILLUMINATION, MANUSCRIPT.)

**LIME,** or calcium oxide or hydroxide. See

CALCIUM.

**LIMERICK,** Irish Atlantic port on Shannon R estuary. Near the cliffs of Moher, Limerick features a number of ancient structures, including the legendary Treaty Stone, St. Mary's Cathedral (9th century), and King John's Castle (13th century). Its name is given to a five-line comic verse form, popularized by Edward LEAR.

**LIMESTONE,** sedimentary rock consisting mainly of calcium carbonate (see CALCIUM), in the forms of CALCITE and aragonite. Some limestones, such as CHALK, are soft but others are hard enough for use in building. Limestone may be formed inorganically (oolites) by evaporation of seawater or freshwater containing calcium carbonate, or organically from the shells of mollusks or skeletons of coral piled up on sea beds and compressed. In such limestone fossils usually abound.

**LIMÓN, José** (1908–1972), Mexican-US dancer and choreographer. In the 1930s he danced with the Humphrey-Weidman company. With Doris HUMPHREY as artistic director, he formed his own company in 1946 and choreographed for it *Moor's Pavane* (1949), *The Visitation* (1952) and *A Choreographic Offering* (1963).

**LIMPOPO RIVER,** or Crocodile R, some 1,100mi long, rising in South Africa, and flowing in a great arc N, E and then SE through Mozambique to the Indian Ocean. It forms South Africa's NW frontier with Botswana and its N frontier with Zimbabwe.

**Born:** February 12, 1809
**Died:** April 15, 1865
**Term of office:** March 4, 1861–April 15, 1865
**Political party:** Republican

**LINCOLN, Abraham** (1809–1865), 16th president of the US who, while leading the North in the Civil War, preserved the Union which he saw as a bastion of democratic government. By his EMANCIPATION PROCLAMATION in 1863, he prepared the abolition of slavery in the US. He was not free from faults and vacillations, but his patience, fortitude and fierce devotion to the Union made him one of America's greatest presidents.

Lincoln was born in a log cabin in backwoods Ky., and raised in poverty. His father Thomas, and stepmother Sarah Bush Johnston Lincoln, were barely literate. In 1831 Abraham set up house in New Salem, Ill., and taught himself law in his spare time, eventually becoming one of the leading lawyers in the state. From 1834 to 1841 he served in the Ill. state legislature. He retained something of his rough frontier manner, even after a well-connected marriage, in 1842, to Mary Todd.

Lincoln entered the House of Representatives in 1847 as a Whig, but his opposition to the MEXICAN WAR lost him his seat in 1849. Returning to politics in 1854 he took his stand on slavery. Though not an abolitionist, he opposed the KANSAS-NEBRASKA ACT of Senator Stephen DOUGLAS, which by repealing part of the MISSOURI COMPROMISE seemed likely to introduce slavery into the new Western territories. Lincoln's speeches against slavery in 1854 aligned him with the new REPUBLICAN PARTY, which he joined in 1856. In 1858 he contested a senate seat with Douglas, challenging him in a series of historic debates in which, though he lost the election, Lincoln emerged as an orator of national stature. In 1860 he was nominated as a compromise presidential candidate, winning against a split Democratic vote.

Before he took office as president seven Southern states had already seceded from the Union. Determined to hold FORT SUMTER in S.C. for the Union, Lincoln ordered supplies to its beleaguered garrison. War broke out on April 12, 1861 (see CIVIL WAR, AMERICAN). At first the North suffered numerous reverses, but Lincoln built up the army, blockaded southern ports and personally directed strategy as commander in chief until, in March 1864, he gave Ulysses S. GRANT command of the armies in the field. Grant and gifted subordinates like William T. SHERMAN carried out Lincoln's grand strategy of multiple coordinated offensives against the numerically inferior South. In the continuing debate on slavery, Lincoln put the Union before abolition, but in response to increasing demands made the EMANCIPATION PROCLAMATION on Jan. 1, 1863. It was to be followed by the 13th Amendment to the CONSTITUTION, sponsored by Lincoln.

The tide turned with Grant's victory at VICKSBURG and LEE's defeat at GETTYSBURG (1863), where Lincoln made his famous address. In 1864 came the victories of the

HENANDOAH VALLEY, ATLANTA and MOBILE
AY, and Lincoln, who had lost some
olitical ground, was reelected. In his
cond inaugural address in March, 1865,
e made plain his lenient intentions towards
e South. Within four weeks Grant took
ichmond, and on April 9 Lee surrendered.
ve days later Lincoln was shot in his box
the theater by John Wilkes BOOTH, and
ed early on April 15.

INCOLN, capital of Neb., named for
braham LINCOLN. A transportation hub
d a commercial and industrial city, it is
so a trade center for livestock and grain.
op 171,932.

INCOLN CENTER FOR THE PER-
ORMING ARTS, in New York City, a
mplex of buildings, designed by leading
odern architects, to accommodate such
ltural organizations as the New York
hilharmonic Orchestra, Metropolitan
pera, theaters, and a library of the
rforming arts.

INCOLN MEMORIAL, marble memor-
l to Abraham Lincoln at the end of the
all in Washington, D.C., dedicated in
922. Its 36 Doric columns represent the
ates of the Union when Lincoln was
esident. The great hall contains a huge
atue of Lincoln by Daniel Chester
ENCH.

NCOLN TUNNEL, road tunnel, 8,216ft
ng, under the Hudson R from Manhattan
land, New York City, to Weehawken,
ew Jersey. The first tube was opened in
937; the second and third in 1945 and
57.

ND, Jenny (1820–1887), Swedish
prano, the "Swedish Nightingale." With
voice of exceptional flexibility and clarity,
e had brilliant success in opera, and after
49 in oratorio and concert recitals.

NDBERGH, Anne Morrow
906– ), US author and wife of
harles A. LINDBERGH, noted for popular
oks about the environment, works of
etry, and writings that eloquently express
r personal philosophy, gathered in two
tobiographies and three volumes of
aries and letters (1972–1980).

NDBERGH, Charles Augustus (1902–
74), US aviator who made the first solo
nstop flight across the Atlantic, in 33½
urs, on May 20, 1927, in "The Spirit of
. Louis." A hero overnight, he became an
line consultant and made many goodwill
ghts. The kidnapping and murder of his
n in 1932 led to a federal law on
napping, popularly known as the
ndbergh Act. Criticized for his pro-
rman, isolationist stance 1938–41, he
er flew 50 combat missions in WWII. His

autobiography, *The Spirit of Saint Louis*
(1953), won a Pulitzer Prize.

LINDSAY, Howard (1889–1968), US
playwright, producer and actor. With
Russel Crouse he wrote *State of the Union*
(1945), which won a Pulitzer Prize, *Life
with Father* (1939, adapted from Clarence
Day's book) and scripts for *Call Me
Madam* (1950) and *The Sound of Music*
(1959).

LINDSAY, John Vliet (1921– ), US
political leader. Elected to Congress 1958,
he was mayor of New York City 1966–74,
the first Republican to win the office in 21
years. A liberal reformer, in 1971 he
became a Democrat. Held partly to blame
for New York's deep fiscal crisis of the
1970s, he lost campaigns for president
(1972) and the Senate (1980).

LINDSAY, (Nicholas) Vachel (1879–1931),
US poet of rhythmic, ballad-like verse
designed to be read out loud. Among the
best known are "The Congo" (1914) and
"Abraham Lincoln Walks at Midnight"
(1914).

LINEN, yarn and fabric manufactured
from the fibers of the FLAX plant. The stems
of the flax plant must first be softened by
soaking in water (retting). Next, the fibers
are separated from the woody core in a
"scutching" mill. The short fibers (tow) are
combed out from the long fibers (line) in the
"hackling" mills. The tow is finally spun
into yarn.

LINGUISTICS, the scientific study of
language. Interest in how language works
and the differences among languages
extends back to ancient times (witness the
attention given to grammar in the classical
curriculum). In the late Middle Ages and
Renaissance, the study of biblical and other
ancient texts marked the emergence of what
is now called historical, or diachronic,
linguistics. In the 19th-century, comparative language studies (comparative
PHILOLOGY) and analyses of grammatical
systems led the way to modern synchronic
linguistics (i.e., the study of contemporary
language use); the great 19th-century
theorist Karl Wilhelm von HUMBOLDT.
anticipated structuralist and behaviorist
concepts vital in the 20th-century linguistics. The first modern linguist was
Ferdinand de SAUSSURE, whose major work
(1916) introduced linguistic structuralism,
i.e., the thesis that there exists a structure
underlying a language distinct from the
sounds or utterances made; elaboration of
this view has dominated all later linguistics.
In Europe, the influential PRAGUS SCHOOL of
linguists has tried to combine study of
structure with study of the many functions

performed by language. American linguists (including Franz BOAS, Edward SAPIR, Benjamin Lee WHORF, and Leonard BLOOMFIELD) emphasized descriptive methods of analyzing languages; American structuralism also became distinctly behavioristic, and thus deliberately excluded SEMANTICS (study of meaning) or theories about if or how the mind produced language. With Zellig S. HARRIS and his student Noam CHOMSKY (the most influential contemporary linguist), the tide turned. Chomsky's system of TRANSFORMATIONAL-GENERATIVE GRAMMAR, as he developed it in the 1960s, postulates a deep structure to language that corresponds to universal features of the human mind, and the rules of the system aim to demonstrate how sound is related to meaning. Technically, linguistics may be considered as having three aspects: the studies of sound (phonology), of word formation (morphology), and of syntax and vocabulary (which are called the "lexicon"). Many branches of linguistics reach into other fields of study, including **psycholinguistics** (concerned mainly with language acquisition), **anthropological** and **sociolinguistics** (which relate language to culture and to socialization), **applied linguistics** (which focuses on methods of teaching languages), **dialectology** and **geographical linguistics**, and so on.

**LINNAEUS, Carolus** (1707–1778), later Carl von Linné, Swedish botanist and physician, the father of TAXONOMY, who brought system to the naming of living things. His classification of plants was based on their sexual organs (he was the first to use the symbols ♂ and ♀ in their modern sense), an artificiality dropped by later workers; but many of his principles and taxonomic names are still used today.

**LINOTYPE**, technique of letterpress printing in which characters are cast from molten type-metal (see ALLOY) a line at a time. Keying by the operator assembles the matrices (molds) for the characters in the correct order, wedge-shaped space bands being placed between the words: when the line is nearly full, pressure is applied to these so that they force apart the words and justify the line (align the right-hand margin). The slug of type is cast from the completed line. If a single character is wrong, the whole line must be recast. (See also MONOTYPE.)

**LIN PIAO** (1907–1971), Chinese communist general and statesman. He was a leader in the LONG MARCH (1934–35) and, by his capture of Manchuria in 1948, crucial in the final defeat of CHIANG KAI-SHEK. Minister of defense from 1959, he was a leader of the

"Cultural Revolution" (1965–69). In 196 he was designated the successor of MA TSE-TUNG. He was killed in an air crash, an the Chinese press later reported that he ha been escaping to Russia after an abortiv coup.

**LINTON, Ralph** (1893–1953), US anthro pologist best known for the eclecticism o his studies in cultural ANTHROPOLOGY, a expressed in *The Study of Man* (1936) an *The Tree of Culture* (1955).

**LIN YUTANG** (1895–1976), Chines author and translator who promote Western understanding of China in suc books as *My Country and My Peopl* (1935), and the novel *Moment in Pekin* (1939). After 1935 he lived in the US.

**LION**, *Panthera Leo*, one of the largest o the big cats, distributed through Africa an Asia. They live in family groups loosel associated into large social units or pride which share a range. Lionesses usually ki for the pride, though the big-maned male are well able to kill for themselves, an frequently do so—particularly those i bachelor groups of immature male Amazingly powerful animals, they ar characteristic of bush or veld, killing zebr wildebeest, even buffalo by dragging on th neck, bringing the prey to the ground an breaking its neck. The roar of a male lion a territorial proclamation.

**LIONS CLUBS INTERNATIONA** organization of business and profession men dedicated to community servic founded in Chicago in 1917. Today the are some 25,000 clubs with a tot membership of more than 1 million in ov 140 countries.

**LIPCHITZ, Jacques** (1891–1973 Russian-born sculptor whose early works Paris were constructed in terms of spac and volumes, as in CUBISM. From 1925 produced a series he called "transparents in which, as in the *Harpist* (1928), conto was emphasized. His later work was mo romantic and metaphorical.

**LIPPI**, name of two Italian ear RENAISSANCE painters in Florence. F Filippo Lippi (c1406–1469) was influence by MASACCIO, DONATELLO and by Flemis painting. His frescoes in Prato cathedr have a prettiness derived from F ANGELICO. Filippino Lippi (c1457–1504 his son, influenced by BOTTICELLI, painte the brilliantly-detailed *Adoration of t Magi* (1496).

**LIPPMANN, Walter** (1889–1974), i fluential US political columnist and forei affairs analyst. His column, "Today a Tomorrow," first appeared in the *New Yo Herald-Tribune* in 1931, and eventual won two Pulitzer prizes (1958, 1962). Books include *Public Opinion* (1922) and *The Good Society* (1937).

**LIPSCOMB, William Nunn, Jr.** (1919– ), US chemist. A professor at Harvard (from 1959), Lipscomb won the 1976 Nobel Prize in Chemistry for his work with boranes (compounds of boron and hydrogen), which yielded basic information about the chemical BOND.

**LIQUID CRYSTAL**, a state of matter, exhibited by certain chemical compounds, resembling both the liquid and the solid crystalline state. The molecules of liquid crystals are free to move around, as in liquids, but they tend to orient themselves spatially in a regular way, as in crystalline solids. The first known observation of this phenomenon was made by an Austrian botanist, Friedrich Reinitzer, in 1888, while working with cholesteryl benzoate. Compounds that have a liquid-crystal phase at ordinary environmental temperatures have been put to a variety of uses, since they are sensitive to minute changes in temperature, pressure, or applied electrical or magnetic fields. Some, which can change from clear to opaque in response to changes in electric current, are widely used in image displays such as in calculators and digital watches. Others that change color in response to small changes in temperature can be applied to surfaces to reveal patterns of temperature variation.

**LISBON**, capital and largest city of Portugal, on the Tagus R estuary. Its fine harbor handles the bulk of the country's foreign trade. Reconquered from the Moors in 1147, Lisbon became the capital c1260. Much of the city was rebuilt after the disastrous earthquake of 1755. Industries include steelmaking, petroleum refining, textiles, chemicals, paper and metal products. Pop 859,200.

**LISSITZKY, Eliezer (El) Markovich,** 1890–1941), Russian abstract painter, designer and architect, proponent of CONSTRUCTIVISM and SUPREMATISM. His series of paintings and drawings, *Proun*, applied geometric forms to art and architecture.

**LIST, Friedrich** (1789–1846), German-US economist and author of *The National System of Political Economy* (1841). Exiled in 1825 for his liberalism, in 1832 he returned to Germany as US consul at Leipzig. He argued for a German customs union, but advocated tariffs to protect developing industries.

**LISTER, Joseph Lister, 1st Baron** 1827–1912), British surgeon who pioneered antiseptic SURGERY, perhaps the greatest single advance in modern medicine. PASTEUR had shown that microscopic organisms are responsible for PUTREFACTION, but his STERILIZATION techniques were unsuitable for surgical use. Lister experimented and, by 1865, succeeded by using carbolic acid (see PHENOL).

**LISTON, Charles "Sonny"** (c1932–1970), heavyweight boxing champion of the world 1962–64. He won the title by beating Floyd PATTERSON, but lost it to Cassius Clay (now Muhammad ALI) in 1964.

**LISZT, Franz** (1811–1886), Hungarian Romantic composer and virtuoso pianist who revolutionized keyboard technique and became a public idol. He was director of music at Weimar 1843–61, and then lived in Rome where he took minor holy orders in 1865. His highly programmatic music includes 13 symphonic poems, a form he invented; program symphonies such as *Faust* (1854); the great B minor piano sonata (1853); *Transcendental Studies* for piano (1852); and 20 *Hungarian Rhapsodies*. His daughter Cosima married WAGNER.

**LITHOGRAPHY.** See PRINTING.

**LITHOSPHERE**, the worldwide rigid outer shell of the EARTH extending to a depth of 70km and overlying the ASTHENOSPHERE; it includes the continental and oceanic crust and the uppermost part of the MANTLE. Seismically, the zone is one of high velocity and efficient wave propagation, suggesting solidity and strength. In plate tectonic theory, the lithosphere consists of a number of plates in motion over the soft asthenosphere. (See also PLATE TECTONICS.)

**LITHUANIA**, constituent republic of the USSR, bounded N by Latvia, E by Belorussia, S by Poland and W by the Baltic. The country is mainly flat with many lakes and forests, and is drained by the Neman R. The climate is generally mild and humid in summer, cold in winter. The population is 80% LITHUANIAN.

Although timber and agricultural produce remain important, Lithuania is now 60% urban, with machinery manufacture, shipbuilding, and building materials the most important industries. The chief cities and industrial centers are Vilnius, the capital, Kaunas and Klaipeda, the main port. Roman Catholicism is the traditional religion.

Fourteenth-century Lithuania, comprising Belorussia and parts of the Ukraine and Russia, was central Europe's most powerful state. In 1386 Lithuania and Poland were united under Grand Duke JAGIELLO. In 18th-century partitions of Poland Lithuania became a Russian province. From 1918 to 1940, when it was reabsorbed by Russia, it had an independent regime. (See USSR.)

**LITHUANIAN**, the most ancient of the BALTIC LANGUAGES and the official language of Lithuania. It has a modified Latin alphabet, and has been a literary language since the 16th century, experiencing a revival in the 19th. Its literary traditions are rich in folklore.

**LITTLE DIPPER** (Ursa Minor, the Little Bear), N Hemisphere circumpolar constellation containing POLARIS, the N polestar.

**LITTLE LEAGUE BASEBALL**, junior baseball organization for teams aged 8–12 years, founded in 1939. The playing area is two-thirds full size, and six rather than nine innings are played; there is a World Series and over 7,500 member leagues, some of them in other countries.

**LITTLE ROCK**, capital and principal commercial and manufacturing city of Ark., on the Arkansas R. It achieved notoriety in 1957 when federal troops were sent in to enforce INTEGRATION at the Central High School after Governor Faubus had ordered the state militia to stop black pupils entering. Pop 158,461.

**LITTLE TURTLE** (c1752–1812), Miami Indian chief, orator and warrior. He won resounding victories against the whites in 1790 and 1791, but shared in the defeat of FALLEN TIMBERS, and in 1795 ceded Indian lands in the Ohio valley to the US.

**LITURGY**, services of public worship, especially in Christianity and Judaism; often applied specifically to Holy COMMUNION (the chief worship service) and to the texts that prescribe the order of services, such as the BREVIARY or the BOOK OF COMMON PRAYER. The 20th-century **Liturgical Movement** in most churches has emphasized reform of the liturgy, use of the vernacular, and lay participation.

**LITVINOV, Maxim Maximovich** (1876–1951), Russian revolutionary and commissar for foreign affairs from 1930–39. He maintained a policy of cooperation with the West, negotiating US recognition of the USSR in 1933 and taking Russia into the League of Nations in 1934. From 1941–43 he was ambassador to the US.

**LIU SHAO-CHI** (1898–1969), Chinese communist leader, who succeeded MAO TSE-TUNG as chairman of the Chinese People's Republic (1959) and came to be seen as his heir. But in 1968 he was publicly denounced for "taking the capitalist road" and dismissed. He died in mysterious circumstances. In 1980 he was rehabilitated and exonerated by China's new leaders.

**LIVER**, the large organ lying on the right of the ABDOMEN beneath the DIAPHRAGM and concerned with many aspects of METABOLISM. It consists of a homogeneous mass of cells arranged round blood vessels and bile ducts. Nutrients absorbed in the GASTROINTESTINAL TRACT pass via the portal VEINS to the liver and many are taken up by it; they are converted into forms (e.g., GLYCOGEN) suitable for storage and release when required. PROTEINS, including ENZYMES, PLASMA proteins and CLOTTING factors, are synthesized from amino acids. The liver converts protein breakdown-products into urea and detoxifies or excretes other substances (including drugs) in the blood. Bilirubin, the HEMOGLOBIN break-down product is excreted in the BILE; this also contains bile salts, made in the liver from CHOLESTEROL and needed for the DIGESTIVE SYSTEM.

Diseases of the liver include CIRRHOSIS and HEPATITIS, while abnormal function is manifested as JAUNDICE, EDEMA, ascites (excessive peritoneal fluid), and a variety of BRAIN and NERVOUS SYSTEM disturbances including DELIRIUM and COMA. Chronic liver disease leads to SKIN abnormalities, a bleeding tendency and alterations in routes of BLOOD CIRCULATION, which may in turn lead to HEMORRHAGE. Hepatitis may be caused by VIRUSES (e.g., infectious and serum hepatitis); their high infectivity has made them a hazard in hospital dialysis units. Many drugs may damage the liver, causing disease similar to hepatitis, and both drugs and severe hepatitis can cause acute liver failure.

**LIVERIGHT, Horace** (1886–1933), US publisher. An influential figure in the literary world of the 1920s, he published (with partner Charles Boni) The Modern Library series of reprinted classics (1917–25) and helped further the careers of such writers as O'NEILL, DREISER, T.S. ELIOT, and HEMINGWAY.

**LIVERPOOL**, industrial city and second largest port in Britain, on the Mersey R., 3mi from the Irish Sea. The borough was chartered in 1207; in the 18th century it was a major slave-trading port. Its extensive docks are now among Europe's finest. Pop 520,200.

**LIVERPOOL AND LONDON RIOTS**, a series of outbreaks, led mostly by white youths, that swept more than 30 cities and towns in Britain in July 1981. Thousands were arrested and hundreds, including many policemen, were injured. Property damage was extensive. Although some of the violence was racially motivated, much of it was attributed to high unemployment, which opposition leaders blamed on the conomic policies of Prime Minister ʜᴀᴛᴄʜᴇʀ's government.

**ᴸIVINGSTON, Robert R.** (1746–1813), ᴜS statesman. He was a delegate at the ᴄᴏɴᴛɪɴᴇɴᴛᴀʟ ᴄᴏɴɢʀᴇss and assisted in rafting the ᴅᴇᴄʟᴀʀᴀᴛɪᴏɴ ᴏғ ɪɴᴅᴇᴘᴇɴᴅᴇɴᴄᴇ. n 1777 he helped draft the N.Y. state ᴏnstitution. As chancellor of N.Y. state 777–1801, he administered the presidenal oath of office to George Washington. In ᴸ801–04 he negotiated the ʟᴏᴜɪsɪᴀɴᴀ ᴜʀᴄʜᴀsᴇ. The Livingston family was ʀominent in N.Y. and national affairs ᴸ680–1823.

**ᴸIVINGSTONE, David** (1813–1873), Scotsh missionary and explorer in Africa, from ᴸ841. He discovered the Zambesi R in 1851 ᴎd explored it in three remarkable ᴐurneys (1852–56, 1858–63, 1866–73). In ᴸ855 he reached the waterfall he was to ᴎame as Victoria Falls. His historic meeting ith the ' New York journalist Henry ᴸorton sᴛᴀɴʟᴇʏ took place in 1871. ᴸivingstone was a sworn enemy of the slave ʀade. He died in central Africa; his body ᴎas carried to the coast by two African ᴏllowers.

**ᴸIVY**, or Titus Livius (c59 BC–17 AD), ᴎportant Roman historian. Of his ᴸ42-book *History of Rome* 35 books ᴎrvive, with fragments and an outline of ᴎe rest. This work, which set out to praise ᴎe ancient republican virtues, won the ᴏpproval of ᴀᴜɢᴜsᴛᴜs.

**ᴸIZARDS**, a diverse group of ʀᴇᴘᴛɪʟᴇs, ᴎaced with sɴᴀᴋᴇs and amphisbaenids in ᴎe order Squatama. Lizards usually ᴐssess well-developed limbs, though these ᴎe reduced or absent in some species. In ᴐme families the tail vertebrae have a ʀedetermined plane of fracture where the ᴎil can be cast if seized by a predator. The ᴎissing portion of tail can usually be ᴎgenerated. The various groups are ᴎapted to a wide variety of environments, ᴎd lizards are found even in dry or desert ᴏnditions. A number of African species of ᴎcertid lizards live in tropical forest where ᴎey climb among trees. Some of these have ᴎattened flaps of skin which can be ʀetched between hind and fore limbs, ʀmitting the lizard to glide down from ᴎe to tree. Lizards are typically ᴎsectivorous though some will take eggs or ᴎall mammals. The group includes ᴇᴄᴋᴏᴇs, ᴄʜᴀᴍᴇʟᴇᴏɴs, sᴋɪɴᴋs, true ᴧᴄᴇʀᴛɪᴅ ʟɪᴢᴀʀᴅs and ᴍᴏɴɪᴛᴏʀs.

**ᴸAMA**, domestic form of a *Lama* species, ᴎe generic name for humpless New World ᴎmellids including the llama and ᴀʟᴘᴀᴄᴀ, ith the wild ɢᴜᴀɴᴀᴄᴏ and ᴠɪᴄᴜɴᴀ. It has ᴎick fleece which may be used for wool,

and is the principal beast of burden of Indians from Peru to Chile, thriving at altitudes of 2,300–4,000m (7,500–13,000ft).

**LLOYD, Harold Clayton** (1894–1971), US comedian of the silent screen. He is famous for his role as the naive young man in glasses and straw hat, forever teetering on the brink of disaster only to be saved at the last moment. Among his best-known films are *Safety Last* (1923), *The Kid Brother* (1927) and *Feet First* (1930).

**LLOYD GEORGE, David,** 1st Earl of Dwyfor (1863–1945), Welsh statesman, British prime minister from 1916–22, one of Britain's greatest war leaders and a brilliant orator. He was elected a Liberal member of Parliament in 1890 and served the same Welsh constituency for 54 years. As chancellor of the exchequer he forced through the so-called "people's budget" 1910–11, virtually founding British welfare legislation. The budget was at first rejected by the House of Lords, an incident which led to effective curtailment of their power of veto. In WWI, Lloyd George became successively minister of munitions, minister of war, and in 1916 prime minister of a coalition government. He was one of "the Big Four" at the Paris Peace Conference, 1919. His later policies, particularly over Ireland, lost him support; he was forced to resign in 1922. In the 1930s he opposed policies of appeasement towards Nazi Germany.

**LLOYD'S OF LONDON,** the world's largest marine insurance association, also involved in other types of insurance. Risks are assured by individual "underwriters," grouped in some 300 "syndicates." The underwriters assume unlimited personal liability for their portion of any given claim.

**LOBACHEVSKI, Nikolai Ivanovich** (1792–1856), Russian mathematician who, independently of ʙᴏʟʏᴀɪ, developed the first ɴᴏɴ-ᴇᴜᴄʟɪᴅᴇᴀɴ ɢᴇᴏᴍᴇᴛʀʏ, hyperbolic or ʟᴏʙᴀᴄʜᴇᴠsᴋɪᴀɴ ɢᴇᴏᴍᴇᴛʀʏ, publishing his developments from 1826 onward.

**LOBACHEVSKIAN GEOMETRY,** or **hyperbolic geometry,** the branch of ɴᴏɴ-ᴇᴜᴄʟɪᴅᴇᴀɴ ɢᴇᴏᴍᴇᴛʀʏ based on the hypothesis that for any point P not lying on a line L, there are at least two lines that can be drawn through P parallel to L.

**LOBBYING,** the attempt to influence legislation by personal persuasion and propaganda outside official hearings or channels. Corporations, professions and trade associations maintain expensive operations to this end. Lobbying abuses are controlled in the US by the Regulation of Lobbying Act (1946).

**LOBOTOMY**, operation in which the FRONTAL LOBES are separated from the rest of the BRAIN, used in the past as treatment for extremely severe and chronic psychiatric conditions. It leads to a characteristically disinhibited type of behavior and is now rarely used.

**LOBSTERS**, large marine decapod crustaceans with the first pair of legs bearing enormous claws. True lobsters, genus *Homarus*, are animals of shallow water living among rocks in crannies feeding on carrion, small crabs and worms. The two large claws differ in both structure and function, one of them always adapted for crushing, the other adapted as a fine picking or scraping claw. The dark blue pigment of the living lobster is a complex compound broken down by heat to the familiar red.

**LOCARNO TREATIES**, a series of pacts drawn up in Locarno, Switzerland, in 1925, among seven European nations, guaranteeing existing borders in E and W Europe. They also established arbitration procedures to solve disputes, notably between France and Germany, the latter being treated as an equal among the European powers for the first time since WWI. The "spirit of Locarno" died in 1936 when Germany denounced the pacts and occupied the Rhineland.

**LOCHNER, Stephan** (c1400–1451), German painter of the Cologne school who brought a new feeling of naturalism and pure color to the Gothic traditions. His most famous work is the triptych altarpiece (1440s) in Cologne Cathedral, in which the central panel depicts the Adoration of the Magi.

**LOCKE, John** (1632–1704), English empiricist philosopher whose writings helped initiate the European Enlightenment. His *Essay Concerning Human Understanding* (1690) is one of the highlights of English philosophy. In it he opposed innate ideas, offered a critique of our ideas on the basis of how we get them, and stressed the limitation of human knowledge. His *Second Treatise of Civil Government* (1690) presents a classical statement of social contract theory. His *A Letter Concerning Toleration* (1689) and *The Reasonableness of Christianity* (1695) were seminal for British religious thought of the 18th century.

**LOCKJAW.** See TETANUS.

**LOCKS AND KEYS.** The earliest known mechanical lock is from ancient Egypt, c2000 BC. The bolt was hollow, with a number of holes bored in its top; one of the bolt staples held a number of wooden pegs which fell into the holes in the bolt, holding it in place. The key could be fitted into the bolt; it had spikes in the same pattern as the holes, and thus could lift the pegs clear. The ancient Greeks situated their locks on the inside of the door, access being achieved *via* a keyhole to whose shape the key conformed. The Romans improved the Egyptian design by having pegs of different shapes and using springs to drive the pegs home; and invented the **warded lock**, whose key must be slotted to clear wards, obstacles projecting from the back of the lock. Early portable locks, and later padlocks, also used this principle. The modern *lever-tumbler lock* was invented by Robert Barron (1778); levers fit into a slot in the bolt patterned such that each lever must be raised a different distance by the key to free the bolt. Jeremiah Chubb added another lever to jam the lock if the wrong key were tried (1818). The *Bramah lock*, invented by Joseph BRAMAH (1784), has a cylindrical key slotted to push down sprung slides, each of which must be depressed a different distance to clear an obstacle. Most domestic locks are now *Yale locks*, invented by Linus YALE (1861). An inner cylindrical plug has hole into which sprung drivers press pins of different lengths. The key is patterned to raise each pin so that its top is flush with the cylinder, which can then turn. Modern safes have combination locks and time devices so that they can only be opened at certain times.

**LOCOMOTIVE**, originally locomotive engine, power unit used to haul railroad trains. The earliest development of the railroad locomotive took place in the UK where R. TREVITHICK built his first engine c1804. R. STEPHENSON's famous *Rocket* of 1829 proved that locomotive engines were far superior to stationary ones and provided a design that was archetypal for the remainder of the steam era. Locomotives were first built in the US c1830. These pioneered many new design features including the leading truck, a set of wheels preceding the main driving wheels, guiding the locomotives over the usually lightly constructed American tracks. For most of the rest of the 19th century, locomotives of the "American" type (4-4-0) were standard on US passenger trains, though towards the end of the century, progressively larger types came to be built. Although electric locomotives have been in service in the US since 1895, the high capital cost of converting tracks to electric transmission have prevented their widespread adoption. Since the 1950s, however, most US locomotives have been built with DIESEL ENGINES. Usually the axles are driven by ectric motors mounted on the trucks, the ain diesel engine driving a generator hich supplies power to the motors iesel-electric transmission). Elsewhere in e world, particularly in Europe, much eater use is made of electric traction, the comotives usually collecting power from erhead cables via a PANTOGRAPH. lthough some GAS-TURBINE locomotives e in service in the US, this and other novel wer sources do not seem to be making uch headway at present.

**OCUST**, a name restricted to about 50 ecies of tropical GRASSHOPPERS which have swarming, gregarious stage in the life cle. In the arid regions where they occur ey have become opportunists, breeding in rge numbers where conditions are itable, then flying in huge swarms to herever food may be abundant. Here they n rapidly effect an agricultural disaster. hey lay their eggs in bare earth just after in. The young hoppers which hatch thus ave new vegetation on which to feed when ey emerge. Then they form into bands hich march across the country eating the aves of grasses, herbs and bushes as they . Once they fledge, a swarm of Desert custs can cover 50km (30mi) a day, on a ont 50km wide, devastating the vegetation it proceeds.

**ODGE**, name of two US statesmen. **Henry abot Lodge** (1850–1924), senator from ass. 1893–1924, known for his successful position to US membership of the LEAGUE NATIONS, which he felt threatened US vereignty. Instructor in American history Harvard 1876–79, he was a prominent storian even during his Senate career. His andson, the diplomat **Henry Cabot Lodge** 902– ), was a Republican senator 37–44 and 1947–52, when he lost his seat John F. KENNEDY. In 1960 he was ichard Nixon's vice-presidential can- date. He served as ambassador to the UN 53–60 and ambassador to South Vietnam 63–64 and 1965–67. As ambassador to est Germany 1968–69, he was chief gotiator at the Vietnam peace talks in ris.

**ODGE, Sir Oliver Joseph** (1851–1940), itish physicist best known for his work on e propagation of ELECTROMAGNETIC DIATION, devising an early instrument e coherer) for detecting it. He also did portant work on PARAPSYCHOLOGY.

**EB, Jacques** (1859–1924), German- rn US biologist best known for his work PARTHENOGENESIS, especially his induc- n of artificial parthenogenesis in sea chins' and frogs' eggs, thereby highlight- g the biochemical nature of

FERTILIZATION.

**LOEB, William** (1905–1981), US news- paper publisher known for his outspoken, conservative views. As publisher from 1946 of the *Manchester Union Leader* in N.H., to which he regularly contributed hard- hitting, front-page editorials, Loeb exerted a nationwide influence, particularly on presidential primaries. He was credited with ruining Senator Edmund S. MUSKIE'S campaign for the 1972 Democratic nomination.

**LOESS**, fine-grained, unstratified, uncon- solidated, wind-deposited SILT found world- wide in deposits up to 50m thick. Its main components are QUARTZ, FELDSPAR, CALCITE and clay minerals. Extremely porous, it forms highly-fertile topsoil, often CHERNOZEM. It is able to stand intact in cliffs.

**LOESSER, Frank** (1910–1969), US composer and lyricist who wrote "Praise the Lord and Pass the Ammunition," one of the most famous songs of WWII. He was a Hollywood songwriter before writing the words and music for such hit Broadway musicals as *Guys and Dolls* (1950) and *The Most Happy Fella* (1956).

**LOEW, Marcus** (1870–1927), US film producer and exhibitor who developed an extensive chain of theaters that featured, first, vaudeville and film shows, and, later, movies only. He purchased several film companies and, in 1924, formed Metro- Goldwyn-Mayer (MGM), the largest of the film-producing "major studios."

**LOEWE, Frederick** (1904– ), Austrian-born US composer of musical plays, usually to lyrics by Alan Jay LERNER. After *Brigadoon* (1947) and *Paint Your Wagon* (1951), their major successes were *My Fair Lady* (1956) and *Camelot* (1960).

**LOEWY, Raymond Fernand** (1893– ), French-born US industrial designer famous for his pioneering automobile designs, which were both functional and visually attractive. His firm designed many hundreds of different products, from refrigerators to passenger ships.

**LOFTING, Hugh** (1886–1947), English- born US author and illustrator of the famous *Dr. Dolittle* stories, begun in letters to his children. *The Voyages of Dr. Dolittle* (1922), the second in the series, won him the Newbery medal in 1923.

**LOGAN, James John** (1725–1780), or Tah-Gah-Jute, prominent Cayuga Indian. Originally a friend of white men, he took the name of a white friend. During an attempt by John DUNMORE to seize the Ohio area Logan's family was massacred, which made him an impassioned foe of the white man.

**LOGAN, Joshua** (1908– ), US theater and film director, producer and writer. Among his many stage productions are *Mister Roberts* (1948), the Pulitzer Prize-winning musical *South Pacific* (1949), filmed in 1958, and *Fanny* (1954).

**LOGARITHMS,** a method of computation using EXPONENTS. A logarithm is the power (see ALGEBRA) to which one number, the base, must be raised in order to obtain another number. For example, since $10^2 = 100$, $\log_{10} 100 = 2$ (read as 'log to the base 10 of 100 equals $2^c$). The most common bases for logarithms are 10 (common logarithms) and (natural logarithms).

Since $a^0 = 1$ for any $a$, $\log 1 = 0$ for all bases. In order to multiply two numbers together, one uses the fact that $a^x \cdot a^y = a^{x+y}$, and hence $\log (x.y) = \log x + \log y$. We therefore look up the values of $\log x$ and $\log y$ in logarithmic tables, add these values, and then use the tables again to find the number whose logarithm is equal to the result of the addition. Similarly, since

$$\left(\frac{a^x}{a^y}\right) = a^{x-y}, \log\left(\frac{x}{y}\right) = \log x - \log y;$$

and since $(a^x)^y = a^{xy}$, $\log x^y = y.\log x$. Log$_x$ $x = 1$ since $x^1 = x$. The antilogarithm of a number $x$ is the number whose logarithm is $x$; that is, if $\log y = x$, then $y$ is the antilogarithm of $x$. A *logarithmic curve* is the plotting of a FUNCTION of the form $f(x) = g x$.

**LOGIC,** the branch of PHILOSOPHY concerned with analyzing the rules that govern correct and incorrect reasoning, or inference. It was created by ARISTOTLE, who analyzed terms and propositions and in his *Prior Analytics* set out systematically the various forms of the SYLLOGISM; this work has remained an important part of logic ever since. Aristotle's other great achievement was the use of symbols to expose the form of an argument independently of its content. Thus a typical Aristotelian syllogism might be: all A is B; all B is C; therefore all A is C. This formalization of arguments is fundamental to all logic.

From the 12th century onward Latin translations of Aristotle's logical works (collectively called the *Organon*) were intently studied, and a kind of program emerged, which was based on Aristotle and included much that would nowadays be regarded as GRAMMAR, EPISTEMOLOGY and linguistic analysis. Among the most important medieval logicians were WILLIAM OF OCKHAM, Albert of Saxony and Jean BURIDAN. After the Renaissance an anti-Aristotelian reaction set in, and logic was given a new turn by Petrus RAMUS and by Francis BACON's prescription that induction (and not deduction) should be the method of the new science. In the work of George BOOLE and Gottlob FREGE the 19th century saw a vast extension in the scope and power of logic. In particular, logic became as bound up with mathematics as it was with philosophy. Logicians became interested in whether particular logical systems were either consistent or complete. (A consistent logic is one in which contradictory propositions cannot be validly derived). The climax of 20th-century logic came in the early 1930s when Kurt GÖDEL demonstrated both the completeness of Frege's first-order logic and that no higher-order logic could be both consistent and complete.

**LOGICAL POSITIVISM,** the doctrines of the "Vienna Circle," a group of philosophers founded by M. SCHLICK. At the heart of logical positivism was the assertion that apparently factual statements that were not sanctioned by logical or mathematical convention were meaningful only if they could conceivably be empirically verified. In this sense only mathematics, logic and science were deemed meaningful; ethics, metaphysics and religion were meaningless. The influence of logical positivism tended to decline after WWII.

**LOHENGRIN,** in German myth, a knight sworn to the service of the HOLY GRAIL. The son of PARSIFAL, he was allowed to champion and marry a mortal princess but when she forced him to reveal his identity he sailed away forever in his swan-drawn boat. The legend is most fully treated in the 13th-century epic *Lohengrin*, an anonymous continuation of WOLFRAM VON ESCHENBACH's *Parzival*, and in WAGNER's opera based on it (1872).

**LOIRE RIVER,** at 627mi the longest river of France. It rises in the Cévenne mountains and flows NW to Orléans, then SW to the ports of Nantes and Saint-Nazaire to empty into the Bay of Biscay. It drains an area of 44,000sq m more than a fifth of all France. Canals link the Loire with the Saône, Rhône and Seine rivers.

**LOLLARDS** ("idlers" or "babblers"), derisory name given to the 14th-century followers of the English religious reformer John WYCLIFFE. Wandering preachers, the Lollards sought to base their beliefs solely on the Bible and simple worship, rejecting the organized Church altogether. Although considered to have declined during the 15th century, Lollard beliefs were linked with adical social unrest and remained as underground influences on later movements.

**LOMAX, John Avery** (1867–1948), pioneering US folk musicologist. His collections of American folksongs include *Cowboy Songs and other Frontier Ballads* (1910) and *Our Singing Country* (1938).

**LOMBARDI, Vince** (1913–70), US football coach. He became coach and general manager of the hapless Green Bay Packers in 1959, and led them to five NFL championships between 1961 and 1967. He also coached the Packers to victories in the first two Super Bowls ever played (1967–68).

**LOMBARDS**, Germanic people who moved down from NW Germany in the 4th century AD towards Italy; in 568 they crossed the Alps and conquered most of N Italy, dividing it into dukedoms until 584, when they united into a kingdom against the threat of Frankish invasion. The kingdom reached its height under LIUTPRAND in the 8th century, but was soon overrun by the Franks c770.

**LOMBARDY**, region of N Italy, once a kingdom of the Lombards, for whom it is named. The country's main industrial and commercial region, it also has efficient and prosperous agriculture. Its capital, Milan, is a major transport hub and commercial center. In area Lombardy is 9,202sq mi and has about 16% of Italy's total population.

**LOMBROSO, Cesare** (1836–1909), Italian physician who pioneered scientific criminology. His view that criminals were throwbacks to earlier evolutionary stages (see ATAVISM) has now been generally discarded. In retrospect his most valuable work is seen to have been his defense of the rehabilitation and more humane treatment of criminals.

**LOMOND, Loch**, Scotland's largest lake, lies at the S extremity of the Highlands. About 24mi long, it is flanked by the Grampian Mts to the NE, and is famous for the beauty of its scenery.

**LOMONOSOV, Mikhail Vasilievich** (1711–1765), Russian scientist and man of letters, best known for his corpuscular theory of matter, in the course of developing which he made an early statement of the KINETIC THEORY.

**LONDON, Jack** (1876–1916), US writer of novels and short stories, many set during the Yukon GOLD RUSH, that treat the struggles of men and animals to survive as romantic conflicts with nature. The best examples are *The Call of the Wild* (1903), *White Fang* (1906) and *Burning Daylight* (1910), but perhaps his finest work is the autobiographical novel *Martin Eden* (1909).

**LONDON, Treaties of,** many important international treaties signed in London during the 19th and 20th centuries. The most important are dealt with here. In the Treaty of 1827 Great Britain, France and Russia supported Greek independence in her struggle against Turkey. The Treaty of 1913 ended the First Balkan War (1912) but led to the Second (1913). Defeated, Turkey lost Macedonia, Crete and most of Thrace to Greece, Serbia and Bulgaria. The Treaty of 1915, signed secretly by Great Britain, France, Russia and Italy, promised Italy the South Tyrol, Istria, Gorizia and north Dalmatia if she entered WWI against Germany. The Treaty of 1930 (London Naval Treaty) was signed by the US, Great Britain, France, Italy and Japan; it imposed limits on naval armaments and regulated submarine warfare.

**LONDON**, capital of the UK. Divided into 33 boroughs, Greater London covers over 650sq mi along both banks of the Thames R in SE England, all the historic city and county of London. The national center of government, trade, commerce, shipping, finance and industry, it is also one of the cultural centers of the world.

The Port of London handles over 33% of UK trade. London is also an important industrial region in its own right, with various manufacturing industries. Many of the most important financial and business institutions such as the BANK OF ENGLAND, the Stock Exchange and LLOYD'S OF LONDON, as well as many banking and shipping concerns, are concentrated in the single square mile known as the City; the ancient nucleus of London, it has its own Lord Mayor and corporation. To the W of it are the Law Courts and the INNS OF COURT, and the governmental area in Westminster centered on the HOUSE OF COMMONS and HOUSE OF LORDS.

London is also a historic city with many beautiful buildings: the TOWER OF LONDON, WESTMINSTER ABBEY and BUCKINGHAM PALACE are major tourist attractions. Home of universities, colleges and some of the world's greatest museums and libraries, it also has a flourishing night life and many cinemas. London's art galleries, concert halls, theaters and opera houses are world-famous. Distant areas of London are linked by the complex and highly efficient subway system known as the Underground. Pop 6,916,500.

**LONDON COMPANY**, joint stock company chartered by James I in 1606 to found an English colony on the Atlantic coast of North America. It settled Jamestown, Va., but was never a success; in 1624 the charter was canceled, its interests vested in the Crown, and Jamestown became a royal colony.

**LONDONDERRY,** or **Derry,** seaport in Northern Ireland, on the Royle R. It has a traditional shirtmaking industry, and some light manufacturing industries. Since 1968 it has been a center of violent conflict between Protestants and Roman Catholics (see IRELAND, NORTHERN). Pop 51,617.

**LONDON SCHOOL OF ECONOMICS AND POLITICAL SCIENCE,** London, England, institution of higher learning founded 1895 which became a branch of the University of London in 1900. Highly influential in the development of modern economic and political knowledge and theory, it also publishes several authoritative journals.

**LONG, Crawford Williamson** (1815–1878), US physician who first discovered the surgical use of diethyl ETHER as an ANESTHETIC (1842). His discovery followed an observation that students under the influence of ether at a party felt no pain when bruising or otherwise injuring themselves.

**LONG, Huey Pierce** (1893–1935), US political leader of La., called the "Kingfish." He entered the state administration in 1918. Governor after a landslide victory in 1928, he put through economic and social reforms, but virtually suspended the democratic process and ruthlessly used his powers of patronage to create what some saw as a semi-fascist system of state government. A US senator from 1931, he attacked President Roosevelt's NEW DEAL policies, advocating his own "share-the-wealth" program and openly proclaiming his presidential ambitions. He was assassinated at Baton Rouge by Dr. Karl Weiss. The "Long machine" dominated La. politics for a generation.

**LONGBOW,** a large bow, about six feet long, generally made of yew. Probably first used in Wales during the late 13th century, it was employed with great effect by the English in the HUNDRED YEARS' WAR and challenged the supremacy of the CROSSBOW until both were superseded by the advent of firearms.

**LONGFELLOW, Henry Wadsworth** (1807 –1882), the most popular US poet of his age. A contemporary of HAWTHORNE at Bowdoin College, he became a professor there and then at Harvard (1836–54). His principal works were *Ballads and Other Poems* (1841) and the narrative poems *Evangeline* (1847), *The Golden Legend* (1851), *The Courtship of Miles Standish* (1858) and above all *The Song of Hiawatha* (1855), which created romantic American legends. Famous individual poems are "The Wreck of the Hesperus" and "Excelsior."

**LONGHI, Pietro** (1702–1785), Venetian painter best known for his small-scale GENRE works of Venetian life, like *The Exhibition of a Rhinoceros* (1750) and *The Family Concert* (1741).

**LONGHORN CATTLE,** a Mexican breed of cattle. It became the basic stock of the US ranch herds during the 19th century. They are known as strong and hardy animals; however they have nearly been bred out of existence in favor of meatier types.

**LONG ISLAND,** island off the SE coast of N.Y., extending E from the mouth of the Hudson R. It is about 118mi long and 12–23mi wide, and covers an area of 1,723sq mi. Brooklyn and Queens Co. at the W end are part of New York City, and many residents of the island work there. Nassau Co. and Suffolk Co., formerly predominantly agricultural, now have much residential and light industrial development. Its beaches and bays make it a popular resort and fishing center.

**LONGITUDE.** See LATITUDE AND LONGITUDE.

**LONG MARCH,** 1934–35, the epic march of the Chinese communists, from Kiangsi in the SE to Shensi in the extreme NW, which saved the movement from extermination by the Nationalist (Kuomintang) forces of CHIANG KAI-SHEK. The communists were surrounded by the Kuomintang. Led by MAO TSE-TUNG, CHOU EN-LAI and LIN-PIAO, the Red Army of some 100,000 broke the trap to begin a 6,000mi trek which took them over 18 mountain ranges and 24 rivers under constant air and land attack by Kuomintang troops and local warlords. Thousands were killed but the heroism and determination of the survivors made the Long March the founding legend of Revolutionary China.

**LONG PARLIAMENT,** English legislative assembly that met between 1640 and 1660. Convened by CHARLES I, it immediately tried to check his power. The conflict culminated in the attempted arrest of John PYM, and the CIVIL WAR (1642), during which the parliament remained in session. In 1648 it was "purged" (see RUMP PARLIAMENT), and in 1653 abolished altogether under the PROTECTORATE. It was briefly reconvened in 1660 prior to the RESTORATION.

**LONSDALE, Dame Kathleen** (1903–1971), British chemist who did pioneering research in the field of X-RAY crystallography. She headed the Depart-

ient of Crystallography at University
College, London (1949–68).

**.OPE DE VEGA.** See VEGA, LOPE DE.

**.OPEZ MATEOS, Adolfo** (1910–1969),
resident of Mexico (1958–64) after being
successful minister of labor (1952–58).
tis presidency was characterized by
grarian reform and a vast industrialization
rogram.

**.OPEZ-MELTON, Nancy** (1957–    ),
JS golfer. She broke the rookie earnings
ecord for men and women in 1977. In 1978
he set an LPGA record with five
onsecutive victories.

**.OPEZ PORTILLO, José** (1920–    ),
resident of Mexico (1976–82), during a
eriod of rapid economic growth, especially
n the energy field, he was notably assertive
n his relationship with the US.

**.ORAN** (*long range navigation*) a
AVIGATION system in which an aircraft
ilot may determine his position by
omparing the arrival times of pulses from
wo pairs of RADIO transmitters. Each pair
ives him enough information to draw a line
f possible positions on a map, the
ntersection of the two lines marking his
rue position.

**.ORCA, Federico García** (1898–1936),
elebrated Spanish poet and dramatist
ispired by his native Andalusia and by
ypsy folklore. He made his reputation with
*ypsy Ballads* (1928) and surrealism
ifluenced *Poet in New York* (published
940), but he returned to folk themes in the
lays *Blood Wedding* (1933), *Yerma*
1935) and *The House of Bernarda Alba*
1936). He was also a talented musician and
heater director. He was murdered by the
Vationalists in the Civil War.

**.ORELEI,** rock on the Rhine R in
iermany, between Koblenz and Bingen. It
ses some 430ft above a point where the
iver narrows. The legend of its river maiden
rho lured boatmen to their death by her
inging is the subject of HEINE's famous
oem, "Die Lorelei."

**.OREN, Sophia** (1934–    ), Italian
creen actress whose combination of
tatuesque beauty and real dramatic ability
on her international acclaim, including an
cademy Award for her performance in
*wo Women* (1961). She married producer
:arlo Ponti.

**.ORENTZ, Pare** (1905–    ), US film
ritic and director, who founded and ran a
overnment documentary film unit,
935–41. *The Plow That Broke The Plains*
1936), on the creation of the DUST BOWL,
nd *The River* (1937), on the TENNESSEE
ALLEY AUTHORITY, were classic and
ifluential documentaries.

**LORENZ, Konrad** (1903–    ), Austrian
zoologist and writer, the father of
ETHOLOGY, awarded for his work the 1973
Nobel Prize for Physiology or Medicine
with FRISCH and TINBERGEN. He is
best-known for his studies of bird behavior
and of human and animal AGGRESSION. His
best known books are *King Solomon's Ring*
(1952) and *On Aggression* (1966).

**LORRE, Peter** (1904–1964), Hungarian-
born actor. He played the child murderer in
the classic German film *M* (1931), made
eight Hollywood films as the oriental
detective Mr. Moto (1937–39), and had key
roles in such memorable films as *The
Maltese Falcon* (1941) and *Casablanca*
(1943).

**LOS ALAMOS,** town in N.M., 25mi NW of
Santa Fe. It grew up around the scientific
laboratory (1943) where the world's first
atomic and hydrogen bombs were
developed. Pop 11,039.

**LOS ANGELES,** city in S Cal., third largest
in the US. It is a sprawling city of some
464sq mi dominated by freeways and the
automobile, and the center of a metropolitan area with a population of over 7 million.
Situated between sea and mountains, it has
no extremes of temperature, which average
55°F in January and 73°F in July. It is the
third largest industrial center in the US,
producing among other things aircraft,
electrical equipment, automobiles, glass,
furniture, rubber, canned fish and refined
oils (but industrialization has made smog a
serious problem). It is the world capital of
the motion-picture and television industry
(see HOLLYWOOD) and also a distribution
and commercial center for the nearby
mining regions, oilfields and rich farm
areas. Its port, San Pedro, handles more
tonnage than any other US Pacific port, and
accommodates a large fishing fleet.
Tourism is another source of wealth. The
city is dominated by fine buildings,
including a number by Frank Lloyd
WRIGHT. It has several museums, many fine
churches and libraries, and four universities. Taken from the Mexicans in 1846, it
was incorporated in 1850. It was linked with
the transcontinental railroad system in the
1870s and 1880s. Oil was discovered in the
region in the 1890s. Pop. 2,966,763.

**LOSEY, Joseph** (1909–    ), US-born
film director. Blacklisted during the
McCarthy era, he migrated to England
(1952) where he made several memorable
films with actor Dirk Bogarde and writer
Harold Pinter, including *The Servant*
(1963) and *Accident* (1967). He also
directed *The Damned* (1961) and *The
Go-Between* (1971).

**LOST COLONY**, an English settlement (1587) on Roanoke Island off the coast of N.C., which disappeared without trace. It was founded by 117 settlers led by John White, sponsored by Sir Walter RALEIGH. Supplies ran out and White visited England for help. When he returned in 1590, the colony had disappeared, possibly having been wiped out by hostile Indians.

**LOST GENERATION**, a term for the US writers of the post-WWI generation, coined in a remark by Gertrude STEIN to Ernest HEMINGWAY. Besides him they included Scott FITZGERALD, John DOS PASSOS, E. E. CUMMINGS and others. Their ideals shattered by the war, they felt alienated from the materialism of America in the 1920s, and many lived bohemian expatriate lives in Paris.

**LOUDSPEAKER**, or **speaker**, device to convert electrical impulses into sound. It commonly comprises a rigid conical diaphragm attached to a coil held such that it may move backward and forward; within the cylinder of the coil is a fixed permanent magnet. Changes in the current supplied to the coil alter its magnetic field so that it, and the cone, vibrate to produce the compression waves that are SOUND. (See also AMPLIFIER; ELECTRICITY; ELECTRO-MAGNETISM; MAGNETISM.) HIGH FIDELITY sets use two or more loudspeakers of different sizes for more accurate reproduction.

**LOUIS**, name of 18 kings of France. **Louis I** (778–840), Holy Roman Emperor 814–40, known as "the Pious." He was the third son of CHARLEMAGNE. He divided the empire among his sons, thereby contributing to its fragmentation, but laying the foundations of the state of France. **Louis II** (846–879), reigned 877–79. **Louis III** (c863–882), reigned 879–82. As king of N France he defeated Norman invaders. **Louis IV** (c921–954), reigned 936–54. He was called "Transmarinus" because of his childhood exile in England. **Louis V** (c966–987), reigned 986–87. The last Carolingian ruler of France, he was known as "the Sluggard." **Louis VI** (1081–1137), reigned 1108–37. He subdued the robber barons around Paris, granted privileges to the towns and aided the Church. He engaged in war against Henry I of England (1104–13 and 1116–20). **Louis VII** (c1120–1180), reigned 1137–80. He joined the second Crusade (1147–49) in defiance of a papal interdict. From 1157 onwards, Louis was at war with Henry II of England who had married Louis' former wife, Eleanor of Aquitaine. **Louis VIII** (1187–1226), reigned 1223–26. Nicknamed "the Lion," he was a great soldier and was at first successful in his attempts to aid the barons rebelling against King John of England. **Louis IX, Saint** (1214–1270), reigned 1226–70. He repelled an invasion by Henry III of England (1242), and led the sixth Crusade (1248), but was defeated and captured in Egypt and had to be ransomed. In 1270 he led another crusade, but died of plague after reaching N Africa. A just ruler, he was regarded as an ideal Christian king and was canonized in 1297. His feast day is Aug. 25. **Louis X** (1289–1316), reigned 1314–16, a period in which the nobility reasserted their strength. **Louis XI** (1423–1483), reigned 1461–83. A cruel and unscrupulous king, he had plotted against his father for the throne, but unified most of France. **Louis XII** (1462–1515), reigned 1498–1515. Nicknamed "Father of the People," he was a popular ruler who inaugurated reforms in finance and justice and was ambitious for territorial gains. **Louis XIII** (1601–1643), reigned 1610–43. A weak king, he was greatly influenced by his chief minister Cardinal RICHELIEU. **Louis XIV** (1638–1715), reigned 1643–1715, known as "Louis the Great" and "the Sun King." The archetypal absolute monarch, he built the great palace at VERSAILLES. "The state is myself," he is said to have declared. His able ministers, MAZARIN and COLBERT, strengthened France with their financial reforms. But Louis squandered money in such escapades as the War of DEVOLUTION (1667–68) and the War of the SPANISH SUCCESSION (1701–13), which broke the military power of France. **Louis XV** (1710–1774), reigned 1715–74, nicknamed "the Well-Beloved." He was influenced by Cardinal Fleury until the cardinal's death in 1743. A weak king dependent on mistresses (especially Madame de POMPADOUR), his involvement in foreign wars ran up enormous debts. **Louis XVI** (1754–1793), reigned 1774–92. Although he accepted the advice of his ministers TURGOT and NECKER on the need for social and political reform, Louis was not strong enough to overcome the opposition of his court and his queen, MARIE ANTOINETTE. This led to the outbreak of the FRENCH REVOLUTION in 1789 with the formation of the National Assembly and the storming of the Bastille. In 1791 Louis attempted to escape but was brought back to Paris and guillotined on Jan. 21, 1793. **Louis XVII** (1785–1795), son of Louis XVI, king in name only. He was imprisoned in 1793 and was reported dead in 1795. **Louis XVIII** (1755–1824), brother of Louis XVI. He escaped from France in 1791. For more than 20 years he remained in exile, but after the final defeat of Napoleon in the Battle of WATERLOO (1815), he became firmly stablished. He proclaimed a liberal constitution, but· on his death the reactionary Ultraroyalists gained control under Charles X.

**LOUIS, Joe** (1914–1981), known as the "Brown Bomber," heavyweight boxing champion of the world 1937–49. Louis, who defended his title 25 times, was only ever beaten three times, finally by Rocky MARCIANO.

**LOUISE, Lake,** in Banff National Park, SW Alberta, Canada. It is sheltered by the Rockies and is a popular tourist center.

Name of state: Louisiana
Capital: Baton Rouge
Statehood: April 30, 1812 (18th state)
Familiar name: Pelican State
Area: 48,523sq mi
Population: 4,203,972
Elevation: Highest— 535ft, Driskill Mountain. Lowest—5ft below sea level, at New Orleans
Motto: Union, Justice and Confidence
State flower: Magnolia
State bird: Brown pelican
State tree: Bald cypress
State song: "Give Me Louisiana"

**LOUISIANA,** state, S central US, on the Gulf of Mexico, at the mouth of the Mississippi R, bounded to the E by Miss., and to the W by Tex., and to the N by Ark.

**Land.** Louisiana can be divided into three geographical regions: the E and W Gulf coastal plains, and between them the Mississippi alluvial plain. The two coastal plains are mainly composed of rolling hills and prairie. The flat and fertile alluvial plain extends into the Mississippi delta which covers about a third of the state's land area. Louisiana has long, hot and humid summers, and brief cool winters.

**People.** About two-thirds of Louisiana's population live in urban areas, about one-third of the population is black. The port of New Orleans is the largest city. The N of the state is a Protestant Anglo-Saxon area, but the people of the S are descended from French and Spanish settlers, and this has clearly influenced the area's culture.

**Economy.** Louisiana is the nation's leading producer of rice and sweet potatoes. Livestock and dairy products are of importance, as are soybeans, cotton, corn and sugarcane. Louisiana is also one of the country's largest producers of petroleum; natural gas, sulfur and salt are also produced. The most important industries are chemicals, foodstuffs, paper and paper products and electronic and transportation equipment. Tourism and commercial fishing are also important.

**History.** In the 18th century, Louisiana was controlled alternately by the French and the Spanish, but in 1803 was sold to the US as part of the LOUISIANA PURCHASE. Louisiana was admitted to the Union in 1812 and quickly prospered. Her population increased almost tenfold between 1812 and the Civil War; but at the outbreak of the war, half the population was composed of slaves. The pre-Civil War period saw the heyday of the great Mississippi steamboats. Louisiana's prosperity, however, was checked by the Civil War and the harsh policies of RECONSTRUCTION. The discovery of oil and natural gas early in the 20th century brought new investment to Louisiana, but she remained basically a poor state, particularly during the 1930s depression. Governors Huey P. Long in the 1920s and Earl K. Long (elected 1948 and 1956) ran the state in a notoriously monarchistic manner but from populist platforms. Since WWII, industrialization has increased markedly, and in the 1970s the population grew by more than 15%. In 1980, the first Republican governor in more than a century was inaugurated.

**LOUISIANA PURCHASE,** the huge territory purchased by the US from France in 1803. It stretched from the Mississippi R to the Rockies, and from the Canadian border to the Gulf of Mexico, some 828,000sq mi. Its acquisition more than doubled the area of what was then the US.

From 1762 the old French province of Louisiana, roughly where Louisiana is today, had been held by Spain. In 1800 Napoleon persuaded the Spanish to return the province to France. President Jefferson received reports of this with alarm, realizing that Napoleon hoped to establish an empire in North America. Jefferson instructed Livingston and Monroe to purchase New Orleans and other strategic parts of the Louisiana province from France. Much to their surprise, Napoleon, who was expecting renewed war with England, in April 1803 offered to sell the huge Louisiana Territory to the US, and the envoys quickly accepted the offer for a total price of $15 million. The purchase had greatly exceeded Jefferson's instructions, and there was some opposition from US businessmen, but most Americans saw the doubling of their territory as a triumph.

**LOUIS PHILIPPE** (1773–1850), king of the French 1830–48. Exiled from France in 1793, he traveled in Europe and the US until 1815, when he was accepted as a compromise candidate for the crown. As king from 1830 he was unwilling to extend the voting franchise, and the revolution of Feb., 1848, led to his abdication.

**LOURDES,** center of Roman Catholic pilgrimage, in SW France where, in 1858, the Virgin is said to have appeared to a 14-year-old peasant girl, now ST. BERNADETTE. Lourdes is visited by some three million pilgrims annually.

**LOURENÇO MARQUES.** See MAPUTO.

**LOUSE.** See LICE.

**L'OUVERTURE, Toussaint.** See TOUSSAINT L'OUVERTURE.

**LOUVRE,** historic palace in Paris, mostly built during the reign of LOUIS XIV. Now one of the world's largest and most famous art museums, its treasures include paintings by Rembrandt, Rubens, Titian and Leonardo da Vinci, whose *Mona Lisa* is there. Other masterpieces in its collection are the painting *Arrangement in Gray and Black*, called "Whistler's Mother," and the famous ancient greek statues, the *Venus de Milo* and *Winged Victory of Samothrace*.

**LOVEBIRDS,** eight or nine species in a genus of African PARROTS, *Agapornis*, so-called because of their close pair-bond and the frequency with which paired birds preen each other.

**LOVE CANAL,** site of a toxic-waste dumping ground in Niagara Falls, N.Y., used by the Hooker Chemicals and Plastics Corp. from the 1940s. In 1953, Hooker sold the 16-acre tract to the local Board of Education for $1; the land was subsequently developed with a school and surrounding residential housing. From 1976, families began to report symptoms of chemical poisoning, as chemicals bubbled up out of the ground; in one (later controversial) study done in 1980, 30% of a sample of the population was found to have chromosome damage. In 1978, N.Y. state evacuated 237 families; in 1980, President Jimmy Carter declared a state of emergency in the area, and 710 families were relocated by the government. Hooker Chemicals has disclaimed any responsibility in the case.

**LOVECRAFT, H(oward) P(hillips)** (1890–1937), US writer of horror tales and science-fiction stories. His works include *The Outsider and Others* (1939) and *Beyond the Wall of Sleep* (1943).

**LOVEJOY,** surname of two American brothers, both dedicated advocates of ABOLITIONISM. **Elijah Parish Lovejoy** (1802–1837) published newspapers in St Louis and in Alton, Ill., advocating abolitionism. He was killed while defending his press from a mob. **Owen Lovejoy** (1811–1864), pastor, and later abolitionist leader in Illinois. A supporter of Abraham Lincoln, he was elected to Congress in 1856 and constantly denounced slavery there.

**LOVELACE, Richard** (1618–1657?), English Royalist soldier and one of the CAVALIER POETS. His poems, in two volumes, entitled *Lucasta*, were published in 1649 and 1660. They are noted at their best for a fine melodic line.

**LOVELL, James Arthur, Jr.** (1928– ) US astronaut. He first flew in Gemini 7 (1965) and Gemini 12 (1966) before joining Apollo 8 (1968), the first manned flight around the moon. In 1970 he commanded the nearly disastrous Apollo 13, when an explosion in the spacecraft prevented a moon landing.

**LOVELL, Sir (Alfred) Bernard** (1913– ), British astronomer who was a pioneer in the field of RADIO ASTRONOMY. As director of the Jodrell Bank Experimental Station (now Nuffield Radio Astronomy Laboratories) he was instrumental in constructing one of the world's largest steerable radio telescopes (1957).

**LOW, Juliette Gordon** (1860–1927), founder of the Girl Scouts in the US. She organized the first troop in her home town, Savannah, Ga., in 1912. By the time of her death there were 140,000 Girl Scouts in the US.

**LOW, Seth** (1850–1916), US politician and educator. Born in Brooklyn, N.Y., he was president of Columbia College 1889–1901 and mayor of New York from 1901–03.

**LOW, Sir David** (1891–1963), New Zealand-born British political cartoonist whose work appeared for decades in the London *Star* and *Evening Standard*. He created brilliant caricatures of British political figures and foreign dictators, notably Hitler and Stalin.

**LOW COUNTRIES.** See BELGIUM; NETHERLANDS; LUXEMBOURG.

**LOWELL, Amy** (1874–1925), US critic and poet of the IMAGIST school. Her collections of verse include *Sword Blade and Poppy Seed* (1914), *Men, Women and Ghosts* (1916) and *What's O'Clock* (1925), which was awarded the Pulitzer prize.

**LOWELL, Francis Cabot** (1775–1817), US cotton manufacturer. In 1812 he founded the Boston Manufacturing Company—the first mill in the US to convert raw cotton into finished cloth in a single plant.

**LOWELL, James Russell** (1819–1891), US poet, editor, essayist and diplomat. His best poems, including the famous *Vision of Sir Launfal* (1848), were written before his wife's death in 1853. His reputation as a political satirist was made by the witty *Bigelow Papers* (1848 and 1867). In 1855 he became professor of modern languages at Harvard, and was minister to England 1877–85.

**LOWELL, Percival** (1855–1916), US astronomer and writer who predicted the existence of and initiated the search for PLUTO; but who is best known for his championing the theory (now discarded) that the "canals" of MARS were signs of an irrigation system built by an intelligent race.

**LOWELL, Robert** (1917–1977), US poet and playwright. For his collection *Lord Weary's Castle* (1946) he won the Pulitzer Prize. Later books, *The Mills of the Kavanaughs* (1951), the autobiographical *Life Studies* (1959) and *For the Union Dead* (1964), established his reputation as a major poet. His dramatic trilogy *The Old Glory* was published in 1965. His free adaptations of Greek tragedy and various European poets brought him acclaim as a translator.

**LOWIE, Robert H.** (1883–1957), Austrian-born US anthropologist who was best known for his studies of the North American Indian, *The Crow Indians* (1935) and *Indians of the Plains* (1954). His classic theoretical studies were *Primitive Society* (1920) and *Social Organization* (1948).

**LOWRY, Malcolm** (1909–1957), English novelist. While living on the coast of British Columbia (1940–54) he published his greatest work, *Under the Volcano* (1947), concerned in part with the problem of alcoholism, which eventually proved fatal to the author. Two volumes of short stories were published posthumously.

**LOYALTY PROBES,** a series of government investigations, 1947–1951, to discover and root out federal employees who might be actual or potential traitors. The investigations were made possible by an executive order of President Harry S. Truman. The means used were distasteful and probably unconstitutional (including, for example, accusations by unnamed informers), but the president considered the order a necessary concession to the nation's fanatic Communist hunters.

**LOYOLA, Saint Ignatius of.** See IGNATIUS OF LOYOLA, SAINT.

**LSD,** lysergic acid diethylamide, a HALLUCINOGENIC DRUG based on ERGOT alkaloids. It may lead to psychotic reaction and bizarre behavior.

**LUBITSCH, Ernst** (1892–1947), German film director, noted chiefly for the sophisticated comedies he made after his emigration to Hollywood in 1923. Among his films are *Forbidden Paradise* (1924), *Ninotchka* (1939), *The Merry Widow* (1939), *The Shop Around the Corner* (1940) and *Heaven Can Wait* (1943).

**LUBLIN,** historic city in SE Poland, on the Bystrzyca R. An important trade center since the 13th century, it is now a manufacturing town and a transport hub. Lublin was the site of a concentration camp during World War II, and served briefly as the Polish capital after the war, as the provisional seat of the Polish Committee of National Liberation. Pop. 235,900.

**LUBRICATION,** the introduction of a thin film of lubricant—usually a semiviscous fluid—between two surfaces moving relative to each other, in order to minimize FRICTION and abrasive wear. In particular, BEARINGS are lubricated in engines and other machinery. Liquid lubricants are most common, usually PETROLEUM fractions, being cheap, easy to introduce, and good at cooling the parts. The VISCOSITY is tailored to the load, being made high enough to maintain the film yet not so high that power is lost. Multigrade oils cover a range of viscosity. The viscosity index represents the constancy of the viscosity over the usual temperature range—a desirable feature. Synthetic oils, including SILICONES, are used for high-temperature and other special applications. Greases—normally oils thickened with soaps, fats or waxes—are preferred where the lubricant has to stay in place without being sealed in. Solid lubricants, usually applied with a binder, are soft, layered solids including graphite, molybdenite, talc and boron nitride. TEFLON, with its uniquely low coefficient of friction, is used for self-lubricating bearings. Rarely air or another gaseous substance is used as a lubricant. Additives to liquid lubricants include antioxidants, detergents, pour-point depressants (increasing low-temperature fluidity), and polymers to improve the viscosity index.

**LUCAN** (39–65 AD), Marcus Annaeus Lucanus, Roman poet best known for his *Bellum Civile* (or, incorrectly, *Pharsalia*), an epic poem on the clash between Julius Caesar and Pompey. He was a protégé of Nero's but eventually aroused the latter's jealousy. Lucan joined the Pisonian conspiracy against Nero and when this failed, committed suicide.

**LUCAS, George** (1944– ), US director, screenwriter, and producer whose *Star Wars* (1977) set box-office attendance records. His film *American Graffiti* (1973) was also extremely successful.

**LUCAS VAN LEYDEN** (c1494–1533), foremost Dutch painter of his day. A noted engraver and printmaker, he was as highly regarded as his acquaintance DÜRER. He painted biblical themes, such as *Lot and His Daughters* (c1509); some of his work foreshadows that of the great GENRE painters.

**LUCE, Clare Boothe** (1903– ), US dramatist, editor and politician. She worked for *Vogue* magazine and was managing editor of *Vanity Fair* 1933–34, marrying Henry LUCE in 1935. Her play *The Women* (1936), was the first of several successes. She served in Congress 1943–47 and was appointed US ambassador to Italy 1953–56, the first American woman to hold high diplomatic office. Named ambassador to Brazil, in 1959, she resigned when the appointment was attacked in the Senate.

**LUCE, Henry Robinson** (1898–1967), US editor and publisher of *Time*, which he founded with Briton Hadden in 1923. He also produced *Fortune* (1930), *Life* (1936) and *Sports Illustrated* (1954), as well as many books, radio series and newsreels.

**LUCERNE** (or Luzern), historic capital city of Lucerne canton, on the NW shore of Lake Lucerne in central Switzerland. It contains a number of 15th- and 16th-century houses, along with several medieval covered bridges. It is a major resort center, serves a rich dairying area and also has some light industries. Pop 69,879.

**LUCIAN** (c125–c190 AD), Syrian-Greek satirist. Among his best-known works are *Dialogues of the Gods*, a parody of mythology; *Dialogues of the Dead*, a biting satire on human vanities; and the *True History*, a lampoon of fantastic travellers' tales, which influenced RABELAIS and Jonathan SWIFT.

**LUCIANO, Charles** (1896–1962), Sicilian-born US gangster who received the nickname "Lucky" when he escaped from a gangland attempt on his life. Arrested over 25 times on a variety of felony charges, he was convicted only once, on vice charges (1936). His 30–50-year prison sentence was eventually commuted by N.Y. Gov. Thomas E. DEWEY on the condition that he leave the US; he returned to Italy in 1946.

**LUCRETIUS** (c95–55 BC), Roman poet, the author of *De rerum natura*, and the last and greatest classical exponent of ATOMISM. His description of atoms in the void and his vision of the progress of man suffered undeserved neglect on account of his antireligious reputation.

**LUDDITES**, bands of English textile workers who destroyed labor-saving textile machinery in the early 19th century. They were protesting against unemployment and low wages which resulted wherever the new machinery was introduced and also against the poor quality of goods produced on the machines. Repressive government measures and an improving economic climate combined to end the rioting by 1816.

**LUDENDORFF, Erich** (1865–1937), German general who with Hindenburg did much to defeat the invading Russian armies in WWI, particularly at TANNENBERG. He was responsible for much German policy 1917–18 and for the request of an armistice in 1918. After the war he led a nationalist movement; he took part in Hitler's abortive coup in Munich in 1923, but severed relations with him soon after.

**LUDLUM, Robert** (1927– ), US author. His best-selling novels of international conspiracy and suspense include *The Osterman Weekend* (1972) and *The Bourne Identity* (1980).

**LUDWIG, Emil** (1881–1948), German writer of plays, history, and biography including *Goethe* (1920) and *Napoleon* (1924).

**LUENING, Otto** (1900– ), US composer, conductor and flutist known primarily for his innovative use of taped and electronic music both alone and in combination with live performance, as in *Gargoyles* (1961) for violin and synthesizer.

**LUFTWAFFE** (German: air arm), title of the German air force. Formed in 1935 under Hitler, it was commanded by Herman GOERING during WWII.

**LUGOSI, Bela** (1888–1956), Hungarian-born US actor who appeared as Dracula in a 1927 Broadway production and a classic 1931 film. He subsequently was typecast as a horror-film villain in such movies as *Mark of the Vampire* (1935) and *The Wolf Man* (1941).

**LUKACS, Gyorgy** (1885–1971), Hungarian-born leading Marxist literary critic. He was made professor of aesthetics at Budapest U. in 1945. After the 1956 Hungarian uprising, Lukacs fell from political favor. Among his major works are *Studies in European Realism* (1946) and *The Historical Novel* (1955).

**LUKE, Saint**, by tradition the author of the third GOSPEL and its sequel, the Acts of the Apostles. Luke was a Gentile and worked as a physician, probably in Antioch. He was influenced by his friend, St. Paul, whom he accompanied on his missionary journeys. The Gospel, written for Gentiles, claims to be based on eyewitness accounts.

**LUKS, George Benjamin** (1867–1933), US realist painter, one of the ASHCAN SCHOOL. Primarily a painter of figures, his bold and vigorous style in such works as *The Wrestlers* (1905) may have owed something to his work as a cartoonist.

**LULLY, Jean-Baptiste** (1632–1687), Italian-born French composer who became Louis XIV's favorite musician. He wrote much stage music, for MOLIÈRE among others, and his operas, particularly *Alceste* (1674) and *Armide* (1686), founded a French operatic tradition.

**LUMBER,** cut wood, especially when prepared for use ("dressed"). Lumbering, the extraction of timber from the forest, is a major industry in the US, which still has vast natural forests. In world timber production, the USSR is first, followed by the US, Japan, and Canada. The demand for lumber is vast; it takes as many as 20 trees to make a ton of paper and the annual US paper production exceeds 35 million tons. The forests would soon be depleted without modern conservation and reforestation programs.

Trees used for lumber are classed as either softwoods or hardwoods. Softwoods, which thrive in cold regions, are the evergreen conifers such as fir, pine, cedar and spruce. Hardwoods, which thrive in temperate regions, include the deciduous trees like oak, birch, aspen and beech. The softwoods, used in building, make up 75% of the US timber market.

In the vast softwood forests of the US lumbering has become a mechanized industry, using power saws to fell and cut to size the trees, and cable. Since forests are often located in inaccessible tractor winches to drag logs to a central clearing by cable. Since forests are often located in inaccessible regions, new roads and new railroads may have to be built to transport the logs. Logs are often floated down mountain streams to broader rivers and lakes on whose banks sawmills are often located. Great masses of logs can be towed by tug down river, inside huge floating collars or booms. Once at the mill they may be stored until needed in a huge log pond, or millpond, protected by the water from fire and disease. After sorting, the logs are fed onto a conveyor belt and into the mill. Each log is clamped to a carriage and fed back and forth against a vertical bandsaw. The boards then pass to an edger, to remove the bark, and a trimmer which cuts them to standard lengths. Other logs are cut into sheets or veneer, for plywood. The newly-cut wood, still green with moisture, is then seasoned (dried) oefore it is used commercially. (See FORESTRY; PAPER; TREE.)

**LUMIÈ, Louis** (1864–1948), French pioneer of motion PHOTOGRAPHY who, with his brother Auguste (1862–1954), invented an early motion-picture system (patented 1895), the *cinématographe*; and made what is regarded as the first movie (1895).

**LUMINESCENCE,** the nonthermal emission of ELECTROMAGNETIC RADIATION, particularly LIGHT, from a PHOSPHOR. Including both fluorescence and phosphorescence (distinguished according to how long emission persists after excitation has ceased, in fluorescence emission ceasing within 10ns but continuing much longer in phosphorescence), particular types of luminescence are named for the mode of excitation. Thus in photoluminescence, PHOTONS are absorbed by the phosphor and lower-energy radiations emitted; in CHEMILUMINESCENCE the energy source is a chemical reaction; cathodoluminescence is energized by cathode rays (ELECTRONS), and BIOLUMINESCENCE occurs in certain biochemical reactions. (See also ELECTROLUMINESCENCE.)

**LUMUMBA, Patrice Emergy** (1925–1961), first prime minister of the Republic of the Congo (Zaire). He negotiated independence from Belgium (1960). Soon after, the army mutinied and Katanga seceded. Following his dismissal by President Joseph Kasavubu in Sept. 1960, he was arrested by General Joseph Mobutu and killed in mysterious circumstances some time later.

**LUNAR ORBITER MISSIONS,** a series of seven unmanned US probes, launched in 1966–67, that went into orbit around the moon, providing thousands of photographs of potential landing sites for the unmanned Surveyor and manned Apollo missions. Lunar Orbiter 1, launched Aug. 10, 1966, made the first photograph of the earth as seen from the moon.

**LUNGS,** in vertebrates, the (usually) two largely airfilled organs in the CHEST concerned with RESPIRATION, the absorption of OXYGEN from and release of carbon dioxide into atmospheric air. In man, the right lung has three lobes and the left, two. Their surfaces are separated from the chest wall by two layers of *pleura*, with a little fluid between them; this allows free movement of the lungs and enables the forces of expansion of the chest wall and DIAPHRAGM to fill them with air. Air is drawn into the TRACHEA via MOUTH or NOSE;

the trachea divides into the BRONCHI which divide repeatedly until the terminal airsacs or *alveoli* are reached. In the alveoli, air is brought into close contact with unoxygenated BLOOD in lung CAPILLARIES; the BLOOD CIRCULATION through these comes from the right ventricle and returns to the left atrium of the HEART. Disorders of ventilation or of perfusion with blood leads to abnormalities in blood levels of carbon dioxide and oxygen. Lung DISEASES include ASTHMA, BRONCHITIS, PNEUMONIA, PLEURISY, PNEUMOTHORAX, PNEUMOCONIOSIS, EMBOLISM, CANCER and TUBERCULOSIS; lungs may also be involved in several systemic diseases (e.g., sarcoidosis, LUPUS ERYTHEMATOSUS). Symptoms of lung disease include COUGH, sputum, blood in the sputum, shortness of breath and wheeze. Sudden failure of breathing requires prompt ARTIFICIAL RESPIRATION. Chest X RAY and estimations of blood gas levels and of various lung volumes aid diagnosis.

**LUNT AND FONTANNE,** famous US acting couple. Alfred Lunt (1892–1977) and Lynn Fontanne (c1887–  ) married in 1922 and co-starred in plays in Europe and the US for nearly 40 years. Best known for sophisticated comedies such as COWARD's *Design for Living* (1933), they also appeared in classics such as *The Taming of The Shrew* in 1935, and in modern works, mostly DÜRRENMATT's *The Visit*, with which they opened their own theater in 1958.

**LURIA, Aleksandr Romanovich** (1902–1977), Soviet neuropsychologist. A world-renowned authority on the human brain, he made important advances in brain surgery and postsurgical restoration of brain function. Among his books were *Higher Cortical Function in Man* (tr. 1966; rev. ed. tr. 1977) and *The Working Brain* (tr. 1974).

**LURIA, Salvador Edward** (1912–  ), Italian-born US biologist who shared with DELBRÜCK and HERSHEY the 1969 Nobel Prize for Physiology or Medicine for research on BACTERIOPHAGES.

**LUTE,** fretted stringed instrument related to the guitar, played by plucking the strings with the fingers. It was perhaps the most popular single instrument between 1400 and 1700, both for solo playing and as accompaniment to songs and madrigals; the great 16th-century composer DOWLAND wrote mostly for the lute.

**LUTHER, Martin** (1483–1546), German REFORMATION leader and founder of LUTHERANISM. Following a religious experience he became an Augustinian friar, was ordained 1507, and visited Rome (1510),

where he was shocked by the worldliness of the papal court. While professor of Scripture at Wittenberg U. (from 1512) he wrestled with the problem of personal salvation, concluding that it comes from the unmerited grace of God, available through faith alone (see JUSTIFICATION BY FAITH). When Johann TETZEL toured Saxony 1517 selling papal INDULGENCES, Luther denounced the practice in his historic 95 Theses, for which he was fiercely attacked, especially by Johann ECK. In 1520 he published *To the Christian Nobility of the German Nation.* It denied the pope's final authority to determine the interpretation of Scripture, declaring instead the priesthood of all believers; and it rejected papal claims to political authority, arguing for national churches governed by secular rulers. Luther denied the special spiritual authority of priests, advocated clerical marriage and denied the doctrine of TRANSUBSTANTIATION, adhering to CONSUBSTANTIATION. In Dec. 1520 he publicly burned a papal bull of condemnation and a copy of the canon law; he was excommunicated 1521. Summoned by Emperor Charles V to renounce his heresies at the Diet of WORMS (1521), he refused, traditionally with the words, "Here I stand: I can do no other." He was outlawed but, protected by Frederick III of Saxony, he retired to the WARTBURG castle. There, in six months, he translated the New Testament into German and began work on the Old. His hymns have been translated into many languages, and he wrote two catechisms (1529), the basis of Lutheranism. Against ERASMUS he wrote *The Bondage of the Will* (1525). He directed the reform movement from Wittenberg, aiming to moderate more extreme elements (see ANABAPTISTS), and opposed the PEASANTS' WAR, condoning princely repression of the revolt. In 1525 he married a former nun; they had six children.

**LUTHERAN CHURCHES,** the churches adhering to LUTHERANISM and springing from the German REFORMATION. From the beginning they were state churches ruled by the local princes; national Lutheran churches also formed in the Scandinavian countries. (See also THIRTY YEARS' WAR.) In 1817 Frederick William III of Prussia enforced union between the Prussian Lutheran and Reformed Churches, provoking the first of several schisms to form free Lutheran churches. A united German Lutheran Church was formed in 1949. Lutheran migrants to the US and Canada formed numerous churches now merged into three: the American LUTHERAN CHURCH, the LUTHERAN CHURCH IN AMERICA and the LUTHERAN CHURCH—MISSOURI SYNOD. The Lutheran World Federation has about 53 million members. Lutherans have played a major formative role in modern theology.

**LUTHERANISM**, Protestant doctrinal system based on the teachings of Martin LUTHER. It regards the Bible as the only source of doctrine; stresses JUSTIFICATION BY FAITH alone; and recognizes only two SACRAMENTS: baptism and Holy Communion (see also CONSUBSTANTIATION). Luther's two catechisms (1529) and the AUGSBURG CONFESSION (1530) were collected with other basic standards in the *Book of Concord* (1580), consolidating Lutheranism against both Roman Catholicism and CALVINISM. (See also PIETISM.)

**LUTHULI, Albert John** (1898–1967), Rhodesian-born Christian leader in South Africa, an unyielding opponent of APARTHEID. A Zulu chief, he was elected president of the AFRICAN NATIONAL CONGRESS (1952). In 1959 he was confined to his village by the South African government. He won the 1960 Nobel Peace Prize.

**LUTOSLAWSKI, Witold** (1913–    ), Polish composer whose work allowed for improvisation on the part of the individual members of the orchestra (as in *Venetian Games*) or chorus (as in *Three Poems by Henri Michaux*). He is best known for his *Little Suite* (1951), *Mourning Music* (1958) and *Concerto for Orchestra* (1954).

**LUXEMBOURG, Grand Duchy of**, constitutional monarchy of W Europe, bounded by West Germany, Belgium and France. It is about 55mi long and 35mi wide. Luxembourg extends into the rugged ARDENNES upland in the N; the agriculturally fertile "Good Country" is in the S lowlands; the SE region along the Moselle R produces wine and fruit. The industrial SW, rich in iron ore, provides the bulk of the national income. Agriculture and tourism are other major industries. The people, chiefly Roman Catholic, speak French, German and Letzeburgesch, the local dialect. Formerly including the Luxembourg province of Belgium, the country was a duchy of the medieval empire; a Hapsburg possession 1482–1795; and a French possession 1795–1815. In 1815 it became a Grand Duchy under the King of the Netherlands. The present ruling house of Nassau came to the throne in 1890. Luxembourg formed an economic union with Belgium in 1922; it is a member of NATO and since the 1950s a member of BENELUX and the COMMON MARKET.

**LUXEMBURG, Rosa** (1871?–1919), Polish-born German Marxist revolutionary, cofounder with Karl LIEBKNECHT of the SPARTACUS LEAGUE, Germany's first communist party. In the 1918 Berlin revolution she edited their journal, *Red Flag*. She and Liebknecht were arrested and murdered in 1919.

**LUXOR**, city in Upper Egypt on the E bank of the Nile R on part of the site of the ancient city of THEBES (see also KARNAK). Its famous temple of Amon, built by AMENHOTEP III, is 623ft long and has a colonnade and hall of hypostyle columns. Pop 84,600.

**LUYTENS, Sir Edwin Landseer** (1869–1944), British architect and President of the Royal Academy. A designer of Edwardian country homes, he was commissioned as planning supervisor of New Delhi, the new Indian capital, where his design for the Viceroy's residence (1915–30) combined classical and Mogul Indian features.

**LUZ, Arturo** (1926–    ), Philippine artist equally adept at painting and sculpture. His neorealist paintings contain colors of his own invention, positioned uniquely. His sculpting is sophisticated and semiabstract, featuring marble, metal, hardwood and even glass creations.

**LVOV**, industrial city and transportation center in the W Ukraine, USSR. A historic university city and cultural center, Lvov was founded in 1256 and has belonged to Poland, Austria, and the USSR, serving as the capital of Austrian Galicia. Its industries include machinery, textiles and oil refining. Pop 553,000.

**LVOV, Prince Georgi Yevgenyevich** (1861–1925), Russian liberal statesman, prime minister of the first provisional government 1917 (see RUSSIAN REVOLUTION). After the Bolshevik Revolution he fled to Paris.

**LYCEUM MOVEMENT**, US associations for popular ADULT EDUCATION, influential in the 19th century. The first was founded by Josiah Holbrook in 1826 in Millbury, Mass. (See also CHAUTAUQUA MOVEMENT.)

**LYDIA**, ancient kingdom of W Asia Minor, of legendary wealth. The Lydians invented metal coins in the 7th century BC. During the 6th century BC its magnificent capital, Sardis, was the cultural center of a growing empire. Its zenith came under CROESUS, but he was defeated c546 BC by Cyrus of Persia.

**LYELL, Sir Charles** (1797–1875), British geologist and writer whose most important work was the promotion of geological UNIFORMITARIANISM (originally developed by James HUTTON) as an alternative to the CATASTROPHISM of CUVIER and others. The prime expression of these views came in his *Principles of Geology* (1830–33). His other works included the *Elements of Geology* (1838), and *Geological Evidence of the Antiquity of Man* (1863). Here he expressed guarded support for DARWIN's theory of evolution.

**LYLY, John** (c1554–1606), English author best known for his *Euphues* (part I, 1578; II, 1580), a prose romance in a highly artificial and allusive style (see EUPHUISM). Lyly also wrote elegant comedies on classical themes, and was influential on other Elizabethan playwrights.

**LYME DISEASE**, a temporary form of arthritis, typically inflaming a knee joint. It is accompanied by fever and a red, ring-shaped skin rash commonly surrounding what is thought to be a tick bite. The cause of the disease is believed to be a yet-unidentified bacterium transmitted by ticks. The disease is named for Lyme, Conn., where it was first described in 1974.

**LYMPH**, fluid which drains from extracellular fluid via lymph vessels and nodes (glands). Important node sites are the neck, axilla, groin, CHEST and ABDOMEN. Fine ducts carry lymph to the nodes, which are filled with lymphocytes and reticulum cells. These act as a filter, particularly for infected debris or PUS and for CANCER cells, which often spread by lymph. The lymphocytes are also concerned with development of IMMUNITY. From nodes, lymph may drain to other nodes or directly into the major thoracic duct which returns it to the BLOOD. Specialized lymph ducts or lacteals carry FAT absorbed in the GASTROINTESTINAL TRACT to the thoracic duct. In addition, there are several areas of lymphoid tissue at the portals of the body as a primary defense against infection (TONSILS, ADENOIDS. Peyer's patches in the gut). Lymph node enlargement may be due to INFLAMMATION following DISEASE in the territory drained (SKIN, PHARYNX), or to development of an ABSCESS in the node (STAPHYLOCOCCUS. TUBERCULOSIS) due to INFECTIOUS DISEASE, secondary spread of cancer and the development of LYMPHOMA or LEUKEMIA. BIOPSY is valuable in diagnosis.

**LYMPHOMA**, malignant proliferation of LYMPH tissue, usually in the lymph nodes, SPLEEN or GASTROINTESTINAL TRACT. The prototype is HODGKIN'S DISEASE, but a number of other forms occur with varying HISTOLOGY and behavior. Cancer CHEMOTHERAPY and RADIATION THERAPY have much to offer in these disorders.

**LYNCHING**, illegal "execution" conducted by a self-appointed body, or a killing by mob violence; probably named for Charles Lynch, a Va. magistrate who in 1780 dispensed summary justice to Tory conspirators. Vigilante bodies in pioneer communities sometimes authorized lynchings. Lynchings in this century have occurred mainly in the South, often instigated by the KU KLUX KLAN, where blacks were usually the victims; always rare, the practice seems to have died out.

**LYNN, Loretta** (1935–    ), US country-and-western singer whose autobiography (1976) was the basis of the popular film *Coal Miner's Daughter* (1980). She recorded the first gold album by a female country singer and was frequently named female country music vocalist of the year.

**LYNX**, bobtailed members of the CAT family, of both Old and New Worlds. Tawny yellow cats, lynxes live in forests, especially of pine, leading solitary lives, hunting by night for small deer, badgers, hares, rabbits and small rodents—as well as occasionally raiding domestic stock.

**LYON, Mary** (1797–1849), US pioneer of women's higher education. A teacher from the age of 17, she was founder and first president of Mount Holyoke Female Seminary (1837), South Hadley, Mass.

**LYRE**, STRINGED INSTRUMENT originating in ancient Greece and the FERTILE CRESCENT. The strings, usually plucked, stretch between the body and a crossbar joining two arms. (See also KITHARA.)

**LYRIC POETRY**, originally poetry sung to the accompaniment of the LYRE. It now denotes any poem, usually short, such as the SONNET, expressing strongly felt personal emotion. Lyric poetry is particularly associated with the ROMANTICS, such as KEATS, SHELLEY and WORDSWORTH.

**LYSENKO,    Trofim    Denisovich** (1898–1976), Soviet agronomist whose antipathy for GENETICS and position of power under the Stalin regime led to the stifling of any progress in Soviet biological studies for 25 years or more. Refusing on ideological grounds to believe in GENES, he adopted a peculiar form of Lamarckism (see LAMARCK; MICHURIN), and forced other Soviet scientists to support his views. He was removed from power in 1964.

**M**

13th letter of the English ALPHABET. It corresponds to the Semitic letter *mem* and the Greek *mu*. It represents a labial nasal sound.

**MACADAM,** road-building system devised by the Scots engineer **John Loudon McAdam** (1756–1836). The soil beneath the road, rather than foundations, takes the load, the road being waterproof and well-drained to keep this soil dry. For modern highways a first layer of larger rocks is laid, then smaller rocks and gravel, the whole being bound with, usually, ASPHALT or TAR.

**MACAO,** Portuguese overseas territory in SE China, on the estuary of the Canton (Pearl) R, area 6sq mi. The territory came into Portuguese possession in 1557 and was granted broad autonomy in 1976. It comprises the peninsula of Macao and adjacent islands of Taipa and Colôane. Macao is a popular resort and gambling center and major commercial port. Fishing is a major economic activity. Pop 282,000.

**MacARTHUR, Charles** (1895–1956), US playwright who won a Pulitzer Prize for *The Front Page* (1928), written with Ben HECHT. They also collaborated on *Twentieth Century* (1933), *Swan Song* (1946) and the screen play *The Scoundrel* (1935).

**MacARTHUR, Douglas** (1880–1964), US general and hero of WWII. He commanded the 42nd (Rainbow) Division in WWI, and was superintendent of West Point (1919–22). In 1930 he became chief of staff of the US army, the youngest man ever to hold the post, and was promoted to general. He retired from the army in 1937, but was recalled in 1941 as commander of US army forces in the Far East. In 1942 he became Allied supreme commander of the Southwest Pacific Area and in 1944 general of the army. Signatory of the Japanese surrender, he led the reconstruction of Japan as Allied supreme commander (1945–54). When the KOREAN WAR broke out (1950) he was selected commander of the UN forces sent to aid South Korea. His unwillingness to obey President TRUMAN's orders to restrict the war to Korea led to his dismissal the following year.

**MACAULAY, Dame Rose** (1881–1958), English author who won recognition as a social satirist with such novels as *Told by an Idiot* (1923) and *Staying with Relatives* (1930). Her works include outstanding travel books, poems and literary criticism.

**MACAULAY, Thomas Babington** (1800–1859), English historian and essayist. He sacrificed a flourishing political career to undertake his *History of England* (5 vols, 1849–61), but he died before completing it. Its clarity and readability made it an immediate success. Like the *History*, his *Essays* display great range brilliance and supreme confidence of judgment.

**MACBETH** (d. 1057), king of Scotland, formerly chief of the province of Moray, who killed King Duncan in battle (1040) and took the throne. SHAKESPEARE's famous tragedy *Macbeth*, based on Holinshed's *Chronicles*, gives a historically inaccurate picture of him as a villainous usurper.

**MACCABEES, Books of,** two books of the Old Testament APOCRYPHA which tell the story of the Maccabees or HASMONEANS, Jewish rulers of the 2nd and 1st centuries BC who fought for the independence of Judea from Syria. 1 Maccabees, a prime historical source, was written c100 BC. 2 Maccabees is a devotional work of low historical value, written before 70 AD. Two other books, 3 and 4 Maccabees, are among the PSEUDEPIGRAPHA.

**MacDIARMID, Hugh** (1892–1978), Scottish poet, born Christopher Murray Grieve. Founder of the Scottish Nationalist Party, he gave fresh impetus to Scottish literature. He is best known for the long rhapsodic poem *A Drunk Man Looks at the Thistle* (1926).

**MACDONALD, Sir John Alexander** (1815–1891), Canadian statesman, first premier of the Dominion of Canada. Elected to the Ontario legislature in 1844, he became premier in 1857 as head of a Conservative coalition which was joined (1864) by George BROWN and others. He led subsequent negotiations which resulted (1867) in the confederation of Canada. The PACIFIC SCANDAL (1873) caused his government's resignation, but he was again premier from 1878 until his death.

**MacDOWELL, Edward Alexander** (1861–1908), US composer and pianist. He is most remembered for his lyrical piano works and for the orchestral *Indian Suite* (1897). His wife founded the MacDowell Colony in Peterborough, N.H., a retreat for creative artists.

**MACEDONIA,** mountainous region of SE Europe, the ancient Macedon. It extends from the NW Aegean coast into the central Balkan peninsula. Divided among GREECE, YUGOSLAVIA and BULGARIA, it covers 25,636sq mi. Ethnically it is very mixed, but there are mainly Slavs in the N and Greeks in the S. The region is primarily agricultural, with tobacco, grains and cotton the chief crops. One of the great powers of the ancient world under ALEXANDER THE GREAT, Macedonia was later ruled by Romans, Byzantines, Bulgars and Serbs. From 1389 to 1912 it was part of the OTTOMAN EMPIRE. The present boundaries derive from the BALKAN WARS (1912–13).

**MACH, Ernst** (1838–1916), Austrian physicist and philosopher whose name is commemorated in the Mach number, defined as speed (as of an airplane) expressed as a multiple of the speed of sound under the same conditions. His greatest influence was in philosophy, where he rejected from science all concepts which could not be validated by experience. This freed EINSTEIN from the absoluteness of Newtonian space-time (and thus helped him toward his theory of RELATIVITY) and helped inform the LOGICAL POSITIVISM of the Vienna Circle.

**MACHAUT, Guillaume de** (c1300–1377), French poet and composer. He was a leading figure in the 14th-century Ars Nova ("new art") school of music, which developed many new forms. His *Mass for Four Voices* was the first complete polyphonic setting by a single composer.

**MACHIAVELLI, Niccolò** (1469–1527), Florentine statesman and political theorist. He served the Republic of Florence, and was its emissary on several occasions. When the MEDICI family returned to power in 1512 he was imprisoned; on his release he devoted himself principally to writing. Despite his belief in political morality and his undoubted love of liberty, as revealed in his *Discourses on Livy* (1531), his master work, *The Prince* (1532; written 1513), describes the amoral and unscrupulous political calculation by which an "ideal" prince maintains his power. It is often seen as a cynical guide to power politics, although Machiavelli's motives in writing it are much debated. He also wrote a brilliant *History of Florence* (1532).

**MACHINE**, a device that performs useful work by transmitting, modifying or transforming motion, forces and energy. There are three basic machines, the inclined plane, the lever, and the wheel and axle: from these, and adaptations of these, are built up all true machines, no matter how complex they may appear. There are two essential properties of all machines: *mechanical advantage*, which is the ratio load/effort, and *efficiency*, the ratio of actual performance to theoretical performance. Mechanical advantage can be less than, equal to or greater than 1; while efficiency, owing to such losses as FRICTION, is always less than 100% (otherwise a PERPETUAL MOTION machine would be possible). (See also EFFICIENCY; ENERGY; FORCE; LEVER; WHEEL; WORK.)

Simple machines derived from the three basic elements include: from the inclined plane, the *wedge* (effort at the top being translated to force at the sides), and the *screw* (an inclined plane in spiral form); from the lever, the wrench or spanner (the BALANCE also uses the principle of the lever), and from the wheel and axle, the PULLEY, (which can also be viewed as a type of lever).

**MACHINE GUN**, a GUN that can fire a number of rounds in rapid succession, a weapon that has changed the face of war in our century. Such guns are known from as early as the 14th century, and LEONARDO DA VINCI produced designs for several. These early guns were little more than a number of single guns arranged so that they could be set off by a single spark. James Puckle patented (1718) the precursor of the modern machine gun: it had a single barrel and a rotating stock holding square bullets: it fired about 9 rounds/min. FLINTLOCK was discarded with the invention of the percussion cap (c1816), and firing reliability much increased. By 1862 GATLING had developed a single-barreled machine gun, used in the Civil War, and later a multi-barreled gun that fired 3,000 rounds/min. MAXIM devised the first fully automatic machine gun around 1884; closely followed by John BROWNING, many of whose designs are in use today.

Three power sources are tapped to operate modern guns: the pressure of the expanding gases in the barrel; the recoil of the bolt and barrel; and the sprung return of a barrel that has recoiled. (See also AMMUNITION; FIREARMS.)

**MACHINE TOOLS**, nonportable, power-driven tools used industrially for working metal components to tolerances far finer than those obtainable manually. The fundamental processes used are cutting and grinding, individual machines being designed for boring, broaching, drilling (see DRILLS), milling, planing and sawing. Essentially a machine tool consists of a jig to hold both the cutting tool and the workpiece, and a mechanism to allow these to be moved relative to each other in a controlled fashion. A typical example is the

LATHE. Auxiliary functions facilitate the cooling and lubrication of the tool and workpiece while work is in progress using a cutting fluid. The rate at which any piece can be worked depends on the material being worked and the composition of the cutting point. High-speed STEEL, TUNGSTEN carbide and CORUNDUM are favored materials for cutting edges. Where several operations have to be performed on a single workpiece, time can be saved by using multiple-function tools such as the turret lathe, particularly if numerically rather than manually controlled. Modern industry would be inconceivable without machine tools. It was only when these began to be developed in the late 18th century that it became possible to manufacture interchangeable parts and thus initiate MASS PRODUCTION.

**MACH NUMBER,** ratio of the speed of an object or fluid to the local speed of SOUND, which is temperature dependent. Speeds are subsonic or supersonic depending on whether the mach number is less than or greater than one.

**MACHU PICCHU,** ancient (15th-century?) INCA city in Peru, an impressive ruin dramatically situated on a high ridge of the Andes. It was discovered in 1911 by the American explorer Hiram BINGHAM.

**MACK, Connie** (1862–1956), famous US baseball player and manager. As owner and manager of the Philadelphia Athletics from 1901 to 1950, he led his team to victory in five world series.

**MACKENZIE, Sir Alexander** (c1764–1820), Canadian fur trader and explorer, the first white man to cross the northern part of North America to the Pacific. Born in Scotland, he emigrated to Canada and in 1789 made an expedition down the MACKENZIE RIVER (named for him). In 1793 he crossed the Rockies to the Pacific coast.

**MACKENZIE RIVER,** in NW Canada, flowing from Great Slave Lake to the Arctic Ocean. The Mackenzie itself is 1,060mi in length, the total length of the system about 2,500mi, the second largest in North America. It is named for Sir Alexander MACKENZIE.

**MACKINAC BRIDGE,** 7,400ft long, connects Upper and Lower Michigan. It is one of the longest suspension bridges in the world, with a main span of 3,800ft.

**MacLEISH, Archibald** (1892–     ), US poet and playwright. *Conquistador* (1932), a narrative poem on the conquest of Mexico, *Collected Poems* (1952), containing his best lyrical verse, and *J.B.* (1958), a verse drama based on Job, all won Pulitzer prizes. Cultural adviser to President ROOSEVELT, he

was Librarian of Congress 1939–44.

**MacMAHON, Marie Edmé Patrice Maurice de** (1808–1893), marshal of France and president of the French Republic (1873–79). A successful army officer, he became governor general of Algeria (1864–70). In 1871 he suppressed the PARIS COMMUNE. His conservative, royalist views led to conflict with the republican majority in parliament, and he was finally obliged to resign the presidency.

**MACMILLAN, Kenneth** (1929–     ), Scottish choreographer and dancer. From 1946–66 he danced and choreographed for the Sadler's Wells companies and from 1966–70 directed the Deutsche Opera Ballet in Berlin. He succeeded Frederick ASHTON in 1970 as director of the Royal Ballet, where he created the full-length *Anastasia* (1971) and *Manon* (1974).

**MACMILLAN, (Maurice) Harold** (1894–     ), British statesman and Conservative prime minister from 1957 to 1963. He entered Parliament in 1924, and was an opponent of APPEASEMENT. Having served in ministerial posts in WWII and the 1950s, he became prime minister after the SUEZ affair. He restored Anglo-US relations, tried to take Britain into the COMMON MARKET and presided over an economic boom, which, however, was already over when he resigned in ill health.

**MacNIECE, Louis** (1907–1963), British poet, born in Northern Ireland. His low-keyed, socially committed poetry links him with the "Oxford Group" of the 1930s, which included W. H. AUDEN and Stephen SPENDER. His *Collected Poems* appeared in 1949.

**MACPHERSON, James** (1736–1796), Scottish poet and member of Parliament from 1780, famous for his purported translations of the Gaelic bard OSSIAN, published 1760–75. Disputed by Samuel JOHNSON and others, they appear to have been Macpherson's own work, loosely based on contemporary Gaelic verse.

**MACROECONOMICS,** the study of aggregates in the national economy, as opposed to that part of economics concerned with the constituent elements, MICROECONOMICS. Macroeconomics studies key economic quantities (such as National Income, SAVINGS, INVESTMENT and BALANCE OF PAYMENTS), the factors determining them and the relationships between them.

**MADAGASCAR,** formerly **Malagasy Republic,** Democratic Republic in the Indian Ocean comprising the large island of Madagascar and several small islands.

**Land.** It is separated from the SE African mainland by the Mozambique Channel.

The island has rugged central highlands and fertile low-lying coastal plains. The highlands have several extinct volcanoes and mountain groups which rise to over 9,000ft. They have a pleasantly cool, and occasionally cold, climate. The coastal plains tend to be hot and humid, with luxuriant tropical vegetation. Soil erosion is a serious problem, and destructive hurricanes may occur between December and April.

**People.** The island's population can be broadly divided into two groups: those of Indonesian-Polynesian descent (Merinas), living mainly in the highlands, and those of African Negro descent (côtiers), living mainly in the coastal regions. Traditional antagonisms exist between the two groups. French, Indian and Chinese nationals are prominent in commerce. Over 90% of the people live in rural areas. The main cities are Antananarivo (Tananarive), the capital and largest city, Antsirabe, Diégo-Suarez, Majunga and Tuléar.

**Economy.** The island is predominantly farming and stock-raising country. Coffee, cloves and vanilla are principal foreign-exchange earners. Meat and prawns are also exported. Chromite, graphite, mica and phosphates are important minerals. Oil and gas deposits have been discovered. Industries include food processing, oil refining, vehicle assembly and textile making.

**History.** Portuguese, French and English rivalry for control of Madagascar ended in French invasion and annexation (1885–1905). In 1947, a revolt against French rule was crushed, but in 1958 the island gained self-government within the French community as the Malagasy Republic. It achieved full independence in 1960. In 1972 the civilian government handed over power to the military, which continues to rule.

**Official name:** Democratic Republic of Madagascar
**Capital:** Tananarive
**Area:** 229,233sq mi
**Population:** c8,549,000

**Languages:** Malagasy, French. Hova spoken
**Religions:** Christian, Animist, Muslim
**Monetary unit(s):** 1 Malagasy franc (FMG) = 100 centimes

**MADARIAGA, Salvador de** (1886–1978), Spanish diplomat and writer. A liberal historian and political philosopher, he settled in England after the Spanish Civil War. His works include *The Genius of Spain* (1923) and *Victors, Beware* (1946).

**MADEIRA,** archipelago in the N Atlantic some 360mi W of Morocco, constituting the Funchal district of Portugal. Madeira, the largest island, is mountainous; settlement, including the capital Funchal, is largely on the coast. The islands produce sugarcane, bananas and the famous Madeira wine. Their scenic beauty and warm climate make them a year-round tourist resort.

**MADERNO, Carlo** (1556–1629), Italian architect of the early BAROQUE. Chief architect of St. Peter's, Rome, from 1603, he designed the nave and facade. He designed the church of Sta. Maria della Vittoria (1620) and began the Palazzo Barberini for URBAN V in 1625.

**MADERO, Francisco Indalecio** (1873–1913), president of Mexico 1911–13. A democratic idealist, he opposed Porfirio DÍAZ in the 1910 election and was imprisoned. He escaped to Tex. and there declared a revolution; joined by Francisco VILLA and ZAPATA, he deposed Díaz in 1911 and was elected president. His administration was marred by his own ineptitude, and division and corruption among his followers. In the face of widespread revolt he was deposed and murdered by Gen. Victoriano HUERTA.

**MADISON, James** (1751–1836), 4th president of the US 1809–17. Born at Port Conway, Va., he graduated from the College of New Jersey (Princeton U.) in 1771. In 1776 he helped draft Va.'s constitution and served in the CONTINENTAL CONGRESS 1780–83. He pressed the need for a stronger central government than was possible under the ARTICLES OF CONFEDERATION. In the Va. house of delegates 1784–86 he advocated federal unity; he promoted the ANNAPOLIS CONVENTION which led in turn to the Federal Constitutional Convention (1787). He submitted a series of proposals to it, the general framework of which is reflected in the US CONSTITUTION adopted by the Convention. This and his skillful conduct in the debates has earned him the title of "father of the Constitution." He was one of the authors of the FEDERALIST PAPERS. As a congressman 1789–97 he advocated the

LL OF RIGHTS.

An influential secretary of state under EFFERSON 1801–08, he was chosen by efferson as his successor. As president mself from 1809 Madison took a firm grip affairs, writing all major state papers in e first two years. In foreign affairs, he ught to free US shipping of the trade straints imposed by Britain and France in e NAPOLEONIC WARS. Trusting dubious rench assurances, Madison imposed an nbargo on trade with Britain in 1810. This d a popular desire to conquer Canada ovoked the WAR OF 1812 in which adison's prestige suffered, especially ter the burning of the White House by the ritish in 1814. After the war Madison esided over a period of new prosperity and pansion. He retired in 1817 to his Va. antation Montpelier. Rector of the niversity of Virginia from 1826, he came interested in the abolition of avery.

**ADISON**, capital city of Wis. and seat of ane Co. A commercial and administrative nter, its main manufactures are meat and iry products. It is the site of U. of isconsin. Pop 170,616.

**ADRID**, capital of Spain and of Madrid ovince, on the Manzanares R in New astile. A 10th-century Moorish fortress ptured by Castile in 1083, it was made the pital by PHILIP II (1561). Now Spain's ministrative and financial headquarters, has a wide range of industries. A cultural nter, its landmarks include the Prado art llery, the royal palace and the university ty. Pop 3,146,000.

**AEGHT**, Aimé (1906–1981), French art aler who represented such artists as hagall, Miro, Giacometti, Matisse, aque and Bonnard and was a major fluence on 20th-century art. He ran lleries in Paris, New York, Barcelona and urich and established the Fondation arguerite et Aimé Maeght, a major art useum at St. Paul-de-Vence, France.

**AETERLINCK**, Maurice (1862–1949), lgian poet and playwright. His early work as influenced by SYMBOLISM; he is best own for the tragedy *Pelléas and élisand* (1892), set as an opera by BUSSY, and the dramatic fable *The Blue rd* (1908). He was awarded the Nobel ize for Literature in 1911.

**AFIA**, Italian-American criminal organ-ation. Its name derives from 19th-century cilian bandits who dominated the asantry through terrorism and the dition of the VENDETTA. Despite pression by successive governments, cluding MUSSOLINI, the Mafia remains

very powerful in Italy. *Mafiosi* emigrated to the US and set up sophisticated criminal bodies there, organized in "families." These prospered during PROHIBITION, and diver-sified from bootlegging into gambling, narcotics, vice, labor unions and more recently into some legitimate business. In the 1950s and 1960s attention was drawn to the Mafia by the fruitless trial of 60 of its leaders, caught in conference at Apalachin, N.Y., in 1957, and the disclosures of former *mafioso* Joseph Valachi. *Mafiosi* may refer to the organization as *Cosa Nostra* (Italian: our affair) but usually deny its existence.

**MAGDALENIAN**, upper-Paleolithic cul-ture named for La Madeleine cave, Dordogne, France, noted for the quality of its painting and bone engraving (see also ALTAMIRA; STONE AGE.)

**MAGELLAN, Ferdinand** (c1480–1521), Portuguese navigator who commanded the first expedition to sail round the world. Accused of embezzlement during his service in the Portuguese Indian army, he fell from favor at court and so sought Spanish backing for his proposed voyage in search of a western route to the Spice Islands or East Indies, then believed to be only a few hundred miles beyond America. Financed by Charles I, Magellan sailed from Sanlúca de Barrameda with five ships on Sept. 20, 1519. In Jan. 1520 he discovered the Río de la Plata and sailed S to Patagonia, where Magellan had to put down a mutiny. Then with only three ships, he sailed to the Pacific through the straits now named for him. For two months no land was sighted and the expedition was near starvation; in March 1521 they reached Guam, and in April the Philippines. Magellan was killed in a skirmish with natives there on April 27. Only one ship, the *Victoria*, under Juan del CANO, returned to Spain, having sailed around the world. Although he did not survive the journey, Magellan was undoubtedly responsible for its success.

**MAGELLAN, Strait of,** separates main-land South America from Tierra del Fuego and islands to the S. Around 330mi long, and an important route before the building of the Panama Canal, it was first navigated by Ferdinand MAGELLAN in 1520.

**MAGI**, Persian priestly caste or tribe. Little is known of them beyond their reputation for wisdom and supernatural powers. Zoroaster was probably a Magus; the Magi headed ZOROASTRIANISM, which may have been based upon their original religion. The Three Wise Men were reputedly Magi.

**MAGIC**, in entertainment, conjuring tricks or manipulated feats of illusion, such as making flowers appear, pulling rabbits out of hats, levitation, or sawing a person in half. Included are spectacular escapes—from strait jackets, handcuffs, locked trunks—of the kind that made Harry HOUDINI the best known of magician-entertainers.

**MAGIC SQUARE,** square array of numbers such that the sums along each row, column and diagonal are equal; e.g.:

$$\begin{array}{ccc} 6 & 7 & 2 \\ 1 & 5 & 9 \\ 8 & 3 & 4 \end{array}$$

**MAGMA,** molten material formed in the upper mantle or crust of the EARTH, composed of a mixture of various complex SILICATES in which are dissolved various gaseous materials, including WATER. On cooling magma forms IGNEOUS ROCKS, though any gaseous constituents are usually lost during the solidification. Magma extruded to the surface forms LAVA. The term is loosely applied to other fluid substances (e.g., molten salt) in the earth's crust. (See also HOT SPRINGS; VOLCANISM.)

**MAGNA CARTA** (Latin: great charter), major British constitutional charter forced on King JOHN I by a baronial alliance at Runnymede in June 1215. The barons rebelled because of John's heavy taxation to finance wars and his exclusion of them from government. He sought to repudiate the charter but died soon after. It falls into 63 clauses, designed to prevent royal restriction of baronial privilege and feudal rights. It also safeguarded church and municipal rights and privileges. Altered forms of it were issued on John's death in 1216, in 1217 and 1225. In fact a reactionary measure, its vagueness allowed many later commentators to find in it the roots of whatever civil rights they wished to defend, such as HABEAS CORPUS and JURY trial. It did, however, pave the way for constitutional monarchy by implicitly recognizing that a king may be bound by laws enforceable by his subjects.

**MAGNANI, Anna** (1908–1973), Italian film actress acclaimed for her portrayals of tempestous characters insuch Italian neorealist films as *Open City* (1945). She won an academy award for her performance in the US film *The Rose Tattoo* (1955).

**MAGNETIC FIELD,** what is said to exist where electric charges (see ELECTRICITY) experience a FORCE proportional to their VELOCITY but at right angles to it, or where magnetic dipoles (see MAGNETISM) experience a TORQUE. The field is defined in the direction of zero torque, with a strength equal to the torque on a unit dipole at right angles to the field. Magnetic fields originate at magnetic dipoles or electric currents.

**MAGNETIC STORM,** an occasional disturbance in the earth's MAGNETIC FIELD correlated with SUNSPOT activity. A high energy PLASMA ejected from a solar flare se up large currents in the MAGNETOSPHERE c reaching the earth, causing a rapid rise around 0.2% in the magnetic field at th surface. The plasma subsequently move around the earth, often accompanied b auroral displays, while the field drops about 0.5% below its normal valu recovering over several days.

**MAGNETISM,** the phenomena associate with "magnetic dipoles," commonly e countered in the properties of the famili horseshoe (permanent) magnet and applie in a multitude of magnetic devices.

Man first learned of magnetism throug the properties of the *lodestone*, a shape piece of MAGNETITE that had the property aligning itself in a roughly north-sou direction. Eventually he found how to use lodestone to magnetize a steel bar, th making an artificial **permanent magnet.** Th power of a magnet was discovered to concentrated in two "poles," one of whic always sought the north, and was called north-seeking pole, or north pole, the oth being a south-seeking pole, or south pole. was early learned that, given two permane magnets, the unlike poles were attracted each other and the like poles repelled eac other according to an inverse-square la Furthermore, dividing a magnet in tw never resulted in the isolation of a individual pole, but only in the creation two shorter two-poled magnets. Th explanation of these properties in terms magnetic "lines of force" was an ear achievement of the science magnetostatics.

Today, physicists explain magnetism terms of *magnetic dipoles*. Magnetic dipo moment is an intrinsic property fundamental particles. ELECTRONS, f example, have a moment of $0.928 \times 10^-$ $A \cdot m^2$ parallel or antiparallel to th direction of observation. The forces betwee magnetic dipoles are identical to tho between electric dipoles (see ELECTRICITY This leads scientists often to regard th dipoles as consisting of two magnet charges of opposite type, the poles traditional theory. But unlike electr charges, magnetic poles are believed nev to be found in isolation.

In **ferromagnetic materials** such as IRO and COBALT, spontaneous dipole alignmen over relatively large regions known *magnetic domains* occurs. Magnetization such materials involves a change in th relative size of domains aligned in differe ections, and can multiply the effect of the magnetizing field a thousand times. Other materials show much weaker, nonpermanent magnetic properties.

Magnetism is intimately associated with electricity (see ELECTROMAGNETISM). Electric currents generate MAGNETIC FIELDS circulating around themselves—the EARTH's magnetic field is maintained by large currents in its liquid core—and small current loops behave like magnetic dipoles with a moment given by the product of the loop current and area.

MAGNETOHYDRODYNAMICS (MHD), the DYNAMICS of conducting fluids such as liquid metals or PLASMAS, in ELECTRIC and MAGNETIC FIELDS. It is a macroscopic form of ELECTRODYNAMICS, deriving from fluid dynamics such concepts as magnetic pressure and magnetic viscosity. Its equations often defy exact solution. The most important applications are in magnetohydrodynamic GENERATORS and controlled nuclear FUSION processes. The extremely hot plasma produced by the fusion is contained by strong circulating magnetic fields; various designs are possible, the stability of each being the paramount consideration.

MAGNET SCHOOL, a superior public school, designed to attract white students to schools in districts predominantly populated by minorities. Magnet schools have been used since 1971 as a means of achieving school integration. With respect to this goal, their success has been limited.

MAGNITUDE, Stellar, a measure of a star's brightness. The foundations of the system were laid by HIPPARCHUS (c120 BC), who divided stars into six categories, from 1 to 6 in order of decreasing brightness. Later the system was extended to include fainter stars which could be seen only by telescope, and brighter stars, which were assigned negative magnitudes (e.g., Sirius, −1.5). Five magnitudes were defined as a 100-times increase in brightness. These *apparent magnitudes* depend greatly on the distances from us of the stars. *Absolute magnitude* is defined as the apparent magnitude a star would have were it at a distance of 10pc from us: Sirius then has magnitude +1.4. Absolute magnitudes clearly tell us far more than do apparent magnitudes. Stars are also assigned red, infrared, bolometric and photographic magnitude.

MAGRITTE, René (1898–1967), Belgian surrealist painter. He was an adherent of SURREALISM from about 1925, developing a style which often juxtaposed realistically portrayed subjects in a deeply disconcerting manner.

MAGYARS, speakers of the Hungarian language. A nomadic warrior people, originally from the Urals, they entered central Europe in the 9th century and settled in the region which is now Hungary. The Magyar language belongs to the Ugro-Finnic linguistic group. (See also HUNGARY.)

MAHABHARATA, great Hindu epic poem, comprising some 110,000 32-syllable couplets, probably written before 500 BC, though with many later passages. It concerns the lengthy feud between two related tribes, the Pandavas and the Kauravas, and has as its central episode the BHAGAVAD-GĪTĀ, a later insertion. There are numerous editorial passages on mythology, religion, philosophy and morals.

MAHAN, Alfred Thayer (1840–1914), US naval officer and historian. His works on the historical significance of sea power are classics in their field. They include *The Influence of Sea Power upon History, 1660–1783* (1890) and *The Influence of Sea Power upon the French Revolution and Empire, 1793–1812* (1892). His work stimulated worldwide naval expansion.

MAHAYANA (Sanskrit: Great Vehicle), school of BUDDHISM founded c200 BC; its teachings were aimed more at a spiritual elite (i.e., those who aspired to Buddhahood or enlightenment) than were those of the Hinayana (Lesser Vehicle), a rival school.

MAHDI (Arabic: the guided one), the prophet or savior who Sunni Muslims believe will bring peace and justice to the world. A notable claimant was 'Ubayd Allah (reigned 909–34), founder of the Egyptian Fatimid dynasty. Another was Muhammad Ahmad (d. 1885), who raised a revolt against Egyptian rule in the Sudan and fought the British 1883–85.

MAHLER, Gustav (1860–1911), Austrian composer and conductor. He wrote nine symphonies (a tenth was unfinished) and a number of song cycles. The symphonies are a culmination of 19th-century Romanticism, but their startling harmonic and orchestral effects link them with early 20th-century works. Among other positions, Mahler was director of the Imperial Opera in Vienna 1897–1907.

MAILER, Norman (1923– ), US novelist and journalist. After the great success of his first novel, *The Naked and the Dead* (1948), he became a trenchant critic of the American way of life. He developed an amalgam of journalism, fiction and autobiography, first evident in his collection *Advertisements for Myself* (1959). He shared a 1969 Pulitzer Prize for *The Armies of the Night* (1968), an account of the 1967 Washington peace march. Later works include *Marilyn* (1973) and *The Executioner's Song* (1979).

**MAILLOL, Aristide** (1861–1944), French sculptor and painter. His chief subject was the female nude, which he sculpted in monumental, static forms that represent a revival of Classical ideals. In the early 1900s he was linked with the NABIS, as a painter; but when he was nearly 40 years old he took up sculpture.

**MAIMAN, Theodore** (1927–    ), US physicist who built the first practical laser (1960).

**MAIMONIDES, Moses** (1135–1204), Moses ben Maimon, or Rambam, the foremost medieval Jewish philosopher. He was born in Muslim Spain, but persecution drove his family to leave the country. They eventually settled near Cairo in Egypt, where Maimonides became renowned as court physician to Saladin. Two of his major works were the *Mishneh Torah* (1180), a codification of Jewish doctrine, and *Guide to the Perplexed* (1190), in which he attempted to interpret Jewish tradition in Aristotelian terms. His work influenced many Jewish and Christian thinkers.

**MAINBOCHER,** (Main Rousseau Bocher; 1890–1976), US fashion designer, the first American to achieve success in the high-fashion world of 1920s Paris. His glamorous evening wear was worn by clients such as Mrs. Wallis Simpson. He also designed women's uniforms for the women's services during WWII.

**Name of state:** Maine
**Capital:** Augusta
**Statehood:** March 15, 1820 (23rd state)
**Familiar name:** Pine Tree State
**Area:** 33,215 sq mi
**Population:** 1,124,660
**Elevation:** Highest—5,268ft, Mount Katahdin. Lowest—sea level, Atlantic Ocean
**Motto:** Dirigo (I direct)
**State flower:** White-pine cone and tassel
**State bird:** Chickadee
**State tree:** White pine
**State song:** "State of Maine Song"

**MAINE,** the northeasternmost state of the US, bounded to the N and E by New Brunswick, to the S by the Atlantic Ocean and to the W by NH and Quebec.

**Land.** There are three distinct land regions in the state—the Seaboard (coastal) Lowlands, the New England Uplands running SW–NE and the White Mountain region in the NW.

**People.** Maine is among the least urbanized of the states with less than 54% of the population living in urban areas in 1980. Portland is the largest city, followed by Lewiston and Bangor. Under the much amended 1820 constitution, there is a 33-member Senate and 151-member House of Representatives. There are several Indian tribal reservations.

**Economy.** Some 80% of the state is forested and much of its economy is based on wood and wood products. The scenic forests, lakes, hills, rivers and coastal regions make tourism an important industry, bringing in about $475 million every year. But the most important branch of Maine's economy is manufacturing which employs nearly 30% of the state's labor force. Major products in addition to paper and wood items include textiles, leather goods and processed food. Maine is also famous for its lobsters and potatoes. The state's isolated location and sparse population have kept it relatively free of pollution and urban blight.

**History.** In the early 1600s the Algonquin Indians who inhabited the region offered little resistance to the establishment of the first white settlements on the coast and along the navigable rivers. But Maine was the scene of many conflicts during the FRENCH AND INDIAN WARS and came under English control after the Treaty of Paris in 1763. Settlement began to increase, but remained low in comparison with other states until the 19th century.

Maine's soldiers played an active part in the Revolutionary War and the first naval engagement of the war took place off the state's coast, near Machias. In 1775 the British burned the town of Falmouth (now Portland). During the WAR OF 1812 the British easily captured and held the eastern portion of the state. In 1820, Maine, which had been a part of Mass. since 1691, became a separate state. In 1980, the Penobscot Indians reached a settlement over their claim to half of Maine's territory.

**MAISTRE, Joseph Marie, Comte de** (1753–1821), French philosopher, author and founder of the Ultramontanist movement. A staunch conservative, he believed papal and royal power should be absolute and was an inveterate opponent of the French evolution.

**MAITLAND, Frederic William** (1850–1906), English jurist and legal historian. He as particularly concerned with early nglish law and founded the Selden Society 1887). Notable among his works is *The History of English Law before the Time of Edward I* (1895), written with Sir Frederick Pollock.

**MAIZE.** See CORN.

**MAJORCA,** or Mallorca, largest of the Balearic Islands of Baleares province, Spain. Majorca lies in the W Mediterranean, 115mi E of the Spanish coast. It is a major tourist center with many resorts, including its capital, Palma.

**MAKARIOS III, Archbishop** (1913–1977), born Michael Christodoulos Mouskos, the first president of independent Cyprus (from 1959), archbishop and primate of the Cypriot Orthodox Church from 1950. During British rule he led the movement for *nosis* (union with Greece). He had links with the EOKA terrorist group and was exiled by the British 1956–57. He fled temporarily during the political disturbances of 1974.

**MAKAROVA, Natalia Romanovna** (1940–      ), Soviet dancer who defected to the West in 1970. From 1959 she danced with the Kirov Ballet in Leningrad, where she starred in classical roles after her first *iselle* (1961). In the West she won acclaim in both classical and modern roles at the American Ballet Theatre, the London Royal Ballet and other companies throughout the world.

**MAKEBA, Miriam** (1932–      ), South African-born singer who appeared in the anti-apartheid film *Come Back Africa* (1958). She won acclaim abroad as a folk singer with an international repertoire.

**MALABAR CHRISTIANS,** or St. Thomas Christians, a group mostly found in Kerala state, SW India. Considered heretics by the Portuguese, though traditionally aligned with Rome since the 6th century, they broke with Rome in 1653. The majority reverted to Catholicism in 1661 but some joined the Syrian Orthodox Church.

**MALACCA,** or Melaka, port and capital city of Malacca, a state of Malaysia, SE Asia. It is a trade center for rice and rubber. It was ruled by the Portuguese from 1511, who made it the center of the East Indian spice trade, by the Dutch, 1641–1824, and then by the British until Malaysian independence, 1957. Pop 86,357.

**MALAGASY REPUBLIC.** See MADAGASCAR.

**MALAMUD, Bernard** (1914–      ), US novelist and short story writer. He won a National Book Award for his stories in *The*

*Magic Barrel* (1958) and the Pulitzer Prize for his novel *The Fixer* (1966). Malamud's work deals mainly with Jewish life and traditions in the US. The heroes of his books are often humble, solitary individuals, though *Dubin's Lives* (1979) marked a departure in subject matter.

**MALAPARTE, Curzio** (1898–1957), pen name of Kurt Suckert, Italian writer with a penchant for the grotesque. His war correspondent experiences with the German army in Russia formed the background of *Kaputt* (1944); those with the US army in Italy were transmitted into *The Skin* (1949).

**MALARIA,** tropical PARASITIC DISEASE causing malaise and intermittent FEVER and sweating, either on alternate days or every third day; bouts often reoccur over many years. One form, cerebral malaria, develops rapidly with ENCEPHALITIS, COMA and SHOCK. Malaria is due to infection with *Plasmodium* carried by mosquitos of the genus *Anopheles* from the BLOOD of infected persons. The cyclic fever is due to the parasite's life cycle in the blood and LIVER; diagnosis is by examination of blood. QUININE and its derivatives, especially CHLOROQUINE and primaquine, are used both in prevention and treatment but other chemotherapy (ATABRINE, pyrimethamine) may also be used. Mosquito control, primarily by destroying their breeding places (swamps and pools), provides the best method of combating the disease.

**MALAY,** general term for a group of about 100 million people who live on the Malay Peninsula and on islands of the Philippines and Indonesia. They are a short, brown-skinned, Mongoloid people. They probably emigrated originally from central Asia. By the 2nd century AD, the powerful Malay kingdom of Srivijaya ruled in Sumatra, Indonesia.

**MALAY ARCHIPELAGO,** formerly the East Indies, the world's largest group of islands, off the coast of SE Asia, between the Indian and Pacific Oceans. They include the 3,000 islands of Indonesia, the 7,000 islands of the Philippines, and New Guinea. Pop 162,838,000.

**MALAYO-POLYNESIAN LANGUAGES,** or **Austronesian Languages**, family of some 500 languages found throughout the Central and S Pacific (except New Guinea and Australia, but including New Zealand) and especially in Malaysia and the Indonesian islands. There are two main groups, Oceanic to the E and Indonesian to the W.

**MALAY PENINSULA,** the southernmost peninsula in Asia, comprising West

Malaysia and SW Thailand. It is one of the world's richest producers of rubber and tin.

**Official name:** Malaysia
**Capital:** Kuala Lumpur
**Area:** 127,581sq mi
**Population:** 13,250,000
**Languages:** Malay; English, Chinese, Tamil
**Religions:** Muslim, Buddhist, Hindu
**Monetary units(s):** 1 Malaysian dollar = 100 cents

**MALAYSIA,** independent federation in Southeast Asia, comprising West Malaysia on the Malay Peninsula and, 400mi away across the South China Sea, East Malaysia, formed by Sabah and Sarawak on the island of Borneo.
**Land.** The landscape of Malaya (West Malaysia) is mainly mountainous (rising to over 7,000ft) with narrow coastal plains and lush equatorial forests. The climate is hot and very humid. Sarawak and Sabah also have mountainous interiors and large areas of rain forest. Many rivers flow from central Borneo to the coastal swamps. Malaysia's highest mountain, Mt. Kinabalu (13,455ft), is in Sabah.
**People.** The predominantly rural population is over 40% Malay, under 40% Chinese and 10% Indian and Pakistani. Whereas in West Malaysia the population comprises more than 50% Malay and 35% Chinese, in East Malaysia the Chinese and Ibans together form 33% and the Malays about 10%. The largest cities are Kuala Lumpur, the capital, Penang (George Town) and Ipoh, in the W, and Kota Kinabalu in Sabah, and Kuching in Sarawak. Government is by constitutional monarchy, a paramount ruler being elected from among the hereditary rulers of nine of the fourteen states for five-year terms.
**Economy.** Malaysia has rich natural resources. It is one of the world's leading producers of natural rubber and tin. The forests also provide valuable timber, palm oil and coconuts. Rice is the chief food crop, and bananas, yams, cocoa, pepper, tea and tobacco are also grown. Malaysia produces petroleum, iron ore, bauxite, coal and gold.

The principal exports are petroleum, rubber, tin, palm oil and timber.
**History.** In the 9th century Malaya was the seat of the Buddhist Srivijaya empire. Beginning in the 14th century the population was converted to Islam. The Portuguese took Malacca in 1511 but were ousted by the Dutch in 1641. The British formed a trading base of the East India Company in Penang in 1786, and in 1827 united Penang, Singapore and Malacca into the Straits Settlement. Between 1888 and 1909 the British established many protectorates in Malaya and Borneo. After the WWII Japanese occupation (1941–45) Malaya was reorganized as the Federation of Malaya (1948), gaining independence within the British Commonwealth (1957). In 1963 the union of Malaya with Singapore, Sarawak and Sabah formed the Federation of Malaysia. Indonesia waged guerrilla warfare against the Federation during 1963–65. In 1965 Singapore seceded to become an independent republic. Parliament was suspended for 22 months in 1969 after racial riots broke out between Malays and Chinese in West Malaysia. Abdul Razak, premier of the Nation Front coalition government from 1974 until his death in 1976, was succeeded by his deputy Datuk Hussein bin Onn. Racial and religious strife again broke out between Malays, Chinese and Hindus in the late 1970s and early 1980s.

**MALCOLM X** (Malcolm Little, 1925–1965), US black radical leader. While in prison 1946–52, he was converted to the BLACK MUSLIMS and became their leader in 1963. In 1964 he formed the rival Organization of Afro-American Unity, pleading for racial brotherhood instead of separation. He was assassinated at an OAAU meeting in New York City.

**Official name:** Republic of Maldives
**Capital:** Malé
**Area:** 115sq mi
**Population:** 148,000
**Languages:** Divehi (Maldivian)
**Religions:** Muslim
**Monetary unit(s):** 1 Maldivian rupee = 100

**MALDIVES, Republic of,** formerly the Maldive Islands, a group of 19 coral atolls in the Indian Ocean. They lie about 400mi SW of Ceylon and comprise some 2,000 islands, of which about 220 are inhabited. The people are Muslims and their language, Divehi, is related to Old Sinhalese. The capital, Malé, lies on the island of the same name. The chief industry is fishing, although coconuts and some grains are grown on a limited scale. From the 12th century the Maldive Islands were governed as a sultanate. The Islands were under British protection 1887–1965, becoming independent in 1965, and a republic in 1968.

**MALEBRANCHE, Nicolas** (1638–1715), French philosopher, scientist and Roman Catholic priest, noted for the doctrine of "occasionalism" as an explanation of causation and the mind-body relation. In both philosophy and science he was much influenced by the thought of DESCARTES, in the former field attempting to reconcile Cartesian philosophy with that of St. Augustine, in the latter field researching LIGHT, VISION and the CALCULUS.

**MALENKOV, Georgy Maksimilianovich** (1902–    ), Soviet premier 1953–55, after STALIN's death. Malenkov was replaced in 1955, then expelled from the PRESIDIUM (1957), accused of forming an "antiparty" group, and from the Party in 1961.

**MALEVICH, Kasimir** (1878–1935), Russian painter, a pioneer of ABSTRACT ART. In 1913 he began painting works based on geometric shapes and published a manifesto to propagate SUPREMATISM. Among his works is *White on White*, 1918.

**MALHERBE, François de** (1555–1628), French court poet to Henry IV and Louis XIII. A critic of the classical style of the PLÉIADE poets, he emphasized the importance of French classic language and of a precise form of writing.

**Official name:** Republic of Mali
**Capital:** Bamako
**Area:** 478,767sq mi

**Population:** c6,661,000
**Languages:** French; Tribal languages
**Religions:** Muslim, Animist
**Monetary unit(s):** Mali franc = 100 centimes

**MALI,** landlocked republic in W Africa, lying to the S of Algeria.

**Land.** Mali is largely desert, but the great Niger R flows across S Mali, and its channels and marshy lakes form an "inland delta" suitable for rice and cotton growing. Without irrigation from the Niger and Senegal Rivers agriculture would be impossible. Middle Mali is arid, with shrub, thorn and acacia. The NE and SW regions are mountainous.

**People.** Mali has many ethnic groups, negroid farming peoples in the S like the Bambara and Malinké, the Dogon in central Mali, the Peuls (Fulani) in the Niger Valley and white nomadic pastoralists, the Tuareg, Moors and Arabs in the N. The capital and largest town is Bamako in the S on the Niger R.

**Economy.** Mali, whose economy depends on agriculture and livestock, has recently faced acute food shortages as a result of drought. Major cash crops are cotton and peanuts; industry is largely restricted to processing these and other agricultural products. Mineral resources are being developed on a limited basis and dependence on imported oil has strained the economy.

**History.** In the 14th century the MALI EMPIRE was at its height and, as late as 1507, TIMBUKTU was still a flourishing cultural center. By the mid-17th century Mali had crumbled under external attacks and internal rivalries. In 1896 the area came under French rule, and in 1904 became the French Sudan. In 1958 the colony accepted autonomy within the French community. During 1959–60, with Senegal, it composed the Sudanese Republic. In 1960 Mali became fully independent under President Keita. In 1968 a military coup gave power to the National Liberation Committee. In 1979 the country returned to civilian rule, but the military remained influential.

**MALI EMPIRE,** greatest of the Sudanese empires of Africa. Founded in the 13th century, it reached its height under Mansa Musa who reigned c1312–37. He and his successors were devout Muslims. The towns of Mali and TIMBUKTU became centers both of the caravan trade and of Islamic culture. The empire declined in the 15th century, mainly because of SONGHAI expansion.

**MALINOWSKI, Bronislaw Kasper** (1884–1942), Polish-born British anthropologist, generally accepted as the founder of social ANTHROPOLOGY. In his functional theory all the mores, customs or beliefs of a society perform a vital function in it. From 1927 to 1938 he was a professor at London University; from 1939 until his death, a professor at Yale.

**MALIPIERO, Gian Francesco** (1882–1973), Italian composer who, with Alfredo Casella, was a leader of the Italian school of modern classical music. He wrote many operas, eight major symphonies, seven quartets, and five oratorios, including the avant-garde *Impressioni dal Vero* (1910). He directed the Venice Conservatory, 1940–52.

**MALLARMÉ, Stéphane** (1842–1898), French Symbolist poet (see SYMBOLISM). He held that the subject of poetry should be the ideal world which language would suggest or evoke, but not describe. Although the syntactical and grammatical structure of his poems are difficult, he had considerable influence on French poetry. His works include *The Afternoon of a Faun* (1876), which inspired DEBUSSY, and *A Throw of the Dice Will Never Eliminate Chance* (1897).

**MALLE, Louis** (1932–    ), French film director. A member of the French NEW WAVE, he later made a successful transition to American films. His films include *Zazie dans le Métro* (1961), *Murmur of the Heart* (1971), *Lacombe, Lucien* (1975), *Pretty Baby* (1978) and *Atlantic City* (1981).

**MALLON, Mary** (1870–1938), US cook, known as Typhoid Mary. Using assumed names, she worked in various households in New York City. A carrier of the typhoid fever bacillus, she spread the disease to more than 50 persons, three of whom died, before she was found by authorities and quarantined in 1915.

**MALNUTRITION**, inadequate nutrition, especially in children, which may involve all parts of diet (marasmus), or may be predominantly of PROTEINS (KWASHIORKOR) or VITAMINS (PELLAGRA, BERIBERI, SCURVY). In *marasmus*, essential factors for METABOLISM are derived from the breakdown of body TISSUES; extreme wasting and growth failure result. In adults, starvation is less rapid in onset, as the demands of growth are absent, but similar metabolic changes occur.

**MALONE, Dumas** (1892–    ), US historian who was editor of the *Dictionary of American Biography* (1931–36) and author of the massive biography, *Jefferson and His Time* (5 vols., 1948–74).

**MALORY, Sir Thomas** (d. 1471), English writer and adventurer, author of *The Book of King Arthur and His Noble Knights of the Round Table*, which CAXTON published

as *Morte d'Arthur*, 1485. Much of the wo is based on French versions of tl ARTHURIAN LEGENDS.

**MALPIGHI, Marcello** (1628–1694 Italian physician and biologist, the father microscopic ANATOMY, discoverer of tl CAPILLARIES (1661), and a pioneer in sever fields of medicine and biology.

**MALRAUX, André** (1901–1976), Fren writer, critic and politician. He fought China, in the Spanish CIVIL WAR and in tl resistance in WWII. He was minister information 1945–46 and 1958, and culture 1955–69. His novels *Man's Fa* (1933) and *Hope* (1938) reflect h experiences in China and Spain; nonfictio works such as *The Voices of Silence* (195 and *The Metamorphosis of the Go* (1960) are concerned with art a civilization.

**MALT**, the product made from any cere grain by steeping it in water, germinati and then drying it. This activates dorma ENZYMES such as DIASTASE, which conve the kernel STARCH to MALTOSE. Malt is us as a source of enzymes and flavoring.

**Official name:** Malta
**Capital:** Valletta
**Area:** 121.9sq mi
**Population:** 316,850
**Languages:** Maltese, English; Italian wid spoken
**Religion:** Roman Catholic
**Monetary unit(s):** 1 pound (M) = 100 cer

**MALTA**, independent country strategica placed in the central Mediterranean. comprises the islands of Malta, Go Comino and two uninhabited islets.

Malta has almost no natural resourc The economy depends on light indust tourism, ship-building and ship-repairir and agriculture.

Inhabited since the 4th millennium B Malta was visited by Phoenicians, Gre and Carthaginians before succumbing Roman control in 218 BC. In c60 AD Paul was shipwrecked on Malta. In 15 after occupation by the Arabs, Norma and Spaniards, the islands were granted the KNIGHTS OF SAINT JOHN. The Knig defeated the Turks in the Great Siege of 1565 and built Valletta. In 1798 they were briefly ousted by the French and in 1814 the British took over the islands. In 1942 Malta was awarded the British George Cross for the courage of its people under siege and bombardment in WWII. The country became an independent member of the British Commonwealth in 1964, and a republic in 1974. The last British troops were withdrawn in 1979.

**MALTESE,** Semitic language of the inhabitants of Malta. Punic-Arabic in origin, it contains elements of several other Mediterranean languages.

**MALTHUS, Thomas Robert** (1766–1834), English clergyman best known for his *Essay on the Principle of Population* (1798; second, larger edition, 1803). In this he argued that the population of a region would always grow until checked by famine, pestilence or war. Even if agricultural production were improved, the only result would be an increase in population and the lot of the people would be no better. Although this pessimistic view held down the provision of poor relief in England for many decades, it also provided both C. DARWIN and A. R. WALLACE with a vital clue in the formulation of their theory of EVOLUTION by natural selection.

**MAMELUKES,** or Mamlūks, originally non-Arab slaves forming the personal bodyguard of the Egyptian caliphs and sultans. In 1250 the Mamelukes overthrew the sultanate and ruled until defeated by the Ottomans (1517). They then became an important part of the Turkish army. But in 1811 the Egyptian pasha Muhammad Ali ordered a massacre of all Mamelukes. A very few escaped to Lower Nubia, but soon dispersed.

**MAMMALS,** a class of VERTEBRATES distinguished by the possession of mammary glands in the female for suckling the young, and of body hair. Living mammals are divided into MONOTREMES, egg-laying mammals; MARSUPIALS, pouched mammals that bear their young in an undeveloped state, and PLACENTAL MAMMALS that nourish the young in the uterus with a PLACENTA. Monotremes, ECHIDNAS and the duck-billed PLATYPUS are a very divergent group with many reptilian characteristics. Placental mammals and marsupials show closer affinities. Mammals evolved from Synapsid reptiles; these diverged early from the main reptilian stem and have no living representatives. Thus the actual origin of mammals is a matter for speculation. Certainly many groups of late synapsids independently developed mammal-like characteristics, and it is probable that more than one group crossed the "mammal line," i.e., that mammals are of polyphyletic origin.

**MAMMOTH,** a name that properly applies to only one species of large hairy elephant, the woolly mammoth, *Elephas primigenius*, which lived in the late Pliocene, but is now used for a whole group of large, extinct ELEPHANTS. These resembled modern forms but were covered with reddish hair and bore tusks far longer than any of today.

**MAMMOTH CAVE,** limestone cavern about 85mi SW of Louisville, Ky., containing a series of vast subterranean chambers. It includes lakes, rivers, stalactites, stalagmites and formations of gypsum crystals. The mummified body of a pre-Columbian man has been found there. It is part of Mammoth Cave National Park.

**MAN,** *Homo sapiens*, the most widespread, numerous, and reputedly the most intelligent (see INTELLIGENCE) of the PRIMATES. For man's evolutionary history see PREHISTORIC MAN; for the varieties of man see RACE, and for his earliest social development see PRIMITIVE MAN.

**MAN, Isle of,** island in the Irish Sea off the NW coast of England. It became the base for Irish missionaries after St. Patrick, and at one time was a Norwegian dependency sold to Scotland in 1266. It is now a British dependency with its own legislature (Court of Tynwald) and representative assembly (House of Keys). Tourism is the main industry. The Manx language is now virtually extinct.

**MANAGEMENT AND BUDGET, Office of,** US government office established in 1970 by executive order as part of the Executive Office of the President. It helps the president prepare the federal budget and formulate fiscal programs.

**MANATEES,** large and fully-aquatic herbivorous mammals of tropical and subtropical Atlantic coasts and large rivers. With the DUGONGS they are the only living sea-cows (order: Sirenia). Heavily-built and torpedo-shaped, they have powerful rounded tails which are flattened horizontally. The forelimbs are small and hindlimbs completely absent; the tail provides all propulsion.

**MANCHESTER SCHOOL,** a group of English businessmen and members of Parliament, c1820–1860, mostly from Manchester, who advocated worldwide free trade. They were led by John BRIGHT and Richard COBDEN. In 1839 Cobden formed the Anti-Corn-Law League, which brought about the repeal of the corn laws in 1846.

**MANCHURIA,** also Dongbei or Manchow, a region of NE China comprising Heilungkiang (Heilongjiang), Kirin (Jilin), and Liaoning provinces. It is an important agricultural and industrial area.

Historically, Manchuria was the home of the MANCHUS. Chinese settlement in the area increased rather steadily, especially after 1900. It was a barren steppe until Western exploitation of its vast mineral resources began in the 19th century. In the 1890s Russia had declared an interest in the province; but Russia's defeat in the 1904–05 Russo-Japanese War brought Japanese domination, first of S Manchuria, then, in 1932, of the whole country. The puppet state of MANCHUKUO was created and it was rapidly industrialized. In 1945 Russian forces occupied the area and dismantled the industries upon their withdrawal. Bitterly contested in the Chinese civil war, Manchuria was captured in 1948 by the communists who redrew the provincial boundaries. The name Manchuria is no longer used in China. Pop 100,000,000.

**MANCHUS,** a Manchurian people who conquered China and formed the Ta Ch'ing dynasty (1644–1912). They originated from the Jurchen tribe of the TUNGUS and were originally a nomadic, pastoral people. The Manchus have now been racially and culturally absorbed by the Chinese and their language is virtually extinct.

**MANDALAY,** capital of the Mandalay division and district, N Burma on the Irrawaddy R. It is a Buddhist center with numerous pagodas and a trade point with air, railroad and river connections. Mandalay was founded in the mid-19th century and served (1860–65) as the last capital of the kingdom of Burma. Pop 417,266.

**MANDARIN,** name of nine grades of important civil servants or military officials in imperial China. Mandarin Chinese, formerly an upper-class language, is now the official national language of China, though many dialects still exist.

**MANDELSTAM, Osip Emilievich** (1891–1938?), Russian poet. At first a member of the neoclassicist Acmeist school, he was arrested in 1934 and exiled until 1937. Rearrested in 1938, he reportedly died soon afterwards in a Siberian prison. His works include *Stone* (1913) and *Tristia* (1922). After his death, his widow, Nadezhda Mandelstam (1899–1981) spent many years collecting his verse and smuggling it to the West. Her memoirs, *Hope Against Hope* (1970) and *Hope Abandoned* (1972) were powerful indictments of Stalinism.

**MANDEVILLE, Bernard** (c1670–1733), Dutch-born English philosopher and satirist. Best-known as the author of a work in verse, *The Fable of the Bees* (1714), he attempted to establish that every virtue is based on self-interest.

**MANET, Édouard** (1832–1883), French painter. Though partly influenced by GOYA and VELÁZQUEZ, his work introduced a new pictorial language, and was often severely criticized by the artistic establishment. His paintings *Olympia* and *Le Déjeuner sur l'Herbe* (both 1863) were thought scandalously bold. He strongly influenced the Impressionists, though he refused to exhibit with them.

**MANGANESE NODULES,** heavy concretionary masses of chemically precipitated manganese (average=24%) and lesser amounts of iron, nickel, cobalt and copper, often deposited concentrically around a hard submarine object that serves as a nucleus. Found on the deep ocean floor, they are considered a potentially valuable submarine deposit where they are numerous. It is estimated that 20 to 50% of the Pacific Ocean floor is covered by manganese nodules. (See also DEEP-SEA MINING; OCEANOGRAPHY.)

**MANHATTAN PROJECT,** US project to develop an explosive device working by nuclear FISSION. It was established in Aug. 1942, and research was conducted at Chicago, California and Columbia universities, as well as at Los Alamos, N.M., and other centers. By Dec. 1942 a team headed by FERMI initiated the first self-sustaining nuclear CHAIN REACTION. On July 16, 1945 the first ATOMIC BOMB was detonated near Alamogordo, N.M., and similar bombs were dropped the following month on Hiroshima (Aug. 6) and Nagasaki (Aug. 9). (See also NUCLEAR WARFARE.)

**MANICHAEISM,** religion founded by **Mani** (c216–c276 AD), a Persian sage who preached from c240 and claimed to be the Paraclete (intercessor) promised by Christ. Mani borrowed ideas from BUDDHISM, CHRISTIANITY, GNOSTICISM, Mithraism and ZOROASTRIANISM. A form of DUALISM, Manichaeism contained an elaborate cosmic mythology of salvation. Man was created by Satan, but had particles of divine light in him, which had to be released. St. AUGUSTINE with a Manichaean in his youth. In the Middle Ages, Manichee doctrines surfaced among the BOGOMILS and CATHARI.

**MANIFEST DESTINY,** a phrase coined in 1845. It implied divine sanction for the US "to overspread the continent allotted by Providence for the free development of our multiplying millions." The concept was used to justify most US territorial gains.

**MANILA,** city on the E shore of Manila Bay in SW Luzon, Philippines. It is the commercial, industrial and cultural center and chief port of the islands. Manila was occupied by the Japanese 1942–45 and almost completely rebuilt after the war. It is the country's seat of government, though not its capital. Pop 1,377,000.

**MANITOBA,** easternmost of central Canada's "prairie" provinces.

**Land.** Manitoba comprises four regions. The Saskatchewan Plain is a rich farming area. The Manitoba Lowland is a region of forests, lakes and swamps. Both are part of the W Interior Plains. The Hudson Bay Lowland is a flat, thinly populated plain extending 50–100mi inland from the bay's S shore. The fourth region is an area of lakes, rivers, forests, muskeg (sphagnum bog) and mineral-rich rock; it covers 60% of Manitoba and is part of the vast Canadian Shield area. About 60% of the province is forested and about 15% is covered by rivers and over 100,000 lakes.

**People.** Most people live in the S, and more than 75% are urban. Winnipeg is the largest city. About 43% of the population is of British origin; other ethnic groups include Germans, Ukrainians, Dutch, Scandinavians, Finns, French Canadians and Indians.

**Economy.** Manitoba is one of Canada's more prosperous provinces with growing agricultural, mining and manufacturing sectors. Manufactures include processed food (especially meat packing), metals, machinery and transportation equipment and clothing. Agriculture focuses on wheat and livestock production, with Winnipeg being Canada's leading grain market. Important minerals include nickel, zinc and copper; there are oil deposits near the town of Virden.

**History.** Manitoba's first white settlers were fur traders of the HUDSON'S BAY COMPANY (1670) and the NORTH WEST COMPANY (1783). There was intermarriage with native Indian women, the offspring being called Métis. In 1812 Thomas Douglas founded the first farming settlement along the Red R. The Métis rebelled against this interference with the fur trade, but by 1821 peace was restored. When the Dominion of Canada gained Manitoba from the Hudson's Bay Company in 1869, the Métis again rebelled (under Louis RIEL). They were afraid of losing their lands to British-Canadian settlers. Their rights were respected in the 1870 Manitoba Act, but waves of immigrants did come from Britain, Scandinavia and Central

Europe. Today over half Manitoba's total population lives in the Winnipeg metropolitan area.

**Name of province:** Manitoba
**Joined Confederation:** July 15, 1870
**Capital:** Winnipeg
**Area:** 251,000sq mi
**Population:** 1,028,000

**MANLEY, Michael** (1924–    ), prime minister of Jamaica (1972–80). Failure of his economic policies and leftist sympathies led to his rejection by the voters.

**MANN, Horace** (1796–1859), US educator, lawyer and politician. He served in the Mass. house of representatives (1827–33), and was state senator (1835–37), secretary of the state board of education (1837–48) and US congressman (1848–53). Mann, who published 12 annual reports (1837–48) promoting public education for all children, greatly raised educational standards in Mass.

**MANN, Thomas** (1875–1955), German novelist, essayist and winner of the 1929 Nobel Prize for Literature. He left Germany (1933), settled in the US (1938) and became a US citizen (1944). His works include *Buddenbrooks* (1901), *Death in Venice* (1912), *The Magic Mountain* (1924) and *Joseph and His Brothers* (4 novels; 1933–43). His literary themes are often concerned with the effects of a changing world on people's inner thoughts and lives; with death in the midst of life; and with the artist's isolation.

**MANNERISM,** the artistic and architectural style between the RENAISSANCE and the BAROQUE. It was developed in Bologna, Florence and Rome during the early 16th century and flourished until the century's end. Marked by strained (though apparently executed with great facility) human postures and crowded compositions, the style was a reaction against the Renaissance's classical principles. Mannerists included PARMIGIANINO and PONTORMO.

**MANNHEIM, Karl** (1893–1947), Hungarian-born sociologist. His *Man and Society in an Age of Reconstruction* (1940) stressed the importance of science in effecting sociological change. He taught in Britain at London U., from 1933.

**MANNING, Henry Edward** (1808–1892), English cardinal. He was an Anglican priest 1833–50 and a member of the OXFORD MOVEMENT. In 1851 he entered the Roman Catholic Church and in 1865 became archbishop of Westminster, being made a cardinal in 1875. He founded the League of the Cross temperance movement and mediated in the 1889 London dock strike.

**MANOLETE** (1917–1947), famous Spanish bullfighter. He was recognized as a true professional at Seville (1939) and remained the world's leading matador until fatally gored.

**MAN O' WAR,** legendary US racehorse. Known as "Big Red," he won 20 of 21 races, including the Belmont and Preakness stakes, in 1920 (he was not entered in the Kentucky Derby). His prize money amounted to a then-record $249,465.

**MANSART, Nicolas François** (1598–1666), French architect who popularized, but did not invent, the high-pitched mansard roof. He helped initiate the purity of the French classical style of architecture.

**MANSFIELD, Katherine** (1888–1923), born Kathleen Mansfield Beauchamp, New Zealand-born British short story writer, poet and essayist: The short stories collected in *The Garden Party* (1922) are among her finest mature work.

**MANSHIP, Paul** (1885–1966), US sculptor. He is best known for his interpretations of classical mythological subjects, among which is his statue of *Prometheus* (1934) at Rockefeller Center, New York.

**MANSON FAMILY,** community of young drifters and losers, dominated by Charles Milles Manson and characterized by drug use, perversion and cruelty. Manson and three of his women (Patricia Krenwinkel, Susan Atkins, Leslie Van Houten) were convicted in 1970 of the 1969 murders of movie actress Sharon Tate and four others in her home in Los Angeles and of the murders of Leno and Rosemary LaBianca the next night; another follower, Charles Watson, was convicted in a separate trial in 1971. In 1975, Lynette Alice ("Squeaky") Fromme, once acting head of the Manson family, was convicted of trying to assassinate President Gerald R. Ford. The total number of Manson murder victims was estimated by prosecutor Vincent Bugliosi at 35–40.

**MANTEGNA, Andrea** (c1431–1506), Italian painter and engraver. He was a member of the Paduan school, acclaimed for his mastery of anatomy and illusionistic perspective. Among his most famous works are the cartoons of the *Triumph of Caesar* (c1495). His frescoes in the Eremitani church, Padua (1448–57), were almost totally destroyed by bombing in 1944.

**MANTISES,** long, narrow, carnivorous insects usually found in the tropics. Most species are well-camouflaged as leaves or twigs. Mantids feed on other insects and sit motionless waiting for prey to approach within striking distance when the long front legs are shot out at great speed to catch it.

Many sit "praying" with forelegs raised and clasped together when awaiting prey. The female usually devours the male after mating.

**MANTLE,** zone of the earth's interior underlying the crust and surrounding the core. The mantle is found from continental depths of about 40km (MOHOROVIČIĆ DISCONTINUITY) to 2900km (Gutenberg Discontinuity) and includes the ASTHENOSPHERE and lowermost LITHOSPHERE in its upper part. Forming 82.3% of the volume and 67.8% of the mass of the EARTH, the mantle is thought to be composed of dense iron- and magnesium-rich silicates.

**MANTLE, Mickey Charles** (1931–   ), US baseball player with the New York Yankees, possessing the rare combination of speed afoot and power at the plate. A switch-hitting outfielder, he won the 1956 triple batting crown, leading the American League in average, runs batted in, and homeruns.

**MANTRA,** in HINDUISM and BUDDHISM, sacred utterance believed to possess supernatural power. The constant repetition of *mantras* is used to concentrate the mind on an object of meditation; e.g. the syllable OM, said to evoke the entire VEDA.

**MANX,** Celtic dialect of the Isle of Man. See CELTIC LANGUAGES.

**MANX CAT,** breed of cat with no tail, popularly believed to come from the Isle of Man (hence Manx) but a widely distributed mutation. In addition to its rounded rump, which should show no vestige of tail, it has a special double coat and long hind legs. The mutation causing taillessness affects the whole spine and continuous breeding of Manx to Manx can produce other abnormalities and dead births.

**MANZONI, Alessandro Francesco Tommaso Antonio** (1785–1873), Italian novelist and poet. He was a leading figure in the Romantic movement and his novel *The Betrothed* (1825–27) influenced many later writers. Manzoni's death inspired VERDI's *Requiem* (1874).

**MAORIS,** the pre-European inhabitants of New Zealand. They are a Polynesian people who migrated to New Zealand c1200–1400 AD. When the first Europeans arrived, the Maoris were a well-organized Neolithic tribal society. Some of their tribes fought the British in the Maori Wars of the 1860s. The Maoris have full political rights, and intermarriage with whites is widespread. (See also NEW ZEALAND.)

**MAO TSE-TUNG** (1893–1976), Chinese communist leader, a founder of the People's Republic of China. Son of an educated peasant in Shao-shan, Hunan province, he

**MAP** 765

became interested in various political creeds, including anarchism; in 1921 he joined the newly-founded Shanghai Communist Party, and in 1927 led the Autumn Harvest uprising. This was crushed by the local KUOMINTANG militia, and Mao fled to the mountains. There he built up the Red Army, and in 1931 proclaimed a republic in Kiangsi. Surrounded by Kuomintang forces in 1934, the army was forced to embark on the famous LONG MARCH to Yenan, Shensi. The appalling rigors of the march united the communists behind Mao, and he was elected chairman. In 1937 an uneasy alliance was made with the Kuomintang under CHIANG KAI-SHEK against the Japanese; after WWII Mao's forces drove the Kuomintang to Taiwan. Mao then became chairman of the new People's Republic. During the 1950s and 1960s he steered China ideologically further away from the USSR. In 1966 he launched the "Cultural Revolution" to clear the party of "revisionists." In the 1970s Mao appeared to favor a degree of détente with the West, especially Europe. In 1972, his meeting with President Nixon signaled better relations with the US. From 1974 age and ill-health forced him increasingly to withdraw from public life. It is uncertain how much influence his wife CHIANG CH'ING had on his rule. (See also CHINA.)

**MAP,** diagram representing the layout of features on the earth's surface or part of it. Maps have many uses, including routefinding; marine or aerial NAVIGATION (such maps are called *charts*); administrative, political and legal definition, and scientific study, an exact art. **Cartography,** or mapmaking, is thus an exact art. The techniques of SURVEYING and GEODESY are used to obtain the positional data to be represented. Since the EARTH is roughly spheroidal— the GEOID being taken as the reference level—and since the surface of a sphere cannot be flattened without distortion, no plane map can perfectly represent its original, the distortion becoming worse the larger the area. But spherical maps or *globes* are impractical for large-scale work. Thus plane maps use various **projections,** geometrical algorithms for transforming the spherical coordinates into plane ones. The choice of projection depends on the purpose of the map; one may aim for correct size or correct shape, but not both at once: a suitable compromise is generally reached. Projections fall into three main classes: *Cylindrical projections* are obtained by projection from the earth's axis onto a cylinder touching the equator. MERCATOR's Projection from the center of the earth, is a well-known example: its graticule (net of parallels and meridians) takes the form of a rectangular grid with the scale increasing toward the poles, which are infinitely distant; straight lines represent RHUMB LINES. *Conic projections,* best suited middle latitudes, are obtained by projection onto a cone that caps the earth, touching a given parallel. *Azimuthal projections* are from a single point onto a plane. The *gnomonic* projection, having the point at the center of the earth, represents GREAT CIRCLE ROUTES by straight lines. The *orthographic* projection has the point at infinity, the projective rays being parallel; distortion is great, but the map looks like the globe. These geometric projections are now seldom used as such, but are modified to give correct relative areas, distances or shapes. The *scale* of a map (assuming it to be constant) is the ratio of a distance on the map to the distance that it represents on the earth's surface. It may be expressed directly as the ratio or representative fraction (1:63,360), as a unit ratio (1in to 1mi), or by a graphic graduated scale. Maps use standard symbols and colors to show features, giving the maximum information clearly. Types of map include physical, political, economic, demographic, historical, geological and meteorological maps; there are also star maps (see CELESTIAL SPHERE).

Maps have been drawn from earliest times, but until the Middle Ages most were little more than sketch maps based on impressions and guesswork, except for those of the Greek geographers, notably PTOLEMY of Alexandria. In the 14th century, Mediterranean sea charts were in use which were remarkably accurate, owing to the introduction of the COMPASS and good estimates of distances sailed. The great voyages of discovery, the rediscovery of Ptolemy's map, and accurate surveying in the Low Countries revolutionized cartography in the 16th and 17th centuries, the work of Gerardus MERCATOR and Abraham Ortelius (who produced the first modern atlas) being well-known. Louis XIV promoted a national survey of France, the British Ordnance Survey (1791) followed suit, and in the 19th century most developed countries produced extensive maps. REMOTE SENSING data is increasingly used in modern cartography.

**MARAT, Jean Paul** (1743–1793), French Revolutionary politician and demagogue. A doctor and journalist, he was elected to the National Convention in 1792, and came to lead the radical faction. Chief instigator of the September Massacre (1792) at which over 1,200 died, he was an active supporter of the REIGN OF TERROR. Marat was murdered in his bath by Charlotte CORDAY.

**MARATHON**, famous plain in Greece, about 25mi NE of Athens, where in 490 BC MILTIADES led an Athenian force of about 11,000 to victory over 20,000 Persians led by DARIUS I. Fearing Athens might surrender prematurely, to the Persian fleet, Miltiades sent the runner Pheidippides to report the victory. On reaching Athens, he delivered the message, collapsed and died. The modern OLYMPIC GAMES marathon race commemorates this incident.

**MARBLE, Alice** (1913–      ), US tennis player who won the US singles championship four times (1936; 1938–40) and the Wimbledon singles title (1939) before becoming a professional in 1940.

**MARBLES**, a children's game played on the ground with small spheres of glass, ceramic, or metal. The player's object is to dislodge as many of his opponents' marbles as possible from an encircled area by shooting at them with his own. Those dislodged become his property. A game very much like modern marbles was known in ancient Egypt and in pre-Christian Rome.

**MARBURY v. MADISON**, historic US Supreme Court decision. In 1803, William Marbury sued James Madison, then secretary of state, for failure to deliver a commission given by the previous administration. Chief Justice John Marshall held the act upon which Marbury relied to be unconstitutional, thus establishing the judicial right to review the constitutionality of legislation.

**MARC, Franz** (1880–1916), German expressionist painter, with KANDINSKY a cofounder of the BLAUE REITER group. His work is characterized by vigorous lines and a vivid and symbolic use of color.

**MARCEAU, Marcel** (1923–      ), perhaps the greatest modern MIME. Born in France, he studied drama in Paris, rising to fame with a brief mime role in the film Les Enfants du paradis (1944). His most famous characterization is the white-faced

clown, Bip. He became world famous with stage appearances in the 1950s.

**MARCH**, third month of the Gregorian CALENDAR. It corresponds to the Roman month Martius (after Mars, god of war), first month of the Roman calendar until 153 BC, when Jan. 1 was made New Year's Day. March has 31 days; the spring equinox occurs on March 21.

**MARCH, Fredric** (1897–1975), US film actor who distinguished himself equally in light comedy and drama. His major films include A Star is Born (1937), The Best Years of Our Lives (1946), for which he won the Academy Award, and Death of a Salesman (1952).

**MARCIANO, Rocky** (1923–1969), US boxer, world heavyweight champion 1952–56, when he retired. He is the only major prizefighter to have remained undefeated throughout his professional career. Born Rocco Marchegiane, Marciano fought 49 bouts in 9 years, winning 43 by knockout. He was killed in an air crash.

**MARCION** (d. c160 AD), founder of a heretical Christian sect. He joined the church in Rome c140 but was excommunicated in 144. Influenced by GNOSTICISM, he taught that there were two rival Gods: one, the tyrannical creator and lawgiver of the Old Testament; the other, the unknown God of love and mercy who sent Jesus to purchase salvation from the creator God. Marcion rejected the Old Testament wholly, and of the New Testament accepted only expurgated versions of Luke's Gospel and 10 of St. Paul's Letters. This forced the orthodox Church to fix its canon of Scripture. Marcionites spread widely but by the end of the 3rd century had mostly been absorbed by MANICHAEISM.

**MARCONI, Guglielmo** (1874–1937), Italian-born inventor and physicist, awarded (with K. F. BRAUN) the 1909 Nobel Prize for Physics for his achievements. On learning of Hertzian (RADIO) waves in 1894, he set to work to devise a wireless TELEGRAPH. By the following year he could transmit and receive signals at distances of about 2km. He went to the UK to make further developments, and in 1899 succeeded in sending a signal across the English Channel. On Dec. 12, 1901 in St. John's, Newfoundland, he successfully received a signal sent from Poldhu, Cornwall, thus heralding the dawn of transatlantic radio communication.

**MARCOS, Ferdinand Edralin** (1917–      ), president of the Philippines since 1966. A lawyer and war hero, he gave the country considerable progress in agriculture, industry and education. He declared martial law in 1971, after a bomb attack on a political rally, and in 1972 introduced emergency powers under a new constitution. Despite his forceful rule, a left-wing guerilla movement grew during the 1970s.

**MARCUS AURELIUS** (121–180 AD), one of the greatest of Roman emperors. Adopted at 17 by his uncle ANTONINUS PIUS, he succeeded him as emperor in 161 AD, after a distinguished career in public service. During this he wrote his famous *Meditations*, his personal philosophy; he was one of the major exponents of STOICISM. His reign was marred by plague, rebellion, barbarian attacks along the Rhine and Danube, and his own savage persecution of Christians, to whom he had taken a dislike strange in so humane a man. His government was otherwise noted for social reform, justice and generosity.

**MARCUSE, Herbert** (1898–1979), German-born US political philosopher who combined Freudianism and Marxism in his social criticism. According to Marcuse modern society is automatically repressive and requires violent revolution as the first step towards a Utopian society. He became a cult figure of the New Left in the US in the 1960s.

**MARDI GRAS,** (literally "fat Tuesday"), festivities on Shrove Tuesday, the last day of carnival before the start of Lent. Celebrated as a holiday in various Catholic countries, it was introduced into the US by French settlers and is now observed in many places, most particularly in New Orleans.

**MARGARINE,** a spread high in food value, prepared from vegetable or animal fats together with milk products, preservatives, emulsifiers, butter and salt. It was first developed in the late 1860s by the French chemist Hippolyte Mège-Mouriès, inspired by a competition launched by Napoleon III to find a cheap BUTTER substitute. The fats used were, early on, primarily animal, with whale oil being particularly popular in Europe, but recently vegetable oils (especially soybean and corn) have been used almost exclusively.

**MARGINAL UTILITY.** In classical economics utility is defined as the psychological satisfaction derived from consuming a particular good or service, whose demand was therefore explained by the amount of utility it afforded. Total utility increases as more of the given good is consumed, and the amount of extra utility derived by consuming each additional unit is called marginal utility.

**MARIANA ISLANDS,** group of islands in the W Pacific. Lying 1,500mi E of the Philippines, their total area is 184sq mi. Discovered by MAGELLAN in 1521, they were named the Ladrones (Thieves) Islands until renamed in 1668 by Jesuit missionaries. After WWI they were under a Japanese mandate until seized by the US in WWII. They became part of the UN Trust Territory of the Pacific Islands in 1947. In 1978 the northern islands became the NORTHERN MARIANAS and became a Commonwealth of the US. The majority of the population lives on the largest and southernmost island, Guam, a US outlying territory. The group's economy rests on subsistence agriculture, copra export and government and military installations.

**MARIA THERESA** (1717–1780), Empress, archduchess of Austria, Queen of Hungary and of Bohemia and wife of the Holy Roman Emperor Francis I, one of the most able of Hapsburg rulers. Despite the PRAGMATIC SANCTION, its signatories launched the War of the AUSTRIAN SUCCESSION against her as soon as she succeeded her father in 1740. This lost Silesia to Prussia; she allied with France in the SEVEN YEARS WAR against Prussia, but was defeated. A capable ruler, she introduced administrative and fiscal reforms and maintained a strong army. Married to Francis of Lorraine in 1736, she arranged his election as emperor.

**MARIE ANTOINETTE** (1755–1793), queen of France from 1774. Daughter of Maria Theresa and the Emperor Francis I, she married the Dauphin in 1770 and became queen on his accession as Louis XVI. Youthful extravagances made her many enemies, as did her unwitting involvement in a confidence trick perpetrated on the Cardinal de Rohan. When the French Revolution broke out she advised the attempted escape of the royal family which ended with its capture at Varennes. Imprisoned with Louis, she was guillotined nine months after him, in Oct. 1793.

**MARIJUANA,** term applied to any part of the HEMP plant (*Cannabis sativa*) or extract from it. The intoxicating drug obtained from the flowering tops is also called cannabis or HASHISH. This drug is usually smoked in cigarettes or pipes, but can also be sniffed or taken as food. It is mainly used for the mild euphoria it produces, although other symptoms include loss of muscular coordination, increased heart beat, drowsiness and hallucination. Its use, the subject of much medical and social debate, is widespread throughout the world.

**MARIN, John** (1870–1953), US painter and print maker best known for his expressionistic watercolors (influenced by

CÉZANNE and the German Expressionists) of Manhattan and the Maine coast, such as *Singer Building* (1921) and *Maine Islands* (1922).

**MARINE BIOLOGY,** the study of the flora and fauna in the sea, from the smallest PLANKTON to massive WHALES. It includes the study of the complex interrelationships between marine organisms that make up the food chains (see ECOLOGY) of the sea. It has become apparent in recent years that if the sea is to remain a major and increasing source of food for man, CONSERVATION measures must be taken, particularly to retain adequate stocks of breeding fish. POLLUTION must also be controlled.

**MARINE CORPS, United States,** armed service within the Department of the Navy providing troops trained for land, sea and air operations. The Corps was founded by the Continental Congress in 1775 and established by act of Congress on July 11, 1798. It served in the REVOLUTIONARY WAR. the naval war with France 1798–1801, the war with Tripoli 1801–05 and all subsequent major conflicts in which the US has been involved. Nearly 79,000 Marines served in WWI; they played a major role in the Pacific theater in WWII, first with their heroic stands at Wake, Guam, Bataan, Corregidor and Midway, and later the assault at Guadalcanal and the Pacific campaign. Over 475,000 Marines fought in WWII. Subsequently the Corps fought in Korea, preserved order in the Lebanon in 1958, and ended fighting in the Dominican Republic in 1965. In Vietnam they developed a new technique of riverine warfare. The Marine Corps has made in all over 300 landings on enemy territory. Between 1943 and 1945, the Marine Corps Women's Reserve numbered over 23,000. With the passing of the Women's Armed Services Integration Act in 1948, the women reservists became full-fledged members of the regular Marine Corps.

**MARINER PROGRAM,** US unmanned space probes which have made close "fly-by" observations of VENUS, MARS and MERCURY. Mariner 9 orbited Mars 1971–72, sending back a detailed surface survey. Mariner 10 flew by Venus in 1974, and took the first pictures of Mercury's surface during three fly-bys 1974–75.

**MARINETTI, Filippo Tommaso** (1876–1944), Italian writer, progenitor of FUTURISM. His *Manifesto* (1909), published in *Le Figaro* in Paris, called for the abandonment of art of the past and the creation of a new art based on continual revolution and change. He came to support Fascism as the best means of revolution.

**MARION, Francis** (c1732–1795), guerrilla leader in the REVOLUTIONARY WAR. Commander of S.C. troops, he fought at Charleston in 1776. In 1780 he and his men were forced to take refuge in the swamps, from which they waged a ceaseless guerrilla warfare on Loyalist farms and on British troops, who nicknamed Marion "the Swamp Fox." He served in the state senate 1782–90, and on the state constitutional convention.

**MARIONETTE.** See PUPPET.

**MARIS, Roger** (1934–    ), US baseball player. An outfielder with the New York Yankees (1960–66), he made sports history by hitting 61 homeruns in 1961, breaking Babe Ruth's single-season homerun mark of 60 set in 1927.

**MARISOL          (Marisol          Escobar)** (1930–    ), Venezuelan-born US sculptor, who satirized and caricatured human society by creating POP ART-type figures, usually from wood and clay. Reminiscent of South American folk art, her sculptures are stark representations, with many of the details drawn on them.

**MARITAIN, Jacques** (1882–1973), leading French Neo-Thomist philosopher. He turned to the study of THOMISM after his conversion to Catholicism in 1906. Professor of modern Philosophy at the Catholic Institute, Paris, 1914–39, he was French ambassador to the Vatican 1945–48 and a professor at Princeton U. 1948–60.

**MARITIME LAW,** body of law, based on custom, court decisions and statutes, seeking to regulate all aspects of shipping and ocean commerce such as insurance, salvage and contracts for carriage of goods by sea. It is international to the extent that firm general principles exist, but these have no legal force except as they are incorporated by individual countries into their own legal systems; they are often modified in the process. Many derive from decisions of medieval maritime courts. In the US maritime law is administered by the federal district courts.

**MARIVAUX, Pierre Carlet de Chamblain de** (1688–1763), French playwright and novelist, best known for his witty comedies. Sparkling    dialogue    is    still    termed *marivaudage*. His most famous works are the comedy *A Game of Love and Chance* (1730) and the novel *The Parvenu Peasant* (1735–36).

**MARK, Saint** (John Mark; flourished 1st century AD), Christian evangelist, traditional author of the second GOSPEL, which derived information from St. Peter in Rome. The Gospel is the earliest and simplest and was a source for the other

SYNOPTIC GOSPELS. Mark accompanied Barnabas (his cousin) and Paul on their missionary journeys.

**MARKHAM, (Charles Edward Anson) Edwin** (1852–1940), US poet and lecturer whose poem of social protest, *The Man with the Hoe* (1899), based on a painting by MILLET, brought him a fortune and worldwide acclaim.

**MARKOVA, Dame Alicia** (1910– ), leading English ballerina, born Lilian Alicia Marks. Having appeared with most of the world's major companies, she founded her own with Anton DOLIN, 1935–38. This grew into the London Festival Ballet, which they headed 1944–52. She also directed the Metropolitan Opera Ballet, 1963–69, and taught at the University of Cincinnati, 1969–74.

**MARK TWAIN.** See TWAIN, MARK.

**MARLBOROUGH, John Churchill, 1st Duke of** (1650–1722), British soldier and statesman, one of the country's greatest generals. He helped suppress MONMOUTH's rebellion for James II, but transferred his allegiance to William of Orange in 1688 and was made an earl and a member of the Privy Council. His wife was Sarah Jennings, a friend and attendant of Princess (later Queen) Anne; together they had great influence with the queen. After her accession in 1702 Marlborough commanded English, Dutch and German forces in the war of the SPANISH SUCCESSION. In 1704 he won a great victory over the French at BLENHEIM; a palace of that name was built for him at the queen's expense. Further victories followed at Ramillies (1706), Oudenarde (1708) and Malplaquet (1709). His wife fell from favor with the Queen in 1711 and Marlborough was dismissed; in 1714, however, he was restored to favor by George I.

**MARLOWE, Christopher** (1564–1593), English poet and dramatist, a major influence on Shakespeare. He developed the use of dramatic blank verse in a rhetorically rich and splendid language. In *Dr. Faustus* (c1589) he developed a new concept of tragedy, the struggle of a great personality doomed to inevitable failure by its own limitations. In *Tamburlaine* (c1581) he created a heroic theme without the depth of characterization that appears in his most mature work, *Edward II* (c1592). Often accused of homosexuality, atheism and of being a government spy, he was stabbed to death in a tavern brawl.

**MARNE RIVER,** chief tributary of the Seine R in France. About 325mi in length, it rises on the Langres plateau, flowing NW to Épernay and from there W to join the Seine at Charenton. It is navigable for about 220mi, much of which has been canalized. The Marne valley was the scene of heavy fighting during WWI.

**MARONITES,** a sect of eastern Christians who in the 7th century espoused MONOTHELETISM. In the 12th century they became affiliated with the Roman Catholic Church (see UNIATE CHURCHES). Although some Maronites have settled in Cyprus, Syria and Egypt, their largest community is still in the Lebanon, where their immediate spiritual head under the pope, the Maronite patriarch, also resides.

**MARQUAND, John Phillips** (1893–1960), US novelist best known for his detective stories centered around the Japanese agent Mr. Moto, and for his gentle satires of New England society, such as *The Late George Apley* (1937), for which he won a 1938 Pulitzer Prize, and *Point of No Return* (1949).

**MARQUESAS ISLANDS,** two clusters of mountainous and volcanic islands in the S Pacific, 740mi NE of Tahiti. Their total area is about 492sq mi; the largest islands are Hiba Oa and Nuku Hiva. The S group was discovered by the Spanish in 1595; both were annexed by France in 1842. The islands are fertile, producing breadfruit, coffee, vanilla and copra for export.

**MARQUETTE, Jacques** (1637–1675), French Jesuit missionary and explorer. With Louis JOLIET he left St. Ignace mission, Mich., in 1673 on a search for the mouth of the Mississippi. They traced its course as far as the mouth of the Arkansas R and learned that it entered the Gulf of Mexico. In 1674 Marquette went back to Ill. to found a mission among Indians who had befriended him, but his health deteriorated. He died on the E shore of Lake Michigan while returning to St. Ignace.

**MARQUIS, Don** (Donald Robert Perry; 1878–1937), US literary journalist, poet and playwright, best known as the creator of "archy," a poet reincarnated as a cockroach, and his friend "mehitabel," a disreputable cat, who appeared in Marquis's columns in the *New York Sun* 1912–22 and *Tribune* 1922–25, and in subsequent books.

**MARRIAGE,** durable union between man and woman for the purpose of cohabitation and usually also for raising children. In the broadest sense it is not an exclusively human institution; some animal pair bonds may endure for life. Most human marriages are at least intended to last for life, but most societies have some provision for DIVORCE, ranging from the easy to the almost impossible. The modern trend is towards **monogamy,** union between one man and one woman only. Many societies still permit POLYGAMY, but it is increasingly rare, even among Muslims. Forms of group and communal marriage have been tried from time to time, though with little success or social acceptance.

Marriage is in some senses a contract, often involving property and in some societies a DOWRY or a bride-price. In US law today marriage creates special ownership rights in marital property. It is, however, still also a religious matter in many countries; marriage is a minor sacrament of the Roman Catholic Church.

Most societies limit marriage in certain ways. It is forbidden in most countries between partners who have too close a blood relationship, or consanguinity, though the degree permissible varies widely between countries, religions and even between US states. In US COMMON LAW a purported marriage involving BIGAMY is void; other conditions, such as non-consummation, render marriage void or voidable, generally through the courts. A marriage is also void if not carried out in the prescribed legal form, although in some states common-law marriage may arise after long cohabitation without any formality. Marriages in the US are performed either by civil authority or by a religious ceremony with civil authorization; the ceremonies of most denominations are so authorized in most states. In general a marriage valid in one state is recognized in the others. Some states require a waiting period, and some religions require banns to be posted.

**MARROW, Bone,** the material in the center of BONES, in which ERYTHROCYTES, white blood cells and platelets are made. Mature cells only are released unless the marrow is diseased, as in LEUKEMIA, secondary CANCER or in serious infections. Bone marrow aspiration or BIOPSY is often valuable in diagnosis.

**MARS,** the fourth planet from the sun, with a mean solar distance of 228Gm (about 1.52AU) and a "year" of 687 days. During the Martian day of about 24.62h, the highest temperature at the equator is about 30°C; the lowest, just before dawn, is about −100°C Mars has a mean diameter of 6,750km, with a small degree of polar flattening, and at its closest to earth (see CONJUNCTION) is some 56Gm distant. Its tenuous atmosphere consists mainly of carbon dioxide, nitrogen and NOBLE GASES, and the distinctive Martian polar caps are composed of frozen carbon dioxide and water ice.

Telescopically, Mars appears as an ocher-red disk marked by extensive dark areas: these latter have in the past been erroneously termed *maria* (seas). Several observers in the past reported sighting networks of straight lines on the Martian surface—the famous canals— but observations with large telescopes and the photographs sent back by MARINER and VIKING probes showed these to be an optical illusion. Mars actually has a cratered surface marked with canyons, ancient volcanoes, and jumbled terrains. No probe has yet found evidence that life ever existed on the planet. Mars has two moons, PHOBOS and DEIMOS.

**MARSEILLAISE,** French national anthem composed in 1792 by Claude Rouget de Lisle, a Revolutionary engineer captain. Named for its popularity with the Marseilles soldiers, it was banned by NAPOLEON I, LOUIS XVIII and NAPOLEON III until 1879.

**MARSEILLES,** city in SE France, the second largest city in the country, its chief Mediterranean seaport and a major industrial center. It was originally the Greek settlement of Massilia, annexed by Rome in 49 BC. The city's recent expansion began with the conquest of Algeria and the opening of the SUEZ CANAL in the 19th century. It has a wide range of industries; its port handles around 25% of French maritime trade. Pop 914,400; met pop 1,070,900.

**MARSH, (Edith) Ngaio** (1899–    ), New Zealand theatrical producer and writer of detective novels which have been praised as among the best of their kind. They include *Death of a Peer* (1940), *Hand in Glove* (1962) and *Killer Dolphin* (1966).

**MARSH, Reginald** (1898–1954), US painter. A newspaper illustrator, he later turned to the realistic depiction of New York City life in egg TEMPERA paintings such as *Twenty-Cent Movie* (1936).

**MARSHALL, Alfred** (1842–1924), British economist, professor of political economy at Cambridge 1885–1908. His *Principles of Economics* (1890) systematized economic thought up to that time, and was the standard text for many years. Through his work on cost and value Marshall developed a viable concept of MARGINAL UTILITY.

**MARSHALL, George Catlett** (1880–1959), US general and statesman. As chief of staff 1939–45 he influenced Allied strategy in WWII. Special ambassador to China in 1945, he was then made secretary of state (1947–49) by President TRUMAN. He introduced the European Recovery Program, or MARSHALL PLAN. He was active in the creation of the NORTH ATLANTIC TREATY ORGANIZATION, serving as

US secretary of defense 1950–51. He was awarded the 1955 Nobel Peace Prize.

**MARSHALL, John** (1755–1835), fourth chief justice of the US, known as the "Great Chief Justice." He established the modern status of the SUPREME COURT. Born in Va., he served in the REVOLUTIONARY WAR, studied law and was elected to the Va. legislature in 1782. A staunch Federalist, he supported acceptance of the Constitution. He declined ministerial posts but became one of the US negotiators who resolved the XYZ AFFAIR. Elected to Congress 1799, he was made secretary of state by President ADAMS 1800–01; in 1801 he became chief justice. He labored to increase the then scant power and prestige of the Supreme Court. In MARBURY V. MADISON he established its power to review a law and if necessary declare it unconstitutional. An opponent of STATES' RIGHTS, he established in McCULLOCH V. MARYLAND and GIBBONS V. OGDEN (and incidentally in the DARTMOUTH COLLEGE CASE) the superiority of federal authority under the Constitution. In 1807 he presided over the treason trial of Aaron BURR.

**MARSHALL, Thurgood** (1908–    ), US judge, first black member of the US SUPREME COURT. Chief counsel for the NATIONAL ASSOCIATION FOR THE ADVANCEMENT OF COLORED PEOPLE 1938–61 and solicitor general 1965–67, he was appointed to the Supreme Court by President JOHNSON in 1967.

**MARSHALL PLAN,** the European Recovery Program 1947–52, named for its originator, US Secretary of State George C. MARSHALL. In general it succeeded in its design, which was to help Europe's economic recovery after WWII and so check Eastern bloc communist influence. Material and financial aid amounting to almost 13 billion dollars was sent to the 17 European countries who formed the Organization for European Economic Cooperation. The plan was administered by the US Economic Cooperation Administration, headed by Paul G. Hoffmann.

**MARSH GAS.** See METHANE.

**MARSILIUS OF PADUA** (c1275–1343), Italian political philosopher whose *Defensor pacis* (Latin: defender of peace; 1324) denied the Church's temporal power and proposed its subjugation to the sovereign, who ruled by popular mandate. He was protected from papal attacks by his patron, Emperor LOUIS IV.

**MARSTON, John** (1576–1634), English playwright best known for his tragicomedy *The Malcontent* (1604) and his rivalry with Ben JONSON. Both were imprisoned for offending JAMES I in their collaboration

*Eastward Ho!* (1605). Marston was ordained 1609.

**MARSUPIALS,** MAMMALS with a double womb, giving birth to incompletely developed young which continue development attached to the mother's teats. Differences in the reproductive system are the only infallible way of separating marsupials from true mammals: in marsupials the urinary ducts from the kidneys separate the developing sex ducts, so that in the female both uterus and vagina are double structures. In the male, the urinary ducts lie between the sperm ducts; in PLACENTAL MAMMALS, they lie outside them. The pouch, or marsupium, is not an exclusive or even universal feature of the group. Marsupials are at their most developed in Australia, where, in the absence of placental mammals, they achieved great diversity of form. In addition, there remain a number of groups in the Americas.

**MARTHA'S VINEYARD,** island off the coast of SE Mass. About 100sq mi in area, it is separated from Cape Cod by Vineyard Sound. Discovered and named by Bartolomew Gosnold (1602), it was settled c1632. A major whaling center in the 18th and 19th centuries, it is now a popular summer resort.

**MARTI, José Julian** (1853–1895), major Cuban poet and hero of the anti-Spanish independence movement. He founded the Cuban Revolutionary Party in the US 1881–95. His best known poems appear in *Ismaelillo* (1882), *Versos libres* (1913) and *Versos sencilles* (1891). A leader of the 1895 independence campaign, Marti was killed at the battle of Dos Rios.

**MARTIAL** (Marcus Valerius Martialis; c40–c104 AD), Spanish-born Latin epigrammatic poet. He lived in Rome 64–98 AD, and was favored by emperors TITUS and DOMITIAN and befriended by PLINY the Younger, JUVENAL and QUINTILIAN. Martial wrote in all 15 books of EPIGRAMS.

**MARTIAL LAW,** temporary superimposition of military on domestic civil government, usually in wartime or other national emergency. The army takes over executive and judicial functions, and civil rights such as HABEAS CORPUS may be suspended. When an invading army assumes control of a country it is said to act not under martial law but as a military government; law applying only to those in military service is not martial but military.

**MARTIN, Glenn Luther** (1886–1955), pioneering US aircraft designer and manufacturer. A former barnstorming flyer, he developed various military designs after WWI, one of which became the famous B-26 bomber. Many of his other planes and flying boats were used in WWII.

**MARTIN, Mary** (1913–    ), US musical comedy star, famous for her stage appearances in *One Touch of Venus* (1945), *South Pacific* (1949), *Peter Pan* (1954; on TV, 1955) and *The Sound of Music* (1959). She also played many film roles in the 1940s.

**MARTIN DU GARD, Roger** (1881–1958), French novelist known for his objective but somber exploration of human relationships and the large backgrounds in which he sets them. In *Jean Barois* (1913) it is the DREYFUS AFFAIR; in *The Thibaults* (1922–40) it is WWI. In 1937 he won the Nobel Prize for Literature.

**MARTINIQUE**, island in the Windward group in the E Caribbean, an overseas department of France since 1946. Discovered by COLUMBUS c1493, it was colonized by France as a sugar-growing center after 1635; slave labor was used until 1848, and much of the present population is of African descent. The economy still rests on sugar, and also rum, fruit and tourism. The island is volcanic, and so is rugged and mountainous but very fertile. Its main town is Fort-de-France.

**MARTIN OF TOURS, Saint** (d. 397), patron saint of France. Son of a pagan, he served in the Roman army but after a vision of Christ sought a religious life. Bishop of Tours from c372, he encouraged monasticism and opposed execution of heretics.

**MARTINŮ, Bohuslav** (1890–1959), Czech composer who lived in Paris 1923–40, and the US 1940–46. Although incorporating Czech folk themes, his highly individual work is usually neoclassical in style, as in the ballet *Istar* (1922) and the powerful *Double Concerto* (1940).

**MARVELL, Andrew** (1621–1678), English METAPHYSICAL POET. Assistant to John MILTON from 1657, he was a member of Parliament from 1659. A Puritan, he was known as a wit and satirist, but is today best remembered for his lyric poetry such as "To His Coy Mistress" and "The Garden."

**MARX, Karl Heinrich** (1818–1883), German philosopher and social and economic theorist, the most important of socialist thinkers. Born at Trier of Jewish parents, Marx studied at Bonn and Berlin. When the Cologne newspaper he edited was suppressed (1843) he moved with his wife Jenny von Westphalen to Paris, Brussels and London, where he spent most of his life in great poverty.

With Friedrich ENGELS, his lifelong friend and collaborator, Marx published the

COMMUNIST MANIFESTO (1848) on the eve of the REVOLUTIONS OF 1848. It summarizes Marx's social philosophy. In London Marx cofounded (1864) and led the International Workingmen's Association (First INTERNATIONAL). But most of his energy went into his writing, of which *Capital* (3 volumes: 1867, 1885, 1894) is the most important.

In developing DIALECTICAL MATERIALISM Marx adapted HEGEL's dialectic to his own economic interpretation of history. Ethics, politics and religion are the products of socioeconomic relations. Accepting the labor theory of value of RICARDO, Marx argued that the surplus value, or profit, extracted by the capitalist from his workforce would in time inevitably decline. CAPITALISM, the inevitable successor to FEUDALISM, would in turn inevitably be replaced by SOCIALISM and eventually COMMUNISM. The class war between the capitalist and the worker he exploits would end in the overthrow of capitalism. (See MARXISM.)

**MARX BROTHERS**, Groucho, Harpo and Chico, famous US film comedy team. The original team consisted of Chico (Leonard; 1887–1961), Groucho (Julius; 1890–1977), Gummo (Milton; c1892–    ), Harpo (Arthur; 1887–1964) and Zeppo (Herbert; 1901–1979). Gummo and Zeppo left the team by 1934. After appearing on Broadway, the Marx brothers made about a dozen movies (1933–46). Their anarchic humor is seen to best advantage in *Duck Soup* (1933) and *A Night at the Opera* (1935). Groucho also starred as a popular TV game show host in the 1950s and 1960s.

**MARXISM**, the foundation philosophy of modern COMMUNISM, originating in the work of Karl MARX and Friedreich ENGELS. Three basic concepts are: that productive labor is the fundamental attribute of human nature; that the structure of any society is determined by its economic means of production; and that societies evolve by a series of crises caused by internal contradictions, analyzable by DIALECTICAL MATERIALISM. Marx held that 19th-century industrial CAPITALISM, the latest stage of the historical process, had arisen from FEUDALISM by class struggle between the aristocracy and the rising bourgeois capitalist class. Dialectical materialism predicted conflict between these capitalists and the working class, or PROLETARIAT, on which the new industrialism depended. The triumphant dictatorship of the proletariat, an idea further developed by LENIN, would give way to a classless, stateless communist society where all would be equal, contributing according to their abilities and receiving according to their needs. A key concept of Marxist economics is the LABOR THEORY OF VALUE, that value is created by labor and profit is surplus value creamed off by the capitalist. The fact that he owns the means of production makes this exploitation possible. It also means that the worker cannot own the product of his labor and thus suffers ALIENATION from part of his own humanity and the social system. Marx believed capitalism would be swept away by the last of a catastrophic series of crises. Among numerous later Marxist theorists are Karl KAUTSKY and Rosa LUXEMBURG. In *The Accumulation of Capital* (1913), Luxemburg argued that capitalism was able to adapt and survive by exploitation of its colonial empires. In Russia STALIN proclaimed Marxist-Leninism, an active philosophy of society in forced evolutionary conflict. In China MAO TSE-TUNG adapted Marxism to an agricultural peasant situation. Yugoslavia's TITO gave Marxism a nationalist bias, still more marked in the thinking of Fidel CASTRO of Cuba. Western economists, sociologists and historians have been widely influenced by Marxism.

**MARY,** the mother of JESUS CHRIST, also called the Blessed Virgin. The chief events of her life related in the Gospels are her betrothal to JOSEPH; the ANNUNCIATION of Christ's birth; her visit to her cousin Elizabeth, mother of John the Baptist; the birth of Christ, and her witnessing his crucifixion. In the Roman Catholic Church Mary is accorded a special degree of veneration, called hyperdulia, superior to that given to other saints, and is regarded as mediatrix of all graces and coredemptress. Roman Catholic doctrine holds she was born free from sin, remained always a virgin, and was assumed bodily into heaven (see IMMACULATE CONCEPTION; ASSUMPTION OF THE VIRGIN.)

**MARY,** name of two English queens. **Mary I** (1516–1558), daughter of HENRY VIII and Catherine of Aragon, succeeded EDWARD VI in 1553. She tried to restore Roman Catholicism in England. Some 300 Protestants were burnt as heretics—a persecution unparalleled in England, which earned her the name "Bloody Mary." Her unpopular alliance with and marriage to PHILIP II of Spain (1554) led to war with France and the loss of Calais (1558). **Mary II** (1662–1694), was the Protestant daughter of JAMES II and wife of her cousin WILLIAM III. She was proclaimed joint sovereign with him in 1689.

**MARYKNOLL FATHERS,** popular name for the Catholic Foreign Mission Society of America. It was founded in 1911 with headquarters at Maryknoll, N.Y. It has sent missions to Asia, Latin America and the Pacific islands.

**Name of state:** Maryland
**Capital:** Annapolis
**Statehood:** April 28, 1788 (7th state)
**Familiar name:** Old Line State, Free State
**Area:** 10,577sq mi
**Population:** 4,216,446
**Elevation:** Highest—3,360ft., Backbone Mountain. Lowest—sea level, Atlantic Ocean
**Motto:** Fatti Maschii, Parole Femine (Manly deeds, womanly words)
**State flower:** Black-eyed susan
**State bird:** Baltimore oriole
**State tree:** White oak
**State song:** "Maryland, My Maryland"

**MARYLAND,** state, E US, on the Atlantic Ocean, one of the original 13 colonies, bounded to the N by Pa., to the NE by Del., to the S and SW by Va. and Washington, D.C., and to the W by W.V.

**Land.** Maryland has three major regions: the Atlantic coastal plain in the E, the Piedmont-Blue Ridge region in the center, and the Appalachian-Allegheny Mts in the W. The Potomac R, forming the state's W border, flows into CHESAPEAKE BAY which divides Md. from N to S, separating the E Shore from the rest of the state. Much of the state is covered by forests, including 12 state forests. The average annual temperature is 53°F.

**People.** Maryland's population is heavily urban (over 75%). The principal urban areas are Baltimore and the suburbs of

Washington, D.C.

**Economy.** A diversified economy is dominated by shipbuilding and the manufacture of iron and steel, transportation equipment, electrical and electronic products, and processed foods. There are also large livestock, horsebreeding and fishing industries.

**History.** Maryland was first explored by John Smith in 1608. In 1632 George CALVERT, Lord Baltimore, was granted the territory and founded a colony named for Henrietta Maria, wife of Charles I of England. The colony's initial religious freedom was eroded by the Puritans' ascendancy. The MASON-DIXON line set the boundary between Md. and Pa. Staunchly anti-loyalist during the War of Independence, Md. was the seventh state to ratify the US Constitution (1788). In 1790–91 it ceded a tract of land along the Potomac R for the new national capital, Washington, D.C. In the 19th century an extensive transportation system was constructed and Baltimore became a major US shipbuilding center. Although locally divided, Md. remained in the Union during the Civil War.

The opening in 1952 of the Chesapeake Bay Bridge-Tunnel led to the industrialization of the Eastern Shore. Md.'s historic sites include Fort McHenry (see WAR OF 1812), the state house in Annapolis and the ANTIETAM National Battlefield site. The US Naval Academy is in Annapolis.

In recent years, Maryland has undergone some economic difficulties, reflected in a low population growth in the 1970s (5.7%) and a population shift from the cities to the suburbs. On the other hand, beginning in the late 1970s, Baltimore was basking in a much-publicized "Renaissance," emanating from the restored and redesigned inner harbor district.

**MARY QUEEN OF SCOTS** (1542–1587), queen of Scotland (1542–67), daughter of JAMES V (d. 1542) and MARY OF GUISE. Brought up in France, she married (1558) the Dauphin, king as FRANCIS II (d. 1560). Returning to Scotland (1561) she married (1565) Lord DARNLEY. In 1566 he murdered her favorite David Rizzio, but was himself later murdered, supposedly by the Earl of BOTHWELL, whom Mary married. Public outrage and Presbyterian opposition forced her abdication and in 1568 she fled to England. Mary, heir presumptive of ELIZABETH I and a Roman Catholic, soon became the natural focus of plots against the English throne. Parliament demanded her death, but it was only in 1587, after the BABINGTON plot, that Elizabeth reluctantly

agreed. Mary's trial and execution at Fotheringay castle inspired SCHILLER's tragedy *Maria Stuart*.

**MASACCIO** (Tommaso Guidi; 1401–1428), Florentine painter of the RENAISSANCE, one of the great innovators of western art. He was possibly a pupil of MASOLINO. By taut line, austere composition, and inspired use of light Masaccio created expressive monumental paintings, notably in the Brancacci chapel, S. Maria del Carmine, Florence.

**MASADA**, rock fortress near the SE coast of the Dead Sea, Israel, the historic scene of Jewish national heroism. The castle-palace complex, built largely by Herod the Great, was siezed from Roman occupation by Jewish ZEALOTS in 66 AD. A two-year siege, 72–73, was needed to recover it but the garrison committed suicide rather than surrender. The site has been excavated and restored.

**MASCAGNI, Pietro** (1863–1945), Italian opera composer of the *verismo* (realist) school, known for the one-act *Cavalleria Rusticana* (Rustic Chivalry, 1890). In 1929 he became musical director of La Scala, Milan.

**MASAI**, a people of E Africa who speak the Masai language of the Sudanic group. The nomadic pastoral Masai of Kenya, the largest Masai tribe, practice polygyny and organize their society on a system of male age sets, graded from junior warrior up to tribal elder. They subsist almost entirely on livestock.

**MASARYK**, name of two Czechoslovakian statesmen. **Thomas Garrigue Masaryk** (1850–1937), was chief founder and first president of Czechoslovakia (1918–35). Professor of philosophy at Prague from 1882, he was a fervent nationalist. During WWI he lobbied western statesmen for Czech independence and helped delimit the frontiers of the new state. His son **Jan Garrigue Masaryk** (1886–1948) was foreign minister of the Czech government in exile in London in WWII, broadcasting to his German-occupied country. He continued as foreign minister in the restored government (1945). Soon after the communist coup (1948) he was said to have committed suicide.

**MASEFIELD, John** (1878–1967), English poet, novelist and playwright. As a youth he served on a windjammer ship, and love of the sea pervades his poems. He won fame with such long narrative poems as *The Everlasting Mercy* (1911), *Dauber* (1913) and *Reynard the Fox* (1919). In 1930 he became POET LAUREATE.

**MASER**, a device used as a MICROWAVE

oscillator or amplifier, the name being an acronym for "*microwave* (or *molecular*) *amplification* by *stimulated emission* of *radiation*." As OSCILLATORS they form the basis of extremely accurate ATOMIC CLOCKS; as AMPLIFIERS they can detect feebler signals than any other kind, and are used to measure signals from outer space.

ATOMS and MOLECULES can exist in various states with different energies; changes from one ENERGY LEVEL to another are accompanied by the emission or absorption of ELECTROMAGNETIC RADIATION of a particular frequency. Maser action is based on the fact that irradiation at the frequency concerned stimulates the process. If more atoms are in the higher energy (excited) state than in the lower state, incident waves cause more emission than absorption, resulting in amplification of the original wave.

The main difficulty is one of maintaining this arrangement of the states, as the EQUILIBRIUM configuration involves more atoms being in the lower than in the excited state. In the AMMONIA gas maser, molecules in the lower state are removed physically through their different response to an ELECTRIC FIELD, while in solid-state masers, often operated at low temperatures, a higher frequency "pumping" wave raises atoms into the excited state from some state not involved in the maser action.

**MASLOW, Abraham** (1908–1970), US psychologist, the major figure in the humanistic school of psychology. Rejecting BEHAVIORISM and PSYCHOANALYSIS, he saw man as a creative being striving for self-actualization. His books included *Motivation and Personality* (1954) and *Toward a Psychology of Being* (1960).

**MASOCHISM**, mental state in which individual gains erotic pleasure from experiencing PAIN. In PSYCHOANALYSIS, analogously, masochism describes the unconscious desire to bring humiliation upon oneself, and may again have an erotic basis.

**MASOLINO DA PANICALE** (1383–1447?), Florentine painter, born Tommaso di Cristoforo Fini. His decorative Gothic style was modified to greater realism under the influence of MASACCIO (possibly his pupil), with whom he executed notable frescoes in the Brancacci chapel, Florence.

**MASON, George** (1725–1792), American statesman who helped draft the US constitution but refused to sign it because of its compromise on slavery and other issues. His Va. declaration of rights became the basis for the BILL OF RIGHTS. Much of the Va. constitution was also his work.

**MASON, James** (1909–     ), English actor noted for the brooding intensity of his characterizations. He became a Hollywood star of the 1950s. His major films include *Odd Man Out* (1946), *Five Fingers* (1952), *A Star is Born* (1954) and *Lolita* (1962).

**MASON AND SLIDELL**, two Confederate statesmen, **James Murray Mason** (1798–1871), and **John Slidell** (1793–1871), sent to obtain help for the South from Britain and France respectively in 1861. Their interception by a US ship led to the TRENT AFFAIR.

**MASON-DIXON LINE**, the S boundary of Pa., surveyed by two English astronomers, Charles Mason and Jeremiah Dixon, in the 1760s. It settled a dispute between the proprietary families of Pa. and Md. In 1779 it was extended westward to become the boundary between Va. and Pa. Up to the Civil War the line was popularly taken as the boundary between free and slave states.

**MASONRY**, or **Freemasonry**, common name for the practices of the order of Free and Accepted Masons, one of the world's largest and oldest fraternal organizations. Members participate in elaborate, secret rituals and are dedicated to the promotion of brotherhood and morality. Membership, of which there are several grades, is restricted to men and allegiance to some form of religious belief is required. Modern Masonry emerged with the Grand Lodge of England, founded in 1717, though masons trace their ancestry to the craft associations or "lodges" of medieval stone masons. The first US lodge was founded in Philadelphia, Pa. in 1730. The basic organization of Masonry is the blue lodge. In the US each state has a grand lodge and grand master, who presides over all the blue lodges in the state. There are associated organizations for women, boys and girls. The worldwide membership is more than six million, including one million in the US.

**MASQUE**, or **mask**, a dramatic entertainment popular at the early 17th-century English court. It concentrated on spectacle rather than plot. Members of the aristocracy often took part with the actors and masks were generally worn (hence the name). Ben JONSON was the most famous masque writer and Inigo JONES designed many of the lavish sets.

**MASS**, a measure of the linear INERTIA of a body, i.e., of the extent to which it resists ACCELERATION when a FORCE is applied to it. Alternatively, mass can be thought of as a measure of the amount of MATTER in a body. The validity of this view seems to receive corroboration when one remembers that bodies of equal inertial mass have identical WEIGHTS in a given gravitational field. But the exact equivalence of inertial mass and gravitational mass is only a theoretical assumption, albeit one strongly supported by experimental evidence. According to EINSTEIN's special theory of RELATIVITY, the mass of a body is increased if it gains ENERGY; according to the famous Einstein equation: $\Delta m = \Delta E/c^2$ where $\Delta m$ is the change in mass due to the energy change $\Delta E$,, and $c$ is the electromagnetic constant. It is an important property of nature that in an isolated system mass–energy is conserved. The international standard of mass is the international prototype KILOGRAM.

**MASS,** term for the celebration of Holy COMMUNION in the Roman Catholic Church and in Anglo-Catholic churches, derived from the final words of the Latin rite: *Ite, missa est* (Go, you are dismissed). Roman Catholics believe that the bread (HOST) and the wine become Christ's body and blood (see TRANSUBSTANTIATION), which are offered as a sacrifice to God. The priest both drinks the wine and eats the wafer; the laity are permitted only the latter. The text consists of the "ordinary," spoken or sung at every celebration, and the "proper," sections which change according to the day (Gospel, including Collect and Epistle) or occasion—for example the REQUIEM mass has its own proper. In high mass, celebrated with priest, deacon and choir, the text is sung to plainchant with choral responses. The ordinary comprises the Kyrie, Gloria, Creed, Sanctus and Benedictus, Agnus Dei, and the Missa est. Medieval choral settings of it are the first great masterpieces of western music; it remained a major musical form into the 20th century. Low mass, said by a single priest, is the basic Roman Catholic service. In 1965 the Vatican sanctioned the use of vernacular languages in place of Latin.

**Name of state:** Massachusetts
**Capital:** Boston
**Statehood:** Feb. 6, 1788 (6th state)
**Familiar name:** Bay State
**Area:** 8,257sq mi
**Population:** 5,737,037

**Elevation:** Highest—3,491ft., Mount Greylock. Lowest—sea level, Atlantic Ocean.
**Motto:** Ense petit placidam sub libertate quietem (By the sword we seek peace, but peace only under liberty)
**State flower:** Mayflower
**State bird:** Chickadee
**State tree:** American elm
**State Song:** "Hail Massachusetts"
**MASSACHUSETTS,** state, NE US, on the Atlantic Ocean, bounded to the S by R.I and Conn., to the W by N.Y., and to the N by Vt. and N.H.; one of the 13 colonies.
**Land.** Massachusetts consists of a coastal plain, and a central hilly region which is separated from the more rugged Berkshire Hills and Taconic Mts in the W by the Connecticut R valley. The climate is temperate, with the hillier regions in the W being colder than the eastern plains.
**People.** Massachusetts is small and densely populated, with a majority of its citizens and principal industries located along the E coastal plain. BOSTON is the seat of government and other large cities include Worcester, Springfield and Cambridge. Mass.'s public school system dating from the 1630s is the oldest in the nation, and its universities and colleges, including HARVARD UNIVERSITY and MASSACHUSETTS INSTITUTE OF TECHNOLOGY, rank among the world's foremost.
**Economy.** Principal manufactures include electrical and nonelectrical machinery, fabricated metal products, foodstuffs, textiles, printed materials and leather products. Agriculture, fishing and mining, once of prime importance to the state's economic base, are now minor branches of the economy. Electronics industries serving communications and space research and development, and tourism have become increasingly important since the 1950s.
**History.** The first permanent colony in Mass. was founded by the PILGRIM FATHERS in 1620. (See also MAYFLOWER; MAYFLOWER COMPACT.) In 1629 a group of English Puritans was granted a charter (see MASSACHUSETTS BAY COMPANY), and the following year they established a settlement at Boston. The colony remained a Puritan theocracy until its original charter was revoked by the English crown in 1684.

The expansion of white settlement aroused Indian resistance, culminating in KING PHILIP'S WAR (1675–76). Mass. played a major role in the events leading up to the American Revolution (see BOSTON MASSACRE; BOSTON TEA PARTY). The depression which followed the revolution fell most heavily on the farmers and led to SHAY'S REBELLION in 1786, which influenced the state's leaders to ratify the Federal Constitution. As farmers moved W in the 19th century, shipbuilding and whaling became leading industries, but by the end of the century manufacturing was the basis of the state's economy. Mass. played a leading role in abolitionism, under such leaders as William Lloyd GARRISON and Wendell PHILLIPS. Between the Civil War and WWI, thousands of European immigrants, notably Irish, came to Mass., and gradually they wrested political power from the established families, creating a powerful Democratic machine. In recent years, Massachusetts has suffered from the steep rise in energy costs and the general economic shift to the Sun Belt; population growth in the 1970s was less than 1%. In the 1980 presidential election, the state went Republican for the first time in 25 years. The state is rich in cultural facilities, historic sites and magnificent vacation areas.

**MASSACHUSETTS BAY COMPANY,** joint stock company set up by royal charter in 1629 and styled the "Governor and Company of the Massachusetts Bay in New England." This gave the company self-government subject only to the king; the charter effectively became the constitution of the colony. In 1630 almost 1000 immigrants landed in Mass., led by John WINTHROP, who became the first governor. The franchise was then restricted to Puritan "freemen" and the colony became an independent Calvinistic theocracy; it coined its own money and restricted freedom of worship. As a result the charter was revoked in 1684 and Massachusetts became a royal colony.

**MASSASOIT,** or Ousamequin (d. 1661), powerful Wampanoag Indian chief who signed a treaty with the PILGRIM FATHERS of Plymouth in 1621. He befriended the Plymouth colony, teaching the settlers much that they needed to know to survive. When he fell ill in 1623, the Pilgrims nursed him back to health, and he kept up friendly relations until his death.

**MASSENET, Jules Émile Frédéric** (1842–1912), French composer, best known for his operas *Manon* (1884), *Esclarmonde* (1889), *Werther* (1892) and *Thais* (1894). He also wrote oratorios and stage music, and over 200 songs. He was a very influential teacher of composition at the Paris Conservatory from 1878.

**MASSEY, Raymond** (1896– ), Canadian-born US actor. A commanding film presence with a wide range, he is best remembered for his portrayals of Abraham LINCOLN. His films include *The Prisoner of Zenda* (1937), *Arsenic and Old Lace*

(1944) and *East of Eden* (1955).

**MASSINE, Léonide** (1896–1979), Russian-born US dancer and choreographer. He made his early career with the DIAGHILEV company, and was choreographer, dancer and director of the Ballet Russe de Monte Carlo 1932–41.

**MASSINGER, Philip** (1583–1640), English dramatist best known for satirical comedies such as *A New Way to Pay Old Debts* (1626?) and romantic tragedies such as *The Duke of Milan* (1621–22). He wrote many works in collaboration with others such as DEKKER and John FLETCHER.

**MASSON, André** (1896– ), French painter and graphic artist. Influenced by SURREALISM, he developed a style of drawing ("automatic drawing") intended to be spontaneous and without conscious intent to portray a specific subject.

**MASS SPECTROSCOPY,** spectroscopic technique in which electric and magnetic fields are used to deflect moving charged particles according to their mass, employed for chemical ANALYSIS, separation, ISOTOPE determination or finding impurities. The apparatus for obtaining a mass spectrum (i.e., a number of "lines" of distinct charge-to-mass ratio obtained from the beam of charged particles) is known as a mass spectrometer or mass spectrograph, depending on whether the lines are detected electrically or on a photographic plate. In essence, it consists of an ion source, a vacuum chamber, a deflecting field and a collector. By altering the accelerating voltage and deflecting field, particles of a given mass can be focused to pass together through the collecting slit.

**MASS TRANSIT,** system for conveying large numbers of people in and around cities, especially by bus, train and subway. The recent deterioration of mass transit systems, particularly in the older cities of the NE US, is partly the function of America's love affair with the car, which caused most transportation funds in the post-WWII years to be poured into concrete for highways. It also reflects the financial troubles of many cities as their tax bases erode. Cities have increased fares to compensate for higher operating costs, but the higher fares cause decreases in ridership, which lead to greater operating deficits, which necessitate still more fare hikes in the face of still poorer service and, in the end, still fewer riders. To help the cities break this cycle, the federal government in 1980 began to set aside 15% of "windfall profits" on oil companies (est. $227.3 billion over 10 years) for energy development and mass transit improvements.

**MASTECTOMY**, removal of a BREAST including the skin and nipple; LYMPH nodes from the armpit and some CHEST wall muscles may also be excised. Mastectomy, often with RADIATION THERAPY, is used for breast CANCER.

**MASTERS, Edgar Lee** (1869–1950), US poet, novelist, biographer and playwright whose best-known work is *Spoon River Anthology* (1915), which reveals the life of a small town as seen through the epitaphs of its inhabitants. He also wrote critical biographies of Lincoln and Mark Twain.

**MASTERS, William H.** (1915– ), and Virginia E. JOHNSON, (1925– ), US sex researchers whose book, *Human Sexual Response* (1966) was the first complete study of the physiology and anatomy of sexual activity.

**MASTERSINGER.** See MEISTERSINGER.

**MASTERSON, William Barclay "Bat"** (1853–1921), US frontiersman. Son of a farmer, he was a professional gambler and law officer in early life; he is most famous as Wyatt EARP's assistant at Tombstone, Ariz. in 1880. In 1902 he became a sports journalist in New York.

**MASTERS TOURNAMENT,** a prestigious annual golf event, held since 1934 at the Augusta, Ga. National Golf Course, one of the most difficult and most beautiful in the world. Invitations are issued on the basis of past achievement. Jack NICKLAUS, with five victories, has the best Masters record.

**MASTIFF,** large and powerful English breed of dog, now much used as guard dogs although usually gentle by nature. Their short coat is usually fawn or fawn and black. They have blunt muzzles and drooping ears, both dark, and can be up to 30in tall and weigh up to 185 pounds.

**MASTODONS,** ELEPHANTS intermediate between the earliest elephant types and those of today. In North America, mastodons survived alongside the elephants into postglacial times. *Mastodon americanus* even outlived elephants in this part of the world.

**MASTOID,** air spaces lined by MUCOUS MEMBRANE lying behind the middle EAR and connected with it; they are situated in the bony protuberance behind the ear. Mastoid infection may follow middle ear infection; block to its drainage by INFLAMMATION and PUS may make eradication difficult. ANTIBIOTICS have reduced its incidence and SURGERY to clear or remove the air spaces is now infrequent.

**MATA HARI** (1866–1917), pseudonym of Margaretha Zelle, Dutch-born dancer, courtesan and spy. Having lived in Indonesia, she appeared as Mata Hari in Paris in 1905; her Oriental erotic dances soon made her world famous. She became the mistress of many French officials, and began to spy for Germany before and during WWI, for which she was tried and executed.

**MATERIALISM,** in philosophy, as opposed to IDEALISM, any view asserting the ontologic primacy of MATTER; in psychology any theory denying the existence of MIND, seeing mental phenomena as the mere outworking of purely physico-mechanical processes in the BRAIN; in the philosophy of religion, any synthesis denying the existence of an immortal soul in man. The earliest thoroughgoing materialists were the classical ATOMISTS, in particular DEMOCRITUS and LUCRETIUS. The growth of modern science brought a revival of materialism which many have argued is a prerequisite for scientific thought, particularly in the field of psychology. Other philosophers, however, have argued against this view, recognizing the arbitrariness of the materialist hypothesis. (See also DIALECTICAL MATERIALISM.)

**MATHEMATICAL LOGIC,** or symbolic logic. See BOOLEAN ALGEBRA; LOGIC.

**MATHEMATICS,** the fundamental, interdisciplinary tool of all science. It can be divided into two main classes, pure and applied mathematics, though there are many cases of overlap between these. Pure mathematics has as its basis the abstract study of quantity, order and relation, and thus includes the sciences of NUMBER, ARITHMETIC and its broader realization ALGEBRA—as well as the subjects described collectively as GEOMETRY (e.g., ANALYTIC GEOMETRY, EUCLIDEAN GEOMETRY, NON-EUCLIDEAN GEOMETRY, TRIGONOMETRY and sometimes TOPOLOGY) and the subjects described collectively as ANALYSIS (of which the most elementary part is CALCULUS). In modern mathematics, many of these subjects are treated in terms of SET THEORY. Abstract algebra (see ALGEBRA, ABSTRACT) deals with generalizations of number systems, such as GROUPS, and has important relationships to other parts of mathematics. Applied mathematics deals with the applications of this abstract science. It thus has particularly close associations with PHYSICS and ENGINEERING. Specific subjects that come under its aegis are BOOLEAN ALGEBRA; GAME THEORY; INFORMATION THEORY; PROBABILITY; STATISTICS, and VECTOR analysis.

**MATHER,** family of American colonial divines. **Richard Mather** (1596–1669) emigrated to Mass. in 1635 and then became an influential preacher. A coauthor of the BAY PSALM BOOK, he wrote the *Platform of Church Discipline* (1649), the basic creed of Massachusetts Congregationalism. **Increase Mather** (1639–1723), son of Richard, was president of Harvard 1685–1701. A renowned preacher and scholar, he helped negotiate the colony's new charter with William III in 1692. In that year he also intervened to mitigate the witchcraft persecution. **Cotton Mather** (1663–1728), son of Increase, was also a famous preacher and scholar; his early work contributed to the witchcraft hysteria, which he always defended in part. His *Magnalia Christi Americana* (1702) is a brilliant religious history of the colonies. He helped found Yale U.; his wide scientific interests made him the first native American to be elected to the Royal Society of London.

**MATHEWSON, Christopher "Christy"** (1880–1925), US baseball player, one of the most successful of pitchers. During a 17-year career he won 373 games while losing 188 and set the National League strikeout record of 2,499. He pitched three shutouts in six days against the Philadelphia Athletics in 1905. Gassed in WWI, he died of tuberculosis.

**MATHIAS, Bob** (1930–    ), US athlete. The first man to win two Olympic decathlon gold medals, he won the first in 1948 at age 17, also a record. He broke the world decathlon record in 1950 and twice more prior to winning at the 1952 Olympics.

**MATISSE, Henri Émile Benôit** (1869–1954), French painter, one of the most important artists of the 20th century. He studied under MOREAU and was much influenced by IMPRESSIONISM. The brilliance of color in such paintings as *Woman with a Hat* (1905) and *Joy of Life* (1906) caused the style of his circle to be dubbed FAUVISM. He visited and exhibited in the USSR and US, and in 1917 settled in Nice, France. A prolific painter, he also produced lithographs, etchings, designs, illustrations and much sculpture. He himself considered the decor of the Dominican Nunnery chapel at Vence, France, his masterpiece.

**MATRIX**, rectangular array of symbols such as

$$A = \begin{pmatrix} a_{11} \, a_{12} \cdots a_{1n} \\ a_{21} \, a_{22} \cdots a_{2n} \\ \cdot \quad \cdot \quad \cdots \cdot \\ a_{m1} \, a_{m2} \cdots a_{mn} \end{pmatrix}$$

which may be abbreviated $A = (a^{ij})$ where $i$ takes the values $1, 2, \ldots, m$ and $j$ the values $1, 2, \ldots, n$. Each element $a^{ij}$ of the matrix is a number, or occasionally some other kind of mathematical object. Matrices form an algebraic system in which two matrices $A$ and $B$ with the same number of rows, $m$, and the same number of columns, $n$, can be added element by element, the elements of the sum being $a^{ij} + b^{ij}$; and in which two matrices of which the first has the same number of columns as the second has rows are multiplied by the rule $c^{ij} = \Sigma_k a^{ik} b^{kj}$, where $C$ is the product of $A$ and $B$ and $\Sigma_k$ denotes the sum over all values of $k$. Matrices are much used in mathematics and in physics and engineering to represent abstract algebraic objects or operations in terms of specific numbers. (See also ALGEBRA, ABSTRACT.)

**MATSUO BASHO**, pseudonym of Matsuo Munefusa (1644–1694), the greatest Japanese exponent of HAIKU poetry. A follower of ZEN, he introduced this philosophy into the formerly trivial *haiku* form with compact and delicate imagery. He is also remembered for his *renga* verses and his accounts of travels.

**MATSUOKA, Yosuke** (1880–1946), Japanese businessman and statesman, educated in the US. He was an extreme nationalist; he headed the delegation to the LEAGUE OF NATIONS that walked out in 1932. Foreign minister 1940–41, he brought about the Tripartite Pact with the Axis powers in 1940. He died before his impending trial as a war criminal.

**MATTEI, Enrico** (1906–62), Italian industrialist. One of the most powerful and controversial figures in post-WWII Italy, he headed the state-run Italian General Petroleum Industry (1945–53) and the Italian National Hydrocarbon Authority (1953–62) which together controlled the nation's oil and gas resources. A major force in Italian political life, he died in a plane crash at the height of his power.

**MATTER**, material substance, that which has extension in space and time. All material bodies have inherent INERTIA, measured quantitatively by their MASS, and exert gravitational attraction on other such bodies. Matter may also be considered as a specialized form of ENERGY. There are three physical states of matter: solid, liquid and gas. An ideal solid tends to return to its original shape after forces applied to it are removed. Solids are either crystalline or amorphous; most melt and become liquids when heated. Liquids and gases are both FLUIDS: liquids are only slightly compressible but gases are easily compressed. On the molecular scale, the state of matter is a balance between attractive intermolecular forces and the disordering thermal motion of the molecules. When the former predominate, MOLECULES vibrate about fixed positions in a solid crystal LATTICE. At higher temperatures, the random thermal motion of the molecules predominates, giving a featureless gas structure. The short-range intermolecular order of a liquid is an intermediate state between solid and gas.

**MATTERHORN** (French: Mont Cervin; Italian: Monte Cervino), 14,691ft high mountain in the Alps on the Swiss-Italian frontier. It was first climbed by Edward WHYMPER in 1865.

**MATTHEW, Saint**, or Levi, one of the twelve APOSTLES, traditionally the author of the first GOSPEL. He was a tax-collector before Jesus called him; little more is known of him. The gospel, the fullest of the four, was written probably c80 AD for Jewish Christians. By many Old Testament quotes it shows Jesus as the promised MESSIAH. (See also SYNOPTIC GOSPELS.)

**MATTHIAS, Saint**, APOSTLE chosen by lot to replace JUDAS ISCARIOT (Acts 1:21–26). Little otherwise is known of him.

**MAUCHLY, John William** (1907–1980) and **John Presper Eckert, Jr.** (1919– ), US engineers. Mauchly, a University of Pennsylvania professor, and Eckert, a graduate engineer, were granted a War Department contract during WWII to develop a high speed computer, and by 1946 had built ENIAC, the first electronic COMPUTER. They subsequently formed their own firm (1947) and built the improved BINAC (1949) and UNIVAC I (1951) computers.

**MAUGHAM, William Somerset** (1874–1965), British author. After qualifying as a medical student he became a successful playwright and novelist; in WWI he served as a secret agent. His plays are no longer popular, and his fame rests on his many short stories and four of his novels, *Of Human Bondage* (1915); *The Moon and Sixpence* (1919), inspired by the life of GAUGUIN; *Cakes and Ale* (1930); and *The Razor's Edge* (1944). These reveal a cynical but sometimes compassionate view of humanity.

**MAULDIN, Bill (William Henry Mauldin)** (1921– ), US cartoonist who rose to fame with his sympathetic caricatures of G.I. life in WWII. After 1945 he became a political cartoonist well known for his biting but sensitive wit. He was awarded two Pulitzer prizes in 1945 and 1958.

**MAUNA LOA** (long mountain), highly active volcano in the HAWAII VOLCANOES NATIONAL PARK, which erupts about once every 3.5 years. It is 13,680ft in height and has several other large craters on its SW slope.

**MAUNDY THURSDAY**, the Thursday before EASTER (see HOLY WEEK), commemorating Christ's washing of his disciples' feet and institution of Holy COMMUNION at the LAST SUPPER. The English monarch distributes special "Maundy money" to poor persons on this day.

**MAUPASSANT, (Henri René Albert) Guy de** (1850–1893), French short-story writer and novelist. A pupil of FLAUBERT, from 1880 to 1891 he produced some 300 short stories of outstanding quality, which excel in the unsentimental portrayal of the less attractive aspects of life and human nature. His direct style, pessimism and NATURALISM are seen at their best in "Boule de suif" (1880) and "The House of Madame Tellier" (1881).

**MAURIAC, François** (1885–1970), French writer whose novels of middle-class life concern man's vulnerability to sin and evil; they reflect his deeply-held Roman Catholic faith. In 1952 he won the Nobel Prize for literature. His works include *A Kiss for the Leper* (1922), *Génitrix* (1923), *The Desert of Love* (1925), *Thérèse Desqueyroux* (1927) and *Vipers' Tangle* (1932).

**Official name:** Islamic Republic of Mauritania
**Capital:** Nouakchott
**Area:** 397,956sq mi
**Population:** c1,664,000
**Languages:** Arabic, French
**Religion:** Muslim
**Monetary unit(s):** 1 CFA franc = 100 centimes

**MAURITANIA**, Islamic republic on the NW coast of Africa, bounded by Western Sahara on the NW, Algeria NE, Mali E and S and Senegal SW.

**Land.** The interior is largely desert and rocky plateau at an average height of 500ft. The climate is hot, with average rainfall less than 4in except in the fertile Senegal R valley in the S, where it rises to 24in.

**People.** Moors of Arab-Berber descent, mostly nomadic herdsmen, form some 80%

of the population; FULANI form about 13% and Negro groups such as the Soninke, Bambara and Wolof, most of whom live in the S, make up the remainder. Nouakchott, the capital and largest town, has a population of 180,000.

**Economy.** Basic crops, grown in the S, are millet, sorghum, rice and other cereals and vegetables; sheep, goats, cattle and camels are raised. There are large iron ore, gypsum and copper deposits, and oil exploration has been undertaken. Iron exports account for about 80% of the value of all exports.

**History.** In the 11th century the Ghanaian empire, to which most of Mauritania then belonged, was shattered by invading nomad Berbers of the Almoravid group (see ALMOHAD AND ALMORAVID). In the 13th century S Mauritania fell to the MALI EMPIRE and Islam was firmly established. The Portuguese probed the coast in the 15th century; the French penetrated the interior in the 19th century. A French colony by 1921, Mauritania left the FRENCH COMMUNITY at full independence in 1960. In 1968 military officers overthrew the government. During the 1970s a war against the Polisario over claims to the Western Sahara brought political and economic instability. Mauritania relinquished its claims to the territory in 1979. Soon after, Mauritania's head of state was deposed and a new leader assumed power.

**Official name:** Mauritius
**Capital:** Port Louis
**Area:** 790sq mi
**Population:** c952,000
**Languages:** English, French, Creole
**Religions:** Hindu, Christian, Muslim
**Monetary unit(s):** 1 Mauritian rupee = 100 cents

**MAURITIUS,** island republic of the British Commonwealth, 500mi E of the island of Madagascar in the Indian Ocean, comprising the islands of Mauritius and Rodrigues and associated archipelagos. Its warm and humid climate has average temperatures of 79°F from Nov. to April and 72°F in winter. The wet season, Dec. to March, is a time of dangerous cyclones.

**People.** Indians, descended from indentured laborers brought in to work the sugar plantations, form about 67% of the population, and Creoles about 30%. Europeans, French, Africans and Chinese constitute the remainder. Rapid population increase, coupled with unemployment and ethnic rivalries, has exacerbated political problems.

**Economy.** Sugar is the single most important export, and manufacturing centers around sugar processing, which makes the economy very sensitive to fluctuations in world market prices for sugar. Clothing is the second-largest export. Tea and tobacco are also cash crops. The capital, Port Louis, is the chief port.

**History.** Formerly uninhabited, Mauritius was settled by the Portuguese in the early 1500s but then abandoned. After a period of Dutch occupation in the 17th century, the French settled the island in 1715, founding the sugar industry. When slavery was abolished in the colonies in 1831, the planters turned to India for labor. The British took Mauritius during the Napoleonic wars (1810), initiated moves to representative government in the late 19th century and granted independence in 1968.

**MAUROIS, André** (born Émile Herzog, 1885–1967), French novelist and biographer, notably of Shelley (1923), Byron (1930), George Sand (1952) and Proust (1949). His first success was *The Silence of Colonel Bramble* (1918), a humorous study of the English, and his novels include *Climats* (1929).

**MAURRAS, Charles** (1868–1952), French poet, journalist and political theorist of "integral nationalism," a forerunner of fascism; he led the "romane" school of anti-SYMBOLIST poets (1891), and helped found *L'Action française* (1899), a promonarchist journal which became a vehicle for his ideas.

**MAX, Peter** (1937– ), German-born US artist, a favorite during the HIPPIE era. In his psychedelic paintings, often verging on OP ART, brilliant colors and flowing lines filled his compositions. He produced very popular posters and also designed upholstery fabrics.

**MAXIM,** US family of inventors, best known for work on FIREARMS and EXPLOSIVES. **Sir Hiram Stevens Maxim** (1840–1916), invented the Maxim MACHINE GUN (c1884) and contributed to the development of CORDITE. He patented hundreds of other inventions. His brother **Hudson Maxim** (1853–1927), a chemist, developed explosives much used in WWII, and notably the high explosive maximite.

Sir Hiram's son **Hiram Percy Maxim** (1869–1936), invented the Maxim silencer for firearms and the Maxim MUFFLER for automobiles.

**MAXIMILIAN** (1832–1867), Austrian archduke and emperor of Mexico from 1864. Liberal and idealistic, he was offered the throne as a result of NAPOLEON III's imperial intrigues. He believed the Mexicans would welcome him, and attempted to rule liberally and benevolently, but found French troops essential against popular support for President JUAREZ. After US pressure had secured his recall he was defeated by Juarez's forces and executed.

**MAXWELL, James Clerk** (1831–1879), British theoretical physicist whose contributions to science have been compared to those of Newton and Einstein. His most important work was in ELECTROMAGNETISM, THERMODYNAMICS, and STATISTICAL MECHANICS. **Maxwell's equations,** four linked differential equations, extend the work of FARADAY and others and completely define the classical theory of the ELECTROMAGNETIC FIELD. The fact that they remain unchanged by LORENTZ transformations of space and time was the principal inspiration for EINSTEIN's theory of RELATIVITY.

**MAY,** fifth month of the year, with 31 days. The name is perhaps derived from Maia, the Roman goddess of growth. (See also MAY DAY.)

**MAY, Cape.** See CAPE MAY.

**MAY, Rollo** (1909– ), US psychologist. An existential psychotherapist, he was a leader of the humanistic movement in psychology and wrote several popular books including *The Meaning of Anxiety* (1950), *Love and Will* (1969) and *Power and Innocence* (1972).

**MAYAKOVSKY, Vladimir Vladimirovich** (1893–1930), Soviet futurist poet and playwright whose powerful, declamatory verse, innovative in rhythm and diction, expresses his sense of being a new man in a revolutionary epoch. Notable works are the elegiac lament for *Lenin* (1924), *Very Good!* (1927) on a decade of Soviet successes and the play *The Bedbug* (1928), satirizing Soviet bureaucracy. He committed suicide.

**MAYAS,** American Indians whose brilliant civilization in central America was at its height c300–c900 AD. The Maya confederation covered the Yucatán peninsula, E Chiapas state in Mexico, most of Guatemala and the W parts of El Salvador and Honduras. They were a farming people of the rain forests and grew corn, cassava, cotton, beans and sweet potatoes and kept bees for wax and honey. The hierarchy of priest-nobles under a hereditary chief had an involved, hieroglyphic form of writing, still undeciphered, and a remarkable knowledge of mathematics, astronomy and chronology. The priests devised two calendars: a 365-day civil year astronomically more accurate than the western Gregorian CALENDAR and a sacred year of 260 days. Mayan art comprises fine sculpture in the round and relief, painted frescoes and manuscripts, ceramics and magnificent architecture. The chief feature of their great cities was the lofty stone pyramid, topped by a temple. By 900 AD their main centers, such as Palenque, Peidras and Copán, were abandoned to the jungle for reasons unknown. A "post-classical" tradition, under TOLTEC influence, sprang up in new centers, notably Chichén Itzá but in the early 1500s the whole region came under Spanish rule.

**MAY DAY,** spring festival on May 1. Traces of its pagan origins survive in the decorated maypoles and May queens of England. Declared a socialist labor festival by the Second INTERNATIONAL in 1889, it is celebrated, particularly in communist countries, by parades and demonstrations.

**MAYER, Julius Robert von** (1814–1878), German physician and physicist who contributed to the formulation of the law of conservation of ENERGY.

**MAYER, Louis Burt** (1885–1957), Russian-born US motion picture producer and tycoon. As head of the Metro-Goldwyn-Mayer Corporation, MGM (1924–51), he "discovered" such stars as Greta Garbo, Joan Crawford and Clark Gable.

**MAYFLOWER,** the ship that carried the PILGRIM FATHERS to America in 1620, leaving Plymouth, England, on Sept. 21 and reaching Provincetown, Mass., on Nov. 21; the Pilgrims sailed on to settle what is now PLYMOUTH, Mass., after signing the MAYFLOWER COMPACT. A two-decker, probably some 90ft long and weighing about 180 tons, the ship has not survived but an English-built replica, *Mayflower II,* sailed the Atlantic in 1957 and is now at Plymouth, Mass.

**MAYFLOWER COMPACT,** agreement signed by 41 of the PILGRIM FATHERS on Nov. 21, 1620. Having landed outside any civil jurisdiction, and fearing that their group might split up, they undertook to form a "civil body politic" and to "frame just and equal laws." The compact became the basis of the government of the colony of Plymouth.

**MAYHEW, Henry** (1812–1887), British journalist, miscellaneous writer, social commentator, and a founder of the magazine *Punch* (1841). His 4-volume *London Labour and the London Poor* (1851–62), a sympathetic and penetrating study, is an invaluable source of social history.

**MAYO, George Elton** (1880–1949), Australian pioneer of industrial sociology and psychology. Teaching at the Harvard Graduate School of Business Administration (1926–47), he organized a classic study of labor-management relations at the Western Electric Co. (1927).

**MAYO CLINIC**, one of the world's largest medical centers, founded in 1889 at Rochester, Minn., as a voluntary association of physicians. It developed from an emergency hospital set up by Dr. William W. MAYO to help cyclone victims. The Clinic treats about 175,000 patients a year and is financed by the Mayo Foundation.

**MAYS, Willie Howard Jr.** (1931–     ), baseball player who joined the New York Giants in 1951. A great hitter and spectacular outfield player, he won four National League home run titles and two Most Valuable Player awards before retiring in 1973.

**MA YUAN** (c1160–c1225), Chinese SUNG period artist, one of China's greatest landscape painters. He was noted for his spare and dramatically asymmetrical compositions.

**MAZARIN, Jules** (1602–1661), Italian-born French statesman and cardinal who strengthened the French monarchy and by successful diplomacy increased France's influence abroad. After the deaths of RICHELIEU (1642) and LOUIS XIII (1643), he became the trusted chief minister of the regent, ANNE OF AUSTRIA, and educator of her son, the future LOUIS XIV. His policy of centralized power and his imposition of taxes provoked the revolts known as the FRONDE (1648–53), which he eventually crushed decisively. In foreign policy he gained favorable terms in the treaties that ended the THIRTY YEARS' WAR (1648) and the war with Spain (1659). He amassed a huge fortune, and was a patron of the arts.

**MAZZINI, Giuseppe** (1805–1872), Italian patriot and a leading propagandist of the RISORGIMENTO. A member of the CARBONARI, he was exiled in 1831, formed the "Young Italy" societies, and from France, Switzerland and England promoted his ideal of a united, democratic Italy. In 1849 he became a leader of the short-lived republic of Rome, but was soon in exile again, continuing his revolutionary propaganda and organizing abortive uprisings. His relations with the moderate CAVOUR were strained, and the actual unification of Italy, in which he took little part, fell short of his popular republican ideals.

**MBOYA, Tom** (1930–1969), Kenyan political leader. General secretary of the Kenya Federation of Labor (1953–63), and a member of the colonial legislative assembly (1957), he played a key role in securing Kenya's independence. Economics minister from 1964, he was established as a likely successor to KENYATTA, and his assassination led to rioting and political tension.

**McALLISTER, Samuel Ward** (1827–1895), US society leader. In 1892 he claimed that there were "only about 400 people in New York society," and his phrase the "Four Hundred" passed into American idiom. He wrote *Society as I Have Found It* (1890).

**McBRIDE, Mary Margaret** (1899–1976), US radio personality, journalist and author who, from 1934, was radio's first "Martha Deane," dispenser of helpful household hints. She was later a talk-show hostess under her own name, retiring in 1954.

**McCARRAN, Patrick Anthony** (1876–1954), US Democratic senator from Nevada (1933–54). He sponsored two controversial measures, the McCarran-Wood Act (1950), requiring the registration of all communists, and the McCarran-Walter Act (1952), which tightened controls over aliens and immigrants.

**McCARTHY, Eugene Joseph** (1916–     ), US Democratic senator from Minn. (1959–71). A consistent opponent of the VIETNAM WAR, he campaigned for the presidential nomination in 1968 and attracted considerable support. He lost the nomination to Hubert HUMPHREY, but his campaign helped to consolidate public opposition to the war.

**McCARTHY, Joseph Raymond** (1908–1957), US Republican senator from Wis. (1947–57) who created the "McCarthy era" in the mid-1950s through his sensational investigations into alleged communist subversion of American life. These investigations were first made (1950) into federal departments, then into the army and among prominent civilians. McCarthyism became a word for charges made without proof and accompanied by publicity. After the national publicity directed on his activities by the Army-McCarthy hearings (1954), McCarthy was formally censured by fellow senators, and his influence steadily diminished.

**McCARTHY, Mary** ((1912–     ), US

writer, best known for her satirical novel *The Group* (1963), about the lives of a generation of Vassar graduates. Her nonfiction works include *Memoirs of a Catholic Girlhood, Vietnam* (1967) and a body of outstanding literary criticism.

**McCLELLAN, George Brinton** (1826–1885), controversial Union general in the American Civil War. In July 1861 he was given command of the Army of the Potomac, and later that year the supreme command. His hesitation in taking the offensive, and his failure to take Richmond and to follow up his success at the Battle of ANTIETAM, brought his dismissal in 1862. In 1864 he ran unsuccessfully for the presidency against Abraham LINCOLN.

**McCLURE, Samuel Sidney** (1857–1949), US editor and publisher who founded (1884) the first US newspaper syndicate. *McClure's Magazine*, of which he was founder (1893) and editor, presented many famous writers to the American public.

**McCONE, John Alex** (1902–    ), US government official, director of the CENTRAL INTELLIGENCE AGENCY (1961–65). He was chairman of the Atomic Energy Commission (1958–60) and succeeded Allen DULLES at the CIA after the unsuccessful BAY OF PIGS landing in Cuba.

**McCORMACK, John** (1884–1945), Irish-American tenor. He began his operatic career in London, first appearing in the US in 1909. He gained his greatest popularity as a concert singer, especially of Irish songs.

**McCORMICK, Anne O'Hare** (1882–1954), US journalist. A prominent foreign correspondent for the *New York Times* during the interwar period, she achieved fame for her exclusive interviews with world leaders. She was the first woman on the *Times* editorial board (1936) and the first to win a Pulitzer Prize (1937).

**McCORMICK, Cyrus Hall** (1809–1884), US inventor and industrialist who invented an early mechanical REAPER (patented 1834), the first models appearing under license from 1841 onward.

**McCORMICK, Robert Rutherford** (1880–1955), US newspaper publisher who became sole owner of the Chicago *Tribune* after WWI. Pursuing an extreme right-wing policy, it won the largest circulation of any paper in the Midwest.

**McCRAE, John** (1872–1918), Canadian physician and poet of WWI, famous for his poem "In Flanders Fields," which was written under fire. It was first published in *Punch* in December 1915.

**McCULLERS, Carson** (1917–1967), US novelist. Her novels, set in her native South, deal with the problems of human isolation.

Her best known book is *The Member of the Wedding* (1946).

**McCULLOCH v. MARYLAND,** case before the US Supreme Court in 1819 in which it was ruled that Congress has implied powers other than those specifically granted by the Constitution. The case involved the Baltimore branch of the US bank which refused to pay a tax imposed by Maryland. The court ruled that the tax was unconstitutional as it interfered with an arm of the federal government.

**McDOUGALL, William** (1871–1938), British psychologist best known for his fusion of the disciplines of PSYCHOLOGY and ANTHROPOLOGY in order to obtain a better understanding of the roots of social behavior. He also conducted important researches into PARAPSYCHOLOGY.

**McENROE, John** (1959–    ), US tennis player, the first man in 60 years to win three straight US tennis championships (1979–81). The feisty, left-handed American was 18 in 1979, when he became the youngest Wimbledon male semifinalist in 100 years.

**McGILL, Ralph** (1898–1969), US journalist and publisher who edited (from 1942) and published (from 1960) the Atlanta *Constitution*. Called "the conscience of the South," he was a champion of civil rights and supporter of school desegregation.

**McGOVERN, George Stanley** (1922–    ), US Senator from South Dakota and the 1972 Democratic presidential candidate. A leading advocate of an end to the Vietnam War, he campaigned for a broad program of social and political reforms. He attracted initially substantial support from liberals, but with serious party divisions his campaign went badly and Richard NIXON won with a record 61% of the popular vote.

**McGRAW, John Joseph** (1873–1934), US professional baseball player and manager. A star third baseman for the Baltimore Orioles, he became manager of Baltimore's American League team (1901). He went to the New York Giants as manager in 1902 and by his retirement in 1932 his team had won ten league championships and three World Series.

**McGUFFEY, William Holmes** (1800–1873), US educator. His series of six *Eclectic Readers* (1836–57) sold an estimated 122 million copies. Almost universal readers for elementary schools in the Middle West and South, they had an immense influence on public education.

**McKAY, Claude** (1890–1948), US black poet and novelist born in Jamaica. His was the first and most militant voice of the New York Negro movement in the 1920s. His works include *Harlem Shadows* (1922) and the novel *Home to Harlem* (1927).

**McKAY, Donald** (1810–1880), US naval architect, master builder of clipper ships. His *Great Republic* (1853) was at 4,555 tons the biggest clipper ever built. The use of steam brought a decline in business that forced him to close his Boston shipyards in 1855.

**McKIM, Charles Follen** (1847–1909), US architect, founder of his own firm (1878) and of the American Academy in Rome. His best-known projects, such as the University Club in New York City (1900), are in neoclassical style.

**McKINLEY, Mount,** highest peak (20,320ft) in North America. Part of Mount McKinley National Park in S central Alaska, much of it is covered by permanent snowfields and glaciers. It was first climbed in 1913.

**McKINLEY, William** (1843–1901), 20th president of the US. The son of a small ironfounder in Niles, Ohio, he enlisted as a private in the 23rd Ohio Volunteers at the outbreak of the CIVIL WAR, at the age of 18. By the end of the war he had reached the rank of brevet major. He then studied law in Albany, N.Y., and set up practice in Canton, Ohio, where, in 1871, he married Ida Saxton. Although she became a chronic invalid after the early deaths of their two daughters, the marriage was a happy one.

McKinley was elected to Congress as a Republican in 1876 and stayed there, except for one term, until 1891. He sponsored the Tariff Act of 1890, which set record-high protective duties. This unpopular measure contributed to his defeat in the 1890 congressional elections. He had, however, attracted the backing of the wealthy Cleveland irondealer, Marcus Alonzo HANNA, with whose help he was elected governor of Ohio in 1891, and again in 1893. Again with Hanna's backing, he was chosen Republican presidential candidate in 1896. His Democratic opponent, William Jennings BRYAN, had early successes with his chosen issue of FREE SILVER, but with the help of $3.5 million that Hanna collected, McKinley's "front porch" campaign was effective enough to gain him a decisive victory.

Immediately after his inauguration he called a special session of Congress, which raised duties still higher, though without the reciprocal measures that McKinley wanted. The Gold Standard Act of 1899 killed Free Silver. With prosperity rising at home, he turned hs attention to foreign affairs. The SPANISH–AMERICAN WAR over Spanish outrages in Cuba was followed by a revolt against American rule in the Philippine Islands, and in 1899 the "Open Door" policy on trade with China was introduced. Reelected in 1900, McKinley was assassinated in 1901 by the anarchist Leon CZOLGOSZ. He had presided over a period characterized by rapidly growing prosperity and the emergence of the US as a world power.

**McKUEN, Rod** (1933–     ), US singer, songwriter and author of over two dozen collections of poems including *Listen to the Warm* (1967) and *Coming Close to the Earth* (1978). He has also composed musical scores for films, including *The Prime of Miss Jean Brodie* (1969) and *A Boy Named Charlie Brown* (1970).

**McLUHAN, (Herbert) Marshall** (1911–     ), Canadian professor of humanities and mass communications specialist, best known for his book *Understanding Media* (1964), which contains the famous phrase "the medium is the message"; that is, the content of communication is determined by its means, with the implication that modern mass communications technology, particularly television, is transforming our way of thinking and perceiving.

**McNAMARA, Robert Strange** (1916–     ), secretary of defense under presidents KENNEDY and JOHNSON (1961–68), who played an important part in the shaping of US defense policy, including Vietnam policy. Before this he had been president of the Ford Motor Company, and in 1968 he became president of the World Bank, serving until 1981.

**McPHERSON, Aimee Semple** (1890–1944), US evangelist, famed for her flamboyant preaching. She worked as a missionary in China, then returned to the US to become an itinerant preacher and faith-healer, eventually founding the Foursquare Gospel Church in Los Angeles. She was married three times, and involved in numerous legal actions.

**McQUEEN, Steve** (1930–1981), US actor whose ingratiating virility made him the star of many action films, among them, *The Magnificent Seven* (1960), *Bullitt* (1968) and *Papillon* (1973).

**MEAD, George Herbert** (1863–1931), US social psychologist and philosopher. Initially influenced by HEGEL, he then moved toward PRAGMATISM. He attempted to explain social psychology in terms of the evolution of the self, and through analyses of spoken language.

**MEAD, Margaret** (1901–1978), US cultural anthropologist best known for books such as *Coming of Age in Samoa*

(1928), *Growing Up in New Guinea* (1930), *The Mountain Arapesh* (3 vols., 1938–49), and *Male and Female* (1949). A first autobiography, *Blackberry Winter*, appeared in 1972. She was associated with New York's American Museum of Natural History, from 1926 until her death.

**MEADE, George Gordon** (1815–1872), Union general in the US CIVIL WAR who, as commander of the Army of the Potomac, won the Battle of GETTYSBURG. Criticized for not following up his victory, he kept his command but served under Grant's direction.

**MEALEY, Denis** (1917–    ), British political leader. He served as secretary of state for defense (1964–70) and chancellor of the Exchequer (1974–79) in Labour governments. He lost a contest for party leader (1980), serving as deputy leader thereafter.

**MEAN, MEDIAN AND MODE,** three terms concerned with different types of averaging processes.

An average, in the simplest arithmetical sense, of *n* terms is the SUM of those terms divided by *n*. Hence the average of 4, 6 and 9 is $^{19}/_3$ or 6.333 .... The average value A of a FUNCTION between $x=a$ and $x=b$ is defined as the AREA under the curve of the function (see CALCULUS) divided by $(b-a)$:

$$A = \frac{\int_a^b f(x)dx}{b-a}$$

**Mean.** The simple arithmetical average described above is an arithmetic mean (see also PROGRESSION). The geometric mean of *n* numbers is defined as the *n*th ROOT of their PRODUCT. The geometric mean of 4, 6 and 9 is thus $\sqrt[3]{4 \times 6 \times 9} = \sqrt[3]{216} = 6$. That of *x* and *y* is $\sqrt{xy}$. The geometric mean of a set of positive terms is always less than their arithmetic mean.

**Median and Mode.** In STATISTICS, ranking all the observations of a sample in increasing order of frequency, the frequency of the middle observation (or, if there is an even number of observations, the arithmetic mean of the two middle observations), is described as the median. The observation with the highest frequency is termed the mode: should a sample contain two (or three) observations of equal frequency greater than that of any of the other observations, it is termed bimodal (or trimodal).

**MEANS, Russell** (1939–    ), US Indian leader. A member of the Oglala SIOUX, he founded a chapter of the militant American Indian Movement (see RED POWER). Using

confrontation tactics to gain national attention, in 1973 he and supporters seized, and for two months held, the town of Wounded Knee, S.D., near the site of the Sioux defeat in 1890.

**MEANY, George** (1894–1980), US labor leader, president (1955–79) of the AMERICAN FEDERATION OF LABOR AND CONGRESS OF INDUSTRIAL ORGANZATIONS (AFL-CIO). He was president of the N.Y. state Federation of Labor (1934) and secretary-treasurer (1939) and president (1952) of the AFL.

**MEARES, John** (c1756–1809), English naval officer and explorer of the Alaskan coast (1786–87). Further expeditions of discovery in 1788–89 advanced British settlement of the NW Coast of America.

**MEASLES,** common INFECTIOUS DISEASE, caused by a VIRUS. It involves a characteristic sequence of FEVER, HEADACHE and malaise followed by CONJUNCTIVITIS and RHINITIS, and then the development of a typical rash, with blotchy ERYTHEMA affecting the SKIN of the FACE, trunk and limbs. COUGH may indicate infections in small BRONCHI and this may progress to virus PNEUMONIA. Secondary bacterial infection may lead to middle EAR infection or pneumonia. ENCEPHALITIS is seen in a small but significant number of cases and is a major justification for VACCINATION against this common childhood disease. Recently, an abnormal and delayed IMMUNITY to measles virus has been associated with a number of BRAIN diseases, including MULTIPLE SCLEROSIS.

**MEAT,** the flesh of any animal, in common use usually restricted to the edible portions of cattle (beef and veal), sheep (lamb) and swine (pork), and less commonly applied to those of the rabbit, horse, goat and deer (venison). Meat consists of skeletal MUSCLE, connective TISSUE, FAT and BONE; the amount of connective tissue determines the toughness of the meat. Meat is an extremely important foodstuff. A daily intake of 100g (3½ oz) provides 45% of daily PROTEIN, 36% of daily iron and important amounts of B VITAMINS, but only 9% of daily energy. Meat protein is particularly valuable as it supplies eight of the AMINO ACIDS which human beings cannot make for themselves. The meat-packing industry employs about 350,000 people in the US.

**MECCA,** Arabic Makka, chief city of the Hejaz region of Saudi Arabia, birthplace of MUHAMMAD and the most holy city of ISLAM. Non-Muslims are not allowed in the city. The courtyard of the great Haram mosque encloses the sacred shrine, the KAABA; nearby is the holy Zem-Zem well.

Pilgrimage to Mecca, the *hajj*, is a duty for all Muslims able to perform it, and each year over 1,000,000 pilgrims arrive. The economy of Mecca depends on the pilgrims. The population includes Muslims of many nationalities. Pop 366,801.

**MECHANICAL DRAWING**, or engineering drawing, the representation of a component or structure in such a way that it can be formed or assembled by someone else without error or misunderstanding. To this end, various projections are used—isometric and orthographic being the most important (see DESCRIPTIVE GEOMETRY; PROJECTIVE GEOMETRY). A person who executes mechanical drawings is a draftsman. (See also PERSPECTIVE.)

**MECHANICS**, the branch of applied mathematics dealing with the actions of forces on bodies. There are three branches: kinematics, which deals with relationships between distance, time, velocity and acceleration; dynamics, dealing with the way forces produce motion, and statics, dealing with the forces acting on a motionless body.

**Kinematics**. In kinematics we deal with distance and time, which are scalar quantities (having no direction), and with VELOCITY and ACCELERATION, which are VECTOR quantities. Velocity is the rate of change of position of a body in a particular direction with respect to time: it thus has both magnitude and direction. Its magnitude is the scalar quantity speed ($S$), related to distance ($s$) and time ($t$) by the equation $S=s/t$; similarly velocity ($v$) is related to distance and time by $v=ds/dt$ (see CALCULUS). Acceleration is rate of change of velocity with respect to time: $a = dv/dt = d^2s/dt^2$. Thus, if velocity is measured in km/s, acceleration is measured in km/s².

**Dynamics** is based on NEWTON's three laws of motion: that a body continues in its state of motion unless compelled by a force to act otherwise; that the rate of change of motion (acceleration) is proportional to the applied force and occurs in the direction of the force, and that every action is opposed by an equal and opposite reaction. The first gives an idea of INERTIA, which is proportional to the MASS and opposes the change of motion: combining the first with the second, we find that F is proportional to $ma$, where F is the force, $m$ the mass of the body and $a$ the acceleration produced by the FORCE. In practice we choose units such that $F=ma$. (See also MOMENTUM.)

**Statics**. We can combine forces much as we do velocities. If forces $P_1$ and $P_2$, with resultant R, act at a point, there must be a third force, $P_3$, equal and opposite to R, for equilibrium. We can combine forces similarly over more complex structures. For a bridge whose weight ($w$) acts as a downward force W at the center, the upward reactions $R_1$ and $R_2$ at the piers must be such that $R_1 + R_2 = -$ W for it to be in EQUILIBRIUM. Similarly, we examine the members of the bridge to determine the stresses acting on each.

**MECHANIZATION AND AUTOMATION**, the use of machines wholly or partly to replace human labor. The two words are often used synonymously, but it is of value to distinguish mechanization as requiring human aid, automation as self-controlling.

The most familiar automated device is the domestic THERMOSTAT. This is set to switch off the heating circuit if room temperature exceeds a certain value, to switch it on if the temperature falls below a certain value. Once set, no further human attention is required: a machine is in full control of a machine.

The thermostat is a sensing element; the information it detects is fed back to the production mechanism (the heater), which adjusts accordingly. All automated processes work on this principle. In fact, fully automated processes are still rare: most often the role of sensing element will be taken over by a human being, who will check the accuracy of the machine and adjust it if needed.

The most versatile devices we have are COMPUTERS: very often, the complexity of their physical construction is more than matched by that of the network of subprograms which they contain. Data can be fed in automatically or by human operators and the computer can be programmed to respond in many ways: to present information; adjust and control other machines, or even to make decisions. Computerized automation plays a larger role in our lives than most of us realize: airline and theater agents often book seat reservations with a computer, not a staffed box office; food manufacture is often automatically controlled from raw materials to packaged product; atomic energy is controlled automatically where radiation prohibits the presence of humans, possible leaks or even explosions being forestalled by machine; the justification of the columns of this book has been performed by a fully automated process. In addition, man would not have reached the moon had it not been for computerized automation.

Since mechanization and automation emerged in the "Second Industrial Revolution," they have been associated with all kinds of sociological problems and upheavals. And this is more than ever true today. Long-term benefits to the human race have to be balanced against short-term evils such as unemployment and its attendant human sufferings. (See also LINEAR PROGRAMMING; MASS PRODUCTION; MACHINE TOOLS; SERVOMECHANISM.)

**MECHNIKOV, Ilya.** See METCHNIKOFF, ÉLIE.

**MEDAWAR, Sir Peter Brian** (1915–   ), British zoologist who shared with F. M. BURNET the 1960 Nobel Prize for Physiology or Medicine for their work on immunological tolerance. Inspired by Burnet's ideas, Medawar showed that if fetal mice were injected with cells from eventual donors, skin grafts made onto them later from those donors would "take," thus showing the possibility of acquired tolerance and hence, ultimately, organ TRANSPLANTS.

**MEDES,** ancient INDO-EUROPEAN people of W Asia. Originally nomadic warrior herdsmen, they settled Media (in modern NW Iran) c900 BC. They controlled PERSIA by 700 BC, and in 612 BC, in alliance with Babylonia, destroyed the Assyrian empire (see BABYLONIA AND ASSYRIA). c550 BC CYRUS THE GREAT captured Ecbatana, the Median capital, and made Media a Persian province.

**MEDIAN.** See MEAN, MEDIAN AND MODE.

**MEDIATION.** See ARBITRATION.

**MEDICAID,** US government-financed system of medical aid to people under 65 who are of low income, introduced along with the MEDICARE legislation in 1965. The federal government pays from 50% to about 80% of the costs for anyone eligible, as determined by each state separately.

**MEDICARE,** US government-financed system of medical and hospital insurance for people aged 65 and over. It was set up in 1965 by legislation supported by President Johnson. It was opposed by the American Medical Association, which objected on principle to possible government intervention, although the cost of private treatment had risen beyond the means of most older people. Medicare helps underwrite the cost of hospital care and some nursing-home care. Medicare insurance covering doctor's fees, outpatient care and home care is optional. In 1972 Medicare was extended to cover disabled Social Security beneficiaries and persons of any age suffering from chronic kidney disease.

**MEDICI,** Italian family of bankers, princes and patrons of the arts who controlled Florence almost continually from the 1420s to 1737, and provided cardinals, popes LEO X, CLEMENT VII and LEO XI and two queens of France. The French spelling of the name is Médicis. The foundations of the family's power were laid by **Giovanni di Bicci de' Medici** (1360–1429). His son **Cosimo de' Medici** (1389–1464), was effectively ruler of Florence from 1434 and was voted "Father of the Country" after his death. He founded the great Laurentian Library and patronized such artists as DONATELLO and GHIBERTI. His grandson **Lorenzo** (1449–1492), called "the Magnificent," was Italy's most brilliant Renaissance prince. Himself a fine poet, he patronized BOTTICELLI, GHIRLANDAIO, the young MICHELANGELO and many other artists. His son **Piero** (1471–1503), was expelled from Florence (1494) by a popular rising led by SAVONAROLA. The family was restored in 1512; **Lorenzo** (1492–1519), ruled from 1513 under the guidance of his uncle **Giovanni** (1475–1521), who as Pope Leo X was a magnificent patron of the arts in Rome. The ruthless **Cosimo I** (1519–1574), doubled Florentine territory and power and was created grand duke of Tuscany in 1569. The later Medicis were less distinguished, and the line died out with **Gian Gastone** (1671–1737).

**Catherine de Médicis** (1519–1589), wife of HENRY II of France, was regent from 1560 for her second son CHARLES IX, and helped plan the SAINT BARTHOLOMEW'S DAY MASSACRE. **Marie de Médicis** (1573–1642), second wife of HENRY IV of France (1600), was powerful regent for her son LOUIS XIII (1610–17), but was forced into exile (1630) by Cardinal RICHELIEU.

**MEDICINE,** the art and science of healing. Within the last 150 years or so medicine has become dominated by scientific principles. Prior to this, healing was mainly a matter of tradition and magic. Many of these prescientific attitudes have persisted to the present day.

The earliest evidence of medical practice is seen in Neolithic (see STONE AGE) skulls in which holes have been bored, presumably to let evil spirits out, a practice called trepanning (see TREPHINE). Treatment in primitive cultures was either empirical or magical. Empirical treatment included bloodletting, dieting, primitive surgery and the administration of numerous potions, lotions and herbal remedies (some used in modern medicines). For serious ailments, magical treatment, involving propitiation of the gods, special rituals or the provision of charms, was performed by the medicine man or witch doctor, who was usually both doctor and priest (see SHAMANISM). Exorcism, the casting out of devils, and FAITH HEALING are still practiced in modern societies. ACUPUNCTURE and OSTEOPATHY, both being ancient and empirical, are also practiced today.

The growth of scientific medicine began with the Greek philosophy of nature. The great Greek physician HIPPOCRATES, with whose name is associated the Hippocratic oath which codifies the physician's ideals of humanity and service, has justly been called the father of medicine. Galen of Pergamum, the encyclopedist of classical medicine, clearly distinguished ANATOMY from PHYSIOLOGY. Medieval medicine was basically a corrupted Galenism. The 16th century saw the dawn of modern medicine. Men such as FABRICIUS, VESALIUS and William HARVEY revived the critical, observational approach to medical research. Perhaps the most far-reaching advances since then have been in preventive medicine, anesthesia and drug therapy. Preventive medicine was attempted in medieval times when ships arriving in Europe during the Black Death were "quarantined" for 40 days. More recent major milestones have been Edward JENNER'S work on VACCINATION and the "germ theory of disease" proposed by Louis PASTEUR and developed by Robert KOCH. ANESTHESIA and ASEPSIS (see LISTER, JOSEPH) made possible great advances in SURGERY. Crawford LONG and James SIMPSON were both pioneers of their use. Drug therapy originated with herbal remedies, but perhaps the two most important discoveries in this field both came in the 20th century: that of INSULIN by Frederick BANTING and Charles BEST, and that of PENICILLIN by Alexander FLEMING. (See also ANTIBIOTICS; CHEMOTHERAPY; DRUGS; SULFA DRUGS.)

Medical training to high set standards is used to protect society against charlatans and is usually undertaken in universities and hospitals. Since the progress of medical knowledge is very rapid, doctors today undergo continual retraining to keep them up to date. Socialized medicine, under the name MEDICARE, was set up in the S in 1965 and helps to pay the costs of medical care. However, several other countries have more comprehensive programs of socialized medicine.

The success of medicine in preventing disease is largely responsible for today's population explosion. This has stimulated an extensive re-examination of traditional attitudes to medical ethics, particularly in the areas of CONTRACEPTION, ABORTION and EUTHANASIA. (See also DISEASE.)

**MEDILL, Joseph** (1823–1899), Canadian-born US editor and publisher of the *Chicago Tribune*, and a founder of the REPUBLICAN PARTY. A strong emancipationist and admirer of Lincoln, he was elected mayor of Chicago in 1871.

**MEDINA,** holy Muslim city and place of pilgrimage in Hejaz, Saudi Arabia, 210mi N of Mecca. The prophet Mohammed came to Medina after his HEGIRA (flight) from Mecca (622 AD), and the chief mosque contains his tomb. A walled city, Medina stands in a fertile oasis noted for its dates, grains and vegetables. Pop 198,186.

**MEDITERRANEAN FRUIT FLY,** *Ceratitis capitata*, a serious pest of fruit in Africa, Australia and South America, attacking, in particular, peaches, apricots and citrus fruits. The larvae completely destroy the fruits and whole harvests may be lost. The maggots are capable of prodigious leaps of about 100mm (4in) high and over distances of 200mm (8in).

**MEDITERRANEAN SEA,** intercontinental sea between Europe, Asia and Africa, connected to the Atlantic Ocean in the west by the Strait of Gibraltar and to the Black Sea by the Dardanelles and Bosporus. The man-made Suez Canal provides the link with the Indian Ocean via the Red Sea. Peninsular Italy, Sicily, Malta, Pantelleria and Tunisia's Cape Bon mark the dividing narrows between the eastern and western basins. The many islands of the western basin include Sicily, Sardinia, Elba, Corsica and the Balearics. Crete, Cyprus, Rhodes and the numerous Aegean islands are contained in the eastern basin. Geologically, the Mediterranean is a relic of Tethys, an ocean which separated Eurasia from Africa 200 million years ago and was partially uplifted to form the Alps, S Europe, and the Atlas Mts. Its name, given by the Romans, reflects its central position and importance in the ancient world. The limited access from the Atlantic and the confined entries to both the Black and Red seas, have given it through history great strategic importance.

**MEDUSA,** in Greek mythology, most celebrated of the GORGON sisters, the very sight of whom turned men to stone. Medusa was eventually decapitated by PERSEUS, who avoided her fatal gaze by looking at her reflection in his bronze shield.

**MEGALITHIC MONUMENTS,** large, usually undressed stone monuments found principally in Europe but also in many other parts of the world, believed to date usually from the late STONE AGE and early BRONZE AGE. They are of four main types: the menhir (from Breton *hir*, long, and *men*, stone) or single standing stone; the stone circle, or circles, as exemplified by STONEHENGE; the chamber or room, usually associated with a tomb, the most ancient of which is the

DOLMEN; and the **alignment**, or row of stones, such as those at CARNAC.

**MEHMET ALI** (or Mohammed Ali; c1769–1849), an Albanian soldier who in 1806 became pasha (governor) of the Turkish province of Egypt and founder of the dynasty which ruled until 1952. He extended Egypt's borders and improved the economy. His power rivaled that of his overlord, the Sultan of Turkey.

**MEHTA, Zubin** (1936–　　), Indian-born conductor who studied at the Vienna Academy of Music and later acted as musical director of the Montreal Symphony (1961–67), Los Angeles Philharmonic (1962–78), and New York Philharmonic (from 1978).

**MEIKLEJOHN, Alexander** (1872–1964), British-born US educator who advocated the intensive study of classical Greek civilization and championed the Great Books approach to higher education. He was president of Amherst College (1912–24) and headed the Experimental College at the U. of Wisconsin (1927–32). His books include *The Liberal College* (1920) and *Education Between Two Worlds* (1942).

**MEIR, Golda** (1898–1978), Israeli leader, prime minister of Israel 1969–74. Born Golda Mabovitch in Kiev, USSR, she was raised in the US and emigrated to Palestine in 1921. She was a prominent figure in the establishment of the State of Israel (1948). Elected to the KNESSET in 1949, she became foreign minister in 1956 and in 1966 was elected general secretary of the dominant Mapai party, later the Israel Labor Party (1968). In 1969 she succeeded Levi Eshkol as premier and formed a broad coalition government. She visited Washington on three occasions to strengthen US support and in 1973 helped Israel to fight off a surprise Egyptian-Syrian attack. In 1974 Mrs. Meir resigned.

**MEISTERSINGER,** a coveted title taken by poets and singers belonging to certain 15th-century German guilds who had perfected their art in accordance with an elaborate set of rules and traditions. WAGNER'S opera DIE MEISTERSINGER VON NÜRNBERG touches on the lives of these artists.

**MEITNER, Lise** (1878–1968), Austrian physicist who worked with Otto HAHN to discover PROTACTINIUM. Following their experiments bombarding URANIUM with NEUTRONS, Meitner and her nephew, **Otto Robert Frisch** (1904–　　), correctly interpreted the results as showing nuclear FISSION and predicted the chain reaction.

**MEKONG RIVER,** one of the chief rivers of SE Asia. Rising in the Tibetan highlands, it flows 2,600mi southward through the Yunnan province of China and Laos, along the Thailand border and through Kampuchea to its wide fertile delta in S Vietnam, on the South China Sea. The lower 340mi can accommodate medium-sized vessels and PHNOM-PENH is an important port.

**MELANCHTHON, Philipp** (1497–1560), German scholar and humanist, second to LUTHER in initiating and leading the Protestant REFORMATION in Germany. His *Loci communes* (1521), a systematic statement of Lutheran beliefs, was the first great Protestant work on religious doctrine; and his *Augsburg Confession* (1530) was one of the principal statements of faith in the Lutheran Church.

**MELANESIA,** one of three main ethnographic divisions of the Pacific islands, the other two being MICRONESIA and POLYNESIA. (See also OCEANIA.)

**MELANIN,** black pigment which lies in various SKIN layers and is responsible for skin color, including the racial variation. It is concentrated in MOLES and FRECKLES. The distribution in the skin determines skin coloring and is altered by light and certain HORMONES.

**MELBA, Dame Nellie** (1861–1931), Australian soprano, born Helen Porter Mitchell. For almost 40 years (1887–1926) hers was one of the most celebrated coloratura voices on the operatic stage. She made her debut as Gilda in Verdi's *Rigoletto* in Brussels in 1887.

**MELBOURNE,** second largest city in Australia and state capital of Victoria, on the Yarra R. Founded by settlers in 1835, the city is now one of the nation's chief ports and ranks with Sydney as a major industrial center. Manufactures include textiles, leather goods and aircraft, and oil refineries have been built. Met pop 2,739,700.

**MELBOURNE, William Lamb, 2nd Viscount** (1779–1848), British statesman. A member of the House of Commons from 1806, he served as chief secretary to Ireland 1827–1828, entered the House of Lords (1829) and as home secretary (1830–34) suppressed agrarian unrest. He became prime minister briefly in 1834 and again 1835–41, when he instructed the young Queen Victoria in her duties.

**MELCHIOR, Lauritz** (1890–1973), Danish-American tenor. He was originally a baritone, but achieved fame as a Wagnerian tenor—notably in the role of SIEGFRIED—and appeared frequently at BAYREUTH.

**MÉLIÈS, Georges** (1861–1938), French movie pioneer, a Paris theater owner and stage illusionist. Impressed by the LUMIÈRE cinematograph, he invented his own camera and mastered its trick possibilities in a number of short films on exotic subjects produced at the turn of the century.

**MELLON, Andrew William** (1855–1937), US financier and industrialist who was an outstandingly able US treasury secretary (1921–31). He served under three presidents, and reduced the national debt by some $9 billion. He was US ambassador to Britain (1932–33). A multimillionaire himself, he founded the Mellon Institute of Industrial Research. His vast art collection formed the basis of the NATIONAL GALLERY OF ART.

**MELVILLE, Herman** (1819–1891), one of the greatest of US writers. His world reputation rests mainly on the masterpiece, *Moby Dick* (1851), and the short novel *Billy Budd*, published posthumously (1924). His whaling and other voyages provided material for several of his earlier, very popular books. *Typee* (1846), his first, was based on his adventures after jumping ship in the Marquesas Islands. *Moby Dick* is a deeply symbolic work, combining allegory with adventure. Too profound and complex for its audience, the novel was not successful and subsequent books did not recapture his former popularity. It was not until the 1930s that his talent was fully recognized.

**MEMBRANES,** layers that form part of the surface of CELLS and which enclose organelles within the cells of all animals and plants. The membranes of the cell wall function to allow some substances into the cell; to exclude others, and actively to transport others into the cell even though the direction of movement may be against existing concentration gradients. Membranes are composed of layers of LIPID or FAT molecules which sandwich a layer of PROTEIN molecules. The protein layer is double but appears as a single layer when viewed under the ELECTRON MICROSCOPE. Thus most membranes appear to be triple-layered, although some appear to be composed of a single layer. Triple-layered membranes are normally 5–10mm thick.

**MEMLING, Hans** (c1430–1494), Flemish painter famous for his portraits and religious works, among which the paneled *Shrine of St. Ursula* (c1489) is one of the most famous. He worked in Bruges, Belgium, and was probably a pupil of Roger van der WEYDEN.

**MEMORIAL DAY,** or Decoration Day, a US holiday, honoring the dead of all wars, observed on the last Monday in May. Traditionally, Memorial Day originated in the South after the Civil War when the graves of both Confederate and Union soldiers were decorated.

**MEMORY,** the sum of the mental processes that result in the modification of an individual's behavior in the light of previous experience. There are several different types of memory. In rote memory, one of the least efficient ways of storing information, data is learned by rote and repeated verbatim. Logical memory is far more efficient: only the salient data are stored, and each may be used in its original or in a different context. Mnemonics, which assist rote memory, superimpose what is in effect an artificial logical structure on not necessarily related data. (See also EIDETIC IMAGE.) Testing of the efficiency of memory may be by recall (e.g., remembering a string of unrelated syllables); recognition (as in a multiple-choice test, where the candidate recognizes the correct answer among alternatives); and relearning, in which comparison is made between the time taken by an individual to commit certain data to memory, and the time taken to recommit it to memory after a delay. Though recent studies of certain COMPUTER functions have thrown light on some of the workings of memory (see also CYBERNETICS), little is known of its exact physiological basis. It appears, however, that chemical changes in the brain, particularly in the composition of RNA (see NUCLEIC ACIDS), alter the electrical pathways there. Moreover, it seems that some form of initial learning takes place in the NERVOUS SYSTEM before data are stored permanently in the BRAIN. (See also ELECTROENCEPHALOGRAPH; INTELLIGENCE; LEARNING.)

**MEMPHIS,** capital of the Old Kingdom of ancient Egypt until c2200 BC. Probably founded by MENES, the first king of a united Upper and Lower Egypt, c3100 BC, the city stood on the W bank of the Nile some 15mi S of modern Cairo. Excavations have revealed the temple of Ptah, god of the city, and the two massive statues of RAMSES II.

**MENANDER** (c342–c291 BC), leading Greek writer of New Comedy. Out of over 100 plays, only *Dyscolos* (The Grouch) survives complete, though there are adaptations by PLAUTUS and TERENCE. His plots are based on love-affairs and he's noted for his elegant style and deft characterization.

**MENCIUS** (c370–c290 BC), Chinese philosopher, a follower of CONFUCIUS. He held that man is naturally good and that the principles of true moral conduct are inborn. He was a champion of the ordinary people and exhorted rulers to treat their subjects well.

**MENCKEN, Henry Louis** (1880–1956), US journalist and author, caustic critic of American society and literature. He wrote for the Baltimore *Sun* and founded and edited the *American Mercury* (1924). His collected essays appeared in *Prejudices* (1919–27), and he wrote an authoritative study, *The American Language* (1919).

**MENDEL, Gregor Johann** (1822–1884), Austrian botanist and Augustinian monk who laid the foundations of the science of GENETICS. He found that self-pollinated dwarf pea plants bred true, but that under the same circumstances only about a third of tall pea plants did so, the remainder producing tall or dwarf pea plants in a ratio about 3:1. Next he crossbred tall and dwarf plants and found this without exception resulted in a tall plant, but one that did not breed true. Thus, in this plant, both tall and dwarf characteristics were present. He had found a mechanism justifying DARWIN's theory of EVOLUTION by NATURAL SELECTION; but contemporary lack of interest and his later, unsuccessful experiments with the hawkweeds discouraged him from carrying this further. It was not until 1900, when H. de VRIES and others found his published results, that the importance of his work was realized. (See also HEREDITY; POLLINATION.)

**MENDELEYEV, Dmitri Ivanovich** (1834–1907), Russian chemist who formulated the Periodic Law, that the properties of elements vary periodically with increasing atomic weight, and so drew up the PERIODIC TABLE (1869). (See also MEYER, J. L.)

**MENDELSOHN, Erich** (1887–1953), German-born expressionist architect, designed "sculptured" and functional buildings, notably the Einstein Tower, Potsdam (1921). He worked in England 1933–37, Palestine 1937–41 and the US, where he was naturalized.

**MENDELSSOHN, Moses** (1729–1786), Jewish philosopher, a leading figure of the Enlightenment in Prussia and a promoter of Jewish assimilation into German culture. He was the model for the hero of LESSING's play *Nathan the Wise*, and a grandfather of the famous composer.

**MENDELSSOHN(-BARTHOLDY), (Jacob Ludwig) Felix** (1809–1847), German Romantic composer. He wrote his concert overture to *A Midsummer Night's Dream* when only 17. Other works include his *Hebrides Overture* (also known as "Fingal's Cave"), *Italian* (1833) and *Scotch* (1842), violin concerto, chamber music and the oratorio *Elijah*. He was also a celebrated conductor, of the Leipzig Gewandhaus

orchestra, and revived interest in BACH.

**MENDES-FRANCE, Pierre** (1907–    ), French political leader. As center-left prime minister (1954–55), he ended France's war in Indochina and kept France out of a projected European Defense Community. He granted Tunisia internal self-government, but was defeated over his liberal Algerian policy.

**MENELIK II** (1844–1913), emperor of Ethiopia from 1889, founder of the modern Ethiopian nation. He unified Ethiopia and doubled its territory, crushed invading Italian forces at ADWA (1896) and instituted reforms and modernization.

**MÉNIÈRE'S DISEASE**, disorder of the cochlea and labyrinth of the EAR, causing brief acute episodes of VERTIGO, with nausea or VOMITING, ringing in the ears and DEAFNESS. Ultimately permanent deafness ensues and vertigo lessens. It is a disorder of inner-ear fluid and each episode causes some destruction of receptor cells. Drugs can reduce the vertigo.

**MENINGITIS**, INFLAMMATION of the meninges (see BRAIN) caused by BACTERIA (e.g., meningococcus, pneumococcus, hemophilus) or VIRUSES. **Bacterial meningitis** is of abrupt onset with HEADACHE, vomiting, FEVER, neck stiffness and avoidance of light. Early and appropriate ANTIBIOTIC treatment is essential as permanent damage may occur in some cases, especially in children. **Viral meningitis** is a milder illness with similar signs in a less ill person; symptomatic measures only are required. **Tuberculous meningitis** is an insidious chronic type which responds slowly to antituberculous drugs. Some FUNGI, unusual bacteria and syphilis (see VENEREAL DISEASES) may also cause varieties of meningitis.

**MENNIN, Peter** (Peter Mennini) (1923–    ), US composer whose distinctive works are characterized by dissonant harmonies and lively rhythms. He served as president of Baltimore's Peabody Conservatory of Music and of New York City's Juilliard School of Music.

**MENNINGER, Karl Augustus** (1893–    ), US psychiatrist who, with his brother **William Claire Menninger** (1899–1966) and father **Charles Frederick Menninger** (1862–1953), set up the Menninger Foundation (1941), a nonprofit organization dedicated to the furtherance of psychiatric research in Topeka, Kan.

**MENNONITES**, Protestant sect originating among the ANABAPTISTS of Zurich, Switzerland. They became influential particularly in the Netherlands, and are named for the Dutch reformer Menno

SIMONS. They base their faith solely on the Bible, believe in separation of Church and State, pacifism, and baptism only for adults renouncing sin. Despite persecution, the sect spread and now totals about 550,000 with some 89,000 members in Canada and 20,000 in the US. They are known for the strict simplicity of their life and worship. (See also AMISH; HUTTERITES.)

**MENOMINEE INDIANS,** North American Indian tribe of the ALGONQUIAN linguistic group. Most lived in upper Mich. and Wis., along the W shore of Green Bay, gathering wild rice (*Menominee* means "wild rice people"). In 1854 they were settled on a reservation on the Wolf and Oconto rivers in Wis., now a county, where their descendants (about 4,000) still live.

**MENOPAUSE.** See MENSTRUATION.

**MENOTTI, Gian Carlo** (1911–     ), Italian-born US composer of dramatically powerful operas with his own librettos, and founder (1958) of the Two Worlds festival at Spoleto, Italy. His works include *The Medium* (1946) and the television opera *Amahl and the Night Visitors* (1951). *The Consul* (1950) and *The Saint of Bleecker Street* (1954) won Pulitzer prizes.

**MENSHEVIKS,** minority group in the Russian Social Democratic Workers' Party, opposed to the Bolsheviks, the majority group led by LENIN (see BOLSHEVISM). Unlike Lenin, the Menshevik theoretician Georgi PLEKHANOV favored mass membership and thought a spell of bourgeois rule must precede communism. Led by L. Martov, the Mensheviks emerged in 1903, backed KERENSKY'S government and opposed the Bolshevik seizure of power. By 1921 they had been eliminated.

**MENSTRUATION,** specifically the monthly loss of BLOOD (period), representing shedding of WOMB endometrium, in women of reproductive age; in general, the whole monthly cycle of hormone, structural and functional changes in such women, punctuated by menstrual blood loss. After each period, the womb-lining endometrium starts to proliferate and thicken under the influence of GONADOTROPHINS (FOLLICLE STIMULATING HORMONE) and ESTROGENS. In midcycle a burst of LUTEINIZING HORMONE secretion, initiated by the HYPOTHALAMUS, causes release of an egg from an ovarian follicle (*ovulation*). More PROGESTERONE is then secreted and the endometrium is prepared for IMPLANTATION of a fertilized egg. If the egg is not fertilized, PREGNANCY does not ensue and blood-vessel changes occur leading to the shedding of the endometrium and some blood; these are lost through the vagina for several days,

sometimes with pain or COLIC. The cycle then restarts. During the menstrual cycle, changes in the BREASTS, body temperature, fluid balance and mood occur, the manifestations varying from person to person. Cyclic patterns are established at PUBERTY (*menarche*) and end in middle life (age 45–50) at the *menopause*, the "change of life." Disorders of menstruation include heavy, irregular or missed periods; bleeding between periods or after the menopause, and excessively painful periods. They are studied in GYNECOLOGY.

**MENTAL ILLNESS,** or psychiatric disorders, is characterized by abnormal functioning of the higher centers of the BRAIN responsible for thought, perception, mood and behavior. Although some mental disorders are organically based (e.g. KORSAKOV'S PSYCHOSIS), others, such as NEUROSES and most SCHIZOPHRENIAS, are considered to be functional or learned. The borderline between disease and the range of normal variability is indistinct and may be determined by cultural factors. Crime may result from mental disease, but modern Western society is careful to eliminate it as far as possible before subjecting a criminal to justice. However, in certain repressive regimes, political or ideological nonconformity can be grounds for admission to a mental hospital. Mental disease has been recognized since ancient times, and both HIPPOCRATES and GALEN evolved theories as to its origins; but in many cultures, over the centuries, madness has been equated with possession by evil spirits and sufferers were often treated as witches. In the 15th century, PARACELSUS proposed that the moon determined the behavior of mad people (hence "lunacy"), while in the 18th century MESMER favored the role of animal magnetism (from which HYPNOSIS is derived). The first humane *asylum* for the mentally ill was founded in Paris by PINEL (1795). Originally only socially intolerable cases were admitted to such hospitals, but today voluntary admission is more common. The *Viennese school* of psychology, in particular Sigmund FREUD and his pupils, emphasized the importance of past, especially childhood experiences, sexual attitudes and other functional factors. PSYCHOANALYSIS and many modern psychotherapies derive from this school. On the other hand, the influence of subtle organic factors (e.g., brain biochemistry) was favored by others; this led to using LOBOTOMY, SHOCK THERAPY and DRUGS.

Mental illness may be classified into PSYCHOSIS, NEUROSIS and personality disorder. **Schizophrenia** is a psychosis causing disturbance of thought and perception in which mood is characteristically flat and behavior withdrawn. Features include: auditory hallucinations; delusions of identity ("I'm the King of Spain"), of surroundings, and about other people (e.g., suspicion of conspiracy in PARANOIA); blocking, insertion and broadcasting of thought, and knight's-move thinking, or nonlogical sequence of ideas. Conversation lacks substance and may be in riddles and neologisms; speech or behavior may be imitative, stereotyped, repetitive or negative. Phenothiazine drugs, especially chlorpromazine and long-acting analogues, are particularly valuable in schizophrenia.

In **affective psychoses**, disturbance of mood is the primary disorder. Subjects usually exhibit DEPRESSION with loss of drive and inconsolably low mood, either in response to situation (exogenous) or for no apparent reason (endogenous). Loss of appetite, CONSTIPATION and characteristic sleep disturbance also commonly occur. ANTIDEPRESSANTS and SHOCK THERAPY are valuable, but psychotherapy may also be needed. In hypnomania or MANIA, excitability, restlessness, euphoria, ceaseless talk, flight of ideas and loss of social inhibitions occur. Financial, sexual and alcohol excesses may result. Chlorpromazine, haloperidol and lithium are effective. **Neuroses** include ANXIETY, the pathological exaggeration of a physiological response, which may coexist with depression but responds to benzodiazepines (Valium) and psychotherapy; obsessional and compulsive neuroses, manifested by extreme habits, rituals and fixations (which may be recognized as irrational); PHOBIAS, excessive and inappropriate fears of objects or situations (e.g. AGORAPHOBIA); and HYSTERIA, the last two of which are helped by behavior therapy. Psychopathy is a specific disorder of personality characterized by failure to learn from experience. Irresponsibility, inconsiderateness and lack of foresight result, and may lead to crime. Other **personality disorders** are exhibited by a variety of people, often with unstable backgrounds, who seem unable to cope with the realities of everyday adult life; attempted suicide is a common gesture. In sexual disorders with antisocial or perverse sexual fixations, behavior therapy may be of value. (See also ALCOHOLISM; ANOREXIA NERVOSA; DRUG ADDICTION.)

**MENTAL RETARDATION**, low intellectual capacity arising, not from MENTAL ILLNESS, but from impairment of the normal development of the BRAIN and NERVOUS SYSTEM. Causes include genetic defect (as in MONGOLISM); infection of the EMBRYO or FETUS; HYDROCEPHALUS or inherited metabolic defects (e.g., CRETINISM), and injury at BIRTH including cerebral HEMORRHAGE and fetal ANOXIA. Disease in infancy such as ENCEPHALITIS may cause mental retardation in children with previous normal development. Retardation is initially recognized by slowness to develop normal patterns of social and learning behavior and is confirmed through intelligence measurements. It is most important that affected children should receive adequate social contact and education, for their development is retarded and not arrested. In particular, special schooling may help them to achieve a degree of learning and social competence.

**MENUHIN, Yehudi** (1916–    ), US violinist and conductor. He made his concert debut at seven, played to Allied forces in WWII, and later to raise cash for war victims. He has revived forgotten masterpieces, aroused interest in Eastern music and directed festivals. In 1963 he opened a school for musically gifted children in England.

**MENZIES, Sir Robert Gordon** (1894–1978), Australian prime minister 1939–41, 1949–66. He was attorney general 1935–39 and leader of the opposition 1943–48. As leader of the Liberal-Country Party coalition 1949–66, he pursued a conservative anti-communist policy and encouraged rapid industrial growth.

**MEO** (MIAO), a non-Chinese people of SW China, N Laos, Vietnam and Thailand. They live in mountain villages and practice shifting cultivation. Many groups raise opium as a cash crop. Numbering about 2,500,500, they have virtually no political organization, and minimal contact with governments and other peoples.

**MEPHISTOPHELES**, in medieval legend, the devil to whom FAUST sold his soul. He is primarily a literary creation, and appears in the famous plays by MARLOWE and GOETHE.

**MERCANTILISM**, in economic history, theories prevailing in 16th- to 18th-century W Europe, reflecting the increased importance of the merchant. Mercantilists favored TARIFFS to secure a favorable INTERNATIONAL TRADE balance and maintain reserves of precious metals, considered essential to a nation's wealth. Their PROTECTIONISM was succeeded by the FREE TRADE arguments of the French PHYSIOCRATS.

**MERCATOR, Gerardus** (1512–1594), Flemish cartographer and calligrapher, best known for Mercator's Projection (see MAP), which he first used in 1569 for a world map.

The PROJECTION is from a point at the center of the earth through the surface of the globe onto a cylinder that touches the earth around the equator.

**MERCER, Johnny** (1909–1976), US songwriter and singer who teamed with several popular composers to write dozens of the most enduring songs of the 1930s, 1940s and 1950s including "That Old Black Magic," "Blues in the Night" and "Moon River."

**MERCHANT SHIPPING,** non-military sea transportation. Until the Industrial Revolution most ships were small and carried cargoes of high-value goods like gold, silks and spices. Today huge tonnages of foods, coal, ores, machinery and petroleum travel in vast merchant vessels. Without this traffic industry would run down and millions would starve. Since 1800, merchant ships have enormously increased in speed, size and number. In 1819 the first US steamship to cross the Atlantic, the *Savannah*, took 29 days. In 1952 the *United States* crossed in 3 days. In 1847 the *Washington* displaced 1,720 tons and was then a large ship. The modern Japanese-built oil tanker, *Globtik London*, is 483,939 dwt (dwt = deadweight tons, measured by the weight of cargo a ship can carry) and 1,243ft long. In 1886 the world's merchant fleets totaled 21 million gross tons (1 gross ton = 100cu ft of ship space), half of which was under sail. In 1973, the world's merchant fleets totaled 290 million gross tons shared out among some 60,000 vessels. Patterns of ownership have also changed. Britain owned half of the world's cargo ships a century ago. In 1973 the flags of Liberia, Japan, Britain, Norway, Greece, the USSR and the US (in that order) led the list of tonnages. (For tax purposes, many American and Greek-owned vessels are registered under Liberian and Panamanian flags of convenience.)

**Types of Ships.** The main types of merchant ship are the tramps that roam the world picking up cargoes and sailing where required, and liners that travel fixed routes on regular schedules. Passenger liner traffic has declined in competition with air travel, but the growth in cargo traffic has produced today's super-tankers and bulk carriers that have led to big new port developments. (See also HARBOR.) The latest advance in cargo transport is the container ship carrying huge rectangular containers preloaded with assorted cargo. (See also SHIPS AND SHIPPING.)

**MERCURY,** the planet closest to the sun with a mean solar distance of 58Gm. Its highly eccentric ORBIT brings it within 46Gm of the sun at perihelion and takes it 70Gm from the sun at aphelion. Its diameter is about 4,870km, its mass about 0.054 that of the earth. It goes around the sun in just under 88 days and rotates on its axis in about 59 days. The successful prediction by Albert EINSTEIN that Mercury's orbit would be found to advance by 43in per century is usually regarded as a confirmation of the General Theory of RELATIVITY. Night surface temperature is thought to be about 110K, midday equatorial temperature over 600K. The airless planet's average density (5.2 grams per cubic centimeter) indicates a high proportion of heavy elements in its interior. In 1974 and 1975, a MARINER space probe revealed that Mercury has a moonlike heavily cratered surface, and a slight magnetic field.

**MERCURY (Hg),** or **quicksilver,** silvery-white liquid metal in Group IIB of the PERIODIC TABLE; an anomalous TRANSITION ELEMENT. It occurs as CINNABAR, calomel and rarely as the metal, which has been known from ancient times. It is extracted by roasting cinnabar in air and condensing the mercury vapor. Mercury is fairly inert, tarnishing only slowly in moist air, and soluble in oxidizing acids only; it is readily attacked by the HALOGENS and sulfur. It forms $Hg^{2+}$ and some $Hg_2^{2+}$ compounds, and many important organometallic compounds. Mercury and its compounds are highly toxic. The metal is used to form AMALGAMS; for electrodes, and in barometers, thermometers, diffusion PUMPS, and mercury-vapor lamps (see LIGHTING, ARTIFICIAL). Various mercury compounds are used as pharmaceuticals. AW 200.6, mp −39°C, bp 357°C, sg 13.546 (20°C). **Mercury (II) cyanate** ($Hg[ONC]_2$), or **mercury fulminate,** is a white crystalline solid, sensitive to percussion, and used as a detonator. **Mercury (II) chloride** ($HgCl_2$), or **corrosive sublimate,** is a colorless crystalline solid prepared by direct synthesis. Although highly toxic, it is used in dilute solution as an ANTISEPTIC, and also as a fungicide and a polymerization catalyst. mp 276°C, bp 302°C. **Mercury (I) chloride** ($Hg_2Cl_2$), or **calomel,** is a white rhombic crystalline solid, found in nature. It is used in ointments and formerly found use as a LAXATIVE. A calomel/mercury cell with potassium chloride electrolyte (the Weston cell) is used to provide a standard ELECTROMOTIVE FORCE. mp 303°C, bp 384°C.

**MERCURY PROGRAM,** first US manned space flights 1960–63, using the one-man Mercury capsule. In 1961 Alan Shepard and Virgil Grissom were launched on suborbital flights by the Redstone carrier missile. In 1962 John GLENN made the first US orbital flight, followed by M. Scott Carpenter, Walter Schirra and Leroy Cooper; orbital missions were launched by Atlas carriers. (See also SPACE EXPLORATION.)

**MEREDITH, George** (1828–1909), English novelist and poet. His best-known novel is the tragicomic *Ordeal of Richard Feverel* (1859). The sonnet sequence *Modern Love* (1862) grew out of the breakdown of his marriage. Other well-known works are *The Egoist* (1879) and *Diana of the Crossways* (1885).

**MEREZHKOVSKI, Dmitri Sergeyevich** (1865–1941), influential Russian author and critic. A mystic, he saw life and literature as divided between seers of the flesh and of the spirit. An opponent of both tsarism and bolshevism, he emigrated after the Revolution.

**MERGENTHALER, Ottmar** (1854–1899), German-born US inventor of the first linotype PRINTING machine (1884), first put to commercial use in 1886.

**MERIDIAN**, on the celestial sphere, the great circle passing through the celestial poles and the observer's ZENITH. It cuts his HORIZON N and S. (See also CELESTIAL SPHERE; TRANSIT.) The term is used also for a line of terrestrial longitude.

**MERIMÉE, Prosper** (1803–1870), French author, historian, archaeologist and linguist. He is best known for short stories such as *Mateo Falcone* (1829) and the romance *Carmen* (1847), source of BIZET's opera.

**MERMAN, Ethel** (Ethel Zimmerman; 1909–    ), US singer and actress. She began in vaudeville with the team of Clayton, Jackson and Durante, then brought her powerful voice to such hit musicals as *Annie Get Your Gun* (1946–49), *Call Me Madam* (1950), and *Gypsy* (1959).

**MEROVINGIANS**, dynasty of Frankish kings 428–751. They were named for the fifth century king Merovech; his grandson CLOVIS I first united much of France. The kingdom was later partitioned, but enlarged and reunited (613) under Clotaire II. The Merovingians governed through the remnants of the old Roman administration and established Catholic Christianity. After DAGOBERT I in the 7th century the kings became known as *rois-Fainéants* (do-nothings) and power passed to the mayors of the palace, nominally high officials; the last of these, PEPIN THE SHORT, deposed the last Merovingian, Childeric III. (See also AUSTRASIA; NEUSTRIA.)

**MERRIAM, Charles Edward, Jr.** (1874–1953), US political scientist who advocated empirical research and was considered the father of behaviorism in political science. A professor at the U. of Chicago (1900–40), he helped expand the role of social science and academics in American life and wrote *New Aspects of Politics* (1925) and *Political Power* (1934).

**MERRICK, David** (David Margulies; 1912–    ), US theatrical producer who was responsible for dozens of Broadway hits, among them *Gypsy* (1958), *Becket* (1960), *Hello Dolly* (1964), *Marat/Sade* (1965), and *42nd Street* (1980).

**MERTON, Thomas** (1915–1968), US religious writer of poetry, meditative works and the autobiography *The Seven Storey Mountain* (1948). Converted to Roman Catholicism, he became a Trappist monk (1941) and later a priest.

**MESA VERDE NATIONAL PARK,** area of 52,074 acres in SW Col., established in 1906. It contains extensive pueblo ruins built by the CLIFF DWELLERS over 1,300 years ago, and much distinctive wild life.

**MESCALINE,** HALLUCINOGENIC DRUG, derived from a Mexican cactus, whose use dates back to ancient times when "peyote buttons" were used in religious ceremonies among American Indians. The hallucinations experienced during its use were among the first to be described (by Aldous HUXLEY) and resemble those of LSD.

**MESMER, Franz Anton** (1734–1815), German physician, controversy over whose unusual techniques and theories sparked in CHARCOT and others an interest in the possibilities of using "animal magnetism" (or mesmerism, i.e., HYPNOSIS) for psychotherapy.

**MESOPOTAMIA** (Greek: between the rivers), ancient region between the Tigris and Euphrates rivers in SW Asia, home of many early civilizations. (See also FERTILE CRESCENT.) Most of it lies in Iraq, between the Armenian and Kurdish Mts in the N and the Persian Gulf in the S; the N is mainly grassy, rolling plateau; the S is a sandy plain leading to marshes. Since ancient times the rivers have been used to irrigate the area, most notably under ABBASIDE rule (749–1285 AD), but the ancient systems degenerated under Mongol invasion and OTTOMAN rule, and were not replaced until the 20th century. Neolithic farming peoples were settling Mesopotamia by 6000 BC followed by the Tell Halaf and al'Ubaid cultures after 4000 BC. By 3000 BC the SUMERIANS had created a civilization of independent city-states in the S. From c3000–625 BC Mesopotamia was successively dominated by SUMER, AKKAD, the Sumerian dynasty of UR, the empires of BABYLONIA AND ASSYRIA and CHALDEA. In 539 BC the Persian Empire absorbed Mesopotamia; in 331 BC it was conquered by Alexander the Great. It then came under Roman, Byzantine and Arab rule. The Abbaside caliphs made BAGHDAD their capital in 762 AD, but prosperity collapsed with the Mongol invasion of 1289. Mesopotamia was under Ottoman rule 1638–1918, when it was largely incorporated into IRAQ.

**MESOSPHERE,** the layer of the ATMOSPHERE immediately above the stratosphere, between ALTITUDES 48km and 53km. IC Eon, lasting from 225 until 65 million years ago. It has three periods: the TRIASSIC, JURASSIC and CRETACEOUS. (See GEOLOGY.)

**MESSERSCHMITT, Wilhelm "Willy"** (1898–1978), German pioneer aircraft designer famous for his fast monoplane fighters used in WWII. They included the Me-109 (1934) and the Me-262, the first jet plane used in war (1944).

**MESSIAEN, Olivier Eugène Prosper Charles** (1908–    ), influential French composer and organist. His music is extremely personal, such works as *The Ascension* (1955) being influenced by Roman Catholic mysticism. Others such as the *Turangalila* symphony (1949) are based on oriental music, or birdsong as in the *Catalog of Birds* (1959).

**MESSIAH** (Hebrew: anointed one), according to Israelite prophets, especially ISAIAH, the ruler whom God would send to restore Israel and begin a glorious age of peace and righteousness (see ESCHATOLOGY). He would be a descendant of King DAVID. Christians recognize Jesus of Nazareth as the Messiah (or CHRIST); his role as "suffering servant" was alien to Jewish hopes of a political deliverer. The concept of a forthcoming divine redeemer is common to many religions.

**MESSINA,** historic seaport city in NE Sicily opposite mainland Italy. Sicily's third largest city and capital of Messina Province, Messina's industries include chemical and food manufacturing. It was founded as a Greek colony c700 BC. Its cathedral and church of Annunciata Dei Catalani probably date from the Byzantine period; they were rebuilt by the Normans in the 13th century. Earthquakes in 1783 and 1908 almost entirely destroyed the city. Pop 261,500.

**MESTROVIĆ, Ivan** (1883–1962), Yugoslav-born US sculptor. He studied at Vienna and Rome, and was influenced by classical Greek styles and RODIN. Professor of fine arts at Notre Dame U. from 1955, he executed mainly religious subjects and portraits.

**METABOLISM,** the sum total of all chemical reactions that occur in a living organism. It can be subdivided into **anabolism** which describes reactions which build up more complex substances from smaller ones, and **catabolism** which describes reactions which break down complex substances into simpler ones. Anabolic reactions require ENERGY while catabolic reactions liberate energy. Metabolic reactions are catalysed by ENZYMES in a highly integrated and finely controlled manner so that there is no overproduction or underutilization of the energy required to maintain life. All energy required to maintain life is ultimately derived from sunlight by PHOTOSYNTHESIS, and most organisms use the products of photosynthesis either directly or indirectly. The energy is stored in most living organisms in a specific chemical compound, adenosine triphosphate (ATP—see NUCLEOTIDES). ATP can transfer its energy to other molecules by a loss of phosphate, later regaining phosphate from catabolic reactions. (See also BASAL METABOLIC RATE.)

**METAL,** an element with high specific gravity; high opacity and reflectivity to light (giving a characteristic luster when polished); that can be hammered into thin sheets and drawn into wires (i.e., is malleable and ductile), and is a good conductor of heat and electricity, its electrical conductivity decreasing with temperature. Roughly 75% of the chemical elements are metals, but not all of them possess all the typical metallic properties. Most are found as ores and in the pure state are crystalline solids (mercury, liquid at room temperature, being a notable exception), their atoms readily losing electrons to become positive IONS. ALLOYS are easily formed because of the nonspecific nondirectional nature of the metallic bond.

**METALLOID,** or **semimetal,** an ELEMENT that has properties—physical and chemical—intermediate between those of METALS and those of NONMETALS. The metalloids—BORON, SILICON, GERMANIUM, ARSENIC, ANTIMONY, SELENIUM and TELLURIUM—form a diagonal band in the PERIODIC TABLE. They do not have high ELECTRONEGATIVITY or electropositivity, and form amphoteric OXIDES; they are SEMI-CONDUCTORS.

**METALLURGY,** the science and technology of METALS, concerned with their extraction from ores, the methods of refining, purifying and preparing them for use and the study of the structure and physical properties of metals and ALLOYS. A few unreactive metals such as silver and gold are found native (uncombined), but most metals occur naturally as MINERALS (i.e., in chemical combination with nonmetallic elements). Ores are mixtures of minerals from which metal extraction is commercially viable. Over 5,000 years man has developed techniques for working ores and forming alloys, but only in the last two centuries have these methods been based on scientific theory. The production of metals from ores is known as process or extraction metallurgy; fabrication metallurgy concerns the conversion of raw metals into alloys, sheets, wires etc., while physical metallurgy covers the structure and properties of metals and alloys, including their mechanical working, heat treatment and testing. Process metallurgy begins with ore dressing, using physical methods such as crushing, grinding and gravity separation to split up the different minerals in an ore. The next stage involves chemical action to separate the metallic component of the mineral from the unwanted nonmetallic part. The actual method used depends on the chemical nature of the mineral compound (e.g., if it is an oxide or sulfide, its solubility in acids etc.) and its physical properties. Hydrometallurgy uses chemical reactions in aqueous solutions to extract metal from ore. Electrometallurgy uses electricity for firing a furnace or electrolytically reducing a metallic compound to a metal. Pyrometallurgy covers roasting, SMELTING and other high-temperature chemical reactions. It has the advantage of involving fast reactions and giving a molten or gaseous product which can easily be separated out. The extracted metal may need further refining or purifying: electrometallurgy and pyrometallurgy are again used at this stage. Molten metal may then simply be cast by pouring into a mold, giving, e.g., pig iron, or it may be formed into ingots which are then hot or cold worked, as with, e.g., wrought iron. Mechanical working, in the form of rolling, pressing or FORGING, improves the final structure and properties of most metals; it tends to break down and redistribute the impurities formed when a large mass of molten metal solidifies. Simple heat treatment such as ANNEALING also tends to remove some of the inherent brittleness of cast metals. (See also BLAST FURNACE; BRAZING; ROLLING MILLS; SINTERIN; STEEL.)

**METAMORPHIC ROCKS,** one of the three main classes of rocks of the earth's crust. They consist of rocks that have undergone change owing to heat, pressure or chemical action. In plate tectonic theory, the collision of lithospheric plates leads to widespread *regional metamorphism*. Igneous intrusion leads to changes in the rocks close to the borders or contacts of the cooling magma and these changes, largely due to the application of heat, constitute *contact (thermal) metamorphism*. Common metamorphic rock types include MARBLE, QUARTZITE, SLATE, SCHIST and GNEISS. Some occurrences of GRANITE are also thought to be of metamorphic origin.

**METAMORPHOSIS,** in animals (notably FROGS, TOADS and INSECTS), a marked and relatively rapid change in body form. This alteration in appearance is associated with a change in habits. Perhaps the best known example is the change which occurs when a tadpole becomes a frog.

**METAPHYSICAL POETS,** early 17th-century English lyric poets characterized by an involved style relying on the metaphysical *conceit*, an elaborate metaphorical image. Most famous among them is John DONNE; others include Andrew MARVELL, George HERBERT, Richard CRASHAW, Henry VAUGHAN and Thomas CAREW. The Metaphysicals (a term first used by Samuel JOHNSON) extended the range of lyric poetry by writing about death, decay, immortality and faith. They declined in popularity after about 1660, but their complex intellectual content and rich exploration of feeling has made them a major influence on 20th century poetry.

**METAPHYSICS,** the branch of philosophy concerned with the fundamentals of existence or reality, such as the existence and nature of God, the immortality of the soul, the meaning of evil, the problem of freedom and determinism, and the relationship of mind and body. Metaphysical thinking was criticized by KANT, who claimed that traditional metaphysics sought to go beyond the limits of human knowledge.

**METASTASIO, Pietro** (born Pietro Antonio Domenico Bonaventura Trapassi; 1698–1782), Italian poet and dramatist. He is best known for his melodramas used as opera librettos, including *Artaxerxes* and *La Clemenza di Tito.*

**METAXAS, Ioannis** (1871–1941), Greek general and from 1936 ultra-royalist premier and dictator of Greece. He made important social and economic reforms. He tried to maintain Greek neutrality in WWII, but after successfully resisting the Italian invasion in 1940 joined the Allied powers.

**METEOR,** the visible passage of a

meteoroid (a small particle of interplanetary matter) into the earth's atmosphere. Due to friction it burns up, showing a trail of fire in the night sky. The velocity on entry lies in the range 11–72km/s.

**Meteoroids** are believed to consist of asteroidal and cometary debris. Although stray meteoroids reach our atmosphere throughout the year, for short periods at certain times of year they arrive in profuse numbers, sharing a common direction and velocity. It was shown in 1866 by SCHIAPARELLI that the annual Perseid meteor shower was caused by meteoroids orbiting the sun in the same orbit as a comet observed some years before; moreover, since their period of orbit is unrelated to that of the earth, the meteoroids must form a fairly uniform "ring" around the sun for the shower to be annual. Other comet-shower relationships have been shown, implying that these streams of meteoroids are cometary debris.

**Meteors** may be seen by a nighttime observer on average five times per hour: these are known as sporadic meteors or shooting stars. Around twenty times a year, however, a meteor shower occurs and between 20 and 35,000 meteors per hour may be observed. These annual showers are generally named for the constellations from which they appear to emanate: e.g., Perseids (Perseus), Leonids (LEO). Large meteors are called Fireballs, and those that explode are known as bolides.

**Meteorites** are larger than meteors, and are of special interest in that, should they enter the atmosphere, they at least partially survive the passage to the ground. Many have been examined. They fall into two main categories: "stones," whose composition is not unlike that of the earth's crust; and "irons," which contain about 80%–95% iron, 2–5% nickel and traces of other elements. Intermediate types exist. Irons display a usually crystalline structure which implies that they were initially liquid, cooling over long periods of time. Sometimes large meteorites shatter on impact, producing large craters like those in Arizona and Siberia.

**METEOROLOGY,** the study of the ATMOSPHERE and its phenomena, weather and climate. Based on atmospheric physics, it is primarily an observational science, whose main application is WEATHER FORECASTING AND CONTROL. The RAIN gauge and WIND vane were known in ancient times, and the other basic instruments— ANEMOMETER, BAROMETER, HYGROMETER and THERMOMETER—had all been invented by 1790. Thus accurate data could be collected; but simultaneous observations over a wide area were impracticable until the development of the telegraph. Since WWI observations of the upper atmosphere have been made, using airplanes, balloons, RADIOSONDE, and since WWII (when meteorology began to flourish) ROCKETS and artificial SATELLITES. RADAR has been much used. Observed phenomena include CLOUDS, PRECIPITATION and HUMIDITY, WIND and air pressure, air temperature, STORMS, CYCLONES, AIR MASSES and FRONTS.

**METER (m),** the SI base unit of length, defined as the length equal to 1,650,763.73 times the wavelength of radiation corresponding to the transition between the ENERGY LEVELS $2p_{10}$ and $5d_5$ of the krypton-86 atom (see SI UNITS). It was originally intended that the meter represent one ten millionth of the distance from the N Pole to the equator on the MERIDIAN passing through Paris. But the surveyors got their sums wrong and for 162 years (to 1960), the meter was defined as an arbitrary distance marked on a metal bar (from 1889–1960, the "international prototype meter," a bar of platinum-iridium which is still kept under controlled conditions near Paris).

**METHANE ($CH_4$),** colorless, odorless gas; the simplest alkane (see HYDROCARBONS). It is produced by decomposing organic matter in sewage and in marshes (hence the name *marsh gas*), and is the "firedamp" of coal mines (see DAMP). It is the chief constituent of NATURAL GAS, occurs in coal gas and water gas, and is produced in PETROLEUM refining. Methane is used as a FUEL, for making carbon-black, and for chemical synthesis. MW 16.0, mp −183°C, bp −164°C.

**METHANOL (CH₃OH),** or methyl alcohol, or wood alcohol, colorless liquid, the simplest ALCOHOL. Formerly made by destructive distillation of wood, it is now almost all made by catalytic reaction of carbon monoxide and hydrogen. It is used to make FORMALDEHYDE and other industrial chemicals, in ANTIFREEZE, rocket fuels, as a solvent and experimentally as automobile fuel, either pure or mixed in a 1-to-9 ratio with gasoline (see GASOHOL). It is highly toxic. MW 32.0, mp −94°C, bp 65°C.

**METHOD ACTING.** See STANISLAVSKI, Konstantin; STRASBERG, Lee.

**METHODISTS,** members of Protestant churches that originated in the 18th-century EVANGELICAL REVIVAL led by John and Charles WESLEY. The name "Methodist" was used first in 1729 for members of the "Holy Club" of Oxford U., led by the Wesleys, who lived "by rule and method." Influenced by the MORAVIAN CHURCH,

Methodism began as an evangelical movement in 1738 when the Wesleys and George WHITEFIELD began evangelistic preaching; banned from most Anglican pulpits, they preached in the open air and drew vast crowds. Converts were organized into class meetings and itinerant lay preachers appointed. Wesleyan Methodism was ARMINIAN; Whitefield's followers were CALVINIST but predominated only in Wales. After Wesley's death in 1791 the societies formally separated from the Church of England and became the Wesleyan Methodist Church. The American Methodist movement was established after 1771 by Francis ASBURY and Thomas Coke. Methodist polity in Britain is in effect presbyterian; in the US it is episcopal. Methodism traditionally stresses conversion, holiness and social welfare. In both the US and England Methodist groups have often seceded from the main church, but most have since reunited. Worldwide there are more than 43 million Methodists.

**METRIC SYSTEM,** a decimal system of WEIGHTS AND MEASURES devised in Revolutionary France in 1791 and based on the METER, a unit of LENGTH intended to equal a ten-millionth part of the distance from the equator to either geographic pole. The original unit of MASS was the GRAM, the mass of a cubic centimetre of water at 4°C, the TEMPERATURE of its greatest DENSITY. Auxiliary units were to be formed by adding Greek prefixes to the names of the base units for their decimal multiples and Latin prefixes for their decimal subdivisions. The metric system forms the basis of the physical units systems known as CGS UNITS and MKSA UNITS, the present International System of Units (SI UNITS) being a development of the latter. SI also provides the primary standards for the US Customary System of units. This means that exact interconversion can be easily accomplished.

**METROPOLITAN MUSEUM OF ART,** the world's largest and most comprehensive art museum. Founded in 1870 in New York City, its collections include art from ancient Egypt, Greece, Rome, Babylonia and Assyria and it has outstanding collections of musical instruments, prints, and of famous paintings and sculpture from all periods. Medieval art is housed in the Cloisters, constructed from actual medieval buildings.

**METROPOLITAN OPERA,** leading US and world opera company. The old Metropolitan Opera House was built in New York City in 1883 but in 1966 the company moved to LINCOLN CENTER. "The Met" has been as famous for its directors, such as Gatti-Casazza and Rudolf BING, as for its operas and singers, or for conductors like MAHLER and TOSCANINI.

**METTERNICH, Clemens Wenzel Nepomuk Lothar, Prince of** (1773–1859), Austrian statesman. After a diplomatic career in Saxony, Prussia and France he became Austrian foreign minister in 1809. He gradually dissociated Austria from France and organized an alliance of Austria, Russia and Prussia against Napoleon. However at the CONGRESS OF VIENNA, 1814–15, he reestablished a system of power whereby Russia and Prussia were balanced by the combined power of Austria, France and England. Appointed state chancellor in 1821, his authority declined after 1826 and he was overthrown in 1848 (see REVOLUTIONS OF 1848). The period 1815–48 is often called the "Age of Metternich."

**MEUSE RIVER,** river in W Europe, rising in the Langres Plateau, France and flowing N for about 580mi across Belgium and the Netherlands, where it is named Maas, into the North Sea. It is an important thoroughfare and line of defense for France and Belgium.

**MEXICAN WAR** (1846–1848), conflict between the US and Mexico. Its immediate cause was the question of US annexation of Texas. In 1835 Americans in the Mexican state of Texas rebelled against SANTA ANNA's dictatorship. On his defeat Texas became an independent republic and the US annexed it in 1845. Mexico claimed that the Texas boundary was the Nueces R, and the US that it was the Rio Grande. President POLK sent John Slidell to negotiate this question and to discuss the purchase of California and New Mexico from Mexico. The Mexicans refused to negotiate and in March 1846 Gen. Zachary TAYLOR was sent with troops to the Rio Grande. A Mexican force met him, and Congress declared war in May. It has been debated whether Polk's motives in promoting hostilities were based on a sincere grievance or on his desire to annex California.

US strategy was to invade N.M. and Cal.; to advance along the Rio Grande; and to invade Mexico City from the N. The American forces were successful in all these campaigns and General Taylor defeated Santa Anna in Feb. 1847 at BUENA VISTA. General Winfield SCOTT landed troops at Veracruz, defeated the Mexicans at CERRO GORDO, CONTRERAS and CHURUBUSCO, and after the battle of CHAPULTEPEC captured Mexico City in Sept. 1847.

By the Treaty of GUADALUPE HIDALGO,

Feb. 1848, Mexico ceded to the US the territory N of the line formed by the Rio Grande, the Gila R., and across the Colorado R to the Pacific. The US agreed to pay $15 million and settle all claims by US citizens against Mexico. Americans were divided over the war, mainly because the extension of territory involved the problem of extending slavery, and debates on this point brought to the forefront of political conflict issues which led to the Civil War.

**Official name:** United Mexican States
**Capital:** Mexico City
**Area:** 761,605sq mi
**Population:** 66,944,000
**Languages:** Spanish, Indian languages
**Religions:** Roman Catholic
**Monetary unit(s):** 1 Mexican peso = 100 centavos

MEXICO, the third-largest country in Latin America, lies in southernmost North America. Straddling the Central American isthmus, it is bounded on the N by the US, about two-thirds of the border following the Rio Grande (Río Bravo in Mexico). In the S it borders on Guatemala and Belize. On the E lies the Gulf of Mexico and on the W, the Gulf of California, which separates Baja (Lower) California from the rest of Mexico and the Pacific Ocean.

Land. About 75% of Mexico is occupied by a central plateau with low hills, basins and mountains and bounded by the Sierra Madre Occidental and Sierra Madre Oriental. Its S edge is formed by volcanoes, some still active, including Popocatépetl (17,887ft), Iztaccíhuatl (17,343ft) and Citlaltépetl or Orizaba (18,700ft, highest peak in Mexico). S of the central plateau is another high and rugged region. On the E and W escarpments drop steeply to the coastal plains, the broader being the Gulf Coast plain extending from the Río Bravo to the Yucatán peninsula and consisting mainly of swamps and lagoons. N Mexico is arid and has few rivers. Three main rivers drain the central plateau: the Santiago-Lerma, the Pánuco-Moctezuma and the upper Balsas R.

There are four climatic zones: tierra

caliente (hot land) lying between sea level and 2,500ft and embracing the Yucatán, coastal lowlands and part of Baja California; tierra templada of the central plateau; and tierra fría (cold land, 6,000–12,000ft). Above 12,000ft is tierra helada (frozen land). Rainfall, heaviest in the SE, decreases inland and to the N.

People. The population continues to increase rapidly due to the high birthrate. Over 60% live in the towns and cities, the largest being Mexico City, the capital. Guadalajara is the second-largest city. About 60% of Mexicans are mestizos (of mixed Indian and white stock), 30% are pure Indians, and 10% whites. Spanish is the official language, but there are many Indian dialects. Though education has progressed, some 12% of the population are still illiterate.

Economy. The economy has expanded since WWII, but though industrialization has made great progress, agriculture remains the most important sector, which employs 40% of the labor force. Less than 15% of the land surface is cultivable. Most cultivated land is on the central plateau. Since the revolution of 1910, most large estates have been expropriated and the land redistributed among the peasants, organized in landholding communities (ejidos). The chief subsistence crops are corn and beans. The main commercial crops are wheat, corn, beans, cotton, coffee, sugarcane and sisal. Tropical crops are grown on the coastal lowlands. Irrigation projects have transformed parts of the arid N. Cattle are reared in the N and in the rugged region S of the central plateau. There are valuable forests (pine, mahogany, cedar) and fisheries (sardines, tuna, shrimps).

Mexico is rich in minerals, especially silver, zinc, lead, copper, coal, natural gas and sulfur. Huge petroleum reserves (possibly second-largest in the world) were discovered in mid-1970s. Abundant reserves of iron ore and uranium await development. Large hydroelectric plants have been constructed on some rivers. Major industries include iron and steel (Monterrey, Monclova and the new, much larger Las Truchas project), and textiles (Mexico City and nearby Puebla and Toluca). Mexico also makes chemicals, electric goods, ceramics, paper, footwear, glass, processed foods and other products. Tourism is a major industry which has stimulated highway improvement and new resort centers.

History. People were living in Mexico by 10,000 BC and maize cultivation led to a farming culture (c1000 BC). Later advanced Indian civilizations developed (see AZTECS; MAYAS; MIXTECS; TEOTIHUACÁN; TOLTEC; ZAPOTEC). The arrival of Hernán CORTÉS (1519) and his destruction of Aztec power (1521) brought Mexico under Spanish rule, which was challenged in 1810 by Father Miguel HIDALGO Y COSTILLA. Independence was achieved in 1821 under the leadership of Agustín de ITURBIDE. The federal republic was created in 1824. Texas broke free of Mexico in 1836 and in the MEXICAN WAR, the republic lost NW territories to the US (1848). During 1864–67 Mexico was ruled by MAXIMILIAN of Austria, a puppet emperor supported by France. He was defeated and executed by Benito JUÁREZ. Then followed the long reformist dictatorship of Porfirio DÍAZ (1876–80, 1884–1911) and the MADERO revolution of 1910. A liberal constitution was introduced by President CARRANZA (1917) and further reforms by later presidents, notably Lázaro CÁRDENAS (1934–40). The National Revolutionary Party, formed from all major political groups in 1929 and later renamed the Institutional Revolutionary Party (PRI), remains the effective political force and is still reformist in character. The presidency of Luis Echeverría (1970–76) was marked by a shift to the left, especially in foreign relations, but his follower, José López Portillo, adopted more moderate policies.

**MEXICO CITY,** capital of Mexico. Located at an altitude of 7,347ft and at the S end of Mexico's central plateau, it is surrounded by the mountain ranges of Iztaccíhuat and Popocatépetl. The climate is cool and dry, but the city, built on land reclaimed from Lake Texcoco, has often been damaged by local floods. Subsidence has caused heavy buildings to sink up to 12in in a year. Mexico City is on the site of the old AZTEC capital of TENOCHTITLAN founded in 1176. CORTES captured the city in 1521 and for the next 300 years it was the seat of the viceroyalty of New Spain and it consequently possesses some of the finest Spanish colonial architecture. Pop 9,618,346.

**MEYER, Adolf** (1866–1950), Swiss-born US psychiatrist best known for his concept of *psychobiology*, the use in psychiatry of both psychological and biological processes together.

**MEYER, Eugene** (1875–1959), US banker, government official and publisher. A former investment banker and governor of the Federal Reserve Board (1930–33), he became publisher (1933–46) and editor (1940–46) of the *Washington Post*, which he built into one of the most influential

newspapers in the US.

**MEYERBEER, Giacomo** (1791–1864), German composer, born Jakob Liebmann Meyer Beer. His work for the romantic and spectacular Paris operas, with librettos by SCRIBE, set the vogue for French opera. Most famous are his operas *Robert le Diable* (1831), *Les Huguenots* (1836) and *L'Africaine* (1865.)

**MEYERHOLD, Vsevolod Yemilyevich** (1874–1942), Russian theatrical director and actor, whose work revolutionized the Russian theater. Rejecting stage illusionist conventions, he adopted abstract "constructivist" settings and advocated "biomechanics"—a system of acting methods and responses.

**MIAMI,** second-largest city in Fla., the seat of Dade Co., located at the mouth of the Miami R on Biscayne Bay. Its fine climate and beaches have made it a world famous resort center. Miami is also a major manufacturing center with a huge port and international airport. Pop 346,931.

**MIAMI INDIANS,** an ALGONQUIAN-speaking North American Indian group, of the Great Lakes region. They hunted buffalo and grew crops. In the 18th century they numbered not more than 1,750. They were allies of the French during the FRENCH AND INDIAN WARS and aided the British during the American Revolution.

**MIASKOVSKY, Nikolai Yakovlevich** (1881–1950), Russian composer and teacher. A professor at the Moscow Conservatory (from 1921), he was the most prominent teacher of composition in the USSR. His 27 symphonies conformed to the esthetic dictates of the Stalin regime.

**MICAH, Book of,** the sixth of the Old Testament MINOR PROPHETS, the oracles of the Judean prophet Micah (flourished late 8th century BC). Chapters 4 through 7 are thought to be later. Ethical in tenor, the book prophesies judgment for sin and restoration by the MESSIAH, centered on Zion.

**MICHAEL** (1596–1645), first ROMANOV czar of Russia, 1613–45. During his rule, peace was made with Sweden and Poland, and some western ideas on army organization and industrial methods were introduced. However the peasants were forced further into serfdom.

**MICHELANGELI, Arturo Benedetti** (1920–    ), Italian pianist, one of the most technically brilliant of the post-WWII generation. He is noted for his interpretations of BACH and SCARLATTI.

**MICHELANGELO** (1475–1564), one of the world's most famous artists. Italian sculptor, painter, architect and poet,

Michelangelo Buonarroti was probably the greatest artistic genius of the Renaissance. As a child he was apprenticed to the Florentine painter GHIRLANDAIO. He went to Rome in 1496 where his beautiful and poignant marble *Pieta* in Saint Peter's (1498–99), established him as the foremost living sculptor. In Florence he sculpted the magnificent *David* (1501–04), the largest marble statue carved in Italy since the end of the Roman empire. In 1505 Michelangelo went to Rome to work on a gigantic tomb for Pope JULIUS II. In Rome he painted the ceiling of the SISTINE CHAPEL, and this work has been one of the most influential in the history of art. After living in Florence (1515–34) and building the New Sacristy and library for the MEDICI family, he moved permanently to Rome. He painted the *Last Judgment* in the Sistine Chapel (1536–41), and his last very great work was rebuilding SAINT PETER'S BASILICA (1546–64). His architectural designs were influential throughout Italy, and in France and England.

**MICHELOZZO MICHELOZZI** (1396–1472), Florentine sculptor and architect of the early Renaissance. His architectural works include the Palazzo Medici-Riccardi in Florence (1444–59) which influenced later palace and town house architecture in Italy.

**MICHELS, Robert** (1876–1936), German political sociologist. He formulated the "iron law of OLIGARCHY" which postulated that political parties and organizations tend to elitist rule even in a democracy. His most famous work, *Political Parties* (1911), sets forth his ideas.

**MICHELSON-MORLEY EXPERIMENT,** important experiment whose results, by showing that the ETHER does not exist, substantially contributed to EINSTEIN's formulation of RELATIVITY theory. Its genesis was the development by Albert Abraham Michelson (1852–1931) of an INTERFEROMETER (1881) whereby a beam of light could be split into two parts sent at right angles to each other and then brought together again. Because of the earth's motion in space, the "drag" of the stationary ether should produce INTERFERENCE effects when the beams are brought together: his early experiments showed no such effects. With E. W. MORLEY he improved the sensitivity of his equipment, and by 1887 was able to show that there was no "drag," and therefore no ether. Michelson, awarded the Nobel Prize for Physics in 1908, was the first US Nobel prizewinner.

**MICHENER, James Albert** (1907– ), US author. His Pulitzer prize-winning *Tales of the South Pacific* (1947), based on his US Navy experience in WWII, inspired the famous musical *South Pacific* (1949) by RODGERS and HAMMERSTEIN. He also wrote such ambitious, historically based novels as *Hawaii* (1959), *Centennial* (1974) and *Chesapeake* (1978).

**Name of state:** Michigan
**Capital:** Lansing
**Statehood:** Jan. 26, 1837 (26th state)
**Familiar name:** Wolverine State
**Area:** 58,216sq mi
**Population:** 9,258,344
**Elevation:** Highest—1,980ft, Mt. Curwood. Lowest—572ft, Lake Erie
**Motto:** Si quaeris peninsulam amoenam, circumspice (If you seek a pleasant peninsula, look around you)
**State flower:** Apple blossom
**State bird:** Robin
**State tree:** White pine
**State song:** "Michigan, My Michigan"

**MICHIGAN,** state, N midwest US, bounded to the E by Canada and Lakes Huron and Erie, to the S by Oh. and Ind., to the W by Wis. and Lake Michigan, and to the N by Lake Superior.

**Land.** Michigan consists of two separate land areas, the Upper Peninsula and the mitten-shaped Lower Peninsula. The two are connected by the Mackinac Bridge. The W half of the Upper Peninsula is a part of the Superior upland regions, a rugged, forested area which possesses some of the nation's richest iron and copper deposits. It is a popular vacation area. The E half of the Upper Peninsula and the entire Lower Peninsula lie in the Great Lakes plain region. While winters in the Upper Peninsula may be extremely severe, the Lower Peninsula has a damp, relatively milder, climate, with hot summers and snowy winters. The Lower Peninsula contains most of the state's industry and fertile farmland.

**People.** About three-fourths of the population lives in urban area, and about 90% live in the Lower Peninsula. Detroit is the state's largest city, famous as the "automobile capital of the world."

**Economy.** Michigan's economy is highly industrialized. The state's automobile industry produces about two-fifths of the total US output of motor vehicles and parts. Other leading products are processed foods, machine tools, chemicals and metal and plastic goods. The rich soil of the Lower Peninsula supports livestock and dairy farming. Corn, wheat, hay, dry beans and fruit are also important. Michigan provides about 15% of the nation's iron ore. Tourism and mining are also important to the state's economy, both in winter and summer.

**History.** The first settlement in what is now Michigan was established by the French in 1668. In 1763 the area came under British control. After the War of 1812 the Michigan area came permanently under the control of the US, and pioneers began to settle the Lower Peninsula in greater numbers. Michigan was admitted to the Union in 1837. The REPUBLICAN PARTY was organized at Jackson (1854). At the end of the 19th century Michigan's population was about 2.4 million, but the state was still primarily rural. This was changed by Henry Ford and others who set up factories in the early 1900s for the mass production of automobiles. By 1920 the population had increased to almost 3.7 million. Apart from very bad years in the 1930s depression, Michigan (still dominated by the automobile industry) prospered into the 1970s. Then the decline of domestic auto sales brought the state to the brink of another true depression. In 1980, unemployment was 14%, more than 800,000 people were receiving public assistance, and the population of Detroit had dropped precipitously. In a desperate attempt to save jobs, the state that year loaned the Chrysler Corporation $150 million.

**MICHIGAN, Lake,** third largest of the GREAT LAKES, in North America. It is the largest freshwater lake wholly within the US, with an area of 22,178sq mi. In the N, Lake Michigan empties into Lake Huron by the Straits of Mackinac. It is part of the navigable Great Lakes-SAINT LAWRENCE SEAWAY, and there is also a series of connections linking it to the Mississippi R and the Gulf of Mexico. Important ports on the lake include Milwaukee, Wis., Chicago, Ill. and Gary, Ind.

**MICHURIN, Ivan Vladimirovich** (1855–1935), Russian horticulturalist whose theories of heredity, including the inheritance of ACQUIRED CHARACTERISTICS (see also LAMARCK), officially displaced GENETICS in Soviet science from 1948 until LYSENKO's fall from power in 1964.

**MICROBIOLOGY,** the study of microorganisms, including BACTERIA, VIRUSES, FUNGI and ALGAE. Departments of microbiology include the traditional divisions of ANATOMY, PHYSIOLOGY, GENETICS, TAXONOMY and ECOLOGY, together with various branches of MEDICINE, VETERINARY SCIENCES and PLANT PATHOLOGY, since many microorganisms are pathogenic by nature. Microbiologists also play an important role in the food industry, particularly in BAKING and BREWING. In the pharmaceutical industry, they supervise the production of ANTIBIOTICS.

**MICROCHEMISTRY,** branch of CHEMISTRY in which very small amounts ($1\mu g$ to $1mg$) are studied. Special techniques and apparatus have been developed for weighing and handling such minute quantities. Tracer methods, especially labeling with radioactive ISOTOPES, are useful, as are instrumental methods of ANALYSIS. Microanalysis is the chief part of microchemistry; another important aspect is the study of rare substances such as the TRANSURANIUM ELEMENTS.

**MICROECONOMICS,** the study in economics of the basic constituent elements of an economy, the individual consumers (households) and producers (firms). By analyzing their behavior and interaction, microeconomics seeks to explain the relative prices of goods and the amount produced and demanded. (See also MACROECONOMICS.)

**MICROENCAPSULATION,** technique for enclosing minute portions of a substance (often a drug or a dye) in tiny capsules from which it is released when these are ruptured or dissolved. Its uses include NCR (no carbon required) copy paper, and the production of slow-release drugs and pesticides.

**MICRON** ($\mu$), unit of length in the CGS system (see CGS UNITS), equal to one millionth of a METER. In SI UNITS it is replaced by the micrometer ($\mu$m).

**MICRONESIA,** a NW subdivision of the Pacific islands of OCEANIA, N of MELANESIA and divided from POLYNESIA by the international date line. The 2,250 small islands and atolls have a total land area of less than 1,500sq mi, and include the Caroline, Marshall, Marianas and Gilbert islands, Wake Island, Marcus Island and Nauru.

**Official name:** Federated States of Micronesia
**Capital:** Kolonia
**Area:** 273sq mi
**Population:** 76,050

**Languages:** English, indigenous dialects
**Religions:** Christian
**Monetary unit(s):** 1 US dollar = 100 cents
**MICRONESIA, FEDERATED STATES OF,** self-governing islands consisting of four constituent states—Yap, Truk, Ponape and Kosrae, each state made up of small islands, many uninhabited—located in the W Pacific just N of the equator.

**Land and People.** The states, part of the Caroline Island group, extend for a length of about 2,000mi. They are composed of both low-lying coral islands and higher volcanic ones that reach a peak elevation of 1,234ft on Truk. Ponape—the largest island—and Kosrae, the most fertile, are wooded and well watered. The climate is hot with little temperature variation. Rainfall reaches 118in per year and severe storms and typhoons may occur.

**People.** The indigenous people are Micronesian, although some speak Malayan languages, and Polynesians live on two isolated atolls in Ponape state. On Yap traditional culture survives more strongly than elsewhere.

**Economy.** Taro, sweet potatoes, bananas, copra and breadfruit are grown on small subsistence holdings, supplemented by fishing. Coconuts and fish constitute virtually the only exports. Little industry takes place and the people rely heavily on US aid.

**History.** The islands, some of which have been inhabited for over 2,000 years, were largely ignored by Europeans until the end of the 18th century. Spain claimed the islands but sold them to Germany in 1898 and in 1914 they were occupied by Japan. In 1945 the US assumed control and they were incorporated into the US Trust Territory of the Pacific Islands in 1947. The Federated States were established in 1979 and termination of the trusteeship was scheduled for the early 1980s.

**MICROPHONE,** device for converting sound waves into electrical impulses. The **carbon microphone** used in TELEPHONE mouthpieces has a thin diaphragm behind which are packed tiny carbon granules. SOUND waves vibrate the diaphragm, exerting a variable pressure on the granules. This varies their RESISTANCE, so producing fluctuations in a DC current (see ELECTRICITY) passing through them. The **crystal microphone** incorporates a piezoelectric crystal in which pressure changes from the diaphragm produce an alternating voltage (see PIEZOELECTRICITY). In the **electrostatic microphone** the diaphragm acts as one plate of a CAPACITOR, vibration producing changes in capacitance. In the moving-coil microphone the diaphragm is attached to a coil located between the poles of a permanent magnet: movement induces a varying current in the coil (see INDUCTANCE). The **ribbon microphone** has, rather than a diaphragm, a metal ribbon held in a magnetic field; vibration of the ribbon induces an electric current in it.

**MICROPROCESSOR,** an INTEGRATED CIRCUIT that performs the functions of a COMPUTER on a tiny "chip" of silicon. Unlike a computer, which can be programmed to solve many different problems, a microprocessor is designed for a specific task. Microprocessors are used in a great variety of "smart" devices, including home appliances that remember instructions and the popular ELECTRONIC GAMES.

**MICROSCOPE,** an instrument for producing enlarged images of small objects. The simple microscope or magnifying glass, comprising a single converging LENS, was known in ancient times, but the first compound microscope is thought to have been invented by the Dutch spectacle-maker Zacharias Janssen around 1590. However, because of the ABERRATION unavoidable in early lens systems, the simple microscope held its own for many years, Anton van LEEUWENHOEK constructing many fine examples using tiny near-spherical lenses. Compound microscopes incorporating ACHROMATIC LENSES became available from the mid 1840s.

In the compound microscope a magnified, inverted image of an object resting on the "stage" is produced by the objective lens (system). This image is viewed through the eyepiece (or ocular) lens (system) which acts as a simple microscope, giving a greatly magnified virtual image. In most biological microscopy the object is viewed by transmitted light, illumination being controlled by mirror, diaphragm and "substage condenser" lenses. The near-transparent objects are often stained to make them visible. As this usually proves fatal to the specimen, phase-contrast microscopy, in which a "phase plate" is used to produce a DIFFRACTION effect, can alternatively be employed. Objects which are just too small to be seen directly can be made visible in darkfield illumination. In this an opaque disk prevents direct illumination and the object is viewed in the light diffracted from the remaining oblique illumination. In mineralogical use objects are frequently viewed by reflected light.

Although there is no limit to the theoretical magnifying power of the optical microscope, magnifications greater than about 2000 × can offer no improvement in resolving power (see TELESCOPE) for light of visible wavelengths. The shorter wavelength of ULTRAVIOLET LIGHT allows better resolution and hence higher useful magnification. For yet finer resolution physicists turn to electron beams and electromagnetic focusing (see ELECTRON MICROSCOPE). The FIELD-ION MICROSCOPE, which offers the greatest magnifications, is a quite dissimilar instrument.

**MICROWAVES,** ELECTROMAGNETIC RADIATIONS of wavelength between 1mm and 30cm; used in RADAR, telecommunications, SPECTROSCOPY and for cooking (microwave ovens). Their dimensions are such that it is easy to build ANTENNAS of great directional sensitivity and high-efficiency WAVEGUIDES for them.

**MIDDLE AGES,** the period in W European history between the fall of the Roman Empire and the dawn of the RENAISSANCE—roughly the 5th to the 15th centuries AD. The centuries preceding the 11th century are often called the DARK AGES. In the 5th century the W half of the Roman Empire broke up. Trade declined, cities shrank in size, law and order broke down. By the 10th century Europe was fragmented into numerous small kingdoms in which economic life for the masses of people was reduced to subsistence level.

**Church, feudalism and society.** The single unifying institution throughout the Middle Ages was the Christian Church. It provided some care for the poor and sick and its monasteries preserved the writings of the Greeks and Romans. But while the Church provided the spiritual foundations of the Middle Ages, society was ordered according to FEUDALISM. Its most important feature was the idea of service in return for land, protection and justice. At the top of the feudal pyramid was the Holy Roman Emperor (see HOLY ROMAN EMPIRE); then kings and princes, then warrior knights and at the bottom were the peasants. Each had a duty to pay homage to those above him and to provide military service when required to do so. In return each vassal was allowed by his suzerain or overlord to exercise control over his own domain and provided protection and justice for those below him.

**Breakup of the old order.** Around the 11th century the long phase of European decline was reversed and population began to grow again. Trade revived and cities grew (see GUILDS). During the 13th and 14th centuries the cities became powerful, and allied themselves with the emerging centralized monarchies against the Church and the feudal barons. New centers of learning, the universities, emerged. By the end of the

16th century LUTHER had set Europe aflame with his criticisms of the Catholic Church, GUTENBERG had invented the printing press and COLUMBUS had discovered a New World.

**MIDDLE EAST,** a large region, mostly in SW Asia but extending into SE Europe and NE Africa. Today the term usually includes the following countries: Bahrain, Cyprus, Egypt, Lebanon, Libya, Syria, Iran, Iraq, Israel, Jordan, Kuwait, Turkey, Sudan, Saudi Arabia and the other countries of the Arabian peninsula. Politically, other countries of predominantly Islamic culture like Algeria, Morocco and Tunisia are sometimes included. The Middle East was the cradle of early civilization. (See EGYPT, ANCIENT; BABYLONIA AND ASSYRIA; MESOPOTAMIA). It was also the birthplace of JUDAISM, CHRISTIANITY and ISLAM. It has been the seat of many great empires, including the OTTOMAN EMPIRE which survived into the present century. Today the Middle East has assumed tremendous geopolitical importance as the world's primary oil-producing region.

**MIDDLETON, Thomas** (c1580–1627), English dramatist. He wrote lively, natural comedies, the Lord Mayor of London's pageants and various masques, and two outstanding tragedies concerning human corruption: *The Changeling* (1653) and *Women beware Women* (1657). *A Game at Chess* (1624) was his satire on political marriages with Spain, suppressed under James I.

**MIDDLE WEST,** a term which usually refers to the following US states: Ohio, Ind., Ill., Mo., Mich., Ia., Wis., Minn., Kan., Neb., N.D. and S.D. The term is often shortened to Midwest. The region includes seven of the 10 leading agricultural states and six of the 10 leading manufacturing states. Although often scorned by Easterners as an area lacking in cultural amenities, Middle West cities have many great universities, museums and orchestras.

**MIDGLEY, Thomas** (1889–1944), US chemist who developed a procedure for increasing the OCTANE rating of GASOLINE, and discovered FREON, a gas used in refrigerators, freezers and air conditioners.

**MIES VAN DER ROHE, Ludwig** (1886–1969), German-American architect, famous for his functional but elegant buildings in the INTERNATIONAL STYLE, constructed of brick, steel and glass. His work includes the Illinois Institute of Technology campus in Chicago, and the Seagram Building (with Philip JOHNSON) in New York. Although he had no formal training, he was a director of the BAUHAUS and one of the 20th century's leading architects.

**MIFFLIN, Thomas** (1744–1800), American soldier and political leader. A member of the First Continental Congress, during the Revolutionary War he rose to the rank of quartermaster general. He was later a delegate to the Constitutional Convention (1787), and the first governor of Pa. (1790–99).

**MIGRANT LABOR,** workers who move from place to place, usually in search of seasonal agricultural employment. Although found elsewhere, migrant labor is primarily a US phenomenon, particularly in the W and SW. The workers, without fixed homes and unprotected by trade unions or governments, often live in sub-standard conditions. Since 1970, however, California migrant workers organized by Cesar CHAVEZ have secured improvement in their status and working conditions.

**MIGRATION,** long-distance mass movements made by animals of many different groups, both vertebrate and invertebrate, often at regular intervals. Generally animals move from a breeding area to a feeding place, returning as the breeding season approaches the following year. This is the pattern of annual movements of migratory birds and fishes. Migrations of this nature may be over great distances, up to 11,000km (7,000mi) in some birds. Navigation is extremely accurate: birds may return to the same nest site year after year; migratory fish return to the exact rivulet of their birth to spawn. In other cases, migrations may follow cycles of food abundance. Gnu in E Africa follow in the wake of the rains grazing on the new grass; CARIBOU in Canada show similar movements. Certain carnivore species may follow these migrations, others capitalize on a temporary abundance as the herds move through their ranges.

**MIKAN, George** (1929?–    ), US basketball player. One of the earliest professional stars and the first "big" center, he led the Minneapolis Lakers to five NBA championships in the 1940s.

**MIKI, Takeo** (1907–    ), Japanese prime minister from 1974–76. The ruling Liberal Democratic Party's compromise choice after the resignation of Kakuei TANAKA's scandal-ridden administration, he at once began a program of vigorous political reform.

**MIKOYAN, Anastas Ivanovich** (1895–1978), Soviet public official, deputy premier under KHRUSHCHEV 1955–57, 1958–64, and chairman of the Presidium of the Supreme Soviet (i.e., head of state)

1964–65. From 1926 his career was largely in departments of trade. In 1956 he took a lead in denouncing STALIN's regime. He retired from public life in 1974.

**MILAN,** city in N Italy. An important European trade and transportation hub, it is Italy's major industrial and commercial center, producing automobiles, airplanes, textiles, chemicals, electrical equipment, machinery and books. Milan was a major late Roman city, and the principal city state of LOMBARDY under the Visconti (1277–1447) and SFORZA families. Spanish from 1535, it fell to Austria in 1713, and became a center of the 19th-century RISORGIMENTO. Artistic treasures include the cathedral, LEONARDO DA VINCI's *Last Supper*, the Brera palace and art gallery and LA SCALA opera house. Pop 1,693,400.

**MILDEW,** general name for the superficial growth of many types of fungi often found on plants and material derived from plants. Powdery mildews are caused by fungi belonging to the Ascomycetes order Erysiphales, the powdery effect being due to the masses of spores. These fungi commonly infest roses, apples, phlox, melons etc. Downy mildews are caused by Phycomycetes. They commonly infest many vegetable crops. Both types of disease can be controlled by use of FUNGICIDES.

**MILE,** name of many units of length in different parts of the world. The statute mile (st mi) is 1,760 yards (exactly 1,609.344m); the international (US) nautical mile is 1.150,78st mi; the UK nautical mile, 1.151,51st mi. The name derives from the Roman (Latin) *milia passuum*, a thousand paces.

**MILHAUD, Darius** (1892–1974), French composer, one of Les SIX, noted for his polytonality (the simultaneous use of different keys). His vast output includes the jazz-influenced ballet, *Creation of the World* (1923), *Saudades do Brasil* (1921) for piano, symphonies, chamber music and operas, among them *Christophe Colombe* (1930).

**MILK,** a white liquid containing water, PROTEIN, FAT, SUGAR, VITAMINS and inorganic salts which is secreted by the mammary glands of female mammals. The secretion of milk (LACTATION) is initiated immediately after birth by the hormone PROLACTIN. The milks produced by different mammals all have the same basic constituents but the proportion of each ingredient differs from species to species and within species. In any species the milk produced is a complete food for the young until weaning. Milk is of high nutritional value and man has used the milk of other animals as a food for at least 5,000 years. Milk for use by man is produced in the largest volume by cows and water buffalo (especially in India); goat milk is also produced in some areas, particularly the Middle East. Milk is an extremely perishable liquid which must be cooled to 10°C within two hours of milking and maintained at that temperature until delivery. The storage life of milk is greatly improved by PASTEURIZATION. Because of the perishable nature of milk large quantities are processed to give a variety of products including BUTTER; CHEESE; cream; evaporated, condensed and dried milk; YOGHURT; milk protein (CASEIN) and LACTOSE.

**MILKY WAY**, our GALAXY. It is a disk-shaped spiral galaxy containing some 100 billion stars, and has a radius of about 15kpc. Our SOLAR SYSTEM is in one of the spiral arms and is just over 9kpc from the galactic center, which lies in the direction of SAGITTARIUS. The galaxy slowly rotates about a roughly spherical nucleus (diameter about 1.5kpc), though not at uniform speed; the sun circles the galactic center about every 230 million years. The galaxy is surrounded by a spheroidal halo some 50kpc in diameter composed of gas, dust, occasional stars and GLOBULAR CLUSTERS. The Milky Way derives its name from our view of it as a hazy milk-like band of stars encircling the night sky. Irregular dark patches are caused by intervening clouds of gas and dust.

**MILL, James** (1773–1836) and **John Stuart** (1806–1873), distinguished British economists and philosophers. James Mill rose from humble origins to a senior position in the East India Company. He was an able apologist for the UTILITARIANISM of his friend Jeremy BENTHAM. A famous account of the education James imposed on his son John Stuart can be found in the latter's *Autobiography* (1873). The younger Mill is noted for his strictly empiricist *A System of Logic* (1843), his *Principles of Political Economy* (1848), and for his essays *On Liberty* (1854) and *Utilitarianism* (1861). J. S. Mill's circle included F. D. Maurice, Thomas CARLYLE and, later, Herbert SPENCER.

**MILLAIS, Sir John Everett** (1829–1896), English painter, a founder of the PRE-RAPHAELITE BROTHERHOOD (1848). His *Christ in the Carpenter's Shop* (1850) caused a scandal by its realism; later works such as *The Blind Girl* (1856) and *Bubbles* (1886) became more sentimental.

**MILLAY, Edna St. Vincent** (1892–1950), US poet of bohemian rebellion. Her reputation was established with *A Few Figs*

*from Thistles* (1920), and *The Harp Weaver* (1922) won a Pulitzer Prize. Other works include *Wine from these Grapes* (1934) and the verse drama *Aria da Capo* (1921).

**MILLENNIUM**, in Christian ESCHATOLOGY, a 1000-year period in which Jesus Christ will reign gloriously. The doctrine, occurring in Revelation 20, ties in with Old Testament prophecies of the MESSIAH's reign. Millenarianism takes two forms: postmillennialists believe in a golden age of righteousness preceding Christ's SECOND COMING; premillennialists believe in a literal reign of Christ on earth after the Second Coming. Many in the early Church were millenarians (or chiliasts), but the idea was spiritualized by St. AUGUSTINE and recurred mainly in enthusiast Protestant sects, FUNDAMENTALISM and among ADVENTISTS.

**MILLER, Arnold Ray** (1923–    ), US labor leader, the reform president of the UNITED MINE WORKERS 1972–79).

**MILLER, Arthur** (1915–    ), US playwright. A committed liberal, he explores individual and social morality in such plays as *Death of a Salesman* (1949; Pulitzer Prize), *The Crucible* (1953) on the witch trials in SALEM, Mass., *A View from the Bridge* (1955; Pulitzer Prize), the partly autobiographical *After the Fall* (1964) and the screenplay *The Misfits* (1961), for his second wife Marilyn MONROE.

**MILLER, Glenn** (1904–1944), US trombonist and band leader in the big band "swing" era of the late 1930s and early 1940s. His blend of instrumental colors, the "Glenn Miller sound," had immense success. Among his most popular recordings were *In the Mood, Moonlight Serenade,* and *Chattanooga Choo-Choo*. He died in a plane crash while touring troop bases in Europe in WWII, but his popularity continues.

**MILLER, Henry** (1891–1980), US writer, noted for his candid treatment of sex and his espousal of the "natural man." *Tropic of Cancer* (1934) and *Tropic of Capricorn* (1939) were banned as obscene in America until 1961. Other books include the trilogy *The Rosy Crucifixion* (1949–60). He was a major influence on the BEAT GENERATION of writers.

**MILLER, Perry Gilbert** (1905–1963), US historian and professor at Harvard (1931–63), whose extensive writings on colonial New England history led to a resurgence of interest in Puritan life and thought. His best known works were *The New England Mind* (2 vols., 1939–53), and intellectual biographies of Jonathan Edwards (2 vols., 1948–49) and Roger Williams (1953).

**MILLER, Stanley Lloyd** (1930– ), US biochemist who carried out the first experiment (1953) replicating primitive conditions of the earth's atmosphere. He demonstrated that AMINO ACIDS, basic to the existence of LIFE, could have been produced when lightning struck a primordial mixture of METHANE, AMMONIA, water vapor and HYDROGEN.

**MILLER, William** (1782–1849), US religious leader who prophesied the second coming of Christ for 1843. His followers, called Millerites or Adventists, laid the foundations of modern ADVENTIST sects.

**MILLET, Jean François** (1814–1875), French painter. His famous peasant subjects like *The Gleaners* (1857) and *The Angelus* (1859) are naturalistic in style if somewhat romanticized.

**MILLETT, Kate** (1934– ), US feminist author, a theoretician of the WOMEN'S LIBERATION MOVEMENT. In *Sexual Politics* (1970) she argued that men as a class have dominated women and demonstrated the sexist attitudes underlying the work of prominent male novelists. In *The Basement* (1979) she explores child abuse.

**MILLIGAN, Ex parte,** 1866, a US Supreme Court ruling defining the limits of military courts. The civilian Milligan had been condemned to death by a military tribunal in 1864 for pro-South COPPERHEAD agitation. The court ruled that a civilian cannot be tried by military courts, even in wartime, if the civil courts are functioning. Milligan was freed.

**MILLIKAN, Robert Andrews** (1868–1953), US physicist awarded the 1923 Nobel Prize for Physics for his determination of the charge on a single ELECTRON (the famous oil-drop experiment) and his work on the PHOTOELECTRIC EFFECT. He also studied and named COSMIC RAYS.

**MILLS, C(harles) Wright** (1916–1962), US sociologist and penetrating critic of US capitalism and militarism whose work was influential with radical social scientists of the 1970s. His books include *White Collar* (1951), *The Power Elite* (1956), *The Causes of World War Three* (1958) and *The Sociological Imagination* (1959), which argues that sociologists should not be passive observers but active agents of social change.

**MILLS, Robert** (1781–1855), US architect and engineer. From 1836 official architect of public buildings in Washington, D.C., he aimed at an American neo-classical style. He designed the Washington Monument, the Treasury and the old Post Office building.

**MILNE, A. A.** (Alan Alexander Milne; 1882–1956), English writer and dramatist, famous for the children's stories and poems he wrote for his son Christopher Robin. They were *Winnie-the-Pooh* (1926), *The House at Pooh Corner* (1928), *When We Were Very Young* (1924) and *Now We are Six* (1927).

**MILNES, Sherrill** (1935– ), US baritone. Starting his operatic career in 1959 with the Santa Fe (N.M.) Opera Company, he joined the NY City Opera in 1964 and the Metropolitan Opera in 1965. His powerful voice, fine technique and dramatic talent have won him an international reputation.

**MILOSZ, Czeslaw** (1911– ), Polish poet, critic, translator, and diplomat. A leading leftist poet in the 1930s, he left Poland for the West in 1951 and has taught at the U. of Cal. in Berkeley for many years. His *The Captive Mind* (Eng. ed., 1953) condemns the spiritually repressive nature of Communism. In 1980 he won the Nobel Prize for Literature.

**MILSTEIN, Nathan** (1904– ), Russian-born US violinist who studied under Leopold Auer in St. Petersburg and left the USSR in 1925. Known for his dazzling technique and intense virtuosity, he performed publicly for more than 50 years and made numerous recordings.

**MILTON, John** (1608–1674), English poet whose blank-verse epic *Paradise Lost* (1667), detailing Lucifer's revolt against God and the fall of Adam and Eve in the Garden of Eden, is one of the masterpieces of English literature. His major early works are the ode *On The Morning of Christ's Nativity* (1629), *L'Allegro* and *Il Penseroso* (c1631), *Comus,* (c1632) and *Lycidas* (1638). A Puritan supporter during the English Civil War, he wrote many political pamphlets and the famous prose piece in defense of freedom of the press, *Areopagitica* (1644). In retirement after the Restoration (1660), and now totally blind, he dictated his final great works: *Paradise Lost, Paradise Regained* (1671) and *Samson Agonistes* (1671).

**MILWAUKEE FOURTEEN.** See HARRISBURG SEVEN.

**MIME,** the dramatic art of gesture and facial expression, also any silent acting. Mime was popular in classical times, often featuring topical or obscene subjects. It played an important part in the improvised Italian COMMEDIA DELL' ARTE of the 16th century and in the silent movie era, which produced such subtle masters of the art as CHAPLIN and KEATON. A theater of the mime has an especially strong tradition in France, where BARRAULT and MARCEAU are major contemporary mimes.

**MIMICRY,** the close resemblance of one organism to another which, because it is unpalatable and conspicuous, is avoided by certain predators. The mimic will thus gain a degree of protection on the strength of the predator's avoidance of the mimicked. Mimicry is well developed among insects. (See also BATES, HENRY W.)

**MINDSZENTY, József** (1892–1975), Hungarian Roman Catholic cardinal who was sentenced (1949) to life imprisonment for his opposition to communism. Released in the uprising of 1956, he took refuge in the US Legation in Budapest. He refused to leave until the charges against him were withdrawn. This condition was met in 1971 by arrangement between the Vatican and the Hungarian government, and Mindszenty left for Rome.

**MINERALS,** naturally-occurring substances obtainable by MINING, including COAL, PETROLEUM and NATURAL GAS; more specifically in geology, substances of natural inorganic origin, of more or less definite chemical COMPOSITION, CRYSTAL structure and properties, of which the ROCKS of the earth's crust are composed. (See also GEMS; ORE.) Of the 3,000 minerals known, fewer than 100 are common. They may be identified by their color (though this often varies because of impurities), HARDNESS, luster, SPECIFIC GRAVITY, crystal forms and CLEAVAGE; or by chemical ANALYSIS and X-RAY DIFFRACTION. Minerals are generally classified by their ANIONS—in order of increasing complexity: elements, SULFIDES, OXIDES, HALIDES, CARBONATES, NITRATES, SULFATES, PHOSPHATES and SILICATES. Others are classed with those which they resemble chemically and structurally, e.g. arsenates with phosphates. A newer system classifies minerals by their topological structure (see TOPOLOGY).

**MING DYNASTY,** Chinese dynasty which ruled from 1368 to 1644, between the Mongol and the Manchu dynasties. The first Ming emperor was Chu Yüanchang. At its zenith, Ming rule extended from S Mongolia and Korea in the north to Burma in the south. Among the great cultural achievements of the era is the famous Ming porcelain.

**MINGUS, Charlie** (1922–1979), American jazz composer, bassist and one of the pioneers of BOP. From the 1960s, he has attempted to widen further the scope of JAZZ with compositions of daring TONALITY.

**MINIMALISM,** an art movement initiated in the 1960s that stresses pure color and geometry. In both painting and sculpture—generally executed with great precision—it rejects emotionalism, striving for a "exclusive, negative, absolute and timeless" quality. Minimalism comprises; among styles and techniques, COLOR-FIELD PAINTING, HARD-EDGE PAINTING, OP ART, th shaped canvas, serial imagery and primar structures.

**MINIMUM WAGE,** a basic wage whic employers are obliged by law to pa employees. They may pay more than thi bottom limit, but not less. It is designed t protect the lowest paid workers, who ma not have powerful unions to act on thei behalf. In 1981, the minimum wage i America stood at $3.35 per hour.

**MINING,** the means for extractin economically important MINERALS and ORE from the earth. Where the desired mineral lie near the surface, the most economic forr of mine is the *open pit*. This usually consist of a series of terraces, which are worke back in parallel so that the mineral is alway within convenient reach of the excavatin machines. *Strip mining* refers to strippin off a layer of overburden to reach a usuall thin mineral seam (often COAL). Th excavating machines used in open-p mining are frequently vast. Soft mineral such as KAOLIN can be recovere hydraulically—by directing heavy wate jets at the pit face and pumping out th resulting slurry. Where a mineral is foun in alluvial (river bed) deposits, bucket c suction dredgers may be used. But whe minerals lie far below the surface, variou deep mining techniques must be use Sulfur is mined by pumping superheate water down boreholes into the mineral be This melts the sulfur which is then pumpe to the surface (see FRASCH PROCESS Watersoluble minerals such as SALT a often mined in a similar way (*solutio mining*). But most often, deep minerals an ores must be won from underground mine Access to the mineral-bearing strata obtained via a vertical *shaft* or slopin *incline* driven from the surface, or via horizontal *adit* driven into the side of mountain. The geometry of the actu mining area is determined by the type mineral and the strength of the surroundir material. All underground mines requir adequate ventilation and lighting, faciliti for pumping out any groundwater or tox gases seeping into the workings, and mea (railroad or conveyor) for removing the o and waste to the surface. As in open-p mining, the rock is broken mechanically with explosives. However, particular ca must be exercised when using explosiv underground. Several occupational diseases (e.g., PNEUMOCONIOSIS) are associated with mining and extraction metallurgy, particularly where high dust levels and toxic substances are involved. About 900,000 persons are employed in the mineral industries in the US. (See also SEA-BED MINING.)

**MINISTRY**, in the Christian Church, those ordained (see ORDINATION) to functions of leadership, preaching, administering the SACRAMENTS, pastoral care, etc. The Anglican churches recognize a "threefold ministry" of BISHOPS, PRIESTS (or presbyters) and DEACONS. The Roman Catholic and Eastern churches have recognized also subdeacons, and the "Minor Orders" of acolytes, readers, exorcists and porters; subdeacons and porters no longer exist in the Roman Catholic Church, and only subdeacons, readers and cantors are retained in the Eastern churches. Other churches usually recognize only pastors (or ministers), elders (or presbyters) and deacons.

**MINK**, semiaquatic carnivores of the WEASEL family. There are two species, one (*Mustela lutreda*) of European distribution, the other (*M. vison*) originating in North America but now widely distributed throughout Europe where it has escaped from fur farms. Feeding on small fish, eggs, fledgeling birds and small mammals, they are fearless hunters, and often kill more than they can eat—creating havoc when they raid domestic chicken farms. Mink are extensively farmed for their prized fur.

**MINNEAPOLIS**, city in E Minn., the largest in the state, seat of Hennepin Co., on the Mississippi R. With its twin city, St. Paul, it is a trading and manufacturing center, notable for grain-processing and the production of electronic equipment. Pop 370,951.

**MINNELLI, Vincente** (1910– ), US film director best known for his stylish musicals *Meet Me in St. Louis* (1944), *An American in Paris* (1951), *The Band Wagon* (1953) and *Gigi* (1958). He was married at one time to film star Judy GARLAND. Their daughter, **Liza Minnelli** (1946– ), also became a singer and star, winning an Academy Award for her performance in *Cabaret* (1972).

**MINNESINGER**, minstrel-poet of medieval Germany who composed and sang songs of courtly love (*minne*). The Minnesingers, heirs to the Provençal TROUBADOURS, flourished from c1150 to c1350. They included WALTHER VON DER VOGELWEIDE and TANNHÄUSER.

**Name of state:** Minnesota
**Capital:** St. Paul
**Statehood:** May 11, 1858 (32nd state)
**Familiar name:** Gopher State
**Area:** 84,068sq mi
**Population:** 4,077,148
**Elevation:** Highest—2,301ft Eagle Mountain. Lowest—602ft, Lake Superior
**Motto:** L'Etoile du Nord (The Star of the North)
**State flower:** Pink and white lady's-slipper
**State bird:** Common loon
**State tree:** Norway pine
**State song:** "Hail! Minnesota"

**MINNESOTA**, state, N midwest US, bounded to the E by Lake Superior and Wis., to the S by Ia., to the W by S.D. and N.D., and to the N by Canada. It is one of the most scenic regions of the nation, with about 15,000 lakes and extensive forests. Its vast wheat fields, flour mills and dairy products have given it the nickname "Bread and Butter State."

**Land.** The state lies within two major geographical regions: its NE part belongs to the Superior Upland (the S tip of the CANADIAN SHIELD); the remainder belongs to the Central Lowland Region of North America, mostly a treeless, gently rolling plain, where glaciers have deposited fertile topsoil. Three great river systems rise in Minnesota: the Mississippi, flowing SE from Lake Itasca and joined by the Minnesota R in St. Paul-Minneapolis; the Red R system flowing N into Hudson Bay; and the St. Louis R (source of the St. Lawrence R) flowing into Lake Superior.

**People.** Two thirds of the population live in urban areas. Major cities include Minneapolis, St. Paul, Duluth and Rochester. Extensive Scandinavian immigration in the late 19th century made a strong cultural impact on the state. Among Minnesota's approximately 65 institutions of higher education is the University of Minnesota, one of the largest US universities.

**Economy.** The manufacture of nonelectrical machinery is the largest single industry in the state. Other leading industries include food processing, printing and publishing, and the manufacture of pulp and paper products, chemicals and electrical and electronic equipment. Livestock and dairy products are prominent, and major crops are corn, hay, spring wheat, alfalfa, soybeans, sugar beet, sunflowers, and barley. Rich in natural resources, Minnesota contains deposits of iron ore, copper and nickel.

**History.** First settled by French missionaries and trader-explorers in the 17th century, for over 100 years Minnesota was noted chiefly as a rich fur-trading area. Immigrant settlement began in the early 1800s and accelerated rapidly throughout the century as land was taken from the Indians. The state's prosperity rested on timber until manufacturing expanded in the 20th century. The present economy, which is stable and diversified, has stood up well, even in recent years. Politically, the state is known for producing liberals (despite the Republican majority), including Hubert Humphrey, Eugene McCarthy, and Walter Mondale.

**MINNESOTA FATS** (nickname oof Rudolph Walter Wanderone, Jr., 1912–    ), US pocket billiards player, known both for his talent and his colorful personality. He was portrayed by Jackie Gleason in the film *The Hustler*.

**MINNOWS,** a term used loosely in the US for any small carplike fishes, from over 40 genera. In Europe it is restricted to *Phoxinus phoxinus*, a small freshwater fish, common in rivers and streams with sandy or gravel bottoms. Although mainly known as the "tiddlers" caught by small boys, minnows play an important part in freshwater ECOLOGY, as food for KINGFISHERS, HERONS and larger fish.

**MINOAN LINEAR SCRIPTS,** two written languages, samples of which, inscribed on clay tablets, were found in Crete by Sir Arthur EVANS (1900), and named Linear A and B. Linear B was deciphered (1952) by Michael Ventris (1922–1956) and shown to be very early Greek (from c1400 BC). Linear A is yet to be deciphered, though some symbols have been assigned phonetic values. (See also AEGEAN CIVILIZATION.)

**MINSTREL SHOW,** form of entertainment native to the US, in which white performers blacked their faces in imitation of Negroes and alternated jokes with Negro songs, many of which thus became well-known American folksongs. The entertainers, led by a "Mister Interlocutor," sat in a semicircle with the "end men" at each end.

**MINT, United States Bureau of the,** a bureau of the Department of the Treasury responsible for the manufacture of domestic coins and for the handling of gold and silver bullion. The first US Mint was established at Philadelphia in 1792, and the present bureau in 1873.

**MINUET,** a French dance in three-quarter time with delicate mincing steps. It became very popular first at the court of Louis XIV and then throughout Europe in the 17th and 18th centuries. It also became a form of lively musical composition, particularly in the works of HAYDN and MOZART.

**MINUIT, Peter** (1580–1638), colonial administrator in North America. He was the first director-general of NEW NETHERLAND for the Dutch West India Company, and is remembered for buying Manhattan Island from the Indians for about $24 in trinkets in 1626. He founded New Amsterdam, now New York City, and later established NEW SWEDEN on the Delaware R for the Swedes.

**MINUTEMEN,** volunteer militia in the American REVOLUTIONARY WAR, who were ready to take up arms "at a minute's notice." Mass. minutemen fought at the battles of LEXINGTON and CONCORD, Mass. (1775). Md., N. H. and Conn. also adopted the system.

**MIOCENE,** the penultimate epoch of the TERTIARY, which lasted from 25 to 10 million years ago. (See GEOLOGY.)

**MIQUELON.** See SAINT PIERRE AND MIQUELON.

**MIRABEAU, Honoré Gabriel Victor Riqueti, Comte de** (1749–1791), French Revolutionary leader. A powerful orator, he became an early moderate leader of the JACOBINS and represented the third estate (the commoners) in the STATES-GENERAL (the French parliament). He worked secretly to establish a constitutional monarchy, but was mistrusted by both revolutionaries and royalists. He was elected president of the National Assembly in 1791, but died a few months later.

**MIRACLE PLAY.** See MYSTERY PLAY.

**MIRAGE,** optical illusion arising from the REFRACTION of light as it passes through air layers of different densities. In *inferior mirages* distant objects appear to be reflected in water at their bases: this is because light rays traveling initially toward the ground have been bent upward by layers of hot air close to the surface. In *superior mirages* objects seem to float in the air: this commonly occurs over cold surfaces such as ice or a cold sea where warmer air overlies cooler, bending rays downward.

**MIRANDA, Carmen** (1913–1955), Portuguese-born Brazilian entertainer, popular in the US musical films of the 1940s and 1950s. She sang and danced to Latin rhythms, wearing extravagant tunics and turbans topped with tropical fruit.

**MIRANDA, Francisco de** (1750–1816), Venezuelan patriot who fought for the forces of freedom on three continents. While an officer in the army of Spain he served in the American Revolution, receiving the British surrender at Pensacola, Fla. He later joined the French revolutionary forces, fighting in several major battles. When in 1810 patriots in Venezuela formed a provisional government, he returned home, where he and Simón Bolivar proclaimed the first South American republic, in Caracas on July 5, 1811. Captured by royalists, he died in prison in Spain.

**MIRANDA VS. ARIZONA,** case establishing the rights of a criminal suspect whom the police or other officials seek to interrogate, as defined by the US Supreme Court in 1963. In its 5-4 ruling the Court specified that prior to any sort of questioning a suspect must be told that he has the right to remain silent, that anything he says can be used against him, and that he has the right to have a lawyer present. Thereafter, if the suspect waives these rights, questioning may proceed.

**MIRÓ, Joan** (1893–    ), Spanish abstract painter. A pioneer of SURREALISM, his imaginative works are freely drawn and are characterized by bright colors and clusters of symbolic forms. His work includes murals and large ceramic decorations for UNESCO in Paris.

**MISCARRIAGE,** popular term for spontaneous ABORTION.

**MISES, Ludwig Edler von** (1881–1973), Austrian-born US economist, a professor at Vienna, 1913–38, and New York U., 1945–69. His most famous work is *The Capitalistic Mentality* (1956) on intellectual opposition to mass demand in a free market place.

**MISHIMA, Yukio** (1925–1970), Japanese author, born Kimitake Hiraoka into a SAMURAI family. His writing is obsessed with the conflict between traditional and post-WWII Japan. He formed a private army devoted to ancient martial arts and committed HARA KIRI. His work includes the novels *The Temple of the Golden Pavilion* (1956), *Sun and Steel* (1970), *Sea of Fertility* (4 vols., 1970), *Patriotism* (1966), on ritual suicide, and modern Kabuki and Nō plays.

**MISSILE,** anything that can be thrown or projected. In modern usage the word most often describes the self-propelled weapons

developed during and since WWII, properly called guided missiles.

The first rocket missiles were used by the Chinese in the 13th century, but the ancestors of the modern missile were the German V-1 and V-2 rockets used to bombard London in WWII. There was no defense against the V-2 which could reach 3500mph. Captured V-2s gave Russia and the US the starting point for further development culminating in intercontinental missiles capable of delivering nuclear warheads to any spot on the globe—and also of launching mankind in space.

Missiles can be classified according to their range, by the way they approach their target (unguided, guided or ballistic), by their use (surface-to-surface [SSM], surface-to-air [SAM], etc.), or by their target (as with antitank missiles). The *Minuteman III*, for example, is an intercontinental ballistic missile (ICBM), with a range of more than 8,000 miles and a ballistic arc trajectory, after burnout of its last stage, of a shell from a gun. The newer guided missiles fall into the category of 'smart' or precision-guided weapons, non-nuclear munitions that can be remotely guided to their target after launch. The first of these, the wire-guided, manually controlled French SS10 antitank missile was used in the Arab-Israeli war of 1956.

Missiles are normally propelled by solid-fueled rockets equipped with an oxidant that allows the fuel to burn outside the atmosphere. Liquid propellants are more volatile and not generally used. Larger missiles, such as the *Minuteman*, comprise several stages, each with its own motor. This gives the missile increased speed, range and lifting capacity. The same system is generally used in spacecraft-launching missiles such as *Atlas* or *Saturn*. A few missiles, such as the *Hound Dog* air-to-surface missile carried by the B-52 and the cruise missiles are powered by jets. Britain's *Bloodhound* is driven by a ramjet (see JET PROPULSION).

Guidance systems vary from wire guidance for short-range missiles to elaborate homing systems which eliminate almost all possibility of escape. Wire guidance allows the operator to control the course of the missile through two fine wires paid out behind it. More complex guidance systems rely on radio beams, television, infrared sensors, radar and laser "designator" beams. Computers fed by laser or radar track missiles and correct their courses. Homing systems involve devices which detect waves emitted by or reflected from the target. Some home in on heat in the form of infrared rays; others use radar. To prevent jamming, systems are being provided with Electronic Counter Counter Measures circuitry allowing them to operate on alternating frequencies. Some systems are pre-set with a complete flight plan to guide the missile to a selected target, and to correct any deviation from course. Most long-range missiles have an INERTIAL GUIDANCE system to detect changes in course and Inertial guidance systems do not rely on information obtained outside the missile. They contain elements that sense the magnitude of direction of the acceleration vector and from that compute velocity, then distance covered and direction.

The emergence of the MULTIPLE INDEPENDENTLY TARGETED REENTRY VEHICLE (MIRV) in the 1960s greatly increased missile lethality. MIRV'd missiles contain multiple Warheads in their first stage or "bus." Each reentry vehicle can be directed to a different target.

Missile launchers range from the simple tube of the BAZOOKA to the fully tracked mobile carrier used for *Lance*. Larger missiles such as ICBMs require so much elaborate support equipment that they must be stored in heavily defended underground silos. Nuclear-powered missile submarines are more difficult to detect and destroy. The US has over 40 such vessels carrying POLARIS, POSEIDON, and TRIDENT missiles. Surface vessels may also use missiles, gyro-stabilized to allow for the movement of the ship. Aircraft launched missiles usually have a guidance system enabling the aircraft itself to remain a considerable distance from the target. Planes taking off from aircraft carriers more than 1,000 miles from target should be able to launch sea-launched cruise missiles (SLCM) at a distance of 700 miles from their objective. The SALT talks between the US and Russia are the result of the crippling expense and high risks involved in the uncontrolled development of nuclear missiles and antimissile systems. (See also NUCLEAR WARFARE.)

**MISSIONS**, organizations for propagating a religious faith. Found from time to time in most religions, they are most characteristic of Christianity. The basis of Christian mission lies in the saving action of God to all men, found in Hebrew prophetic writings and especially in the New Testament, and in Jesus' commission to his APOSTLES to "make disciples of all nations." Vigorous missionary activity, pioneered by St. PAUL, spread Christianity through the Roman Empire and beyond. From the 5th to the 10th centuries the rest of Europe was converted (sometimes by force), though N Africa was lost to ISLAM. There was then little missionary activity until after the Council of TRENT, when the Roman Catholic Church sent missionaries, especially JESUITS, to the Far East and the empires of Spain, Portugal and France; such work has been administered since 1622 by the Congregation for the Propagation of the Faith (see PROPAGANDA). Protestant missionary work began in the 17th century among the American Indians (see ELIOT, JOHN; BRAINERD, DAVID), but became a major enterprise only after the EVANGELICAL REVIVAL, when numerous missionary societies, denominational and voluntary, were formed, starting with the Baptist Missionary Society (1792). Today, missions operate in most countries of the world, aiming to help native churches and to do medical and educational work.

Name of state: Mississippi
Capital: Jackson
Statehood: Dec. 10, 1817 (20th state)
Familiar name: Magnolia State
Area: 47,716sq mi
Population: 2,520,638
Elevation: Highest—806ft, Woodall Mountain, Lowest—sea level, Gulf of Mexico
Motto: Virtute et Armis (By Valor and Arms)
State flower: Magnolia
State bird: Mockingbird
State tree: Magnolia
State song: "Go, Mississippi"

**MISSISSIPPI**, state, S US, bounded to the E by Ala., to the W by La. and Ark. across the Mississippi R., and to the N by Tenn. On the S it borders on the Gulf of Mexico, and includes a chain of small islands separated from the mainland by the Mississippi Sound.

**Land.** The W edge of the state is in the fertile Mississippi alluvial plain known as the Delta, which has numerous streams, rivers and lakes. The rest of the state lies in the Gulf coastal plain. Pine forests cover much of the S area (about 55% of the state is commercial woodland), and the NE is hilly agricultural land. The general climate is subtropical with some 200 to 300 days of growing season and average rainfall of 50in per year.

**People.** The present population is about 50% rural. The white population is more than 98% native-born with primarily British, Irish and N European ancestors, while the black population (about 35% of the total) is also almost wholly native-born, partly descended from the former slave population. **Economy.** In the 1960s for the first time Mississippi's income from agriculture came second to that from industry. Although cotton is no longer "king" in what was virtually a one-crop economy until the 1860s, it is still produced in large quantities. Other important produce includes soybeans, pecans, sweet potatoes, rice, sugarcane, poultry, livestock and seafood from the Gulf. Petroleum and natural gas are the main natural resources besides timber. Major manufacturing is concerned with clothing and textiles, paper and wood products, food processing, chemicals and electrical and transportation equipment.

**History.** Mississippi was discovered by Hernando DE SOTO in 1540. Part of the area was claimed by Britain and was ceded by the French to Britain in 1763. Spanish claims in the S were not relinquished until 1798. Mississippi became a slave-based agricultural economy and was the second state to secede from the Union (Jan. 1861) before the CIVIL WAR. The state suffered severely from the war and RECONSTRUCTION. After WWII agriculture in the state was boosted with federal funds and farm programs. During the 1960s Mississippi experienced a period of intense change which brought increasing industrial employment and also bitter protests over black civil rights. By the 1970s the state's economy was more prosperous than it had ever been and its racial problems were generally being confronted in a more balanced atmosphere.

**MISSISSIPPIAN,** the antepenultimate period of the PALEOZOIC, lasting from about 345 to 315 million years ago. (See also CARBONIFEROUS; GEOLOGY.)

**MISSISSIPPI RIVER,** the chief river of the North American continent and one of the world's great rivers. It divides the US from N to S between Lake Itasca in NW Minn. and the Gulf of Mexico below New Orleans, La. Known as the "father of waters," it drains an area of approximately 1,247,000sq mi. With the MISSOURI and OHIO rivers (its chief tributaries) and the Jefferson-Beaverhead-Red Rock system it forms the world's third longest river system

(some 3,710mi). Its main course is some 2,348mi. It receives more than 250 tributaries. The Mississippi is noted for sudden changes of course; its length varies by 40–50mi per year. The river's average discharge is 1,640,000cu ft per sec, but in high water season this soars to some 2,300,000cu ft per sec. Flooding is a serious problem, but dikes and levees have been built to contain its periodic massive overflows. The river is a major transportation artery of the US and was of fundamental importance in the development of the American continent.

**Name of state:** Missóuri
**Capital:** Jefferson City
**Statehood:** Aug. 10, 1821 (24th state)
**Familiar name:** Show Me State
**Area:** 69,686sq mi
**Population:** 4,917,444
**Elevation:** Highest—1,772ft, Taum Sauk Mountain. Lowest—230ft, St. Francis River in Dunklin County
**Motto:** Salus populi suprema lex esto (Let the welfare of the people be the supreme law)
**State flower:** Hawthorn
**State bird:** Bluebird
**State tree:** Flowering dogwood
**State song:** 'Missouri Waltz"

**MISSOURI,** a W central US state, bounded by Ia. to the N, Ark. to the S, Kan., Neb. and Okla. to the W; on the E it is separated from Ill., Ky. and Tenn. by the Mississippi R. Its largest cities are St. Louis; Kansas City; Springfield; and Independence, the home of former President Harry S. TRUMAN.

**Land.** The state's development has been shaped by its two principal rivers. The Missouri was an early pioneering route to the West, while the Mississippi linked the state to the South. The N third of the state above the Missouri lies in the Midwest "corn belt," while the SE corner lies in the fertile Mississippi alluvial plain. In the central and S portion of the state is the forested Ozark plateau, which has poor, stony soil but great scenic beauty and is a popular tourist region.

**People.** About 65% of the people now live in urban areas and the population continues to move from rural areas. In 1980 blacks formed about 11% of the state's total population.

**Economy.** Agriculture has always been an important factor of the state's economy. Livestock raising is a prime source of income as is the production of soybeans, corn, wheat and cotton. Manufacturing is heavily concentrated around the St. Louis-Kansas City area which is a major mid-continental transportation crossroads and industrial center. Production of transportation equipment (automobile assembly, railroad cars, airplanes, rocket engines, space capsules and other aerospace technology) ranks first; the second-largest industry is food processing. Electrical and electronic equipment and chemicals are also produced. Missouri is a leading iron ore and lead producer. Banking (with Federal Reserve banks in St. Louis and Kansas City) and tourism are also important to the state's economic base.

**History.** Missouri was explored by the Spanish in the mid-16th century, but claimed for France by LA SALLE in 1682 and was subsequently developed by French fur traders. It was acquired by the US in the LOUISIANA PURCHASE (1803). Under the MISSOURI COMPROMISE, the state entered the Union as a slave state in 1821. Historically, the state was a central point of departure for traders, explorers and pioneers moving westward. It was also a border state between N and S, conservative in politics but generally northern in sympathies. During the Civil War many battles were fought on its territory. Industry expanded with the arrival of German, Irish, Polish and Jewish immigrants.

In 1839, the U. of Mo. was the first state university to be founded W of the Mississippi. Its world-famous School of Journalism (established 1908) was the first in the world. Since WWII technological industrialization has displaced agriculture in the economy and many new industries have created new jobs.

A boundary dispute with Ill. settled in 1970, resulted in Mo. receiving Cottonwoods and Roth Islands. In the 1970s, population growth was a modest 5.1%. Entering the 1980s, despite a diversified economy, the state faced a variety of fiscal problems and a disturbing rise in unemployment.

**MISSOURI COMPROMISE,** a measure adopted by the US Congress in 1820, to resolve the issue of Missouri's admission to the Union as a slave state. At the time of Missouri's first petition (1819), there were 11 free and 11 slave states in the Union. The addition of Missouri would have changed the balance of power in the US Senate and reopened the bitterly contested issue between N and S as to whether slavery should be permitted and allowed to spread in the US. Action on Missouri's petition was delayed until Maine (formerly a part of Massachusetts) requested admission as a free state. A series of maneuvers led by Henry CLAY resulted in Missouri being admitted as a state in which slavery was legal, while Maine was admitted as a state in which it was not, with the added proviso that slavery would not be permitted in the rest of the territory of the LOUISIANA PURCHASE (of which Missouri had been part) N of 36° 30'. The compromise was later repealed in 1854 by the KANSAS-NEBRASKA ACT, which introduced the doctrine of popular sovereignty.

**MISSOURI RIVER,** longest river in the US (about 2,466mi) and the chief tributary of the MISSISSIPPI, with which it forms the major waterway of the US. Formed in SE Mont. by the Jefferson, Madison and Gallatin rivers in the Rocky Mts, it flows N and then E through Mont. and then enters N Dak. continuing generally SE to empty into the Mississippi R N of St. Louis. Its main tributaries along the way include the Cheyenne, Kansas, Osage, Platte and Yellowstone, James and Milk rivers. The Missouri was explored by JOLIET and MARQUETTE in 1673 and the LEWIS AND CLARK EXPEDITION in 1804–05. Like the Mississippi, it has been subject to disastrous flooding, which has been brought under control in the past three decades (see MISSOURI RIVER BASIN PROJECT).

**MISTI, El,** a volcano, rising 19,031ft high in the Andes Mts, S Peru, near Arequipa. Its last eruption was in 1600. El Misti has been the source of many legends and played a part in the religion of the INCAS.

**MISTRAL, Frédéric** (1830–1914), French poet. He won the 1905 Nobel Prize for Literature and for his work as leader of a movement to restore the former glories of the Provençal language and culture. Among his works are the epic poems *Mireio* (1859), *Calendau* (1867), *Nerto* (1884) and *Lou Pouém dúo Rose* (1897).

**MISTRAL, Gabriela** (1889–1957), pen name of Chilean poet, educator and diplomat, Lucila Godoy Alcayaga, awarded the Nobel Prize for Literature in 1945. Her simple, lyrical poems express a deep sympathy with nature and mankind. Her work includes *Desolation* (1922) and *Tenderness* (1924).

**MITCHELL, John** (1870–1919), US labor leader; president of the UNITED MINE WORKERS (1898–1908) and vice-president of the AFL (1899–1914). He was a conservative whose advocacy of harmonious relations between labor and capital alienated him from many union members.

**MITCHELL, John Newton** (1913–   ), US lawyer and public official. A law partner of Richard Nixon, he served as Nixon's attorney general 1969–72, and as chairman of Nixon's reelection campaign (1972). In that position he became involved in WATERGATE. Convicted of conspiracy, obstruction of justice, and perjury, he was sentenced to 2½ years in prison. He was released in 1979 after serving 19 months.

**MITCHELL, Margaret** (1900–1949), US writer. Her best selling and only novel *Gone With the Wind* (1936) won the 1937 Pulitzer Prize and was made into a phenomenally successful film (1939).

**MITCHELL, Maria** (1818–1889), US astronomer, who discovered a comet in 1847. She was the first woman to be elected to the American Academy of Arts and Sciences (1848) and was professor of astronomy at Vassar College (1865–88).

**MITCHELL, Wesley Clair** (1874–1948), US economist and educator. He helped organize the National Bureau of Economic Research (1920) and was its research director, 1920–45. He served on many government boards and was a leading authority on business cycles.

**MITCHELL, William ("Billy") Lendrum** (1879–1936), US army officer and aviator. After leading US air services in WWI, he became an active champion for a strong air force independent of army or naval control. Court-martialed for insubordination, and suspended from duty for five years in 1925, he resigned from the army in 1926.

**MITFORD, Jessica** (1917–   ), English-born US writer known as the "Queen of the Muckrakers." In addition to her exposé of the funeral industry in *The American Way of Death* (1963), she has excoriated the Famous Writers School, "fat farms" for wealthy women, and the US prison system. A sister of Nancy Mitford, she has chronicled her eccentric family in *Daughters and Rebels* (1960) and *A Fine Old Conflict* (1977).

**MITFORD, Nancy** (1904–1973), English author known for her witty, sophisticated portrayals of the English upper classes in such novels as *Love in a Cold Climate* (1949) and *Don't Tell Alfred* (1960). She also wrote biographies: *Madame de Pompadour* (1954, 1968), *Voltaire in Love* (1957) and *Frederick the Great* (1970).

**MITHRA,** or Mithras, Indo-Iranian sun-god, also Mitra, one of the ethical lords or gods in ZOROASTRIANISM. By 400 BC, he was the chief Persian deity. His cult spread over most of Asia Minor and, according to Plutarch, reached Rome in 68 BC. Mithraism was especially popular among the Roman legions. Roman Mithraism, which amounted to a virtual parody of Christianity, declined after 200 AD and was officially suppressed in the 4th century.

**MITOCHONDRIA.** See CELL.

**MITOSIS,** the normal process by which a CELL divides into two. Initially the CHROMOSOMES become visible in the nucleus before longitudinally dividing into a pair of parallel *chromatids*. The chromosomes shorten and thicken and arrange themselves on a spindle across the equator of the cell. The cell then divides so that each daughter contains a full complement of chromosomes.

**MITTERAND, François** (1916–   ), writer, political leader and president of France (1981–   ). A cabinet minister in 11 governments during the Fourth Republic, he opposed De Gaulle's establishment of the Fifth Republic in 1958. Candidate of the non-Communist left he first ran for the presidency in 1965 and was defeated by De Gaulle. He became head of the Socialist Party in 1971 and again ran unsuccessfully for the presidency in 1974. He finally won in 1981. His party also won a majority in the French Assembly and initiated a program of nationalizing certain banks, abolishing the death penalty and creating new public jobs.

**MIX, Tom** (1880–1940), US film actor and director whose popular westerns featured spectacular photography and daring horsemanship. He starred in such silent films as *Desert Love* (1920) and *Riders of the Purple Sage* (1925) and in numerous films of the 1930s.

**MIXTECS,** or Mixtecas, Indian people occupying Guerrero, Puebla and Oaxaca states, in SW Mexico. They were one of the most important and culturally advanced pre-Columbian peoples in Mesoamerica. They eclipsed the ZAPOTEC INDIANS by the 14th century, but were themselves overshadowed by the AZTECS prior to the arrival of the Spanish who defeated the last Mixtec kingdom c1550. The Mixtec language is today spoken by some 300,000 Mexican people.

**MOBILE,** a moving, three-dimensional abstract sculpture. The form was invented by Alexander CALDER c1930 and named by Marcel DUCHAMP. A mobile consists of a group of shapes connected together by rods or wires, and suspended to move freely in the air, changing the spatial relationships between each piece as they turn.

**MOBILE BAY, Battle of,** Civil War conflict on Aug. 5, 1864, in which Union admiral FARRAGUT'S command broke through the Confederate defensive forts and torpedo lines and destroyed key units of the South's fleet. The battle formed part of the North's wider strategy to encircle the Confederacy.

**MÖBIUS STRIP,** a topological space (see TOPOLOGY) formed by joining the two ends of a strip of paper or other material after having turned one of the ends through an ANGLE of 180°. It is of interest in that it has only one side: if a line is drawn from a point A on the surface parallel to the edges of the strip it will eventually pass through a point A' directly through the paper from A. This circle is known as a nonbounding cycle since it does not bound an area of the surface.

**MOBUTU SESE SEKO** (1930–      ), born Joseph Désiré Mobutu, president of the Republic of Zaire (formerly the Belgian Congo) from 1965. He ousted President KASAVUBU.

**MOBUTU SESE SEKO, Lake.** See ALBERT, LAKE.

**MOCKINGBIRDS,** a family, Mimidae, of songbirds of the Americas; or, certain species within that family. They are long-tailed birds with short, rounded wings and well-developed legs, which skulk in low scrub feeding on insects and fruit. Certain species may flick their wings when searching for food, perhaps to disturb insects that would otherwise remain undetected.

**MODE,** in music, the method of tone selection as a basis for melody and harmony. Starting on any "home" note to designate key, each mode follows a fixed progression of tones and semitones to form a SCALE. By about 1600 Western music retained only the Major and Minor modes of 14 that grew from the eight Plainsong modes of Medieval church music. The eight Greek modes, ancestors of these, were conceived from the top note down.

**MODEL CITIES,** or Concentrated Community Development, a US government program (1966–1973) that sought to plan new housing and redevelop cities. It was established by the Demonstration Cities and Metropolitan Development Act. The US Department of Housing and Urban Development administered the program.

**MODEL PARLIAMENT,** an English parliament set up in 1295 by Edward I. The Model Parliament's wide representation of clergy, earls, barons, two knights from each county and two burgesses from each borough indicated Parliament's developing representational role, although these principles of membership were by no means strictly observed through much of the 14th century.

**MODERNISM,** in Christian theology, a movement in the late 19th and early 20th centuries that aimed to reinterpret traditional doctrine to align it with modern trends in philosophy, history and the sciences. It espoused the liberal, critical view of the Bible, was skeptical about the historicity of Christian origins, and downgraded traditional credal dogma. Modernism became dominant in Protestantism (though opposed by FUNDAMENTALISM). The similar movement in Roman Catholicism was formally condemned by Pius X (1907) and largely disappeared.

**MODERNISMO,** a movement in Latin American and Spanish poetry in the late 19th and early 20th centuries, influenced by SYMBOLISM and the PARNASSIANS. The exoticism of the Nicaraguan poet Rubén Darío provided the impetus for the movement.

**MODIGLIANI, Amedeo** (1884–1920), Italian painter and sculptor. He is best known for studies of nudes and for portraits, works characterized by elongated forms and elegant draftsmanship. He was influenced by African sculpture and by BRANCUSI.

**MOGILEV,** capital of Mogilev Oblast in the Belorussian republic of the USSR. It is an important industrial city and transportation center, on the Dnieper R. Pop 202,000.

**MOGUL EMPIRE,** 16th- and 17th-century empire in India, founded by BABUR, who invaded India from Afghanistan in 1526. His son Humayun was defeated by the Afghan Sher Shah Sur, but Mogul power was restored by AKBAR (1556–1605). He established firm, centralized government throughout Afghanistan and N and central India. The Mogul "golden age" was in the reign of SHAH JEHAN (1628–58). During this time, the TAJ MAHAL, the Pearl Mosque of Agra and many of Delhi's finest buildings were erected. In the 1700s, the rising power of the MAHRATTAS weakened the empire. In 1803 the British occupied Delhi and in 1857 they deposed the last puppet Mogul emperor, Bahadur Shah II.

**MOHACS, Battles of,** name of two Turkish battles. In 1526 the Ottoman Sultan Suleiman I defeated the Hungarians, killing Louis II of Hungary and about 25,000 of his army. In 1687 the Turks were routed by forces under Charles V of Lorraine.

**MOHAMMED,** or **Muhammad** or **Mahomet** (c570–632), "the Praised One," founder of ISLAM, the Muslim faith. He was born in Mecca and was a member of its ruling tribe. He became a merchant and his trade from Mecca brought him into contact with Judaism and Christianity. At the age of 40, he had a vision of the archangel Gabriel which bade him go forth and preach. This, and subsequent visions, were recorded in the KORAN, the Muslim sacred book. Mohammed proclaimed himself God's messenger and called on the Meccans to accept Allah as the only god. At first, he made few converts. Among the earliest were his wife Khadija, his daughter FATIMA, her husband and his cousin, ALI and his friend ABU BAKR. As Mohammed's influence increased, the Meccans began to fear he might gain political control of the city. They persecuted his followers and plotted to murder him. In 622, he fled to Yathrib, which he subsequently renamed MEDINA, "City of the Prophet," with Abu Bakr and some followers. This event is known as the HEGIRA (departure). Muslim calendars are dated from the Hegira. In Medina, Mohammed formed an Islamic community based upon religious faith rather than tribal or family loyalties. He rapidly extended his territory by conquest and conversion. In 630, after a long period of warfare with Mecca and winning the battles of Badr (624) and Uhud (625) he captured Mecca with little bloodshed, making it both the political and religious capital of Islam. He proclaimed the KAABA a mosque and laid down the ceremonies of the *Hadj* (pilgrimage) to Mecca.

**MOHAMMED REZA PAHLAVI** (1919–1980), shah of Iran. The British forced his pro-German father to abdicate as shah in 1941, and put the son in his place. He left the country briefly during a period of left-wing domination (1953), but returned to consolidate his power. He was crowned in 1967. He instituted sweeping social reforms, which some of his people were not ready to accept, and he also imprisoned many opponents. A rising tide of Islamic fundamentalist opposition forced him into exile (1979). His trip to the US for medical treatment later that year precipitated Iran's seizure of the US Embassy and more than 60 hostages.

**MOHAMMED V** (Sidi Mohammed ben Youssef; 1909–1961), first king of Morocco, 1957–61. He became sultan in 1927 and was exiled by the ruling French authorities, 1953–55.

**MOHAWK INDIANS**, North American tribe of Indians, members of the IROQUOIS League. They aided the British in their victories at Lake George, 1755, and Fort Niagara, 1759, and during the Revolutionary War.

**MOHAWK VALLEY**, fertile valley of the Mohawk R. It was the home of the IROQUOIS League and the site of various Revolutionary War skirmishes. The Revolutionary victory at Oriskany (1777) won the valley for the Americans.

**MOHO**, abbreviation for MOHOROVIČIĆ DISCONTINUITY.

**MOHOROVIČIĆ DISCONTINUITY**, a seismic boundary of the earth originally regarded as separating the crust and mantle (see EARTH), evidenced by rapid increase in the velocity of seismic waves (see EARTHQUAKE). The US project Mohole, designed to drill through the "Moho," was abandoned in 1966. More important are the discontinuities between the core and the mantle (Gutenberg or Oldham Discontinuity), with a radius of about 3,500km; and between the inner and outer cores, with a radius of about 1,200km to 1,650km.

**MOIRÉ PATTERN**, a family of CURVES formed by the INTERSECTIONS of one family of curves with another over which it has been superimposed. Moiré patterns may be seen by looking through the folds of a gauze or nylon curtain: motion of the curtain or observer will cause dramatic changes in the patterns observed. They are of particular note in color printing, where special techniques are employed to prevent their appearance in HALFTONES; and are used in industry to determine, for example, the degree of flatness of a surface. They are used also as mathematical models of physical phenomena, and occasionally in the solution of mathematical problems. Their disturbing optical properties are of interest in psychology.

**MOJAVE DESERT**, or Mohave Desert, an area of barren mountains and desert valleys in S Cal. It is swept by strong winds; average annual rainfall is 5in. It includes DEATH VALLEY in the N, and the Joshua Tree National Monument in the S. It is a rich source of minerals.

**MOLASSES**, yellow to dark brown syrup, usually obtained as a byproduct in the production of SUGAR from SUGARCANE juice. It was originally used for FERMENTATION of industrial ethyl alcohol, but is now mainly used in animal feeds, adhesives, fertilizers and the pharmaceutical industry.

**MOLASSES ACT**, prohibitive duties introduced by England in 1733 in an attempt to force the American colonies to import molasses, sugar, rum and other spirits exclusively from the British West Indies. Rendered ineffective through smuggling, it was replaced by the SUGAR ACT

(1764).

**MOLD,** general name for a number of filamentous FUNGI that produce powdery or fluffy growths on fabrics, foods and decaying plant or animal remains. Best known is the blue bread mold caused by *Penicillium*, from which the ANTIBIOTIC. PENICILLIN, was first discovered.

**MOLDAU RIVER.** See VLTAVA.

**MOLE,** pigmented spot or nevus in the SKIN, consisting of a localized group of special cells containing MELANIN. Change in a mole, such as increase in size, change of color and bleeding should lead to suspicion of MELANOMA.

**MOLE (mol),** the SI base unit of amount of substance, defined as the amount of substance of a system which contains as many elementary entities (of a specified kind) as there are atoms in 0.012kg of carbon-12 (i.e., the AVOGADRO Number). One mole of a compound is its MOLECULAR WEIGHT in grams. The molarity of a solution is its concentration in moles per litre; a solution whose molarity is 1 is called molar. (See SI UNITS.)

**MOLECULAR BIOLOGY,** the study of the structure and function of the MOLECULES which make up living organisms. This includes the study of PROTEINS, ENZYMES. CARBOHYDRATES, FATS and NUCLEIC ACIDS. (See also BIOCHEMISTRY; BIOLOGY; BIO-PHYSICS.)

**MOLECULAR WEIGHT,** the sum of the ATOMIC WEIGHTS of all the atoms in a MOLECULE. It is an integral multiple of the empirical FORMULA weight found by chemical ANALYSIS. and of the EQUIVALENT WEIGHT. Molecular weights may be found directly by MASS SPECTROSCOPY, or deduced from related physical properties including gas DENSITY; effusion; osmotic pressure (see OSMOSIS), and effects on solvents; lowering of vapor pressure and freezing point, and raising of boiling point; for large molecules the ultracentrifuge is used. (See also MOLE.)

**MOLECULE,** entity composed of ATOMS linked by chemical BONDS and acting as a unit; the smallest particle of a chemical compound which retains the COMPOSITION and chemical properties of the compound. The composition of a molecule is represented by its molecular FORMULA. Elements may exist as molecules, e.g. oxygen $O_2$, phosphorus $P_4$. FREE RADICALS and IONS are merely types of molecules. Molecules range in size from single atoms to macromolecules—chiefly PROTEINS and POLYMERS—with MOLECULAR WEIGHTS of 10,000 or more. The chief properties of molecules are their structure (bond lengths and angles)—determined by electron diffraction, X-RAY DIFFRACTION and SPECTROSCOPY—spectra, and DIPOLE MOMENTS.

**MOLES,** small insectivores adapted to an underground digging existence, family Talpidae. The family includes a number of species of European and American distribution. All have large spade-shaped hands projecting sideways from the body and long, mobile muzzles. The eyes are small and there is no external ear. They are solitary animals and live in a complicated system of burrows, feeding on soil invertebrates, largely earthworms. Parallel evolution has produced identical adaptations in Marsupial moles and GOLDEN MOLES.

**MOLEY, Raymond Charles** (1886–1975), US expert on government and public law. He became a member of Roosevelt's BRAIN TRUST and was appointed assistant secretary of state in 1933. Resigning shortly after, he founded the magazine *Today* and became a critic of the NEW DEAL.

**MOLIÈRE,** stage name of Jean-Baptiste Poquelin (1622–1673), France's greatest comic dramatist, renowned for his satire on hypocrisy and his characters personifying particular vices and types. After touring the provinces as actor-manager and playwright for many years, he eventually became established in Paris with the success of *Les Précieuse ridicules* in 1659. Among his best-known works are *Tartuffe* (1664), *Le Misanthrope* (1666), *Le Bourgeois gentil-homme* (1670) and *Le Malade imaginaire* (1673).

**MOLLET, Guy** (1905–1975), French statesman, wartime resistance leader and secretary general of the French socialist party 1946–69. He was premier in the center-left government of Jan. 1956–May 1957, and minister of state under De Gaulle 1958–59.

**MOLLUSKS,** soft-bodied INVERTEBRATES. typically having a calcareous shell into which the body can withdraw. They include SLUGS and SNAILS, LIMPETS, winkles, CLAMS MUSSELS and OYSTERS, as well as the apparently dissimilar OCTOPUSES and SQUIDS. Mollusks have adapted to an incredible variety of niches in the sea, in fresh water and on land. This has resulted in equal diversity of structure and habit. Major groups of mollusks include BIVALVES. CEPHALOPODA, CHITONS and GASTROPODA.

**MOLNÁR, Ferenc** (1878–1952), Hungarian author and playwright, who lived in the US from 1940. His play *Liliom* (1909) was adapted as the musical *Carousel* (1945). He also wrote novels and short stories.

**MOLOCH,** or Molech, the Canaanite god

of fire, to whom children were sacrificed, identified in the Old Testament as a god of the Ammonites. His worship, introduced by King Ahaz, was condemned by the prophets, and his sanctuary at Tophet near Jerusalem later became known as GEHENNA.

**MOLOTOV, Vyacheslav Mikhailovich** (1890–   ), born Vyacheslav Mikhailovich Skriabin, Russian diplomat. He became a Bolshevik in 1906, and after the RUSSIAN REVOLUTION quickly rose to power in the Communist Party. He was Soviet premier 1930–41 under Stalin. As foreign minister 1939–49 and 1953–56, he negotiated the 1939 nonaggression pact with Germany and played an important role in the USSR's wartime and postwar relations with the West. Under Khruschev, he lost power and held only minor posts, and in 1964 it was revealed that he had been expelled from the Communist Party.

**MOLTING,** the shedding of the skin, fur or feathers by an animal. It may be a seasonal occurrence, as a periodic renewal of fur or plumage in mammals and birds, or it may be associated with GROWTH, as in insects or crustaceans. In birds and mammals the molt is primarily to renew worn fur or feathers so that plumage or pelage is kept in good condition for waterproofing, insulation or flight. In addition it may serve to shed breeding plumage in birds, or to change between summer and winter coats. In invertebrates the rigid external skeleton must be shed and replaced to allow growth within. In larval insects the final molts are involved in the METAMORPHOSIS to adult form.

**MOLYBDENUM (Mo),** silvery-gray metal in Group VIB of the PERIODIC TABLE; a TRANSITION ELEMENT. It is obtained commercially by roasting MOLYBDENITE in air and reducing the oxide formed with carbon in an electric furnace or by the THERMITE process to give ferromolybdenum. Because of its high melting point, it is used to support the filament in electric lamps and for furnace heating elements. It also finds use in corrosion-resistant, high-temperature STEELS and ALLOYS. Molybdenum is unreactive, but forms various covalent compounds. Some are used as industrial CATALYSTS. Molybdenum is a vital trace element in plants and a catalyst in bacterial NITROGEN FIXATION. AW 95.9, mp 2610°C, bp 5560°C, sg 10.2 (20°C).

**MOMBASA,** capital of Coast Province, Kenya, on an island in an inlet of the Indian Ocean. It is an industrial center, major market and the chief port for Kenya, Uganda and Ethiopia. From 8th–16th century, it was an important Arab trading center. Pop 371,000.

**MOMENTUM,** the product of the MASS and linear VELOCITY of a body. Momentum is thus a VECTOR quantity. The linear momentum of a system of interacting particles is the sum of the momenta of its particles, and is constant if no external forces act. The rate of change of momentum with time in the direction of an applied force equals the force (Newton's second law of motion—see MECHANICS). In rotational motion, the analogous concept is **angular momentum,** the product of the moment of inertia and the angular velocity of a body relative to a given rotation axis. If no external forces act on a rotating system, the direction and magnitude of its angular momentum remain constant.

**Official name:** Principality of Monaco
**Capital:** Monaco
**Area:** 0.7sq mi
**Population:** 25,029
**Languages:** French
**Religions:** Roman Catholic
**Monetary unit(s):** 1 French franc = 100 centimes.

**MONACO,** independent principality on the Mediterranean near the French-Italian border, about 370 acres in area. It is a tourist center with a yachting harbor and a world-famous casino.

The reigning constitutional monarch, Prince Rainier III, succeeded to the throne in 1949 and married the US film actress Grace Kelly in 1956. In 1962, after a crisis with France over Monaco's tax free status, he proclaimed a new constitution, guaranteeing fundamental rights, giving the vote to women and abolishing the death penalty. The government consists of three councillors, headed by a minister of state who must be French. There is an 18-member National Council elected for five-year terms by universal suffrage, which shares legislative powers with the Prince.

Monaco's towns are MONTE CARLO, Monaco-Ville (capital), La Condamine (commercial center) and Fontvieille (small industrial area).

**MONADNOCK,** isolated hill formed of erosion-resistant bedrock in an area otherwise well eroded (see EROSION; PENEPLAIN); named for Mt Monadnock, Cheshire Co., N.H.

**MONARCH BUTTERFLY,** *Danaus plexippus,* an American BUTTERFLY remarkable for its size and coloration, and because it is one of those species of butterfly that undertake long MIGRATIONS. In spring it flies north to Canada, returning along exactly the same route in the fall. Monarchs have an unpleasant taste; their coloration is mimicked for protection by other less distasteful species.

**MONARCHY,** form of government in which sovereignty is vested in one person, usually for life. The office may be elective but is usually hereditary. A monarch who has unlimited power is an *absolute monarch*; one whose power is limited by custom or constitution is a *constitutional monarch*. In modern parliamentary democracies a monarch is usually a non-party political figure and a symbol of national unity. (See also DIVINE RIGHT OF KINGS.)

**MONASTICISM,** way of life, usually communal and celibate, always ascetic, conducted according to a religious rule. It is found in all major religions. Christian monasticism aims at holiness by fulfilling vows of poverty, chastity and obedience. It was founded in Egypt by St. ANTONY OF THEBES, and spread rapidly. Most early monks were HERMITS or lived in small groups; later, CENOBITES predominated, engaging in prayer, manual work, and sometimes in teaching and scholarship. In W Christianity, under the pervasive rule of St. BENEDICT OF NURSIA, communities were contemplative and "enclosed" (see BENEDICTINE ORDERS), as e.g. CISTERCIANS are today; but AUGUSTINIAN, DOMINICAN and FRANCISCAN friars abandoned enclosure in the 13th century. Important monastic centers included Mount ATHOS, CLUNY and MONTE CASSINO. Monasticism was abolished where the REFORMATION succeeded, but has revived and spread since the mid-19th century.

**MONCK, Charles Stanley, 1st Baron** (1819–1894), Irish peer and British Liberal MP. As governor general of British North America (1861–67), he promoted confederation of the Canadian provinces and became the first governor general of the Dominion of Canada (1867–68).

**MONCK (or Monk), George, 1st Duke of Albermarle** (1608–1670), English general and naval commander. At first supporting CHARLES I in the English CIVIL WAR, he later became CROMWELL's commander-in-chief in Scotland (1650–52; 1654–60). After Cromwell's death he was the architect of the RESTORATION of Charles II. He was a successful commander of the fleet in the DUTCH WARS (1652–54; 1666).

**MONDRIAN, Piet** (1872–1944), Dutch painter and theorist, a founder of the DE STIJL movement. At first a symbolist, he was influenced by CUBISM, and evolved a distinctive abstract style relating primary colors and black and white in grid-like arrangements.

**MONET, Claude** (1840–1926), French painter, leading exponent of IMPRESSIONISM, a term coined after his picture *Impression, Sunrise* (1872). He worked in and around Paris, in poverty in his early years. Always fascinated by varying light effects, around 1889 he began painting series of pictures of a subject at different times of day, such as those of *Rouen Cathedral* (1892–94). His last pictures of *Water Lilies* are virtually abstract.

**MONETARISM,** theoretical position in economics, chiefly associated with the work of Milton FRIEDMAN of the University of Chicago. This contemporary theory is based on the 19th-century "quantity-of-money" theory, which directly related changes in price levels to changes in the amount of money in circulation. Monetarism, which stands generally in opposition to Keynesianism, advocates curing inflation and depression not by fiscal measures but rather by control of the nation's money supply—for instance, by varying the interest rate charged by the FEDERAL RESERVE SYSTEM and expanding or limiting the sale of Treasury bills.

**MONEY,** in any economic system, is a medium of exchange, of labor and products, or for payment of debts. In primitive societies, BARTER, direct physical exchange, was commonly used. The precise origin of money is unknown. It evolved gradually out of the needs of commerce and trade. A wide variety of objects have at one time or other been used as money: shells, nuts, beads, stones etc. Gradually, metal was adopted because of its easy handling, durability, divisibility, and—especially with gold or silver—for its own value. The oldest coinage dates back to about 700 BC, when COINS of gold and silver alloys were made in Lydia (Asia Minor). Paper money was known in China as early as the 9th century, but it did not develop in Europe until the 17th century. The banknote and the modern BANKING system evolved when goldsmiths began, for safekeeping, to store gold and coins for others. Money thus deposited or invested could be re-used by the borrower, who therefore paid INTEREST as a fee for its availability. The realization that available money could make more money overthrew the medieval Church's view that money was barren and usury wrong. An over-reaction led to MERCANTILISM, in which money was preferred to all other forms of wealth.

The stability and value of paper currency is usually guaranteed by governments or banks (those invested with legal authority to issue currency) with some bullion holdings. However, it is tempting for governments to over-issue money as an easy way to pay their debts. This can lead to INFLATION and DEVALUATION of the currency. (See also FEDERAL RESERVE SYSTEM.)

In the last 20 or 30 years, there has emerged a school of economists who argue that monetary policies (controlling the volume of money in circulation) should be utilized to achieve MACROECONOMIC objectives, such as growth rates, employment levels and curbing inflation.

The monetary system of the US during most of the 19th century was based on BIMETALISM, with the dollar defined as 371.25 grains of fine silver or 24.75 grains of fine gold. From 1900, the dollar was defined in terms of gold, with the passing of the GOLD STANDARD Act of 1900 and the Gold Reserve Act of 1934. However, in 1970 the dollar's dependency on gold was ended when the requirement set by the Treasury of 25% gold backing for all Federal Reserve notes was dropped. (See also FIAT MONEY.)

**MONEY MARKET,** system of institutions and of means for trading in short-term credit instruments, such as US Treasury bills, commercial paper, and banker's acceptances. Traditionally, money-market investment has been undertaken primarily by commercial banks and other specialists, but recently high interest rates have attracted ordinary investors into the market, especially via money-market mutual funds. This has drained assets from the stock and bond markets, savings and loan associations, and savings banks.

**MONGOL EMPIRE,** founded in the 1200s by GENGHIS KHAN who united the Mongol tribes of central Asia. Already superb horsemen and archers, the Mongols were united by Genghis Khan into a huge, well-disciplined, swiftly-moving army, which had conquered N China by 1215, and then swept W to engulf Bukhara, Samarkand, Gurgan and S Russia in a wave of terror and destruction. After his death, the bloody Mongol invasions were continued under his son Ogotai. During 1237–40, the Mongol general BATU KHAN, a grandson of Genghis Khan, crossed the Volga, crushed the Bulgars and Kumans, devastated central Russia and invaded Poland and Hungary. Further conquest was halted only by the death of Ogotai in 1241.

By about 1260 the Empire was organized into four Khanates: the Il Khanate (Persia); the Kipchak Khanate, founded by the GOLDEN HORDE (Russia); the Jagatai (Turkestan); and the Great Khanate (China). During KUBLAI KHAN'S rule (1260–94) the Great Khanate became the YÜAN DYNASTY of China. The Empire

stretched from the China Seas to the Danube R. After his death, it disintegrated. But the Mongol tradition of conquest was revived by TAMERLANE in the 1300s and BABUR in the 1500s.

**Official name:** Mongolian People's Republic
**Capital:** Ulan Bator
**Area:** 604,095sq mi
**Population:** 1,667,000
**Languages:** Mongolian
**Religions:** No official religion
**Monetary unit(s):** 1 Togrog = 100 mongo
**MONGOLIAN PEOPLE'S REPUBLIC,** previously known as Outer Mongolia, republic in Central Asia between China and the USSR, set up in 1921.
**Land.** The country is a steppe plateau fringed on the N and W by mountains. Much of the SE is part of the Gobi desert. The climate is dry, with harsh extremes of temperature, and the country is very thinly populated. There are forests in the mountainous north.
**People.** Over 50% of the population live on state collective farms, and almost 25% in the capital, Ulan Bator. Many people continue to practice Tibetan Buddhism (Lamaism), with monasteries allowed to function.
**Economy.** The economy is based on livestock farming, principally of sheep and goats, but also of horses, cattle, yaks and (in the desert) camels. There is some agriculture, and hunting of sable and other wild animals for fur. Coal, iron ore, gold and other minerals are mined. Industry is developing at Choybalsan, Darkhan and Ulan Bator, but is limited to felts, furniture, and other consumer goods. Chief exports are of livestock, wool, hides, meat and ores. The Trans-Mongolian railroad links the country with the USSR (her chief trading partner) and China; roads and communications are poor.
**History.** Formerly the heartland of the MONGOL EMPIRE and a Chinese province since 1691, Mongolia declared itself independent in 1911, but was reoccupied by China in 1919. With Soviet support the

country declared its independence again in 1921, and in 1924 adopted its present name and became the world's second communist state. Its communist government has since maintained close links with the USSR, with the government patterned after that of the USSR and led, since 1940, by Yumjaagiyn Tsedenbal.

**MONGOLISM,** or Down's syndrome, a relatively common (1 in 600 births) congenital disorder due to a chromosomal abnormality, usually of CHROMOSOME 21. It causes characteristic facial appearance (resembling that of a Mongolian), HAND shape and SKIN patterns; floppiness in the baby; MENTAL RETARDATION, and delayed growth. Congenital diseases of the HEART and GASTROINTESTINAL TRACT are common, as is CATARACT. These persons also have an increased incidence of LEUKEMIA. As the average age of parenthood advances, mongolism is becoming increasingly common.

**MONGOLOID,** one of the three major divisions of the human RACE. Mongoloids generally have straight black hair, little facial hair, yellow to brown skin and the distinctive epicanthic fold, a fold of skin over the eyes which gives them a slanting appearance. The AMERINDS, Eskimos, Polynesians and Patagonians are Mongoloid peoples, as are the Chinese, Japanese, Koreans, Indochinese and many other Asian peoples.

**MONGOOSES,** small carnivores of the Viverridae, with a reputation for killing snakes and stealing eggs. There are about 48 species occupying a variety of habitats around the Mediterranean, in Africa and southern Asia. Most of them are diurnal, feeding on lizards, snakes, eggs and small mammals. They are usually solitary although a few species form colonies, often in burrows in termite mounds. All mongooses have great immunity to snake venom. One of the best known species is the Common or Egyptian mongoose sometimes known as the ICHNEUMON.

**MONISM,** any philosophical system asserting the essential unity of things—that all things are matter (see MATERIALISM), or mind (see IDEALISM), or of some other essence. Monism is contrasted with various kinds of DUALISM or pluralism.

**MONITOR AND MERRIMACK,** two pioneer ironclad warships famous for the first battle fought by iron armored vessels during the US CIVIL WAR at Hampton Roads, Va., on March 9, 1862. The *U.S.S. Merrimack* was a scuttled Union steam frigate, salvaged by the Confederates, renamed the *C.S.S. Virginia* and reinforced with iron plate. The *U.S.S. Monitor* was designed by John ERICSSON and equipped with a revolving gun turret. The ships' battle had little real effect on the war except to boost morale on both sides.

**MONK, Thelonious Sphere** (1920–    ), US jazz pianist and composer; with Dizzy GILLESPIE and Charlie PARKER, he was a leading innovator of modern jazz from the mid-1940s and 1950s. His jazz ballad *'Round Midnight* and compositions *Epistrophy, Straight No Chaser* and *Blue Monk* are standard in modern jazz repertoires.

**MONKEY,** a term used to describe any higher PRIMATE, suborder *Anthropoidea,* that is not an ape or a man. It includes both New World and Old World forms. There is thus little uniformity in the group; monkeys have adapted to a variety of modes of life. All have flattened faces, the Old and New World groups being distinguished by nose shape. New World, platyrrhine monkeys, family Cebidae, have broad, flat noses with the nostrils widely separated. Old World, catarrhines, family Cercopithecidae, have the nostrils separated by only a thin septum. Monkeys are normally restricted to tropical or subtropical areas of the world. Old World forms include LANGURS, Colobines, MACAQUES, GUENONS, MANGABEYS and BABOONS. Monkeys of the New World include Sakis, UAKARIS, HOWLERS, Douroucoulis, SQUIRREL MONKEYS and CAPUCHINS. (See also ANTHROPOID APES.)

**MON-KHMER LANGUAGES,** a linguistic subfamily and geographical language group of the so-called Austro-Asiatic or Southeast Asian language family, spoken by some 35 million to 45 million people. Khmer is spoken in Cambodia and Mon in Burma; related dialects are used in South Vietnam, the Malay peninsula, the Nicobar islands and India. (See also MALAYO-POLYNESIAN LANGUAGES.)

**MONNET, Jean** (1888–1979), French economist and statesman; known as the architect of a united W Europe. He created the Monnet Plan (1947) to help France's economic recovery from WWII, planned and served as first president of the EUROPEAN COAL AND STEEL COMMUNITY (ECSC) and helped plan the COMMON MARKET.

**MONOD, Jacques Lucien** (1910–1976) French biochemist who, with F. JACOB and A. LWOFF, received the 1965 Nobel Prize for Physiology or Medicine for his work with Jacob on regulatory GENE action in BACTERIA.

**MONONUCLEOSIS, Infectious,** or **glandular fever,** common VIRUS infection o adolescence causing a variety of symptoms including severe sore throat, HEADACHE, FEVER, malaise and enlargement of LYMPH nodes and SPLEEN. Skin rashes, hepatitis (see LIVER) with JAUNDICE, pericarditis (see PERICARDIUM) and involvement of the NERVOUS SYSTEM may also be prominent. Atypical lymphocytes in the BLOOD and specific agglutination reactions (see ANTIBODIES AND ANTIGENS) are diagnostic. Severe cases may require STEROIDS and convalescence may be lengthy. It can be transmitted in SALIVA and has thus been nicknamed the "kissing disease."

**MONOPHYSITE CHURCHES**, branches of the EASTERN CHURCH formed in the 6th century by the schismatic adherents of MONOPHYSITISM: the ARMENIAN, COPTIC and JACOBITE CHURCHES. Their doctrine is now essentially orthodox.

**MONOPHYSITISM** (from Greek *monos*, one, and *physis*, nature), heretical doctrine that in the Person of Christ there is but one (divine) nature. It arose in opposition to the orthodox Council of CHALCEDON (451). A confused controversy resulted, and despite reconciliation attempts the schism hardened. (See also INCARNATION.)

**MONOPOLY**, an economic term describing significant control or ownership of a product or service (and thereby its price) because of command of the product's supply, legal privilege or concerted action. There are different kinds of monopoly. PATENTS and COPYRIGHTS are legal monopolies granted by a government to individuals or companies. A nationalized industry or service such as the US Post Office has a monopoly. A FRANCHISE granted by government to a public company to run a public utility (such as an electrical company) creates a monopoly. Trading and industrial monopolies have the power to decide upon supply and price of goods. Sometimes labor unions act as monopolies in the supply of workers' services. In the case of national monopolies, it is considered that they can provide mass-produced goods or services at a lower price, or more efficiently, than could be provided in a competitive situation; in practice this is not always true. Business or manufacturing monopolies may often discourage competitors from entering the field of competition. There is legislation designed to control monopolies that conspire to restrain price or trade (see SHERMAN ANTITRUST ACT; CLAYTON ANTITRUST ACT; FEDERAL TRADE COMMISSION).

**MONOPOLY**, a famous trademarked board game for two to eight players. Its object is to become the richest player and drive opponents into bankruptcy. Profit is gained through the selling, buying and trading of property. Play money, property, cards, tiny blocks representing buildings, counters and dice are used. The designations of properties on the board were taken from street names in Atlantic City, N.J. in 1933, the year the game was invented.

**MONOTHEISM**, belief in one God, contrasted with POLYTHEISM, PANTHEISM or ATHEISM. Classical monotheism is held by Judaism, Christianity and Islam; some other religions, such as early Zoroastrianism and later Greek religion, are monotheistic to a lesser degree. In the theories of E. B. TYLOR, religions have evolved from animism through polytheism and henotheism (the worship of one god, ignoring others in practice) to monotheism. There is, however, evidence for residual monotheism (the "High God") in primitive religions.

**MONOTYPE**, technique of letterpress printing in which each character is individual and fresh-cast out of molten type metal (see ALLOY). Keying by the operator encodes a ribbon with perforations that represent characters and spaces, with special codes punched after sets of characters that almost fill a line to instruct the machine to justify (align the right-hand margin). In response to the perforations, matrices (molds) are drawn from the matrix case, and from these the characters are cast. (See also LINOTYPE.)

**MONROE, Bill** (1911–    ), US country musician who performed both with his older brothers, Birch and Charlie, and later with his band, The Bluegrass Boys (from 1938). His driving syncopated rhythms and complex harmonies are credited with being the earliest examples of BLUEGRASS music.

**MONROE, James** (1758–1831), fifth president of the US, 1817–25. Promulgated the MONROE DOCTRINE, one of the most fundamental statements of foreign policy in the history of American diplomacy.

Monroe was born in Westmoreland Co., Va. He fought in the Revolution, was wounded at Trenton, commended for gallantry and became a lieutenant colonel. In 1780 he began to study law under Thomas JEFFERSON, and with his sponsorship was elected to the Virginia House of Delegates (1782), beginning a career of public service which would last over 40 years. He served in the Congress of the Confederation (1783–86) and began his law practice in 1788. Elected by Va. in 1790 for the US Senate, he joined Jefferson and James MADISON in forming the DEMOCRATIC-

REPUBLICAN PARTY.

Monroe's first diplomatic foray as minister to France (1794) went badly when he criticized the JAY TREATY and was recalled. He withdrew into Virginia politics, becoming governor from 1799 to 1802. During Jefferson's presidency, he was envoy extraordinary to France (1803) where he and Robert LIVINGSTON arranged the terms of the LOUISIANA PURCHASE, but was less successful in Madrid, with the Spaniards, who refused to consider American claims to W Fla. As minister to Great Britain (1806), he was unsatisfactory and an attempt to secure the presidential candidacy from Madison in 1808 was a failure. In 1811 he was once again elected governor of Va., and in the same year became Madison's secretary of state. After the British burned Washington, D.C., in the WAR OF 1812, he added the duties of secretary of war to those of secretary of state (1814). In 1816 he easily defeated his Federalist opponent for the presidency and was reelected unopposed four years later.

Monroe's administration years were called the "era of good feeling." The country prospered after the war and expanded westward. Monroe was a moderate man who believed in a decentralized federal government. During his presidency, Fla. was purchased from Spain (1819), Mo. was admitted to the Union (1821) under the MISSOURI COMPROMISE, the RUSH-BAGOT agreement was concluded with Great Britain, the 49th parallel was established as the US-Canadian boundary, the MONROE DOCTRINE guaranteed that European interference would not be tolerated in the Americas and the Santa Fe Trail to the SW was opened. Monroe retired after his presidency, but served as regent of the U. of Virginia and in 1829 presided over Va.'s constitutional convention.

**MONROE, Marilyn** (1926–1962), US movie star, Norma Jean Baker, who became world-famous as a blond sex-symbol. A comic actress of considerable talent, her films include *Gentlemen Prefer Blondes* (1953), *The Seven-Year Itch* (1955), *Bus Stop* (1956) and *Some Like It Hot* (1959).

**MONROE DOCTRINE,** a declaration of American policy toward the newly independent states of Latin America, issued by President James MONROE before the US Congress on Dec. 2, 1823. It stated in effect that any attempt by European powers to interfere with their old colonies in the western hemisphere would not be tolerated by the US and that the Americas were "henceforth not to be considered as subjects for further colonization by any European powers." The declaration relied for its force on British reluctance, backed by her naval supremacy, to see her own New World position threatened by other European states. President Theodore Roosevelt's corollary to the doctrine (1904) asserted that the US had the power and the right to control any interference in the affairs of the hemisphere by outside governments, and to ensure that acceptable governments were maintained there (this became known as the "big stick" policy; it was repudiated in 1928 by the Clark memorandum). Although the doctrine was mostly ignored until the last decade of the 19th century, it has remained a fundamental policy of the US.

**MONSOON,** wind system where the prevailing WIND direction reverses in the course of the seasons, occurring where large temperature (hence pressure) differences arise between oceans and large landmasses. Best known is that of SE Asia. In summer moist winds, with associated HURRICANES, blow from the Indian Ocean into the low-pressure region of NW India that is caused by intense heating of the land. In winter, cold dry winds sweep S from the high-pressure region of S Siberia.

**MONTAGNA, Bartolomeo** (c1450–1523) Italian early Renaissance painter. His stark, somber works were influenced by MANTEGNA and BELLINI and he founded a school of painting at Vicenza. His works include a *Madonna and Child* at the Venice Academy and an *Ecce Homo* in the Louvre, Paris.

**MONTAGU, Lady Mary Wortley** (1689–1762), English writer. She is noted for her so-called Embassy Letters, written from Turkey, and her society verse. Alexander POPE satirizes her under the name Sappho. She is also remembered as a pioneer in the use of smallpox inoculation, to which she submitted her children.

**MONTAIGNE, Michel Eyquem, seigneur de** (1533–1592), French writer, generally regarded as the originator of the personal essay. The first two books of his *Essays*, published in 1580, were written in an informal style and display an insatiable intellectual curiosity—his motto was always *Que sais-je?* (What do I know?). A third book of essays appeared in 1588, and the posthumous edition of 1595 includes his last reflections. He studied law, held various provincial political offices in Bordeaux and engaged in diplomacy during the French religious civil wars.

**Name of state:** Montana
**Capital:** Helena
**Statehood:** Nov. 8, 1889 (41st state)
**Familiar name:** Treasure State
**Area:** 147,138sq mi
**Population:** 786,690
**Elevation:** Highest—12,799ft, Granite Peak. Lowest—1,800ft Kootenai River in Lincoln County
**Motto:** Oro y Plata (Gold and Silver)
**State flower:** Bitterroot
**State bird:** Western meadowlark
**State tree:** Ponderosa pine
**State song:** "Montana"

MONTANA, state, NW US, in the Rocky Mts, bounded on the N by Canada along the 49th parallel, on the E by N.D. and S.D., on the S by Wyo. and on the SW and W by Ida.

**Land.** The fourth largest state, it can be divided into two physiographic regions: the mountains to the W, rising to Granite Peak (12,799ft), which cover two-fifths of the state and the Great Plains to the E. The state's major rivers include the Missouri (its headwaters are in SW Mont.) the Yellowstone, and the Clark Fork, Flathead and Kootenai in the W; there are many other rivers and lakes. About half the state is grassland, and about one-quarter is forest lands (22,400,000 acres). Climatic differences between E and W are marked, but the yearly average temperature ranges are 14°–70°F in the E and 20°–64°F in the W. Annual rainfall averages 15½in, while snow varies from 15in to 300in. The state has an abundance of wildlife and protected herds of buffalo.

**People.** About 75% of the population lives in rural areas. The largest urban centers are Billings, Great Falls and Missoula. The state contains over 37,250 American Indians (about 5% of the state's total population).

**Economy.** The economy is dominated by agriculture; livestock brings in about half of the agriculture income, while the other half comes from crops, notably durum wheat, barley, hay, sugar beets, rye, oats and potatoes. Montana is rich in mineral resources including coal, petroleum, copper, gold, lead, zinc and silver. Numerous other minerals are also mined. Lumbering, food processing and the smelting and refining of nonferrous metals are major industries. Natural power resources are supplemented by large-scale hydroelectric power schemes. Tourism is also important throughout the state. Principal attractions include Glacier National Park, Flathead Lake, and the Custer Battlefield National Monument.

**History.** Under the LOUISIANA PURCHASE, E Mont. became a US territory (1803). The first recorded exploration was undertaken by the LEWIS AND CLARK EXPEDITION in 1805–06, but except for fur traders and missionaries to the Indians, settlement did not begin until the discovery of gold at Grasshopper Creek (1852). The resulting lawlessness led to the creation of the Montana Territory (1864). Escalating conflict between the settlers and the Indians culminated in the massacre of Gen. CUSTER and his troops by the Sioux at the Battle of the Little Bighorn (1876), but the Sioux surrendered by 1881. The NEZ PERCÉ INDIANS made a dramatic march to freedom across Mont., but surrendered before reaching Canada. In 1889 the territory, formed in 1864, became a state. At the end of the century there were feuds between mine-owners for control of the copper industry and of state politics. Agriculture prospered until the 1930s. After the depression, industry began to expand and natural resources were further developed with construction of large dams and many federal reclamation projects. In the early 1980s, the state faced difficult policy decisions in the conflict between mining and industrial interests and concern for the environment.

MONTANUS (flourished 2nd century AD), Phrygian founder of the heretical Christian sect of **Montanism**. Claiming direct inspiration by the Holy Spirit, he prophesied the fulfilment of PENTECOST and the MILLENNIUM. The sect had a strict ascetic discipline, sought ecstatic religious experiences (including GLOSSOLALIA), and was puritan and anti-intellectual. It separated from the Catholic Church and was denounced, but spread widely; TERTULLIAN was a member. Montanism largely died out in the 5th century.

**MONT BLANC.** See BLANC, MONT.

**MONTCALM, Louis Joseph de** (1712–1759), French general; military commander in Canada from 1756 during the FRENCH AND INDIAN WARS. He captured Fort Ontario (1756) and Fort William Henry (1757) and repulsed the British at Ticonderoga (1758). He was defeated and killed on the Plains of Abraham (Sept. 13, 1759) while defending Quebec against the British General James WOLFE, who was also killed.

**MONTE CARLO,** town in the independent principality of MONACO, on the Mediterranean coast known as the French Riviera. It is an international resort with a gambling casino, a yacht harbor and an annual automobile rally and the Monaco Grand Prix car race. It is the home (and tax haven) of many international firms. Pop 9,948.

**MONTE CASSINO,** an Italian monastery founded by St. BENEDICT OF NURSIA c529 AD, which was the ruling house of the BENEDICTINE ORDERS and an influential cultural and religious center for centuries. Its buildings were destroyed for the fourth time in their history in WWII by bombardment but have since been rebuilt; the abbey is now a national monument.

**MONTENEGRO,** the smallest of Yugoslavia's six constituent republics, at the S end of the Dinaric Alps on the Adriatic Sea. Its capital is Titograd. Its former capital, Cetinje, was absorbed into Serbia after WWI. The area is mountainous with heavy forests. Mining and the raising of livestock are its chief occupations. Pop 530,361.

**MONTESQUIEU, Charles Louis de Secondat, Baron de la Brède et de** (1689–1755), French political philosopher who profoundly influenced 19th and 20th century political and social philosophy. His theory that governmental powers should be separated into legislative, executive and judicial bodies to safeguard personal liberty was developed in his most important work *The Spirit of the Laws* (1748), which influenced the US Constitution and others. Montesquieu's *Persian Letters* (1721) satirized contemporary French sociopolitical institutions.

**MONTESSORI, Maria** (1870–1952), Italian psychiatrist and educator. The first woman to gain a medical degree in Italy (1894), she developed a system of preschool teaching, the Montessori Method, in which children of 3 to 6 are given a wide range of materials and equipment which enable them to learn by themselves. There are about 600 schools in the US using this method which encourages individual initiative.

**MONTEUX, Pierre** (1875–1964), French-American conductor. He is remembered especially for his performance of the music of Stravinsky, Debussy and Ravel, as conductor of DIAGHILEV'S Ballet Russe (1911–14). Later he was conductor of the Boston Symphony Orchestra (1919–24), the San Francisco Symphony (1935–52) and the London Symphony Orchestra (1960–64).

**MONTEVERDI, Claudio** (1567–1643), Italian composer. His innovative operas were the predecessors of modern opera, in which aria, recitative and orchestral accompaniment all enhance dramatic characterization. *Orfeo* (1607) is considered the first modern opera. His other compositions include the ornate *Vespers* (1610) and much other sacred music, the operas *The Return of Ulysses to his Country* (1641) and *The Coronation of Poppea* (1642), and many MADRIGALS.

**MONTEVIDEO,** capital and largest city of Uruguay and of Montevideo department, located in the S on the Río de la Plata. It is the industrial, cultural and transportation center for the country, as well as a seaport and popular resort. Founded 1724. Pop 1,229,748.

**MONTEZUMA,** name of two Aztec rulers of Mexico before its conquest. **Montezuma I** (c1390–1469), was a successful conqueror who ruled from 1440. His descendant **Montezuma II** (1466–1520), was the last Aztec emperor (1502–20). When the Spanish conquistadors arrived, Montezuma failed to resist them because he believed CORTES to be the white god QUETZALCOATL, and he became a hostage. The Aztecs rebelled and Montezuma II was killed in the struggle.

**MONTEZUMA CASTLE NATIONAL MONUMENT,** site of pre-Columbian (c1100 AD) cliff dwellings of the PUEBLO INDIANS. The monument's 843 acres are in central Ariz. in the Verdi R valley. Established in 1906, it features a well-preserved five-story "castle" constructed in the shelter of limestone cliffs and named by settlers in the mistaken belief that it had been built by refugees from Mexico.

**MONTFORT, Simon de, Earl of Leicester** (c1208–1265), Anglo-French leader who mounted a revolt to limit Henry III's power by law. The BARONS' WAR followed which ended in the capture of the king (1264). The famous parliament of 1265, summoned by Montfort, was a landmark in English history with representatives from every shire, town and borough. In fighting that followed Montfort was killed at the Battle of Evesham.

**MONTGOLFIER, Joseph Michel** (1740–1810) and **Jacques Étienne** (1745–1799), French brothers noted for their invention of the first manned aircraft, the first practical (hot-air) BALLOON, which they flew in 1783. Later that same year Jacques assisted Jacques CHARLES in the launching of the first gas (hydrogen) balloon.

**MONTGOMERY,** capital city of Ala., seat of Montgomery Co., about 90mi SE of Birmingham. It is the marketing center for a fertile blacksoil farm region and has a large livestock market, as well as diversified industry. It is known as the "Cradle of the Confederacy" because the CONFEDERATE STATES OF AMERICA was formed in the city in Feb., 1861. Pop 178,157.

**MONTGOMERY, Bernard Law, 1st Viscount Montgomery of Alamein** (1887–1976), British army leader known as the commander who never lost a battle. He defeated ROMMEL at El Alamein (1942) driving the Germans out of N Africa. Promoted to field marshal, he commanded the British forces in the invasion of Normandy (1944) and later became deputy supreme commander of NATO, 1951–58.

**MONTGOMERY, Robert** (1904–1981), US actor, star of films such as *Night Must Fall* (1937) and *Here Comes Mister Jordan* (1941). He was president of the Screen Actors Guild, and, in the 1950s, produced a TV dramatic series and served as media advisor to President EISENHOWER.

**MONTGOMERY BUS BOYCOTT** (1955–56), tactic used by blacks, led by Rev. Martin Luther KING, Jr., to end segregation of bus passengers by race. King was convicted of violating an ordinance forbidding boycotts, but the blacks won when the US Supreme Court affirmed a lower-court ruling invalidating state and local laws requiring segregation on intrastate buses.

**MONTH,** name of several periods of time, mostly defined in terms of the motion of the MOON. The synodic month (lunar month or lunation) is the time between successive full moons; it is 29.531 DAYS. The sidereal month, the time taken by the moon to complete one revolution about the earth relative to the fixed stars, is 27.322 days. The anomalistic month, 27.555 days, is the time between successive passages of the moon through perigee (see ORBIT). The solar month, 30.439 days, is one twelfth of the solar YEAR. Civil or calendar months vary in length throughout the year, lasting from 28 to 31 days (see CALENDAR). In popular usage, the (lunar) month refers to 28 days.

**MONTHERLANT, Henri-Marie Joseph Millon de** (1896–1972), French novelist and playwright. His work stressed masculine as opposed to feminine virtues and his characters are heroic idealists. His many works include the novels *The Girls* (1936–39) and *Chaos and Night* (1963) and the plays *Malatesta* (1946) and *La guerre civile* (1965).

**MONTICELLO,** a 640-acre estate planned by Thomas JEFFERSON in Va., 3mi from Charlottesville. Construction of the neoclassical mansion atop a small mountain began in 1770; Jefferson moved in before it was completed and lived there for 56 years. His tomb is nearby and the house became a national shrine in 1926, and is open to the public.

**MONTMARTRE,** the highest hill (432ft) in Paris, France, on the right bank of the Seine. Topped by the famous Sacré-Coeur church, the hill was celebrated as the bohemian haunt of artists and writers and for its night life.

**MONTPELIER,,** capital of Vt. and the seat of Washington Co. Its industries include life insurance, granite quarrying and lumbering. It is a winter tourist resort. Pop 8,241.

**MONTREAL,** city in S Quebec, Canada, located on the island of Montreal at the confluence of the St. Lawrence and Ottawa rivers. It is a huge inland port, despite its distance of 1000mi from the sea, Canada's second-largest city and the second-largest French-speaking city in the world. A French mission was built on the site in 1642 and then became an important fur trading center. Ceded to Britain in 1763, the city retained much of its French character. In the 19th century Montreal grew into an important transportation and industrial center aided by its many natural resources and abundance of hydroelectric power. It is the site of McGill U., the U. of Montreal and Sir George Williams U. Pop 1,080,545.

**MONTREUX CONVENTION,** an international agreement, which gave Turkey military control of the DARDANELLES, signed in 1936. Ratified by Turkey, Great Britain, France, USSR, Germany, Greece, Bulgaria and Yugoslavia (and Japan, with reservations), it closed the straits to warships if Turkey was at war and allowed passage of merchant ships in peace and war (if the countries were neutral to Turkey). The convention still stands.

**MONTSERRAT** ("saw-toothed mountain"), mountain in Catalonia, NE Spain, rising from the plain NW of Barcelona to a height of 4,054ft. The Benedictine monastery there contains a celebrated wooden statue of the Virgin Mary.

**MOODY, Dwight Lyman** (1837–1899), US evangelist, who toured the US and Britain on missions with the hymn writer Ira D. SANKEY. He founded several schools and set up a Bible Institute in Chicago (1889) to promote religious learning.

**MOODY, Helen Newington Wills** (1906–   ), US tennis star. Between 1923 and 1938 she won seven US singles titles and eight Wimbledon championships.

**MOOG, Robert Arthur** (1934–   ), US electrical engineer. He invented the "Moog Synthesizer," the most famous of the early electronic musical instruments, which he marketed from 1965.

**MOON,** a SATELLITE, in particular, the earth's largest natural satellite. The moon is so large relative to the earth (it has a diameter two thirds that of MERCURY) that earth and moon are commonly regarded as a double planet. The moon has a diameter of 3,476km and a mass 0.0123 that of the earth; its ESCAPE VELOCITY is around 2.4km/s. The orbit of the moon defines the several kinds of MONTH. The distance of the moon from the earth varies between 363Mm and 406Mm (perigee and apogee) with a mean of 384.4Mm. The moon rotates on its axis every 27.322 days, hence keeping the same face constantly toward the earth; however, in accordance with KEPLER'S second law, the moon's orbital velocity is not constant and hence there is exhibited the phenomenon known as *libration*: to a particular observer on the earth, marginally different parts of the moon's disk are visible at different times. There is also a very small physical libration due to slight irregularities in its rotational velocity.

The moon is covered with craters, whose sizes range up to 200km diameter. These sometimes are seen in chains up to 1Mm in length. Other features include rilles, trenches a few kilometers wide and a few hundred kilometers long; the *maria* (Latin: seas) or great plains; the bright rays which emerge from the large craters, and the lunar mountains. There are also lunar hot spots, generally associated with those larger craters showing bright rays: these remain cooler than their surroundings during lunar daytime, warmer during the lunar night. It has been shown, both by the samples brought back by the Apollo 11 (1969) and subsequent lunar expeditions (see SPACE EXPLORATION) and measurements of crater circularities carried out in 1968, that the smaller lunar craters are in general of meteoritic (see METEOR) origin, the larger of volcanic origin. It is believed that the earth and the moon formed simultaneously, the greater mass of the earth accounting for its

higher proportion of metallic iron; the heat of the young earth's atmosphere, which evaporated silicates, accounting for their higher proportion on the moon.

**MOONEY, Thomas J.** (1883–1942), US labor activist. A key figure in labor's struggle for recognition on the West Coast, he was sentenced to death for his part in a bomb outrage in San Francisco, Cal., in 1916. He was widely believed to be innocent, and his sentence was commuted in 1918. He was pardoned in 1939.

**MOONIES,** common name for members of the Unification Church, an organization founded by the Reverend Sun Myung Moon in 1954 in Korea. This church, known for its great wealth, large real-estate holdings, business ventures, high-pressure conversion tactics and strict control of members, has been a prominent US institution since the mid-1970s. It is estimated to have more than a million members worldwide; it advocates a sort of fundamentalist Christianity. In 1981, Rev. Moon was charged with income tax evasion.

**MOORE, Barrington, Jr.** (1913–   ), US political scientist, a specialist in comparative politics and a member of the Russian Research Center at Harvard U. His books include *Terror and Progress in the USSR* (1954), *Social Origins of Dictatorship and Democracy* (1966) and *Reflections on the Causes of Human Misery* (1970).

**MOORE, Brian** (1921–   ), Irish-born Canadian novelist. In such works as *The Lonely Passion of Judith Hearne* (1955) and *The Luck of Ginger Coffey* (1960), Moore focused on "insignificant" characters who suffer because of their inability to change their lives.

**MOORE, Clement Clarke** (1779–1863), US educator and poet. He wrote the popular Christmas poem *A Visit from St. Nicholas,* which begins "Twas the night before Christmas" (1823), and was a professor of Oriental and Greek literature at New York City's General Theological Seminary for 29 years.

**MOORE, George Augustus** (1852–1933), Irish writer. He spent his youth in Paris and came under the influence of BALZAC and ZOLA, returning to England to stir literary society with realistic novels such as *Esther Waters* (1894) and his masterpiece *Héloise and Abélard* (1921). He contributed much to the Irish literary revival and the ABBEY THEATRE's success.

**MOORE, George Edward** (1873–1958), English philosopher who led the 20th-century reaction against IDEALISM and is known for his "ordinary language" approach to philosophy. In his main work,

*Principia Ethica* (1903) he held that "good" was not an aspect of the natural world as investigated by science but a simple, indefinable concept.

**MOORE, Henry** (1898–    ), English sculptor and artist, one of the outstanding sculptors of the 20th century. His inspiration comes from natural forms such as stones, roots and bones and often expresses itself in curving abstract shapes perforated with large holes. His work, with repeated themes such as mother and child, is monumental and full of humanity and includes *Family Group* (1949) and *Reclining Figure* (1965).

**MOORE, Marianne Craig** (1887–1972), US poet, winner of the 1952 Pulitzer Prize for her *Collected Poems*. She edited the *Dial* magazine (1925–29) and translated La Fontaine's *Fables* (1954). Her subjects and themes are often taken from nature.

**MOORE, Mary Tyler** (1937–    ), US actress who attracted national attention as the costar of the TV series, *The Dick Van Dyke Show* (1961–66), and as the producer and star of her own *Mary Tyler Moore Show* (1970–77), one of the most successful situation comedies ever broadcast. She also appeared in dramatic roles on Broadway, in *Whose Life is it Anyway?* (1980) and the film *Ordinary People* (1980).

**MOORE, Thomas** (1779–1852), Irish poet. He is remembered for his *Irish Melodies* 1808–34), including "The Last Rose of Summer" and other lyrics. Extremely popular in his own day, he also wrote an oriental romance *Lalla Rookh* (1817) and lives of Sheridan (1825) and of Byron 1830).

**MOORS**, N African people of mixed Berber and Arabic stock who in the 8th century conquered much of Spain and Portugal, basing their rule in Córdoba and Granada. Philosophy and the sciences flourished under their patronage, as did architecture. After losing ground throughout the 13th century, they were finally driven from the peninsula in 1492. (See also ALMOHAD and LMORAVID.)

**MOOSE**, *Alces alces*, a large long-legged DEER of cold climates, known as the ELK in N Europe and Asia, and Moose in North America. It is characterized by its large size, long legs and overshot muzzle. The males have large, palmate antlers, as much as 2m (6.6ft) across. Often living near water, the moose feeds on aquatic plants as well as browsing from bushes and mature trees.

**MOOSE, Loyal Order of**, a fraternal organization with a broad scope of community service activities, operating in the US, Canada and Great Britain. Founded in 1888, it has over 4,000 local lodges and a membership of over one million. The Moose are similar to the ELKS and other fraternal groups.

**MORAINE**, heterogenous accumulation of debris called TILL carried or dropped by a glacier. *Ground moraine* is DRIFT left in a sheet as the GLACIER retreats. *Terminal moraines* are ridges deposited when the ice is melting prior to the glacial retreat; a series of ridges may mark pauses in the retreat. *Lateral moraines* are formed of debris that falls onto the glacier: when two glaciers merge their lateral moraines may unite to form a *medial moraine*.

**MORALITY PLAY**, form of drama popular in the Middle Ages from about the 14th to the 16th centuries. It was intended to instruct its audience on the eternal struggle between good and evil for human souls. The characters were personifications of virtues and vices. The most noted English example is *Everyman* (from the 1500s) which is still sometimes performed. Morality plays grew out of earlier religious pageants and were an important step in the secularization of drama. (See also MYSTERY PLAY.)

**MORAL MAJORITY**, strictly, the religious-political organization headed by the Rev. Jerry FALWELL; loosely, the entire religious constituency of the NEW RIGHT. In this second sense, the Moral Majority is the same as the New Christian (or Religious) Right; led chiefly by TV evangelists, it represents fundamentalist Christian beliefs, and proved a potent force in the 1980 presidential and congressional campaigns, especially in the Sun Belt and West. In Sept., 1980, their favored candidate, Ronald Reagan, appeared at a convention in Dallas, Tex., for Protestant and Catholic clergy, sponsored by the Religious Roundtable, and endorsed the political and religious goals of the movement. The Moral Majority also supported many of the 33 new representatives and 16 new senators (who gave the Republicans control of the Senate for the first time since 1955). The Moral Majority has been widely criticized, even by such conservatives as Sen. Barry Goldwater, for being racist, bigoted, socially divisive and intent upon intruding into people's private lives. Following his election, Reagan postponed action on the Moral Majority's major aims, including outlawing abortion, introducing prayers and religious teachings into public schools, suppressing pornography and so on.

**MORAVIA, Alberto** (1907–    ), Italian novelist, born Alberto Pincherle, whose detached and colloquial style lends realism to his theme of disaffection and aridity in modern life. His novels include *The Woman of Rome* (1947) and *Two Women* (1957).

**MORAVIAN CHURCH,** Protestant church also known as the Church of the Brethren or *Unitas Fratrum*, formed (1457) by Bohemian followers of Jan HUS, believers in simple worship and strict Christian living, with the Bible as their rule of faith. They broke with Rome in 1467. During the THIRTY YEARS WAR (1618–48), they were persecuted almost to extinction, but revived in Silesia and in 1732 began the missionary work for which they are still known. The first American settlements were in Pa. (1740) and N.C. (1753). In 1969 the Moravian Church had 353,228 members but its influence, especially in shaping modern Protestantism, has been far greater than its numbers suggest. (See also ZINZENDORF.)

**MORE, Paul Elmer** (1864–1937), US scholar and literary critic, an exponent (with Irving BABBITT) of the New Humanism. His works include *Shelburne Essays* (1904–21) and *The Greek Tradition* (1921–31).

**MORE, Sir Thomas** (1478–1535), English statesman, writer and saint who was executed for his refusal to take the oath of supremacy recognizing Henry VIII as head of the English Church. A man of brilliance, subtlety and wit, he was much favored by the king. When Cardinal WOLSEY fell in 1529 More was made lord chancellor. Probably because of Henry's determination to divorce Catherine of Aragon in defiance of the pope, More resigned only three years later. Considered dangerously influential even in silence and retirement, More was condemned for high treason. More's best-known work is *Utopia*, a description of an ideal society based on reason. Long recognized as a martyr by the Catholic Church, More was canonized in 1935.

**MOREAU, Gustave** (1826–1898), French painter noted for his highly dramatic studies of mythological and supernatural scenes, such as *Oedipus and The Sphinx* (1864). As a teacher he greatly influenced MATISSE and ROUAULT.

**MORGAN,** US banking family famous for its immense financial power and its philanthropic activities. The banking house of J. S. Morgan and Co. was founded by **Junius Spencer Morgan** (1813–1890), and developed into a vast financial and industrial empire (J. P. Morgan & Co.) under his son, **John Pierpont Morgan** (1837–1913). Many of J. P. Morgan's commercial activities aroused controversy,

and in 1904 his Northern Securities Company was dissolved as a violation of the SHERMAN ANTITRUST ACT. Notable philanthropic legacies include part of his art collection to the Metropolitan Museum of Art, and the Pierpont Morgan Library, which was endowed by his son. **John Pierpont Morgan, Jr.** (1867–1943) was American agent for the Allies during WWI, when he raised huge funds and organized contracts for military supplies. Most of the large postwar international loans were floated by the house of Morgan.

**MORGAN, Edmund Sears** (1916– ), US historian. A specialist in colonial American history, he taught at Brown (1946–55) and Yale (after 1955) and wrote several popular yet scholarly works including *The Puritan Family* (1944) and *The Puritan Dilemma* (1958).

**MORGAN, Lewis Henry** (1818–1881), US ethnologist best known for his studies of kinship systems and for his attempts to prove that the AMERINDS had migrated into North America, and to discover their place of origin. His techniques and apparently successful results have earned him regard as a father of the science of cultural ANTHROPOLOGY.

**MORGAN, Sir Henry** (c1635–1688), notorious English adventurer and leader of the West Indies BUCCANEERS. The destruction (1671) of Panama City, his most daring exploit, took place after the signing of a treaty between England and Spain. Recalled under arrest, he was subsequently pardoned, knighted (1673) and made lieutenant governor of Jamaica.

**MORGAN, Thomas Hunt** (1866–1945), US biologist who, through his experiments with the fruit fly *Drosophila*, established the relation between GENES and CHROMOSOMES and thus the mechanism of HEREDITY. For his work he received the 1933 Nobel Prize for Physiology or Medicine.

**MORGENTHAU, Hans** (1904–1980), German-born US political scientist. He advocated a realistic approach to foreign policy and gained international attention for his opposition to US involvement in Vietnam during the 1960s and 1970s. Among his books are *Politics Among Nations* (1948) and *A New Foreign Policy for the United States* (1969).

**MÖRIKE, Eduard** (1804–1875), major German lyric poet. His poetry, first collected in the volume *Gedichte* (1838), is small in quantity but richly varied in theme and technique. He also wrote a novel and some short stories.

**MORISON, Samuel Eliot** (1887–1976), US historian and Harvard professor who wrote the official 15-volume history (1947–62) of the US Navy during WWII. He won Pulitzer Prizes for his *Admiral of the Ocean Sea* (1942), a life of Christopher Columbus, and *John Paul Jones* (1959).

**MORLEY, Thomas** (c1557–?1603), English composer noted especially for his madrigals. A pupil of William BYRD and organist of St. Paul's Cathedral, he also wrote *A Plaine and Easie Introduction to Practicall Musicke* (1597), an invaluable source of information on Elizabethan musical practice.

**MORMONS**, members of the Church of Jesus Christ of Latter-Day Saints founded (1830) by Joseph SMITH. Mormons accept Smith as having miraculously found and translated a divinely-inspired record of the early history and religion of America, the *Book of Mormon*. With Smith's own writings and the Bible, this forms the Mormon scriptures. Smith's teachings quickly gained a following, but the Mormons' attempts to settle met with recurrent persecution, culminating in the murder of Smith in 1844. It was Brigham YOUNG who led the Mormons in 1847 beyond the frontier to what is now Salt Lake City (still the location of their chief temple). In 1850 Congress granted them the Territory of Utah with Young as Governor. Hostility to the flourishing agricultural community which then developed focused on the Mormon sanction of polygamy and came to a climax with the "Utah War" (1857–58). In 1890 the Mormons abolished polygamy, and Utah was admitted to the Union in 1896. The Mormons have no professional priesthood, but a president and counselors. They stress repentance and believe in the afterlife and the Last Judgment. The Mormons are notably temperate and law-abiding; their religion is an integral part of their lives. They have a membership of over 3 million.

**MORO, Aldo** (1916–1978), Italian political leader. First elected as a Christian Democrat to the Chamber of Deputies in 1948, he headed five Italian governments as prime minister during the 1960s and 1970s. He was generally expected to be elected Italy's president in 1978 but was kidnapped by the terrorist Red Brigades only weeks before the election. He was found murdered in a car in Rome.

**MOROCCO**, country in NW Africa, on the Mediterranean and the Atlantic, bordering Algeria (S and E) and the Spanish Sahara (S). Its topography varies from the fertile coastal region (which includes the RIF Mts along the Mediterranean) to barren desert, with the great ATLAS mountain chain

enclosing extensive plains W to E across the center. N Morocco has a Mediterranean climate.

**People.** Most Moroccans are of Arab descent but about one third are BERBERS, and there are Jewish, French and Spanish communities. Less than a third of the people are town dwellers. The largest cities are CASABLANCA, MARRAKESH and RABAT (the capital).

**Economy.** About 30% of the Gross National Product is provided by agriculture. Wheat, barley, corn, beans, dates, citrus and other fruits are grown. Timber, livestock and fishing are also sources of income, and tourism is increasingly important. The chief mineral is phosphate. Coal, manganese, iron ore, lead, cobalt, zinc, silver and some oil are also produced. There are leather, textile and cement industries. Traditional Moroccan handicrafts are world-famous.

**History.** The Arabs swept into N Africa from the east (c683 AD), converting the native Berbers to Islam and enlisting their aid in the 8th-century conquest of Spain, but lengthy Arab-Berber strife followed under a succession of dynasties. European (chiefly Portuguese) penetration of Morocco, beginning in 1415, was checked in 1660, but resumed in the 19th and 20th centuries by France, Spain and Germany. Independent since 1956, Morocco is now ruled by King Hassan II. It is a member of the ARAB LEAGUE, the ORGANIZATION OF AFRICAN UNITY, and the United Nations. Polisario Front guerrillas have been battling Morocco for control of the Western Sahara since 1975.

**Official name:** Kingdom of Morocco
**Capital:** Rabat
**Area:** 172,413sq mi
**Population:** 20,938,000
**Languages:** Arabic. French, Spanish also spoken
**Religion:** Muslim
**Monetary unit(s):** 1 Tugrik = 100 centimes

**MORPHINE**, OPIUM derivative used as a NARCOTIC ANALGESIC and also commonly in DRUG ADDICTION. It depresses RESPIRATION and the COUGH reflex, induces sleep and may cause VOMITING and CONSTIPATION. It is valuable in HEART failure and as a premedication for ANESTHETICS; its properties are particularly valuable in terminal malignant DISEASE (see also HEROIN). Addiction and withdrawal syndromes are common.

**MORRIS, Gouverneur** (1752–1816), American statesman responsible for planning the US decimal coinage system. He was a member of the New York provincial congress (1775–77). At the Constitutional Convention of 1787 he argued for a strong, property-based federal government, and was responsible, as a literary adviser, for much of the wording of the US Constitution. He was minister to France (1792–94) and later played a leading part in promoting the Erie Canal.

**MORRIS, William** (1834–1896), English artist, poet and designer. One of the PRE-RAPHAELITES, he sought to counteract the effects of industrialization by a return to the aesthetic standards and craftsmanship of the Middle Ages. In 1861 he set up Morris and Co. to design and make wallpaper, furniture, carpets and other home furnishings. Influenced by RUSKIN, he formed the Socialist League (1884). His founding (1890) of the Kelmscott Press had a primary impact on typographical and book design.

**MORRIS DANCE,** English folk dance associated with ancient ritual festivals such as May Day. Literary references to the Morris Dance occur from the 1400s, and it still survives today. The dancers performed in groups, often centered around a man symbolically disguised as an animal.

**MORRISON, Jim** (1946–1971), singer and lyricist for the late 1960s rock music quartet, *The Doors.* The suggestive content of his songs and his eroticized method of delivery have made him a cult figure.

**MORRISON, Toni** (1931–    ), black US novelist admired for the precise, vivid style of her prose, which often approaches poetry. Her works include *The Bluest Eye* (1969), *Sula* (1973), *The Black Book* (1974), *Song of Solomon* (1977) and *Tar Baby* (1981).

**MORSE, Samuel Finley Breese** (1791–1872), US inventor of an electric TELEGRAPH. His first crude model was designed in 1832, and by 1835 he could demonstrate a working model. With the considerable help of Joseph HENRY (which later he refused to acknowledge) he developed by 1837 electromagnetic relays to extend the range and capabilities of his system. WHEATSTONE'S invention had preceded Morse's, so that he was unable to obtain an English patent, and in the US

official support did not come until 1843. His famous message, "What hath God wrought!", was the first sent on his Washington-Baltimore line on May 24, 1844. For this he used MORSE CODE, devised in 1838. In early life, Morse was a noted portrait painter.

**MORSE CODE,** signal system devised (1838) by Samuel MORSE for use in the wire TELEGRAPH, now used in radiotelegraphy and elsewhere. Letters, numbers and punctuation are represented by combinations of dots (brief taps of the transmitting key) and dashes (three times the length of dots).

**MORTAR,** short-barreled gun which fires a shell in a high trajectory. Developed for trench warfare in WWI, it consists of a mounted tube into which the shell is dropped for firing. It has become a universally-used infantry weapon, and its lightness, simplicity and high trajectory make it suitable for GUERRILLA WARFARE in confined spaces and difficult terrain.

**MORTGAGE,** loan given on the security of the borrower's property. A mortgage is sometimes taken out on property already owned, but is more often used to help finance the purchase of property. If the loan is not repaid on time the mortgage may be foreclosed: that is, the person who loaned the money may obtain a court order to sell the property, and take what he is owed from the proceedings. Mortgages taken out for the purchase of a home usually run for 20 years or more. In the US, most mortgages are granted by banks or savings and loan societies. Mortgages are also issued for the purchase of machinery (especially farm machinery), when property other than real estate is often used as security.

**MORTON, Ferdinand "Jelly Roll"** (1885–1941), US jazz composer, pianist and bandleader of the Red Hot Peppers, born Ferdinand Joseph La Menthe. He was a pioneer of the original New Orleans jazz style.

**MOSAIC,** general name for VIRUS DISEASES of plants such as tobacco, tomatoes, potatoes, soybeans and peas, which produce a characteristic leaf mottling and stunted growth. A number of viruses cause this type of disease, for example, tobacco mosaic virus. Transmission of the disease may be via aphids or by mechanical contact. Control may be achieved by use of INSECTICIDES and by careful cultivation techniques.

**MOSAIC,** ancient mode of decorating surfaces (mainly floors and walls) by inlaying small pieces of colored stone, marble, or glass, fitted together to form a design. Greek pebble mosaics survive from about 400 BC. There are fine Roman mosaics at Pompeii near Naples and outstanding Byzantine examples may be seen in Ravenna, Italy. American Indian stone mosaics have been found at Chichén Itza in Mexico.

**MOSCA, Gaetano** (1858–1941), Italian politician and jurist who held that all governments are run by entrenched elitist groups and that majority rule is therefore a myth. His ideas, set out in *The Ruling Class* (1896) and other writings, were distorted to suit apologists of FASCISM.

**MOSCONI, Willie** 1923–        ), US pocket billiards champion. He won his first world title in 1941, and captured 13 thereafter. He set several world records, including high average and high run.

**MOSCOW ART THEATER,** influential Russian repertory theater famed for its ensemble acting and its introduction of new techniques in stage realism. Founded in 1897 by Konstantin STANISLAVSKY and Vladimir NEMIROVICH-DANCHENKO, it introduced plays by such authors as CHEKHOV and GORKI.

**MOSCOW** (Moskava), capital of the Soviet Union (USSR) and of the Russian Soviet Federated Socialist Republic, administrative center of Moscow region, on both banks of the Moskva R. It is the USSR's largest city, and its political, cultural, commercial, industrial and communications center. Some leading industries are chemicals, textiles, wood products and a wide range of heavy machinery including aircraft and automobiles. Moscow became the capital of all Russia under IVAN IV in the 16th century. Superseded by St. Petersburg (now LENINGRAD) in 1713, it regained its former status in 1918, following the Russian Revolution. At the city's heart is the KREMLIN, location of the headquarters of government and containing notable architectural relics of tsarist Russia. Immediately east of the Kremlin, from which wide boulevards radiate in all directions, lies Red Square, the site of parades and celebrations, overlooked by the Lenin Mausoleum and St. Basil's Cathedral. Among outstanding cultural and educational institutions are the BOLSHOI THEATER, the MOSCOW ART THEATER, the Maly Theater, Moscow University, the Academy of Sciences, the Tchaikovsky Conservatory and the Lenin State Library. Pop 8,099,000.

**MOSES** (c13th century BC), Hebrew lawgiver and prophet who led the Israelites out of Egypt. According to the Bible, the infant Moses, hidden to save him from being killed, was found and raised by the pharaoh's daughter. After killing a tyrannical Egyptian, he fled to the desert. From a burning bush, God ordered him to return and demand the Israelites' freedom under threat of the PLAGUES. On PASSOVER night Moses led them out of Egypt (the "exodus"); the Red Sea was parted to let them cross. On Mt. Sinai he received the TEN COMMANDMENTS. After years of ruling the wandering Israelites in the wilderness, Moses died within sight of the promised land. Traditionally he was the author of the PENTATEUCH.

**MOSES, Grandma** (Anna Mary Robertson Moses; 1860–1961), US artist of the so-called primitive style. Self-taught, she began painting at age 76 and won wide popularity with her lively, unpretentious pictures of rural life in the upstate N.Y. of her youth.

**MOSES, Robert** (1888–1981), US administrator who helped plan the N.Y. state and city parks and parkways and the N.Y. World's Fair (1964–65). He exercised sweeping authority to build bridges, tunnels and highways, often brushing aside objections from governors and mayors.

**MOSLEMS.** See MUSLIMS.

**MOSLEY, Sir Oswald Ernald** (1896–        ), British politician who formed (1932) the British Union of Fascists, popularly called the Blackshirts. He was interned during WWII. In 1948 he founded the extreme right-wing British Union Movement.

**MOSQUE,** Muslim place of worship. The name derives from the Arabic *masjid*, meaning "a place for prostration" (in prayer). Mosques are typically built with one or more MINARETS; a courtyard with fountains or wells for ceremonial washing; an area where the faithful assemble for prayers led by the *imam* (priest); a *mihrah* (niche) indicating the direction (*qiblah*) of MECCA; a *mimbar* (pulpit) and sometimes, facing it, a *maqsurah* (enclosed area for important persons). Some mosques include a *madrash* (religious school). (See also ISLAM; ISLAMIC ART AND ARCHITECTURE.)

**MOSQUITOES,** two-winged flies of the family Culicidae, with penetrating, sucking mouthparts. The females of many species feed on vertebrate blood, using their needle-like stylets to puncture a blood capillary, but usually only when about to lay eggs. The males, and the females at other times, feed on sugary liquids such as nectar. Both the larvae and pupae are entirely aquatic, breathing through spiracles at the tip of the abdomen. In all but the Anopheline mosquitoes, the spiracles are at the tip of a tubular siphon, and the larva's body is suspended from this below the surface film. Mosquitoes are involved in the transmission of many diseases in man including YELLOW FEVER, FILARIASIS, and MALARIA.

**MOSSADEGH, Mohammed** (c1880–1967), Iranian prime minister (1951–53) who nationalized Iran's British-controlled oil industry. A subsequent boycott by foreign consumers brought Iran near to economic disaster, and Mossadegh was forced out of office and imprisoned (1953–56).

**MÖSSBAUER EFFECT**, the recoilless emission of GAMMA RAYS from certain CRYSTALS, discovered by Rudolf Ludwig Mössbaue (1929– ) in 1957. When gamma rays are emitted from most nuclei, the latter recoil to a variable extent, giving the emitted PHOTONS a broad ENERGY spectrum. Mössbauer found that certain crystals, e.g. Fe$^{57}$, recoiled as a whole, i.e., their effective recoil was negligible. Gamma rays of closely specified frequency are thus produced and can be used for nuclear clocks and for testing RELATIVITY theory predictions.

**MOSSES**, large group of plants belonging to the class Musci, of the division BRYOPHYTA. Each moss plant consists of an erect "stem" to which primitive "leaves" are attached. The plants are anchored by root-like rhizoids. Mosses have worldwide distribution and are usually found in woods and other damp habitats. They are often early colonizers of bare soil and play an important role in preventing soil erosion. SPHAGNUM debris is an important constituent of PEAT. (See also ALTERNATION OF GENERATIONS; HORNWORTS; LIVERWORTS.)

**MOSTEL, Zero** (1915–1977), US actor noted for his comic portrayals. He enjoyed great success on Broadway, as Leopold Bloom in *Ulysses in Nightown* (1958) and as Tevye in *Fiddler on the Roof* (1964). His films include *A Funny Thing Happened on the Way to the Forum* (1966) and *The Producers* (1968).

**MOTET**, polyphonic vocal music, usually unaccompanied, which has occupied a place in sacred services, largely Roman Catholic, analogous to that of the Protestant ANTHEM. Like the MADRIGAL, its secular counterpart, the motet reached its zenith in the 16th and 17th centuries. Notable composers of motets include PALESTRINA and BACH.

**MOTHER GOOSE**, fictitious character to whose authorship many collections of fairy tales and nursery rhymes have been ascribed. The name seems to have been first associated with Charles PERRAULT'S *Tales of Mother Goose* (1697).

**MOTHER-OF-PEARL**, or **nacre**, the iridescent substance of which PEARLS and the inner coating of bivalved mollusk shells are made. It consists of alternate thin layers of aragonite (CALCIUM carbonate) and conchiolin, a horny substance. Valued for its beauty, it is used in thin sheets for ornament, jewelry and for buttons.

**MOTHER'S DAY**, holiday observed in the US on the second Sunday in May to honor motherhood. It was officially recognized by Congress in 1914. Similar days of remembrance are observed in Canada, Australia and Britain.

**MOTHERWELL, Robert** (1915– ), US painter and theoretician, a leading exponent of ABSTRACT EXPRESSIONISM. His work is characterized by restrained colors and large indefinite shapes.

**MOTHS**, insects which, together with the BUTTERFLIES, constitute the order LEPIDOPTERA. The differences between moths and butterflies are not clearly defined. Butterflies usually fly by day and rest with the wings raised over the back. Moths are mostly nocturnal and rest with the wings outspread. The antennae of butterflies are usually simple and end in a knob; this is rare in moths, where the antennae, at least in the males, are often feathery. This confers powerful long-range scent perception. In many species females produce "pheromones"—chemical sexual attractants. The males can detect even a single molecule of this, sensing females as far as 1.6km (1mi) away. In many species, melanistic forms (see MELANISM) have developed or increased in numbers in industrial areas. Darker coloration provides a better camouflage against birds on the blackened trees of these regions, an example of evolution in progress.

**MOTION PICTURES**, a succession of photographs projected rapidly onto a screen to create the illusion of continuous movement. Modern "movies" project 24 frames per second. Film may be 8mm, 16mm, 35mm or 70mm wide and may have a sound track (see SOUND RECORDING).

Research into persistence of vision, using drawings, in the 19th century, and the development of photography, culminated in Thomas EDISON'S Kinetoscope (1894), a peep show version of the movies. Projection of motion pictures, using Edison's Vitascope (1896), was a success in vaudeville. Static camera work soon gave way to the creative use of both camera and film-editing processes and in 1903 Edwin S. Porter exploited these in the one-reel narrative film, *The Great Train Robbery*. The success of this movie helped establish NICKELODEONS in the US, and this led in turn to the building of movie palaces. By 1913 the American film industry was established, aimed at satisfying a mass popular craving. Independent producers moved to Cal. to escape the power of distribution trusts. Cecil B. DE MILLE's *The Squaw Man* (1914) and Mack Sennett's comedies helped finance the establishment of the Hollywood studios. D. W. GRIFFITH was the creative genius of the era. From 1908, he explored the possibilities of film and created "stars" to increase the appeal of his work. He made the first feature length films (1913), and his epics *The Birth of a Nation* (1915) and *Intolerance* (1917) are considered landmarks of cinema history. WWI had stopped film production in Europe, but afterwards German cinema attained influence with films such as *The Cabinet of Dr. Caligari* (1919), and the work of G. W. PABST and Fritz LANG. Russia's Sergei EISENSTEIN and the Scandinavians Carl Dreyer and Victor Sjorström were among those directors who achieved major reputations in a medium which, despite the employment of many technicians, writers and actors, is ultimately controlled artistically by the director and film editor—except in the case of a few extraordinarily creative producers such as David O. SELZNICK and Irving THALBERG.

The use of motion pictures for other than narrative purposes was established early. Newsreels were produced by Charles PATHÉ in Paris by 1909; Robert FLAHERTY's *Nanook of the North* (1922) consolidated the appeal of documentary films; cartoons became popular features of cinema programs, especially after Walt DISNEY created Mickey Mouse in the late 1920s.

The coming of sound in *The Jazz Singer*, 1927, briefly set film back as an art: the camera was immobilized, but regained its fluidity when sound techniques were improved and it was realized that sound was merely a useful adjunct. Color techniques were finally established with such films as *The Wizard of Oz* (1939) and the epic *Gone With the Wind* (1939), among the first in which color was an integral part of the effect and not a mere novelty. After WWII the industry experimented with Cinerama, Cinemascope, Vista Vision and even 3-D, but cinema still achieved its most powerful results with techniques of editing and photography used since the silent era.

The great age of Hollywood (1930–1950) occurred partly because of its ability to provide cheap entertainment during the Depression and because of the dominance of totalitarian censorship, which crippled filmmaking in much of Europe (Lang and von STERNBERG were among those who fled to America). The Western and the musical were recognized as uniquely successful North American film genres. The British film industry produced notable successes under Alexander KORDA's production and Alfred HITCHCOCK's direction, while French directors René CLAIR and Jean RENOIR were among the most acclaimed of the era.

Since WWII the split has grown between "art" and popular film. Distribution has become more truly international. Television has drastically reduced audiences for all but a few films, and producers try to win them back by producing wide-screen spectaculars or specific-appeal films, whether the appeal is violence, sex or intellectual content. Yet film distribution has become more truly international. Directors such as FELLINI, DE SICA, Satyajit RAY, KUROSAWA, ROSSELINI BUÑEL, TRUFFAUT and Ingmar BERGMAN have made exciting contributions to cinematic art. Hollywood's dominance has been superseded by many independent productions worldwide, and the vigor and popularity of film, both as art and as entertainment, continues unabated, despite competition from television.

**MOTION SICKNESS,** nausea and VOMITING caused by rhythmic movements of the body, particularly the head, set up in automobile, train, ship or airplane travel. In susceptible people, neither stimulation of the EAR labyrinths nor their action on the vomiting centers in the BRAIN stem are adequately suppressed. Hyoscine and phenothiazines can prevent it if taken before travel.

**MOTLEY, John Lothrop** (1814–1877), US historian known for his books on Dutch history, *The Rise of the Dutch Republic* (1856) and *History of the United Netherlands* (1860–67). He was also sent as a diplomat to Russia, Austria and England.

**MOTOR, Electric,** a device converting electrical into mechanical energy. Traditional forms are based on the FORCE experienced by a current-carrying wire in a magnetic field (see ELECTROMAGNETISM). Motors can be, and sometimes are, run in reverse as GENERATORS.

Simple direct-current (see ELECTRICITY) motors consist of a magnet or ELECTROMAGNET (the *stator*) and a coil (the *rotor*) which turns when a current is passed through it because of the force between the current and the stator field. So that the force keeps the same sense as the rotor turns, the current to the rotor is supplied via a *commutator*—a slip ring broken into two semicircular parts, to each of which one end of the coil is connected, so that the current direction is reversed twice each revolution.

For use with alternating-current supplies, small DC motors are often still suitable, but **induction motors** are preferred for heavier duty. In the simplest of these, there is no electrical contact with the rotor, which consists of a cylindrical array of copper bars welded to end rings. The stator field, generated by more than one set of coils, is made to rotate at the supply frequency, including (see INDUCTION, ELECTROMAGNETIC) currents in the rotor when (under load) it rotates more slowly, these in turn producing a force accelerating the rotor. Greater control of the motor speed and torque can be obtained in "wound rotor" types in which the currents induced in coils wound on the rotor are controlled by external resistances connected via slip-ring contacts.

In applications such as electric clocks, **synchronous motors**, which rotate exactly in step with the supply frequency, are used. In these the rotor is usually a permanent magnet dragged round by the rotating stator field, the induction-motor principle being used to start the motor.

The above designs can all be opened out to form **linear motors** producing a lateral rather than rotational drive. The induction type is the most suitable, a plate analogous to the rotor being driven with respect to a stator generating a laterally moving field. Such motors have a wide range of possible applications, from operating sliding doors to driving trains, being much more robust than rotational drive systems, and offering no resistance to manual operation in the event of power cuts. A form of DC linear motor can be used to pump conducting liquids such as molten metals, the force being generated between a current passed through the liquid and a static magnetic field around it.

**MOTORBOATING,** the recreational or competitive sport of driving a motorboat. Motorboats are usually powered by one or more internal combustion engines, driving submerged propellers, and can travel up to 175mph. Smaller motorboats, between 10ft and 20ft long, are usually powered by outboard motors and are known as runabouts. They usually have "planing" or "gliding" hulls which enable the boat to skim across the water with its bow in the air, thus reducing water resistance and allowing high speeds to be achieved. Whereas runabouts have seating facilities only, the larger inboard cruisers, 20ft to 60ft long, are often fitted with luxurious cabins. Motorboat design first evolved in 1885 and in 1887 Gottlieb DAIMLER built a gasoline-powered motorboat. Jet-propelled speed boats have also been designed and have attained speeds of more than 300mph.

**MOTORCYCLE,** a motorized bicycle, first developed in 1885 by Gottlieb DAIMLER. The engine of a motorcycle may be either two-stroke or four-stroke and is usually air cooled. Chain drive is almost universal. In lightweight machines, ignition is often achieved by means of a MAGNETO inside the flywheel. Motorcycles were first widely used by despatch riders in WWI. Between the wars, the motorcycle industry was dominated by simple, heavy British designs. After WWII, Italy also developed the motor scooter, designed for convenience and economy, with 150cc two-stroke engines. In the 1960s the Japanese introduced a series of highly sophisticated, lightweight machines, which are now seen all over the world. (See IGNITION SYSTEM; INTERNAL COMBUSTION ENGINE.)

**MOTOWN,** name of the first major black recording company, founded in Detroit (the "Motor Town") in 1960. Such stars as Stevie WONDER, The Jackson Five, and Diana ROSS began their careers as Motown singers.

**MOTT, Lucretia Coffin** (1793–1880), US reformer who was one of the first pioneers of women's rights. A Quaker by religion, she founded the Philadelphia Female Anti-Slavery Society (1833), and with Elizabeth STANTON organized the first women's rights convention at Seneca Falls, N.Y., in 1848.

**MOULIN ROUGE,** a Paris music hall. It was opened in 1889 in Montmartre, a section of Paris renowned for its night life. It became the favorite haunt of the painter and lithographer TOULOUSE-LAUTREC, whose posters of its dancers and habitués soon made the Moulin Rouge the rage of Paris. A hall bearing the name remains in Paris today.

**MOUNTAIN,** a landmass elevated substantially above its surroundings. The difference between a mountain and a hill is essentially one of size: the exact borderline is not clearly defined. Plateaus, or table-mountains, unlike most other mountains, have a large summit area as compared with that of their base. Most mountains occur in groups, ranges or chains (see also MASSIF). The processes involved in mountain building are termed orogenesis. OROGENIES can largely be explained in terms of the theory of PLATE TECTONICS. Thus the Andes have formed where the Nazca oceanic plate is being subducted beneath (forced under) the South American continental plate, and the Himalayas have arisen at the meeting of two continental plates.

Mountains are traditionally classified as Volcanic, Block or Folded. **Volcanic mountains** occur where LAVA and other debris (e.g., PYROCLASTIC ROCKS) build up a dome around the vent of a VOLCANO. They are found in certain well-defined belts around the world, marking plate margins. **Block mountains** occur where land has been uplifted between FAULTS in a way akin to that leading to the formation of RIFT VALLEYS. **Folded mountains** occur through deformations of the EARTH's crust (see FOLD), especially in geosynclinal areas (see GEOSYNCLINE), where vast quantities of sediments whose weight causes deformation, accumulate (see also SEDIMENTATION). EROSION eventually reduces all mountains to plains. But it may also play a part in the creation of mountains, as where most of an elevated stretch of land has been eroded away, leaving a few resistant outcrops of rock (see MONADNOCK).

**MOUNTAIN LION.** See PUMA.

**MOUNTAIN MEN,** pioneer fur trappers and traders in the Rockies in the 1820s and 1830s. Early mountain men included John COLTER, who stayed in the area after the LEWIS AND CLARK EXPEDITION of 1804–06, Thomas Fitzpatrick, Jedediah SMITH and W. S. WILLIAMS. Many mountain men, including James BRIDGER took part in William ASHLEY's expedition up the Missouri R in 1822. The mountain men were the first to begin opening up the Rockies and make the area's potential known. They were quickly followed by the big fur companies such as the Rocky Mountain Fur Company and the American Fur Company.

**MOUNTAIN SHEEP.** See BIGHORN.

**MOUNTBATTEN, Louis Francis Albert Victor Nicholas, 1st Earl Mountbatten of Burma** (1900–1979), British admiral and statesman. In WWII he was supreme allied commander in SE Asia and liberated Burma from the Japanese. After WWII he was the last British viceroy of India, and led the negotiations for India's and Pakistan's independence. He later served as first sea lord, admiral of the fleet and chief of the defense staff. He was killed by Irish Republican Army terrorists.

**MOUNT SAINT HELENS,** active volcano in the Cascade Range of SW Wash. Long considered dormant, the volcano became seismically active in Mar. 1980 and erupted for the first time in 120 years on May 18, 1980. The eruption was preceded by two magnitude 5 earthquakes (see RICHTER SCALE) and was the first in the 48 conterminous states since Mt Lassen erupted in 1915. More than 60 people were killed, and there were widespread floods and mudslides. Surrounding forests were scorched or devastated and much of Wash., Ore., Ida. and Mont. were blanketed with volcanic ash.

**MOUNT VERNON,** the restored Georgian home (1747–99) of George WASHINGTON on the Potomac R in Va., S of Washington. The tomb of Washington and his wife Martha is nearby.

**MOUSE,** a term applied loosely to almost any small RODENT. The majority however fall into two groups: Old World mice, family Muridae, and New World mice of the family Cricetidae. Very active animals, often nocturnal, they are characteristically shortlived. Feeding on berries and grain, they are, in terms of biomass, extremely important herbivores, and in turn important as prey for many birds and mammals.

**MOVIES:** See MOTION PICTURES.

**Official name:** People's Republic of Mozambique
**Capital:** Maputo
**Area:** 303,070sq mi
**Population:** 10,270,000
**Languages:** Portuguese, Bantu languages
**Religions:** Animist, Christian, Muslim
**Monetary unit(s):** 1 metical = 100 centavos

**MOZAMBIQUE,** republic in SE Africa on the Indian Ocean between Tanzania and South Africa. A hot, humid coastal plain and low plateaus cover about two-thirds of the country, rising to mountainous regions in the N and W. Most of the coastal plain is infertile except in the Zambezi, Save, Limpopo and small river areas.

**People.** The population comprises over 60 Bantu tribes and a small group with African-Portuguese ancestry. There are some Europeans and Asians, though their numbers have sharply decreased since independence.

**Economy.** Mozambique is a poor country, almost completely dependent on agriculture, including forestry, fishing and hunting. Main exports are cashews, seafood and cotton. The government has encouraged collective farming; in the late 1970s drought created acute food shortages. The economy also suffered at that time as a result of Mozambique's support for Zimbabwe nationalists during the Rhodesian war. Good relations with Zimbabwe and the expansion of port facilities are expected to increase Mozambique's trade and transport opportunities. Although Mozambique is ideologically opposed to its neighbor, South Africa, the countries have strong economic and commercial ties.

**History.** The first European to reach Mozambique was VASCO DA GAMA (1498). During the 1500s and 1600s the Portuguese set up small trading settlements. From the mid-18th until the early-19th century their great source of wealth was the black slave trade. Mozambique became a Portuguese colony in 1910 and Portugal placed controls on its economic growth and the Africans' social advancement. In 1962 the Mozambique nationalists formed the Mozambique Liberation Front (Frelimo) which engaged in fierce guerrilla warfare with Portuguese troops for 1964–74. After the 1974 coup in Portugal negotiations led to the formation in June 1975 of an independent socialist republic in Mozambique. Since independence, elements hostile to the government have committed sporadic sabotage.

**MOZART, Wolfgang Amadeus** (1756–1791), Austrian composer whose brief career produced some of the world's greatest music. He was a child prodigy of the harpsichord, violin and organ at the age of four and toured the European courts. He soon became a prodigious composer. Between 1771–81 he was concertmaster to the archbishop of Salzburg. Much of Mozart's early music is in a pure and elegant classical style, which is also extremely lively and spontaneous. In 1781 he moved to Vienna where he became Court Composer to Joseph II, in 1787. He became a close friend of HAYDN and set DA PONTE's opera librettos *The Marriage of Figaro* (1786) and *Don Giovanni* (1787) to music. In a three-month period during 1788 he wrote three of his greatest symphonies, numbers 39–41. Mozart wrote over 600 works, including 50 symphonies, over 20 operas, nearly 30 piano concertos, 27 string quartets, about 40 violin sonatas and many other instrumental pieces. In all these genres his work shows great expressive beauty and technical mastery, and he advanced the styles and musical forms of each.

**MUBARAK, Hosni** (1928–    ), president of Egypt (1981–    ). A graduate of Egypt's military academy, he was trained as a bomber pilot and rose in rank to air force chief of staff (1969) and air force commander (1972). He launched the surprise air attack in the 1973 war with Israel. Chosen by President Sadat to be Egypt's vice president in 1975, Mubarak thereafter concentrated his attention on domestic and international affairs. He became president, by public referendum, after Sadat was assassinated.

**MUCKRAKERS**, term coined in 1906 by President Theodore Roosevelt to condemn journalists specializing in sensational exposés of corrupt businesses and political procedures. The name was adopted by a group of contemporary reformist writers and journalists. The "Muckrakers" included Lincoln STEFFENS who wrote about political corruption, Ida TARBELL who exposed the exploitative practices of an enormous oil company, and Upton SINCLAIR who uncovered deplorable conditions in the Chicago meat-packing industry.

**MUGWUMPS**, term for independent voters, or sometimes political fence straddlers. Particularly used for Republicans who voted for Democrat Grover CLEVELAND in 1884.

**MUHAMMAD, Elijah** (1897–1975), US Black Muslim leader. In 1931 he met Wali "Prophet" Farad, founder of the first Temple of Islam in Detroit, Mich. Elijah became a prominent disciple and on Farad's disappearance (1934) became leader of the movement. He advocated black separatism.

**MUHAMMAD ALI.** See ALI, MUHAMMAD.

**MUIR, John** (1838–1914), Scottish-American naturalist and writer, an advocate of US forest conservation. He described his walking journeys in the NW US and Alaska in many influential articles and books. Yosemite and Sequoia national parks and MUIR WOODS NATIONAL MONUMENT were established as a result of his efforts.

**MUIR WOODS NATIONAL MONUMENT**, a park of 503 acres 15mi NW of San Francisco, Cal., established in 1908 to preserve a large stand of virgin coastal redwoods (*Sequoia sempervirens*) some of which are more than 2,000 years old.

**MUKDEN.** See SHENYANG.

MULATTO, person with one Negro and one white parent; often used to describe a person of mixed Negro and Caucasian ancestry. A child of a true mulatto and a white was traditionally called a quadroon (one-quarter Negro ancestry).

MULE, a term now commonly used to describe infertile hybrids between various species. The name is properly restricted to the offspring of a male DONKEY and a mare. Mules have the shape and size of a HORSE, and the long ears and small hooves of a donkey. They are favored for their endurance and surefootedness as draft or pack animals. (See also HINNY.)

MULLIGAN, Gerry (Gerald Joseph Mulligan; 1927– ), US jazz musician. Technically accomplished rather than just intuitive, he played baritone saxophone and piano for many leading JAZZ bands after WWII, formed a pianoless quartet in 1952 and arranged and composed pieces with a new tone color.

MULLIN, Willard (1908–1978), US sports cartoonist whose work appeared in the New York World Telegram six days a week from 1934 to 1966. He created the Brooklyn Bum, the character who came to symbolize the Brooklyn Dodgers baseball team. The National Cartoonist Society cited Mullin as "Sports Cartoonist of the Century."

MULTINATIONAL COMPANY, business organization that owns manufacturing facilities or other types of enterprises in more than one country. Since the end of WWII the economic power of such firms—usually giant corporations—has grown enormously. Direct US investment overseas, for example, increased from a nominal amount in the 1930s to $192 billion in 1979. The growing power of multinationals has long been a controversial issue. They are recognized as a positive force in enlarging job opportunities and improving the industrial structures of the countries where they operate. But they are also accused of acting in their own interests rather than those of their host countries, and some US multinationals have been charged with corruption in dealing with foreign governments. A few host countries—notably, Canada and Australia—have adopted strict legislation to regulate the movement of foreign investment in their economies.

MULTIPLE BIRTH, the delivery of more than one child at the end of PREGNANCY. Twins, the commonest type of multiple birth, are of two distinct varieties. Monozygotic or identical twins originate in a single fertilized egg (zygote) which divides, each half (containing identical genetic material) developing independently into EMBRYO and FETUS, although they may share a common PLACENTA. Dizygotic or nonidentical twins originate in the release of two eggs at ovulation (see MENSTRUATION), each being fertilized, implanting (see IMPLANTATION) and developing separately. There is no more relation between their GENES than between those of other siblings. Higher orders of multiple births (triplets, quadruplets, quintuplets, etc.) usually arise from multiple ovulation and are rare unless ovarian follicle stimulants (e.g., GONADOTROPHINS) have been used in the treatment of infertility; here the dosage is critical. Multiple pregnancy may run in families. Prematurity, toxemia, ANEMIA and other complications are more common in multiple pregnancy.

MULTIPLE INDEPENDENTLY TARGETED REENTRY VEHICLE (MIRV), a missile with the capability of shooting at many targets. MIRVs contain payloads, consisting of two or more warheads, in their final stage or "bus." Upon ejection, the warheads follow a pre-programmed set course. Each can be directed toward a different target. The first US MIRVs were tested in 1968. Currently the US MIRV arsenal consists of land-based Minuteman IIIs and submarine-based Poseidons and Tridents. The proposed MX (missile experimental), a MIRV device, will carry 10 nuclear warheads.

MULTIPLE SCLEROSIS, or disseminated sclerosis, a relatively common disease of the BRAIN and SPINAL CORD in which MYELIN is destroyed in plaques of INFLAMMATION. Its cause is unknown although slow VIRUSES, abnormal ALLERGY to viruses and abnormalities of FATS are suspected. It may affect any age group, but particularly young adults. Symptoms and signs indicating disease in widely separate parts of the NERVOUS SYSTEM are typical. They occur episodically, often with intervening recovery or improvement. Blurring of VISION, sometimes with EYE pain; double vision; VERTIGO; abnormal sensations in the limbs; PARALYSIS; ATAXIA, and BLADDER disturbance are often seen, although individually these can occur in other brain diseases. STEROIDS, certain DIETARY FOODS, and DRUGS acting on spasticity in muscles and the bladder are valuable in some cases. The course of the disease is extremely variable, some subjects having but a few mild attacks, while others progress rapidly to permanent disability and dependency.

MUMFORD, Lewis (1895– ), US social critic and historian, concerned with the relationship between man and his environment, especially in urban planning. His books include *The Brown Decades* (1931), *The Culture of Cities* (1934), *The City in History* (1961) and *The Pentagon of Power* (1971).

**MUMPS**, common VIRUS infection causing swelling of the parotid salivary GLAND, and occasionally INFLAMMATION of the PANCREAS, an OVARY or a TESTIS. Mild FEVER, HEADACHE and malaise may precede the gland swelling. Rarely a viral MENINGITIS and less often ENCEPHALITIS complicates mumps. Very rarely a bilateral and severe testicular inflammation can cause STERILITY.

**MUNCH, Charles** (1891–1968), French orchestra conductor. He conducted the Paris Conservatory orchestra (1936–46) and, the Boston (Mass.) Symphony orchestra (1949–62), and was director of its Berkshire Music Center (1951–62).

**MUNCH, Edvard** (1863–1944), Norwegian painter and printmaker. His work foreshadowed EXPRESSIONISM and was influential in the development of modern art. His powerful, often anguished pictures show his obsession with the themes of love, death and loneliness.

**MÜNCHHAUSEN, Karl Friedrich Hieronymus, Freiherr von** (1720–1797), German soldier and country gentleman. His exaggerated adventure tales were the basis of fantastic "tall tales" compiled by R. E: Raspe, published in London (1785). These stories became widely popular. The English *Adventures of Baron Munchhausen* (1793) is the standard edition.

**MUNICH**, capital of Bavaria, West Germany, on the Isar R about 30mi N of the Alps. A cultural center with a cathedral and palace, it is also heavily industrialized (beer, textiles, publishing), and is Germany's third largest city. Founded in 1158 by Duke Henry the Lion, it was ruled 1255–1918 by the Wittelsbach family (dukes and kings of Bavaria). Munich was the birthplace and headquarters of NATIONAL SOCIALISM and the scene of Hitler's attempted "beer hall putsch" of 1923. Munich hosted the 1972 OLYMPIC GAMES. Pop 1,299,700.

**MUNICH AGREEMENT**, a pact, signed Sept. 30, 1938, prior to WWII, which forced Czechoslovakia to surrender its SUDETENLAND to Nazi Germany. The Sudetenland in W Czechoslovakia contained much of the nation's industry, about 700,000 Czechs as well as 3 million German-speaking citizens, the pretext for Hitler's demands for occupation. The agreement, which allowed an immediate German takeover, was signed by Adolph

HITLER, Neville CHAMBERLAIN (Britain), Edouard DALADIER (France) and Benito MUSSOLINI (Italy). Neither the Czechs no their Russian allies were consulted. The Allies hoped this would be Hitler's "las territorial claim," and that the pact woul avert war, but in March 1939 he occupie the rest of Czechoslovakia.

**MUÑOZ MARÍN, Luis** (1898–1980), Puerto Rican political leader, the firs elected governor of the island (1948–64) founder of the Popular Democratic Part (1938). Elected to the legislature in 1932 he favored social reforms and ties with th US. He led the campaign for Puerto Rica self-government status, achieved in 1952.

**MUNRO, Hector Hugh** (pseudonym, Saki 1870–1916), British writer, known for hi inventive, satirical and often fantastic shor stories. Among his published works ar stories collected in *Reginald* (1904) an *Beasts and Super-Beasts* (1914) and novel, *The Unbearable Bassington* (1912).

**MUNSEY, Frank Andrew** (1854–1925) US newspaper publisher. *Munsey' Magazine* (founded 1889) pioneered cheap illustrated mass circulation periodicals. H also built a profitable empire based o prominent New York City daily papers.

**MÜNZER, Thomas** (c1490–1525), radica German Protestant reformer. Originally follower of LUTHER, he preached revolutio and the establishment of a godl communistic state. He was executed as leader of the PEASANTS' WAR (1524–25).

**MUPPETS**, a cross between marionette and puppets created by Jim HENSON. The first achieved wide popularity as regulars o the PBS education program *Sesame Stree* in the 1970s and from 1976 appeared in th successful TV series *The Muppet Show* The enormous cast of cloth-covere characters includes an everyman, Kerm the Frog, and the flamboyant, Ma West-like Miss Piggy.

**MURAL PAINTING**, any kind of paintin executed on a wall. The earliest are the cav paintings of reindeer and bison at ALTAMIRA Spain, and LASCAUX, France, which wer probably a form of magic to Paleolith man. Early Roman FRESCO murals wer found in POMPEII. Wall paintings of sacre subjects were the chief form of religiou instruction in the Byzantine Empir medieval Europe and India. The fresc technique was adopted by Italian artists lik GIOTTO at Padua and Assisi, MICHELANGEL for the ceiling of the SISTINE CHAPEL an TIEPOLO in N Italian palaces, and also by th 20th-century Mexican artist OROZCO.

**MURASAKI, Shikibu** (c978–1026? Japanese court lady and author of *Gen*

Monogatari, or the *Tale of Genji*, the greatest Japanese classic and probably the world's first novel.

**MURAT, Joachim** (1767–1815), French marshal under Napoleon Bonaparte and king of Naples 1808–15. Murat gained his reputation as a brilliant cavalry leader in the Italian and Egyptian campaigns (1796–99), and contributed to French successes in the NAPOLEONIC WARS. He married Napoleon's sister Caroline. As king of Naples he fostered the beginnings of Italian nationalism. Although he joined the Allies in 1814, he supported Napoleon during the HUNDRED DAYS, and was executed after an attempt to recapture Naples.

**MURCHISON, Clinton Williams** (1895–1969), US businessman who made a fortune exploiting Texas oil and natural gas in the 1920s. A man with a Midas touch, he diversified his holdings and investments and eventually controlled more than 115 companies with assets of $600 million.

**MURCHISON FALLS**, famous waterfall in the Victoria Nile R, 20mi E of Lake Albert, NW Uganda. Discovered in the mid-1860s, it is 130ft high and is the central attraction of Kabarega National Park.

**MURDOCH, (Jean) Iris** (1919–    ), Irish-born British novelist. Her novels such as *Under the Net* (1954), *A Severed Head* (1961), *The Red and the Green* (1965), *A Fairly Honourable Defeat* (1970) and *Henry Cato* (1976) display wit and a gift for analyzing human relations.

**MURILLO, Bartolomé Estéban** (1618–1682), Spanish BAROQUE painter, known as the "Raphael of Seville." The most famous painter of his time in Spain, Murillo produced religious narrative scenes expressing deep piety and gentleness, works of realism and fine portraits. Among his many famous paintings are the *Visions of St. Anthony*, the *Two Trinities* (known as the *Holy Family*) and *Beggar Boy*.

**MURNAU, Friedrich Wilhelm** (1889–1931), German motion picture director, born Friedrich Wilhelm Plumpe. A pioneer in camera technique, he used close-ups to further action and to interpret mood and emotion. His films included *Nosferatu* (1922), *The Last Laugh* (1924) and *Tabu* (1931) with co-director Robert FLAHERTY.

**MURRAY, George Gilbert Aimé** (1866–1957), British classical scholar, best known for his translations of ancient Greek playwrights. He actively promoted the LEAGUE OF NATIONS.

**MURRAY, Philip** (1886–1952), Scottish-born US labor leader. President of the CONGRESS OF INDUSTRIAL ORGANIZATIONS (CIO) from 1940; prominent leader of the UNITED MINE WORKERS, 1912–42; organizer and head of the UNITED STEELWORKERS from 1942. In 1949–50 he helped rid the CIO of communist unions.

**MURRAY RIVER**, chief river of Australia; an important source of irrigation. It rises in the mountains of New South Wales and flows for 1,609mi, passing through Hume reservoir and Lake Victoria, on to Encounter Bay on the Indian Ocean.

**MURROW, Edward R.** (Edward Egbert Roscoe Murrow; 1908–1965), US broadcaster. He was head of Columbia Broadcasting System's European bureau during WWII; from 1947–60 he produced many acclaimed radio and TV programs, including an exposé of Senator Joseph MCCARTHY (1954). He directed the US INFORMATION AGENCY 1961–63.

**MUSCLE**, the tissue whose contraction produces body movement. In man and other vertebrates there are three types of muscle. **Skeletal or striated muscle** is the type normally associated with the movement of the body. Its action can either be initiated voluntarily, through the central NERVOUS SYSTEM, or it can respond to REFLEX mechanisms. Under the microscope this muscle is seen to be striped or striated. It consists of cylinders of tissue 0.01mm in diameter, showing great variation in length (1–150mm) and containing many nuclei. Each cylinder consists of thousands of filaments, each bathed in cytoplasm (known as sarcoplasm) which is their source of nutrition. Energy for contraction is derived by the OXIDATION of GLUCOSE brought by the BLOOD and stored as granules of GLYCOGEN in the sarcoplasm. The oxidation and breakdown of the glucose takes place in the mitochondria (see CELL), the net result being the formation of adenosine triphosphate (ATP—see NUCLEOTIDES). This molecule provides a "high-energy" bond which enables actin and myosin, two proteins in the muscle filament, to slide into each other, an action which, repeated many times throughout the muscle, results in its contraction. The behavior of a particular fiber is governed by an "all-or-none" law, in that it will either contract completely or not at all. Therefore the extent to which a muscle contracts is dependent solely on the number of individual fibers contracting. If a muscle is starved of oxygen, a process termed GLYCOLYSIS provides the energy. However, glycolysis involves LACTIC ACID production with the consequent risk of CRAMP. Skeletal muscle functions by being attached via TENDONS to two parts of the SKELETON which move relative to each other. The larger attachment is known as the muscle's origin. Contraction of the muscle attempts to draw together the two parts of the skeleton. Muscles are arranged in antagonistic groups so that all movements involve the contraction of some muscles at the same time as their antagonists relax. **Smooth or involuntary muscle** is under the control of the autonomic nervous system and we are rarely aware of its action. Smooth muscle fibers are constructed in sheets of cells, each with a single nucleus. They are situated in hollow structures such as the gut, BRONCHI, uterus and BLOOD vessels. Smooth muscle uses the property of "tone" (continual slight tension) to regulate the diameter of tubes such as blood vessels. Being responsive to HORMONES, notably ADRENALINE, it can thus decrease blood supply to nonessential organs during periods of stress. In the gut, the muscle also propels the contents along by contracting along its length in waves (PERISTALSIS). **Cardiac muscle**, found only in the HEART, has the property of never resting throughout life. It combines features of both skeletal and smooth muscle, for it is striped but yet involuntary. The fibers are not discrete but branching and interlinked, thus enabling it to act quickly and in unison when stimulated.

**MUSCULAR DYSTROPHY**, a group of inherited DISEASES in which MUSCLE fibers are abnormal and undergo ATROPHY. Most develop in early life or adolescence. *Duchenne dystrophy* occurs in males although the genes for it are carried by females. It starts in early life and some swelling (pseudohypertrophy) of calf and other muscles may be seen. A similar disease can affect females. Other types, described by muscles mainly affected, include *limb-girdle* and *facio-scapulo-humeral* dystrophies. There are many diverse variants, largely due to structural or biochemical abnormalities in muscle fibers. *Myotonic dystrophy* occurs in older men, causing BALDNESS, CATARACTS, TESTIS atrophy and a characteristic myotonus, in which contraction is involuntarily sustained. Muscular dystrophies usually cause weakness and wasting of muscles, particularly of those close to and in the trunk; a waddling gait and exaggerated curvature of the lower spine are typical. The muscles of RESPIRATION may be affected, with resulting PNEUMONIA and respiratory failure; HEART muscle, too, can also be affected. These two factors in particular may lead to early death in severe cases. Mechanical aids, including, if necessary, ARTIFICIAL RESPIRATION, may greatly improve well-being, mobility and life-span.

**MUSES,** in Greek mythology, nine patron goddesses of the arts, worshiped especially near Mt HELICON. Daughters of ZEUS and the goddess of memory (MNEMOSYNE), they were attendants of APOLLO, god of poetry. The chief muse was Calliope (epic poetry); the others were Clio (history), Euterpe (lyric poetry), Thalia (comedy, pastoral poetry), Melpomene (tragedy), Terpsichore (choral dancing), Erato (love poetry), Polyhymnia (sacred song) and Urania (astronomy).

**MUSEUM,** institution that collects, preserves and exhibits objects—natural or manmade—for cultural and educational purposes. A museum was originally a place sacred to the MUSES; the most famous ancient museum, at Alexandria, Egypt (founded c280 BC), was a center for Greek scholars. Public museums did not exist in the ancient world or in medieval Europe; they developed from private Renaissance collections. The royal collections of works of art at the LOUVRE in Paris were made public in 1793, and the English physician and naturalist Sir Hans SLOANE's widely varied collections were bought by the British government which then opened the BRITISH MUSEUM (1759). In the late 19th and 20th centuries numerous public museums were established, tending to specialize in particular subjects or time periods. Museums and their collections are of several kinds: general, art and picture galleries, historical, scientific, natural history, outdoors, specialized (industrial, commercial or professional) and regional or local.

**MUSHROOM,** popular name given to many gill fungi or AGARICS. In general, mushrooms are considered to be edible, while poisonous or inedible agarics are called toadstools. The common field mushroom (*Agaricus campestris*) is the most frequent wild species eaten, while *Agaricus bisporus* is the cultivated mushroom. Some mushrooms are serious parasites of wood, plantation trees and garden plants. Although mainly eaten for their flavor, mushrooms are of some food value, containing 5% protein. (See also AMANITA; FUNGI.)

**MUSIAL, Stanley Frank** (1920–    ) known as "Stan the Man," famous US baseball player. A left-hand-hitting outfielder for the St. Louis Cardinals, he had a career batting average of .331 (1941–63) He was elected the National League's most valuable player three times, was its batting champion seven times and entered the Baseball Hall of Fame in 1969. His 3,630 hits set a league career record that stood until 1981. He also hit 475 home runs.

**MUSIC,** the art of arranging sound. Music cannot be defined merely as the art of arranging pleasing sounds; discords (see DISSONANCE) have long been used, and many modern composers experiment with almost any kind of sound.

One of the most important elements of western music is HARMONY, the interaction of tones. An elaborate theory and technique of harmony has been evolved and can be used to great effect by a skilled composer. Eastern music, however, has largely developed without harmony and tends to rely more on complex melodic or rhythmic structures, as in the Indian *raga* or *tala*. Here the performer's ability to improvise within the traditional musical framework is important. Chinese musical theory depends on a single note, the *huang chung*, from which arises a series of twelve notes (*lue*), each of which is the basis of a pentatonic SCALE. RHYTHM is the one element common to music of all cultures. Music probably grew up as a rhythmical accompaniment to man's natural urge to dance.

Music has existed in every culture, and often seems to have developed in conjunction with religion. Music was used in Sumerian temple ceremonies c4000 BC. The ancient Greeks used music for religious and dramatic purposes. The Romans made much use of music for ceremonial occasions. The early history of western music is largely that of church music, with secular music taking a significant but secondary place until the Renaissance. Modern NOTATION was developed by the Benedictine monk GUIDO D'ARREZO in the 11th century, allowing a complex musical tradition to evolve. The current repertoire consists largely of music written after 1600, divided roughly into RENAISSANCE, BAROQUE, CLASSICAL, ROMANTIC and modern styles. Recently this has been extended to cover much earlier music, music of other cultures and less traditionally "serious" forms such as JAZZ and BLUES, POP MUSIC and FOLK MUSIC. The last has grown up as a separate tradition from formal music (though interacting with it) in almost all cultures, and has been transmitted orally from generation to generation.

Many people have tried to evolve a philosophy of music, but none has ever satisfactorily explained its power to heighten feeling and to communicate on a deeper level than language. What is certain is that a liking for music in one form or another is one of mankind's most natural and universal instincts. (See also ATONALITY; COUNTERPOINT; HOMOPHONY; POLYPHONY; SOUND; TONALITY.)

**MUSICAL COMEDY,** stage play, often witty and sentimental, using song, dance and dialogue. Related to OPERETTA, VAUDEVILLE and musical revues, the "musical" was developed mainly in the US after 1900. Integral use of ballet was pioneered by Agnes DE MILLE. Landmarks in musicals include *Oklahoma!*, Jerome KERN's *Show Boat*, Irving BERLIN's *Annie Get Your Gun*, Leonard BERNSTEIN's *On the Town* and *West Side Story*. Notable book and music collaborators have included RODGERS and HART, RODGERS and HAMMERSTEIN, and LERNER and LOEWE. MOTION PICTURES have had great success adapting and creating musicals.

**MUSICAL NOTATION.** See NOTATION.

**MUSIL, Robert** (1880–1942), Austrian writer. He is known for *The Man without Qualities*, 3 vols., 1930–43, an encyclopedic novel about the ills of pre-war Austria.

**MUSK,** a strongly-scented substance used in the manufacture of perfume. The term is strictly applied to that obtained from the musk glands of the male MUSK DEER, but also covers other similar secretions, e.g., civet musk, badger musk.

**MUSKET,** smoothbore, muzzle-loaded FIREARM developed by the Spanish in the early 16th century; a heavier HARQUEBUS. It was not very accurate and was at first fired from a forked rest by two men. Later muskets were lighter and more satisfactory, but they were superseded by the RIFLE.

**MUSKIE, Edmund Sixtus** (1914– ), US political leader. He was governor of Maine (1954–58), then elected its first Democratic senator (1958– ). On the Democratic ticket with Hubert HUMPHREY, he ran for vice-president 1968; in 1972 his bid for the presidential nomination failed. In the Senate he espoused liberal and environmental causes. He left the Senate to serve as Jimmy Carter's secretary of state (1980–81).

**MUSKOGEAN,** one of the nine language families of the major North American Indian language group called Macro-Algonkian (see ALGONQUIAN). Muskogean has four languages. Today about 20,000 people speak the Choctaw, Chickasaw, Creek and Seminole dialects of Muskogean.

**MUSK-OX,** *Ovibos moschatus*, a heavily-built bovid from the Arctic of North America, not a true ox but related to sheep and goats. Musk-oxen have thick, shaggy coats and a pronounced hump over the shoulders. They are highly aggressive animals living in herds of up to 100. When threatened, herds form a circle of adults around the calves, with horns facing outward. Musk-oxen have always been hunted for their fur, but now they are also farmed commercially.

**MUSKRAT, or Musquash,** *Ondatra zibethica*, of North America, the largest of the VOLES, measuring up to 600mm (23.6in). It is an aquatic animal living in fresh water or salt marshes, feeding mainly on water plants. The feet are broad, the hindfeet being webbed, and the fur is thick and waterproof. Musk rats are frequently hunted for their fur.

**MUSLIM LEAGUE,** political group (originally the All-India Muslim League) founded in 1906 to protect the rights of MUSLIMS in India. From 1940 the league backed the idea of an independent Muslim state; PAKISTAN was formed (1947) and the league became its predominant political party until it split into factions in the 1960s.

**MUSLIMS** (Arabic: ones who submit), adherents of the religion of ISLAM. (See also ABBASIDS; ARAB; ARAB LEAGUE; CALIPHATE; CRUSADES; ISLAMIC ART AND ARCHITECTURE; OTTOMAN EMPIRE; SELJUKS.)

**MUSSET, Louis Charles Alfred de** (1810–1857), French Romantic poet and playwright (see ROMANTICISM). After an affair with George SAND, he wrote "Les Nuits" (1835–37), some of the finest love poetry in French, and the autobiographical *Confession d'un enfant du siècle* (1836). His witty plays are often produced today.

**MUSSOLINI, Benito** (1883–1945) Italian founder of FASCISM, dictator of ITALY, 1924–43. Editor of the socialist party paper 1912–14, Mussolini split with the Socialists when he advocated Italy's joining the Allies in WWI. In 1919 he formed a Fascist group in Milan which, in that time of political unrest, attracted many Italians with its blend of nationalism and socialism. The Fascist Party was nationally organized 1921; in 1922 the Fascist militia conducted the march on Rome which led the king to make Mussolini premier. He consolidated his position, eliminated opponents, signed the LATERAN TREATY and began an aggressive foreign policy. He brutally conquered Ethiopia 1935–36 (see ITALO-ETHIOPIAN WAR), and annexed Albania 1939. He joined Hitler (see AXIS POWERS) and in 1940 declared war on the ALLIES. Italy suffered defeats in Greece, Africa and at home. Mussolini was captured by the Allies (1943). When rescued by the Germans he headed the fascist puppet regime in German-occupied N Italy; on its collapse he was shot by Italian PARTISANS. (See also CORPORATE STATE.)

**MUSSORGSKY, Modest Petrovich,** or Moussorgsky (1839–1881), major Russian composer. His *Boris Godunov* (1874) is one of the finest Russian operas. He developed a highly original style around characteristically Russian idioms, as in the song cycle *Songs and Dances of Death* (1875–77) and the piano suite *Pictures from an Exhibition* (1874). An alcoholic, Mussorgsky left many unfinished works.

**MUSTANG,** small feral HORSE of the W US, descended from horses of N African stock brought over by the Spaniards. Well adapted to plains conditions, they were popular as cow ponies. A **bronco** was an untamed mustang.

**MUTATION,** a sudden and relatively permanent change in a GENE or CHROMOSOME set, the raw material for evolutionary change. Chemical or physical agents which cause mutations are known as *mutagens*. Mutations can occur in any type of CELL at any stage in the life of an organism but only changes present in the GAMETES are passed on to the offspring. A mutation may be dominant or recessive, viable or lethal. The majority are changes in individual genes (gene mutations) but in some cases changes in the structure or numbers of chromosomes may be seen. The formation of structural chromosome changes is used to test drugs for mutagenic activity. Mutation normally occurs very rarely but certain mutagens—X-RAYS, GAMMA RAYS, NEUTRONS and MUSTARD GAS—greatly accelerate mutation.

**MUTE.** See DUMBNESS.

**MUTSUHITO** (1852–1912), emperor of Japan from 1867, with regnal name Meiji. The long isolation of Japan under the SHOGUNS ended 1868 with the restoration of imperial power. Mutsuhito guided the transformation of Japan- from a feudal empire into a modern nation. He established industries, promoted education, gave farmers titles to their land, and modernized the armed forces.

**MUTUAL FUNDS,** investment companies which pool their shareholders' funds and invest them in a broad range of stocks and shares. This spreads the risks for a small investor, who receives dividends for his shares in the fund (rather than for individual company shares) and who can always sell his fund shares back to the company at net asset value (see also STOCKS AND STOCK MARKET).

**MUYBRIDGE, Eadweard** (Edward James Muggeridge; 1830–1904), English-born US photographer. He pioneered studies of human and animal movement using a series of cameras with special shutters, and invented a precursor of the cinema projector to display his results, published in his *Animal Locomotion* portfolio (1887).

**MX,** a proposed four-stage rocket with an 8000-mile range. Destined to replace the *Minuteman* which it exceeds in size, it measures 70 ft long, has a 92-inch diameter and weighs 192,000 lbs. (The *Minuteman* is 60 ft long, 66 inches in diameter and weighs 78,000lbs.) The MX, or missile experimental, would be the largest ICBM allowable under SALT. Advocates say it would be less vulnerable and more flexible and accurate than the silo-based *Titans* and *Minutemen* that are the present backbone of the US land-based nuclear arsenal.

The MX will carry 10 MIRV warheads in its final-stage, liquid-fueled "bus." These could be aimed at separate targets. The yield of the first warheads (335 kilotons) and their accuracy (about 600 feet at a range of 6000 miles) would be similar to that of the improved *Minuteman III*. Later models would have yields of 500 kilotons. The MX, guided by on-board computers and other advanced electronic equipment, would threaten enemy nuclear missile-launching sites.

Considerable controversy has surrounded the basing of the MX. The Carter administration's plan to shuttle 200 mobile missiles among 4,600 shelters in the Western desert as part of a giant "shell game" was cancelled in October 1981. Present plans are to house the MX in specially hardened *Titan* and *Minuteman* silos. They may later be launched from aircraft in continuous flight or from bases built far below ground.

**MYASTHENIA GRAVIS,** a DISEASE of the junctions between the peripheral NERVOUS SYSTEM and the MUSCLES, probably due to abnormal IMMUNITY, and characterized by the fatigability of muscles. It commonly affects EYE muscles, leading to drooping lids and double VISION, but it may involve limb muscles. Weakness of the muscles of RESPIRATION, swallowing and coughing may lead to respiratory failure and aspiration or bacterial PNEUMONIA. Speech is nasal, regurgitation into the nose may occur and the FACE is weak, lending a characteristic snarl to the MOUTH. It is associated with disorders of THYMUS GLAND and THYROID GLAND. Treatment is with cholinesterase inhibitors; STEROIDS and thymus removal may control the causative immune mechanism.

**MYCENAE,** city of ancient Greece and a late Bronze Age site, 7mi N of Argos in the NE Peloponnesus. The city of HOMER's King Agamemnon, it was destroyed by the Dorian invasion of 1100 BC. Historically the city is important as the center of Mycenaean civilization (see AEGEAN CIVILIZATION). The remains of the city include the Treasury of Atreus and royal beehive and shaft tombs and the Lion Gate of the citadel wall. Heinrich SCHLIEMANN excavated the site (1876–78) and uncovered weapons, jewels, ornaments, gold and silverware.

**MYCOLOGY,** the scientific study of FUNGI.

**MYDANS, Carl** (1907–    ), and **Shelley Smith Mydans** (1915–    ), US photojournalists for *Life* magazine. They were assigned to Europe in 1939 and to the Far East in 1940, where their 22-month internment became the subject of Shelley Mydans' novel, *The Open City* (1945). They collaborated on *The Violent Peace* (1968).

**MY LAI,** a hamlet in South Vietnam where nearly 350 Vietnamese civilians were massacred by US soldiers in March 1968. Subsequent revelations (autumn, 1969) led to army and congressional investigations. Lt. William Calley, in immediate command during the incident, was convicted of killing 22 persons and imprisoned for three years. Two generals were censured for failing to conduct an adequate investigation. Charges against other soldiers were dismissed.

**MYOCARDITIS,** a rare INFLAMMATION of the HEART muscle caused by VIRUSES, BACTERIA, some metal poisons and drugs. It is a serious complication of acute RHEUMATIC FEVER. Treatment involves bed rest, but the heart may be permanently damaged.

**MYOPIA,** or near- or shortsightedness, a defect of VISION in which light entering the EYE from distant objects is brought to a focus in front of the retina. The condition may be corrected by use of a diverging spectacle LENS.

**MYRDAL, Gunnar** (1898–    ), Swedish economist who wrote a classic work on race relations, *An American Dilemma* (1944), and an influential study of Third World economic development, *Asian Drama* (1968). He won the 1974 Nobel Prize in Economic Science.

**MYRON** (5th century BC), Greek sculptor best-known for his *Discobulus* (The Discus Thrower), a marble reconstruction of which is housed in Rome's National Museum. His work, almost exclusively in bronze, marks the apogee of early classical art. It is predominantly concerned with the human figure at critical moments of poise and balance in the course of generally strenuous, often athletic actions.

**MYRRH,** the fragrant resin obtained from

small thorny trees of the genus *Commiphora* from the family Burseraceae. Myrrh has been used for embalming, in medicines and as incense and is now an important constituent of some PERFUMES.

**MYSTERIES,** secret religious rites of ancient Greece and Rome. Revealed only to initiated persons, they were called mysteries from the Greek word *mystes*, meaning an initiate. Disclosure of the secrets of the rites was punishable by death, hence the fragmentary nature of our knowledge of them. Of the Classical mysteries the most famous were the ELEUSINIAN MYSTERIES held at Eleusis and later in Athens. These involved purification rites, dance, drama and the display of sacred objects such as an ear of corn. The Orphic mysteries were said to have been founded by ORPHEUS. Other mysteries were connected with nature deities and those of eastern cults such as CYBELE, ATTIS, ISIS, OSIRIS and MITHRA.

**MYSTERY PLAY,** medieval religious drama based on biblical themes, chiefly those concerning the Nativity, the Passion and the Resurrection. The form is closely related to that of the Miracle play, which is generally based on non-biblical material, such as, for example, the saints' lives. The distinction between the two forms is not clearcut and some authorities refer to both as Miracle plays. Mystery plays, which are liturgical in origin, can be extraordinarily ambitious in scale, treating the whole of man's spiritual history from the Creation to Judgment Day in vast cycles which required communal cooperation to perform. Important examples are the English York and Wakefield cycles, the French cycle *Miracle of Notre Dame* and the famous OBERAMMERGAU Passion, of Bavaria. (See also MORALITY PLAY.)

**MYSTICISM,** belief that man can experience a transcendental union with the divine in this life through meditation and other disciplines. It is at the core of most eastern religions, though it may be only loosely linked with them. The path to this union is usually seen as three stages: cleansing away of physical desires, purification of will and enlightenment of mind. Mysticism is important in some forms of Christianity. The goal is union and communion with God in love and by intuitive knowledge in prayer; mystical experience can be expressed only in metaphors, especially of love and marriage.

**MYSTIC SEAPORT,** a 20–acre village, at the mouth of the Mystic R, on Long Island Sound, part of Stonington, Conn. This popular tourist attraction is a recreated mid-19th century whaling port, with early American buildings, cobbled streets, old ships and marine and other museums.

**MYTHOLOGY,** the traditional stories of a people which collectively constitute their folk history and that of their gods and heroes, embody their beliefs and ideas, and represent an affirmation of their culture. Most major mythologies originated in pre-literate societies and were passed on orally. The stories within a mythology fall into three main types: myths proper, which take place in a timeless past and are serious attempts to rationalize the mysterious and unknowable—i.e., the creation of the world, the origin of the gods, death and afterlife, the seasonal renewal of the earth; folk tales, narratives set in historical time and more social than religious in their concerns; and legends and sagas, which recount the embellished exploits of racial heroes.

Comparative studies have revealed fundamental similarities of theme and action among many widely separated mythologies. These similarities are thought by some to be the result of cultural interchanges. For others they constitute evidence of universal archetypes, the embodiments of the unconscious racial memories common to all humanity (see Carl G. JUNG). Sir James FRAZIER's *The Golden Bough* (1890) is the most famous work of comparative mythology.

The mythologies that have had the most profound influence on western thought and literature are those of the ancient Near East (Mesopotamian, Egyptian and Canaanite); classical, or Greco-Roman; Norse, including the Icelandic and Scandinavian sagas (see EDDA) and the Germanic NIBELUNGENLIED; and Celtic, especially Irish mythology.

# N

14th letter of the English alphabet, corresponding with the 14th Semitic letter nū and the Greek nū. N is the abbreviation for name, noun, neuter and north, among others. (See ALPHABET.)

**NAACP.** See NATIONAL ASSOCIATION FOR THE ADVANCEMENT OF COLORED PEOPLE.

**NABOKOV, Vladimir** (1899–1977), Russian-US novelist and critic. Born in St.

Petersburg (now Leningrad), he became a US citizen in 1945. Noted for his originality and satiric wit, he published poetry, essays, short stories and novels in Russian and in English. His first English novel was *The Real Life of Sebastian Knight* (1938); he became famous for *Lolita* (1958), the story of a middle-aged man's passion for a young girl. His works include *Pnin* (1957), *Pale Fire* (1962), *Ada* (1969) and an English translation of *Eugene Onegin* (1964).

**NADELMAN, Elie** (1882–1946), Polish-born US sculptor. He interpreted the human form through the eyes of 18th century folk-artists and doll-makers, but was also influenced by "classic" sculptors such as RODIN. Among his more amusing sculptures was *Man in the Open Air*.

**NADER, Ralph** (1934– ), US consumer crusader and lawyer. The controversy which greeted his book *Unsafe at Any Speed* (1965), a criticism of safety standards in the auto industry, enabled him to gain widespread support for investigations into other areas of public interest, including chemical food additives, X-ray leakage and government agencies. His work has resulted in Congressional hearings and remedial legislation.

**NAGASAKI,** capital of Nagasaki prefecture, a major port, on W Kyushu Island, Japan, and a foreign trading center since 1571. In WWII about 40,000 residents were killed when the US dropped the second atomic bomb (Aug. 9, 1945). Today shipbuilding is the city's major industry. Pop 446,900.

**NAGY, Imre** (1896–1958) Hungarian communist leader and premier (1953–55). His criticism of Soviet influence led to his removal from office; but during the Oct. 1956 revolution he became premier again briefly. After Soviet troops crushed the uprising, the Russians tried and executed Nagy in secret.

**NAHUM, Book of,** the seventh of the Old Testament MINOR PROPHETS, the oracles of the prophet Nahum. It graphically relates the fall of Nineveh (612 BC) and is dated shortly before or after this.

**NAIPAUL, Vidiadhar Surajprasad** (1932– ), cosmopolitan Indian writer, born in Trinidad. A brilliant critic and essayist, Naipaul has been especially praised for his novels of life in the Third World, including *A House for Mr. Biswas* (1961) and *A Bend in the River* (1979).

**NAMATH, Joe** (1943– ), US football player. During a career made brief by knee injuries, the gifted quarterback passed for a record 4,007yds in 1967, and led the New York Jets to a 16–7 victory over Baltimore

in Super Bowl III (1969), the first time an AFL team had won the event.

**Official name:** Namibia (South West Africa)
**Capital:** Windhoek
**Area:** 318,259sq mi
**Population:** 1,075,000
**Languages:** Afrikaans, English, Bantu
**Religions:** Christian, Animist
**Monetary unit(s):** 1 South African Rand = 100 cents

**NAMIBIA,** or South West Africa, a territory under the control of the Republic of South Africa, is bordered by the S Atlantic Ocean, Angola, Zambia, Botswana and South Africa.
**Land.** The land rises from the Namib Desert, which stretches N to S on the Atlantic coast, to a plateau averaging 3,500ft above sea level covered by rough grass and scrub. The Kalahari, a desert region, lies to the E. The climate is hot and dry and there are only two important rivers.
**People.** The population is overwhelmingly Bantu. Ovambos, the single largest ethnic group, Bushmen and Kavango live in Ovamboland, to the N. The Hereros, Nama and Damara live in the S plateau, chiefly around Windhoek, the capital, which is home to most of the country's Europeans, about 12% of the population. The Rehoboths, or Coloureds, of African and European ancestry, are also an important group. All these groups—except the Bushmen—farm, raise cattle or work in mines.
**Economy.** The mineral sector accounts for most exports, diamonds and uranium being the leading commodities. Livestock dominates the agricultural sector. Fishing is also an important economic activity. Meat processing and fish canning are the main industries.
**History.** The territory was annexed by Germany in 1884, and mandated to South Africa after WWI by the League of Nations in 1920. After WWII South Africa refused to place it under UN trusteeship; the UN in 1966 declared the original mandate terminated and tried to bring South West

Africa under its control, later renaming it Namibia. In 1971 the International Court of Justice reversed its earlier rulings in favor of South Africa, stating that South Africa's practice of *apartheid* (separation of the races) violated its mandate. South Africa rejected the court's ruling. The UN continued to seek the country's independence into the 1980s. To defend against Namibian guerrillas, South Africa maintains a military presence.

**NANSEN, Fridtjof** (1861–1930), Norwegian explorer, scientist and humanitarian, awarded the 1922 Nobel Peace Prize, best known for his explorations of the Arctic. His most successful attempt at reaching the NORTH POLE was in 1895, when he achieved latitude 86° 14′, the farthest north then reached. He also designed the Nansen Bottle, a device for obtaining water samples at depth.

**NANTES, Edict of,** proclamation of religious toleration for French Protestants (HUGUENOTS) issued in the city by Henry IV in 1598. Protestants were granted civil rights and freedom of private and public worship in many parts of France (but not in Paris). In 1685 Catholic pressure brought Louis XIV to revoke the edict.

**NANTUCKET ISLAND,** popular summer resort, 25mi S of Cape Cod, Mass., across Nantucket Sound. The 15mi-long island has a mild climate and 88mi of beaches. It was a world famous 18th-century whaling center. Pop 3,774.

**NAPALM,** a SOAP consisting of the aluminum salt of a mixture of CARBOXYLIC ACIDS, with aluminum hydroxide in excess. When about 10% is added to GASOLINE it forms a GEL, also called napalm, used in flame throwers and incendiary bombs; it burns hotly and relatively slowly, and sticks to its target. Developed in WWII, it was used in the Vietnam War and caused great havoc. (See also CHEMICAL AND BIOLOGICAL WARFARE.)

**NAPIER, John** (1550–1617), Scottish mathematician credited with the invention of LOGARITHMS (before 1614). Natural logarithms (to the base $e$) are often called Napierian Logarithms for him. He also developed the modern notation for the DECIMAL SYSTEM.

**NAPLES,** third-largest city in Italy, capital of Naples province and of the Campania region, on N shore of the Bay of Naples, 120mi SE of Rome. Founded by the Greeks (c600 BC), it was the capital of the Kingdom of NAPLES and later the TWO SICILIES. The historic city has a 13th-century cathedral and university (1224), and medieval castles and palaces. Nearby

are the ruins of POMPEII. Naples is the financial and intellectual center of S Italy. A major seaport, its industries vary from heavy engineering and textiles to wine and glass manufacture. Pop 1,225,400.

**NAPLES, Kingdom of.** It comprised all of Italy S of the Papal States, including Sicily. It emerged after the conquests of the Norman Robert Guiscard in the 1000s; his nephew Roger II took the title King of Sicily and Apulia (1130). Naples was ruled in turn by the HOHENSTAUFENS, the ANGEVINS, the Aragonese (see ARAGON) and the Spanish Crown. The Austrians conquered the kingdom in 1707, but it was taken by the Spanish BOURBON kings in 1734. NAPOLEON I annexed the kingdom to his empire and made his brother Joseph king (1806) followed by his brother-in-law MURAT. In 1815, after Napoleon's defeat, the Bourbon Ferdinand IV was restored; he reunited Naples and Sicily as the Kingdom of the TWO SICILIES. Bourbon rule collapsed before the advance of the revolutionary forces of GARIBALDI (1860). When VICTOR EMMANUEL was confirmed by the Italian parliament as king of all Italy (Feb. 1861), Naples became a part of the new Italian state, ending 700 years as an independent kingdom.

**NAPOLEON I** (1769–1821), general and emperor of the French (1804–14). Napoleon Bonaparte was born in Corsica, went to military schools in France and became a lieutenant in the artillery (1785). He associated with JACOBINS on the outbreak of the FRENCH REVOLUTION, drove the British from Toulon (1793), and dispersed a royalist rebellion in Paris (Oct. 1795). Soon after his marriage to Joséphine de BEAUHARNAIS, he defeated the Austro-Sardinian armies in Italy (1796–7) and signed the treaty of Campo Formio extending French territory. He returned to Paris a national hero. He then campaigned in Egypt and the Middle East, threatening Great Britain's position in India. Although he won land battles, the French fleet was destroyed in the Battle of the Nile (ABOUKIR) Aug. 1798. Napoleon later returned to Paris and helped to engineer the coup d'etat of Nov. 9, 1799, which established a CONSULATE with himself as First Consul and virtual dictator. He reorganized the government, established the Bank of France and the CODE NAPOLÉON, which is still the basis of French law.

Continuing hostilities with Austria and Great Britain resulted in the Treaty of Lunéville which recognized French dominance on the Continent. The Treaty of Amiens with Britain (March 1802) meant that Europe was at peace for the first time in ten years. Napoleon became first consul for life (1802) and crowned himself emperor (1804). In the NAPOLEONIC WARS he then won a series of great victories over the European alliance at Austerlitz (1805), Jena (1806) and Friedland (1807), dissolving the HOLY ROMAN EMPIRE (1806) and becoming ruler of almost the whole continent. After Jena he inaugurated the CONTINENTAL SYSTEM whereby he hoped to keep European ports closed to British trade, but the battle of TRAFALGAR (1805) established the dominance of Britain at sea.

In 1809 Napoleon divorced Joséphine and married MARIE LOUISE who bore him an heir, NAPOLEON II. The PENINSULAR WAR revealed growing French weakness, and in 1812 Napoleon began his disastrous campaign against Russia. A new alliance of European nations defeated the French at Leipzig (1813); in 1814 France was invaded, Napoleon abdicated and was exiled to the island of Elba. In March 1815 he escaped, returned to France and ruled for the HUNDRED DAYS, which ended in French defeat at WATERLOO (1815). Napoleon was then exiled to SAINT HELENA where he died in 1821. His remains were brought to Paris in 1840 and buried under the dome of Les Invalides.

**NAPOLEON II** (1811–1832), son of Napoleon and MARIE LOUISE, proclaimed king of Rome at birth. After his father's abdication (1814), he lived in Austria as Duke of Reichstadt. He died of tuberculosis.

**NAPOLEON III** (Louis Napoleon; 1808–1873), emperor of the French (1852–70); son of Louis Bonaparte, king of Holland, and nephew of Napoleon I. He attempted several coups against King LOUIS PHILIPPE, was jailed but escaped to England (1846). After the 1848 revolution, he was elected president of France; he dissolved the legislature and made himself emperor (1852). His regime promoted domestic prosperity but by the 1860s opposition to his repressive, corrupt government had grown. He joined in the CRIMEAN WAR (1854–56),

but failed to make MAXIMILIAN emperor of Mexico. In 1870 his ill-judged war with Prussia ended in defeat, capture and the collapse of his empire; he died in exile in England.

**NAPOLEONIC CODE.** See CODE NAPOLÉON.

**NAPOLEONIC WARS** (1804–15), fought by France after NAPOLEON I became emperor. After the Treaty of Amiens (1802) which had ended the FRENCH REVOLUTIONARY WARS (1792–1802), Britain declared war on France in May, 1803, maintaining that Napoleon was not keeping to the treaty. Napoleon planned to invade Britain but the British fleet proved too strong for him, especially after TRAFALGAR. The British, Austrians and Russians formed an alliance in July 1805; Napoleon defeated the Austrians and Russians at Austerlitz (Dec. 1805); the Prussians at Jena (1806) and the Russians at Friedland (1807); the Peace of Tilsit (1807) left him nearly master of Europe. Meanwhile Britain had secured supremacy of the seas at the Battle of Trafalgar (1805). The CONTINENTAL SYSTEM begun after Jena was Napoleon's attempt to blockade British trade; on the pretext of enforcing it he invaded Portugal (1807) and Spain (1808). During the defeat of his armies by the British in the PENINSULAR WAR (1808–14), he signed the Peace of Schönbrunn (1809) with the defeated Austrians. In 1812 Napoleon invaded Russia with a grand army some 500,000 strong. He barely won the Battle of Borodino (1812) and marched unchallenged to Moscow, but his troops suffered from lack of supplies and the cold weather. Their retreat from Moscow and Russia was horrifying; only about 30,000 of Napoleon's soldiers returned. The French, by now drained of manpower and supplies, were decisively beaten at Leipzig (1813). Paris fell, and on April 6, 1814, Napoleon abdicated. The victorious allies signed the Treaty of Paris with the Bourbons. After Napoleon's escape from Elba and return (The HUNDRED DAYS) and his defeat at Waterloo (1815), the second Treaty of Paris was signed in 1815 (see PARIS, TREATIES OF).

**NARAYAN, R. K.** (1906–    ), Indian novelist writing in English who created the fictitious South Indian town of Malgudi in a series of novels which dealt with the ironies of daily life in contemporary India. These include *The Bachelor of Arts* (1937), *The Financial Expert* (1952) and *The Vendor of Sweets* (1967).

**NARODNIKI** (Russian: populists), members of a socialist movement in 19th-century Russia. They ineffectually spread political propaganda among the peasants; failure and police repression turned them to terrorism, culminating in Tsar Alexander II's assassination (1881). They were succeeded by the Socialist Revolutionary Party (1901).

**NARWHAL,** *Monodon monoceros,* a "toothed whale" of the Arctic. The teeth are completely absent in both sexes except for a single spiral tusk in the male on the left-hand side of the jaw. This tusk may be up to 2.5m (8.2ft) long; its function is unknown. It is believed that narwhal tusks were once thought to be the horns of unicorns.

**NASA.** See NATIONAL AERONAUTICS AND SPACE ADMINISTRATION.

**NASH, John** (1752–1835), British architect, famous for his development of Regent's Park and Regent St, London, begun 1811. He built the Royal Pavilion, Brighton, Sussex; redesigned St. James's Park, London; and began alterations to Buckingham Palace (1821). (See REGENCY STYLE.)

**NASH, Ogden** (1902–1971), US humorous poet with a witty, sometimes satirical style, punctuated by puns, asides, unconventional rhymes and unexpectedly long lines. He published 20 volumes of verse and wrote lyrics for musicals.

**NASHVILLE,** capital city of Tenn., seat of Davidson Co., on the Cumberland R in N central Tenn. The last major battle of the Civil War was fought nearby (Dec. 1864). Nashville is a commercial, industrial and agricultural city; the center of the country music recording industry; and a religious educational and publishing center. Pop 455,651.

**NASSAU,** capital city of the Bahama Islands, a port on NE New Providence Island. Long a pirate haunt, it is now a world-famous tourist resort. Met pop 138,500.

**NASSER, Gamal Abdel** (1918–1970), Egyptian president and Arab leader. He led the military coup d'etat which overthrew King FAROUK I (1952), then ousted General NAGUIB and named himself prime minister (1954). He ended British military presence in Egypt (1954) and seized the SUEZ CANAL (1956). He was elected president of Egypt unopposed (1956), and was president of the UNITED ARAB REPUBLIC 1958–61. His "Arab socialism" policy brought new land ownership laws and agricultural policies, more schools, increased social services and widespread nationalization. He fought a brief war with Israel in 1956; after the disastrous 1967 ARAB-ISRAELI WAR with Israel, he resigned but resumed office by popular demand.

**NAST, Condé** (1874–1942), US publisher who bought *Vogue* magazine (1909) and transformed it into an elegant and sophisticated fashion journal. He also published *Vanity Fair, House and Garden* and *Glamour* magazines.

**NAST, Thomas** (1840–1902), German-born US cartoonist, creator of the symbols for the Democratic Party (donkey) and the Republican Party (elephant). His attacks on the TAMMANY HALL political machine, symbolized as a tiger, contributed to its disintegration. Nast's drawings of SANTA CLAUS set a US popular image.

**NATAL,** province of South Africa, on the Indian Ocean, 33,578sq mi in area, with capital Pietermaritzburg. It produces sugar, fruit, cereals and coal and manufactures fertilizers and textiles, mainly near Durban, the chief city. Natal was a British colony 1856–1910.

**NATCHEZ TRACE,** old road from Natchez, Miss., to Nashville, Tenn.; developed from Indian trails, it was of great importance c1780–1830. The Natchez Trace National Parkway, about 450mi long, follows the old route.

**NATHAN, George Jean** (1882–1958), US editor and drama critic, author of numerous essays and of *The Theatre Book of the Year,* an annual 1943–51. With H. L. MENCKEN he edited *The Smart Set* and founded *American Mercury.*

**NATION, Carry Amelia** (1846–1911), US temperance agitator. She began her campaign against liquor bars in the "dry" state of Kan. Formidable in size and appearance, from 1901 she smashed several saloons with a hatchet. Arrested on about 30 occasions, she paid fines by selling souvenir hatchets and lecturing. She was not supported by the national PROHIBITION movement.

**NATIONAL ACADEMY OF DESIGN,** US fine arts association, founded 1825. Membership is limited to 125 painters, 50 sculptors, 25 architects, 25 graphic artists and 25 aquarellists; associate membership is unlimited. It has a School of Fine Arts in New York City.

**NATIONAL ACADEMY OF SCIENCES,** private US organization of scientists and engineers, founded 1863. It officially advises the government on scientific questions, and coordinates major programs. Members are elected for distinguished research achievements.

**NATIONAL AERONAUTICS AND SPACE ADMINISTRATION (NASA),** US government agency responsible for nonmilitary SPACE EXPLORATION and related research. Founded by President Eisenhower (1958) as successor to the National Advisory Committee for Aeronautics (NACA), it has numerous research stations, laboratories and space flight launching centers, including Cape CANAVERAL and the Houston control center. Its headquarters are in Washington, D.C. The annual budget is about $3½ billion.

**NATIONAL ASSOCIATION FOR THE ADVANCEMENT OF COLORED PEOPLE (NAACP),** US voluntary interracial organization, founded in New York City (1909) to oppose RACISM and racial segregation and discrimination, and to ensure CIVIL RIGHTS AND LIBERTIES for black Americans. It works for the enactment and enforcement of civil rights laws, supports education programs and engages in direct action. An early success was the ending of LYNCHING. The NAACP Legal Defense and Education Fund was set up (1939) as its legal arm. NAACP's membership in 1980 was about 450,000.

**NATIONAL ASSOCIATION OF MANUFACTURERS (NAM),** US organization of manufacturing companies, founded 1895 to coordinate their policies and represent them to the government and the public.

**NATIONAL BUREAU OF STANDARDS (NBS),** bureau of the US Department of Commerce, established 1901. It determines national WEIGHTS AND MEASURES, tests products and materials, and carries on research in science and technology. It also advises government agencies and industries on safety codes and technical specifications.

**NATIONAL COLLEGIATE ATHLETIC ASSOCIATION (NCAA),** US advisory body founded 1906 to establish eligibility and competition rules for intercollegiate athletics. After 1921 most other college sports came under its jurisdiction. The NCAA compiles statistics on college sports and publishes rule books and guides. It has over 800 member institutions.

**NATIONAL CONFERENCE OF CHRISTIANS AND JEWS,** US organization founded 1928 to fight prejudice, intolerance and bigotry and to promote interfaith harmony. The conference sponsors BROTHERHOOD WEEK. It has about 260,000 members.

**NATIONAL COUNCIL OF THE CHURCHES OF CHRIST IN THE USA,** organization of 32 Protestant and Eastern Orthodox churches (with combined membership of 40 million), founded 1950 to promote interdenominational cooperation and understanding. It has educational, evangelistic, ecumenical, political and relief programs, and has allied itself with many other church bodies and missionary societies.

**NATIONAL DEBT,** the amount of money owed by a government, borrowed to pay expenses not covered by taxation revenue. The US national debt totaled more than $1 trillion by 1982. National debts are incurred to pay for wars, public construction programs, etc. To obtain money, governments sell BONDS or short-term certificates to banks, other organizations and individuals. Some governments in crisis have defaulted or devalued the currency. The **public debt** includes not only the national debt but also debts of individual states, cities, etc. (See also FUNDED DEBT.)

**NATIONAL EDUCATION ASSOCIATION (NEA),** organization of professional school teachers and administrators. Established 1857 to raise professional standards, it was chartered by Congress in 1907. The NEA works to improve education and to promote the welfare of its members.

**NATIONAL GALLERY OF ART,** US museum of nationally-owned works of art, opened 1941, in Washington, D.C. It is part of the SMITHSONIAN INSTITUTION. The initial collection was donated by Andrew MELLON (1937). The gallery possesses Jan van Eyck's *The Annunciation* and Raphael's *The Alba Madonna*; it has many works by Italian, French and American artists.

**NATIONAL GEOGRAPHIC SOCIETY,** nonprofit scientific and educational organization, established in Washington, D.C. (1888) "for the increase and diffusion of geographic knowledge." It publishes *National Geographic* magazine, books, maps and school bulletins, and sponsors expedition and research projects.

**NATIONAL GUARD,** volunteer reserve groups of the US Army and Air Force, with a combined authorized strength of about 500,000, originating in the volunteer militia organized in 1792. Each state, territory, and the District of Columbia has its National Guard units. Army units are directed by the National Guard Bureau of the Department of the Army and air units by the Department of the Air Force. The National Defense Acts of 1920 and 1933 empower the president to call up units in time of national crisis. Governors may call up state units during strikes, riots, disasters and other emergencies—in recent years National Guard units have checked civil disturbances, often amid controversy. A guardsman takes a dual oath—to the federal government and to his state. In peacetime he attends 48 drill sessions and a two-week training camp annually.

**NATIONAL INSTITUTES OF HEALTH (NIH)**, research agency of the US Public Health Service, Department of Health, Education and Welfare. It supports over one-third of the nation's medical research through nine institutes, a clinical center, fellowships and grants to medical and dental schools and universities. It also distributes biological and medical information.

**NATIONALISM**, political and social attitude of groups of people who share a common culture, language and territory as well as common aims and purposes, and thus feel a deep-seated loyalty to the group to which they belong, as opposed to other groups. Nationalism in the modern sense dates from the FRENCH REVOLUTON, but had its roots in the rise of strong centralized monarchies, in the economic doctrine of MERCANTILISM and the growth of a substantial middle class. Nationalism today is also associated with any drive for national unification or independence. It can represent a destructive force in multinational states.

**NATIONALITY**, in law, recognized membership of a particular country. Nations themselves determine who their nationals are. Two basic principles for deciding nationality are acknowledged by most countries: *jus sanguinis*, the right of blood, based on the nationality of a parent; and *jus soli*, the right of place of birth. (See also CITIZENSHIP; NATURALIZATION.)

**NATIONAL LABOR RELATIONS BOARD (NLRB)**, independent US government agency designed to prevent or correct unfair labor practices. Originally set up to administer the National Labor Relations Act of 1935 and protect fledgling unions from illegal interference, the board has since been granted power to police both illegal union and management practices. Its actions are subject, however, to approval by the federal courts.

**NATIONAL MEDIATION BOARD**, independent US federal agency which mediates and arbitrates in labor disputes threatening to disrupt interstate (airline and railroad) commerce. Its arbitration decisions are legally binding.

**NATIONAL MERIT SCHOLARSHIP CORPORATION**, nonprofit, independent corporation, started with a $20 million investment by the FORD FOUNDATION in 1955. The Carnegie Corporation was a leading initial contributor and many philanthropies, businesses, and educational institutions now also are donors. The corporation runs two nationwide scholarship programs; one provides college scholarship grants, ranging from $1,000 to $6,000, to some 3,800 high school graduates annually; the other provides similar scholarships for outstanding black students. Awards are based on scores in tests run by the corporation, on extracurricular achievements, school standing and so on.

**NATIONAL ORGANIZATION FOR WOMEN (NOW)**, founded 1966 to promote full equality between men and women in all walks of life. With some 150,000 members, NOW has focused its efforts since 1978 on passage of the EQUAL RIGHTS AMENDMENT. Its first president was Betty FRIEDAN, its current president Eleanor Smeal.

**NATIONAL PARK SYSTEM**, system administered by the US National Park Service, a bureau of the Department of the Interior, whereby land of outstanding scenic or historical interest is protected "for the benefit and enjoyment of the people". The national park idea originated in the US; descriptions in 1870–71 of the wild country at the headwaters of the Yellowstone R in Wyo. led in 1872 to an Act of Congress creating Yellowstone National Park (2,221,733 acres). In Cal., Sequoia and Yosemite were declared parks in 1890, but few other sites were brought under protection until 1916, when President Woodrow Wilson instituted the Park Service. Today it administers more than 46,000sq mi of parkland, comprising about 300 protected areas—and the number is still growing. Of this land, 38 outstanding scenic areas are known simply as national parks. Another 82, combining scenery with precolonial history, natural or man-made objects, or geological, zoological or botanical phenomena, are called national monuments. The other 178 areas include battlefields (such as Gettysburg), forts and trading posts, pioneer trails, cemeteries, recreation areas, scenic lake shores and waterways, important birthplaces (Washington's, Lincoln's), the National Scientific Reserve, the Statue of Liberty, memorials such as the Washington Monument and Mt Rushmore, and the White House. The service also protects shorelines in danger of erosion. (See also NATIONAL CAPITAL PARKS.)

**NATIONAL REPUBLICAN PARTY**, American political party formed when the Democratic–Republican Party split up in the 1828 presidential election. The party's candidate in 1832, Henry CLAY, was routed and during JACKSON's presidency, in 1836, the party merged with other political groups to form the WHIG party.

**NATIONAL RIFLE ASSOCIATION OF AMERICA (NRA)**, US organization composed of people interested in firearms, founded 1871. It promotes the use of firearms for sport and self-defense, safety and wildlife conservation, and maintains all national records of shooting competitions. The organization is a major lobbying group opposed to gun-control legislation. It has 1½ million members.

**NATIONAL ROAD,** famous old paved road for settlers emigrating to the West. It ran from Cumberland, Md., through Vandalia, Ill., to St. Louis, Mo. The first section, as far as Wheeling, W Va. (the Cumberland Road) was opened in 1818. Today's US Highway 40 closely follows the original route.

**NATIONAL SCIENCE FOUNDATON (NSF),** US federal agency set up in 1950. It promotes research, education and international exchange in the sciences and funds fellowships, projects such as the International Decade of Ocean Exploration, and several permanent observatories.

**NATIONAL SECURITY COUNCIL (NSC),** US defense council created by Congress in 1947 as part of the executive office of the president, to advise him on a wide range of matters relating to national security and defense policies. Chaired by the president, its permanent members include the vice-president and the secretaries of state and defense.

**NATIONAL WAR COLLEGE,** school for selected army, navy, air force, state department and other governmental personnel, established (1949) in Washington, D.C., and now under the authority of the JOINT CHIEFS OF STAFF.

**NATIONAL WILDLIFE FEDERATION,** US organization founded in 1936 to educate and interest the public in preservation of the country's wildlife and nature heritage. It issues relevant publications and helps finance local conservation projects and research. There are over 4 million members.

**NATIVISM,** turning in of a country or society towards its own culture through movements rejecting foreign influences, ideas or immigrants; largely an anthropological term. Nativism is brought on by social stress or disintegration, as with primitive peoples faced by Western civilization. For notable examples of nativist movements in American history see KNOW-NOTHING PARTY; KU KLUX KLAN. (See also CHAUVINISM.)

**NAT TURNER'S REBELLION,** or the Southampton Insurrection, the largest slave uprising in US history, leading to harsher slave laws in the South and the eclipse of emancipation societies. On Aug. 21, 1831, Nat Turner, a Negro slave and Baptist preacher, believing himself called to free his fellow slaves, murdered his master, John Travis of Southampton Co., Va., and led a brief campaign in which 55 whites were killed. He was captured on Oct. 22, tried and hanged.

**NATURAL GAS,** mixture of gaseous HYDROCARBONS occurring in reservoirs of porous rock (commonly sand or sandstone) capped by impervious strata. It is often associated with PETROLEUM, with which it has a common origin in the decomposition of organic matter in sedimentary deposits. Natural gas consists largely of METHANE and ETHANE, with also propane and butane (separated for BOTTLED GAS), some higher ALKANES (used for GASOLINE), nitrogen, oxygen, carbon dioxide, hydrogen sulfide, and sometimes valuable HELIUM. It is used as an industrial and domestic FUEL, and also to make carbonblack and in chemical synthesis. Natural gas is transported by large pipelines or (as a liquid) in refrigerated tankers.

**NATURALISM,** attempt to apply the scientific view of the natural world to philosophy and the arts. There is nothing real beyond nature; man is thus a prisoner of his environment and heredity. This aesthetic movement, inspired by Émile ZOLA's argument for a scientific approach to literature in *The Experimental Novel* (1880), had a profound affect on the fine arts, literature and drama. Zola's ideas influenced many writers—Guy de MAUPASSANT, as well as Stephen CRANE and Theodore DREISER in the US; dramatists from Scandinavia's Henrik IBSEN and August STRINDBERG to Russia's Maxim GORKI and the modern American playwrights Arthur MILLER and Tennessee WILLIAMS; and painters such as the Frenchman Gustave COURBET.

**NATURALIZATION,** process whereby a resident alien, obtains citizenship of a country. In the US, under the Immigration and Nationality Act of 1952, an alien is eligible for naturalization if he is over 18, entered the country legally and has resided there for at least five years, is of "good moral character," names two referees who can vouch for his qualifications, can demonstrate familiarity with written and spoken English and American history and government, and is prepared to renounce all foreign allegiances and take an oath of loyalty and service to his new country. Citizenship may be granted on the recommendation of the immigration service after a court hearing. Alien wives of Americans may normally apply for naturalization after three years' residence. Naturalization of resident aliens in Canada proceeds on much the same lines as in the US, except that the minimum age is 21, and two court hearings are required before the citizenship oath is taken.

**NATURAL LAW,** the body of law supposed to be innate, discoverable by natural human reason, and common to all mankind. Under this philosophy, man–made or *positive* law, though changeable and culturally dependent, must—if truly just—be derived from the principles of natural law. The concept was rooted in Greek philosophy (see STOICISM) and Roman law, and particularly in the Christian philosophy of Thomas AQUINAS, where natural law—the sense of right and wrong implanted in men by God—is contrasted with revealed law (see REVELATION). It lay behind GROTIUS' ideas on international law (17th century). It was used as a basis for ethics, morality, and even for protests against tyranny by SPINOZA, LEIBNIZ, LOCKE, ROUSSEAU and many others, but with the development of scientific philosophies in the 19th century, natural law largely lost its influence.

**NATURAL SELECTION,** mechanism for the process of EVOLUTION discovered by Charles DARWIN in the late 1830s, but not made public until 1858. According to Darwin, evolution occurs when an organism is confronted by a changing environment. A degree of variety is always present in the members of an interbreeding population. Normally, the possession of a variant character by an individual confers no particular advantage on it, and the proportion of individuals in the population with a given variation remains constant. But if it ever arises in a changed environment that a given variation increases the chances of an individual's survival, then individuals possessing that character will be more liable to survive—and breed. The frequency with which the variant character occurs in future generations of the organism will thus increase, and, over a large number of generations, the general form of the population will change. The name "natural selection" derives from the analogy Darwin saw between this selection on the part of "Nature" and the "artificial selection" practiced by animal breeders.

**NAURU,** independent island republic in the W Pacific Ocean, 40mi S of the equator. The Polynesian population's revenue comes from phosphate rock which covers the central plateau and is the chief resource and export.

**History.** The island was discovered in 1798 and annexed by Germany in 1888.

**Official name:** Republic of Nauru
**Capital:** No official capital
**Area:** 8.2sq mi
**Population:** 7,254
**Languages:** Nauruan, English
**Monetary unit:** Australian Dollar (A$)=100 cents

Australia captured it in WWI and administered it as a trust territory until independence was achieved in 1968.

**NAVAHO INDIANS** (or Navajo), migrants from the N who settled around 1000 AD in Ariz. and N.M.; cousins to the APACHE Indians. They learned agriculture, weaving and sand painting from the PUEBLO Indians. After the Spanish introduced sheep in the 1600s, they became pastoralists. Inveterate raiders of Spanish and American settlements in the SW, they were finally subdued (1864) by Kit CARSON and held at Fort Sumner, N.M., until their resettlement on a reservation in 1868. Today there are about 100,000 Navahos. The Navaho culture has an elaborate mythology and religion; their folk art includes painting, silver-working and the weaving of rugs and blankets.

**NAVAL OBSERVATORY, US,** source of official standard time in the US. Founded in Washington, D.C., in 1833, the observatory has moved several times to obtain better observing conditions. Since 1955 its main station has been in Flagstaff, Ariz.

**NAVIGATION,** the art and science of directing a vessel from one place to another. Originally navigation applied only to marine vessels, but now air navigation and, increasingly, space navigation are also important. Although the techniques and applications of navigation have lost. But soon they learned to use sunset and sunrise, the hence the principles, have remained much the same.

**Marine Navigation.** Primitive sailors could not venture out of sight of land without the risk of getting lost. But soon they learned to use sunset and sunrise, the prevailing winds, the POLE STAR and so forth as aids to direction. Early on, the first FATHOMETER, a weighted rope used to measure depth, was developed. Before the 10th century AD the magnetic COMPASS had appeared. But it was not until the 1730s that the inventions of the SEXTANT and CHRONOMETER heralded the dawn of accurate sea navigation. Both LATITUDE AND LONGITUDE could now be determined within reasonable tolerances. (See also ASTROLABE; GREENWICH OBSERVATORY.)

Modern navigation uses electronic aids such as LORAN and the radiocompass; celestial navigation, the determination of position by sightings of celestial bodies, and dead reckoning where, by knowing one's position at a particular past time, the time that has elapsed since, one's direction and speed (see LOG), one can tell one's present position. (See also DIRECTION FINDER; ECHO SOUNDER; MAP; SONAR; SUBMARINE.)

Air Navigation uses many of the principles of marine navigation. In addition, the pilot must work in a third dimension, must know his altitude (see ALTIMETER), and in bad visibility must use aids like the INSTRUMENT LANDING SYSTEM. RADAR is also used.

Space Navigation is a science in its infancy. Like air navigation, it works in three dimensions, but the problems are exacerbated by the motions both of one's source (the earth) and one's destination, as well as by the distances involved. But, prior to developments in new areas, it seems that SPACE EXPLORATION has inaugurated a new era in navigation by the stars. (See also CELESTIAL SPHERE; GYRO-COMPASS; GYROPILOT; INERTIAL GUIDANCE; REMOTE CONTROL.)

**NAVIGATION ACTS,** laws regulating navigation at sea or in port, or restricting commercial shipping in the national interest. More specifically, regulations promulgated (from 1650) by the British during the American colonial period to try to insure that benefits of commerce would accrue to England (and to a lesser extent, the colonies) rather than to England's enemies. After 1763, strict enforcement of the acts caused friction between England and the American colonies and was a major factor leading to the outbreak of the REVOLUTIONARY WAR.

**NAVY,** a seaborne armed force maintained for national defense or attack. In ancient times, armed men often put to sea to explore or raid distant territories. Assyria, Egypt and Phoenicia each deployed merchant fleets on military tasks. Among the first to create a permanent naval force were the Athenians. Their armed *triremes* (galleys with three tiers of oars) defeated the Persians at SALAMIS (480 BC) and were adopted by Carthage and later Rome, after

the naval battle at ACTIUM in 31 BC, ruled the Mediterranean for 400 years. In Scandinavia, the VIKINGS created marauding fleets which ravaged the coasts of Europe from c800 AD for over 200 years. Only ALFRED THE GREAT withstood their raids by creating an English naval task force. Byzantium, Genoa, Venice and other Italian republics, the Arabs and Turks developed powerful navies in the Mediterranean. By the late 16th century most western European nations had acquired naval forces. Spain emerged as the leading naval power, but after her ARMADA was defeated by the English in 1588, England had mastery of the seas. Her naval supremacy was challenged by Holland (see DUTCH WARS) and France, but the Battle of TRAFALGAR in 1805 restored it for another 100 years. A powerful navy ensured that a country could maintain an overseas empire and world influence. Large armored BATTLESHIPS (called *dreadnoughts*) were built from before WWI, until they were outmoded in WWII, although some are presently being reinstated. The submarine and the aircraft carrier then took over. In the postwar period, Britain was overshadowed as a leading naval power by the US and the USSR. The strike power of modern navies, capable of nuclear warfare, assures them a prominent place in the superpowers' armed forces in the future. (See also NAVY, UNITED STATES.)

**NAVY, United States,** the branch of the US armed forces designed to maintain command of the sea, especially in regions considered vital to the defense of the US. It began in the American Revolution, when the Continental Congress voted (1775) the first naval budget to outfit ships designed to harry British naval ships. After the Revolution the US Navy was disbanded, but in 1794 Congress authorized six frigates to be built and used against the persistent attacks of pirates on American shipping off the North African coast. By 1798 the Navy Department was established. US navy ships helped suppress piracy and some slave trading, and were active in the MEXICAN WAR. In the American CIVIL WAR the Union navy was active in blockading Confederate ports. (See MONITOR AND MERRIMACK.) The outbreak of the SPANISH-AMERICAN WAR in 1898 brought the US to the forefront of the world's seapowers, second only to Great Britain. America entered WWII when much of the US Pacific fleet had been destroyed at PEARL HARBOR. The US Navy played a decisive role in halting the Japanese advance in the Pacific, in the Battle of the CORAL SEA and the Battle of

MIDWAY (1942). Leading developments after the war were the nuclear-powered submarine (the US Navy commissioned the first, called *Nautilus*) and missiles (*Polaris* and *Poseidon*) carried on surface ships and submarines. By 1965, US fleets covered the oceans of the world. (See NAVY; NAVY, DEPARTMENT OF THE; see also MARINE CORPS, UNITED STATES.)

**NAZARETH,** historic town in N Israel, lower Galilee, where Jesus Christ lived as a youth. A place of Christian pilgrimage, the town has many shrines and churches. It also has some light industry and is an agricultural market center. Pop 40,400.

**NAZISM,** or National Socialism, the creed of the National Socialist German Workers' Party (Nazi Party) led by Adolf HITLER from 1921 to 1945. The Nazi movement began (1918–19) when Germany was humiliated and impoverished by defeat in WWI and by the severe terms of the Treaty of VERSAILLES. There was growing economic, political and social chaos, and fear of increasing communist influence. The Nazi Party emerged as a political force during the worldwide GREAT DEPRESSION. From a membership of around 100,000 in 1928, the party increased in strength to 920,000 in 1932. Using Hitler's powerful talent for public oratory and propaganda, the Nazis set forth a program designed to appeal to the grievances of as wide a range of German society as possible. The ideas behind the program were rooted in nationalism, racism (especially ANTI-SEMITISM), authoritarianism and militarism. They were expressed by Hitler in *Mein Kampf* (*My Struggle*, 1923). Recovery of the German nation was to be accomplished by rearmament, territorial expansion to acquire *lebensraum* (living space) for the Teutonic *herrenrasse* (master race) and the restoration of self-respect under a unified military regime—*Ein Reich, Ein Volk, Ein Führer* (one state, one nation, one leader). The movement continued to grow, aided by publicity techniques, military pageantry and intimidation and terrorization of opponents by the party's brownshirted militia, the *Sturm-Abteilung* (S.A.). In 1932 the Nazi party won more than one-third of the seats in the German parliament (*Reichstag*) and in Jan. 1933 politicians who hoped to be able to manipulate Hitler and use his political power base made him chancellor. In 1933–34 he reversed the situation by establishing a Nazi dictatorship. With the aid of the secret police (GESTAPO) and the S.A., Hitler began systematically to intern Jews, other non-Aryans and any opposing

groups including labor unions and political parties in CONCENTRATION CAMPS. In the 1940s many of these were used for the systematic extermination of millions of Jews. Hitler's Nazi program of expansionism temporarily improved the German economic position, but led to WORLD WAR II, which resulted in the defeat of Germany and its allies and the end of the Nazi Party. (See also GERMANY; FASCISM.)

**NCAA.** See NATIONAL COLLEGIATE ATHLETIC ASSOCIATION.

**NE.** See ANNABA.

**NEARSIGHTEDNESS.** See MYOPIA.

**Name of state:** Nebraska
**Capital:** Lincoln
**Statehood:** March 1, 1867 (37th state)
**Familiar name:** Cornhusker state
**Area:** 77,227sq mi
**Population:** 1,570,006
**Elevation:** Highest—5,424ft, Kimball County; Lowest—840ft, Richardson County
**Motto:** Equality Before the Law
**State flower:** Goldenrod
**State bird:** Western meadowlark
**State tree:** Cottonwood
**State song:** "Beautiful Nebraska"

**NEBRASKA,** W central state of the US, bounded on the E by Ia. and Mo. across the Missouri R, on the S by Kan., and Col., to the W by Wyo. and on the N by S.D.

**Land.** Nebraska is an undulating plain which slopes gradually from NW to SE. Over half of the state's area is covered with fertile soil. Most of W Nebraska consists of semiarid high plains, often broken by rugged hills called buttes. In the NW corner of the state lie about 1,000sq mi of BADLANDS, used mostly for grazing. The state is crossed by many rivers (notably the Platte) and contains over 2,000 lakes. The climate is marked by extremes of very cold winters and very hot summers.

**People.** Although Nebraska is primarily an agricultural state, just over half its people live in urban areas. About 97% of the population is native born. About one-third have German ancestors; other large groups which settled the state were the English and the Irish.

**Economy.** The state's chief field crop is corn, followed by wheat, hay, grain and sorghum. The state contains one of the world's largest cattle markets and is a principal producer of beef cattle. Food processing is the most important industry; other major manufactures include electrical machinery, chemicals, metal products, printed material and electronic and transportation equipment.

**History.** During the 17th and 18th centuries the French established fur-trading centers there. Nebraska became part of the US with the LOUISIANA PURCHASE (1803), was set up as a territory under the KANSAS–NEBRASKA ACT (1854) and joined the Union in 1867. When the railroad crossed the state in that year, hordes of settlers began to move in. In the next two decades the pioneer farmers were active in the GRANGER and POPULIST movements. The state's prosperity depended upon agricultural productivity, and natural disasters and the Great Depression in the 1930s brought much hardship. In 1937 Nebraska adopted a unicameral (one-house) legislative system. After WWII increasing farm mechanization and new industries benefited the state's economy. At the start of the 1980s, Nebraska was in a quiet way doing very well. In 1980, a bad year economically nationwide, Nebraska's unemployment rate was low and her per capita income was a respectable $8,684.

**NEBULA,** an interstellar cloud of gas or dust. The term is Latin, meaning "cloud," and was initially used to denote any fuzzy celestial object, including COMETS and external GALAXIES: this practice has now largely been abandoned. There are two main types of nebula. **Diffuse nebulae** are large, formless clouds of gas and dust and may be either bright or dark. *Bright nebulae*, such as the ORION Nebula, appear to shine due to the proximity or more usually presence within them of bright stars, whose light they either reflect (reflection nebula) or absorb and re-emit (emission nebula). *Dark nebulae*, such as the Horsehead Nebula, are not close to, or do not contain, any bright stars, and hence appear as dark patches in the sky obscuring the light from stars beyond them. Study of diffuse nebulae is particularly important since it is generally accepted that they are in the process of condensing to form new STARS. **Planetary nebulae** are very much smaller, and are always connected with a star that has gone NOVA some time in the past. They are, in fact, the material that has been cast off by the star. They are usually symmetrical, forming an expanding shell around the central star, which is often still visible within. The Ring Nebula is an outstanding example.

**NEEDLEWORK,** work using a needle either for plain sewing like mending, darning, sewing seams or hemming, or for decorative embroidery such as smocking, needlepoint or canvas work (needlework on canvas backing), and drawn-thread work. Quilting involves sewing together two layers of material with padding between; appliqué is attaching small pieces of material to a backing material. LACE may be made with a needle and thread, being then called needlepoint lace; TATTING employs shuttles, CROCHET employs a hook and KNITTING employs needles: all four are usually termed needlework. Samplers are traditional forms of recording various embroidery stitches and designs; one of the earliest, Jane Bostocke's (1598), includes satin, chain, ladder, buttonhole, arrowhead and cross stitches in metal thread and silk.

**NEFERTITI,** or Nefretete (XVIII dynasty), queen of ancient Egypt, and subject of a famous painted limestone portrait bust now in the Berlin Museum. She was the wife of Pharaoh AKHENATON (reigned c1379–62 BC).

**NEGEV,** also Negeb, a triangular region of hills, plateaus and desert in S Israel, extending S from Beersheba to Elath on the Gulf of Aqaba. It covers an area of around 5,000sq mi, or more than half of Israel. Although it is mainly an arid region, irrigation has made many areas fertile. It is rich in mineral and natural gas resources.

**NEGROES, American,** descendants of Negro slaves brought from Africa to North America from the 16th to the 19th centuries. They belong to the Negroid race, although about one third of American Negroes possess some Caucasoid genes. Today there are about 24 million Negroes in the US, roughly the same number in South America and about 32,000 in Canada.

**History.** During the nearly 400 years of the slave trade, some 10–15 million slaves were brought to the Americas. The slaves were first brought over by the Spanish and Portuguese and then by the American colonists. The slave trade reached its height in the 18th century. After the Revolutionary War, however, it seemed for a time that slavery was dying out, with at least six states passing anti-slavery laws. This was all changed by Eli WHITNEY's invention of the cotton gin in 1793, for this made cotton a viable cash crop. The admission into the Union of the state of Louisiana (1812), quickly followed by Mississippi (1817) and

Alabama (1819), opened up new lands for cotton and sugarcane. Although Congress prohibited the further importation of slaves (1808), the slave trade continued to flourish illegally, and by 1860 about half the population of the South were slaves. When the Civil War broke out there were nearly 4 million slaves in the US, plus about half a million freed slaves. However, the freed slaves never had a place in American society, and attempts were made to repatriate them to LIBERIA, on the W coast of Africa. The slavery issue was, of course, one of the main causes of the Civil War. While the slave-based cotton industry of the South had been booming, the North had been rejecting slavery. Of note are the founding of the American Anti-Slavery Society in 1833 (see ABOLITIONISM), and the publication in 1852 of Harriet Beecher STOWE's *Uncle Tom's Cabin*. The Civil War saw an end to slavery in the US, but it did little to improve the position of the freed Negro in American society. With the withdrawal of federal troops in 1877, the Negro in the South was soon reduced to a condition little better than that of slavery—it must be remembered that until the early 20th century, 90% of US Negroes lived in the South. Some Negro writers (e.g., Booker T. WASHINGTON) were willing to accept the position of the Negro as a second-class citizen, but others, including W. E. B. DU BOIS, a co-founder of the NATIONAL ASSOCIATION FOR THE ADVANCEMENT OF COLORED PEOPLE (1909), believed in fighting for Negro equality. Basic socioeconomic change was to prove the precursor to social and political change.

In the first half of the 20th century, some five million Negroes left the South for the overcrowded cities of the North. There the Negro could begin to have some political effect, and some individual Negroes were able to distinguish themselves professionally. However, it was not until the historic Supreme Court decision of May 17, 1954, ordering the integration of all schools, that the position of the Negro in American society began to change fundamentally. Under the leadership of Martin Luther KING, the civil rights movement spread all over the South, leading eventually to the Voting Rights Act of 1960, and the Civil Rights Act of 1964 and 1968. In northern cities, however, unemployment and poverty loomed as the most pressing problems for the Negroes, and between 1965 and 1967 many of the "black ghettos" exploded into violence. The late 1960s saw the emergence of the BLACK POWER movement, with groups like the BLACK MUSLIMS and the BLACK PANTHERS. These groups rejected civil rights activity and wished to organize blacks into separate social and economic communities within a white America. By the mid-1970s the more violent aspects of Black Power had dissipated themselves. American Negroes nevertheless asserted their own social and cultural identity. An indication of this was the rejection of the old term "Negro" in favor of "Black" or "Afro-American." In the 1980s black progress continued to be promoted by AFFIRMATIVE ACTION but otherwise slowed as a result of budget cuts in many of the 1960s social and economic programs that had benefited disadvantaged blacks as a group.

**NEGROID**, one of the racial divisions of man. The RACE is characterized by woolly hair and yellow, dark brown or black skin. Most negroid peoples originated in Africa, but Melanesians and Negritos are also negroid.

**NEHEMIAH** (flourished 5th century BC), Jewish leader of the return from the BABYLONIAN CAPTIVITY. As described in the OLD TESTAMENT Book of Nehemiah (written with the Book of EZRA by the author of CHRONICLES), he rebuilt Jerusalem's walls and enforced moral and religious reforms.

**NEHRU, Jawaharlal** (1889–1964), first prime minister of independent India. An English-educated lawyer, he embraced the cause of India's freedom after the massacre at AMRITSAR (1919). In 1929 he became president of the Indian National Congress. He spent most of 1930–36 in prison for his part in civil disobedience campaigns. By 1939 his Marxist outlook had brought conflict to his long association with GANDHI, but during WWII the two leaders united in their opposition to aiding Britain unless India was freed. Released in 1945 after three years' imprisonment, Nehru began negotiations with Britain which culminated, in 1947, in the establishment of independent India. He was prime minister until his death, successfully guiding his country through the difficult early years of freedom. Although the eventual compromise of his neutralist and non-aggressive policies evoked some criticism, he never lost the profound devotion of his countrymen.

**NELSON, Byron** (1912–    ), US professional golfer. A US Open and two-time PGA and Masters' champion, he won 18 pro tournaments in 1945, 11 of them consecutively.

**NELSON, Horatio, Admiral Lord Nelson** (1758–1805), great British naval hero who defeated the French and Spanish Fleets at the Battle of TRAFALGAR. He entered the navy at age 12, was rapidly promoted, and given his first command in the French Revolutionary Wars. He was instrumental in defeating the Spanish fleet off Cape St. Vincent (1797). His destruction of the French fleet off Aboukir (1798) brought him fame and honors. Official disapproval caused by the scandal of his liaison with Emma, Lady HAMILTON, was dispelled by his defeat of the Danes at Copenhagen (1801). His pursuit of the French fleet on the renewal of the war in 1803 culminated in the Battle of Trafalgar, the occasion of his now-famous flag signal, "England expects that every man will do his duty." The victory cost Nelson his life, but ensured British naval supremacy for 100 years.

**NEMEROV, Howard** (1920– ), US poet, novelist and critic noted for his satiric power. His *Collected Poems* (1977) won The National Book Award and Pulitzer Prize in 1978. Among his novels are *The Melodramatists* (1949) and *The Homecoming Game* (1957).

**NEMIROVICH-DANCHENKO, Vladimir Ivanovich** (1858–1943), Russian novelist, playwright and producer, cofounder, with Stanislavsky, of the MOSCOW ART THEATER. As a producer, Nemirovich-Danchenko was a great patron of the works of Ibsen and Chekhov.

**NEOCLASSICISM,** in the visual arts and architecture, a movement, c1750–1850, to return to the style and spirit of classical times. A reaction against the BAROQUE, its ideals of simplicity and proportion were particularly successful in architecture. Leading figures included Thomas JEFFERSON in America, and Inigo JONES and Christopher WREN in England. In music, it was a movement from c1920 looking back to 18th-and 19th-century "classical" composers.

**NEOCONSERVATISM,** political philosophy of an influential group of former liberals, who in the late 1960s began to oppose many of the policies and principles associated with President Lyndon Johnson's Great Society programs. In particular, the neoconservatives (or new conservatives) objected to affirmative-action programs based on racial quotas, and they deplored a perceived trend toward lower standards and loss of individual initiative. The movement, often characterized as elitist, was first publicized in *Public Interest*, a quarterly edited by Irving Kristol and Daniel Bell. Norman Podhoretz, editor of *Commentary*, took the lead in calling for a strong anti-Soviet, pro-Israel foreign policy.

**NEOPLATONISM,** a school of philosophy based on the work of Plato and dominant from the 3rd to the 6th centuries AD. It was

developed by PLOTINUS and formulated in his *Enneads*. Neoplatonic philosophy set forth a systematized order which contained all levels and states of existence. From God, or the One, emanates the Divine Mind, from which the World Soul proceeds, and which in turn comprehends the visible world. Man's ideal is to rise upward toward union with the One. Neoplatonic philosophy greatly influenced early Christian theology through St. Augustine and others.

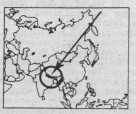

**Official name:** Nepal
**Capital:** Kathmandu
**Area:** 54,600sq mi
**Population:** 14,000,000
**Languages:** Nepali, Hindu, Tibeto-Burman dialects
**Religions:** Hindu, Buddhist
**Monetary unit(s):** 1 Nepali rupee=100 pice
**NEPAL,** independent kingdom of S Asia. It is a land of strongly contrasting climate and terrain, with the Himalayas in the N, the temperate Valley of Nepal in the center, and the low-lying swamplands and forests of the Terai region in the S. Its major rivers rise in Tibet.

**People.** The population of Nepal is of mixed Mongolian and Indo-Aryan origin. Its main ethnic groups are the Newars, the Bhotias (who include the Sherpas) and the GURKHAS. Hinduism, numerically the dominant religion, has long coexisted with Buddhism. Tribal and caste distinctions retain considerable importance. In spite of rapid educational expansion since 1951, the illiteracy rate is still about 85%.

**Economy.** Nepal's economy is predominantly agricultural. Crops include rice, wheat, corn, oilseeds, potatoes, jute, tobacco, opium and cotton. Livestock is important. The forests of the Terai provide wood, and medicinal herbs are exported from the slopes of the Himalayas. Nepal's few industries, employing only about 1% of the labor force, rely chiefly on the processing of agricultural products, but include wood and metal handicrafts. Means of transportation, though still severely limited in the remoter areas, now include roads linking the Valley of Nepal with both

Tibet and India, and several airports including an international facility at Kathmandu and smaller fields in towns like Pokhara.

**History.** Nepal comprised numerous principalities until it was conquered by the Gurkhas in 1768. Political power was in the hands of the RANA family from 1846 to 1951, when it returned to the monarchy. The first democratically-elected government came to power in 1959, but a conflict in 1962 resulted in King Mahendra's banning all political parties. The present king, Birendra, came to the throne in 1972 and continued his father's policies. In 1980 a referendum resulted in the continuance of the partyless government, Panchayat.

**NEPHRITIS,** INFLAMMATION affecting the KIDNEYS. The term **glomerulonephritis** covers a variety of diseases, often involving disordered IMMUNITY, in which renal glomeruli are damaged by immune complex deposition (e.g., BRIGHT'S DISEASE); by direct autoimmune attack (Goodpasture's syndrome), or sometimes as a part of systemic disease (e.g., LUPUS, endocarditis, DIABETES or hypertension). Acute or chronic renal failure or nephrotic syndrome may result. The treatment is immunosuppressive or with STEROIDS. Acute **pyelonephritis** is bacterial infection of the kidney and renal pelvis, following SEPTICEMIA or lower urinary tract infection. Typically, this involves FEVER, loin pain and painful, frequent urination. The treatment requires ANTIBIOTICS. Chronic pyelonephritis includes recurrent kidney infection with permanent scarring and functional impairment.

**NEPHROSIS,** or nephrotic syndrome, EDEMA associated with kidney disease (see NEPHRITIS).

**NEPTUNE,** the fourth-largest planet in the SOLAR SYSTEM and the eighth in position from the sun, with a mean solar distance of 30.07AU. Neptune was first discovered in 1846 by J. G. Galle using computations by LEVERRIER based on the perturbations of URANUS' orbit. The calculation had been performed independently by John Couch ADAMS in England but vacillations on the part of the then Astronomer Royal had precluded a rigorous search for the planet. Neptune has two moons, Triton and Nereid, the former having a circular, retrograde orbit, the latter having the most eccentric orbit of any moon in the solar system. Neptune's "year" is 164.8 times that of the earth, its day being 15.8h. Its diameter is about 51Mm and its mass 17.45 times that of the earth. Its structure and constitution are believed to resemble those of JUPITER.

**NERNST, Walther Hermann** (1864–1941), German physical chemist awarded the 1920 Nobel Prize for Chemistry for his discovery of the Third Law of THERMODYNAMICS.

**NERO** (37–68 AD), infamous Roman emperor. Born Lucius Domitius Ahenobarbus, he was adopted by his stepfather, emperor Claudius, whom he succeeded in 54 AD. Nero had Claudius' son Britannicus murdered in 55. In 59 he killed his mother Agrippina, and in 62 his wife Octavia, Claudius' daughter. The wise rule of SENECA and Burrus, to whom Nero had left affairs of state, ended in 62. Nero rebuilt Rome after the fire in 64 AD. Not himself responsible, he attributed the fire to the Christians, and the first Roman persecution followed. His cruelty, instability, and imposition of heavy taxes led to a revolt. Deserted by the PRAETORIAN GUARD, Nero committed suicide.

**NERUDA, Pablo** (1904–1973), born Neftalí Ricardo Reyes Basualto, influential Chilean poet, diplomat and communist leader. He won the 1971 Nobel Prize for Literature. His verse collections, written in the surrealist vein, include *Twenty Love Poems and a Song of Despair* (1924) and the highly-regarded *Canto general* (1950).

**NERVAL, Gérard de** (1808–1855), born Gérar Labrunie, French romantic writer who anticipated the symbolist and surrealist movements in French Literature. His works include a collection of sonnets, *Les Chimère* (1854); some short stories, *Les Filles du Feu* (1854), and his autobiography, *Aurélia* (1853–54).

**NERVI, Pier Luigi** (1891–1979), Italian civil engineer and architect. In the 1940s he invented *ferrocemento,* a new form of reinforced concrete. Notable among his bold and imaginative designs are the Turin exposition hall, the railway station in Naples, the Olympic buildings in Rome, and (in collaboration) the UNESCO headquarters in Paris.

**NERVOUS SYSTEM,** the system of tissues which coordinates an animal's various activities with each other and with external events by means of nervous impulses conducted rapidly from part to part via nerves. Its responses are generally rapid, whereas those of the endocrine system with which it shares its coordinating and integrating function are generally slow (see GLANDS, HORMONES).

The nervous system can be divided into two parts. The **central nervous system** (CNS), consisting of BRAIN and SPINAL CORD, stores and processes information and sends messages to muscles and glands. The **peripheral nervous system,** consisting of 12 pairs of cranial nerves arising in and near the medulla oblongata of the brain and 31 pairs of spinal nerves arising at intervals from the spinal cord, carries messages to and from the central nervous system.

A third system, the autonomic nervous system, normally considered part of the peripheral nervous system, controls involuntary actions such as heartbeat and digestion. It is divisible into two complementary parts: the *sympathetic system* prepares the body for "fight or flight," and the *parasympathetic system* controls the body's vegetative functions. Most internal organs are innervated by both parts.

The nervous system's basic anatomical and functional unit is the highly specialized nerve cell or NEURON, the shape of which varies greatly in different regions. It possesses two kinds of processes: *dendrites* which together with the cell body receive impulses from other neurons, and an *axon* which conducts impulses to other neurons. Axons vary greatly in length (up to a few meters) and speed of conduction (up to about 90m/s).

Sensory or *afferent neurons* carry information to the central nervous system from sensory receptors (such as skin receptors and muscle stretch receptors), whereas *efferent neurons* carry information away from it. Efferent neurons passing to muscle are called *motor neurons*.

Nerves are formed from many axons, both afferent and efferent, surrounded by their associated sheaths which insulate them from each other. Axons surrounded by a fat and protein sheath, called a MYELIN sheath, conduct fastest. Just prior to entering the spinal cord each spinal nerve divides into a *dorsal root* containing afferent axons only and a *ventral root* containing efferent axons only.

Adjacent neurons communicate through specialized contact points or *synapses* which are either excitatory or inhibitory. The elaborate neural circuitry arising from synaptic contact in the central nervous system is responsible for much of behavior, from simple reflex action to complex thought-communication patterns.

The nerve impulse, or action potential, is an electrical signal conducted at speeds far slower than ELECTRICITY. An electrical potential difference of about 70mV, called the resting potential, exists between the inside and outside of the neuron due to the ionic concentration imbalance between inside and outside, and a metabolic pump moving IONS across the cell membrane. If the resting potential is reduced below a

certain threshold level, as may occur when impulses are received from other neurons, an impulse is initiated. Impulses are all the same strength ("all-or-none" law), and travel to the end of the axon to the synapse where a chemical transmitter substance (see ACETYLCHOLINE) is released which initiates a new electrical signal in the next neuron. (See also NEURALGIA; NEURITIS; NEUROLOGY.)

**NEST,** a structure prepared by many animals for the protection of their eggs and young, or for sleeping purposes. In social insects, the nest provides the home of the whole colony, and may have special structures for temperature control and ventilation. The sleeping nests of, for example, the great apes, are commonly no more than crudely woven hammocks of twigs and branches. The sleeping nests of other mammals (which may be used for hibernation) are as complex and woven as any breeding nest. Both these and the nests used by birds and mammals for breeding, must protect the animals within from both weather and predators. Nests can be built of mud, leaves, twigs, down, paper and various human garbage.

**NESTORIANS,** members of the heretical Christian sect named for Nestorius (Patriarch of Constantinople 428–431), who was condemned by the Council of Ephesus (431) for rejecting the title "Mother of God" for the Virgin MARY, and teaching the existence of two persons—divine and human—in Jesus Christ. The Nestorians expanded vigorously for 800 years, but were persecuted by the Mongols and—in recent times—by the Turks. The modern Nestorian (Assyrian) Church has about 100,000 members, mainly in Iraq, Iran, and Syria

**Official name:** Kingdom of the Netherlands
**Capital:** Amsterdam
**Seat of government:** The Hague
**Area:** 15,785sq mi
**Population:** 14,091,000
**Language:** Dutch
**Religions:** Protestant, Roman Catholic
**Monetary unit(s):** 1 Guilder = 100 cents

**NETHERLANDS, The,** kingdom in W Europe, commonly known as Holland. The land is mostly flat, about 38% is below sea-level. It is protected from the sea by a narrow belt of dunes bordering the North Sea coast and a vast complex of dikes forming POLDERS. The major cities of the Netherlands are located in the polders region, which, with its rich clay soil, contains the finest agricultural land. The higher inland region has natural drainage but relatively poor, sandy soil, except where it is traversed by the Lower Rhine, Waal and Maas (Meuse) rivers. The climate of the Netherlands is mild and damp.

**People.** The Netherlands is one of the world's most densely populated countries. Nearly half the population lives close to the three largest cities—Amsterdam (the capital), The Hague (the seat of government) and Rotterdam. Schooling is compulsory for children between the ages of 7 and 15. The literacy rate is one of the highest in the world. There are 11 universities, including the famous public universities at Leiden, Utrecht, Groningen and Amsterdam. There is no official religion.

**Economy.** Industry now provides 40% of the Netherlands' GNP, and employs over a million people. There are reserves of oil, natural gas and coal, but most raw materials must be imported. Major industries include oil-refining, iron and steel textiles, machinery, electrical equipment and plastics. Dairy produce, the basis of Holland's intensive agriculture, sustains a large food-processing industry. Financial and transportation services contribute significantly. Tourism is also important. A highly advanced transportation system includes about 4,000mi of natural and artificial waterways. The Netherlands is a member of the EUROPEAN COMMON MARKET.

**History.** The Low Countries' seven northern provinces (now the Netherlands) broke away from Spanish rule under William the Silent, Prince of Orange, to form the Union of Utrecht in 1579. Independence was declared in 1581 but not recognized by Spain until the Treaty of Westphalia (1648), which ended the THIRTY YEARS' WAR. The 17th century saw the golden age of the Netherlands: made prosperous by overseas trading and colonizing, it was also famed for its religious tolerance and cultural life (see REMBRANDT; VERMEER; SPINOZA). In the 18th century Holland was outrivalled by England and France. Popular sympathy with the French Revolution led (1795) to the establishment of the French-ruled Batavian Republic.

After the defeat of Napoleon (1814), the United Kingdom of the Netherlands was formed, joining Holland with present-day Belgium. The latter broke away in 1830. Holland's subsequent history, under its constitutional monarchy, has been marked by a steady growth of prosperity and liberalism. Neutral in WWI, the Dutch recovered rapidly after the devastating German occupation in WWII. Since the war, they have taken a leading part in European integration.

**NETHERLANDS ANTILLES** (the Dutch West Indies), two groups of islands in the Caribbean Sea. They are an autonomous part of the Netherlands. The S group comprises Curacao (location of the capital, Willemstad), Aruba, and Bonaire, about 50mi off Venezuela. The N group, 500mi to the NE, comprises Saba, St. Eustacius, and St. Maarten. The processing of petroleum from Venezuela accounts for 98% of exports. There is also some tourism. The S group came under Dutch control in 1634, the N group in 1815. They became self-governing in 1954. Independence referenda are scheduled for the 1980s, present evidence indicating that Aruba favors independence while other islands favor continued Dutch rule for economic reasons. Pop 246,540.

**NEUMANN, Johann Balthasar** (1687–1753), leading German architect of the late BAROQUE style. He designed palaces churches, houses, bridges and water systems. Especially notable are the church in Vierzehnheiligen and the Residenz at Würzburg.

**NEURITIS,** or peripheral neuropathy, any disorder of the peripheral NERVOUS SYSTEM which interferes with sensation, the nerve control of MUSCLE, or both. Its causes include DRUGS and heavy metals (e.g., gold) infection or allergic reaction to it (as with LEPROSY or DIPHTHERIA); inflammatory disease (rheumatoid ARTHRITIS); infiltration, systemic and metabolic disease (e.g. DIABETES or PORPHYRIA); VITAMIN deficiency (BERIBERI); organ failure (e.g., of the LIVER or KIDNEY); genetic disorders, and the nonmetastatic effects of distant CANCER Numbness, tingling, weakness and PARALYSIS result, at first affecting the extremities. Diagnosis involves electrical studies of the nerves as well as the procedure of nerve BIOPSY.

**NEURON,** or nerve cell, the basic unit of the NERVOUS SYSTEM (including the BRAIN and SPINAL CORD). Each has a long AXON specialized for transmitting electrical impulses and releasing chemical transmitters that act on MUSCLE or effector cells or other neurons. Branched processes called dendrites integrate the input to neurons.

**NEUROSIS,** originally any NERVOUS SYSTEM activity; later, any disorder of the nervous system; though in PSYCHOANALYSIS, those mental disorders (e.g., HYSTERIA) unconnected with the nervous system. It is usually seen as based in UNCONSCIOUS conflict, with an unconscious attempt to conform to reality (not escape from it, as in PSYCHOSIS). **Actual neurosis** is based in disorders of current sexual behavior (see SEX); **psychoneurosis** is rooted in the past life; **anxiety neurosis** is characterized by exaggerated ANXIETY. (See OBSESSIONAL NEUROSIS.)

**NEUTRA, Richard Joseph** (1892–1970), Austrian born US architect who brought the INTERNATIONAL STYLE of architecture to the US. The Tremaine House (1947) in Santa Barbara, Calif., demonstrates his skill in relating a building to its setting.

**NEUTRALITY,** the status of a country which elects not to participate in a war between other countries. Under international law, a neutral state has the right to have its boundaries and territorial waters respected, and the obligation to remain impartial towards belligerents in its actions. The two World Wars, however, brought many violations of neutrality, e.g. Germany's invasion of Belgium in WWI. Before the US entered WWII, her neutrality was effectively nullified by her support of the Allies. With the need for would-be neutral countries to defend their status by aggression (as America in WWI), the viability of neutrality became questionable. Membership in the United Nations is not compatible with neutrality, since members may be called upon to act against aggressors.

**NEUTRINO.** See SUBATOMIC PARTICLES.

**NEUTRON (n),** uncharged SUBATOMIC PARTICLE with rest mass $1.6748 \times 10^{-27}$hg (slightly greater than that of the PROTON) and SPIN ½. A free neutron is slightly unstable, decaying to a proton, an ELECTRON and an antineutrino with HALF-LIFE 680s:

$$n \rightarrow p^+ + e^- + \bar{v}$$

But neutrons bound within the nucleus of an ATOM are stable. All nuclei save hydrogen contain neutrons, which contribute to the nuclear cohesive forces and separate the mutually repulsive protons. Free neutrons are produced in many nuclear reactions, including nuclear FISSION, and hence nuclear reactors and particle ACCELERATORS are used as sources. The neutron was discovered in 1932 by Sir James CHADWICK, who bombarded beryllium with ALPHA PARTICLES emitted by a radioisotope.

Neutrons are highly penetrating, and are moderated (slowed down) by colliding with the nuclei of light atoms. They induce certain heavy atoms to undergo fission. Shielding requires thick concrete walls. Neutrons are detected by counting the ionizing particles or GAMMA RAYS produced when they react with nuclei. Neutrons have wave properties, and their DIFFRACTION is used to study crystal structures and magnetic properties.

**NEUTRON BOMB,** or neutron weapon, technically known as the enhanced radiation weapon, a tactical nuclear armament fashioned to release energy as subatomic radiation rather than blast or heat. Slated for anti-tank use, its "bullets," high radiation neutrons, can penetrate armor, causing tank personnel to die of radiation sickness.

Neutron bombs are in effect H-bombs stripped of their outer shell of uranium 238. In a typical H-bomb, the heat created by the explosion of a fission device (A-bomb) causes a fusion reaction in the surrounding fusion materials (deuterium and tritium). In the process, a barrage of high energy neutrons are released. During a second fissioning process, these neutrons cause a chain reaction in the uranium 238 coating the bomb, resulting in added explosive yield. Since the neutron weapon lacks a uranium shell, the high energy neutrons are released directly in the form of intense radiation which destroys human cells particularly those of the central nervous system.

Pro-neutron bomb factions tout the weapon for its lower blast effect, resulting in reduced toll to land, property and surrounding civilians. They also cite its deterrent quality in creating "a more certain NATO capacity". Opponents counter that neutron bombs have in fact a significant blast effect and that their so-called "cleanliness" could increase the credibility of initial use of nuclear weapons in combat.

The neutron bomb has been tested by the US, USSR and France. In August 1981, President Reagan decided to produce and stockpile neutron bombs in the form of Lance missile warheads and eight-inch artillery shells.

**NEVADA,** US western state, situated between the Rocky Mts and the Sierra Nevada, bounded to the E by Ut. and Ariz., to the S and W by Cal., and to the N by Ore. and Ida.

**Land.** Most of the state lies in the Great Basin, an arid plateau at about 5,000ft above sea level which is broken by many short mountain ranges running from N to S.

**Name of state:** Nevada
**Capital:** Carson City
**Statehood:** Oct. 31, 1864 (36th state)
**Familiar name:** Silver State, Sagebrush State
**Area:** 110,540sq mi
**Population:** 799,184
**Elevation:** Highest—13,140ft, Boundary Peak; Lowest—470ft, Colorado River in Clark County
**Motto:** All for Our Country
**State flower:** Sagebrush
**State bird:** Mountain bluebird
**State tree:** Single-leaf piñon
**State song:** "Home Means Nevada"

Nevada's longest river is the Humboldt and the major lakes are the Mead (formed by the Hoover Dam), Tahoe, Pyramid and Walker. The state has the lowest average annual rainfall in the US, and because of its altitude, temperatures drop considerably at night. There are extremes of heat in summer and cold in winter. Much of the state is arid desert.

**People.** Most of the population of Nevada, which ranks 47th in state populations, is concentrated in Las Vegas and Reno. Over 90% of the population is white, the rest are Negro or Indian and there are a number of Indian reservations. Carson City is the smallest state capital in the US.

**Economy.** The Nevada economy depends heavily on tourism, which its liberal gambling and divorce laws support. Mining, especially of copper and iron ore, is also important. The manufacturing sector is gradually expanding. Principal products include gaming devices, electronic equipment, chemicals and wood and glass items.

**History.** Nevada was first explored by the Spanish in the 1770s. In 1827 Jedediah SMITH crossed Nevada toward Cal. and in the 1840s John FRÉMONT explored it extensively. It first became a US possession by the treaty of GUADELOUPE-HIDALGO after the MEXICAN WAR. In 1859, the discovery of the COMSTOCK LODE, rich gold and silver deposits, attracted thousands of prospectors to the area. In 1864 Nevada was made the 36th state, largely to secure its precious metal resources for the Union in the Civil War. In the late 19th century prosperity declined when the gold and silver mines were depleted. But copper mining and tourism have brought new wealth to the state, and in the 1970s it was one of the fastest-growing states in the US, with a high average per capita income of over $10,000 annually. Entering the 1980s, the state focused on the issues of control and reparation of damage to the environment.

**NEVELSON, Louise** (1900–    ), Russian-born US sculptor. She is famous for her intricate wooden constructions, both free-standing and wall-hung, which suggest vast ranges of box-like shelves with found objects on them.

**NEVINS, Allan** (1890–1971), US historian, whose best-known work is the Civil War series, *The Ordeal of the Union* (1947–60). Nevins received Pulitzer Prizes for his biographies, *Grover Cleveland* (1932) and *Hamilton Fish* (1936). His many other works include the biography *John D. Rockefeller* (1953).

**NEWBERY MEDAL,** an annual award for the most distinguished contribution to American children's literature published in the preceding year. The medal is named for John Newbery (1713–1767), an English publisher and bookseller who made a specialty of books for children.

**NEW BRUNSWICK,** second largest of the Canadian Atlantic provinces, one of the Maritime Provinces. Its coast runs some 750mi along the Chaleur Bay, the Gulf of St. Lawrence, Northumberland Strait and the Bay of FUNDY.

**Land and People.** About 88% of the province is forested. The center is high land and there is a coastal plain in the NE. The province is well-drained by many swift-flowing rivers and streams. The fertile valley of the St. John R provides an excellent farming region. The climate is continental and ocean breezes moderate extremes along the coast. About half the population live in cities, the largest being Saint John, Moncton and the capital Fredericton. Over 50% of the population is of British origin, and 33% of French. French is the language of instruction in public schools. New Brunswick had been losing population to central Canada, notably Ontario, but in recent years population has grown at a rate of about 1%.

**Economy.** The economy is largely based on forest industries, pulp and paper manufacturing, food processing, fishing and tourism. Copper, lead, silver and particularly zinc mining are being developed in the NE. Since WWII hydroelectric power has been exploited on an increasing scale. During the past 10 years, the work force has expanded by more than 60,000 people and the manufacturing sector has diversified. Manufactures include fabricated metals, machinery, plastics, and electrical products. An important renewable energy resource of potential value is the tidal power of the Bay of Fundy.

History. Jacques CARTIER explored the region in 1534. Samuel de CHAMPLAIN established a settlement in 1604 in what became known as French ACADIA. Britain gained control of the region in 1713, but it was not until the arrival of Loyalists from the US after the Revolution that New Brunswick became a separate province (1784). The boundary with Maine was settled after the AROOSTOOK WAR by the WEBSTER-ASHBURTON TREATY of 1842. New Brunswick was one of the four original provinces to join the Dominion of Canada in 1867. The province developed slowly, inhabitants emigrated and it was an under-privileged area. However the discovery of mineral deposits, the growing importance of the port of Saint John and large federal financial support have helped in economic expansion.

**Name of province:** New Brunswick
**Joined Confederation:** July 1, 1867
**Capital:** Fredericton
**Area:** 28,354sq mi.
**Population:** 707,000

NEW CALEDONIA, French overseas territory in the SW Pacific, formed by the islands of New Caledonia, Isle of Pines, LOYALTY ISLANDS and smaller groups, and covering 8,548sq mi. The economy rests on nickel mining, coffee and copra. The capital, Nouméa, is on the principal island, New Caledonia (area 6,530sq mi), which is mountainous, temperate, but not widely fertile. New Caledonia island was discovered by Captain COOK in 1774 and annexed by the French in 1853.

NEWCOMEN, Thomas (1663–1729), British inventor of the first practical STEAM ENGINE (before 1712). His device, employed mainly to pump water from mines, used steam pressure to raise the piston and, after condensation of the steam, atmospheric pressure to force it down again: it was thus called an "atmospheric" steam engine.

NEW DEAL, program adopted by President Franklin D. ROOSEVELT to alleviate the effects of the GREAT DEPRESSION. On his election in 1933, Roosevelt initiated a dramatic program of relief and reform, known as "the first hundred days." He called an immediate BANK HOLIDAY and restored confidence in those banks which

were allowed to reopen by the EMERGENCY BANKING ACT. Bank funds and practices were overseen by the FEDERAL DEPOSIT INSURANCE CORPORATION and the FEDERAL RESERVE board. Measures were taken to control the Stock Exchange (see SECURITIES AND EXCHANGE COMMISSION).

Farm recovery was helped by the creation of credit facilities, subsidies, rural electrification programs and the resettlement of some farmers in more productive areas. The NATIONAL RECOVERY ADMINISTRATION (NRA) and the CIVILIAN CONSERVATION CORPS (CCC) were set up to boost business and ensure jobs, though many of the NRA's functions were later declared unconstitutional by the Supreme Court. Unions were protected by the Labor Relations Act (1935), and the FAIR LABOR STANDARDS ACT (1938) set a national MINIMUM WAGE. Measures were taken to relieve poverty and unemployment. The SOCIAL SECURITY system was established in 1935 and jobs were created by the WORKS PROJECTS ADMINISTRATION (WPA), including the massive TENNESSEE VALLEY AUTHORITY (TVA) project. The Home Loan Corporation and the FEDERAL HOUSING ADMINISTRATION (FHA) helped home owners and aided recovery in the construction industry.

After its initial popularity, the New Deal met increasing opposition in Congress and the Supreme Court. It ended in 1939 as the economy expanded to meet the demands of WWII. The question of its success remains controversial; many believe that only WWII finally ended the Great Depression. Its influence however was permanent; it changed the direction of social legislation, centralized control of the economy and altered the US public's attitude to the role of the federal government.

NEW DELHI, capital of India, on the Jumna R, in the N central part of the country. It was built by the British in 1912–29 to the S of Delhi, when the capital was transferred from Calcutta. New Delhi, a spacious city, was designed by the architect Sir Edwin Lutyens. Since independence in 1947 new official buildings, shops and industrial quarters have been added to the city. Pop 302,000.

NEW FEDERALISM, a term used by some US political leaders to suggest a changed relationship between the federal and state governments, with functions and powers exercised primarily by the federal government becoming more widely shared with the states. A concept set forth by Republican Presidents NIXON and REAGAN, among others, it appealed to supporters of states' rights and to those who, in general, wanted to get the federal government "off their backs." The New Federalism found practical application in revenue sharing and block grants.

**NEWFOUNDLAND,** largest Canadian Atlantic province, comprising Newfoundland Island and Labrador and their adjacent islands.

**Land.** Newfoundland Island has a long (6,000mi) indented coastline with many islands, which is most rugged in the S and E coast; the land rises from the E lowlands to a plateau and mountains, the highest being the Lewis Hills (2,672ft). The central plateau has many lakes and bogs. Avalon peninsula is the most densely populated part of the province, and contains the capital, St. John's. Labrador is a rugged, forested plateau (mountain peaks reaching 5,160ft) with a rocky coast and many fiords. Its climate is harsher than that of Newfoundland island; winters are severe throughout the whole province. More than 56% of Newfoundland province is forested.

**People.** The province is sparsely populated and most of the people live close to the sea. Only 3% live in Labrador, and 10% of these are of Indian or Eskimo descent.

**Economy.** The economy is gold, are very large iron-ore mines in Labrador; copper, gold, lead, silver and zinc are also mined. In the 1970s more than half of Canada's output of iron was produced in western Labrador. The province still contains large reserves of mineral wealth. Exploration began in 1965 of the continental shelf, and in 1979 high-quality crude oil was discovered on the southeastern Grand Banks. Fishing is Newfoundland's best-known industry. Fishermen from Europe and Japan are attracted to the famous GRAND BANKS, which abound in cod, haddock and other fish. Fishstocks were seriously depleted in 1977 but are being restored. Manufacturing accounts for some 44% of the economy; industries include paper, steel, textiles and clothing manufacture and food processing. Electricity is mostly provided by hydroelectric plants, the most recent being the gigantic Churchill Falls project; completed in 1974, it is one of the largest generating plants in the world. The province's strategic position has made it important in transatlantic air travel; there are large air terminals at Gander and Goose Bay.

**History.** Remains of 10th-century Viking settlements have been found on Newfoundland Island. John CABOT rediscovered the island in 1497 and Sir Humphrey GILBERT claimed it for England in 1583. It was not until 1763, after the SEVEN YEARS' WAR, that England gained firm control, although France retained the "French shore" on the W coast until 1904. Newfoundland gained fully responsible government in 1855, but Britain took control again in 1934 when the island's economy was hit by the Great Depression. Newfoundland chose to join the Dominion of Canada in 1949 and became Canada's tenth province. Since then federal aid and the boom in mining have dramatically raised the standard of living and reduced unemployment.

**Name of province:** Newfoundland
**Capital:** St. John's
**Joined confederation:** March 31, 1949
**Area:** 156,185sq mi
**Population:** 580,000

**NEWFOUNDLAND DOG,** a large water dog, probably originating from crossbreeding of native with European dogs. It has a broad head, stands about 28in high and has a dull jet black coat. The dog's webbed feet and oily coat make it a powerful swimmer.

**NEW FRANCE,** North American territories held by France from the 16th century to 1763 which extended W beyond the St. Lawrence to the Great Lakes and NE areas. France lost these territories in a series of colonial wars with Britain.

**NEW FREEDOM,** program adopted by President WILSON in 1912 which aimed to establish more political and economic opportunities in the US and to free the US economy from tariffs and other restrictions. He passed the UNDERWOOD TARIFF Act, the Federal Reserve Act (see FEDERAL RESERVE SYSTEM) and the Antitrust Act in 1913–17.

**NEW FRONTIER,** collective name for the policies of the administration of President John F. Kennedy, derived from Kennedy's acceptance speech after winning the Democratic nomination in 1960 when he said that the nation stood on "the edge of a new frontier." Characteristic New Frontier programs aimed at space exploration, improved science education, extension of civil-rights protections, and better medical care for the elderly.

**NEW GRANADA,** Spanish colony in NW South America which included present–day Colombia, Panama, Ecuador and Venezuela, established in the first half of the 16th century. It was named by Gonzalo JIMÉNEZ DE QUESADA in 1537 and attached to the vice-royalty of Peru until 1717 when it became a vice-royalty itself until independence in 1819.

**NEW GUINEA,** world's second largest island. It lies in the SW Pacific just S of the equator and is separated from N Australia by the Torres Strait and the Arafura and

Coral Seas. The island covers an area of 319,713sq mi, and comprises a series of high central mountain ranges and densely-forested tropical lowlands. Djaja Peak is the highest mountain at 16,535ft. Politically, New Guinea is divided into two parts: IRIAN JAYA, a province of Indonesia, and PAPUA NEW GUINEA, self-governing since 1973.

Melanesians and Papuans are the two largest population groups in New Guinea. In remote mountain areas there are primitive Negrito groups and Papuans some of whom are head-hunting tribes. Some animals such as the opossum are related to Australian species. There are more than 70 species of snakes, many species of butterflies and birds of paradise.

New Guinea was discovered by the Portuguese in the 16th century and named for Guinea, West Africa. It was colonized by the Dutch, Germans and British; after WWI, Australia gained the German sector. The island was bitterly contested by the Japanese and the Allies during WWII.

**Name of state:** New Hampshire
**Capital:** Concord
**Statehood:** June 21, 1788 (9th state)
**Familiar name:** Granite State
**Area:** 9,304sq mi
**Population:** 920,610
**Elevation:** Highest—6,288ft, Mount Washington; Lowest—sea level, Atlantic Ocean
**Motto:** Live Free or Die
**State flower:** Purple lilac
**State bird:** Purple finch
**State tree:** White birch
**State songs:** "New Hampshire, My New Hampshire," "Old New Hampshire"

NEW HAMPSHIRE, state, NE US, one of the New England states and one of the original 13 colonies, bounded to the E by Me. and the Atlantic Ocean, to the S by Mass., to the W by Vt. across the Connecticut R and to the N by Canada. Forests cover four-fifths of New Hampshire's surface, and it contains mountains, lakes and streams. Despite its rural appearance and fame as a tourist center it is also one of the most intensively industrialized states of the union.

**Land.** New Hampshire can be divided into three main areas: the White Mountains in the N third of the state; the coastal lowlands in the extreme SE corner; and the New England Upland, a rolling plateau that covers the central and S portions of the state. The 86-peak Presidential Range includes the highest point in New England, Mount Washington (6,288ft); and the Franconia Range includes Profile Mountain and the steep chasm of the Flume. The Merrimack R drains southward from the White Mountains, and most of the state's major cities, industries and farms are located along its hilly, uneven valley.

**People.** Most of New Hampshire's people and industries are concentrated in the S, but the scenic beauty of the White Mountains attracts thousands of skiers, hikers, campers and sightseers. About 40% of the population is urban. Cities include Manchester, Nashua and Concord.

**Economy.** The original importance of agriculture, textiles and leather goods has declined, but under the farsighted planning of the New Business Development Corporation, the development of new and varied industries more than outweighs these losses. Principal manufactures include leather, wood and paper goods, electrical equipment, machinery and metal products. Part of the population commutes to jobs in neighboring Mass.

**History.** The first settlements were established along the coast in the 1620s, and in 1629 Capt. John MASON was granted the land between the Merrimack and Piscataqua rivers, which he named New Hampshire. Inland settlement was slow and began on a large scale only after the FRENCH AND INDIAN WARS. New Hampshire was the first colony to declare itself independent of British rule and to adopt a new constitution, 1776. New Hampshire plays a national bellwether role in presidential election campaigns by virtue of holding the first primaries.

NEW HARMONY, town in SW Ind., the site of two cooperative communities in the early 1800s. "Harmonie" was settled in 1814 by George Rapp, leader of the HARMONY SOCIETY. In 1824 the colony was sold to Robert OWEN, and renamed New Harmony. The community, based on socialism and Owen's theories of human freedom, was a noted scientific and cultural center but broke up in 1828. Pop 945.

NEWHART, Bob (1929–    ), US comedian. A master of the "telephone monologue," he recorded the first of several successful comedy albums, *The Button-Down Mind of Bob Newhart*, in 1960. His television series, a situation comedy, won him an Emmy Award in 1962.

**NEW HAVEN**, third-largest city in Conn., its chief port, and famous as the seat of YALE UNIVERSITY. It is a noted cultural center and important for its varied industrial products. It was founded in 1638 by Puritans from Boston led by John DAVENPORT and Theophilus EATON. It was a flourishing port at the end of the 18th century, and only revived as such when a deep water channel was dredged in 1927. Pop 126,109.

**NEW HEBRIDES.** See VANUATU.

**NE WIN** (formerly Shu Maung; 1911– ), Burmese general, political leader and president of Burma since 1974. After serving as prime minister, he assumed power in 1962 in an army coup and attempted to establish a form of socialist republic in Burma.

**Name of state:** New Jersey
**Capital:** Trenton
**Statehood:** Dec. 18, 1787 (3rd state)
**Familiar name:** Garden State
**Area:** 7,836sq mi
**Population:** 7,364,158
**Elevation:** Highest—1,803ft, High Point
Lowest—sea level, Atlantic Ocean
**Motto:** Liberty and Prosperity
**State flower:** Purple violet
**State bird:** Eastern goldfinch
**State tree:** Red oak
**State song:** None

**NEW JERSEY**, state, E US, bounded on the E by N.Y. and the Atlantic Ocean and on the W by Del. and Pa. across the Delaware R, the nation's most highly urbanized and most densely populated state, and one of the original 13 colonies.

**Land.** New Jersey can be divided into four natural regions: the Appalachian Valley in the NW; the Appalachian Highlands running NE-SW; the low-lying Piedmont Plateau; and the Atlantic coastal plain. The state's major rivers are the Delaware, Hudson, Passaic, and Raritan.

**People.** More than 90% of New Jersey's population lives in urban areas, the largest cities being Newark, Trenton, Jersey City, Paterson, and Elizabeth. Blacks constitute 12.5% of the total population.

**Economy.** One of the leading industrial states, New Jersey contains a number of small but highly efficient farms. Strategically located amid many rich markets, it has exceptional transport facilities and the most concentrated rail and road network in the nation. After WWII a large number of industrial research centers were established, and these plants play an important role in the state's industrial importance. The leading branch of manufacturing is the chemical industry, followed by the production of electrical machinery, processed food, metal goods, transportation equipment, and clothing. Tourism is also a major industry, bolstered in the late 1970s by the legalization of gambling in Atlantic City.

**History.** On a voyage for the Dutch East India Company, Henry HUDSON sailed up the Hudson R in 1609, and Dutch trading posts were soon established, but the first permanent settlement in present-day New Jersey was not founded until the 2nd half of the 17th century. In 1664 the Dutch possessions in North America were captured by the English (see NEW NETHERLAND), and New Jersey was divided and subdivided among various owners until 1702, when it became a single crown colony. After the British captured New York in 1776, New Jersey became the "cockpit of the Revolution," as armies crossed and recrossed the state, fighting nearly 100 engagements.

Today, New Jersey is a state profoundly divided, two-thirds being farm land and woods, while the highly-industrialized NE corner of the state is more densely populated than Japan. This area is also plagued by air pollution, urban blight, toxic wastes, and water management problems. The environment generally, especially the coastline, has been little protected. Local governments have at times been notoriously corrupt; and in 1980–81, New Jersey figured prominently in the ABSCAM investigations. In sum, New Jersey faces a range of critical challenges and opportunities.

**NEW JERUSALEM, Church of the.** See SWEDENBORG, Emanuel.

**NEW JOURNALISM,** a style of informal, personal, emotional, and often florid reporting that emerged in the 1960s, principally in the US, where it was especially encouraged by editor Clay Felker of *New York Magazine.* The journalists Tom Wolfe, Gail Sheehy, Gay Talese, and Jack Newfield were considered among its major practicioners. Although it provided an antidote to stodgy, uncritical, Establishment-oriented news, it was to be increasingly criticized for promoting inaccurate, distorted and sometimes totally fictitious versions of real events.

**NEW LEFT,** the radical, typically youthful US dissenters of the 1960s, who opposed the VIETNAM WAR, racial discrimination, economic injustice, the capitalist-government establishment, liberal orthodoxy, and sometimes most existing forms of society and culture. The movement was originally largely pacifist. Early prominent organizations were the STUDENT NONVIOLENT COORDINATING COMMITTEE (SNCC) and STUDENTS FOR A DEMOCRATIC SOCIETY (SDS). More violent and/or antisocial organizations included the BLACK PANTHER PARTY and the theatrical YIPPIES. Finally, there emerged some underground splinter groups which carried out violent acts, particularly the WEATHERMEN and the Symbionese Liberation Army. The New Left, which was a significant force in the 1960s, never found a practical mode of political expression to assure continuing attention to its concerns, and as a distinct movement expired early in the 1970s.

**NEWMAN, John Henry** (1801–1890), English clergyman and a founder of the OXFORD MOVEMENT in 1833. A Church of England vicar and tutor at Oxford University, he was converted to Roman Catholicism in 1845, becoming a cardinal in 1879. Much of his thought was controversial, opposed by Cardinal Henry MANNING and Charles KINGSLEY. He was a master stylist. His writings include *Apologia pro vita sua* (1864), a religious autobiography that remains his monument.

**NEWMAN, Paul,** (1925–    ), US film actor who starred in such dramas as *The Hustler* (1961), *Sweet Bird of Youth* (1962) and *Hud* (1963) and costarred with Robert Redford in popular comedy-adventure films such as *Butch Cassidy and the Sundance Kid* (1969) and *The Sting* (1973).

**Name of state:** New Mexico
**Capital:** Santa Fe

**Statehood:** Jan. 6, 1912 (47th state)
**Familiar name:** Land of Enchantment
**Area:** 122,666sq mi
**Population:** 1,299,968
**Elevation:** Highest—13,160ft, Wheeler Peak; Lowest—2,817ft, Red Bluff Reservoir
**Motto:** *Crescit eundo* (It grows as it goes)
**State flower:** Yucca
**State bird:** Roadrunner
**State tree:** Piñon, or nut pine
**State song:** "O, Fair New Mexico"

**NEW MEXICO,** state, S US, bounded to the E by Tex., to the S by Tex. and Mexico, to the W by Ariz., and to the N by Col. It is a mixture of three distinct cultures—Anglo-American, Spanish and Indian. Side by side with reminders of the old Indian and Spanish cultures are modern industries and research stations for atomic energy and space travel. The world's first atomic bomb, developed during WWII at the Los Alamos Laboratories north of Santa Fe, was exploded near Alamogordo in July 1945.

**Land.** New Mexico's varied topography and geological history make the area of great interest to geologists. Innumerable fossils have been found in the various geological strata, including many extinct species of plants and animals. The state has an average elevation of about 5,700ft. New Mexico includes parts of four main regions: the Colorado Plateaus in the NW, the Rocky Mountain System in the N central area, the Great Plains in the E and the Basin and Range Region in the central and SW area of the state. The state is generally arid with limited water resources, but it has two important rivers, the Rio Grande and the Pecos, both of which help to provide irrigation.

**People.** In 1980 there were more than 104,000 Indians in New Mexico, many of whom lived on reservations. Spanish-Americans account for over 30% of the population, and Spanish influence is evident in architecture and place names as well as in the wide use of the Spanish language. By the early 1970s, some 70% of New Mexico's population was concentrated in urban areas, the largest being Albuquerque and Santa Fe.

**Economy.** New Mexico is basically a mining state with rich deposits of many minerals, particularly uranium. Other important mineral resources are oil, natural gas, and potash. Atomic and space research is heavily funded by the federal government and is of great importance to the state's economy. Ranching is the state's most important agricultural activity. Crops include hay, sorghum, grain, onions, cotton, and corn. Tourism is also important.

**History.** Indians have inhabited what is now New Mexico for perhaps 20,000 years. In the 16th century the Spaniards conquered the Indians and colonized the area. In 1821 Mexico won its independence from Spain and took control over New Mexico, only to lose it to the US after the MEXICAN WAR (1846–48). Settlement continued, and in 1859 the GADSDEN PURCHASE was made. In 1980 the state's per capita income was relatively low and unemployment was high. These factors put added strain on the state's meager tax base and contributed to tensions among the Anglo, Spanish and Indian communities. The conviction of some Hispanics that the original Spanish land grants in New Mexico are still valid has sometimes provoked armed conflict. Although still small in comparison to most states, New Mexico's population increased 27.8% during the 1970s.

**NEW NATIONALISM,** Theodore ROOSEVELT's political philosophy (about 1910) proclaimed in opposition to Woodrow WILSON's Democratic manifesto, the NEW FREEDOM. His ideas included increased federal intervention to regulate the economy and promote social justice, honest government and conservation of natural resources.

**NEW NETHERLAND,** Dutch colonial territory extending roughly from Albany, N.Y., to Manhattan Island, and including parts of New Jersey, Connecticut and Delaware. It was granted in 1621 by the government of Holland to a group of merchants known as the DUTCH WEST INDIA COMPANY. In 1626 the company purchased Manhattan Island from the Indians and called it New Amsterdam. In 1664, under the British, New Amsterdam became New York City.

**NEW ORLEANS,** historic city in La., seat of Orleans parish, on the banks of the Mississippi R 107mi from the river's mouth. One of the world's great ports, New Orleans is the business and financial capital of the South. Excellent transport facilities serve the port, which is also the main gateway for trade with Latin America. New Orleans is surrounded by oil and natural gas deposits. It is a center of huge aerospace, shipbuilding, oil and chemical industries, and has many manufacturing and processing plants. The city is famed for its picturesque French Quarter (*Vieux Carré*) and Mardi Gras Carnival, and as the birthplace of JAZZ. Its varied population includes French-speaking Creoles who are descended from early French and Spanish settlers (see LOUISIANA PURCHASE). The

Creole cookery of New Orleans is famous. Pop 557,482.

**NEW ORLEANS, Battle of,** British attempt in 1815 to occupy New Orleans during the WAR OF 1812. The result was more of a massacre than a battle for the British, whom Andrew JACKSON repulsed in a terrible defeat. Jackson became a national hero for this, and eventually president.

**NEWPORT,** historic resort city in SE R.I., seat of Newport Co., and an important naval base. Founded in 1639, it became a refuge from religious persecution for Quakers and Jews. It was a wealthy resort in the 19th century, and its jazz festivals in the 1950s were famous. Pop 29,259.

**NEW REALISM,** modern art movement which, in rejecting various painterly schools and the principles of ABSTRACT ART, advocated works that incorporated real materials and artifacts. Based on a manifesto entitled *The New Realism* (Milan, 1960) and related to DADA, it has also been dubbed "junk art."

**NEW RIGHT,** ultraconservative US political movement, comprising several popular and powerful religious organizations as well as extreme right-wing politicians and political groups. Formerly relegated to the fringe of political life, the New Right came into its own during the presidential campaign of 1980, in which it enthusiastically and effectively supported Republican candidate Ronald Reagan. The movement's leaders helped to rout Democrats in the US Senate, giving Republicans a 53–46 majority, with some 15 senators in the New Right camp. Senator Jesse HELMS of N.C. is the unofficial political leader of the movement, and TV evangelist the Rev. Jerry FALWELL is the chief religious spokesman. Influential New Right organizations include the Congressional Club (originally a Helms campaign committee) and Falwell's MORAL MAJORITY. The New Right opposes abortion (see ABORTION CONTROVERSY), sex education, equal rights for homosexuals, the EQUAL RIGHTS AMENDMENT for women, school BUSING to achieve integration, government regulation of business, and almost all government programs to aid the poor. It favors arms spending, a militant anticommunist, antisocialist stance abroad, CAPITAL PUNISHMENT, prayers in schools, a balanced budget, and SUPPLY-SIDE ECONOMICS generally. The New Right differs from NEOCONSERVATISM in being anti-intellectual and at times anti-semitic. It differs from the traditional right, as represented by Sen. Barry GOLDWATER, in its desire to govern people's private sexual and religious behavior.

**NEW SOUTH WALES,** the most populous (5,078,000) and fourth largest (309,433sq mi) of Australia's six states, situated in the SE. It is the most highly-developed industrial and agricultural state in Australia, steel, wheat, wool and meat being the principal products. The state has rich mining resources. Sydney is the state capital and chief port.

**NEWSPAPER,** daily or weekly publication of current domestic and foreign news. In addition newspapers often contain information, humor and advice on a great variety of subjects. In 59 BC Julius Caesar ordered the daily publication of a newssheet, the *Acta Diurna,* which was posted in public places. The first Chinese newspaper was published in the 8th century. Johann GUTENBERG'S invention of movable type in the mid-15th century was an important step in the development of newspapers, and newspaper sheets appeared in Venice and Cologne in the 16th century. In 1620 fact-sheets printed in Amsterdam were sold in England. The *London Gazette* (1665) was the first paper issued regularly in a newspaper format. The first English daily, the *London Daily Courant,* appeared in England in 1702. The first regularly printed American paper was the *Boston Newsletter* (1704). Early newspapers were too expensive for the ordinary reader, but the gap was later filled by James Gordon BENNETT and Horace GREELEY publishing daily penny papers, such as *The New York Sun* (1833), the *New York Herald* (1835) and the *New York Tribune* (1841).

An era of fierce competitive journalism began with the end of the Civil War, when newspaper initiative took the form of stunts, crusades, scandal and increasing sensationalism. In the late 19th and early 20th centuries Joseph PULITZER, a pioneer of fiercely competitive, less–than–responsible YELLOW JOURNALISM, William Randolph HEARST, Colonel Robert MC CORMICK and Joseph Medill Patterson, and Lords BEAVERBROOK and NORTHCLIFFE in England, were the tsars of vast newspaper empires, and the media was an important force in national life and international politics. Newspapers in general have since toned down, although the traditions of yellow journalism continue to be followed by some major publishers, notably Australia's Rupert MURDOCH.

Radio, and later television, together with rising production costs, forced many newspapers out of business in recent years, with urban afternoon dailies in the US being especially hard-hit.

**NEW SWEDEN,** Swedish colony on the Delaware R extending from the site of Trenton, N.J., to the mouth of the Delaware R. In 1633 the New Sweden Company was organized, and in 1638 two Swedish vessels arrived and Peter MINUIT founded Fort Christina (later Wilmington, Del.). The Dutch, led by Peter STUYVESANT, annexed the colony in 1655.

**NEW TESTAMENT,** the part of the Bible which is distinctively Christian. In it are recorded the life and teachings of JESUS CHRIST and the beginnings of CHRISTIANITY. It comprises the four GOSPELS, the ACTS OF THE APOSTLES, the Epistles and the Book of REVELATION, numbering 27 books in all (for list see BIBLE). The Gospels (lives of Christ) are named for their traditional authors: Saints MATTHEW, MARK, LUKE and JOHN. The Epistles are early evangelical letters, written to local churches or individuals. Thirteen are ascribed to St. PAUL; the others (except the anonymous HEBREWS), are named for their traditional authors. The New Testament is written in everyday 1st-century Greek. The earliest copy fragments date from the early 2nd century. (See also CANON, BIBLICAL.)

**NEWTON, Sir Isaac** (1642–1726), the most prestigious natural philosopher and mathematician of modern times, the discoverer of the CALCULUS and author of the theory of universal GRAVITATION. Newton went up to Trinity College, Cambridge, in 1661, retiring to Woolsthorp, Lincolnshire, during the Plague of 1665–66, but becoming a fellow in 1667 and succeeding Isaac BARROW in the Lucasian Chair of Mathematics in 1669. He was elected Fellow of the ROYAL SOCIETY in 1672, on the strength of his optical discoveries. In Cambridge, Newton spent much time in alchemical experiments, though, toward the end of the century, he tired of the academic life and accepted a position at the Royal Mint, becoming Master of the Mint in 1699. He resigned his chair and entered Parliament in 1701 and two years later began his presidency of the Royal Society, which he retained until his death. His whole life was one of ceaseless energy— investigating mathematics, optics, chronology, chemistry, theology, mechanics, dynamics and the occult—broken only by a period of mental illness about 1693. His achievements were legion: the method of FLUXIONS and fluents (calculus); the theory of universal gravitation and his derivation of KEPLER'S LAWS; his formulation of the concept of FORCE as expressed in his three laws of motion (see MECHANICS); the corpuscular theory of LIGHT, and the

BINOMIAL THEOREM, among many others. These were summed up in his two greatest works: *Philosophiae Naturalis Principia Mathematica*(1687)—the "Principia," which established the mathematical representation of nature as the paradigm of what counted as "science"—and the *Opticks* (1704). Newton's often bitter controversies with his fellow scientists (notably HOOKE and LEIBNIZ) are famous, but his influence is undoubted, even if, in the cases of optical theory and the Newtonian calculus notation, it retarded rather than accelerated the advance of British science.

**NEW WAVE,** in CINEMA, denotes a film style of the late 1950s and early '60s identified with such French directors as François TRUFFAUT and Jean Luc GODARD, who exercised an unusual degree of control over all phases of the filmmaking process and whose films, such as Truffaut's semiautobiographical *The 400 Blows* (1959), represented strongly personal statements.

New Wave in **rock music** refers to a late 1970s movement back to the more basic, rhythmically simple rock modes of the 1960s.

**Name of state:** New York
**Capital:** Albany
**Statehood:** July 26, 1788 (11th state)
**Familiar name:** Empire State
**Area:** 49,576sq mi
**Population:** 17,364,158
**Elevation:** Highest—5,344ft, Mt. Marcy; Lowest—sea level, Atlantic Ocean
**Motto:** *Excelsior* (Ever Upward)
**State flower:** Rose
**State bird:** Bluebird
**State tree:** Sugar maple
**State song:** "I Love New York"

**NEW YORK,** state, E US, one of the original 13 colonies, location of the nation's largest metropolis, NEW YORK CITY. It is bounded on the N by Canada and Lake Ontario, E by Vt., Mass., and Conn., S by Pa., N.J., and the Atlantic Ocean, and W by Pa., Lake Erie and Canada.

**Land.** The topography of N.Y. is rich in variety and scenic beauty. The Appalachian Plateau, its largest land region, slopes upward (NW to SE) from Niagara Falls to the Catskill Mts. In the NE is the Adirondack Upland. There are 1,637sq mi of inland waters in addition to those of the Great Lakes. The Hudson R with its tributary the Mohawk, the St. Lawrence R and the Delaware R all form important transport routes.

**People.** Almost 90% of the population is urban. New York has traditionally been the immigration center of the nation. The numerically dominant immigrant groups are from Italy, Germany, the Soviet Union, Poland, Ireland and Puerto Rico. New York has the largest black population of any state in the US.

**Economy.** New York is one of the nation's leading manufacturing and trading states. Major industries include printing and publishing, clothing, electronic equipment, metal goods and food products. New York's intensive agriculture produces milk, grain, potatoes, apples and grapes. The state's varied natural resources are far from sufficient to supply manufacturing needs, but hydroelectricity is provided by the St. Lawrence and Niagara power plants. Tourism, finance and government operations are also important to New York's economic base.

**History.** Home of the IROQUOIS and ALGONQUIN INDIANS, the roots of present-day New York were established (1624) as the colony of NEW NETHERLAND by Dutch settlers. In 1664 Peter STUYVESANT, under whose administration the colony had flourished, was forced to surrender to British claims, when the state together with its capital New Amsterdam was renamed for the Duke of York (later James II of England). New York was a major battlefield during the FRENCH AND INDIAN WARS (1689–1763), and during the REVOLUTIONARY WAR was the scene of the decisive Battle of SARATOGA. The state contributed significantly to Union success during the CIVIL WAR.

The late 19th and early 20th centuries saw increased industrialization and immigration, making New York for many years the leading manufacturing state as well as the most populous. Though now shrinking in population (−3.8% in the 1970s), the state remains the 2nd largest after California, while New York City continues as the nation's largest metropolis. Because of its size, the city tends to experience urban problems sooner—and on a larger scale—than other municipalities. Thus, its near-bankruptcy in 1975 presaged the troubles of other cities, as did the stringent cure of layoffs of government workers and cutbacks in a host of social and economic programs. The continuing erosion of the city's tax base as middle- and upper-income people leave for the suburbs (to which many corporations also are moving) is likely to lead to greater demands for aid from the state, especially as federal funding diminishes, but it occupies a central position in the nation's—and the world's—cultural and business affairs.

**NEW YORK CITY,** city in SE N.Y., the largest in the US. It is divided into five boroughs: Manhattan, the Bronx, Brooklyn, Queens and Richmond. The long, narrow island of Manhattan, upon which New York's complex network of bridges and tunnels all converge, is the city's economic and cultural heart. New York is the nation's richest port, and a world leader in trade and finance. It is also a manufacturing (notably garments), communications (broadcasting, printing and publishing), and performing arts center.

In 1626, Dutch settlers of NEW NETHERLAND purchased Manhattan from the resident Indians, reputedly for $24 worth of goods, and it became the site of their major city, New Amsterdam. The city, which had flourished under the firm administration of its last Dutch governor, Peter STUYVESANT, was surrendered to the British in 1664, and renamed New York. Over the next hundred years it developed rapidly as a prosperous trade center. In the late Colonial period New Yorkers were among the most outspoken opponents of British rule, but after the defeat (1776) of George Washington at the Battle of Long Island (see LONG ISLAND, BATTLE OF) the city remained in the hands of English troops until the end of the REVOLUTIONARY WAR, after which it served briefly (1789–90) as the nation's capital. As early as the first census of 1790, New York was the largest city in the US, and by 1860 its population was almost a million. Already suffering from its rapid, unplanned growth, the city's population was doubled in the great wave of immigration between 1880 and 1900. Housing and transport problems caused by this influx were partly eased by the construction of the first elevated railway in 1867, Brooklyn Bridge in 1883, and the first subway system in 1904. Scarcity of land and subsequent high land prices produced a new architectural form—the skyscraper, which was to be for long the very symbol of modernity.

Around the turn of the century bitter conflicts between labor and management resulted in highly progressive labor laws.

New York's political leadership, at times notoriously corrupt, has included such notable reformers as Theodore ROOSEVELT and Fiorello LA GUARDIA.

New York has over 100 parks, some of them achieving a striking atmosphere of serenity within the often hectic bustle of activity which surrounds them. The city's cultural and sporting facilities offer an enormous range of interest and opportunity. Pop 7,071,030.

**NEW YORK MARATHON,** annual ROAD RACING event inaugurated in 1970. Run at the marathon distance (26 miles, 385 yards), it follows a course that takes the runners into each of New York City's five boroughs. The event has become phenomenally popular, attracting some 30,000 applicants in 1981, of which about 14,000 were permited to compete. Alberto Salazar of the US established a world marathon record of 2hrs, 8min, 13sec in 1981 as he won the race for the second successive year, while Allison Roe of New Zealand established a new women's mark of 2:25:26.74.

**NEW YORK PUBLIC LIBRARY,** major US research facility and largest library system in the world, established in New York City in 1895 through consolidation of the Astor, Lenox and Tilden libraries. The landmark main building on Fifth Avenue was completed in 1911, and Andrew CARNEGIE provided for 39 branch libraries. The system has since absorbed or opened many general and specialized libraries. Its vast holdings include nearly four million books and thousands of rare editions, manuscripts, maps and prints.

**NEW YORK SCHOOL,** a diverse group of painters active in New York City from the early 1940s through the late 1950s. Its initial members included Arshile GORKY, Hans HOFMANN, Willem DE KOONING, Robert MOTHERWELL, Jackson POLLOCK, Mark ROTHKO, and Clyfford STILL. All abstractionists, they can be subdivided into "action painters" and painters of the "color field."

**NEW YORK STOCK EXCHANGE,** largest securities market in the US, located at Broad and Wall streets in the financial district of New York City. This world-famous trading market has 1,350 members and handles 1,900 issues. It was founded in 1792 and received its present name in 1863.

**NEW ZEALAND,** sovereign state within the British Commonwealth, 1,200mi SE of Australia, in the S. Pacific Ocean. The country comprises North Island, South Island (the two principal islands), Stewart

Island and the Chatham Islands, with other small outlying islands.

**Land.** Both major islands are mountainous, with fertile coastal plains. North Island has some volcanic ranges, a region of hot springs surrounding Lake Taupo in the center, and the country's major river, the Waikato. South Island includes large areas of forest, and many glaciers and lakes. Plants include subtropical species. There are hardly any native mammals, but many rare birds, such as the KIWI. The climate is temperate.

**People.** About 10% of New Zealand's population are MAORIS, and about 90% are descended from settlers who came from Britain. Over 40% of the population live in urban areas—notably Auckland, Christchurch, and the capital, Wellington.

**Economy.** Sheep and cattle are the main sources of income. Principal exports are frozen meat (mainly lamb), wool and dairy products. The country's varied light industry is dominated by food-processing. Some minerals are produced. New Zealand's beauty and diversity, and its famous fishing and winter sports attract growing numbers of tourists.

**History.** The chief Maori migrations (1200–1400) led to the eclipse of the earlier Moriori tribes in New Zealand. The islands were sighted by the Dutch seaman Abel TASMAN in 1642, and named for the Netherlands province of Zeeland. In the 1770s Captain James COOK visited New Zealand and claimed it for England. Missionaries became active in the early 19th century, and systematic colonization was begun in 1840 by the New Zealand Company. Maori chiefs acknowledged British sovereignty in exchange for recognition of their territorial rights at the Treaty of Waitangi (1840), but over the

**Official name:** New Zealand
**Capital:** Wellington
**Area:** 103,883
**Population:** 3,100,100
**Languages:** English; Maori also spoken
**Religions:** Protestant, Roman Catholic
**Monetary unit(s):** 1 New Zealand dollar = 100 cents

next 30 years the treaty was contravened by white settlers who fought Maoris for their land. It achieved self-government in 1852, became a dominion under the British crown in 1907, and was made completely independent in 1931. A pioneer in social reform, New Zealand was the first country to give women the vote (1893) and inaugurated a progressive social security system in 1898. WESTERN SAMOA gained independence in 1962, and internal self-government was granted to the Cook Islands (1965) and Niue (1974).

**NEY, Michel** (1769–1815), French Napoleonic marshal and military hero. His rear-guard defense during NAPOLEON I's retreat from Moscow (1812) was the most notable achievement of a brilliant career. Though he helped persuade Napoleon to abdicate, Ney's allegiance to the Bourbon Louis XVIII did not outlive Napoleon's return from exile. Ney fought with Napoleon at WATERLOO, and afterward was condemned to death for treason by the British.

**NEZ PERCÉ INDIANS** (French: pierced nose), American Indian tribe of present-day central Idaho. Noted horse-breeders, they ceded (1855) much of their territory to the US. Fraudulently-enforced cession of a further 75% of their land (1863) and many land disputes led to the Nez Percé War of 1877, in which 300 Indians held out for five months against 5,000 US troops before surrendering.

**NIACIN.** See VITAMINS.

**NIAGARA FALLS,** cataract in the Niagara R. between W N.Y. and S Ontario, Canada, world-famous spectacle and an important source of hydroelectric power. The river is divided into the American Falls (1,060ft wide and 167ft high) and the Canadian, or Horseshoe Falls (2,600ft wide and 158ft high), by Goat Island before plunging into the deep gorge with its Whirlpool Rapids. Some 212,000cu ft of water per second pass over the Falls, which are gradually moving upstream as they erode the rock.

**NIBELUNGENLIED** ("Song of the Nibelungs"), German epic written c1200 AD, partly based on Scandinavian myths. It tells how SIEGFRIED who had gained the treasure of the Nibelungen dwarfs, is given Kriemhild in marriage as a reward for helping Gunther win BRUNHILD by trickery. Brunhild in revenge has Siegfried killed by Hagen, who hides the treasure in the Rhine. Kriemhild's subsequent vow to avenge Siegfried ends in a holocaust. The story inspired WAGNER'S operatic tetralogy *The Ring of the Nibelungs.*

**NICAEA, Councils of,** the first and seventh

ECUMENICAL COUNCILS. The first Nicaean Council, called in 325 AD by the Emperor CONSTANTINE, condemned ARIANISM, and drew up the NICENE CREED. The second Nicaean Council in 787 ruled in favor of the restoration of images in churches (see ICONOCLASTIC CONTROVERSY).

**Official name:** Republic of Nicaragua
**Capital:** Managua
**Area:** 57,143sq mi
**Population:** 2,325,000
**Language:** Spanish
**Religion:** Roman Catholic
**Monetary unit(s):** 1 Córdoba = 100 centavos

**NICARAGUA,** largest of the Central American republics, bounded on the N by Honduras, E by the Caribbean Sea, S by Costa Rica, and W by the Pacific Ocean.

**Land.** Nicaragua is a country of volcanoes, lakes and forested plains. A prominent physical feature is the long, eastern lowland belt running diagonally across the country, which embraces two large lakes: Nicaragua and Managua. This lowland belt contains all the large towns and 90% of Nicaragua's relatively sparse population. Earthquakes, such as the one which devastated the capital Managua in 1972, are not uncommon.

**People.** The people are predominantly (70%) of mixed Spanish-Indian descent, but include pure Spanish, pure Negroes and pure Indians. About half of the population is illiterate.

**Economy.** Only 10% of land is cultivated, but agriculture is the mainstay of the economy. Forestry and mining also play an important part. The main exports are raw cotton, meat, coffee, gold, timber and rice.

**History.** Before the arrival of the Spanish conquistador Gil González de Avila (1522) the country was inhabited by various Indian communities. Another Spanish expedition founded León and Granada in 1524. From 1570 the country was ruled as part of Guatemala. Nicaragua won independence from Spain in 1821, and was then annexed to Mexico, after which it became (1825) part of the Central American Federation Independent from 1838, the country became convulsed by power struggles. In 1912 the US was asked for aid, and US Marines occupied the country almost continuously until 1933. Ostensibly a democracy, Nicaragua was ruled by members of the powerful Somoza family from 1937 until 1979 when Sandinist guerrillas forced Anastasio Somoza Debayle to resign and leave the country. A socialist Government of National Reconstruction was installed.

**NICENE CREED,** either of two early CREEDS. The first was issued by the first Council of Nicaea (325) to state orthodoxy against ARIANISM. The second was perhaps issued by the Council of Constantinople.

**NICHOLAS, Saint,** 4th-century patron saint of children, scholars, merchants and sailors and probably bishop of Myra in Lycia, Asia Minor. In many European countries he traditionally visits children and gives them gifts on his feast day (Dec. 6). The custom was brought to America by the Dutch, whose Sinter Klaas became the SANTA CLAUS of Christmas.

**NICHOLAS,** name of two Russian tsars: **Nicholas I** (1796–1855), emperor and tsar 1825–55, notorious for his despotic rule. His succession was challenged by a liberal revolt (see DECEMBRIST REVOLT) which was quickly crushed. A determined absolutist, he opposed all liberal reform or independence. He expanded Russian territory at the expense of Turkey and was only checked by the CRIMEAN WAR. **Nicholas II** (1868–1918), tsar 1894–1917, whose inflexibility and misgovernment helped bring about the RUSSIAN REVOLUTION and the overthrow of his dynasty. His wife, the empress ALEXANDRA, filled the court with irresponsible favorites of whom the monk RASPUTIN was the most influential. Russian defeats in the RUSSO-JAPANESE WAR (1904–05) led to a popular uprising and Nicholas granted limited civil rights and called the first representative DUMA (1905). The military defeats of WWI led to his abdication and eventual execution.

**NICHOLS, Mike** (1931–    ), German-born US comedian and director. He gained national attention with partner Elaine May for their brilliantly satiric dialogues performed (from 1957) in nightclubs, on TV, on Broadway (1960), and on recordings. He turned to directing in the early 1960s and was responsible for such shows as *The Odd Couple* (1965) and *The Gin Game* (1977), and such movies as *Who's Afraid of Virginia Woolf?* (1965), *The Graduate* (Academy Award, 1967) and *Carnal Knowledge* (1971).

**NICHOLSON, Ben** (1894–    ), British abstract sculptor and painter of landscapes and still-lifes. His reliefs, like *White Relief,*

1939, are composed in an elegant pure linear style.

NICHOLSON, Jack (1937– ), US actor who emerged from B-films of the 1950s and 1960s to become one of the screen's most compelling figures, usually portraying outsiders and misfits. His films include *Easy Rider* (1969), *Carnal Knowledge* (1971), *One Flew Over the Cuckoo's Nest* (1975), for which he won the Academy Award, and The Shining (1980).

NICKEL (Ni), hard, gray-white, ferromagnetic (see MAGNETISM) metal in Group VIII of the PERIODIC TABLE; a TRANSITION ELEMENT. About half the total world output comes from deposits of pyrrhotite and pentlandite at Sudbury, Ontario; garnierite in New Caledonia is also important. Roasting the ore gives crude nickel oxide, refined by electrolysis or by the Mond process. Nickel is widely used in ALLOYS, including MONEL METAL, INVAR and GERMAN SILVER. In many countries "silver" coins are made from cupronickel (an alloy of copper and nickel). Nickel-chromium alloys ("nichrome"), resistant to oxidation at high temperatures, are used as heating elements in electric heaters, etc. Nickel is used for nickel plating and as a catalyst for HYDROGENATION. Chemically nickel resembles IRON and COBALT, being moderately reactive, and forming compounds in the $+2$ oxidation state; the $+4$ state is known in LIGAND complexes. AW 58.7, mp 1453°C, bp 2732°C, sg 8.902 (25°C).

NICKELODEON, early motion-picture theater. The first one opened in 1905 in McKeesport, Pa., and offered for five cents a screen program with piano accompaniment. It was so popular that there were 5,000 nickelodeons in the US by 1907. The name was subsequently applied to coin-operated, automatic phonographs.

NICKLAUS, Jack William (1940– ), US golfer, the outstanding professional of the 1960s and 1970s. After winning the US amateur title in 1961, he joined the tour and by 1982 had won four US Open titles and five Masters tournaments, including three in the four-year span 1963–66.

NICOLSON, Sir Harold (1886–1968), British writer and diplomat. After 20 years' diplomatic service (1909–29), he became a member of Parliament (1935–45). He wrote biographies of Verlaine, Byron, Tennyson, Swinburne and King George V, and many reviews.

NICOTINE, colorless oily liquid, an ALKALOID occurring in tobacco leaves and extracted from tobacco refuse. It is used as an insecticide and to make nicotinic acid (see VITAMINS). Nicotine is one of the most toxic substances known; even the small dose ingested by SMOKING causes blood-vessel constriction, raised blood pressure, nausea, headache and impaired digestion.

NIEBUHR, Reinhold (1892–1971), American Protestant theologian. An active socialist in the early 1930s, he turned back after WWII to traditional Protestant values, relating them to modern society in his "conservative realism." His *Nature and Destiny of Man* (1941–43) greatly influenced American theology.

NIELSEN, Carl August (1865–1931), Danish composer. His six symphonies are most notable for their original harmonic structure. He also wrote operas, concertos for flute, clarinet and violin and chamber music.

NIEMEYER, Oscar (Oscar Niemeyer Soares Filho; 1907– ), Brazilian architect whose outstanding work in Brazil culminated in that country's capital city, BRASILIA, 1956–60. His most characteristic style is the curved, sculptural use of reinforced concrete.

NIEMÖLLER, Martin (1892– ), German Lutheran pastor who opposed the Nazis and Adolf Hitler. He was confined in concentration camps (1937–1945). In 1945 he organized the "Declaration of Guilt" in which German Churches admitted their failure to resist the Nazis.

NIEPCE, Joseph Nicéphore (1765–1833), French inventor who in 1826 made the first successful permanent photograph. The image, recorded in asphalt on a pewter plate, required an 8hr exposure in a camera obscura (see CAMERA LUCIDA AND CAMERA OBSCURA). The method used derived from heliography, Niepce's photoengraving process. In 1829 Niepce went into partnership with DAGUERRE.

NIETZSCHE, Friedrich (1844–1900), German philosopher, classical scholar and critic of Christianity. In *Thus Spake Zarathustra* (1833–92) he introduced the concept of the "Superman," a great-souled hero who transcends the slavish morality of Christianity and whose motivating force is the supreme passion of "will to power," which is directed towards creativity. This passion distinguishes him from inferior human beings. Nietzsche's ideas have been much misrepresented, particularly by the Nazis who misappropriated the concept of the "Superman" to justify their own concepts of Aryan racial superiority.

NIGER, the largest state in W Africa, is surrounded by seven countries, with Algeria and Libya to the N and Nigeria and Benin to the S.

Land. Despite its vast area, the country is

**Official name:** Republic of Niger
**Capital:** Niamey
**Area:** 489,190sq mi
**Population:** 5,501,000
**Languages:** French, Hausa, Fulani
**Religions:** Muslim, Animist, Christian
**Monetary unit(s):** 1 CFA franc=100
centimes

thinly populated. Most of the country is desert: the N is typically Saharan and the NE is virtually uninhabitable. Moderate rainfall in the S and SW permit cultivation. The Niger R flows through the SW corner and farmers plant crops there when the river floods. The Air Mts are in N central Niger.
**People.** The people are divided into several different groups: the Hausa, who form over half the population, Djerma-Songhai and Beriberi-Manga in the S are mainly farmers; the Fulani, Tuareg and others in the N are nomadic pastoralists.
**Economy.** Niger is presently one of the world's poorest countries; however, it is rich in mineral potential. Principal exports are uranium, livestock and vegetables. Chief food crops are millet, cassava, sorghum, vegetables, rice and peanuts.
**History.** Areas of what is now Niger were part of the Mali and Songhai empires. In 1922 Niger became a French colony; in 1960 it gained independence. In 1974 widespread unrest caused by food shortages brought about the overthrow of the government, which was taken over by the military.
**NIGERIA,** federal republic in West Africa, the most populous country in the African continent. Nigeria is one of Africa's most powerful nations and plays a major role in international affairs.
**Land.** Bordering on the Gulf of Guinea, it lies between Cameroon on the E and Benin on the W. Behind the coastal strip are lowlands which rise to the Jos Plateau and fall away to sandy high plains in the N. In the S Nigeria has a 475mi coastline of sandbars, mangroves and lagoons, with the great delta of the Niger R as the most prominent natural feature. The N is hot and dry; the S is humid with the rainfall

averaging more than 150in per year.
**People.** The country has over 200 tribes and languages. There are three major tribal groups: the Yorubas in the W, the Ibos in the E, and the Hausa-Fulani in the N; the minority tribes are more or less equal in number to these three groups. The population is concentrated mainly in the Muslim N, although the S is also heavily populated. Most Nigerians are farmers, herders or fishermen. Despite widespread illiteracy, Nigeria has a relatively large number of university graduates, many of whom have studied abroad. The government has introduced free primary education. Nigeria is one of the most urbanized countries in Africa; the largest cities are Ibaden, Lagos, Ogbomosho, Kano and Oshogbo. There is a large community of expatriates, most of whom are employed by foreign companies, including oil companies.
**Economy.** Nigeria is the second largest supplier of oil to the US, after Saudi Arabia. The economy gricultural production has declined substantially since independence. Manufacturing includes vehicle assembly, food processing, textiles, building materials and furniture.
**History.** The Nok culture of Negro settlers on the Jos Plateau, c800 BC–200 AD is the earliest known in Nigeria. Small trading city-states arose c1000 AD, especially in the N and by the 1300s became powerful empires such as the Kanem, Mali and the BENIN in the S. The Portuguese reached Nigeria in 1483. Britain annexed areas of Nigeria, establishing it in 1914 as a colony and protectorate. In 1960 Nigeria became independent, and a republic in 1963. Political parties had long developed on regional lines, and after disputes over the 1964 election the collapse of law and order led to a series of military regimes until 1966,

**Official name:** Federal Republic of Nigeria
**Capital:** Lagos
**Area:** 356,669sq mi
**Population:** 76,982,000
**Languages:** English, Hausa, Ibo, Yoruba
**Religions:** Muslim, Christian, Animist
**Monetary unit(s):** 1 Naira = 100 kobo

when General GOWON set up a military government. Gowon reorganized Nigeria into 12 states but the Ibo seceded to form the independent republic of BIAFRA. Civil war between Biafra and the rest of Nigeria broke out in 1967 and continued until Biafra surroundered in 1970. In 1975 Gowon was deposed and exiled by a military coup led by Brig. Murtala Muhammed, who was later assassinated in an abortive coup. He was succeeded by Lt. Gen. Olusegun Obasanjo. In 1976 Nigeria increased the number of its states to 19, and in 1979 Shehu Shagari was elected president.

**NIGER RIVER,** the third longest river in Africa, 2,600mi long. With its eastern branch, the Benue, it drains an area of more than 1 million sq mi. Rising in SW Guinea, it curves NE, E then SE into Nigeria and finally S towards the Gulf of Guinea where it forms a 14,000sq mi delta.

**NIGHT BLINDNESS,** or nyctalopia, inability to accommodate in or adapt to darkness. It may be a hereditary defect or an early symptom of VITAMIN A deficiency in adults. It is due to a defect in rod VISION.

**NIGHTINGALE,** *Luscinia megarhynchos,* bird of the thrush subfamily Turdinae, renowned for its beautiful song. A small brown bird, feeding on insects and other invertebrates, it lives in deciduous woodlands throughout most of Europe.

**NIGHTINGALE, Florence** (1820–1910), English founder of modern nursing, known as the "Lady with the Lamp" because she worked night and day during the Crimean War. She determined to make a career out of nursing the sick and traveled in Europe in the 1840s studying methods of nursing. In 1854 the British government asked her to tend the wounded of the CRIMEAN WAR. She sailed with 38 nurses to Scutari and established sanitary methods and discipline in the two huge army hospitals. In 1860 she set up a nurses' training school in London.

**NIHILISM,** a doctrine that denies all values, questions all authority, and advocates the destruction of all social and economic institutions. The movement arose in 19th-century Russia in reaction against all authority, especially that of the tsar. It is romantic in origin and anarchist in outlook; its most noted exponent was KROPOTKIN.

**NIJINSKY, Vaslav** (1890–1950), famous Russian dancer whose outstanding technique and magnetic stage presence contributed greatly to the impact of Russian ballet on the West, when Sergei DIAGHILEV brought a company to Paris in 1909. With Diaghilev's encouragement, Nijinsky devised original choreography, based on Greek vase paintings, for DEBUSSY'S *Afternoon of a Faun.* Mental illness ended his career in 1919.

**NILE RIVER,** the longest river in the world, flowing generally N about 4,145mi from central Africa to the Mediterranean. Its remotest headstream is the Luvironza R in Burundi above Victoria Nyanza (Lake Victoria), from which flows the White Nile. The Blue Nile rises above Lake Tana in NW Ethiopia, and joins the White Nile at Khartoum, Sudan, to form the Nile proper. N of Cairo it fans out into a 115mi-wide delta with principal outlets at Rosetta near Alexandria and Damietta near Port Said. Silt deposited by the Nile's annual overflow brought agricultural prosperity throughout Egypt's history. The river is now being harnessed, notably at the ASWAN HIGH DAM, to supply hydroelectricity as well as constant irrigation. The Nile is navigable the year round from its mouth to ASWAN, and in full spate is generally navigable as far south as Uganda.

**NILSSON, Birgit** (1918–    ), Swedish soprano, widely regarded as the greatest Wagnerian soprano of her time; famed as Brünnhilde in *Der Ring des Nibelungen,* but known also for other roles, notably PUCCINI'S Turandot and STRAUSS' Elektra.

**NIMITZ, Chester William** (1885–1966), US admiral who commanded naval operations in the Pacific after America entered WORLD WAR II in 1941. Credited with originating the strategy of "island hopping," he had an outstandingly successful command. On Sept. 2, 1945, the Japanese surrender was signed aboard his flagship, U.S.S. *Missouri.*

**NIN, Anaïs** (1903–1977), French-born US author whose novels and stories depict the inner worlds of women in surrealistic and psychoanalytic fashion. Her novels include *The House of Incest* (1936) and *Collages* (1964). She is best known, however, for *The Diaries of Anaïs Nin* (7 vols., 1966–80), which span the years 1931–74 and include portraits of such contemporaries as Lawrence Durrell, Henry Miller, William Carlos Williams, and Marguerite Young.

**NINEVEH,** capital of ASSYRIA in the 7th century BC, on the Tigris R, opposite modern Mosul, Iraq. Invaluable remains survive from its period of greatness under SENNACHERIB and ASHURBANIPAL. Its destruction by invaders in 612 BC ended the Assyrian Empire. (See also BABYLONIA AND ASSYRIA.)

**NIRENBERG, Marshall Warren** (1927–    ), US biochemist who shared with HOLLEY and KHORANA the 1968 Nobel Prize for Physiology or Medicine for his major contributions toward the decipherment of the genetic code (see GENETICS).

**NITROGEN** (N), nonmetal in Group VA of the PERIODIC TABLE; a colorless, odorless gas ($N_2$) comprising 78% of the ATMOSPHERE, prepared by fractional distillation of liquid air. Combined nitrogen occurs mainly as NITRATES. As a constituent of AMINO ACIDS, it is vital (see also NITROGEN CYCLE). Molecular nitrogen is inert because of the strong triple bond between the two atoms, but it will react with some elements, especially the ALKALINE-EARTH METALS, to give nitrides; with oxygen; and with hydrogen. Activated nitrogen, formed in an electric discharge, consists of nitrogen atoms and is much more reactive. Nitrogen is used in NITROGEN FIXATION and to provide an inert atmosphere; liquid nitrogen is a CRYOGENIC refrigerant. AW 14.0, mp −210°C, bp −196°C.

Nitrogen forms mainly trivalent and pentavalent compounds. **Nitric oxide** (NO), is a colorless gas formed in the electric-arc process; it is readily oxidized further to nitrogen dioxide, mp−164°C, bp−152°C. **Nitrites** are salts (or esters) of **Nitrous Acid** ($HNO_2$) and are mild reducing agents. **Nitrous Oxide** ($N_2O$), or laughing gas, is a colorless gas with a sweet odor, prepared by heating ammonium nitrate, and used as a weak anesthetic, sometimes producing mild hysteria, and also as an aerosol propellant. mp −91°C, bp−88°C. **Nitrogen Dioxide** ($NO_2$), a red-brown toxic gas in equilibrium with its colorless dimer ($N_2O_4$), is a constituent of automobile exhaust and smog. A powerful oxidizing agent, it is used in the manufacture of SULFURIC ACID and in rocket fuels. It is also an intermediate in the manufacture of NITRIC ACID. mp −11°C, bp 21°C. See also AMMONIA; HYDRAZINE.

**NITROGLYCERIN** ($C_3H_5(ONO_2)_3$), properly called glyceryl trinitrate, the NITRATE ester of GLYCEROL, made by its nitration. Since it causes VASODILATION, it is used to relieve ANGINA PECTORIS. Its major use, however, is as a very powerful high EXPLOSIVE, though its sensitivity to shock renders it unsafe unless used in the form of DYNAMITE or blasting gelatin. It is a colorless, oily liquid. AW 227.1, mp 13°C.

**NIXON, Richard Milhous** (1913–   ), 37th president of the US (1969–74). Nixon was born into a Quaker family in Yorba Linda, Cal., and trained and practiced (1937–42) as a lawyer. An aviation ground officer in the navy in WWII, he began his political career with election to congress in 1946. As a congressman he became a prominent member of the House's anti-communist UN-AMERICAN ACTIVITIES COMMITTEE. In 1950 he was elected to the

Senate, where his continued and aggressive anti-communist stance probably influenced Dwight D. Eisenhower's choice of Nixon as running-mate in 1952. As Eisenhower's vice-president (1953–61) Nixon was given an unusually prominent role both at home and abroad. In 1960 he was chosen as the Republican presidential nominee, but was narrowly defeated by John KENNEDY. After running unsuccessfully for the governorship of California in 1962, he announced his retirement to pursue his career in law. Reentering political life in 1964, however, Nixon gradually won wide backing and, with Spiro AGNEW as his running-mate, won the presidency in 1968. He was reelected in 1972 with a large majority.

Nixon had pledged withdrawal from the VIETNAM WAR, which had plagued the presidencies of his two predecessors. Although his actions did not always seem consistent with his electoral promise (notably his ordering of the invasions of Cambodia and Laos and of saturation bombing in North Vietnam), he began pulling US troops out of Vietnam almost at once. Eventually, with Secretary of State Henry KISSINGER as Nixon's chief negotiator, a cease-fire agreement was reached (1973). In the meantime COLD WAR tensions were eased by arms-limitation talks with the USSR in 1969, and again when Nixon visited Moscow (he was the first US president to do so) in 1972. This followed his historic state visit to the People's Republic of China, which reopened contact with the mainland Chinese for the first time in more than 20 years. In domestic affairs, Nixon introduced the "New Federalism," which in principle sought a more balanced relationship between the federal and state governments. A major element of this concept was revenue-sharing, the return to the states of some federal tax money for use as the states saw fit. Nixon also imposed wage and price controls to help offset the nation's severe economic problems of recession and inflation.

Nixon's second term of office was aborted by the scandal of the WATERGATE affair, which led to revelations of widespread corruption, misinforming the public, and an unprecedented increase in the power of the White House at the expense of congress and the judiciary. Several of Nixon's top aides were tried and imprisoned, and a House judiciary committee recommended that Nixon be impeached. On August 9, 1974, Nixon resigned office, the first US president ever to do so.

A month later, Nixon was given a pardon by his successor, Gerald Ford, for any illegal acts he may have committed while president. Barred from practicing law, Nixon wrote his memoirs and other books.

**NKRUMAH, Kwame** (1901–1972), Ghanian who led his country to independence, and a champion of pan-Africanism. After the electoral victory (1951) of his Convention People's party, he became first prime minister of the then Gold Coast, in which role he established (1957) the independent Republic of Ghana. As president from 1960, his gradual assumption of dictatorial powers won him enemies, and his government was overthrown by a military coup in 1966.

**NOBEL, Alfred Bernhard** (1833–1896), Swedish-born inventor of dynamite and other explosives. About 1863 he set up a factory to manufacture liquid NITROGLYCERIN, but when in 1864 this blew up, killing his younger brother, Nobel set out to find safe handling methods for the substance, so discovering DYNAMITE, patented 1867 (UK) and 1868 (US). Later he invented gelignite (patented 1876) and ballistite (1888). A lifelong pacifist, he wished his explosives to be used solely for peaceful purposes, and was much embittered by their military use. He left most of his fortune for the establishment of the Nobel Foundation and this fund has been used to award Nobel Prizes since 1901.

**NOBLE GASES,** the elements in Group 0 of the PERIODIC TABLE, comprising HELIUM, NEON, ARGON, KRYPTON, XENON and RADON. They are colorless, odorless gases, prepared by fractional distillation of liquid air (see ATMOSPHERE), except helium and radon. Owing to their stable filled-shell electron configurations, the noble gases are chemically unreactive: only krypton, xenon and radon form isolable compounds. They glow brightly when an electric discharge is passed through them, and so are used in advertising signs: neon tubes glow red, xenon blue, and krypton bluish-white; argon tubes glow pale red at low pressures, blue at high pressures.

**NOBLE METALS,** the corrosion–resistant precious metals comprising the PLATINUM GROUP, SILVER and GOLD, and sometimes including RHENIUM.

**NOGUCHI, Isamu** (1904–  ), US abstract sculptor whose works, especially those created for specific architectural settings such as the UNESCO building in Paris, have won international recognition. He was a student of BRANCUSI.

**NOH,** or **Nō,** the classical drama of Japan, developed under court patronage in the 14th century. Typically, a Noh play dramatizes the spiritual life of its central character, employing speech, singing, instrumental music, dancing and mime in a highly ritualized style. The performers are all male, and traditional wooden masks are used. Noh gave rise to the more popular KABUKI theater.

**NOISE,** in electronics, any unwanted or interfering current or voltage in an electrical device or system. Its presence in the amplifying circuits of RADIOS, TELEVISION receivers, etc., may mask or distort signals. Unpredictable random noise exists in any component with RESISTANCE because of the thermal motion of the current-carrying ELECTRONS, and in electron tubes due to random CATHODE emission. Thermal radiations and variations in the atmosphere also cause random noise. Nonrandom noise arises from spurious oscillations and unintended couplings between components.

**NOISE,** unwanted SOUND. As far as man is concerned this is a subjective definition: people vary in their sensitivity to noise; many sounds are agreeable to some and noisy to others. Blasts or explosions can cause sudden damage to the ear and prolonged exposure to impulsive sounds such as pneumatic drill may cause gradual HEARING impairment. In general, any sound that is annoying, interferes with speech, damages the hearing or reduces concentration or work efficiency may be considered as noise. From the physical viewpoint, sound waves (either in air or vibrations in solid bodies) that mask required signals or cause fatigue and breakdown of equipment or structures are noise and should be minimized. In air, sound is radiated spherically from its source as a compressional wave, being partly reflected, absorbed or transmitted on hitting an obstacle. Noise is usually a nonperiodic sound wave, as opposed to a periodic pure musical tone or a sine-wave combination. It is characterized by its intensity (measured in DECIBELS or NEPERS), frequency and spatial variation; a sound level meter and frequency analyzer measure these properties. Noise may be controlled at source (e.g., by a MUFFLER), between it and the listener (e.g., by sound absorbing material) or at the listener (e.g., by wearing ear plugs).

**NOLAND, Kenneth** (1924–    ), US painter whose work featured bands of color. With Morris Louis, he developed a technique of employing thinned paints for staining and became one of the best-known color field painters.

**NOLDE, Emil** (1867–1956), born Emil Hansen, German expressionist, engraver and painter, notably of landscapes and figures, whose bold, visionary and highly emotional style is typified in his *Marsh Landscape* (1916). (See also EXPRESSIONISM.)

**NOMINALISM**, in philosophy, usually as opposed to REALISM, the view that the names of abstract ideas (e.g., beauty) used in describing things (as in, a *beautiful* table) are merely conventions or conveniences, and should not be taken to imply the actual existence of universals corresponding to those names.

**NONCONFORMISTS, or Dissenters,** those who will not conform to the doctrine or practice of an established church; especially the Protestant dissenters from the Church of England (mainly PURITANS) expelled by the Act of Uniformity (1662). They now include Baptists, Brethren, Congregationalists, Methodists, Presbyterians and Quakers.

**NON-EUCLIDEAN GEOMETRY**, those branches of GEOMETRY that challenge EUCLIDEAN GEOMETRY'S tenet that through any POINT A not on a LINE L there passes one and only one line parallel to L, but which accept in general all other Euclidean axioms with at most minor changes. The geometry based on the hypothesis that no lines pass through A parallel to L is RIEMANNIAN GEOMETRY; that based on the hypothesis that there is more than one such line is LOBACHEVSKIAN GEOMETRY. The first mathematician to open the doors for non-Euclidean geometry was GAUSS in the 19th century. He did not publish his work, however, and the fathers of non-Euclidean geometry are usually considered to be BOLYAI, Jáns and LOBACHEVSKY.

**NONO, Luigi** (1924–    ), Italian composer of serial or TWELVE-TONE MUSIC. His choral and instrumental works, often political in content, include *Epitaffo per Federico García Lorca* (1952), *Il canto sospeso* (1956) and *Intolleranza* (1961), an antifascist opera. Word sounds and electronic tape and equipment are important elements in much of his music.

**NONPARTISAN LEAGUE**, political association of farmers and farmworkers founded (1915) and centered in the Dakotas. Formed in response to the power of banking, grain and railroad bosses, the league campaigned for state-run elevators, mills, banks and insurance. Dominating N.D. government 1916–21, it realized most of its demands.

**NORDHOFF AND HALL**, US novelists best known for *Mutiny on the Bounty* (1932). **Charles Bernard Nordhoff** (1887–1947) and **James Norman Hall** (1887–1951) met as pilots in WWI. Their first joint work was a history, *The Lafayette Flying Caps* (1920). The "Bounty" trilogy was completed by *Men Against the Sea* (1933) and *Pitcairn's Island* (1934). (See also BOUNTY, MUTINY ON THE).

**NORMAN CONQUEST**, conquest of England by William, Duke of Normandy, following the Battle of HASTINGS (Oct. 14, 1066) when William defeated and killed England's Saxon king, HAROLD. Although illegitimate, William claimed the English throne as EDWARD THE CONFESSOR'S cousin and named successor. Crowned WILLIAM I in London, he quickly crushed revolts, building castles as he advanced. The land of the English nobles was distributed to NORMANS in return for their agreement to supply the king with mounted soldiers. The great DOMESDAY BOOK (1086) listed landholdings. The conquerors also brought to England the influence of their French language and innovations in architecture and methods of warfare.

**NORMANDY**, region of NW France facing the English Channel, noted for dairy products, fruit, brandy, wheat and flax. Le Havre, Dieppe and Cherbourg are the main ports; Rouen and Caen are historic cathedral and university cities. Shipbuilding, steel, iron and textiles are the main industries. Home of the NORMANS, it was later much contested with England before finally going to France in 1450. In WWII it was chosen for the Allied landing, June 6, 1944.

**NORMANS**, inhabitants of NORMANDY, the former province of NW France. In 911 Rollo, leader of the VIKING raider-settlers, was recognized as duke of the area. Strong, warlike and excellent administrators, the Normans ("Northmen") became Christians in the 10th century and completed the NORMAN CONQUEST of England in the 11th. They were active in the CRUSADES, in the reconquest of Spain, in S Italy and Sicily.

**NORRIS, Frank** (Benjamin Franklin Norris; 1870–1902), US novelist and newspaperman. His best-known novels are his first, naturalistic *McTeague* (1899) about life in San Francisco slums and his uncompleted trilogy *The Epic of Wheat* (*The Octopus*, 1901 and *The Pit*, 1903), in which he foreshadowed the MUCKRAKERS.

**NORRIS, George William** (1861–1944), noted US congressman (1902–42) and reformer. Elected to the House as a Republican from Neb., he led the fight which ousted Speaker Joseph CANNON. In 1912 he moved to the Senate. There his progressive, nonpartisan crusades embraced election reform, setting up the TENNESSEE VALLEY AUTHORITY, labor disputes (the Norris–La Guardia Act), farm relief, the 20th or LAME DUCK AMENDMENT which he authored, and POLL TAX abolition.

**NORTH, Frederick, Lord North**, (later Earl of Guildford; 1732–1792), British Tory prime minister. His policies precipitated the break with the American colonies. A tool of George III, North answered the BOSTON TEA PARTY with the INTOLERABLE ACTS (1774), including the QUEBEC ACT, which kept Canada loyal to Britain. He resigned in 1782, and in 1783 formed a brief coalition with Charles James FOX.

**NORTH AMERICA**, third-largest continent, bounded in the N by the Arctic Ocean, in the S by South America, in the W by the Pacific and Bering Sea, and in the E by the Atlantic. It includes the US, Canada, Mexico, Central America, the Caribbean Islands and Greenland—one-sixth of the earth's land surface (9,361,791sq mi), with over 95,000mi of coastline.

**Land.** Its regions differ immensely: in the W coastal ranges from Alaska to the Gulf of California parallel to the Rocky Mts, the continent's backbone. Between lies the Intermountain Region, with the Great Basin and Mexican Plateau. E of the Rockies is the vast Interior Plain which includes the Great Plains, the Canadian Prairies, the US Midwest and the Great Lakes and in the NE the ancient rocks of the Canadian (Laurentian) Shield. In the SE lie the Piedmont and Atlantic Coastal Plain and Appalachian Mts. The CONTINENTAL DIVIDE, created by the Rockies, directs the main rivers: the Colorado, Columbia, Fraser and Yukon flow W to the Pacific; the Mackenzie, St. Lawrence, Rio Grande, Missouri and Mississippi flow E to the Atlantic and Arctic oceans. The climate ranges from polar to tropical. Most of the interior has cold winters and hot summers; rainfall can reach 140in a year on the NW Pacific coast and in S Central America. Vegetation varies widely, with northern tundra in Greenland, Alaska and N Canada, desert in SW US and Mexico, and jungle in Central America. Wildlife is rich

and diverse. North America has enormous mineral wealth and a large proportion of the land has a hospitable climate and fertile soils.

**People.** The continent ranks third in population, which is densest in the E US, SE Canada, the W coast of both, and in Mexico. The people are mainly Caucasians of European descent, speaking English and French in the N, and Spanish in Mexico and Central America. Their ancestors emigrated following the first permanent European contacts made in the 1490s by Columbus in the Caribbean and the Cabots in Newfoundland. The settlers found Indians, descendants of the Mongoloid peoples who are thought to have moved E from Asia across the Bering Strait some 25,000 years ago (see ESKIMO; INDIANS, CENTRAL AND SOUTH AMERICAN; INDIANS, NORTH AMERICAN.) Negroes were brought in from Africa as slaves, and are now concentrated in the Caribbean and the US, where every European nation is represented and 10% of the population are NEGROES or MULATTOES. Of Mexicans 60% are MESTIZOS. Varied backgrounds have brought wide differences in culture, religion and standards of living. (See also CANADA; MEXICO; UNITED STATES and other countries.)

**NORTH AMERICAN AIR DEFENSE COMMAND (NORAD)**, combined command responsible for global aerospace surveillance and the defense of North America against ballistic and air attack. It employs US and Canadian air force units and US army and navy air units. Set up in 1958, NORAD's present capabilities with which to circumvent air and ballistic missile attack are limited to early warning.

**NORTH ATLANTIC TREATY ORGANIZATION (NATO)**, defense organization of nations adhering to the North Atlantic Treaty. An extension of the 1948 Brussels Treaty for military cooperation among five European nations, the treaty is directed at the threat of armed communist attack in Europe or the N Atlantic or Mediterranean area. The new treaty was signed in April 1949 by Belgium, Canada, Denmark, France, Great Britain, Iceland, Italy, Luxembourg, the Netherlands, Norway, Portugal and the US, by Greece and Turkey in 1951 and by West Germany in 1954. Article 5 states that an armed attack on any one or two members will be taken as an attack on all; other clauses cover military, political and economic cooperation. The supreme body is the North Atlantic Council, backed up by committees. It coordinated with its executive branch, the Military Committee, in Brussels. The

Presidency of the Military Committee annually rotates among member nations. NATO has three commands: Europe, the Atlantic, and the English Channel and North Sea. The Canada–United States Regional Planning Group coordinates North American defense with NATO. France expelled NATO forces in 1966 and the US, which resents its disproportionate share of cost, is accused of acting unilaterally in political matters, but the alliance holds through mutual self-interest among the members. Its corresponding alliance system is the Soviet-dominated WARSAW PACT.

**Name of state:** North Carolina
**Capital:** Raleigh
**Statehood:** Nov. 21, 1789 (12th state)
**Familiar name:** Tar Heel State
**Area:** 52,586sq mi
**Population:** 5,874,429
**Elevation:** Highest—6,684ft, Mt Mitchell Lowest—sea level, Atlantic Ocean
**Motto:** Esse quam videri (To Be, Rather Than to Seem)
**State flower:** Dogwood
**State bird:** Cardinal
**State tree:** Pine
**State song:** "The Old North State"

**NORTH CAROLINA,** state, E US, bounded to the E by the Atlantic Ocean, to the S by S.C. and Ga., to the W by Tenn. and to the N by Va.; one of the original 13 colonies.

**Land.** The Atlantic coastal plain of swamps and rich farmland, shielded in the N by a long chain of barrier islands, gives way on the W to the rolling hills of the Piedmont, where industry has centered at Raleigh, the capital, the urban complex of Greensboro/Winston-Salem and Charlotte, the biggest city. Farther W lie the BLUE RIDGE and GREAT SMOKY MOUNTAINS areas; Mt Mitchell is the highest peak E of the Mississippi R. The many rivers provide for hydroelectric power. Forests cover over half of the state. The mild climate has a mean annual temperature of 59°F and rainfall of about 50in.

**People.** Almost all the citizens of North Carolina are US-born. Approximately 23% of the population is black and more than 45% of the total lives in urban communities. Baptists are the largest religious group, followed by Methodists and Presbyterians.

**Economy.** Industry, intensified after WWII, now accounts for a major proportion of North Carolina's income. The state continues to be one of the leading US manufacturers of textiles, cigarettes and furniture. Chemicals, electrical machinery, processed foods and pulp and paper products are also important to North Carolina's economic base. In agriculture, tobacco leads, followed by soybeans, corn, peanuts and cotton. Tourism, supported by the scenic beauty in the W, five national forests and many historical sites, brings increasing revenue. Mining centers on construction materials, but North Carolina is also the main source of felspar, lithium and mica in the US.

**History.** Sir Walter Raleigh failed twice in the 1580s to settle the area, inhabited by CATAWBA, CHEROKEE and TUSCARORA INDIANS (see LOST COLONY). Grants from Charles I (hence *Carolina*) and II were followed in 1677 by CULPEPER'S REBELLION by settlers. North Carolina became a separate colony in 1712 and a royal colony in 1729. It was the first to instruct its delegates to vote for independence and in 1789 became the twelfth state of the US. It seceded in 1861 when it failed in efforts to preserve the Union. Development was spurred in the 1900s by a major expansion in education and after WWII by industrial diversification and provision of hydroelectric power. North Carolina is now a pioneer in social legislation and a major industrial force in the South. Despite this, per capita income of $7,385 in 1979 was only five-sixths of the national average, and a wide gap continued to exist between the incomes of whites and blacks. The state has a healthy mix of manufacturing and agricultural resources, though its farmers still depend unduly on tobacco production. In recent years, the state's textile industry has been hurt by imports and some mills have closed. Nonetheless, the population increased 15.5% in the 1970s, and urban expansion is rapidly changing the state.

**NORTHCLIFFE, Alfred Charles William Harmsworth, Viscount** (1865–1922), creator of modern British journalism. On a basis of popular journals starting with *Answers* (1888), he built the world's biggest newspaper empire. He founded or bought the *London Evening News*, *Daily Mail*, *Sunday Dispatch*, *Daily Mirror*, *Observer* and the *Times*.

**Name of state:** North Dakota
**Capital:** Bismarck
**Statehood:** Nov. 2, 1889 (39th state)
**Familiar name:** Flickertail State, Sioux State
**Area:** 70,665sq mi
**Population:** 652,695
**Elevation:** Highest—3,506ft, White Butte Lowest—750ft, Red River in Pembina County
**Motto:** Liberty and Union, Now and Forever, One and Inseparable
**State flower:** Wild prairie rose
**State bird:** Western meadowlark
**State tree:** American elm
**State song:** "North Dakota Hymn"

**NORTH DAKOTA,** N central US state, bounded to the E by Minn., to the S by S.D., to the W by Mont. and to the N by Canada. The state lies at the center of the North American land mass.

**Land.** The most populous part is the flat, fertile Red R valley in the E. The Red R of the North forms the E border with Minn. It drains E N.D. and flows N to Lake Winnipeg. The Drift Plains, with fertile glacial deposits and many lakes, roll W some 70mi in the S and 200mi in the N to the Missouri escarpment. The Missouri Plateau, part of the Great Plains, covers the SW of the state. The Missouri R enters N.D. from Montana in the W and flows SE via the huge Garrison hydroelectric dam and reservoir to S.D. Near the W border lie the spectacularly eroded BADLANDS. The continental climate has temperatures averaging 70°F in the summer and 10°F in winter. The rain (only 20in in the E and 14in in the W), falls mostly in the growing season. Only 1% of the land is forested.

**People.** The people are nearly all native-born, of European descent. Less than 25% of the total population lives in urban areas. The largest cities are Fargo, Grand Forks, Bismarck and Minot. Lutherans and Roman Catholics are the largest religious groups.

**Economy.** A major part of North Dakota's economy is based on agriculture. Wheat, grown in all 53 counties, is by far the most important crop, followed by flax, barley, rye, potatoes and oats. Earnings from livestock products of the W are second to those of wheat. Oil (discovered 1951 in the NW) and lignite (the US's largest deposits, in the SW) are the chief minerals exploited. Natural gas and uranium are also mined. Tourism and manufacturing (food processing and oil refining) roughly equal mineral exploitation in value.

**History.** The state was part of the 1803 LOUISIANA PURCHASE. Even after the LEWIS AND CLARK expedition, few homesteaders settled there until the arrival of railroads in the 1870s and the 1881 defeat of the SIOUX chief SITTING BULL. Friction between farmers and grain monopolies led to the forming of the NONPARTISAN LEAGUE in 1915. WWII brought recovery from the drought, dust storms and depression of the 1930s. The manufacturing sector remains modest, while agriculture has gradually consolidated, with farms now averaging more than 1,000 acres in size. The enlargement of farms, and the accompanying mechanization of farm work, has reduced the already sparse population of North Dakota's rural areas—a trend that is expected to continue. The local economy benefited from the building in the 1960s and 1970s of air bases and missile and anti-missile sites in the state. Any future breakthrough in the exploitation of lignite for synthetic fuels would have profound implications for North Dakota.

**NORTHEAST PASSAGE,** sea passage linking the Atlantic and Pacific oceans. It passes N of the Eurasian mainland along the Arctic coast of Norway and the USSR. Adolf Nordenskjöld, the Swedish explorer, was first to sail its length, 1878–79, although its exploration dates from the 15th century. Explorers of the area have included Willem Parents, Henry Hudson, Captain James Cook, and Vitus Bering.

**NORTHERN IRELAND.** See IRELAND, NORTHERN.

**NORTHERN LIGHTS.** See AURORA.

**NORTHERN MARIANA ISLANDS,** a commonwealth of the US, comprises 16 islands in the W Pacific.

**Land.** Although GUAM is geographically part of the Marianas, it has long been administered separately and is not considered part of the group. Of these volcanic and coral islands, only six are inhabited, with more than 85% of the population living on Saipan, the largest island and administrative center, which is followed in size by Tinian and Rota.

**People.** About 75% of the people are

descended from the Chamorro, the indigenous Micronesian group of the Marianas; most of the others are Caroline Islanders. Roman Catholicism predominates.

**Economy.** The US government is the largest employer, as Saipan continues to serve as the administrative center of the Trust Territory of the Pacific Islands despite the Northern Marianas' separate status. The leading crops include coconuts, sugar, coffee, taro, breadfruit and yams; cattle raising is of growing importance. Tourism is also a leading source of income.

**History.** After Spain assumed control of the Marianas in 1565 they moved all the Chamorros to Guam and the other islands remained uninhabited until some resettlement began during the late 17th century. In 1898 control of Guam passed to the US and the other Marianas were sold to Germany, and occupied in 1914 by Japan, which developed commercial sugar plantations. US forces successfully invaded the islands in 1944 after heavy fighting, and they subsequently became part of the US Trust Territory of the Pacific Islands. Northern Mariana voters approved separate status as a commonwealth in 1975, which became effective in 1978.

**Official name:** Commonwealth of the Northern Mariana Islands
**Capital:** Saipan
**Area:** 298sq mi
**Population:** 16,758
**Languages:** English, Chamorro
**Religion:** Christian
**Monetary unit(s):** 1 US dollar = 100 cents

**NORTH PLATTE RIVER,** river, 680mi long, which rises in N Col., flows N into central Wyo., E and SE into W central Neb., uniting with the South Platte R in SW Neb. to become the Platte. The pioneer Overland Trail followed the river valley.

**NORTH POLE,** the point on the earth's surface some 750km N of Greenland through which passes the earth's axis of rotation. It does not coincide with the earth's N Magnetic Pole, which is over 1,000km away (see EARTH). The Pole lies roughly at the center of the Arctic Ocean, which is permanently ice-covered, and experiences days and nights each of six months. It was first reached by Robert E. Peary (April 6, 1909). (See also CELESTIAL SPHERE; MAGNETISM; SOUTH POLE.)

**NORTH SEA,** arm of the Atlantic Ocean lying between Britain, Scandinavia and NW Europe, rich in fish, gas and oil. Almost 600mi long, it covers 222,125sq mi with an average depth of 300ft, falling to 2,400ft off Norway. Long a rich

commercial fishing ground for flatfish and herring, the North Sea since the early 1960s has been prospected by more than 20 international companies for oil and gas. The first productive gas field was found in 1965, 42mi E of Britain's Humber estuary. Since then, major gas and oil deposits have been found off the Dutch.

**NORTH STAR.** See POLARIS.

**NORTHUMBRIA,** English Anglo-Saxon kingdom of the 6th–9th centuries, extending from the Mersey and Humber Rivers on the S to the Firth of Forth in the N. It became the cultural center of England due to the civilizing work of monks (see BEDE, SAINT). The kingdom was absorbed by England during the NORMAN CONQUEST.

**NORTHWEST ORDINANCE,** ordinance adopted by Congress in 1787, which established the government of the NORTHWEST TERRITORY and provided a form for future territories to follow. It stated that Congress should appoint a territorial governor, a secretary and three judges. Once the territory had a voting population of 5,000 it could elect a legislature and send a non-voting representative to Congress. When the population reached 60,000, the territory could seek full admission to the Union. It barred slavery, guaranteed basic rights and encouraged education.

**NORTHWEST PASSAGE,** inland water route from the E coast of North America to the Pacific, and thus to the Orient. This was unsuccessfully sought for centuries. John CABOT explored the coast around Newfoundland in 1497 thinking it was China; Henry HUDSON sailed as far as Hudson Bay and beyond (1609–11); William BAFFIN and Robert Bylot found a way between Baffin Island and Greenland. Explorations opened up important new lands, but not until Robert McCLURE's expedition of 1850–54 was the existence of a passage weaving among the Arctic islands proved. The first complete journey was made when Roald AMUNDSEN sailed W from Baffin Bay through Lancaster Sound, 1903–06. The entire Atlantic–Pacific crossing was not accomplished until the US Navy navigated the Northwest Passage by atomic submarine in 1958.

**NORTHWEST TERRITORIES,** federally administered region of Canada comprising the mainland N of 60°N between Yukon Territory and Hudson Bay, the islands in Hudson, James and Ungava Bays and all islands N of the mainland.

**Land.** It is an immense, low-lying thinly-populated area: about half the region lies within the Arctic Circle. Two thirds of the mainland are covered by the Mackenzie

R, its tributaries, and by lakes such as the Great Bear and Great Slave. The Mackenzie Mts to the W rise to 9,000ft. There is permanent sea ice N of Melville Island where the winter temperature sinks to −40°F compared with −18°F in the Mackenzie delta.

**People.** More than 60% of the population are Inuit (Eskimo) and Indians. Most of the Indians and whites are in the Mackenzie District, which is the most developed area and where the largest towns, Yellowknife, the capital, Fort Smith and Inuvik are.

**Economy.** The principal industries are fishing, mining and trapping. Of these, mining is the most important, the territory producing all of Canada's tungsten, 44% of its lead, 26% of its zinc, 20% of its silver, and 13% of its gold. Uranium exploration is continuing. Oil and gas exploration boomed in the 1970s, with the Beaufort Sea project and oil drilling in the Arctic Islands. Farming in the region is still in an experimental stage.

**History.** Early explorers include Sir Martin FROBISHER who reached Baffin Island in 1576, and the trader-explorers of the HUDSON'S BAY COMPANY. Sir Alexander MACKENZIE explored in the 1780s. The region was part of a larger area sold to Canada in 1870 by the Hudson's Bay Company. The Territories' boundaries were established in 1912.

**Name of territory:** The Northwest Territories (Districts: Mackenzie, Keewatin, Franklin)

**Joined Confederation:** 1870 (as Rupert's Land, purchased by Canada from the Hudson's Bay Company; present boundaries set in 1912)

**Capital:** Yellowknife (since 1967; previously Ottawa)

**Area:** 1,304,903sq mi

**Population (including districts):** 43,000

**NORTHWEST TERRITORY,** region between the Ohio and Mississippi rivers, extending N around the Great Lakes. It was the first national territory of the US, eventually forming Ohio (1803), Ind. (1816), Ill. (1818), Mich. (1837), Wis. (1848) and part of Minn. Won by Britain from the French who explored it in the 1600s, it was ceded to the US by the Treaty of Paris 1783, and its future determined by the Ordinance of 1787 (see NORTHWEST ORDINANCE). The first governor was Arthur St. Clair and settlement soon followed. Indians were defeated by General Anthony WAYNE at the battle of FALLEN TIMBERS and most of their lands taken by the Treaty of Greenville, 1795. Ind., Mich., and Ill. became territories prior to statehood.

**Official name:** Norway
**Capital:** Oslo
**Area:** 125,020sq mi
**Population:** 4,079,000
**Languages:** Norwegian; Lappish, Finnish spoken in the North
**Religion:** Evangelical Lutheran
**Monetary unit(s):** 1 krone = 100 øre

**NORWAY,** European constitutional monarchy in the W Scandinavian peninsula between the Atlantic, on the W, and Sweden. Finland and the USSR are to the NE. Norwegian territory also includes thousands of coastal islands.

**Land.** It is a rugged, mountainous land famous for its beautiful fiords, with many deep lakes and swift rivers. The mountains covering over half of Norway, extend nearly its whole length. It has the highest peak in Scandinavia (Galdhøpiggen, 8,098ft) and the largest ice field in mainland Europe, the Jostedalsbreen. Because of its maritime situation and on-shore winds, the climate is mild. Rainfall varies from 100in on the coast to 40in inland. Pine and spruce forests cover about a fourth of Norway.

**People.** The majority of the population are of the fair Nordic type, but there are some Lapps and Finns in the N. The S is the most heavily populated, the largest towns there being Oslo, the capital, Bergen and Stavanger and in the N, Trondheim. There are two official languages, Nynorsk and Bokmål (see NORWEGIAN LANGUAGE), although the Lapps in the N have their own Finnish-Ugric speech.

**Economy.** Norway's natural resources are sparse: mineral deposits are minimal and less than 3% of the land is under cultivation. Norway has developed a thriving economy since WWII by restricting imports and promoting industrialization, particularly in aluminum production, chemicals, textiles, machinery, paints and furniture. Agriculture, based on farms of 25 acres or less, give high yields of oats, hay, barley, potatoes, fruits and vegetables, and livestock are raised in the mountains. Forestry and fishing, particularly of mackerel and cod, are very important industries.

**History.** Norway's separate history began about 800 AD when the VIKINGS began to raid European coastal towns. Until the 14th century there was a long series of civil wars. In 1397 Norway merged with Denmark (becoming a Danish province in 1536) and in 1814 with Sweden. In 1905 it became an independent constitutional monarchy under HAAKON VII. Germany occupied all of Norway 1940–45. Norway is a member of the NORTH ATLANTIC TREATY ORGANIZATION and of the EUROPEAN FREE TRADE ASSOCIATION, but refused in a 1972 referendum to join the COMMON MARKET.

**NORWEGIAN LANGUAGE,** language of Norway, developed from the NORSE and influenced by union with Denmark 1397–1814. There are two official versions: *Nynorsk* or *Landsmål*, based on native dialects, and *Bokmål* or *Riksmål*, a Dano-Norwegian used by writers and the press. Differences between them are diminishing.

**NOTATION,** method of writing down music formalized between the 10th and 18th centuries into a system of stave notation, now in general use. It consists of five horizontal lines or staves as the framework on which eight notes are written—A, B, C, D, E, F, G (in ascending order of pitch) and thence to A again an octave higher (see also SCALE). Each note's special place on or between the lines depends on its pitch: in the base clef, if low, the treble clef if higher. A middle or alto clef is sometimes used. The KEY of the music is indicated by sharps and flats on the staves next to the clef sign at the beginning of the score. The length of the notes relative to each other is shown by their form. There are commonly seven forms of note from the longest held to the shortest. The beat of the music is shown by dividing the staves by vertical lines into *bars* and marking at the outset how many beats there are to each bar (see also RHYTHM). Other notations are the *tonic sol-fa* in which notes are related to each other, not to the established pitch of the written stave; and *tablature* in which a diagram indicates where to place the fingers on various instruments to obtain notes. New signs for use in ELECTRONIC MUSIC are being invented.

**NOTOCHORD,** the primitive longitudinal skeletal element characterizing the class Chordata, the first stage in the development of a flexible internal skeleton. All chordates possess a notochord at some time during life. Though replaced by cartilage or bone in the adult VERTEBRATE and absent in the adults of other chordate groups, e.g., TUNICATES, it is well developed in the embryos or larvae of all these groups, confirming evolutionary relationships within the class.

**NOTRE DAME DE PARIS,** cathedral church of Paris, on the Ile de la Cité in the Seine R. Begun in 1163, it was finished in 1313 and is one of the finest examples of early Gothic architecture, especially for the ROSE WINDOW of the west facade and the sculptured portals. Some restoration was necessary after the French Revolution. (See also GOTHIC ART.)

**NOUVELLE CUISINE,** a reformed approach to certain aspects of French cookery that achieved international popularity in the 1970s. The "new" cuisine, promoted in France by such restaurant chefs as Paul Bocuse, Michael Guérard and the Troisgros brothers, Jean and Pierre, rejected thickened sauces and featured scarcely cooked vegetables and raw fish, unusual combinations such as meat and fruit, and artfully arranged small portions on outsized plates.

**NOVA,** a star which over a short period (usually a few days) increases in brightness by 100 to 1,000,000 times. This is thought to be due to the star undergoing a partial explosion: that is to say, part of the star erupts, throwing out material at a speed greater than the ESCAPE VELOCITY of the star. The initial brightness fades quite rapidly though it is usually some years before the star returns to its previous luminosity, having lost about 0.0001 of its mass. At that time a rapidly expanding planetary NEBULA may be seen to surround the star. Recurrent novae are stars which go nova at irregular periods of a few decades. Dwarf novae are subdwarf stars which go nova every few weeks or months. Novae have been observed in other galaxies besides the MILKY WAY. (See also SUPERNOVA.)

**NOVALIS,** the pen name of Friederich Leopold, Freiherr von Hardenberg (1772–1801), German poet. His works, notably the myth-romance *Heinrich von Ofterdingen* (1802), influenced later European exponents of ROMANTICISM. He attempted to unite poetry, philosophy and science into an allegory of the world.

**NOVA SCOTIA,** one of the four original provinces of the Dominion of Canada; it includes Cape Breton Island to the NE. It is also one of the MARITIME PROVINCES on the Atlantic seaboard. Linked to the mainland by the narrow Chignecto Isthmus, it is bounded on the N by New Brunswick and is separated from Prince Edward Island on the NW by Northumberland Strait; otherwise it is bounded by the Bay of Fundy and the Atlantic Ocean.

**Land.** Nova Scotia has an area of 21,425sq mi (1,023sq mi of inland water). There are many short rivers, the longest being the Mersey and St. Mary's (both run about 72mi). The Atlantic Upland is a distinctive feature of the landscape and is divided into five areas separated by fertile valleys and lowlands, notably the Annapolis Valley, famous for its apple orchards. The province generally has a cool climate, intensified by the cold Labrador Current; average temperatures are 24°F in Jan. with heavy snowfall and 65°F in July. Rainfall ranges from an average of 55in in the E to 40in in the W. About 84% of the province is forested; wildlife and birdlife are abundant.

**People.** Most Nova Scotians are of British or French ancestry, but important minority groups are descendants of Irish and German immigrants and of former West Indian slaves, and about 3,000 Micmac Indians live in the province. About 16% of the land is occupied by small farms averaging around 190 acres and while 6% of the people live on farms, 35% live in nonfarm rural areas. In coastal areas farming is combined with fishing and inland it is combined with dairying.

**Economy.** Lumbering is an important industry in the province, which has numerous other natural resources including coal, gypsum, barite and natural gas. There are rich fisheries and farmlands. Apples are the chief fruit crop; hay, oats, barley, wheat and vegetables are grown in substantial quantities. Manufacturing is diversified and chiefly concentrated around Halifax (which is also the main port), Sydney, Pictou County and on the Strait of Canso. The leading industries are coal mining, petroleum refining, food and beverage processing, transportation–equipment manufacturing and paper industries. Coal, lead, zinc, gypsum, salt, sand and gravel are mined. Recent finds suggest the possibility of offshore oil and natural gas deposits. The most important exports are from lumber mills and from fish-processing and agricultural processing plants. The province has turned from imported coal to native coal and is assessing hydroelectric potential. Tidal power may be its key to meeting future energy needs.

**History.** Leif ERICSON may have visited Nova Scotia as early as 1000 AD, but it is certain that John CABOT discovered Cape Breton Island in 1497. Canada's first permanent settlement was established in 1605 on the site of Annapolis Royal. In the 17th century the area was contested by the British and the French, but after the FRENCH AND INDIAN WARS it was gained by England.

Nova Scotia became the first Canadian colony to gain responsible government in 1848 and in 1867 it formed the original Dominion with Quebec, Ontario and New Brunswick. Since then, Nova Scotia has been concerned with establishing its rightful place in the nation, alongside much larger and richer provinces. Much economic and social progress has been achieved, aided by large-scale industrial development around the Sydney area and construction of a deep-water port on the Strait of Canso.

**Name of province:** Nova Scotia
**Joined Confederation:** July 1st, 1867
**Capital:** Halifax
**Area:** 21,425sq mi
**Population:** 841,200

**NOVAYA ZEMLYA,** a group of islands (including two main ones) in NW USSR in the Arctic Ocean between the Barents Sea on the W and the Kara Sea on the E. Used as a Soviet nuclear testing site, the islands have a small native population which fishes and hunts in the S tundra areas.

**NOVEL,** a work of prose fiction (usually over 60,000 words long) generally portraying in one or more plot lines the interrelationship of a number of characters. Rudimentary forms of novel appear to have existed in ancient Egypt as long ago as 2000 BC; the Greek *Daphnis and Cloë* and the eclectic *The Golden Ass* by the Roman APULEIUS are the earliest known in the West. The Japanese *Tale of Genji* (c1000) by Lady MURASAKI is a sophisticated and startlingly modern love novel. The modern European novel developed out of the Italian Renaissance *novella* form, typified by BOCCACCIO'S *Decameron*. RABELAIS' *Gargantua and Pantagruel* (1532–52) and CERVANTES' *Don Quixote* (1605–15) are prototypes of the European novel. In English literature the form was established in the works of DEFOE, and in the mid-18th century with the contrasting work of RICHARDSON and FIELDING. The 19th-century novel was a major form of mass entertainment throughout Europe and the Americas; it was also a forum for the discussion of politics and special problems, and so recorded them for posterity. The novels of GOETHE, Sir Walter SCOTT and others inspired much Romantic drama and music. In France George SAND and Victor HUGO were among the first post-Revolutionary novelists of standing. In the US the novel contributed to the development of a national identity and the defining of a specifically American experience.

Giants of the form in both stature and output emerged in the 19th century such as

BALZAC, DICKENS, George ELIOT, TOLSTOY, DOSTOYEVSKY and Herman MELVILLE who exploited the vast possibilities of the form. From the time of FLAUBERT there has been less emphasis on "story-telling"; the novel came to be seen as an intense psychological artifact with aesthetic aspirations akin to poetry. Henry JAMES, Marcel PROUST, James JOYCE, Virginia WOOLF and others have elaborated this emphasis, often at the expense of any easy accessibility. Writers such as Thomas HARDY and D. H. LAWRENCE, and HEMINGWAY and other US writers have, in their different styles, favored a more direct and passionate approach, while writers like ORWELL, KOESTLER and even SOLZHENITSYN emphasized political stance and almost documentary reportage. Despite contrary prophecies the novel's vitality appears to remain undiminished today.

**NOVEMBER,** the 11th month of the year, the ninth in the original Roman CALENDAR; its name derives from the Latin *novem*, nine. It now has 30 days, and the 4th Thurs. is THANKSGIVING DAY in the US.

**NOVGOROD,** historic city and capital of Novgorod oblast, NW USSR. Located on the Volkhov R, it long formed a trade link between the Baltic and the Orient. The city was important as an ancient VARANGIAN capital, a cultural and a commercial center, and was later a trading center of the HANSEATIC LEAGUE. The kremlin (citadel) includes a number of 15th-century churches and watchtowers. Pop 128,000.

**NOVOCAINE,** alternative name for PROCAINE, a local anesthetic.

**NOVOTNÝ, Antonín** (1904–1975), Czechoslovakian Communist Party leader, president of Czechoslovakia, 1957–68. As a Stalinist and supporter of Moscow, Novotný ll from power in Jan. 1968 after years of economic stagnation and political unrest. He was succeeded by a liberal regime led by Alexander DUBČEK and others.

**NOYES, Alfred** (1880–1958), English poet, a traditionalist known for his popular, vigorous rhythmic ballads like *The Highwayman* and patriotic sea poems such as *Drake* (1908). His other works include the blank verse *Torch-Bearers* (1922–30) praising scientific progress, and *Collected Poems* (1947).

**NOYES, Frank Brett** (1863–1948), US newspaper publisher who was a founder of the Associated Press. He was also editor and publisher of the Chicago *Record-Herald* (from 1902) and president of the Washington *Star* (from 1910).

**NOYES, John Humphrey** (1811–1886), US religious reformer, founder of the ONEIDA COMMUNITY, 1848. He preached so-called "perfectionism" in his communities at Putney, Vt. and Oneida, N.Y., but "Bible Communism" and a form of polygamy aroused opposition and he fled to Canada in 1879.

**NUBIA,** ancient region of NE Africa, now mostly in the republic of Sudan, along both banks of the Nile R from Aswan nearly to Khartoum. Called CUSH by the Egyptians, its rulers overran Upper Egypt in 750 BC and Lower Egypt in 721 BC. The Assyrians drove the Cushites out about 667 BC. Around 200 AD the Nobatae, a Negro people, settled in Nubia and by 600 AD their powerful kingdom was Christianized, but eventually it disintegrated under Muslim pressure in the later 14th century.

**NUCLEAR ENERGY,** energy released from an atomic nucleus during a nuclear reaction in which the atomic number (see ATOM), MASS NUMBER or RADIOACTIVITY of the nucleus changes. The term atomic energy, also used for this energy, which is produced in large amounts by NUCLEAR REACTORS and NUCLEAR WEAPONS, is not strictly appropriate, since nuclear reactions do not involve the orbital ELECTRONS of the atom. Nuclear energy arises from the special forces (about a million times stronger than chemical bonds) that hold the PROTONS and NEUTRONS together in the small volume of the atomic nucleus (see NUCLEAR PHYSICS). Lighter nuclei have roughly equal numbers of protons and neutrons, but heavier elements are only stable with a neutron:proton ratio of about 1.5:1. If one could overcome the electrostatic repulsion between protons and assemble them with neutrons to form a stable nucleus, its mass would be less than that of the constituent particles by the *mass defect*, $\Delta m$, of the nucleus, and the *binding energy*, BE, given by $BE = \Delta mc^2$ (where $c$ is the speed of light), would be released. Because $c$ is large, a vast amount of energy would be released, even for a very small value of the mass defect. The binding energy (equivalent to the work needed to split up the nucleus into separate protons and neutrons) is always positive—nuclei are always more stable than their separate nucleons (protons or neutrons)—but is greatest for nuclei of medium mass, decreasing slightly for lighter and heavier elements. The low binding energy of very light elements means that energy can be released by combining e.g., two DEUTERIUM nuclei to form a helium nucleus. This combination of two protons and two neutrons is particularly stable (see FUSION, NUCLEAR). For heavy elements the decrease in binding energy indicates that the more positively charged the nucleus becomes, the less stable it is, even though it contains more neutrons than protons. This sets a limit on the number of elements, and also explains why the nuclear-fission process, in which a heavy nucleus splits into two or more medium-mass nuclei with higher total binding energy, releases energy. The first nuclear reaction was performed experimentally in 1919 by RUTHERFORD who exposed NITROGEN to ALPHA PARTICLES (helium nuclei) from the radioactive element RADIUM, producing OXYGEN and HYDROGEN:

$$N^{14} + He^{14} \rightarrow 3^{\Psi^*} + H^1$$

But, because nuclei are positively charged and repel each other, it was found difficult to bring them close enough together to react with each other. The discovery of the neutron in 1932 helped overcome this problem. Being uncharged and heavy (on the atomic scale), the neutron has high energy even when moving slowly and is good for initiating nuclear reactions. By 1939 many nuclear reactions had been studied, but none seemed feasible as an energy source. Although energy might be released in a reaction, more energy was expended in producing particles able to initiate the reaction than could be recovered from it. Moreover, only a small fraction of the reagent particles would react as desired and any product particles would have little chance of reacting again. The situation was like trying to set fire to a damp forest with a box of matches! A breakthrough came around 1939 when the violent reaction of the heavy element uranium on bombardment with slow neutrons (first observed experimentally by FERMI in 1934) was successfully interpreted. It was realized that this was an example of nuclear fission, the slow neutrons delivering enough energy to the small proportion of $U^{235}$ nuclei in natural uranium to split them into two parts. This split does not always occur in the same way, and many radioactive fission products are formed, but each fission is accompanied by the release of much energy and two or three neutrons (these because the lighter nuclei of the fission products have a lower neutron:proton ratio than uranium). These neutrons were the key to the large scale production of nuclear energy; they could make the uranium "burn" by setting up a chain reaction. Even allowing for the loss of some neutrons, sufficient are left to produce other fissions, each producing two or three more neutrons, and so on, leading to an explosive release of energy. The first controlled chain reaction took place in Chicago in 1942, using pure graphite as a moderator to slow down neutrons and natural uranium as fuel. Rods of neutron-absorbing material kept the reaction under control by limiting the number of neutrons available to cause fissions. The possibilities of nuclear energy as a weapon were exploited at once and WWII ended shortly after the United States dropped two ATOMIC BOMBS on Japan. Later, more powerful bombs exploiting nuclear fusion were developed. An increasing quantity of man's energy is produced in NUCLEAR REACTORS from nuclear fission, although the earth's natural supplies of fissionable material are surprisingly limited. Moreover, because the fission products from these reactors are radioactive with long HALF-LIVES, atomic waste disposal is a major environmental problem. At present the waste is stored in concrete vaults lined with stainless steel, though the possibilities of converting waste to an insoluble glass are being explored. Disposal in space, in geologically stable parts of the earth's crust or by chemical conversion to safer materials are ideas for the future. Nuclear fusion seems to offer much better long-term prospects for energy supply, although fusion reactors have not yet progressed beyond the research stage.

**NUCLEAR PHYSICS**, the study of the physical properties and mathematical treatment of the atomic nucleus and SUBATOMIC PARTICLES. The subject was born when RUTHERFORD postulated the existence of the nucleus in 1911. The nature of the short-range exchange forces which hold together the nucleus, acting between positively charged protons and neutral neutrons is still uncertain. Experimental data from MASS SPECTROSCOPY and scattering experiments have enabled various partially successful theoretical models to be devised. Despite the special techniques required to produce nuclear reactions, the subject has rapidly grown with the technical exploitation of NUCLEAR ENERGY.

**NUCLEAR REACTOR**, device containing sufficient fissionable material, arranged so that a controlled chain reaction may be started up and maintained in it. Many types of reactor exist; all produce NEUTRONS, GAMMA RAYS, radioactive fission products and HEAT, but normally use is made of only one of these. Neutrons may be used in nuclear research or for producing useful RADIOISOTOPES. Gamma rays are dangerous to man and must be shielded against, but have some uses (see IRRADIATION). The fragments produced by fission of a heavy nucleus have a large amount of energy and the heat they produce may be used for carrying out a variety of high-temperature processes or for heating a working fluid (such as steam) to operate a TURBINE and produce ELECTRICITY. This is the function of most commercial reactors, although a number are used to power ships and submarines, since a small amount of nuclear fuel gives these a very long range. In an electricity-generating reactor, the fuel is normally uranium pellets surrounded by a moderator and the cooling fluid heavy water or liquid sodium (which in turn heats the turbine fluid). There is much insulation and radiation shielding. The fuel is expensive, but produces several thousand times the heat of the same weight of coal. After some time it must be replaced (although only partly consumed) because of the build-up of neutron-absorbing fission products. This replacement, and the reprocessing of the radioactive products, needs costly remote handling equipment. New fast breeder reactors with no moderator avoid this problem, since as well as producing fission of $U^{235}$, they convert nonfissionable $U^{238}$ to plutonium which also undergoes fission chain reactions—they effectively breed fuel! Research is continuing into more efficient reactors as power sources for the future.

Questions relating to nuclear safety and the disposal of nuclear wastes (see WASTE DISPOSAL) are still unresolved, however. The 1979 accident at Pennsylvania's Three Mile Island reactor—involving a partial fuel-core meltdown and the release of radioactive gases into the atmosphere—brought the issue of nuclear safety into the public arena. Since that year, studies of nuclear plants have revealed that in some, machinery is rusting; in a few, the steel shell that surrounds the fuel core has been made brittle by radiation; and in some cases, welds are not strong enough to withstand thermal shock, the rapid cooling that occurs when fuel cores are replaced.

**NUCLEAR REGULATORY COMMISSION (NRC),** independent US government agency set up in 1975 to take on all the licensing and regulatory functions formerly assigned to the Atomic Energy Commission. (See also THREE MILE ISLAND NUCLEAR ACCIDENT.)

**NUCLEAR WARFARE,** the use of nuclear weapons—the ATOMIC BOMB, the HYDROGEN BOMB and its variant, the NEUTRON BOMB—in warfare. The possible appalling consequences of large-scale nuclear warfare have overshadowed world politics since soon after WWII. Following FERMI's discovery of nuclear FISSION, preliminary experiments were done in the US starting in 1939, owing largely to fears of Germany's developing the

atomic bomb first. With the US entry into the war, the MANHATTAN PROJECT was started, culminating in the atomic bombs dropped on Hiroshima and Nagasaki. The USSR tested its first such weapon in 1949; from then on an arms race between those two "great powers" escalated until the late 1960s. The US exploded its first hydrogen bomb in 1952: the USSR in 1953. The UK, France and China have also developed nuclear weapons; certain other countries may well have done so without testing them. Development and deployment of nuclear weapons has been dictated by the theory of the nuclear deterrent, the aim being the capability of "assured destruction" of the enemy nation, a stable strategic balance achieved. Essential to this is the protection of a country's missiles against destruction in a "first strike," i.e., before any can be used in retaliation; thus the guided missiles are sited underground and in nuclear-powered SUBMARINES. The problem of radioactive FALLOUT pollution from nuclear tests led to the partial Nuclear Test-Ban Treaty, signed by the UK, US and USSR in 1963: this bans tests in space, in the atmosphere and underwater, but permits underground explosions that do not release fission products beyond national frontiers. Enforcement of the treaty requires explosions to be detected: this is done by detecting seismic or acoustic disturbances, radiation, or radioactive debris. Further disarmament negotiations led to the Treaty on the Non-Proliferation of Nuclear Weapons, ratified 1970 by 43 nations. There have also been attempts to limit delivery systems, especially intercontinental ballistic missiles (ICBMs), and defensive systems. Strategic arms limitation talks (SALT) began in 1969 and have achieved some limitation. Very stringent precautions are taken to prevent accidental or irresponsible use of nuclear weapons. Several persons validly authorized are required, and there is an electronic fail-safe system. Military strategy in recent years has been directed toward limited nuclear warfare, using tactical nuclear weapons in the battle zone, and toward preventing middle-scale nuclear wars from escalating to a total nuclear holocaust.

**NUCLEIC ACIDS,** the vital chemical constituents of living things; a class of complex threadlike molecules comprising two main types: the deoxyribonucleic acid (DNA) and the ribonucleic acids (RNA). DNA is found almost exclusively in the nucleus of the living CELL, where it forms the chief material of the CHROMOSOMES. It is the DNA molecule's ability to duplicate itself (replicate) that makes cell reproduction possible; and it is DNA, by directing PROTEIN SYNTHESIS, that controls HEREDITY in all organisms other than certain VIRUSES which contain only RNA. RNA performs several important tasks connected with protein synthesis, and is found throughout the cell.

In both DNA and RNA the backbone of the molecule is a chain of alternate phosphate and sugar groups. To each sugar group is bonded one or other of four nitrogonous side groups, which are either purines or pyrimidines. Each unit consisting of a side group, a sugar and a phosphate is called a NUCLEOTIDE. DNA differs chemically from RNA in that its sugar group has one less oxygen atom (hence the prefix "deoxy-") and one of its side groups, thymine, is replaced in RNA by uracil. DNA molecules are usually very much longer than RNA and may contain a million or so phosphate-sugar links.

It is the sequence in which the side groups are arranged along the DNA molecule that constitutes stored genetic information and so makes the difference between one inherited characteristic and another. This information, in the form of coded instructions for the synthesis of particular protein molecules, is carried outside the cell nucleus by molecules of "messenger RNA," each incorporating a side-group sequence determined by DNA. Floating freely outside the nucleus are AMINO ACIDS, the "building blocks" of proteins, and molecules of another, smaller kind of RNA, "transfer RNA." Each of these RNA molecules is able to capture an amino acid molecule of a particular type and locate it in its proper place in a sequence dictated by messenger RNA.

The DNA molecule has not one but two sugar-phosphate chains twisted around each other to form a double helix. Linking the chains rather like the rungs of a ladder are the side groups, each interlocking with its appropriate opposite number, for a particular side group can be partnered by a side group of only one other kind. The molecule replicates by splitting down the middle, whereupon the side groups of each half bond with the appropriate side groups of free phosphate-sugar units to form a pair of identical DNA molecules. The elucidation of DNA structure, one of the greatest advances of 20th-century biology, is chiefly associated with the work of the Nobel Prize-winners James WATSON, Francis CRICK and Maurice WILKINS.

**NUCLEOTIDES,** organic chemicals of central importance in the life chemistry of all plants and animals. Some nucleotides provide the basic molecular units for the synthesis of various more complex molecules, notably the NUCLEIC ACIDS—DNA and RNA; others— preeminently adenosine triphosphate (ATP)—provide a means of storing and releasing the ENERGY needed to drive biochemical processes.

The nucleotide molecule is a three-part structure, comprising a phosphate group linked to a 5-carbon sugar group (pentose) linked in turn to a nitrogenous side group (base). The five commonest bases are the purines adenine and guanine, and the pyrimidines cytosine, thymine and uracil. Adenine, guanine, cytosine and thymine serve in the DNA molecule as the four key "letters" of the genetic code. The nucleotide's pentose is either ribose or deoxyribose, the latter differing from the former only in having one less oxygen atom. The base-pentose component of a nucleotide is called a nucleoside.

The phosphate group consists of one or a combination of two or three phosphate units, and is accordingly termed a mono-, di- or triphosphate. The nucleotide adenosine triphosphate (ATP) is a nucleoside consisting of adenine and ribose bonded to a triphosphate group. The importance of ATP as an energy store depends on the third phosphate unit. When a third unit is added to adenosine diphosphate (ADP) to form ATP, an energy-rich chemical bond is formed; and it is this energy, released when ATP is converted back to ADP, that the CELL utilizes. (The human body daily builds up and breaks down approximately its own weight in ATP.) By releasing its energy, ATP activates or accelerates the action of ENZYMES, the catalysts of biochemical reactions, and so belongs to a class of substances called coenzymes. Most coenzymes are nucleotides.

**NULLIFICATION,** in US history, an act by which a state suspends a federal law within its borders. An extreme interpretation of STATES' RIGHTS, the tactic was particularly used by southern states to protect their minority status. First raised in the KENTUCKY AND VIRGINIA RESOLUTIONS of 1798, the doctrine was forcibly urged by John C. CALHOUN, whose *exposition* argued that the state of S.C. could nullify the so-called "Tariff of Abominations," passed in 1828. When another protective tariff passed in 1832, S.C. declared it null and void, threatening secession if coerced. President Jackson and Congress were ready to enforce the law by military action, but a compromise tariff was passed before the state's nullification order came into effect. The doctrine died when the South lost the Civil War. (See also HARTFORD CONVENTION; PROTECTIONISM; TARIFF.)

**NUMBER,** an expression of quantity. In everyday terms, numbers are usually used with UNITS: e.g., "three meters" (or 3m); "6.5893 kilograms" (or 6.5893kg).

For ways of expressing numbers see CUBE; FRACTION; ROOTS. For systems of expressing numbers see BINARY NUMBER SYSTEM; DECIMAL SYSTEM; DUODECIMAL SYSTEM. Types and systems of numbers include IMAGINARY NUMBERS; INTEGERS; IRRATIONAL NUMBERS; NATURAL NUMBERS; RATIONAL NUMBERS; REAL NUMBERS; TRANSCENDENTAL NUMBERS. (See also ALGEBRA; CARDINAL NUMBER; ORDINAL NUMBER; TRANSFINITE CARDINAL NUMBER and PERFECT NUMBER; PRIME NUMBER.)

**NUMBERS,** the fourth book of the PENTATEUCH, so called because it records two censuses of the Israelites. It narrates their wanderings in the wilderness until they reached Canaan.

**NUMISMATICS,** the study of coins, including their origin, history, use, mythology and manufacture. A coin is a medium of exchange, usually made in metal and issued by government authority. In its widest sense, numismatics includes a study of medals, tokens, counters and earliest money forms as well as the coinage of all countries from earliest times to the present.

**NUREMBERG TRIALS,** a series of WAR CRIMES trials held in Nuremberg, West Germany, 1945–1949, by the victors of WWII—the US, USSR, Great Britain and France. The accused, including von RIBBENTROP, GOERING, HESS and heads of the German armed forces, were tried for three kinds of crime: *Crimes Against Peace* (planning and waging aggressive war); *War Crimes* (murder or mistreatment of civilians or prisoners of war, killing of hostages, plunder of property, wanton destruction of communities, etc.); *Crimes Against Humanity* (extermination or enslavement of any civilian population before or during a war on political, racial or religious grounds; see GENOCIDE). The trials established new principles in the law of nations, above all that every person is responsible for his own acts.

**NUREYEV, Rudolf** (1938–   ), Russian virtuoso ballet dancer who sought asylum in the West when touring with the Kirov Ballet in 1961. As guest artist of the Royal Ballet, London, he became famed as a leading classical and modern dancer and for his partnership with Margot FONTEYN. He also staged several ballets.

**NURSERY SCHOOLS,** preschool care and early education for children from about three to five years old. Nursery schools developed from 19th-century infant-care programs for factory women's children, launched by Robert OWEN in Great Britain and copied in Europe as the Industrial Revolution spread. Johann PESTALOZZI (1746–1827), Friedrich FROEBEL (1782–1852) and Maria MONTESSORI (1870–1952) all pioneered preschool methods of nursery education. In the US the first nursery schools opened in the 1850s in large cities like New York and Philadelphia to release mothers for factory work. The first American effort to combine early care and educational projects began in 1915 at the U. of Chicago. Nursery schools today have developed programs in which the young learn by experience and through play to understand others, the world around them and themselves.

**NURSING,** care of the sick, injured or handicapped. Until the 19th century nursing was considered a charitable activity and was administered by religious bodies such as the Sisters of CHARITY (founded in 1634). In 1860 Florence NIGHTINGALE opened a school in London where experienced nurses and physicians gave instruction in nursing skills. This helped to establish nursing as a career rather than a religious vocation. In the US, nursing schools opened in New York City, Boston and New Haven, Conn., in the 1870s. Until then all nurses had been volunteers. Dorothea DIX was named by the US government as the first superintendent of nurses during the Civil War, after organizing 2,000 women into the Women's Central Association of Relief. By the 1970s there were about 1,350 schools of professional nursing in the US and an estimated 723,000 trained nurses employed. A nursing career today requires a high school education followed by a choice of three training programs: 1. a diploma after three years' training in hospitals and independent schools in the theory and practice of nursing and in the sciences; 2. a four-year nursing course and general education from a university, leading to a bachelor's degree (B.Sc.); and 3. a similar but shorter two-year junior college course. After training a state licensing examination (each state sets its own standards) must be passed to obtain registration. "Practical nursing" after one year of study is becoming increasingly popular and valuable, relieving the registered nurse (R.N.), now in short supply, of routine chores. (See also HOSPITAL; MEDICINE.)

NUTRITION, the process by which living organisms take in and utilize nutrients—the substances or foodstuffs required for GROWTH and the maintenance of LIFE. Vital substances that cannot be synthesized within the CELL and must be present in the food are termed "essential nutrients." Organisms such as green plants can derive ENERGY from sunlight and synthesize their nutritional requirements from simple inorganic chemicals present in the soil and air (see PLANT; PHOTOSYNTHESIS). Animals, on the other hand, depend largely on previously synthesized organic materials obtainable only by eating plants or other animals (see ANIMAL; DIGESTIVE SYSTEM; METABOLISM; ECOLOGY).

Human nutrition involves five main groups of nutrients: PROTEINS, FATS, CARBOHYDRATES, VITAMINS and minerals. Proteins, fats and carbohydrates are the body's sources of energy, and are required in relatively large amounts. They yield this energy by OXIDATION in the body cells, and nutritionists measure it in heat units called food CALORIES (properly called kilocalories, each equalling 1,000 gram calories). Carbohydrates (food STARCHES and SUGARS) normally form the most important energy source, contributing nearly half the calories in a well-balanced diet. Cereal products and potatoes are rich in starch; SUCROSE (table sugar) and LACTOSE (present in milk) are two common sugars. Fats, which provide about 40% of the calorie requirement, include butter, edible oils and shortening, and are present in such foods as eggs, fish, meat and nuts. Fats consist largely of fatty acids (see carboxylic acids), which divide into two main classes: saturated and unsaturated. Certain fatty acids are essential nutrients; but if there is too much saturated fatty acid in the diet, an excess of CHOLESTEROL may accumulate in the blood. Proteins supply the remaining energy needs, but their real importance lies in the fact that the body tissues, which are largely composed of protein, need certain essential AMINO ACIDS, found in protein foods, for growth and renewal. Protein-rich foods include meat, fish, eggs, cereals, peas and beans. Too little protein in the diet results in malnutritional diseases such as KWASHIORKOR.

Minerals (inorganic elements) and vitamins (certain complex organic molecules) provide no energy, but have numerous indispensable functions. Some minerals are components of body structures. Calcium and phosphorus, for example, are essential to BONES and TEETH. Iron in the BLOOD is vital for the transport of oxygen to the tissues: an iron deficiency results in ANEMIA. Milk and milk products are good sources of calcium and phosphorus; liver, red meat and egg yolk, of iron. Other important minerals, normally well supplied in the Western diet, include chlorine, iodine, magnesium, potassium, sodium and sulfur. Vitamins, which are present in small quantities in most foods, are intimately associated with the action of ENZYMES in the body cells, and particular vitamin deficiencies accordingly impair certain of the body's synthetic or metabolic processes. A chronic lack of vitamin A, for example, leads to a hardening and drying of the skin and can result in irreversible damage to the conjunctiva and cornea of the eye. BERIBERI is caused by a vitamin $B_1$ deficiency, SCURVY by a vitamin C deficiency; RICKETS by a lack of vitamin D.

Despite the fact that the nutritionists now understand the basic requirements of a healthy diet, the difficulty of applying their knowledge world-wide is immense. About two-thirds of the world's population remains severely undernourished and subject to deficiency diseases. Even in the richer countries malnutrition occurs but here it is likely to be due to an ill-chosen rather than impoverished diet. In the US, the Food and Nutrition Board of the United States Academy of Sciences National Research Council publishes a table of recommended daily nutrient allowances. (See also DIETETIC FOODS; DIETING; OBESITY.)

NYAD, Diana (1949–    ), US marathon swimmer. In 1979 she became the first person ever to swim the 89mi from the Bahamas to the US. She gained world notice the year before with an unsuccessful attempt to swim from Cuba to Florida.

NYASA, Lake. See MALAWI, LAKE.

NYASALAND. See MALAWI.

NYERERE, Julius Kambarage (1921–    ), founder and first president of the East African state of Tanzania. He led Tanganyika to independence (1961) and united it with Zanzibar, forming Tanzania (1964). A supporter of nonalignment, he nonetheless accepted aid from communist China. He espoused belief in a one-party socialist democracy. His military intervention helped overthrow Ugandan dictator Amin.

NYLON, group of POLYMERS containing AMIDE groups recurring in a chain. The commonest nylon is made by condensation of adipic acid and hexamethylene diamine. Nylon is chemically inert, heat-resistant, tough and strong, and is extruded and drawn to make SYNTHETIC FIBERS, or cast and molded into bearings, gears, zippers etc.